J. W. M

Bo

12 Stoneleigh Park Road
Ewell, Epsom, Surrey KT19 0QT
England

Tel: 0011 44 208 393 7700   Fax: 0011 44 208 393 1694
email: jwmck@netcomuk.co.uk
website: www.mckenzie-cricket.co.uk

*Specialists in Antiquarian,
Secondhand Cricket Books
Wisdens, and Memorabilia*

Catalogues Issued

*We are always pleased to hear of Books and
Collections for Sale*

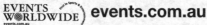

5TH EDITION

WISDEN

CRICKETERS' ALMANACK

AUSTRALIA

—— 2002-03 ——

HARDIE GRANT BOOKS

Published in 2002 by
Hardie Grant Books
12 Claremont Street, South Yarra, Victoria 3141, Australia
www.hardiegrant.com.au

Copyright © John Wisden & Co Ltd, 2002
"Wisden" is a registered trademark of John Wisden & Co Ltd.

Cased edition ISBN 1 74066 004 8
Leather bound edition ISBN 1 74066 005 6
(Limited edition of 100)
ISSN 1441-1725

Typeset by Melbourne Media Services
Printed in Australia by McPherson's Printing Group

PREFACE

As I write, we are being reminded of how the little kingdom of cricket is being affected by the political dynamics of the post-September 11 world. Should Australia honour its commitment to tour Pakistan or is it unreasonable to expect that sportspeople should be exposed to possible danger? Readers will know the decision by the time they read these words and will be able to scrutinise it, but the comfortable old assertions that sport and politics do not mix are now permanently buried. Even a conservative Australian government enthusiastically endorsed the cancellation of the Zimbabwe tour in April as being a timely and appropriate tool for dramatising its disapproval of the regime in Harare.

Yet, beyond this unknown lies another Ashes visit by an England team with its sense of history and tradition. Seventy years since the Bodyline series, a century since possibly the most exciting Ashes series ever; the resonances go ringing back to the beginnings of Test cricket. The question of the tour to Pakistan and the Ashes series in Australia crystallise the task of *Wisden Australia*: to be a force for continuity in a time of dramatic flux, yet record and analyse the processes of change which affect the game.

In this edition, Western Australian cricket historian Bill Reynolds encapsulates that sense of continuity and change in his examination of the MacGill and Meuleman families and their far-reaching contributions to cricket in the west over three generations. Ian Diehm pays tribute to another figure of continuity, the gracious and graceful Bill Brown, currently Australia's oldest living Test cricketer. In addition, he is a reminder of our own history, now being the only surviving Cricketer of the Year from pre-World War II *Wisden*.

During the 1970s and 1980s, there was a fatally easy acceptance of the new phenomenon of sledging as an orchestrated tool of what the current Australian captain is pleased to call the "mental destabilisation" of the opposition. After all, giving your opponents a verbal spray was part of that aggressive larrikinism which was supposed to be quintessentially Australian, any rough edges of which could be smoothed over by a beer with the opposition after play. Increasingly, it is being seen for the boorish, cretinous blight on the game that it is, and Brian Booth gives a considered analysis of its growth and challenges its continued presence. Booth, it goes without saying, brings to his writing the credibility and respect generated by his own personal integrity and cricketing prowess.

It is salutary to remember that, away from the ivory tower of international cricket, each summer weekend thousands of Australians take to suburban parks and country ovals to play their version of the game. Jim Young comments on the state of the grassroots in his customarily wry and ironic way and reminds us that this form of cricket is too vital to the health of the game to be left to starve from neglect or to drown in the morass of user-pays charges.

Steven Carroll continues the long association between cricket and literature with an account of how the game has fed the writing of his last two novels. This essay tells gently and movingly, of the ways in which cricket has seeped into the fabric of Australian life and how it is one of the factors that help to shape our sense of ourselves as Australians.

Wisden has the luxury of time to enable it to take a longer view than the incessant demands of daily journalism allow. Greg Baum utilises this space to analyse the current situation of the Australian team so that we might ponder the links between current practice and performance and future trends.

The bulk of the volume records the breadth and depth of Australian cricket across levels, region and gender. This year, we have introduced a survey of Newcastle grade cricket in order to give an account of the strong competition in Australia's largest non-capital-city centre. In addition, we have included an account of the performance in the previous year of the substantial brigade of Australians contracted to play county cricket in England. While they are part of a long tradition, the practice has now become so important to the individual and such a formalised part of the county scene that it is worth recording separately.

It is a sporting axiom that a champion team will always beat a team of champions. As Executive Editor, I had the luxury and privilege of having both. George Thomas continued to weave his skill with copy and to be an invaluable source of sound and creative advice and support. I value the experience of John Ross, and I wish to emphasise that it was the unfailing expertise, energy and commitment of Mary Small that made the appearance of this volume possible. I would also wish to record my thanks to Hugh Chevallier, Tim de Lisle and Christopher Lane, our colleagues at John Wisden & Co Ltd in England, the ever-vigilant and knowledgeable Ross Dundas for his indispensable statistical work, proof-reader and fact-checker Nabila Ahmed, and to Neil Conning and David Spratt for their immense technical skills which literally made the production happen. Thanks are also due to Ken Piesse for his intimate knowledge of the cricket world which allowed him to obtain advertising copy so expeditiously.

WARWICK FRANKS
Executive Editor

CONTRIBUTORS

Greg Baum is an author and senior sports journalist with *The Age*, Melbourne.

Brian Booth, MBE, is a former Test batsman (debut 1961, 29 Tests) who captained both Australia and New South Wales, and is a retired lecturer.

Jack Brown is secretary of the Wallsend Cricket Club, Newcastle.

Alex Buzo is an author, dramatist, humorist, cricket-lover and captain of the Metros in Sydney. He is also the co-editor of *The Longest Game*.

Steven Carroll is a Melbourne novelist, author of *The Art of the Engine Driver* and *The Gift of Speed*.

Ken Casellas was chief cricket writer for the *West Australian* for 27 years.

Colin Chung is a cricket writer for Hobart's *Mercury* newspaper.

Lawrie Colliver, a former grade cricketer in South Australia, is a broadcaster for 5AA in Adelaide.

Michael Crutcher is an AAP sports writer, based in Brisbane.

Andrew Dawson is a senior sports writer with the *Courier-Mail*, Brisbane.

Philip Derriman is the author of many cricket books and writes on cricket and rugby union for the *Sydney Morning Herald*. He edited the *Australian Cricket Almanac* from 1990 to 1996.

Ian Diehm is a Brisbane lawyer and the author of the Queensland Cricket Association history, *From Green Hills to Gabba*.

Ross Dundas is Australia's only full-time cricket statistician.

Shane Erickson is a sports writer/presenter with Melbourne radio station Gold FM.

Ric Finlay is a cricket statistician and historian, and a senior secondary college mathematics teacher in Hobart.

Warwick Franks is co-editor of the *Oxford Companion to Australian Cricket*, and teaches English and Sports History at Charles Sturt University, Bathurst.

David Frith is author and editor of more than 20 books on cricket, and former editor of *Cricketer* and *Wisden Cricket Monthly*.

Stephen Gibbs is a cricket collector and bibliophile, and co-editor of *Early Cricket in Sydney*.

Jamie Grant is a poet, reviewer and co-editor of *The Longest Game*.

Stephen Gray is media manager for Queensland Cricket.

Gideon Haigh is a Melbourne journalist, and a former editor of *Wisden Cricketers' Almanack Australia*. He has written ten books about sport and business, bowls off-spin and lives with a cat called Trumper.

Catherine Hanley is a post-doctoral research associate at the University of Sheffield, a Somerset supporter and a contributor to Wisden.com.

Rajesh Kumar is an Indian cricket statistician and historian.

Jim Maxwell is a senior ABC radio cricket commentator and the editor of the *ABC Cricket Book*.

Greg McKie is a secondary school teacher, VCA delegate and the Australian Cricket Board's statistician for under-age cricket.

Kersi Meher-Homji is the Sydney-based author of many cricket books, including a biography of the Waugh twins.

Adam Morehouse is the statistician for the ACT Cricket Association and the author of *From Country to Comets*, a statistical study of ACT cricket.

Ken Piesse is a journalist and prolific cricket author, and former editor of *Cricketer* and *Australian Cricket*.

Mark Ray is a cricket author and journalist. His second book of photographs will be published in late 2002, and he is currently a staff member of the *Sydney Morning Herald*.

Bill Reynolds is a Western Australian cricket historian.

Erica Sainsbury is the statistician for Women's Cricket Australia and scorer for the Commonwealth Bank Southern Stars.

Geoff Sando is an Adelaide cricket historian and secretary of the East Torrens Cricket Club.

David Stockdale is a senior sports journalist with Hobart's *Mercury* newspaper.

Warwick Torrens is a statistician and author of a history of the National Country Cricket Championships.

Bernard Whimpress is a historian of cricket and Australian Rules football, and curator of the South Australian Cricket Association museum. He is the author of *Passport to Nowhere*, a pioneering study of the relationship between Aboriginal Australians and cricket

Phil Wilkins spent three decades as chief cricket writer for the *Sydney Morning Herald*, the *Sun-Herald* and the *Australian*, and now writes on cricket and rugby union for the John Fairfax group.

Ken Williams is a Melbourne-based cricket writer and statistician.

Jim Young is the author of *Any Old Eleven*, a hilarious look at the Australian institution of park cricket.

CONTENTS

Part One: Comment

Part Two: The Players

Part Three: Records

Part Four: Australian Cricket in 2001-02

Part Five: Australians Overseas in 2001-02

Part Six: Administration and Laws

Part Seven: Miscellaneous

Index of Fillers and Inserts

ACKNOWLEDGEMENTS

Black and white photographs:

Rick Smith pp 69, 72, 74, 75, 88, 97, 107, 108, 110, 402, 439, 440, 450, 813, 825; Getty Images pp 404, 658; Queensland Cricket Association pp 77, 79, 81, 82, 84, 86, 415, 416; South Australian Cricket Association pp 427, 428; New South Wales Cricket Association p 404. Tasmanian Cricket Association p 95; Victorian Cricket Association pp 104, 450, 452; Western Australian Cricket Assocociation pp 115, 121, 463, 464.

Colour photographs are credited in the colour section.

The publisher acknowledges the work done over many years by the Association of Cricket Statisticians and Historians and offers thanks for the assistance of members in compiling information for *Wisden Australia*.

PART ONE: COMMENT

NOTES BY THE EDITOR

The old order changeth ...

On paper, Australian cricket had a satisfying 12 months. At the Test level, England were summarily dealt with, the series against New Zealand suffered from poor weather, while South Africa never looked like being seriously competitive until the fifth of the summer's six Tests. Australia won nine of the 14 Tests played and lost only two, a record of success which was a fair reflection of what actually happened on the field. In the limited-overs internationals, Australia cruised to an easy win in the triangular series in England and finished the season by crushing the South Africans. These successes were punctuated by such an indifferent beginning to the limited-overs series in Australia that the home side made a rare non-appearance in the finals.

Yet, despite this record, periodic undercurrents of ill-ease and mutterings that all was not well led the more excitable sections of the press and a portion of the cricket public to feed off one another. This brouhaha grew out of an over-hasty dismissal of the capabilities of the New Zealand side and a feeling that an Australian victory in the series would be the merest of formalities. In Brisbane, however, New Zealand almost succeeded in snatching a win after the two captains refused to let rain consign the match to a dull draw, while the Hobart Test was drowned by bad weather. In the final Test, at Perth, the New Zealanders gave an excellent account of themselves in a rousingly contested match. A series of three draws was interpreted as a sign that something was amiss, as the intrusion of the weather dropped from mind. Despite Australia's comfortable win in the Tests against South Africa, the subsequent slow start to the limited-overs series produced another attack of hand-wringing and a demand that the selectors do something.

In mid-February, the something turned out to be the removal of Steve Waugh as captain of the Australian limited-overs side in South Africa. Public reaction was immediate and passionate, its continual theme being that this was scurvy treatment after Waugh's distinguished career of 325 limited-overs matches for Australia. By contrast, a number of knowledgeable insiders had been quietly observing the infinitesimal slowing of his reflexes and shuffling footwork, which are fatal at the highest level of the limited-overs game. Nevertheless, the reaction continued, a number of editorials fulminated against the dastardly deed, and chairman of selectors Trevor Hohns was ridiculed for the apparently laughable achievement of having played only seven Tests. It was as if we could hear T.S. Eliot's J. Alfred Prufrock muttering forlornly: "That is not what I meant at all."

The crucial dimensions of both this episode and the subsequent dropping of Mark Waugh from the limited-overs side were the ones which received the least public attention. Australia's cricketers are now very highly paid professionals, tied to the Australian Cricket Board by contractual obligations and commercial commitments which are part of the modern landscape of cricket. Properly free of the former need to find and develop a secure job which saw the likes of Richie Benaud and Bob Simpson leave cricket in their early thirties, today's players have handsome contracts which help to prolong their cricketing careers. They also now have a legitimate financial incentive to extend their careers as far as possible, as a decision to retire voluntarily could be tantamount to an act of economic self-mutilation.

The age structure of the present Australian team makes it likely that this issue will be a recurring one in the near future. Of the current regular Test players, only Ricky Ponting, Jason Gillespie and Brett Lee are under 30 years of age, which raises the question of how and when changes can and should be made to the side, particularly if it continues its current rate of success. One direct consequence of prolonged stability could be a lost generation of potential Test cricketers as the likes of Simon Katich and Stuart MacGill find the first hints of the chill winds of autumn beginning to blow on their careers. So, the selectors are faced with the sensitive issue of managing change in a way that prevents stability from becoming hardening of the arteries, yet avoids the giddiness of change for its own sake.

Yet the public reaction to Steve Waugh's sacking revealed a hankering for a traditional set of values, expressed in a feeling that Waugh's service, commitment and loyalty to Australian cricket had been devalued by the decision to drop him from part of the national game. This reaction was yet another reminder of the complicated set of forces operating on contemporary cricket, where commerce and morality co-exist in often uneasy tension. Professional sport, cricket included, has become a commodity where the rules of the market place hold sway, so that a contract is a commercial arrangement in which it is difficult to place moral considerations of the kind which caused such public anguish in the Waugh affair. On the one hand, we now have an environment in which no highly paid cricketer can complain if lack of performance leads to loss of income or contract. On the other hand, if these matters are not handled with care and tact, and there is no place for non-material values, then we may plumb new depths of public cynicism.

Virtual cricket

Mention of cynicism is a good starting place for the three-match limited-overs tournament against Pakistan in June. Washed over by the focus on the Rugby League's State of Origin series in New South Wales and Queensland, inundated by the passion for Australian Rules football in the other states and drowned by the spectacle of soccer's World Cup, this wretched travesty of cricket sank without trace. While there were no recorded cases of exposure, many of the spectators looked pinched and drawn as they braced themselves against the rigours of winter. Various official handouts intoned solemnly about the importance of the series, most laughably in the insistence that it was a vital cog in Australian preparations for the World Cup in South Africa at the end of next summer. The players did their best to provide some entertainment but, understandably, they struggled to look any more than mildly interested in proceedings. But, as the Demtel advertisements assure us: "There's more." The series' principal sponsor, Tower, made $25,000 available for each match which was to be divided between bowlers who could legally exceed 160.9 km/h (100 mph) or batsmen who could make a century within 100 deliveries. A similar amount was made available for lucky members of the crowd, but the intricacy of the process was such that it seemed to mix Bob Dyer's old television show *Pick a Box* with the process of electing a pope. Its effect was to have the punters scurrying off to look up the meaning of the word "risible".

Sadly, this was virtual cricket being played in the cyberspace of television advertising revenue from the subcontinent. It was an occurrence which sprang from nowhere, went nowhere and had nothing hanging on it, and the public showed its preference for a warm bed on a cold night. For such a tournament to have any substance, it needs to have at least a semblance of meaning about it, developing from a sense of vitality and reality. It needs to be linked to the wider purposes of a tour or a larger competition and it needs the nourishment of the summer season on which cricket in Australia depends. The fiasco in June was such a cynically meaningless exercise that it should not be repeated unless the Australian Cricket Board is prepared to be brutally frank about its reasons for mounting a winter folly. Hopefully, the administrators will realise that such frankness is now unnecessary, as a savvy cricket public knows the dubious article when it sees it. Worst of all, in divorcing cricket from a real context there is the risk of providing an atmosphere in which disinterest and meaninglessness combine to provide ideal conditions for nurturing the kind of temptations that the Condon Report investigated.

The Ministry of Truth

In May 2002, Adam Gilchrist spoke at a lunch meeting before an AFL game at Melbourne's Optus Oval, home of the Carlton Football club. The club's president, John Elliott, asked him if he thought that the action of Sri Lankan off-spinner Muttiah Muralitharan was illegal. Gilchrist's reported reply was "Yes", although he added to his comment by saying: "Technically, if you read the rules, I think he's probably not quite within them." He also went on to suggest that the problem of suspect bowling actions is one that is given little attention on the subcontinent. After his response became public ACB chief executive James Sutherland charged Gilchrist under rule 10 of his body's player code of behaviour which deals with media comments "detrimental to the interests of the game". A few days later, the Board's code of conduct commissioner Alan Sullivan QC issued Gilchrist with a reprimand, the mildness of the penalty reflecting, according to Sutherland, the Australian vice-captain's "outstanding behavioural record". In between, the ACB was pilloried by both public and press as a kind of politburo of ageing hacks intent on ensuring that its chattels toed the party line and said nothing controversial.

The onward march of the football season soon obscured the episode, but it is worth examining because of what it reveals about some of the ways in which Australian cricket is organised and reported. Initially, of course, there is the distinction between the realm of the public and the private and whether it was ethical of the journalist to have publicised comments made at what was portrayed in sections of the press as a private function. In this context, an example could be drawn from the practice of one of Australia's greatest cricket journalists, Ray Robinson, who built relationships with players founded on absolute trust, yet whose discretion never robbed him of the faculty of critical analysis.

The very existence of a code of conduct and rule 10's notion of "the interests of the game" point to that continuing issue of the relationship between administrators and players in the governing of cricket. Traditionally, the predecessors of the ACB exercised their power ruthlessly, as the likes of Sid Barnes found to their cost. Yet the challenge of contemporary corporatised cricket is to define "the interests of the game" in a way that preserves the proper organisation and running of cricket while allowing players to be more than puppets with a limited string of clichés which produce antiseptic commentaries on the game and its issues.

The most alarming aspect of the incident, though, was the ignorantly strident quality of some of the commentary on Gilchrist's remarks. This kind of response involved an assertion that he was only saying what everyone knows but that frank opinions on Muralitharan's action have been driven underground by a conspiracy of political correctness because of the bowler's nationality. Like most conspiracy theories, this one generates more heat than light as it ignores the exhaustive investigation and analysis to which Muralitharan has been subjected in clearing his action. Of course, the rabid conspiracist will quickly point to the fact that only in Australia have umpires been courageous and truthful enough to call Muralitharan, acting in that great Australian tradition of fearless honesty. Rhetoric like this is a reminder that there is still plenty of myopia and insularity in the way in which we approach the cricket of other nations, particularly those of the subcontinent, and even more particularly, Sri Lanka's. Australian cricket needs to be mindful of the fact that while the Australian crawl was a distinctively Australian swimming stroke, the Australian whine is much less productive.

More on the whine industry

The problem with rules, as any school pupil can tell you, is that the more there are, the easier it is to subvert them. For the 2001-02 triangular limited-overs tournament, the VB Cup, a bonus point was offered to a team which scored at more than 1.25 times the rate of their opponents. Of course, this incentive was justified by the ancient incantation to Brighter Cricket which, it goes without saying, is a Good Thing. The only problem was that the new rule came back to bite the home side when New Zealand conceded a bonus point to South Africa and then, shortly afterwards, South Africa deliberately aimed at a target which would lose the match but deny Australia the bonus point that they needed to make the finals. Both captains had calculated that their chances of winning the series would be better if they did not have to play Australia and they took a course which the rules allowed. We were then treated to a great deal of moral outrage directed against what was claimed to be a per-version of Australian understandings of fair play in which the spirit, if not the letter, of the law was being flouted. Steve Waugh wanted the situation examined so that similar occurrences would not affect the 2002-03 World Cup, but much of the reaction was singularly unconvincing, particularly from a country whose cricket has always prided itself on its pragmatism and adaptability. Malcolm Gray, chairman of the International Cricket Council, summarised the situation pithily with his observation that "the more you introduce artificial rules to a competition, the more chance there is to have contrived, unusual or even silly results".

It was also ironic that notions of fair play were being invoked not long before the Australian talent and propensity for sledging was justified by the captain on the grounds that no action had been taken against any Australian player by the International Cricket Council. Similarly, the ACB chief executive James Sutherland argued that "If Australian players are breaking the code of conduct, I'm sure the officials at the match would take appropriate action." Both comments sounded like an assurance that the letter of the law was being observed without its spirit being mentioned.

A different kind of coach

In June 2002, the Australian cricket coach, John Buchanan, led a three-day forum in Brisbane involving each of the state coaches, the

Australian selectors and team management, which aimed at ensuring the national sharing of cricket knowledge and resources in the development of Australian cricket. The agenda moved far beyond the technical aspects of coaching and included such issues as sport science, the impact of technology, and player welfare. It repeated a similar exercise held in 2000 and is a proper and vital recognition of the needs of cricket and cricketers in the contemporary game.

Traditionally, the value of coaching in Australia has been decried as a pedantic stifling of natural and intuitive talent which bred the technically correct but overly timid English batting which many Australians claimed was the hallmark of the English approach. Part of the appeal of Bradman came from the image of the stump, the golf ball and the tank stand with its overtones of practicality, ingenuity and self-sufficiency which linked him and his Bowral world into a version of Australia's bush legend.

Even in earlier times, though, there were plenty of coaches in Australia, such as George Garnsey in Sydney, who had extensive, systematically organised coaching programmes, designed to find and develop youthful talent. More recently, the position of coach has been formalised and developed at both state and national levels, typically involving a well-performed ex-player, but Buchanan's appointment as Queensland and then Australian coach signalled a different kind of approach. Traditionally, the coach's credentials were based on the weight of his first-class performance; but Buchanan, with just seven appearances for Queensland, brought a new combination of technical analysis, psychological insight and statistical thoroughness whose results were both tangible and widely accepted by players. Queensland continued this approach by appointing Bennett King to succeed Buchanan as its coach in 1999-00, and reaffirmed its commitment to the practice by installing Terry Oliver when King left to take up the position at the Cricket Academy in 2002 after coaching the side to successive Pura Cup victories. Tasmania have announced the appointment as their coach for 2002-03 of Brian McFadyen who, like King, has played no first-class cricket. Of course, it needs emphasising that all of these coaches have played plenty of good cricket in many different contexts, so that they are not cricketing incompetents at a practical level.

This trend, though, indicates an important development in Australian cricket where the position of coach is one of increasing subtlety, complexity and sophistication, which in turn reflects the evolution of the game itself. It will be interesting to see how this new group moulds the job and the extent to which they develop and transform it. The development of first-class cricket into a commercial commodity means that we are already seeing the managerial and organisational elements of the position receiving greater attention, but the challenge that cricket faces, along with most other major team sports, is to move appropriately with the times without losing that human and personal dimension which makes the game worth playing and watching.

New umpires from old players

In July 2002, the Australian Cricket Board announced that former Victorian Test player Paul Reiffel and former New South Wales and Tasmanian all-rounder Rod Tucker were to be fast-tracked as umpires. The plan involves appointing them to a project panel aimed at attracting ex-players with first-class experience into the ranks of umpires. They will start by officiating in first-grade matches, with the prospect of elevation to first-class level as an endorsement of those who show aptitude.

This innovation could be an interesting development in Australian cricket. In the modern era, the number of ex-first-class players who donned the white coat has been very small. Men like Jack Scott, the ferocious fast-bowler, Mick Harvey, who opened the batting for two states, and Bruce Oxenford, a former Queensland leg-spinner, who is on the current Australian first-class list, are the exceptions rather than the rule. By contrast, English umpires such as Nigel Plews and Don Oslear, who had not played first-class cricket, were highly unusual. The issue is not whether having played first-class cricket makes for a better umpire, nor is it to devalue the enormous service rendered to cricket by a legion of devoted officials who have not played the game at any high level. Rather, it represents a possible way of allowing ex-players to continue a practical involvement in the game and, in so doing, enhance that sense of continuity which is so important to the health of cricket.

The Miller's tale

With the departure of Colin Miller from the first-class scene, Australian cricket has lost one of its most refreshing and interesting players. Having first appeared for Victoria back in the mists of the mid-1980s, he subsequently moved to South Australia and then Tasmania as a quickish bowler who never shirked hard work. It seemed that his would be a state career of honest endeavour, but a sudden development as an off-spinner in 1997-98 propelled him into the national team for a productive career of 18 Tests and 69 wickets.

Miller was such an engaging figure because there was a refreshing and genuine individuality about him in the environment of Test cricket, whose contemporary face sometimes seems bland and homogenised. He communicated a sense of relishing the unexpected opportunity in Test cricket which had come his way, but the laconic, self-deprecating quality of his public self kept a sense of perspective about it. He celebrated Australia's centenary of Federation by turning out in brilliant blue hair for the occasion at Sydney in January 2001, its startling quality reducing Courtney Walsh to paroxysms of genuine laughter. This ability to laugh at himself, though, never degenerated into his becoming a pre-packaged "character" and nor did it involve a denigration of his own considerable skills. The ability to learn quickly and the willingness to work assiduously in honing his off-spinning skills were shaped by the sense of perspective brought by the experience of the long seasons on the Sheffield Shield circuit. In February 2001, he was named Australia's Test Cricketer of the Year after taking 20 wickets in three Tests against the West Indies, including a match-winning five in each innings at Adelaide. Season 2002-03 will see him back in Melbourne as vice-captain of Footscray–Victoria University's district side, where he can continue to pass on his accumulated knowledge.

Yet, to paraphrase C. L. R. James, Miller knew more about cricket because he knew more than just cricket. First-class cricket, like all professional sport, can seem both self-regarding and self-absorbed, but Miller put it into a wider perspective where it was but one of many interests and passions which made him such a well-rounded person. As such, he is a great role model for younger cricketers and deserves the thanks of all those who love and follow the game.

THE MacGILLS AND THE MEULEMANS

By BILL REYNOLDS

It is very rare for three generations of one family to excel at their given sport. In the first-class cricket world it has happened only five times. The most famous are the Hutton family of Yorkshire, Middlesex and England, and the Headley family of Jamaica, West Indies, Middlesex, Worcestershire, Kent and England. The other three families are Australian, two of them Western Australian: the MacGills and the Meulemans; the third is the Victorian trio of leg-spinning Raysons who between them played 27 games across 40 years from the mid-1920s.

Although each Western Australian generation played cricket at about the same time, none of the MacGills played in a state team alongside any of the Meulemans. The first member of the sextet to grace a cricket field was Charlie MacGill, born in Perth in 1916 and educated at Perth Boys' High School. He made his first-grade pennant debut as an 18-year-old batting all-rounder with the Subiaco club. A broad-shouldered lad of medium height, he was able to open the bowling or come on first-change with his medium-paced swingers. To complete his adaptability, he was also a very good off-spinner and could bat anywhere in the top order.

An excellent all-round club season of 361 runs and 43 wickets led to his state debut against Victoria in Perth in March 1939, before Western Australia had attained Sheffield Shield status. In that game he opened the batting with another debutant, Arthur "Hubba" Read, and made a solid 48. In the second innings he opened the bowling due to an injury to Ron Halcombe, but he was no-balled for throwing by square-leg umpire Buttsworth. In the second match he bowled admirably to capture 4/45, but, while batting, he was badly injured when struck on the hand by an Ernie McCormick thunderbolt.

The next season MacGill was selected against South Australia in Perth. He claimed the wicket of Don Bradman in the first innings, but suffered at his hands in the second. World War II intervened and robbed him of his prime years. He enlisted in the army, but was seconded into the air force where he used his skill as a carpenter in Melbourne making aeroplane frames. There at the Essendon club he first encountered and played with Ken Meuleman, the patriarch of the other dynasty. In Melbourne, too, he met his future wife. In early January 1946, the family, now numbering three, returned to Perth where Charlie continued to play club cricket, becoming an integral member of the powerful North Perth team.

He was overlooked for state honours in favour of more recognised opening batsmen, but was recalled in 1950-51, as a bowler, when Charlie Puckett was injured. In the second innings of the match against Queensland he deputised as an opening bat and contributed a solid 38. Then, in conjunction with Harry Price, he took 4/56 and bowled Western Australia to an exciting victory. His final first-class match came at the end of that season when captain Keith Carmody was injured, but from then on younger bowlers were preferred. In 1955, Charlie retired from competitive cricket and took up a coaching position, having completed 16 seasons in Perth cricket, where he made 3,583 runs at 19.31 with one century, took 422 wickets at 15.71 and held 58 catches. In later life, the quietly spoken MacGill joined the Repatriation Department, where he assisted fellow ex-servicemen.

The MacGills began their second generation in 1945 with the birth of Terry who, like his father, showed a liking for cricket and hockey. While a 16-year-old Tuart Hill High School student, he made his first-grade debut for North Perth. Unlike his father, however, he was a bowling all-rounder. He came under the guidance of former state spinner Tony Zimbulis, who encouraged him to bowl leg-spin. Of medium height, he was more a finger-spinner with an arm action that came straight over the top, making him a purveyor of accuracy rather than sharp spin or flight. On his Western Australian debut he was an important contributor to his side's victory over South Australia, batting sensibly and then bowling judiciously in tandem with the experienced Tony Lock. In 1970, wishing to broaden his experience, he took the adventurous step, at the time, to play in the Lancashire League, for Todmorden.

As the second Western Australian spinner, he was playing in the shadow of the redoubtable Lock. This gave MacGill limited state opportunities, particularly as fellow leg-spinner Tony Mann was getting the selectors' nod because of his brilliant fielding in the covers and his ability to bowl the wrong'un. Further complicating the situation was the Western Australian selectors' ingrained belief that the bouncy Perth wickets were more conducive to pace bowlers. By the early 1970s, MacGill had a young family, and was concerned about the effects that the demands for time away from the classroom for first-class cricket were having on his career as a schoolteacher.

He had a similar pennant career to that of his father, playing 20 seasons from 1962-63 to 1982-83, principally with North Perth. He scored 3,935 runs at 19.68 with two centuries, took 431 wickets at 19.60 and held 109 catches. The differences between father and son in their approach to batting were obvious: Charlie was an attacking batsman with a wide range of strokes, whereas Terry was a more defensive player who could swing the bat effectively when the situation demanded. Terry also turned his hand to coaching late in his career, becoming the playing coach for both the Nedlands and Subiaco–Floreat clubs. With a strong personality and voice to match, he was able to get his point across to his charges with force and conviction.

The third member of the family arrived in 1971. Stuart MacGill readily took to cricket, as bats and balls were part of the household furniture. Educated at Christ Church Grammar School, where his father was on the teaching staff, he made his first-grade debut in 1989-90 at the age of 18 with the family club, North Perth. While he carried on the leg-spinning tradition of his father, his batting lacked the application of the previous two generations.

Like his father, when Stuart commenced his bowling career he was not a big turner of the ball, relying instead on accuracy. In 1991, however, he came under the tutelage of the master spinning coach Peter Philpott in Adelaide during a stint at the Cricket Academy. They had such a rapport that Stuart was prepared to follow his teacher after leaving the academy and move to Sydney to gain more experience in a club scene that encouraged spin bowlers. He had played one Shield match for Western Australia with little success.

With this move came some dramatic changes. First he forced his way into the New South Wales team in 1996-97 on the back of good club performances with Sutherland and North Sydney. He still had the straight-arm action of a finger-spinner but was now developing the ability to spin the ball quickly and viciously. He obtained his first Australian cap against the 1997-98 South Africans, bowling in tandem with Shane Warne at Adelaide. An injury to Warne opened the door for him to tour Pakistan in early 1998 as the principal spinner, his 15 wickets in the Tests including figures of 5/66 and 4/47 in Australia's innings victory at Rawalpindi. Warne was still injured for the ensuing Ashes series in Australia and MacGill returned a remarkable 27 wickets at 17.70 in four Tests, including a match-winning 5/57 and 7/50 in the Fifth Test at Sydney. By this stage, he had extended his bowling weaponry with the addition of a fizzing topspinner and a well-controlled, though sparingly used, wrong'un, and often bamboozled the Englishmen. A return to fitness by Warne has meant that MacGill has had to play second fiddle, but he remains the supremely accomplished spinner in the wings.

Charlie MacGill was seven years old when Ken Meuleman was born in suburban Melbourne. Spotted by Essendon cricket officials, he made the progression into their first team just after World War II. With a sound defence and copybook footwork, he found his way into the Victorian team once hostilities ended and interstate cricket resumed. The Australian selectors liked what they saw and marked him down as one of the leading new talents. Meuleman was picked for the short 1946 tour of New Zealand but was dismissed without scoring in the Test at Wellington. He was twelfth man in the first two Tests of the 1946-47 Ashes series, but the Morris–Barnes opening partnership had cemented itself, so Meuleman returned to Sheffield Shield ranks.

In club cricket he batted at number four and expected to do so for his state. The Victorian selectors, however, saw his technical and temperamental soundness as the answer to their prayers for a reliable opener. Meuleman did not enjoy the experience and, always forthright in his opinions, told the Victorian selectors so. The result was that after six productive seasons for Victoria he was overlooked for the 1951-52 season. At that time, Western Australia were struggling for batting stability, so he took the plunge in 1952-53 and went west on a year's trial. He had a good season for Western Australia and accepted an invitation to tour India with the Commonwealth team in 1953-54, returning from the tour as the best-performed batsman, with 1,158 runs at 52.63 and three centuries. The break also gave him time to assess his cricketing future, and seeing the potential in Western Australia, he decided to settle there.

A small but solid man with strong wrists and forearms, Meuleman became the backbone of the Western Australian batting. His presence in the team gave the selectors the opportunity to groom young players such as Barry Shepherd and Murray Vernon who were to lay the foundations of a new era of success in the west. Able to master slow bowling by using nimble footwork, he showed by example how to deal with an attack and became an ideal mentor for the younger brigade. After the retirement of the foundation Western Australian Sheffield Shield captain, Keith Carmody, Meuleman was the logical skipper and led the team from 1956-57 until he retired in 1959-60.

The success of the Meuleman experiment gave Western Australia the confidence to offer other players from outside the state, and country, the opportunity to play in Perth. The "imported" player was encouraged to stay and contribute to the west's cricket, but only Tony Lock decided to do so. The benefit to Western Australian cricket, however, was such that the state became the trendsetters in interstate cricket from the early 1970s onwards.

Like many sportsmen, Ken found himself in the sports goods business. In the late 1950s, he harnessed his skills at squash and involved the whole family in the sport when they took over the running of a squash centre. Expansion gave him the room to coach young cricketers in the winter. His expertise was drawn on to assist the Western Australian team with coaching and advice. Sometimes his frankness upset the authorities, but no one doubted his knowledge or motives. Both sons, Robert and John, were state under-age squash champions.

Robert Meuleman, born in 1949, followed his father into pennant cricket and began as a 16-year-old with the Nedlands club, making his Sheffield Shield debut three years later. By the time he was 20, he was captain-coach of Fremantle, an appointment that revealed an astute cricketing mind. His slight build, however, gave the state selectors the conviction that he lacked the power to pierce the field. Consequently, his first-class career was confined to four seasons and one century, a patient innings in Sydney that enabled Western Australia to gain an advantage. With Rod Marsh entering the state team, Ross Edwards relinquished the gloves to play as a specialist batsman, squeezing Robert out of the team to concentrate on squash and business.

Both father and son continued to coach young cricketers, emphasising a philosophy that was simple but traditional. Having excellent footwork themselves, they based their batting instruction around that skill so effectively that the fruits of the Meuleman tuition were obvious in a generation of Perth batsmen. Ken and Robert both served at club and state level as coaches and selectors.

In fact, when the West Perth club vacated the WACA Ground and relocated to Willetton, Robert was enticed out of retirement to lead them. He had not played serious cricket for eight seasons; a young family and business commitments curtailed any long-term return to playing and he soon retired, having scored 2,889 runs at 28.89 in pennant cricket.

Like most youngsters from sporting families, Robert's children had access to a cornucopia of sporting equipment and opportunities. Two, Justin and Scott, chose cricket as their principal sport. Justin became a proficient club player and is currently the captain of Melville. His temperament and footwork have the classic Meuleman stamp, but it is his younger brother Scott, born in 1980, who shows more flair. He made his first-grade debut as a 17-year-old leg-spinner whose batting pretensions were limited. Since then, however, he has shown such aptitude at batting that he has developed that skill in favour of bowling. Of medium height, but with strong wrists, he has moulded his style on good defence and, not surprisingly, correct footwork. He finished the 2000-01 club season with scores of 104, 98 and 121 to demonstrate his development. This showed the state selectors that he was capable of higher honours, and he made his first-class debut two weeks later.

A proud Meuleman family was on hand to see Scott on that debut in March 2001. Apart from the helmet, which neither father nor grandfather wore, there were many similarities in style. Early in his innings he played a perfect off-drive to the boundary that was reminiscent of a bygone era. The technique of foot forward for early positioning and an easy flow of the bat was exactly how his grandfather and father had played.

Scott opened the 2001-02 club season in a blaze of runs, scoring 175 not out and 118 not out in his first two innings. Showing the benefit of a spell at the Australian Cricket Academy, he scored his first first-class century, 109, against the South Africans in December. The Hutton family is the only other case of three generations each scoring a first-class century. Scott Meuleman is on the threshold of a lengthy cricket career provided he continues his current development. A quiet lad, he may take some time to adjust to the hurly-burly of professional cricket.

The reliable pitches and the summer climate in the west encourage cricketers onto the playing fields. Maybe there is something special about the clean air, sparkling light and excellent environment in

Perth; but for two cricketing dynasties to be produced in this one small part of the world is certainly worthy of note.

Career records

	M	R	HS	Avge	W	BB	Avge	Ct
C. W. T. MacGill (1938-39 – 1950-51)								
For WAust	6	250	78	25.00	19	4/45	29.42	5
T. M. D. MacGill (1968-69 – 1972-73)								
For WAust	12	210	34	15.00	23	4/94	40.04	7
S. C. G. MacGill (1993-94 – 2001-02)								
For WAust	1	11	9	11.00	0	–	–	0
Career	69	729	53	9.72	286	7/29	29.24	40
Tests	17	228	43	10.86	82	7/50	25.01	12
K. D. Meuleman (1945-46 – 1960-61)								
For WAust	48	3,398	234*	51.48	10	2/58	63.70	13
Career	117	7,855	234*	47.60	19	3/7	50.31	35
Tests	1	0	0	0.00	0	–	–	0
R. D. Meuleman (1968-69 – 1971-72)								
For WAust	14	545	101*	28.68	0	–	–	6
S. W. Meuleman (2000-01 – 2001-02)								
For WAust	10	384	109	22.59	0	–	–	3

* Denotes not out.

QUEEN'S BIRTHDAY HONOURS LIST, 2002

The following cricketers and administrators were honoured:

Member (AM) in the General Division
Norman Carlyon, who kept wickets for Victoria in 1961-62 and again in 1969-70, for service to the horse racing and breeding industries in Victoria, and to the community.
Wendy Weir, who played two Tests for Australia between 1974-45 and 1978-79 and had a long career with NSW, for service to cricket as an administrator, particularly through the New South Wales Women's Cricket Association

Medal (OAM) in the Division
Eric Freeman, who played 11 Tests for Australia between 1967-68 and 1969-70 and was a stalwart of the South Australian side between 1964-65 and 1973-74, for service to sport, particularly cricket as a player, administrator and commentator.
Austen Hughes, for service to cricket, particularly as President of the Northern District Cricket Club in Sydney.

THE CURSE OF SLEDGING

By BRIAN BOOTH

The sun was setting behind the Mount Panorama racing track at Bathurst as my father and I rode our bikes the 12 kilometres back to Perthville from All Saints College. Earlier in the day, at the urging of my team-mates, I had run out a batsman when he left the crease before I bowled. My father said, "Son, according to the rules that boy was run out today, but never, ever do that again – especially when I'm the umpire!" I learnt a most valuable lesson that day in 1946. I was to learn other equally valuable lessons about sports-manship and the spirit in which cricket should be played, not only from my father, but also from my marvellous teachers and other encouraging mentors from the Bathurst district from 1946 to 1952.

Many years later, as coach of the St George A.W. Green Shield Under-16s cricket team in 1999-00, I was observing one of my young batsmen being continually harassed by a fast bowler much taller than himself. In his follow-through the bowler continued until he was within three metres of the batsman. His position, with associ-ated verbalisation, could only be described as confrontational.

On his eventual dismissal, I said to the young batsman, "You seemed to be copping a mouthful from that fast bowler. What did he have to say to you?" I could see he did not want to elaborate but said, "Not much, Mr Booth, but he has a very limited vocabulary. He just kept saying f— this and f— that." "What did you do in reply?" I asked. "Nothing," he said, "I just smiled at him." My heart warmed at his response. I thought, here is a young man of character. I was also proud of him because my team had been instructed to do the hard thing and not sledge back.

Three things disappointed me that day and continue to do so: first that I was continuing to see such behaviour; second that the oppos-ing coach showed no concern; and third that the umpires did nothing to correct the situation. I was sure my father and my other Bathurst mentors would have had something of value to say to that fast bowler, his captain and his coach.

These two anecdotes illustrate to me how cricket has changed at the grassroots level. I am reminded of how little one got away with in 1946, and how much some are getting away with now. Much of this unpleasant behaviour is covered by the term "sledging". The

Macquarie Dictionary, (third edition 1997) refers to sledging specifically in the context of cricket as "the practice among bowlers and fielders of heaping abuse and ridicule on the batsman". It would be fair to say that some batsmen also use the practice when provoked. This practice is the focus of this article.

In March 2002, Malcolm Speed, CEO of the International Cricket Council, announced a new system of code-of-conduct disciplinary penalties. These penalties are designed to counter what the ICC regards as "declining standards of on-field behaviour" at the first-class level and "the inconsistencies that have occurred in dealing with it".

At the time of writing this article, details of the disciplinary penalties had not been finalised. In brief, however, the new system proposes four levels of breaches of the code of conduct, with minimum and maximum penalties at each level. Level 1 involves dissent, where a first-time breach could bring the minimum penalty of a reprimand, while the maximum penalty might be a fine of 50 per cent of the player's match fee. Serious offences, such as threats of violence, are covered by Level 4 code breaches. Depending on the nature of the offence, these are likely to incur a minimum ban of five Tests or ten limited-overs internationals, or a maximum life ban. No suspended sentences are proposed for the more serious Level 3 or 4 offences.

This new system of penalties shows a response by administrators to negative trends in the modern game. These include sledging, associated abusive language, excessive and unnecessary appealing, charging towards umpires on appeals, excessive clapping and talking, and dissent to the umpire's decision. All of these issues are seen by many as contrary to the spirit of cricket. As I understand it, the ICC's proposed new system of penalties is based on the hope that standards of on-field behaviour might revert to the more traditional and acceptable standards of the past. These values are worth holding on to.

Importantly, the new code will not only be in the context of the spirit of cricket, but also will come under the interpretation of Law 42, "Fair and Unfair Play". The premise underlying this proposed new system of code of conduct is that the ICC will then be better able to "clamp down" on sledging and associated verbal abuse. Umpires and referees will not only have the power to take stronger action, but will be provided with specific guidelines to assist them in eliminating the inconsistencies which may have occurred in the interpretation and application of the previous system.

Additionally, players will be put on notice as to what the penalties are and why they are there. Under the MCC's revised 2000 code of Laws, players have no excuse for stepping outside these boundaries. In my view it has always been unacceptable for captains, players and coaches to say sledging and verbal abuse or intimidation are justifiable tactics as long as you are playing according to the rules.

The truth is that sledging as a practice, and its associated histrionics, are now unacceptable because they are contrary to the spirit of cricket according to the rules. The preamble to the revised code, and Law 42, "Fair and Unfair Play", are quite clear on this point. The ICC is to be applauded on its initiative.

I often hear it said that although sledging is a recent term, it has always existed in one form or another. However, sledging in its modern form as a premeditated and acceptable practice certainly did not exist in my playing days, at least not in the matches in which I was involved.

'The truth is that sledging as a practice, and its associated histrionics, are now unacceptable because they are contrary to the spirit of cricket according to the rules.'

Although as patron of the St George District Cricket Club I could be called a "patron Saint", I want to make the point that I am not arguing that cricket in the past was made up of angels or saints. It wasn't. In my playing days from 1946 to 1977, there were a number of aggressive players at all levels. The aggression, however, was not verbally directed personally at players.

Two of the most aggressive fast bowlers I encountered in Sheffield Shield cricket in the late 1950s and early 1960s were the Western Australians Des Hoare and Ron Gaunt. Ron also played for Victoria, and both played Test cricket for Australia. They were wonderful men off the field and great competitors on it. Graham McKenzie was another speedster from the west who had an outstanding Test career. In contrast, he was a quieter man, both on and off the field, but a wonderful team man and a much underrated bowler. He was even more lethal than Gaunt and Hoare, because he pitched the ball up more. However, his bumper – when he bowled it – was very effective.

Although bumpers were quite prolific in Sheffield Shield cricket in the 1950s and 1960s, the bean ball (head-high full toss) was not. In a match between New South Wales and Western Australia at the SCG in the 1960s I recall receiving a bean ball and a bumper from successive balls from Des Hoare. I do not think the bean ball was deliberate. There was no doubt about the bumper. There was no verbal exchange on that occasion, but there was considerable feeling and an intense atmosphere. Des was letting the ball do the work for him and I was attempting to let the bat do the work for me.

It was not that these bowlers said all that much, but their body language and aggressive bowling let you know you were in a contest. When batting against them, there was little respite for a batsman, especially if you were wearing a New South Wales cap and batting on the bouncy pitch at the WACA. It seemed there was no limit to short-pitched bowling in those days (and we did not wear helmets).

As I reflect on the various phases of my playing days there was a definite absence of sledging in the modern sense. There were pointed comments from time to time, but these were not personal or prolonged. There was no premeditated sledging, nor was sledging, or anything like it, a policy. The term itself was not in use. Any verbal comments that arose were more a response to a given situation and then left at that. There was no need for referees or penalties. Umpires and respected captains ensured situations did not get out of control. In fact, acts of sportsmanship and courtesy were commonplace.

Roy Sitch from Bathurst was captain of the Western District Country Week team in 1950-51. The team was playing another country team at Jubilee Oval, Kogarah, in Sydney. Roy was bowling and at one point a batsman fell over while attempting a quick single. On his hands and knees, he was attempting to scramble back to the non-striker's end. The ball was returned to Roy but he just stood at the stumps and allowed the batsman to make the safety of his crease. When asked why he had not run the batsman out Roy replied, "How could I? He forgot his boots and I've loaned him a pair of mine. They are two sizes too big for him, and he caught his toe and tripped. It would be unfair of me to run him out in those circumstances." I thought this a most generous act of sportsmanship, and it made a considerable impact on me. Although trying to win the game was important, there seemed to be a balance between winning and playing the game in a sporting spirit.

My introduction to Sydney first-grade cricket was for St George against Gordon at Chatswood Oval in 1952. It did not take me long to find out that there were some tough, wily characters of vast experience and guile playing the game. As I nervously approached the crease, Test batsman Sid Barnes greeted me. "So you are young Booth from Bathurst. I've been reading about you in the paper during the week. Welcome to Sydney grade cricket, son, and all the best." He gripped my hand and shook it warmly. It mattered little that shortly afterwards he had me leg-before for 11. Sid Barnes was recognised as being as tough a competitor as they come. Yet this same player extended courtesy and encouragement to me as a new player.

To play that day in the same team as Test batsman Arthur Morris and against Test batsman Sid Barnes was a marvellous introduction to grade cricket. To have Sid Barnes actually talk to you, shake your hand and wish you well was a real bonus. Ken Gulliver, captain of the neighbouring Mosman Club, was well known for doing the same thing when a new player was making his debut. The spirit of cricket was alive and well in the 1950s in Sydney.

Not all talking on the field, however, was encouraging to opposing batsmen. Most first-grade teams had members who were more talkative than others. Some teams had more than one. I sensed that for captains these players provided a considerable challenge in keeping them under control.

There is a story told about Ron James, captain of Cumberland in the 1950s, which illustrates the point. Ron was a very strong character, an aggressive batsman and an astute captain. He represented both South Australia and New South Wales at Sheffield Shield level and was a New South Wales selector for many years. He was chairman of the New South Wales selection panel when I was captain of the Shield team in the mid-1960s. Ron evidently had some talkers in his Cumberland team. On one occasion, before a first-grade game, he called his players together and said, "Today, if you are a bowler, I want you to let the ball do the talking for you. If you are a batsman, let the bat do the talking for you. And as I am the captain, let me do the talking for you."

In Sheffield Shield cricket also some players were more outspoken than others. New South Wales and Victoria are traditional rivals. In my first Sheffield Shield match against Victoria at the SCG I was batting against the experienced leg-spinner Jack Hill. I played forward, meeting the ball with the full face of the bat. Jack appealed like a thunderclap for leg-before. The umpire rightly said not out. Jack turned towards me and gave a short verbal blast with one or two "b" words included. I was bemused. This had never happened to me before. On reflection, I think it was Jack's way of saying, "Welcome to Sheffield Shield cricket, son – you are in the big league now." Perhaps it was to test my temperament or possibly it was to put some pressure on the umpire. I regarded it as no more than gamesmanship from an older to a younger player. It ended quickly and was not repeated.

Sometimes the talk was related to good-natured by-play between players who knew and respected each other and had toured overseas together. The relationship between New South Wales and South Australia in Sheffield Shield matches in the 1950s and 1960s was always competitive but cordial. Both teams played attacking cricket. In a match at the Adelaide Oval in the early 1960s, when both teams were at full strength, there was an interesting piece of by-play.

Les Favell, captain and opening batsman for South Australia, had reached 87. Richie Benaud, captain of New South Wales, said to Les, "Favellie, have you seen your score on the board?" Les retorted, "Eighty-seven, but not for long." The score of 87 was, and probably still is, regarded superstitiously by some cricketers as an unlucky 13 away from 100. Les immediately got out on 87.

When Les arrived at the crease to open South Australia's second innings, he was immediately reminded by members of the baseball fraternity in the New South Wales team that he was still on 87. Les replied confidently, "I'll soon fix that!" In the first over he got a short-pitched ball, attempted to hook it over the Victor Richardson Gates, and was caught at backward square leg for a duck.

As he left the crease there was a chorus from a number of New South Wales players, who good-naturedly farewelled Les by saying, "Don't forget Favellie, next innings you are still on 87." Les chirped back, "Your day today, boys, but my day will come." It was a good-natured piece of by-play. In no way was it disrespectful, nor were the comments tinged with animosity or abusiveness.

As one would expect, Test cricket was the toughest contest of all. I played 29 Tests for Australia from 1961 to 1966 and eight unofficial Tests against New Zealand, four in 1960 and four in 1967. In none of these was I aware of sledging or abusive language as a tactic. In that sense, the atmosphere on the field was similar to grade and Sheffield Shield cricket – some gamesmanship, a terse comment occasionally, some humour, hard but fair competitive contests, played within the spirit of cricket.

In the 1965-66 season, regular captain Bob Simpson was injured before the First Test, and I had the honour of captaining Australia against Mike Smith's England team at the Gabba. During England's first innings, opening batsman Geoff Boycott played a defensive stroke at a delivery from leg-spinner Peter Philpott. The ball spun back off the pitch and stopped between the crease and the stumps. Boycott bent down and brushed the ball away with his right hand. Ever alert, wicket-keeper Wally Grout warned him, "Don't do that again, matey, or you'll be out." There was no appeal, but when Boycott queried the umpires, Lou Rowan and Colin Egar, on the point, he was told this was correct. Geoff apologised. According to the rules he would have been given out on appeal. However, since the ball was stationary and not rolling towards the stumps, the team did not want Geoff to lose his wicket that way. As far as I was concerned the spirit of that law was not designed for those circumstances.

Test matches are often characterised by drama and high tension on the field. The 1965 tour of the West Indies was no exception. In the First Test in Jamaica and the Second Test in Trinidad, batsmen faced the ferocious fast bowling of Wesley Hall and Charlie Griffith. Keith Miller, who was covering the tour for the press, wrote of the Trinidad Test that "Bumpers were hurled down like hail-stones in a torrential downpour." Despite the tension of these two Tests in particular, I do not recall any verbal abuse from any of the West Indian players.

The nearest I came to getting anything like a sledge in that series was in the Third Test at Georgetown. I was batting late in the day. Off-spinner Lance Gibbs came on to bowl and uncharacteristically presented me with two full tosses which I hit through the covers to the boundary. As Seymour Nurse sauntered past at the end of the over he said rather laconically, "Boot [sic], you are the best bat against bad bowling." I accepted the remark positively and appreciated the wit behind the comment.

The Second Test at Bombay in 1964 was another tension-packed occasion. The team had been away from home for six months on the United Kingdom leg of the tour and still had six weeks to go. Players were tired and somewhat homesick. We still had a four-Test commitment on the subcontinent, three in India and one in Pakistan.

India were batting. It was a stifling hot and humid day at Brabourne Stadium. A number of decisions had not gone in our favour, and a high level of frustration was evident among the team. The Indian captain, the Nawab of Pataudi, "Pat" to us, was at the crease. He played a ball just wide of me in the covers and called for a run. There was hesitation between the batsmen. I threw the wicket down with Pataudi some three metres out of his crease. There seemed hardly any reason to appeal but the umpire at square leg said, "Not out!" I could not believe the decision but had to accept it. The very next ball was played to me as well. In my frustration I fired the ball back to wicket-keeper Barry Jarman, who was standing over the stumps. The ball narrowly missed the Nawab's head. Two balls later the umpire called over, and as I changed fielding position I went to the Nawab and said, "I'm sorry, Pat. I wasn't trying to hit you with the ball." To which he most graciously replied, "That's okay, Brian, I quite understand. What you must remember is that here in India, when you are given not out, you stay!" I replied, "The problem is, Pat, we don't seem to be having that choice." There the situation ended and composure was regained.

I realised that Pataudi and I had something in common. We were both subjected to the same frustrations as any other player. However, we also had the same responsibility as any other player of not letting that frustration spoil the spirit of the game.

Although my competitive playing days ended in 1977, I have maintained contact with the game. Essentially this has been at the grassroots level of grade cricket in Sydney through my involvement with St George, of which I have been an active patron since 1982. For the past 11 seasons I have been selector and coach-manager of St George's Under-16s A.W. Green Shield team. Additionally, for the past five seasons I have been the batting skills coach for the grade club, and a grade team selector for the past two seasons. Over the past 11 seasons I have observed a considerable amount of club practice and match play.

One of the reasons I got back into coaching was that I felt with my experience I might be able to make some contribution to the education of young players who eventually move into grade and higher representative levels. I was concerned at some of the negative trends I was observing at the first-class level, which I felt were contrary to the spirit of the game. I saw this behaviour being emulated by younger players at the grassroots level.

Towards the end of my playing days in the late 1970s I did note a more win-at-all-costs attitude developing, with increased talk and "geeing up" on the field. It did not impress me to hear of Australian teams of the 1970s and 1980s being referred to as "the ugly Australians".

In 1983 I wrote a book with Dr Paul White called *Booth to Bat*, for which Sir Donald Bradman kindly wrote the foreword. We said to Sir Donald that the intention of the book was "to present the positive values of cricket that we hold dear to our hearts ... and to tell a life story that hopefully will be of encouragement to others". The book was also a response to what I regarded as increasing examples of poor sportsmanship at the first-class level. We hoped the book would provide experiences that would show younger people in particular that a player did not have to play that way to be successful.

In the mid-1990s I received a letter from an 11-year-old boy requesting my autograph. In the letter he said that when he grew up he wanted to be a bowler like one of the Australian players. Then he added a phrase that both alarmed me and warmed my heart. He wrote, "But I want to be a better sportsman." I was impressed that here was a young boy who could tell the difference between good and poor sportsmanship. It reminded me of the impact that Australian Test and first-class players had on the players of the future.

In response to similar correspondence and increasing teacher and parental concern, a booklet I had written called *Sport and Sportsmanship* was published in 1998. It was designed for discussion among students of secondary age on a number of sporting issues including poor sportsmanship, sledging and win-at-all-costs attitudes.

By the late 1990s sledging had indeed seeped into the ethos of cricket and other sports. It was apparent at all levels. Over these recent years I have observed an increase in sledging as a practice, accompanied by excessive talking, clapping, appealing and inappropriate gestures – in sum, a severe deterioration in the spirit of cricket. I have noted this also at Green Shield and grade cricket levels. I should hasten to say, however, that such behaviour is more apparent with some clubs than others and more with some players than others. Fortunately, not all clubs and not all players have deteriorated to this level.

It seems that sledging is coached into young players by some well-meaning coaches. In their enthusiasm for success, they observe trends at the highest level and either transfer or condone such practices to their younger players. While these coaches may be good at developing skills, often they have not played a high standard of cricket themselves, or their experience has not allowed them to develop an understanding of the true spirit of the game. Winning at all costs seems to have become an obsession with them.

During the 1999-00 A.W. Green Shield competition I encountered a team where even before the first ball was bowled every player was "talking it up" and clapping excessively. The noise was deafening. It continued, prompted from time to time by the coach from the pavilion. The sad part was that the experienced umpire officiating did nothing to correct the situation.

However, in nine matches at Green Shield level in 2001-02, I encountered only one team that exhibited similar behaviour, and thankfully not to the same extent. On this occasion one of the umpires was a former first-grade player. We had played against each other on a number of occasions and I knew him to be a very fair player with a positive attitude to the spirit of the game. At the afternoon tea break I said to him, "How do you like all this excessive talk and clapping?" He replied, "I don't like it at all." I said, "Neither do I. I have told my batsmen that if it continues they have my permission to pull away from the crease and wait for it to stop." When play resumed after tea, this umpire stopped play and spoke to two opposing players in quick succession. I do not know what he said, or how he said it, but the clapping and excessive talking became far less noticeable.

In my coaching at the Green Shield and grade levels I discourage sledging as a practice. In fact I have nothing good to say about sledging at any level of cricket. Before the Green Shield competition begins I give my players a handout covering the administrative details, but more importantly how cricket is to be played. I deal with sledging in this way:

> Sledging opposition players or umpires will not be tolerated. It is a
> blight on the game and totally unnecessary. Sledging is against the Spirit
> of Cricket, does not make you a better player and certainly does not

reflect appropriate behaviour or character. Improved skill makes you a better player.

Some teams or individual players will sledge you. The easy thing is to sledge back. The hard thing is to IGNORE IT. Opposing players only do this to distract your concentration. If you ignore it they will only distract themselves.

Scoring runs, batting in partnerships, taking wickets and catches, or making a run out is the best way to answer the sledgers. They soon become very quiet.

In my view sledging is unsportsmanlike. It is bad manners and an example of discourtesy in sport. It is an admission, by those who use it, that they do not believe they can win fairly. There is no place in cricket for this kind of pettiness or lowbrow psychology. There are more positive ways of getting the mental edge over opponents that are in keeping with the spirit of cricket. However, human nature being what it is, sledging will occur. The question is how to cope with sledging as a player and how to deal with this cancer administratively in order to preserve the spirit of the game.

While I totally support the ICC in its proposed new system of disciplinary penalties to deal with sledging, abusive language and other behaviour contrary to the spirit of cricket, I am disappointed

> **•It is an admission, by those who use it, that they do not believe they can win fairly.•**

that such action is needed. Along with the need for referees, it is a sad indictment on the declining standards of on-field behaviour at the first-class level. As a former Test captain I am disappointed when I read that Australian Test and limited-overs players now have the reputation of being the "world's best sledgers". I believe the real answer to stamping out the sledging cancer comes back, not only to administrative responsibility in providing a punitive system of penalties, but also to a combined, co-operative approach by administrators, coaches, captains, players, umpires, referees and all associated with the game.

In my view, however, the real issue with sledging is what happens on the field. I totally endorse the preamble to the Laws of Cricket (2000) code. Captains are responsible for their team's on-field behaviour. Therefore, they shoulder the major responsibility.

While umpires do not make the laws, it is their responsibility to interpret them on the field of play. Umpires must be vigilant and ready when necessary to interpret and apply Law 42, which is crystal clear on the sledging issue and on what is regarded as within and outside the spirit of cricket.

I do believe, however, that sledging and abusive language could be eliminated overnight if captains and coaches wanted to do so and willingly accepted the spirit of the code. However, this will require a changed attitude by some captains and their coaches. If common sense prevails, the code may prove to be a catalyst which initiates a change of attitude at the captaincy level.

During the 2001-02 season I sensed a trend back towards the more traditional spirit of cricket. At the grade and Green Shield matches I observed in Sydney most matches were played in excellent spirit. The Manly second-grade captain declared a ban on sledging for his team. I now hear more coaches, former players and parents openly denigrating sledging.

At a recent sports-star award night in the St George area, I made the comment that although we had a very good Australian team, I could not condone some of their on-field behaviour. I evidently touched an important issue, as there was spontaneous and sustained applause from sports stars of the past, the young stars of the future and their parents. I concluded my short address by requesting all parents to make every endeavour to put "sportsmanship back into sport". This comment also drew instant applause.

The ethos of the 1990s could well be described at the highest level as "Winning isn't everything, it's about how much money is in it." If the trend I have noted at the grassroots level during 2001-02 continues, we may be able to look back and say that the next decade, and beyond to the 2020s, returned to the spirit of cricket, where the ethos was "It's not whether you win or lose but how you win or lose that's important." A starting point in that process is to give sportsmanship the green light and sledging the red – sportsmanship is in, sledging is out.

BILL BROWN – ELDER STATESMAN OF AUSTRALIAN CRICKET

By IAN DIEHM

On July 31 this year, Bill Brown, Australia's oldest living Test cricketer and sole surviving *Wisden* Cricketer of the Year from those distant days before World War II, celebrated his 90th birthday. Well-wishers enquiring after his health these days are greeted with a chirpy, "Well, I'm still here." Indeed he is. In his eighties, Bill discovered a new career. As a member of the famous 1948 Invincibles and colleague of Sir Donald Bradman, he was suddenly in great demand to autograph memorabilia and to make guest appearances on television chat shows and at cricket society meetings, dinners and lunches. Exhibiting a ready wit and excellent recall, Bill regales audiences with whimsical reminiscences of another golden age of cricket. His infectious slow smile readily engages the audience. At dinners and lunches, he is so besieged for autographs that Barbara, his wife of more than 60 years, has to insist that he be given space to eat his meal. Since Bradman's retirement from public comment and subsequent death, Bill Brown has become the venerable elder statesman of Australian cricket, revered most of all by the younger generation of Australian cricketers.

A courteous gentleman, Bill relates his anecdotes with an unpretentiousness that belies the wonderful contribution he made to Australian teams. Bradman, never one to laud a player lightly, commented in a 1995 interview: "Bill Brown was a very good player indeed. He was a nice looking batsman, a good style of player. I had a lot of time for Bill." High praise from the hardest marker of all.

Brown had the essential orthodoxy and conventional approach characteristic of the sound opening batsman, complemented by an admirable temperament, so that nothing flurried or upset him. True to type, he paid every bowler a certain amount of respect yet reserved the right to give the loose ball the treatment it deserved. A predominantly back-foot player, Brown was noted for his strength off his pads, turning anything on middle and leg to the on side. He cut or hooked short deliveries but is particularly remembered for his elegant leg glance.

That he lacked powerful off-side shots could be traced to the backyard cricket of his childhood when, as a six or seven-year-old, he was induced to change to batting right-handed, even though he was a natural left-hander and later played golf, tennis and billiards left-handed. This alteration to his batting left him unable to play the powerful off-side shots that form part of the repertoire of the attacking batsman.

Bill Brown's batting encapsulated the character of the man himself – measured and full of charm. In 22 Test matches between 1934 and 1948, he made 1,592 runs at 46.82 with four centuries. His greatest performances for Australia occurred overseas, for a series of hand injuries caused him to miss all but five of the 15 home Test matches played during his career.

Bill was born in Toowoomba, but his father's dairy farm and hotel business failed and the family moved to Sydney in search of employment when Bill was just three years old. This proved to be to Bill's great advantage because it enabled him to go through the New South Wales junior coaching system, which was then far superior to anything Queensland could offer. He came under the influence of George Garnsey, a former New South Wales leg-spinner, who taught the youngster to use his feet to slow bowling and helped make him a complete batsman.

Chosen as an opener for New South Wales as a 20-year-old, his initial partnership with Jack Fingleton ended in disaster when Brown mistook Fingleton's habit of taking a few steps forward after playing a shot as an invitation to run and was run out by a direct hit from Charlie Andrews without facing a ball. The pair recovered from that disaster to find that their games melded. Jack gave Bill tremendous help and encouragement, and Bill regarded him as a marvellous batting partner because he never took a backward step.

A fighting innings against Douglas Jardine's 1932-33 MCC team followed by some heavy scoring the next season saw Bill preferred to the more experienced Fingleton for the 1934 tour of England. Somewhat unexpectedly, the 21-year-old Brown, who hailed from the working-class suburb of Marrickville, found himself travelling first-class on an ocean liner with the Australian cricket team to England. If he departed Australia a callow youth among the giants of the game, Brown returned as their peer after winning his spurs at Trent Bridge with 22 and 73 followed by a century in his first Test at Lord's.

Fingleton and Brown finally appeared together in a Test in the 1935-36 tour of South Africa. They built up a great understanding and formed one of Australia's most successful opening partnerships, particularly in South Africa, where they had stands of 12 and 93, 105 and 17, 233, 99 and 162. This tour under the buccaneering Vic Richardson was Bill's happiest.

Like his elder brother Bob, who was a champion athlete, Bill was a fine runner and a magnificent fielder, initially in the outfield and, later, pairing with Fingleton in the famous O'Reilly two-man legtrap. Neville Cardus once described the Fingleton–Brown fielding combination as "crouching low and acquisitively, each with as many arms as an Indian God".

If *Wisden* could describe the South African tour as the apogee of Fingleton's career, then the 1938 tour of England was the apogee of Bill Brown's. In the First Test at Trent Bridge, Brown hit 48 and 133 as Australia fought to avoid defeat after England led off with eight declared for 658. Stan McCabe's inspirational 232 provided the stimulus for Brown's second-innings defiance as he and Bradman (144 not out) ensured that McCabe's glorious innings was not in vain. On his favourite ground at Lord's, Brown found all around him succumbing to the English attack. On he batted, calm and imperturbable, until he found an unlikely partner in Bill O'Reilly. Brown shielded O'Reilly from the fast bowlers as the pair added 85 runs and averted the follow-on. Last man in, Fleetwood-Smith, stayed long enough for Brown to reach 206 not out, which was just the tenth time a Test player had carried his bat. In the next match against Derbyshire, he hit his highest first-class score of 265.

The Fourth Test at Headingley turned when Brown's sharp reflex catch off O'Reilly dismissed Hammond for a duck in England's second innings and Australia went on to win a tense encounter by five wickets. At The Oval, Brown wore out a spot at short leg fielding to Len Hutton for three days as England amassed seven for 903 before declaring. When play resumed, Brown emerged with Jack Badcock to start Australia's reply. Toiling through Australia's first innings only to be last out for 69 to part-time spinner Maurice Leyland, Brown just failed to join Bill Woodfull in carrying his bat for a second time. Ten minutes later, Brown was back in the centre opening Australia's second innings. He finished the tour with 1,854 runs at 57.93, second only to Bradman in averages and aggregate, his performances earning him recognition as one of *Wisden*'s Five Cricketers of the Year.

Returning to Australia, Brown continued his remarkable form, scoring 1,057 runs in the 1938-39 season, including an innings of 168 against New South Wales at Sydney when he and Geoff Cook set a Queensland record opening partnership of 265 that stood for 44 years. With his scores reaching Bradmanesque proportions, it seemed that Bill Brown would scale great heights in the next few years when he was at his peak. Alas, war intervened. Bill joined the RAAF and fitted in a game of cricket when he could.

After the war, aged 33, Bill led a powerful Australian team to New Zealand in early 1946, where they played one Test against a side captained by Walter Hadlee, sire of the famous Hadlee clan, who was to become a lifelong friend of the Browns, a match not regarded as a Test until 1948. Still, as the incumbent captain of Australia, Bill was well in the running to continue in that role against England should Bradman not continue in Test cricket. Then Bill's Australian jinx struck again and a broken thumb put him out for the 1946-47 season.

He returned the following year against the Indians but suffered another finger injury after opening with Arthur Morris in the first two Tests. Brought back for the Fifth Test at Melbourne, he thought it wiser to be run out for 99 than to send back the young Neil Harvey, who was playing in his first Test before his home crowd. As Brown returned to the pavilion, he noted with some irony that he had been run out by Vinoo Mankad. Earlier in the tour, Mankad had run him out twice for backing up too far at the bowler's end. After it happened in the Second Test, Bill had phoned Mankad to invite him for a drink with the Australians. Mankad politely declined but said, "Bill, I'll tell you one thing, I'll never run you out like that again."

A third tour of England followed but to Bill's disappointment, Barnes and Morris were now Australia's opening pair and he batted uncomfortably in the middle order for the first two Test matches before the selectors decided on new blood. Although Bill had a successful tour, he now had to devote more time to his business so he asked the selectors not to consider him for the South African tour of 1949-50. However, he did take a second Australian team to New Zealand in early 1950, a tour that launched the career of Alan Davidson.

When Brown returned from South Africa in 1936, the Great Depression was raging. Jobs, even for Australian cricketers, were not plentiful, so when the president of the Queensland Cricket

Association, Jack Hutcheon, offered him the post of Queensland cricket coach, Bill accepted. He was not Hutcheon's first choice – he had negotiated unsuccessfully with Arthur Chipperfield in 1934 – but Bill Brown came to Queensland and served the state faithfully from 1936 to 1950, scoring 3,493 runs at 56.33, an average second only to Greg Chappell's 69.00 among Queensland Shield cricketers.

After the war, Bill had to find a career. By now, he was married to Barbara and they had three sons. His good friends, Stan McCabe and Bill O'Reilly, were up from Sydney and suggested that Bill, the only Australian player in Queensland, should open a sports store. So Bill Brown's Sports Store opened in George Street, just opposite McDonnell and East. Ray Thompson, a very good businessman, ran the shop, while Bill went to the schools and clubs to obtain their custom and took cricket teams on tour to promote his business.

On retiring from first-class cricket, Bill became a state selector and, in 1952-53, an Australian selector. After Don Tallon was not chosen for the Gabba Test against South Africa, local enthusiasts vented their spleen by daubing uncomplimentary signs on his sports store. When Bill expanded the store by taking over the entire building in 1959, he stood down as a selector and thereafter played no official role in cricket; however, he would, when requested, help out with coaching from time to time.

Although the QCA did not hold testimonial matches for past champions as other states did, the Association did its humble best for Bill, inviting him to Test matches and functions, but not until 1992, when he was 80, was Bill awarded life membership – and then only after Queensland Cricket's CEO, Barry Richards, had urged recognition of past champions to bring them back into the fold. He had previously been awarded life membership of the Queensland Cricketers Club. Then, two years ago, Bill was honoured with the Order of Australia Medal for services to cricket – a fitting reward for a lifetime of cricket.

GRASSROOTS CRICKET

By JIM YOUNG

"It doth endure vicissitude and season as the grass"

About 18 months ago I published a small volume, *Any Old Eleven*, a memoir of my days as a park cricketer of very modest achievement. The tone of the book was whimsical, though any book about sport written by someone no longer playing is bound to be an elegy for lost youth.

Self-published, the book attracted an audience predictably small, but (I told myself) discerning, and gave me direct contact with those interested enough to pursue whatever they might have heard. Letters, telephone conversations, meetings in convenient pubs have brought in stories and recollections that have the odour of gumleaves about them.

Park cricket has a distinctive aura, and those who are drawn into it never lose their attachment. One new acquaintance, with whom I spent a very pleasant day at the MCG, showed me a number of notebooks he had kept over the years, one of which was devoted to his own career, firstly at school, later in the park. One could only admire such dedication in sustaining the record over so many years, but even more so the enthusiasm undimmed by so complete and comprehensive a history of failure. Overwhelmingly the most common entry was the zero, and very seldom was the tens column called for. It was a good season when the average rose above three.

There was also provision for partnerships of twenty or more. Partnerships are a complex entry. You need to record the number of the wicket – since 20 at the top of the order is just a beginning, but heroic with numbers ten and 11 out there. Courtesy requires the name of the batsman who shared your triumph, individual scores for both of you, the partnership tally, and the team total to which you (in tandem) had for once materially contributed. The pages of the notebook were narrow, so it was fortunate for the neatness of the bookkeeping, though not for the prestige of the scribe, that very few entries had been made.

What was more surprising was that this notably unsuccessful cricketer was actually quite good at a rival sport. It would not be accurate to say that Tim was a serious contender for the national athletic team, but he was good enough to compete against those who were. So, with the appropriate adjustments, that made him about District firsts level, worthy to tread the same turf as Shield and Test players – as against his actual cricketing ability, which was D-Grade in the local churches comp – always provided there wasn't an E or F to accommodate him. But running around in a circle for 400 metres is boring compared to the variety and subtlety of cricket, where someone even of limited ability can always contrive new forms of self-humiliation.

Hanging on in spite of fading (or non-existent) powers is a notable feature of park cricket. As for instance the gentleman who rang me a few days ago – at 64 years old he's still playing local club cricket, banished to a quiet corner of the outfield you would imagine, except that this is a wicket-keeper. Just imagine how many squats that means since you discovered your vocation at, say, ten or 12 years of age. His orthopaedic surgeon has told him there must be absolutely no more operations on those knees, but he's only three games short of 200 for his club and desperate to make the milestone. Fortunately he has a mate who is the medical consultant for an Australian Football League club who's said to him, "No worries! I've got a pill that'll get you across the line." So that's how some of my winter heroes front up, proppy but game, after a week of news reports on cartilages and ligaments. And one hopes that by now in the lower grades at Hampton, one stalwart has raised the double-century.

Recently, as Test selectors and the nation's media went through agonies about deposing ageing champions, park cricket proceeded in its usual manner, resting on a cushion of old buffers – players who even themselves would not try to argue they were still close to their peak. A useful standby for any club is the old hand who comes along to watch the new generation (even more reliable if one of them happens to be his son) – and of course brings along his creams just in case one of the feckless young lets everyone down.

Such parental devotion perhaps explains one sporting triumph by a senior park cricketer in Melbourne, who took a bag of seven wickets bowling in his carpet slippers. His son Paul, keen but less competent, was the main point of contact with the club, but Dad was clearly of more value. Spurning the mealy-mouthed description "medium pacer", he still called himself a fast bowler, but even he conceded that, well into his fifties, a new pair of cricket boots was an extravagance. On the day in question, the old boots packed it in early and the only fall-back option was the slippers he always wore driving to the ground. The match-winning haul lifted the team into the semi-finals, and of course made him an automatic selection, requiring an emergency visit to the cobbler on Monday, since the slippers didn't seem appropriate to the dignity of the occasion.

The family's sad decline in sporting talent was also evident on the occasion Paul, perfectly suited to the No. 11 spot, went out to join his father, who was on 90. He regards it as a mark of his father's dignity and restraint that he has never taken him to task for losing his stumps spectacularly when the old man had reached 98.

Cricket is very revealing of innate character – though only those terminally deluded by the game's propaganda have ever believed it does anything to improve what nature and heredity bestowed on you to start with. More commonly it underlines and emphasises existing weaknesses.

At the highest levels of cricket, whenever a run-out occurs commentators are quick to advise the audience that the survivor (especially if he's the guilty party) should beware of losing his concentration, thus allowing his self-recrimination to turn one mistake into two. Park cricketers need no such urging. If you run someone out, you know you'd better stay in the middle as long as you possibly can. The good of the team has little to do with it. One celebrated Melbourne footballer recalled running out a team-mate known as Louie the Fly and sticking in till stumps in the hope Louie might have cooled down enough to prevent physical repercussions.

In fact, most park cricketers concentrate exclusively on personal achievement ahead of team performance. It can put you one up on everyone you'll be drinking with that night and give temporary respite from the truly hurtful sledging we are exposed to – what you have to put up with from your best mates.

The brother of one very serious park bowler (who appears prominently elsewhere in the pages of this volume) provided details of an occasion when young brother was driven into the outfield for an easy two. The bowler turned and stalked indignantly back to his mark muttering about the luck and temerity of mere batsmen. He accepted with exasperation the return from the fieldsman and was pretty well back to the top of his run before the shouts of team-mates broke in on his private reverie and he became aware that mid-pitch confusion had stranded both batsmen at the far end and the easiest of run-outs had been missed by the time he woke up.

But a bowler is there primarily to do one thing, and that was what he was concentrating on. In any case run-outs do not go onto a bowler's analysis, so what's the point?

Park cricket teams are held together by a shared mythology, a fund of stories always to the discredit of one or other member of the group, elaborated out of all recognition, or simply invented to memorialise the spirit of the individual's contribution, so it is only fair to record that the subject of the above story has no recollection of any such incident. He does, however, remember an on-field coup against his captaincy led by his two brothers in a successful effort to remove him from the bowling crease.

In any case, the self-absorption alleged against him is appropriate, because, in spite of the elaborate apparatus of a team composed of living persons and an equally real set of opponents, park cricketers are wrapped up in fantasies that are taking place on far nobler turf. For instance, as an aspiring leg-spinner growing up in the fifties and sixties, I was Richie Benaud – despite all appearances to the contrary. I saw quite a bit of Benaud and made a close study. I particularly admired his habit as he walked back to his mark of dragging the front sprig of his right boot along the ground in the last wheeling stride as he turned to run in to bowl. Despite the complete absence of sprigs on sandshoes (the best thing on offer before the present garish explosion of podiatric possibilities) I quite mastered this aspect of the demanding science of wrist-spin bowling. After that, my action tended to fall apart somewhat, but many a batsman, deceived by the lack of subtlety of flight, struck heavy blows at apparently innocuous deliveries, unaware of how authentic my action was five or six yards before I reached the bowling crease.

In the absence of any concrete achievement, many of us are forced to make do entirely with the world of the imagination, though an occasional episode allows us to cosset ourselves in delusions that have no basis in reality. One correspondent related an episode from his final school year. He was passing the oval where the first eleven were at practice. Though his own ability did not make him a contender, these were his mates, so he jumped the fence, got hold of a ball and sent down just one delivery, which skittled the stumps of the school's undoubted star cricketer – in fact, future Test player Peter Taylor. At this point the public address system erupted and the irate voice of the Phys Ed teacher – remote but alert, and equipped with binoculars to keep an eye on interlopers

– bellowed: "McDonald – get off the oval in those shoes." A brief public humiliation, but in hindsight the very brevity of the moment enhances speculation on what might have been.

The contests in which park cricketers engage may not deserve the attention of anyone within spectator distance, but for those involved they are of passionate importance. In the last club for which I turned out a relatively new player for us dropped a catch in a semi-final with the opposition nine wickets down and four runs behind. After the game he was seen spreadeagled on the bonnet of his car, alternately clasping his hands behind his neck, then beating his fists against the drumming metalwork.

No one had the heart to tell him that one of the central identities in the club – best player, immediate past captain, everyone's great mate – was getting married the next Saturday. More than half that day's side and most of the possible replacements had already sent in their RSVPs, so if we'd made the grand final it would probably have been a forfeit anyway. (No one in our team ever knocked back a social invitation – especially when someone else was paying for the drinks – on the off-chance that we might have fluked it into a cricket final.)

This club, Naughton's Old Boys, about which I wrote *Any Old Eleven*, certainly approached the game in a manner that was on the relaxed side of casual, but Mick's very genuine distress on this occasion was a reminder to us of the proper attitude to the game, which we very seldom attained.

In writing about such a club a flippant tone was unavoidable, but in the years since NOBs' demise park cricket has come to seem less sunny than it did. The first screw to be turned went by the name of "cost recovery". No longer do local councils feel the community's money is usefully invested in facilities the community can enjoy. User pays, and ground rents have spiralled as a result.

But now even direr threats hang over our convivial Saturdays. This time it's the familiar concept of insurance that has spooked the civil administrators of the nation and baffled the finest minds our collective governments can scrape together. A strolling citizen stung by a passing bee induces nervous breakdowns among those responsible for calculating unfunded liabilities.

One local council hit upon the expedient of making sporting clubs guilty of anything that could be hung on them, so if a child falls off a slippery-dip while the cricketers are practising over the other side of the park a causal connection will be found and the responsibility sheeted home to the hapless sportsmen. When it became clear that no insurance company would write such a policy the council tried to ban all organised sport on grounds under its control. In consequence, one club proudly celebrating its centenary year (an event conducted in the Town Hall) faced the real possibility of having to withdraw from the competition – not for lack of players or flagging enthusiasm, but because the ground it had used for 30 and more years would be unavailable, though continuing to be assiduously mown and maintained. Every competition with a club or two in that municipality risked last-minute withdrawals by clubs perfectly viable, except that they lacked a home ground. Very reluctantly, and for one season only, the council agreed not to enforce its hard line.

Residents of Melbourne are familiar with its dry belt, where peculiarities of local politics mean there's no point in looking for the local pub anywhere from Camberwell through Box Hill. Now a little to the south another administration is doing its best to ensure that the young men of the city don't work up a thirst on Saturday afternoons. It used to be local government that supported community activities. The higher you go the less likely it is that money will be wasted on anything that won't get pictures in the paper, but now even grassroots politicians shun our company.

The grassroots metaphor is one that appeals to park cricketers. Regularly cut down to size, our stunted ambitions remain green and robust for all that. And without us, there is no firm footing for those who are chosen to tread on hallowed ground.

As the 1980s proved, Australian cricket can survive a decade of gloom at the elite level. It is more doubtful that it can do without the anonymous thousands who throng our public parks on summer weekends. Whatever their personal level of competence, they constitute the game itself, and their activity and their passion define its place in the national character.

THE ART OF CRICKET FICTION

By STEVEN CARROLL

The novelist John Fowles once said of his friend the playwright Harold Pinter that everything Pinter wrote was about cricket. This might surprise most Pinter followers and would certainly make *The Dumb-Waiter* one of the subtlest cricket plays ever written. Fowles never explained this enigmatic comment, but, odd as it sounds, I think there's something to be drawn from it.

The novel I'm writing at the moment (which I've called *The Gift of Speed*) is set against the backdrop of the 1960-61 West Indies tour of Australia. Although not a cricket novel, the book is deeply informed by cricket. It is the second book in a trilogy – a chronicle of a post-war Australian suburb, from the mid-1950s to the early 1970s – which began with *The Art of the Engine Driver*. Cricket was an integral part of suburban life in the 1950s and 1960s, and cricket is an integral part of the book.

A central character in the book is a 16-year-old boy who – for various reasons – is obsessed with fast bowling. But it's the idea of speed that I'm exploring. Fast bowling is the motif, though not necessarily the subject. The characters in the book live in an age of speed, and the boy's obsession with speed is emblematic of that age. In this sense the book is a meditation on both cricket and post-war suburban life. There are really no models that I'm aware of for this book, since most cricket fiction is either yarn or comedy and *The Gift of Speed* is neither.

The best books about places – Paris, Venice and so on – are careful not to lay on the details too heavily. In fact, it's usually a sign of insecurity on a writer's part if a book is weighed down with factual detail about a place. It's a way of convincing readers that the writer knows a place well enough to write about it. There is a similar temptation in writing a book about cricket. In the long run though, less is more. I'm not interested in statistics, and, to an extent, I'm not even interested in the facts. And, so far, I've done virtually no research. In fact, research needs to be finely judged. Too much research can also weigh a novel down and just gets in the way of the imagination. When I interviewed British novelist Kazuo Ishiguro, he told me that he did no research for his Booker Prize-winning novel *Remains of the Day*. He never researches anything. Yet, when *Remains of the*

Day was published – it is about the archetypal English butler on a five-day motoring holiday – he received letters from butlers all over England telling him how right he got it.

Every writer works differently. I think research can actually enhance memories, and if researched details are sufficiently telling or compelling they can work with the same force as memories. We can forget things, and research can fire the imagination by firing the memory. Above all what I want to create in this novel is a sense of cricket the way I grew up with it.

Crucial to the whole novel, then, is the creation of a peculiarly Australian experience of cricket. And I won't get that from the statistics of Test matches – even Test matches as famous as those played in the summer of 1960-61. I need to draw on my memories of cricket and, often, the idiosyncratic touches of a game – both the suburban experience and the Test series that provides the novel with its time frame. But it's not enough just to draw on memories. They need to be fashioned into the kind of fiction that is consistent with the style of the novel. And sometimes, when your memories aren't strong enough or resonant enough, you need to make them up.

In *The Art of the Engine Driver* there is a chapter called "Studying Ray Lindwall". The boy, who is 12 years old in this earlier volume, bowls an old cork ball against his back fence where he has painted three white stumps. I'm sure it was a common practice at the time and I suspect it was also a practice responsible for the demolition of many a back fence. He takes his bowling style from a series of newsreel stills showing Lindwall approaching the crease, reaching delivery stride, bowling and following through. To the boy – and to most other observers of Lindwall – he had the perfect action; a combination of grace and devastating speed. I did bowl against my back fence, but I never studied Ray Lindwall in such a manner. In many ways, this scene wasn't really about cricket. It was about writing. Cricket provided me with a focus, a metaphor or motif, but the subject was fiction itself; about how to slowly build a novel, about how to keep all the moving parts functioning as smoothly and unobtrusively as possible and how to get the maximum impact with what you've got.

Often, it's not the actual playing of the game that provides you with the resonating memories which are the stuff that can be used for fiction. Blow-by-blow accounts of games long gone are often the most tedious form of cricket writing. Often, it's the seemingly incidental memories that have the most legs: the nauseating, sickly scent of Juicy Fruit chewing gum in crowded cars on the way to Saturday afternoon matches, a song that was playing on the radio at the time, or a short conversation about politics that has stayed with me long after memories of the match itself are gone.

In fact a scene in the novel *The Gift of Speed* is about precisely that: a long, hot drive in a crowded car (usually driven by a church official). The car reeks of chewing gum and the church official gives everybody a lecture on the evils of socialism as they go. I remember just such a drive (although I've totally forgotten the game), and remember questioning the driver's views. The car then fell into silence for the rest of the drive. One of the thematic avenues this led me to explore was the question of just who my character was playing for. Cricket literature is full of talk of playing the game -- as in Newbolt's famous poem -- or about playing for the team. In fact the idea of the team is often just as important as the idea of the game itself. But my character doesn't play for the team. He doesn't even like the team. He is playing for himself. And not just for his bowling figures either.

In the late 1950s and early 1960s, working-class children -- and the novel is set in a distinctly working-class suburb -- usually had two ways of escaping the confines of working-class life. They could either be good at art, or they could be good at sport. To an extent, nothing much has changed, except that sport in those days meant cricket and footy, whereas today there is a far greater range. In this way *The Gift of Speed* draws on a tradition of working-class film and literature about sport as a means of escape. Two of these stand out for me: David Storey's *This Sporting Life* (about a Yorkshire coal-miner who attempts to climb the social ladder through professional football) and Alan Sillitoe's *The Loneliness of the Long Distance Runner* (about a young athlete whose running prowess -- the one activity that gives him a sense of freedom -- is used by a reform school for its own propagandist purposes). Neither of these is about cricket. But that doesn't matter. The point is they connect with a major theme in the book, that an activity such as fast bowling can give the character's life a sense of meaning as well as provide a way out of working-class suburbia.

Stylistically, these writers are also important because I've always admired their no-nonsense prose -- although a lot has happened since then, of course, and many other stylistic influences come into play, as it were, in my book. But it should be said that the title of Sillitoe's novella has always resonated with me and is quite possibly the distant template of titles such as *The Art of the Engine Driver* and *The Gift of Speed*.

This political strain also informs other aspects of the book. Michael reads everything he can about cricket. He keeps scrapbooks and journals, labelling and annotating everything meticulously – which I never did. Naturally, he pays special attention to the fast bowlers of cricket history and discovers that the fast bowlers quite often come from lower-class backgrounds: Trueman, Lindwall and Larwood. In fact his loyalties often reside with the bowlers, not with countries or teams. Rather than hate Larwood, as many Australians would, he admires him. And a whole chapter – "The Lesson of Harold Larwood" – is a reflection on the way Larwood was used by the English establishment and thrown away when he became an embarrassment. The situation in reality was a lot more complex than that – but to the 16-year-old Michael it's not. To Michael, Larwood played for the team and his loyalty was rewarded with betrayal. And this, not the way he bowled, is his ultimate lesson.

In Michael's world these two means of escape – art and sport – fuse, mainly because he has a keen sense of the aesthetics of the game. The small, incidental aspects of a Test can open up all sorts of fictional doors. In the Third Test against West Indies in Sydney in 1961, for example, Alan Davidson spoke briefly in an interview about one particular shot that Frank Worrell played off his bowling. It was, to Davidson, the perfect cover drive. And although he was the bowler, as he followed through even he was able to see the sheer grace of the shot, so perfectly was it executed. It may seem like a small event in the overall context of the game, but for a writer it provides an occasion and an opportunity to explore the aesthetics of the game. It is also an opportunity to explore the relationship between bowler and batsman, for rivalries in cricket – it seems to me – are sometimes more like collaborations. A great bowler and a great batsman, can, in concert, produce magnificent spectacles.

Take Worrell's cover drive. Davidson never says that there was anything wrong with the ball he bowled to Worrell. In fact, in replay, it looks like a very good ball – just a bit short. Had the ball been a lesser ball, the shot would have been a lesser shot. In order to create what many observers at the time saw as a perfect cricketing moment, a ball of unquestionably high quality was required so that the perfect cover drive could be executed. Of course, Davidson was trying his hardest to get Worrell out – and Worrell's innings probably won the game for West Indies – but Davidson ended up being an indispensable part of one of the most aesthetically pleasing moments of the tour. And this, paradoxically, is when rivalry becomes collaboration: albeit, unwitting collaboration. Davidson's initial disappointment at being hit for four aside, his subsequent observations about that shot suggest that he knew straight away that he had just been part of something special.

This may seem like poetic licence taken to the extreme – but that's what a licence is for. And it's at the extremes of possibility that we get to explore the poetics and aesthetics of the game in a way that we normally wouldn't.

As the book progresses, memories and details from research rise to surface above the mass of memories and details associated with that time. And, as usual, what announces itself as fictional material can be surprising. Recently I read a short biographical study of Lindsay Hassett by Melbourne writer Laurie Clancy. After reading the piece, memories of Hassett's basement shop at 52 Swanston Street, Melbourne, started coming back quite strongly. The coolness of the shop in summer returned to me, along with the trepidation of descending the stairs – for Hassett was often there. And he was often found walking about the shop chatting to customers, usually young cricket fans like myself who couldn't afford to buy anything, but came to see what an Australian cricket captain looked like. And as I wrote the chapter, simply titled "Lindsay Hassett's Sports Store", it became clear to me that the importance of the place was that it brought dreams near by placing them in the context of the everyday. In such a place the dream of playing Test cricket for Australia was imaginable. Not only because of the cricketers from all over the country – and overseas – who sometimes visited the store, but because of what the store contained. Here were the kinds of sweaters and boots and shirts that real cricketers wore. For Michael, while standing in that shop, there is a distinct sense that his dreams don't belong to another world after all.

The novel, I imagine, finishes in Melbourne on the final day of the West Indies tour. Half a million people turn out in the streets of the city to farewell the West Indies team. People hang from office windows, confetti and ticker-tape are showered on the visiting players, and Michael, one of the crowd, stands in the main thoroughfare of the city waving farewell to the stuff of his adolescent dreams.

For one unforgettable summer, the closed community of his suburb opens to the outside world. And it is not – as in the past – a war that has opened the community (and the country) to this outside world, but a veritable carnival of cricket, music and colour; an explosion of joy in which a community discovers the best in itself.

ICC TEST CHAMPIONSHIP TABLE, JULY 31, 2002

	Team	Played	Won	Lost	Drawn	Points	Average
1	Australia	13	9	2	2	20	1.54
2	South Africa	16	11	3	2	24	1.50
3	New Zealand	17	8	5	4	20	1.18
4	Sri Lanka	16	8	6	2	18	1.13
5	England	16	7	6	3	17	1.06
6	West Indies	15	6	8	1	13	0.87
7	Pakistan	16	4	7	5	13	0.81
8	India	14	4	7	3	11	0.79
9	Zimbabwe	16	3	11	2	8	0.50
10	Bangladesh	5	–	5	–	0	–

Points System: 2 – series win, 1 – series draw, 0 – series loss.
Sides ranked on average (points divided by series played).

Only series consisting of two Tests or more are counted. The most recent series between the two sides, home and away, are counted. The initial table was constructed only considering series starting during or after the initial five-year cut-off date of May 1996. Thereafter series replace one another under the ICC ten-year programme with no fixed cut-off period. If, for any reason, a scheduled series is not played or completed, no points will be awarded. This decision has been taken to act as an incentive for members to fulfil all fixtures. Bangladesh will not be allocated an average score until they have completed nine Test series of the maximum 18. This is expected to be completed in April 2003. The table will revert to a straight points system once every side has played each other home and away. This is expected to be completed in 2005. The leading side will hold the ICC Test Championship trophy, produced in silver and gold by Asprey & Garrard and valued at more than £30,000. The trophy will automatically pass from leader to leader. If two sides are tied at the top of the table the holder will retain the ICC Test Championship trophy.

WISDEN AUSTRALIA
CRICKETER OF THE YEAR

ADAM GILCHRIST

By MARK RAY

Some great cricketers change the game forever. Others possess a talent so rare that those who follow cannot emulate their feats, and when they retire the game reverts to its former self. Don Bradman did things no one before or since has been able to repeat. Garry Sobers scaled heights as an all-rounder that have not been approached by succeeding generations.

Shane Warne has had it both ways. He changed cricket in the 1990s by reinvigorating spin bowling. The likes of India's Anil Kumble and Pakistan's Mushtaq Ahmed have not only sought Warne's advice on technique but also acknowledged the inspiration they have drawn from his brilliant career. Yet as Warne's friend and coach Terry Jenner has argued, Warne will not leave behind a generation of gifted leg-spinners simply because his is such a rare gift. No one before him was able to combine such accuracy and so many subtle variations with such prodigious turn. Leg-spinners who follow Warne will be willing in spirit but the likelihood is that the flesh just will not be up to the task.

Adam Gilchrist looks set to dominate the first decade of the new millennium as Warne did the 1990s. For some years before his rise, wicket-keepers had to bat well. The English selectors, for instance, have preferred Alec Stewart, a modestly talented keeper but a fine batsman, to a specialist gloveman like Jack Russell. What Gilchrist has done is to stretch that trend beyond expectation. He is already the greatest wicket-keeper-batsman in history and, surely, the greatest No. 7 batsman. He is the first wicket-keeper to rate as a genuine all-rounder, one who would demand a place in his team in either role. As such he will leave a legacy, but will his successors be good enough to bat the way he does?

Gilchrist's Test captain, Steve Waugh, has said Gilchrist will change the game because the next generation will follow his lead by batting aggressively in first-class matches as if they were playing in limited-overs cricket. There might be some embarrassing dismissals if too many try to play that way. As Jenner asks, will the next generation be good enough to pull it off? Gilchrist's talent with the bat should not be underestimated. His current Test average of 60.00 from 31 matches (with a brilliant strike-rate of 81.63 runs per 100 balls faced) is phenomenal, and his ability to constantly savage bowling attacks unprecedented by all-rounders, with the sole exception of Sobers. As well as his excellent batting figures, he has taken 122 catches in Tests and made ten stumpings. Gilchrist's is the sort of talent that does not appear as often as once in a generation.

Gilchrist's brilliant 2001-02 was recognised in July with the award of cricketer of the year by the Federation of International Cricketers' Associations. By the time he received that honour, he was sitting comfortably on top of the PricewaterhouseCoopers ratings as the best batsman in the world, ahead of such luminaries as Sachin Tendulkar and Brian Lara.

The nuts and bolts of Gilchrist's brilliant year included a stunning counter-attack on the Indians in the First Test in Mumbai in February 2001, a thrilling 152 against England in the First Test at Edgbaston in July – in which his third 50 came off 25 balls as he and Glenn McGrath added 63 for the last wicket to which the fast bowler contributed one run – and two maulings of the South Africans in February and March 2002. Gilchrist's undefeated 204 in the First Test in Johannesburg featured the fastest Test double-century to that point in cricket history, off 212 balls against Ian Botham's 220-ball effort against India in 1982 – although remarkably it was bettered by New Zealander Nathan Astle's assault on England weeks later. Gilchrist followed his double-century with a frenetic 108-ball 138 in the Second Test in Cape Town. South Africa's rather fanciful hopes of unseating Australia as the best team in the world flew away with the left-hander's first six at the Wanderers. In the 12 months beginning with the Ashes series, Gilchrist scored 1,166 runs in 14 Tests at an average of 77.73, including four centuries.

The raw figures are highly impressive but it is the way Gilchrist does it that makes him such a popular and entertaining player. On a softish pitch in Mumbai he joined Matthew Hayden with the first innings score a perilous five for 99, and proceeded to counter-attack off-spinner Harbhajan Singh. Both left-handers hit against the spin deep into the on side, Hayden with huge sweep shots, Gilchrist mostly with thunderous lofted drives. At Edgbaston Gilchrist reached his century, on Ashes debut, with an improvised glide over the wicket-keeper's head. There is great joy and enviable simplicity as well as awesome power in his play.

Yet Gilchrist's year was not without setbacks. His form in limited-overs cricket was nowhere near as impressive as in Test cricket. After his century in Mumbai he made a pair in the Second Test and two singles in the Third as Harbhajan played upon his nerves. Admittedly umpiring decisions went against him, but he seemed at a loss once Harbhajan regained confidence after Mumbai. In the Fourth Test at Headingley his captaincy, in the absence of the injured Steve Waugh, ended in a rare defeat and some criticism of his handling of his bowlers on the final day.

Off the field, Gilchrist was overlooked for the Australian limited-overs captaincy despite having been Waugh's deputy before Ricky Ponting was appointed. At a football club function in Melbourne in May 2002, Gilchrist somewhat naively answered a leading question about the legitimacy of Muttiah Muralitharan's action by saying he thought it outside the rules. The Australian Cricket Board reprimanded him for a breach of its disciplinary rules, declining to fine him due to his blameless record and impressive work in improving the image of the national team. Soon after, Gilchrist was one of several Australians accused by young South African batsman Graeme Smith of excessive sledging during the series in the republic. Critics who berated the other accused Australians ignored Gilchrist's alleged involvement, further evidence of the strength of his popularity and clean image. Nevertheless, some people saw these misdemeanours as reassuring evidence that the man was not the perfect cricket citizen, that he was flesh and blood as well as a very rare talent.

Gilchrist's affable, modest behaviour off the field is one thing; his impact on it quite another. Before his Test debut, the Australians were the best team in the world with the wicket-keeper widely regarded as the best keeper-batsman Australia had produced. Yet soon after Gilchrist replaced Ian Healy, the team gained in power and confidence. His nerveless century in his second match, during the historic run chase with Justin Langer on the last day of the Second Test against Pakistan in Hobart, had a profound effect on team belief. After that, no situation seemed lost. The security Gilchrist's presence at No. 7 gave the six batsmen above him allowed them to play freely, to play shots and try to maintain the stated aim of scoring 300 runs in a day. Scoring at such a brisk rate provides the bowlers with time to take 20 wickets for a win. It is a simple game plan, but one usually honoured more in theory than in practice. Other Test teams have now seen that it can be done and are at least aspiring to something similar.

Although Steve Waugh has said he believes that four specialist bowlers are enough, Gilchrist's stature as a batsman at least allows the selectors to consider choosing him at number six and including a fifth bowler should conditions or circumstances warrant. It may never happen but it is now a viable option, and less of a gamble than it would be for weaker sides.

Gilchrist is an intelligent man, brought up by sports-loving parents who instilled discipline, modesty and common sense in their children. His father Stan was a school inspector and leg-spinner who made it as far as the New South Wales seconds. Stan coached many junior teams but his greatest contribution to Australian cricket was surely his attitude towards Adam's play in the family's backyard. Stan always encouraged Adam to hit the ball. Early on he saw his son's sharp eye and gift for clean hitting and allowed it to develop with minimal technical advice. Stan kept his coaching simple and Adam, now the best player in the world, still plays a simple game.

When asked before the limited-overs series in South Africa about his recent modest returns in that form of the game, Gilchrist said: "I need to bat exactly the same way as I bat in Test cricket. That is, not to be worried about field restrictions, early boundaries and run-rates – just focus with a clear mind on every ball." That clear mind is the key to his game. Generally he has the knack of being able to play every ball as he sees its merits. If he thinks he can hit it for four, or six, he will try to do so – no second-guessing, no complications. This is also the way he responds to match situations. He knows his best game is attack, so he pursues it even if his team is in trouble.

Can Gilchrist improve? Does he have deficiencies?

Two of the greatest attacking batsmen of the modern era, Ian Botham and Mark Waugh, played great defensive innings in the later stages of their careers, innings constructed with the sole purpose of saving a match; runs were not an issue. Gilchrist has not yet been able to do that. He had opportunities in India but could not survive the first few overs he received from Harbhajan. However, counter-attack had worked for Gilchrist in the Mumbai Test. Also, Steve Waugh's preference is to attack when in trouble and Gilchrist is one of his main weapons in this largely successful plan. As Gilchrist gains experience he may well play a great defensive innings. If he does not, he will still be considered a player of the highest quality. If he does, he will have enhanced his status as one of the finest players of the modern era.

Nor has Gilchrist had to cope with a prolonged form slump, one in which failures eat away at his natural confidence. Presumably, that will come. How he handles it will say much about his temperament, but the indications are that he will force his way through in impressive style.

Michael Holding has said that he would need only an over to dismiss Gilchrist. One can easily imagine how: a bouncer to shake him up, a few deliveries angled across him towards the slips followed by one that moves back in and finds the gap between bat and pad. The late Malcolm Marshall might not have needed a full over. Gilchrist's technique is not perfect but one thing is certain: while bowlers are trying to find a way through it he will be redirecting some of the pressure by scoring quick runs.

Most worryingly, will the demands of his heavy workload as wicket-keeper and batsman take their toll on his body?

The answers await us down the track. For now, we can sit back and enjoy the spectacle of a rare talent – Adam Gilchrist in full flight.

A PROLONGED HAT-TRICK

On the weekend of 16 and 17 March 2002, Melbourne cricketer Stephen Hickman achieved a rare hat-trick which was spread over three overs, two days, two innings and involved the same batsman twice, all observed by the same non-striker. Playing in the Mercantile Cricket Association's C grade semi-final at Fawkner Park, South Yarra, Gunbower had reached eight for 109 when Hickman came on to bowl his gentle off-spinners. He took a wicket with the last ball of his third over and then bowled number 11 batsman Richard Higgins with the first ball of his next over to finish the innings, leaving Chris Taylor as the not out batsman.

Power House scored a convincing 361 to leave Gunbower little but pride to play for on the second day. In a reconfigured batting order, Taylor opened and was joined by Higgins at the fall of the fourth wicket. Aware of the possibilities, the captain brought Hickman brought back into the attack immediately; the hapless Higgins was again clean bowled to give him a pair of golden ducks for the match, the proceedings again observed by Taylor. Gunbower struggled to eight for 139 in what quickly became known as Hickman's match. – WARWICK FRANKS

CRICKETER OF THE YEAR

Getty Images

Adam Gilchrist

PURA CUP CRICKETER OF THE YEAR

Jimmy Maher

TRANS-TASMAN CAPTAINS

Steve Waugh captained the Australian Test team to undisputed world supremacy, but his replacement as captain of the Australian limited-overs team suggested that an illustrious career may be drawing to a close.

Stephen Fleming of New Zealand reaches 100 on the first day of the Third Test against Australia at the WACA, Perth.

SPEED WEAPON

A typically aggressive Brett Lee in action in the series against New Zealand,
in which he took 14 wickets.

TEST SERIES STARS

Getty Images

Ricky Ponting, the new Australian vice-captain, catches South Africa's Gary Kirsten
off Shane Warne in the First Test, Adelaide.

Getty Images

Rejuvenated opener Justin Langer had a magnificent summer with a domestic Test average
of 76.50, and a share in two double-century opening stands with Matthew Hayden.

BIG HITTERS

New Zealand's master of the mighty hit, Chris Cairns, thrilled the crowds with his work, scoring 102 not out from 99 balls in Brisbane, and 27 off one over in Perth.

Getty Images

Australia's limited-overs team had a new leader in Ricky Ponting after Australia failed in the VB triangular series against New Zealand and South Africa. Here he takes runs with a square cut against South Africa.

Getty Images

QUEENSLAND CHAMPIONS

Getty Images

After a seemingly permanent drought, Queensland continued to dominate the Pura Cup competition, taking their third successive victory. Here the scene is set at the magnificent Brisbane Cricket Ground at Woolloongabba, with its reconstruction phase complete.

Getty Images

The Pura Cup-winning Queensland players in their victory pose after defeating Tasmania.

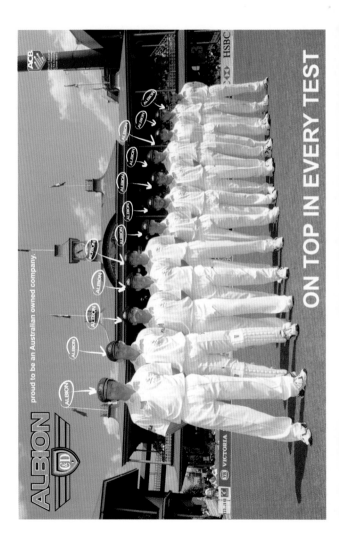

WISDEN AUSTRALIA
PURA CUP CRICKETER OF THE YEAR

JIMMY MAHER

By ANDREW DAWSON

Of the 1,721 runs Queensland opener Jimmy Maher scored last season, a relatively paltry 37 in a limited-overs match at the Adelaide Oval probably sums up his coming of age as a batsman. In Pura Cup cricket, Maher had scored 209 against South Australia in Brisbane, 198 against New South Wales in Sydney, 174 against Western Australia in Perth and 96 against Victoria at Punt Road. Yet this little 39-ball cameo in an ING Cup match against South Australia, watched intently by Australian chairman of selectors Trevor Hohns, said everything about Maher's batting evolution.

In short, 20 of Maher's 37 runs were gloriously gathered with drives that ran either side of the stumps at the non-striker's end. With dead-still stance, and leaning slightly forward into the delivery, Maher had perfected an ability to play straighter than at any other time during his career. Gone was the high-risk tendency to flick the ball across the line of his body. Instead, straight balls were played back down the pitch, more often than not just beyond the fingernails of a flustered bowler, and beyond the grasp of either a mid-on or mid-off fieldsman.

During the off-season of 2000 Maher, in consultation with Queensland's Pura Cup-winning coach Bennett King, had tirelessly addressed his shortcomings. Queensland had won the Pura Cup, but did it with limited contributions from Maher, who averaged an alarming 25.93. "He realised he had a problem and he wanted to do something about it," said former Test No. 3 Dean Jones, who has a soft spot for Maher. "He spoke to me and AB [Allan Border] to work it out. I told him the best players in the world play straight. I told him, 'Keep trying to whip it backward of square and you will average 32.'"

The result was instant. Maher started the 2000-01 season by amassing 175 against Western Australia in Perth, and his batting in the first-class arena has not missed a beat since then. When his outstanding start to that summer demanded his inclusion in the Australia A side to confront the West Indians in Hobart, Maher responded with 150 and 46.

The Australian selectors took note, but more was required. He finished the 2000-01 summer with 1,142 runs at 63.44, then enjoyed the English summer to the tune of 1,133 runs at 53.95 playing county cricket for Glamorgan. Woven through his first-class deeds was a continuation of his supreme domestic limited-overs form which, over 61 matches, has yielded 2,434 runs at an average of 46.80. When the Australian selectors knocked again on Maher's door, this time in January 2002, looking to build an Australia A side to confront South Africa and New Zealand in limited-overs matches, Maher gained a second chance. He scored 42 against the Kiwis and then 94 against South Africa in Adelaide. One suspects Maher's performance in a run-chase against the Proteas was the one which provided him with a down payment on Australian selection.

Before the searching eyes of Australia A coach Allan Border, Maher produced under pressure, under lights. As a result, when the Australian selectors decided it was time to cull Mark Waugh from the national limited-overs outfit, Maher had positioned himself at the head of the queue. "I am totally overcome with emotion," Maher said on the day he was recalled to the Australian side after dipping his toe unsuccessfully in the swirling waters of international cricket for two matches in 1997-98.

Border's role in voting Maher onto the Australian side was an ultimate forgiveness for Maher's unforgettable performance in his first-ever match for the state against Tasmania in 1993. Without facing a ball, Maher managed to run out Border, the Australian captain. Border drove into the covers and Maher set off from the non-striker's end as if the sound of ball on bat was akin to a starter's gun in an Olympic sprint final. Maher, the startled hare, was safe, but Border was hopelessly stranded. Maher recalls: "I'll never forget David Boon laughing his head off. He said: 'What a way to start off your career, running out AB.'" Maher finished on 24 not out, and as he walked back to the dressing room with butterflies swirling in his stomach he thought: "Oh no. I've run out AB and I'm going back to face him." However, rather than berate the apologetic teenager, Border walked up to him and offered encouragement.

Border was Maher's hero and the Australian Test great remains his cricket idol. Border once said to Maher: "Never take anything for granted." And when Maher led Queensland onto the famous Adelaide Oval as captain and a 100-game player last season, he vowed it would be a moment he would never forget. Maher wears his heart on his sleeve, and said: "This milestone means a lot because I love everything about playing for Queensland. I love the look of the maroon cap on my head."

Maher is the "Babinda Boy", Babinda being a town south of Cairns, where summer raindrops appear the size of a bucket. Locals live with crocodiles, snakes, cane fires, floods and more rain. One day when Maher was a boy he crossed the Mulgrave River to play cricket but by the time stumps were called just after midday, the muddy river had burst its banks and he was stranded with relatives for several days. Maher, originally from Cairns and then from Babinda, finished his schooling at Brisbane's Nudgee College, arguably the most successful rugby union breeding ground in Queensland. Yet Maher and Australian team-mate Nathan Hauritz, along with young state players Brendan Nash and Scott Brant, have given the school an almost instant cricketing tradition as well.

Maher and his former Australian Under-19s team-mate Martin Love have been Queensland's lucky charms. They have been playing with or against each other since they were 12 years old, and together have seen the northerners bury the ghosts of failed Sheffield Shield campaigns which stretched back to the 1920s. Since Maher and Love entered the first-class ranks in 1993-94, Queensland have won five titles. When they won their first-ever Shield in 1994-95, Maher remarked in typical fashion, "I am as happy as a fat spider."

Maher has a stump from each of the first four triumphs, and is aiming for a set of six stumps so his children can have "one hell of a game of backyard cricket". His love of his state is such that when he was selected to play for Australia, part of him was disappointed he would miss out on helping Queensland win their third successive first-class title. At that time if you had given Maher one wish, it would have been that he be in two places at once. During the final against Tasmania he nearly drove the Queensland dressing room mad with phone calls from South Africa. At one stage he instructed coach Bennett King to ring and wake him in the South African night every hour, on the hour, to give him progressive scores.

Part of Queensland's success has been built on passion and belief. Ability has played an enormous role as well, but self-belief and passion have also been instilled in the team. Front and centre was

Matthew Hayden, who refused to be intimidated by opponents, even in the pre-Sheffield Shield-winning days. Significantly, early in his career, Maher formed cricket's odd couple with Hayden. The pair lived together, the smoking, beer-drinking Maher contrasting sharply to the clean-living Hayden, who treated his body like a temple.

They are both country boys, born to an ethic of hard work, but have different personalities. Hayden never has his mobile phone on and likes to retreat from the outside world, spending a lot of time at either Moreton or Stradbroke Islands, just offshore from Brisbane. In contrast, Maher can generally be contacted and loves the feeling of his friends being able to talk with him. However, the pair laugh together, sometimes fish together and, during off-season, have tramped through North Queensland together. They have developed a bond which is apparent every time they bat together. When Maher was married last year, he asked Hayden to be his best man.

The imposing Hayden, tall, with broad shoulders and straight drive as powerful as any batsman in world cricket, gave Maher confidence. There were times when Maher would jump into Hayden's slipstream and benefit from Hayden's demolition of opposition attacks. Now Maher stands firmly on his own two feet, an international player in his own right. His match-winning 96 against South Africa early in the year, and then a nerveless, unbeaten 40-odd to enable Australia to tie against the Proteas, are compelling evidence that Maher has come of age. He was Player of the Match in both games.

He has grown in maturity, aided by his loving wife and confidante Debbie, who was a rock when Maher needed comforting prior to his elevation to one of the country's elite batsmen. It said everything about Maher's new-found responsibility that he could find no comfort in scoring a double-century during a loss to South Australia at the Gabba in January. He followed the late Peter Burge, who said his one sporting regret was that his state-record 283 against New South Wales was in a losing side. Not even a message from his father, Warren, in North Queensland, during the tea break could give Maher the strength to carry his bat through the last session and guide the side to a draw. "No matter what score you are on, you are accountable for each ball you face," Maher said after a tired cover drive led to his dismissal. "I had to bat for another 30 minutes. Scoring 200 is fine, but the fact is I was in control and I got out."

That comment sums up Maher's ruthless approach. Gone is the batsman who would effortlessly reach scores of between 25 and 70, only to spray his bat across the line and end up bowled or leg-before. In his place is a run machine who was as disappointed to be dismissed for 198 in his last game of the season for Queensland against New South Wales, as he was for 96 in his first at Punt Road against Victoria. However, the happy-go-lucky character has remained, a chirpy voice in the corner whether the team has had a good day or a bad day. Attending Maher's wedding was like winning a ticket to a comedy club. Joke after joke, gag after gag, ricocheted between Maher and the master of ceremonies, Scott Thompson. Indeed his sprightly personality was part of the appeal to the Australian selectors looking for more energy in the dressing room of the limited-overs outfit.

When he first played for his country in 1997-98 against New Zealand, Maher was a shock choice picked from outside the "system". Overcome by the occasion, he scored just eight and 13. Unlike in his second coming as an international batsman in South Africa early this year, an uncertain Maher never looked as if he belonged on the international stage. He said he played his innings in his head before he actually went out to bat.

Several years on, Maher has forced his way in through consistency in both forms of the game. He is more mature both as a person and a batsman, knowing his limitations and his strengths. Such maturity has been noted by the state selectors, who recommended Maher be named Queensland captain for the 2002-03 season. The Queensland board accepted their recommendation despite the claims of Hayden, Love and Wade Seccombe. "It is not going to be the Jimmy Maher run show. I am the sort of person that will listen to a lot of people's ideas, whether they have played one game or 100 games," Maher said. His appointment is as much for the future as it is for next season, because he is seen as the perfect link between the elite players and emerging players like Nathan Hauritz, James Hopes and Mitchell Johnson. Maher's captaincy of a young and inexperienced side in February, when Queensland defeated South Australia in Adelaide in the last few minutes of play, was noted by the state selectors. Just as he earned Australian selection and captaincy through hard work, he also earned his award as *Wisden Australia* Pura Cup Cricketer of the Year.

CAN THE AUSTRALIAN EMPIRE LAST?

By GREG BAUM

Australian cricket can be compared with a great empire, like those of the Romans, Moghuls and Ottomans, ruling almost all the known world. The comparison holds down to the detail of a pocket of resistance, India, that heroically refuses to bend to Australia's sovereignty. The Australian dynasty has its roots in the dark ages following the simultaneous retirements of Greg Chappell, Dennis Lillee and Rod Marsh at the end of 1983-84. To those who lived through it, that time seemed interminable. In fact, the worst was over by the time of the 1987-88 World Cup, and from the signal Ashes tour of 1989 Australia rose irresistibly to become the paramount force in the game. Compare this history with that of England, which cannot claim to have been the best team in the world since the 1960s, and whose own dark ages began with that 1989 Ashes humiliation and are running still. That is a galvanising thought.

The Australian empire, far from waning, looks to be at its zenith. Australia is detested for its might, but like the greatest fiefdoms is also envied and imitated – if not quite as obsequiously as was Don Bradman by the 1947-48 Indian team, who felt honoured and proud to have him score his 100th century against them. Colonising powers have this contradictory effect. Now every country has an academy or is creating one, and squads of elite players, and codes of behaviour, and is looking to establish more competitive domestic competitions from which will emerge more competitive Test teams. England have introduced numbered shirts and caps for Test players in the very image of Australia.

Twenty years ago, English county clubs wanted only West Indians, but now Australians are in hot demand. They sign up Australians whenever and however they can get them. This most recent northern summer Gloucestershire called in Jo Angel at short notice at the age of 34 for a three-week locum. Australians are also in demand as coaches and administrators. This is an empire with tentacles everywhere.

Steve Waugh is Australia's last link with its subjugated past. He is the last Australian cricketer of a generation driven not primarily by striving for perfection, but by the horror and loathing of constant defeat and the desperation not to relive it. It became a motivating force that would not slacken until the world was brought to heel. Waugh's passing from the game, when it comes, will be a watershed to compare with 1983-84. Will the end of his era also be the end of the empire? Will it be overrun, crumble or – historically the most likely – fall because of dissent, apathy or sloth within? Mark Waugh, Shane Warne and Glenn McGrath must also finish in the near future, on their own terms or others'. Will that destabilise Australia? Will all be lost when this current great team has had its day?

The probable answer is no. For a start, these elder statesmen understand as well as everyone else that their time is coming. In a previous, less professional era, the Waughs might have gone already to day jobs, family and Saturdays at the racetrack. Now that it is as much a matter of livelihood as lifestyle, they cannot be so blithe.

The selectors grasped this long ago. Since dropping Dean Jones in 1992, they eased a player a year out of the Test team, at least until Mark Waugh thwarted their best-laid plans by playing too well two summers ago. The process has been calculated, sustained and mostly unwavering; Australia will not be caught again as it was in 1983-84. The selectors have brought in new players regularly, persevered with some, discarded others, recycled occasionally and kept the side fresh. They have been careful not to confuse stability with stagnation. Now they have a pool of experienced and capable players to provide for a smooth succession, at least in the short term.

Some of the changes have prompted a wringing of hands and a "woe is us" from the cricket public. Remember the apprehension when Allan Border was dumped for Mark Taylor as captain, and then when Taylor was stood aside for Steve Waugh? But the players themselves are the least sentimental about the turnover; professionalism has seen to that. Typically, there is a minute's sombreness for the departed one, and then it is on with the show. A new loyalty applies, observable also in football, belonging to the moment rather than the institution. Border was reluctant to go into the media upon his retirement because he did not want to put himself in the position of paid critic of long-time team-mates. Now newly retired players fall over one another in their efforts to get to the microphone. They swap one loyalty for another. The team goes on, greater always than the sum of its parts.

Taylor's belief that he was worth an extra player to the team because of his inspired captaincy was an understandable conceit, but was quickly debunked upon his retirement. Waugh as captain has always said publicly that the team of the moment was the best team for the job. The point was made more bluntly than even he would have cared for when he was stood aside for Ricky Ponting for the limited-overs series in South Africa early in 2002, and Australia's progress did not miss a beat.

The Australian team has kept itself invigorated by other types of striving. Since major sport was subsumed into the entertainment industry, it has been judged by high and harsh standards. Victory of itself, unaccompanied by flair, is not enough. The Australians, recognising this, have sought not merely to dominate, but to play in a spectacular style. There can have been few cricketers in history as watchable as Warne, Mark Waugh or Adam Gilchrist. Together, they have set new standards for the way cricket ought to be played. Gilchrist made the fastest double-century in Test cricket early in 2002, only for New Zealand's Nathan Astle to trump him with an astonishing rearguard action against England a week later. Run-a-minute is now the rule, not the exception.

The Australians do not have the look of a team content to rest on its laurels. The Australian cricket establishment has not fallen for the empire's trap of sitting on its hands. As it has led the change in cricketing times, so it has adapted to them. The board was modernised under Malcolm Speed, the administration professionalised and – not before a bitter battle – the players empowered. James Sutherland, the new chief executive, has a demeanour that suggests he would rather drop a line over the side of the boat than rock it, but this is a time of consolidation rather than reformation. As a former fast bowler, he also knows that, much as anyone would like to send the stumps cartwheeling, sometimes it is important to nag away on a line and length.

The academy, that fundament of success, has been broadened and regionalised. New frontiers are being established in the north. The interstate competition functions more than ever as a feeder for the Test team rather than as its own entity. The inevitable corollary is that there has never been less interest in or fuss about the competition's intrinsic worth. None the less, it remains the cornerstone of Australia's success, for in no other country is the path from the park to the Test team as clear and logical for those who are good enough to make the journey.

Principles are observed, but sacred cows no longer honoured. David Hookes, having long advocated that the states divide up a virtual pool of likeliest Test players, suddenly found himself as coach of Victoria, once the most parochially proud of all the states. You can be sure that the next Gilchrist will not have to wait five years and move the width of the country just to get into first-class cricket, for you can be sure that the next Phil Emery will not be allowed to detain him. Sentimentality is a thing of the past.

Australia can never be too careful. The truth about empires is that even the greatest, no matter how invulnerable and eternal they seem, fall eventually. Australia's vigil cannot be relaxed. Rod Marsh, as he left to coach in England, said bowlers were still plentiful in Australian junior ranks, but warned that batting stocks were thinning alarmingly.

Cricket's battle with the several football codes, but especially Australian rules, for the hearts and minds of the young grows ever harder to win. Football offers more opportunities and more money, sooner, to more players. Appeals to juniors on the grounds that cricket is a nobler game played on a bigger stage will fall on deaf ears, for as we have already observed, only dollars make sense now. Three players picked in Victoria's Under-17s team two years ago had given the game away by the next year to pursue flourishing football careers; they are unlikely to be seen in creams again. Cricket will not be able to withstand this recruiting imbalance forever. Again, it is instructive to look at England, where soccer has overwhelmed all sensibilities. In Manchester, the two Old Traffords lie a kilometre apart, the football ground a gleaming palace and shrine, the cricket ground host to a thousand memories, but careworn, old and cold.

The place of cricket and cricketers in our culture has changed. We see, hear and know far more about our summer heroes than ever before, and that familiarity breeds, if not contempt, then a lesser mystique. Close up, a coarseness can sometimes be seen and heard that is far from endearing. None of this has turned Australians away from the game. Crowds for international matches remain healthy, television ratings high, the Cricket Board wealthy and the levels of junior participation consistently strong. The Australian team is still the talk of the country in summer and when on tour, for Australians have a famously inexhaustible appetite for winners and winning.

Thus, warts and all, is the empire propagated from one generation to the next.

The threat from without is muted. South Africa's progress has slowed because of complicated and delicate internal politics. England is marshalling its resources and determination, but is yet to recover from the withering of the game in the schools, previously its strength. The West Indians ruled for 20 years until the introduction of laws to proscribe the intimidatory power of their fast bowling, which at length exposed the flimsiness of their coalition. Now they look a rabble. The countries of the subcontinent, though all capable of stunning periodic feats, do not seem able to mount a concerted attack on Australia's ascendancy. The others cannot compete for scale.

The most industrious force working against Australia just now is the International Cricket Council. It is not ICC policy to see Australia brought low, but it is part of the ICC's philosophy to see wider and more even competition. Australia's domination is antithetical. It is instructive that the ICC's two most senior figures are Australians who helped to create the empire and whose best interests now lie in curbing its power. One maintains privately that there could be no greater fillip for cricket just now than the toppling of Australia.

But the gravest danger to Australia, as to all empires, is from itself. Steve Waugh said upon arriving for a short stint with Kent recently that he wanted to use the chance to remind himself of what had so drawn him to cricket when he was a child. He wanted to remember the game's essential beauty. Implicitly and subconsciously, his words were a warning about the stifling and suffocating effect professionalism can have on even the purest sporting soul. They ought not to be dismissed lightly.

More than at any previous time in history, the best players are piling up the spoils. At the time of writing, Australia's leading cricketers were battling the ICC over their lucrative personal endorsements, a battle that was threatening the approaching World Cup. The players' concern with their income streams was not new, nor restricted to Australia, and in any case hardly constituted Romans lying about on beds being fed grapes by their servants while the Visigoths and Vandals rattle and howl at the gates. But at the same time as this battle was being fought, outspoken Manchester United captain Roy Keane said his famous club had not won trophies last season because its players had been more preoccupied with their Rolex watches, big houses and fast cars than with the sweat and toil that had brought them these fruits in the first place. Australia must beware, for a decline, once started, is desperately hard to arrest. The bottom and the past are murky places, and Australia still has Steve Waugh to say that it does not want to go there.

PURLEWAUGH'S FIFTH STRAIGHT PREMIERSHIP

In 2001-02, Purlewaugh Cricket Club won a record fifth consecutive premiership in the Coonabarabran District Cricket Association competition in north-western New South Wales. Purlewaugh is a farming community 25 kilometres east of Coonabarabran, a town of 3,000, which nestles in the foothills of the Warrumbungle Ranges, home to the Siding Spring Observatory. Once possessing a school, general store and post office/telephone exchange, Purlewaugh has been all but wiped out by economic change, except for its community hall and the cricket ground, a kilometre along the road towards Long Ridge. The cricket club has a continuous history since its formation in 1922 under the captaincy of George Border, whose great-nephew, Allan, was to make his mark in Australian cricket. Until the formation of the Coonabarabran association in the mid-1950s, Purlewaugh's cricket consisted mainly of contesting the local examples of the challenge cups which were the staple of country cricket in those days. The current captain, David Sullivan, is the third generation of his family to lead the side: his father, Ron, and grandfather, Tom, were both successful captains and leading batsmen of their time. The previous record number of successive wins in the Coonabarabran competition was three, achieved twice by the Merrygoen club, which has since folded. – WARWICK FRANKS.

THE BOYDS OF POMBORNEIT

Mark Boyd continued a remarkable family tradition when he captured five wickets with the first five balls of his fifth over for Pomborneit against Simpson in Victoria's South West Association's A-Grade competition in February 2002. Simpson were dismissed for 78 with Boyd taking 7/14, having been promoted that week from the seconds. His grandfather, Geoff, 81, was among the small crowd present to witness the rare feat. In his own career he took six hat-tricks, including four in seven games for Pomborneit in the Timboon–Stonyford Cricket Association in 1939, a feat which prompted a letter of congratulation from Don Bradman. Four generations of Boyds have been closely involved in cricket at Pomborneit, situated in the Stony Rises, east of Camperdown. Seven of them are life members. Geoff's son Brian has played more than 700 senior games, made almost 10,000 runs and taken 1,000 wickets over a 43-year period. He says his proudest moment was playing in the same Pomborneit team as his four sons, Rodney, Stuart, Mark and Craig. His brother Ian also played that day. "All of us are very grateful for the opportunities the club has offered us over the years," he said. "If it hadn't had such a stable administration we may have folded like a lot of other clubs." – KEN PIESSE

PART TWO: THE PLAYERS

INDEX TO PLAYER PROFILES

The players listed in this section are those who participated in first-class and/or domestic limited-overs competitions during the 2001-02 season.

First-class cricket is defined in accordance with Regulations of the International Cricket Council 2.1, 2.2 and 2.3. It includes Test matches, three or four-day matches played by Australia against first-class sides while on tour, four-day matches between touring international teams and the states, four-day matches between touring international teams and Australian Elevens, four-day matches between the states for the Sheffield Shield or the Pura Cup, and some games played by the AIS Cricket Academy that fulfill the ICC's definitions.

International limited-overs cricket is defined in accordance with the Regulations of the International Cricket Council.

Domestic first-class cricket refers to matches between the states for either the Sheffield Shield or the Pura Cup.

Domestic limited-overs cricket refers to matches between the states for the ING Cup or any earlier equivalent competition.

PLAYER PROFILES

The players listed in this section are all Australian players who participated in the 2001-02 season.

Note: First-class statistics and limited-overs international statistics are current to June 30, 2002.

* Denotes not out.

NEW SOUTH WALES
By Phil Wilkins

BEVAN, Michael Gwyl
Born: May 8, 1970 Belconnen (Australian Capital Territory)
Left-handed batsman, left-arm slow 'chinaman' bowler

To emphasise his prodigious talents yet again, Bevan sculpted the 50th first-class century of his career on the Sydney Cricket Ground in New South Wales' initial game of the Pura Cup against Tasmania. He also hit two further Pura Cup centuries, against Victoria and a match-saving 203 not out against Western Australia at the SCG, and then an unbeaten 183 against the touring South Africans. Bevan eclipsed former Test batsman Alan Kippax's New South Wales 8,005-run record aggregate during the season and automatically moved into Australia's limited-overs side for the VB Series. Against New Zealand in Melbourne, Bevan manufactured a miracle. With his team apparently fatally stricken at six for 82 in pursuit of 246, Bevan made 102 not out from 95 balls to create a two-wicket victory. Australia failed to reach the finals, but the performance reminded all of his rare temperament and rich talent. In eight first-class games for New South Wales, he made 868 runs at 72.33.

	M	I	NO	R	HS	100s	50s	Avge	Ct	St	W	Avge	BB
First-class	203	340	61	15,858	203*	55	69	56.84	110	0	115	44.74	6/82
Dom. first-class	91	162	31	7,549	203*	29	32	57.63	42	0	21	64.10	3/40
Test	18	30	3	785	91	0	6	29.07	8	0	29	24.24	6/82
Int'l limited-overs	178	156	53	5,751	108*	6	38	55.83	57	0	36	45.97	3/36
Dom. limited-overs	54	54	19	2,146	135*	1	19	61.31	14	0	5	38.80	2/24

BRACKEN, Nathan Wayne
Born: September 12, 1977 Penrith (New South Wales)
Right-handed batsman, left-arm fast-medium bowler

This was not the season of advancement and acclaim which had been expected for the 2000-01 Sir Donald Bradman Young Cricketer of the Year. Missing New South Wales' first three games through injury, Bracken immediately brought himself to the selectors' attention with 11 wickets in Pura Cup games against Tasmania and South Australia. He played with distinction in New South Wales' ING Cup team as it retained the limited-overs trophy, capturing a hat-trick against Victoria. Bracken also bowled well with Jason Gillespie for the Australia A team in its defeats of both touring teams, but his first-class performances began to cause concern and puzzlement for his lack of sustained endeavour. The national selectors ignored him for the VB Series and the tour of South Africa and though Bracken was again included in the contracted list and the Australia A team to South Africa, he must show more resilience in the four-day game or be overlooked as a Test candidate.

	M	I	NO	R	HS	100s	50s	Avge	Ct	St	W	Avge	BB
First-class	22	33	15	247	38	0	0	13.72	8	0	69	27.70	5/22
Dom. first-class	21	31	13	237	38	0	0	13.17	7	0	64	28.91	5/22
Int'l limited-overs	9	0	0	0	–	0	0	–	2	0	10	30.30	2/21
Dom. limited-overs	23	7	1	30	9	0	0	5.00	6	0	34	24.35	5/38

BRADSTREET, Shawn David
Born: February 28, 1972 Wollongong (New South Wales)
Right-handed batsman, right-arm medium bowler

All but discarded by the New South Wales selectors as a first-class player, the tough, dedicated all-rounder enjoyed his finest moment at the Gabba after bringing Queensland's innings to a dramatic end in the ING Cup final with 4/6 from 13 deliveries of accurate, probing medium-pacers, justifying the selectors' high regard for his competitive limited-overs cricket. Bradstreet is well thought of as a shrewd captain, but has been unable to convince the selectors of his all-round value for the Pura Cup, having failed to register a century or five-wicket performance in four seasons of first-class cricket. He made a solitary first-class appearance against the touring South Africans without compelling a change of opinion.

	M	I	NO	R	HS	100s	50s	Avge	Ct	St	W	Avge	BB
First-class	8	15	3	253	60	0	1	21.08	6	0	12	57.08	2/32
Dom. first-class	7	14	3	238	60	0	1	21.64	6	0	11	46.82	2/32
Dom. limited-overs	29	23	10	389	75*	0	1	29.92	6	0	23	34.87	4/23

CLARK, Anthony Michael
Born: March 23, 1977 St Leonards (New South Wales)
Right-handed batsman, right-arm off-spin bowler
Domestic limited-overs debut 2001-02

Clark's encouraging start to his first-class career in 2000-01 ground to a disappointing halt during the season with New South Wales' selectors eventually preferring Dale Turner as Stuart MacGill's slow bowling partner. Clark was relegated to the state Second XI after an early-season appearance against Victoria in a Pura Cup match at Richmond, a game in which he bowled just seven wicketless overs. He enjoyed greater success at the SCG in mid-December, taking a career-best 4/130 from 36 overs against Western Australia, but then bowled only one more over for New South Wales for the season in an ING Cup game in Melbourne. Clark contributed significantly to Fairfield–Liverpool club's initial Belvidere Cup premiership. His career should rise again after this season of setbacks.

	M	I	NO	R	HS	100s	50s	Avge	Ct	St	W	Avge	BB
First-class	6	6	1	71	24	0	0	14.20	3	0	10	43.70	4/130
Dom. first-class	6	6	1	71	24	0	0	14.20	3	0	10	43.70	4/130
Dom. limited-overs	1	1	1	3	3*	0	0	–	0	0	0	–	–

CLARK, Stuart Rupert
Born: September 28, 1975 Caringbah (New South Wales)
Right-handed batsman, right-arm fast-medium bowler

New South Wales' Player of the Year was a slow developer. For years the selectors had expected much from the tall pace man, and this season, from the first ING Cup game, Clark's bowling developed from its customary clinical precision and placement to a genuine weapon of aggression and threat as he maintained pace and movement off the seam and through the air. Never a tearaway, Clark had a sufficiently sharp edge to his bowling and enough bounce to keep batsmen on the defensive. Two respectable ING Cup games at Bankstown Oval began his season and then, with Brett Lee out injured, Clark claimed his first five-wicket innings haul. His 5/64 from 32 overs against

Tasmania was all the more significant for he outshone Sutherland club team-mate Glenn McGrath. With McGrath, Lee and Nathan Bracken available for the Pura Cup match against South Australia, Clark was made twelfth man but did not miss out again. Claiming six wickets in the Pura Cup defeat of Victoria at Richmond, he became a model of consistency and menace, a bowler to whom his captain could always turn for an important breakthrough. Six times in nine first-class matches, Clark took four wickets or more in an innings, finishing with 45 wickets at 23.27. He was a front-line bowler throughout New South Wales' successful ING Cup campaign, and deservedly won an ACB contract at the end of the season.

	M	I	NO	R	HS	100s	50s	Avge	Ct	St	W	Avge	BB
First-class	19	31	9	235	31*	0	0	10.68	5	0	59	33.92	5/42
Dom. first-class	19	31	9	235	31*	0	0	10.68	5	0	59	33.92	5/42
Dom. limited-overs	33	6	3	27	11	0	0	9.00	6	0	36	30.42	4/26

CLARKE, Michael John
Born: April 2, 1981 Liverpool (New South Wales)
Right-handed batsman, left-arm orthodox bowler

The time is fast approaching when Michael Clarke will explode across the Australian cricketing landscape. The Australian selectors may have done him a favour by excluding him from the end-of-season tour to South Africa, adding new incentive to his ambitions. Approaching his third season for New South Wales and now established as the team's number four batsman, his glittering driving and brilliant throwing from the deep could twist the selectors' arms for national recognition, perhaps for Australia's defence of the World Cup in South Africa. That he is under consideration is shown by his selection for the Australia A limited-overs tour of South Africa. Clarke grabbed his chance in the absence of the Waugh brothers to post his second first-class century against Victoria. He was tried as an opening batsman midway through the ING Cup, but it was at number four that he made his match-winning 132-ball century against Western Australia, his first in the domestic limited-overs competition. A Pura Cup hundred in Adelaide added lustre to his reputation without being able to stave off outright defeat. Clarke has the hallmarks of an international, but must strive for even greater consistency. His left arm orthodox spinners were infrequently used, but as first change for New South Wales in the ING Cup match against Tasmania he claimed three quick wickets. He might well have been bowled more advantageously.

	M	I	NO	R	HS	100s	50s	Avge	Ct	St	W	Avge	BB
First-class	21	40	2	1,245	132	3	6	32.76	16	0	3	42.33	2/25
Dom. first-class	19	36	1	1,183	132	3	6	33.80	15	0	3	40.67	2/25
Dom. limited-overs	15	13	2	377	101*	1	3	34.27	5	0	3	21.33	3/57

HADDIN, Bradley James
Born: October 23, 1977 Cowra (New South Wales)
Right-handed batsman, wicket-keeper

This proved a season of acute frustration for Haddin, whatever his accomplishments. He started the ING Cup with a phenomenal 74-ball century against Tasmania at Bankstown Oval, a record for the domestic limited-overs competition, but scored only two more half-centuries in eight games of the competition. The Australian selectors' decision to bypass him for the Western Australian Ryan Campbell as Adam Gilchrist's national understudy for the Australia A team's games against New Zealand and South Africa proved a devastating blow. Haddin has never lacked ambition or dedication and he continued to toil in the nets with New South Wales' coach, former Test wicket-keeper Steve Rixon. His batting at number seven in the Pura Cup was often exceptional, the purity of his driving and pulling as attractive to watch as that by any batsman in Australia. In ten first-class matches, he had six innings over 40 as well as registering his maiden first-class hundred against Queensland. Wicket-keepers invariably perform better as they mature. Haddin surely falls into that category.

	M	I	NO	R	HS	100s	50s	Avge	Ct	St	W	Avge	BB
First-class	31	56	4	1,587	102	1	12	30.52	77	7	0	–	–
Dom. first-class	27	50	3	1,415	102	1	11	30.11	67	5	0	–	–
Int'l limited-overs	1	1	0	13	13	0	0	13.00	0	1	0	–	–
Dom. limited-overs	35	35	0	1,152	133	2	9	32.91	48	15	0	–	–

HEATH, Jamie Matthew
Born: April 25, 1977 Belmont (New South Wales)
Right-handed batsman, right-arm fast bowler

The tall, gaunt pace bowler began the season so encouragingly, maintaining his pace and accuracy for Manly–Warringah and the New South Wales Second XI that he came into reckoning for a state position. However, Stuart Clark suddenly developed into the essential member of the state attack and although the overall performances of Nathan Bracken and Don Nash deteriorated, so, regrettably, did those of Heath. He played against the South Africans at the SCG when Clark was rested, and bowled sufficiently well to claim 3/72 in the tourists' first innings from 23 overs without persuading the selectors to call on him again.

	M	I	NO	R	HS	100s	50s	Avge	Ct	St	W	Avge	BB
First-class	6	10	5	38	15	0	0	7.60	4	0	13	45.54	3/37
Dom. first-class	5	10	5	38	15	0	0	7.60	3	0	10	48.10	3/37

HIGGS, Mark Anthony
Born: June 30, 1976 Queanbeyan (New South Wales)
Left-handed batsman, left-arm slow 'chinaman' bowler

An intensely disappointing season for a player of exceptional talent ended with Higgs being dropped by New South Wales only two months after representing Australia A. It has been apparent for two seasons that Higgs' variations of spin bowling, essentially orthodox but occasionally over-the-wrist, were proving a major distraction. When his bowling was expensive, it threw more pressure on him to succeed in batting. When his batting failed, it created more tension in his bowling. His superb unbeaten 63 from just 39 deliveries against Queensland in the ING Cup in Sydney was evidence of his strike-power. It was the fastest half-century of the competition and ensured New South Wales victory. Despite opportunities, Higgs failed to provide selectors with enough convincing innings or sufficient wickets to justify his retention, although he managed to remain a member of the limited-overs team long enough to take part in the ING Cup final victory at the Gabba. In the off season he moved to South Australia, and was later selected in the Australia A limited-overs team to South Africa.

	M	I	NO	R	HS	100s	50s	Avge	Ct	St	W	Avge	BB
First-class	22	36	4	974	181*	1	4	30.44	14	0	16	64.88	3/59
Dom. first-class	21	35	4	951	181*	1	4	30.68	13	0	14	66.57	3/59
Dom. limited-overs	34	30	5	722	77	0	3	28.88	18	0	26	25.54	4/15

JAQUES, Philip Anthony
Born: May 3, 1979 Wollongong (New South Wales)
Left-handed batsman

Jaques was another in the battalion of batsmen who failed to grasp an opportunity offered by the state selectors. Having performed splendidly in an emergency in the final 2000-01 Pura Cup game, he looked likely to receive early opportunities in the new season. In fact, Jaques remained out of the front line until the end of the Pura Cup competition again, when he was chosen for the match against Tasmania at Bellerive in Hobart, only to make a duck and 23. He is a batsman well-regarded among his peers, and has the time and talent to show the selectors he deserves a longer trial.

	M	I	NO	R	HS	100s	50s	Avge	Ct	St	W	Avge	BB
First-class	2	4	0	86	40	0	0	21.50	2	0	0	–	–
Dom. first-class	2	4	0	86	40	0	0	21.50	2	0	0	–	–
Dom. limited-overs	2	2	0	59	40	0	0	29.50	0	0	0	–	–

LAMBERT, Grant Michael
Born: August 5, 1977 Parramatta (New South Wales)
Right-handed batsman, right-arm fast-medium bowler
First-class, domestic first-class and domestic limited-overs
debut 2001-02

Persistence and consistency eventually paid off for the strong
Fairfield–Liverpool all-rounder. Having won the Bill O'Reilly
Medal as the best player of the Sydney competition two years
previously, Lambert became a regular member of the New South
Wales Second XI. He gradually overcame a perception that he was
not sufficiently dynamic as either new-ball bowler or middle-order
batsman to become the bowling all-rounder and fourth pace man in an attack of Stuart
Clark, Don Nash and Nathan Bracken for the Pura Cup game against Western Australia
in Perth. Earlier in the week, Lambert made his debut in New South Wales' last-over
ING Cup defeat of Western Australia, taking 2/33 from six overs. He had the unexpected
promotion of opening the batting in both Pura Cup innings when Brett Van Deinsen
sustained a back injury. An occasional opener for his club, Lambert made a gritty 29 and
11 and bowled with enough spirit to earn another game in Hobart against Tasmania, this
time in the more suitable batting position of number eight where he made a brave
unbeaten 45 in a failed attempt to stave off defeat.

	M	I	NO	R	HS	100s	50s	Avge	Ct	St	W	Avge	BB
First-class	2	4	1	88	45*	0	0	29.33	0	0	4	41.25	3/86
Dom. first-class	2	4	1	88	45*	0	0	29.33	0	0	4	41.25	3/86
Dom. limited-overs	1	1	1	3	3*	0	0	–	0	0	2	16.50	2/33

LEE, Brett
Born: November 8, 1976 Wollongong (New South Wales)
Right-handed batsman, right-arm fast bowler

Having established himself as part of the Australian pace trident with Glenn McGrath
and Jason Gillespie, Lee was inevitably lost for long periods to New South Wales. The
demands on his physique have been excessive despite adjusting his delivery action to a
more square-on approach to reduce strain on his back and spinal column. Lee missed
New South Wales' first three games due to a side strain, took 5/56 in the second innings
of South Australia's outright loss and returned immediately to the Test team against New
Zealand. He played in all six home Tests of the summer, his venom yielding him 14
wickets in the three-Test series against New Zealand. In the six Tests, he took 23 wickets
at 28.96. Lee was at times a boisterous number nine in Australia's batting order, making
61 from 93 balls against New Zealand in Brisbane and 41 from 55 balls in the Hobart
Test. In an ING Cup game in Adelaide, Lee smashed three sixes and two fours in a
violent innings of 44 not out to win the Man of the Match award. In South Africa, his
lack of accuracy in the limited-overs series caused concern and he appeared in only
three of the seven games.

	M	I	NO	R	HS	100s	50s	Avge	Ct	St	W	Avge	BB
First-class	47	53	11	739	79	0	3	17.60	11	0	192	24.50	6/25
Dom. first-class	14	19	3	177	34	0	0	11.06	6	0	56	25.71	5/42
Test	21	21	5	384	62*	0	2	24.00	3	0	84	26.83	5/47
Int'l limited-overs	39	18	5	206	51*	0	1	15.85	2	0	69	24.67	5/27
Dom. limited-overs	12	4	2	74	44*	0	0	37.00	0	0	17	28.06	3/41

LEE, Shane
Born: August 8, 1973 Wollongong (New South Wales)
Right-handed batsman, right-arm fast-medium bowler

As captain of a team which won the ING Cup and finished last in the Pura Cup, this was a season which Lee would review with much personal dissatisfaction. After a rousing start with a Man of the Match performance of 83 from 93 balls in the ING Cup win over Victoria, Lee sustained an injury to his right knee in December, and was never the same force. He missed seven weeks of mid-summer representative cricket during which period he aggravated the injury, requiring surgery. He returned to lead the team in February, but was unable to bowl for long, even during the ING Cup final. The selectors persisted with him, only for Lee to withdraw before the final Pura Cup match in Hobart. By the season's end, Lee was fortunate to be under consideration at all, having made a single innings higher than 50 and two two-wicket returns. He must regain full fitness or face a bleak future.

	M	I	NO	R	HS	100s	50s	Avge	Ct	St	W	Avge	BB
First-class	91	149	22	4,991	183*	12	24	39.30	74	0	150	40.47	4/20
Dom. first-class	67	113	16	3,391	183*	7	17	34.96	52	0	97	39.88	4/20
Int'l limited-overs	45	35	8	477	49	0	0	17.67	23	0	48	25.94	5/33
Dom. limited-overs	57	51	6	1,405	115	2	7	31.22	30	0	54	31.39	4/59

MacGILL, Stuart Charles Glyndwr
Born: February 25, 1971 Mount Lawley (Western Australia)
Right-handed batsman, right-arm leg-spin bowler

It is a supreme irony that having established himself as one of the three outstanding leg-spinners of international cricket with Shane Warne and Anil Kumble, MacGill has been so seldom able to ply his trade at the highest level. In his only Test for the summer, MacGill took 7/174 from a marathon 65.2 overs against South Africa, bowling in effective tandem with Warne, who took 6/179 from 61.5 overs. MacGill was not required for the VB Series limited-overs games, although he played in both Australia A games against New Zealand and South Africa. He toured South Africa but was again overlooked in the Tests. Typically, MacGill took five wickets when given his opportunity against South Africa A in Port Elizabeth. For the second season in a row he was the leading wicket-taker in the ING Cup, and was one of New South Wales' potent weapons in the successful campaign. His Pura Cup bowling returns, however, were meagre, but as some compensation his unorthodox batting was occasionally very useful, as his first-class figures of 177 runs at 19.66, scored at nearly a run a ball, attest.

	M	I	NO	R	HS	100s	50s	Avge	Ct	St	W	Avge	BB
First-class	69	95	20	729	53	0	1	9.72	40	0	286	29.24	7/29
Dom. first-class	40	60	14	421	53	0	1	9.15	21	0	133	36.07	6/64
Test	17	23	2	228	43	0	0	10.86	12	0	82	25.01	7/50
Int'l limited-overs	3	2	1	1	1	0	0	1.00	2	0	6	17.50	4/19
Dom. limited-overs	30	9	4	44	18	0	0	8.80	8	0	63	20.59	5/40

MAIL, Gregory John
Born: April 29, 1978 Penrith (New South Wales)
Right-handed batsman, wicket-keeper, right-arm medium bowler

New South Wales' selectors were confronted with a number of difficult decisions as the contradictions of the season's competitions mounted, none more so than their omission of Greg Mail. A player of tremendous determination, Mail was predictably ignored for the ING Cup games, but began the Pura Cup with splendid consistency, scoring an unbeaten 150 against South Australia in the second game and having six innings of 40 or better in New South Wales' first five first-class matches, including two half-centuries against South Africa. The selectors' concerns centred on his inability to lift the scoring tempo. Their suspicion that Mail's slow scoring thrust more pressure on his batting partners became a conviction, and when he failed in consecutive games in January, they dropped him. Like Geoffrey Boycott, who was dropped by England for slow scoring and returned triumphant, Mail is capable of a successful return.

	M	I	NO	R	HS	100s	50s	Avge	Ct	St	W	Avge	BB
First-class	24	44	2	1,456	176	2	10	34.67	20	0	1	30.00	1/6
Dom. first-class	22	40	2	1,302	176	2	8	34.26	20	0	0	–	–
Dom. limited-overs	3	2	1	29	19*	0	0	29.00	2	1	0	–	–

McGRATH, Glenn Donald
Born: February 9, 1970 Dubbo (New South Wales)
Right-handed batsman, right-arm fast bowler

McGrath remained the finest fast bowler of international cricket, a relentless and scheming craftsman, utilising his pace, bounce and seaming skills to reinforce his reputation as one of the best of all time. If he was not taking wickets, he was exerting pressure for his bowling allies to exploit. He appeared in all six home Tests against New Zealand and South Africa and in seven of the eight VB Series matches, his only absence due to a one-game suspension for dissent. McGrath took 19 Test wickets at an unusually high average of 35.63, his best return being 6/107 against South Africa in Adelaide, but he was clearly Australia's best in the VB Series with 14 wickets at an extraordinary 16.14 average despite the team's elimination from the finals. McGrath was seen in better light in the three Tests in South Africa, his eight-wicket haul in Johannesburg promoting him to 385 Test wickets, the eighth-highest in the game's history. He bowled in New South Wales' first four representative games when clearly eliminating rust from his engine after the tour of England.

	M	I	NO	R	HS	100s	50s	Avge	Ct	St	W	Avge	BB
First-class	143	147	49	717	55	0	1	7.32	39	0	639	20.83	8/38
Dom. first-class	21	21	8	111	26	0	0	8.54	3	0	81	26.74	5/36
Test	84	96	33	411	39	0	0	6.52	25	0	389	21.91	8/38
Int'l limited-overs	156	47	25	88	11	0	0	4.00	18	0	236	23.40	5/14
Dom. limited-overs	18	0	0	0	–	0	0	–	4	0	21	26.71	4/17

NASH, Don Anthony
Born: March 29, 1978 Dubbo (New South Wales)
Right-handed batsman, right-arm fast-medium bowler

The burly fast bowler's inclusion in the Australia A team in 2000-01 soon faded from memory as Nash joined the line of players who failed to respond to New South Wales' needs. Dropped to make way for the side's international trio of pace men for two of the first three Pura Cup games, Nash rarely revealed the genuine speed or killer instinct he had shown in his first two seasons, and took 21 wickets at 43.29 in nine first-class games. There was criticism that Nash, as the fastest bowler, was not automatically given the new ball, but he failed to make the most of an SCG pitch that at times was sufficiently well-grassed to bring out the beast in a fast bowler. Forced to miss three ING Cup matches with injury, he returned in time for the final in Brisbane. His deteriorating confidence was reflected in his slide down to number ten in the batting list, after some fine hitting the previous season had elevated him almost to all-rounder status. A one-game suspension for an on-field confrontation with former New South Wales batsman Richard Chee Quee did not prevent his taking the new ball for Fairfield–Liverpool's initial Sydney club premiership.

	M	I	NO	R	HS	100s	50s	Avge	Ct	St	W	Avge	BB
First-class	27	45	2	469	46	0	0	10.91	4	0	68	35.03	7/54
Dom. first-class	24	42	2	439	46	0	0	10.98	4	0	61	34.16	7/54
Dom. limited-overs	12	7	2	97	61*	0	1	19.40	1	0	12	32.58	3/31

O'BRIEN, Aaron Warren
Born: October 2, 1981 St Leonards (New South Wales)
Left-handed batsman, slow-left arm orthodox bowler
First-class, domestic first-class and domestic limited-overs
debut 2001-02

When Stuart MacGill was called into the Test squad, 20-year-old
Aaron O'Brien was chosen as his state replacement. A Cricket
Academy graduate from Narara Valley on the Central Coast, an
impressive century-maker at club level for Northern District in
Sydney, and a left-arm finger-spinner considered to have a good
future, he had a whirlwind rise through the ranks to become the
spin partner of Anthony Clark against Western Australia. O'Brien had a prolonged
bowling session in the first innings when he delivered 33 overs, developing a nice loop
with an easy action. He batted in the middle order without success and a failure in the
ING Cup in Melbourne in January satisfied the selectors that he needed time to adjust
to representative cricket. O'Brien has received a rookie contract with Cricket New South
Wales for the new season.

	M	I	NO	R	HS	100s	50s	Avge	Ct	St	W	Avge	BB
First-class	1	1	0	6	6	0	0	6.00	0	0	1	134.00	1/134
Dom. first-class	1	1	0	6	6	0	0	6.00	0	0	1	134.00	1/134
Dom. limited-overs	1	1	0	0	0	0	0	0.00	0	0	0	–	–

PHELPS, Matthew James
Born: September 1, 1972 Lismore (New South Wales)
Right-handed batsman

A robust, quiet-natured batsman from the village of Clunes, which produced the great
Sam Trimble, on New South Wales' far North Coast, Phelps is finally justifying the
selectors' long-held expectations. Having broken into first-class cricket in 1998-99
without securing a permanent position in the side, he has continued to score heavily for
Manly–Warringah – strong off his pads, driving and pulling fluently – to fight his way
back into representative contention. Phelps performed impressively in the ACB Cup
competition, contributing significantly to the New South Wales Second XI's overall
success, at one stage captaining the team impressively. With prominent batsmen again
failing, the selectors turned back to Phelps. He batted at number seven in the ING Cup
final and contributed an important, steely 31 from 44 balls. Confidence boosted, he
proceeded to play four resolute Pura Cup innings, his innings of 84 and 65 not out
against Queensland promising more substantial performances ahead and enabling him
to head New South Wales' batting averages with 243 runs at 81. He begins the new
season with the selectors' full confidence to become a senior batsman.

	M	I	NO	R	HS	100s	50s	Avge	Ct	St	W	Avge	BB
First-class	10	20	1	734	192	1	5	38.63	5	0	0	–	–
Dom. first-class	10	20	1	734	192	1	5	38.63	5	0	0	–	–
Dom. limited-overs	7	7	0	91	31	0	0	13.00	2	0	0	–	–

PILON, Nathan Steven
Born: October 27, 1976 Dubbo (New South Wales)
Right-handed batsman, wicket-keeper
Domestic limited-overs debut 2001-02

In every way Pilon resembles a first-class wicket-keeper, few though his opportunities
have been. Thick-set, dependable, with swift hands and possessing the spirit necessary
for long hours in the game's most thankless, most vulnerable position behind the stumps,
he was one of the outstanding performers in the New South Wales Second XI's ACB
Cup win. He also showed he could wield a punishing bat. Of country rugby league

stock, Pilon was called up for the Pura Cup game against South Australia at the SCG when Brad Haddin was sidelined with a chipped thumb, and the selectors had no qualms about turning to him again when Haddin required a pin in his left little finger for the ING Cup game against Tasmania in Devonport. On this occasion, Pilon was promoted to number three, making a tidy 28 and keeping smartly again in the seven-wicket win. New South Wales are fortunate to have an understudy of Pilon's talents and will be even more fortunate if they can retain him.

	M	I	NO	R	HS	100s	50s	Avge	Ct	St	W	Avge	BB
First-class	2	3	0	24	16	0	0	8.00	14	0	0	–	–
Dom. first-class	2	3	0	24	16	0	0	8.00	14	0	0	–	–
Dom. limited-overs	1	1	0	28	28	0	0	28.00	1	0	0	–	–

RICHARDS, Corey John
Born: August 25, 1975 Camden (New South Wales)
Right-handed batsman, right-arm medium bowler

Richards made a splendid resurgence to regain a state position through weight of runs. After consecutive pairs in the Pura Cup in 2000-01, Richards' New South Wales career appeared finished. In mid-October, the neat right-hander gave notice that he was not a spent force with a sweetly-timed 78 from 108 balls for the New South Wales Second XI against a full-strength Tasmanian team in Sydney. His opportunity came when Michael Slater severely sprained an ankle in the nets before New South Wales' match against the South Africans. It was the stepping stone Richards needed. Though he tested the selectors' patience through January, his gradually mounting confidence led to a match-dominating 151 as opener in the ING Cup game in Perth. Richards opened in the ING Cup final at the Gabba with 34 in an 82-run stand with Brad Haddin which propelled the side to victory. Richards and Matthew Phelps then shared an opening partnership of 166 in the Pura Cup match against Queensland, reinforcing the belief that New South Wales have found a reliable opening combination.

	M	I	NO	R	HS	100s	50s	Avge	Ct	St	W	Avge	BB
First-class	50	92	5	2,847	164	7	15	32.72	25	0	0	–	–
Dom. first-class	43	81	3	2,321	164	5	13	29.76	19	0	0	–	–
Dom. limited-overs	39	36	4	1,090	151	2	6	34.06	13	0	0	–	–

RUMMANS, Graeme Clifford
Born: December 13, 1976 Camperdown (New South Wales)
Left-handed batsman, left-arm medium

The career of this rising cricketer was cast into turmoil late in the season when, acting on medical advice, he received treatment for a slow-healing boil on his shoulder only to learn after a random test that he had tested positive to the masking agent probenecid. Following a lengthy ACB hearing in Melbourne, Rummans was fined $2,000 and suspended for one month. In an age of increasing drug menace, it appeared Rummans was made an example in order that other cricketers might be constantly vigilant about medication. The suspension was doubly punishing for Rummans in that it interrupted his representative career just as it was beginning to blossom, and he might well have captained New South Wales in the final Pura Cup match. In January, batting at number five, Rummans made a resolute 73 not out from 107 balls while team-mates fell in disarray in the ING Cup game in Coffs Harbour, and then two half-centuries in Pura Cup games in Sydney and Perth. The masking agent episode ruined what was to be a season of important development for Rummans. During the off season he announced that he was moving to Victoria.

	M	I	NO	R	HS	100s	50s	Avge	Ct	St	W	Avge	BB
First-class	21	34	4	857	119	1	5	28.57	13	0	5	23.80	3/24
Dom. first-class	19	32	4	660	67	0	4	23.57	11	0	2	46.50	2/71
Dom. limited-overs	25	23	3	669	75	0	4	33.45	7	0	0	–	–

SLATER, Michael Jonathon
Born: February 21, 1970 Wagga Wagga (New South Wales)
Right-handed batsman, right-arm bowler

A time of despair for Slater, as his international career closed, his ACB contract was not extended and his representative future with New South Wales was unclear following his omission from both the ING Cup and Pura Cup teams, ended with the surprise of his temporary appointment to the state captaincy for the first time. Batting at number three as captain, Slater made 50 and seven against Tasmania in the Pura Cup match at Bellerive, and was unable to save his team from a three-day defeat. He was used in the middle order rather than in his favoured opening position in early ING Cup matches, and was more successful opening in the first five Pura Cup games, in each contributing a score of 40 or better with a top score of 58 not out from 66 balls against Victoria. But his ING Cup failures mounted and selectors omitted him from the limited-overs side. On the eve of New South Wales' game against the touring South Africans in December, Slater severely sprained his ankle while bowling in the nets, the injury preventing him from playing for a critical month. He played one more match before being dropped from the Pura Cup team. Stunned by the decision, Slater took temporary leave from cricket before returning to his club, University of New South Wales. Then, extraordinarily, he was appointed captain of New South Wales, a promotion which may yet inspire one of the game's entertainers to write an exciting new chapter in his career.

	M	I	NO	R	HS	100s	50s	Avge	Ct	St	W	Avge	BB
First-class	203	360	19	14,036	221	33	68	41.16	110	0	3	37.33	1/4
Dom. first-class	56	106	3	4,014	143	9	24	38.97	35	0	0	–	–
Test	74	131	7	5,312	219	14	21	42.84	33	0	1	10.00	1/4
Int'l limited-overs	42	42	1	987	73	0	9	24.07	9	0	0	–	–
Dom. limited-overs	39	39	0	910	96	0	7	23.33	10	0	0	–	–

THORNELY, Dominic John
Born: October 1, 1978 Albury (New South Wales)
Right-handed batsman, right-arm medium bowler
Domestic limited-overs debut 2001-02

A raw-boned, sandy-haired all-rounder who emerged from the Cricket Academy as one of its finest graduates as a top-order batsman, Thornely is beginning to fulfil coach Rod Marsh's glowing predictions. By the end of the season, Thornely had entrenched himself in New South Wales' limited-overs side so proficiently that he won the Man of the Match award when the team claimed the ING Cup final against Queensland at the Gabba. In his initial ING Cup game, in stifling conditions in Coffs Harbour, Thornely was responsible for an outstanding running catch to end Darren Lehmann's century, after which two tidy slow-medium bowling efforts in Sydney and Devonport confirmed his position. In the final, Thornely made a stubborn 20 not out from 41 balls at No. 9 and then cut into Queensland's batting heart, finishing with 3/36 from eight overs. Thornely seems set to become a New South Wales regular, especially if his medium-paced deliveries continue to develop.

	M	I	NO	R	HS	100s	50s	Avge	Ct	St	W	Avge	BB
Dom. limited-overs	5	3	1	26	20*	0	0	13.00	3	0	5	38.20	3/36

TURNER, Dale Andrew
Born: January 30, 1974 Bankstown (New South Wales)
Right-handed batsman, right-arm off-spin bowler
First-class and domestic first-class debut 2001-02

Returning to his original home base in Sydney after breaking into
representative cricket with the Queensland limited-overs side in
1999-00, Turner played his maiden first-class match for New South
Wales in an unexpected late-season selection. Turner came into the
team as a result of the selectors' search for a spin bowling partner
for Stuart MacGill, but neither spinner claimed a wicket as Victoria
gained a comprehensive victory. Given a second opportunity against Queensland, Turner
again failed to take a wicket, but he contributed a valuable innings of 39. A wiry,
competitive player, Turner is a fine fieldsman and busy late-order batsman.

	M	I	NO	R	HS	100s	50s	Avge	Ct	St	W	Avge	BB
First-class	2	4	0	51	39	0	0	12.75	0	0	0	–	–
Dom. first-class	2	4	0	51	39	0	0	12.75	0	0	0	–	–
Dom. limited-overs	7	2	0	16	16	0	0	8.00	1	0	6	42.17	2/13

VAN DEINSEN, Brett Paul
Born: December 28, 1977 Bankstown (New South Wales)
Right-handed batsman, right-arm medium bowler
Domestic limited-overs debut 2001-02

Since his first-class debut in 1999-00, the selectors have awaited the transition of the
opener from strapping club century-maker into a powerful first-class representative. It
was not until Michael Slater was injured before Christmas that Van Deinsen was recalled
to the New South Wales team, making an encouraging start with a second innings of 61
against the South Africans. He was tried in the ING Cup, made a duck and then had more
convincing innings of 60 and 23 in the Pura Cup in Adelaide, only to fail against Victoria
and lose his place. Recalled to open in the Pura Cup match in Perth, Van Deinsen injured
his back while bowling his medium-pacers, batting under difficulties at number eight for
27 and a duck in the second innings. He is a batsman of considerable appeal with his
driving and resounding stroke-play and one who cannot be discarded when, back
permitting, he should be in his prime.

	M	I	NO	R	HS	100s	50s	Avge	Ct	St	W	Avge	BB
First-class	11	21	0	375	61	0	2	17.86	15	0	3	36.33	3/42
Dom. first-class	10	19	0	313	60	0	1	16.47	15	0	3	36.33	3/42
Dom. limited-overs	1	1	0	0	0	0	0	0.00	1	0	0	–	–

WAUGH, Mark Edward
Born: June 2, 1965 Canterbury (New South Wales)
Right-handed batsman, right-arm off-spin bowler

The Test series in South Africa in 2002 brought one of the game's most elegant and
prolific batsmen face-to-face with the reality that his international career was nearing its
end. With his feet no longer gliding automatically into position, Waugh had had a poor
limited-overs tournament at home after the Tests against New Zealand and South Africa,
his innings of 55 not out from 62 balls against South Africa in Sydney being his top score
in seven games. In the six home Tests he scored only 269 runs at 33.63. When his 53 in
Johannesburg proved to be his highest Test score in South Africa, the writing was on the
wall. He was omitted from the limited-overs series in South Africa and his international
future remains uncertain despite an extension of his ACB contract. For one who has been
such a champion, the World Cup is temptingly close and would be a fitting arena for him
to end his career. His season began auspiciously in October with 123 off 103 balls in the

ING Cup against Tasmania, and 168 off 211 balls against a similar Tasmanian attack in the Pura Cup, but his state form did not carry over into the international matches.

	M	I	NO	R	HS	100s	50s	Avge	Ct	St	W	Avge	BB
First-class	344	550	70	25,473	229*	80	125	53.07	413	0	208	39.39	6/68
Dom. first-class	74	124	13	6,172	229*	23	24	55.60	85	0	51	36.78	4/130
Test	125	205	17	7,949	153*	20	46	42.28	173	0	59	39.97	5/40
Int'l limited-overs	244	236	20	8,500	173	18	50	39.35	108	0	85	34.56	5/24
Dom. limited-overs	45	44	4	1,477	123	3	9	36.93	25	0	19	31.26	3/23

WAUGH, Stephen Rodger
Born: June 2, 1965 Canterbury (New South Wales)
Right-handed batsman, right-arm medium bowler

The twin brothers made the same flight home after the Test series in South Africa, aware that their limited-overs international careers were, in all likelihood, finished. Steve Waugh learned his fate some weeks earlier before the team left for South Africa, whereas Mark was informed after the Test series. Suffering from a minor form of deep vein thrombosis, Waugh missed New South Wales' first five matches, but the selectors, satisfied with his fitness, chose him for the First Test against New Zealand and were reassured when he made 101 not out in the ING Cup against Queensland a week later in Sydney. It proved his only hundred in the Australian season. Waugh led Australia in all six home Tests, but scored only 219 runs at 27.38. Likewise, his VB Series return of 187 runs in eight games at 31.16 was poor by his standards. His Test performances in South Africa were no better, with a top score of 42 in Durban. Waugh's captaincy remained as astute and hard-edged as ever, Australia's 3-0 and 2-1 series wins over South Africa confirming his team's No. 1 ranking in Test cricket.

	M	I	NO	R	HS	100s	50s	Avge	Ct	St	W	Avge	BB
First-class	315	486	80	21,126	216*	67	88	52.03	248	0	243	32.09	6/51
Dom. first-class	70	119	13	5,390	216*	17	21	50.85	72	0	82	30.78	6/51
Test	148	233	41	9,600	200	27	44	50.00	102	0	89	35.92	5/28
Int'l limited-overs	325	288	58	7,569	120*	3	45	32.91	111	0	195	34.69	4/33
Dom. limited-overs	39	38	8	1,548	131	3	9	51.60	14	0	34	24.85	4/32

WILLIAMS, Vaughan Morgan
Born: December 19, 1977 Blaxland (New South Wales)
Right-handed batsman

First-class and domestic first-class debut 2001-02

This chunky opening batsman has curbed the aggression of his early career to become one of the most consistent run-scorers in the Sydney competition with Bankstown–Canterbury, hitting three centuries in 858 runs at 47.66 for the season. Chosen for his first-class debut in the last Pura Cup game, Williams batted at number six, failing in both innings as Tasmania won comfortably in three days in Hobart but he will be better for the experience. He has kept wickets at first-grade level.

	M	I	NO	R	HS	100s	50s	Avge	Ct	St	W	Avge	BB
First-class	1	2	0	4	4	0	0	2.00	0	0	0	–	–
Dom. first-class	1	2	0	4	4	0	0	2.00	0	0	0	–	–

QUEENSLAND

By Stephen Gray

BICHEL, Andrew John
Born: August 27, 1970 Laidley (Queensland)
Right-handed batsman, right-arm fast-medium bowler

Andy Bichel enjoyed a prolific English county season for Worcestershire in 2001 and earned their Player of the Year award. He resumed duties for Queensland before occupying the familiar position of twelfth man for the three Tests against New Zealand. He briefly returned to the Queensland side after missing the First Test against South Africa in Adelaide, before yo-yoing back into the team for the Boxing Day Test, where he broke with his usual tradition and played. The selectors allowed him to play a few matches in the limited-overs series, where his moment in the sun came with 5/19 against South Africa in Sydney. With all his expert pushing of the drinks trolley he played only five first-class matches for the season, hardly a just reward for this whole-hearted cricketer. He claimed another career-best on his return to Worcestershire for the 2002 season, snaring 9/93 in an innings against Gloucestershire.

	M	I	NO	R	HS	100s	50s	Avge	Ct	St	W	Avge	BB
First-class	96	126	11	2,380	110	1	10	20.70	51	0	406	24.30	9/93
Dom. first-class	51	68	5	1,321	110	1	5	20.97	28	0	244	22.18	6/45
Test	6	8	0	63	18	0	0	7.88	4	0	13	39.77	5/60
Int'l limited-overs	30	20	6	191	27*	0	0	13.64	6	0	35	34.09	5/19
Dom. limited-overs	43	23	9	362	59*	0	1	25.86	14	0	45	35.20	4/45

BRANT, Scott Andrew
Born: January 26, 1983 Harare (Zimbabwe)
Right-handed batsman, left-arm fast-medium bowler
First-class, domestic first-class and domestic limited-overs
debut 2001-02

Something of a "Boys' Own" quality attaches itself to Scott Brant. The tale of a Zimbabwean teenager who relocates to Brisbane with his mother, brother and sisters to avoid the deteriorating conditions in his home country, leaving his father to continue running the family business, only to burst into prominence as a cricketer, has a romantic ring to it. Family, friends and cricket officials struggled to get the news of his selection to him in a lecture theatre at Bond University on the Gold Coast, where he is studying sports management, in order to get him to the airport to fly to Adelaide to play the next day. The athletic Brant is also a proficient swimmer, golfer, runner and hockey player. He has the potential to mature into a left-arm fast-medium bowler with the ability to swing the new ball both ways and then bowl long, economical spells. A more than handy bat, the highlight of his Pura Cup final (where he suffered a side strain early) was the massive six that he hit into the second tier of the Gabba's Northern Stand.

	M	I	NO	R	HS	100s	50s	Avge	Ct	St	W	Avge	BB
First-class	3	3	2	35	19*	0	0	35.00	3	0	7	18.00	3/23
Dom. first-class	3	3	2	35	19*	0	0	35.00	3	0	7	18.00	3/23
Dom. limited-overs	1	0	0	0	–	0	0	–	1	0	1	33.00	1/33

CARSELDINE, Lee Andrew
Born: November 17, 1975 Nambour (Queensland)
Left-handed batsman, left-arm medium

A brace of double-centuries in minor state cricket made it a season to remember for the lithe Carseldine, who looks set to thrust himself above the growing pack of batsmen contending for a state spot. After attending the Australian Cricket Academy in 1997, he has wandered in the wilderness longer than expected. But Carseldine blasted an extraordinary 200 not out against a near Test-strength New Zealand team at Allan Border Field, and a few months later he slammed a remarkable 234 out of 345 in an ACB Cup match against Australian Capital Territory. His key innings for Queensland came in their win over Victoria at the Gabba in March when he top-scored with 39 in a wobbly first innings total of 107. A fielder of the highest quality, he represents a tantalising all-round prospect if the cards fall into place. His left-arm pace bowling produced a best of 8/37 for his club side Valley, which he captained last season.

	M	I	NO	R	HS	100s	50s	Avge	Ct	St	W	Avge	BB
First-class	10	16	3	281	39	0	0	21.62	10	0	0	–	–
Dom. first-class	10	16	3	281	39	0	0	21.62	10	0	0	–	–
Dom. limited-overs	15	14	2	224	34	0	0	18.67	6	0	1	96.00	1/32

CASSELL, Jerry Lee
Born: January 12, 1975 Mona Vale (New South Wales)
Right-handed batsman, slow-left arm orthodox bowler

Cassell's fortunes did not unfold as he would have hoped, with a broken hand curtailing his season just as he was primed to move into the opening spot with Matthew Hayden and Jimmy Maher away for the final matches. He played five Pura Cup games, scoring 211 runs at 23.44 with a highest score of 86 in Perth. His high point came early in the season when he scored 163 for the Queensland Academy of Sport team against the touring New Zealanders. Hand injuries continued to dog him in the off season, with a stint playing Lancashire League cricket for Todmorden cut short due to a broken finger. A relaxed character, he has a good temperament for an opener and can bat for a long period when set. He is strongest square of the wicket. Before the 2001-02 season he left his position as a crane driver on the Brisbane wharves to pursue his cricket career full-time.

	M	I	NO	R	HS	100s	50s	Avge	Ct	St	W	Avge	BB
First-class	14	23	1	585	136	1	2	26.59	9	0	0	–	–
Dom. first-class	13	22	1	563	136	1	2	26.81	8	0	0	–	–
Dom. limited-overs	1	1	0	13	13	0	0	13.00	0	0	0	–	–

DALE, Adam Craig
Born: December 30, 1968 Greensborough (Victoria)
Left-handed batsman, right-arm fast-medium bowler

The impact of a spectacular outfield catch four years earlier finally hit Adam Dale last season. The right shoulder that had revolved through thousands of deliveries since his magnificent diving effort in the Gabba outfield to dismiss Phil Emery in October 1997, required major surgery after just one game. Although Dale hoped to return before the end of the season, the extent of the injury restricted him to the role of spectator. A positive thinker, Dale likened the operation to the restorative work he had done on his lovingly resurrected Valiant sedan that easily holds down the title of the oldest car in the team carpark. While attempting to force his way back into the state side he will captain-coach Wynnum–Manly in the Brisbane first-grade competition, where his assistant will be Australian and Queensland women's wicket-keeper Julia Price.

	M	I	NO	R	HS	100s	50s	Avge	Ct	St	W	Avge	BB
First-class	55	64	11	783	55	0	1	14.77	12	0	231	20.66	7/24
Dom. first-class	40	48	7	644	48	0	0	15.71	10	0	170	22.06	7/40
Test	2	3	0	6	5	0	0	2.00	0	0	6	31.17	3/71
Int'l limited-overs	30	12	8	78	15*	0	0	19.50	11	0	32	30.59	3/18
Dom. limited-overs	27	11	6	55	14*	0	0	11.00	6	0	36	23.39	4/26

DAWES, Joseph Henry
Born: August 29, 1970 Herston (Queensland)
Right-handed batsman, right-arm fast-medium bowler

After a deluge of wickets in 2000-01, Joe Dawes suffered cricket's equivalent of an El Nino effect, claiming 19 wickets from eight matches as a nagging knee injury dried up his prospects and opened the door for others. Nevertheless, Dawes reinforced his value as a consummate team and squad player, acting as a mature commissar for the young cadre of pace bowlers in the state squad. He still had firepower to offer, with his 3/4 from nine hostile overs against Tasmania at the Gabba a hint of what he can produce. Although not the most fashionable quick, he bowls well to left-handers in particular with his ability to take the ball away off the wicket. He ended a 12-year career with the Queensland Police Force to take on the role of community relations and media manager for the Federal Member for Dickson, Peter Dutton, a former police colleague. A badly broken nose stymied Dawes' off-season after he crashed his mountain bike, but he recovered to tour Malaysia and Singapore with the MCC, with whom he is a playing member.

	M	I	NO	R	HS	100s	50s	Avge	Ct	St	W	Avge	BB
First-class	34	43	13	252	26	0	0	8.40	7	0	132	24.09	7/98
Dom. first-class	32	40	12	240	26	0	0	8.57	7	0	119	24.82	7/98
Dom. limited-overs	9	1	1	1	1*	0	0	–	0	0	15	22.33	3/26

HAURITZ, Nathan Michael
Born: October 18, 1981 Wondai (Queensland)
Right-handed batsman, right-arm off-spin bowler
First-class, domestic first-class and international limited-overs
debut 2001-02

Hauritz enjoyed a dizzying 12-month period. He made his first-class debut early in 2001-02 against Victoria and subsequently played seven Pura Cup games for Queensland, taking 16 wickets at 30.25. It was in the limited-overs game that he excelled, finishing as the second among the wicket-takers in the ING Cup behind Stuart MacGill and distinguishing himself with his control and anticipation of batsmen. He was chosen both on potential and performance for the limited-overs leg of the South Africa tour, where he justified the faith in him by taking a wicket in his first over for Australia, finishing with 2/31. Like most Australian finger-spinners, he is not a huge turner of the ball but makes up for that with discipline and variety in pace and flight. A calm individual, he also held his own with the bat, combining with Jimmy Maher to tie the third match in South Africa. An ACB contract followed and he will hold strong hopes for a World Cup berth. He aspires to be considered an all-rounder and his 61 in a practice match for Queensland against Pakistan in June suggests this desire might not be unrealistic. He also took a hat-trick for Norths in Brisbane cricket.

	M	I	NO	R	HS	100s	50s	Avge	Ct	St	W	Avge	BB
First-class	7	9	1	102	41	0	0	12.75	5	0	16	30.25	4/119
Dom. first-class	7	9	1	102	41	0	0	12.75	5	0	16	30.25	4/119
Int'l limited-overs	4	2	2	13	11*	0	0	–	1	0	3	48.67	2/31
Dom. limited-overs	16	7	2	41	18*	0	0	8.20	7	0	22	23.41	4/47

HAYDEN, Matthew Lawrence
Born: October 29, 1971 Kingaroy (Queensland)
Left-handed batsman, right-arm medium bowler

Increasingly at ease with the rigours of international cricket, Hayden has won over doubters with his steadfastness at the top of the Australian order. Following a steady Ashes tour, Hayden prepared for the season with a regular diet of fishing and surfing mixed with some gruelling physical fitness sessions on the sand dunes of Moreton Island. Centuries in the opening two games for Queensland suggested he had found the right formula and signalled the onset of a golden summer. Hayden went on to dominate New Zealand and South Africa in Australia and scored 1,243 first-class runs at 82.86 in the season. He eclipsed Bob Simpson's Australian record for the most Test runs in a calendar year before carrying on his feats in South Africa. But for an overly ambitious cut when he was 96 in the Second Test in South Africa, Hayden would have scored five Test centuries in a row against the same opponents. Omitted from the Australian limited-overs team during the summer, he batted his way back into the side for the South African tour and the June series against Pakistan. In June he and his wife Kellie became parents to a baby girl, Grace Kellie.

	M	I	NO	R	HS	100s	50s	Avge	Ct	St	W	Avge	BB
First-class	209	362	36	17,362	235*	55	74	53.26	181	0	17	39.47	3/10
Dom. first-class	82	149	17	7,323	234	24	30	55.48	75	0	3	31.00	2/17
Test	30	52	4	2,354	203	8	9	49.04	29	0	0	–	–
Int'l limited-overs	37	35	2	1,113	111	1	9	33.73	16	0	0	–	–
Dom. limited-overs	51	51	9	2,231	152*	8	11	53.12	16	0	3	10.67	2/16

HOPES, James Redfern
Born: October 24, 1978 Townsville (Queensland)
Right-handed batsman, right-arm fast-medium bowler
First-class and domestic first-class debut 2001-02

A genuine all-round talent, Hopes emerged as an increasingly vital member of the Queensland squad in 2001-02. His ING Cup appearances brought 16 wickets at 21.68 and 213 runs at 26.62, with key performances coming despite a stress fracture in his foot that he defied to play the final three matches. The injury ruled him out for the last month of the season. He is by no means a fanciful tip as a World Cup long-shot, with his accuracy and variety already earning him the role as the Queenslanders' "closer" in the limited-overs game. His first-class debut was less auspicious than his limited-overs season, however, and his three matches brought little success. His batting should continue to develop, boasting as he does a fine array of attacking strokes on both sides of the wicket. He has centuries to his credit in minor cricket. Despite mischievous rumours, his middle name Redfern was not inspired by a parental love of seventies pop star Jamie Redfern or a particular affinity with the Sydney suburb, but is an ancestral family name from England.

	M	I	NO	R	HS	100s	50s	Avge	Ct	St	W	Avge	BB
First-class	3	5	0	40	14	0	0	8.00	0	0	3	99.67	2/50
Dom. first-class	3	5	0	40	14	0	0	8.00	0	0	3	99.67	2/50
Dom. limited-overs	16	14	1	246	52*	0	1	18.92	5	0	27	19.85	5/29

JOHNSON, Mitchell Guy
Born: November 2, 1981 Townsville (Queensland)
Left-handed batsman, left-arm fast bowler
First-class and domestic first-class debut 2001-02

Rarely has a young player had to bowl his first ball in first-class cricket under so much scrutiny. A blizzard of expectation has swirled about Johnson ever since Dennis Lillee and Rod Marsh tipped the teenage Townsville pace man to be Australia's next "express" fast bowler after discovering him in 1999. Lillee went so far as to state just before his debut last season that the quietly-spoken teen was "one of those natural talents who come along once in a lifetime". In his two first-class matches he took six wickets and displayed sharp pace with good bounce and a knack for swinging the ball. His season was cut short by a back stress fracture, an injury he has already overcome once. As he develops, Johnson should also grow into a more than useful batsman on the strength of the evidence to date. He has scored a second-grade century, his first scoring shot in first-class cricket was a hook for six, and a cameo innings of 33 against Pakistan in a practice match in June almost took his team to victory.

	M	I	NO	R	HS	100s	50s	Avge	Ct	St	W	Avge	BB
First-class	2	2	2	18	12*	0	0	–	0	0	6	36.00	2/64
Dom. first-class	1	1	1	12	12*	0	0	–	0	0	3	36.67	2/66

KASPROWICZ, Michael Scott
Born: February 10, 1972 South Brisbane (Queensland)
Right-handed batsman, right-arm fast bowler

With his regular partners Andy Bichel and Adam Dale missing for large chunks of the season, the big-hearted Kasprowicz took it upon himself to imprint his sizeable presence on the first-class scene. He finished as the leading domestic wicket-taker with 49 Pura Cup scalps at 22.08, including a first innings 5/60 in the Pura Cup final that spiked Tasmania's guns by removing Jamie Cox, Michael Dighton and Michael Di Venuto. His nine wickets for the final (4/103 in the second innings) would normally have attracted greater acclaim but for Shayne Jurgensen's remarkable 11-wicket haul. He returned to England in 2002 where he had previously appeared for Essex and Leicestershire, this time joining Glamorgan.

	M	I	NO	R	HS	100s	50s	Avge	Ct	St	W	Avge	BB
First-class	161	210	44	2,854	92	0	8	17.19	63	0	624	27.07	7/36
Dom. first-class	74	96	17	1,173	52*	0	2	14.85	28	0	316	24.58	6/47
Test	17	23	5	234	25	0	0	13.00	6	0	47	37.00	7/36
Int'l limited-overs	16	8	6	60	28*	0	0	30.00	3	0	22	32.23	3/50
Dom. limited-overs	52	27	12	208	34	0	0	13.87	12	0	62	31.10	4/21

LAW, Stuart Grant
Born: October 18, 1968 Herston (Queensland)
Right-handed batsman, right-arm medium bowler

Law made the courageous decision to stand down as state captain just days after leading Queensland to their fifth domestic title in eight seasons and their third Pura Cup title in a row. It was an unexpected announcement after another triumphant summer and another crucial innings in the final – but Law has always been his own man. He aims to play on as a batsman and be a senior figure in the Queensland dressing-room, much as Allan Border did in the gloaming of his career. Law's batting returns slipped in 2001-02, a broken finger ruling him out of two Pura Cup games. Coming off 1,311 runs in his final season with Essex in 2001, Law's Australian haul of 280 runs would have galled him, especially as it was the first time since 1991-92 that he did not score a century. But his first innings 69 in the final would have given some solace, combining with Andrew Symonds combining to take the side from an unsteady four for 98 to the comfort of 253 before the fall of the next wicket. He returned to England to join Lancashire where he made a typically bright start before breaking a thumb in July.

	M	I	NO	R	HS	100s	50s	Avge	Ct	St	W	Avge	BB
First-class	249	416	45	18,225	263	54	88	49.12	283	0	81	48.99	5/39
Dom. first-class	123	202	24	7,812	216	22	40	43.89	109	0	51	45.25	5/39
Test	1	1	1	54	54*	0	1	–	1	0	0	–	–
Int'l limited-overs	54	51	5	1,237	110	1	7	26.89	12	0	12	52.92	2/22
Dom. limited-overs	71	65	6	1,916	159	5	5	32.47	30	0	20	28.95	4/33

LOVE, Martin Lloyd
Born: March 30, 1974 Mundubbera (Queensland)
Right-handed batsman

Quietly building an impressive case for himself for higher honours, the dependable Love could well make a noisy entry into international cricket in the next 12 months. He has yet to make a big impact on the greater cricketing public, even if his peers and the more knowledgeable fans are well aware of his ability. At 28, he is approaching the peak of his powers, and added to his repertoire last season by making his captaincy debut for Queensland and leading them to victory in that match. He was the leading run-scorer in the Pura Cup with 1,108 runs at 65.17 with two hundreds and six other scores over 50, including a 93 in the second innings in the final. His unflustered approach also works effectively in the harum-scarum limited-overs arena. He led the way for the Bulls in the ING Cup, scoring 423 runs at 42.30, with a career-best 127 not out off 127 balls against New South Wales at the Gabba. Love has put his career as a physiotherapist on hold for the moment, returning to England in 2002 to play his second season for Durham. At Lord's against Middlesex he reeled off 251, his highest first-class score, but a broken finger hindered the second half of his season. The national selectors awarded him an ACB contract for the second year in a row for 2002-03.

	M	I	NO	R	HS	100s	50s	Avge	Ct	St	W	Avge	BB
First-class	123	212	17	9,412	251	22	46	48.27	143	0	1	5.00	1/5
Dom. first-class	83	142	11	6,201	228	15	27	47.34	93	0	1	5.00	1/5
Dom. limited-overs	58	55	7	1,744	127*	3	9	36.33	20	0	0	–	–

MacKENZIE, Damien Robert
Born: July 21, 1980 Brisbane (Queensland)
Right-handed batsman, right-arm fast-medium bowler
First-class, domestic first-class and domestic limited-overs debut 2001-02

The solidly built pace man made his debut for Queensland against Tasmania in Hobart, taking three wickets. He had shown promise in taking 4/52 against the New Zealanders at Albion in October. MacKenzie emerged from the Queensland youth scheme and came to notice in the 1998-99 national Under-19s championships when he took a hat-trick against South Australia. He was an Australian Cricket Academy scholar in 1999 before he suffered a serious knee injury that required a reconstruction. He performs best when he is hitting the wicket hard, which enables him to extract good bounce and pace off most wickets. He is also a handy lower-order batsman.

	M	I	NO	R	HS	100s	50s	Avge	Ct	St	W	Avge	BB
First-class	1	2	0	21	17	0	0	10.50	0	0	3	15.00	3/45
Dom. first-class	1	2	0	21	17	0	0	10.50	0	0	3	15.00	3/45
Dom. limited-overs	2	2	0	11	9	0	0	5.50	0	0	3	16.67	2/21

MAHER, James Patrick
Born: February 27, 1974 Innisfail (Queensland)
Left-handed batsman, right-arm medium bowler

It all came up smelling of roses for Jimmy Maher in 2001-02, with a string of personal and sporting highlights for the livewire left-hander. A return of 1,000-plus runs for Glamorgan in county cricket was followed by his second 1,000-run season in Australia in a row (1,194 at 66.33). He also made a telling debut as Queensland captain in the absence of Stuart Law, leading the side to crucial wins against South Australia in Adelaide in the Pura and ING Cups. Along with Brad Hodge, he was the joint Pura Cup player of the year. After an experimental call to arms for Australia in 1998, Maher was given a more structured return for the South Africa tour. In front of parents Warren and Marie, he celebrated his return to the green and gold with Man of the Match performances in his first two games, including 95 and then 56 as he steered a wobbling Australia to victory. He was named Queensland captain for the 2002-03 season just before he and his wife Deb welcomed their daughter Lily Matilda.

	M	I	NO	R	HS	100s	50s	Avge	Ct	St	W	Avge	BB
First-class	116	204	25	7,816	217	17	36	43.66	120	0	10	50.00	3/11
Dom. first-class	90	159	18	5,761	209	10	28	40.86	100	0	10	30.20	3/11
Int'l limited-overs	8	7	2	193	95	0	1	38.60	5	0	0	–	–
Dom. limited-overs	61	61	9	2,426	128	4	15	46.65	28	0	2	43.50	2/43

MULLER, Scott Andrew
Born: July 11, 1971 Herston (Queensland)
Right-handed batsman, right-arm fast-medium bowler

Operations to both knees over the past two years have kept the former Test bowler's cricket opportunities to a bare minimum, with the 2001-02 season providing little respite. He played two ING Cup games for the Queenslanders but was overlooked for a first-class return when the selectors opted to blood Scott Brant. Without a Queensland contract for 2002-03, his future remains up in the air. However, his career has never followed a traditional path and he may yet again bubble to the top. On his day he is a match-winner, with his ability to swing the new ball at pace representing a challenge for most batsmen.

	M	I	NO	R	HS	100s	50s	Avge	Ct	St	W	Avge	BB
First-class	30	34	13	210	26	0	0	10.00	12	0	102	23.50	5/35
Dom. first-class	24	28	8	183	26	0	0	9.15	8	0	76	23.49	5/35
Test	2	2	2	6	6*	0	0	–	2	0	7	36.86	3/68
Dom. limited-overs	7	2	1	5	5*	0	0	5.00	1	0	12	20.67	5/43

NASH, Brendan Paul
Born: December 14, 1977 Bentley (Western Australia)
Left-handed batsman

Dubbed a "street-fighter" by his captain Stuart Law, himself a grizzled veteran of many a stoush in the first-class arena, Nash finished his second season with many more admirers than he started with. Gone was the nervy figure of the 2000-01 Pura Cup final, with this season's steelier version narrowly missing the honour of a century in a final, scoring 96. His season returns of 395 runs at 43.88 were noteworthy, with a maiden first-class century (157 in Adelaide) that featured as part of a 296-run partnership with Martin Love, a third-wicket record for Queensland against South Australia. Perhaps the smallest first-class cricketer in Australia, he has a tidy, unhurried technique and is particularly forceful off the back foot. He is also a nimble fielder who made a difficult running outfield catch against Victoria in an ING Cup match at the Gabba look simple. In a team brimming with internationals, Nash found himself uniquely placed when a group of Brisbane university students formed the Brendan Nash Fan Club during the season, complete with e-mail mailing list and distinctive members' t-shirts. He played League cricket in Kent during the 2002 English summer.

	M	I	NO	R	HS	100s	50s	Avge	Ct	St	W	Avge	BB
First-class	9	16	1	463	157	1	2	30.87	4	0	0	–	–
Dom. first-class	9	16	1	463	157	1	2	30.87	4	0	0	–	–
Dom. limited-overs	10	9	2	171	63	0	1	24.43	4	0	0	–	–

NOFFKE, Ashley Allan
Born: April 30, 1977 Nambour (Queensland)
Right-handed batsman, right-arm fast bowler

A severe ankle injury suffered during a match on the 2001 Ashes tour troubled Noffke on more than one occasion in the 2001-02 season. Still, his 39 first-class wickets at 28.46 made him the second-highest wicket-taker for Queensland, and he will assume increasing importance for the side in coming seasons. Overlooked for an ACB contract, Noffke made the most of a guest stint with Middlesex as a substitute pro for Abdul Razzaq early in the 2002 English summer, taking a career-best 7/100 on the way to 19 wickets in three first-class matches. Waspishly quick, he has often been likened to Glenn McGrath in style, and shapes as a long-term prospect for the national team. He is a more than capable batsman, as evidenced by his 275 runs at 27.50 with a highest score of 73 against Victoria in 2001-02, and was even touted by one good judge as a temporary solution at the top of the Queensland order when Matthew Hayden, Jimmy Maher and Jerry Cassell were missing late in the season.

	M	I	NO	R	HS	100s	50s	Avge	Ct	St	W	Avge	BB
First-class	23	24	5	443	73	0	1	23.32	8	0	88	27.86	7/100
Dom. first-class	15	17	5	325	73	0	1	27.08	5	0	59	27.66	5/31
Dom. limited-overs	19	5	2	49	22*	0	0	16.33	7	0	23	32.61	4/32

PAYNE, Daniel Martin
Born: October 27, 1978 Brisbane (Queensland)
Right-handed batsman
First-class and domestic first-class debut 2001-02

Payne is the latest fresh face to burst into the Queensland ranks seemingly from nowhere. But whereas previous mystery men have mostly been pace bowlers, Daniel Payne is a batsman, and one of the braver punts by the Queensland selection panel. A Beaudesert junior who represented Queensland in schools cricket teams, he was on track to be a golfer until cricket took hold of him again once he left school. Included in the Queensland Academy squad for the first time last season, he was consistent without dominating until surprisingly picked to open the batting for Queensland in their last match before the Pura Cup final. In his four first-class innings he had a top score of 35 and will benefit greatly from the experience. Quick on his feet, his pull shot is a feature of his batting once set, while in the field he is another of the Queensland fielding dynamos who make opposition batsmen nervous. He traces Japanese, Javanese, Aboriginal and Greek elements in his ancestry. Awarded a Cricket Academy scholarship for 2002, he was also contracted to Queensland for 2002-03.

	M	I	NO	R	HS	100s	50s	Avge	Ct	St	W	Avge	BB
First-class	2	4	0	82	35	0	0	20.50	3	0	0	–	–
Dom. first-class	2	4	0	82	35	0	0	20.50	3	0	0	–	–

PERREN, Clinton Terrence
Born: February 22, 1975 Herston (Queensland)
Right-handed batsman, right-arm fast-medium bowler

Perren had a largely unfulfilled season. When the right-hander is on song, he is a stroke-maker of the calibre of Stuart Law or Martin Love, with his back-foot square driving in the virtuoso league. But he struggled to find consistency in the first-class arena in 2001-02, and spoiled an otherwise fine limited-overs season in the final. He was Queensland's third-highest run-scorer in the ING Cup with 317 at 35.22, including a sumptuous 96 against Tasmania at the Gabba, yet came up short in the final against New South Wales, falling to a rash shot when steadiness was required (although he was not the only culprit on that regard). He played Central Lancashire League cricket for Milnrow in the English summer, and has returned from such playing stints in the past with renewed confidence.

	M	I	NO	R	HS	100s	50s	Avge	Ct	St	W	Avge	BB
First-class	21	33	4	733	153	2	1	25.28	23	0	1	42.00	1/15
Dom. first-class	20	31	3	652	153	2	1	23.29	21	0	0	–	–
Dom. limited-overs	26	22	3	606	96	0	4	31.89	9	0	3	23.67	1/13

SECCOMBE, Wade Anthony
Born: October 30, 1971 Murgon (Queensland)
Right-handed batsman, wicket-keeper

The day when a Queensland team takes the field without the familiar figure of Wade Seccombe behind the stumps will surely be one to stick in the memory. Seccombe's resilience in missing just one match in seven seasons has provided his team-mates with a rock-solid foundation. With 391 scalps to his credit already, he should record his 400th first-class dismissal for his state sometime in 2002-03. He had the most dismissals for the season with 52 (all caught) last season and should again be in the minds of the national selectors should an emergency arise or insurance be needed, as was the case on the 2001 Ashes tour. A free spirit away from the field, he is a harsh taskmaster on himself when he dons the keeper's gloves. Aside from Victoria's Darren Berry, he is almost without peer standing up to the stumps against medium-fast bowling, a skill he has mastered through many hours of hard work. A confidence player with the bat, Seccombe lost some momentum last season, scoring just 171 runs at 11.40, although he hit a spectacular 151 for his club team University of Queensland. He resigned his position in the marketing department of Queensland Cricket in 2001 and returned to study, undertaking a Masters of Business (Marketing) at Queensland University of Technology.

	M	I	NO	R	HS	100s	50s	Avge	Ct	St	W	Avge	BB
First-class	85	123	20	2,417	151	2	6	23.47	385	16	0	–	–
Dom. first-class	74	108	18	2,100	151	2	5	23.33	352	10	0	–	–
Dom. limited-overs	49	39	10	549	64*	0	1	18.93	69	12	0	–	–

SIPPEL, Michael
Born: November 1, 1975 Ipswich (Queensland) (Queensland)
Left-handed batsman, slow-left arm orthodox bowler
Domestic limited-overs debut 2001-02

An unexpected addition to Queensland's ranks last season, Sippel
made his debut as a replacement for Stuart Law in the ING Cup
match against Tasmania in Hobart. A clean-hitting left-hander who
has represented Queensland at Under-19s, Colts and ACB Cup
levels, Sippel finished with a duck and two catches as a member of
the winning team. However, his form at grade level, where he was
the leading run-scorer with 675, suggests the selectors will keep their eyes on him. A
second cousin of Andy Bichel, he lives at Gatton in the Brisbane Valley area and
commutes to Brisbane to play for Souths.

	M	I	NO	R	HS	100s	50s	Avge	Ct	St	W	Avge	BB
Dom. limited-overs	1	1	0	0	0	0	0	0.00	2	0	–	–	–

SYMONDS, Andrew
Born: June 9, 1975 Birmingham, West Midlands (England)
Right-handed batsman, right-arm medium-off spin bowler

The enigmatic Symonds continued to baffle both supporters and detractors last season.
His early season featured two blazing nineties for Queensland that brought wins against
Western Australia in the Pura and ING Cups. His 91 off 57 balls in the ING Cup would
have smashed the record for the fastest domestic limited-overs century if he had not been
caught on the third-man boundary. Spun out of form by the Australian limited-overs
team rotation policy, he returned to prominence in the Pura Cup final, where his first-
day 91 was the stuff that turns matches from "may be" to "will be". While Symonds is
primarily a batsman, former Australian spinner Greg Matthews swears he could turn him
into a Test off-spinner. However, his most important scalps came as a medium-pace
bowler with the ability to sneak an in-dipper past even the best players. Although he
spent another winter in 2002 with Kent, the laid-back Symonds would no doubt have
yearned for the opportunity to drop a few crab pots near the mouth of the Logan River,
as is his wont when cricket is not calling. His English sojourn included a career-best
6/105 bowling off-spin. Retaining his ACB contract but relegated to the Australia A
limited-overs squad for the moment, his time of reckoning may be near.

	M	I	NO	R	HS	100s	50s	Avge	Ct	St	W	Avge	BB
First-class	140	235	21	8,762	254*	25	35	40.94	95	0	119	37.96	6/105
Dom. first-class	63	103	8	3,397	163	9	12	35.76	38	0	70	30.69	4/39
Int'l limited-overs	48	34	6	707	68*	0	2	25.25	20	0	43	30.21	4/11
Dom. limited-overs	48	45	4	973	91	0	3	23.73	23	0	22	31.77	3/32

SOUTH AUSTRALIA
By Geoff Sando

ADCOCK, Nathan Tennyson
Born: April 22, 1978 Campbelltown (South Australia)
Right-handed batsman, right-arm fast-medium bowler

South Australian selectors have shown faith in Nathan Adcock. He appeared destined
for a career of achievement from the time he scored centuries in his first two A-Grade
matches for Sturt as an 18-year-old. A first-class century for the Australian Cricket

Academy in Zimbabwe in 1998-99 gave further encouragement. For South Australia, though, Adcock has failed to produce similar results. At times his form in Grade cricket has also disappointed and he has owed his selection for the state to a belief that his part-time off-spinners could enhance the balance of the team. In 2001-02, however, Adcock earned his recall with a string of substantial Grade and ACB Cup innings commencing at the end of November. Thereafter he was a regular member of the ING Cup team but failed to consolidate his place in the Pura Cup team. In first-class matches his top score of 46 came in the second innings against Victoria at Melbourne.

	M	I	NO	R	HS	100s	50s	Avge	Ct	St	W	Avge	BB
First-class	11	19	1	453	114	1	0	25.17	11	0	2	104.50	1/19
Domestic first-class	9	17	1	338	48	0	0	21.13	5	0	2	104.50	1/19
Dom. limited-overs	15	14	0	252	57	0	2	18.00	6	0	0	–	–

BLEWETT, Gregory Scott
Born: October 29, 1971 North Adelaide (South Australia)
Right-handed batsman, right-arm medium bowler

As one of the numerous batsmen on the periphery of the Australian team, Blewett is under self-imposed pressure to perform. His output for 2001-02 was satisfying with five centuries featuring among over 1,000 first-class runs. In limited-overs matches he tied for the award for the ING Player of the Year, losing to team-mate Darren Lehmann on a countback. For Australia A, Blewett managed 42 against South Africa and 50 against New Zealand. The New Zealanders also conceded an innings of 41 when Blewett represented the Prime Minister's XI at Manuka. To complete the season, Blewett helped his Kensington club to the SACA premiership with a spell of 6/28 against Sturt. There were also low points. He secured a pair against Western Australia at Adelaide. More seriously, Blewett was convicted for driving with a blood alcohol reading above the legal limit. He was on the way to a club match at Henley Reserve, where he top-scored with 56 and claimed 3/38 to lead his team to victory over West Torrens.

	M	I	NO	R	HS	100s	50s	Avge	Ct	St	W	Avge	BB
First-class	190	340	25	14,633	268	40	70	46.45	160	0	118	42.19	5/29
Domestic first-class	83	157	9	7,365	268	20	35	49.76	58	0	71	40.21	4/39
Test	46	79	4	2,552	214	4	15	34.03	45	0	14	51.43	2/9
Int'l limited-overs	32	30	3	551	57*	0	2	20.41	7	0	14	46.14	2/6
Dom. limited-overs	60	58	5	2,033	101*	1	14	38.36	21	0	45	34.36	4/33

DAVIES, Christopher James
Born: November 15, 1978 Bedford Park (South Australia)
Right-handed batsman

It is hard not to enjoy Chris Davies' successes. He is a fluent, upright batsman who strikes the ball with a natural flair that is reminiscent of his state coach Greg Chappell. Thus far, though, injuries and inconsistency have stood in the way of a permanent place in the South Australian team. An epic innings of 233 not out in 455 minutes for the South Australian Second XI against Australian Capital Territory at the Adelaide Oval was the springboard for his season. He was thereafter a fixture in South Australia's team for Pura Cup and ING Cup matches. At Brisbane he scored his initial first-class century, 119 not out against Queensland. Davies' form for Adelaide was also encouraging, as he managed 92 against Sturt, 95 against University and 130 against Woodville.

	M	I	NO	R	HS	100s	50s	Avge	Ct	St	W	Avge	BB
First-class	20	38	3	993	119*	1	6	28.37	7	0	0	–	–
Domestic first-class	18	35	3	906	119*	1	6	28.31	7	0	0	–	–
Dom. limited-overs	33	32	0	908	125	1	5	28.38	10	0	0	–	–

DEITZ, Shane Alan
Born: May 4, 1975 Bankstown (New South Wales)
Left-handed batsman – wicket-keeper

Deitz's often stoic batting in 2000-01 had earned him a position as an opener in South Australia's Pura Cup team. His work was undone by failures in the opening 2001-02 matches against Victoria and New South Wales, which led to his omission from the team. Deitz reacted in the best possible manner, scoring consistently for his club and in ACB Cup matches. He scored 627 runs at 57.00 in minor round matches for Southern District to top the SACA Grade batting aggregates. Deitz's recall to the South Australian team as wicket-keeper for the final Pura Cup match in Perth was well earned. By scoring 86 in the middle order and 43 as an opener he did his prospects for the ensuing season no harm.

	M	I	NO	R	HS	100s	50s	Avge	Ct	St	W	Avge	BB
First-class	17	34	0	1,075	114	2	5	31.62	16	0	2	46.50	2/17
Domestic first-class	16	32	0	1,063	114	2	5	33.22	14	0	2	46.50	2/17
Dom. limited-overs	6	6	0	134	44	0	0	22.33	3	0	0	–	–

DEMPSEY, Darren Michael
Born: October 17, 1975 Mt Gambier (South Australia)
Right-handed batsman, right-arm off-spin bowler
First-class and domestic first-class debut 2001-02

Tall and strongly built, Dempsey arrived in South Australia with strong credentials. He was joint winner of the VCA's Jack Ryder Medal in 2000-01 and had averaged 50 for his 4,000 runs in club cricket. Early indications were that this form would continue in South Australia, as he scored a commanding 100 against the Australian Cricket Academy and 78 not out against Victorian Second XI in early ACB Cup matches. On his first-class debut against Victoria he had the unfortunate experience of being the middle victim in Ian Harvey's hat-trick. Dempsey failed to adequately redeem himself in subsequent matches against New South Wales and Tasmania and was omitted from the team. Despite scores of 139 against New South Wales Second XI, 64 against the England National Academy team and 96 in the Grade cricket final for Kensington against Sturt, Dempsey was not rewarded with a contract for 2002-03.

	M	I	NO	R	HS	100s	50s	Avge	Ct	St	W	Avge	BB
First-class	3	5	0	38	21	0	0	7.60	5	0	0	–	–
Domestic first-class	3	5	0	38	21	0	0	7.60	5	0	0	–	–

FITZGERALD, David Andrew
Born: November 30, 1972 Osborne Park (Western Australia)
Right-handed batsman, right-arm medium bowler

There are countless reasons for cricketers' seasons to be disrupted. David Fitzgerald, like Ray Lindwall in 1946-47, succumbed to chickenpox, making 2001-02 a second successive abbreviated season for him. An epic innings of 139 in 422 minutes against Queensland at Adelaide was the high point of Fitzgerald's summer. He will remember the final Pura Cup match at Perth with less enthusiasm. Opening as usual, he was struck in the face by a swift delivery from Brad Williams. He retired hurt and, though he resumed later in the South Australian innings, chose to bat in the middle order in the second innings.

	M	I	NO	R	HS	100s	50s	Avge	Ct	St	W	Avge	BB
First-class	50	94	3	3,016	167	9	13	33.14	31	0	0	–	–
Domestic first-class	48	90	2	2,848	167	8	12	32.36	30	0	0	–	–
Dom. limited-overs	35	35	1	1,042	114	2	6	30.65	12	0	0	–	–

GILLESPIE, Jason Neil
Born: April 19, 1975 Darlinghurst (New South Wales)
Right-handed batsman, right-arm fast-medium bowler

An established member of the Australian juggernaut, Gillespie appeared for South Australia in only two Pura Cup and four ING matches. The highlight was a fiery 8/50 against New South Wales at Sydney. Playing a season for once relatively unscathed by major injuries, Gillespie confirmed his place as a vital component in Australia's Test attack. He invariably claimed wickets at key times, though it often appeared that his figures were a poor reward for the tribulations his accurate aggression imposed on the batsmen. A pleasing aspect of Gillespie's bowling was the manner in which he settled into Australia's limited-overs team. Having gained promotion during the VB Series, he retained his place in the subsequent matches in South Africa and in the June Tower Challenge squad.

	M	I	NO	R	HS	100s	50s	Avge	Ct	St	W	Avge	BB
First-class	77	99	22	1,066	58	0	3	13.84	29	0	279	24.89	8/50
Domestic first-class	24	39	5	446	58	0	2	13.12	11	0	96	23.59	8/50
Test	33	42	12	404	46	0	0	13.47	10	0	123	26.06	7/37
Int'l limited-overs	37	22	6	158	26	0	0	9.88	1	0	51	29.29	4/26
Dom. limited-overs	19	11	4	41	15	0	0	5.86	2	0	34	22.00	4/46

HARRIS, Ryan James
Born: October 11, 1979 Nowra (New South Wales)
Right-handed batsman, right-arm fast-medium bowler
First-class and domestic first-class debut 2001-02

Following a free-scoring innings of 100 in the ACB Cup against Australian Capital Territory at Adelaide, the strongly built Northern Districts all-rounder gained inclusion in the Pura Cup team for the match against Tasmania at Bellerive. He will not remember his first-class debut with a great deal of affection as he strained a pectoral muscle after claiming two early wickets. On his recovery, Harris performed well in Grade matches, scoring 102 not out and claiming 4/46 against Tea Tree Gully and adding 4/49 against Southern District and 5/74 against West Torrens. Having regained his place for the final Pura Cup match at Perth he had a dismal match, securing a pair and failing to take a wicket. Solace came in selection for the Australian Cricket Academy tour to India in April 2002.

	M	I	NO	R	HS	100s	50s	Avge	Ct	St	W	Avge	BB
First-class	2	2	0	0	0	0	0	0.00	0	0	2	49.50	2/26
Domestic first-class	2	2	0	0	0	0	0	0.00	0	0	2	49.50	2/26
Dom. limited-overs	10	5	3	60	31*	0	0	30.00	6	0	7	41.14	2/29

HARRITY, Mark Andrew
Born: March 9, 1974 Semaphore (South Australia)
Right-handed batsman, left-arm fast-medium bowler

Early injuries to Paul Wilson and Brett Swain and the regular absence of Jason Gillespie meant that Harrity became South Australia's senior front-line bowler. He accepted the challenge, notably when an injury to Ryan Harris during the match against Tasmania at Bellerive further depleted the South Australian attack and he responded with a hostile second innings performance of 5/65. Thereafter, Harrity found wickets harder to come by in Pura Cup matches and was omitted from the final match in Perth. He was South Australia's leading wicket-taker in ING Cup matches. On several occasions during the season his much-maligned batting proved useful. Harrity survived for 55 minutes against Victoria in Melbourne to add 19 of a 71-run partnership for the tenth wicket with Ben

Johnson. Because of state commitments, he did not bowl a ball for his Grade club, Port Adelaide, during 2001-02.

	M	I	NO	R	HS	100s	50s	Avge	Ct	St	W	Avge	BB
First-class	70	85	43	220	19	0	0	5.24	25	0	192	37.88	5/65
Dom. first-class	59	75	41	181	19	0	0	5.32	23	0	161	38.67	5/65
Dom. limited-overs	33	4	2	7	4*	0	0	3.50	9	0	52	24.15	5/42

HIGGINS, Benjamin Hugh
Born: March 8, 1972 Rose Park (South Australia)
Left-handed batsman, left-arm bowler

Higgins' debut as a middle-order batsman in 2000-01 came a decade after he was a key bowler in South Australia's championship-winning Under-19s team in 1990-91. In the meantime, he had progressed slowly up the West Torrens batting order before thrusting his name before the state selectors with a stunning century in the 1999-00 Grade final. A further century in a state Second Eleven match earned a well-deserved promotion to the South Australian team. Perhaps the fact that Higgins had rarely batted in the first four in minor matches encouraged sceptics to predict a brief stay at first-class level. By consistent, sensible batting, however, Higgins did much to retain his place. Five half-centuries in Pura Cup matches in 2001-02 yielded a highest score of 80 against New South Wales at Adelaide. Perhaps the conversion of one of those innings to a more substantial score may have prevented his omission from the season's final match. Higgins' batting in Grade matches reflected a new confidence gained from becoming a first-class cricketer, and he scored 105 not out against Glenelg and 128 against Port Adelaide.

	M	I	NO	R	HS	100s	50s	Avge	Ct	St	W	Avge	BB
First-class	13	24	2	689	80	0	8	31.32	3	0	1	80.00	1/49
Domestic first-class	12	22	2	668	80	0	8	33.40	3	0	1	80.00	1/49
Dom. limited-overs	7	6	2	65	36	0	0	16.25	2	0	0	–	–

JOHNSON, Benjamin Andrew
Born: August 1, 1973 Naracoorte (South Australia)
Left-handed batsman, right-arm medium bowler

There were murmurs that South Australia's poor 2000-01 season had one benefit: it revealed those players who were not up to the task. Johnson's omission from early Pura Cup matches in 2001-02 was therefore telling. Only the coinciding unavailability of Jeff Vaughan and David Fitzgerald, and the lack of form of Shane Deitz, provided Johnson with an opportunity to resume his early role of opening batsman. He took the chance by carrying his bat through the innings in scoring 121 not out against Western Australia at Adelaide and then repeating the feat in scoring 138 not out against Victoria at Melbourne. Not since Bill Lawry had an Australian opener batted through complete innings in consecutive first-class matches. Johnson almost repeated the feat in a later match, being the ninth man dismissed after scoring 138 in 418 minutes of resistance against Tasmania at Adelaide. His medium-pace bowling gave him a pivotal role in South Australia's ING Cup team but this aspect of his game was inconsequential in Pura Cup matches.

	M	I	NO	R	HS	100s	50s	Avge	Ct	St	W	Avge	BB
First-class	60	113	13	3,602	168	8	16	36.02	30	0	44	42.82	3/16
Domestic first-class	56	106	13	3,448	168	8	15	37.08	30	0	42	42.31	3/16
Dom. limited-overs	43	42	7	870	83	0	3	24.86	18	0	19	29.79	3/46

KING, Matthew Denham
Born: June 26, 1977 Port Pirie (South Australia)
Left-handed batsman, right-arm medium bowler
Dom. limited-overs debut 2001-02

In three seasons following his debut for Sturt in 1998-99, Matthew King has accumulated a record that commanded consideration for higher honours, his 89 wickets coming at a cost of 14.92. Having played a key role in the competitive nature of a young Sturt team, he was rewarded by selection in South Australia's Second Eleven for early season ACB matches in 2001-02, taking wickets freely. Injuries to incumbent bowlers allowed him to represent South Australia in an ING Cup match against Western Australia at Adelaide, but he took no wickets while conceding 43 runs in six overs and yielded his place to Paul Wilson. Without producing any outstanding performances, King collected 22 wickets at 16.23 in minor round Grade matches but found the going tough in the competition final against Kensington.

	M	I	NO	R	HS	100s	50s	Avge	Ct	St	W	Avge	BB
Dom. limited-overs	1	0	0	0	–	0	0	–	0	0	0	–	–

LEHMANN, Darren Scott
Born: February 5, 1970 Gawler (South Australia)
Left-handed batsman, slow left-arm orthodox bowler

Darren Lehmann continues to make first-class cricket appear an absurdly simple game. He accumulates runs in prolific quantities at a rapid rate, relying not only on powerful hitting (and he does give the ball a thump) but also on inventive strokeplay. The leg glance, which he plays while walking across his stumps, is now a specialty. He seems intent at times, particularly during the final stages of his masterful double-century at Bellerive, on developing the deflection over the wicket-keeper's head as a legitimate weapon. Four times recipient of the Man of the Match award in eight games, Lehmann won the ING Player of the Year for the third time. He is the leading run-scorer in the history of this competition and during the season also surpassed Jamie Siddons as the leading run-scorer in Sheffield Shield/Pura Cup matches. Lehmann was recalled to the Australian team for the VB Series and retained his place in the team for subsequent internationals in South Africa. He now appears philosophical about his future in the Australian team, having shown signs that his alternative lifestyle as a Yorkshire cricketer is a satisfying one. In the 2002 English season, this time captaining the county side, he was once again one of the leading batsmen in the country, as well as one of the best limited-overs players.

	M	I	NO	R	HS	100s	50s	Avge	Ct	St	W	Avge	BB
First-class	205	350	23	18,447	255	60	82	56.41	110	0	60	40.28	4/42
Domestic first-class	119	215	13	10,936	255	37	43	54.14	73	0	21	50.57	3/42
Test	5	8	0	228	98	0	2	28.50	3	0	2	22.50	1/6
Int'l limited-overs	78	71	14	2,047	110*	2	11	35.91	16	0	22	32.68	2/4
Dom. limited-overs	67	66	9	2,623	142*	6	17	46.02	23	0	10	36.70	3/16

MANOU, Graham Allan
Born: April 23, 1979 Modbury (South Australia)
Right-handed batsman, wicket-keeper

Since his inclusion in the South Australian team, the skills of Manou's wicket-keeping have been acclaimed by team-mates and selectors alike. He has retained his place despite the superior batting credentials of Shane Deitz and, at times, Darren Reeves. Manou's cause has been helped by occasional glimpses of batting skills in minor matches. From time to time there were hints that this form would translate to the first-class level. A massive final-over six in a tense conclusion to an ING Cup match against Victoria at

Richmond indicated a sound temperament. Later he contributed an innings of 62 in a Pura Cup match against New South Wales at Adelaide. In the end, though, a couple of irresponsible dismissals at vital times tested the selectors, who preferred Shane Deitz for the season's final match at Perth. The coming season will reveal if the omission has long-term ramifications.

	M	I	NO	R	HS	100s	50s	Avge	Ct	St	W	Avge	BB
First-class	32	54	9	818	78	0	3	18.18	88	12	0	–	–
Domestic first-class	28	47	7	722	78	0	3	18.05	78	12	0	–	–
Dom. limited-overs	25	20	8	203	42*	0	0	16.92	39	1	0	–	–

McINTYRE, Peter Edward
Born: April 27, 1966 Gisborne (Victoria)
Right-handed batsman, right-arm leg-spin bowler

As the season progressed, it was apparent that McIntyre would play a role for South Australia only in first-class games on pitches receptive to spin. A match-winner in the tour match against New Zealand at Adelaide, where he claimed 3/101 and 6/75, he subsequently found wickets harder to come by. Brad Young was preferred because of his batting proficiency. McIntyre remained a force in Grade cricket for Tea Tree Gully, taking 5/95 against Woodville and 4/7 against Kensington. He announced his retirement at the end of the season, citing the increasing demands of his employment.

	M	I	NO	R	HS	100s	50s	Avge	Ct	St	W	Avge	BB
First-class	97	134	35	798	43	0	0	8.06	33	0	322	39.66	6/43
Domestic first-class	74	107	30	647	43	0	0	8.40	26	0	236	43.45	6/64
Test	2	4	1	22	16	0	0	7.33	0	0	5	38.80	3/103
Dom. limited-overs	5	3	0	1	1	0	0	0.33	0	0	7	30.57	4/39

ROFE, Paul Cameron
Born: January 16, 1981 Adelaide (South Australia)
Right-handed batsman, right-arm fast bowler

Though he had appeared in three first-class matches for South Australia in 2000-01 when injuries depleted the attack, it was widely expected that similar circumstances would be required for Rofe to be a regular member of the team in 2001-02. By claiming 5/81 in an early ACB Cup match against the Australian Cricket Academy, he shaped as a logical replacement for the injured Paul Wilson for the opening ING Cup match in Perth. He took no wickets and conceded 50 runs in six overs, and owed his retention in the team to a further injury to Brett Swain. After that he began to make an impact. His performances in Pura Cup matches soon brought comparisons with Glenn McGrath – a consistent line and length, coupled with awkward bounce from a high action, often stifled the scoring. Figures of 3/31 off 23 overs against Western Australia were exemplary but paled in the light of his subsequent haul of 6/60 and 7/52 against New South Wales at Adelaide. At the end of the season, the East Torrens pace man could look back in the knowledge that he had done much of the groundwork required to put his name before the Australian selectors.

	M	I	NO	R	HS	100s	50s	Avge	Ct	St	W	Avge	BB
First-class	14	21	8	105	18	0	0	8.08	3	0	44	30.02	7/52
Domestic first-class	13	19	7	100	18	0	0	8.33	3	0	44	28.93	7/52
Dom. limited-overs	13	3	3	2	1*	0	0	–	0	0	13	40.92	3/44

SMITH, Michael John
Born: July 17, 1973 Rose Park (South Australia)
Right-handed batsman, right-arm medium bowler

With the increasing emphasis placed on interstate Second Eleven matches, Under-19s and Under-17s carnivals and Australian Cricket Academy matches, many players now progress to first-class honours with little experience of Grade cricket. An exception is Mike Smith, who began with East Torrens as far back as 1991-92. He first appeared for South Australia in 1999-00 but failed to secure a regular berth. Further prominent performances for University, notably a spell of 5/31 against Kensington, earned a recall in the tour match against New Zealand. Smith retained his place in both ING and Pura Cup matches, initially due to sporadic hints that he could play a role as both a batsman and a bowler. The promise was fulfilled in the Pura Cup match against Queensland in Brisbane. He added a rapid 40 to South Australia's imposing first innings before providing the decisive blows in the second innings with a haul of 7/98. By the end of the season he had established himself in both Pura Cup and ING Cup competitions as a bowling all-rounder.

	M	I	NO	R	HS	100s	50s	Avge	Ct	St	W	Avge	BB
First-class	12	23	2	497	76	0	1	23.67	10	0	37	34.62	7/98
Domestic first-class	11	21	2	472	76	0	1	24.84	10	0	34	35.65	7/98
Dom. limited-overs	11	10	4	71	30*	0	0	11.83	6	0	14	27.36	3/32

SWAIN, Brett Andrew
Born: February 14, 1974 Stirling (South Australia)
Left-handed batsman, left-arm fast-medium bowler

Although hampered by injuries over recent seasons, Brett Swain had established his position as an automatic selection for South Australia. The injuries continued in 2001-02, when he hurt his shoulder in a fielding mishap during South Australia's opening ING Cup match against Western Australia in Perth. A hat-trick for West Torrens against East Torrens in January, uniquely his fourth in SACA Grade matches, suggested a recovery, but he failed to impress in a subsequent ACB Cup match against New South Wales Second XI. With the acquisition of rival swing bowler Damien Fleming, Swain has not been offered a contract for South Australia's 2002-03 campaign.

	M	I	NO	R	HS	100s	50s	Avge	Ct	St	W	Avge	BB
First-class	23	35	7	264	36*	0	0	9.43	8	0	72	28.47	5/59
Domestic first-class	22	34	7	255	36*	0	0	9.44	8	0	71	27.99	5/59
Dom. limited-overs	19	7	2	84	35*	0	0	16.80	4	0	13	48.46	2/16

VAUGHAN, Jeffrey Mark
Born: March 26, 1974 Blacktown (New South Wales)
Right-handed batsman, right-arm fast-medium bowler

Season 2001-02, which was always going to be a pivotal one in the career of Jeff Vaughan, began promisingly when, in his club's first match against Port Adelaide, he hit 204 not out in an innings total of eight for 297 in 60 overs. A knock of 69 in the second innings against New South Wales in Sydney gave further encouragement. Things, however, went wrong at Bellerive. Opening the innings on a mischievous wicket, Vaughan was struck in the face when a ball from David Saker reared from a good length. Retiring hurt with severe concussion, he was hampered by headaches for several weeks, missing two first-class matches. Following failures in two ING Cup matches and the Pura Cup fixture at Melbourne, an innings of 96 in a club match against Tea Tree Gully was not enough to save his place in the state team. Vaughan failed to gain a contract for 2002-03.

	M	I	NO	R	HS	100s	50s	Avge	Ct	St	W	Avge	BB
First-class	27	50	5	1,416	157*	3	9	31.47	18	0	0	–	–
Domestic first-class	25	47	5	1,316	157*	3	8	31.33	18	0	0	–	–
Dom. limited-overs	20	19	1	246	57	0	2	13.67	11	0	0	–	–

WILSON, Paul
Born: January 12, 1972 Newcastle (New South Wales)
Right-handed batsman, right-arm fast-medium bowler

For the big University fast bowler, 2001-02 did not get off to a good start. Wilson missed the opening matches when arthroscopic surgery was required to remove damaged cartilage behind his right knee. Having been the dominant opening bowler in the South Australian squad for several seasons, he may have expected an automatic return to the team as soon as he had regained fitness, but the form of Harrity and Rofe delayed matters. Wilson bowled without success in two ACB Cup matches and had to wait until the penultimate Pura Cup match to play his only first-class game of the season. He fared better in limited-overs matches, where he has always been a dominant force. Evidence that Wilson remained a lethal force came in the closing minor round Grade match when he took 11/38 to destroy Port Adelaide. Seeking greater opportunities in 2002-03, Wilson accepted an approach from Western Australia.

	M	I	NO	R	HS	100s	50s	Avge	Ct	St	W	Avge	BB
First-class	40	54	17	332	32*	0	0	8.97	6	0	125	29.79	6/106
Domestic first-class	35	47	13	312	32*	0	0	9.18	6	0	112	29.48	5/68
Test	1	2	2	0	0*	0	0	–	0	0	0	–	–
Int'l limited-overs	11	5	2	4	2	0	0	1.33	1	0	13	34.62	3/39
Dom. limited-overs	46	25	8	146	16	0	0	8.59	3	0	70	23.94	4/23

YOUNG, Bradley Evan
Born: February 23, 1973 Semaphore (South Australia)
Right-handed batsman, slow left-arm orthodox bowler

After injury ruined Brad Young's 2000-01 season, 2001-02 assumed an important test for the former Australian limited-overs all-rounder. A hat-trick in West Torrens' opening match against Glenelg augured well, but this was somewhat negated when Young himself became the third victim of Ian Harvey's hat-trick in South Australia's opening Pura Cup match. An innings of 122 against New South Wales at Adelaide Oval improved Young's highest in first-class matches but, like a generation of South Australian spinners before him, he found it difficult to take wickets with match-winning frequency. Selection for the Prime Minister's XI against New Zealand at Manuka provided a reminder that it was only two years since Young had represented Australia in limited-overs internationals. However, neither his batting nor his bowling was productive enough for him to be confident of his state spot in the long term, let alone a return to the national team.

	M	I	NO	R	HS	100s	50s	Avge	Ct	St	W	Avge	BB
First-class	50	85	16	1,978	122	2	8	28.67	41	0	135	44.37	6/85
Domestic first-class	44	76	15	1,808	122	2	8	29.64	37	0	124	44.81	6/85
Int'l limited-overs	6	3	1	31	18	0	0	15.50	2	0	1	251.00	1/26
Dom. limited-overs	36	34	5	485	56	0	1	16.72	25	0	38	32.95	4/24

TASMANIA

By David Stockdale

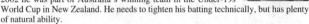

BAILEY, George John
Born: September 7, 1982 Launceston (Tasmania)
Right-handed batsman
Domestic limited-overs debut 2001-02

A Cricket Academy scholarship winner, the versatile Bailey has also represented Tasmania in football and tennis. In his only game for Tasmania, he made a promising ING Cup debut with 33 off 52 balls against Victoria at the Melbourne Cricket Ground. Early in 2002 he was part of Australia's winning team in the Under-19s World Cup in New Zealand. He needs to tighten his batting technically, but has plenty of natural ability.

	M	I	NO	R	HS	100s	50s	Avge	Ct	St	W	Avge	BB
Dom. limited-overs	1	1	0	33	33	0	0	33.00	0	0	0	–	–

CLINGELEFFER, Sean Geoffrey
Born: May 9, 1980 Hobart (Tasmania)
Left-handed batsman, wicket-keeper

In only his second first-class season, Clingeleffer blossomed with both bat and gloves to a point where he must now have front running to succeed Australia's incumbent, Adam Gilchrist. A tall and affable character, "Clinger" scored 517 first-class runs at 47, hitting his maiden century of 141 against South Australia at Bellerive and following it up with 112 in the next game there against Victoria. He took 36 catches, including a record nine in the Hobart rout of Queensland. The former Australian Under-19s representative comes from a family of keepers, with his brother Matthew at Clarence and before that his father Rod, who is chief executive of the Tasmanian Racing Club at Burnie.

	M	I	NO	R	HS	100s	50s	Avge	Ct	St	W	Avge	BB
First-class	21	29	5	720	141*	2	2	30.00	57	4	0	–	–
Dom. first-class	21	29	5	720	141*	2	2	30.00	57	4	0	–	–
Dom. limited-overs	20	12	6	130	30	0	0	21.67	21	2	0	–	–

COX, Jamie
Born: October 15, 1969 Burnie (Tasmania)
Right-handed batsman, right-arm medium bowler

By his own high standards, it was not a great season for the veteran opener. A strong finish again enabled Cox to be Tasmania's leading first-class run-getter with 660 at 38.82 with two centuries and three fifties. With captain Ricky Ponting away on national duties for most of the season, Cox was still effectively the leader. There were times when it looked as though the continuing grind of playing cricket all year round at home and in England as captain of Somerset appeared to leave him mentally and physically drained. Yet in the main he retained his amicable nature and added to his laurel of being Tasmania's highest first-class run-maker with 10,592 at 43.77 with 33 centuries by eclipsing David Boon's record of most games for the state.

	M	I	NO	R	HS	100s	50s	Avge	Ct	St	W	Avge	BB
First-class	201	353	26	14,955	245	44	64	45.73	90	0	4	80.75	3/46
Dom. first-class	134	244	16	9,601	245	29	41	42.11	61	0	0	–	–
Dom. limited-overs	62	60	4	1,537	99	0	12	27.45	17	0	0	–	–

CUNNINGHAM, Graeme Timothy
Born: January 25, 1975 Goulburn (New South Wales)
Right-handed batsman, right-arm off-spin bowler

It was another unfulfilled summer for Cunningham, who moved to Tasmania two seasons ago after the Australian Capital Territory team was axed from the old Mercantile Mutual Cup competition. Little was seen of his awesome hitting power, his eight ING Cup games yielding only 112 runs at 16.00. The brightest spot was a typically punishing 46 off 49 balls with five fours batting at number seven in the high-scoring season opener against New South Wales at Bankstown. He has had two good seasons with New Town in the TCA, and may yet carry that form over into the interstate arena.

	M	I	NO	R	HS	100s	50s	Avge	Ct	St	W	Avge	BB
Dom. limited-overs	25	23	1	597	76	0	3	27.14	6	0	0	–	–

DENTON, Gerard John
Born: August 7, 1975 Mt Isa (Queensland)
Right-handed batsman, right-arm fast-medium bowler

Despite his delayed return to the side late in the season, Denton showed encouraging signs that he could be over the recurring back problems which have forced him to miss so many games over the past three seasons. The former Australia A speedster took 2/41 and 1/66 in the last-round home win over New South Wales, which earned him a spot in the final against Queensland at the Gabba. With Damien Wright carrying a side injury, he stood up well to the extra workload, taking 3/67 off 22 overs in the first innings. His 23 wickets at 8.82 helped Kingborough reach the TCA final.

	M	I	NO	R	HS	100s	50s	Avge	Ct	St	W	Avge	BB
First-class	21	28	8	85	14	0	0	4.25	2	0	46	43.00	4/39
Dom. first-class	19	27	7	83	14	0	0	4.15	2	0	41	45.34	4/53
Dom. limited-overs	8	0	0	0	–	0	0	–	1	0	8	44.00	3/53

DI VENUTO, Michael James
Born: December 12, 1973 Hobart (Tasmania)
Left-handed batsman

It was an injury-plagued and disappointing season for the dashing left-hander, who has never fully cashed in on the riches of his talent. After turning down an offer to play for South Australia during the winter, he missed the first four Pura Cup matches after injuring an ankle in an informal game of soccer on the eve of the season opener against New South Wales at the Sydney Cricket Ground. Dropped mid-season along with other regulars Shaun Young and Dene Hills in the wake of the humiliating loss to Queensland at the Gabba, his five games produced a modest 273 runs at 39.00. Injudicious shot selection too often cut short his blossoming starts in both Pura Cup and ING Cup. He retained his form in the slips and took nine Pura Cup catches. After a successful season with Derbyshire in 2001 he returned for a third season in 2002 and began with an innings of 230.

	M	I	NO	R	HS	100s	50s	Avge	Ct	St	W	Avge	BB
First-class	147	252	13	9,736	230	18	63	40.74	135	0	5	81.20	1/0
Dom. first-class	85	149	6	5,798	189	9	42	40.55	73	0	2	96.50	1/0
Int'l limited-overs	9	9	0	241	89	0	2	26.78	1	0	0	–	–
Dom. limited-overs	57	55	7	1,443	129*	2	6	30.06	20	0	3	28.67	1/10

DIGHTON, Michael Gray
Born: July 24, 1976 Toowoomba (Queensland)
Right-handed batsman

Dighton was recruited from Western Australia, where he had struggled to recapture the form of his career-best 182 not out against Queensland two seasons before. He made a horror start for his new state with 23 runs in his first four innings, due mainly to his inability to cope with the rising ball outside the off stump. But he showed a determination which belied his easy-going nature and was rewarded with 594 briskly-scored Pura Cup runs at 39.60 with a century in each match against Victoria. A tall and elegant number three, he drove powerfully off the front foot and dispatched the short ball well.

	M	I	NO	R	HS	100s	50s	Avge	Ct	St	W	Avge	BB
First-class	21	34	2	1,199	182*	3	5	37.47	19	0	0	–	–
Dom. first-class	20	32	1	1,149	182*	3	5	37.06	17	0	0	–	–
Dom. limited-overs	11	10	1	126	52	0	1	14.00	4	0	0	–	–

DOHERTY, Xavier John
Born: November 22, 1982 Scottsdale (Tasmania)
Right-handed batsman, slow-left arm orthodox bowler
First-class, domestic first-class and domestic limited-overs
debut 2001-02

Doherty made his debut against Victoria at Bellerive to the odd statistical revelation that he was the only player in domestic first-class cricket history with a first name beginning with X. By game's end there were far more substantive things to say about the young left-arm orthodox spinner after he took 2/23 from 8.3 overs and 1/55 from 28. An Australian Cricket Academy scholar, he showed good control, tactical acumen and a willingness to try and turn the ball rather than just roll it out like so many orthodox left-armers. He appeared in two Pura Cup matches and two ING Cup matches, and showed both maturity and promise. He played a key role in Australia's victory in the Under-19s World Cup in New Zealand by taking 16 wickets, more than anyone else in the tournament.

	M	I	NO	R	HS	100s	50s	Avge	Ct	St	W	Avge	BB
First-class	2	2	1	10	6	0	0	10.00	0	0	5	39.40	2/23
Dom. first-class	2	2	1	10	6	0	0	10.00	0	0	5	39.40	2/23
Dom. limited-overs	2	1	0	3	3	0	0	3.00	1	0	1	65.00	1/36

DOWNTON, Andrew Graham
Born: July 17, 1977 Auburn (New South Wales)
Right-handed batsman, left-arm fast-medium bowler

The success of pace trio David Saker, Shane Jurgensen and Damien Wright restricted Downton to two first-class games in which he managed only two expensive wickets. He was dropped after being plundered for 100 off 22 overs in Western Australia's run orgy in Perth. Unfortunately, the left-armer, who is at his best when the conditions favour swing, did not get the chance to exploit the new-found life in the Bellerive wicket.

	M	I	NO	R	HS	100s	50s	Avge	Ct	St	W	Avge	BB
First-class	16	16	2	89	19	0	0	6.36	4	0	45	34.47	6/56
Dom. first-class	14	15	1	88	19	0	0	6.29	4	0	37	38.05	6/56
Dom. limited-overs	2	0	0	0	–	0	0	–	0	0	2	43.00	1/26

HILLS, Dene Fleetwood
Born: August 27, 1970 Wynyard (Tasmania)
Left-handed batsman

With another disappointing set of numbers from Hills and his contract not renewed for
2002-03, it looks as though his union with boyhood mate Jamie Cox, which made them
the most prolific opening pair in Australian domestic first-class history, is over. The
likeable left-hander could get nowhere near the form which made him the 1997-98
Sheffield Shield Player of the Year, and he was dumped after four games which yielded
a meagre 186 runs at 23.25. Again Hills paid a heavy price for cutting on the up to a
cordon of expectant slips. The only glimpse of his halcyon days was his 136 in an
opening partnership of 205 with Cox in the first game against New South Wales at
the SCG.

	M	I	NO	R	HS	100s	50s	Avge	Ct	St	W	Avge	BB
First-class	112	207	10	7,894	265	21	43	40.07	80	0	2	26.50	2/20
Dom. first-class	100	187	8	6,887	265	18	36	38.47	67	0	2	23.50	2/20
Dom. limited-overs	42	39	3	1,137	81	0	8	31.58	10	0	0	–	–

JURGENSEN, Shane John
Born: April 28, 1976 Redcliffe (Queensland)
Right-handed batsman, right-arm fast bowler
Domestic limited-overs debut 2001-02

A little-known journeyman trying his luck in his third state, the lanky paceman
succeeded beyond his wildest dreams. Despite missing the first three Pura Cup matches,
Jurgensen was Tasmania's second-highest wicket-taker with 36 at 19.72, including an
11-wicket haul and a hat-trick against New South Wales at Bellerive to clinch
Tasmania's berth in the final. He repeated that effort in the final against Queensland at
the Gabba, his 11/103 off a back-breaking 69 overs setting a record for the number of
wickets in a final. Jurgensen backed up a deadly cocktail of swing and seam with great
reserves of stamina, and his sunny and determined nature in adversity earned him the
nickname of the "Smiling Assassin". He also found time to take 31 wickets at the
remarkable average of 7.32 for Lindisfarne in the TCA.

	M	I	NO	R	HS	100s	50s	Avge	Ct	St	W	Avge	BB
First-class	13	15	7	148	56	0	1	18.50	2	0	44	26.89	6/65
Dom. first-class	12	14	6	135	56	0	1	16.88	1	0	43	25.47	6/65
Dom. limited-overs	5	1	1	3	3*	0	0	–	0	0	3	52.00	2/41

KREMERSKOTHEN, Scott Paul
Born: January 5, 1979 Launceston (Tasmania)
Left-handed batsman, right-arm medium bowler

A horrendous injury from a bouncer by New South Wales pace man Stuart Clark in the
season opener at the Sydney Cricket Ground restricted the promising young all-rounder
to five first-class games. The ball passed between the peak of his helmet and the lowered
visor, and the damage required major plastic surgery. Not surprisingly, when he returned
after two months it took some time for him to regain confidence and form, and he
finished with 228 Pura Cup runs at 32.57 and six wickets at 28.17. His fielding skills
were undiminished and a couple of his nine catches were superb. His ING Cup form fell
away, and after taking 14 wickets in 2000-01 he bowled only 4.2 fruitless overs in five
matches.

	M	I	NO	R	HS	100s	50s	Avge	Ct	St	W	Avge	BB
First-class	26	37	9	928	82*	0	4	33.14	19	0	23	44.39	3/64
Dom. first-class	25	36	8	927	82*	0	4	33.11	18	0	21	45.10	3/64
Dom. limited-overs	23	17	4	291	47	0	0	22.38	6	0	15	29.53	3/33

MARQUET, Joshua Phillip
Born: December 3, 1968 Melbourne (Victoria)
Right-handed batsman, right-arm fast-medium bowler

After doing well with nine wickets at 25.11 in six limited-overs matches for the Tasmanians the previous season, the veteran pace man was called up only twice. Big in build and quiet of voice, Marquet could not recapture that form and took only four wickets at 36.67 as the selectors chopped and changed in a desperate effort to find a winning mix. The joint TCA Medal winner in 1999-00 continued his fine form for University and was the leading wicket-taker in the association with 47 at 14.70 with a best of 7/37.

	M	I	NO	R	HS	100s	50s	Avge	Ct	St	W	Avge	BB
First-class	22	18	9	28	10	0	0	3.11	9	0	60	42.48	5/94
Dom. first-class	21	18	9	28	10	0	0	3.11	9	0	59	41.46	5/94
Dom. limited-overs	16	5	2	7	6	0	0	2.33	4	0	24	28.08	5/23

MARSH, Daniel James
Born: June 14, 1973 Subiaco (Western Australia)
Right-handed batsman, slow-left arm orthodox bowler

Since shrugging off the tag of being the son of Rod Marsh by winning Tasmania's Player of the Year in 1999-00, his career has stalled. After injury had shortened an otherwise successful season with Leicestershire in 2001, the chunky all-rounder returned to perform only modestly with the bat (443 runs at 28.87), and his orthodox left-arm spin bowling (eight wickets at 50.14 from 155 overs) failed to make much of an impact on opposing batting line-ups. In the ING Cup he was the Tasmanians' equal-highest run-scorer with 243 at 34.71, including a spectacular century against New South Wales. If he can get back to something like his best, he has the makings of a future captain. He fielded superbly at first slip with 20 catches in the Pura Cup, including a record-equalling seven in the home game against New South Wales.

	M	I	NO	R	HS	100s	50s	Avge	Ct	St	W	Avge	BB
First-class	77	126	22	3,897	157	7	20	37.47	87	0	128	42.55	7/57
Dom. first-class	65	106	18	2,983	134	4	15	33.90	73	0	117	42.26	7/57
Dom. limited-overs	52	45	12	1,042	101*	1	5	31.58	21	0	26	50.23	3/47

MASON, Scott
Born: July 27, 1976 George Town (Tasmania)
Left-handed batsman

With the decline of Dene Hills, the diminutive Mason was recalled to open with Jamie Cox. While his 187 runs at 20.78 from ten innings was statistically a modest return, Mason did occupy the crease for long periods to take the shine off the new ball and was always an encouraging voice on the field. In making his top score of 41 in the home victory over New South Wales he showed he has shots in his kitbag to bring out after playing himself in. But he must get over the hump of scoring his first fifty, because Tasmania now have former South Australian opener Luke Williams waiting in the wings.

	M	I	NO	R	HS	100s	50s	Avge	Ct	St	W	Avge	BB
First-class	11	17	1	287	41	0	0	17.94	3	0	0	–	–
Dom. first-class	10	15	1	248	41	0	0	17.71	3	0	0	–	–
Dom. limited-overs	8	7	0	66	16	0	0	9.43	3	0	0	–	–

PASCOE, Matthew David
Born: January 10, 1977 Camperdown (NSW)
Right-handed batsman, right-arm fast bowler

The big pace man performed well enough on debut for Tasmania – a last-round ING Cup game against Victoria at the Melbourne Cricket Ground – taking 2/38 from eight overs, to suggest he should be persevered with. Pascoe was the equal leading wicket-taker in the ACB Cup with 17 at 24.41 from four matches, but his batting made no impression whatsoever. He was recruited from Queensland, where in 1998-99 he made a first-class debut more befitting of an all-rounder by taking 3/67 and 1/26 and scoring 62 and 38 against South Australia. His bowling was a key ingredient in North Hobart's premiership win in the TCA.

	M	I	NO	R	HS	100s	50s	Avge	Ct	St	W	Avge	BB
First-class	2	3	1	120	62	0	1	60.00	1	0	4	34.75	3/67
Dom. first-class	2	3	1	120	62	0	1	60.00	1	0	4	34.75	3/67
Dom. limited-overs	3	0	0	0	–	0	0	–	0	0	6	19.67	3/43

POLKINGHORNE, Adam William
Born: August 23, 1975 Karoonda (South Australia)
Left-handed batsman

A former Bradman Medal winner in Adelaide cricket, Polkinghorne could not reproduce his outstanding club form for South Hobart–Sandy Bay in the ING Cup, scoring only 35 runs in five innings and taking two wickets at 118.50. His meagre returns were typical of the state's welter of all-rounders who were unable to perform up to standard in either discipline. He was compensated somewhat by winning his second consecutive TCA Medal, racking up 425 runs at 38.64 and taking 33 wickets at 11.27 with a mix of medium-pace and leg-spin.

	M	I	NO	R	HS	100s	50s	Avge	Ct	St	W	Avge	BB
Dom. limited-overs	8	7	0	57	14	0	0	8.14	1	0	3	86.33	1/22

PONTING, Ricky Thomas
Born: December 19, 1974 Launceston (Tasmania)
Right-handed batsman, right-arm medium bowler

This was the season in which the one-time naughty boy of Australian cricket became a leader. Ponting matured into an astute captain of first his state and then his country, along the way marrying Rianna Cantor, the woman whose influence he says had helped turn him around. Ponting took over the reins of Tasmania from Jamie Cox and led by example in the few state games available to him before leaving for international duties at home and abroad. In two Pura Cup games "Punter" racked up 367 runs at 91.75 with two centuries and was just as awesome in three ING Cup sorties with 203 at 67.67 with one century. In the Second Test against New Zealand at Hobart, Ponting hit a masterly 157 not out from 218 balls, and his Test summer was crowned by a superb series-winning century in Port Elizabeth. In February he was asked to captain the Australian limited-overs team, taking over when Steve Waugh was forced to abdicate. Quickly proving himself to be a natural leader and a smart tactician, he led Australia to a resounding 5-1 series win over South Africa, winning the Player of the Series award in the process.

	M	I	NO	R	HS	100s	50s	Avge	Ct	St	W	Avge	BB
First-class	143	240	35	11,218	233	39	48	54.72	144	0	13	52.08	2/10
Dom. first-class	47	87	13	4,749	233	20	14	64.18	31	0	5	73.40	1/7
Test	56	89	12	3,505	197	10	16	45.52	72	0	4	40.00	1/0
Int'l limited-overs	141	141	16	5,110	145	9	29	40.88	47	0	3	34.67	1/12
Dom. limited-overs	30	30	4	930	102	1	6	35.77	12	0	5	23.80	3/34

SAKER, David James
Born: May 29, 1966 Oakleigh (Victoria)
Right-handed batsman, right-arm fast-medium bowler

Like fellow former Victorian pace man Mark Ridgway before him, Saker showed there was plenty of life in the old dog yet. His sustained fire from a shortish run, his enviable stamina, and his ability to move the ball away from the right-handers made him the side's leading first-class wicket-taker with 38 at 26.39. A popular winner of the Tasmanian Player of the Year award, he formed a lethal union with Shane Jurgensen to propel Tasmania into the Pura Cup final. He also played some vital innings down the order, capped by an unbeaten 66 in a last-wicket stand of 114 with Jurgensen which kick-started the charge to the final.

	M	I	NO	R	HS	100s	50s	Avge	Ct	St	W	Avge	BB
First-class	70	96	28	1,356	66*	0	4	19.94	16	0	246	29.63	7/32
Dom. first-class	66	90	26	1,250	66*	0	3	19.53	15	0	230	30.31	7/32
Dom. limited-overs	43	23	7	255	47*	0	0	15.94	4	0	46	32.83	4/35

THOMAS, Brad John
Born: January 18, 1972 Hobart (Tasmania)
Right-handed batsman, right-arm medium bowler
First-class and domestic first-class debut 2001-02

Thomas struggled to reproduce the form which had won him three TCA Medals. In his only first-class game, against South Australia at Bellerive, the University all-rounder made 21 and four and took one expensive wicket, being one of many bowlers to suffer at the hands of rampant double-century-maker Darren Lehmann. In two ING Cup appearances, Thomas made 16 not out in his only innings and took no wickets. Batting as low as eight and nine did not give him much chance to show his wares with the bat, while his bowling was too loose in width and length.

	M	I	NO	R	HS	100s	50s	Avge	Ct	St	W	Avge	BB
First-class	1	2	0	25	21	0	0	12.50	0	0	1	52.00	1/52
Dom. first-class	1	2	0	25	21	0	0	12.50	0	0	1	52.00	1/52
Dom. limited-overs	4	3	1	48	16*	0	0	24.00	1	0	1	74.00	1/15

TUBB, Shannon Benjamin
Born: May 11, 1980 Bracknell (Tasmania)
Right-handed batsman, left-arm slow 'chinaman' bowler
Domestic limited-overs debut 2001-02

Given that the changing nature of the Bellerive wicket assisted the Tasmanian battery of pace men, it was not surprising that Tubb's opportunities to master spin bowling's most esoteric art were very limited. Despite that, he did well to take five wickets at 16.00 apiece and showed improved control. The much-travelled former Australian Cricket Academy scholar played a vital role in the away win over South Australia by taking 3/57 off 18 overs, including the prize wicket of century-maker Ben Johnson. He also showed handy form batting in the tail, hitting a top score of 33. In the ACB Cup he took 6/55 in the second innings against Australian Capital Territory at Manuka.

	M	I	NO	R	HS	100s	50s	Avge	Ct	St	W	Avge	BB
First-class	5	7	0	99	42	0	0	14.14	1	0	5	35.80	3/57
Dom. first-class	5	7	0	99	42	0	0	14.14	1	0	5	35.80	3/57
Dom. limited-overs	1	1	0	13	13	0	0	13.00	0	0	0	–	–

WATSON, Shane Robert
Born: June 17, 1981 Ipswich (Queensland)
Right-handed batsman, right-arm medium bowler
International limited-overs debut 2001-02

The husky blond all-rounder has enjoyed the sort of meteoric rise that you would only expect to read in a Boys' Own Annual. Plucked by Tasmania from the Cricket Academy in the middle of the 2000-01 season after being ignored by Queensland, his vigorous middle-order batting and aggressive pace bowling led to his selection in the Australian team to tour South Africa in early 2002. The catalyst was his amazing match figures of 11/78 off 20.5 overs of blistering pace against the Queenslanders at Bellerive in front of national selectors Trevor Hohns and David Boon. In seven matches, Watson took 22 wickets at 23.26 and scored a more modest 292 runs at 29.20 with three fifties. He was Tasmania's equal top run-getter in the ING Cup with 243 at 30.38, also with three fifties. He scored a whirlwind century against South Africa A at Port Elizabeth and later showed promise in his appearances for Australia in limited-overs matches. A hard worker who listens to his elders, he could develop into the all-rounder Australia has not seen since the days of Alan Davidson.

	M	I	NO	R	HS	100s	50s	Avge	Ct	St	W	Avge	BB
First-class	13	20	4	701	105	2	5	43.81	4	0	36	23.97	6/32
Dom. first-class	12	19	3	601	105	1	5	37.56	4	0	33	24.33	6/32
Int'l limited-overs	7	6	1	89	44*	0	0	17.80	2	0	2	123.50	1/38
Dom. limited-overs	15	14	2	346	96	0	3	28.83	5	0	7	64.86	2/46

WRIGHT, Damien Geoffrey
Born: July 25, 1975 Casino (New South Wales)
Right-handed batsman, right-arm fast-medium bowler

It was another productive season for the popular blond pace man, although his 23 first-class wickets came at a rather costly 40.52 each. It is something of an oddity that in bowling the second-highest number of overs after David Saker he also produced the most maidens, with 114. That may be explained by the fact that once Shayne Jurgensen turned into a match-winner as the season progressed, Wright was asked to play a more stock role. He also began to fulfil his promise as a valuable batsman down the order, shaming some of those above him by scoring 409 runs at 34.08 with four fifties. He was again the Tasmanians most economical bowler in the ING Cup, his 13 wickets coming at 29.46 and 3.83 an over, and he was rewarded with selection in the Australia A limited-overs side to tour South Africa.

	M	I	NO	R	HS	100s	50s	Avge	Ct	St	W	Avge	BB
First-class	30	42	11	702	63	0	4	22.65	13	0	70	40.74	4/54
Dom. first-class	29	42	11	702	63	0	4	22.65	13	0	68	40.66	4/54
Dom. limited-overs	27	16	7	150	40	0	0	16.67	7	0	37	24.68	4/23

YOUNG, Shaun
Born: June 13, 1970 Burnie (Tasmania)
Left-handed batsman, right-arm fast-medium bowler

Dropped in the middle of the season and with no contract renewal for 2002-03, the hard-bitten all-rounder's long and impressive first-class career may have come to an end. His was one of three heads to roll after the debacle against Queensland at the Gabba, even though his batting (259 runs at 32.38) had been solid, if not his bowling (one wicket for 156). After winning the Mercantile Mutual Player of the Year award in 2000-01, his limited-overs form also dropped away alarmingly. He took only three wickets in seven matches and conceded more than five an over. "China" has been a great servant of Tasmanian cricket, being one of only four to play 100 first-class games, the second-highest wicket-taker (201 at 39.22) and the fifth-highest run-scorer (5,565 at 37.86 with ten centuries).

	M	I	NO	R	HS	100s	50s	Avge	Ct	St	W	Avge	BB
First-class	138	227	37	7,212	237	14	44	37.96	82	0	274	35.82	7/64
Dom. first-class	104	176	29	5,565	175*	10	35	37.86	62	0	201	39.22	5/26
Test	1	2	1	4	4*	0	0	4.00	0	0	0	–	–
Dom. limited-overs	64	56	6	1,428	96	0	9	28.56	23	0	43	43.35	3/16

VICTORIA

By Ken Williams

ARNBERGER, Jason Lee
Born: November 18, 1972 Penrith (New South Wales)
Right-handed batsman

Troubled by a back injury that he aggravated while playing club cricket in Scotland during the winter, Jason Arnberger had a disappointing season in which he made only two fifties in 16 first-class innings. Although he and Matthew Elliott took part in some useful opening partnerships, with two century stands and three others over 50, his eight Pura Cup appearances produced a modest 401 runs at 28.64, a far cry from 2000-01, when his confident and aggressive strokeplay brought him 1,006 runs. His injury eventually caused him to miss the last two Pura Cup matches. He played in the first two ING Cup games, but after dropping out with a groin strain, he appeared only once more, scoring 55 runs in three innings.

	M	I	NO	R	HS	100s	50s	Avge	Ct	St	W	Avge	BB
First-class	55	105	7	3,538	214	5	22	36.10	41	0	0	–	–
Dom. first-class	52	100	7	3,396	214	5	21	36.52	38	0	0	–	–
Dom. limited-overs	22	21	1	348	75	0	2	17.40	0	0	0	–	–

BARTLETT, Robert Andrew
Born: January 2, 1972 Melbourne (Victoria)
Right-handed batsman, right-arm medium bowler
Domestic limited-overs debut 2001-02

Following a century for the Victorian Second XI and good form at club level, Robbie Bartlett was recalled to the Victorian side for five ING Cup matches. His only previous appearance for the state was nine seasons earlier, when Glenn McGrath dismissed him for nought and seven in a Shield game at Sydney. A polished stroke-maker with a wide range of shots, and an excellent field, it was hoped his inclusion would lift the one-day side, reeling after the loss of its first four matches. On his ING Cup debut, against Tasmania, he batted attractively for 40 and took part in an opening stand of 85 with Matthew Elliott, easily Victoria's best start for the season in the competition. However, he failed to reach double figures in his next four matches and was dropped. Although a useful medium-pacer at club level, he was not called upon to bowl for the state. He had an excellent season in Premier cricket for Fitzroy–Doncaster, scoring 851 runs at 47.27, and helping them to the premiership by top-scoring with 73 in the final after making a century in the semi-final.

	M	I	NO	R	HS	100s	50s	Avge	Ct	St	W	Avge	BB
First-class	1	2	0	7	7	0	0	3.50	0	0	0	–	–
Dom. first-class	1	2	0	7	7	0	0	3.50	0	0	0	–	–
Dom. limited-overs	5	5	0	57	40	0	0	11.40	2	0	0	–	–

BERRY, Darren Shane
Born: December 10, 1969 Melbourne (Victoria)
Right-handed batsman, wicket-keeper

Darren Berry again gave fine service behind the stumps. After losing the vice-captaincy of Victoria's Pura Cup and ING Cup sides, his place in the team looked insecure. However, he was one of only two players (with Matthew Elliott) to appear in all Victoria's matches, and showed he had lost none of his skill behind the stumps. His seven catches against Queensland in the last Pura Cup match took his total number of catches in first-class cricket to 500, a total reached previously by only two Australian keepers, Rod Marsh and Ian Healy. He was equally effective in the ING Cup, where his 19 dismissals was a state record and only two short of the record set by Ryan Campbell. Berry has completed more dismissals than any other player in the Sheffield Shield/Pura Cup (488) and domestic one-day competitions (120). With 382 runs at 29.38 in first-class matches, he had his best season with the bat for some years, mainly due to his spirited 148 against New South Wales, his fourth first-class hundred, all of which have been made against New South Wales. During the season he passed Dean Jones's record of 104 Sheffield Shield/Pura Cup appearances for the state.

	M	I	NO	R	HS	100s	50s	Avge	Ct	St	W	Avge	BB
First-class	138	210	31	3,835	166*	4	9	21.42	500	45	0	–	–
Dom. first-class	124	191	28	3,525	166*	4	8	21.63	447	41	0	–	–
Dom. limited-overs	73	55	15	660	64*	0	1	16.50	93	27	0	–	–

CARR, William Niall
Born: June 1, 1976 Box Hill (Victoria)
Right-handed batsman, right-arm fast bowler
First-class and domestic first-class debut 2001-02

The success of fast bowler Will Carr was one of the few bright spots in Victoria's poor season. Called up for the last three Pura Cup matches following the retirement of Paul Reiffel and a spate of injuries to other bowlers, he bowled with pace and hostility to capture 16 wickets at 17.25, including figures of 6/46 against Queensland in the last match. Tall and broad-shouldered, he takes a relatively short and straight approach to the wicket, with a high delivery and powerful shoulder action which enable him to gain deceptive speed and sharp lift. A relative latecomer to first-class cricket at 25, he learnt his cricket at Berwick in Melbourne's outer south-east before joining Premier club Dandenong four seasons ago. Only modestly successful in his first two seasons, his record improved markedly in 2000-01 when he made his state Second XI debut. A six-wicket haul in a Second XI game against Western Australia in early February led to his promotion to the Pura Cup side. For Dandenong in Premier cricket he captured 38 wickets at 20.89.

	M	I	NO	R	HS	100s	50s	Avge	Ct	St	W	Avge	BB
First-class	3	3	1	4	4	0	0	2.00	0	0	16	17.25	6/46
Dom. first-class	3	3	1	4	4	0	0	2.00	0	0	16	17.25	6/46

CRAIG, Shawn Andrew Jacob
Born: June 23, 1973 Carlton (Victoria)
Left-handed batsman, right-arm leg-spin bowler

Although his steady batting is better suited to the four-day game, Shawn Craig played in two ING Cup matches early in the season in which he made six (run out) and 11. Early in the new year a scan revealed that he had been playing for some weeks with a cracked bone in his foot and he was unable to play again for the season. He had been in excellent form for the state Second XI, scoring 397 runs at 99.25. In May it was announced that his Victorian contract would not be renewed.

	M	I	NO	R	HS	100s	50s	Avge	Ct	St	W	Avge	BB
First-class	20	36	6	936	128*	1	4	31.20	20	0	8	83.00	2/89
Dom. first-class	17	31	5	807	128*	1	3	31.04	15	0	7	87.00	2/89
Dom. limited-overs	20	18	4	346	60	0	2	24.71	4	0	7	23.57	3/56

DART, Simon Paul
Born: February 3, 1978 Melbourne (Victoria)
Right-handed batsman, right-arm medium bowler

Still to make his first-class debut, Simon Dart appeared in five ING Cup matches in which he confirmed the good impression he had made in 2000-01. A busy and tidy batsman, his best effort was a bright 51 not out against Western Australia, his first half-century for the state. In mid-January he was picked for the Pura Cup match against Western Australia at Perth but unfortunately, on the Saturday before the game, his right index finger was broken while batting in a club match. This kept him out of action for six weeks, ruling him out of state selection for the rest of the season. In Premier cricket for Hawthorn–Monash University, he scored 444 runs at 49.33.

	M	I	NO	R	HS	100s	50s	Avge	Ct	St	W	Avge	BB
Dom. limited-overs	10	9	2	192	51*	0	1	27.43	3	0	0	–	–

ELLIOTT, Matthew Thomas Gray
Born: September 28, 1971 Chelsea (Victoria)
Left-handed batsman, slow-left arm orthodox bowler

Having lost his ACB contract, Matthew Elliott was anxious to score heavily in order to impress the national selectors. However, although rarely troubled by the new ball and batting confidently throughout the season, his Pura Cup record of 780 runs at 43.33 fell below expectations. Although he reached fifty on seven occasions, he only once went on to a century, a match-saving 135 not out against Tasmania in Hobart, his 23rd century for the state. His inability to convert more fifties into hundreds was frustrating, as he frequently seemed set for a big score before falling to what was often his first false shot. He was easily Victoria's most successful batsman in the ING Cup, scoring 431 runs at 47.88 with one century, also against Tasmania in Hobart. Named as captain of Victoria's limited-overs side and vice-captain of its four-day side, he was called upon to lead the Pura Cup side in six of its ten matches after the retirement of Paul Reiffel. Despite his lack of experience, for he had not even captained his club side before the season, he settled into the job well. He topped the Premier Cricket batting averages for the second successive season, scoring 483 runs at 80.50 for Camberwell Magpies.

	M	I	NO	R	HS	100s	50s	Avge	Ct	St	W	Avge	BB
First-class	131	242	19	11,016	203	34	51	49.40	154	0	9	62.56	1/3
Dom. first-class	74	144	12	6,973	203	23	33	52.83	102	0	7	50.86	1/3
Test	20	34	1	1,171	199	3	4	35.48	13	0	0	–	–
Int'l limited-overs	1	1	0	1	1	0	0	1.00	0	0	0	–	–
Dom. limited-overs	52	50	4	1,587	118*	5	7	34.50	22	0	0	–	–

FLEMING, Damien William
Born: April 24, 1970 Bentley (Western Australia)
Right-handed batsman, right-arm fast-medium bowler

Damien Fleming experienced a frustrating season during which he fell victim to a range of injuries. A member of the Australian team in England during the winter, he appeared only twice in the triangular international limited-overs competition because of a calf strain and was not chosen for any of the Tests, although his effective swing bowling in county games suggested that he was unlucky not to have replaced the out-of-form Brett Lee for at least one Test. He began the Australian season by bowling impressively in Victoria's opening Pura Cup match against South Australia, but thereafter was dogged by injury. A bruised and blistered foot kept him out of an ING Cup match in late October and a month later he broke down with a torn hamstring on the opening day of a Pura Cup game against Tasmania. Despite appearing in two ING Cup games in January and declaring himself to be fully fit, he did not return to the Pura Cup side until the return match against Tasmania in mid-February. Troubled by tendonitis, he took only one wicket and immediately after the game underwent surgery to repair a torn cartilage in his right shoulder. This brought an early end to an unsatisfactory season in which he captured 13 wickets at 30.08 in five Pura Cup matches and six wickets in seven ING Cup appearances. In May the ACB decided not to renew his contract and soon after the Victorian selectors announced that he would not be offered a state contract. Keen to continue playing cricket at the top level, he accepted an offer to play for South Australia in 2002-03.

	M	I	NO	R	HS	100s	50s	Avge	Ct	St	W	Avge	BB
First-class	112	134	38	1,437	71*	0	4	14.97	54	0	376	27.95	7/90
Dom. first-class	67	87	26	819	45*	0	0	13.43	29	0	221	30.20	7/90
Test	20	19	3	305	71*	0	2	19.06	9	0	75	25.89	5/30
Int'l limited-overs	88	31	18	152	29	0	0	11.69	14	0	134	25.39	5/36
Dom. limited-overs	46	25	12	152	21	0	0	11.69	10	0	48	33.00	3/25

HARVEY, Ian Joseph
Born: April 10, 1972 Wonthaggi (Victoria)
Right-handed batsman, right-arm fast-medium bowler

Although Ian Harvey came second in Victoria's Pura Cup batting averages and topped their ING Cup bowling averages, he produced only patches of the all-round brilliance which has earned him the nickname "Freak". His record in limited-overs internationals was especially disappointing. In the VB Series he appeared in only three of Australia's eight matches, contributing a modest 23 runs and capturing four wickets. In South Africa, he played in five of the seven matches, but scored only 43 runs in four innings and took five wickets at 46.40 and at the unusually uneconomical rate of nearly six runs per over. He was omitted from the Australian squad for the series against Pakistan in June. In seven Pura Cup matches for Victoria he scored 432 runs at 48.00 and was runner-up to Brad Hodge in the batting averages. On his day there are few more fluent and clean strikers of the ball, as he revealed in his 87 against Tasmania, the highest of his four half-centuries. He was less successful with the ball, capturing 17 wickets at 36.65 and failing to capture more than three wickets in an innings, despite taking a hat-trick against South Australia in the opening match. He was more effective as a bowler in the ING Cup, capturing 12 wickets at 14.50 in six matches. Against Queensland, despite being on the losing side he made a quickfire 72 off 66 balls and took 3/19 off his ten overs. After a successful season with Gloucestershire in 2001 he returned in 2002 for his fourth season with the county.

	M	I	NO	R	HS	100s	50s	Avge	Ct	St	W	Avge	BB
First-class	102	170	13	4,913	136	7	29	31.29	74	0	289	26.94	7/44
Dom. first-class	62	108	10	3,352	136	4	23	34.20	42	0	145	33.43	7/44
Int'l limited-overs	43	32	8	429	47*	0	0	17.88	13	0	47	34.60	4/28
Dom. limited-overs	53	48	3	892	72	0	5	19.82	16	0	63	26.22	5/34

HARWOOD, Shane Michael
Born: March 1, 1974 Ballarat (Victoria)
Right-handed batsman, right-arm fast-medium bowler
Domestic limited-overs debut 2001-02

A tearaway right-arm fast bowler with good control, 27-year-old Shane Harwood impressed when given a trial in the ING Cup side mid-season. Originally from Ballarat, he represented Victoria at several national country championships, but repeatedly turned down offers to play in Melbourne until he agreed to play for Melbourne Cricket Club in 1999-00. He captured 46 wickets in his first season of Premier cricket, and was included in the following year's state squad, but was hampered by injury. Again troubled by injury at the start of 2001-02, he came into Victoria's ING Cup side soon after taking 6/41 in a Second XI match against Tasmania. His debut match was ruined by rain and he did not bowl, but in the next two games he impressed with his pace and control, especially against New South Wales in Melbourne where he captured 3/22 in a hostile ten-over spell. A week later he broke a bone in his ankle in a club game, which kept him out of the Victorian side for the rest of the season. A fierce competitor, he is a capable lower-order batsman who hits hard and plays straight.

	M	I	NO	R	HS	100s	50s	Avge	Ct	St	W	Avge	BB
Dom. limited-overs	3	1	0	0	0	0	0	0.00	0	0	4	15.25	3/22

HEWETT, Ian Stephen Louis
Born: January 24, 1976 East Melbourne (Victoria)
Left-handed batsman, left-arm fast-medium bowler

Ian Hewett was a regular member of the state's ING Cup side and made a single Pura Cup appearance in late January, his first match at first-class level since he played two Shield games at the age of 19 in 1995-96. His best performance was in an ING Cup match against Western Australia shortly before Christmas, when he captured 4/22 to set Victoria on the way to their first win of the season. In his next match, against New South Wales, he turned likely defeat into a remarkable victory by hitting out bravely. In the Pura Cup match against New South Wales at Sydney in late January, he opened the attack with fellow left-armer Mathew Inness, capturing 3/63 in the second innings, his best first-class figures. Lower back problems, which kept him out of the final ING Cup match, also prevented him from playing in the remaining Pura Cup games. In Premier cricket he topped Richmond's batting averages with 393 runs at 49.12 but captured only eight wickets.

	M	I	NO	R	HS	100s	50s	Avge	Ct	St	W	Avge	BB
First-class	3	3	2	41	34*	0	0	41.00	1	0	6	51.83	3/63
Dom. first-class	3	3	2	41	34*	0	0	41.00	1	0	6	51.83	3/63
Dom. limited-overs	17	14	4	86	29*	0	0	8.60	3	0	21	25.71	4/22

HODGE, Bradley John
Born: December 29, 1974 Sandringham (Victoria)
Right-handed batsman, right-arm off-spin bowler

Brad Hodge capped off a fine season when he was named as the joint Pura Cup Player of the Year. He began the season brilliantly, scoring 140 and 110 not out against South Australia in Adelaide. After passing 50 only once in the next six matches, he had another burst of fine form late in the season when he reeled off successive scores of 85 and 109 against Tasmania and 121 against Western Australia. Possessing a classical technique, he is one of the most attractive batsman in the country, and is a far more mature and composed player than the brilliant but rash stroke-maker who burst onto the first-class scene nine years ago. He was less successful in ING Cup matches, compiling 227 runs at 25.22. Appointed vice-captain of the state's ING side at the start of the season, he was elevated to the vice-captaincy of the Pura Cup side after the retirement of Paul Reiffel. In Premier Cricket for Melbourne, whom he captained for the first time, he scored 446 runs at 63.71. He replaced the injured Martin Love as Durham's overseas professional for the second half of the 2002 English season. He is still young enough to achieve higher honours.

	M	I	NO	R	HS	100s	50s	Avge	Ct	St	W	Avge	BB
First-class	86	159	17	5,646	140	16	26	39.76	46	0	36	38.75	4/17
Dom. first-class	78	145	14	5,057	140	13	24	38.60	43	0	27	48.81	4/92
Dom. limited-overs	56	54	5	1,739	118*	2	13	35.49	23	0	6	50.00	2/25

INNESS, Mathew William Hunter
Born: January 13, 1978 East Melbourne (Victoria)
Left-handed batsman, left-arm fast-medium bowler

Mathew Inness confirmed his reputation as one of the most under-rated bowlers in the country with an excellent season in which he captured 31 wickets at 19.25 in the Pura Cup, which enabled him to top the national bowling averages for bowlers with 20 or more first-class wickets. He commanded respect from opposing batsmen with his lively pace, accurate off-stump line and the ability to move the ball either way. Against New South Wales at Sydney in late January he routed the home side for 109 with career-best figures of 7/19, including a spell of 5/7 with his last 28 balls. His match figures of 11/86 represented his second ten-wicket haul for the state. A broken big toe kept him out of the next two Pura Cup matches, but he returned to capture 4/37 against Queensland in the last match. He also bowled effectively when called up for Victoria's last three ING Cup matches. He has the unusual distinction of having taken nearly twice as many wickets for the state as he has scored runs.

	M	I	NO	R	HS	100s	50s	Avge	Ct	St	W	Avge	BB
First-class	41	43	16	77	27	0	0	2.85	12	0	148	24.56	7/19
Dom. first-class	38	42	16	74	27	0	0	2.85	11	0	137	24.46	7/19
Dom. limited-overs	9	0	0	0	–	0	0	–	2	0	4	73.00	2/36

JEWELL, Nicholas
Born: August 27, 1977 East Melbourne (Victoria)
Right-handed batsman, left-arm fast-medium bowler
First-class, domestic first-class and domestic limited-overs
debut, 2001-02

A hard-hitting middle-order batsman, Nick Jewell was one of several new players tried by Victoria late in the season. Tall and strongly built, he is a powerful driver off the front foot with a liking for the on side. Following two centuries for the state's Second XI, he appeared the last two ING Cup matches, and created a favourable impression with scores of 31 against Queensland and 39 against Tasmania. He was then chosen for the last two Pura Cup matches, but seemed less assured at first-class level, making 49 runs in four innings. In Premier cricket for St Kilda he scored 457 runs at 28.56 including two centuries and took 18 wickets at 27.11. He is the son of Tony Jewell, the former VFL footballer and coach. A promising footballer himself, he played one AFL game for Richmond in 1997 before concentrating on cricket.

	M	I	NO	R	HS	100s	50s	Avge	Ct	St	W	Avge	BB
First-class	2	4	0	49	26	0	0	12.25	0	0	0	–	–
Dom. first-class	2	4	0	49	26	0	0	12.25	0	0	0	–	–
Dom. limited-overs	2	2	0	70	39	0	0	35.00	0	0	0	–	–

KLINGER, Michael
Born: July 4, 1980 Kew (Victoria)
Right-handed batsman

Michael Klinger was one of several top-order Victorian batsmen to experience a lean year. Despite working hard during the winter to overcome a tendency to play across the line, his output of runs fell well below that expected from a number five batsman. He failed to play a long innings, his top score in 21 innings for the state in both competitions being 58. He played in the first seven Pura Cup matches, scoring 251 runs at 27.88, while his ten ING Cup appearances produced a moderate tally of 211 runs at 23.44. He also had a lean year in Premier cricket for St Kilda, scoring 272 runs at 24.72. Still only 21, he has time to regain form and fulfil his promise a talented stroke-maker and brilliant fieldsman.

	M	I	NO	R	HS	100s	50s	Avge	Ct	St	W	Avge	BB
First-class	20	31	4	761	99*	0	6	28.19	10	0	0	–	–
Dom. first-class	17	28	4	630	99*	0	5	26.25	9	0	0	–	–
Dom. limited-overs	21	21	3	473	80*	0	3	26.28	3	0	0	–	–

LEWIS, Michael Llewellyn
Born: June 29, 1974 Greensborough (Victoria)
Right-handed batsman, right-arm fast-medium bowler

Although his record of 16 wickets at 38.81 in seven Pura Cup matches was unremarkable, Mick Lewis bowled better than these figures indicate. Normally bowling at first change, he delivered some fine spells, especially against top-order batsmen, and was unlucky with missed chances. His best performance was a seven-wicket haul against South Australia in Melbourne in mid-December which took Victoria to its first win for the season. For the second year running he appeared in every ING Cup match, picking up a useful 13 wickets at 24.61 with best figures of 4/41 against Western Australia at Perth. Hard-working and fit, he was one the few Victorian bowlers to go through the season without injury. No longer a tearaway fast bowler, he now relies more on control and movement, with good variations of pace. Hitherto regarded as a rank tail-ender, his batting improved to such an extent that he made a first-class fifty, an undefeated 54 against New South Wales in Sydney.

	M	I	NO	R	HS	100s	50s	Avge	Ct	St	W	Avge	BB
First-class	19	27	9	188	54*	0	1	10.44	4	0	54	33.70	5/57
Dom. first-class	19	27	9	188	54*	0	1	10.44	4	0	54	33.70	5/57
Dom. limited-overs	24	4	3	25	15*	0	0	25.00	6	0	29	29.14	4/41

McDONALD, Andrew Barry
Born: June 5, 1981 Wodonga (Victoria)
Right-handed batsman, right-arm fast-medium bowler
First-class, domestic first-class and domestic limited-overs
debut 2001-02

A talented 20-year-old all-rounder, Andrew McDonald was one of four Victorians to make his first-class debut in the new year. Tall and red-headed, he is a middle-order batsman with a good technique and a wide range of strokes, and a lively medium-paced bowler who is especially good at picking up wickets near the end of limited-overs games. He played grade cricket in both Melbourne and Sydney before joining the Melbourne Cricket Club in 1999. In January 2000 he was a member of the Australian team in the Under-19s World Cup in Sri Lanka and he went on to attend the Cricket Academy in 2000-01. A regular member of the state's Second XI , he appeared in three ING Cup and two Pura Cup matches towards the end of the season. Dismissed without scoring in his first innings in both competitions, his contributions were modest, although he picked up a few useful wickets and shaped well to make 26 against Queensland in the final Pura Cup match. He was in fine all-round form for Melbourne in Premier cricket, scoring 598 runs at 42.71 and capturing 23 wickets at 21.52.

	M	I	NO	R	HS	100s	50s	Avge	Ct	St	W	Avge	BB
First-class	2	4	1	43	26	0	0	14.33	3	0	2	10.00	1/6
Dom. first-class	2	4	1	43	26	0	0	14.33	3	0	2	10.00	1/6
Dom. limited-overs	3	3	1	21	19*	0	0	10.50	1	0	1	75.00	1/44

McGAIN, Bryce Edward
Born: March 25, 1972 Mornington (Victoria)
Right-handed batsman, right-arm leg-spin bowler
First-class and domestic first-class debut 2001-02

Making a late debut at 29 years of age, leg-spinner Bryce McGain bowled tidily in two Pura Cup matches late in the season. His selection came after a number of good hauls in Premier cricket and some useful spells for the state's Second XI. An accurate and probing bowler, he relies on well-concealed variations of flight and spin to deceive batsmen rather than sharp turn. He is a smart fieldsman, especially off his own bowling, but has no pretensions with the bat. Chosen for the Pura Cup match against New South Wales in Sydney to replace the out-of-form Colin Miller, he bowled with good control to capture two wickets in the second innings. After being left out for the next match, he was brought back to play against Western Australia in Melbourne, and again bowled accurately, capturing three wickets cheaply in Western Australia's first innings. In Premier cricket he was the season's second-highest wicket-taker, capturing 48 wickets for Prahran at 18.89. Captaining them for the first time, he made such an impression that he was named as captain of the Premier cricket team of the season. He spent the winter of 2002 playing club cricket in Denmark.

	M	I	NO	R	HS	100s	50s	Avge	Ct	St	W	Avge	BB
First-class	2	2	0	3	3	0	0	1.50	2	0	6	33.67	3/46
Dom. first-class	2	2	0	3	3	0	0	1.50	2	0	6	33.67	3/46

MILLER, Colin Reid
Born: February 6, 1964 Footscray (Victoria)
Right-handed batsman, right-arm medium-off spin bowler

Colin Miller's loss of form, following a season in which he was named as Australia's Test Player of the Year, came as a big disappointment. At the start of the season he featured in advertisements for the newly-named ING Cup competition, his hair dyed bright orange to match the sponsor's colour, but ironically he did not play a single game in the competition. His first appearance for Victoria was in a Pura Cup match against South Australia in Adelaide. He found wickets hard to take, capturing just one in each innings. After taking only one wicket in each of the next two matches, he was relegated, much to his annoyance, to 12th man for the next two games. His replacement, leg-spinner Cameron White, at 18, almost 20 years his junior. Miller was recalled to play against Western Australia at Perth in January. Bowling mainly medium pace on a pitch that did not favour spin, he captured only two wickets, and was left out of the state side for the rest of the season. Having taken just six wickets 72.50 in four Pura Cup matches, his omission was hardly surprising. It became clear that his career was over when his ACB contract was not renewed and he was not offered a state contract. Despite these setbacks he continued to toil hard in Premier cricket for Footscray–Victoria University, finishing with the solid return of 33 wickets at 23.69.

	M	I	NO	R	HS	100s	50s	Avge	Ct	St	W	Avge	BB
First-class	126	150	31	1,533	62	0	3	12.88	39	0	446	30.97	7/49
Dom. first-class	84	106	22	1,145	60*	0	2	13.63	25	0	304	32.03	7/49
Test	18	24	3	174	43	0	0	8.29	6	0	69	26.16	5/32
Dom. limited-overs	45	27	6	232	32	0	0	11.05	9	0	46	36.46	4/36

MOSS, Jonathan
Born: May 4, 1975 Manly (New South Wales)
Right-handed batsman, right-arm fast-medium bowler

In his second season with Victoria after moving from Sydney, Jon Moss again proved a valuable all-rounder, especially after he was brought into the Pura Cup team for the second half of the season. Replacing Ian Harvey, he made an immediate impact. In his first three innings he scored two determined half-centuries in a low-scoring match against Western Australia, and a disciplined maiden first-class hundred against New South Wales after Victoria had slumped to five for 50 on a Sydney green-top. His five Pura Cup appearances produced 378 runs at 42.00 and by the end of the season he was promoted to No. 4. His lively medium-pace bowling was used sparingly, despite often proving effective, his best figures being 3/35 from 26 overs against Western Australia. He was a regular member of the ING Cup side, scoring 162 runs at 23.14, but was again little used as a bowler. Hard-working and enthusiastic, he has fitted well into the Victorian side. In Premier cricket with Prahran he again won both the batting and bowling averages, with 449 runs at 49.88 and 27 wickets at 14.96.

	M	I	NO	R	HS	100s	50s	Avge	Ct	St	W	Avge	BB
First-class	8	14	0	514	109	1	4	36.71	4	0	11	28.82	3/35
Dom. first-class	8	14	0	514	109	1	4	36.71	4	0	11	28.82	3/35
Dom. limited-overs	12	10	1	197	64*	0	1	21.89	2	0	9	20.78	5/47

MOTT, Matthew Peter
Born: October 3, 1973 Charleville (Queensland)
Left-handed batsman, right-arm medium bowler

Matthew Mott's Pura Cup output of 378 runs at 23.62 fell well short of that expected from a top-order batsman. Occupying the number three position for the first seven games, he reached 50 only once, with a highest first innings score of just 35. After being omitted for one match, he was brought back to open the batting in the last two games when Jason Arnberger was ruled unfit. Playing with more freedom, he marked his recall with a well-made 84 against Western Australia, putting on 145 for the first wicket with Matthew Elliott, the state's best opening stand of the season. As usual he fielded well close to the wicket but his medium-paced bowling was little used. He appeared only once in the ING Cup, as a last-minute replacement when Brad Hodge was injured. In Premier cricket, he headed Frankston Peninsula's batting averages for the fourth year in a row with 550 runs at 55.00, his average boosted by an undefeated double-century in the last match. Although his gritty batting has served Victoria well in recent years his place is likely to come under challenge.

	M	I	NO	R	HS	100s	50s	Avge	Ct	St	W	Avge	BB
First-class	57	101	4	3,193	154	6	17	32.92	48	0	7	63.71	3/35
Dom. first-class	53	95	4	3,027	154	6	15	33.26	43	0	7	61.29	3/35
Dom. limited-overs	18	16	1	275	55*	0	2	18.33	7	0	4	27.50	2/2

OLIVER, Benjamin Carl
Born: October 24, 1979 Castlemaine (Victoria)
Right-handed batsman, right-arm fast-medium bowler

Promising all-rounder Ben Oliver's appearances for Victoria were cut short by injury, which limited him to just the first two ING Cup matches. Diagnosed with osteitis pubis during the winter, it was initially felt that with careful management of his condition he would be fit enough to complete a full season. However, by November he required surgery, followed by a rehabilitation programme which kept him out of action for the rest of the season. In May he signed a two-year contract to play for Tasmania, a decision which disappointed Victorian cricket officials, as in 2000-01 he had won the Best New Talent award in the Mercantile Mutual Cup.

	M	I	NO	R	HS	100s	50s	Avge	Ct	St	W	Avge	BB
First-class	1	1	0	0	0	0	0	0.00	1	0	3	15.00	2/13
Dom. limited-overs	12	10	2	150	39*	0	0	18.75	5	0	6	51.17	2/36

REIFFEL, Paul Ronald
Born: April 19, 1966 Box Hill (Victoria)
Right-handed batsman, right-arm fast-medium bowler

Paul Reiffel captured 4/71 against Tasmania in Hobart to take his tally of first-class wickets for the state to 331, one more than Alan Connolly's 330, which had stood as the Victorian record since 1970. Only two games later, following Victoria's defeat in Perth, he announced his retirement from all cricket. It had been widely expected that he would retire at the end of the season, and the timing of his announcement came as a surprise, for he had taken ten wickets in his last three Pura Cup appearances and in the previous match had played a punishing innings of 75. However, citing a lack of motivation and the constant pain resulting from years of wear and tear as a fast bowler, he felt he would have been cheating himself and the team had he kept on playing. Somewhat controversially, he had not been picked for any ING Cup games, following his replacement by Matthew Elliott as captain of the limited-overs side. Although his undemonstrative nature meant that his performances always tended to be overshadowed by those of his team-mates, Reiffel gave outstanding service at both state and national levels. His Test highlights were his match-winning bowling on the 1993 and 1997 Ashes tours of England and his seven wickets against West Indies at Kingston in 1995 to help Australia regain the Frank Worrell Trophy. He has agreed to take part in an ACB programme designed to encourage former first-class players to take up umpiring.

	M	I	NO	R	HS	100s	50s	Avge	Ct	St	W	Avge	BB
First-class	167	208	59	3,690	86	0	18	24.77	77	0	545	26.41	6/57
Dom. first-class	86	116	30	1,819	86	0	6	21.15	42	0	318	25.92	6/57
Test	35	50	14	955	79*	0	6	26.53	15	0	104	26.96	6/71
Int'l limited-overs	92	57	21	503	58	0	1	13.97	25	0	106	29.20	4/13
Dom. limited-overs	40	26	10	251	44	0	0	15.69	12	0	37	32.46	4/14

WARNE, Shane Keith
Born: September 13, 1969 Ferntree Gully (Victoria)
Right-handed batsman, right-arm leg-spin bowler

By capturing 74 wickets in the course of his 14 Tests for Australia between July 2001 and March 2002, Shane Warne climbed to second place on the overall list of Test wicket-takers. After his injury-plagued season in 2000-01, many felt that the exertion of ten years at international level was taking its toll and that his best days were behind him. Such an assessment proved false. After a lean series against New Zealand, in which he captured just six expensive wickets, he tormented South Africa's batsmen, capturing 37 wickets in the six Tests. His enthusiasm for bowling remained undimmed, and in South

Africa he sent down 50 overs more than any other Australian bowler, including a marathon spell of 70 overs in the second innings of the Second Test at Cape Town where his 6/161 represented his 21st five-wicket haul in Tests. He also made some significant contributions with the bat, including 99 against New Zealand after a middle-order collapse. His 63 at Cape Town, in his 100th Test, helped Adam Gilchrist in a century stand after Australia were in some difficulty. During this innings became only the second Australian, after Richie Benaud, to achieve the double of 2,000 runs and 200 wickets in Tests. His bowling proved less effective in limited-overs internationals than in the past. In the VB Series against New Zealand and South Africa in January he captured only six wickets in eight matches and in the series in South Africa, after missing the first four matches with a hamstring strain, he conceded more than six runs per over in the remaining three. Nevertheless he bowled effectively in the three matches against Pakistan in June. He was available for only a handful of games for Victoria, all early in the season, in which he captured six wickets in two Pura Cup appearances and four in the ING Cup.

	M	I	NO	R	HS	100s	50s	Avge	Ct	St	W	Avge	BB
First-class	192	257	34	3,930	99	0	14	17.62	153	0	803	26.59	8/71
Dom. first-class	33	43	7	594	69	0	2	16.50	25	0	112	36.55	6/42
Test	101	139	13	2,091	99	0	7	16.60	83	0	450	26.52	8/71
Int'l limited-overs	181	101	27	946	55	0	1	12.78	74	0	278	25.67	5/33
Dom. limited-overs	20	16	1	190	32	0	0	12.67	9	0	29	26.00	5/35

WHITE, Cameron Leon
Born: August 18, 1983 Bairnsdale (Victoria)
Right-handed batsman, right-arm leg-spin bowler
Domestic limited-overs debut 2001-02

The high point of Cameron White's hectic season came in February when he led Australia to victory in the Under-19s World Cup in New Zealand. His leadership was widely praised, team manager Brian Freedman describing him as the most mature young captain he had seen since Steve Waugh in his early days at Bankstown–Canterbury. He was the tournament's leading run-scorer with 423 runs at 70.50, but he took only two wickets from 54 overs. He appeared in five Pura Cup matches for Victoria, displacing Colin Miller. Although his brisk leg-breaks captured only seven wickets at 57.85, he produced some good spells in which he obtained bounce and revealed variations of flight and spin. His best innings was a punishing 91 against South Australia in Melbourne, his first half-century for the state – had he reached three figures he would have been the youngest Victorian to make a century in the Sheffield Shield/Pura Cup. He made his ING Cup debut during the season, but made no impact. He also appeared for the Prime Minister's XI in its matches against the New Zealanders and the ATSIC Chairman's XI. At the end of the season, after visiting India as part of a training squad sent to gain experience of conditions on the subcontinent, he was named in the squad of 24 players to attend the Australian Cricket Academy.

	M	I	NO	R	HS	100s	50s	Avge	Ct	St	W	Avge	BB
First-class	7	11	2	156	91	0	1	17.33	4	0	11	49.18	4/65
Dom. first-class	7	11	2	156	91	0	1	17.33	4	0	11	49.18	4/65
Dom. limited-overs	4	3	1	1	1*	0	0	0.50	0	0	1	89.00	1/37

WESTERN AUSTRALIA

By Ken Casellas

ANGEL, Jo
Born: April 22, 1968 Mt Lawley (Western Australia)
Left-handed batsman, right-arm fast bowler

Like Old Man River, Jo Angel just keeps rolling along, continuing to defy the doubters by producing high-quality performances with the ball. He was Western Australia's most consistent and reliable bowler, heading the averages and aggregates for the 2001-02 season. The burly right-hander took 44 Pura Cup wickets at an average of 24.40, and his seven wickets in the final match against South Australia in Perth took his tally of wickets in the domestic first-class competition to 387, putting him into second place on the all-time Australian list, behind Clarrie Grimmett's 513. During the season Angel produced his best figures, 6/52 off 25.3 overs in Victoria's second innings in Perth. He was a better bowler at home than away, taking 30 wickets at 19.63 in five matches at the WACA Ground. Angel also produced his best figures in the limited-overs domestic competition when he snapped up 5/16 off 6.3 overs against Victoria in Perth, and he finished the ING series with 14 wickets at 23.71 and a career record of 73 wickets to be the leading wicket-taker in the history of the domestic limited-overs competition. He won the Excalibur award (for upholding the spirit of the Western Australians) for a record fourth time. Angel wound down after a strenuous Australian summer by playing for Leigh in a Liverpool league competition.

	M	I	NO	R	HS	100s	50s	Avge	Ct	St	W	Avge	BB
First-class	108	139	40	1,299	84*	0	4	13.12	27	0	449	24.32	6/52
Dom. first-class	94	122	33	1,148	84*	0	4	12.90	19	0	387	24.14	6/52
Test	4	7	1	35	11	0	0	5.83	1	0	10	46.30	3/54
Int'l limited-overs	3	1	0	0	0	0	0	0.00	0	0	4	28.25	2/47
Dom. limited-overs	62	13	5	63	19*	0	0	7.88	5	0	73	28.14	5/16

BAKER, Robert Michael
Born: July 24, 1975 Osborne Park (Western Australia)
Right-handed batsman, slow-left arm orthodox bowler

After missing the entire 2000-01 season with chronic fatigue syndrome, Rob Baker fought his way back into the state side. He appeared in Western Australia's final four limited-overs ING Cup matches, but did not enjoy much luck and managed only 55 runs at an average of 13.75. He had a fair season for Scarborough, scoring two first-grade centuries and a total of 485 runs at 37.31, and took 13 wickets at 20.23.

	M	I	NO	R	HS	100s	50s	Avge	Ct	St	W	Avge	BB
First-class	30	53	7	1,308	111*	1	6	28.43	25	0	24	37.13	6/53
Dom. first-class	27	48	7	1,168	111*	1	5	28.49	24	0	18	42.89	2/26
Dom. limited-overs	27	25	7	360	55	0	1	20.00	6	0	7	46.14	3/25

CAMPBELL, Ryan John
Born: February 7, 1972 Osborne Park (Western Australia)
Right-handed batsman, wicket-keeper
International limited-overs debut 2001-02

After a miserable 2000-01 season, Campbell batted superbly and kept wickets in grand style, and was rewarded with selection in several Australia A sides. He relished these opportunities, opening and smashing a rapid-fire 46 (run out) against New Zealand and a 16-ball unbeaten 20 against South Africa, including a square-driven six. Those efforts

GUTS, GRACE AND GLORY

GARRY
SOBERS
MY AUTOBIOGRAPHY

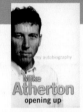

GARRY SOBERS:
MY AUTOBIOGRAPHY
One man changed the
face of West Indian
cricket forever.
Regarded as the
world's finest all-
rounder, Garry Sobers
talks passionately
about his life and
the game. $49.95

OPENING UP -
MY AUTOBIOGRAPHY
Mike Atherton,
England Captain and
the most consistently
successful English
cricketer of the last
two decades, gives
us the inside story
in this revealing
autobiography. $49.95

earned him a place in the Australian limited-overs side to replace the unavailable Adam Gilchrist against New Zealand at the Sydney Cricket Ground in which he opened and scored 38 off 52 deliveries and took two catches and a stumping. He also took over from Gilchrist in Pura Cup and ING Cup matches and performed at a high standard. A dynamic, clean striker of the ball, Campbell scored 576 quick first-class runs at 41.14, including a dashing 133-ball 121 at No. 5 against New South Wales in Perth. After missing the first three ING Cup matches, he did well to score 181 runs at 36.20. He hit two centuries among his 451 runs at 75.17 for his new first-grade club, Joondalup.

	M	I	NO	R	HS	100s	50s	Avge	Ct	St	W	Avge	BB
First-class	61	107	3	3,859	203	8	23	37.11	154	3	0	–	–
Dom. first-class	55	97	2	3,502	203	7	22	36.86	135	1	0	–	–
Int'l limited-overs	1	1	0	38	38	0	0	38.00	2	1	0	–	–
Dom. limited-overs	48	47	1	1,033	108	1	6	22.46	59	6	0	–	–

CARY, Sean Ross
Born: March 10, 1971 Subiaco (Western Australia)
Right-handed batsman, right-arm fast-medium bowler

In the twilight of his career, Sean Cary had limited opportunities in interstate cricket in 2001-02 despite another fruitful season with Willetton in the first-grade competition, where his 54 wickets cost only 12.99 runs each. Cary lost his place in the Western Australian side after taking three expensive wickets in three matches. He worked hard with bowling coach Bruce Reid to improve his follow-through and therefore obtain better late swing and in January, after five-wicket hauls for Willetton in three successive matches, he was recalled to the limited-overs side for the first time in two years, playing in two ING Cup matches and bowling accurately and economically.

	M	I	NO	R	HS	100s	50s	Avge	Ct	St	W	Avge	BB
First-class	39	40	19	178	13	0	0	8.48	14	0	102	36.02	4/9
Dom. first-class	36	38	19	168	13	0	0	8.84	13	0	93	36.15	4/9
Dom. limited-overs	14	4	3	8	7*	0	0	8.00	3	0	9	50.44	2/25

CLARK, Michael Wayne
Born: March 31, 1978 Perth (Western Australia)
Right-handed batsman, left-arm fast-medium bowler
First-class, domestic first-class and domestic limited-overs
debut 2001-02

The son of former Test opening bowler Wayne Clark, Michael Clark, a tall, willowy left-armer, came back from adversity after serious setbacks in his football career to break into top-level cricket. He had two shoulder reconstructions and a knee reconstruction in an AFL career that spanned five years but only one senior game for Fremantle. At the Subiaco–Floreat club he received expert tuition from former Western Australian fast-medium left-armer Jim Hubble, and after good form with the state Second XI and first-grade hauls of 6/35 and 5/41, he was chosen in an ING Cup match against Victoria at the WACA Ground in which he made a dream debut, taking 3/34 off his ten overs. He then played in Western Australia's final five Pura Cup matches, taking seven wickets at 46.26. He swung the ball in his early interstate matches, but then lost that ability by going too wide on the crease.

	M	I	NO	R	HS	100s	50s	Avge	Ct	St	W	Avge	BB
First-class	5	5	4	11	6	0	0	11.00	2	0	7	46.29	3/49
Dom. first-class	5	5	4	11	6	0	0	11.00	2	0	7	46.29	3/49
Dom. limited-overs	3	1	0	7	7	0	0	7.00	2	0	5	21.80	3/34

GILCHRIST, Adam Craig
Born: November 14, 1971 Bellingen (New South Wales)
Left-handed batsman, wicket-keeper

Adam Gilchrist continued his meteoric rise in international cricket as he maintained his superb form with the bat and behind the stumps. He began the Australian summer with 118 in the First Test against New Zealand at the Gabba. In February he notched his fifth Test hundred, a dazzling unbeaten 204 against South Africa in Johannesburg, reaching 200 off 212 deliveries to record the fastest Test double-century, and followed it up with another blazing century in the Second Test. He also scored an unbeaten century in a limited-overs international against South Africa in Durban. In May, Gilchrist moved to the top of the official world batting rankings, ahead of Brian Lara and Sachin Tendulkar. He was the most successful Test wicket-keeper in the calendar year of 2001, with 52 catches and five stumpings. International duties kept Gilchrist's appearances for Western Australia to a minimum. He played in Western Australia's first two Pura Cup matches, scoring 98 against Queensland in Brisbane, and also played in the first four ING Cup matches, scoring 117 runs at 29.25, with a highest score of 84 against South Australia in Perth.

	M	I	NO	R	HS	100s	50s	Avge	Ct	St	W	Avge	BB
First-class	118	178	33	6,640	204*	19	26	45.79	474	28	0	–	–
Dom. first-class	59	94	13	3,117	203*	8	11	38.48	253	8	0	–	–
Test	31	44	8	2,160	204*	6	11	60.00	122	10	0	–	–
Int'l limited-overs	136	131	5	4,279	154	7	24	33.96	187	32	0	–	–
Dom. limited-overs	36	33	3	988	115	1	7	32.93	56	6	0	–	–

GOODWIN, Murray William
Born: December 11, 1972 Salisbury (Rhodesia)
Right-handed batsman, right-arm leg-spin bowler

After a bountiful season in English county cricket with Sussex in 2001 (1,654 first-class runs at 61.25) Murray Goodwin failed to live up to expectations for Western Australia and was dropped from both the first-class and limited-overs sides. His early-season form was good, with innings of 141 against Tasmania, 68 against Queensland and 61 against South Africa. He missed Pura Cup matches against New South Wales (at home and away) and Victoria and he failed to reach 40 in his final five Pura Cup innings to finish the season with 474 first-class runs at 36.46. His form in ING Cup matches was disappointing, and after scoring 112 runs at 18.66 from the first six matches he lost his spot in the side. Her knuckled down to play some important innings for Subiaco–Floreat late in the season and he finished with 607 first-grade runs at 50.58 before heading off to England for another stint with Sussex.

	M	I	NO	R	HS	100s	50s	Avge	Ct	St	W	Avge	BB
First-class	87	154	13	6,179	203*	17	28	43.82	59	0	7	48.14	2/23
Dom. first-class	27	48	4	1,316	141	2	6	29.91	23	0	0	–	–
Test	19	37	4	1,414	166*	3	8	42.85	11	0	0	–	–
Int'l limited-overs	71	70	3	1,818	112*	2	8	27.13	20	0	4	52.50	1/12
Dom. limited-overs	19	18	3	667	167	1	4	44.47	5	0	0	–	–

HARVEY, Kade Murray
Born: October 7, 1975 Subiaco (Western Australia)
Right-handed batsman, right-arm fast-medium bowler

After failing to play a first-class match in the two previous seasons, Kade Harvey was given further opportunities and appeared in five Pura Cup matches. His best effort was his 4/43 in the first innings against New South Wales in Perth and he finished with nine wickets at 37.55 and 134 runs at 22.33, with a top score of 59 against Victoria in Perth. A whole-hearted competitor, he was again a permanent member of Western Australia's limited-overs side, but he took only six wickets at an average of 53.16 and conceded 5.06 runs an over. He was dismissed three times in eight innings which produced 106 runs at 35.33. He had a best return of 6/37 in his 26 wickets at 15.19 in first-grade ranks for Scarborough, and also scored 260 runs at 43.33.

	M	I	NO	R	HS	100s	50s	Avge	Ct	St	W	Avge	BB
First-class	15	19	4	323	79	0	2	21.53	11	0	31	34.16	4/43
Dom. first-class	11	15	3	228	59	0	1	19.00	9	0	26	30.92	4/43
Dom. limited-overs	50	30	15	369	31	0	0	21.71	7	0	61	27.69	4/8

HOGG, George Bradley
Born: February 6, 1971 Narrogin (Western Australia)
Left-handed batsman, left-arm slow 'chinaman' bowler

The livewire Brad Hogg bounced back in emphatic style as a key member of the Western Australian first-class side. Despite missing the opening three matches and the game against Tasmania in Hobart later in the season (when suspended for swearing in a club match), Hogg enjoyed his best season with the bat and one of his best with the ball in both forms of the game. He scored a fine 90 against South Africa and his Pura Cup scores included 84, 77 not out, 62, 61 and 56 not out for a first-class aggregate of 575 runs at 65.62. He bowled with greater confidence and control and thoroughly deserved his 17 wickets at 33.82. In the ING Cup he scored 128 runs at 25.60 and took 12 wickets at 25.66. As usual, his fielding and catching were of the highest order. His 455 runs at 75.83 in first-grade matches for Willetton included an unbeaten 220. The Australian selectors noticed his improvement and named him in the Australia A limited-overs side (along with fellow Western Australians Justin Langer, Ryan Campbell, Mike Hussey and Brad Williams) to tour South Africa.

	M	I	NO	R	HS	100s	50s	Avge	Ct	St	W	Avge	BB
First-class	61	92	20	2,151	111*	2	13	29.88	36	0	77	47.03	5/53
Dom. first-class	53	81	17	1,890	111*	1	12	29.53	34	0	68	44.82	5/53
Test	1	2	0	5	4	0	0	2.50	0	0	1	69.00	1/69
Int'l limited-overs	7	7	4	38	11*	0	0	12.67	2	0	3	72.67	1/23
Dom. limited-overs	54	44	19	761	59	0	2	30.44	27	0	38	26.89	4/50

HUSSEY, Michael Edward Killeen
Born: May 27, 1975 Mt Lawley (Western Australia)
Left-handed batsman, right-arm medium bowler

For the second successive season Mike Hussey under-achieved as an opening batsman, but he continued to make great strides as a fast-scoring and innovative middle-order limited-overs batsman. So good was his form in the limited-overs arena that he was chosen in the Australia A side and was rewarded with an ACB contract in May after losing it a year earlier. The high point of his 440 runs at 55.00 in ING Cup matches was his 103 not out against Tasmania in Hobart. But his most memorable innings was his 45 against New South Wales at the WACA Ground when he swept a ball from medium-pacer Dominic Thornely into a sponsor's sign to earn a $200,000 jackpot. After scoring 2,055 first-class runs at 79.03 for Northamptonshire in his first season of county cricket in 2001, Hussey looked set for a big season with the bat with Western Australia. However, he was dismissed under 20 eight times in first-class cricket and his 19 innings produced only 621 runs at 34.50. He reached 50 only five times and had a highest score of 100 against New South Wales in Sydney. In first-grade club cricket, Hussey hit two centuries in his 442 runs at 63.14 for Wanneroo. He took over as captain of

Player Profiles – Western Australia

Northamptonshire in 2002, and was the first player in the English season to reach 1,000 first-class runs.

	M	I	NO	R	HS	100s	50s	Avge	Ct	St	W	Avge	BB
First-class	108	196	14	8,984	329*	22	40	49.36	103	0	5	53.80	2/21
Dom. first-class	75	137	7	5,371	187	12	24	41.32	65	0	3	56.33	2/21
Dom. limited-overs	45	42	5	1,538	103*	2	11	41.57	27	0	3	23.67	3/52

KARPPINEN, Stuart James
Born: June 13, 1973 Townsville (Queensland)
Right-handed batsman, right-arm fast-medium bowler

Karppinen's season was ruined by a stress fracture of the lower back. The athletic new-ball bowler conceded only 3.8 runs an over in five early ING Cup matches, but did not take a wicket from his 37 overs. His only first-class appearance came against the touring South Africans at the WACA Ground when he gave a spirited display to take five wickets. His back injury curtailed his activities after Christmas and he was unable to continue in club cricket with South Perth.

	M	I	NO	R	HS	100s	50s	Avge	Ct	St	W	Avge	BB
First-class	2	3	0	18	17	0	0	6.00	0	0	10	26.30	4/110
Dom. first-class	1	2	0	18	17	0	0	9.00	0	0	5	13.60	3/34
Dom. limited-overs	16	10	3	93	23	0	0	13.29	6	0	11	50.36	2/35

KATICH, Simon Matthew
Born: August 21, 1975 Middle Swan (Western Australia)
Left-handed batsman, slow-left arm orthodox bowler
International limited-overs debut 2001-02

After making his Test debut on the 2001 Ashes tour, Katich was chosen to captain Western Australia in the absence of Adam Gilchrist and Justin Langer. But his form deteriorated, he became disenchanted with some controversial selections, he lost his lucrative ACB contract, and finally stunned local officials by deciding to quit his home state to continue his career with New South Wales. He had threatened to quit as captain after the selectors dropped Murray Goodwin, but he denied that his move to Sydney had anything to do with unrest in the team. Katich was dismissed for 25 or less in eight of his 18 first-class innings for Western Australia in the 2001-02 season. His solitary century was 131 against New South Wales at the SCG and he finished with 651 runs at 36.16. Seven of his ten ING Cup match innings were 20 or less. His only substantial limited-overs scores were his 70 against Queensland and his 118 against Victoria, both at the WACA Ground. In first-grade matches for Midland–Guildford he scored two centuries from four innings that produced 333 runs at 111.00. He will be sorely missed by his home state.

	M	I	NO	R	HS	100s	50s	Avge	Ct	St	W	Avge	BB
First-class	73	129	21	5,346	228*	16	24	49.50	75	0	20	53.80	3/21
Dom. first-class	46	83	10	3,498	228*	11	15	47.92	37	0	11	46.27	3/46
Test	1	2	1	15	15	0	0	15.00	1	0	0	–	–
Int'l limited-overs	1	0	0	0	–	0	0	–	0	0	0	–	–
Dom. limited-overs	38	37	3	1,178	118	2	8	34.65	10	0	0	–	–

LANGER, Justin Lee
Born: November 21, 1970 Subiaco (Western Australia)
Left-handed batsman, right-arm medium bowler

The fighting spirit and unswerving faith in his ability enabled Justin Langer to make one of Test cricket's great comebacks. At The Oval in 2001, Langer grasped his opportunity with both hands and scored 102 before being forced to retire hurt. His opening partnership of 158 with Matthew Hayden was the first of a series of magnificent stands between the left-handers. He scored 104 in the First Test against New Zealand at the Gabba and followed it with 123 in the Second Test in Hobart and 75 in the Third Test in Perth. His good form continued into the series against South Africa, with centuries in the First and Third Tests to take his tally to 12 Test centuries, a record by a Western Australian batsman. Langer began the domestic season in grand style, with 96 against Queensland at the Gabba and 133 against Tasmania at the WACA Ground in Western Australia's opening Pura Cup contests. He played in four of his state's ten Pura Cup matches, scoring 345 runs at 57.50, and he again proved a highly efficient limited-overs batsman with scores of 107 against New South Wales in Sydney and 57 against Tasmania in Hobart in the ING Cup competition. That he cannot break into the Australian limited-overs side is Langer's major regret in cricket, but his selection to captain the Australia A limited-overs side to tour South Africa suggests that the selectors have not forgotten him.

	M	I	NO	R	HS	100s	50s	Avge	Ct	St	W	Avge	BB
First-class	212	372	40	17,012	274*	55	63	51.24	182	0	5	39.80	2/17
Dom. first-class	71	130	11	6,438	274*	20	22	54.10	61	0	0	–	–
Test	51	85	5	3,516	223	12	15	43.95	34	0	0	–	–
Int'l limited-overs	8	7	2	160	36	0	0	32.00	2	1	0	–	–
Dom. limited-overs	61	59	5	2,063	146	2	17	38.20	24	0	0	–	–

MARTYN, Damien Richard
Born: October 21, 1971 Darwin (Northern Territory)
Right-handed batsman, right-arm medium bowler

A more mature Damien Martyn turned the corner in 2001 when he re-established himself as a permanent member of the Australian Test side. He enjoyed a splendid Ashes series in England in 2001, scoring 382 runs at 76.40. Back in Australia, he failed in the first two Tests against New Zealand before scoring 60 and 30 in the Third Test and then starring against South Africa, with centuries in the First and Third Tests. These were followed by his 133 in the First Test in Johannesburg. A batsman with a flawless defensive technique and quicksilver footwork, Martyn now places a far higher value on his wicket than he did in his somewhat irresponsible youth. Martyn's appearances for Western Australia were rare in 2001-02 when he played in two Pura Cup matches, hitting 189 against Tasmania at the WACA Ground. In three ING Cup matches he scored 224 runs at 74.66, including 108 against Tasmania in Perth.

	M	I	NO	R	HS	100s	50s	Avge	Ct	St	W	Avge	BB
First-class	153	260	38	10,945	203*	34	55	49.30	126	2	35	41.20	4/30
Dom. first-class	92	162	16	6,639	203*	20	32	45.47	87	1	32	38.69	4/30
Test	25	40	9	1,559	133	5	9	50.29	10	0	1	75.00	1/3
Int'l limited-overs	97	83	27	2,202	144*	3	10	39.32	34	0	11	53.36	2/21
Dom. limited-overs	51	48	7	1,879	140	3	13	45.83	14	0	18	16.33	3/3

MEULEMAN, Scott William
Born: July 17, 1980 Subiaco (Western Australia)
Right-handed batsman, right-arm leg-spin bowler
Domestic limited-overs debut 2001-02

A compact opener with an excellent technique and sound defensive skills as well as an array of attacking shots, Scott Meuleman notched his maiden first-class century, an impressive 109 against a formidable South African attack at the WACA Ground, in December. After missing the first two Pura Cup matches when the side's international players were available, Meuleman became Mike Hussey's opening partner, but managed only one half-century (60 against New South Wales at the Sydney Cricket Ground) from 12 Pura Cup innings that produced 198 runs at 16.55. He was dropped for the final match. However, he remains one of the state's brightest batting prospects and is assured of many more opportunities. He started the first-grade season for Melville with 175 not out against Gosnells and 118 against Fremantle and finished with 641 runs at 53.41.

	M	I	NO	R	HS	100s	50s	Avge	Ct	St	W	Avge	BB
First-class	10	17	0	384	109	1	1	22.59	3	0	0	–	–
Dom. first-class	9	16	0	275	60	0	1	17.19	3	0	0	–	–
Dom. limited-overs	5	5	0	157	49	0	0	31.40	0	0	0	–	–

NICHOLSON, Matthew James
Born: October 2, 1974 St Leonards (New South Wales)
Right-handed batsman, right-arm fast-medium bowler

With the retirements of Tom Moody and Brendon Julian, Matthew Nicholson decided to try to improve his batting and be chosen for Western Australia as an all-rounder, not just as a fast bowler. Indeed, his batting, at times, was impressive. Revealing an excellent mixture of defence and aggression, he scored his maiden first-class century when he went in at number eight and hit three sixes and 13 fours in an unbeaten 101 off 139 deliveries against South Africa at the WACA Ground. And that came after he had taken 5/68 off 20.3 overs in South Africa's first innings. In other sound batting displays, he scored 59 not out against Queensland in Perth and a splendid 49 against Victoria at the MCG to finish the season with 33 first-class wickets at 28.36 and 334 runs at 30.36. He played in five of Western Australia's ten ING Cup matches, but took only two wickets at 83.50 and conceded 5.38 runs an over.

	M	I	NO	R	HS	100s	50s	Avge	Ct	St	W	Avge	BB
First-class	35	51	11	1,028	101*	1	3	25.70	17	0	119	29.73	7/77
Dom. first-class	29	45	9	796	59*	0	1	22.11	16	0	95	31.41	5/49
Test	1	2	0	14	9	0	0	7.00	0	0	4	28.75	3/56
Dom. limited-overs	6	4	1	28	14	0	0	9.33	3	0	2	83.50	1/30

NORTH, Marcus James
Born: July 28, 1979 Melbourne (Victoria)
Left-handed batsman, right-arm off-spin bowler

Despite scoring his maiden first-class century (106 against Queensland in Perth) in November and 71 against the South Africans the following month, Marcus North was dropped for two Pura Cup matches in January following a run of four low scores. However, his heavy scoring in club cricket earned him another chance late in the season, and he finished in a blaze of glory with a remarkable unbeaten second-innings 200 against Victoria at the Melbourne Cricket Ground, which enabled Western Australia to win after following on, and 111 against South Australia in Perth. This gave him satisfactory season's figures of 633 runs at 45.21. He had another good season in first-grade ranks for Bayswater–Morley, scoring 536 runs at 67.00. After playing for Colne in the Lancashire League in 2001, North decided to play for Gateshead Fell in the North-East Premier League in 2002.

	M	I	NO	R	HS	100s	50s	Avge	Ct	St	W	Avge	BB
First-class	21	34	2	1,090	200*	3	5	34.06	17	0	13	47.62	3/23
Dom. first-class	18	30	2	956	200*	3	3	34.14	15	0	12	44.42	3/23
Dom. limited-overs	7	6	1	47	17	0	0	9.40	1	0	0	–	–

OLDROYD, Bradley John
Born: November 5, 1973 Bentley (Western Australia)
Left-handed batsman, slow-left arm orthodox bowler

Brad Oldroyd is well and truly at the crossroads of his cricketing career after appearing in only three first-class matches in 2001-02 and taking a solitary wicket for 276 runs. The Western Australian selectors considered Brad Hogg the side's premier spinner and Oldroyd played only one home match, against South Africa, and failed to take a wicket.

He bowled tightly at Adelaide Oval and Bellerive Oval but with scant success. His only appearance in a limited-overs match was against Tasmania in Hobart where he was expensive, taking 1/43 off eight overs. However, Oldroyd still has excellent potential, as he showed by taking 39 wickets at 23.35 in first-grade matches for South Perth. He excelled in a semi-final against Melville, taking 6/69.

	M	I	NO	R	HS	100s	50s	Avge	Ct	St	W	Avge	BB
First-class	30	41	14	289	47	0	0	10.70	8	0	56	40.71	4/68
Dom. first-class	26	38	12	257	47	0	0	9.88	6	0	50	37.32	4/68
Dom. limited-overs	8	2	2	8	5*	0	0	–	2	0	6	45.33	2/36

ROGERS, Christopher John Llewellyn
Born: August 31, 1977 Kogarah (New South Wales)
Left-handed batsman

Rogers enjoyed a wonderful summer with the bat and was rewarded for a mountain of runs in first-grade and state Second XI matches with a recall to the Western Australian side after being overlooked for the entire previous season. Not a polished left-hander, he is more of a street fighter who gets the job done. He was chosen to play in a Pura Cup match against New South Wales at the Sydney Cricket Ground, replacing Murray Goodwin, and scored 53 in Western Australia's only innings. He was then dropped for the next two Pura Cup matches before returning for the final three in which he struck a purple patch: 96 and 18 against New South Wales in Perth, 26 and 15 at the MCG and 101 not out and 102 not out against South Australia at the WACA Ground. This gave him a season's tally of 411 first-class runs at 82.20. He also got an opportunity in ING Cup matches in which he scored 100 runs at 25.00. In club matches for South Perth, he scored two centuries and 664 runs at 60.36. He then spent the English winter playing for Exeter in the Devon League.

	M	I	NO	R	HS	100s	50s	Avge	Ct	St	W	Avge	BB
First-class	11	18	2	544	102*	2	2	34.00	10	0	0	–	–
Dom. first-class	10	17	2	530	102*	2	2	35.33	10	0	0	–	–
Dom. limited-overs	5	5	1	119	39	0	0	29.75	0	0	0	–	–

RONCHI, Luke
Born: April 23, 1981 Dannevirke (New Zealand)
Right-handed batsman, wicket-keeper
Domestic limited-overs debut 2001-02

Luke Ronchi arrived in Perth from New Zealand with his family as a seven-year-old and started his cricket as a lad with the Wanneroo club before switching to Perth and gaining a cricket scholarship at Kent Street High School. He learnt much about wicket-keeping from Rod Marsh at the Australian Cricket Academy and from Adam Gilchrist, a clubmate at Perth. An aggressive batsman, Ronchi impressed in scoring 704 runs at 41.41 in first-grade matches with Perth in 2001-02, with a highest score of 178 against Melville. He also scored 203 for Perth in a colts quarter-final against Scarborough. Ronchi made his senior interstate debut in an ING Cup match against Victoria at the WACA Ground. He went to England in 2002 to play another season for Bashley–Rydal in the Southern Electric Premier League.

	M	I	NO	R	HS	100s	50s	Avge	Ct	St	W	Avge	BB
Dom. limited-overs	1	1	0	0	0	0	0	0.00	1	0	0	–	–

SWAN, Gavin Graham
Born: October 30, 1970 Subiaco (Western Australia)
Right-handed batsman, right-arm fast-medium bowler

A wholehearted competitor used to fill injury gaps early in the season, Swan appeared in three first-class matches, taking four wickets at 88.00. Now in the veteran class, his first-class future is doubtful. However, he continues to excel in club cricket and he led Subiaco–Floreat to its second successive first-grade premiership in 2001-02. His seven wickets in the final earned him the Man of the Match award, and he finished the season with 45 first-grade wickets at 17.91. He played for the Philadelphia club in the North-East Premier League in England in the off season.

	M	I	NO	R	HS	100s	50s	Avge	Ct	St	W	Avge	BB
First-class	11	10	5	8	8*	0	0	1.60	6	0	28	39.96	5/54
Dom. first-class	9	9	5	8	8*	0	0	2.00	6	0	22	40.77	5/54

WATES, Darren Jude
Born: July 2, 1977 Subiaco (Western Australia)
Right-handed batsman, right-arm fast-medium bowler

A highly-competent all-rounder, Darren Wates has yet to realise his full potential. He did not add to his tally of two first-class matches in 2001-02 and was disappointing in ING Cup matches. He played in the first three rounds, and after taking one wicket for 122, was dropped for the next three matches. He then made the most of a last-minute call-up for the game against Queensland in Perth in which he took 3/32. He finished the ING Cup season with five wickets at 54.20 off 52 overs, but had few opportunities with the bat. Wates performed solidly in first-grade for South Perth, scoring 455 runs at 30.33 and taking 45 wickets at 18.82.

	M	I	NO	R	HS	100s	50s	Avge	Ct	St	W	Avge	BB
First-class	2	4	1	104	62	0	1	34.67	1	0	2	50.00	1/31
Dom. first-class	2	4	1	104	62	0	1	34.67	1	0	2	50.00	1/31
Dom. limited-overs	19	9	4	36	11	0	0	7.20	3	0	20	35.15	3/32

WILLIAMS, Bradley Andrew
Born: November 20, 1974 Frankston (Victoria)
Right-handed batsman, right-arm fast bowler

Williams' excellent season was stalled at the halfway mark when he suffered a broken thumb when batting for Australia against New Zealand in his international debut in a VB Series match at the Melbourne Cricket Ground. This prevented him from making further limited-overs appearances for Australia and kept him out of two Pura Cup matches. After injury forced Jason Gillespie out of the Australian side for the Boxing Day Test, Williams was called into the squad and acted as twelfth man. The former Victorian tearaway who came to Perth in 1999 is a spirited bowler who gives 100 per cent all the time. In 2001-02 he became more consistent with his line and length to be one of Australia's most destructive fast bowlers. He sustained his consistency throughout the summer, forming a formidable pace partnership with Jo Angel, and finished with 32 first-class wickets at 28.31. He also shone in the ING Cup, taking 18 wickets at 16.38 and winning the match against South Australia in Adelaide with a six in the last over.

	M	I	NO	R	HS	100s	50s	Avge	Ct	St	W	Avge	BB
First-class	43	58	16	638	41*	0	0	15.19	14	0	156	30.48	6/74
Dom. first-class	35	48	14	506	41*	0	0	14.88	12	0	132	30.51	6/74
Int'l limited-overs	1	1	1	13	13*	0	0	–	0	0	0	–	–
Dom. limited-overs	24	4	3	23	16	0	0	23.00	3	0	33	27.30	4/44

AUSTRALIAN TEST CRICKETERS

Note: The Third Test at the Melbourne Cricket Ground from December 31–January 5, 1971 has been sanctioned by the Australian Cricket Board as an official Test match. The Australian Cricket Board in consultation with the MCC tour management declared the Test a draw. This decision was determined as the two teams had been officially announced, including the 12th men, and the toss had been made. The umpires were walking out to the ground when rain began to fall and prevented any further play in the match.

FULL LIST FROM 1876-77 TO JULY 1, 2002

Abbreviations: *Eng* (England), *Ind* (India), *NZ* (New Zealand), *Pak* (Pakistan), *SAf* (South Africa), *SL* (Sri Lanka), *WI* (West Indies), *Zim* (Zimbabwe).

Number of Test Cricketers: 384

a'BECKETT, Edward Lambert (4)

Debut: 1928-29	Eng	Ind	NZ	Pak	SAf	SL	WI	Zim	Total
Tests at home	2	–	–	–	1	–	–	–	3
Tests abroad	1	–	–	–	–	–	–	–	1

ALDERMAN, Terence Michael (41)

Debut: 1981	Eng	Ind	NZ	Pak	SAf	SL	WI	Zim	Total
Tests at home	5	–	1	5	–	2	7	–	20
Tests abroad	12	–	4	1	–	–	4	–	21

ALEXANDER, George (2)

Debut: 1880	Eng	Ind	NZ	Pak	SAf	SL	WI	Zim	Total
Tests at home	1	–	–	–	–	–	–	–	1
Tests abroad	1	–	–	–	–	–	–	–	1

ALEXANDER, Harry Houston (1)

Debut: 1932-33	Eng	Ind	NZ	Pak	SAf	SL	WI	Zim	Total
Tests at home	1	–	–	–	–	–	–	–	1

ALLAN, Francis Erskine (1)

Debut: 1878-79	Eng	Ind	NZ	Pak	SAf	SL	WI	Zim	Total
Tests at home	1	–	–	–	–	–	–	–	1

ALLAN, Peter John (1)

Debut: 1965-66	Eng	Ind	NZ	Pak	SAf	SL	WI	Zim	Total
Tests at home	1	–	–	–	–	–	–	–	1

ALLEN, Reginald Charles (1)

Debut: 1886-87	Eng	Ind	NZ	Pak	SAf	SL	WI	Zim	Total
Tests at home	1	–	–	–	–	–	–	–	1

ANDREWS, Thomas James Edwin (16)

Debut: 1921	Eng	Ind	NZ	Pak	SAf	SL	WI	Zim	Total
Tests at home	3	–	–	–	–	–	–	–	3
Tests abroad	10	–	–	–	3	–	–	–	13

ANGEL, Jo (4)

Debut: 1992-93	Eng	Ind	NZ	Pak	SAf	SL	WI	Zim	Total
Tests at home	1	–	–	–	–	–	1	–	2
Tests abroad	–	–	–	2	–	–	–	–	2

ARCHER, Kenneth Alan (5)

Debut: 1950-51	Eng	Ind	NZ	Pak	SAf	SL	WI	Zim	Total
Tests at home	3	–	–	–	–	–	2	–	5

ARCHER, Ronald Graham (19)

Debut: 1952-53	Eng	Ind	NZ	Pak	SAf	SL	WI	Zim	Total
Tests at home	4	–	–	–	1	–	–	–	5
Tests abroad	8	–	–	1	–	–	5	–	14

ARMSTRONG, Warwick Windridge (50)

Debut: 1901-02	*Eng*	*Ind*	*NZ*	*Pak*	*SAf*	*SL*	*WI*	*Zim*	*Total*
Tests at home	22	–	–	–	5	–	–	–	27
Tests abroad	20	–	–	–	3	–	–	–	23

BADCOCK, Clayvel Lindsay (7)

Debut: 1936-37	*Eng*	*Ind*	*NZ*	*Pak*	*SAf*	*SL*	*WI*	*Zim*	*Total*
Tests at home	3	–	–	–	–	–	–	–	3
Tests abroad	4	–	–	–	–	–	–	–	4

BANNERMAN, Alexander Chalmers (28)

Debut: 1878-79	*Eng*	*Ind*	*NZ*	*Pak*	*SAf*	*SL*	*WI*	*Zim*	*Total*
Tests at home	17	–	–	–	–	–	–	–	17
Tests abroad	11	–	–	–	–	–	–	–	11

BANNERMAN, Charles (3)

Debut: 1876-77	*Eng*	*Ind*	*NZ*	*Pak*	*SAf*	*SL*	*WI*	*Zim*	*Total*
Tests at home	3	–	–	–	–	–	–	–	3

BARDSLEY, Warren (41)

Debut: 1909	*Eng*	*Ind*	*NZ*	*Pak*	*SAf*	*SL*	*WI*	*Zim*	*Total*
Tests at home	12	–	–	–	5	–	–	–	17
Tests abroad	18	–	–	–	6	–	–	–	24

BARNES, Sydney George (13)

Debut: 1938	*Eng*	*Ind*	*NZ*	*Pak*	*SAf*	*SL*	*WI*	*Zim*	*Total*
Tests at home	4	3	–	–	–	–	–	–	7
Tests abroad	5	–	1	–	–	–	–	–	6

BARNETT, Benjamin Arthur (4)

Debut: 1938	*Eng*	*Ind*	*NZ*	*Pak*	*SAf*	*SL*	*WI*	*Zim*	*Total*
Tests abroad	4	–	–	–	–	–	–	–	4

BARRETT, John Edward (2)

Debut: 1890	*Eng*	*Ind*	*NZ*	*Pak*	*SAf*	*SL*	*WI*	*Zim*	*Total*
Tests abroad	2	–	–	–	–	–	–	–	2

BEARD, Graeme Robert (3)

Debut: 1979-80	*Eng*	*Ind*	*NZ*	*Pak*	*SAf*	*SL*	*WI*	*Zim*	*Total*
Tests abroad	–	–	–	3	–	–	–	–	3

BENAUD, John (3)

Debut: 1972-73	*Eng*	*Ind*	*NZ*	*Pak*	*SAf*	*SL*	*WI*	*Zim*	*Total*
Tests at home	–	–	–	2	–	–	–	–	2
Tests abroad	–	–	–	–	–	–	1	–	1

BENAUD, Richard (63)

Debut: 1951-52	*Eng*	*Ind*	*NZ*	*Pak*	*SAf*	*SL*	*WI*	*Zim*	*Total*
Tests at home	15	–	–	–	8	–	6	–	29
Tests abroad	12	8	–	4	5	–	5	–	34

BENNETT, Murray John (3)

Debut: 1984-85	*Eng*	*Ind*	*NZ*	*Pak*	*SAf*	*SL*	*WI*	*Zim*	*Total*
Tests at home	–	–	–	–	–	–	2	–	2
Tests abroad	1	–	–	–	–	–	–	–	1

BEVAN, Michael Gwyl (18)

Debut: 1994-95	*Eng*	*Ind*	*NZ*	*Pak*	*SAf*	*SL*	*WI*	*Zim*	*Total*
Tests at home	3	–	–	–	1	–	4	–	8
Tests abroad	3	1	–	3	3	–	–	–	10

BICHEL, Andrew John (6)

Debut: 1996-97	*Eng*	*Ind*	*NZ*	*Pak*	*SAf*	*SL*	*WI*	*Zim*	*Total*
Tests at home	–	–	–	–	2	–	4	–	6

BLACKHAM, John McCarthy (35)

Debut: 1876-77	*Eng*	*Ind*	*NZ*	*Pak*	*SAf*	*SL*	*WI*	*Zim*	*Total*
Tests at home	19	–	–	–	–	–	–	–	19
Tests abroad	16	–	–	–	–	–	–	–	16

BLACKIE, Donald Dearness (3)

Debut: 1928-29	Eng	Ind	NZ	Pak	SAf	SL	WI	Zim	Total
Tests at home	3	–	–	–	–	–	–	–	3

BLEWETT, Gregory Scott (46)

Debut: 1994-95	Eng	Ind	NZ	Pak	SAf	SL	WI	Zim	Total
Tests at home	2	3	3	6	3	–	4	–	21
Tests abroad	6	3	2	–	3	3	7	1	25

BONNOR, George John (17)

Debut: 1880	Eng	Ind	NZ	Pak	SAf	SL	WI	Zim	Total
Tests at home	7	–	–	–					
Tests abroad	10	–	–	–	–	–	–	–	10

BOON, David Clarence (107)

Debut: 1984-85	Eng	Ind	NZ	Pak	SAf	SL	WI	Zim	Total
Tests at home	15	8	10	5	3	6	13	–	60
Tests abroad	16	3	7	6	3	3	9	–	47

BOOTH, Brian Charles (29)

Debut: 1961	Eng	Ind	NZ	Pak	SAf	SL	WI	Zim	Total
Tests at home	8	–	–	1	4	–	–	–	13
Tests abroad	7	3	–	1	–	–	5	–	16

BORDER, Allan Robert (156)

Debut: 1978-79	Eng	Ind	NZ	Pak	SAf	SL	WI	Zim	Total
Tests at home	22	11	13	13	3	3	21	–	86
Tests abroad	25	9	10	9	3	4	10	–	70

BOYLE, Henry Frederick (12)

Debut: 1878-79	Eng	Ind	NZ	Pak	SAf	SL	WI	Zim	Total
Tests at home	7	–	–	–	–	–	–	–	7
Tests abroad	5	–	–	–	–	–	–	–	5

BRADMAN, Donald George (52)

Debut: 1928-29	Eng	Ind	NZ	Pak	SAf	SL	WI	Zim	Total
Tests at home	18	5	–	–	5	–	5	–	33
Tests abroad	19	–	–	–	–	–	–	–	19

BRIGHT, Raymond James (25)

Debut: 1977	Eng	Ind	NZ	Pak	SAf	SL	WI	Zim	Total
Tests at home	1	3	1	–	–	–	1	–	6
Tests abroad	9	3	2	5	–	–	–	–	19

BROMLEY, Ernest Harvey (2)

Debut: 1932-33	Eng	Ind	NZ	Pak	SAf	SL	WI	Zim	Total
Tests at home	1	–	–	–	–	–	–	–	1
Tests abroad	1	–	–	–	–	–	–	–	1

BROWN, William Alfred (22)

Debut: 1934	Eng	Ind	NZ	Pak	SAf	SL	WI	Zim	Total
Tests at home	2	3	–	–	–	–	–	–	5
Tests abroad	11	–	1	–	5	–	–	–	17

BRUCE, William (14)

Debut: 1884-85	Eng	Ind	NZ	Pak	SAf	SL	WI	Zim	Total
Tests at home	9	–	–	–	–	–	–	–	9
Tests abroad	5	–	–	–	–	–	–	–	5

BURGE, Peter John Parnell (42)

Debut: 1954-55	Eng	Ind	NZ	Pak	SAf	SL	WI	Zim	Total
Tests at home	9	–	–	–	5	–	2	–	16
Tests abroad	13	8	–	3	1	–	1	–	26

BURKE, James Wallace (24)

Debut: 1950-51	Eng	Ind	NZ	Pak	SAf	SL	WI	Zim	Total
Tests at home	9	–	–	–	–	–	1	–	10
Tests abroad	5	3	–	1	5	–	–	–	14

BURN, Edwin James Kenneth (2)

Debut: 1890	*Eng*	*Ind*	*NZ*	*Pak*	*SAf*	*SL*	*WI*	*Zim*	*Total*
Tests abroad	2	–	–	–	–	–	–	–	2

BURTON, Frederick John (2)

Debut: 1886-87	*Eng*	*Ind*	*NZ*	*Pak*	*SAf*	*SL*	*WI*	*Zim*	*Total*
Tests at home	2	–	–	–	–	–	–	–	2

CALLAWAY, Sydney Thomas (3)

Debut: 1891-92	*Eng*	*Ind*	*NZ*	*Pak*	*SAf*	*SL*	*WI*	*Zim*	*Total*
Tests at home	3	–	–	–	–	–	–	–	3

CALLEN, Ian Wayne (1)

Debut: 1977-78	*Eng*	*Ind*	*NZ*	*Pak*	*SAf*	*SL*	*WI*	*Zim*	*Total*
Tests at home	–	1	–	–	–	–	–	–	1

CAMPBELL, Gregory Dale (4)

Debut: 1989	*Eng*	*Ind*	*NZ*	*Pak*	*SAf*	*SL*	*WI*	*Zim*	*Total*
Tests at home	–	–	–	1	–	1	–	–	2
Tests abroad	1	–	1	–	–	–	–	–	2

CARKEEK, William (6)

Debut: 1912	*Eng*	*Ind*	*NZ*	*Pak*	*SAf*	*SL*	*WI*	*Zim*	*Total*
Tests abroad	3	–	–	–	3	–	–	–	6

CARLSON, Phillip Henry (2)

Debut: 1978-79	*Eng*	*Ind*	*NZ*	*Pak*	*SAf*	*SL*	*WI*	*Zim*	*Total*
Tests at home	2	–	–	–	–	–	–	–	2

CARTER, Hanson (28)

Debut: 1907-08	*Eng*	*Ind*	*NZ*	*Pak*	*SAf*	*SL*	*WI*	*Zim*	*Total*
Tests at home	12	–	–	–	5	–	–	–	17
Tests abroad	9	–	–	–	2	–	–	–	11

CHAPPELL, Gregory Stephen (88)

Debut: 1970-71	*Eng*	*Ind*	*NZ*	*Pak*	*SAf*	*SL*	*WI*	*Zim*	*Total*
Tests at home	21	3	6	14	–	–	12	–	56
Tests abroad	15	–	8	3	–	1	5	–	32

CHAPPELL, Ian Michael (76)

Debut: 1964-65	*Eng*	*Ind*	*NZ*	*Pak*	*SAf*	*SL*	*WI*	*Zim*	*Total*
Tests at home	17	4	3	4	–	–	12	–	40
Tests abroad	14	5	3	–	9	–	5	–	36

CHAPPELL, Trevor Martin (3)

Debut: 1981	*Eng*	*Ind*	*NZ*	*Pak*	*SAf*	*SL*	*WI*	*Zim*	*Total*
Tests abroad	3	–	–	–	–	–	–	–	3

CHARLTON, Percie Chater (2)

Debut: 1890	*Eng*	*Ind*	*NZ*	*Pak*	*SAf*	*SL*	*WI*	*Zim*	*Total*
Tests abroad	2	–	–	–	–	–	–	–	2

CHIPPERFIELD, Arthur Gordon (14)

Debut: 1934	*Eng*	*Ind*	*NZ*	*Pak*	*SAf*	*SL*	*WI*	*Zim*	*Total*
Tests at home	3	–	–	–	–	–	–	–	3
Tests abroad	6	–	–	–	5	–	–	–	11

CLARK, Wayne Maxwell (10)

Debut: 1977-78	*Eng*	*Ind*	*NZ*	*Pak*	*SAf*	*SL*	*WI*	*Zim*	*Total*
Tests at home	–	5	–	1	–	–	–	–	6
Tests abroad	–	–	–	–	–	–	4	–	4

COLLEY, David John (3)

Debut: 1972	*Eng*	*Ind*	*NZ*	*Pak*	*SAf*	*SL*	*WI*	*Zim*	*Total*
Tests abroad	3	–	–	–	–	–	–	–	3

COLLINS, Herbert Leslie (19)

Debut: 1920-21	*Eng*	*Ind*	*NZ*	*Pak*	*SAf*	*SL*	*WI*	*Zim*	*Total*
Tests at home	10	–	–	–	–	–	–	–	10
Tests abroad	6	–	–	–	3	–	–	–	9

CONINGHAM, Arthur (1)
Debut: 1894-95	*Eng*	*Ind*	*NZ*	*Pak*	*SAf*	*SL*	*WI*	*Zim*	*Total*
Tests at home	1	–	–	–	–	–	–	–	1

CONNOLLY, Alan Norman (30)
Debut: 1963-64	*Eng*	*Ind*	*NZ*	*Pak*	*SAf*	*SL*	*WI*	*Zim*	*Total*
Tests at home	3	3	–	–	3	–	5	–	14
Tests abroad	5	7	–	–	4	–	–	–	16

COOK, Simon Hewitt (2)
Debut: 1997-98	*Eng*	*Ind*	*NZ*	*Pak*	*SAf*	*SL*	*WI*	*Zim*	*Total*
Tests at home	–	–	2	–	–	–	–	–	2

COOPER, Bransby Beauchamp (1)
Debut: 1876-77	*Eng*	*Ind*	*NZ*	*Pak*	*SAf*	*SL*	*WI*	*Zim*	*Total*
Tests at home	1	–	–	–	–	–	–	–	1

COOPER, William Henry (2)
Debut: 1881-82	*Eng*	*Ind*	*NZ*	*Pak*	*SAf*	*SL*	*WI*	*Zim*	*Total*
Tests at home	2	–	–	–	–	–	–	–	2

CORLING, Grahame Edward (5)
Debut: 1964	*Eng*	*Ind*	*NZ*	*Pak*	*SAf*	*SL*	*WI*	*Zim*	*Total*
Tests abroad	5	–	–	–	–	–	–	–	5

COSIER, Gary John (18)
Debut: 1975-76	*Eng*	*Ind*	*NZ*	*Pak*	*SAf*	*SL*	*WI*	*Zim*	*Total*
Tests at home	3	4	–	3	–	–	3	–	13
Tests abroad	–	–	2	–	–	–	3	–	5

COTTAM, John Thomas (1)
Debut: 1886-87	*Eng*	*Ind*	*NZ*	*Pak*	*SAf*	*SL*	*WI*	*Zim*	*Total*
Tests at home	1	–	–	–	–	–	–	–	1

COTTER, Albert (21)
Debut: 1903-04	*Eng*	*Ind*	*NZ*	*Pak*	*SAf*	*SL*	*WI*	*Zim*	*Total*
Tests at home	8	–	–	–	5	–	–	–	13
Tests abroad	8	–	–	–	–	–	–	–	8

COULTHARD, George (1)
Debut: 1881-82	*Eng*	*Ind*	*NZ*	*Pak*	*SAf*	*SL*	*WI*	*Zim*	*Total*
Tests at home	1	–	–	–	–	–	–	–	1

COWPER, Robert Maskew (27)
Debut: 1964	*Eng*	*Ind*	*NZ*	*Pak*	*SAf*	*SL*	*WI*	*Zim*	*Total*
Tests at home	4	4	–	1	–	–	–	–	9
Tests abroad	5	2	–	1	5	–	5	–	18

CRAIG, Ian David (11)
Debut: 1952-53	*Eng*	*Ind*	*NZ*	*Pak*	*SAf*	*SL*	*WI*	*Zim*	*Total*
Tests at home	–	–	–	–	1	–	–	–	1
Tests abroad	2	2	–	1	5	–	–	–	10

CRAWFORD, William Patrick Anthony (4)
Debut: 1956	*Eng*	*Ind*	*NZ*	*Pak*	*SAf*	*SL*	*WI*	*Zim*	*Total*
Tests abroad	1	3	–	–	–	–	–	–	4

DALE, Adam Craig (2)
Debut: 1997-98	*Eng*	*Ind*	*NZ*	*Pak*	*SAf*	*SL*	*WI*	*Zim*	*Total*
Tests abroad	–	1	–	–	–	–	1	–	2

DARLING, Joseph (34)
Debut: 1894-95	*Eng*	*Ind*	*NZ*	*Pak*	*SAf*	*SL*	*WI*	*Zim*	*Total*
Tests at home	13	–	–	–	–	–	–	–	13
Tests abroad	18	–	–	–	3	–	–	–	21

DARLING, Leonard Stuart (12)
Debut: 1932-33	*Eng*	*Ind*	*NZ*	*Pak*	*SAf*	*SL*	*WI*	*Zim*	*Total*
Tests at home	3	–	–	–	–	–	–	–	3
Tests abroad	4	–	–	–	5	–	–	–	9

DARLING, Warrick Maxwell (14)

Debut: 1977-78	*Eng*	*Ind*	*NZ*	*Pak*	*SAf*	*SL*	*WI*	*Zim*	*Total*
Tests at home	4	1	–	1	–	–	–	–	6
Tests abroad	–	5	–	–	–	–	3	–	8

DAVIDSON, Alan Keith (44)

Debut: 1953	*Eng*	*Ind*	*NZ*	*Pak*	*SAf*	*SL*	*WI*	*Zim*	*Total*
Tests at home	13	–	–	–	–	–	4	–	17
Tests abroad	12	6	–	4	5	–	–	–	27

DAVIS, Ian Charles (15)

Debut: 1973-74	*Eng*	*Ind*	*NZ*	*Pak*	*SAf*	*SL*	*WI*	*Zim*	*Total*
Tests at home	1	–	3	3	–	–	–	–	7
Tests abroad	3	–	5	–	–	–	–	–	8

DAVIS, Simon Peter (1)

Debut: 1985-86	*Eng*	*Ind*	*NZ*	*Pak*	*SAf*	*SL*	*WI*	*Zim*	*Total*
Tests abroad	–	–	1	–	–	–	–	–	1

DE COURCY, James Harry (3)

Debut: 1953	*Eng*	*Ind*	*NZ*	*Pak*	*SAf*	*SL*	*WI*	*Zim*	*Total*
Tests abroad	3	–	–	–	–	–	–	–	3

DELL, Anthony Ross (2)

Debut: 1970-71	*Eng*	*Ind*	*NZ*	*Pak*	*SAf*	*SL*	*WI*	*Zim*	*Total*
Tests at home	1	–	1	–	–	–	–	–	2

DODEMAIDE, Anthony Ian Christopher (10)

Debut: 1987-88	*Eng*	*Ind*	*NZ*	*Pak*	*SAf*	*SL*	*WI*	*Zim*	*Total*
Tests at home	1	–	1	–	–	1	2	–	5
Tests abroad	–	–	–	3	–	2	–	–	5

DONNAN, Harry (5)

Debut: 1891-92	*Eng*	*Ind*	*NZ*	*Pak*	*SAf*	*SL*	*WI*	*Zim*	*Total*
Tests at home	2	–	–	–	–	–	–	–	2
Tests abroad	3	–	–	–	–	–	–	–	3

DOOLAND, Bruce (3)

Debut: 1946-47	*Eng*	*Ind*	*NZ*	*Pak*	*SAf*	*SL*	*WI*	*Zim*	*Total*
Tests at home	2	1	–	–	–	–	–	–	3

DUFF, Reginald Alexander (22)

Debut: 1901-02	*Eng*	*Ind*	*NZ*	*Pak*	*SAf*	*SL*	*WI*	*Zim*	*Total*
Tests at home	9	–	–	–	–	–	–	–	9
Tests abroad	10	–	–	–	3	–	–	–	13

DUNCAN, John Ross Frederick (1)

Debut: 1970-71	*Eng*	*Ind*	*NZ*	*Pak*	*SAf*	*SL*	*WI*	*Zim*	*Total*
Tests at home	1	–	–	–	–	–	–	–	1

DYER, Gregory Charles (6)

Debut: 1986-87	*Eng*	*Ind*	*NZ*	*Pak*	*SAf*	*SL*	*WI*	*Zim*	*Total*
Tests at home	2	–	3	–	–	1	–	–	6

DYMOCK, Geoffrey (21)

Debut: 1973-74	*Eng*	*Ind*	*NZ*	*Pak*	*SAf*	*SL*	*WI*	*Zim*	*Total*
Tests at home	7	–	1	1	–	–	2	–	11
Tests abroad	–	5	2	3	–	–	–	–	10

DYSON, John (30)

Debut: 1977-78	*Eng*	*Ind*	*NZ*	*Pak*	*SAf*	*SL*	*WI*	*Zim*	*Total*
Tests at home	5	6	3	–	–	–	5	–	19
Tests abroad	5	–	3	3	–	–	–	–	11

EADY, Charles John (2)

Debut: 1896	*Eng*	*Ind*	*NZ*	*Pak*	*SAf*	*SL*	*WI*	*Zim*	*Total*
Tests at home	1	–	–	–	–	–	–	–	1
Tests abroad	1	–	–	–	–	–	–	–	1

EASTWOOD, Kenneth Humphrey (1)

Debut: 1970-71	Eng	Ind	NZ	Pak	SAf	SL	WI	Zim	Total
Tests at home	1	–	–	–	–	–	–	–	1

EBELING, Hans Irvine (1)

Debut: 1934	Eng	Ind	NZ	Pak	SAf	SL	WI	Zim	Total
Tests abroad	1	–	–	–	–	–	–	–	1

EDWARDS, John Dunlop (3)

Debut: 1888	Eng	Ind	NZ	Pak	SAf	SL	WI	Zim	Total
Tests abroad	3	–	–	–	–	–	–	–	3

EDWARDS, Ross (20)

Debut: 1972	Eng	Ind	NZ	Pak	SAf	SL	WI	Zim	Total
Tests at home	5	–	–	2	–	–	–	–	7
Tests abroad	8	–	–	–	–	–	5	–	13

EDWARDS, Walter John (3)

Debut: 1974-75	Eng	Ind	NZ	Pak	SAf	SL	WI	Zim	Total
Tests at home	3	–	–	–	–	–	–	–	3

ELLIOTT, Matthew Thomas Gray (20)

Debut: 1996-97	Eng	Ind	NZ	Pak	SAf	SL	WI	Zim	Total
Tests at home	–	–	3	–	3	–	2	–	8
Tests abroad	6	–	–	–	3	–	3	–	12

EMERY, Philip Allen (1)

Debut: 1994-95	Eng	Ind	NZ	Pak	SAf	SL	WI	Zim	Total
Tests abroad	–	–	–	1	–	–	–	–	1

EMERY, Sidney Hand (4)

Debut: 1912	Eng	Ind	NZ	Pak	SAf	SL	WI	Zim	Total
Tests abroad	2	–	–	–	2	–	–	–	4

EVANS, Edwin (6)

Debut: 1881-82	Eng	Ind	NZ	Pak	SAf	SL	WI	Zim	Total
Tests at home	4	–	–	–	–	–	–	–	4
Tests abroad	2	–	–	–	–	–	–	–	2

FAIRFAX, Alan George (10)

Debut: 1928-29	Eng	Ind	NZ	Pak	SAf	SL	WI	Zim	Total
Tests at home	1	–	–	–	–	–	5	–	6
Tests abroad	4	–	–	–	–	–	–	–	4

FAVELL, Leslie Ernest (19)

Debut: 1954-55	Eng	Ind	NZ	Pak	SAf	SL	WI	Zim	Total
Tests at home	6	–	–	–	–	–	4	–	10
Tests abroad	–	4	–	3	–	–	2	–	9

FERRIS, John James (8)

Debut: 1886-87	Eng	Ind	NZ	Pak	SAf	SL	WI	Zim	Total
Tests at home	3	–	–	–	–	–	–	–	3
Tests abroad	5	–	–	–	–	–	–	–	5

FINGLETON, John Henry Webb (18)

Debut: 1931-32	Eng	Ind	NZ	Pak	SAf	SL	WI	Zim	Total
Tests at home	8	–	–	–	1	–	–	–	9
Tests abroad	4	–	–	–	5	–	–	–	9

FLEETWOOD-SMITH, Leslie O'Brien (10)

Debut: 1935-36	Eng	Ind	NZ	Pak	SAf	SL	WI	Zim	Total
Tests at home	3	–	–	–	–	–	–	–	3
Tests abroad	4	–	–	–	3	–	–	–	7

FLEMING, Damien William (20)

Debut: 1994-95	Eng	Ind	NZ	Pak	SAf	SL	WI	Zim	Total
Tests at home	7	3	–	3	–	–	–	–	13
Tests abroad	–	1	–	3	–	2	–	1	7

FRANCIS, Bruce Colin (3)

Debut: 1972	*Eng*	*Ind*	*NZ*	*Pak*	*SAf*	*SL*	*WI*	*Zim*	*Total*
Tests abroad	3	–	–	–	–	–	–	–	3

FREEMAN, Eric Walter (11)

Debut: 1967-68	*Eng*	*Ind*	*NZ*	*Pak*	*SAf*	*SL*	*WI*	*Zim*	*Total*
Tests at home	–	2	–	–	–	–	4	–	6
Tests abroad	2	1	–	–	2	–	–	–	5

FREER, Frederick Alfred William (1)

Debut: 1946-47	*Eng*	*Ind*	*NZ*	*Pak*	*SAf*	*SL*	*WI*	*Zim*	*Total*
Tests at home	1	–	–	–	–	–	–	–	1

GANNON, John Bryant (3)

Debut: 1977-78	*Eng*	*Ind*	*NZ*	*Pak*	*SAf*	*SL*	*WI*	*Zim*	*Total*
Tests at home	–	3	–	–	–	–	–	–	3

GARRETT, Thomas William (19)

Debut: 1876-77	*Eng*	*Ind*	*NZ*	*Pak*	*SAf*	*SL*	*WI*	*Zim*	*Total*
Tests at home	15	–	–	–	–	–	–	–	15
Tests abroad	4	–	–	–	–	–	–	–	4

GAUNT, Ronald Arthur (3)

Debut: 1957-58	*Eng*	*Ind*	*NZ*	*Pak*	*SAf*	*SL*	*WI*	*Zim*	*Total*
Tests at home	–	–	–	–	1	–	–	–	1
Tests abroad	1	–	–	–	1	–	–	–	2

GEHRS, Donald Raeburn Algernon (6)

Debut: 1903-04	*Eng*	*Ind*	*NZ*	*Pak*	*SAf*	*SL*	*WI*	*Zim*	*Total*
Tests at home	1	–	–	–	4	–	–	–	5
Tests abroad	1	–	–	–	–	–	–	–	1

GIFFEN, George (31)

Debut: 1881-82	*Eng*	*Ind*	*NZ*	*Pak*	*SAf*	*SL*	*WI*	*Zim*	*Total*
Tests at home	18	–	–	–	–	–	–	–	18
Tests abroad	13	–	–	–	–	–	–	–	13

GIFFEN, Walter Frank (3)

Debut: 1886-87	*Eng*	*Ind*	*NZ*	*Pak*	*SAf*	*SL*	*WI*	*Zim*	*Total*
Tests at home	3	–	–	–	–	–	–	–	3

GILBERT, David Robert (9)

Debut: 1985	*Eng*	*Ind*	*NZ*	*Pak*	*SAf*	*SL*	*WI*	*Zim*	*Total*
Tests at home	–	2	3	–	–	–	–	–	5
Tests abroad	1	2	1	–	–	–	–	–	4

GILCHRIST, Adam Craig (31)

Debut: 1999-00	*Eng*	*Ind*	*NZ*	*Pak*	*SAf*	*SL*	*WI*	*Zim*	*Total*
Tests at home	–	3	3	3	3	–	5	–	17
Tests abroad	5	3	3	–	3	–	–	–	14

GILLESPIE, Jason Neil (33)

Debut: 1996-97	*Eng*	*Ind*	*NZ*	*Pak*	*SAf*	*SL*	*WI*	*Zim*	*Total*
Tests at home	1	–	3	–	1	–	6	–	11
Tests abroad	9	3	–	–	6	1	3	–	22

GILMOUR, Gary John (15)

Debut: 1973-74	*Eng*	*Ind*	*NZ*	*Pak*	*SAf*	*SL*	*WI*	*Zim*	*Total*
Tests at home	1	–	2	3	–	–	5	–	11
Tests abroad	1	–	3	–	–	–	–	–	4

GLEESON, John William (30)

Debut: 1967-68	*Eng*	*Ind*	*NZ*	*Pak*	*SAf*	*SL*	*WI*	*Zim*	*Total*
Tests at home	6	4	–	–	–	–	5	–	15
Tests abroad	8	3	–	–	4	–	–	–	15

GRAHAM, Henry (6)

Debut: 1893	*Eng*	*Ind*	*NZ*	*Pak*	*SAf*	*SL*	*WI*	*Zim*	*Total*
Tests at home	2	–	–	–	–	–	–	–	2
Tests abroad	4	–	–	–	–	–	–	–	4

GREGORY, David William (3)

Debut: 1876-77	Eng	Ind	NZ	Pak	SAf	SL	WI	Zim	Total
Tests at home	3	–	–	–	–	–	–	–	3

GREGORY, Edward James (1)

Debut: 1876-77	Eng	Ind	NZ	Pak	SAf	SL	WI	Zim	Total
Tests at home	1	–	–	–	–	–	–	–	1

GREGORY, Edward Sydney (58)

Debut: 1890	Eng	Ind	NZ	Pak	SAf	SL	WI	Zim	Total
Tests at home	23	–	–	–	–	–	–	–	23
Tests abroad	29	–	–	–	6	–	–	–	35

GREGORY, Jack Morrison (24)

Debut: 1920-21	Eng	Ind	NZ	Pak	SAf	SL	WI	Zim	Total
Tests at home	11	–	–	–	–	–	–	–	11
Tests abroad	10	–	–	–	3	–	–	–	13

GREGORY, Ross Gerald (2)

Debut: 1936-37	Eng	Ind	NZ	Pak	SAf	SL	WI	Zim	Total
Tests at home	2	–	–	–	–	–	–	–	2

GRIMMETT, Clarence Victor (37)

Debut: 1924-25	Eng	Ind	NZ	Pak	SAf	SL	WI	Zim	Total
Tests at home	9	–	–	–	5	–	5	–	19
Tests abroad	13	–	–	–	5	–	–	–	18

GROUBE, Thomas Underwood (1)

Debut: 1880	Eng	Ind	NZ	Pak	SAf	SL	WI	Zim	Total
Tests abroad	1	–	–	–	–	–	–	–	1

GROUT, Arthur Theodore Wallace (51)

Debut: 1957-58	Eng	Ind	NZ	Pak	SAf	SL	WI	Zim	Total
Tests at home	12	–	–	–	5	–	5	–	22
Tests abroad	10	5	–	4	5	–	5	–	29

GUEST, Colin Ernest James (1)

Debut: 1962-63	Eng	Ind	NZ	Pak	SAf	SL	WI	Zim	Total
Tests at home	1	–	–	–	–	–	–	–	1

HAMENCE, Ronald Arthur (3)

Debut: 1946-47	Eng	Ind	NZ	Pak	SAf	SL	WI	Zim	Total
Tests at home	1	2	–	–	–	–	–	–	3

HAMMOND, Jeffrey Roy (5)

Debut: 1972-73	Eng	Ind	NZ	Pak	SAf	SL	WI	Zim	Total
Tests abroad	–	–	–	–	–	–	5	–	5

HARRY, John (1)

Debut: 1894-95	Eng	Ind	NZ	Pak	SAf	SL	WI	Zim	Total
Tests at home	1	–	–	–	–	–	–	–	1

HARTIGAN, Michael Joseph (2)

Debut: 1907-08	Eng	Ind	NZ	Pak	SAf	SL	WI	Zim	Total
Tests at home	2	–	–	–	–	–	–	–	2

HARTKOPF, Albert Ernest Victor (1)

Debut: 1924-25	Eng	Ind	NZ	Pak	SAf	SL	WI	Zim	Total
Tests at home	1	–	–	–	–	–	–	–	1

HARVEY, Mervyn Roye (1)

Debut: 1946-47	Eng	Ind	NZ	Pak	SAf	SL	WI	Zim	Total
Tests at home	1	–	–	–	–	–	–	–	1

HARVEY, Robert Neil (79)

Debut: 1947-48	Eng	Ind	NZ	Pak	SAf	SL	WI	Zim	Total
Tests at home	20	2	–	–	5	–	9	–	36
Tests abroad	17	8	–	4	9	–	5	–	43

HASSETT, Arthur Lindsay (43)

Debut: 1938	Eng	Ind	NZ	Pak	SAf	SL	WI	Zim	Total
Tests at home	10	4	–	–	5	–	4	–	23
Tests abroad	14	–	1	–	5	–	–	–	20

HAWKE, Neil James Napier (27)

Debut: 1962-63	Eng	Ind	NZ	Pak	SAf	SL	WI	Zim	Total
Tests at home	5	1	–	1	4	–	–	–	11
Tests abroad	7	1	–	1	2	–	5	–	16

HAYDEN, Matthew Lawrence (30)

Debut: 1993-94	Eng	Ind	NZ	Pak	SAf	SL	WI	Zim	Total
Tests at home	–	–	3	–	3	–	8	–	14
Tests abroad	5	3	1	–	7	–	–	–	16

HAZLITT, Gervys Rignold (9)

Debut: 1907-08	Eng	Ind	NZ	Pak	SAf	SL	WI	Zim	Total
Tests at home	3	–	–	–	–	–	–	–	3
Tests abroad	3	–	–	–	3	–	–	–	6

HEALY, Ian Andrew (119)

Debut: 1988-89	Eng	Ind	NZ	Pak	SAf	SL	WI	Zim	Total
Tests at home	15	5	7	6	6	5	15	–	59
Tests abroad	18	4	4	8	6	6	13	1	60

HENDRY, Hunter Scott Thomas Laurie (11)

Debut: 1921	Eng	Ind	NZ	Pak	SAf	SL	WI	Zim	Total
Tests at home	5	–	–	–	–	–	–	–	5
Tests abroad	4	–	–	–	2	–	–	–	6

HIBBERT, Paul Anthony (1)

Debut: 1977-78	Eng	Ind	NZ	Pak	SAf	SL	WI	Zim	Total
Tests at home	–	1	–	–	–	–	–	–	1

HIGGS, James Donald (22)

Debut: 1977-78	Eng	Ind	NZ	Pak	SAf	SL	WI	Zim	Total
Tests at home	6	2	3	–	–	–	1	–	12
Tests abroad	–	6	–	–	–	–	4	–	10

HILDITCH, Andrew Mark Jefferson (18)

Debut: 1978-79	Eng	Ind	NZ	Pak	SAf	SL	WI	Zim	Total
Tests at home	1	–	1	2	–	–	2	–	6
Tests abroad	6	6	–	–	–	–	–	–	12

HILL, Clement (49)

Debut: 1896	Eng	Ind	NZ	Pak	SAf	SL	WI	Zim	Total
Tests at home	25	–	–	–	5	–	–	–	30
Tests abroad	16	–	–	–	3	–	–	–	19

HILL, John Charles (3)

Debut: 1953	Eng	Ind	NZ	Pak	SAf	SL	WI	Zim	Total
Tests abroad	2	–	–	–	–	–	1	–	3

HOARE, Desmond Edward (1)

Debut: 1960-61	Eng	Ind	NZ	Pak	SAf	SL	WI	Zim	Total
Tests at home	–	–	–	–	–	–	1	–	1

HODGES, John Robart (2)

Debut: 1876-77	Eng	Ind	NZ	Pak	SAf	SL	WI	Zim	Total
Tests at home	2	–	–	–	–	–	–	–	2

HOGAN, Tom George (7)

Debut: 1982-83	Eng	Ind	NZ	Pak	SAf	SL	WI	Zim	Total
Tests at home	–	–	–	1	–	–	–	–	1
Tests abroad	–	–	–	–	–	1	5	–	6

HOGG, George Bradley (1)

Debut: 1996-97	Eng	Ind	NZ	Pak	SAf	SL	WI	Zim	Total
Tests abroad	–	1	–	–	–	–	–	–	1

HOGG, Rodney Malcolm (38)

Debut: 1978-79	Eng	Ind	NZ	Pak	SAf	SL	WI	Zim	Total
Tests at home	9	2	2	6	–	–	6	–	25
Tests abroad	2	6	–	–	–	1	4	–	13

HOHNS, Trevor Victor (7)

Debut: 1988-89	Eng	Ind	NZ	Pak	SAf	SL	WI	Zim	Total
Tests at home	–	–	–	–	–	–	2	–	2
Tests abroad	5	–	–	–	–	–	–	–	5

HOLE, Graeme Blake (18)

Debut: 1950-51	Eng	Ind	NZ	Pak	SAf	SL	WI	Zim	Total
Tests at home	4	–	–	–	4	–	5	–	13
Tests abroad	5	–	–	–	–	–	–	–	5

HOLLAND, Robert George (11)

Debut: 1984-85	Eng	Ind	NZ	Pak	SAf	SL	WI	Zim	Total
Tests at home	–	1	3	–	–	–	3	–	7
Tests abroad	4	–	–	–	–	–	–	–	4

HOOKES, David William (23)

Debut: 1976-77	Eng	Ind	NZ	Pak	SAf	SL	WI	Zim	Total
Tests at home	6	2	2	–	–	–	1	–	11
Tests abroad	5	–	–	1	–	1	5	–	12

HOPKINS, Albert John Young (20)

Debut: 1901-02	Eng	Ind	NZ	Pak	SAf	SL	WI	Zim	Total
Tests at home	7	–	–	–	–	–	–	–	7
Tests abroad	10	–	–	–	3	–	–	–	13

HORAN, Thomas Patrick (15)

Debut: 1876-77	Eng	Ind	NZ	Pak	SAf	SL	WI	Zim	Total
Tests at home	14	–	–	–	–	–	–	–	14
Tests abroad	1	–	–	–	–	–	–	–	1

HORDERN, Herbert Vivian (7)

Debut: 1910-11	Eng	Ind	NZ	Pak	SAf	SL	WI	Zim	Total
Tests at home	5	–	–	–	2	–	–	–	7

HORNIBROOK, Percival Mitchell (6)

Debut: 1928-29	Eng	Ind	NZ	Pak	SAf	SL	WI	Zim	Total
Tests at home	1	–	–	–	–	–	–	–	1
Tests abroad	5	–	–	–	–	–	–	–	5

HOWELL, William Peter (18)

Debut: 1897-98	Eng	Ind	NZ	Pak	SAf	SL	WI	Zim	Total
Tests at home	10	–	–	–	–	–	–	–	10
Tests abroad	6	–	–	–	2	–	–	–	8

HUGHES, Kimberley John (70)

Debut: 1977	Eng	Ind	NZ	Pak	SAf	SL	WI	Zim	Total
Tests at home	14	5	3	10	–	–	10	–	42
Tests abroad	8	6	3	6	–	–	5	–	28

HUGHES, Mervyn Gregory (53)

Debut: 1985-86	Eng	Ind	NZ	Pak	SAf	SL	WI	Zim	Total
Tests at home	8	6	2	3	–	3	9	–	31
Tests abroad	12	–	3	–	2	–	5	–	22

HUNT, William Alfred (1)

Debut: 1931-32	Eng	Ind	NZ	Pak	SAf	SL	WI	Zim	Total
Tests at home	–	–	–	–	1	–	–	–	1

HURST, Alan George (12)

Debut: 1973-74	Eng	Ind	NZ	Pak	SAf	SL	WI	Zim	Total
Tests at home	6	1	1	2	–	–	–	–	10
Tests abroad	–	2	–	–	–	–	–	–	2

HURWOOD, Alexander (2)

Debut: 1930-31	*Eng*	*Ind*	*NZ*	*Pak*	*SAf*	*SL*	*WI*	*Zim*	*Total*
Tests at home	–	–	–	–	–	–	2	–	2

INVERARITY, Robert John (6)

Debut: 1968	*Eng*	*Ind*	*NZ*	*Pak*	*SAf*	*SL*	*WI*	*Zim*	*Total*
Tests at home	–	–	–	–	–	–	1	–	1
Tests abroad	5	–	–	–	–	–	–	–	5

IREDALE, Francis Adams (14)

Debut: 1894-95	*Eng*	*Ind*	*NZ*	*Pak*	*SAf*	*SL*	*WI*	*Zim*	*Total*
Tests at home	9	–	–	–	–	–	–	–	9
Tests abroad	5	–	–	–	–	–	–	–	5

IRONMONGER, Herbert (14)

Debut: 1928-29	*Eng*	*Ind*	*NZ*	*Pak*	*SAf*	*SL*	*WI*	*Zim*	*Total*
Tests at home	6	–	–	–	4	–	4	–	14

IVERSON, John Brian (5)

Debut: 1950-51	*Eng*	*Ind*	*NZ*	*Pak*	*SAf*	*SL*	*WI*	*Zim*	*Total*
Tests at home	5	–	–	–	–	–	–	–	5

JACKSON, Archibald (8)

Debut: 1928-29	*Eng*	*Ind*	*NZ*	*Pak*	*SAf*	*SL*	*WI*	*Zim*	*Total*
Tests at home	2	–	–	–	–	–	4	–	6
Tests abroad	2	–	–	–	–	–	–	–	2

JARMAN, Barrington Noel (19)

Debut: 1959-60	*Eng*	*Ind*	*NZ*	*Pak*	*SAf*	*SL*	*WI*	*Zim*	*Total*
Tests at home	3	4	–	1	–	–	4	–	12
Tests abroad	4	3	–	–	–	–	–	–	7

JARVIS, Arthur Harwood (11)

Debut: 1884-85	*Eng*	*Ind*	*NZ*	*Pak*	*SAf*	*SL*	*WI*	*Zim*	*Total*
Tests at home	7	–	–	–	–	–	–	–	7
Tests abroad	4	–	–	–	–	–	–	–	4

JENNER, Terrence James (9)

Debut: 1970-71	*Eng*	*Ind*	*NZ*	*Pak*	*SAf*	*SL*	*WI*	*Zim*	*Total*
Tests at home	4	–	–	–	–	–	1	–	5
Tests abroad	–	–	–	–	–	–	4	–	4

JENNINGS, Claude Burrows (6)

Debut: 1912	*Eng*	*Ind*	*NZ*	*Pak*	*SAf*	*SL*	*WI*	*Zim*	*Total*
Tests abroad	3	–	–	–	3	–	–	–	6

JOHNSON, Ian William Geddes (45)

Debut: 1945-46	*Eng*	*Ind*	*NZ*	*Pak*	*SAf*	*SL*	*WI*	*Zim*	*Total*
Tests at home	13	4	–	–	1	–	4	–	22
Tests abroad	9	2	1	1	5	–	5	–	23

JOHNSON, Leonard Joseph (1)

Debut: 1947-48	*Eng*	*Ind*	*NZ*	*Pak*	*SAf*	*SL*	*WI*	*Zim*	*Total*
Tests at home	–	1	–	–	–	–	–	–	1

JOHNSTON, William Arras (40)

Debut: 1947-48	*Eng*	*Ind*	*NZ*	*Pak*	*SAf*	*SL*	*WI*	*Zim*	*Total*
Tests at home	9	4	–	–	5	–	5	–	23
Tests abroad	8	–	–	–	5	–	4	–	17

JONES, Dean Mervyn (52)

Debut: 1983-84	*Eng*	*Ind*	*NZ*	*Pak*	*SAf*	*SL*	*WI*	*Zim*	*Total*
Tests at home	11	5	4	3	–	3	3	–	29
Tests abroad	6	3	1	3	–	3	7	–	23

JONES, Ernest (19)

Debut: 1894-95	*Eng*	*Ind*	*NZ*	*Pak*	*SAf*	*SL*	*WI*	*Zim*	*Total*
Tests at home	8	–	–	–	–	–	–	–	8
Tests abroad	10	–	–	–	1	–	–	–	11

JONES, Samuel Percy (12)

Debut: 1881-82	Eng	Ind	NZ	Pak	SAf	SL	WI	Zim	Total
Tests at home	8	–	–	–	–	–	–	–	8
Tests abroad	4	–	–	–	–	–	–	–	4

JOSLIN, Leslie Ronald (1)

Debut: 1967-68	Eng	Ind	NZ	Pak	SAf	SL	WI	Zim	Total
Tests at home	–	1	–	–	–	–	–	–	1

JULIAN, Brendon Paul (7)

Debut: 1993	Eng	Ind	NZ	Pak	SAf	SL	WI	Zim	Total
Tests at home	–	–	–	–	–	1	–	–	1
Tests abroad	2	–	–	–	–	–	4	–	6

KASPROWICZ, Michael Scott (17)

Debut: 1996-97	Eng	Ind	NZ	Pak	SAf	SL	WI	Zim	Total
Tests at home	1	1	3	1	2	–	2	–	10
Tests abroad	3	4	–	–	–	–	–	–	7

KATICH, Simon Matthew (1)

Debut: 2001	Eng	Ind	NZ	Pak	SAf	SL	WI	Zim	Total
Tests abroad	1	–	–	–	–	–	–	–	1

KELLEWAY, Charles (26)

Debut: 1910-11	Eng	Ind	NZ	Pak	SAf	SL	WI	Zim	Total
Tests at home	15	–	–	–	5	–	–	–	20
Tests abroad	3	–	–	–	3	–	–	–	6

KELLY, James Joseph (36)

Debut: 1896	Eng	Ind	NZ	Pak	SAf	SL	WI	Zim	Total
Tests at home	15	–	–	–	–	–	–	–	15
Tests abroad	18	–	–	–	3	–	–	–	21

KELLY, Thomas Joseph Dart (2)

Debut: 1876-77	Eng	Ind	NZ	Pak	SAf	SL	WI	Zim	Total
Tests at home	2	–	–	–	–	–	–	–	2

KENDALL, Thomas Kingston (2)

Debut: 1876-77	Eng	Ind	NZ	Pak	SAf	SL	WI	Zim	Total
Tests at home	2	–	–	–	–	–	–	–	2

KENT, Martin Francis (3)

Debut: 1981	Eng	Ind	NZ	Pak	SAf	SL	WI	Zim	Total
Tests abroad	3	–	–	–	–	–	–	–	3

KERR, Robert Byers (2)

Debut: 1985-86	Eng	Ind	NZ	Pak	SAf	SL	WI	Zim	Total
Tests at home	–	–	2	–	–	–	–	–	2

KIPPAX, Alan Falconer (22)

Debut: 1924-25	Eng	Ind	NZ	Pak	SAf	SL	WI	Zim	Total
Tests at home	7	–	–	–	4	–	5	–	16
Tests abroad	6	–	–	–	–	–	–	–	6

KLINE, Lindsay Francis (13)

Debut: 1957-58	Eng	Ind	NZ	Pak	SAf	SL	WI	Zim	Total
Tests at home	2	–	–	–	–	–	2	–	4
Tests abroad	–	3	–	1	5	–	–	–	9

LAIRD, Bruce Malcolm (21)

Debut: 1979-80	Eng	Ind	NZ	Pak	SAf	SL	WI	Zim	Total
Tests at home	2	–	–	3	–	–	6	–	11
Tests abroad	1	–	3	6	–	–	–	–	10

LANGER, Justin Lee (51)

Debut: 1992-93	Eng	Ind	NZ	Pak	SAf	SL	WI	Zim	Total
Tests at home	5	3	3	3	3	–	9	–	26
Tests abroad	1	3	6	4	3	3	4	1	25

LANGLEY, Gilbert Roche Andrews (26)

Debut: 1951-52	Eng	Ind	NZ	Pak	SAf	SL	WI	Zim	Total
Tests at home	2	–	–	–	5	–	5	–	12
Tests abroad	7	2	–	1	–	–	4	–	14

LAUGHLIN, Trevor John (3)

Debut: 1977-78	Eng	Ind	NZ	Pak	SAf	SL	WI	Zim	Total
Tests at home	1	–	–	–	–	–	–	–	1
Tests abroad	–	–	–	–	–	–	2	–	2

LAVER, Frank (15)

Debut: 1899	Eng	Ind	NZ	Pak	SAf	SL	WI	Zim	Total
Tests at home	2	–	–	–	–	–	–	–	2
Tests abroad	13	–	–	–	–	–	–	–	13

LAW, Stuart Grant (1)

Debut: 1995-96	Eng	Ind	NZ	Pak	SAf	SL	WI	Zim	Total
Tests at home	–	–	–	–	–	1	–	–	1

LAWRY, William Morris (68)

Debut: 1961	Eng	Ind	NZ	Pak	SAf	SL	WI	Zim	Total
Tests at home	16	4	–	1	5	–	5	–	31
Tests abroad	14	8	–	1	9	–	5	–	37

LAWSON, Geoffrey Francis (46)

Debut: 1980-81	Eng	Ind	NZ	Pak	SAf	SL	WI	Zim	Total
Tests at home	6	–	4	5	–	1	7	–	23
Tests abroad	15	–	–	3	–	–	5	–	23

LEE, Brett (21)

Debut: 1999-00	Eng	Ind	NZ	Pak	SAf	SL	WI	Zim	Total
Tests at home	–	2	3	–	3	–	2	–	10
Tests abroad	5	–	3	–	3	–	–	–	11

LEE, Philip Keith (2)

Debut: 1931-32	Eng	Ind	NZ	Pak	SAf	SL	WI	Zim	Total
Tests at home	1	–	–	–	1	–	–	–	2

LEHMANN, Darren Scott (5)

Debut: 1997-98	Eng	Ind	NZ	Pak	SAf	SL	WI	Zim	Total
Tests at home	2	–	–	–	–	–	–	–	2
Tests abroad	–	1	–	2	–	–	–	–	3

LILLEE, Dennis Keith (70)

Debut: 1970-71	Eng	Ind	NZ	Pak	SAf	SL	WI	Zim	Total
Tests at home	13	3	3	14	–	–	11	–	44
Tests abroad	16	–	5	3	–	1	1	–	26

LINDWALL, Raymond Russell (61)

Debut: 1945-46	Eng	Ind	NZ	Pak	SAf	SL	WI	Zim	Total
Tests at home	15	5	–	–	4	–	5	–	29
Tests abroad	14	5	1	3	4	–	5	–	32

LOVE, Hampden Stanley Bray (1)

Debut: 1932-33	Eng	Ind	NZ	Pak	SAf	SL	WI	Zim	Total
Tests at home	1	–	–	–	–	–	–	–	1

LOXTON, Samuel John Everett (12)

Debut: 1947-48	Eng	Ind	NZ	Pak	SAf	SL	WI	Zim	Total
Tests at home	3	1	–	–	–	–	–	–	4
Tests abroad	3	–	–	–	5	–	–	–	8

LYONS, John James (14)

Debut: 1886-87	Eng	Ind	NZ	Pak	SAf	SL	WI	Zim	Total
Tests at home	8	–	–	–	–	–	–	–	8
Tests abroad	6	–	–	–	–	–	–	–	6

McALISTER, Peter Alexander (8)

Debut: 1903-04	Eng	Ind	NZ	Pak	SAf	SL	WI	Zim	Total
Tests at home	6	–	–	–	–	–	–	–	6
Tests abroad	2	–	–	–	–	–	–	–	2

MACARTNEY, Charles George (35)

Debut: 1907-08	Eng	Ind	NZ	Pak	SAf	SL	WI	Zim	Total
Tests at home	8	–	–	–	4	–	–	–	12
Tests abroad	18	–	–	–	5	–	–	–	23

McCABE, Stanley Joseph (39)

Debut: 1930	Eng	Ind	NZ	Pak	SAf	SL	WI	Zim	Total
Tests at home	10	–	–	–	5	–	5	–	20
Tests abroad	14	–	–	–	5	–	–	–	19

McCOOL, Colin Leslie (14)

Debut: 1945-46	Eng	Ind	NZ	Pak	SAf	SL	WI	Zim	Total
Tests at home	5	3	–	–	–	–	–	–	8
Tests abroad	–	–	1	–	5	–	–	–	6

McCORMICK, Ernest Leslie (12)

Debut: 1935-36	Eng	Ind	NZ	Pak	SAf	SL	WI	Zim	Total
Tests at home	4	–	–	–	–	–	–	–	4
Tests abroad	3	–	–	–	5	–	–	–	8

McCOSKER, Richard Bede (25)

Debut: 1974-75	Eng	Ind	NZ	Pak	SAf	SL	WI	Zim	Total
Tests at home	6	–	–	3	–	–	5	–	14
Tests abroad	9	–	2	–	–	–	–	–	11

McDERMOTT, Craig John (71)

Debut: 1984-85	Eng	Ind	NZ	Pak	SAf	SL	WI	Zim	Total
Tests at home	9	7	8	3	3	4	9	–	43
Tests abroad	8	2	5	2	3	3	5	–	28

McDONALD, Colin Campbell (47)

Debut: 1951-52	Eng	Ind	NZ	Pak	SAf	SL	WI	Zim	Total
Tests at home	7	–	–	–	5	–	6	–	18
Tests abroad	8	7	–	4	5	–	5	–	29

McDONALD, Edgar Arthur (11)

Debut: 1920-21	Eng	Ind	NZ	Pak	SAf	SL	WI	Zim	Total
Tests at home	3	–	–	–	–	–	–	–	3
Tests abroad	5	–	–	–	3	–	–	–	8

McDONNELL, Percy Stanislaus (19)

Debut: 1880	Eng	Ind	NZ	Pak	SAf	SL	WI	Zim	Total
Tests at home	12	–	–	–	–	–	–	–	12
Tests abroad	7	–	–	–	–	–	–	–	7

MacGILL, Stuart Charles Glyndwr (17)

Debut: 1997-98	Eng	Ind	NZ	Pak	SAf	SL	WI	Zim	Total
Tests at home	4	–	–	–	2	–	4	–	10
Tests abroad	–	–	–	3	–	–	4	–	7

McGRATH, Glenn Donald (84)

Debut: 1993-94	Eng	Ind	NZ	Pak	SAf	SL	WI	Zim	Total
Tests at home	7	3	6	6	6	3	10	–	41
Tests abroad	11	4	3	5	8	3	8	1	43

McILWRAITH, John (1)

Debut: 1886	Eng	Ind	NZ	Pak	SAf	SL	WI	Zim	Total
Tests abroad	1	–	–	–	–	–	–	–	1

McINTYRE, Peter Edward (2)

Debut: 1994-95	Eng	Ind	NZ	Pak	SAf	SL	WI	Zim	Total
Tests at home	1	–	–	–	–	–	–	–	1
Tests abroad	–	1	–	–	–	–	–	–	1

MACKAY, Kenneth Donald (37)

Debut: 1956	Eng	Ind	NZ	Pak	SAf	SL	WI	Zim	Total
Tests at home	8	–	–	–	–	–	5	–	13
Tests abroad	8	8	–	3	5	–	–	–	24

McKENZIE, Graham Douglas (61)

Debut: 1961	Eng	Ind	NZ	Pak	SAf	SL	WI	Zim	Total
Tests at home	13	2	–	1	5	–	5	–	26
Tests abroad	13	8	–	1	8	–	5	–	35

McKIBBIN, Thomas Robert (5)

Debut: 1894-95	Eng	Ind	NZ	Pak	SAf	SL	WI	Zim	Total
Tests at home	3	–	–	–	–	–	–	–	3
Tests abroad	2	–	–	–	–	–	–	–	2

McLAREN, John William (1)

Debut: 1911-12	Eng	Ind	NZ	Pak	SAf	SL	WI	Zim	Total
Tests at home	1	–	–	–	–	–	–	–	1

MACLEAN, John Alexander (4)

Debut: 1978-79	Eng	Ind	NZ	Pak	SAf	SL	WI	Zim	Total
Tests at home	4	–	–	–	–	–	–	–	4

McLEOD, Charles Edward (17)

Debut: 1894-95	Eng	Ind	NZ	Pak	SAf	SL	WI	Zim	Total
Tests at home	11	–	–	–	–	–	–	–	11
Tests abroad	6	–	–	–	–	–	–	–	6

McLEOD, Robert William (6)

Debut: 1891-92	Eng	Ind	NZ	Pak	SAf	SL	WI	Zim	Total
Tests at home	3	–	–	–	–	–	–	–	3
Tests abroad	3	–	–	–	–	–	–	–	3

McSHANE, Patrick George (3)

Debut: 1884-85	Eng	Ind	NZ	Pak	SAf	SL	WI	Zim	Total
Tests at home	3	–	–	–	–	–	–	–	3

MADDOCKS, Leonard Victor (7)

Debut: 1954-55	Eng	Ind	NZ	Pak	SAf	SL	WI	Zim	Total
Tests at home	3	–	–	–	–	–	–	–	3
Tests abroad	2	1	–	–	–	–	1	–	4

MAGUIRE, John Norman (3)

Debut: 1983-84	Eng	Ind	NZ	Pak	SAf	SL	WI	Zim	Total
Tests at home	–	–	–	1	–	–	–	–	1
Tests abroad	–	–	–	–	–	–	2	–	2

MAILEY, Arthur Alfred (21)

Debut: 1920-21	Eng	Ind	NZ	Pak	SAf	SL	WI	Zim	Total
Tests at home	10	–	–	–	–	–	–	–	10
Tests abroad	8	–	–	–	3	–	–	–	11

MALLETT, Ashley Alexander (39)

Debut: 1968	Eng	Ind	NZ	Pak	SAf	SL	WI	Zim	Total
Tests at home	9	–	3	2	–	–	8	–	22
Tests abroad	8	5	3	–	1	–	–	–	17

MALONE, Michael Francis (1)

Debut: 1977	Eng	Ind	NZ	Pak	SAf	SL	WI	Zim	Total
Tests abroad	1	–	–	–	–	–	–	–	1

MANN, Anthony Longford (4)

Debut: 1977-78	Eng	Ind	NZ	Pak	SAf	SL	WI	Zim	Total
Tests at home	–	4	–	–	–	–	–	–	4

MARR, Alfred Percy (1)

Debut: 1884-85	Eng	Ind	NZ	Pak	SAf	SL	WI	Zim	Total
Tests at home	1	–	–	–	–	–	–	–	1

MARSH, Geoffrey Robert (50)

Debut: 1985-86	Eng	Ind	NZ	Pak	SAf	SL	WI	Zim	Total
Tests at home	11	7	3	2	–	1	5	–	29
Tests abroad	6	3	4	3	–	–	5	–	21

MARSH, Rodney William (97)

Debut: 1970-71	Eng	Ind	NZ	Pak	SAf	SL	WI	Zim	Total
Tests at home	22	3	6	14	–	–	12	–	57
Tests abroad	21	–	8	6	–	–	5	–	40

MARTIN, John Wesley (8)

Debut: 1960-61	Eng	Ind	NZ	Pak	SAf	SL	WI	Zim	Total
Tests at home	–	–	–	–	1	–	3	–	4
Tests abroad	–	2	–	1	1	–	–	–	4

MARTYN, Damien Richard (25)

Debut: 1992-93	Eng	Ind	NZ	Pak	SAf	SL	WI	Zim	Total
Tests at home	–	–	3	–	5	–	5	–	13
Tests abroad	5	–	4	–	3	–	–	–	12

MASSIE, Hugh Hamon (9)

Debut: 1881-82	Eng	Ind	NZ	Pak	SAf	SL	WI	Zim	Total
Tests at home	8	–	–	–	–	–	–	–	8
Tests abroad	1	–	–	–	–	–	–	–	1

MASSIE, Robert Arnold Lockyer (6)

Debut: 1972	Eng	Ind	NZ	Pak	SAf	SL	WI	Zim	Total
Tests at home	–	–	–	2	–	–	–	–	2
Tests abroad	4	–	–	–	–	–	–	–	4

MATTHEWS, Christopher Darrell (3)

Debut: 1986-87	Eng	Ind	NZ	Pak	SAf	SL	WI	Zim	Total
Tests at home	2	–	–	–	–	–	1	–	3

MATTHEWS, Gregory Richard John (33)

Debut: 1983-84	Eng	Ind	NZ	Pak	SAf	SL	WI	Zim	Total
Tests at home	9	3	3	2	–	–	3	–	20
Tests abroad	1	3	3	–	–	3	3	–	13

MATTHEWS, Thomas James (8)

Debut: 1911-12	Eng	Ind	NZ	Pak	SAf	SL	WI	Zim	Total
Tests at home	2	–	–	–	–	–	–	–	2
Tests abroad	3	–	–	–	3	–	–	–	6

MAY, Timothy Brian Alexander (24)

Debut: 1987-88	Eng	Ind	NZ	Pak	SAf	SL	WI	Zim	Total
Tests at home	3	–	3	–	3	–	4	–	13
Tests abroad	5	–	–	5	1	–	–	–	11

MAYNE, Lawrence Charles (6)

Debut: 1964-65	Eng	Ind	NZ	Pak	SAf	SL	WI	Zim	Total
Tests abroad	–	1	–	–	2	–	3	–	6

MAYNE, Richard Edgar (4)

Debut: 1912	Eng	Ind	NZ	Pak	SAf	SL	WI	Zim	Total
Tests abroad	1	–	–	–	3	–	–	–	4

MECKIFF, Ian (18)

Debut: 1957-58	Eng	Ind	NZ	Pak	SAf	SL	WI	Zim	Total
Tests at home	4	–	–	–	1	–	2	–	7
Tests abroad	–	5	–	2	4	–	–	–	11

MEULEMAN, Kenneth Douglas (1)

Debut: 1945-46	Eng	Ind	NZ	Pak	SAf	SL	WI	Zim	Total
Tests abroad	–	–	1	–	–	–	–	–	1

MIDWINTER, William Evans (8)

Debut: 1876-77	Eng	Ind	NZ	Pak	SAf	SL	WI	Zim	Total
Tests at home	5	–	–	–	–	–	–	–	5

| Tests abroad | 3 | – | – | – | – | – | – | – | 3 |

MILLER, Colin Reid (18)

Debut: 1998-99	*Eng*	*Ind*	*NZ*	*Pak*	*SAf*	*SL*	*WI*	*Zim*	*Total*
Tests at home	3	–	–	–	–	–	3	–	6
Tests abroad	–	1	3	3	–	3	1	1	12

MILLER, Keith Ross (55)

Debut: 1945-46	*Eng*	*Ind*	*NZ*	*Pak*	*SAf*	*SL*	*WI*	*Zim*	*Total*
Tests at home	14	5	–	–	4	–	5	–	28
Tests abroad	15	–	1	1	5	–	5	–	27

MINNETT, Roy Baldwin (9)

Debut: 1911-12	*Eng*	*Ind*	*NZ*	*Pak*	*SAf*	*SL*	*WI*	*Zim*	*Total*
Tests at home	5	–	–	–	–	–	–	–	5
Tests abroad	1	–	–	–	3	–	–	–	4

MISSON, Francis Michael (5)

Debut: 1960-61	*Eng*	*Ind*	*NZ*	*Pak*	*SAf*	*SL*	*WI*	*Zim*	*Total*
Tests at home	–	–	–	–	–	–	3	–	3
Tests abroad	2	–	–	–	–	–	–	–	2

MOODY, Thomas Masson (8)

Debut: 1989-90	*Eng*	*Ind*	*NZ*	*Pak*	*SAf*	*SL*	*WI*	*Zim*	*Total*
Tests at home	–	1	1	1	–	2	–	–	5
Tests abroad	–	–	–	–	–	3	–	–	3

MORONEY, John (7)

Debut: 1949-50	*Eng*	*Ind*	*NZ*	*Pak*	*SAf*	*SL*	*WI*	*Zim*	*Total*
Tests at home	1	–	–	–	–	–	1	–	2
Tests abroad	–	–	–	–	5	–	–	–	5

MORRIS, Arthur Robert (46)

Debut: 1946-47	*Eng*	*Ind*	*NZ*	*Pak*	*SAf*	*SL*	*WI*	*Zim*	*Total*
Tests at home	14	4	–	–	5	–	4	–	27
Tests abroad	10	–	–	–	5	–	4	–	19

MORRIS, Samuel (1)

Debut: 1884-85	*Eng*	*Ind*	*NZ*	*Pak*	*SAf*	*SL*	*WI*	*Zim*	*Total*
Tests at home	1	–	–	–	–	–	–	–	1

MOSES, Henry (6)

Debut: 1886-87	*Eng*	*Ind*	*NZ*	*Pak*	*SAf*	*SL*	*WI*	*Zim*	*Total*
Tests at home	6	–	–	–	–	–	–	–	6

MOSS, Jeffrey Kenneth (1)

Debut: 1978-79	*Eng*	*Ind*	*NZ*	*Pak*	*SAf*	*SL*	*WI*	*Zim*	*Total*
Tests at home	–	–	–	1	–	–	–	–	1

MOULE, William Henry (1)

Debut: 1880	*Eng*	*Ind*	*NZ*	*Pak*	*SAf*	*SL*	*WI*	*Zim*	*Total*
Tests abroad	1	–	–	–	–	–	–	–	1

MULLER, Scott Andrew (2)

Debut: 1999-00	*Eng*	*Ind*	*NZ*	*Pak*	*SAf*	*SL*	*WI*	*Zim*	*Total*
Tests at home	–	–	–	2	–	–	–	–	2

MURDOCH, William Lloyd (18)

Debut: 1876-77	*Eng*	*Ind*	*NZ*	*Pak*	*SAf*	*SL*	*WI*	*Zim*	*Total*
Tests at home	11	–	–	–	–	–	–	–	11
Tests abroad	7	–	–	–	–	–	–	–	7

MUSGROVE, Henry Alfred (1)

Debut: 1884-85	*Eng*	*Ind*	*NZ*	*Pak*	*SAf*	*SL*	*WI*	*Zim*	*Total*
Tests at home	1	–	–	–	–	–	–	–	1

NAGEL, Lisle Ernest (1)

Debut: 1932-33	*Eng*	*Ind*	*NZ*	*Pak*	*SAf*	*SL*	*WI*	*Zim*	*Total*
Tests at home	1	–	–	–	–	–	–	–	1

NASH, Laurence John (2)

Debut: 1931-32	Eng	Ind	NZ	Pak	SAf	SL	WI	Zim	Total
Tests at home	1	–	–	–	1	–	–	–	2

NICHOLSON, Matthew James (1)

Debut: 1998-99	Eng	Ind	NZ	Pak	SAf	SL	WI	Zim	Total
Tests at home	1	–	–	–	–	–	–	–	1

NITSCHKE, Holmesdale Carl (2)

Debut: 1931-32	Eng	Ind	NZ	Pak	SAf	SL	WI	Zim	Total
Tests at home	–	–	–	–	2	–	–	–	2

NOBLE, Montague Alfred (42)

Debut: 1897-98	Eng	Ind	NZ	Pak	SAf	SL	WI	Zim	Total
Tests at home	19	–	–	–	–	–	–	–	19
Tests abroad	20	–	–	–	3	–	–	–	23

NOBLET, Geffery (3)

Debut: 1949-50	Eng	Ind	NZ	Pak	SAf	SL	WI	Zim	Total
Tests at home	–	–	–	–	1	–	1	–	2
Tests abroad	–	–	–	–	1	–	–	–	1

NOTHLING, Otto Ernest (1)

Debut: 1928-29	Eng	Ind	NZ	Pak	SAf	SL	WI	Zim	Total
Tests at home	1	–	–	–	–	–	–	–	1

O'BRIEN, Leo Patrick Joseph (5)

Debut: 1932-33	Eng	Ind	NZ	Pak	SAf	SL	WI	Zim	Total
Tests at home	3	–	–	–	–	–	–	–	3
Tests abroad	–	–	–	–	2	–	–	–	2

O'CONNOR, John Denis Alphonsus (4)

Debut: 1907-08	Eng	Ind	NZ	Pak	SAf	SL	WI	Zim	Total
Tests at home	3	–	–	–	–	–	–	–	3
Tests abroad	1	–	–	–	–	–	–	–	1

O'DONNELL, Simon Patrick (6)

Debut: 1985	Eng	Ind	NZ	Pak	SAf	SL	WI	Zim	Total
Tests at home	–	–	1	–	–	–	–	–	1
Tests abroad	5	–	–	–	–	–	–	–	5

OGILVIE, Alan David (5)

Debut: 1977-78	Eng	Ind	NZ	Pak	SAf	SL	WI	Zim	Total
Tests at home	–	3	–	–	–	–	–	–	3
Tests abroad	–	–	–	–	–	–	2	–	2

O'KEEFFE, Kerry James (24)

Debut: 1970-71	Eng	Ind	NZ	Pak	SAf	SL	WI	Zim	Total
Tests at home	3	–	3	5	–	–	–	–	11
Tests abroad	3	–	5	–	–	–	5	–	13

OLDFIELD, William Albert Stanley (54)

Debut: 1920-21	Eng	Ind	NZ	Pak	SAf	SL	WI	Zim	Total
Tests at home	22	–	–	–	5	–	5	–	32
Tests abroad	16	–	–	–	6	–	–	–	22

O'NEILL, Norman Clifford (42)

Debut: 1958-59	Eng	Ind	NZ	Pak	SAf	SL	WI	Zim	Total
Tests at home	10	–	–	–	4	–	5	–	19
Tests abroad	9	7	–	3	–	–	4	–	23

O'REILLY, William Joseph (27)

Debut: 1931-32	Eng	Ind	NZ	Pak	SAf	SL	WI	Zim	Total
Tests at home	10	–	–	–	2	–	–	–	12
Tests abroad	9	–	1	–	5	–	–	–	15

OXENHAM, Ronald Keven (7)

Debut: 1928-29	Eng	Ind	NZ	Pak	SAf	SL	WI	Zim	Total
Tests at home	3	–	–	–	1	–	3	–	7

PALMER, George Eugene (17)

Debut: 1880	Eng	Ind	NZ	Pak	SAf	SL	WI	Zim	Total
Tests at home	10	–	–	–	–	–	–	–	10
Tests abroad	7	–	–	–	–	–	–	–	7

PARK, Roy Lindsay (1)

Debut: 1920-21	Eng	Ind	NZ	Pak	SAf	SL	WI	Zim	Total
Tests at home	1	–	–	–	–	–	–	–	1

PASCOE, Len Stephen (14)

Debut: 1977	Eng	Ind	NZ	Pak	SAf	SL	WI	Zim	Total
Tests at home	2	3	3	–	–	–	2	–	10
Tests abroad	4	–	–	–	–	–	–	–	4

PELLEW, Clarence Everard (10)

Debut: 1920-21	Eng	Ind	NZ	Pak	SAf	SL	WI	Zim	Total
Tests at home	4	–	–	–	–	–	–	–	4
Tests abroad	5	–	–	–	1	–	–	–	6

PHILLIPS, Wayne Bentley (27)

Debut: 1983-84	Eng	Ind	NZ	Pak	SAf	SL	WI	Zim	Total
Tests at home	–	3	3	5	–	–	2	–	13
Tests abroad	6	–	3	–	–	–	5	–	14

PHILLIPS, Wayne Norman (1)

Debut: 1991-92	Eng	Ind	NZ	Pak	SAf	SL	WI	Zim	Total
Tests at home	–	1	–	–	–	–	–	–	1

PHILPOTT, Peter Ian (8)

Debut: 1964-65	Eng	Ind	NZ	Pak	SAf	SL	WI	Zim	Total
Tests at home	3	–	–	–	–	–	–	–	3
Tests abroad	–	–	–	–	–	–	5	–	5

PONSFORD, William Harold (29)

Debut: 1924-25	Eng	Ind	NZ	Pak	SAf	SL	WI	Zim	Total
Tests at home	10	–	–	–	4	–	5	–	19
Tests abroad	10	–	–	–	–	–	–	–	10

PONTING, Ricky Thomas (56)

Debut: 1995-96	Eng	Ind	NZ	Pak	SAf	SL	WI	Zim	Total
Tests at home	3	3	6	3	6	3	7	–	31
Tests abroad	8	7	–	1	3	3	2	1	25

POPE, Roland James (1)

Debut: 1884-85	Eng	Ind	NZ	Pak	SAf	SL	WI	Zim	Total
Tests at home	1	–	–	–	–	–	–	–	1

RACKEMANN, Carl Grey (12)

Debut: 1982-83	Eng	Ind	NZ	Pak	SAf	SL	WI	Zim	Total
Tests at home	2	–	1	5	–	1	1	–	10
Tests abroad	–	–	1	–	–	–	1	–	2

RANSFORD, Vernon Seymour (20)

Debut: 1907-08	Eng	Ind	NZ	Pak	SAf	SL	WI	Zim	Total
Tests at home	10	–	–	–	5	–	–	–	15
Tests abroad	5	–	–	–	–	–	–	–	5

REDPATH, Ian Ritchie (67)

Debut: 1963-64	Eng	Ind	NZ	Pak	SAf	SL	WI	Zim	Total
Tests at home	14	3	–	3	1	–	11	–	32
Tests abroad	10	7	3	1	9	–	5	–	35

REEDMAN, John Cole (1)

Debut: 1894-95	Eng	Ind	NZ	Pak	SAf	SL	WI	Zim	Total
Tests at home	1	–	–	–	–	–	–	–	1

REID, Bruce Anthony (27)

Debut: 1985-86	Eng	Ind	NZ	Pak	SAf	SL	WI	Zim	Total
Tests at home	9	5	2	–	–	–	1	–	17
Tests abroad	–	2	3	3	–	–	2	–	10

REIFFEL, Paul Ronald (35)

Debut: 1991-92	*Eng*	*Ind*	*NZ*	*Pak*	*SAf*	*SL*	*WI*	*Zim*	*Total*
Tests at home	–	1	5	3	4	2	3	–	18
Tests abroad	7	2	3	–	1	–	4	–	17

RENNEBERG, David Alexander (8)

Debut: 1966-67	*Eng*	*Ind*	*NZ*	*Pak*	*SAf*	*SL*	*WI*	*Zim*	*Total*
Tests at home	–	3	–	–	–	–	–	–	3
Tests abroad	–	–	–	–	5	–	–	–	5

RICHARDSON, Arthur John (9)

Debut: 1924-25	*Eng*	*Ind*	*NZ*	*Pak*	*SAf*	*SL*	*WI*	*Zim*	*Total*
Tests at home	4	–	–	–	–	–	–	–	4
Tests abroad	5	–	–	–	–	–	–	–	5

RICHARDSON, Victor York (19)

Debut: 1924-25	*Eng*	*Ind*	*NZ*	*Pak*	*SAf*	*SL*	*WI*	*Zim*	*Total*
Tests at home	10	–	–	–	–	–	–	–	10
Tests abroad	4	–	–	–	5	–	–	–	9

RIGG, Keith Edward (8)

Debut: 1930-31	*Eng*	*Ind*	*NZ*	*Pak*	*SAf*	*SL*	*WI*	*Zim*	*Total*
Tests at home	3	–	–	–	4	–	1	–	8

RING, Douglas Thomas (13)

Debut: 1947-48	*Eng*	*Ind*	*NZ*	*Pak*	*SAf*	*SL*	*WI*	*Zim*	*Total*
Tests at home	–	1	–	–	5	–	5	–	11
Tests abroad	2	–	–	–	–	–	–	–	2

RITCHIE, Gregory Michael (30)

Debut: 1982-83	*Eng*	*Ind*	*NZ*	*Pak*	*SAf*	*SL*	*WI*	*Zim*	*Total*
Tests at home	4	2	3	–	–	–	1	–	10
Tests abroad	6	3	3	3	–	–	5	–	20

RIXON, Stephen John (13)

Debut: 1977-78	*Eng*	*Ind*	*NZ*	*Pak*	*SAf*	*SL*	*WI*	*Zim*	*Total*
Tests at home	–	5	–	–	–	–	3	–	8
Tests abroad	–	–	–	–	–	–	5	–	5

ROBERTSON, Gavin Ron (4)

Debut: 1997-98	*Eng*	*Ind*	*NZ*	*Pak*	*SAf*	*SL*	*WI*	*Zim*	*Total*
Tests abroad	–	3	–	1	–	–	–	–	4

ROBERTSON, William Roderick (1)

Debut: 1884-85	*Eng*	*Ind*	*NZ*	*Pak*	*SAf*	*SL*	*WI*	*Zim*	*Total*
Tests at home	1	–	–	–	–	–	–	–	1

ROBINSON, Richard Daryl (3)

Debut: 1977	*Eng*	*Ind*	*NZ*	*Pak*	*SAf*	*SL*	*WI*	*Zim*	*Total*
Tests abroad	3	–	–	–	–	–	–	–	3

ROBINSON, Rayford Harold (1)

Debut: 1936-37	*Eng*	*Ind*	*NZ*	*Pak*	*SAf*	*SL*	*WI*	*Zim*	*Total*
Tests at home	1	–	–	–	–	–	–	–	1

RORKE, Gordon Frederick (4)

Debut: 1958-59	*Eng*	*Ind*	*NZ*	*Pak*	*SAf*	*SL*	*WI*	*Zim*	*Total*
Tests at home	2	–	–	–	–	–	–	–	2
Tests abroad	–	2	–	–	–	–	–	–	2

RUTHERFORD, John Walter (1)

Debut: 1956-57	*Eng*	*Ind*	*NZ*	*Pak*	*SAf*	*SL*	*WI*	*Zim*	*Total*
Tests abroad	–	1	–	–	–	–	–	–	1

RYDER, John (20)

Debut: 1920-21	*Eng*	*Ind*	*NZ*	*Pak*	*SAf*	*SL*	*WI*	*Zim*	*Total*
Tests at home	13	–	–	–	–	–	–	–	13
Tests abroad	4	–	–	–	3	–	–	–	7

SAGGERS, Ronald Arthur (6)

Debut: 1948	Eng	Ind	NZ	Pak	SAf	SL	WI	Zim	Total
Tests abroad	1	–	–	–	5	–	–	–	6

SAUNDERS, John Victor (14)

Debut: 1901-02	Eng	Ind	NZ	Pak	SAf	SL	WI	Zim	Total
Tests at home	8	–	–	–	–	–	–	–	8
Tests abroad	4	–	–	–	2	–	–	–	6

SCOTT, Henry James Herbert (8)

Debut: 1884	Eng	Ind	NZ	Pak	SAf	SL	WI	Zim	Total
Tests at home	2	–	–	–	–	–	–	–	2
Tests abroad	6	–	–	–	–	–	–	–	6

SELLERS, Reginald Hugh Durning (1)

Debut: 1964-65	Eng	Ind	NZ	Pak	SAf	SL	WI	Zim	Total
Tests abroad	–	1	–	–	–	–	–	–	1

SERJEANT, Craig Stanton (12)

Debut: 1977	Eng	Ind	NZ	Pak	SAf	SL	WI	Zim	Total
Tests at home	–	4	–	–	–	–	–	–	4
Tests abroad	3	–	–	–	–	–	5	–	8

SHEAHAN, Andrew Paul (31)

Debut: 1967-68	Eng	Ind	NZ	Pak	SAf	SL	WI	Zim	Total
Tests at home	2	4	2	2	–	–	5	–	15
Tests abroad	7	5	–	–	4	–	–	–	16

SHEPHERD, Barry Kenneth (9)

Debut: 1962-63	Eng	Ind	NZ	Pak	SAf	SL	WI	Zim	Total
Tests at home	2	–	–	1	4	–	–	–	7
Tests abroad	–	–	–	–	–	–	2	–	2

SIEVERS, Morris William (3)

Debut: 1936-37	Eng	Ind	NZ	Pak	SAf	SL	WI	Zim	Total
Tests at home	3	–	–	–	–	–	–	–	3

SIMPSON, Robert Baddeley (62)

Debut: 1957-58	Eng	Ind	NZ	Pak	SAf	SL	WI	Zim	Total
Tests at home	9	8	–	1	5	–	5	–	28
Tests abroad	10	3	–	1	10	–	10	–	34

SINCOCK, David John (3)

Debut: 1964-65	Eng	Ind	NZ	Pak	SAf	SL	WI	Zim	Total
Tests at home	1	–	–	1	–	–	–	–	2
Tests abroad	–	–	–	–	–	–	1	–	1

SLATER, Keith Nichol (1)

Debut: 1958-59	Eng	Ind	NZ	Pak	SAf	SL	WI	Zim	Total
Tests at home	1	–	–	–	–	–	–	–	1

SLATER, Michael Jonathon (74)

Debut: 1993	Eng	Ind	NZ	Pak	SAf	SL	WI	Zim	Total
Tests at home	10	3	3	6	3	3	5	–	33
Tests abroad	10	7	3	6	3	3	8	1	41

SLEEP, Peter Raymond (14)

Debut: 1978-79	Eng	Ind	NZ	Pak	SAf	SL	WI	Zim	Total
Tests at home	4	–	3	2	–	1	–	–	10
Tests abroad	–	2	–	2	–	–	–	–	4

SLIGHT, James (1)

Debut: 1880	Eng	Ind	NZ	Pak	SAf	SL	WI	Zim	Total
Tests abroad	1	–	–	–	–	–	–	–	1

SMITH, David Betram Miller (2)

Debut: 1912	Eng	Ind	NZ	Pak	SAf	SL	WI	Zim	Total
Tests abroad	2	–	–	–	–	–	–	–	2

SMITH, Stephen Barry (3)

Debut: 1983-84	*Eng*	*Ind*	*NZ*	*Pak*	*SAf*	*SL*	*WI*	*Zim*	*Total*
Tests abroad	–	–	–	–	–	–	3	–	3

SPOFFORTH, Frederick Robert (18)

Debut: 1876-77	*Eng*	*Ind*	*NZ*	*Pak*	*SAf*	*SL*	*WI*	*Zim*	*Total*
Tests at home	11	–	–	–	–	–	–	–	11
Tests abroad	7	–	–	–	–	–	–	–	7

STACKPOLE, Keith Raymond (44)

Debut: 1965-66	*Eng*	*Ind*	*NZ*	*Pak*	*SAf*	*SL*	*WI*	*Zim*	*Total*
Tests at home	9	–	3	1	–	–	5	–	18
Tests abroad	5	5	3	–	9	–	4	–	26

STEVENS, Gavin Byron (4)

Debut: 1959-60	*Eng*	*Ind*	*NZ*	*Pak*	*SAf*	*SL*	*WI*	*Zim*	*Total*
Tests abroad	–	2	–	2	–	–	–	–	4

TABER, Hedley Brian (16)

Debut: 1966-67	*Eng*	*Ind*	*NZ*	*Pak*	*SAf*	*SL*	*WI*	*Zim*	*Total*
Tests at home	–	–	–	–	–	–	1	–	1
Tests abroad	1	5	–	–	9	–	–	–	15

TALLON, Donald (21)

Debut: 1945-46	*Eng*	*Ind*	*NZ*	*Pak*	*SAf*	*SL*	*WI*	*Zim*	*Total*
Tests at home	10	5	–	–	–	–	–	–	15
Tests abroad	5	–	1	–	–	–	–	–	6

TAYLOR, John Morris (20)

Debut: 1920-21	*Eng*	*Ind*	*NZ*	*Pak*	*SAf*	*SL*	*WI*	*Zim*	*Total*
Tests at home	10	–	–	–	–	–	–	–	10
Tests abroad	8	–	–	–	2	–	–	–	10

TAYLOR, Mark Anthony (104)

Debut: 1988-89	*Eng*	*Ind*	*NZ*	*Pak*	*SAf*	*SL*	*WI*	*Zim*	*Total*
Tests at home	15	5	7	6	6	5	11	–	55
Tests abroad	18	4	4	6	5	3	9	–	49

TAYLOR, Peter Laurence (13)

Debut: 1986-87	*Eng*	*Ind*	*NZ*	*Pak*	*SAf*	*SL*	*WI*	*Zim*	*Total*
Tests at home	2	2	–	2	–	1	2	–	9
Tests abroad	–	–	1	2	–	–	1	–	4

THOMAS, Grahame (8)

Debut: 1964-65	*Eng*	*Ind*	*NZ*	*Pak*	*SAf*	*SL*	*WI*	*Zim*	*Total*
Tests at home	3	–	–	–	–	–	–	–	3
Tests abroad	–	–	–	–	–	–	5	–	5

THOMS, George Ronald (1)

Debut: 1951-52	*Eng*	*Ind*	*NZ*	*Pak*	*SAf*	*SL*	*WI*	*Zim*	*Total*
Tests at home	–	–	–	–	–	–	1	–	1

THOMSON, Alan Lloyd (4)

Debut: 1970-71	*Eng*	*Ind*	*NZ*	*Pak*	*SAf*	*SL*	*WI*	*Zim*	*Total*
Tests at home	4	–	–	–	–	–	–	–	4

THOMSON, Jeffrey Robert (51)

Debut: 1972-73	*Eng*	*Ind*	*NZ*	*Pak*	*SAf*	*SL*	*WI*	*Zim*	*Total*
Tests at home	10	5	–	5	–	–	9	–	29
Tests abroad	11	–	3	3	–	–	5	–	22

THOMSON, Nathaniel Frampton Davis (2)

Debut: 1876-77	*Eng*	*Ind*	*NZ*	*Pak*	*SAf*	*SL*	*WI*	*Zim*	*Total*
Tests at home	2	–	–	–	–	–	–	–	2

THURLOW, Hugh Motley (1)

Debut: 1931-32	*Eng*	*Ind*	*NZ*	*Pak*	*SAf*	*SL*	*WI*	*Zim*	*Total*
Tests at home	–	–	–	–	1	–	–	–	1

TOOHEY, Peter Michael (15)

Debut: 1977-78	Eng	Ind	NZ	Pak	SAf	SL	WI	Zim	Total
Tests at home	6	5	–	–	–	–	1	–	12
Tests abroad	–	–	–	–	–	–	3	–	3

TOSHACK, Ernest Raymond Herbert (12)

Debut: 1945-46	Eng	Ind	NZ	Pak	SAf	SL	WI	Zim	Total
Tests at home	5	2	–	–	–	–	–	–	7
Tests abroad	4	–	1	–	–	–	–	–	5

TRAVERS, Joseph Patrick Francis (1)

Debut: 1901-02	Eng	Ind	NZ	Pak	SAf	SL	WI	Zim	Total
Tests at home	1	–	–	–	–	–	–	–	1

TRIBE, George Edward (3)

Debut: 1946-47	Eng	Ind	NZ	Pak	SAf	SL	WI	Zim	Total
Tests at home	3	–	–	–	–	–	–	–	3

TROTT, Albert Edwin (3)

Debut: 1894-95	Eng	Ind	NZ	Pak	SAf	SL	WI	Zim	Total
Tests at home	3	–	–	–	–	–	–	–	3

TROTT, George Henry Stephens (24)

Debut: 1888	Eng	Ind	NZ	Pak	SAf	SL	WI	Zim	Total
Tests at home	13	–	–	–	–	–	–	–	13
Tests abroad	11	–	–	–	–	–	–	–	11

TRUMBLE, Hugh (32)

Debut: 1890	Eng	Ind	NZ	Pak	SAf	SL	WI	Zim	Total
Tests at home	15	–	–	–	–	–	–	–	15
Tests abroad	16	–	–	–	1	–	–	–	17

TRUMBLE, John William (7)

Debut: 1884-85	Eng	Ind	NZ	Pak	SAf	SL	WI	Zim	Total
Tests at home	4	–	–	–	–	–	–	–	4
Tests abroad	3	–	–	–	–	–	–	–	3

TRUMPER, Victor Thomas (48)

Debut: 1899	Eng	Ind	NZ	Pak	SAf	SL	WI	Zim	Total
Tests at home	20	–	–	–	5	–	–	–	25
Tests abroad	20	–	–	–	3	–	–	–	23

TURNER, Alan (14)

Debut: 1975	Eng	Ind	NZ	Pak	SAf	SL	WI	Zim	Total
Tests at home	–	–	–	3	–	–	6	–	9
Tests abroad	3	–	2	–	–	–	–	–	5

TURNER, Charles Thomas Byass (17)

Debut: 1886-87	Eng	Ind	NZ	Pak	SAf	SL	WI	Zim	Total
Tests at home	9	–	–	–	–	–	–	–	9
Tests abroad	8	–	–	–	–	–	–	–	8

VEIVERS, Thomas Robert (21)

Debut: 1963-64	Eng	Ind	NZ	Pak	SAf	SL	WI	Zim	Total
Tests at home	4	–	–	1	3	–	–	–	8
Tests abroad	5	3	–	1	4	–	–	–	13

VELETTA, Michael Robert John (8)

Debut: 1987-88	Eng	Ind	NZ	Pak	SAf	SL	WI	Zim	Total
Tests at home	1	–	3	1	–	1	2	–	8

WAITE, Mervyn George (2)

Debut: 1938	Eng	Ind	NZ	Pak	SAf	SL	WI	Zim	Total
Tests abroad	2	–	–	–	–	–	–	–	2

WALKER, Maxwell Henry Norman (34)

Debut: 1972-73	Eng	Ind	NZ	Pak	SAf	SL	WI	Zim	Total
Tests at home	7	–	1	4	–	–	3	–	15
Tests abroad	9	–	5	–	–	–	5	–	19

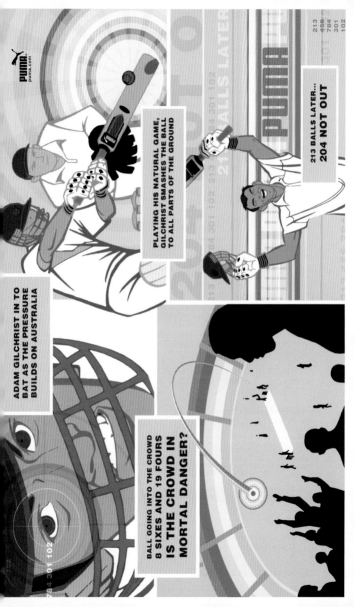

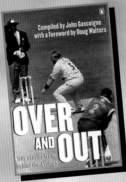

WALL, Thomas Welbourn (18)

Debut: 1928-29	Eng	Ind	NZ	Pak	SAf	SL	WI	Zim	Total
Tests at home	5	–	–	–	3	–	1	–	9
Tests abroad	9	–	–	–	–	–	–	–	9

WALTERS, Francis Henry (1)

Debut: 1884-85	Eng	Ind	NZ	Pak	SAf	SL	WI	Zim	Total
Tests at home	1	–	–	–	–	–	–	–	1

WALTERS, Kevin Douglas (75)

Debut: 1965-66	Eng	Ind	NZ	Pak	SAf	SL	WI	Zim	Total
Tests at home	19	5	6	4	–	–	4	–	38
Tests abroad	18	5	5	–	4	–	5	–	37

WARD, Francis Anthony (4)

Debut: 1936-37	Eng	Ind	NZ	Pak	SAf	SL	WI	Zim	Total
Tests at home	3	–	–	–	–	–	–	–	3
Tests abroad	1	–	–	–	–	–	–	–	1

WARNE, Shane Keith (101)

Debut: 1991-92	Eng	Ind	NZ	Pak	SAf	SL	WI	Zim	Total
Tests at home	6	5	9	6	9	3	9	–	47
Tests abroad	17	6	6	3	9	5	7	1	54

WATKINS, John Russell (1)

Debut: 1972-73	Eng	Ind	NZ	Pak	SAf	SL	WI	Zim	Total
Tests at home	–	–	–	1	–	–	–	–	1

WATSON, Graeme Donald (5)

Debut: 1966-67	Eng	Ind	NZ	Pak	SAf	SL	WI	Zim	Total
Tests abroad	2	–	–	–	3	–	–	–	5

WATSON, William James (4)

Debut: 1954-55	Eng	Ind	NZ	Pak	SAf	SL	WI	Zim	Total
Tests at home	1	–	–	–	–	–	–	–	1
Tests abroad	–	–	–	–	–	–	3	–	3

WAUGH, Mark Edward (125)

Debut: 1990-91	Eng	Ind	NZ	Pak	SAf	SL	WI	Zim	Total
Tests at home	12	7	9	6	9	3	15	–	61
Tests abroad	17	7	5	6	9	6	13	1	64

WAUGH, Stephen Rodger (148)

Debut: 1985-86	Eng	Ind	NZ	Pak	SAf	SL	WI	Zim	Total
Tests at home	19	5	13	9	7	5	18	–	76
Tests abroad	22	9	10	8	9	3	10	1	72

WELLHAM, Dirk Macdonald (6)

Debut: 1981	Eng	Ind	NZ	Pak	SAf	SL	WI	Zim	Total
Tests at home	1	–	–	2	–	–	1	–	4
Tests abroad	2	–	–	–	–	–	–	–	2

WESSELS, Kepler Christoffel (24)

Debut: 1982-83	Eng	Ind	NZ	Pak	SAf	SL	WI	Zim	Total
Tests at home	4	–	1	5	–	–	5	–	15
Tests abroad	6	–	–	–	–	1	2	–	9

WHATMORE, Davenell Frederick (7)

Debut: 1978-79	Eng	Ind	NZ	Pak	SAf	SL	WI	Zim	Total
Tests at home	–	–	–	2	–	–	–	–	2
Tests abroad	–	5	–	–	–	–	–	–	5

WHITNEY, Michael Roy (12)

Debut: 1981	Eng	Ind	NZ	Pak	SAf	SL	WI	Zim	Total
Tests at home	–	3	1	–	–	–	2	–	6
Tests abroad	2	–	–	–	–	2	2	–	6

WHITTY, William James (14)

Debut: 1909	Eng	Ind	NZ	Pak	SAf	SL	WI	Zim	Total
Tests at home	2	–	–	–	5	–	–	–	7
Tests abroad	4	–	–	–	3	–	–	–	7

WIENER, Julien Mark (6)

Debut: 1979-80	Eng	Ind	NZ	Pak	SAf	SL	WI	Zim	Total
Tests at home	2	–	–	–	–	–	2	–	4
Tests abroad	–	–	–	2	–	–	–	–	2

WILSON, John William (1)

Debut: 1956-57	Eng	Ind	NZ	Pak	SAf	SL	WI	Zim	Total
Tests abroad	–	1	–	–	–	–	–	–	1

WILSON, Paul (1)

Debut: 1997-98	Eng	Ind	NZ	Pak	SAf	SL	WI	Zim	Total
Tests abroad	–	1	–	–	–	–	–	–	1

WOOD, Graeme Malcolm (59)

Debut: 1977-78	Eng	Ind	NZ	Pak	SAf	SL	WI	Zim	Total
Tests at home	7	4	3	4	–	–	11	–	29
Tests abroad	12	2	3	6	–	1	6	–	30

WOODCOCK, Ashley James (1)

Debut: 1973-74	Eng	Ind	NZ	Pak	SAf	SL	WI	Zim	Total
Tests at home	–	–	1	–	–	–	–	–	1

WOODFULL, William Maldon (35)

Debut: 1926	Eng	Ind	NZ	Pak	SAf	SL	WI	Zim	Total
Tests at home	10	–	–	–	5	–	5	–	20
Tests abroad	15	–	–	–	–	–	–	–	15

WOODS, Samuel Moses James (3)

Debut: 1888	Eng	Ind	NZ	Pak	SAf	SL	WI	Zim	Total
Tests abroad	3	–	–	–	–	–	–	–	3

WOOLLEY, Roger Douglas (2)

Debut: 1982-83	Eng	Ind	NZ	Pak	SAf	SL	WI	Zim	Total
Tests abroad	–	–	–	–	–	1	1	–	2

WORRALL, John (11)

Debut: 1884-85	Eng	Ind	NZ	Pak	SAf	SL	WI	Zim	Total
Tests at home	4	–	–	–	–	–	–	–	4
Tests abroad	7	–	–	–	–	–	–	–	7

WRIGHT, Kevin John (10)

Debut: 1978-79	Eng	Ind	NZ	Pak	SAf	SL	WI	Zim	Total
Tests at home	2	–	–	2	–	–	–	–	4
Tests abroad	–	6	–	–	–	–	–	–	6

YALLOP, Graham Neil (39)

Debut: 1975-76	Eng	Ind	NZ	Pak	SAf	SL	WI	Zim	Total
Tests at home	6	1	–	7	–	–	4	–	18
Tests abroad	7	6	–	3	–	1	4	–	21

YARDLEY, Bruce (33)

Debut: 1977-78	Eng	Ind	NZ	Pak	SAf	SL	WI	Zim	Total
Tests at home	9	3	–	4	–	–	3	–	19
Tests abroad	–	3	3	2	–	1	5	–	14

YOUNG, Shaun (1)

Debut: 1997	Eng	Ind	NZ	Pak	SAf	SL	WI	Zim	Total
Tests abroad	1	–	–	–	–	–	–	–	1

ZOEHRER, Timothy Joseph (10)

Debut: 1985-86	Eng	Ind	NZ	Pak	SAf	SL	WI	Zim	Total
Tests at home	4	–	–	–	–	–	–	–	4
Tests abroad	–	3	3	–	–	–	–	–	6

BIRTHS AND DEATHS OF CRICKETERS

The following list details information on the 3,151 players to have represented an Australian first-class cricket team.

The compiler of this section welcomes any information from readers regarding the details contained therein.

Key to abbreviations

Australian states and territories: ACT – Australian Capital Territory, NSW – New South Wales, NT – Northern Territory, Qld – Queensland, SAust – South Australia, Tas – Tasmania, Vic – Victoria, WAust – Western Australia.

*Denotes Test player.

**Denotes Test player for two countries.

There is a full list of Australian Test players from page 123.

a'Beckett, Edward Clive (Vic) b Jan. 18, 1940 East Melbourne (Vic)

a'Beckett, Edward Fitzhayley (Vic) b April 16, 1836 Holborn, London, (England) d March 25, 1922 Upper Beaconsfield (Vic)

* a'Beckett, Edward Lambert (Vic) b Aug. 11, 1907 East St Kilda (Vic) d June 2, 1989 Terang (Vic)

a'Beckett, Malwyn (Vic) b Sept. 26, 1834 London, Middlesex (England) d June 25, 1906 Sale (Vic)

Abell, William (Qld) b c. 1874 d c. 1955 (Qld)

Achurch, Claude Septimus (NSW) b Aug. 16, 1896 Dubbo (NSW) d Aug. 15, 1979 Nambour (Qld)

Adams, Edward William (NSW) b July 10, 1896 Bathurst (NSW) d May 25, 1977 Bexley (NSW)

Adams, Francis (NSW) b Feb. 12, 1835 Doohat, County Fermanagh (Ireland) d Feb. 10, 1911 North Sydney (NSW)

Adams, James William (Qld) b Feb. 22, 1904 Toowong (Qld) d Jan. 8, 1988 Willoughby (NSW)

Adamson, Charles Young (Qld) b April 18, 1875 Neville's Cross, Durham (England) d Sept. 17, 1918 Salonica (Greece)

Adcock, Nathan Tennyson (SAust) b April 22, 1978 Campbelltown (SAust)

Addison, Alexander Gollan (Tas) b Sept. 29, 1877 Adelaide (SAust) d Oct. 12, 1935 Double Bay (NSW)

Ainslie, James (Vic) b June 9, 1880 Elsternwick (Vic) d Dec. 31, 1953 St Kilda (Vic)

Albury, William Douglas (Qld) b Feb. 9, 1947 Herston (Qld)

* Alderman, Terence Michael (WAust) b June 12, 1956 Subiaco (WAust)

Aldridge, Keith John (Tas) b March 13, 1935 Evesham, Worcestershire (England)

Alexander, Francis James (WAust) b April 15, 1911 Perth (WAust)

* Alexander, George (Vic) b April 22, 1851 Oxfordshire (England) d Nov. 6, 1930 East Melbourne (Vic)

* Alexander, Harry Houston (Vic) b June 9, 1905 Ascot Vale (Vic) d April 15, 1993 East Melbourne (Vic)

Alexander, Leonard James (Tas) b Sept. 1, 1922 Hobart (Tas)

Alexander, William Colin (SAust) b Sept. 14, 1907 Gawler (SAust) d Feb. 8, 1993 Melbourne (Vic)

* Allan, Francis Erskine (Vic) b Dec. 2, 1849 Allansford (Vic) d Feb. 9, 1917 East Melbourne (Vic)

Allan, George Harold (Tas) b Feb. 18, 1887 Albury (NSW) d Nov. 2, 1932 Adelaide (SAust)

Allan, Henry Alexander (NSW) b Jan. 6, 1846 Westminster, London, Middlesex (England) d Apr. 26, 1926 East Melbourne (Vic)

* Allan, Peter John (Qld) b Dec. 31, 1935 Coorparoo (Qld)

Allanby, Nicholas John (Tas) b Aug. 24, 1957 Hobart (Tas)

Allanby, Richard Andrew (Tas) b July 26, 1971 Hobart (Tas)

Allanson, Noel Laurence (Vic) b Dec. 25, 1925 North Carlton (Vic)

Allardice, Geoffrey John (Vic) b May 7, 1967 Melbourne (Vic)

Allee, Charles George (Vic) b Feb. 10, 1848 Melbourne (Vic) d June 7, 1896 East Melbourne (Vic)

Allen, Donald John (Qld) b Feb. 26, 1947 Lismore (NSW)

Allen, Donald Radford (Vic) b Dec. 13, 1926 East St Kilda (Vic)

Allen, Harold Eric (Tas) b Oct. 13, 1886 Invercargill (New Zealand) d July 9, 1939 West Hobart (Tas)

Allen, Harold Hedley (Tas) b Nov. 15, 1940 Latrobe (Tas)

Allen, Jeremy Michael (WAust) b June 11, 1971 Subiaco (WAust)

Allen, Leslie Graham (Tas) b Sept. 13, 1954 Wynyard (Tas)

* Allen, Reginald Charles (NSW) b July 2, 1858 Glebe (NSW) d May 2, 1952 Sydney (NSW)

Allen, Ross Thomas (Qld) b Aug. 12, 1939 Toowoomba (Qld)

Allen, Thomas (Qld) b Sept. 5, 1912 Toowoomba (Qld) d March 18, 1954 Cambooya (Qld)

Allen, Thorpe (Qld) b March 7, 1870 Oxley (Qld) d Jan. 25, 1950 East Brisbane (Qld)

Allen, William Miller (Vic) b July 7, 1889 Ballarat (Vic) d Nov. 13, 1948 Ringwood (Vic)

Alley, Phillip John Sydney (SAust & NSW) b July 26, 1970 Orange (NSW)

Alley, William Edward (NSW) b Feb. 3, 1919 Hornsby (NSW)

Alleyne, John Placid (NSW) b Aug. 1, 1908 Glebe (NSW) d June 24, 1980 Glebe (NSW)

Allison, Henry (Tas) b July 14, 1828 Campbell Town (Tas) d May 12, 1881 Coupeville Island, Washington (USA)

Allsopp, Arthur Henry (NSW & Vic) b March 1, 1908 Lithgow (NSW) d Feb. 6, 1993 Chadstone (Vic)

Alsop, Charles James (Vic) b Nov. 24, 1868 Moonee Ponds (Vic) d Sept. 17, 1948 Melbourne (Vic)

Amalfi, Anthony John (Vic) b Jan. 19, 1967 East Melbourne (Vic)

Ambler, Albert Mark (SAust) b Sept. 27, 1892 Murray Bridge (SAust) d Nov. 27, 1970 Prospect (SAust)

Amos, Gordon Stanley (NSW & Qld) b April 4, 1905 Newtown (NSW) d April 7, 1995 Labrador (Qld)

Amos, William (SAust) b April 20, 1860 Glen Osmond (SAust) d May 14, 1935 North Adelaide (SAust)

Anderson, Allan David (NSW) b April 22, 1949 Greenwich (NSW)

Anderson, Dale Thomas (Tas) b June 10, 1931 Latrobe (Tas)

Anderson, David John (Vic) b Jan. 26, 1940 Warrnambool (Vic)

Anderson, James William Falconer (Qld) b Feb. 25, 1889 birth place and death details unknown

Anderson, John Gregory (Vic) b Feb. 15, 1955 East Melbourne (Vic)

Anderson, John Theodore (WAust) b Aug. 10, 1878 Warrnambool (Vic) d Aug. 29, 1926 South Yarra (Vic)

Anderson, Matthew Allen (Qld) b Oct. 30, 1976 Darwin (NT)

Anderson, Peter Gordon (NSW) b Oct. 4, 1933 Camberwell (Vic)

Anderson, Peter McKenzie (Vic) b Sept. 17, 1968 Geelong (Vic)

Anderson, Peter William (Qld & SAust) b May 22, 1961 South Brisbane (Qld)

Andrew-Street, Alfred Gordon (Vic) b April 8, 1914 Bondi (NSW) d Dec. 13, 1984 Concord (NSW)

* Andrews, Thomas James Edwin (NSW) b Aug. 26, 1890 Newtown (NSW) d Jan. 28, 1970 Croydon (NSW)

Andrews, Wayne Stewart (WAust) b Nov. 19, 1958 Melbourne (Vic)

Andrews, William Charles (NSW & Qld) b July 14, 1908 West Maitland (NSW) d June 9, 1962 Bombay (India)

* Angel, Jo (WAust) b April 22, 1968 Mt Lawley (WAust)

Antill, Thomas Wills (Vic) b Nov. 20, 1830 Jarvisfield (NSW) d May 11, 1865 Nelson (New Zealand)

Appleton, Leslie Joseph Francis (Tas) b Sept. 28, 1947 Hobart (Tas)

Archer, Daniel John Lancelot (Tas) b June 17, 1939 Launceston (Tas)

* Archer, Kenneth Alan (Qld) b Jan. 17, 1928 Yeerongpilly (Qld)

* Archer, Ronald Graham (Qld) b Oct. 25, 1933 Highgate Hill (Qld)

Armstrong, Edward Killeen (Qld) b Feb. 15, 1881 Milton (Qld) d April 29, 1963 Brisbane (Qld)

Armstrong, George Gort (Qld) b Dec. 29, 1882 Milton (Qld) d Jan. 12, 1956 Brisbane (Qld)

Armstrong, Glenarvon Huntley (SAust) b Nov. 17, 1969 Hobart (Tas)

Armstrong, Thomas Goldsmith (Vic) b Oct. 31, 1889 Caulfield (Vic) d April 15, 1963 Bairnsdale (Vic)

* Armstrong, Warwick Windridge (Vic) b May 22, 1879 Kyneton (Vic) d July 13, 1947 Darling Point (NSW)

Armstrong, William Anthony (Qld) b May 2, 1886 Milton (Qld) d May 29, 1955 Brisbane (Qld)

Arnberger, Jason Lee (NSW & Vic) b Nov. 18, 1972 Penrith (NSW)

Arnold, Colin Robert (Tas) b Aug. 19, 1957 Devonport (Tas)

Arnold, Evan Matthew Campbell (SAust) b Aug. 20, 1974 North Adelaide (SAust)

Arnold, Weller (Tas) b Sept. 23, 1882 North Hobart (Tas) d Oct. 28, 1957 Hobart (Tas)

Arnott, Percival Sinclair (NSW) b July 9, 1889 Newcastle (NSW) d Dec. 23, 1950 Camperdown (NSW)

Arthur, Charles (Tas) b Feb. 5, 1808 Plymouth, Devon (England) d July 29, 1884 Longford (Tas)

Arthur, George Henry (Tas) b March 10, 1849 Longford (Tas) d Nov. 13, 1932 Longford (Tas)

Arthur, Gerald Charles (WAust) b July 25, 1913 Yarloop (WAust)

Arthur, John Lake Allen (Tas) b April 7, 1847 Longford (Tas) d April 26, 1877 Longford (Tas)

Asher, Oswald Philip (NSW) b May 21, 1891 Paddington (NSW) d July 16, 1970 Waverton (NSW)

Ashley, Nathan William (Cricket Academy) b Oct. 3, 1973 St Leonards (NSW)

Astley, Graeme Patrick (Tas) b March 31, 1957 Sydney (NSW)

Atkins, Arthur Alfred (Qld & NSW) b April 22, 1874 (NSW) death details unknown

Atkinson, James Archibald (Vic & Tas) b April 4, 1896 North Fitzroy (Vic) d June 11, 1956 Beaconsfield (Tas)

Atkinson, Mark Neville (Tas) b Feb. 11, 1969 Sydney (NSW)

Atkinson, Mark Peter (WAust) b Nov. 27, 1970 Bentley (WAust)

Attenborough, Geoffrey Robert (SAust) b Jan. 17, 1951 Mile End (SAust)

Austen, Ernest Thomas (Vic) b Sept. 23, 1900 Hawthorn (Vic) d June 21, 1983 Melbourne (Vic)

Austen, Victor Cecil (SAust) b Nov. 30, 1918 Kew (Vic)

Austin, Harold MacPherson (Vic) b March 8, 1903 Skipton (Vic) d July 31, 1981 Timboon (Vic)

Austin, Sydney Walter (NSW & Qld) b Nov. 16, 1866 Sydney (NSW) d Sept. 9, 1932 Randwick (NSW)

Auty, Clinton (WAust) b Oct. 29, 1969 Auckland (New Zealand)

Aylett, Allen James (Vic) b April 24, 1934 Melbourne (Vic)

Ayres, Ryall Sydney (Qld) b Sept. 1, 1931 Clayfield (Qld) d Nov. 24, 1991 Sydney (NSW)

Ayres, Sydney William (Qld) b Aug. 7, 1889 Enmore (NSW) d Aug. 7, 1974 Castle Hill (NSW)

Ayres, Warren Geoffrey (Vic) b Oct. 25, 1965 Moorabbin (Vic)

Back, William (WAust) b c. 1856 Rottnest Island (WAust) d Feb. 15, 1911 Perth (WAust)

Backman, Charles James (SAust) b April 14, 1884 birth place unknown d April 25, 1915 Gallipoli (Turkey)

* Badcock, Clayvel Lindsay (Tas & SAust) b April 10, 1914 Exton (Tas) d Dec. 13, 1982 Exton (Tas)

Badcock, Kevin Bruce (Tas) b March 24, 1951 Launceston (Tas)

Bagshaw, Kenneth James (SAust) b Oct. 22, 1920 Kadina (SAust) d Oct. 8, 1985 Watson (ACT)

Bailey, Alfred John Thomas Slater (SAust) b March 3, 1932 North Adelaide (SAust)

Bailey, Bertram Theodore (SAust) b Dec. 5, 1874 Adelaide (SAust) d Oct. 3, 1964 Payneham (SAust)

Bailey, Ernest Albert (SAust) b Nov. 15, 1881 Adelaide (SAust) d Aug. 16, 1966 Northfield (SAust)

Bailey, George Herbert (Tas) b Oct. 29, 1853 Colombo (Ceylon) d Oct. 10, 1926 Hobart (Tas)

Bailey, George Keith Brooke (Tas) b Jan. 3, 1882 Hobart (Tas) d June 17, 1964 Hobart (Tas)

Bailey, Peter George (Vic) b Aug. 16, 1939 Glenhuntly (Vic)

Bailey, Rowland Herbert (Vic) b Oct. 5, 1876 Melbourne (Vic) d March 24, 1950 Ivanhoe (Vic)

Bailey, William Henry (Vic) b July 20, 1898 Condoblin (NSW) d Feb. 27, 1983 Geelong (Vic)

Baird, James George (Vic) b Nov. 9, 1920 Parkville (Vic)

Baird, Keith Hugh (WAust) b Dec. 27, 1911 Perth (WAust) d July 18, 1965 Peppermint Grove (WAust)

Baker, Charles Michael (Vic) b June 18, 1880 Ballarat East (Vic) d May 4, 1962 Ballarat (Vic)

Baker, Charles Ronald (NSW) b March 24, 1939 Islington (NSW)

Baker, Dennis James (WAust & Tas) b Dec. 29, 1947 Norseman (WAust)

Baker, Everard Audley (Vic) b Nov. 9, 1920 Parkville (Vic) d March 30, 1987 Melbourne (Vic)

Baker, Frederick (Vic) b c. 1851 (England) d c. 1925

Baker, Glen George (Qld) b Aug. 9, 1915 Townsville (Qld) d Dec. 15, 1943 Buna (Papua New Guinea) on active service

Baker, Leigh James (Vic) b Sept. 20, 1951 Oakleigh (Vic)

Baker, Robert Michael (WAust) b July 24, 1975 Osborne Park (WAust)

Bakker, Jason Richard (Vic) b Nov. 12, 1967 Geelong (Vic)

Balcam, Leonard Frank (Qld & Vic) b Aug. 20, 1957 Footscray (Vic)

Baldock, Darrel John (Tas) b Sept. 29, 1938 Devonport (Tas)

Baldry, Robert John (Vic) b Nov. 30, 1950 Warragul (Vic)

Ball, Thomas Edward (Qld) b Dec. 3, 1921 Atherton (Qld) d Jan. 13, 2002 Cairns (Qld)

Ballans, David Murray (SAust) b June 30, 1868 at sea d June 26, 1957 Goodwood Park (SAust)

Bandy, Lawrence Henry (WAust) b Sept. 3, 1911 Perth (WAust) d July 18, 1984 Scarborough (WAust)

Banks, Albert James (WAust) b Dec. 10, 1883 Maryborough (Vic) d July 5, 1930 Toodyay (WAust)

* Bannerman, Alexander Chalmers (NSW) b March 21, 1854 Paddington (NSW) d Sept. 19, 1924 Paddington (NSW)

* Bannerman, Charles (NSW) b July 23, 1851 Woolwich, Kent (England) d Aug. 20, 1930 Surry Hills (NSW)

Barbour, Eric Pitty (NSW) b Jan. 27, 1891 Ashfield (NSW) d Dec. 7, 1934 Darlinghurst (NSW)

Barbour, Robert Roy (Qld) b March 29, 1899 Ashfield (NSW) d Dec. 29, 1994 Berwick (Vic)

Bardsley, Raymond (NSW) b Jan. 19, 1894 Glebe Point (NSW) d June 25, 1983 death place unknown

* Bardsley, Warren (NSW) b Dec. 6, 1882 Nevertire (NSW) d Jan. 20, 1954 Collaroy (NSW)

Baring, Frederick Albert (Vic) b Dec. 15, 1890 Hotham East (Vic) d Dec. 10, 1961 Doncaster (Vic)

Baring, Hugh Thomas (Vic) b Aug. 17, 1906 East Melbourne (Vic) d July 9, 1968 Fitzroy (Vic)

Barnard, Francis George Allman (Vic) b Dec. 26, 1857 Kew (Vic) d June 1, 1932 Melbourne (Vic)

Barnes, James Charles (NSW) b Oct. 16, 1882 Alexandria (NSW) death details unknown

Barnes, Jeffrey Robert (SAust) b Jan. 9, 1948 Glenelg (SAust)

Barnes, John Francis (Qld) b Sept. 27, 1916 Rockhampton (Qld)

Barnes, John Robert (Vic) b May 20, 1905 Williamstown (Vic) d Oct. 6, 1999 Williamstown (Vic)

Barnes, Richard Thomas Bygrove (Tas) b Sept. 5, 1852 Hobart (Tas) d April 30, 1902 Heidelberg (Vic)

* Barnes, Sydney George (NSW) b June 5, 1916 Annandale (NSW) d Dec. 16, 1973 Collaroy (NSW)

* Barnett, Benjamin Arthur (Vic) b March 23, 1908 Auburn (Vic) d June 29, 1979 Newcastle (NSW)

Barras, Alexander Edward Owen (WAust) b Jan. 26, 1914 Auburn (Vic) d Aug. 15, 1986 Mt Lawley (WAust)

Barrett, Edgar Alfred (Vic) b June 26, 1869 Emerald Hill (Vic) d April 29, 1959 Kew (Vic)

Barrett, Henry (Tas) b Aug. 19, 1837 Launceston (Tas) d Sept. 10, 1910 Westbury (Tas)

* Barrett, John Edward (Vic) b Oct. 15, 1866 Emerald Hill (Vic) d Feb. 6, 1916 Peak Hill (WAust)

Barsby, Trevor John (Qld) b Jan. 16, 1964 Herston (Qld)

Barstow, Charles Banks (Qld) b March 13, 1883 Brisbane (Qld) d July 12, 1935 Eagle Junction (Qld)

Bartlett, Albert James (SAust) b April 23, 1900 Parkside (SAust) d Oct. 6, 1968 Woodville South (SAust)

Bartlett, Robert Andrew (Vic) b Jan. 2, 1972 Melbourne (Vic)

Bateman, William Augustus (WAust) b Sept. 11, 1866 Fremantle (WAust) d July 27, 1935 South Perth (WAust)

Bates, Barry (NSW) b July 1, 1939 Mayfield (NSW)

Bayles, Robert Charles Alfred Vivian (Tas) b July 7, 1892 Ross (Tas) d May 16, 1959 Launceston (Tas)

Bayles, William Headlam (Tas) b Jan. 8, 1896 Ross (Tas) d Dec. 17, 1960 Launceston (Tas)

Bayliss, Trevor Harley (NSW) b Dec. 21, 1962 Goulburn (NSW)

Bayly, Henry Vincent (Tas) b Nov. 19, 1850 Dulcot (Tas) d Jan. 7, 1903 New Town (Tas)

Beacham, George (Vic) b Oct. 27, 1867 (Qld) d Jan. 11, 1925 South Fitzroy (Vic)

Beagley, John William (SAust) b March 23, 1933 Adelaide (SAust)

Beal, Charles William (Australians) b June 24, 1855 Sydney (NSW) d Feb. 5, 1921 Randwick (NSW)

Beal, James Charles (NSW) b May 26, 1830 Sydney (NSW) d Aug. 24, 1904 Milton (Qld)

Beames, Percy James (Vic) b July 27, 1911 Ballarat (Vic)

Bean, Ernest Edward (Vic) b April 17, 1866 Miner's Rest, near Ballarat (Vic) d March 22, 1939 Hampton (Vic)

Beard, Barry Allan (Tas) b Dec. 21, 1941 Bothwell (Tas) d June 9, 2001 Ulverstone (Tas)

* Beard, Graeme Robert (NSW) b Aug. 19, 1950 Auburn (NSW)

Beath, Neville Ray James (NSW) b Nov. 12, 1921 Goolagong (NSW) d Nov. 22, 1987 Richmond (NSW)

Beattie, Simon Guy (Qld) b Dec. 10, 1958 Junee (NSW)

Beatty, Christopher (NSW) b Oct. 21, 1952 Newcastle (NSW)

Beatty, Reginald George (NSW) b Dec. 24, 1913 Wickham (NSW) d May 27, 1957 Waratah (NSW)

Becker, Gordon Charles (WAust) b March 14, 1936 Katanning (WAust)

Bedford, Albert Austen (SAust) b Sept. 12, 1932 Rose Park (SAust) d March 25, 2001 Noarlunga (SAust)

Bedford, Peter Lawrence Anthony (Vic) b April 11, 1947 Melbourne (Vic)

Bednall, Philip Malcolm (SAust) b Jan. 27, 1931 Burra (SAust)

Beeston, Norman Charles (Qld) b Sept. 29, 1900 Brisbane (Qld) d Feb. 4, 1985 South Brisbane (Qld)

Beetson, John Lievesley (NSW) b c. 1830 Lancashire (England) d June 1, 1873 Newcastle (NSW)

Belcher, Samuel Harborne (NSW) b Nov. 1, 1834 (England) d Aug. 22, 1920 Garroorigang (NSW)

Bell, John Clifford (Qld) b Jan. 18, 1949 Ipswich (Qld)

* Benaud, John (NSW) b May 11, 1944 Auburn (NSW)

* Benaud, Richard (NSW) b Oct. 6, 1930 Penrith (NSW)

Benbow, Ernest Aldred (Qld) b March 14, 1888 Mt Walker (Qld) d Dec. 28, 1940 Springsure (Qld)

Bendixen, Hilton Fewtrell (Qld) b Feb. 21, 1910 Nambour (Qld) d April 15, 1962 Nambour (Qld)

Benjamin, Emmanuel (Tas) b Feb. 2, 1955 Jullundur City (India)

Bennett, Albert (NSW) b May 21, 1910 St Helens, Lancashire (England) d c. 1985 full death details unknown

Bennett, Floyd Chester (SAust & WAust) b April 12, 1919 North Perth (WAust) d Nov. 26, 1997 Stirling (SAust)

Bennett, George Henry (NSW) b Aug. 16, 1906 Brookvale (NSW) d c. 1984 full death details unknown

Bennett, Harry Francis (WAust) b June 22, 1859 Prahran (Vic) d Oct. 4, 1898 Guildford (WAust)

Bennett, Joseph (Vic) birth and death details unknown

* Bennett, Murray John (NSW) b Oct. 6, 1956 Brisbane (Qld)

Bennett, Rex Leland (SAust & Tas) b June 25, 1896 Snowtown (SAust) d Dec. 14, 1963 Collaroy (NSW)

Bennett, Richard John (Tas) b June 5, 1965 Launceston (Tas)

Bennett, Thomas (SAust) b Oct. 11, 1866 Littlehampton (SAust) d Dec. 26, 1942 Northfield (SAust)

Bennetts, Gordon Kissack (Vic) b March 26, 1909 Wellington (NSW) d April 4, 1987 Geelong (Vic)

Benneworth, Anthony John (Tas) b Dec. 12, 1949 Launceston (Tas)

Bennison, James Ernest (Tas) b Feb. 16, 1854 Hobart (Tas) d Nov. 14, 1916 Hobart (Tas)

Bensley, Gary Robert (NSW) b Oct. 17, 1958 Inverell (NSW)

Bensted, Eric Charles (Qld) b Feb. 11, 1901 Killarney (Qld) d March 24, 1980 Brisbane (Qld)

Benton, Jeffrey John (SAust) b Oct. 9, 1953 Mildura (Vic)

Bernard, Stephen Russell (NSW) b Dec. 28, 1949 Orange (NSW)

Berrie, Edward Bruce (NSW) b April 8, 1884 Tomenbil, near Forbes (NSW) d Dec. 8, 1963 Tamworth (NSW)

Berry, Darren Shane (Vic & SAust) b Dec. 10, 1969 Melbourne (Vic)

Berry, Walter Lyall (NSW) b April 9, 1893 Woolwich (NSW) d April 20, 1970 Ettalong Beach (NSW)

Bessen, Mervyn Oscar (WAust) b Aug. 29, 1913 Tambellup (WAust)

Best, Leslie (NSW) b Nov. 20, 1893 Seven Hills (NSW) d Aug. 27, 1925 Sydney (NSW)

Bettington, Brindley Cecil John (NSW) b Sept. 2, 1898 Parramatta (NSW) d Aug. 26, 1931 Merriwa (NSW)

Bettington, Reginald Henshall Brindley (NSW) b Feb. 24, 1900 Parramatta (NSW) d June 24, 1969 Gisborne (New Zealand)

Betts, Arthur John (Tas) b Feb. 26, 1880 Launceston (Tas) d Aug. 4, 1948 Belgrave (Vic)

Bevan, Hubert George (WAust) b Dec. 21, 1932 Perth (WAust)

Bevan, John Lawrence (SAust) b May 10, 1846 Swansea, Glamorgan (Wales) d March 31, 1918 Portland Estate (SAust)

* Bevan, Michael Gwyl (SAust & NSW) b May 8, 1970 Belconnen (ACT)

Beven, Ian Robert (Tas) b Nov. 27, 1958 Hobart (Tas)

* Bichel, Andrew John (Qld) b Aug. 27, 1970 Laidley (Qld)

Bichel, Donald Alan (Qld) b May 4, 1935 Lowood (Qld)

Bidstrup, Trevor Allan (WAust) b Dec. 29, 1937 Midland (WAust)

Biffin, Raymond Leo (Tas) b May 6, 1949 Launceston (Tas)

Biggs, Malcolm (Qld) b July 7, 1904 Caboolture (Qld) d Aug. 1, 1972 Ipswich (Qld)

Bill, Oscar Wendell (NSW) b April 8, 1909 Waverley (NSW) d May 10, 1988 Sydney (NSW)

Bingham, John Edmund (Tas) b July 15, 1864 Forcett (Tas) d July 23, 1946 Hobart (Tas)

Binney, Edgar James (Vic) b May 31, 1885 Port Tremayne (SAust) d Sept. 9, 1978 Brighton (Vic)

Birch, William Thomas (Tas) b Oct. 26, 1849 Hobart (Tas) d Aug. 18, 1897 Hobart (Tas)

Birchall, James Thomas Wardlaw (SAust) b Nov. 23, 1962 North Adelaide (SAust)

Bird, Thomas Robert (Vic) b Aug. 31, 1904 Collingwood (Vic) d April 12, 1979 Thornbury (Vic)

Bishop, Edward George (WAust) b Aug. 4, 1872 birthplace unknown d Feb. 16, 1943 Nedlands (WAust)

Bishop, Glenn Andrew (SAust) b Feb. 25, 1960 North Adelaide (SAust)

Bishop, Henry Symons (Vic) b Dec. 15, 1849 Torrington, Devon (England) d July 18, 1891 Prahran (Vic)

Bitmead, Robert Clyde (Vic) b July 17, 1942 Fitzroy (Vic)

Bizzell, Graham Maurice (Qld) b Nov. 19, 1941 Beenleigh (Qld)

Black, Alfred A. (Vic) birth details unknown d c. 1859

Black, George Gordon (NSW) b Jan. 19, 1885 Darling Point (NSW) d Dec. 6, 1954 Orange (NSW)

Black, Graham Ash (SAust) b May 14, 1924 Unley (SAust)

* Blackham, John McCarthy (Vic) b May 11, 1854 North Fitzroy (Vic) d Dec. 28, 1932 Melbourne (Vic)

* Blackie, Donald Dearness (Vic) b April 5, 1882 Bendigo (Vic) d April 18, 1955 South Melbourne (Vic)

Blackman, Oswald Colin (NSW) b March 9, 1942 Griffith (NSW)

Blackstock, John MacDonald (Qld) b Jan. 16, 1871 Drum, Thornhill, Edinburgh (Scotland) d post-1945 Sydney (NSW)

Blair, Dennis John (Tas) b Sept. 27, 1934 birthplace unknown

Blair, Gregory David (Tas & Vic) b Dec. 15, 1947 Launceston (Tas)

Blanchard, C. O. (Surrey) b c. 1842 d c. 1919 Newtown (NSW)

Blaxland, Marcus Herbert (NSW & Qld) b April 29, 1884 Callan Park (NSW) d July 31, 1958 Clayfield (Qld)

* Blewett, Gregory Scott (SAust) b Oct. 29, 1971 North Adelaide (SAust)

Blewett, Robert Kevin (SAust) b March 30, 1943 Prospect (SAust)

Blinman, Harry (SAust) b Dec. 30, 1861 Adelaide (SAust) d July 23, 1950 Adelaide (SAust)

Blizzard, Phillip Ashley (Tas & NSW) b Feb. 6, 1958 Burnie (Tas)

Bloomfield, George Thomas (SAust) b Feb. 5, 1882 Bowden (SAust) d Nov. 1, 1958 Adelaide (SAust)

Blundell, George Robert (WAust) b April 19, 1896 Perth (WAust) d Feb. 11, 1940 West Perth (WAust)

Blundell, Norman Charles (Vic) b Sept. 2, 1917 North Carlton (Vic)

Blundell, Rex Pole (SAust) b May 8, 1942 Adelaide (SAust)

Blundell, William Walter (Vic) b Dec. 30, 1866 Majorca (Vic) d Feb. 28, 1946 Kensington (Vic)

Boag, Kenneth John (Qld) b Sept. 6, 1914 Toowoomba (Qld) d July 10, 1984 Port Kembla (NSW)

Boddam, Edmund Tudor (Tas) b Nov. 23, 1879 Hobart (Tas) d Sept. 9, 1959 New Town (Tas)

Bogle, James (NSW) b Jan. 4, 1893 Mossgiel (NSW) d Oct. 19, 1963 Southport (Qld)

Bolton, John Turner (Qld) b Oct. 3, 1888 Riverstone (NSW)

* Bonnor, George John (Vic & NSW) b Feb. 25, 1855 Bathurst (NSW) d June 27, 1912 East Orange (NSW)

* Boon, David Clarence (Tas) b Dec. 29, 1960 Launceston (Tas)

* Booth, Brian Charles (NSW) b Oct. 19, 1933 Perthville (NSW)

Booth, Ernest Brian Nelson (Tas) b Sept. 30, 1924 Scottsdale (Tas)

* Border, Allan Robert (NSW & Qld) b July 27, 1955 Cremorne (NSW)

Borgas, Cameron James (SAust) b Sept. 1, 1983 Flinders (SAust)

Bosley, Marcus Williams (NSW) b Aug. 10, 1897 Liverpool (NSW) d June 12, 1982 Newport (NSW)

* Botham, Ian Terence (Qld) b Nov. 24, 1955 Heswall, Cheshire (England)

Botham, Leslie John (Vic) b May 5, 1930 Hawthorn (Vic) d April 17, 1999 Melbourne (Vic)

Bott, Leonidas Cecil (WAust) b July 14, 1889 Adelaide (SAust) d Aug. 21, 1968 Perth (WAust)

Botten, Robert Dyas (SAust) b Oct. 11, 1853 Lewisham, Kent (England) d April 26, 1935 Medindie (SAust)

Boulter, Edward Samuel (Vic) b March 23, 1886 North Fitzroy (Vic) d June 10, 1968 North Balwyn (Vic)

Bourne, Gordon Alister (Qld) b April 21, 1913 Tintenbar (NSW) d Sept. 13, 1993 Goomeri (Qld)

Bovell, Henry Edward Joseph (WAust) b March 15, 1936 East Fremantle (WAust)

Bowden, Albert John (NSW) b Sept. 28, 1874 Sydney (NSW) d Aug. 8, 1943 Northwood (NSW)

Bowden, Samuel Hedskis (Qld) b Sept. 29, 1867 Sydney (NSW) d Aug. 25, 1945 Manly (NSW)

Bowe, Ronald Doig (WAust) b Dec. 10, 1939 Beaconsfield (WAust)

Bower, Rodney John (NSW) b Nov. 30, 1959 Bankstown (NSW)

Bower, Timothy Donald (Tas) b Sept. 10, 1968 Devonport (Tas)

Bowler, Peter Duncan (Tas) b July 30, 1963 Plymouth, Devon (England)

Bowley, Bruce Leonard (SAust) b Jan. 1, 1922 Clare (SAust)

Bowley, Edwin Leonard (SAust) b Feb. 27, 1888 Clare (SAust) d April 22, 1963 Woodville (SAust)

Bowman, Alcon Ninus Ascot (Vic) b May 10, 1862 Ascot Vale (Vic) d June 30, 1938 Surrey Hills (Vic)

Box, Henry (Vic) b c. Sept. 1837 Walsall, London, Staffordshire (England) d June 3, 1916 death place unknown

Boyce, Raymond Charles Manning (NSW) b June 28, 1891 Taree (NSW) d Jan. 20, 1941 Northwood (NSW)

Boyd, David Laurence (WAust) b Nov. 21, 1955 Kalgoorlie (WAust)

Boyd, Trevor Joseph (NSW) b Oct. 22, 1944 Nyngan (NSW)

* Boyle, Henry Frederick (Vic) b Dec. 10, 1847 Sydney (NSW) d Nov. 21, 1907 Bendigo (Vic)

Brabon, George William (Qld) b Aug. 2, 1957 Ayr (Qld)

Bracher, Herbert Henry Gladstone (Vic) b Aug. 28, 1886 Footscray (Vic) d Feb. 25, 1974 Hawthorn (Vic)

Bracken, Nathan Wayne (NSW) b Sept. 12, 1977 Penrith (NSW)

Bradbridge, John Sidney (NSW) b Dec. 1, 1831 Sydney (NSW) d July 14, 1905 Dulwich Hill (NSW)

Bradley, Craig Edwin (SAust & Vic) b Oct. 23, 1964 Ashford (SAust)

Bradley, William Francis (Qld) b Oct. 8, 1867 Brisbane (Qld) d Sept. 7, 1948 Ipswich (Qld)

* Bradman, Donald George (NSW & SAust) b Aug. 27, 1908 Cootamundra (NSW) d Feb. 25, 2001 Kensington Park (SAust)

Bradshaw, Keith (Tas) b Oct. 2, 1963 Hobart (Tas)

Bradstreet, Shawn David (NSW) b Feb. 28, 1972 Wollongong (NSW)

Braid, Rupert Lee (Vic) b March 3, 1888 Talbot (Vic) d Nov. 11, 1963 Upper Ferntree Gully (Vic)

Brain, Desmond Morrah (Tas) b Dec. 16, 1909 Hobart (Tas) d March 1, 1990 Tumut (NSW)

Brain, John Heather (Tas) b Feb. 9, 1905 Hobart (Tas) d June 21, 1961 Hobart (Tas)

Brain, Roy Albert (Tas) b Sept. 2, 1926 Hobart (Tas)

Braithwaite, Arthur (Tas) b Sept. 2, 1880 Rushworth (Vic) d c. 1953 Cheltenham (Vic)

Brakey, Gary Leslie (Combined XI) b Oct. 8, 1942 Wynyard (Tas) d Feb. 3, 1987 Killarney Heights (NSW)

Brant, Scott Andrew (Qld) b Jan. 26, 1983 Harare (Zimbabwe)

Braslin, Leon Anthony (Tas) b May 12, 1938 New Norfolk (Tas)

Bratchford, James Douglas (Qld) b Feb. 2, 1929 Cleveland (Qld) d Oct. 5, 1997 on flight from USA to Australia

Braybrook, Clive (SAust) b Sept. 27, 1901 Goodwood (SAust) d July 16, 1985 Swan Hill (Vic)

Brayshaw, Ian James (WAust) b Jan. 14, 1942 South Perth (WAust)

Brayshaw, James Antony (WAust & SAust) b May 11, 1967 Subiaco (WAust)

Breman, Todd George (WAust) b Oct. 28, 1965 Subiaco (WAust)

Bremner, Colin David (Services) b Jan. 29, 1920 Hawthorn (Vic) d June 13, 2002 Canberra (ACT)

Brew, Francis Malcolm (Qld) b Jan. 5, 1903 Petrie Terrace (Qld) d Jan. 13, 1974 Sandgate (Qld)

Brewster, Robert Colin (NSW) b Aug. 17, 1867 Sydney (NSW) d Nov. 8, 1962 Killara (NSW)

Briant, George William (Tas) b c. 1828 Hackney, London, Middlesex (England) d May 10, 1914 Hobart (Tas)

Brideson, John Holmes (SAust) b July 9, 1856 Rushworth (Vic) d Feb. 1, 1898 Belair (SAust)

Bridgman, Hugh Hossick Mackay (SAust) b Feb. 1, 1890 Findon (SAust) d Dec. 3, 1953 Torrensville (SAust)

Briggs, Ronald Edward (NSW) b Sept. 22, 1929 Belmore (NSW)

* Bright, Raymond James (Vic) b July 13, 1954 Footscray (Vic)

Britt, Harold James (Vic) b May 6, 1911 Doncaster (Vic)

Broad, David John (Vic) b Sept. 25, 1953 Kew (Vic)

Broad, Wayne Ronald (Qld) b June 20, 1956 Herston (Qld)

Broadby, Christopher Laurence (Tas) b March 17, 1959 Hobart (Tas)

Brodie, James Chalmers (Vic) b Sept. 28, 1820 Perth, Perthshire (Scotland) d Feb. 19, 1912 Balwyn (Vic)

Brodie, Richard Sinclair (Vic) b Sept. 9, 1813 County Caithness (Scotland) d Jan. 18, 1872 Bulla Bulla (Vic)

* Bromley, Ernest Harvey (WAust & Vic) b Sept. 3, 1912 Fremantle (WAust) d Feb. 1, 1967 Clayton (Vic)

Brooks, Gordon Victor (SAust) b May 30, 1938 Ceduna (SAust)

Brooks, Thomas Francis (NSW) b March 28, 1919 Paddington (NSW)

Broomby, Reginald Arthur (Tas) b Jan. 6, 1905 Launceston (Tas) d May 10, 1984 Southport (Qld)

Broster, Paul Alexander (Vic) b Jan. 31, 1973 Wangaratta (Vic)

Broughton, Donald Ean (Tas) b Feb. 4, 1931 Hobart (Tas) d Dec. 11, 1987 Hobart (Tas)

Brown, Albert Ernest (Vic) b Dec. 22, 1890 Clifton Hill (Vic) d Nov. 17, 1954 Northcote (Vic)

Brown, Anthony Norman (Qld) b March 30, 1961 Herston (Qld)

Brown, Craig Franklin Archer (Tas) b Jan. 25, 1954 Hobart (Tas)

Brown, Edward (NSW) b c. Jan. 1837 Uppingham, Rutland (England) d full death details unknown

Brown, Edward Keith Faulkner (NSW) b March 7, 1891 Newcastle (NSW) d March 12, 1949 Bowenfels (NSW)

Brown, Graham Campbell (Vic) b May 9, 1944 Burwood (Vic)

Brown, Guy Archibald Loeman (Qld) b July 31, 1884 Dalby (Qld) d March 21, 1958 New Farm (Qld)

Brown, John (Qld) b May 13, 1943 Mt Morgan (Qld)

Brown, Kevin Ronald (Tas) b July 1, 1941 Devonport (Tas)

Brown, Norman Eric (Vic) b April 1, 1889 North Fitzroy (Vic) d July 7, 1962 Carrum (Vic)

Brown, Raymond Kinnear (Tas) b Nov. 3, 1950 New Norfolk (Tas)

Brown, Roger Leedham (Tas) b Aug. 9, 1959 Launceston (Tas)

Brown, Vallancey Kennedy (Vic) b Dec. 7, 1912 Ashfield (NSW) d Oct. 24, 1987 Melbourne (Vic)

Brown, Walter Graham Fairfax (NSW) b April 12, 1899 Summer Hill (NSW) d May 21, 1931 Mosman (NSW)

Brown, Wilfred Martin (Qld) b March 21, 1930 Warwick (Qld)

Brown, William (Tas) b c. 1807 (England) d Aug. 28, 1859 Hobart (Tas)

* Brown, William Alfred (NSW & Qld) b July 31, 1912 Toowoomba (Qld)

Browne, William Creighton (Qld) b Nov. 6, 1898 Toowoomba (Qld) d Oct. 25, 1980 Southport (Qld)

Browning, George Richard (Vic) b Dec. 12, 1858 Hepburn (Vic) d Oct. 9, 1900 North Carlton (Vic)

Brownlow, Bertie b May 22, 1920 Portland (NSW)

* Bruce, William (Vic) b May 22, 1864 South Yarra (Vic) d Aug. 3, 1925 Elwood (Vic)

Bryant, Francis Joseph (WAust) b Nov. 7, 1907 Perth (WAust) d March 11, 1984 Glendalough (WAust)

Bryant, James Mark (Vic) b 1826 birth day and month unknown Caterham, Surrey (England) d Dec. 10, 1881 Sale (Vic)

Bryant, Richard (NSW) b c. 1847 Maitland (NSW) d Oct. 27, 1931 Stockton (NSW)

Bryant, Richard John (WAust) b May 8, 1904 Perth (WAust) d Aug. 17, 1989 Mt Lawley (WAust)

Bryant, William James (WAust) b Jan. 15, 1906 Perth (WAust) d Jan. 1, 1995 Perth (WAust)

Bryce, William Cecil James (Qld) b Aug. 18, 1911 Maryborough (Qld) d Feb. 8, 1986 Spring Hill (Qld)

Bubb, Ernest Reinhard (NSW) b Dec. 6, 1884 Summer Hill (NSW) d Nov. 26, 1946 Neutral Bay (NSW)

Bubb, Roy Alfred Reinhard (NSW) b June 23, 1900 Darlinghurst (NSW) d April 4, 1965 Hamilton (Qld)

Buchanan, John Marshall (Qld) b April 5, 1953 Ipswich (Qld)

Buckingham, Danny James (Tas) b Dec. 2, 1964 Burnie (Tas)

Buckle, Frank (NSW) b Nov. 11, 1891 Pyrmont (NSW) d June 4, 1982 Sydney (NSW)

Buckle, William Harvey (Qld) b June 3, 1943 Wooloowin (Qld)

Buggins, Bruce Leonard (WAust) b Jan. 29, 1935 Perth (WAust)

Bull, Desmond Frederick Earl (Qld) b Aug, 13, 1935 South Brisbane (Qld)

Bull, Eric Alister (NSW) b Sept. 28, 1886 Bourke (NSW) d May 14, 1954 Mt Kuring-Gai (NSW)

Bullough, Walter (SAust) b Oct. 21, 1855 Hunslet, Yorkshire (England) d Sept. 17, 1888 Hindmarsh (SAust)

Burchett, Alfred (Vic) b 1831 birth day and month unknown London (England) d Nov. 12, 1888 St Kilda (Vic)

Burchett, Frederick (Vic) b 1824 birth day and month unknown London (England) d July 16, 1861 Melbourne (Vic)

* Burge, Peter John Parnell (Qld) b May 17, 1932 Kangaroo Point (Qld) d Oct. 5, 2001 Main Beach (Qld)

* Burke, James Wallace (NSW) b June 12, 1930 Mosman (NSW) d Feb. 2, 1979 Manly (NSW)

* Burn, Edwin James Kenneth (Tas) b Sept. 17, 1862 Richmond (Tas) d July 20, 1956 Hobart (Tas)

Burn, James Henry (Tas) b July 31, 1849 Hobart (Tas), death details unknown

Burns, Harold Vincent (Qld) b May 20, 1908 Ebagoolah (Qld) d June 6, 1944 Cairns (Qld)

Burrows, Arthur Owen (Tas) b Oct. 17, 1903 Hobart (Tas) d Jan. 4, 1984 Sandy Bay (Tas)

Burrows, Ian Donald (Combined XI) b Nov. 20, 1944 Hobart (Tas)

Burrows, J. (NSW) b Dec. 12, 1903 Hillgrove (NSW), d Feb. 14, 1959 (NSW)

Burt, Selby John Wright (NSW) b Dec. 12, 1903 Hillgrove (NSW) d Feb. 14, 1959 Camperdown (NSW)

* Burton, Frederick John (NSW & Vic) b Nov. 2, 1865 Collingwood (Vic) d Aug. 25, 1929 Wanganui (New Zealand)

Burton, Garth (SAust) b Jan. 21, 1913 Black Forest (SAust) d Sept. 6, 1993 South Brighton (SAust)

Burton, Jack Richard (SAust) b Nov. 3, 1923 Cleve (SAust) d Oct. 30, 2001 Elizabeth Vale (SAust)

Bush, Giles Edmund Wreford (WAust) b Sept. 9, 1956 Subiaco (WAust)

* Butcher, Roland Orlando (Tas) b Oct. 14, 1953 East Point, St Philip (Barbados)

Butler, Charles William (Tas) b Sept. 18, 1854 Battery Point (Tas) d June 10, 1937 Sandy Bay (Tas)

Butler, Edward Henry (Tas & Vic) b March 15, 1851 Battery Point (Tas) d Jan. 5, 1928 Lower Sandy Bay (Tas)

Butler, Edward Lionel Austin (Tas) b April 10, 1883 Hobart (Tas) d Aug. 23, 1916 Puchevillers (France)

Butler, Frank (Tas) b Nov. 13, 1889 Brighton (Vic) d May 8, 1965 Kew (Vic)

Butler, Walter John (WAust) b May 30, 1882 Port Adelaide (SAust) d March 12, 1966 Bruce Rock (WAust)

Butterworth, Benjamin (Vic) b 1832 birth day and month unknown Rochdale, Lancashire (England) d Jan. 6, 1879 Chiswick, Middlesex (England)

Butterworth, Thomas (Vic) b Dec. 17, 1828 Rochdale, Lancashire (England) d July 15, 1877 Kensington, London, Middlesex (England)

Buttsworth, Frederick James (WAust) b May 29, 1927 North Perth (WAust)

Buttsworth, Frederick Richard (WAust) b April 28, 1880 Wilberforce (NSW) d Feb. 26, 1974 Perth (WAust)

Buttsworth, Wallace Francis (WAust) b Jan. 21, 1917 North Perth (WAust) d May 22, 2002 Milton (NSW)

Byfield, Arnold Stanley (WAust) b Nov. 1, 1923 Northam (WAust)

Byrne, Thomas (Qld) b July 11, 1868 Paterson (NSW) d Dec. 19, 1951 Herston (Qld)

Caban, Timothy Kenneth (Qld) b Feb. 15, 1952 Cessnock (NSW)

Caffyn, William (NSW) b Feb. 2, 1828 Reigate, Surrey (England) d Aug. 28, 1919 Reigate, Surrey (England)

Cahill, Keyran William Jack (Tas) b Dec. 3, 1911 Hobart (Tas) d March 7, 1966 Launceston (Tas)

Cain, William (Qld) b Dec. 17, 1899 Paddington (Qld) d Dec. 24, 1981 Sherwood (Qld)

Calder, Henry (WAust) b July 3, 1906 Guildford (WAust) d Aug. 27, 1970 South Perth (WAust)

Caldwell, Tim Charles John (NSW) b Oct. 29, 1913 Clayfield (Qld) d June 17, 1994 Orange (NSW)

Callachor, John Joseph Casimir (NSW) b Nov. 10, 1857 Woolloomooloo (NSW) d Feb. 20, 1924 Lane Cove (NSW)

Callaway, Norman Frank (NSW) b April 5, 1896 Hay (NSW) d May 3, 1917 Bullecourt (France)

* Callaway, Sydney Thomas (NSW) b Feb. 6, 1868 Redfern (NSW) d Nov. 25, 1923 Christchurch (New Zealand)

* Callen, Ian Wayne (Vic) b May 2, 1955 Alexandra (Vic)

Calvert, Derreck (Tas) b Dec. 22, 1919 South Arm (Tas)

Cameron, Robert Alastair (SAust) b Sept. 6, 1938 North Adelaide (SAust)

Cameron, Verney Lovett (Vic) b c. 1842 Sorrento (Vic) d May 27, 1881 Richmond (Vic)

Campbell, Blair Maismore (Vic & Tas) b Aug. 20, 1946 Kew (Vic)

Campbell, Colin Mansfield (Tas) b Aug. 13, 1872 Cressy (Tas) d April 3, 1907 Winlaton, Northumberland (Eng)

Campbell, Donald (Vic) b Sept. 18, 1851 Loddon Plains (Vic) d Sept. 14, 1887 South Yarra (Vic)

Campbell, Francis Beresford (Tas) b April 20, 1867 Hobart (Tas) d c. 1929 Ryde (NSW)

Campbell, Gordon Cathcart (SAust) b June 4, 1885 Myrtle Bank (SAust) d Aug. 13, 1961 Woodville South (SAust)

* Campbell, Gregory Dale (Tas) b March 10, 1964 Launceston (Tas)

Campbell, Ivan James (WAust) b Oct. 29, 1908 Perth (WAust) d Jan. 22, 1962 Hollywood (WAust)

Campbell, James Norval (NSW) b Sept. 21, 1908 Chatswood (NSW) d Sept. 11, 1973 St Ives (NSW)

Campbell, Leslie Percy (NSW) b Oct. 14, 1902 Marrickville (NSW) d Aug. 19, 1970 Southport (Qld)

Campbell, Malcolm MacDonald (Qld) b Jan. 7, 1881 Ipswich (Qld) d Dec. 14, 1967 Ipswich (Qld)

Campbell, Ryan John (WAust) b Feb. 7, 1972 Osborne Park (WAust)

Campbell, Stoddart William Grylls (Vic) b Sept. 19, 1846 Melbourne (Vic) d Sept. 2, 1903 East Melbourne (Vic)

Camphin, William Joseph (NSW) b Nov. 13, 1867 Sydney (NSW) d Sept. 11, 1942 Quirindi (NSW)

Campling, Campbell Roy (NSW) b April 3, 1892 Burwood (NSW) d April 21, 1977 Greenwich (NSW)

Canning, Tamahau Karangatukituki (Cricket Academy) b April 7, 1977 Adelaide (SAust)

Cannon, William Henry (Vic) b Sept. 11, 1871 Eaglehawk (Vic) d April 29, 1933 North Fitzroy (Vic)

Cantrell, Peter Edward (Qld) b Oct. 28, 1962 Gunnedah (NSW)

Cantwell, Hubert Richard (WAust) b Oct. 24, 1905 Warbleton, Sussex (England) d April 22, 1956 Esperance (WAust)

Capes, Peter Andrew (WAust) b Feb. 26, 1962 East Fremantle (WAust)

Carew, James (Qld) b Jan. 23, 1872 Pine Mountain (Qld) d Sept. 1, 1950 Kelvin Grove (Qld)

Carew, Patrick (Qld) b Sept. 8, 1875 Pine Mountain (Qld) d March 31, 1942 Queanbeyan (NSW)

Carew, Paul John (Qld & SAust) b July 9, 1967 South Brisbane (Qld)

* Carkeek, William (Vic) b Oct. 17, 1878 Walhalla (Vic) d Feb. 20, 1937 Prahran (Vic)

* Carlson, Phillip Henry (Qld) b Aug. 8, 1951 Nundah (Qld)

Carlson, Victor Charles (WAust) b July 16, 1893 Adelaide (SAust) d Feb. 23, 1974 Perth (WAust)

Carlton, Alfred Robert (Vic) b Nov. 13, 1867 Bacchus Marsh (Vic) d Sept. 10, 1941 Camberwell (Vic)

Carlton, John (Vic & Qld) b July 6, 1866 Bacchus Marsh (Vic) d Aug. 13, 1945 Parkville (Vic)

Carlton, Thomas Andrew (Vic & SAust) b Dec. 8, 1890 Footscray (Vic) d Dec. 17, 1973 Brunswick (Vic)

Carlton, William (Vic) b May 22, 1876 Fitzroy (Vic) d Dec. 23, 1959 Parkville (Vic)

Carlyon, Norman Murdoch (Vic) b May 5, 1938 East Melbourne (Vic)

Carmichael, Ian Robert (SAust) b Dec. 17, 1960 Hull, Yorkshire (England)

Carmody, Douglas Keith (NSW & WAust) b Feb. 16, 1919 Mosman (NSW) d Oct. 21, 1977 Concord (NSW)

Carney, Brian William (Tas) b June 2, 1931 Launceston (Tas)

Carr, Charles Seymour (Vic) b Nov. 22, 1849 (Jamaica) d March 30, 1921 East Melbourne (Vic)

Carr, William Niall (Vic) b June 1, 1976 Box Hill (Vic)

Carracher, Arthur James (SAust) b July 7, 1867 Heywood (Vic) d Oct. 15, 1935 North Adelaide (SAust)

Carragher, Edward John (SAust) b May 24, 1891 Broken Hill (NSW) d Nov. 28, 1977 Broken Hill (NSW)

Carrigan, Aubrey Herbert (Qld) b Aug. 26, 1917 Zillmere (Qld)

Carroll, Edmund Louis (Vic) b Oct. 22, 1886 Albert Park (Vic) d June 6, 1959 Ormond (Vic)

Carroll, Eugene Vincent (Vic) b Jan. 17, 1885 South Melbourne (Vic) d Sept. 18, 1965 Elsternwick (Vic)

Carroll, Sidney Joseph (NSW) b Nov. 28, 1922 Willoughby (NSW) d Oct. 12, 1984 Willoughby (NSW)

Carroll, Thomas Davis (Tas) b Feb. 26, 1884 Hobart (Tas) d June 3, 1957 Hobart (Tas)

Carseldine, Lee Andrew (Qld) b Nov. 17, 1975 Nambour (Qld)

Carter, Alfred Snowden (Vic) b March 1, 1869 Kew (Vic) d June 7, 1920 Camberwell (Vic)

Carter, Edmund Sardinson (Vic) b Feb. 3, 1845 Malton, Yorkshire (England) d May 23, 1923 Scarborough, Yorkshire (England)

Carter, Edwin Lewis (Vic) b May 2, 1925 Caulfield (Vic)

* Carter, Hanson (NSW) b March 15, 1878 Halifax, Yorkshire (England) d June 8, 1948 Bellevue Hill (NSW)

Carter, Reginald Clarence (WAust) b March 1, 1888 Brunswick East (Vic) d July 16, 1970 Subiaco (WAust)

Carter, William Jack Sydney (NSW) b Dec. 7, 1907 Randwick (NSW) d Aug. 19, 1995 Penshurst (NSW)

Cartledge, Brian Lewis (Tas) b March 3, 1941 Smithton (Tas)

Cary, Sean Ross (WAust) b March 10, 1971 Subiaco (WAust)

Cass, George Rodney (Tas) b April 23, 1940 Overton, Yorkshire (Eng)

Cassell, Jerry Lee (Qld) b Jan. 12, 1975 Mona Vale (NSW)

Castle, David James (Tas) b May 25, 1972 Launceston (Tas)

Catchlove, Walter Evered (SAust) b Feb. 24, 1907 North Adelaide (SAust) d April 12, 1997 Glen Osmond (SAust)

Caterer, Thomas Ainslie (SAust) b May 16, 1858 Woodville (SAust) d Aug. 25, 1924 Walkerville (SAust)

Causby, Barry Leon (SAust) b Sept. 9, 1948 Adelaide (SAust)

Causby, John Phillip (SAust) b Oct. 27, 1942 Hindmarsh (SAust)

Cavenagh, George (Vic) b June 16, 1836 Sydney (NSW) d Nov. 23, 1922 Albert Park (Vic)

Chadwick, Derek (WAust) b March 21, 1941 Busselton (WAust)

Chamberlain, Cornelius Thomas (SAust) b c. 1882 (Ireland) d Nov. 14, 1943 Rose Park (SAust)

Chamberlain, John Aloysius (WAust) b Aug. 29, 1884 Glanville (SAust) d April 1, 1941 Leabrook (SAust)

Chamberlain, William Leonard (SAust) b Jan. 15, 1889 Port Adelaide (SAust) d March 21, 1956 Darlinghurst (NSW)

Chambers, John Lindsay (Vic) b Oct. 14, 1930 Geelong (Vic)

Chancellor, Frederick Edgar (Tas) b Aug. 28, 1878 Hobart (Tas) d June 16, 1939 Hobart (Tas)

Chapman, Frederick Douglas (Vic) b March 21, 1901 Clifton Hill (Vic) d June 27, 1964 Northcote (Vic)

Chapman, George Arthur Northcote (NSW) b April 21, 1904 Chatswood (NSW) d May 22, 1986 Sydney (NSW)

Chapman, Henry William (Qld) b Jan. 1, 1868 birthplace and death details unknown

Chapman, Lawrence Gordon (Qld) b June 25, 1928 Tingalpa (Qld)

Chapman, Ross Albert (NSW) b Oct. 22, 1952 New Lambton (NSW)

* Chappell, Gregory Stephen (SAust & Qld) b Aug. 7, 1948 Unley (SAust)

* Chappell, Ian Michael (SAust) b Sept. 26, 1943 Unley (SAust)

* Chappell, Trevor Martin (SAust, WAust & NSW) b Oct. 12, 1952 Glenelg (SAust)

Chardon, David Michael (NSW) b Dec. 12, 1951 Newtown (NSW)

Charlesworth, Lester (WAust) b Oct. 11, 1916 Kanowna (WAust) d Jan. 15, 1980 Perth (WAust)

Charlesworth, Richard Ian (WAust) b Dec. 6, 1952 Subiaco (WAust)

* Charlton, Percie Chater (NSW) b April 9, 1867 Surry Hills (NSW) d Sept. 30, 1954 Pymble (NSW)

Chee Quee, Richard (NSW) b Jan. 4, 1971 Camperdown (NSW)

Cheetham, Albert George (NSW) b Dec. 7, 1915 Ryde (NSW) d May 23, 1997 Sandringham (Vic)

Chegwyn, John William (NSW) b March 18, 1909 Botany (NSW) d May 26, 1992 Sydney (NSW)

Chillingworth, Garry Andrew (SAust) b Jan. 23, 1970 Sutherland (NSW)

Chilvers, Hugh Cecil (NSW) b Oct. 26, 1902 Sawbridgeworth, Hertfordshire (England) d Dec. 1, 1994 Sydney (NSW)

Chinner, Hubert George Williams (SAust) b Aug. 30, 1870 Brighton (SAust) d June 12, 1953 Unley Park (SAust)

* Chipperfield, Arthur Gordon (NSW) b Nov. 17, 1905 Ashfield (NSW) d July 29, 1987 Ryde (NSW)

Chittleborough, Henry Carew (SAust) b April 14, 1861 Wallaroo (SAust) d June 25, 1925 Malvern (SAust)

Chivers, Alfred Percy (Vic) b Aug. 15, 1908 Templestowe (Vic) d July 11, 1997 Templestowe (Vic)

Christ, Charles Percival (Qld) b June 10, 1911 Paddington (Qld) d Jan. 22, 1998 Redcliffe (Qld)

Christensen, Robert Thomas (SAust) b Oct. 31, 1959 Hindmarsh (SAust)

Christian, Arthur Hugh (Vic & WAust) b Jan. 22, 1877 Richmond (Vic) d Sept. 8, 1950 Claremont (WAust)

Christy, Frederick Collier (Surrey) b Sept. 9, 1822 birthplace unknown d Jan. 17, 1909 South Yarra (Vic)

* Christy, James Alexander Joseph (Qld) b Dec. 12, 1904 Pretoria (South Africa) d Feb. 1, 1971 Durban (South Africa)

Chyer, Darren Scott (SAust) b July 28, 1966 Glenelg (SAust)

Clark, Anthony Michael (NSW) b March 23, 1977 St Leonards (NSW)

Clark, Donald Jack (Tas) b Jan. 19, 1914 Hobart (Tas) d Aug. 16, 1994 Hobart (Tas)

Clark, Henry Judge (WAust) b April 23, 1892 Sydney (NSW) d Feb. 8, 1973 Perth (WAust)

Clark, James Patrick (Qld) b March 14, 1871 (Qld) d June 6, 1941 Coolangatta (Qld)

Clark, John Lawrence (Qld & NSW) b Oct. 14, 1928 Paddington (NSW)

Clark, Michael Wayne (WAust) b March 31, 1978 Mt Lawley (WAust)

Clark, Stuart Rupert (NSW) b Sept. 28, 1975 Caringbah (NSW)

* Clark, Wayne Maxwell (WAust) b Sept. 19, 1953 Perth (WAust)

Clarke, Alfred Edward (NSW) b April 6, 1868 Surry Hills (NSW) d Sept. 16, 1940 Wellington (New Zealand)

Clarke, David Alexander (SAust) b Jan. 25, 1970 Adelaide (SAust)

Clarke, Gerard John (Vic) b Dec. 31, 1966 Malvern (Vic)

Clarke, Gother Robert Carlisle (NSW) b April 27, 1875 North Sydney (NSW) d Oct. 12, 1917 Zonnebeke (Belgium)

Clarke, Graham Cornelius (SAust) b July 10, 1939 Laura (SAust)

Clarke, John Turner (NSW) b c. 1829 d Feb. 29, 1872 Bourke (NSW)

Clarke, Michael John (NSW) b April 2, 1981 Liverpool (NSW)

Clark, Michael Wayne (WAust) b March 31, 1978 Perth (WAust)

Claxton, Norman (SAust) b Nov. 2, 1877 North Adelaide (SAust) d Dec. 5, 1951 North Adelaide (SAust)

Claxton, William David Hambridge (SAust) b June 2, 1857 Kensington (SAust) d March 12, 1937 Glenelg (SAust)

Clay, Ivor Thomas (Tas) b May 7, 1915 Bendigo (Vic) d Aug. 12, 1958 Essendon (Vic)

Clayton, Nicholas George (Tas) b March 11, 1826 Norfolk Plains (Tas) d April 23, 1867 Auckland (New Zealand)

Cleary, Edward Joseph (Vic) b April 18, 1913 Benalla (Vic) d April 6, 1985 Benalla (Vic)

Cleeve, John Oatley (NSW) b Feb. 14, 1864 Sydney (NSW) d Feb. 8, 1909 Moree (NSW)

Clem, Gordon Rex (Qld) b July 5, 1909 Milora (Qld) d March 3, 1970 Melbourne (Vic)

Clements, Peter John (SAust) b Jan. 23, 1953 Glenelg (SAust)

Clements, Shane Clifton (WAust) b June 28, 1958 Middle Swan (WAust) d April 22, 2001 Inglewood (WAust)

Clews, Mark Lindsay (NSW) b Jan. 13, 1952 Grange (SAust)

Clifford, Peter Stanley (NSW & Qld) b Nov. 4, 1959 Bellingen (NSW)

Clingeleffer, Sean Geoffrey (Tas) b May 9, 1980 Hobart (Tas)

Clingly, Michael Thomas (SAust) b April 18, 1932 Prospect (SAust)

Clough, Peter Michael (Tas & WAust) b Aug. 17, 1956 Sydney (NSW)

Clutterbuck, Stanley Herwin (SAust) b May 27, 1888 Kapunda (SAust) d Jan. 24, 1972 Adelaide (SAust)

Coates, Joseph (NSW) b Nov. 13, 1844 Huddersfield, Yorkshire (England) d Sept. 9, 1896 Sydney (NSW)

Coats, James (Qld) b Feb. 26, 1914 Annerley (Qld) d June 8, 2002 Wynnum West (Qld)

Cobcroft, Leslie Thomas (NSW) b Feb. 12, 1867 Muswellbrook (NSW) d March 9, 1938 Wellington (New Zealand)

Cockburn, James Sydney David (Qld) b May 20, 1916 Maryborough (Qld) d Nov. 13, 1990 Herston (Qld)

Cockburn, William Frederick (Vic) b Nov. 28, 1916 Richmond (Vic)

Cody, Leslie Alwyn (NSW & Vic) b Oct. 11, 1890 Paddington (NSW) d Aug. 10, 1969 Toorak (Vic)

Cohen, Bertram Louis (Vic) b Sept. 25, 1892 London (England) d June 30, 1955 North Caulfield (Vic)

Cohen, Morton Barnett (NSW) b Sept. 19, 1913 Paddington (NSW) d Jan. 14, 1968 Vaucluse (NSW)

Colegrave, Mark David (Tas) b July 1, 1970 Hobart (Tas)

Colgan, Gregory (WAust) b Nov. 5, 1953 Subiaco (WAust)

* Colley, David John (NSW) b March 15, 1947 Mosman (NSW)

Colley, Timothy Peter Michael (SAust) b July 10, 1935 Sydney (NSW)

Collins, Frank Henry Kenneth (SAust) b Dec. 16, 1910 Queenstown (SAust) d Jan 24, 2001 Penola (SAust)

Collins, Frederick Bisset (Vic) b Feb. 25, 1881 Richmond (Vic) d Oct. 4, 1917 Ypres (Belgium)

* Collins, Herbert Leslie (NSW) b Jan. 21, 1888 Randwick (NSW) d May 28, 1959 Little Bay (NSW)

Collins, Ross Phillip (NSW) b Dec. 9, 1945 Paddington (NSW)

Collins, Vincent A (NSW) b c. 1917 Newtown (NSW) d Oct. 30, 1989 Sunnybank (Qld)

Collins, William Anthony (Tas) b Dec. 9, 1837 Launceston (Tas) d Jan. 12, 1876 Launceston (Tas)

Colreavy, Bernard Xavier (NSW) b June 30, 1871 Dripstone (NSW) d Nov. 30, 1946 Dubbo (NSW)

Combes, Geoffrey Arthur (Tas) b May 19, 1913 Greymouth (New Zealand) d Feb. 4, 1997 Woodstock near Huonville (Tas)

Combes, Maxwell James (Tas) b July 29, 1911 Greymouth (New Zealand) d March 10, 1983 Longley (Tas)

* Coningham, Arthur (NSW & Qld) b July 14, 1863 South Melbourne (Vic) d June 13, 1939 Gladesville (NSW)

Connell, Thomas William Christopher (NSW) b March 4, 1869 Invercargill (New Zealand) d Aug. 5, 1916 Mascot (NSW)

* Connolly, Alan Norman (Vic) b June 29, 1939 Skipton (Vic)

Connor, Gerald O'Grady (WAust & Tas) b Sept. 15, 1932 Perth (WAust) d Sept. 5, 1993 Perth (WAust)

Considine, Bernard Thomas (Vic & Tas) b April 8, 1925 Ararat (Vic) d June 4, 1989 (Qld)

Conway, John (Vic) b Feb. 3, 1842 Fyansford (Vic) d Aug. 22, 1909 Frankston (Vic)

Cook, Bernard William (Qld) b March 15, 1879 Torquay, Devon (England) d March 15, 1944 Sherwood (Qld)

Cook, Bruce (NSW) b Oct. 24, 1914 Orange (NSW) d Jan. 2, 1981 Balgowlah (NSW)

Cook, Geoffrey Glover (Qld) b June 29, 1910 Chelmer (Qld) d Sept. 12, 1982 Chelmer (Qld)

Cook, Russell Frederick (Vic) b Sept. 23, 1947 South Melbourne (Vic)

* Cook, Simon Hewitt (Vic & NSW) b Jan. 29, 1972 Hastings (Vic)

Cooke, Colin John (Qld) b Nov. 21, 1947 Harrisville (Qld)

Cooley, Troy James (Tas) b Dec. 9, 1965 Launceston (Tas)

Coombe, Ephraim Henry (SAust) b Aug. 26, 1858 Gawler (SAust) d April 5, 1917 Semaphore (SAust)

Coombe, Percy Howard (SAust) b Jan. 7, 1880 Brompton (SAust) d July 28, 1947 Prospect (SAust)

Coombe, Thomas Melrose (WAust) b Dec. 3, 1873 Gladstone (SAust) d July 22, 1959 London (England)

Cooper, Allan Ferguson (NSW) b March 18, 1916 Sydney (NSW) d Sept. 7, 1970 Concord (NSW)

* Cooper, Bransby Beauchamp (Vic) b March 15, 1844 Dacca (India) d Aug. 7, 1914 Geelong (Vic)

Cooper, Bryce Arnot (NSW) b Dec. 19, 1905 Lewisham (NSW) d May 19, 1995 Gordon (NSW)

Cooper, Duncan Elphinstone (Vic) b c. 1813 (India) d Nov. 22, 1904 Paddington, London (England)

Cooper, George Henry (Qld) b Feb. 15, 1907 Gympie (Qld) d Jan. 3, 2000 Mudgeeraba (Qld)

Cooper, John Richard (Qld) b July 11, 1922 Lilydale (Vic)

Cooper, Lewis Dale (Qld) b May 14, 1937 Mackay (Qld)

* Cooper, William Henry (Vic) b Sept. 11, 1849 Maidstone, Kent (England) d April 5, 1939 Malvern (Vic)

Cooper, William Osborne (SAust) b Feb. 13, 1891 North Adelaide (SAust) d June 28, 1930 Glenelg (SAust)

Corbett, Troy Frederick (Vic) b Oct. 10, 1972 Ouyen (Vic)

Cordner, John Pruen (Vic) b March 20, 1929 Diamond Creek (Vic)

Cordner, Laurence Osmaston (Vic) b Feb. 7, 1911 Warrnambool (Vic) d July 11, 1992 Penshurst (Vic)

* Corling, Grahame Edward (NSW) b July 13, 1941 Newcastle (NSW)

Cormack, Geoffrey Fairhurst (Vic) b Feb. 26, 1929 Camberwell (Vic)

Cornelius, William John (Vic) b Feb. 17, 1915 Port Melbourne (Vic)

Corstorphin, Colin James (Vic) b July 20, 1954 Bairnsdale (Vic) d Sept. 4, 1998 Melbourne (Victoria)

Cosgrave, Bryan (Vic) b March 23, 1903 Clifton Hill (Vic) d Nov. 22, 1992 Melbourne (Vic)

Cosgrave, James (Vic) b March 16, 1932 Parkville (Vic)

* Cosier, Gary John (Vic, SAust & Qld) b April 25, 1953 Richmond (Vic)

Cossart, Charles Edward (Qld) b Sept. 2, 1885 Rosewood (Qld) d June 6, 1963 Boonah (Qld)

Costick, Samuel (Vic & NSW) b Jan. 1, 1836 Croydon, Surrey (England) d April 8, 1896 West Maitland (NSW)

Cottam, John Thomas (NSW) b Sept. 5, 1867 Strawberry Hills (NSW) d Jan. 30, 1897 Coolgardie (WAust)

* Cotter, Albert (NSW) b Dec. 3, 1884 Sydney (NSW) d Oct. 31, 1917 Beersheba (Palestine)

Cotter, Denis Francis (Vic) b c. 1862 Fitzroy (Vic) d Nov. 18, 1905 North Fitzroy (Vic)

Cotton, Edward Kenneth (NSW) b Aug. 8, 1927 Paddington (NSW) d March 26, 2002 Kogarah (NSW)

Cotton, Harold Norman Jack (SAust) b Dec. 3, 1914 Prospect (SAust) d April 6, 1966 Malvern (SAust)

Coulson, Craig Edward (WAust) b June 13, 1967 South Perth (WAust)

Coulstock, Richard (Vic) b c. 1823 Surrey (England) d Dec. 15, 1870 South Melbourne (Vic)

* Coulthard, George (Vic) b Aug. 1, 1856 Boroondara (Vic) d Oct. 22, 1883 Carlton (Vic)

Courtice, Brian Andrew (Qld) b March 30, 1961 South Brisbane (Qld)

Courtney, Nicholas Charles Palliser (Tas) b July 18, 1967 Launceston (Tas)

Coverdale, Miles Colquhoun (Tas) b Aug. 4, 1846 Richmond (Tas) d April 3, 1898 Hobart (Tas)

Cowan, Robert Francis (SAust) b May 3, 1880 Angaston (SAust) d Nov. 11, 1962 Neutral Bay (NSW)

Cowley, Ian Arthur (Tas) b March 20, 1937 Launceston (Tas)

Cowley, Owen William (NSW & Qld) b Dec. 14, 1868 Port Louis (Mauritius) d Feb. 27, 1922 Brisbane (Qld)

Cowley, Terence John (Tas) b July 17, 1928 Evandale (Tas)

Cowmeadow, Garry John (Tas) b Aug. 21, 1954 Huonville (Tas)

Cowper, David Raymond (Vic) b Jan. 25, 1939 Kew (Vic)

Cowper, George (NSW) b c. 1858 full birth and death details unknown

* Cowper, Robert Maskew (Vic & WAust) b Oct. 5, 1940 Kew (Vic)

Cox, Douglas Edward (Qld) b July 9, 1919 West End (Qld) d Jan. 9, 1982 Dakabin (Qld)

Cox, Jamie (Tas) b Oct. 15, 1969 Burnie (Tas)

Cox, John (Tas & Vic) b 1823 birth day and month unknown Norfolk Plains (Tas) full birth and death details unknown

Cox, Michael John (WAust) b April 26, 1957 Newcastle (NSW)

Cox, Peter John (Vic) b Jan. 13, 1954 Mildura (Vic)

Cox, Richard (Tas) b April 21, 1830 Hobart (Tas) d March 27, 1865 Fingal (Tas)

Coyle, Timothy Charles (Tas) b July 22, 1960 Launceston (Tas)

Coyne, Thomas Harold (WAust) b Oct. 12, 1873 Tornagullah (Vic) d April 8, 1955 Christchurch (New Zealand)

* Craig, Ian David (NSW) b June 12, 1935 Yass (NSW)

Craig, Reginald Jack (SAust) b Aug. 3, 1916 North Adelaide (SAust) d April 17, 1985 Walker Flat (SAust)

Craig, Shawn Andrew Jacob (Vic) b June 23, 1973 Carlton (Vic)

Craigie, John Edwin (SAust) b Aug. 25, 1866 Adelaide (SAust) d Oct. 13, 1948 Gilberton (SAust)

Crane, Frederick Robert (Qld) b July 10, 1942 Mullumbimby (NSW)

Cranney, Harold (NSW) b Oct. 23, 1886 Parramatta (NSW) d Jan. 29, 1971 North Rocks (NSW)

* Crawford, John Neville (SAust) b Dec. 1, 1886 Cane Hill, Surrey (England) d May 2, 1963 Epsom, Surrey (England)

* Crawford, William Patrick Anthony (NSW) b Aug. 3, 1933 Dubbo (NSW)

Creevey, Brendan Neville (Qld) b Feb. 18, 1970 Charleville (Qld)

Cresswick, Ernest Albert (Qld) b Oct. 16, 1867 Newcastle (NSW) d Sept. 23, 1939 Waverley (NSW)

Creswick, Henry (Vic) b April 13, 1824 Sheffield, Yorkshire (England) d Oct. 24, 1892 Hawthorn (Vic)

Crippin, Ronald James (NSW) b April 23, 1947 Darlinghurst (NSW)

Cripps, Alan Edward (WAust) b Aug. 11, 1930 Lakemba (NSW)

Cristofani, Desmond Robert (NSW) b Nov. 14, 1920 Waverley (NSW)

Crompton, Colin Neil (Vic) b Aug. 16, 1937 Dandenong (Vic)

Crook, Andrew Richard (SAust) b Oct. 14, 1980 Modbury (SAust)

Crossan, Ernest Eric (NSW) b Nov. 3, 1914 Footscray (Vic)

Crouch, Edward Robert (Qld) b Jan. 11, 1873 Holborn, London, (England) d Aug. 8, 1962 South Brisbane (Qld)

Crouch, George Stanton (Qld) b Aug. 20, 1878 Strand, London, Middlesex (England) d Aug. 21, 1952 Indooroopilly (Qld)

Crow, Thomas Leslie (Vic) b Aug. 23, 1931 Hawthorn (Vic)

Crowden, Ian Bruce (Tas) b Feb. 22, 1933 Deloraine (Tas)

Crowder, Arthur Beaumont (Tas) b July 4, 1892 Sorell (Tas) d Feb. 16, 1964 Hobart (Tas)

* Crowe, Jeffrey John (SAust) b Sept. 14, 1958 Cornwall Park, Auckland (New Zealand)

Cruse, Bruce Andrew (Tas) b April 26, 1967 Launceston (Tas)

Cuff, Alan Gordon (Tas) b June 7, 1908 Launceston (Tas) d April 23, 1995 Launceston (Tas)

Cuff, Leonard Albert (Tas) b March 28, 1866 Christchurch (New Zealand) d Oct. 9, 1954 Launceston (Tas)

Cuffe, John Alexander (NSW) b June 26, 1880 Dubbo (NSW) d April 16, 1931 Burton-on-Trent, Staffordshire (England)

Cullen, Daniel Robert (NSW) b April 27, 1889 Balmain (NSW) d July 21, 1971 Concord (NSW)

Cullen, Geoff Ian (WAust) b March 16, 1977 Claremont (WAust)

Cullen, William (NSW) b c. 1887 Wellington (New Zealand) d May 7, 1945 Double Bay (NSW)

Cullinan, Thomas (WAust) b (SAust) full birth details unknown d July 31, 1907 Fremantle (WAust)

Cumberland, Charles Brownlow (Vic) b c. 1801 d Nov. 27, 1882 Leamington, Warwickshire (England)

Cumming, Kenneth Roy (WAust) b April 12, 1916 East Coolgardie (WAust) d Oct. 11, 1988 Perth (WAust)

Cummins, Frank Septimus (NSW) b Aug. 8, 1906 West Maitland (NSW) d April 27, 1966 North Sydney (NSW)

Cunningham, Kenneth George (SAust) b July 26, 1939 Adelaide (SAust)

Currie, Ernest William (Qld) b April 9, 1873 Dunedin (New Zealand) d Oct. 23, 1932 Randwick (NSW)

Curtin, Barry George (SAust) b June 30, 1951 Rose Park (SAust)

Curtin, Paul (SAust) b May 10, 1954 Rose Park (SAust)

Curtin, Pearce William Edward (WAust) b Sept. 27, 1907 Boulder (WAust) d May 17, 1997 Canberra (ACT)

Curtin, Peter Donald (SAust) b Sept. 22, 1949 Rose Park (SAust)

Curtis, George Thomas (NSW) b Aug. 17, 1837 Sydney (NSW) d April 2, 1885 Darlinghurst (NSW)

Curtis, Louis David (SAust) b Aug. 5, 1928 Loxton (SAust)

Cush, Norman Lloyd (NSW) b Oct. 4, 1911 Glebe Point (NSW) d Jan. 22, 1983 Maroubra (NSW)

Cuthbert, Daniel Charles (Tas) b Feb. 2, 1846 Franklin (Tas) d July 6, 1912 Hobart (Tas)

* Dale, Adam Craig (Qld) b Dec. 30, 1968 Greensborough (Vic)

Daly, Anthony John (Tas) b July 25, 1969 Newcastle (NSW)

Daly, Thomas (Tas) b c. 1847 d Sept. 23, 1887 Inveresk (Tas)

Daniel, Jack (Vic) b Dec. 9, 1923 Leeds, Yorkshire (England)

* Daniel, Wayne Wendell (WAust) b Jan. 16, 1956 Brereton Village, St Philip (Barbados)

Dansie, Hampton Neil (SAust) b July 2, 1928 Nuriootpa (SAust)

D'Arcy, D (NSW) birth and death details unknown

Darke, William Floyd (Vic) b July 24, 1846 Sydney (NSW) d Jan. 24, 1925 Elsternwick (Vic)

* Darling, Joseph (SAust) b Nov. 21, 1870 Glen Osmond (SAust) d Jan. 2, 1946 Hobart (Tas)

* Darling, Leonard Stuart (Vic) b Aug. 14, 1909 South Yarra (Vic) d June 24, 1992 Daw Park (SAust)

* Darling, Warrick Maxwell (SAust) b May 1, 1957 Waikerie (SAust)

Davey, John Richard (SAust) b Aug. 26, 1957 Bournemouth, Hampshire (England)

Davey, John Ryan (SAust) b Sept. 20, 1913 Broken Hill (NSW) d Sept. 6, 1992 Unley (SAust)

Davidson, Alan Andrew (Vic) b July 14, 1897 Brunswick (Vic) d Aug. 1, 1962 Ringwood (Vic)

* Davidson, Alan Keith (NSW) b June 14, 1929 Lisarow (NSW)

Davidson, Hugh Lavery (NSW) b May 17, 1907 South Yarra (Vic) d April 22, 1960 Wamberal (NSW)

Davidson, Thomas Rex (Tas) b July 30, 1927 Campbell Town (Tas)

Davie, Bert Joseph James (Tas & Vic) b May 2, 1899 Hobart (Tas) d June 3, 1979 Melbourne (Vic)

Davies, Christopher James (SAust) b Nov. 15, 1978 Bedford Park (SAust)

Davies, George Arthur (Vic) b March 19, 1892 Maindample (Vic) d Nov. 27, 1957 Essendon (Vic)

Davies, Geoffrey Robert (NSW) b July 22, 1946 Randwick (NSW)

Davies, Gerald Stanley (Tas) b Jan. 29, 1949 Cinderford, Gloucestershire (England)

Davies, John George (Tas) b Feb. 17, 1846 Melbourne (Vic) d Nov. 12, 1913 New Town (Tas)

Davies, Peter John (Vic) b Aug. 18, 1957 Melbourne (Vic)

Davis, Arthur Hugh (Tas) b Nov. 6, 1898 Launceston (Tas) d March 5, 1947 Camberwell (Vic)

Davis, Frank Alexander (Tas) b May 29, 1904 Launceston (Tas) d Sept. 12, 1973 Launceston (Tas)

Davis, Horace Hyman (NSW) b Feb. 1, 1889 Darlinghurst (NSW) d Feb. 4, 1960 Sydney (NSW)

* Davis, Ian Charles (NSW & Qld) b June 25, 1953 North Sydney (NSW)

Davis, Jonas J. (NSW) b May 12, 1859 Goulburn (NSW) d May 18, 1911 Waverley (NSW)

Davis, Neil Wilton (Tas) b Aug. 1, 1900 Launceston (Tas) d April 25, 1974 Evans Head (NSW)

Davis, Reginald Augur (Tas) b Oct. 22, 1892 Invermay (Tas) d July 11, 1957 Launceston (Tas)

* Davis, Simon Peter (Vic) b Nov. 8, 1959 Brighton (Vic)

* Davis, Winston Walter (Tas) b Sept. 18, 1958 Sion Hill, Kingstown (St Vincent)

Davison, Brian Fettes (Tas) b Dec. 21, 1946 Bulawayo (Southern Rhodesia)

Davison, John Michael (Vic) b May 9, 1970 Campbell River, Vancouver Island, British Columbia (Canada)

Davison, Lindsay John (Vic) b Oct. 11, 1941 Malvern (Vic)

Davison, Rodney John (NSW) b June 26, 1969 Kogarah (NSW)

Dawes, Joseph Henry (Qld) b Aug. 29, 1970 Herston (Qld)

Day, Arthur Charles (Vic) b Aug. 8, 1933 Sunshine (Vic)

Day, Herbert John (SAust) b April 1, 1868 Bowden (SAust) d Oct. 14, 1947 Hindmarsh (SAust)

* De Courcy, James Harry (NSW) b April 18, 1927 Newcastle (NSW) d June 20, 2000 Newcastle (NSW)

De Gruchy, Henry William (Vic) b May 15, 1898 Sydney (NSW) d May 2, 1952 Parkville (Vic)

De Jong, Howard Keith (Qld) b Feb. 12, 1956 Mt Lavinia, Colombo (Ceylon)

De Winter, Allister John (Tas) b March 12, 1968 Launceston (Tas)

Dean, Archibald Herbert (Vic) b Oct. 3, 1885 Hawthorn (Vic) d Sept. 3, 1939 Norfolk Island (NSW)

Dean, Arthur Edgar (Vic) b July 23, 1931 Williamstown (Vic)

Dean, Oscar Hessel (NSW) b April 30, 1886 Windsor (NSW) d May 11, 1962 Windsor (NSW)

Deane, Norman Younger (NSW) b Aug. 29, 1875 Neutral Bay (NSW) d Sept. 30, 1950 Lindfield (NSW)

Deane, Sydney Leslie (NSW) b March 1, 1867 Sydney (NSW) d March 20, 1934 New York (USA)

Deely, Patrick Joseph (Vic) b Feb. 18, 1864 North Melbourne (Vic) d Feb. 28, 1925 Brighton (Vic)

Deitz, Shane Alan (SAust) b May 4, 1975 Bankstown (NSW)

Delaney, William (SAust) b Jan. 17, 1866 Kapunda (SAust) d Dec. 16, 1921 Port Augusta (SAust)

* Dell, Anthony Ross (Qld) b Aug. 6, 1945 Lymington, Hampshire (England)

Dell, Christopher Ronald (Tas) b Oct. 27, 1960 Devonport (Tas)

Delves, Thomas Frederick (Vic) b Aug. 23, 1876 Carlton (Vic) d July 28, 1944 Heidelberg (Vic)

Delves, Walter Frederick (Vic) b Feb. 17, 1891 Brunswick (Vic) d May 27, 1955 Canterbury (Vic)

Dempsey, Darren Michael (SAust) b Oct. 17, 1975 Mt Gambier (SAust)

Dempster, Robert Alexander (Vic) b March 11, 1915 Hotham West (Vic) d April 2, 1974 Fitzroy (Vic)

Denton, Gerard John (Tas) b Aug. 7, 1975 Mt Isa (Qld)

Desmazeures, Pitre Cesar (Vic & SAust) b Aug. 17, 1880 Collingwood (Vic) d Oct. 7, 1942 New Norfolk (Tas)

Deveney, Frank Barclay (Vic) b Aug. 16, 1910 Berwick (Vic) d Oct. 30, 1998 Melbourne (Vic)

Devenish-Meares, Frank (WAust & NSW) b April 25, 1873 Surry Hills (NSW) d July 4, 1952 Petersham (NSW)

Deverson, Charles Sydney (SAust) b Nov. 2, 1905 Alberton (SAust) d Feb. 2, 1945 Port Adelaide (SAust)

Di Venuto, Michael James (Tas) b Dec. 12, 1973 Hobart (Tas)

Diamond, Austin (NSW) b July 10, 1874 Huddersfield, Yorkshire (England) d Aug. 5, 1966 Concord (NSW)

Dick, Alexander Williamson (WAust) b Nov. 30, 1922 Boulder (WAust)

Dick, Andrew M. (Vic) birth and death details unknown

Dick, Ian Robinson (WAust) b Aug. 30, 1926 Boulder (WAust)

Dick, William Allan (Vic) b Nov. 10, 1922 Newcastle (NSW)

Dickson, George D. (NSW) birth and death details unknown

Dighton, Michael Gray (WAust & Tas) b July 24, 1976 Toowoomba (Qld)

Dillon, Marshall (Vic) b July 22, 1925 Ballarat (Vic) d Oct. 11, 1979 Beaumaris (Vic)

Dimattina, Michael Gerard David (Vic) b May 11, 1965 Malvern (Vic)

Diprose, Noel Vertigan (Tas) b March 5, 1922 Glenorchy (Tas)

Ditchburn, Albert James (WAust) b Aug. 24, 1908 Boulder (WAust) d March 7, 1964 Perth (WAust)

Dive, Percy William (NSW) b July 10, 1881 Paddington (NSW) d Sept. 17, 1965 Roseville (NSW)

Dixon, Joseph Black (Tas) b Sept. 26, 1836 Hobart (Tas) d March 6, 1882 Battery Point (Tas)

Dixon, Patrick Leslie (Qld) b Jan. 13, 1916 Eagle Junction (Qld) d Nov. 5, 1996 Goulburn (NSW)

Dixon, Troy James (Qld) b Dec. 22, 1969 Geelong (Vic)

Doble, Alan William (Vic) b Dec. 27, 1942 Glenhuntly (Vic)

Docker, Arthur Robert (NSW) b June 3, 1848 Thornthwaite (NSW) d April 8, 1929 Enfield, Middlesex (England)

Docker, Cyril Talbot (NSW) b March 3, 1884 Ryde (NSW) d March 26, 1975 Double Bay (NSW)

Docker, Ernest Brougham (NSW) b April 1, 1842 Thornthwaite (NSW) d Aug. 12, 1923 Elizabeth Bay (NSW)

Docker, Keith Brougham (NSW) b Sept. 1, 1888 Ryde (NSW) d May 16, 1977 Ashfield (NSW)

Docker, Phillip Wybergh (NSW) b April 8, 1886 Ryde (NSW) d Oct. 29, 1978 Concord (NSW)

Docking, Trevor William (Tas) b Dec. 22, 1952 Burnie (Tas)

Dodds, Norman (Tas) b Aug. 30, 1876 Hobart (Tas) d Dec. 15, 1916 Hobart (Tas)

* Dodemaide, Anthony Ian Christopher (Vic) b Oct. 5, 1963 Williamstown (Vic)

Doherty, Xavier John (Tas) b Nov. 22, 1982 Scottsdale (Tas)

Doig, Ronald Oldham (WAust) b July 10, 1909 Fremantle (WAust) d Sept. 17, 1932 Beaconsfield (WAust)

Dollery, Keith Robert (Qld & Tas) b Dec. 9, 1924 Cooroy (Qld)

Dolling, Charles Edward (SAust) b Sept. 4, 1886 Wokurna (SAust) d June 11, 1936 Adelaide (SAust)

Dolman, Michael Charles (SAust) b June 14, 1960 North Adelaide (SAust)

Donahoo, Sydney John (Vic & Qld) b April 14, 1871 St Kilda (Vic) d Jan. 14, 1946 St Kilda (Vic)

Donaldson, John Stuart (SAust) b April 14, 1950 Adelaide (SAust)

Donaldson, William Peter James (NSW) b Oct. 26, 1923 Lilyfield (NSW) d Aug. 8, 1999 Sydney (NSW)

Done, Richard Phillip (NSW) b Aug. 5, 1955 Ryde (NSW)

* Donnan, Harry (NSW) b Nov. 12, 1864 Liverpool (NSW) d Aug. 13, 1956 Bexley (NSW)

Donnelly, James Louis (NSW) b June 24, 1906 Merimbula (NSW) d March 2, 1978 Koorawatha (NSW)

Doolan, Bruce Richard (Tas) b Sept. 9, 1947 Launceston (Tas)

* Dooland, Bruce (SAust) b Nov. 1, 1923 Cowandilla (SAust) d Sept. 8, 1980 Bedford Park (SAust)

Douglas, Adye (Tas) b May 31, 1815 Thorpe-next-Norwich (England) d April 10, 1906 Hobart (Tas)

Douglas, Alfred Jamieson (Tas) b Feb. 4, 1872 Newstead (Tas) d June 9, 1938 Malvern (Vic)

Douglas, John Raymond (Vic) b Oct. 24, 1951 East Brunswick (Vic)

Douglas, Osborne Henry (Tas) b March 14, 1880 Launceston (Tas) d April 24, 1918 Dernancourt, near Albert (France)

Dowling, Gerard Patrick (Vic) b Nov. 10, 1964 Preston (Vic)

Down, Granville James Stuart (SAust) b May 24, 1883 Dubbo (NSW) d May 14, 1970 St Kilda (Vic)

Downes, Francis (NSW) b June 11, 1864 Redfern (NSW) d May 20, 1916 Little Bay (NSW)

Downey, Donnell Raymond (SAust) b April 12, 1907 Parkside (SAust) d Jan. 23, 1966 Adelaide (SAust)

Downey, Joseph Aloysius (Qld) b Feb. 4, 1895 (Qld) d April 18, 1934 Kangaroo Point (Qld)

Downton, Andrew Graham (Tas) b July 17, 1977 Auburn (NSW)

Dowsley, Harcourt (Vic) b July 15, 1919 Essendon (Vic)

Doyle, Bryan Bernard John (Vic) b Oct. 20, 1968 Carlton (Vic)

Draney, John Davis Rodney (Qld) b May 10, 1927 Indooroopilly (Qld)

Drape, Isaac Selby (Vic & Qld) b May 13, 1866 Hotham (Vic) d Feb. 7, 1916 St Kilda (Vic)

Drennan, John (SAust) b Nov. 13, 1932 West Croydon (SAust)

Drew, Albert David (WAust) b Oct. 30, 1906 West Leederville (WAust) d Feb. 20, 1984 Shenton Park (WAust)

Drew, Charles Francis (SAust) b April 24, 1888 Kooringa, now Burra (SAust) d Feb. 19, 1960 Adelaide (SAust)

Drew, James Leggat (Vic) b Jan. 20, 1872 Williamstown (Vic) d Jan. 22, 1944 Maryborough (Vic)

Drew, Thomas Mitchell (SAust) b June 9, 1875 Kooringa, now Burra (SAust) d Jan. 9, 1928 Toowoomba (Qld)

Drewer, Richard Harris (SAust) b June 12, 1946 Parkside (SAust)

Drinnen, Peter John (Qld) b Oct. 5, 1967 Bundaberg (Qld)

Driscoll, Clarence Rheuben (Tas) b Sept. 4, 1895 Glebe (Tas) d May 1, 1948 Hobart (Tas)

Driscoll, Vernon Reginald (Tas) b April 11, 1891 Glebe (Tas) d March 19, 1967 Bellerive (Tas)

Driver, Richard (NSW) b Sept. 16, 1829 Cabramatta (NSW) d July 8, 1880 Moore Park (NSW)

Driver, Walter George (Vic & WAust) b Sept. 25, 1922 Glenhuntly (Vic) d Jan. 11, 1994 Moolooloola (Qld)

Druery, William Lance (Qld) b May 14, 1927 Townsville (Qld) d Aug. 10, 1993 Carina (Qld)

Drysdale, John (Vic) b c. 1862 Castlemaine (Vic) d Feb. 15, 1922 Kew (Vic)

Du Croz, Gervase Bedford (Tas & Vic) b c. 1830 (England) d Feb. 19, 1855 Launceston (Tas)

Ducker, John Robert (SAust) b June 12, 1934 Prospect (SAust)

Dudgeon, Keith Edward (Qld) b Sept. 5, 1946 Cairns (Qld)

Dudley, Walter John (Vic) b May 29, 1918 Carlton North (Vic) d April 5, 1978 Northcote (Vic)

* Duff, Reginald Alexander (NSW) b Aug. 17, 1878 Sydney (NSW) d Dec. 13, 1911 North Sydney (NSW)

Duff, Walter Scott (NSW) b April 22, 1876 Sydney (NSW) d Nov. 11, 1921 Sydney (NSW)

Duffy, Joseph Thomas (Vic) b c. 1860 Ballarat (Vic) d c. 1936 Ballarat (Vic)

Duffy, William Vincent (WAust) b July 8, 1866 Doutta Galla (Vic) d June 13, 1959 Subiaco (WAust)

Dufty, Ross (Tas) b Aug. 13, 1927 Bingara (NSW)

Dugan, Robert Wayne (SAust) b Aug. 10, 1959 Broken Hill (NSW)

Duldig, Lance Desmond (SAust) b Feb. 21, 1922 Eudunda (SAust) d Sept. 14, 1998 Beaumont (SA)

Dulling, Philip (Tas) b May 5, 1909 Launceston (Tas) d Sept. 1, 1974 Launceston (Tas)

Dumaresq, Henry Rowland Gascoigne (Tas) b Feb. 28, 1839 Longford (Tas) d Oct. 31, 1924 Ulverstone (Tas)

Dummett, Arthur William (Vic) b Nov. 18, 1900 Clifton Hill (Vic) d June 4, 1968 Ivanhoe (Vic)

Dummett, William (NSW) b July 18, 1840 Sydney (NSW) d c. 1906 (NSW)

* Duncan, John Ross Frederick (Qld & Vic) b March 25, 1944 Herston (Qld)

Duncan, William (Qld) b Oct. 19, 1912 Brisbane (Qld) d July 27, 1943 South Brisbane (Qld)

Dunn, Martin Matthew Francis (Qld) b May 10, 1884 Maryborough (Qld) d Dec. 31, 1942 Woollahra (NSW)

Dunn, Wallace Peter (WAust) b Aug. 8, 1921 Westonia (WAust)

Dunstan, William John (WAust) b Dec. 4, 1878 Glen Osmond (SAust) d April 11, 1955 Perth (WAust)

Dupain, Francois Henri (NSW) b Aug. 19, 1889 Ashfield (NSW) d Sept. 29, 1959 Burradoo (NSW)

Duperouzel, Bruce (WAust) b April 21, 1950 Northam (WAust)

Dwyer, Christopher (Vic) b c. 1879 Albury (NSW) d July 21, 1961 Kew (Vic)

Dwyer, Edmund Alfred (NSW) b Oct. 19, 1894 Mosman (NSW) d Sept. 10, 1975 Mosman (NSW)

Dwyer, Eric William (Tas) b June 15, 1917 St Helen's (Tas) d May 15, 1997 Canberra (ACT)

Dykes, James Andrew (Tas) b Nov. 15, 1971 Hobart (Tas)

* Dymock, Geoffrey (Qld) b July 21, 1945 Maryborough (Qld)

* Dyson, John (NSW) b June 11, 1954 Kogarah (NSW)

* Eady, Charles John (Tas) b Oct. 29, 1870 Hobart (Tas) d Dec. 20, 1945 Hobart (Tas)

Easton, Frank Alexander (NSW) b Feb. 19, 1910 Waterloo (NSW) d May 5, 1989 Sydney (NSW)

Easton, Robert Peter (Qld) b Oct. 21, 1936 Windsor (Qld)

* Eastwood, Kenneth Humphrey (Vic) b Nov. 23, 1935 Chatswood (NSW)

Eaton, Anthony Mark (SAust) b June 11, 1953 Prospect (SAust)

Eaton, George Melville (Vic) b Oct. 23, 1904 Durban (South Africa) d May 28, 1938 East Melbourne (Vic)

Eaton, Harry Ronald (NSW) b c. 1909 St Leonards (NSW) d May 13, 1960 Castlecrag (NSW)

* Ebeling, Hans Irvine (Vic) b Jan. 1, 1905 Avoca (Vic) d Jan. 12, 1980 East Bentleigh (Vic)

Ebsworth, Norman (NSW) b Jan. 2, 1878 Sydney (NSW) d Nov. 19, 1949 Kirribilli (NSW)

Edmondson, Henry Pudsey Dawson (WAust) b Nov. 25, 1872 Hobart (Tas) d Aug. 18, 1946 Perth (WAust)

Edwards, Alan Robert (WAust) b Dec. 24, 1921 Perth (WAust)

Edwards, Allen Crisp (SAust) b Nov. 18, 1868 Brighton (SAust) d Jan. 1, 1961 Adelaide (SAust)

Edwards, Edmund Keane (WAust) b Jan. 6, 1910 Cottesloe (WAust) d Aug. 18, 1990 Cottesloe (WAust)

Edwards, Frederick Raymond (SAust) b Feb. 28, 1908 Sydney (NSW) d April 27, 1982 St Leonards (NSW)

* Edwards, John Dunlop (Vic) b June 12, 1860 Prahran (Vic) d July 31, 1911 Hawksburn (Vic)

Edwards, John Neild (Vic) b Aug. 16, 1928 Ormond (Vic)

* Edwards, Ross (WAust & NSW) b Dec. 1, 1942 Cottesloe (WAust)

* Edwards, Walter John (WAust) b Dec. 23, 1949 Subiaco (WAust)

Egan, Grahame Maxwell (Qld) b June 8, 1941 Armidale (NSW)

Egan, Thomas Charles Wills (NSW) b Oct. 5, 1906 Warren (NSW) d Nov. 29, 1979 Double Bay (NSW)

Egglestone, John Waterhouse (Vic) b July 7, 1847 Hobart (Tas) d Oct. 17, 1912 Malvern (Vic)

Eime, Andrew Barry (SAust) b July 3, 1971 North Adelaide (SAust)

Elliott, Edward Hudspith (Vic) b April 19, 1851 Sunderland, Durham (England) d March 19, 1885 North Carlton (Vic)

Elliott, Gideon (Vic) b April 17, 1828 Merstham, Surrey (England) d Feb. 15, 1869 Richmond (Vic)

* Elliott, Matthew Thomas Gray (Vic) b Sept. 28, 1971 Chelsea (Vic)

Elliott, Raymond Allister (Tas) b Jan. 1, 1917 New Norfolk (Tas) d Sept. 8, 1997 New Town (Tas)

Elliott, Thomas Henry (Tas) b March 22, 1879 Hobart (Tas) d Oct. 21, 1939 Launceston (Tas)

Ellis, David Leigh (Qld) b Jan. 2, 1951 Herston (Qld)

Ellis, Donald George (Tas) b Oct. 5, 1917 Launceston (Tas) d Sept. 4, 2001 Launceston (Tas)

Ellis, John Albert (Qld) b June 10, 1914 Spring Hill (Qld) d Oct. 17, 1994 Greenslopes (Qld)

Ellis, John Leslie (Vic) b May 9, 1890 Malvern (Vic) d July 26, 1974 Glen Iris (Vic)

Ellis, Leslie George (NSW) b March 2, 1936 New Lambton (NSW)

Ellis, Matthew (Vic) b Feb. 3, 1870 Melbourne (Vic) d Nov. 19, 1940 Fitzroy (Vic)

Ellis, Percy Arthur (Vic) b May 10, 1906 Abbotsford (Vic) d April 25, 1992 Lilydale (Vic)

Ellis, Reginald Newnham (Vic) b Feb. 22, 1891 Randwick (NSW) d May 26, 1959 Cheltenham (Vic)

Ellis, Reginald Sidney (SAust) b Nov. 26, 1917 Angaston (SAust)

* Ellison, Richard Mark (Tas) b Sept. 21, 1959 Willesborough, Kent (England)

Eltham, William Keith (Tas) b Oct. 10, 1886 Hobart (Tas) d Dec. 31, 1916 Lesboeufs (France)

Emerson, David Alan (Vic) b March 10, 1961 Malvern (Vic)

Emerson, Norman Leonard (Vic) b Oct. 26, 1939 Ararat (Vic)

* Emery, Philip Allen (NSW) b June 25, 1964 St Ives (NSW)

* Emery, Sidney Hand (NSW) b Oct. 16, 1885 Macdonaldtown (NSW) d Jan. 7, 1967 Petersham (NSW)

Emery, Victor Rupert (NSW) b Dec. 20, 1920 Redfern (NSW)

Eneberg, Alfred (SAust) b Nov. 30, 1928 Birkenhead (SAust)

England, Ernest James (WAust & SAust) b May 26, 1927 Bunbury (WAust)

Englefield, William (SAust) b Oct. 6, 1917 Leichhardt (NSW) d June 3, 1988 Ryde (NSW)

Epstein, Jan (WAust) b Oct. 1, 1918 West Perth (WAust) d March 24, 1988 Melbourne (Vic)

Evan, Laurence William (SAust) b Oct. 27, 1864 Adelaide (SAust) d Aug. 12, 1894 North Adelaide (SAust)

Evans, Arthur Ernest (SAust) b July 12, 1871 East Adelaide (SAust) d March 26, 1950 Bordertown (SAust)

Evans, Charles F (Tas) birth and death details unknown

* Evans, Edwin (NSW) b March 26, 1849 Emu Plains (NSW) d July 2, 1921 Walgett (NSW)

Evans, George Nicholas (WAust) b Dec. 24, 1915 Boulder (WAust) d April 11, 1965 Hollywood (WAust)

Evans, Henry (Tas) b Aug. 6, 1846 Launceston (Tas) death details unknown

Evans, Richard (SAust) b Sept. 9, 1867 Hindmarsh (SAust) d Nov. 1, 1939 Hindmarsh (SAust)

Evans, Royston Macauley (WAust) b Jan. 13, 1884 Semaphore (SAust) d March 12, 1977 Perth (WAust)

Evans, Walter Allan (WAust) b Sept. 29, 1897 Gympie (Qld) d Jan. 15, 1955 Hollywood (WAust)

Evans, William Thomas (Qld) b April 9, 1876 Indooroopilly (Qld) d July 19, 1964 Woolloongabba (Qld)

Everett, Charles Samuel (NSW) b June 17, 1901 Marrickville (NSW) d Oct. 10, 1970 Concord (NSW)

Everett, Dudley Tabor (WAust) b March 9, 1912 Perth (WAust) d May 3, 1943 Ontario (Canada) on active service

Everett, James Seabrook (WAust) b July 20, 1884 Toodyay (WAust) d June 19, 1968 Nedlands (WAust)

Evers, Harold Albert (NSW & WAust) b Feb. 28, 1876 Newcastle (NSW) d Feb. 6, 1937 Perth (WAust)

Eyres, Gordon (WAust) b Dec. 20, 1912 Kalgoorlie (WAust)

Facy, Ashley Cooper (Tas & Vic) b Jan. 26, 1886 Bellerive (Tas) d Dec. 2, 1954 Hobart (Tas)

Fagan, Arthur Mervyn (NSW) b April 24, 1931 birthplace unknown

Fairbairn, Clive Lindsay (Vic) b Aug. 25, 1919 Geelong (Vic)

* Fairfax, Alan George (NSW) b June 16, 1906 Summer Hill (NSW) d May 17, 1955 Kensington, London (England)

Fairweather, Robert John (NSW) b July 24, 1845 Pyrmont (NSW) d May 31, 1925 Waverley (NSW)

Faithfull, Henry Montague (NSW) b June 16, 1847 Springfield (NSW) d Oct. 22, 1908 Elizabeth Bay (NSW)

Fallowfield, Leslie John (NSW) b March 12, 1914 North Sydney (NSW) d May 29, 1999 North Ryde (NSW)

Fanning, Edward (Vic) b March 16, 1848 Sydney (NSW) d Nov. 30, 1917 St Kilda (Vic)

Farnsworth, Andrew William (NSW) b Jan. 14, 1887 Sydney (NSW) d Oct. 30, 1966 Waterfall (NSW)

Farquhar, Barclay Wallace (NSW) b Feb. 22, 1875 West Maitland (NSW) d May 31, 1960 death place unknown

Farquhar, John Kennedy (Qld) b Jan. 30, 1887 Home Hill (Qld) d July 31, 1977 Chermside (Qld)

Farrar, Frank Martindale (NSW) b March 29, 1893 Rylstone (NSW) d May 30, 1973 Waverley (NSW)

Farrell, Graeme Ian (Tas) b Nov. 2, 1947 Launceston (Tas)

Farrell, Graeme Stanley (SAust) b Feb. 4, 1943 Norwood (SAust)

Farrell, Michael Graeme (Tas) b Sept. 24, 1968 Melbourne (Vic)

Faulkner, Peter Ian (Tas) b April 18, 1960 Launceston (Tas)

Faull, Martin Peter (SAust) b May 10, 1968 Darwin (NT)

Faunce, Thomas Bowman (Qld) b March 19, 1883 (Qld) d May 27, 1968 Greenslopes (Qld)

Favell, Alan Leslie (SAust) b June 6, 1960 North Adelaide (SAust)

* Favell, Leslie Ernest (SAust) b Oct. 6, 1929 Rockdale (NSW) d June 14, 1987 Magill (SAust)

Fennelly, Sidney James (Qld) b March 22, 1887 Sydney (NSW) d Aug. 25, 1964 Brighton (Qld)

Fenton, Arthur (Vic) b Feb. 27, 1870 Tarnagulla (Vic) d May 20, 1950 Melbourne (Vic)

Ferguson, James Alexander (Tas) b Feb. 19, 1848 Launceston (Tas) d May 10, 1913 Brisbane (Qld)

Ferguson, Leslie Drummond (Vic) b Dec. 8, 1892 North Brighton (Vic) d Jan. 30, 1957 East Melbourne (Vic)

Ferrall, Raymond Alfred (Tas) b May 27, 1906 Launceston (Tas) d June 1, 2000 Launceston (Tas)

Ferries, Kenneth Ian (WAust) b May 7, 1936 Wyalkatchem (WAust)

**Ferris, John James (NSW & SAust) b May 21, 1867 Sydney (NSW) d Nov. 21, 1900 Durban (South Africa)

Fett, Frederick (Qld) b May 2, 1886 Toowoomba (Qld) d Aug. 27, 1979 Woolloongabba (Qld)

Fewin, Henry (Qld) b Jan. 25, 1896 Townsville (Qld) d Aug. 25, 1980 Bongaree (Qld)

Fidock, Harold Edward (WAust) b Aug. 24, 1902 Adelaide (SAust) d Feb. 9, 1986 Nedlands (WAust)

Field, William (Tas) b March 17, 1816 Port Dalrymple (Tas) d June 22, 1890 Bishopsbourne (Tas)

Fielke, Noel Robert (SAust) b Dec. 23, 1966 Blackwood (SAust)

Findlay, Algernon Percy (Tas) b March 17, 1892 Launceston (Tas) d Jan. 9, 1956 Launceston (Tas)

* Fingleton, John Henry Webb (NSW) b April 28, 1908 Waverley (NSW) d Nov. 22, 1981 St Leonards (NSW)

Fisher, Alexander (Qld) b March 14, 1908 Gatton (Qld) d Oct. 6, 1968 Maryborough (Qld)

Fisher, Arthur Donnelly Wentworth (NSW) b Dec. 14, 1882 Lavender Bay (NSW) d July 9, 1968 Neutral Bay (NSW)

Fisher, Barry (Qld) b Jan. 20, 1934 Brisbane (Qld) d April 6, 1980 Inverell (NSW)

Fisher, Harry Medcalf (SAust) b May 28, 1899 North Adelaide (SAust) d Oct. 14, 1982 South Launceston (Tas)

Fisher, William Thornton (Qld) b Aug. 31, 1865 Brisbane (Qld) d June 1, 1945 Herston (Qld)

Fitchett, Michael King (Vic) b Nov. 30, 1927 Hawthorn (Vic)

Fitness, Gavin Arthur James (Qld) b June 4, 1968 Maryborough (Qld)

Fitzgerald, David Andrew (WAust & SAust) b Nov. 30, 1972 Osborne Park (WAust)

Fitzgerald, James (Qld) b Feb. 19, 1874 Surry Hills (NSW) d Aug. 20, 1950 Graceville (Qld)

Fitzmaurice, Desmond Michael John (Vic) b Oct. 16, 1917 Carlton (Vic) d Jan. 19, 1981 Prahran (Vic)

Fitzmaurice, Dudley James Anthony (Vic) b May 21, 1913 Carlton (Vic) d June 28, 2001 Frankston (Vic)

Fitzpatrick, Jack Herbert (NSW) b Sept. 18, 1911 Bankstown (NSW) d Jan. 23, 1999 Bankstown (NSW)

Fitzpatrick, John Milling (Vic) b June 26, 1889 Waverley (NSW) d Aug. 16, 1952 Coogee (NSW)

Fleay, Clarence William Edward James (WAust) b Dec. 27, 1886 Gilgering (WAust) d Aug. 6, 1955 Katanning (WAust)

* Fleetwood-Smith, Leslie O'Brien (Vic) b March 30, 1908 Stawell (Vic) d March 16, 1971 Fitzroy (Vic)

Flegler, Shawn Leonard (Qld) b March 23, 1972 Darwin (NT)

* Fleming, Damien William (Vic) b April 24, 1970 Bentley (WAust)

Fletcher, John Henry (Qld) b Oct. 27, 1893 Brisbane (Qld)

Fletcher, John William (Qld) b Jan. 25, 1884 Woollahra (NSW) d March 13, 1965 South Brisbane (Qld)

Flint, Kerry Royce (Tas) b Sept. 17, 1946 Smithton (Tas)

Flockton, Raymond George (NSW) b March 14, 1930 Paddington (NSW)

Flynn, Brian James (Qld) b June 7, 1929 Darlinghurst (NSW) d Aug. 3, 1986 Vesty's Beach, Darwin (NT)

Flynn, John Paul (NSW) b June 29, 1890 Paddington (NSW) d May 28, 1952 Chatswood (NSW)

Foley, Geoffrey Ian (Qld) b Oct. 11, 1967 Jandowae (Qld)

Foley, Maurice Hinton (WAust) b Feb. 4, 1930 Perth (WAust)

Folkard, Bernard James (NSW) b May 17, 1878 Ryde (NSW) d Jan. 31, 1937 Leichhardt (NSW)

Fontaine, Frederick Ernest (Vic) b Dec. 14, 1912 Northcote (Vic) d Oct. 24, 1982 Greensborough (Vic)

Foot, Charles Francis (Vic) b Aug. 14, 1855 Brighton (Vic) d July 2, 1926 East Melbourne (Vic)

Foot, Henry Boorn (Vic) b Nov. 21, 1805 Romsey, Hampshire (England) d May 14, 1857 Brighton (Vic)

Ford, Douglas Allan (NSW) b Dec. 16, 1928 Maryville (NSW)

Forsaith, Geoffrey Milner (WAust) b Jan. 5, 1931 Perth (WAust)

Forssberg, Edward Ernest Brackley (NSW) b Dec. 10, 1894 Sydney (NSW) d May 23, 1953 Bondi (NSW)

Forster, William Robert (Tas) b March 1, 1884 Gateshead-on-Tyne, Durham (England) d Feb. 7, 1930 Richmond (Tas)

Foster, Michael Robert (Vic) b March 5, 1973 East Melbourne (Vic)

Foster, Norman Kelk (Qld) b Jan. 19, 1878 Brisbane (Qld) d March 15, 1960 Clayfield (Qld)

Foster, Thomas Henry (NSW) b Sept. 30, 1883 Glebe (NSW) d June 27, 1947 Leichhardt (NSW)

Fothergill, Desmond Hugh (Vic) b July 15, 1920 Northcote (Vic) d March 16, 1996 Melbourne (Vic)

Fowler, Edwin (Vic) b c. 1841 London (England) d May 31, 1909 St Kilda (Vic)

Fox, Albert Henry Newnham (Vic) b April 20, 1867 Battery Point (Tas) d Dec. 24, 1946 Brighton (Vic)

Fox, Norman Henry (NSW) b July 29, 1904 Longueville (NSW) d May 7, 1972 Castle Cove (NSW)

* Francis, Bruce Colin (NSW) b Feb. 18, 1948 Sydney (NSW)

Francis, Craig Lawrence (SAust) b Nov. 25, 1966 North Adelaide (SAust)

Francis, John Charles (Vic) b June 22, 1908 Hawthorn (Vic) d July 6, 2001 Camberwell (Vic)

Francis, Keith Raymond (NSW) b Nov. 14, 1933 Arncliffe (NSW)

Francis, Stanley George (WAust) b April 14, 1906 Geelong (Vic) d Jan. 25, 1994 Nedlands (WAust)

Francke, Fredrick Malcolm (Qld) b March 21, 1939 Mt Lavinia, Colombo (Ceylon)

Frankish, Ronald Richard (WAust) b Oct. 6, 1925 Perth (WAust)

Fraser, Neville Graham (Qld) b Sept. 28, 1930 Cleveland (Qld)

Fraser, Robert Alexander (SAust) b Feb. 13, 1954 Parkside (SAust)

Frazer, Ian Douglas (Vic) b Sept. 7, 1966 Lilydale (Vic)

Frederick, John (Vic) b Dec. 18, 1910 Armadale (Vic)

Free, Ernest Peardon (Tas) b Sept. 7, 1867 Rokeby (Tas) d July 5, 1946 Hobart (Tas)

Freedman, David Andrew (NSW) b June 19, 1964 Darlinghurst (NSW)

Freeman, Edward John (Tas) b Nov. 7, 1848 Hobart (Tas) d Aug. 11, 1905 Hobart (Tas)

* Freeman, Eric Walter (SAust) b July 13, 1944 Largs Bay (SAust)

Freeman, Harry Septimus (Vic & Qld) b June 11, 1860 Carlton (Vic) d Nov. 7, 1933 Brunswick (Vic)

Freeman, John Edward (Qld) b June 28, 1935 Nundah (Qld)

Freeman, Thomas Daniel (Tas) b June 13, 1894 Hobart (Tas) d June 19, 1965 Heidelberg (Vic)

Freemantle, Leslie Francis (Vic & WAust) b May 11, 1898 Canterbury (Vic) d June 6, 1963 Kew (Vic)

* Freer, Frederick Alfred William (Vic) b Dec. 4, 1915 North Carlton (Vic) d Nov. 2, 1998 Frankston (Vic)

Frei, Harald (Qld) b May 1, 1951 Nuremberg (Germany)

Frick, John (SAust) b March 24, 1957 Medindie (SAust)

Friend, Raymond Grattan (Tas) b April 11, 1898 Prahran (Vic) death details unknown

Frost, Albert Edgar (Tas) b March 19, 1878 Launceston (Tas) d Oct. 25, 1951 Launceston (Tas)

Frost, Allan Russell (SAust) b Dec. 2, 1942 Adelaide (SAust)

Frost, Sydney Robert (Tas) b Jan. 21, 1881 Launceston (Tas) d Dec. 19, 1952 Middle Park (Vic)

Fry, Herbert James (Vic) b Oct. 28, 1870 Morphett Vale (SAust) d Jan. 19, 1953 Hawthorn (Vic)

Furlong, Ronald William (Vic) b May 16, 1936 Ballarat (Vic)

Furness, Arthur John (NSW) b Jan. 11, 1873 Sydney (NSW) d Oct. 31, 1948 Strathfield (NSW)

Gaggin, William Wakeham (Vic) b Nov. 23, 1847 County Cork (Ireland) d July 5, 1925 Elsternwick (Vic)

Gallagher, Ian Noel (Qld) b Nov. 20, 1950 Greenslopes (Qld)

Gallash, Ian (WAust) b June 17, 1936 Perth (WAust)

Galloway, Paul Warren (SAust) b Sept. 14, 1943 North Sydney (NSW) d Aug. 20, 1996 Loxton (SAust)

Gamble, Herbert Spencer (Vic & Qld) b March 2, 1903 Sunbury (Vic) d June 15, 1962 Shorncliffe (Qld)

Gandy, Michael George (Tas) b Aug. 28, 1944 Hobart (Tas)

* Gannon, John Bryant (WAust) b Feb. 8, 1947 Subiaco (WAust)

Gardiner, George Allan (WAust) b Nov. 27, 1914 Perth (WAust)

Gardiner, Grant Bruce (Vic) b Feb. 26, 1965 Melbourne (Vic)

Gardiner, Jack (Tas) b May 20, 1913 Hobart (Tas) d Sept. 11, 1976 Hobart (Tas)

Gardner, Charles Allan (Vic) b Oct. 28, 1908 Brighton East (Vic) d Dec. 9, 2001 Frankston (Vic)

Gardner, Roy (Vic) b Jan. 18, 1914 Hotham West (Vic)

Garland, John George Morton (Vic) b Aug. 22, 1875 Hotham (Vic) d Feb. 23, 1938 Hawthorn (Vic)

Garlick, Paul Anthony (Vic) b Sept. 21, 1968 Sandringham (Vic)

Garnaut, Matthew Stuart (WAust) b Nov. 7, 1973 Subiaco (WAust)

* Garner, Joel (SAust) b Dec. 16, 1952 Enterprise, Christ Church (Barbados)

Garnsey, George Leonard (NSW) b Feb. 10, 1881 Sydney (NSW) d April 18, 1951 Canberra (ACT)

* Garrett, Thomas William (NSW) b July 26, 1858 Wollongong (NSW) d Aug. 6, 1943 Warrawee (NSW)

Gartrell, Kevin Boyd (WAust) b March 4, 1936 Midland (WAust)

Gartrell, Robert Boyd (WAust & Tas) b March 9, 1962 Middle Swan (WAust)

Garwood, Rex Elvyn (Tas) b May 15, 1930 Hobart (Tas)

Gaskell, Mark Andrew (Qld) b Oct. 17, 1956 Herston (Qld)

Gatehouse, George Henry (Tas) b June 20, 1864 Sorell (Tas) d Jan. 25, 1947 Toorak (Vic)

Gatenby, David John (Tas) b Feb. 12, 1952 Launceston (Tas)

Gatenby, Lawrence Frank (Tas) b April 10, 1889 Epping Forest (Tas) d Jan. 14, 1917 Armentieres (France)

Gatenby, Peter Robert (Tas) b May 26, 1949 Launceston (Tas)

* Gaunt, Ronald Arthur (WAust & Vic) b Feb. 26, 1934 Yarloop (WAust)

Geary, Alfred (NSW) b Aug. 8, 1849 birthplace unknown d Oct. 14, 1911 Brisbane (Qld)

Gee, Daniel Albert (NSW) b Sept. 30, 1875 Sydney (NSW) d Jan. 16, 1947 Adelaide (SAust)

Gehan, Rodney Arthur Howard (SAust) b Nov. 12, 1942 Werribee (Vic) d Feb. 8, 2001 Hope Island (Qld)

* Gehrs, Donald Raeburn Algernon (SAust) b Nov. 29, 1880 Port Victor (SAust) d June 25, 1953 Kings Park (SAust)

Geise, Gregory Gordon (NSW) b April 3, 1960 Wallsend (NSW)

Gentle, Steven Robert (SAust) b May 30, 1955 Rose Park (SAust)

George, Shane Peter (SAust) b Oct. 20, 1970 Adelaide (SAust)

Germaine, Lewis (Vic & WAust) b March 1, 1935 Glenhuntly (Vic) d April 8, 1992 Melbourne (Vic)

Geyer, Kevin James (NSW) b Oct. 11, 1973 Bathurst (NSW)

Gibaud, Henry Peter (Vic) b May 1, 1892 Carlton (Vic) d July 29, 1964 Fitzroy (Vic)

Gibbs, Charles H. (SAust) b c. 1841 full birth and death details unknown

* Gibbs, Lancelot Richard (SAust) b Sept. 29, 1934 Georgetown (British Guiana)

Giblin, Vincent Wanostrocht (Tas) b Nov. 13, 1817 Kingston upon Thames, Surrey (England) d May 15, 1884 Milsons Point (NSW)

Gibson, George (Tas) b 1827 birth day and month unknown Norfolk Plains (Tas) d Oct. 8, 1873 Sandy Bay (Tas)

Gibson, George Watson Hogg (Vic) b 1827 birth day and month unknown Thakambau (Jamaica) d Sept. 5, 1910 Carlton (Vic)

Gibson, Gordon Galloway (Tas) b Nov. 1, 1908 Hobart (Tas) d July 7, 1967 Melbourne (Vic)

Gibson, Vincent Roy (SAust) b May 14, 1916 Rose Park (SAust) d Nov. 28, 1983 Neutral Bay (NSW)

* Giffen, George (SAust) b March 27, 1859 Adelaide (SAust) d Nov. 29, 1927 Parkside (SAust)

* Giffen, Walter Frank (SAust) b Sept. 21, 1861 Adelaide (SAust) d June 28, 1949 North Unley (SAust)

Gilbert, Ashley Stephen (Vic) b Nov. 26, 1971 Melbourne (Vic)

* Gilbert, David Robert (NSW & Tas) b Dec. 19, 1960 Darlinghurst (NSW)

Gilbert, Eddie (Qld) b 1904 birth day and month unknown Woodford (Qld) d Jan. 9, 1978 Wacol (Qld)

Gilbert, George Henry Bailey (NSW) b Sept. 2, 1829 Cheltenham, Gloucestershire (England) d June 16, 1906 Summer Hill (NSW)

Gilbourne, Robert James (SAust) b July 16, 1943 Adelaide (SAust)

* Gilchrist, Adam Craig (NSW & WAust) b Nov. 14, 1971 Bellingen (NSW)

Giles, Leonard George (SAust) b June 17, 1921 Yorketown (SAust) d Aug. 23, 1994 Glandore (SAust)

Gill, Lynwood Laurence (Tas & Qld) b Nov. 19, 1891 Macquarie Plains (Tas) d Dec. 4, 1986 Pullenvale (Qld)

Giller, James Frederick (Vic) b May 1, 1870 Melbourne (Vic) d June 13, 1947 Albert Park (Vic)

* Gillespie, Jason Neil (SAust) b April 19, 1975 Darlinghurst (NSW)

Gilmore, Francis Patrick John (NSW) b c. 1909 Yass (NSW) d April 26, 1955 Camperdown (NSW)

* Gilmour, Gary John (NSW) b June 26, 1951 Waratah (NSW)

Gladigau, Peter Wayne (SAust) b May 23, 1965 Whyalla (SAust)

Glassock, Craig Anthony (NSW) b Nov. 29, 1973 Mona Vale (NSW)

* Gleeson, John William (NSW) b March 14, 1938 Kyogle (NSW)

Glew, Steven Adam (Cricket Academy) b March 11, 1977 Perth (WAust)

Glynn, William Thomas (Tas) b c. 1846 d June 18, 1895 Fitzroy (Vic)

Goddard, Henry (NSW) b Nov. 16, 1885 Sydney (NSW) d May 13, 1925 Maroubra (NSW)

Godfrey, Charles George (SAust) b Nov. 17, 1860 Adelaide (SAust) d March 27, 1940 Rose Park (SAust)

Goffet, Gordon (NSW) b March 4, 1941 Speers Point (NSW)

Goggin, Peter John Thomas (Qld) b Oct. 30, 1965 Roma (Qld)

Gogler, Keith Geoffrey (SAust) b May 1, 1923 Port Augusta (SAust) d Aug. 24, 1983 Glenelg (SAust)

Goldman, Albert Edward Arms (Qld) b Oct. 4, 1868 Wee Waa (NSW) d Dec. 31, 1939 Sydney (NSW)

Goldsmith, Louis (Vic) b Sept. 14, 1846 Melbourne (Vic) d Sept. 15, 1911 East Melbourne (Vic)

Gonnella, Peter (WAust) b Jan. 14, 1963 Canberra (ACT)

Good, Robert Norman Scott (WAust) b March 29, 1885 East Melbourne (Vic) d June 16, 1962 Camberwell (Vic)

Goode, Benjamin Ryall (SAust) b Jan. 23, 1924 Port Lincoln (SAust)

Gooden, Henry Alfred (SAust) b Jan. 12, 1858 Adelaide (SAust) d March 30, 1904 North Fitzroy (Vic)

Gooden, James Edward (SAust) b Dec. 23, 1845 Brentford, Middlesex (England) d July 17, 1913 Norwood (SAust)

Gooden, Norman Leslie (SAust) b Dec. 27, 1889 Norwood (SAust) d July 5, 1966 Unley Park (SAust)

Goodfellow, James Edward (SAust) b Aug. 21, 1850 Surrey (England) d July 22, 1924 Malvern (SAust)

Goodman, Gary Weech (Tas & SAust) b Dec. 6, 1953 Sydney (NSW)

Goodrick, Garnet Gordon (Tas) b Feb. 19, 1895 Franklin (Tas) d Jan. 26, 1929 South Melbourne (Vic)

Goodwin, Charles Geoffrey (Tas) b Feb. 12, 1923 Hobart (Tas) d Sept. 20, 1981 Fitzroy (Vic)

* Goodwin, Murray William (WAust) b Dec. 11, 1972 Salisbury (Southern Rhodesia)

Goodwin, Victor Henry Vallance (Qld) b Oct. 26, 1906 Newtown (NSW) d Sept. 22, 1957 Leichhardt (NSW)

Gooma, George Arlington (Qld) b June 25, 1918 Fortitude Valley (Qld) d Oct. 1, 1985 Greenslopes (Qld)

Gooneseena, Gamini (NSW) b Feb. 16, 1931 Mt Lavinia, Colombo (Ceylon)

Gordon, Charles Steward (Vic) b Sept. 8, 1849 Oakleaze, Gloucestershire (England) d March 24, 1930 Nottington, Dorset (England)

Gordon, Evan Shawn (NSW) b Sept. 26, 1960 Pinelands, Cape Town (South Africa)

Gordon, George Birnie (Vic) b Aug. 12, 1860 South Melbourne (Vic) d March 5, 1946 Rose Bay (NSW)

Gordon, George Hollinworth (NSW) b Sept. 20, 1846 New England District (NSW) d May 18, 1923 Darling Point (NSW)

Gordon, Trevor Fairburn (Tas) b Feb. 18, 1915 Hobart (Tas)

Gorman, Frank O. (NSW) birth and death details unknown

Gorringe, Harrison Reginald (WAust) b March 7, 1928 Carlisle (WAust)

Gorry, Charles Richard (NSW) b Sept. 18, 1878 Auckland (New Zealand) d Sept. 13, 1950 Petersham (NSW)

Goss, Edward Alfred (Vic) b Nov. 28, 1875 Richmond (Vic) d Sept. 1, 1955 Camberwell (Vic)

Gostelow, Reginald Edwin Potter (NSW) b July 26, 1900 Darlinghurst (NSW) d Aug. 2, 1984 Darling Point (NSW)

Gott, Douglas Lawrence (Vic) b June 30, 1950 Melbourne (Vic)

Gough, Francis Joseph (Qld) b July 26, 1898 Sandgate (Qld) d Jan. 30, 1980 Sandgate (Qld)

Gould, Fred Keen (SAust) b Sept. 18, 1891 Hindmarsh (SAust) d Feb. 15, 1954 Kingswood (SAust)

Gould, John William (NSW) b Oct. 1, 1868 Sydney (NSW) d Dec. 4, 1908 Lewisham (NSW)

Gouly, Lionel (WAust) b Feb. 12, 1873 Woolloomooloo (NSW) d April 15, 1911 Perth (WAust)

Gourlay, Kenneth Garrett (Tas) b June 27, 1914 Hobart (Tas) d Jan. 28, 1999 Lenah Valley (Tas)

Govan, John Macmillan (Qld) b Dec. 30, 1914 Coorparoo (Qld) d July 20, 1996 South Brisbane (Qld)

Gow, Frederick Kingswood (NSW) b Dec. 18, 1882 Richmond (NSW) d Oct. 11, 1961 Randwick (NSW)

Grace, Brian James David (Qld) b Dec. 30, 1945 Herston (Qld)

Graf, Shaun Francis (Vic & WAust) b May 19, 1957 Somerville (Vic)

* Graham, Henry (Vic) b Nov. 22, 1870 Carlton (Vic) d Feb. 7, 1911 Dunedin (New Zealand)

Grangel, Horace Henry Eric (Vic) b Nov. 23, 1908 Burwood (Vic)

Grant, Bartholomew (Vic) b Aug. 13, 1876 St Kilda (Vic) death details unknown

Grant, Colin Spicer (SAust) b June 22, 1927 Alberton (SAust) d Sept. 3, 1998 Clare (SAust)

Grant, John William (Vic) b Feb. 9, 1941 Essendon (Vic)

Grant, Norman Frederic (Qld) b Jan. 15, 1891 Sydney (NSW) d Sept. 17, 1966 Coorparoo (Qld)

Grant, Thomas Christopher (Vic) b Dec. 20, 1879 St Kilda (Vic) d c. 1934 Kurri Kurri (NSW)

* Graveney, Thomas William (Qld) b June 16, 1927 Riding Mill, Northumberland (England)

Gray, Arthur Thomas (NSW) b June 12, 1892 Glebe (NSW) d July 19, 1977 Glebe (NSW)

Gray, Cecil Douglas (SAust) b April 28, 1902 Henley Beach (SAust) d c. 1976

Gray, Geoffrey Thomas (Qld) b Aug. 27, 1943 Ipswich (Qld)

Greaves, William Henry (Vic) b c. 1830 (England) d Aug. 6, 1869 Warrnambool (Vic)

Green, Albert (SAust) b Jan. 28, 1874 Medindie (SAust) d c. 1913

Green, Braddon Clive (Vic) b Jan. 18, 1958 Benalla (Vic)

Green, Donald William (Vic) b Nov. 22, 1933 Canterbury (Vic)

Green, Douglas Carling (Tas) b May 19, 1902 Hobart (Tas) d Nov. 28, 1990 Hobart (Tas)

Green, Jack Godfrey (Vic) b Oct. 4, 1921 Brighton (Vic)

Green, Randal James (NSW) b July 15, 1961 Hawthorn (Vic)

Gregg, Donald Malcolm (SAust) b Sept. 17, 1924 Tumby Bay (SAust)

Gregg, Norman McAlister (NSW) b March 7, 1892 Burwood (NSW) d July 27, 1966 Woollahra (NSW)

Gregory, Arthur Herbert (NSW) b July 7, 1861 Sydney (NSW) d Aug. 17, 1929 Chatswood (NSW)

Gregory, Charles Smith (NSW) b June 5, 1847 Wollongong (NSW) d April 5, 1935 Chatswood (NSW)

Gregory, Charles William (NSW) b Sept. 30, 1878 Randwick (NSW) d Nov. 14, 1910 Darlinghurst (NSW)

* Gregory, David William (NSW) b April 15, 1845 Fairy Meadow (NSW) d Aug. 4, 1919 Turramurra (NSW)

* Gregory, Edward James (NSW) b May 29, 1839 Waverley (NSW) d April 22, 1899 Randwick (NSW)

* Gregory, Edward Sydney (NSW) b April 14, 1870 Randwick (NSW) d Aug. 1, 1929 Randwick (NSW)

* Gregory, Jack Morrison (NSW) b Aug. 14, 1895 North Sydney (NSW) d Aug. 7, 1973 Bega (NSW)

* Gregory, Ross Gerald (Vic) b Feb. 28, 1916 Malvern (Vic) d June 10, 1942 in action over Ghafargon, Assam (India)

Grew, Ernest Sadler (Qld) b Aug. 11, 1867 Birmingham, Warwickshire (England) d Sept. 4, 1954 Brisbane (Qld)

Grieves, Kenneth John (NSW) b Aug. 27, 1925 Burwood (NSW) d Jan. 3, 1992 Rawtenstall, Lancashire (England)

Griffith, Harold Bickerton (Qld) b Oct. 10, 1879 Manly (NSW) d May 30, 1947 Herston (Qld)

Griffiths, Charles Samuel (Qld) b May 28, 1889 Townsville (Qld) d May 12, 1928 Rockhampton (Qld)

Griffiths, George Edward (NSW & SAust) b April 9, 1938 Glebe (NSW)

Grigg, Henry Tattersall (WAust) b May 24, 1906 Fremantle (WAust) d July 9, 1991 Inglewood (WAust)

* Grimmett, Clarence Victor (Vic & SAust) b Dec. 25, 1891 Caversham, Dunedin (New Zealand) d May 2, 1980 Kensington (SAust)

Grinrod, Barton (Vic) b April 25, 1834 Liverpool , Lancashire (England) d May 23, 1895 Great Crosby, Lancashire (England)

Grosser, John William (NSW) b Aug. 29, 1942 Gunnedah (NSW)

* Groube, Thomas Underwood (Vic) b Sept. 2, 1857 New Plymounth, Taranaki (New Zealand) d Aug. 5, 1927 Hawthorn (Vic)

Grounds, William Thomas (NSW) b Jan. 14, 1878 Surry Hills (NSW) d July 21, 1950 Mortdale (NSW)

* Grout, Arthur Theodore Wallace (Qld) b March 30, 1927 Mackay (Qld) d Nov. 9, 1968 Spring Hill (Qld)

Grove, Percival Brian (SAust) b Feb. 23, 1921 Adelaide (SAust)

* Guest, Colin Ernest John (Vic & WAust) b Oct. 7, 1937 Melbourne (Vic)

Gulliver, Kenneth Charles (NSW) b Aug. 14, 1913 East Maitland (NSW) d June 11, 2001 Collaroy (NSW)

Gumley, William Dudgeon (Qld) b June 28, 1923 Bangalow (NSW) d Aug. 14, 1988 Redcliffe (Qld)

Gun, Lancelot Townsend (SAust) b April 13, 1903 Port Adelaide (SAust) d May 25, 1958 North Adelaide (SAust)

Gunston, Edward Claude (Vic) b May 7, 1913 Brunswick (Vic) d Feb. 28, 1991 Melbourne (Vic)

Gunthorpe, Gilbert Dudley (Qld) b Aug. 9, 1910 Mt Morgan (Qld) d June 3, 1998 Casino (NSW)

Gurr, Gordon Caleb (SAust) b Dec. 22, 1881 Hyde Park (SAust) d Aug. 11, 1960 Loxton (SAust)

Guthrie, Herbert France (Vic) b Sept. 29, 1902 Brisbane (Qld) d Jan. 26, 1951 Bellevue Hill (NSW)

Guttormsen, Maurice Stewart (Qld) b July 29, 1916 Coorpooroo (Qld) d Aug. 8, 1998 Redcliffe (Qld)

Guy, Richard Henry (NSW) b April 4, 1937 St Leonards (NSW)

Gwynne, Leslie William (NSW) b Jan. 26, 1893 Sydney (NSW) d Oct. 25, 1962 Keith (SAust)

Hack, Alfred Thomas (SAust) b June 12, 1905 Glenelg (SAust) d Feb. 4, 1933 Adelaide (SAust)

Hack, Frederick Theodore (SAust) b Aug. 24, 1877 Aldinga (SAust) d April 10, 1939 Brisbane (Qld)

Hack, Norman Reginald (SAust) b Feb. 25, 1907 Glenelg (SAust) d Oct. 13, 1971 Keith (SAust)

Hackett, James Victor (Qld) b Oct. 8, 1917 Perth (WAust)

Haddin, Bradley James (NSW) b Oct. 23, 1977 Cowra (NSW)

Haddrick, Alfred Page (Vic) b July 14, 1868 Adelaide (SAust) d c. 1935 Adelaide (SAust)

Haddrick, Ronald Norman (SAust) b April 9, 1929 Glenelg (SAust)

* Hadlee, Richard John (Tas) b July 3, 1951 St Albans, Christchurch (New Zealand)

Hagdorn, Kim John (WAust) b April 8, 1955 Subiaco (WAust)

Halbert, John Arno (SAust) b Sept. 5, 1937 Hyde Park (SAust)

Halcombe, Ronald Andrewes (SAust & WAust) b March 19, 1906 Petersburg (SAust) d Aug. 1, 1993 Adelaide (SAust)

Haldane, Harry (SAust) b July 13, 1865 Kent Town (SAust) d Aug. 12, 1951 Ararat (Vic)

Hale, David John (Qld) b Nov. 11, 1941 Ashgrove (Qld)

Hale, Harold (Tas) b March 27, 1867 Perth (WAust) d Aug. 2, 1947 Melbourne (Vic)

Hall, Melmoth (Vic) b April 26, 1811 Horringer, Suffolk (England) d Oct. 4, 1885 Ashfield (NSW)

Hall, Richard (NSW) birth and death details unknown

* Hall, Wesley Winfield (Qld) b Sept. 12, 1937 Glebe Land, Station Hill, St Michael (Barbados)

Hallebone, Jeffrey (Vic) b Aug. 3, 1929 East Coburg (Vic)

* Hamence, Ronald Arthur (SAust) b Nov. 25, 1915 Hindmarsh (SAust)

Hamilton, James (Tas) b May 16, 1843 birthplace unknown d July 28, 1881 Launceston (Tas)

Hamilton, Thomas Ferrier (Vic) b c. 1820 Cathlaw (Scotland) d Aug. 7, 1905 St Kilda (Vic)

Hammelmann, Andrew John (Qld) b May 9, 1966 Corinda (Qld)

Hammersley, William Josiah Sumner (Vic) b Sept. 26, 1828 Ash, Surrey (England) d Nov. 15, 1886 Fitzroy (Vic)

Hammond, Ashley James (SAust) b Sept. 27, 1969 Burnside (SAust)

Hammond, Charles Pitt (Tas) b Aug. 31, 1868 Hobart (Tas) d c. 1955 Hollywood, California (United States of America)

* Hammond, Jeffrey Roy (SAust) b April 19, 1950 North Adelaide (SAust)

* Hampshire, John Harry (Tas) b Feb. 10, 1941 Thurnscoe, Yorkshire (England)

Hand, Walter Charles (NSW) b July 22, 1847 Richmond, Surrey (England) death details unknown

Handrickan, Anthony John (SAust) b Jan. 6, 1959 Largs Bay (SAust)

Hanify, Cecil Page (Qld) b Aug. 1, 1887 Brisbane (Qld) d Oct. 28, 1964 Manly (Qld)

Hanlin, David Walter (NSW) b Dec. 8, 1928 Chester (England) d June 6, 2001 Chester (England)

Hanna, Brian Leslie (WAust) b Oct. 7, 1946 Katanning (WAust)

Hansen, Christopher Desmond Petrie (Qld) b May 20, 1912 Childers (Qld)

Hanson, Frederick James (Tas) b April 7, 1872 Hobart (Tas) d Sept. 24, 1917 Moonah (Tas)

Hanson, Leopole Harry (SAust) b Sept. 27, 1883 Woodville (SAust) d April 27, 1952 Kingscote (SAust)

Hantke, Theodore Charles Muncaster (WAust) b Aug. 1, 1875 Blinman (SAust) d May 22, 1931 South Perth (WAust)

Harburn, Colin Malcolm (WAust) b Sept. 3, 1938 Subiaco (WAust)

Hardcastle, Gilbert William (Qld) b Feb. 26, 1910 Bowen Hills (Qld) d Feb. 14, 2000 Currimundi (Qld)

Hardie, Archibald Edward (WAust) b April 14, 1892 Warrnambool (Vic) d March 31, 1976 Nedlands (WAust)

Hardie, J. (Australians) birth and death details unknown

Hargrave, Christopher George (Tas) b Aug. 31, 1951 Kiverton, Yorkshire (England)

Harms, Christopher Louis (SAust) b April 21, 1956 Albury (NSW)

Harper, Barry James (Tas) b Oct. 30, 1938 Launceston (Tas)

Harper, Charles Walter (WAust) b Jan. 27, 1880 Guildford (WAust) d July 1, 1956 South Perth (WAust)

Harper, Laurence Damien (Vic) b Dec. 10, 1970 Deniliquin (NSW)

Harper, Peter Quinton (Vic) b Dec. 11, 1977 Burwood (Vic)

Harris, Daniel Joseph (SAust) b Dec. 31, 1979 Adelaide (SAust)

Harris, David (SAust) b Dec. 19, 1930 Alberton (SAust)

Harris, David Andrew (Vic) b March 17, 1966 Newtown (Vic)

Harris, Douglas James (WAust) b Dec. 20, 1962 Subiaco (WAust)

Harris, Errol John (Tas) b May 2, 1963 Cairns (Qld)

Harris, Gordon William (SAust) b Dec. 11, 1897 Alberton (SAust) d June 30, 1974 Kensington Park (SAust)

Harris, Henry Vere Poulett (Tas & WAust) b April 22, 1865 Hobart (Tas) d March 7, 1933 Perth (WAust)

Harris, Kim Phillip (SAust) b Jan. 24, 1952 North Adelaide (SAust)

Harris, Ryan James (SAust) b Oct. 11, 1979 Nowra (NSW)

Harrison, Colin William (SAust) b May 10, 1928 West Croydon (SAust)

Harrison, Ernest Weedon (Tas) b July 22, 1874 Campbell Town (Tas) d Nov. 14, 1968 New Norfolk (Tas)

Harrity, Mark Andrew (SAust) b March 9, 1974 Semaphore (SAust)

Harrold, Hubert Walton (WAust) b March 9, 1898 East Perth (WAust) d April 14, 1968 Hollywood (WAust)

* Harry, John (Vic) b Aug. 1, 1857 Ballarat (Vic) d Oct. 27, 1919 Surrey Hills (Vic)

Harry, Rex Alexander (Vic) b Oct. 19, 1936 Melbourne (Vic)

Hart, Harold William (Vic) b Jan. 4, 1889 Fitzroy South (Vic) d Jan. 2, 1953 Yarraville (Vic)

Hart, Trevor Herbert (Vic) b Nov. 18, 1935 Morwell (Vic)

Harten, James Thomas (Qld) b Nov. 11, 1924 Brisbane (Qld) d Sept. 11, 2001 Everton Hills (Qld)

* Hartigan, Michael Joseph (NSW & Qld) b Dec. 12, 1879 Chatswood (NSW) d June 7, 1958 Brisbane (Qld)

Hartigan, Thomas Joseph (NSW) b Dec. 8, 1877 Chatswood (NSW) d May 2, 1963 Mosman (NSW)

* Hartkopf, Albert Ernest Victor (Vic) b Dec. 28, 1889 South Fitzroy (Vic) d May 20, 1968 Kew (Vic)

Harvey, Clarence Edgar (Vic & Qld) b March 17, 1921 Newcastle (NSW)

Harvey, Ernest (WAust) b Dec. 14, 1880 Redfern (NSW) d Oct. 19, 1923 Perth (WAust)

Harvey, George Graham (NSW) b May 7, 1885 Mudgee (NSW) death details unknown

Harvey, Ian Joseph (Vic) b April 10, 1972 Wonthaggi (Vic)

Harvey, Kade Murray (WAust) b Oct. 7, 1975 Subiaco (WAust)

* Harvey, Mervyn Roye (Vic) b April 29, 1918 Broken Hill (NSW) d March 18, 1995 Footscray (Vic)

Harvey, Raymond (Vic) b Jan. 3, 1926 Sydney (NSW)

* Harvey, Robert Neil (Vic & NSW) b Oct. 8, 1928 Fitzroy (Vic)

Harvey, Ronald Mason (NSW) b Oct. 26, 1933 Newcastle (NSW)

* Hassett, Arthur Lindsay (Vic) b Aug. 28, 1913 Geelong (Vic) d June 16, 1993 Batehaven (NSW)

Hassett, Richard Joseph (Vic) b Sept. 7, 1909 Geelong (Vic)

Hastings, Edward Percival (Vic) b c. 1849 (England) d May 31, 1905 Brighton East (Vic)

Hastings, Thomas James (Vic) b Jan. 16, 1865 Melbourne (Vic) d June 14, 1938 North Brighton (Vic)

Hatton, Mark Aaron (Tas) b Jan. 24, 1974 Waverley (NSW)

Hauritz, Nathan Michael (Qld) b Oct. 18, 1981 Wondai (Qld)

* Hawke, Neil James Napier (WAust, SAust & Tas) b June 27, 1939 Cheltenham (SAust) d Dec. 25, 2000 Adelaide (SAust)

Hawkins, George William (Vic) b Dec. 7, 1908 Brunswick (Vic) d July 20, 1979 Chiltern (Vic)

Hawson, Edgar Stanley (Tas) b July 25, 1878 Hobart (Tas) d Sept. 29, 1946 Hobart (Tas)

Hawson, Reginald James (Tas) b Sept. 2, 1880 Hobart (Tas) d Feb. 20, 1928 Hobart (Tas)

Hay, Henry (SAust) b March 30, 1874 Adelaide (SAust) d May 16, 1960 Adelaide (SAust)

* Hayden, Matthew Lawrence (Qld) b Oct. 29, 1971 Kingaroy (Qld)

Hayes, William Bede (Qld) b Oct. 16, 1883 Surry Hills (NSW) d Nov. 5, 1926 Corinda (Qld)

Haymes, Frederick George (Tas) b April 5, 1849 Launceston (Tas) d March 12, 1928 Lakes Entrance (Vic)

Hayne, Greg John (NSW) b Oct. 2, 1971 Moree (NSW)

Haysman, Michael Donald (SAust) b April 22, 1961 North Adelaide (SAust)

Hayward, Charles Waterfield (SAust) b June 6, 1867 Norwood (SAust) d Feb. 2, 1934 North Adelaide (SAust)

Haywood, Martin Thomas (NSW) b Oct. 7, 1969 Tamworth (NSW)

* Hazlitt, Gervys Rignold (Vic & NSW) b Sept. 4, 1888 Enfield (NSW) d Oct. 30, 1915 Parramatta (NSW)

Head, Lindsay Hudson (SAust) b Sept. 16, 1935 North Adelaide (SAust)

Headlam, Eustace Slade (Tas) b May 20, 1892 Bothwell (Tas) d May 25, 1958 Launceston (Tas)

Headlam, Felix Emerson (Tas) b June 20, 1897 Bothwell (Tas) d Oct. 5, 1965 Bowral (NSW)

Heairfield, Herbert Venters (SAust) b Feb. 28, 1907 Adelaide (SAust)

Healy, Edwin Francis (Vic) b Sept. 26, 1909 Hawthorn (Vic) d June 14, 1995 Camberwell (Vic)

Healy, Eric Nicholas (WAust) b Nov. 5, 1888 Elizabeth Bay (NSW) d Oct. 9, 1954 Cottesloe (WAust)

Healy, Gerald Edward James (Vic) b March 26, 1885 Prahran (Vic) d July 12, 1946 Armadale (Vic)

* Healy, Ian Andrew (Qld) b April 30, 1964 Spring Hill (Qld)

Healy, John Joseph (Vic) b June 23, 1851 Burra (SAust) d May 17, 1916 East Melbourne (Vic)

Healy, Kenneth James (Qld) b Oct. 15, 1967 South Brisbane (Qld)

Heath, Henry Francis Trafford (SAust) b Dec. 19, 1885 Kadina (SAust) d July 9, 1967 Edinburgh (Scotland)

Heath, Jamie Matthew (NSW) b April 25, 1977 Belmont (NSW)

Heather, Edward Drinkall (Vic) b Oct. 6, 1848 Marylebone, London (England) d July 10, 1935 South Melbourne (Vic)

Heather, Percival Jackson (Vic) b Oct. 6, 1882 Emerald Hill (Vic) d June 29, 1956 Melbourne (Vic)

Hefferan, Francis Urban (Qld) b May 25, 1901 Bowen (Qld) d Sept. 21, 1974 Tweed Heads (NSW)

Heffernan, Ray Leslie (Tas) b Oct. 13, 1935 Hobart (Tas)

Heindrichs, Adolphos Heinrich Julius Carl (WAust) b April 28, 1883 (Germany) d June 24, 1967 Adelaide (SAust)

Henderson, Frank (Vic) b June 1, 1908 Wickham (NSW) d Dec. 6, 1954 Heidelberg (Vic)

Hendricks, Michael (NSW & SAust) b Dec. 12, 1942 Corrimal (NSW)

Hendrie, Charles Richard (Vic) b July 5, 1886 Richmond (Vic) death details unknown

* Hendry, Hunter Scott Thomas Laurie (NSW & Vic) b May 24, 1895 Woollahra (NSW) d Dec. 16, 1988 Rose Bay (NSW)

Hennah, Walter Henry (WAust) b March 16, 1880 Ballarat (Vic) d Aug. 13, 1946 Perth (WAust)

Henri, Harry James Tepapa (Tas) b July 27, 1865 Tauranga (New Zealand) d Feb. 5, 1947 Lindisfarne (Tas)

Henry, Albert (Qld) b c. 1880 Boonah (Qld) d March 13, 1909 Yarrabah (Qld)

Henry, Donald McKenzie (SAust) b June 24, 1885 Parkside (SAust) d July 31, 1973 Felixstow (SAust)

Henschell, Allan Brett (Qld) b June 6, 1961 Dalby (Qld)

Henty, Philip Guy (Tas) b Feb. 4, 1883 Pakenham (Vic) d Oct. 21, 1949 Hobart (Tas)

Henty, William (Tas) b Sept. 23, 1808 West Tarring, Sussex (England) d July 11, 1881 Hove, Sussex (England)

Hepburn, Thomas Robert (Vic) b Dec. 20, 1839 Collingwood (Vic) d April 22, 1921 St Kilda (Vic)

Herbert, Henry James (WAust) b April 24, 1895 Fremantle (WAust) d Nov. 21, 1957 Claremont (WAust)

Herbert, Morgan Uriah (WAust) b Aug. 4, 1918 Albany (WAust) d June 15, 2000 Duncraig (WAust)

Herbert, Peter Jeffrey (SAust) b Jan. 8, 1947 Adelaide (SAust)

Herman, Richard John (Vic) b July 31, 1967 Melbourne (Vic)

Herring, Llewellyn Lloyd (WAust) b April 3, 1871 Clunes (Vic) d Aug. 5, 1922 Fremantle (WAust)

Herring, Robert Wolseley (Vic) b June 8, 1898 Maryborough (Vic) d Oct. 8, 1964 Melbourne (Vic)

Hervey, Matthew (Vic) b Jan. 27, 1820 Glasgow, Lanarkshire (Scotland) d Dec. 1, 1874 Turnbull Plains (Vic)

Herzberg, Steven (WAust & Tas) b May 25, 1967 Carshalton, Surrey (England)

Hetherington, Henry Francisco (Vic) b Sept. 3, 1874 West Melbourne (Vic) d July 11, 1950 Malvern (Vic)

Hewer, William Albert (SAust) b May 7, 1877 Goodwood (SAust) d June 2, 1948 Wayville (SAust)

Hewett, Ian Stephen Louis (Vic) b Jan. 24, 1976 East Melbourne (Vic)

Hewitt, Albert Hedley Vickers (Qld) b Jan. 21, 1866 Nowra (NSW) d July 15, 1947 death place unknown

Hewitt, Richard Child (NSW) b Feb. 13, 1844 Beverley, Yorkshire (England) d c. 1920 Granville (NSW)

Hewson, Robert Henry (WAust) b Aug. 4, 1893 Carlton (Vic) d Oct. 21, 1972 Melbourne (Vic)

* Hibbert, Paul Anthony (Vic) b July 23, 1952 Brunswick (Vic)

* Hick, Graeme Ashley (Qld) b May 23, 1966 Salisbury (Rhodesia)

Hickey, Denis Jon (Vic & SAust) b Dec. 31, 1964 Mooroopna (Vic)

Hickson, Robert Newburgh (NSW) b May 2, 1884 Newcastle (NSW) d June 21, 1963 Armidale (NSW)

Hiddleston, Hugh Charles Stewart (NSW) b c. 1855 full birth details unknown d May 14, 1934 Coolgardie (WAust)

Hide, Jesse Bollard (SAust) b March 12, 1857 Eastbourne, Sussex (England) d March 19, 1924 Edinburgh (Scotland)

Hiern, Barry Neil (SAust) b Aug. 8, 1951 North Adelaide (SAust)

Hiern, Ross Noel (SAust) b Aug. 2, 1922 Parkside (SAust) d Aug. 21, 1999 Morphettville (SAust)

Higgins, Benjamin Hugh (SAust) b March 8, 1972 Rose Park (SAust)

Higgins, Henry James Roy (Qld) b Jan. 27, 1900 Rosalie (Qld) d Feb. 24, 1990 Chermside (Qld)

Higgins, James (Qld) b Nov. 14, 1874 Ormiston (Qld) d Nov. 24, 1957 Sandgate (Qld)

* Higgs, James Donald (Vic) b July 11, 1950 Kyabram (Vic)

Higgs, Mark Anthony (NSW) b June 30, 1976 Queanbeyan (NSW)

* Hilditch, Andrew Mark Jefferson (NSW & SAust) b May 20, 1956 North Adelaide (SAust)

Hill, Arthur (SAust) b May 28, 1871 Adelaide (SAust) d June 22, 1936 Glenelg (SAust)

* Hill, Clement (SAust) b March 18, 1877 Hindmarsh (SAust) d Sept. 5, 1945 Parkville (Vic)

Hill, Clement John (NSW) b July 2, 1904 Beryl (NSW) d May 21, 1988 Belmont (NSW)

Hill, Henry John (SAust) b July 7, 1878 Adelaide (SAust) d Oct. 30, 1906 Kensington Park (SAust)

* Hill, John Charles (Vic) b June 25, 1923 Murrumbeena (Vic) d Aug. 11, 1974 Caulfield (Vic)

Hill, John Gerard (Qld) b Nov. 11, 1956 Waratah (NSW)

Hill, Kenneth Michael (NSW) b Jan. 26, 1945 Merewether (NSW)

Hill, Leon Trevor (SAust & Qld) b Feb. 28, 1936 West Croydon (SAust)

Hill, Leslie Roy (SAust) b April 27, 1884 Adelaide (SAust) d Dec. 15, 1952 North Adelaide (SAust)

Hill, Mark Anthony (Tas) b July 27, 1964 Perth (WAust)

Hill, Percy (SAust) b July 4, 1868 Kent Town (SAust) d July 24, 1950 Adelaide (SAust)

Hill, Peter Distin (SAust) b Jan. 28, 1923 North Adelaide (SAust)

Hill, Roland James (SAust) b Oct. 18, 1868 Parkside (SAust) d Jan. 10, 1929 Glenelg (SAust)

Hill, Stanley (SAust & NSW) b Aug. 22, 1885 Adelaide (SAust) d May 10, 1970 Englefield Green, Surrey (England)

Hill, Wayne Douglas (WAust) b Dec. 5, 1953 Subiaco (WAust)

Hill-Smith, Wyndham (WAust) b Feb. 16, 1909 Angaston (SAust) d Oct. 25, 1990 Angaston (SAust)

Hilliard, Henry (NSW) b Nov. 7, 1826 Sydney (NSW) d March 19, 1914 Willoughby (NSW)

Hills, Dene Fleetwood (Tas) b Aug. 27, 1970 Wynyard (Tas)

Hird, Sydney Francis (NSW) b Jan. 7, 1910 Balmain (NSW) d Dec. 20, 1980 Bloemfontein (South Africa)

Hird, William (Tas) b Sept. 23, 1921 Stanley, Durham (England)

Hiscock, Ernest John (SAust) b April 9, 1868 Penrice (SAust) d Dec. 16, 1895 Alberton (SAust)

Hitchcock, Oswould Charles (Qld) b Sept. 9, 1859 Greenhill, Shoalhaven (NSW) d July 13, 1948 Brisbane (Qld)

Hitchcock, Robert Alan (SAust) b May 14, 1938 North Adelaide (SAust)

* Hoare, Desmond Edward (WAust) b Oct. 19, 1934 Perth (WAust)

Hoare, William (Qld) b Oct. 23, 1868 Brisbane (Qld) d Dec. 16, 1954 Salt Lake City, Utah (USA)

Hodge, Bradley John (Vic) b Dec. 29, 1974 Sandringham (Vic)

Hodge, Malcolm Gordon Fergurson (SAust) b Aug. 28, 1934 Adelaide (SAust)

* Hodges, John Robart (Vic) b Aug. 11, 1855 Knightsbridge (London) death details unknown

Hodgetts, Bruce Frederick (Tas) b Jan. 25, 1947 Burnie (Tas)

Hodgkinson, John Ernest (NSW) b Feb. 7, 1873 Surry Hills (NSW) d Nov. 19, 1939 Burwood (NSW)

Hodgson, Robert William (Tas) b Feb. 22, 1973 Launceston (Tas)

* Hogan, Tom George (WAust) b Sept. 23, 1956 Merredin (WAust)

Hogg, Geoffrey Charles Huxtable (NSW) b Sept. 28, 1909 Goulburn (NSW) d Aug. 14, 1959 Coorparoo (Qld)

* Hogg, George Bradley (WAust) b Feb. 6, 1971 Narrogin (WAust)

Hogg, James Edgar Phipps (NSW & Qld) b Oct. 16, 1906 Goulburn (NSW) d Dec. 2, 1975 West Ryde (NSW)

* Hogg, Rodney Malcolm (SAust & Vic) b March 5, 1951 Richmond (Vic)

Hogg, Thomas (Combined XIII) b March 12, 1845 Hobart (Tas) d July 13, 1890 Trevallyn (Tas)

Hogue, Thomas Herbert (NSW & WAust) b Oct. 5, 1877 Wickham (NSW) d May 6, 1956 Nedlands (WAust)

Hogue, Wallace White (WAust) b Dec. 9, 1879 Wickham (NSW) d June 1, 1946 Cook's Hill (NSW)

* Hohns, Trevor Victor (Qld) b Jan. 23, 1954 Nundah (Qld)

* Holding, Michael Anthony (Tas) b Feb. 16, 1954 Half Way Tree, Kingston (Jamaica)

Holdsworth, Wayne John (NSW) b Oct. 5, 1968 Paddington (NSW)

* Hole, Graeme Blake (NSW & SAust) b Jan. 6, 1931 Concord West (NSW) d Feb. 14, 1990 Kensington Gardens (SAust)

* Holland, Robert George (NSW) b Oct. 19, 1946 Camperdown (NSW)

Holman, Raymond Sidney (SAust) b Sept. 17, 1919 Largs Bay (SAust) d Sept. 19, 1989 Woodville South (SAust)

Holten, Charles Valentine (Vic) b Sept. 15, 1927 Brighton (Vic)

Holton, Leslie George (SAust) b March 13, 1903 Carlton (Vic) d Feb. 1, 1956 Hawthorn (Vic)

Holyman, Josef Michael (Tas) b June 10, 1970 Launceston (Tas)

Homburg, Robert Otto (SAust) b Jan. 31, 1876 Norwood (SAust) d Oct. 21, 1948 Medindie (SAust)

Hone, Brian William (SAust) b July 1, 1907 Semaphore (SAust) d May 28, 1978 Paris (France)

Hone, Garton Maxwell (SAust) b Feb. 21, 1901 Morphett Vale (SAust) d May 28, 1991 Myrtle Bank (SAust)

Honeybone, George Alfred (Vic) b April 2, 1875 London (England) d Nov. 1, 1956 Ashburton (Vic)

Honour, Victor Gerald (Qld) b Oct. 25, 1910 Bierton, Buckinghamshire (England) d Jan. 3, 2001 Brookfield (Qld)

Hook, Benjamin James (SAust) b March 5, 1973 Kingswood (SAust)

Hooker, John Edward Halford (NSW) b March 6, 1898 Summer Hill (NSW) d Feb. 12, 1982 Winmalee (NSW)

* Hookes, David William (SAust) b May 3, 1955 Mile End (SAust)

Hookey, Scott Gregory (NSW & Tas) b Feb. 10, 1967 Sydney (NSW)

Hooper, Kerry (Tas) b June 9, 1942 Launceston (Tas)

Hooper, Victor Leonard (Tas) b April 23, 1905 Mt Stuart (Tas) d Sept. 3, 1990 New Town (Tas)

Hope, Adam (Vic) b c. 1834 (England) d Oct. 9, 1916 East Melbourne (Vic)

Hopes, James Redfern (Qld) b Oct. 24, 1978 Townsville (Qld)

* Hopkins, Albert John Young (NSW) b May 3, 1874 Young (NSW) d April 25, 1931 North Sydney (NSW)

Hopkins, Isaac (Vic) b Nov. 9, 1870 Collingwood (Vic) d Oct. 25, 1913 Richmond (Vic)

Hopkinson, Samuel Good (Vic) b Oct. 1, 1825 Thorne, Yorkshire (England) d June 26, 1887 South Melbourne (Vic)

Horan, James Francis (Vic) b June 8, 1880 Fitzroy (Vic) d Nov. 1, 1945 Malvern (Vic)

Horan, Thomas Ignatius Bernard (Vic) b April 7, 1886 Fitzroy (Vic) d May 26, 1952 East Camberwell (Vic)

* Horan, Thomas Patrick (Vic) b March 8, 1854 Midleton, County Cork (Ireland) d April 16, 1916 Malvern (Vic)

* Hordern, Herbert Vivian (NSW) b Feb. 10, 1883 North Sydney (NSW) d June 17, 1938 Darlinghurst (NSW)

Horley, John Rasalle (SAust) b Jan. 23, 1936 Medindie (SAust)

* Hornibrook, Percival Mitchell (Qld) b July 27, 1899 Obi Obi (Qld) d Aug. 25, 1976 Spring Hill (Qld)

Horrocks, William John (WAust) b June 18, 1905 Warrington, Lancashire (England) d Nov. 15, 1985 Parkdale (Vic)

Horsell, Jack Aymat James (SAust) b July 12, 1914 Stepney (SAust) d April 20, 1985 Sydney (NSW)

Horsfield, Gordon Cameron (NSW) b March 24, 1913 Balmain (NSW) d Aug. 25, 1982 Mosman (NSW)

Horsley, Daniel, Anthony (NSW) b July 20, 1972 Sydney (NSW)

Horsnell, Kenneth George (SAust) b Sept. 3, 1933 Joslin (SAust)

Horton, Arnell Stanley (Tas) b Sept. 21, 1892 Burnie (Tas) d Sept. 15, 1987 Newstead (Tas)

Hosie, Robert (Vic) b Sept. 8, 1858 Collingwood (Vic) d Sept. 29, 1932 Richmond (Vic)

Hosking, Peter Mowat (Vic) b Sept. 30, 1932 Fairfield (Vic)

Hoskings, Arthur G. W. (WAust) b c. 1872 d Sept. 2, 1919 Dunella, New Jersey (United States of America)

Hotchin, Mortimer Douglas (Vic) b May 20, 1889 Prahran (Vic) d June 21, 1958 East Melbourne (Vic)

Hotham, Augustus Thomas (Vic) b c. 1817 (christened Jan. 25) Denningston, Suffolk (England) d Dec. 24, 1896 Tunbridge Wells, Kent (England)

Hourn, David William (NSW) b Sept. 9, 1949 Bondi (NSW)

House, Graham Warwick Charles (WAust & SAust) b Sept. 4, 1950 Busselton (WAust)

Houston, Richard Shinnock (Vic) b June 30, 1863 Brighton (Vic) d Nov. 27, 1921 Williamstown (Vic)

Howard, Craig (Vic) b April 8, 1974 Lilydale (Vic)

Howard, Harry Cecil (WAust) b June 30, 1885 Adelaide (SAust) d Sept. 18, 1960 Perth (WAust)

Howard, Leonard Easther (SAust) b April 18, 1886 Adelaide (SAust) d Aug. 14, 1945 Prospect (SAust)

Howard, Roy (Vic) b Nov. 15, 1922 Terang (Vic)

Howard, Stephen John (Tas) b Feb. 7, 1949 Launceston (Tas)

Howard, Thomas Harris (NSW) b May 2, 1877 Sydney (NSW) d Oct. 6, 1965 Randwick (NSW)

Howe, John Sidney (Tas) b Dec. 27, 1868 Kotree (India) d July 29, 1939 Neutral Bay (NSW)

Howell, George (NSW) b June 9, 1822 Sydney (NSW) d Nov. 18, 1890 Sydney (NSW)

Howell, William Hunter (NSW) b Jan. 12, 1902 Penrith (NSW) d Jan. 23, 1987 Penrith (NSW)

* Howell, William Peter (NSW) b Dec. 29, 1869 Penrith (NSW) d July 14, 1940 Castlereagh (NSW)

Howlett, John Thomas (Vic) b April 8, 1868 North Melbourne (Vic) d June 15, 1931 East Melbourne (Vic)

Howson, Herbert (Vic) b Aug. 11, 1872 Newstead (Vic) d May 8, 1948 Murrumbeena (Vic)

Hubbard, Edward Francis (Qld) b June 27, 1906 Brisbane (Qld) d Oct. 1, 1969 Herston (Qld)

Hubble, James Merrick (WAust) b Aug. 12, 1942 Beaconsfield (WAust)

Huddleston, John (Vic) b Nov. 25, 1837 Nottingham, Nottinghamshire (England) d c. 1904 Brunswick (Vic)

Hudson, Graeme Charles (Tas) b June 16, 1930 Wynyard (Tas) d Sept. 23, 1974 Launceston (Tas)

Hudson, John Lambert (Tas) b July 23, 1882 Launceston (Tas) d March 16, 1961 Hobart (Tas)

Hughes, David Paul (Tas) b April 13, 1947 Newton-le-Willows, Lancashire (England)

Hughes, Glenn Arthur (Tas) b Nov. 23, 1959 Goomalling (WAust)

Hughes, Graeme Christopher (NSW) b Dec. 6, 1955 Stanmore (NSW)

* Hughes, Kimberley John (WAust) b Jan. 26, 1954 Margaret River (WAust)

* Hughes, Mervyn Gregory (Vic) b Nov. 23, 1961 Euroa (Vic)

Hughes, Walter Cecil (WAust) b Aug. 13, 1882 Adelaide (SAust) d Aug. 16, 1917 Perth (WAust)

Hughson, Desmond George (Qld) b May 27, 1941 Herston (Qld)

Hugo, Victor (SAust) b Nov. 25, 1877 Adelaide (SAust) d April 8, 1930 Malvern (SAust)

Hume, Andrew Ernest (NSW) b Feb. 5, 1869 Redfern (NSW) d June 22, 1912 London (England)

Humphreys, Anthony John Rolph (Tas) b June 9, 1971 Launceston (Tas)

Humphreys, John (NSW) birth and death details unknown

Hunt, Horace Charles (Vic) b July 15, 1907 Stawell (Vic) d Oct. 15, 1984 Melbourne (Vic)

* Hunt, William Alfred (NSW) b Aug. 26, 1908 Balmain (NSW) d Dec. 30, 1983 Balmain (NSW)

Huntington, Ian Ross (Vic) b Oct. 18, 1931 Coburg (Vic)

Hurburgh, Clifton Maurice (Tas) b Jan. 15, 1917 Hobart (Tas)

Hurn, Brian Morgan (SAust) b March 4, 1939 Angaston (SAust)

* Hurst, Alan George (Vic) b July 15, 1950 Altona (Vic)

* Hurwood, Alexander (Qld) b June 17, 1902 Kangaroo Point (Qld) d Sept. 26, 1982 Coffs Harbour (NSW)

Hussey, Michael Edward Killeen (WAust) b May 27, 1975 Mt Lawley (WAust)

Hussey, Percival Leitch (WAust) b June 23, 1869 Perth (WAust) d May 13, 1944 Adelaide (SAust)

Hutcheon, Ernest Henry (Qld) b June 17, 1889 Toowoomba (Qld) d June 9, 1937 Brisbane (Qld)

Hutcheon, John Silvester (Qld) b April 5, 1882 Warwick (Qld) d June 18, 1957 Albion Heights (Qld)

Hutchison, Paul James (SAust & Tas) b Feb. 17, 1968 Glen Innes (NSW)

Hutton, Ernest Hamilton (Vic & Qld) b March 29, 1867 Mt Rouse (Vic) d July 12, 1929 Ascot (Qld)

Hutton, Henry George (SAust) b Aug. 26, 1878 Masterton (New Zealand) d Aug. 13, 1968 Norwood (SAust)

Hutton, Maurice Percy (SAust) b March 21, 1903 Parkside (SAust) d Feb. 20, 1940 Mitcham (SAust)

Hutton, Mervyn Douglas (SAust) b Aug. 24, 1911 Port Augusta (SAust) d Sept. 28, 1988 Melbourne (Vic)

Hutton, Norman Harvey (SAust) b Aug. 10, 1911 Unley (SAust) d Aug. 27, 1965 Fullarton (SAust)

Hutton, William Frederick Percy (SAust) b Oct. 2, 1876 Mintaro (SAust) d Oct. 1, 1951 Millswood (SAust)

Hyatt, Roland Shane (Tas) b Dec. 30, 1961 Hobart (Tas)

Hyde, Phillip Andrew (Vic) b Oct. 22, 1958 Melbourne (Vic)

Hyett, Francis William (Vic) b Feb. 9, 1882 Bolwarra (Vic) d April 25, 1919 Fitzroy (Vic)

Hyland, Byron John (Tas) b Jan. 14, 1930 New Norfolk (Tas)

Hynes, Lincoln Carruthers (NSW) b April 12, 1912 Balmain (NSW) d Aug. 7, 1977 Killara (NSW)

Hyslop, Hector Henry (Australians) b Dec. 13, 1840 Southampton, Hampshire (England) d Sept. 11, 1920 Cosham, Hampshire (England)

* Ibadulla, Khalid (Tas) b Dec. 20, 1935 Lahore (Pakistan)

Iceton, Thomas Henry (NSW) b Oct. 12, 1849 Sydney (NSW) d May 19, 1908 Ashfield (NSW)

Illingworth, Edward Philip (Vic) b Nov. 27, 1938 Fairfield (Vic)

Illman, Brian Kevin (SAust) b Oct. 23, 1937 Unley Park (SAust)

* Imran Khan (NSW) b Nov. 25, 1952 Lahore (Pakistan)

Ingleton, Walter George (Vic) b Feb. 16, 1867 Collingwood (Vic) d Feb. 4, 1923 East Melbourne (Vic)

Inkster, Gordon Bradford (SAust) b June 30, 1893 Portland Estate (SAust) d March 22, 1957 Darlinghurst (NSW)

Inness, Mathew William Hunter (Vic) b Jan. 13, 1978 East Melbourne (Vic)

Inverarity, Mervyn (WAust) b Oct. 25, 1907 Claremont (WAust) d March 17, 1979 Cottesloe (WAust)

* Inverarity, Robert John (WAust & SAust) b Jan. 31, 1944 Subiaco (WAust)

Inwood, Bradley Phillip (Qld) b July 23, 1963 Gladstone (Qld)

* Iredale, Francis Adams (NSW) b June 19, 1867 Surry Hills (NSW) d April 15, 1926 Crows Nest (NSW)

Ireland, Gary John (WAust) b Oct. 3, 1961 Collie (WAust)

* Ironmonger, Herbert (Qld & Vic) b April 7, 1882 Pine Mountain (Qld) d June 1, 1971 St Kilda (Vic)

Irvine, John Taylor (WAust) b April 13, 1944 Subiaco (WAust)

* Iverson, John Brian (Vic) b July 27, 1915 Melbourne (Vic) d Oct. 23, 1973 Brighton (Vic)

Ives, William Francis (NSW) b Nov. 14, 1896 Glebe (NSW) d March 23, 1975 Newport Beach (NSW)

Ivory, Wilfred Charles (Rest of Australia) b Sept. 12, 1888 South Yarra (Vic) d Oct. 13, 1975 North Brighton (Vic)

Jack, Keith Mayall (Qld) b April 25, 1927 Tambo (Qld) d Nov. 22, 1982 Buderim (Qld)

Jackman, Darrell (Tas) b May 31, 1921 Hobart (Tas) d April 5, 1991 Cheltenham (Vic)

* Jackson, Archibald (NSW) b Sept. 5, 1909 Rutherglen, Lanarkshire (Scotland) d Feb. 16, 1933 Clayfield (Qld)

Jackson, Arthur Enderby (WAust) b Jan. 6, 1872 Kapunda (SAust) d June 29, 1935 Cottesloe (WAust)

Jackson, Paul William (Vic & Qld) b Nov. 1, 1961 East Melbourne (Vic)

Jackson, Victor Edward (NSW) b Oct. 25, 1916 Woollahra (NSW) d Jan. 30, 1965 Manildra (NSW)

Jacobson, Alan Melville (Tas) b Nov. 12, 1942 Sydney (NSW)

Jacomb, John Newton (Vic) b c. 1843 Melbourne (Vic) d Nov. 5, 1891 Walhalla (Vic)

Jakins, James Albert (Tas) b Oct. 1, 1886 Hawthorn (Vic) d Dec. 12, 1948 Wivenhoe (Tas)

James, Alec Pearce (SAust) b May 22, 1889 Neath, Glamorgan (Wales) d Aug. 14, 1961 Torquay, Devon (England)

James, Eric Lisle (Tas) b Oct. 21, 1881 Low Head (Tas) d c. 1948 Malvern (Vic)

James, Eric Pearse (WAust) b Feb. 27, 1923 Albany (WAust) d March 28, 1999 Albany (WAust)

James, Gerald Thomas Henry (Tas) b March 22, 1908 New Norfolk (Tas) d Dec. 24, 1967 Hobart (Tas)

James, Ronald Victor (NSW & SAust) b May 23, 1920 Paddington (NSW) d April 28, 1983 Auburn (NSW)

James, Sidney Victor Austin (Tas) b Oct. 26, 1895 Adelaide (SAust) d Aug. 3, 1966 Canterbury (Vic)

Jamieson, Dudley Garfield (SAust) b July 4, 1912 Redruth (SAust) d Jan. 14, 1979 Burnside (SAust)

Jamieson, Walter Angus Bethune (Tas) b 1828 birth day and month unknown Plenty (Tas) d Dec. 28, 1881 Plenty (Tas)

Jansan, Ernest William (NSW) b Aug. 26, 1874 Gulgong (NSW) d May 31, 1945 Leichhardt (NSW)

Jaques, Philip Anthony (NSW) b May 3, 1979 Wollongong (NSW)

* Jarman, Barrington Noel (SAust) b Feb. 17, 1936 Hindmarsh (SAust)

Jarvis, Alfred (SAust) b Feb. 15, 1868 Hindmarsh (SAust) d Aug. 12, 1938 Semaphore (SAust)

* Jarvis, Arthur Harwood (SAust) b Oct. 19, 1860 Hindmarsh (SAust) d Nov. 15, 1933 Hindmarsh (SAust)

Jarvis, Carlisle Melrose Byron (WAust) b Dec. 10, 1906 East Fremantle (WAust) d Nov. 6, 1979 Mt Lawley (WAust)

Jarvis, Harwood Samuel Coombe (SAust) b Aug. 30, 1884 Brompton (SAust) d Oct. 10, 1936 Port Pirie (SAust)

Jeffrey, Clifton Linley (Tas) b Jan. 10, 1913 Hobart (Tas) d Feb. 11, 1987 Launceston (Tas)

Jeffrey, Robert Frederick (NSW & Tas) b Sept. 19, 1953 Goulburn (NSW)

Jeffreys, Arthur Frederick (NSW) b April 7, 1848 London (England) d Feb. 4, 1906 Lasham, Hampshire (England)

Jeffreys, John Alan (WAust) b April 17, 1913 Fremantle (WAust) d Nov. 3, 1943 Shipham, Somerset (England)

Jeffreys, Keith Stanley (WAust) b Jan. 18, 1921 Bridgetown (WAust) d May 16, 2000 Mandurah (WAust)

Jelich, Neville (Qld & Tas) b March 11, 1962 Orasje, near Belgrade (Yugoslavia)

* Jenner, Terrence James (WAust & SAust) b Sept. 8, 1944 Mt Lawley (WAust)

* Jennings, Claude Burrows (SAust & Qld) b June 5, 1884 East St Kilda (Vic) d June 20, 1950 Adelaide (SAust)

Jennings, Henry John (Vic) b April 9, 1849 Launceston (Tas) d June 6, 1925 St Kilda (Vic)

Jewell, Nicholas (Vic) b Aug. 27, 1977 East Melbourne (Vic)

Jinks, Allan (Vic) b Dec. 29, 1913 Carlton North (Vic) d Nov. 7, 1997 Melbourne (Vic)

Jinks, Frederick (Vic) b May 6, 1909 Eaglehawk (Vic) d Aug. 16, 1996 Melbourne (Vic)

John, Bruce Duncanson (Tas) b July 20, 1937 Launceston (Tas)

Johns, Alfred Edward (Vic) b Jan. 22, 1868 Hawthorn (Vic) d Feb. 13, 1934 Melbourne (Vic)

Johnson, Benjamin Andrew (SAust) b Aug. 1, 1973 Naracoorte (SAust)

Johnson, Eric Alfred (SAust) b July 11, 1902 North Norwood (SAust) d Jan. 10, 1976 Adelaide (SAust)

Johnson, Francis Barry (NSW) b May 21, 1880 birthplace unknown d May 28, 1951 Longueville (NSW)

* Johnson, Ian William Geddes (Vic) b Dec. 8, 1917 Hotham West (Vic) d Oct. 9, 1998 Malvern (Vic)

Johnson, James William (Vic) b Sept. 22, 1884 Footscray (Vic) d Aug. 14, 1941 Middle Park (Vic)

* Johnson, Leonard Joseph (Qld) b March 18, 1919 Ipswich (Qld) d April 20, 1977 Silkstone (Qld)

Johnson, Mitchell Guy (Qld) b Nov. 2, 1981 Townsville (Qld)

Johnston, Aubrey Edmund (NSW) b Sept. 7, 1882 Canterbury (NSW) d June 16, 1960 Manly (NSW)

Johnston, Clive William (NSW) b Aug. 4, 1925 Petersham (NSW) d May 11, 1991 Petersham (NSW)

Johnston, David Alexander Hughes (NSW) b July 10, 1955 Maitland (NSW)

Johnston, David Allan (SAust) b Dec. 4, 1954 Melbourne (Vic)

Johnston, David Trent (NSW) b April 29, 1974 Wollongong (NSW)

Johnston, Frederick Bourke (NSW) b Sept. 10, 1915 Sydney (NSW) d Sept. 6, 1977 Hillsdale (NSW)

* Johnston, William Arras (Vic) b Feb. 26, 1922 Beeac (Vic)

Johnstone, Richard Gordon (Vic) b Feb. 9, 1885 Malvern (Vic) d Nov. 9, 1961 Geelong (Vic)

Jolly, Harvey Bruce (SAust) b Aug. 1, 1960 Naracoorte (SAust)

Jones, Alan (WAust) b Nov. 4, 1938 Velindre, Glamorgan (Wales)

Jones, Alan Robert (Qld) b June 11, 1948 Greenslopes (Qld)

Jones, Arthur Harold (Qld) b Dec. 17, 1874 Brisbane (Qld) d Dec. 2, 1917 Salisbury Plain, Wiltshire (England)

Jones, Charles Frederick (Vic) b Feb. 9, 1870 Williamstown (Vic) d March 25, 1957 Williamstown (Vic)

* Jones, Dean Mervyn (Vic) b March 24, 1961 Coburg (Vic)

* Jones, Ernest (SAust & WAust) b Sept. 30, 1869 East Auburn (SAust) d Nov. 23, 1943 Norwood (SAust)

Jones, John Raymond (WAust) b May 10, 1899 Clunes (Vic) d March 14, 1991 Hamilton Hill (WAust)

Jones, Neil Richard (NSW) b July 12, 1966 Stourport-on-Severn, Worcestershire (England)

Jones, Ronald Andrew (NSW) b March 28, 1964 Dubbo (NSW)

* Jones, Samuel Percy (NSW & Qld) b Aug. 1, 1861 Sydney (NSW) d July 14, 1951 Auckland (New Zealand)

Jones, Sidney (NSW) birth and death details unknown

Jones, Stephen Alexander (WAust) b July 1, 1949 Sydney (NSW)

Jones, Victor Clarence (WAust) b May 11, 1881 Ballarat (Vic) d July 20, 1923 Mt Lawley (WAust)

Jones, William George (SAust) b May 13, 1864 Hindmarsh (SAust) d July 16, 1924 Adelaide (SAust)

Jordan, Frank Slater (NSW) b Sept. 19, 1905 Darlington (NSW) d Oct. 22, 1995 Vaucluse (NSW)

Jordan, Grant Leigh (Vic) b March 18, 1965 Ivanhoe (Vic)

Jordon, Raymond Clarence (Vic) b Feb. 17, 1936 Melbourne (Vic)

Jose, Anthony Douglas (SAust) b Feb. 17, 1929 Knoxville (SAust) d Feb. 3, 1972 Los Angeles, California (United States of America)

Jose, Gilbert Edgar (SAust) b Nov. 1, 1898 Taichow (China) d March 27, 1942 Changi POW Camp (Singapore)

Joseph, Joel P. (NSW) b c. 1867 d c. 1942 Canterbury (NSW)

* Joslin, Leslie Ronald (Vic) b Dec. 13, 1947 Yarraville (Vic)

Joyce, Robert Eric (Qld) b Dec. 11, 1947 Auchenflower (Qld)

Joynt, Hartley Kelly (WAust) b June 14, 1938 Subiaco (WAust)

* Julian, Brendon Paul (WAust) b Aug. 10, 1970 Hamilton (New Zealand)

Junor, John Leonard (Vic) b April 27, 1914 Thornbury (Vic)

Junor, Robert Johnston (Vic) b Jan. 10, 1888 Marcus Hill (Vic) d July 26, 1957 Heidelberg (Vic)

Jurgensen, Shayne John (WAust & Tas) b April 28, 1976 Redcliffe (Qld)

Kahler, Lance Warren (Qld) b June 27, 1977 Crows Nest (Qld)

* Kallicharran, Alvin Isaac (Qld) b March 21, 1949 Paidama (British Guiana)

* Kanhai, Rohan Bholal (WAust & Tas) b Dec. 26, 1935 Port Mourant, Berbice (British Guiana)

Karppinen, Stuart James (WAust) b June 13, 1973 Townsville (Qld)

* Kasprowicz, Michael Scott (Qld) b Feb. 10, 1972 South Brisbane (Qld)

* Katich, Simon Matthew (WAust) b Aug. 21, 1975 Middle Swan (WAust)

Kay, William Malcolm (Qld) b May 4, 1893 Gympie (Qld) d July 7, 1973 Taringa (Qld)

Keating, James Leslie (Vic) b Oct. 1, 1891 Brunswick East (Vic) d March 13, 1962 Fitzroy (Vic)

Kekwick, Edwin Huntley (SAust) b March 5, 1875 Port MacDonell (SAust) d Aug. 29, 1950 Adelaide (SAust)

* Kelleway, Charles (NSW) b April 25, 1886 Lismore (NSW) d Nov. 16, 1944 Lindfield (NSW)

Kellick, Charles Moore (NSW) b Nov. 21, 1842 Sydney (NSW) d March 27, 1918 Strathfield (NSW)

Kellick, James (NSW) b Aug. 24, 1840 Sydney (NSW) d Aug. 8, 1926 Sydney (NSW)

Kelly, David John (SAust) b Jan. 28, 1959 North Adelaide (SAust)

Kelly, Ian Donald Cameron (Qld) b May 5, 1959 Herston (Qld)

* Kelly, James Joseph (NSW) b May 10, 1867 Sandridge (Vic) d Aug. 14, 1938 Bellevue Hill (NSW)

Kelly, Otto Harvey (WAust) b May 15, 1880 Sandridge (Vic) d July 30, 1946 Mt Lawley (WAust)

Kelly, Peter Charles (NSW & WAust) b April 28, 1942 Mosman (NSW)

Kelly, Richard Terence Bonynge (Vic) b March 21, 1870 Ballan (Vic) d Dec. 27, 1941 St Kilda (Vic)

Kelly, Robert Charles (WAust) b May 18, 1969 Subiaco (WAust)

* Kelly, Thomas Joseph Dart (Vic) b May 3, 1844 County Waterford (Ireland) d July 20, 1893 Hawthorn (Vic)

Kelly, William Harvey (WAust) b March 24, 1883 St Kilda (Vic) d July 3, 1944 Croydon (Vic))

Kelly, William Lucius Usna (Vic) b Jan. 20, 1875 Rosedale (Vic) d Dec. 27, 1968 Bulla (Vic)

Kelton, Matthew David (SAust) b April 9, 1974 Woodville South (SAust)

Kemp, Benjamin Charles Ernest (SAust & Vic) b Jan. 30, 1864 Plymouth, Devon (England) d Dec. 3, 1940 Albert Park (Vic)

Kemp, Leonard Denton (Vic) b June 6, 1909 Malvern (Vic)

Kendall, Keith Harold Dudley (Vic) b March 16, 1929 South Melbourne (Vic)

* Kendall, Thomas Kingston (Vic & Tas) b Aug. 24, 1851 Bedford, Bedfordshire (England) d Aug. 17, 1924 Hobart (Tas)

Kenneally, Cornelius James (SAust) b July 28, 1926 Edwardstown (Vic) d Jan. 18, 1995 Ashford (SAust)

Kenny, Arthur (Vic) b Aug. 9, 1878 Emerald Hill (Vic) d Aug. 2, 1934 South Melbourne (Vic)

Kenny, Justin Dean (NSW) b Sept. 24, 1966 Camperdown (NSW)

* Kent, Martin Francis (Qld) b Nov. 23, 1953 Mossman (Qld)

Keogh, Ernest John (WAust) b c. 1869 South Melbourne (Vic) d c. 1951 South Yarra (Vic)

Kermode, Alexander (NSW) b May 15, 1876 Sydney (NSW) d July 17, 1934 Balmain (NSW)

Kerr, Eric Alan David (Vic) b June 28, 1923 Auburn (Vic) d Feb. 16, 1989 Melbourne (Vic)

* Kerr, Robert Byers (Qld) b June 16, 1961 Herston (Qld)

Kershler, Anthony John (NSW) b July 6, 1968 St Leonards (NSW)

Kessey, Gwilym Taf (WAust) b Jan. 13, 1919 Meekatharra (WAust) d June 25, 1986 Perth (WAust)

Kettle, John Louis (NSW) b Dec. 3, 1830 Sydney (NSW) d Oct. 30, 1891 Newtown (NSW)

Kiernan, Christopher (Vic) b March 23, 1878 Fitzroy (Vic) d Dec. 2, 1925 North Fitzroy (Vic)

Kierse, John Michael (SAust) b Jan. 11, 1918 Nhill (Vic)

Kildey, Edward Keith (Tas) b April 30, 1919 Leeton (NSW)

Killen, Christopher Michael (SAust) b Sept. 23, 1967 Dubbo (NSW)

Kimber, Adam Patrick (SAust) b Sept. 30, 1969 North Adelaide (SAust)

Kimpton, Robert Webb (WAust) b Jan. 5, 1914 Essendon (Vic)

King, Darryl James (Qld) b June 6, 1942 East Brisbane (Qld) d March 3, 2002 Buderim (Qld)

King, Ian Harold (Qld) b June 1, 1943 Herston (Qld)

King, James Francis (SAust) b May 23, 1851 Hindmarsh (SAust) d June 28, 1921 Hindmarsh (SAust)

King, Norman Reginald (SAust) b April 9, 1915 Mile End (SAust) d April 25, 1973 Linden Park (SAust)

King, Percy Macgregor (NSW) b Sept. 2, 1889 Richmond (Vic) d Dec. 9, 1967 Rose Bay (NSW)

King, Peter Denis (Vic) b May 24, 1959 Melbourne (Vic)

King, Stuart Patrick (Vic) b April 22, 1906 Ararat (Vic) d Feb. 28, 1943 in action on the Coral Sea

Kingdon, Darren Robert (Qld) b Sept. 24, 1969 Dubbo (NSW)

Kington, Philip Oliphant (Vic) b Dec. 17, 1832 Clifton, Gloucestershire (England) d July 2, 1892 Dachet, Buckinghamshire (England)

Kinloch, John (NSW) b c. 1833 Dublin (Ireland) d April 9, 1897 Camperdown (NSW)

Kinnear, Joseph David (Vic) b Feb. 12, 1912 West Brunswick (Vic) d Dec. 14, 1981 Moreland (Vic)

Kinnear, William George (Vic) b Aug. 19, 1914 West Brunswick (Vic) d Dec. 7, 1982 West Brunswick (Vic)

* Kippax, Alan Falconer (NSW) b May 25, 1897 Sydney (NSW) d Sept. 5, 1972 Bellevue Hill (NSW)

Kirby, Keith William (Vic) b Oct. 1, 1939 Essendon (Vic)

Kirby, Richard George (Tas) b Jan. 28, 1861 Hobart (Tas) d Aug. 26, 1947 Hobart (Tas)

Kirkman, William Stanley (Tas) b Feb. 14, 1961 Launceston (Tas)

Kirkwood, Harold Peter (SAust) b Sept. 15, 1882 Orroroo (SAust) d May 19, 1943 Unley (SAust)

Kissell, Ronald Keith (NSW) b Aug. 9, 1928 Camperdown (NSW)

Kitson, Eugene Henry (SAust) b Nov. 28, 1889 Adelaide (SAust) d Aug. 4, 1962 Heidelberg (Vic)

* Kline, Lindsay Francis (Vic) b Sept. 29, 1934 Camberwell (Vic)

Klinger, Michael (Vic) b July 4, 1980 Kew (Vic)

Klose, Tom Elliott (SAust) b Jan. 22, 1918 North Adelaide (SAust) d June 13, 1986 Nailsworth (SAust)

* Knight, David Jeffrey (Vic) b Aug. 21, 1956 Coburg (Vic)

Knight, Gary William (Combined XI) b July 20, 1950 Launceston (Tas)

Knight, Robert Leonard (Tas) b Nov. 20, 1957 Launceston (Tas)

Knill, William (SAust) b Jan. 28, 1859 Prospect Village (SAust) d July 8, 1940 North Adelaide (SAust)

* Knott, Alan Philip Eric (Tas) b April 9, 1946 Belvedere, Kent (England)

Knowles, Eric Charles (Qld) b March 9, 1896 Toowoomba (Qld) d Sept. 15, 1978 Southport (Qld)

Kortlang, Henry Frederick Lorenz (Vic) b March 12, 1880 Carlton (Vic) d Feb. 15, 1961 Cottesloe (WAust)

Kowalick, Jeffrey Peter (SAust) b July 22, 1946 Maylands (SAust)

Kremerskothen, Scott Paul (Tas) b Jan. 5, 1979 Launceston (Tas)

Kroger, Henry Jack (Vic) b June 27, 1906 Caulfield (Vic) d July 16, 1987 Malvern (Vic)

Kyle, James Henderson (Vic) b May 29, 1880 Bacchus Marsh (Vic) d Jan. 11, 1919 Albert Park (Vic)

La Frantz, Errold Campbell (Qld) b May 25, 1919 Wooloowin (Qld)

* Laird, Bruce Malcolm (WAust) b Nov. 21, 1950 Mt Lawley (WAust)

Lambert, Daryl John (SAust) b Oct. 8, 1946 Prospect (SAust)

Lambert, Grant Michael (NSW) b Aug. 5, 1977 Parramatta (NSW)

Lambert, Henry Francis (Vic) b July 8, 1918 Bairnsdale (Vic) d June 19, 1995 Grange (SAust)

Lambert, Oswald (NSW) b Aug. 23, 1926 New Lambton (NSW)

Lampard, Albert Wallis (Vic) b July 3, 1885 Richmond (Vic) d Jan. 11, 1984 Armadale (Vic)

Lampe, William Henry Warwick (NSW) b Aug. 29, 1902 Wagga Wagga (NSW) d Dec. 22, 1987 Wagga Wagga (NSW)

Lane, John Bayley (NSW) b Jan. 7, 1886 Petersham (NSW) d Aug. 30, 1937 Manly (NSW)

Lang, Harold King (WAust) b Aug. 23, 1905 Bangena (Vic) d April 23, 1991 Nedlands (WAust)

Langdon, Christopher Walter (WAust) b July 4, 1922 Boulder (WAust)

* Langer, Justin Lee (WAust) b Nov. 21, 1970 Subiaco (WAust)

Langer, Robert Samuel (WAust) b Oct. 3, 1948 Subiaco (WAust)

Langford, Ian Frederick (Vic) b June 2, 1936 Kew (Vic)

* Langley, Gilbert Roche Andrews (SAust) b Sept. 14, 1919 North Adelaide (SAust) d May 14, 2001 Fullarton (SAust)

Langley, Jeffrey Noel (SAust & Qld) b Oct. 28, 1948 Adelaide (SAust)

Lanigan, Emmet Robert (Vic) b Sept. 6, 1909 Maffra (Vic)

Lanigan, Joseph Patrick (WAust) b July 8, 1891 Mogumber (WAust) d Sept. 30, 1972 Glendalough (WAust)

Lansdown, Albert Joseph Walter (Vic) b March 10, 1897 Fitzroy South (Vic) d Jan. 7, 1979 Frankston (Vic)

Lansdown, Harold Charles (Vic) b Feb. 18, 1900 North Fitzroy (Vic) d April 18, 1957 Ivanhoe (Vic)

Larkin, Rohan Patrick (Vic) b Oct. 19, 1969 Seymour (Vic)

* Laughlin, Trevor John (Vic) b Jan. 30, 1951 Nyah West (Vic)

Lavender, Mark Philip (WAust) b Aug. 28, 1967 Madras (India)

* Laver, Frank (Vic) b Dec. 7, 1869 Castlemaine (Vic) d Sept. 24, 1919 East Melbourne (Vic)

Laver, John Francis Lee (Tas) b March 9, 1917 Malvern (Vic)

Law, Ian Kennon (Vic) b Sept. 27, 1938 Richmond (Vic)

Law, Rupert William (Qld) b Feb. 24, 1890 Sydney (NSW) d May 5, 1942 Randwick (NSW)

* Law, Stuart Grant (Qld) b Oct. 18, 1968 Herston (Qld)

Lawes, Charles Henry Wickham (NSW) b Dec. 9, 1899 Cobar (NSW) death details unknown

Lawlor, John (Vic) b Jan. 25, 1864 Castleisland, County Kerry (Ireland) d Jan. 29, 1908 Melbourne (Vic)

Lawrence, Charles (NSW) b Dec. 16, 1828 Hoxton, London (England) d Dec. 20, 1916 Canterbury (Vic)

Lawrence, Rodney John (Qld) b Aug. 8, 1954 Herston (Qld)

* Lawry, William Morris (Vic) b Feb. 11, 1937 Thornbury (Vic)

* Lawson, Geoffrey Francis (NSW) b Dec. 7, 1957 Wagga Wagga (NSW)

Lawson, Robert James (Vic) b March 23, 1901 South Melbourne (Vic) d Nov. 28, 1974 West Brunswick (Vic)

Laycock, Henry (SAust) b Oct. 31, 1901 Edwardstown (SAust) d Aug. 6, 1983 Port Noarlunga (SAust)

Le Couteur, Philip Ridgeway (Vic) b June 26, 1885 Kyneton (Vic) d June 30, 1958 Gunnedah (NSW)

Leabeater, Leonard Raymond (NSW) b July 10, 1906 Parramatta (NSW) d June 1, 1996 Port Macquarie (NSW)

Leak, Brian Headley (SAust) b May 5, 1917 Hawthorn (SAust)

Leak, Ernest Howard (SAust) b Oct. 28, 1872 Finniss Vale (SAust) d Aug. 22, 1945 Adelaide (SAust)

Leak, Stanley Garfield (SAust) b March 12, 1886 Goodwood (SAust) d Jan. 10, 1963 Millswood (SAust)

Leary, John Denis (Qld) b c. 1862 Picton (NSW) d Jan. 16, 1940 Herston (Qld)

Leather, Thomas William (Vic) b June 2, 1910 Rutherglen, Lanarkshire (Scotland) d May 10, 1991 Prahran (Vic)

Ledger, Scott Norman (Qld) b Sept. 1, 1952 Nambour (Qld)

Ledward, John Allan (Vic) b April 22, 1909 East Melbourne (Vic) d July 22, 1997 Box Hill (Vic)

* Lee, Brett (NSW) b Nov. 8, 1976 Wollongong (NSW)

Lee, Clarence Leslie (Tas) b Dec. 28, 1890 Cressy (Tas) d Feb. 5, 1959 Invermay (Tas)

Lee, Ian Somerville (Vic) b March 24, 1914 Brunswick North (Vic) d April 14, 1976 Port Melbourne (Vic)

* Lee, Philip Keith (SAust) b Sept. 15, 1904 Gladstone (SAust) d Aug. 8, 1980 Woodville South (SAust)

Lee, Robert William (SAust) b Jan. 31, 1927 Hindmarsh (SAust) d June 9, 2001 Adelaide (SAust)

Lee, Shane (NSW) b Aug. 8, 1973 Wollongong (NSW)

Lee, Terance Henry (NSW) b Aug. 31, 1940 Manly (NSW)

Leedham, Michael John (Tas) b Feb. 22, 1950 Campbell Town (Tas)

Leehane, John Francis (Vic) b Dec. 11, 1950 Coburg (Vic)

Leehane, John Thomas (Vic) b Oct. 20, 1921 Brunswick (Vic) d July 22, 1991 Caulfield (Vic)

Leeson, Henry Follie (Qld) b July 20, 1908 Mount Morgan (Qld) d June 25, 1950 Logan River (Qld)

Lehmann, Charles Albert (WAust) b Sept. 16, 1878 Caltowie (SAust) d April 27, 1940 Melbourne (Vic)

* Lehmann, Darren Scott (SAust & Vic) b Feb. 5, 1970 Gawler (SAust)

Leslie, Peter Glen (NSW) b Feb. 24, 1947 Bexley (NSW)

Letcher, Charles (Vic) b c. 1869 Collingwood (Vic) d Nov. 30, 1916 Perth (WAust)

Lethborg, Gordon John (Tas) b Nov. 23, 1907 Scottsdale (Tas) d Aug. 31, 1989 Launceston (Tas)

Lette, Henry Elms (Tas) b 1829 birth day and month unknown Curramore (Tas) d Aug. 15, 1892 Launceston (Tas)

* Lever, Peter (Tas) b Sept. 17, 1940 Todmorden, Yorkshire (England)

Levingston, Raydon Charles (Qld) b Jan. 17, 1946 Toowoomba (Qld)

Levy, Graham Bruce (SAust) b Feb. 10, 1938 North Adelaide (SAust)

Levy, Roy Mark (Qld) b April 20, 1906 Waverley (NSW) d Dec. 12, 1965 Clayfield (Qld)

Lewis, Arthur (Vic) b c. 1830 full birth details unknown d June 1, 1907 Alexandra (Vic)

Lewis, John William (Qld) b Nov. 21, 1867 St George (Qld) d Sept. 19, 1939 Brisbane (Qld)

Lewis, Keith (SAust) b Feb. 4, 1923 Prospect (SAust)

Lewis, Kevin John (SAust) b Nov. 27, 1947 Hindmarsh (SAust)

Lewis, Laurence Robert (SAust) b May 24, 1889 Cherry Gardens (SAust) d Sept. 2, 1947 Prospect (SAust)

Lewis, Michael Llewellyn (Vic) b June 29, 1974 Greensborough (Vic)

Lewis, Oswald Hoddle (NSW) b Feb. 28, 1833 Sydney (NSW) d April 28, 1895 Darlinghurst (NSW)

Lewis, Percy Markham (Vic) b March 13, 1864 Hamilton (Vic) d Nov. 24, 1922 St Kilda (Vic)

Lewis, Thomas Harvie (NSW) b c. 1828 London (England) d June 19, 1901 Darlinghurst (NSW)

Liddicut, Arthur Edward (Vic) b Oct. 17, 1891 Fitzroy (Vic) d April 8, 1983 Parkdale (Vic)

Lihou, Jack (Qld) b Sept. 9, 1930 Sandgate (Qld)

Lill, John Charles (SAust) b Dec. 7, 1933 Maylands (SAust)

* Lillee, Dennis Keith (WAust & Tas) b July 18, 1949 Subiaco (WAust)

Lillie, Dennis John (Qld) b Oct. 28, 1945 Auchenflower (Qld)

Lilly, Kenneth Edward (WAust) b Dec. 25, 1959 Perth (WAust)

Limb, Allen (Tas) b Sept. 29, 1886 Gawler (SAust) d July 1, 1975 Battery Point (Tas)

* Lindwall, Raymond Russell (NSW & Qld) b Oct. 3, 1921 Mascot (NSW) d June 22, 1996 Greenslopes (Qld)

Linney, George Frederick (Tas) b Nov. 18, 1869 Guildford, Surrey (England) d Nov. 5, 1927 Weston-super-Mare, Somerset (England)

Lister, Charles (Vic) b Nov. 7, 1811 Armitage Park, Staffordshire (England) d Aug. 18, 1873 Laverstock Asylum, Alderbury, Wiltshire (England)

Liston, George Grieve (SAust) b April 29, 1860 Tanunda (SAust) d June 6, 1929 Kent Town (SAust)

Litster, John Lewis (Qld) b Feb. 2, 1904 Townsville (Qld) d March 11, 1982 Railway Estate, Townsville (Qld)

Little, Raymond Cecil James (NSW) b Oct. 7, 1914 Armidale (NSW) d April 28, 1995 Burwood (NSW)

Living, Gary Francis (Vic) b Oct. 1, 1952 Dandenong (Vic)

Livingston, Bruce Arthur Lionel (NSW) b May 11, 1927 Marrickville (NSW)

Livingston, Leonard (NSW) b May 3, 1920 Hurlstone Park (NSW) d Jan. 16, 1998 Hurlstone Park (NSW)

Lloyd, Robert Grantley (SAust) b Oct. 24, 1940 Gladstone (SAust)

* Loader, Peter James (WAust) b Oct. 25, 1929 Wallington, Surrey (England)

Lochner, Augustus Meyer (Tas) b Oct. 1, 1827 Enfield, Middlesex (England) d Feb. 20, 1865 Plumstead Common, Kent (England)

* Lock, Graham Anthony Richard (WAust) b July 5, 1929 Limpsfield, Surrey (England) d March 29, 1995 Beechboro (WAust)

Lockie, George William (Qld) b Feb. 18, 1910 Mt Morgan (Qld) d Nov. 2, 1971 Northgate (Qld)

Lockwood, William Thomas (WAust) b June 26, 1868 Geelong (Vic) d Aug. 29, 1953 Tuart Hill (WAust)

Lodding, Brent Andrew (Vic) b March 20, 1973 Upper Ferntree Gully (Vic)

Loder, Robert Roy (NSW) b Dec. 17, 1896 East Maitland (NSW) d Feb. 13, 1964 French's Forest (NSW)

Lodge, Arthur Oliver (WAust) b April 7, 1933 Guildford (WAust)

Logan, William (Vic) birth and death details unknown

Lonergan, Albert-Roy (SAust & NSW) b Dec. 6, 1909 Maylands (WAust) d Oct. 22, 1956 Adelaide (SAust)

Loney, Geoffrey Souter (Tas) b March 31, 1894 Campbelltown (NSW) d April 7, 1985 Hobart (Tas)

Long, Edmund James (NSW) b March 28, 1883 Darlinghurst (NSW) d Dec. 8, 1947 Leichhardt (NSW)

Long, Gordon Hillhouse (Combined XI) b May 6, 1934 Hobart (Tas)

Long, Thomas Tasman Thompson (Qld) b Sept. 11, 1875 at sea d Oct. 20, 1926 Spring Hill (Qld)

Longney, Geoffrey Wallace (Vic) b May 25, 1935 Oakleigh (Vic)

Lord, John Carr (Tas) b Aug. 17, 1844 Hobart (Tas) d May 25, 1911 Antill Ponds (Tas)

Lord, Sidney (Tas) b Oct. 20, 1886 birthplace and death details unknown

Loton, Cecil Vernon (WAust) b Jan. 5, 1906 Upper Swan (WAust) d June 8, 1986 Pinjarra (WAust)

Loton, Morris William (WAust) b March 18, 1905 Springhill (WAust) d March 2, 1976 Northam (WAust)

Lough, William David (NSW) b Oct. 31, 1886 Bourke (NSW) d c. 1939 Newtown (NSW)

Loughnan, Austin Robert (Vic) b June 15, 1851 Hobart (Tas) d Oct. 9, 1926 Cheltenham (Vic)

* Love, Hampden Stanley Bray (NSW & Vic) b Aug. 10, 1895 Lilyfield (NSW) d July 22, 1969 Sydney (NSW)

Love, Martin Lloyd (Qld) b March 30, 1974 Mundubbera (Qld)

Lovell, David Cameron (SAust) b Feb. 17, 1955 North Adelaide (SAust)

Lovelock, Oswald Ifould (WAust) b Aug. 28, 1911 Highgate (WAust) d Aug. 1, 1981 Subiaco (WAust)

Loveridge, Eustace Alfred (SAust) b April 14, 1891 Yongala (SAust) d July 29, 1959 Adelaide (SAust)

Loveridge, Walter David (NSW) b Sept. 13, 1867 Redfern (NSW) d Jan. 6, 1940 East Brisbane (Qld)

Lovett, Arthur Frederick (Tas & WAust) b June 1, 1920 St Kilda (Vic) d July 1, 1990 Coffs Harbour (NSW)

Lovett, Henry Charles (Tas) b March 3, 1856 Battery Point (Tas) d May 20, 1937 Hobart (Tas)

Lowe, Frederick (Vic) b Sept. 7, 1827 Holme Pierrepont, Nottinghamshire (England) d Oct. 15, 1887 Ararat (Vic)

Lowry, Jack Brown (Vic) b Nov. 25, 1916 Lambton (NSW)

Loxton, Colin Cameron (Qld) b Jan. 1, 1914 Beecroft (NSW) d Sept. 2, 2000 Greenslopes (Qld)

Loxton, John Frederick Cameron (Qld) b Nov. 26, 1945 Ashgrove (Qld)

* Loxton, Samuel John Everett (Vic) b March 29, 1921 Albert Park (Vic)

Lucas, Clyde Edward (Tas) b Aug. 11, 1898 Kingston (Tas) d Jan. 12, 1988 Palm Beach (Qld)

Lucas, Edward (Tas) b June 16, 1848 Kingston (Tas) d April 19, 1916 Kingston (Tas)

Lucas, Frank Russell (SAust) b Nov. 9, 1888 Port Pirie (SAust) d Aug. 31, 1941 Adelaide (SAust)

Lucas, Michael John (Qld) b April 14, 1944 Ashgrove (Qld)

Lucas, Thomas Turland (SAust) b Feb. 18, 1852 Eyres Flat (SAust) d March 13, 1945 Norwood (SAust)

Lugton, Frank Leslie (Vic) b Nov. 4, 1893 Northcote (Vic) d July 29, 1916 near Villers-Bretonneux (France)

Lukeman, Eric William (NSW) b March 11, 1923 Drummoyne (NSW) d April 18, 1993 Palm Beach (Qld)

Lush, John Grantley (NSW) b Oct. 14, 1913 Prahran (Vic) d Aug. 23, 1985 Sydney (NSW)

* Lyons, John James (SAust) b May 21, 1863 Gawler (SAust) d July 21, 1927 Magill (SAust)

Lyons, Rodney Bernard (Qld) b April 24, 1924 Cairns (Qld)

* McAlister, Peter Alexander (Vic) b July 11, 1869 Williamstown (Vic) d May 10, 1938 Richmond (Vic)

McAllen, Charles (Tas) b July 2, 1860 Hobart (Tas) d Jan. 15, 1924 Hobart (Tas)

McAllister, Donald Ernest (SAust) b Nov. 19, 1936 Hindmarsh (SAust)

McAndrew, John William (Qld) b Nov. 4, 1889 Berrima (NSW) d April 10, 1960 Ipswich (Qld)

McArdle, Brendan Joseph (Vic) b March 2, 1952 Preston (Vic)

* Macartney, Charles George (NSW) b June 27, 1886 West Maitland (NSW) d Sept. 9, 1958 Little Bay (NSW)

McAulay, Kenneth James (WAust) b Sept. 29, 1949 Subiaco (WAust)

McBeath, Arthur (NSW & SAust) b June 17, 1876 Mudgee (NSW) d March 17, 1945 Surry Hills (NSW)

* McCabe, Stanley Joseph (NSW) b July 16, 1910 Grenfell (NSW) d Aug. 25, 1968 Beauty Point (NSW)

McCaffrey, Michael Francis (Qld) b Feb. 18, 1878 Rockhampton (Qld) d March 17, 1949 Brisbane (Qld)

McCaffrey, Victor William (NSW) b Aug. 11, 1918 Goulburn (NSW)

* McCague, Martin John (WAust) b May 24, 1969 Larne (Northern Ireland)

McCarthy, John Edward (Qld) b Feb. 22, 1917 Maryborough (Qld) d Feb. 18, 1998 Southport (Qld)

McCarthy, Kevin Joseph (SAust) b Oct. 11, 1945 Rose Park (SAust)

McCarthy, Patrick Covell Derrick (WAust) b Oct. 24, 1919 (Ceylon)

McCarthy, Richard Charles Arthur Marum (Vic) b Dec. 21, 1961 Geelong (Vic)

McCauley, Bede Vincent (NSW) b June 11, 1909 Coogee (NSW) d Oct. 14, 1994 Sydney (NSW)

McCloy, William Stanley Swain (Qld & NSW) b Nov. 10, 1886 Paddington (NSW) d Nov. 10, 1975 Young (NSW)

McCooke, Steven Milne (Vic) b Jan. 31, 1960 South Caulfield (Vic)

* McCool, Colin Leslie (NSW & Qld) b Dec. 9, 1916 Paddington (NSW) d April 5, 1986 Concord (NSW)

McCoombe, Clarence Arthur (Qld) b Feb. 23, 1904 Cooktown (Qld) d Sept. 6, 1955 Sydney (NSW)

McCormack, William Henry (Vic) b May 5, 1877 St Kilda (Vic) d April 26, 1946 Stawell (Vic)

* McCormick, Ernest Leslie (Vic) b May 16, 1906 North Carlton (Vic) d June 28, 1991 Tweed Heads (NSW)

McCormick, Raymond Vincent (SAust) b Jan. 30, 1931 Mile End (SAust)

* McCosker, Richard Bede (NSW) b Dec. 11, 1946 Inverell (NSW)

McCoy, Bernard Leslie (NSW) b March 26, 1896 Kangaroo Valley (NSW) d June 11, 1970 Sydney (NSW)

McCurdy, Rodney John (Tas, Vic & SAust) b Dec. 30, 1959 Melbourne (Vic)

* McDermott, Craig John (Qld) b April 14, 1965 Ipswich (Qld)

McDonald, Andrew Barry (Vic) b June 5, 1981 Wodonga (Vic)

* McDonald, Colin Campbell (Vic) b Nov. 17, 1928 Glen Iris (Vic)

* McDonald, Edgar Arthur (Tas & Vic) b Jan. 6, 1891 Launceston (Tas) d July 22, 1937 Blackrod, near Bolton, Lancashire (England)

McDonald, Ian Hamilton (Vic) b July 28, 1923 Windsor (Vic)

Macdonald, Kenneth Locke (Tas) b Jan. 3, 1934 Premaydena (Tas) d July 1, 1999 Hobart (Tas)

Macdonald, Robert (Qld) b Feb. 14, 1870 Clunes (Vic) d March 7, 1946 Victoria, British Columbia (Canada)

McDonald, Walter Hugh (Vic, Qld & Tas) b March 24, 1884 Shepparton (Vic) d March 22, 1955 Kew (Vic)

* McDonnell, Percy Stanislaus (Vic, NSW & Qld) b Nov. 13, 1858 Kennington, Kent (England) d Sept. 24, 1896 South Brisbane (Qld)

McDowell, Robert Murray (Tas) b Sheffield, Yorkshire (England) full birth and death details unknown

Mace, Christopher (Vic) b Dec. 24, 1830 Bedale, Yorkshire (England) d Nov. 23, 1907 Sydenham (NSW)

Mace, John (Vic) b Dec. 28, 1828 Bedale, Yorkshire (England) d April 30, 1905 Te Aroha (New Zealand)

Mace, John Cruttenden (Tas) b May 7, 1839 Sydney (NSW) d April 18, 1906 Hawley-with-Minley, Hampshire (England)

McElhone, Frank Eric (NSW) b June 27, 1887 Waverley (NSW) d July 21, 1981 Darlinghurst (NSW)

McEvoy, Daniel Michael (WAust) b Aug. 19, 1946 Mount Lawley (WAust)

McEvoy, Frederick Aloysius (Vic) b July 4, 1856 Gundagai (NSW) d Nov. 5, 1913 Brighton (Vic)

McEvoy, William Joseph (Vic) b c. 1845 Sydney (NSW) d July 14, 1930 (England)

McEwan, Kenneth Scott (WAust) b July 16, 1952 Bedford, Cape Province (South Africa)

McEwan, W. (Tas) b 1815 birth day and month unknown Perth, Perthshire (Scotland) d c. 1862 (Vic)

McFarland, Robert (Vic) b July 9, 1847 Coleraine (Vic) d July 4, 1876 Coleraine (Vic)

McFarlane, Clement Basil Patrick (Qld) b Aug. 20, 1900 New Farm (Qld) d March 2, 1946 Grange (Qld)

McFarlane, Robert Donald (WAust) b Feb. 7, 1955 Corrigin (WAust)

McGain, Bryce Edward (Vic) b March 25, 1972 Mornington (Vic)

McGan, Bryan (Vic) b c. 1848 Melbourne (Vic) d July 9, 1894 South Melbourne (Vic)

McGhee, Robert William (Qld) b March 24, 1963 Richmond (Qld)

MacGill, Charles William Terry (WAust) b June 16, 1916 Perth (WAust) d Oct. 31, 1999 Perth (WAust)

* MacGill, Stuart Charles Glyndwr (WAust & NSW) b Feb. 25, 1971 Mt Lawley (WAust)

MacGill, Terry Mornington David (WAust) b Dec. 22, 1945 Moreland (Vic)

McGilvray, Alan David (NSW) b Dec. 6, 1909 Paddington (NSW) d July 17, 1996 Darlinghurst (NSW)

McGinn, Albert Howard (Qld) b Nov. 11, 1913 Upper Kedron (Qld)

McGinty, Adam David (Vic) b March 24, 1971 Melbourne (Vic)

McGlinchy, William Walter (NSW & Qld) b Jan. 31, 1864 Newcastle (NSW) d July 1, 1946 Sydney (NSW)

* McGrath, Glenn Donald (NSW) b Feb. 9, 1970 Dubbo (NSW)

McGregor, William (Australians) b Feb. 23, 1888 St Kilda (Vic) d Oct. 5, 1980 Benalla (Vic)

McGuire, David Victor (Tas) b Nov. 13, 1931 Hobart (Tas)

McGuirk, Harold Vincent (NSW) b Oct. 17, 1906 Crookwell (NSW) death details unknown

McGuirk, Leo Daniel (NSW) b May 3, 1908 Crookwell (NSW) d June 15, 1974 Sydney (NSW)

* McIlwraith, John (Vic) b Sept. 7, 1857 Collingwood (Vic) d July 5, 1938 Camberwell (Vic)

McInnes, Alan Roderick (Vic) b May 29, 1907 Kensington (Vic) d Sept. 16, 1991 Dandenong (Vic)

McInnes, Mark William (Cricket Academy) b April 16, 1977 Wagga Wagga (NSW)

McIntyre, Ernest John (Vic) b April 19, 1921 Albert Park (Vic)

* McIntyre, Peter Edward (Vic & SAust) b April 27, 1966 Gisborne (Vic)

McIntyre, William Robert (NSW) b April 10, 1877 Forbes (NSW) d c. 1943 Drummoyne (NSW)

Mack, Christopher David (WAust) b June 30, 1970 Subiaco (WAust)

McKay, Douglas Gordon (SAust) b July 2, 1904 North Adelaide (SAust) d April 9, 1994 North Adelaide (SAust)

Mackay, George (Vic) b July 6, 1860 Castlemaine (Vic) d May 22, 1948 Bendigo (Vic)

McKay, Henry James (SAust) b Jan. 1, 1883 Goodwood (SAust) d Feb. 12, 1926 Hawthorn (SAust)

Mackay, James Rainey Munro (NSW) b Sept. 9, 1880 Armidale (NSW) d June 13, 1953 Walcha (NSW)

Mackay, John Robert Edward (Qld) b Nov. 24, 1937 Rockhampton (Qld)

* Mackay, Kenneth Donald (Qld) b Oct. 24, 1925 Windsor (Qld) d June 13, 1982 Point Lookout, Stradbroke Island (Qld)

Mackay, Kerry (NSW) b May 7, 1949 Brighton-Le-Sands (NSW)

MacKenzie, Alexander Cecil Knox (NSW) b Aug. 7, 1870 Sydney (NSW) d April 11, 1947 Epping (NSW)

McKenzie, Colin (Vic) b Dec. 12, 1880 Trawool (Vic) d Aug. 31, 1930 Avenel (Vic)

MacKenzie, Damien Robert (Qld) b July 21, 1980 Brisbane (Qld)

McKenzie, Douglas Charles (WAust) b March 15, 1906 Kew (Vic) d July 1, 1979 Perth (WAust)

McKenzie, Eric Norman (WAust) b Dec. 9, 1910 Kalgoorlie (WAust) d April 28, 1994 Cottesloe (WAust)

* McKenzie, Graham Douglas (WAust) b June 24, 1941 Cottesloe (WAust)

McKenzie, John (SAust) b Oct. 11, 1862 Aldinga (SAust) d June 3, 1944 Hazelwood Park (SAust)

McKenzie, Matthew Stanley (Tas) b May 17, 1890 Launceston (Tas) d Dec. 8, 1915 Alexandria (Egypt)

McKew, Cecil George (NSW) b Aug. 12, 1887 Leichhardt (NSW) d Oct. 12, 1974 Lilli Pilli (NSW)

* McKibbin, Thomas Robert (NSW) b Dec. 10, 1870 Raglan (NSW) d Dec. 15, 1939 Bathurst (NSW)

McKone, John James (NSW) b Oct. 3, 1835 Sydney (NSW) d Aug. 7, 1882 Sydney (NSW)

McLachlan, Ian Murray (SAust) b Oct. 2, 1936 North Adelaide (SAust)

* McLaren, John William (Qld) b Dec. 22, 1886 Toowong (Qld) d Nov. 17, 1921 Highgate Hill (Qld)

McLaughlin, John Joseph (Qld) b Feb. 18, 1930 Corinda (Qld)

McLay, Gregory Francis (NSW) b May 7, 1969 Wagga Wagga (NSW)

McLean, Allan Robert Charles (SAust) b Feb. 1, 1914 Mile End (SAust) d Nov. 9, 1989 Christies Beach (SAust)

McLean, Hugh (Vic) b Nov. 26, 1864 Woodford (Vic) d Feb. 19, 1915 East Melbourne (Vic)

McLean, Ian Robert (SAust) b Jan. 30, 1954 Semaphore (SAust)

* MacLean, John Alexander (Qld) b April 27, 1946 Herston (Qld)

MacLeay, Kenneth Hervey (WAust) b April 2, 1959 Bradford-on-Avon, Wiltshire (England)

McLellan, Ross Malcolm (SAust) b Feb. 20, 1955 Glenhuntly (Vic)

* McLeod, Charles Edward (Vic) b Oct. 24, 1869 Sandridge (Vic) d Nov. 26, 1918 Armadale (Vic)

McLeod, Daniel Hutton (Vic) b March 29, 1872 Sandridge (Vic) d Nov. 25, 1901 Port Melbourne (Vic)

* McLeod, Robert William (Vic) b Jan. 19, 1868 Sandridge (Vic) d June 14, 1907 Middle Park (Vic)

McMahon, John Terrence (Qld) b May 18, 1932 Five Dock (NSW)

McMahon, Vincent Gerald (Qld) b Jan. 18, 1918 Chinchilla (Qld) d Jan. 23, 1988 Greenslopes (Qld)

McMichael, Samuel Albert (Vic) b July 18, 1869 Collingwood (Vic) d July 21, 1923 Elsternwick (Vic)

McNamara, Bradley Edward (NSW) b Dec. 30, 1965 Sydney (NSW)

McNamee, Raymond Leonard Alphonsus (NSW) b Aug. 26, 1895 Orange (NSW) d Sept. 18, 1949 Little Bay (NSW)

McNaughton, John Leonard (Vic) b Jan. 15, 1884 Richmond (Vic) d Dec. 26, 1970 Lower Kingswood, Surrey (England)

MacNish, William George (NSW) b Oct. 29, 1842 Paddington (NSW) d Nov. 29, 1873 Bundaberg (Qld)

McPetrie, William Martin (Vic) b Feb. 15, 1880 Emerald Hill (Vic) d June 30, 1951 Hawthorn (Vic)

McPhee, Mark William (WAust) b Jan. 25, 1964 Katanning (WAust) d Aug. 15, 1999 Gingin (WAust)

McPhee, Peter Thomas (Tas) b July 29, 1963 South Brisbane (Qld)

MacPherson, Herbert James Keele (NSW) b Feb. 20, 1869 Mudgee (NSW) d Nov. 12, 1953 Mudgee (NSW)

McPherson, James Philip (Vic) b Nov. 20, 1842 Moonee Ponds (Vic) d Aug. 23, 1891 Melbourne (Vic)

McPhillamy, Keith (NSW) b June 20, 1882 Bathurst (NSW) d May 3, 1937 Bowral (NSW)

McRae, Donald (SAust) b June 13, 1873 Aldinga (SAust) d Oct. 22, 1940 Prospect (SAust)

McRae, William Alexander (WAust) b June 18, 1904 Geelong (Vic) d July 25, 1973 Subiaco (WAust)

MacRow, William Reginald Fairbairn (Vic) b July 7, 1889 Kew (Vic) d May 19, 1970 Heidelberg (Vic)

* McShane, Patrick George (Vic) b April 18, 1858 Keilor (Vic) d Dec. 11, 1903 Kew (Vic)

Madden, Robert Harold (NSW) b Dec. 12, 1928 Camperdown (NSW)

Maddern, James Gregory (Qld) b March 22, 1914 Crows Nest (Qld) d March 27, 1987 Nambour (Qld)

Madders, Garry James (Qld) b Jan. 21, 1953 Maryborough (Qld)

Maddock, Charles Edward Rokeby (Qld) b Aug. 14, 1887 (Qld) d Feb. 14, 1957 Herston (Qld)

* Maddocks, Leonard Victor (Vic & Tas) b May 24, 1926 Beaconsfield (Vic)

Maddocks, Richard Ivor (Vic) b July 30, 1928 Carnegie (Vic) d Sept. 10, 1968 Blackburn (Vic)

Maddox, George (Tas) b c. 1811 (Ireland) d July 7, 1867 Melbourne (Vic)

Maddox, John Montgomery (Tas) b Dec. 30, 1930 St Mary's (Tas)

Magarey, William Ashley (SAust) b Jan. 30, 1868 North Adelaide (SAust) d Oct. 18, 1929 North Adelaide (SAust)

* Maguire, John Norman (Qld) b Sept. 15, 1956 Murwillumbah (NSW)

Maher, James Patrick (Qld) b Feb. 27, 1974 Innisfail (Qld)

Mahoney, Hector James Henry (Qld) b Sept. 8, 1913 Maryborough (Qld) d Sept. 25, 1991 Maryborough (Qld)

Mail, Gregory John (NSW) b April 29, 1978 Penrith (NSW)

Mailer, David (Vic) b Aug. 18, 1874 Coburg (Vic) d Dec. 21, 1937 Shepparton (Vic)

* Mailey, Arthur Alfred (NSW) b Jan. 3, 1886 Zetland (NSW) d Dec. 31, 1967 Kirrawee (NSW)

Mainhardt, Michael Shane (Qld) b Jan. 6, 1960 Clermont (Qld)

Mair, Frederick (NSW) b April 15, 1901 Balmain (NSW) d Dec. 25, 1959 Sydney (NSW)

Majewski, Neil John (Tas) b May 27, 1954 Footscray (Vic)

* Majid Jahangir Khan (Qld) b Sept. 28, 1946 Ludhiana (India)

Major, Albert George (Vic) b March 20, 1851 Langport, Somerset (England) d Oct. 16, 1921 Caulfield (Vic)

Makin, James Charles (Vic) b Feb. 11, 1904 Collingwood (Vic) d Jan. 15, 1973 Heidelberg (Vic)

Makin, William Samuel (NSW) b Oct. 4, 1889 Mount Keira (NSW) d Jan. 11, 1962 West Kogarah (NSW)

Makinson, Charles (Vic) b c. 1831 Salford, Lancashire (England) d June 12, 1895 Rugeley, Staffordshire (England)

* Mallett, Ashley Alexander (SAust) b July 13, 1945 Chatswood (NSW)

* Malone, Michael Francis (WAust) b Oct. 9, 1950 Perth (WAust)

Maloney, Peter Ivan (NSW) b Nov. 5, 1950 Ballina (NSW)

Mancell, Peter John (Tas) b March 15, 1958 Goulburn (NSW)

* Mann, Anthony Longford (WAust) b Nov. 8, 1945 Middle Swan (WAust)

Mann, John Lewis (SAust) b April 26, 1919 Strathalbyn (SAust) d Sept. 24, 1969 Lockleys (SAust)

Manning, John Stephen (SAust) b June 11, 1923 Ethelton (SAust) d May 31, 1988 Belair (SAust)

Manou, Graham Allan (SAust) b April 23, 1979 Modbury (SAust)

Mansfield, Graeme Edward (Tas) b Dec. 27, 1942 Hobart (Tas)

Mansfield, J. (Tas) birth and death details unknown

Maplestone, Henry Carman (Vic) b Jan. 11, 1870 Parkville (Vic) d Dec. 10, 1949 Moonee Ponds (Vic)

Maranta, Michael Gerard (Qld) b March 20, 1961 South Brisbane (Qld)

Marjoribanks, Hugh Lynch (NSW) b Aug. 12, 1933 Mackay (Qld)

Marks, Alexander Edward (NSW) b Dec. 9, 1910 Toowong (Qld) d July 28, 1983 Wahroonga (NSW)

Marks, Lynn Alexander (NSW & SAust) b Aug. 15, 1942 Randwick (NSW) d Dec. 7, 1997 Mona Vale (NSW)

Marks, Neil Graham (NSW) b Sept. 13, 1938 Randwick (NSW)

Marks, Phillip Henry (NSW) b April 30, 1961 Salisbury (Southern Rhodesia)

* Marks, Victor James (WAust) b June 25, 1955 Middle Chinnock, Somerset (England)

Marquet, Joshua Phillip (Tas) b Dec. 3, 1968 Melbourne (Vic)

* Marr, Alfred Percy (NSW) b March 28, 1862 Pyrmont (NSW) d March 15, 1940 Arncliffe (NSW)

Marriott, Arthur John (Tas) b c. 1821 (England) d March 31, 1866 Nice (France)

Marsden, Albert John (Qld) b June 13, 1887 Maryborough (Qld) d Dec. 17, 1971 Kallista (Vic)

Marsden, Frederick William (Vic) b c. 1819 Lewisham, London (England) d March 20, 1870 Fitzroy (Vic)

Marsh, Daniel James (SAust & Tas) b June 14, 1973 Subiaco (WAust)

* Marsh, Geoffrey Robert (WAust) b Dec. 31, 1958 Northam (WAust)

Marsh, Jack (NSW) b c. 1874 Yugilbar (NSW) d May 25, 1916 Orange (NSW)

* Marsh, Rodney William (WAust) b Nov. 4, 1947 Armadale (WAust)

Marsh, Shaun Edwards (WAust) b July 9, 1983 Narrogin (WAust)

Marshal, Alan (Qld) b June 12, 1883 Warwick (Qld) d July 23, 1915 Imtarfa Military Hospital (Malta)

Marshall, Angus Neil (Qld) b Jan. 27, 1906 Essequibo (British Guiana) d Aug. 29, 1969 Nundah (Qld)

Marshall, George (Tas) b 1832 birth day and month unknown Sorell (Tas) d July 13, 1905 Sorell (Tas)

Marshall, George (Vic) b Dec. 20, 1829 Nottingham, Nottinghamshire (England) d March 6, 1868 Melbourne (Vic)

Marshall, John (Tas) b c. 1796 (England) d Sept. 7, 1876 New Town (Tas)

Martin, Charles (Qld) b May 15, 1867 Ipswich (Qld) d c. 1942 Sydney (NSW)

Martin, Charles Albert (SAust) b March 29, 1863 Adelaide (SAust) d May 14, 1955 St Georges (SAust)

Martin, Charles William Beresford (Tas) b Oct. 6, 1888 Launceston (Tas) d Oct. 30, 1951 Camberwell (Vic)

Martin, Edmund John (WAust) b Sept. 30, 1902 Eaglehawk (Vic)

Martin, Geoffrey Bernard (Tas) b July 16, 1927 Launceston (Tas)

Martin, Geoffrey William (Tas) b March 7, 1896 Launceston (Tas) d March 7, 1968 Launceston (Tas)

Martin, Gordon Francis (Qld) b Jan. 14, 1885 Clunes (Vic) d Aug. 19, 1974 Canberra (ACT)

Martin, Hugh (NSW) b Aug. 3, 1947 Enkeldoorn (Southern Rhodesia)

Martin, James Macfie (Tas) b Feb. 25, 1851 Launceston (Tas) d Oct. 22, 1930 Launceston (Tas)

Martin, John Frank (NSW) b May 8, 1942 Alton, Hampshire (England)

* Martin, John Wesley (NSW & SAust) b July 28, 1931 Wingham (NSW) d July 15, 1992 Burrell Creek (NSW)

Martin, William (Tas) b June 21, 1856 Westbury (Tas) d July 10, 1938 Launceston (Tas)

* Martyn, Damien Richard (WAust) b Oct. 21, 1971 Darwin (NT)

Mason, Matthew Sean (WAust) b March 20, 1974 Claremont (WAust)

Mason, Scott Robert (Tas) b July 27, 1976 George Town (Tas)

Massey, Richard Eric Charles (SAust) b June 5, 1961 Tamworth (NSW)

* Massie, Hugh Hamon (NSW) b April 11, 1854 near Belfast (Vic) d Oct. 12, 1938 Point Piper (NSW)

* Massie, Robert Arnold Lockyer (WAust) b April 14, 1947 Subiaco (WAust)

Massie, Robert John Allwright (NSW) b July 8, 1890 North Sydney (NSW) d Feb. 14, 1966 Mosman (NSW)

Mateljan, Tony (WAust) b Feb. 18, 1934 Middle Swan (WAust)

Mather, Adam (NSW) b Nov. 26, 1860 Paterson (NSW) d Aug. 31, 1917 Singleton (NSW)

Mather, John Henry (Vic) b Nov. 19, 1822 Everton, Lancashire (England) d Aug. 4, 1870 Iquique (Chile)

Mathers, James (Vic) b June 30, 1894 Minmi (NSW) d March 28, 1977 Eastwood (NSW)

Mathieson, Donald Kenneth (Vic) b April 24, 1931 Nhill (Vic)

Matson, George (Tas) b Dec. 5, 1817 Rochester, Kent (England) d July 22, 1898 Brighton, Sussex (England)

* Matthews, Christopher Darrell (WAust & Tas) b Sept. 22, 1962 Cunderdin (WAust)

* Matthews, Gregory Richard John (NSW) b Dec. 15, 1959 Newcastle (NSW)

Matthews, James George Facey (SAust) b Sept. 27, 1876 Roseworthy (SAust) d Oct. 8, 1963 Prospect (SAust)

Matthews, Robert Graham (Vic) b April 17, 1953 Camberwell (Vic)

Matthews, Thomas Harold (Tas) b Feb. 9, 1905 Longley (Tas) d May 11, 1990 Longley (Tas)

* Matthews, Thomas James (Vic) b April 3, 1884 Mt Gambier (SAust) d Oct. 14, 1943 Caulfield (Vic)

Maxwell, Eustace (Tas) b Jan. 20, 1864 Hobart (Tas) d May 18, 1939 Hobart (Tas)

Maxwell, Neil Donald (Vic & NSW) b June 12, 1967 Lautoka (Fiji)

* May, Timothy Brian Alexander (SAust) b Jan. 26, 1962 North Adelaide (SAust)

Mayes, Alexander Dunbar Aitken (NSW & Qld) b July 24, 1901 Toowoomba (Qld) d Feb. 8, 1983 Spring Hill (Qld)

* Mayne, Lawrence Charles (WAust) b Jan. 23, 1942 Westonia (WAust)

* Mayne, Richard Edgar (SAust & Vic) b July 2, 1882 Jamestown (SAust) d Oct. 26, 1961 Richmond (Vic)

* Meckiff, Ian (Vic) b Jan. 6, 1935 Mentone (Vic)

Meech, James Robert (Tas) b Dec. 16, 1884 Hobart (Tas) d Oct. 31, 1955 Hobart (Tas)

Meek, Andrew Bonar (WAust) b Dec. 7, 1889 Gulgong (NSW) d Feb. 13, 1957 Perth (WAust)

Meikle, George Stanley (Vic) b Oct. 22, 1916 Footscray (Vic) d July 25, 1991 Brighton (Vic)

Melville, Paul (Vic) b Dec. 27, 1956 South Shields, Durham (England) d Nov. 21, 1978 Vermont South (Vic)

Menegon, Lyndon John (Tas) b Feb. 11, 1948 Burnie (Tas)

Mengel, Douglas Charles (Qld) b March 2, 1933 Brisbane (Qld)

Metcalfe, Evelyn James (Qld) b Sept. 29, 1865 Kennington, Kent (England) d June 14, 1951 Cambridge, Cambridgeshire (England)

* Meuleman, Kenneth Douglas (Vic & WAust) b Sept. 5, 1923 Melbourne (Vic)

Meuleman, Robert Douglas (WAust) b Sept. 6, 1949 Melbourne (Vic)

Meuleman, Scott William (WAust) b July 17, 1980 Subiaco (WAust)

Michael, Constantine Anthony (WAust) b Jan. 12, 1953 Victoria Park (WAust)

Michael, Leonard (SAust) b June 3, 1921 Medindie (SAust) d March 16, 1996 Adelaide (SAust)

Middleton, Frederick Stewart (NSW) b May 28, 1883 Burrowa (now Booroowa) (NSW) d July 21, 1956 Auckland (New Zealand)

Middleton, Roy Foster (SAust) b Sept. 18, 1889 Kent Town (SAust) d March 19, 1975 Adelaide (SAust)

**Midwinter, William Evans (Vic) b June 19, 1851 St Briavel's, Gloucestershire (England) d Dec. 3, 1890 Kew Asylum (Vic)

Mihell, Robert William (Qld) b Jan. 8, 1937 Lismore (NSW)

* Milburn, Colin (WAust) b Oct. 23, 1941 Burnopfield, Durham (England) d Feb. 28, 1990 Newton Aycliffe, Durham (England)

Miles, Geoffrey John (Vic) b Aug. 7, 1957 Kew (Vic)

Millar, Geoffrey Alan (WAust) b Nov. 22, 1955 Subiaco (WAust)

Millar, Keith James (Vic) b Aug. 15, 1906 Richmond (Vic) d July 13, 1971 Camberwell (Vic)

* Miller, Colin Reid (Vic, SAust & Tas) b Feb. 6, 1964 Footscray (Vic)

Miller, David Lawson (NSW & Qld) b Jan. 30, 1870 Holytown, Lanarkshire (Scotland) d April 12, 1943 Clayfield (Qld)

Miller, Graeme Geoffrey (Combined XI) b Sept. 24, 1940 Launceston (Tas)

Miller, Ivan Derness (Vic) b Dec. 30, 1913 Ivanhoe (Vic) d May 6, 1966 Heidelberg (Vic)

* Miller, Keith Ross (Vic & NSW) b Nov. 28, 1919 Sunshine (Vic)

Miller, Kevin Roy (Tas) b Oct. 12, 1936 Launceston (Tas)

Miller, Leslie Percy Robert (Vic) b June 16, 1880 St Kilda (Vic) d July 2, 1963 death place unknown

Miller, Michael Christian (Qld & SAust) b May 30, 1979 Toowoomba (Qld)

Miller, Noel Keith (NSW) b July 1, 1913 Wyong (NSW)

Miller, William Edward (WAust) b March 9, 1905 East Perth (WAust) d July 24, 1974 Perth (WAust)

Milliken, Geoffrey Scott (NSW) b May 6, 1964 Hay (NSW)

Millns, David James (Tas) b Feb. 27, 1965 Clipstone, Nottinghamshire (England)

Mills, John (NSW) b June 3, 1836 Botley, Hampshire (England) d Feb. 24, 1899 Bisterne, Hampshire (England)

Mills, Rowland Leslie (WAust) b July 14, 1914 Leederville (WAust) d Feb. 27, 2000 Perth (WAust)

Milosz, Stephen Joseph (WAust & Tas) b Dec. 26, 1955 Northam (WAust)

Minagall, Matthew John Peter (SAust) b Nov. 13, 1971 Woodville (SAust)

Minchin, James Melbourne (Vic) b Aug. 15, 1859 Emerald Hill (Vic) d Feb. 13, 1919 Cheltenham (Vic)

Minnett, Leslie Alma (NSW) b May 19, 1883 St Leonards (NSW) d Aug. 8, 1934 Collaroy (NSW)

* Minnett, Roy Baldwin (NSW) b June 13, 1886 St Leonards (NSW) d Oct. 21, 1955 Manly (NSW)

Minnett, Rupert Villiers (NSW) b Sept. 2, 1884 St Leonards (NSW) d June 24, 1974 Cremorne (NSW)

Minter, Eric James (NSW) b Sept. 13, 1917 Kempsey (NSW) d July 1, 1985 Vincentia (NSW)

* Misson, Francis Michael (NSW) b Nov. 19, 1938 Darlinghurst (NSW)

Mitchell, Brian Gordon (SAust) b March 15, 1959 Glenelg (SAust)

Mitchell, Norman Frederick (Vic) b Feb. 19, 1900 Collingwood (Vic) d March 8, 1973 Melbourne (Vic)

Mitchell, Robert (Vic) b April 11, 1863 Campbellfield (Vic) d Sept. 17, 1926 West Preston (Vic)

Moffat, William (SAust) b July 22, 1858 Byethorne (SAust) d July 30, 1922 Jamestown (SAust)

Moffatt, Alfred Augustine (WAust) b March 15, 1870 Perth (WAust) d Dec. 8, 1956 Perth (WAust)

Moir, Bruce Graeme (Vic) b Nov. 10, 1960 Melbourne (Vic)

Monfries, John Elliott (Vic) b Dec. 25, 1873 Gumeracha (SAust) d Sept. 2, 1954 Hobart (Tas)

Monohan, Vincent Clifford (Vic) b April 22, 1896 Collingwood (Vic) d July 9, 1974 Linden Park (SAust)

Monty, Stephen (Qld) b March 3, 1963 Glenelg (SAust)

* Moody, Thomas Masson (WAust) b Oct. 2, 1965 Adelaide (SAust)

Moore, David John Arthur (NSW) b Oct. 16, 1964 Sydney (NSW)

Moore, George (NSW) b April 18, 1820 Ampthill, Bedfordshire (England) d Sept. 29, 1916 West Maitland (NSW)

Moore, George Stanley (NSW & Qld) b April 18, 1886 North Sydney (NSW) d March 22, 1948 Bundaberg (Qld)

Moore, Henry Thomas (SAust) b c. 1860 Plomesgate (England) death details unknown

Moore, James (NSW) b c. 1839 Ampthill, Bedfordshire (England) d April 19, 1890 West Maitland (NSW)

Moore, Leonard David (NSW) b Feb. 8, 1871 West Maitland (NSW) d Sept. 11, 1934 Maitland (NSW)

Moore, William Henry (NSW & WAust) b Oct. 16, 1863 West Maitland (NSW) d Feb. 25, 1956 Lane Cove (NSW)

Morcom, Samuel (Combined XIII) b c. 1847 full birth details unknown d Jan. 15, 1888 Adelaide (SAust)

Morgan, Charles Edward (Vic) b Aug. 10, 1900 Collingwood (Vic) d Dec. 8, 1965 Preston (Vic)

Morgan, Charles William (Qld) b Jan. 10, 1877 Hotham (Vic) d April 15, 1937 death place unknown

Morgan, George (NSW) b July 7, 1844 Bathurst (NSW) d July 17, 1896 Sydney (NSW)

Morgan, John Gordon (NSW) b March 6, 1893 Camperdown (NSW) d May 7, 1967 Concord (NSW)

Morgan, Oliver John (Qld) b June 7, 1945 Herston (Qld)

Morgan, Walter Millard (Vic) b Nov. 1, 1871 Ballarat (Vic) d July 10, 1941 Ballarat (Vic)

Morgan, Wayne Geoffrey (Qld) b July 10, 1955 Greenslopes (Qld)

* Moroney, John (NSW) b July 24, 1917 Macksville (NSW) d July 1, 1999 Orange (NSW)

Moroney, Robert (SAust) b Jan. 23, 1885 Upper Sturt (SAust) d Aug. 4, 1958 Parkside (SAust)

Morres, Thomas Furley (Vic) b Sept. 12, 1829 Wokingham, Berkshire (England) d Sept. 28, 1884 East Melbourne (Vic)

* Morris, Arthur Robert (NSW) b Jan. 19, 1922 Bondi (NSW)

Morris, John Humphrey (NSW) b June 5, 1831 Sydney (NSW) d Dec. 9, 1921 Glebe Point (NSW)

Morris, Maesmore Alfred (Vic) b c. 1868 Northcote (Vic) d Aug. 31, 1917 Heidelberg (Vic)

Morris, Norman O'Neil (NSW) b May 9, 1907 Camperdown (NSW) d July 15, 1982 Leichhardt (NSW)

* Morris, Samuel (Vic) b June 22, 1855 Hobart (Tas) d Sept. 20, 1931 South Melbourne (Vic)

Morris, William Wallace (Qld) b March 6, 1918 Thornleigh (NSW)

Morrisby, Ronald Orlando George (Tas) b Jan. 12, 1915 Hobart (Tas) d June 12, 1995 Hobart (Tas)

Morrissey, Charles Vincent (NSW) b April 26, 1903 Corowa (NSW) d Feb. 20, 1938 Quirindi (NSW)

Morse, Eric George Arnold (Tas) b Aug. 26, 1918 Sheffield (Tas)

Morton, Francis Lonsdale (SAust & Vic) b Dec. 21, 1901 Fullarton (SAust) d Oct. 14, 1971 Caulfield (Vic)

Morton, Hugh Gilbert Stuart (Qld) b Oct. 14, 1881 Maryborough (Qld) d Jan. 28, 1936 Herston (Qld)

* Moses, Henry (NSW) b Feb. 13, 1858 Windsor (NSW) d Dec. 7, 1938 Strathfield (NSW)

* Moss, Jeffrey Kenneth (Vic) b June 29, 1947 Melbourne (Vic)

Moss, Jonathan (Vic) b May 4, 1975 Manly (NSW)

Moss, Ronald Barbar (NSW) b June 13, 1922 Alexandria (NSW)

Mossop, Kenneth Leonard Mario (Qld) b Aug. 15, 1909 New Farm (Qld) d Sept. 18, 1975 Surfers Paradise (Qld)

Mott, Matthew Peter (Qld & Vic) b Oct. 3, 1973 Charleville (Qld)

* Moule, William Henry (Vic) b Jan. 31, 1858 Brighton (Vic) d Aug. 24, 1939 St Kilda (Vic)

Moyes, Alban George (SAust & Vic) b Jan. 2, 1893 Gladstone (SAust) d Jan. 18, 1963 Chatswood (NSW)

Moyle, Charles Rule (SAust) b April 16, 1884 Adelaide (SAust) d Aug. 2, 1952 Adelaide (SAust)

Moyle, Edward James Ross (SAust) b Oct. 15, 1913 Moonta Mines (SAust) d Oct. 24, 1942 Cairo (Egypt) on active service

Moysey, George Bickford (WAust) b May 14, 1874 Battery Point (Tas) d May 18, 1932 Canterbury (NSW)

Muddle, Donald Gordon (Qld) b July 26, 1937 The Grange (Qld)

Mudge, Harold (NSW) b Feb. 14, 1914 Stanmore (NSW)

Mueller, Mervyn Edward Christopher Edgar (SAust) b Oct. 3, 1914 Yatala (SAust)

Muggleton, Mervyn Brian (WAust) b Sept. 4, 1941 Unley (SAust)

Muhl, Arthur Henry (Qld) b Feb. 12, 1913 South Brisbane (Qld) d April 17, 1994 South Brisbane (Qld)

Muir, William Frederick (Vic) b Feb. 8, 1907 Prahran (Vic) d Nov. 27, 1964 Box Hill (Vic)

Mulder, Brett (WAust) b Feb. 6, 1964 Subiaco (WAust)

Mulherin, Wayne Michael (NSW) b June 17, 1957 Canterbury (NSW)

Mullagh, Johnny (Unaarrimin) (Vic) b Aug. 13, 1841 Harrow (Vic) d Aug. 14, 1891 Pine Hills Station (Vic)

* Mullally, Alan David (WAust) b July 12, 1969 Southend-on-Sea, Essex (England)

Mullarkey, Desmond Antony (NSW) b Sept. 19, 1899 Rockdale (NSW) d Sept. 1, 1975 death place unknown

* Muller, Scott Andrew (Qld) b July 11, 1971 Herston (Qld)

Mullett, David Anthony (Tas) b Aug. 18, 1958 Burnie (Tas)

Mullett, Leonard Thomas (Vic) b Nov. 27, 1894 Moonee Ponds (Vic) d April 22, 1944 Toorak (Vic)

Mullooly, Thomas Cade (WAust) b Jan. 30, 1954 Mt Lawley (WAust)

Mundy, David Lloyd (SAust) b June 30, 1947 Enfield (SAust)

Munn, Arthur Reginald (NSW) b Feb. 22, 1888 Paddington (NSW) d Sept. 15, 1975 Sydney (NSW)

Munro, Charles (WAust) b March 21, 1871 Wallan (Vic) d Feb. 7, 1969 North Fremantle (WAust)

Munro, John Knox Ewing (WAust) b Dec. 27, 1928 Perth (WAust)

Munro, William (Qld) b c. 1862 Manchester, Lancashire (England) d Feb. 18, 1896 Stanthorpe (Qld)

Murch, Stewart Nigel Clifford (Vic) b June 27, 1944 Warrnambool (Vic)

**Murdoch, William Lloyd (NSW) b Oct. 18, 1854 Sandhurst (Vic) d Feb. 18, 1911 Melbourne (Vic)

Murfett, Julian Ivor (Tas) b July 2, 1915 Dunorlan (Tas) d April 27, 1982 Hobart (Tas)

Murphy, James Joseph (NSW) b Sept. 29, 1911 Bega (NSW) d May 7, 1984 Glenfield (NSW)

Murphy, Michael Augustus (Vic) b June 12, 1854 Sydney (NSW) d Sept. 2, 1890 Richmond (Vic)

Murray, Alfred Wynyatt (Vic) b Feb. 4, 1868 Long Gully (Vic) d July 27, 1936 Regent (Vic)

Murray, George Ian (WAust) b Nov. 6, 1940 South Perth (WAust)

Murray, John Tinline (SAust) b Dec. 1, 1892 Norwood (SAust) d Sept. 19, 1974 Stirling (WAust)

Murray, Norman Eric (Tas) b Nov. 2, 1908 Perth (WAust) d Aug. 21, 1967 Manly (NSW)

Murray, Richard (NSW) b c. 1831 Sydney (NSW) d Nov. 21, 1861 Manly (NSW)

Murray, William Walter Bruce (Vic) b Sept. 4, 1929 Red Cliffs (Vic)

* Musgrove, Henry Alfred (Vic) b Nov. 27, 1860 Surbiton, Surrey (England) d Nov. 2, 1931 Darlinghurst (NSW)

Musgrove, John (SAust) b July 28, 1861 Adelaide (SAust) d June 9, 1940 death place unknown

Mutton, Howard James Charles (SAust) b Oct. 21, 1924 Angaston (SAust) d Nov. 20, 1992 Adelaide (SAust)

Myers, Hubert (Tas) b Jan. 2, 1875 Yeadon, Yorkshire (England) d June 12, 1944 Hobart (Tas)

* Nagel, Lisle Ernest (Vic) b March 26, 1905 Bendigo (Vic) d Nov. 23, 1971 Mornington (Vic)

Nagel, Vernon George (Vic) b March 26, 1905 Bendigo (Vic) d April 27, 1974 Sandringham (Vic)

Nash, Brendan Paul (Qld) b Dec. 14, 1977 Bentley (WAust)

Nash, Don Anthony (NSW) b March 29, 1978 Dubbo (NSW)

Nash, John Eric (SAust) b April 16, 1950 North Adelaide (SAust)

* Nash, Laurence John (Tas & Vic) b May 2, 1910 Fitzroy (Vic) d July 24, 1986 Heidelberg (Vic)

Neill, Bruce William (Tas) b Feb. 23, 1949 Cabramatta (NSW)

Nettelton, Robert Glanville (Vic) b Sept. 16, 1909 Newport (Vic) d April 6, 1972 Newport (Vic)

Neville, Kevin John (Vic) b March 24, 1968 Numurkah (Vic)

Neville, Warwick John (Qld) b Dec. 31, 1948 Melbourne (Vic)

Newcombe, Henry Charles Edwin (NSW) b c. 1835 Sydney (NSW) d Oct. 26, 1908 Randwick (NSW)

Newell, Andrew Livingstone (NSW) b Nov. 13, 1865 Dungog (NSW) death details unknown

Newland, Philip Mesmer (SAust) b Feb. 2, 1875 Kensington (SAust) d Aug. 11, 1916 Knightsbridge (SAust)

Newman, Charles Frederick (WAust) b Nov. 7, 1909 Fremantle (WAust) d March 28, 1977 Fremantle (WAust)

Newman, Henry Albert (WAust) b March 13, 1907 Fremantle (WAust) d April 23, 1988 Riverton (WAust)

Newman, Richard Nelson (Tas) b Aug. 9, 1924 Brunswick (Vic)

Newstead, George Holt (Vic) b Aug. 11, 1910 Brighton (Vic) d July 21, 2000 Deepdene (Vic)

Newton, Alan Colin (Tas) b April 6, 1894 Longford (Tas) d March 27, 1979 Narrabeen (NSW)

Newton, Percy Allen (NSW) b Dec. 21, 1880 Newtown (NSW) d April 25, 1946 Rose Bay (NSW)

Nichols, Arthur Joseph (NSW) b Sept. 3, 1881 Sydney (NSW) d Nov. 19, 1937 North Sydney (NSW)

Nicholls, Charles Omer (NSW) b Dec. 5, 1901 Freeman's Reach (NSW) d Jan. 14, 1983 Freeman's Reach (NSW)

Nicholls, Paul Allen (WAust) b Nov. 10, 1946 East Fremantle (WAust)

Nicholls, Ronald Charles (Vic) b Sept. 1, 1951 Footscray (Vic)

* Nicholson, Matthew James (WAust) b Oct. 2, 1974 St Leonards (NSW)

Nicolson, John Norman Walter (Tas) b April 14, 1917 Campbell Town (Tas) d Oct. 7, 1992 Launceston (Tas)

Niehuus, Richard Dudley (SAust) b July 6, 1917 St Peters (SAust)

Nielsen, Timothy John (SAust) b May 5, 1968 Forest Gate, London (England)

Nikitaras, Steven (NSW & WAust) b Aug. 31, 1970 Port Kembla (NSW)

* Nitschke, Holmesdale Carl (SAust) b April 14, 1905 Adelaide (SAust) d Sept. 29, 1982 North Adelaide (SAust)

Nobes, Paul Christopher (Vic & SAust) b April 20, 1964 West Heidelberg (Vic)

Noble, Edward George (NSW) b Jan. 16, 1865 Brickfield Hill (NSW) d May 4, 1941 Balmain (NSW)

* Noble, Montague Alfred (NSW) b Jan. 28, 1873 Sydney (NSW) d June 22, 1940 Randwick (NSW)

* Noblet, Geffery (SAust) b Sept. 14, 1916 Evandale (SAust)

Noel, John (SAust) b March 28, 1856 Hindmarsh (SAust) d Jan. 9, 1938 Largs Bay (SAust)

Noffke, Ashley Allan (Cricket Academy) b April 30, 1977 Nambour (Qld)

Nolan, Francis Edward (Qld) b June 27, 1920 Manly (Qld)

Noonan, Daniel Francis (Vic) b May 11, 1873 North Melbourne (Vic) d May 30, 1910 North Melbourne (Vic)

Noonan, David James (NSW) b Jan. 8, 1876 Newtown (NSW) d March 10, 1929 Sydney (NSW)

Norman, Michael John (Tas) b Aug. 17, 1952 Launceston (Tas)

Norman, Hercules Rex (NSW) b 1890 birthplace unknown d Dec. 30, 1961 Parramatta (NSW)

North, Frederic Dudley (WAust) b Nov. 9, 1866 Kensington, London, Middlesex (England) d Aug. 22, 1921 Cottesloe (WAust)

North, Marcus James (WAust) b July 28, 1979 Melbourne (Vic)

* Nothling, Otto Ernest (NSW & Qld) b Aug. 1, 1900 Teutoburg (Qld) d Sept. 26, 1965 Chelmer (Qld)

Noyes, Alfred William Finch (Vic) b c. 1835 Torquay, Devon (England) d Sept. 30, 1902 Deniliquin (NSW)

Noyes, Harold David (Qld) b Aug. 12, 1892 Warwick (Qld) d July 14, 1968 Brisbane (Qld)

Numa, Herbert Leslie (Vic) b June 22, 1925 Carlton (Vic) d April 17, 1984 Heidelberg (Vic)

Nunn, Thomas (NSW) b Jan. 21, 1846 Penshurst, Kent (England) d May 31, 1889 Bexley (NSW)

Nutt, Richard Nathaniel (NSW) b June 25, 1911 Balmain (NSW) d Feb. 5, 1985 Gladesville (NSW)

Oakes, Cecil James Grellis (Tas) b March 1, 1915 Hobart (Tas) d Oct. 10, 1994 Canberra (ACT)

Oakley, Hector Herbert (Vic) b Jan. 10, 1909 North Fitzroy (Vic) d Dec. 19, 1998 Sandringham (Vic)

Oatley, James Napoleon (NSW) b Aug. 12, 1845 Newtown (NSW) d Dec. 17, 1925 Cremorne (NSW)

O'Brien, Aaron Warren (NSW) b Oct. 2, 1981 St Leonards (NSW)

O'Brien, Charles Joseph (NSW) b c. 1921 birthplace unknown d Dec. 15, 1980 Coal Point (NSW)

O'Brien, Ernest Francis (NSW) b Aug. 26, 1900 Paddington (NSW) d Nov. 2, 1935 Newcastle (NSW)

* O'Brien, Leo Patrick Joseph (Vic) b July 2, 1907 West Melbourne (Vic) d March 13, 1997 Mentone (Vic)

O'Brien, Leslie John (NSW) d c. 1968 full birth and death details unknown

O'Brien, M. Evanson (Anderson's XI) birth and death details unknown

O'Brien, Robert (Qld) b July 16, 1869 Redfern (NSW) d Oct. 2, 1922 Brisbane (Qld)

O'Connell, Thomas Reginald (SAust) b March 10, 1916 Parkside (SAust)

O'Connor, Brian Redmond Devereaux (Qld) b July 5, 1913 South Brisbane (Qld) d Dec. 20, 1963 Red Hill (Qld)

O'Connor, Donald Frederick Gregory (SAust & Tas) b July 20, 1958 Gilgandra (NSW)

* O'Connor, John Denis Alphonsus (NSW & SAust) b Sept. 9, 1875 Booroowa (NSW) d Aug. 23, 1941 Lewisham (NSW)

O'Connor, John William (Vic) b Aug. 19, 1868 Geelong (Vic) d Feb. 2, 1952 Windsor (Vic)

O'Connor, Leo Patrick Devereaux (Qld) b April 11, 1890 Murtoa (Vic) d Jan. 16, 1985 Melbourne (Vic)

* O'Donnell, Simon Patrick (Vic) b Jan. 26, 1963 Deniliquin (NSW)

O'Dwyer, Thomas Edmund (WAust) b Nov. 5, 1919 Bridgetown (WAust)

* Ogilvie, Alan David (Qld) b June 3, 1951 Southport (Qld)

Ogilvy, David Skene (NSW) b c. 1859 Wollongong (NSW) d Aug. 6, 1917 Liverpool (NSW)

O'Halloran, Dale Francis (Tas) b Feb. 15, 1955 Smithton (Tas)

O'Halloran, James Patrick (Vic) b Jan. 12, 1872 Richmond (Vic) d April 28, 1943 East Melbourne (Vic)

O'Halloran, William Matthew (Vic) b June 18, 1934 Corowa (NSW) d Dec. 13, 1994 East Melbourne (Vic)

O'Hanlon, William James (NSW) b March 10, 1863 Carlton (Vic) d June 23, 1940 Randwick (NSW)

Ohlstrom, Patrick Andreas Paul (SAust) b Dec. 16, 1890 Warooka (SAust) d June 10, 1940 Adelaide (SAust)

O'Keeffe, Francis Aloysius (NSW & Vic) b May 11, 1896 Waverley (NSW) d March 26, 1924 Hampstead, London (England)

* O'Keeffe, Kerry James (NSW) b Nov. 25, 1949 Hurstville (NSW)

O'Leary, Scott James (Qld) b Dec. 17, 1977 South Brisbane (Qld)

* Oldfield, William Albert Stanley (NSW) b Sept. 9, 1894 Alexandria (NSW) d Aug. 10, 1976 Killara (NSW)

Oldroyd, Bradley John (WAust) b Nov. 5, 1973 Bentley (WAust)

Oliver, Benjamin Carl (Vic) b Oct. 24, 1979 Castlemaine (Vic)

Oliver, Charles Nicholson Jewel (NSW) b April 24, 1848 Hobart (Tas) d June 14, 1920 Manly (NSW)

Oliver, Stuart Bradley (Tas) b March 20, 1972 Launceston (Tas)

O'Meara, Phillip Anthony (WAust) b June 13, 1951 Kellerberrin (WAust)

O'Mullane, George Jeremiah Patrick (Vic) b Dec. 3, 1842 Melbourne (Vic) d Dec. 20, 1866 East Melbourne (Vic)

O'Neill, Kevin Ignatius (SAust) b Aug. 16, 1919 Hectorville (SAust)

O'Neill, Mark Dorian (WAust & NSW) b March 5, 1959 Sutherland (NSW)

* O'Neill, Norman Clifford (NSW) b Feb. 19, 1937 Carlton (NSW)

Onyons, Basil Austin (Vic) b March 14, 1887 Prahran (Vic) d May 31, 1967 Glen Iris (Vic)

O'Regan, James Bernard (NSW) b April 23, 1938 Ashfield (NSW) d May 15, 1998 Randwick (NSW)

O'Reilly, John William (NSW) b Nov. 16, 1930 Mosman (NSW)

* O'Reilly, William Joseph (NSW) b Dec. 20, 1905 White Cliffs (NSW) d Oct. 6, 1992 Sutherland (NSW)

Orr, Herbert Richard (WAust) b Feb. 3, 1865 Kensington, London (England) d May 22, 1940 Sevenoaks, Kent (England)

Osborn, Francis James (SAust) b Feb. 13, 1935 Alberton (SAust)

Osborne, Mark (Vic) b Oct. 8, 1961 Kogarah (NSW)

Osborne, Noton Michael (Vic) b c. 1844 (England) d Dec. 10, 1878 Hobart (Tas)

Osborne, Robert Henry (NSW) b Feb. 4, 1897 Redfern (NSW) d Feb. 21, 1975 Long Jetty (NSW)

Osborne, Robert Moorhead (Vic) b Sept. 29, 1881 St Kilda (Vic) d Nov. 19, 1927 Wesburn (Vic)

O'Shannassy, Robert Martin (SAust) b March 7, 1949 Hindmarsh (SAust)

O'Shaughnessy, Barney (WAust) b Feb. 28, 1912 Wiluna (WAust)

Oswald, Norman Hamilton (SAust) b Oct. 31, 1916 Prospect (SAust) d June 22, 1970 Adelaide (SAust)

Outridge, Thomas Michael (WAust) b Sept. 8, 1927 Perth (WAust)

Over, Willie (Vic) b Jan. 20, 1862 Richmond (Vic) d Nov. 10, 1910 Krugersdorp, Transvaal (South Africa)

Owen, Christopher John (SAust) b Dec. 21, 1963 Henley Beach (SAust)

Owen, Kerry Alfred (NSW) b June 23, 1943 Bondi Beach (NSW)

Oxenford, Bruce Nicholas James (Qld) b March 5, 1960 Southport (Qld)

Oxenford, Ian Bruce (Qld) b Sept. 3, 1932 South Brisbane (Qld)

Oxenham, Lionel Emmanuel (Qld) b Jan. 27, 1888 Nundah (Qld) d Jan. 10, 1970 Clayfield (Qld)

* Oxenham, Ronald Keven (Qld) b July 28, 1891 Nundah (Qld) d Aug. 16, 1939 Nundah (Qld)

Packham, Leonard (WAust) b Sept. 15, 1891 Norwood (SAust) d Oct. 4, 1958 Swanbourne (WAust)

Page, Clive Basil (Qld) b May 25, 1894 Rockhampton (Qld) d July 1, 1967 Greenslopes (Qld)

Palfreyman, Brent Avis Hardcastle (Tas) b Jan. 20, 1945 Hobart (Tas)

* Palmer, George Eugene (Vic & Tas) b Feb. 22, 1859 Mulwala (NSW) d Aug. 22, 1910 Benalla (Vic)

Palmer, George Hamilton (SAust) b Aug. 2, 1903 Eastwood (SAust) d Aug. 24, 1986 Woodville South (SAust)

Palmer, Jack Stirling (SAust) b Oct. 20, 1903 East Adelaide (SAust) d Dec. 11, 1979 Glenelg (SAust)

Panitzki, Robert James (Tas) b April 29, 1948 Hobart (Tas)

Park, Alfred Leath (NSW) b April 15, 1840 Oatlands (Tas) d Jan. 16, 1924 Liverpool (NSW)

* Park, Roy Lindsay (Vic) b July 30, 1892 Charlton (Vic) d Jan. 23, 1947 Middle Park (Vic)

Parker, Alec David (Qld) b June 12, 1955 Dalby (Qld)

Parker, Ernest Frederick (WAust) b Nov. 5, 1883 Perth (WAust) d May 2, 1918 Caestre (France)

Parker, Geoffrey Ross (Vic & SAust) b March 31, 1968 Malvern (Vic)

Parker, John Francis (WAust) b March 13, 1936 South Perth (WAust)

Parker, Robert Ernest (Qld) b Sept. 18, 1942 Toowoomba (Qld)

Parker, Ronald Arthur (SAust) b Feb. 23, 1916 Goodwood (SAust) d Aug. 27, 1993 San Francisco, California (United States of America)

Parker, Russell John (SAust) b Aug. 3, 1952 Sudbury, Middlesex (England)

Parkin, George Thomas (SAust) b Oct. 11, 1864 Adelaide (SAust) d Aug. 6, 1933 Adelaide (SAust)

Parkinson, Henry (Tas) b June 10, 1882 Port Arthur (Tas) d c. 1962 death place unknown

Parkinson, Samuel David Haslam (SAust) b July 8, 1960 Adelaide (SAust)

Parry, Cyril Norman (SAust & Tas) b Oct. 14, 1900 Queenstown (SAust) d July 6, 1984 Kew (Vic)

Parsonage, Thomas Griffiths (NSW) b Nov. 13, 1910 Chatswood (NSW) d Feb. 3, 1951 Manly (NSW)

Parsons, Herbert Fulton (Vic) b May 21, 1875 Hawthorn (Vic) d Dec. 20, 1937 Canterbury (Vic)

* Pascoe, Len Stephen (NSW) b Feb. 13, 1950 Bridgetown (WAust)

Pascoe, Matthew David (Qld) b Jan. 10, 1977 Camperdown (NSW)

Pateman, Robert (Vic) b Aug. 28, 1856 Magpie (Vic) death details unknown

Patfield, Alfred Samuel (WAust) b Sept. 6, 1884 Paterson (NSW) d Nov. 9, 1961 Perth (WAust)

Paton, George Douglas (Tas) b March 1, 1879 Hobart (Tas) d Oct. 5, 1950 Hobart (Tas)

Patrick, Charles Wright (NSW & Qld) b Jan. 13, 1866 Sydney (NSW) d Nov. 29, 1919 Coogee (NSW)

* Patterson, Balfour Patrick (Tas) b Sept. 15, 1961 Portland (Jamaica)

Patterson, Brian Clifford (Tas) b June 28, 1937 Hobart (Tas)

Patterson, Mark Winston (NSW) b Nov. 15, 1966 Dubbo (NSW)

Patterson, Thomas Francis (Tas) b Sept. 16, 1839 Hobart (Tas)

Paulsen, Robert George (Qld & WAust) b Oct. 18, 1947 Herston (Qld)

Pavy, Leonard (WAust) b Aug. 21, 1936 Boulder (WAust)

Pawley, Michael Bernard (NSW) b March 10, 1944 Glen Innes (NSW)

Payne, Charles Percy (Tas) b July 31, 1876 Hobart (Tas) d Jan. 28, 1938 Lower Sandy Bay (Tas)

Payne, Daniel Martin (Qld) b Oct. 27, 1978 Brisbane (Qld)

Peachey, Mark (Qld) b Oct. 31, 1900 Tannymorel (Qld) d Nov. 23, 1987 Ipswich (Qld)

Peake, Clinton John (Vic) b March 25, 1977 Geelong (Vic)

Pearce, Donald Rex (Tas) b Feb. 21, 1941 Ulverstone (Tas) d Feb. 13, 1999 Burnie (Tas)

Pearce, Kevin Dudley (Tas) b Feb. 29, 1960 Devonport (Tas)

Pearce, Reginald Manus (NSW) b April 20, 1918 Tumbarumba (NSW) d June 19, 1995 Sydney (NSW)

Pearsall, Alan Louden (Tas) b May 24, 1915 Hobart (Tas) d March 8, 1941 in action in English Channel

Pearson, Trevor John (SAust) b Oct. 13, 1943 Goodwood (SAust)

Pearson, William Ernest (Vic) b Nov. 10, 1912 Kerang (Vic) d Sept. 11, 1987 Melbourne (Vic)

Pegg, Harry Robert Edgar (Qld) b March 19, 1916 Moorooka (Qld)

Pellew, Arthur Howard (SAust) b Jan. 20, 1878 Riverton (SAust) d Aug. 21, 1948 Rose Park (SAust)

* Pellew, Clarence Everard (SAust) b Sept. 21, 1893 Port Pirie (SAust) d May 9, 1981 Adelaide (SAust)

Pellew, John Harold (SAust) b July 17, 1882 Truro (SAust) d Oct. 17, 1946 Unley (SAust)

Pellew, Lancelot Vivian (SAust) b Dec. 15, 1899 Port Elliott (SAust) d Dec. 8, 1970 Adelaide (SAust)

Penman, Arthur Percival (NSW) b Jan. 23, 1885 Ultimo (NSW) d Sept. 11, 1944 Rockley (NSW)

Pennefather, George Shirley (Tas) b Sept. 28, 1864 Launceston (Tas) d Oct. 16, 1945 Launceston (Tas)

Pennycuick, Rupert James (Tas) b April 11, 1893 Jericho (Tas) d Jan. 17, 1963 Concord (NSW)

Penter, Colin Edward (WAust) b July 20, 1955 Albany (WAust)

Pepper, Cecil George (NSW) b Sept. 15, 1916 Forbes (NSW) d March 24, 1993 Littleborough, Lancashire (England)

Perraton, Jack Oldfield (Vic) b Feb. 26, 1909 Prahran (Vic) d Oct. 1, 1950 Kings Cross (NSW)

Perraton, William Thomas Crooke (Vic) b Aug. 27, 1867 Collingwood (Vic) d Sept. 23, 1952 Elsternwick (Vic)

Perren, Clinton Terrence (Qld) b Feb. 22, 1975 Herston (Qld)

Perrin, Thomas Henry (Vic) b Oct. 27, 1928 Prahran (Vic)

Perrins, Keith Robinson (Qld) b Jan. 17, 1931 Rockhampton (Qld)

Perry, Cecil Thomas Henry (Tas) b March 3, 1846 Battery Point (Tas) d Aug. 4, 1917 Timaru (New Zealand)

Perryman, Charles Henry (Vic) b Jan. 20, 1872 Richmond (Vic) d Aug. 30, 1950 St Kilda (Vic)

Peters, Arthur Ernest (SAust) b March 8, 1872 Adelaide (SAust) d Sept. 24, 1903 Henley Beach (SAust)

Pettiford, Jack (NSW) b Nov. 29, 1919 Freshwater (NSW) d Oct. 11, 1964 North Sydney (NSW)

Pettinger, Aldam Murr (SAust) b July 30, 1859 Kent Town (SAust) d Aug. 18, 1950 Lower Mitcham (SAust)

Phelps, Leslie R. (Tas) birth and death details unknown

Phelps, Matthew James (Tas) b Sept. 1, 1972 Lismore (NSW)

Phillips, Edward George (SAust) b March 1, 1851 Port Adelaide (SAust) d Feb. 8, 1933 North Adelaide (SAust)

Phillips, Edward Lauriston (SAust) b Sept. 2, 1892 North Adelaide (SAust) d Jan. 8, 1971 Adelaide (SAust)

Phillips, James (Vic) b Sept. 1, 1860 Pleasant Creek (Vic) d April 21, 1930 Burnaby, Vancouver, British Columbia (Canada)

Phillips, Joseph (Vic) b April 22, 1840 Parramatta (NSW) d May 7, 1901 Heidelberg (Vic)

Phillips, Norbert Eugene (NSW) b July 9, 1896 Cowra (NSW) d Oct. 3, 1961 Sydney (NSW)

Phillips, Raymond Berry (NSW & Qld) b May 23, 1954 Paddington (NSW)

* Phillips, Wayne Bentley (SAust) b March 1, 1958 Adelaide (SAust)

* Phillips, Wayne Norman (Vic) b Nov. 7, 1962 Geelong (Vic)

Philpott, Albert John William (Vic) b March 14, 1873 Gaffneys Creek (Vic) d Nov. 25, 1950 Kew (Vic)

* Philpott, Peter Ian (NSW) b Nov. 21, 1934 Manly (NSW)

Philpott, Richard Stamper (Vic) b Feb. 7, 1813 West Farleigh, Kent (England) d June 8, 1888 Brenchley, Kent (England)

Philpott, William (Vic) b Jan. 24, 1819 West Farleigh, Kent (England) d Nov. 4, 1891 Linton, Kent (England)

Pickering, George Thomas (Vic) b c. 1832 Sydney (NSW) d Dec. 1, 1858 Sandridge (Vic)

Pickering, Kelby Sinclair (SAust) b Jan. 3, 1973 Lameroo (SAust)

Pickett, Alfred William (Tas) b c. 1871 Ulverstone (Tas) d March 19, 1953 Ulverstone (Tas)

Pickett, Edward Arthur (Tas) b April 2, 1909 Ulverstone (Tas)

Pictet, Francis Stewart (Tas) b June 4, 1866 Bath, Somerset (England) death details unknown

Pierce, Michael (NSW & Qld) b Sept. 3, 1869 Paddington (NSW) d Feb. 4, 1913 Sydney (NSW)

Pilon, Nathan Steven (NSW) b Oct. 27, 1976 Dubbo (NSW)

Pinch, Colin John (NSW & SAust) b June 23, 1921 Brownsville (NSW)

Pinkus, Harold William (Tas) b Sept. 27, 1934 Smithton (Tas)

Pinnington, Todd Andrew (Tas) b March 21, 1971 Hobart (Tas)

Pitcher, Franklyn Joseph (Vic) b June 24, 1879 Collingwood (Vic) d Jan. 23, 1921 Northcote (Vic)

Pite, Walter Edward (NSW) b Sept. 24, 1876 Sydney (NSW) d May 7, 1955 Waverley (NSW)

Pittman, Brian Harold (SAust) b June 17, 1930 Rose Park (SAust)

Plant, Hugh Joseph (Vic) b Oct. 12, 1907 Narrandera (NSW) d Aug. 30, 1993 Geelong (Vic)

* Playle, William Rodger (WAust) b Dec. 1, 1938 Palmerston North (New Zealand)

Plummer, Neil Robert (SAust) b July 6, 1955 Lobethal (SAust)

Pocock, William Johnstone (NSW) b c. 1848 Clifton, Gloucestershire (England) d Sept. 27, 1928 East Brighton (Vic)

Poeppel, George Augustus (Qld) b Nov. 6, 1893 Bundaberg (Qld) d Feb. 2, 1917 Hermies (France)

Poidevin, Leslie Oswald Sheridan (NSW) b Nov. 5, 1876 Merrilla (NSW) d Nov. 19, 1931 Waverley (NSW)

Polzin, Michael Allan (Qld) b June 23, 1964 Wondai (Qld)

* Ponsford, William Harold (Vic) b Oct. 19, 1900 North Fitzroy (Vic) d April 6, 1991 Kyneton (Vic)

* Ponting, Ricky Thomas (Tas) b Dec. 19, 1974 Launceston (Tas)

Poon, Hunter Robert George (Qld) b May 14, 1894 Pimlico (NSW) d Jan. 25, 1980 Greenslopes (Qld)

* Pope, Roland James (NSW) b Feb. 18, 1864 Ashfield (NSW) d July 27, 1952 Manly (NSW)

Porter, Brian Clifford (Vic) b Dec. 20, 1942 Carlton (Vic)

Porter, Graham David (WAust) b March 18, 1955 Middle Swan (WAust)

Potter, Jack (Vic) b April 13, 1938 Melbourne (Vic)

Powell, George (NSW) b April 12, 1918 Newtown (NSW) d April 11, 1994 Clovelly (NSW)

Powell, Ronald Hartley (Tas) b Sept. 27, 1883 New Norfolk (Tas) d Aug. 22, 1922 (Qld)

Powell, Theodore (NSW) b July 10, 1852 Berrima (NSW) d Sept. 3, 1913 Sydney (NSW)

Power, John Francis (Vic) b March 23, 1932 Port Melbourne (Vic)

Power, Laurence James (SAust) b July 31, 1898 Ovingham (SAust) d March 20, 1963 Glenelg (SAust)

Power, Louis Bertrand (SAust) b Oct. 10, 1905 Ovingham (SAust) d Sept. 30, 1988 Bedford Park (SAust)

Power, Robert (Vic) b c. 1833 Galway (Ireland) d Nov. 4, 1914 Toorak (Vic)

Powlett, Frederick Armand (Vic) b Jan. 6, 1811 Shrewsbury, Shropshire (England) d June 9, 1865 Kyneton (Vic)

Pratten, Herbert Graham (NSW) b April 22, 1892 Ashfield (NSW) d Sept. 11, 1979 Neutral Bay (NSW)

Preen, Alan Thomas (WAust) b July 4, 1935 Fremantle (WAust)

Prentice, Warden Selby (NSW) b July 30, 1886 Homebush (NSW) d Feb. 26, 1969 Rosebery (NSW)

Prescott, Shaun St Aubyn (Vic) b Sept. 7, 1966 Melbourne (Vic)

Prestwidge, Scott Arthur (Qld) b May 15, 1968 Bankstown (NSW)

Pretty, Alfred Henry (SAust) b Jan. 29, 1874 Willunga (SAust) d June 21, 1929 Mile End (SAust)

Price, Charles Frederick Thomas (Services) b Feb. 17, 1917 Sydney (NSW) d Jan. 19, 1997 Avalon (NSW)

Price, Henry Alexander (Qld) b March 31, 1913 Spring Hill (Qld) d May 3, 1999 Wavell Heights (Qld)

Price, Reuben Henry (WAust) b April 27, 1923 London (England) d Feb. 26, 1991 Perth (WAust)

Price, Walter Davies (SAust) b March 24, 1886 Hawthorn (Vic) d July 29, 1944 Adelaide (SAust)

Prindiville, Kevin Joseph (WAust) b Sept. 18, 1949 Subiaco (WAust)

Prindiville, Terence John (WAust) b Nov. 20, 1942 Subiaco (WAust)

Prior, Wayne (SAust) b Sept. 30, 1952 Salisbury (SAust)

Pritchard, David Edward (SAust) b Jan. 5, 1893 Queenstown (SAust) d July 4, 1983 Myrtle Bank (SAust)

Prout, James Alexander (Qld) b Aug. 12, 1889 Flemington (Vic) d Feb. 18, 1952 Double Bay (NSW)

Pryor, David Godfrey (NSW) b Feb. 3, 1870 Maitland (NSW) d Jan. 3, 1937 Gosford (NSW)

Puckett, Charles William (WAust) b Feb. 21, 1911 Beddington Corner, Surrey (England) d Jan. 22, 2002 Morphett Vale (SAust)

Puckett, Maxwell Charles (SAust) b June 3, 1935 Unley Park (SAust) d Aug. 25, 1991 North Adelaide (SAust)

Punch, Austin Thomas Eugene (NSW & Tas) b Aug. 16, 1894 North Sydney (NSW) d Aug. 25, 1985 Cremorne (NSW)

Punch, Keith Francis (WAust) b Oct. 19, 1940 Subiaco (WAust)

Putman, Sydney William Leslie (Tas) b March 25, 1912 Hobart (Tas) d Sept. 20, 1947 Hobart (Tas)

Pye, Leslie Walter (NSW) b July 6, 1871 Windsor (NSW) d March 9, 1949 Parramatta (NSW)

Pyke, James Kendrick (SAust) b June 7, 1966 Cottesloe (WAust)

Pyke, Richard Dimond (Qld) b Aug. 15, 1877 Collingwood (Vic) d Dec. 4, 1914 Gympie (Qld)

Pynor, Ernest Ivan (SAust) b April 23, 1920 Essendon (Vic) d Oct. 23, 1999 East Doncaster (Vic)

Quelch, Leslie Norman (Qld) b Feb. 26, 1918 Maryborough (Qld) d April 13, 1987 Paddington (Qld)

Quick, Ian William (Vic) b Nov. 5, 1933 Geelong (Vic)

Quigley, Brian Maxwell (SAust) b Dec. 27, 1935 Henley Beach (SAust)

Quilty, John (SAust) b c. 1860 Adelaide (SAust) d May 9, 1942 Kent Town (SAust)

Quin, Stanley Oldfield (Vic) b April 17, 1908 Caulfield (Vic) d Nov. 27, 1967 Brighton (Vic)

Quinlan, Francis Patrick (WAust) b March 17, 1891 Perth (WAust) d Aug. 15, 1935 Perth (WAust)

Quinn, Michael Brian (Vic) b July 2, 1962 Adelaide (SAust)

Quist, Karl Hugo (NSW, WAust & SAust) b Aug. 18, 1875 Milson's Point (NSW) d March 31, 1957 Plympton (SAust)

* Rackemann, Carl Gray (Qld) b June 3, 1960 Wondai (Qld)

Rahmann, Herbert William (Qld) b Aug. 23, 1886 Maryborough (Qld) d Oct. 12, 1957 Nundah (Qld)

Rainey, Leslie Newburn (Vic) b Jan. 10, 1881 South Yarra (Vic) d Aug. 27, 1962 Melbourne (Vic)

Ramsay, John (Tas) b Dec. 26, 1872 Glasgow, Lanarkshire (Scotland) d Feb. 6, 1944 Launceston (Tas)

Ramsay, Marmaduke Francis (Qld) b Dec. 8, 1860 Cheltenham, Gloucestershire (England) d Dec. 31, 1947 Lee, Canterbury, Kent (England)

Ramshaw, Darrin Joseph (WAust & Vic) b Nov. 29, 1965 Subiaco (WAust)

Randell, Alfred Charles (WAust) b May 10, 1884 Perth (WAust) d Sept. 13, 1958 Sydney (NSW)

Randell, Ernest Arthur (WAust) b Jan. 25, 1873 Perth (WAust) d May 12, 1938 Perth (WAust)

Randell, James Arthur (NSW) b Aug. 4, 1880 birthplace unknown d Dec. 7, 1952 Balgowlah (NSW)

* Ransford, Vernon Seymour (Vic) b March 20, 1885 South Yarra (Vic) d March 19, 1958 Brighton (Vic)

Ratcliffe, Andrew Thomas (NSW) b April 3, 1891 Leichhardt (NSW) d Aug. 31, 1974 Banksia (NSW)

Rathie, David Stewart (Qld) b May 29, 1951 Roma (Qld)

Rawle, Keith Trevillian (Vic) b Oct. 29, 1924 Essendon (Vic)

Ray, Mark (NSW & Tas) b Oct. 2, 1952 Surry Hills (NSW)

Raymer, Vincent Norman (Qld) b May 4, 1918 Toowoomba (Qld)

Raymond, Ralph Cossart (Qld) b Nov. 28, 1912 Boonah (Qld) d Oct. 11, 1982 Murgon (Qld)

Rayson, Maxwell William (Vic) b Aug. 26, 1912 Kew (Vic) d May 11, 1993 Heidelberg (Vic)

Rayson, Roger William (Vic) b Feb. 17, 1942 Windsor (Vic)

Rayson, William Jones (Vic) b Dec. 18, 1889 Malmsbury (Vic) d Sept. 8, 1957 Parkdale (Vic)

Read, Arthur Edwin (WAust) b May 26, 1908 Unley (SAust) d March 1, 2001 Bentley (WAust)

Rebbeck, Phillip Douglas (SAust) b July 31, 1948 North Adelaide (SAust)

Reddrop, Walter William (Vic) b Sept. 9, 1901 Kyneton (Vic) d March 31, 1983 Parkville (Vic)

Redfearn, James (Vic) b c. 1836 Yorkshire (England) d March 10, 1916 Glenhuntly (Vic)

Redgrave, John Sidney (NSW & Qld) b Aug. 5, 1878 North Sydney (NSW) d Aug. 3, 1958 West End (Qld)

* Redpath, Ian Ritchie (Vic) b May 11, 1941 Geelong (Vic)

* Reedman, John Cole (SAust) b Oct. 9, 1865 Taminda (SAust) d March 25, 1924 Gilberton (SAust)

Rees, John Newman Stace (SAust) b Sept. 2, 1880 Hindmarsh (SAust) d Jan. 17, 1959 St Peters (SAust)

Rees, Robert Blackie Colston (SAust) b April 15, 1882 Hindmarsh (SAust) d Sept. 20, 1966 Bowmans Green, Hertfordshire (England)

Rees, William Gilbert (NSW) b April 6, 1827 St Issell's, Pembrokeshire (Wales) d Oct. 31, 1898 Marlborough (New Zealand)

Rees, William Lee (Vic) b Dec. 16, 1836 Bristol, Gloucestershire (England) d May 13, 1912 Gisborne (New Zealand)

Reeves, Damion Albert (SAust) b July 12, 1971 Darwin (NT)

Reeves, William Henry (Vic) b c. 1881 Fitzroy (Vic) d Sept. 13, 1962 Kew (Vic)

Regeling, Donald Carl (Qld) b Aug. 13, 1955 Boonah (Qld)

Reid, Alan Walter (Qld) b June 30, 1931 Maryborough (Qld)

Reid, Basil Stanley (Tas) b May 17, 1924 Launceston (Tas) d July 16, 2000 Launceston (Tas)

* Reid, Bruce Anthony (WAust) b March 14, 1963 Osborne Park (WAust)

Reid, Curtis Alexander (Vic) b July 16, 1836 Inverary Park (NSW) d July 1, 1886 Hawthorn (Vic)

Reid, Douglas Clement (NSW) b Sept. 23, 1886 St Peters (NSW) d Aug. 21, 1959 Wahroonga (NSW)

Reid, Stanley John (Tas) b May 5, 1955 St Helen's (Tas)

Reid, W. (Tas) birth and death details unknown

Reid, William (SAust) b c. 1871 North Adelaide (SAust) full birth and death details unknown

* Reiffel, Paul Ronald (Vic) b April 19, 1966 Box Hill (Vic)

Renfrey, Leslie Cotswold (WAust) b Feb. 15, 1893 Wallaroo Mines (SAust) d Sept. 23, 1958 Mt Lawley (WAust)

* Renneberg, David Alexander (NSW) b Sept. 23, 1942 Rozelle (NSW)

Reynolds, George Raymond (Qld) b Aug. 24, 1936 Bundaberg (Qld)

Rhodes, Brian Leslie (NSW) b March 7, 1951 Paddington (NSW)

Ricci, Brendan Paul (Vic) b April 24, 1965 East Melbourne (Vic)

* Richards, Barry Anderson (SAust) b July 21, 1945 Morningside, Durban, Natal (South Africa)

Richards, Corey John (NSW) b Aug. 25, 1975 Camden (NSW)

Richards, Frank Hitchen (Vic) d Fremantle (WAust) full birth and death details unknown

* Richards, Isaac Vivian Alexander (Qld) b March 7, 1952 St John's (Antigua)

Richards, Thomas Oliver (SAust) b July 5, 1855 Norwood (SAust) d Dec. 14, 1923 Cottonville (Qld)

* Richardson, Arthur John (SAust & WAust) b July 24, 1888 Sevenhills (SAust) d Dec. 23, 1973 Semaphore (SAust)

Richardson, Brian Douglas (Tas) b May 15, 1932 Hobart (Tas)

Richardson, Charles Augustus (NSW) b Feb. 22, 1864 Sydney (NSW) d Aug. 17, 1949 Waipara, Canterbury (New Zealand)

Richardson, Colin George (Tas) b June 6, 1920 Hobart (Tas) d Dec. 22, 1993 Hobart (Tas)

Richardson, Edward Noel (Tas) b Dec. 8, 1929 Hobart (Tas)

Richardson, Frederick William (Tas) b March 29, 1878 Campbell Town (Tas) d March 7, 1955 Campbell Town (Tas)

Richardson, Geoffrey William (Vic) b Dec. 7, 1956 Koo Wee Rup (Vic)

Richardson, George Biggs (NSW) b May 28, 1834 Bathurst (NSW) d May 1, 1911 Dandaloo (NSW)

Richardson, Howard James (Vic) b Oct. 29, 1894 Berwick (Vic) d Dec. 21, 1959 Richmond (Vic)

Richardson, Joseph (SAust) b Feb. 28, 1878 Kooringa (SAust) d June 13, 1951 Glenelg (SAust)

Richardson, Leonard Martin (NSW & Qld) b May 5, 1950 Paddington (NSW)

Richardson, Leslie Lambert (Tas) b Jan. 9, 1887 Ralph's Bay (Tas) d Nov. 15, 1962 Hobart (Tas)

Richardson, Leslie Walter (Tas) b Sept. 5, 1911 New Town (Tas) d Nov. 1, 1981 Hobart (Tas)

Richardson, Reginald Maxwell (Tas) b Oct. 6, 1922 Hobart (Tas)

* Richardson, Victor York (SAust) b Sept. 7, 1894 Parkside (SAust) d Oct. 29, 1969 Fullarton (SAust)

Richardson, Walter Barrett (Tas) b Oct. 24, 1876 Ralph's Bay (Tas) d May 30, 1962 Hobart (Tas)

Richardson, William Alfred (NSW) b Aug. 22, 1866 Sydney (NSW) d Jan. 3, 1930 Mosman (NSW)

Richter, Arthur Frederick (SAust) b Sept. 1, 1908 Telowie (SAust) d Aug. 16, 1936 Adelaide (SAust)

Rickman, Wilfred (Vic) b c. 1856 South Yarra (Vic) d June 6, 1911 Frankston (Vic)

Ridge, Frank Macquarie (NSW) b Jan. 10, 1873 Dubbo (NSW) d May 25, 1959 Manly (NSW)

Ridgway, Mark William (Tas) b May 21, 1960 Warragul (Vic)

Ridings, Kenneth Lovett (SAust) b Feb. 7, 1920 Malvern (SAust) d May 17, 1943 in action over Bay of Biscay, France

Ridings, Phillip Lovett (SAust) b Oct. 2, 1917 Malvern (SAust) d Sept. 13, 1998 Adelaide (SAust)

Rigaud, Stephen (SAust) b Nov. 25, 1856 Kenton Valley, Talunga (SAust) d Nov. 13, 1922 Claremont (WAust)

Rigby, Albert (WAust) b c. 1901 Lancashire (England) d Oct. 10, 1963 Hollywood (WAust)

Rigg, Basil Augustus (WAust) b Aug. 12, 1926 Highgate (WAust)

Rigg, Herbert William Hardy (WAust) b Aug. 18, 1923 Highgate (WAust)

* Rigg, Keith Edward (Vic) b May 21, 1906 Malvern (Vic) d Feb. 28, 1995 Malvern (Vic)

Riley, William Norman (SAust) b April 9, 1894 Hyde Park (SAust) d Oct. 2, 1960 North Adelaide (SAust)

Rimington, Stanley Garnet (Vic) b Jan. 22, 1892 Kew (Vic) d Nov. 23, 1991 Kew (Vic)

* Ring, Douglas Thomas (Vic) b Oct. 14, 1918 Hobart (Tas)

* Ritchie, Gregory Michael (Qld) b Jan. 23, 1960 Stanthorpe (Qld)

Ritossa, David John (SAust) b Jan. 22, 1971 Rose Park (SAust)

* Rixon, Stephen John (NSW) b Feb. 25, 1954 Albury (NSW)

Roach, Peter John (Vic) b May 19, 1975 Kew (Vic)

Roach, William Alexander (WAust) b Dec. 12, 1914 South Fremantle (WAust) d June 8, 1944 in action over Friesian Islands (Netherlands)

* Roberts, Anderson Montgomery Everton (NSW) b Jan. 29, 1951 Urlings Village (Antigua)

Roberts, Kevin Joseph (NSW) b July 2, 1972 North Sydney (NSW)

Roberts, Peter Gerald (Tas) b Feb. 16, 1952 Hobart (Tas)

Roberts, William (NSW) birth and death details unknown

Roberts, William Maurice (SAust) b Aug. 26, 1916 Wallaroo Mines (SAust) d Jan. 21, 1989 Adelaide (SAust)

Robertson, Ashley Peter Scott (Vic) b March 9, 1972 Footscray (Vic)

Robertson, David Alexander (SAust) b March 4, 1959 North Adelaide (SAust)

* Robertson, Gavin Ron (NSW & Tas) b May 28, 1966 St Leonards (NSW)

Robertson, George Pringle (Vic) b Aug. 22, 1842 Hobart (Tas) d June 23, 1895 East Melbourne (Vic)

Robertson, Trevor John (SAust) b Nov. 20, 1947 Rose Park (SAust)

* Robertson, William Roderick (Vic) b Oct. 6, 1861 Deniliquin (NSW) d June 24, 1938 Brighton (Vic)

Robins, Donnell (SAust) b March 7, 1934 Blackwood (SAust)

Robinson, Alexander (WAust) b Aug. 19, 1886 Brighton (Vic) d Oct. 4, 1967 Perth (WAust)

Robinson, Alexander William (WAust) b Aug. 14, 1924 Boulder (WAust)

Robinson, Brian Anthony (Tas) b Nov. 22, 1967 Devonport (Tas)

Robinson, Charles Henry (Tas & WAust) b Feb. 18, 1879 Dubbo (NSW) d Sept. 23, 1951 Ashfield (NSW)

Robinson, David Brian (Tas & Vic) b March 20, 1958 Devonport (Tas)

Robinson, George David (WAust) b Jan. 21, 1921 Boulder (WAust) d March 12, 1999 Kew (Vic)

Robinson, Henry Joseph Wickham (NSW) b March 11, 1864 Watsons Bay (NSW) d March 24, 1931 Mascot (NSW)

* Robinson, Rayford Harold (NSW & SAust) b March 26, 1914 Stockton (NSW) d Aug. 10, 1965 Stockton (NSW)

* Robinson, Richard Daryl (Vic) b June 8, 1946 East Melbourne (Vic)

Robison, William Carr (NSW) b Dec. 14, 1874 Camden (NSW) d July 5, 1916 Darlinghurst (NSW)

Robran, Barrie Charles (SAust) b Sept. 25, 1947 Whyalla (SAust)

Roche, William (Vic) b July 20, 1871 Brunswick (Vic) d Jan. 2, 1950 East Brunswick (Vic)

Rocher, Thomas Walter (Tas) b June 17, 1930 Scottsdale (Tas)

Rock, Claude William (Tas) b June 9, 1863 Deloraine (Tas) d July 27, 1950 Longford (Tas)

Rock, Harry Owen (NSW) b Oct. 18, 1896 Scone (NSW) d March 9, 1978 Manly (NSW)

Rock, Norman Vosper (Tas) b Aug. 30, 1864 Deloraine (Tas) d Feb. 7, 1945 Brighton (Vic)

Rockliffe, Thornton Francis Edward (Tas) b July 5, 1887 Sassafras (Tas) d March 18, 1961 East Devonport (Tas)

Rodwell, Edwin Emerson (Tas) b April 12, 1921 Hobart (Tas)

Roe, Richard (WAust) b Jan. 22, 1913 Geraldton (WAust)

Rofe, Paul Cameron (SAust) b Jan. 16, 1981 Adelaide (SAust)

Rogers, Christopher John Llewellyn (WAust) b Aug. 31, 1977 Kogarah (NSW)

Rogers, John Edward (Vic) b Feb. 8, 1858 Botany (NSW) d July 8, 1935 South Melbourne (Vic)

Rogers, Noel Thomas (Qld) b Dec. 28, 1923 Spring Hill (Qld) d May 27, 1982 Annerley (Qld)

Rogers, Rex Ernest (Qld) b Aug. 24, 1916 Cairns (Qld) d May 22, 1996 Coorparoo (Qld)

Rogers, William John (NSW) b May 7, 1943 Gosford (NSW)

Rolfe, Douglas John (Vic & SAust) b Feb. 26, 1953 Wheelers Hill (Vic)

Ronchi, Luke (WAust) b April 23, 1981 Dannevirke (New Zealand)

Roper, Arthur William (NSW) b Feb. 20, 1917 Petersham (NSW) d Sept. 4, 1972 Woy Woy (NSW)

* Rorke, Gordon Frederick (NSW) b June 27, 1938 Neutral Bay (NSW)

Rose, Robert Peter (Vic) b Feb. 6, 1952 Eastern Hill (Vic) d May 12, 1999 Heidelberg (Vic)

Rosen, Marshall Frederick (NSW) b Sept. 17, 1948 Paddington (NSW)

Rosman, Arthur Victor (SAust) b Nov. 26, 1870 Barossa Goldfields (SAust) d Feb. 10, 1948 Kent Town (SAust)

Ross, Charles Howard (Vic) b May 10, 1863 St Kilda (Vic) d Feb. 5, 1935 Sydney (NSW)

Ross, Graeme Thomson (Vic) b Feb. 5, 1955 Geelong (Vic)

Ross, William A. (Vic) birth and death details unknown

Rosser, John (Vic) b April 22, 1862 Fremantle (WAust) d Dec. 25, 1925 Toowoomba (Qld)

Rothwell, Barry Alan (NSW) b Aug. 18, 1939 Ryde (NSW)

Rothwell, John Wilson (Tas) b Oct. 1, 1913 Hobart (Tas)

Rowan, Robert Keith (Vic) b Sept. 14, 1947 Coburg (Vic)

Rowe, Raymond Curtis (NSW) b Dec. 9, 1913 Harris Park (NSW) d May 14, 1995 Parramatta (NSW)

Rowe, Samuel Harold Drew (WAust) b Nov. 5, 1883 Perth (WAust) d Oct. 29, 1968 Perth (WAust)

Rowe, William Denis (Qld) b Jan. 10, 1892 East Brisbane (Qld) d Sept. 3, 1972 South Brisbane (Qld)

Rowell, Gregory John (NSW, Qld & Tas) b Sept. 1, 1966 Lindfield (NSW)

Rowland, Frank Walter (NSW) b March 1, 1893 Inverell (NSW) d Feb. 25, 1957 Mosman (NSW)

Rowlands, Edward Richard (Vic) b c. 1826 Claines, Worcestershire (England) d c. 1860

Rowlands, William Trevor (WAust) b May 7, 1904 Echuca (Vic) d May 18, 1984 Subiaco (WAust)

Rowley, Francis (NSW) b Sept. 27, 1835 Burwood (NSW) d June 23, 1862 Woolloomooloo (NSW)

Roxby, Robert Charles (NSW & SAust) b March 16, 1926 Newcastle (NSW)

Rummans, Graeme Clifford (NSW) b Dec. 13, 1976 Camperdown (NSW)

Rundell, Joshua Upcott (SAust) b May 6, 1858 Sandhurst (Vic) d Jan. 7, 1922 Alberton (SAust)

Rundell, Percy Davies (SAust) b Nov. 20, 1890 Alberton (SAust) d March 24, 1979 North Adelaide (SAust)

Rush, Edward Reynolds (Vic) b March 29, 1868 Flemington (Vic) d May 6, 1936 Malvern (Vic)

Rush, John (Vic) b April 5, 1910 Malvern (Vic) d Jan. 13, 1982 Adelaide (SAust)

Rush, Thomas Reynolds (Vic) b Dec. 7, 1874 Collingwood (Vic) d Oct. 29, 1926 Malvern (Vic)

Rushbrook, Roy Francis Kerr (Qld) b Sept. 29, 1911 Spring Hill (Qld) d March 31, 1987 Mackay (Qld)

Rushforth, Alfred William (Tas) b April 23, 1898 Hobart (Tas) d Dec. 30, 1985 Taroona (Tas)

Russell, Bernard L. (NSW) b Aug. 1, 1891 Leichhardt (NSW) d July 13, 1961 Belmore (NSW)

Russell, Richard Stevan (WAust) b Jan. 22, 1968 Helensville (New Zealand)

Russen, Charles Gordon (Tas) b May 9, 1886 Launceston (Tas) d Dec. 16, 1969 Newstead (Tas)

* Rutherford, John Walter (WAust) b Sept. 25, 1929 Bungulluping (WAust)

Ryan, Alfred James (SAust) b April 27, 1904 Adelaide (SAust) d July 10, 1990 Semaphore (SAust)

Ryan, Gregory William (NSW) b March 13, 1913 Wallsend (NSW) d May 10, 1986 Randwick (NSW)

Ryan, Peter Andrew (Qld) b Feb. 18, 1951 East Melbourne (Vic)

Ryan, Roderick Thomas (WAust) b Nov. 15, 1909 Cannington (WAust) d Oct. 23, 1979 Toronto, Ontario (Canada)

Ryan, Thomas Patrick (Tas) b May 4, 1865 Hobart (Tas) d April 20, 1921 Hobart (Tas)

* Ryder, John (Vic) b Aug. 8, 1889 Collingwood (Vic) d April 3, 1977 Fitzroy (Vic)

Rymill, Jack Westall (SAust) b March 20, 1901 North Adelaide (SAust) d Feb. 11, 1976 Adelaide (SAust)

Saballus, Andrew William (Tas) b June 1, 1969 Hobart (Tas)

Sacristani, Peter Geoffrey (Vic) b Sept. 5, 1957 Melbourne (Vic)

Saddler, Edward (NSW) d Oct. 28, 1874 full birth and death details unknown

* Sadiq Mohammad (Tas) b May 5, 1945 Junagadh (India)

* Saggers, Ronald Arthur (NSW) b May 15, 1917 Sydenham (NSW) d March 17, 1987 Harbord (NSW)

Sainsbury, Andrew John (NSW) b May 11, 1974 Gosford (NSW)

Saint, John Michael (Tas) b Jan. 31, 1969 Auburn (NSW)

Saker, David James (Vic & Tas) b May 29, 1966 Oakleigh (Vic)

Salmon, Benjamin Melville (NSW) b Jan. 9, 1906 Footscray (Vic) d Jan. 24, 1979 Mosman (NSW)

Salmon, John Lionel (Vic) b March 31, 1934 Canterbury (Vic)

Salvado, John Frederick (Vic) b Nov. 11, 1939 Carlton (Vic)

Salvana, Louis Charles (Vic) b Jan. 20, 1897 Hawthorn (Vic) d Dec. 8, 1974 Mitcham (Vic)

Sams, Louis Robert (Tas) b Sept. 26, 1863 Westbury (Tas) d July 6, 1941 Redcliffe (Qld)

Sams, Richard Horace (Tas) b c. 1864 Westbury (Tas) d March 5, 1933 Roseville (NSW)

Samuels, Edward (NSW) b May 25, 1833 Sydney (NSW)

Sanders, Leyland Arthur (Qld) b Oct. 17, 1927 Sandgate (Qld)

Sandford, Horace Charles Augustus (Vic) b Oct. 14, 1891 St Leonards (NSW) d Aug. 16, 1967 Heidelberg (Vic)

Sands, Ronald Francis (WAust) b Sept. 16, 1921 Perth (WAust) d Sept. 5, 1995 Nedlands (WAust)

Sangster, Christopher Bagot (SAust) b May 1, 1908 Kooringa (SAust) d Feb. 27, 1995 North Adelaide (SAust)

Sangster, John Fraser (SAust) b Jan. 21, 1942 Adelaide (SAust)

Sankey, Clarence Joseph (Tas) b Oct. 27, 1913 Northtown (Tas) d March 12, 1996 Launceston (Tas)

Sargent, Murray Alfred James (SAust) b Aug. 23, 1928 Adelaide (SAust)

Sarovich, Theodor Keith (Vic) b May 20, 1915 Port Melbourne (Vic) d Nov. 23, 1987 Atherton (Qld)

Sarre, Ronald Basil (WAust) b Jan. 20, 1932 Midland (WAust)

Sartori, Ronald Joseph (WAust) b March 23, 1915 Fremantle (WAust) d July 1, 1991 Perth (WAust)

* Saunders, John Victor (Vic) b March 21, 1876 Melbourne (Vic) d Dec. 21, 1927 Toorak (Vic)

Saunders, Stuart Lucas (Tas) b June 27, 1960 Hobart (Tas)

Saunders, Warren Joseph (NSW) b July 18, 1934 Arncliffe (NSW)

Savage, Harold (NSW) b c. 1886 Woollahra (NSW) death details unknown

Savage, Keith Douglas (Qld) b Sept. 19, 1926 Brisbane (Qld) d Jan. 18, 1979 Mt Morgan (Qld)

Savigny, John Horatio (Tas) b Aug. 25, 1867 Bathurst (NSW) d Feb. 11, 1923 Carrick (Tas)

Savigny, William Henry (Tas) b Feb. 17, 1864 Sydney (NSW) d Aug. 6, 1922 Burwood (NSW)

Sawle, Lawrence Michael (WAust) b Aug. 19, 1925 East Fremantle (WAust)

Sayers, Dean Keith (SAust) b June 11, 1954 Hindmarsh (SAust)

Sayers, Mervyn Gerald (WAust) b March 5, 1958 Subiaco (WAust)

Scaife, John Willie (Vic) b Nov. 14, 1908 Haslingden, Lancashire (England) d Oct. 27, 1995 Melbourne (Vic)

Scanes, Albert Edward (NSW) b Aug. 6, 1900 Erskineville (NSW) d Nov. 1, 1969 death place unknown

Scanlan, Edmund (NSW) b c. 1848 Newcastle on Tyne, Northumberland (England) d Jan. 9, 1916 Erskineville (NSW)

Scannell, Timothy Francis (Vic) b Nov. 12, 1882 Hotham (Vic) d July 9, 1939 Royal Park (Vic)

Scarff, Clark Steven (WAust) b Nov. 19, 1948 Subiaco (WAust)

Schade, Matias Anderson (Vic) b March 25, 1887 Huntly (Vic) d June 9, 1959 Williamstown (Vic)

Schenscher, Peter Malcolm (SAust) b May 4, 1962 Murray Bridge (SAust)

Schmidt, Keith Ernest (Tas) b Dec. 19, 1921 Hobart (Tas)

Schneider, Karl Joseph (Vic & SAust) b Aug. 15, 1905 Hawthorn (Vic) d Sept. 5, 1928 Kensington Park (SAust)

Scholes, Mark Bradley (Vic) b July 1, 1957 Carlton (Vic)

Scholes, Walter John (Vic) b Jan. 5, 1950 East Brunswick (Vic)

Schrader, Heinrich Christian (Vic) b Dec. 5, 1893 East Prahran (Vic) d June 10, 1980 Kew (Vic)

Schreiber, Sidney Arthur (Qld) b April 7, 1873 birth and death details unknown

Schuller, Denis Clemenceau (Qld) b May 5, 1948 Herston (Qld)

Schultz, Bruce (SAust) b March 13, 1913 Royston Park (SAust) d Jan. 11, 1980 Modbury (SAust)

Schultz, Julius William Eugene (SAust) b Sept. 25, 1888 Summer Town (SAust) d Aug. 8, 1966 Berri (SAust)

Scott, Darryl Bryan (SAust) b March 9, 1961 Glenelg (SAust)

* Scott, Henry James Herbert (Vic) b Dec. 26, 1858 Prahran (Vic) d Sept. 23, 1910 Scone (NSW)

Scott, Jack A. (SAust) b Jan. 14, 1910 Sydney (NSW) d May 22, 1980 Collaroy Beach (NSW)

Scott, John Drake (NSW & SAust) b Jan. 31, 1888 Petersham (NSW) d April 7, 1964 Springbank (SAust)

Scott, Robert Barrington (Vic & NSW) b Oct. 9, 1916 South Melbourne (Vic) d April 6, 1984 Melbourne (Vic)

Scott, Walter Aubrey (Vic) b Feb. 19, 1907 Camberwell (Vic) d Oct. 23, 1989 death place unknown

Scott, William John (Vic) b June 14, 1882 Hotham (Vic) d Sept. 30, 1965 Ferntree Gully (Vic)

Scrymgour, Bernard Vincent (SAust) b July 31, 1864 Adelaide (SAust) d April 16, 1943 Medindie (SAust)

Scuderi, Joseph Charles (SAust) b Dec. 24, 1968 Ingham (Qld)

Seabrook, Wayne John Stephen (NSW) b Sept. 6, 1961 Ryde (NSW)

Seale, Joseph (NSW) b April 18, 1855 Grafton (NSW) d Aug. 19, 1941 Waratah (NSW)

Searle, James (NSW) b Aug. 8, 1861 Surry Hills (NSW) d Dec. 28, 1936 Manly (NSW)

Searle, Richard Henry (Qld) b Jan. 16, 1934 Red Hill (Qld)

Seccombe, Donald Harry (Qld) b April 3, 1942 Goomeri (Qld)

Seccombe, Wade Anthony (Qld) b Oct. 30, 1971 Murgon (Qld)

Seddon, Cecil Dudley (NSW) b July 3, 1902 Campbelltown (NSW) d April 18, 1978 Dulwich Hill (NSW)

Seib, Ian Martin (Qld) b Sept. 15, 1946 Herston (Qld)

Seitz, John Arnold (Vic) b Sept. 19, 1883 Carlton (Vic) d May 1, 1963 St Kilda (Vic)

Selk, Rudolph Albert (WAust) b Oct. 6, 1871 Omeo (Vic) d Jan. 31, 1940 Pickering Brook (WAust)

Sellers, Michael John (Tas) b July 5, 1952 Launceston (Tas)

* Sellers, Reginald Hugh Durning (SAust) b Aug. 20, 1940 Bulsar (India)

Selth, Victor Poole (SAust) b June 1, 1895 Parkside (SAust) d Sept. 2, 1967 Daw Park (SAust)

* Serjeant, Craig Stanton (WAust) b Nov. 1, 1951 Nedlands (WAust)

Serjeant, David Maurice (Vic) b Jan. 18, 1830 Ramsey, Huntingdonshire (England) d Jan. 12, 1929 Camberwell, London (England)

Sewart, William Isaac (Qld & Vic) b Nov. 12, 1881 Allendale East (SAust) d Dec. 13, 1928 Caulfield (Vic)

Shade, Eric (Vic) b Aug. 27, 1943 Brighton (Vic)

Sharman, Baden Eric (Tas) b Aug. 11, 1939 Beulah (Tas)

* Sharpe, Duncan Albert (SAust) b Aug. 3, 1937 Rawalpindi (India)

Shaw, John Hilary (Vic) b Oct. 18, 1932 Geelong (Vic)

Shaw, Noel Clyde (Vic) b May 10, 1937 Euroa (Vic)

Shawe, Patrick Henry Villiers Washington (Tas) b Bangalore (India) d Sept. 24, 1945 East Melbourne (Vic)

Shea, John Adrian (WAust) b May 8, 1913 Boulder (WAust) d Feb. 7, 1986 Claremont (WAust)

Shea, Morris (NSW) b c. 1869 Campbelltown (NSW) death details unknown

Shea, Patrick Augustus (Vic) b March 17, 1886 Clunes (Vic) d May 29, 1954 Northbridge (NSW)

* Sheahan, Andrew Paul (Vic) b Sept. 30, 1948 Werribee (Vic)

Sheen, Brian Lawrence (Tas) b Dec. 30, 1938 Hobart (Tas)

Shelton, Herbert John (Tas) b Jan. 21, 1924 Launceston (Tas)

Shepard, David John (Vic) b Dec. 30, 1970 Berwick (Vic)

Shephard, Athol Lennard (Tas) b Aug. 16, 1920 Burnie (Tas)

Shepherd, Alan Gordon (SAust) b Sept. 29, 1912 Kilkenny (SAust) d Oct. 9, 1998 Marion (SAust)

* Shepherd, Barry Kenneth (WAust) b April 23, 1937 Donnybrook (WAust) d Sept. 17, 2001 Fremantle (WAust)

Shepherd, David Stanmore (Vic) b Aug. 3, 1956 Melbourne (Vic)

Shepherd, James (NSW) b May 24, 1856 Steiglitz (Vic) death details unknown

Shepherdson, Hartley Robert (SAust) b Sept. 4, 1913 Mt Gambier (SAust) d Aug. 19, 1992 Fitzroy (Vic)

Shepley, Herbert Neil (SAust) b Oct. 7, 1899 Knightsbridge (SAust) d Nov. 14, 1953 Tranmere (SAust)

Sheppard, Benjamin Joseph (Vic) b June 23, 1892 Fitzroy (Vic) d Sept. 9, 1931 Fitzroy (Vic)

Sheppard, James Francis (Qld) b Jan. 16, 1888 Brisbane (Qld) d Dec. 10, 1944 Hendra (Qld)

Sheridan, Edward Orwell (NSW) b Jan. 3, 1842 Sydney (NSW) d Nov. 30, 1923 West End (Qld)

Sherriff, Rowan James (Tas) b July 7, 1951 Sheffield (Tas)

Shewan, Leslie James (Qld) b June 12, 1892 Rushworth (Vic) d Sept. 25, 1977 Windsor (Vic)

Shiell, Alan Bruce (SAust) b April 25, 1945 St Peters (SAust)

Shillinglaw, Harold Arthur Edward (Vic) b Dec. 2, 1927 Fitzroy (Vic)

Shipperd, Gregory (WAust & Tas) b Nov. 13, 1956 Subiaco (WAust)

Short, Henry William (SAust) b March 31, 1874 Morphett Vale (SAust) d May 11, 1916 Lower Mitcham (SAust)

Shortland, Herbert (NSW) b April 7, 1881 Sydney (NSW) d July 17, 1946 death place unknown

Shugg, Albert William (Tas) b July 5, 1894 Hawthorn (Vic) d July 20, 1941 Hobart (Tas)

Siddons, James Darren (Vic & SAust) b April 25, 1964 Robinvale (Vic)

Sidebottom, William Lemuel (Tas) b Sept. 24, 1862 Evandale (Tas) d April 11, 1948 Launceston (Tas)

Sides, Francis William (Qld & Vic) b Dec. 15, 1913 Mackay (Qld) d Aug. 25, 1943 Kunai Spur, Salamaua (Papua New Guinea) in action

Sieler, Alan John (Vic) b July 17, 1948 Arncliffe (NSW)

* Sievers, Morris William (Vic) b April 13, 1912 Powlett River (Vic) d May 10, 1968 Parkville (Vic)

Siggs, Douglas (Qld) b Aug. 11, 1920 Fortitude Valley (Qld)

Sim, Charles Wallace (Qld) b March 30, 1895 Brisbane (Qld) d July 3, 1971 Woodville South (SAust)

Simmonds, W. (Anderson's XI) birth and death details unknown

Simmons, Arthur Harry (NSW) b Nov. 13, 1909 Croydon (NSW) d Feb. 28, 1990 Mirrabooka (NSW)

Simmons, Jack (Tas) b March 28, 1941 Clayton-le-Moors, Lancashire (England)

Simpson, Charles Edward (Qld & NSW) b March 27, 1882 Parramatta (NSW) d June 26, 1956 Sydney (NSW)

* Simpson, Robert Baddeley (NSW & WAust) b Feb. 3, 1936 Marrickville (NSW)

Sims, Alfred Edward (Qld) b Nov. 8, 1875 birthplace and death details unknown

Sims, Arthur (Australians) b July 27, 1877 Spridlington, Lincolnshire (England) d April 27, 1969 East Hoathly, Sussex (England)

Simunsen, Robert Francis (SAust) b June 7, 1941 Adelaide (SAust)

Sinclair, Arthur (NSW) birth details unknown d Nov. 29, 1869 Sydney (NSW)

Sincock, Andrew Thomas (SAust) b June 7, 1951 Adelaide (SAust)

* Sincock, David John (SAust) b Feb. 1, 1942 North Adelaide (SAust)

Sincock, Harrold Keith (SAust) b Dec. 10, 1907 Eastwood (SAust) d Feb. 2, 1982 Plympton (SAust)

Sincock, Peter Damien (SAust) b July 8, 1948 North Adelaide (SAust)

Sincock, Russell John (Vic) b Dec. 28, 1947 Kew (Vic)

Sindrey, Clive Alexander Hazell (Vic) b Aug. 10, 1903 Richmond (Vic) d June 26, 1981 Vermont (Vic)

Single, Clive Vallack (NSW) b Sept. 17, 1888 Penrith (NSW) d July 10, 1931 Woollahra (NSW)

Sismey, Stanley George (NSW) b July 15, 1916 Junee (NSW)

Skilbeck, Andrew John (NSW) b July 21, 1958 St Leonards (NSW)

Skuse, Alan Raymond (Qld) b March 28, 1942 Herston (Qld)

Sladen, Charles (Vic) b Aug. 28, 1816 Walmer, Kent (England) d Feb. 22, 1884 Geelong (Vic)

* Slater, Keith Nichol (WAust) b March 12, 1935 Midland (WAust)

* Slater, Michael Jonathon (NSW) b Feb. 21, 1970 Wagga Wagga (NSW)

* Sleep, Peter Raymond (SAust) b May 4, 1957 Penola (SAust)

Slight, Alexander Frank (SAust) b March 13, 1861 Emerald Hill (Vic) d July 5, 1930 Maylands (SAust)

* Slight, James (Vic) b Oct. 20, 1855 Ashby, Geelong (Vic) d Dec. 9, 1930 Elsternwick (Vic)

Slight, William (Vic & SAust) b Sept. 19, 1858 Emerald Hill (Vic) d Dec. 22, 1941 Toorak Gardens (SAust)

Small, Gladstone Cleophas (SAust) b Oct. 18, 1961 Brighton, St George (Barbados)

Small, Stephen Mark (NSW & Tas) b March 2, 1955 Canterbury (NSW)

Smart, Christopher Boddington (Qld) b Oct. 17, 1958 Port Moresby (Papua New Guinea)

Smart, Hadyn Warren Gavin (SAust) b Nov. 26, 1958 Hobart (Tas)

Smart, Lawrence Maxwell (SAust) b Feb. 16, 1928 Narridy (SAust)

Smith, Adam Matthew (Vic) b April 6, 1976 Greensborough (Vic)

Smith, Alfred Edward Charles (WAust) b Oct. 4, 1908 Prahran (WAust) d Jan. 17, 1989 Fremantle (WAust)

Smith, Andrew (SAust) b Sept. 1, 1889 Port Adelaide (SAust) d May 18, 1983 Adelaide (SAust)

Smith, Carey Kenneth (Vic) b Oct. 16, 1960 Moreland (Vic)

Smith, Cyril Robert (Qld) b Nov. 1, 1926 South Brisbane (Qld)

Smith, Darryl Donald (WAust) b June 8, 1960 Adelaide (SAust)

Smith, David Anthony (Tas) b Sept. 1, 1957 Launceston (Tas)

* Smith, David Betram Miller (Vic) b Sept. 14, 1884 Richmond (Vic) d July 29, 1963 Hawthorn (Vic)

Smith, Douglas Roy (Tas) b Oct. 9, 1880 Fingal (Tas) d Feb. 27, 1933 Port Fairy (Vic)

Smith, Edward Henry (Tas) b July 30, 1911 Nook (Tas) d Dec. 26, 1999 Launceston (Tas)

Smith, George Elms (Vic) b July 22, 1855 Emerald Hill (Vic) d April 7, 1897 St Kilda (Vic)

Smith, Harry Oxley (Tas & Vic) b Oct. 27, 1887 Launceston (Tas) d Aug. 24, 1916 Pinewood, London (England)

Smith, Herbert George (Vic) b March 21, 1914 Richmond (Vic) d c. 1997 Melbourne (Vic)

Smith, Horace Clitheroe (Tas) b Oct. 31, 1892 Sandy Bay (Tas) d April 6, 1977 Hobart (Tas)

Smith, Hubert George Selwyn (Qld) b Oct. 9, 1891 Beaudesert (Qld) d June 7, 1917 Messines (France)

Smith, James (NSW) birth and death details unknown

Smith, John Phillips (Vic) b March 6, 1936 Ballarat (Vic)

Smith, Lavington Albert (SAust) b Oct. 9, 1904 Medindie (SAust) d May 9, 1953 Adelaide (SAust)

Smith, Leonard Angus (Vic) b c. 1882 Hotham (Vic) d c. 1943 Heidelberg (Vic)

Smith, Lloyd Harold James (Tas) b Aug. 5, 1928 Hobart (Tas)

Smith, Michael John (SAust) b July 17, 1973 Rose Park (SAust)

Smith, Peter Julian (Vic) b Feb. 8, 1968 Greensborough (Vic)

Smith, Robert Thomas (Vic) b May 27, 1868 Harrow (Vic) d Aug. 21, 1927 East Melbourne (Vic)

Smith, Stanley Arthur John (Vic) b Jan. 8, 1910 Footscray (Vic) d c. 1984 Ryde (NSW)

* Smith, Stephen Barry (NSW) b Oct. 18, 1961 Sydney (NSW)

Smith, Struan McKinley (Rest of Australia) b June 4, 1907 St Leonards (NSW)

Smith, Thomas Henry (Qld) b Sept. 19, 1898 Talgai (Qld) d March 6, 1926 Warwick (Qld)

Smith, Warren Robert (WAust) b Dec. 29, 1941 Guildford (WAust)

Smyth, Neil Weston (Vic) b June 6, 1928 South Yarra (Vic)

* Sobers, Garfield St Aubrun (SAust) b July 28, 1936 Chelsea Road, Bay Land, Bridgetown (Barbados)

Solomon, Cyril Moss (NSW) b March 11, 1911 Cootamundra (NSW) d July 15, 1995 Manly (NSW)

Soule, Richard Eric (Tas) b Sept. 5, 1966 Launceston (Tas)

Souter, Vernon John (Vic) b Feb. 26, 1894 Uranquinty (NSW) d July 17, 1915 Elsternwick (Vic)

Spalding, Earl George (WAust) b March 13, 1965 South Perth (WAust)

Speirs, Norman Lennox (Vic) b May 31, 1886 Caulfield (Vic) d Aug. 1, 1960 Noosa Heads (Qld)

Spencer, Duncan John (WAust) b April 5, 1972 Burnley, Lancashire (England)

Spencer, Ernest Lott (Vic) b May 1, 1888 Hotham West (Vic) d Nov. 4, 1953 Essendon (Vic)

* Spofforth, Frederick Robert (NSW & Vic) b Sept. 9, 1853 Balmain (NSW) d June 4, 1926 Ditton Hill, Surrey (England)

Spring, Graham Allan (NSW) b April 20, 1961 Sydney (NSW)

Spry, Richard (Qld) b July 18, 1862 Melbourne (Vic) d Nov. 10, 1920 Linville (Qld)

Squires, Philip Horley (SAust) b June 18, 1939 Marden (SAust)

Stacey, Bradley John (Vic) b June 11, 1972 Geelong (Vic)

Stack, George Bagot (NSW) b March 12, 1846 West Maitland (NSW) d Oct. 7, 1930 Orange (NSW)

Stack, Walter Jaques (NSW) b Oct. 31, 1884 Croydon (NSW) d March 26, 1972 Bathurst (NSW)

* Stackpole, Keith Raymond (Vic) b July 10, 1940 Collingwood (Vic)

Stackpole, Keith William (Vic) b July 31, 1916 Melbourne (Vic) d Sept. 19, 1992 Heidelberg (Vic)

Stackpoole, John (Qld) b Nov. 23, 1916 Jundah (Qld)

Stalker, Walter (Vic) b Oct. 29, 1909 Elaine (Vic) d Jan. 13, 1977 Ballarat (Vic)

Stanes, John Gladstone (Vic) b Dec. 15, 1910 South Melbourne (Vic) d Feb. 7, 1983 Ferntree Gully (Vic)

Stanford, Graham Edwin (SAust) b April 25, 1948 Adelaide (SAust)

Stanford, Ross Milton (SAust) b Sept. 25, 1917 Fulham (SAust)

Stapleton, Harold Vincent (NSW) b Jan. 7, 1915 Kyogle (NSW)

Starr, Cecil Leonard Berry (SAust) b July 20, 1907 Quorn (SAust)

Steele, Donald Macdonald (SAust) b Aug. 17, 1892 East Adelaide (SAust) d July 13, 1962 Adelaide (SAust)

Steele, Harry Cornwall (NSW) b April 22, 1901 East Sydney (NSW) d Nov. 9, 1985 Sydney (NSW)

Steele, John Anthony (NSW) b Nov. 13, 1942 Waverley (NSW)

Steele, Kenneth Nagent (SAust) b Dec. 17, 1889 East Adelaide (SAust) d Dec. 19, 1956 North Adelaide (SAust)

Stephens, Jack Lawson (Vic) b Aug. 31, 1913 Majorca (Vic) d Sept. 2, 1967 Daylesford (Vic)

Stephens, John Raymond (Vic) b Sept. 15, 1950 East Melbourne (Vic)

Stephens, Reginald Stanley (Vic) b April 16, 1883 Creswick (Vic) d Sept. 7, 1965 Malvern (Vic)

Stephenson, Franklyn Dacosta (Tas) b April 8, 1959 Halls, St James (Barbados)

Stepto, Paul Douglas (NSW) b Dec. 23, 1966 Sydney (NSW)

* Stevens, Gavin Byron (SAust) b Feb. 29, 1932 Glenelg (SAust)

Stevens, John Grenfell (NSW) b Feb. 22, 1948 Muswellbrook (NSW)

Stevens, John Whitehall (Vic) birth and death details unknown

Stevens, Robert Barry (Vic) b Nov. 5, 1929 Melbourne (Vic)

Stewart, Barry James (Tas) b May 6, 1940 Wynyard (Tas) d July 23, 1975 Wynyard (Tas)

Stewart, Gordon Lionel (NSW) b June 16, 1906 Petersham (NSW) d Oct. 21, 1984 Katoomba (NSW)

Stewart, James (WAust & NSW) b Aug. 22, 1970 East Fremantle (WAust)

Stewart, James C. (Vic) birth and death details unknown

Stewart, Trevor George (Qld) b March 15, 1940 Mt Isa (Qld)

Stewart, William (Vic) b c. 1844 full birth and death details unknown

Stibe, Colin George Reinzi (Qld) b April 22, 1916 Bundaberg (Qld) d Jan. 6, 1970 Sydney (NSW)

Still, Robert Stuart (Tas) b March 15, 1822 Bathurst (NSW) d July 5, 1907 Launceston (Tas)

Still, William Cathcart (NSW) b c. 1820 (England) d July 5, 1910 Sydney (NSW)

Stillman, William Leslie (Vic & SAust) b Oct. 5, 1949 Alexandra (Vic)

Stirling, William Stuart (SAust) b March 19, 1891 Jamestown (SAust) d July 18, 1971 Adelaide (SAust)

Stobo, Richard Montagu (NSW) b June 20, 1965 Toowoomba (Qld)

Stokes, George William (Vic) b Dec. 11, 1857 South Yarra (Vic) d Aug. 16, 1929 Brighton (Vic)

Stokes, Raymond Gordon (Tas) b May 21, 1924 Longford (Tas)

Stokes, William (WAust) b July 28, 1886 Geraldton (WAust) d Oct. 4, 1954 Perth (WAust)

Storey, Stephen Craig (Qld) b Nov. 23, 1964 Mona Vale (NSW)

Stratford, H. E. (Vic) birth and death details unknown

Strauss, Raymond Bernard (WAust) b Nov. 4, 1927 Perth (WAust)

Strudwick, David Charles (SAust) b Jan. 11, 1934 Adelaide (SAust)

Stuart, Anthony Mark (NSW) b Jan. 2, 1970 Waratah (NSW)

Stuart, William Percy (SAust) b March 7, 1871 Goolwa (SAust) d Aug. 20, 1956 Unley Park (SAust)

Stubbs, John Robert Marshall (WAust) b Oct. 15, 1931 Collie (WAust)

Stuckey, George (Vic) b July 6, 1871 Walhalla (Vic) d March 15, 1932 North Melbourne (Vic)

Stuckey, John Henry (Vic) b July 3, 1869 Walhalla (Vic) d Aug. 10, 1952 Cheltenham (Vic)

Such, Bruce Vincent (Qld) b c. 1907 Sydney (NSW) d April 14, 1933 Townsville (Qld)

Sullivan, Alfred Ernest (NSW) b Dec. 10, 1872 Balmain (NSW) d Sept. 25, 1942 Balmain (NSW)

Sullivan, William (Qld) b Aug. 19, 1877 Hotham (Vic) d Aug. 29, 1924 Albury (NSW)

Suppel, James Thomas (NSW) b Oct. 19, 1914 Warren (NSW) d March 9, 1994 Lidcombe (NSW)

* Surti, Rusi Framroz (Qld) b May 25, 1936 Surat (India)

Sutherland, David (Vic) b June 4, 1873 Boroondara (Vic) d Oct. 6, 1971 Hawthorn (Vic)

Sutherland, Donald John (SAust) b Nov. 28, 1949 Adelaide (SAust)

Sutherland, James Alexander (Vic) b July 14, 1965 East Melbourne (Vic)

Swain, Brett Andrew (SAust) b Feb. 14, 1974 Stirling (SAust)

Swan, Gavin Graham (WAust) b Oct. 30, 1970 Subiaco (WAust)

Swanson, John David (Vic) b April 5, 1940 Brunswick (Vic)

Swendsen, Robert Charles (Qld) b Oct. 18, 1929 Charters Towers (Qld)

Swift, John Sheddon (Vic) b Feb. 3, 1852 birthplace unknown d Feb. 28, 1926 Kew (Vic)

Symonds, Andrew (Qld) b June 9, 1975 Birmingham, West Midlands (England)

Symonds, Crawford (SAust) b Feb. 15, 1915 North Adelaide (SAust) d uly 20, 2000 Bedford Park (SAust)

Taaffe, Frederick Herbert (WAust) b Jan. 7, 1899 Deolali (India) d April 2, 1964 Ulladulla (NSW)

Tabart, John Lewis Benjamin (Tas) b Nov. 30, 1827 St Pancras, London (England) d Sept. 9, 1894 Launceston (Tas)

Tabart, Thomas Alfred (Tas) b Aug. 10, 1877 Campbell Town (Tas) d Aug. 29, 1950 East Melbourne (Vic)

* Taber, Hedley Brian (NSW) b April 29, 1940 Wagga Wagga (NSW)

Tait, Alan Houston (Qld) b Feb. 17, 1908 Toowoomba (Qld) d July 27, 1988 Indooroopilly (Qld)

Tait, George (Parr's XI) b April 12, 1844 Parramatta (NSW) d Dec. 21, 1934 East Malvern (Vic)

* Tallon, Donald (Qld) b Feb. 17, 1916 Bundaberg (Qld) d Sept. 7, 1984 Bundaberg (Qld)

Tallon, Leslie William Thomas (Qld) b July 9, 1914 Bundaberg (Qld) d Sept. 18, 1972 Coopers Plains (Qld)

Tamblyn, Geoffrey Leonard (Vic) b April 8, 1949 Melbourne (Vic)

Tamblyn, Gordon Erle (Vic) b April 23, 1918 Wallaroo Mines (SAust)

Tame, Michael Philip (Tas) b Jan. 6, 1956 Hobart (Tas)

Tardif, Joseph Henry (SAust) b May 17, 1860 Gawler (SAust) d June 14, 1920 Prospect (SAust)

Targett, Benjamin Stuart (Tas) b Dec. 27, 1972 Paddington (NSW)

Tarrant, Francis Alfred (Vic) b Dec. 11, 1880 Fitzroy (Vic) d Jan. 29, 1951 Upper Hawthorn (Vic)

Tarrant, William Ambrose (Vic) b Sept. 22, 1866 Fitzroy (Vic) d Nov. 1, 1938 North Fitzroy (Vic)

Tatchell, Thomas (Vic) b June 13, 1867 Inglewood (Vic) d Oct. 18, 1936 East Melbourne (Vic)

Taylor, Bruce William (Qld) b June 14, 1924 Brisbane (Qld) d Oct. 16, 1984 New Farm (Qld)

Taylor, David (NSW) b May 2, 1881 Sydney (NSW) death details unknown

* Taylor, John Morris (NSW) b Oct. 10, 1895 Stanmore (NSW) d May 12, 1971 Turramurra (NSW)

Taylor, Joseph Stanley (NSW) b Nov. 1, 1887 Leichhardt (NSW) d Sept. 3, 1954 Waratah (NSW)

* Taylor, Mark Anthony (NSW) b Oct. 27, 1964 Leeton (NSW)

Taylor, Michael David (Vic & Tas) b June 9, 1955 Chelsea (Vic)

* Taylor, Peter Laurence (NSW & Qld) b Aug. 22, 1956 North Sydney (NSW)

Taylor, Ross Simeon (NSW) b May 8, 1938 Mudgee (NSW) d Dec. 7, 1996 Tamworth (NSW)

Taylor, Stuart Gifford (Tas) b April 13, 1900 Prahran (Vic) d Feb. 2, 1978 Mosman Park (WAust)

Tazelaar, Dirk (Qld) b Jan. 13, 1963 Ipswich (Qld)

Teagle, Reginald Crump (SAust) b Feb. 27, 1909 Parkside (SAust) d June 8, 1987 Adelaide (SAust)

Teece, Richard (Combined XIII) b April 29, 1847 Paihia (New Zealand) d Dec. 13, 1928 Point Piper (NSW)

Teisseire, Francis Lawrence (SAust) b July 8, 1917 Rose Park (SAust) d Nov. 23, 1998 Glenelg (SAust)

Templeton, Robert Ian (Vic) b March 15, 1957 Hamilton (Vic)

Tennent, Hector Norman (Australians) b April 6, 1843 Hobart (Tas) d April 16, 1904 Westminster, London (England)

Tennent, John Pattison (Vic) b July 31, 1846 Hobart (Tas) d Oct. 31, 1893 Clifton Hill (Vic)

Terry, Richard Benjamin (Vic) birth and death details unknown

Thamm, Carl Friedrich Wilhelm (SAust) b Nov. 1, 1874 Nuriootpa (SAust) d July 4, 1944 Subiaco (WAust)

Thatcher, Allen Norman (NSW) b April 17, 1899 Sydney (NSW) d Feb. 12, 1932 Dulwich Hill (NSW)

Theak, Henry John Thomas (NSW) b March 19, 1909 Pyrmont (NSW) d Sept. 14, 1979 Narwee (NSW)

Thollar, Douglas Hugh (Tas) b Feb. 13, 1919 George Town (Tas)

Thomas, Arthur Churchill (SAust) b May 4, 1869 Unley (SAust) d April 28, 1934 Unley (SAust)

Thomas, Brad John (Tas) b Jan. 18, 1972 Hobart (Tas)

Thomas, George Alexander (NSW) b April 22, 1881 Sydney (NSW)

* Thomas, Grahame (NSW) b March 21, 1938 Croydon Park (NSW)

Thomas, Jeffrey Mark (Qld) b Oct. 19, 1971 Toowoomba (Qld)

Thomas, John Oliver (Tas) b April 12, 1852 Merthyr Tydfil (Wales) d May 29, 1915 Carlton (Vic)

Thomas, Josiah (Vic) b Aug. 27, 1910 Golden Square, Bendigo (Vic) d May 28, 1960 Essendon (Vic)

Thomas, Kenneth Bruce (Vic) b Oct. 5, 1942 East Melbourne (Vic)

Thomas, Llewellyn (Tas) b April 1, 1883 Fitzroy (Vic) d Nov. 2, 1962 Evandale (Tas)

Thomas, Maxwell Raymond (Tas) b June 28, 1921 Launceston (Tas) d May 20, 2001 Lenah Valley (Tas)

Thomas, Ramon Cedric (SAust) b Nov. 18, 1932 Mile End (SAust)

Thomas, Ronald Vivian (Tas) b Sept. 21, 1915 Longford (Tas) d May 28, 1987 Launceston (Tas)

Thomlinson, Arthur (Tas) b c. 1887 full birth and death details unknown

Thompson, C.D. (NSW) birth and death details unknown

Thompson, Francis Cecil (Qld) b Aug. 17, 1890 Stanwell (Qld) d Sept. 24, 1963 Southport (Qld)

Thompson, Horace Malcolm (SAust) b Nov. 29, 1913 Malvern (SAust) d March 19, 1936 Kalgoorlie (WAust)

Thompson, James Bogne (Vic) b c. 1829 Yorkshire (England) d July 18, 1877 Melbourne (Vic)

Thompson, Kerry William (NSW) b Dec. 12, 1949 Wallsend (NSW)

Thompson, Scott Michael (NSW) b May 4, 1972 Bankstown (NSW)

Thompson, William James (Qld) b Jan. 2, 1891 (Qld)

* Thoms, George Ronald (Vic) b March 22, 1927 Footscray (Vic)

Thomsett, Harold King (Qld) b Oct. 23, 1913 Yarraman (Qld) d April 12, 1991 Spring Hill (Qld)

* Thomson, Alan Lloyd (Vic) b Dec. 2, 1945 Reservoir (Vic)

Thomson, Alan Ogilvie (Vic) b Sept. 1, 1899 Tibooburra (NSW) d c. 1938 Tibooburra (NSW)

Thomson, Alfred Taddy (Vic) b 1818 birth day and month unknown Paddington, London, Middlesex (England) d Oct. 12, 1895 London (England)

Thomson, Geoffrey David (WAust) b April 21, 1959 Subiaco (WAust)

* Thomson, Jeffrey Robert (NSW & Qld) b Aug. 16, 1950 Greenacre (NSW)

Thomson, Joseph (Qld) b May 27, 1877 South Brisbane (Qld) d Aug. 1, 1953 (Qld)

Thomson, Kenneth Stephen (Tas) b Jan. 5, 1947 Hobart (Tas)

* Thomson, Nathaniel Frampton Davis (NSW) b May 29, 1839 Surry Hills (NSW) d Sept. 2, 1896 Burwood (NSW)

Thorn, Frank Leslie Oliver (Vic) b Aug. 16, 1912 St Arnaud (Vic) d Feb. 11, 1942 Gasmata (New Britain) in action

Thornton, Barry Thomas (WAust) b June 3, 1941 South Perth (WAust)

Thornton, John (Vic) b Jan. 16, 1835 Huddersfield, Yorkshire (England) d Dec. 15, 1919 Camperdown (Vic)

Thorpe, Henry (Combined XI) b c. 1862 Parramatta (NSW) d c. 1937 Artarmon (NSW)

Thorpe, Linsley James (Qld) b Feb. 15, 1923 Alpha (Qld)

Thurgarland, Wilfred John (SAust) b March 11, 1892 Queenstown (SAust) d July 12, 1974 Campbelltown (SAust)

* Thurlow, Hugh Morley (Qld) b Jan. 10, 1903 Townsville (Qld) d Dec. 3, 1975 Rosalie (Qld)

Thwaites, Colin Geoffrey (Vic) b Jan. 23, 1955 Lang Lang (Vic)

Thwaites, Thomas Edwin (Qld) b July 1, 1910 Nindooinbah (Qld) d May 24, 2000 Beaudesert (Qld)

Tilyard, Gregory Almeria Sydney (Tas) b March 19, 1932 Sandford (Tas)

Timbury, Fredrick Richard Vaughan (Qld) b July 12, 1885 Gladstone (Qld) d April 14, 1945 Sydney (NSW)

Tindall, Edwin (NSW) b March 31, 1851 Liverpool (NSW) d Jan. 16, 1926 Marrickville (NSW)

Tobin, Bertrandt Joseph (SAust) b Nov. 11, 1910 North Adelaide (SAust) d Oct. 19, 1969 Adelaide (SAust)

Tobin, William Andrew (Vic) b June 7, 1859 Kensington, London, Middlesex (England) d Feb. 17, 1904 South Melbourne (Vic)

Toby, Frederick James (Tas) b Dec. 9, 1888 Redfern (NSW) d c. 1963 death details unknown

Tolhurst, Edward Keith (Vic) b Oct. 29, 1895 St Kilda (Vic) d May 24, 1982 East Prahran (Vic)

Tooher, John Andrew (NSW) b Nov. 18, 1846 Sydney (NSW) d May 23, 1941 Neutral Bay (NSW)

* Toohey, Peter Michael (NSW) b April 20, 1954 Blayney (NSW)

Tooley, Mark Victor (Qld) b April 29, 1965 Toowoomba (Qld)

Toovey, Ernest Albert (Qld) b May 16, 1922 Warwick (Qld)

* Toshack, Ernest Raymond Herbert (NSW) b Dec. 8, 1914 Cobar (NSW)

Tovey, Edward Richard (Qld) b Dec. 25, 1930 Kings Cross (NSW) d May 31, 2002 St Leonard's (NSW)

Townley, Reginald Colin (Tas) b April 15, 1904 Hobart (Tas) d May 3, 1982 Hobart (Tas)

Townsend, Richard James Bruce (SAust) b Aug. 12, 1886 Mt Torrens (SAust) d Jan. 17, 1960 Waikerie (SAust)

Tozer, Claude John (NSW) b Sept. 27, 1890 Sydney (NSW) d Dec. 21, 1920 Lindfield (NSW)

Tozer, George Bruce (Vic) b June 27, 1926 Hopetoun (Vic)

Trapp, Vincent Burney (Vic) b Jan. 26, 1861 Prahran (Vic) d Oct. 21, 1929 Armadale (Vic)

* Travers, Joseph Patrick Francis (SAust) b Jan. 10, 1871 Adelaide (SAust) d Sept. 15, 1942 Adelaide (SAust)

Traves, Roger Norman (Qld) b Oct. 15, 1961 Cairns (Qld)

Treanor, John Cassimar (NSW) b Aug. 17, 1922 Darlinghurst (NSW) d Nov. 7, 1993 East Ballina (NSW)

Trebilcock, Arthur Joseph (Tas) b Dec. 13, 1907 Zeehan (Tas) d May 2, 1972 Hobart (Tas)

Tregoning, Jack (SAust) b June 13, 1919 West Adelaide (SAust) d June 26, 1989 North Adelaide (SAust)

Trembath, Thomas James (Vic) b Jan. 16, 1912 Moonta (SAust) d April 2, 1978 West Brunswick (Vic)

Trenerry, Edwin (NSW) b Feb. 24, 1897 Queanbeyan (NSW) d July 8, 1983 Woollahra (NSW)

Trenerry, William Leo (NSW) b Nov. 29, 1892 Queanbeyan (NSW) d Sept. 4, 1975 Mosman (NSW)

Trethewey, Peter Grant (SAust & Qld) b May 12, 1935 Croydon (SAust)

* Tribe, George Edward (Vic) b Oct. 4, 1920 Footscray (Vic)

Triffitt, Arthur (Tas) birth and death details unknown

Trimble, Glenn Samuel (Qld) b Jan. 1, 1963 Herston (Qld)

Trimble, Samuel Christy (Qld) b Aug. 16, 1934 Lismore (NSW)

Tringrove, James (Tas) b Nov. 25, 1907 Blackmans Bay (Tas) d Sept. 11, 1979 Blackmans Bay (Tas)

Trinnick, James (Vic) b Dec. 13, 1853 Kingsbridge, Devon (England) d July 12, 1928 Northcote (Vic)

**Trott, Albert Edwin (Vic) b Feb. 6, 1873 Collingwood (Vic) d July 30, 1914 Willesden Green, London (England)

* Trott, George Henry Stephens (Vic) b Aug. 5, 1866 Collingwood (Vic) d Nov. 10, 1917 South Melbourne (Vic)

Trowse, Dean Frederick (SAust) b Oct. 18, 1931 Rose Park (SAust)

Trueman, Geoffrey Stanley (NSW) b Jan. 7, 1926 Double Bay (NSW) d June 28, 1981 Sydney (NSW)

Truman, Frederick George (Vic) b Dec. 6, 1886 Carlton (Vic) d June 17, 1955 Brighton (Vic)

* Trumble, Hugh (Vic) b May 12, 1867 Abbotsford (Vic) d Aug. 14, 1938 Hawthorn (Vic)

* Trumble, John William (Vic) b Sept. 16, 1863 Collingwood (Vic) d Aug. 17, 1944 Brighton (Vic)

Trumper, Victor (NSW) b Oct. 7, 1913 Chatswood (NSW) d Aug. 31, 1981 Sydney (NSW)

* Trumper, Victor Thomas (NSW) b Nov. 2, 1877 Sydney (NSW) d June 28, 1915 Darlinghurst (NSW)

Truscott, William John (WAust) b Oct. 9, 1886 Lithgow (NSW) d June 20, 1966 Bayswater (WAust)

Tubb, Shannon Benjamin (Tas) b May 11, 1980 Bracknell (Tas)

Tucker, Adrian Edward (NSW) b Sept. 19, 1969 Ryde (NSW)

Tucker, Rodney James (NSW & Tas) b Aug. 28, 1964 Auburn (NSW)

Tuckwell, Bertie Joseph (Vic) b Oct. 6, 1882 Carlton (Vic) d Jan. 2, 1943 Wellington (New Zealand)

Tumilty, Leonard Ross (Tas) b June 12, 1884 Launceston (Tas) d March 27, 1962 Launceston (Tas)

Tunks, William (NSW) b April 8, 1816 Castlereagh (NSW) d April 12, 1883 St Leonards (NSW)

* Turner, Alan (NSW) b July 23, 1950 Camperdown (NSW)

* Turner, Charles Thomas Byass (NSW) b Nov. 16, 1862 Bathurst (NSW) d Jan. 1, 1944 Manly (NSW)

Turner, Dale Andrew (NSW) b Jan. 30, 1974 Bankstown (NSW)

Turner, Edward (Vic) b Aug. 8, 1858 Northcote (Vic) d Jan. 26, 1893 Prahran (Vic)

Turner, J. B. (Vic) birth and death details unknown

Turner, Thomas (SAust & Vic) b March 7, 1865 Nuriootpa (SAust) d Oct. 27, 1936 Prospect (SAust)

Turner, Wilfred Herbert (Vic) b July 6, 1921 Woodvale near Bendigo (Vic) d Feb. 24, 2002 Bendigo (Vic)

Tuttle, Roy Thomas (Vic) b Sept. 11, 1920 Carlton (Vic) d c. 1997 Canberra (ACT)

Tweeddale, Ernest Richard (NSW) b Aug. 23, 1895 Newtown (NSW) d April 28, 1956 Dover Heights (NSW)

Twible, Paul William (Qld) b Dec. 14, 1957 Herston (Qld)

Twopenny (Murrumgunarriman) (NSW) b c. 1845 Bathurst (NSW) d March 12, 1883 West Maitland (NSW)

Van Deinsen, Brett Paul (NSW) b Dec. 28, 1977 Bankstown (NSW)

Varis, Leslie (WAust) b May 13, 1947 Kalgoorlie (WAust)

Vaughan, Frederick (Vic) b Nov. 8, 1876 (England) d Sept. 30, 1926 Elsternwick (Vic)

Vaughan, Jeffrey Mark (SAust) b March 26, 1974 Blacktown (NSW)

Vaughan, Leonard J. (NSW) b March 16, 1908 Waverley (NSW) d c. 1960 full death details unknown

Vaughan, Robert (NSW) b c. 1834 d July 12, 1865 at sea between Australia and New Zealand

Vaughton, Roland William (SAust) b May 5, 1914 Ardrossan (SAust) d Jan. 5, 1979 Adelaide (SAust)

Vautin, Charles Edwin (Tas) b June 24, 1867 Sorell (Tas) d Dec. 11, 1942 Moonah (Tas)

Vautin, Douglas Maynard (Tas) b July 26, 1896 Hobart (Tas) d Jan. 11, 1976 Mt Martha (Vic)

Vautin, George James Phillips (Tas & Vic) b April 23, 1869 Orielton (Tas) d Jan. 9, 1949 West Preston (Vic)

Vawser, Bruce Forbes (Vic) b June 17, 1929 Mitcham (Vic)

* Veivers, Thomas Robert (Qld) b April 6, 1937 Beenleigh (Qld)

* Veletta, Michael Robert John (WAust) b Oct. 30, 1963 Subiaco (WAust)

Vernon, Edward Henry George (Vic) b Oct. 11, 1911 Northcote (Vic) d May 8, 1968 Kew (Vic)

Vernon, Leslie Phillip (Vic) b May 29, 1880 Melbourne (Vic) d May 11, 1957 Ashwood (Vic)

Vernon, Murray Trevor (WAust) b Feb. 9, 1937 Kondinin (WAust)

Vidler, Robert Trevor (NSW) b Feb. 5, 1957 Cronulla (NSW)

Vimpani, Graeme Ronald (Vic) b Jan. 27, 1972 Herston (Qld)

Vincent, Brian Alfred (SAust) b Feb. 16, 1960 Unley (SAust)

Vincent, Norman Hill (Tas) b Nov. 10, 1883 (England) d Feb. 12, 1958 Prahran (Vic)

Vincent, Russell George (SAust) b March 25, 1954 Jamestown (SAust)

Vint, William (Vic) b June 30, 1851 Belfast (Ireland) d March 28, 1897 Helens Bay (Ireland)

Waddy, Edgar Lloyd (NSW) b Dec. 3, 1879 Morpeth (NSW) d Aug. 2, 1963 Collaroy (NSW)

Waddy, Ernest Frederick (NSW) b Oct. 5, 1880 Morpeth (NSW) d Sept. 23, 1958 Evesham , Worcestershire (England)

Wade, Frank Hainsworth (NSW) b Sept. 1, 1871 Farsley, Yorkshire (England) d Oct. 4, 1940 Lindfield (NSW)

Wainwright, Edmund George Chalwin (SAust) b May 18, 1903 North Adelaide (SAust) d Aug. 8, 1995 North Geelong (Vic)

* Waite, Mervyn George (SAust) b Jan. 7, 1911 Kent Town (SAust) d Dec. 16, 1985 Georgetown (SAust)

Waldron, Alfred Edward (SAust) b Feb. 26, 1857 Moorooduc (Vic) d June 7, 1929 Adelaide (SAust)

Wales, Isaac (NSW) b Jan. 31, 1865 Auckland Park, near Bishop Auckland, Durham (England) d Jan. 11, 1949 death place unknown

Walford, Sydney Rundle (NSW) b Nov. 19, 1857 Darlinghurst (NSW) d July 2, 1949 Woollahra (NSW)

Walker, Alan Keith (NSW) b Oct. 4, 1925 Manly (NSW)

Walker, Charles William (SAust) b Feb. 19, 1909 Brompton Park (SAust) d Dec. 18, 1942 in action over Soltau (Germany)

Walker, Darren Kenneth (Vic) b June 8, 1966 Bendigo (Vic)

Walker, Jeffrey Milton (Qld) b Sept. 11, 1960 Beaudesert (Qld)

Walker, Kenneth Victor John (Vic) b June 25, 1941 Melbourne (Vic)

* Walker, Maxwell Henry Norman (Vic) b Sept. 12, 1948 West Hobart (Tas)

Walker, Ronald Radford (Vic) b Jan. 1, 1926 Collingwood (Vic)

Walker, William Holden (Tas) b Dec. 16, 1835 Islington, London (England) d June 14, 1886 Hobart (Tas)

Walkerden, Henry Ernest (WAust) b Nov. 20, 1885 Brunswick (Vic) d May 16, 1966 Richmond (Vic)

Walkley, Edwin (SAust) b May 10, 1876 Wallaroo (SAust) d April 18, 1950 Randwick (NSW)

Wall, John Craik Lyall Sydney (NSW) b Oct. 25, 1891 Balmain (NSW) d June 9, 1969 West Pymble (NSW)

* Wall, Thomas Welbourn (SAust) b May 13, 1904 Semaphore (SAust) d March 26, 1981 Adelaide (SAust)

Wallace, Percival Henry (Vic) b Oct. 6, 1891 Bendigo (Vic) d Oct. 3, 1959 Glen Iris (Vic)

Wallace, Richard Miscamble (Tas) b March 22, 1934 Melbourne (Vic)

Walmsley, Walter Thomas (NSW, Tas & Qld) b March 16, 1916 Homebush (NSW) d Feb. 25, 1978 Hamilton (New Zealand)

Walsh, James Michael (Tas) b May 28, 1913 Launceston (Tas) d July 5, 1986 Launceston (Tas)

Walsh, John Edward (NSW) b Dec. 4, 1912 Walcha (NSW) d May 20, 1980 Wallsend (NSW)

Walsh, Lawrence Stanley (SAust) b Feb. 8, 1902 North Adelaide (SAust) d Jan. 12, 1976 St Georges (SAust)

Walsh, Mark Jason (WAust) b April 28, 1972 Townsville (Qld)

Walsh, Norman Arthur (SAust) b Feb. 8, 1902 North Adelaide (SAust) d Dec. 7, 1969 Adelaide (SAust)

Walshe, John Hamilton (Tas) b c. 1841 (England) d April 17, 1893 Sandy Bay (Tas)

* Walters, Francis Henry (Vic & NSW) b Feb. 9, 1860 Richmond (Vic) d June 1, 1922 at sea near Bombay

* Walters, Kevin Douglas (NSW) b Dec. 21, 1945 Dungog (NSW)

Walters, Maxwell John (Qld) b July 28, 1953 Bundaberg (Qld)

Walton, Douglas John (Tas) b April 9, 1927 New Norfolk (Tas) d Feb. 18, 2001 Glenorchy (Tas)

Ward, Edward Wolstenholme (NSW) b Aug. 17, 1823 Calcutta (India) d Feb. 5, 1890 Cannes (France)

* Ward, Francis Anthony (SAust) b Feb. 23, 1906 Leichhardt (NSW) d May 25, 1974 Brooklyn (NSW)

Ward, Harry Alexander (Tas) b Dec. 8, 1924 Hobart (Tas) d Dec. 8, 1993 Sandy Bay (Tas)

Ward, John Charles (Vic) b Nov. 15, 1946 Melbourne (Vic)

Ward, Leonard Keith (Tas) b Feb. 17, 1879 South Kingston (SAust) d Sept. 30, 1964 Heathpool (SAust)

Ward, Maxwell John (NSW) b Feb. 3, 1907 Randwick (NSW) d Oct. 24, 1983 New Lambton Heights (NSW)

Ward, Ronald Egbert (Tas) b May 7, 1905 Adelaide (SAust) d Nov. 8, 2000 Launceston (Tas)

Ward, William George (Tas) b May 15, 1863 West Hobart (Tas) d June 22, 1948 East Malvern (Vic)

Warden, Lester Griffith (Qld) b April 14, 1940 Wooloowin (Qld) d April 3, 1989 Greenslopes (Qld)

Wardill, Benjamin Johnson (Vic) b Oct. 15, 1842 Everton, Lancashire (England) d Oct. 15, 1917 Sandringham (Vic)

Wardill, Richard Wilson (Vic) b Nov. 3, 1840 Everton, Lancashire (England) d Aug. 17, 1873 Melbourne (Vic)

Wardlaw, Douglas McLaren Searl (Tas) b July 19, 1904 Hobart (Tas) d May 20, 1968 St Marys (Tas)

Wardlaw, Robert Bruce Searl (Tas) b Jan. 9, 1914 Hobart (Tas) d Sept. 12, 1986 Launceston (Tas)

Ware, Joseph Maitland (Tas) b Sept. 8, 1822 London (England) d Sept. 21, 1868 Lausanne (Switzerland)

Warne, Frank Belmont (Vic) b Oct. 3, 1906 North Carlton (Vic) d May 29, 1994 Edenvale (South Africa)

* Warne, Shane Keith (Vic) b Sept. 13, 1969 Ferntree Gully (Vic)

Warne, Tom Summerhayes (Vic) b Jan. 13, 1870 North Melbourne (Vic) d July 7, 1944 Carlton (Vic)

Warr, Gerald Gerrard (Qld) b May 17, 1939 Casino (NSW)

Warren, Peter Charles (Tas) b May 13, 1953 Launceston (Tas)

Wasley, Mark Andrew (WAust & Tas) b Oct. 6, 1965 Subiaco (WAust)

Waterman, Leonard William (Qld) b Feb. 18, 1892 Brisbane (Qld) d Jan. 1, 1952 Kangaroo Point (Qld)

Waters, Glen Wayne (Tas) b May 3, 1943 Launceston (Tas)

Waters, Robert William (SAust) b April 29, 1874 Gravesend, Kent (England) d Feb. 20, 1912 Woodville (SAust)

Wates, Darren Jude (WAust) b July 2, 1977 Subiaco (WAust)

* Watkins, John Russell (NSW) b April 16, 1943 Hamilton (NSW)

Watling, Walter Herbert (SAust) b March 13, 1864 Unley (SAust) d Dec. 19, 1928 Randfontein (South Africa)

Watmuff, Frederick John (Vic) b Sept. 16, 1915 St Kilda (Vic) d Aug. 10, 1972 Castlemaine (Vic)

Watsford, Goulburn (SAust) b July 1, 1859 Goulburn (NSW) d May 16, 1951 Melbourne (Vic)

Watson, Alfred Edward (Tas) b Aug. 31, 1888 Carlton (Vic) d May 6, 1957 South Melbourne (Vic)

Watson, Andrew Simon (SAust) b Oct. 14, 1955 Woomera (SAust)

Watson, Bertie Francis (NSW) b March 13, 1898 Maclean (NSW) d Nov. 18, 1987 Canberra (ACT)

* Watson, Graeme Donald (Vic, WAust & NSW) b March 8, 1945 Kew (Vic)

Watson, Gregory George (NSW & WAust) b Jan. 29, 1955 Gulgong (NSW)

Watson, John Wentworth (Tas) b 1828 birth day and month unknown Sorell (Tas) d June 26, 1920 Scottsdale (Tas)

Watson, Roy Clarence William (WAust) b June 21, 1933 Fremantle (WAust)

Watson, Shane Robert (Tas) b June 17, 1981 Ipswich (Qld)

Watson, William (NSW) b Nov. 10, 1881 Lambton (NSW) d Feb. 12, 1926 North Sydney (NSW)

* Watson, William James (NSW) b Jan. 31, 1931 Randwick (NSW)

Watt, Arthur David (WAust) b Nov. 24, 1913 Edinburgh (Scotland)

Watt, Arthur Kenneth Elwyn (Tas) b Dec. 12, 1891 Hobart (Tas) d Oct. 8, 1973 Hobart (Tas)

Watt, Donald (Qld) b March 15, 1920 Southport (Qld)

Watt, John (Tas) b Feb. 16, 1858 Hobart (Tas) d Nov. 14, 1918 Glebe (Tas)

Watt, John Charles (Tas) b July 6, 1884 Hobart (Tas) d Aug. 4, 1961 Hobart (Tas)

Watters, John Charles (Vic) b Oct. 6, 1924 Footscray (Vic)

Watts, Colin Arthur (SAust) b Jan. 9, 1921 St Peters (SAust)

Watts, Gary Maxwell (Vic) b Oct. 22, 1958 Dunolly (Vic)

Waugh, Dean Parma (NSW) b Feb. 3, 1969 Campsie (NSW)

* Waugh, Mark Edward (NSW) b June 2, 1965 Canterbury (NSW)

Waugh, Russell Frederick (NSW & WAust) b Sept. 29, 1941 Sydney (NSW)

* Waugh, Stephen Rodger (NSW) b June 2, 1965 Canterbury (NSW)

Waye, Libby Sibly (SAust) b Jan. 14, 1885 Willunga (SAust) d June 10, 1951 Frewville (SAust)

Wearne, William Stewart (NSW) b Jan. 18, 1857 Campbelltown (NSW) d Jan. 28, 1929 Kalk Bay (South Africa)

Webb, Berrowes Littleton (Qld) b April 15, 1915 Brisbane (Qld) d Feb. 7, 1983 Greenslopes (Qld)

Webb, Colin Ralph (SAust) b Jan. 20, 1926 North Adelaide (SAust)

Webb, Kenneth Norman (SAust) b Feb. 27, 1921 Unley (SAust) d March 7, 1994 Daw Park (SAust)

Webber, Darren Scott (SAust) b Aug. 18, 1971 Burnside (SAust)

Webster, Alexander Miles Clifton (WAust) b Nov. 25, 1908 East Fremantle (WAust) d March 28, 1964 Shenton Park (WAust)

Webster, Harold Wynne (SAust) b Feb. 17, 1887 Randwick (NSW) d Oct. 7, 1949 Randwick (NSW)

Webster, Stuart Edward (NSW) b June 11, 1946 Orange (NSW)

Wedgwood, Walter Bernard (Vic) b Oct. 23, 1912 Clifton Hill (Vic) d Dec. 2, 1977 Mornington (Vic)

Weekley, Leonard Rex (SAust) b July 21, 1922 Port Wakefield (SAust)

Weeks, Albert Edmund (SAust) b July 23, 1864 Bowden (SAust) d April 21, 1948 Hollywood (WAust)

Weir, Alexander John (SAust) b March 5, 1921 Largs Bay (SAust)

Weir, Harold Stanley (Qld) b April 23, 1904 Croydon Junction (Qld) d June 11, 2002 Maryborough (Qld)

Welch, Charles William (Vic) b June 9, 1907 birthplace unknown d April 11, 1983 Melbourne (Vic)

* Wellham, Dirk Macdonald (NSW, Tas & Qld) b March 13, 1959 Marrickville (NSW)

Wellham, Walter Arthur (NSW) b Sept. 17, 1932 Belmont (NSW)

Wellington, Clement Wellesley (WAust) b Aug. 17, 1880 Yongala (SAust) d July 26, 1956 Underdale (SAust)

Wellington, Stephen Leslie (Tas) b July 4, 1899 Beaconsfield (Tas) d June 11, 1974 Scotts Head (NSW)

Wells, Arthur Phillip (NSW) b Sept. 4, 1900 Paddington (NSW) d Dec. 27, 1964 South Coogee (NSW)

**Wessels, Kepler Christoffel (Qld) b Sept. 14, 1957 Bloemfontein, Orange Free State (South Africa)

West, Neville Leonard (Vic) b Nov. 9, 1933 Marysville (Vic) d Aug. 8, 1987 Belrose (NSW)

Westaway, Colin Edward (Qld) b Aug. 27, 1936 Indooroopilly (Qld)

Westbrook, Keith Raymond (Tas) b May 28, 1887 Scottsdale (Tas) d Jan. 20, 1982 Burnie (Tas)

Westbrook, Norman Russell (Tas) b June 25, 1868 Launceston (Tas) d May 29, 1931 Launceston (Tas)

Westbrook, Roy Austin (Tas) b Jan. 3, 1889 Ringarooma (Tas) d Aug. 7, 1961 Wellington (New Zealand)

Westbrook, Thomas (Tas) b 1827 birth day and month unknown Hobart (Tas) d Sept. 13, 1911 Sandy Bay (Tas)

Westbrook, Walter Horatio (Tas) b Nov. 21, 1827 Hobart (Tas) d Jan. 3, 1897 Launceston (Tas)

Whalley, John (Qld) b Nov. 27, 1872 Spring Hill (Qld) d Oct. 29, 1925 Brisbane (Qld)

* Whatmore, Davenell Frederick (Vic) b March 16, 1954 Colombo (Ceylon)

Whiddon, Henry (NSW) b Nov. 20, 1878 Sydney (NSW) d Dec. 19, 1935 Manly (NSW)

White, Alfred Becher Stewart (NSW) b Oct. 4, 1879 Mudgee (NSW) d Dec. 15, 1962 Karuah (NSW)

White, Alfred Henry Ebsworth (NSW) b Oct. 18, 1901 Scone (NSW) d March 6, 1964 Darling Point (NSW)

White, Cameron Leon (Vic) b Aug. 18, 1983 Bairnsdale (Vic)

* White, Craig (Vic) b Dec. 16, 1969 Morley, Yorkshire (England)

White, Edward Clive Stewart (NSW) b April 17, 1913 Mosman (NSW) d Oct. 10, 1999 Hornsby (NSW)

Whiteside, Warren Gregory (Vic) b Nov. 1, 1961 Box Hill (Vic)

Whitesides, Thomas (Tas) b 1836 birth day and month unknown Hobart (Tas) d Sept. 24, 1919 Hobart (Tas)

Whitfield, Henry Edward (SAust) b Feb. 25, 1903 Kent Town (SAust) d Jan. 14, 1937 Royston Park (SAust)

Whitfield, Stephen Bourke John (NSW) b Nov. 21, 1950 Ryde (NSW)

Whitford, Graham Sydney (Vic) b July 25, 1938 Ascot Vale (Vic)

Whiting, Albert William Harley (NSW) b May 31, 1866 Darlinghurst (NSW) death details unknown

Whitington, Richard Smallpeice (SAust) b June 30, 1912 Unley Park (SAust) d March 13, 1984 Sydney (NSW)

Whitlow, Edward Hardmond (Vic) b c. 1832 Manchester, Lancashire (England) d Nov. 29, 1870 South Melbourne (Vic)

Whitney, Gary Reginald (Tas) b March 19, 1951 Campbell Town (Tas)

* Whitney, Michael Roy (NSW) b Feb. 24, 1959 Surry Hills (NSW)

Whitting, William Charles (NSW) b July 9, 1884 Drummoyne (NSW) d Oct. 26, 1936 Bellevue Hill (NSW)

* Whitty, William James (NSW & SAust) b Aug. 15, 1886 Sydney (NSW) d Jan. 30, 1974 Tantanoola (SAust)

Whyte, Graham Keith (Qld) b March 29, 1952 Herston (Qld)

* Wiener, Julien Mark (Vic) b May 1, 1955 Melbourne (Vic)

Wigley, Robert Strangways (SAust) b March 15, 1864 Windsor (Vic) d April 20, 1926 Glenelg (SAust)

Wigney, Bradley Neil (SAust) b June 30, 1965 Leongatha (Vic)

Wilberforce, Robert James (WAust) b July 31, 1910 Subiaco (WAust) d Oct. 10, 1987 Woodlands (WAust)

Wildsmith, Andrew (Vic) b Jan. 9, 1958 East Melbourne (Vic)

Wildsmith, John (Vic) b July 1, 1939 Fitzroy (Vic)

Wilkes, Alfred Ernest (Tas) b Nov. 15, 1922 Launceston (Tas) d Aug. 27, 1998 Evandale (Tas)

Wilkie, Daniel (Vic) b Dec. 1, 1843 Melbourne (Vic) d May 11, 1917 St Kilda (Vic)

Wilkin, John Winstanley Symons (SAust) b April 28, 1924 North Adelaide (SAust)

Wilkins, Roy (Tas) b April 18, 1892 North Hobart (Tas) d July 17, 1965 Hobart (Tas)

Wilkinson, Alfred (SAust) b Jan. 2, 1863 Kooringa (SAust) d Jan. 22, 1922 Lower Mitcham (SAust)

Wilkinson, James Scott (Tas) b Dec. 4, 1951 Hobart (Tas)

Wilkinson, Robert B. (Vic) birth and death details unknown

Wilkinson, William Archer (Vic) b Sept. 1, 1899 Clifton Hill (Vic) d May 5, 1974 Mildura (Vic)

Willcocks, Robert James (Qld) b Dec. 23, 1891 Brisbane (Qld) d March 21, 1965 Toowoomba (Qld)

Williams, Bradley Andrew (Vic & WAust) b Nov. 20, 1974 Frankston (Vic)

Williams, Brett Douglas (SAust) b Dec. 15, 1967 Camden (NSW)

Williams, Douglas Samuel Thomas (WAust) b July 3, 1919 Elwood (Vic)

Williams, Edward Alexander (Vic) b Sept. 18, 1915 North Fitzroy (Vic)

Williams, Luke (SAust) b Dec. 24, 1979 Henley Beach (SAust)

* Williams, Neil Fitzgerald (Tas) b July 2, 1962 Hope Well (St Vincent)

Williams, Norman Leonard (SAust) b Sept. 23, 1899 Exeter (SAust) d May 31, 1947 Semaphore (SAust)

Williams, Owen Charles (Vic) b June 20, 1847 Impression Bay (Tas) d Nov. 18, 1917 Kandy (Ceylon)

Williams, Peter David (Vic) b Feb. 9, 1942 Brighton (Vic)

Williams, Robert Graham (SAust) b April 4, 1911 St Peters (SAust) d Aug. 31, 1978 Medindie (SAust)

Williams, Scott Bradley (Qld) b Feb. 1, 1971 Herston (Qld)

Williams, Vaughan Morgan (NSW) b Dec. 19, 1977 Blaxland (NSW)

Williamson, Cameron John (SAust) b March 26, 1970 Ryde (NSW)

Willis, Carl Bleackley (Vic) b March 23, 1893 Daylesford (Vic) d May 12, 1930 Berrigan (NSW)

Wills, Thomas Wentworth (Vic) b Dec. 19, 1835 Molonglo Plains (NSW) d May 2, 1880 Heidelberg (Vic)

Willsmore, Hurtle Binks (SAust) b Dec. 26, 1889 Beverley (SAust) d Sept. 17, 1985 Kings Park (SAust)

Wilson, Charles Geldart (Vic) b Jan. 9, 1869 Carngham (Vic) d June 28, 1952 Rosenerth (New Zealand)

Wilson, George Lindsay (Vic) b April 27, 1868 Collingwood (Vic) d March 9, 1920 St Kilda (Vic)

Wilson, Gregory James (Tas) b Jan. 4, 1958 Launceston (Tas)

Wilson, Henry (Tas) b March 31, 1865 Westbury (Tas) d Aug. 18, 1914 Sydney (NSW)

Wilson, Horace (WAust) b June 28, 1864 Kadina (SAust) d May 15, 1925 West Perth (WAust)

Wilson, John Thomas (Tas) b Nov. 27, 1868 Westbury (Tas) d July 24, 1906 Launceston (Tas)

Wilson, John Warwick (NSW) b Sept. 1, 1947 Paddington (NSW)

* Wilson, John William (Vic & SAust) b Aug. 20, 1921 Albert Park (Vic) d Oct. 13, 1985 Bayswater (Vic)

Wilson, Joseph Cameron (NSW) b Feb. 11, 1869 Braidwood (NSW) d c. 1938 Wollongong (NSW)

* Wilson, Paul (SAust) b Jan. 12, 1972 Newcastle (NSW)

Wilson, Richard (Qld) b Jan. 14, 1869 Paddington (NSW) d c. 1937 Parramatta (NSW)

Wilson, Stanley Vincent (WAust & SAust) b Sept. 23, 1948 Midland (WAust)

Wilson, William John (Vic) b c. 1912 Mildura (Vic)

Wilson, William Young (Vic) b Dec. 13, 1909 Essendon (Vic) d Sept. 30, 1976 Ascot Vale (Vic)

Windsor, Edward Arthur Cartwright (Tas) b March 9, 1869 Launceston (Tas) d Dec. 23, 1953 Launceston (Tas)

Wingrove, Francis William (Combined XI) b April 20, 1863 Eltham (Vic) d May 27, 1892 Rupanyup (Vic)

Winning, Charles Samuel (AIF) b July 17, 1889 Paddington (NSW) d April 20, 1967 Newport (NSW)

Winser, Cyril Legh (SAust) b Nov. 27, 1884 High Legh, Staffordshire (England) d Dec. 20, 1983 Barwon Heads (Vic)

Winter, Graham John (SAust) b Nov. 6, 1955 Medindie (SAust)

Wishart, Peter William (WAust) b June 18, 1937 Perth (WAust)

Wishart, Warren Keith (WAust) b Feb. 17, 1971 Subiaco (WAust)

Wolfe, Malcolm Frederick (WAust) b July 28, 1952 Gnowangerup (WAust)

Wood, Cecil Clunas (Tas) b April 8, 1896 Erin Bay (Tas) death details unknown

* Wood, Graeme Malcolm (WAust) b Nov. 6, 1956 East Fremantle (WAust)

Wood, Hartley Lionel (SAust) b April 5, 1930 Flinders Park (SAust) d Dec. 16, 1988 Elizabeth Vale (SAust)

Wood, John Robert (NSW) b April 11, 1865 Newcastle (NSW) d Feb. 14, 1928 Putney, London (England)

Wood, Percy Barnes (WAust) b Dec. 22, 1901 Wellington (New Zealand) d June 9, 1941 Litani River (Syria) in action

* Wood, Reginald (Vic) b March 7, 1860 Woodchurch, Cheshire (England) d Jan. 6, 1915 Manly (NSW)

Wood, William (NSW) b Nov. 11, 1849 Forglen, Banffshire (Scotland) d April 12, 1924 Marrickville (NSW)

Woodbury, William Joseph George (Vic) b Dec. 6, 1892 Balmain (NSW) d Aug. 31, 1983 Moe (Vic)

* Woodcock, Ashley James (SAust) b Feb. 27, 1947 Adelaide (SAust)

Woodford, John Robert Herbert (Vic & SAust) b June 23, 1881 Camberwell (Vic) d May 1, 1949 North Fitzroy (Vic)

* Woodfull, William Maldon (Vic) b Aug. 22, 1897 Maldon (Vic) d Aug. 11, 1965 Tweed Heads (NSW)

Woodhead, Derek John (WAust) b Sept. 7, 1934 Subiaco (WAust)

Woods, Julian Augustus (Tas) b Sept. 4, 1887 Oatlands (Tas) d Oct. 11, 1975 Lindisfarne (Tas)

**Woods, Samuel Moses James (Australia) b April 13, 1867 Ashfield (NSW) d April 30, 1931 Taunton, Somerset (England)

Woolcock, Arthur Henry (SAust) b June 10, 1887 Port Pirie (SAust) d June 29, 1975 Adelaide (SAust)

Woolf, Louis Sydney (Vic) b July 28, 1855 Collingwood (Vic) d July 6, 1942 Richmond (Vic)

Woolley, H. (Tas) birth and death details unknown

* Woolley, Roger Douglas (Tas) b Sept. 16, 1954 Hobart (Tas)

Woolmer, Gordon Rae (NSW) b Feb. 24, 1917 Hamilton (NSW) d July 31, 1999 Fairfield (NSW)

Wootton, John Richard (Vic) b Jan. 18, 1906 Rushworth (Vic) d July 18, 1986 death place unknown

Wootton, Stanley Eli (Vic) b April 28, 1895 South Yarra (Vic) d March 20, 1962 Heidelberg (Vic)

Wordsworth, Charles William (NSW) b Sept. 9, 1877 Rotherham, Yorkshire (England) d June 10, 1960 Redfern (NSW)

Workman, James Allen (Services) b March 17, 1917 Peterhead (SAust) d Dec. 23, 1970 Westminster, London (England)

* Worrall, John (Vic) b June 21, 1861 Chinamans Flat, Maryborough (Vic) d Nov. 17, 1937 Fairfield Park (Vic)

Wray, Thomas Fawcett (Vic) b c. 1827 Cleasby, Yorkshire (England) d Sept. 6, 1877 Melbourne (Vic)

Wrigglesworth, Ian Alastair (Vic) b Nov. 29, 1967 Sale (Vic)

Wright, Albert William (SAust) b Sept. 24, 1875 Norwood (SAust) d Dec. 23, 1938 North Adelaide (SAust)

Wright, Bert Harold (Vic) b Dec. 2, 1926 Wonthaggi (Vic) d Nov. 20, 1994 Beaumaris (Vic)

Wright, Damien Geoffrey (Tas) b July 25, 1975 Casino (NSW)

Wright, Francis John (Vic) b March 13, 1874 Ballarat East (Vic) d Oct. 10, 1899 Ballarat East (Vic)

Wright, Gary John (SAust) b Nov. 9, 1970 Henley Beach (SAust)

Wright, Harry Lovegrove (Vic) b April 13, 1870 Ballarat West (Vic) d March 19, 1950 West Melbourne (Vic)

* Wright, Kevin John (WAust & SAust) b Dec. 27, 1953 North Fremantle (WAust)

Wright, Robert Raymond (SAust) b Nov. 11, 1914 Marryatville (SAust) d Jan. 20, 1965 Springfield (SAust)

Wundke, Stephen Christopher (SAust) b July 2, 1961 North Adelaide (SAust)

Wyatt, Alan Edward (NSW) b April 4, 1935 Annandale (NSW)

Wyeth, Ezra Robert Harding (Qld) b March 13, 1910 Toowoomba (Qld) d Oct. 15, 1992 Northbridge, California (United States of America)

Wynne, Lester Alan (Vic) b Oct. 7, 1908 Carlton (Vic) d Nov. 29, 1980 Melbourne (Vic)

Yagmich, Dennis Brian (WAust & SAust) b Aug. 23, 1948 Victoria Park (WAust)

* Yallop, Graham Neil (Vic) b Oct. 7, 1952 Balwyn (Vic)

* Yardley, Bruce (WAust) b Sept. 5, 1947 Midland (WAust)

Yeates, George Walter Carrington (NSW) b May 5, 1918 Erskineville (NSW) d April 8, 1967 Kogarah Bay (NSW)

Yeates, Sydney Fergus Macrae (Qld) b Aug. 20, 1912 Toowoomba (Qld) d March 19, 1992 Auchenflower (Qld)

Yeomans, Frederick Caleb (Vic) b Nov. 11, 1888 Northcote (Vic) d Jan. 16, 1965 Brighton (Vic)

Youill, George Joseph (NSW) b Oct. 2, 1871 Sydney (NSW) d Dec. 21, 1936 Glebe (NSW)

Young, Allan Stanley (Qld) b July 7, 1920 Ipswich (Qld) d Dec. 23, 1974 Albion (Qld)

Young, Bradley Evan (SAust) b Feb. 23, 1973 Semaphore (SAust)

Young, Claye Michael (Tas) b Dec. 31, 1964 Hobart (Tas)

Young, George Albert (WAust) b Feb. 3, 1949 Caulfield (Vic)

Young, Jason Carl (NSW) b Feb. 17, 1971 Wagga Wagga (NSW)

Young, Peter William (Vic) b Dec. 31, 1961 Geelong (Vic)

* Young, Shaun (Tas) b June 13, 1970 Burnie (Tas)

* Younis Mohammad Ahmed (SAust) b Oct. 20, 1947 Jullundur (India)

Zachariah, Harry (Vic) b June 4, 1911 Stirling (SAust)

Zadow, Robert John (SAust) b Jan. 17, 1955 Mannum (SAust)

Zesers, Andris Karlis (SAust) b March 11, 1967 Medindie (SAust)

Ziebell, Keith Percy (Qld) b July 26, 1942 Rosewood (Qld)

Zimbulis, Anthony George (WAust) b Feb. 11, 1918 Perth (WAust) d May 17, 1963 Palm Beach (WAust)

* Zoehrer, Timothy Joseph (WAust) b Sept. 25, 1961 Armadale (WAust)

Zschorn, Paul William (SAust) b July 16, 1886 North Unley (SAust) d June 13, 1953 Glen Iris (Vic)

THE PRICEWATERHOUSECOOPERS RATINGS

Introduced in 1987 as the Deloitte Ratings, and known from 1990 to 1998 as the Coopers and Lybrand Ratings, the PricewaterhouseCoopers Ratings rank Test cricketers on a scale up to 1,000 according to their performances in Test matches. A rating of 900 points is outstanding and rarely achieved. The ratings take into account playing conditions, the quality of the opposition and the result of the matches. A player cannot get a full rating until he has played 30 innings or taken 70 wickets in Tests. The leading ten batsmen and bowlers in the ratings after matches played up to August 26, 2002 were:

Batsmen	Rating	Bowlers	Rating
1. A. C. Gilchrist (Aus)	881	1. G. D. McGrath (Aus)	908
2. S. R. Tendulkar (Ind)	863	2. M. Muralitharan (SL)	899
3. Inzamam-ul-Haq (Pak)	852	3. S. M. Pollock (SAf)	874
4. B. C. Lara (WI)	837	4. S. K. Warne (Aus)	764
5. M. L. Hayden (Aus)	836	5. Saqlain Mushtaq (Pak)	710
6. J. H. Kallis (SAf)	783	6. A. Kumble (Ind)	703
7. D. P. M. D. Jayawardene (SL)	780	7. Waqar Younis (Pak)	695
8. A. Flower (Zim)	776	8. M. J. Hoggard (Eng)	670*
9. H. H. Gibbs (SAf)	764	9. C. L. Cairns (NZ)	667
10. K. C. Sangakkara (SL)	751*	10. D. Gough (Eng)	661

Denotes players still qualifying for 100% of their rating

PART THREE: RECORDS

Because of time constraints in production, all records in this section provided by Ross Dundas cover the period up to and including July 8, 2002. Thus, performances by Australians in England after this date are excluded from this edition.

* Denotes not out or an unbroken partnership.

Key to abbreviations

Australian States: NSW – New South Wales, Qld – Queensland, SAust – South Australia, Tas – Tasmania, Vic – Victoria, WAust – Western Australia.
Countries: Aust – Australia, Ban – Bangladesh, Can – Canada, Eng – England, Ind – India, Ire – Ireland, Kya – Kenya, N Amer – North America, NZ – New Zealand, Pak – Pakistan, SAf – South Africa, Sco – Scotland, SL – Sri Lanka, WI – West Indies, Zim – Zimbabwe.
Australian Grounds: Bel – Bellerive Oval, CS – Colonial Stadium, Ex – Exhibition Ground, LRG – Lower "Railway" Ground, TCA – Tasmanian Cricket Association Ground.
Other Grounds: BS – Brabourne Stadium (Bombay/Mumbai), Corp – Corporation Stadium (Madras/Chennai), EP – Ellis Park, OW – Old Wanderers, PIS – R. Premadasa (Khettarama) International Stadium, PSS – P. Saravanamuttu Stadium, SSC – Sinhalese Sports Club Ground, WS – Wanderers Stadium (Johannesburg), Wankhede Stadium (Bombay/Mumbai).

AUSTRALIAN FIRST-CLASS RECORDS

BATTING RECORDS

BOWLING RECORDS

ALL-ROUND RECORDS

WICKET-KEEPING RECORDS

FIELDING RECORDS

TEAM RECORDS

MISCELLANEOUS

AUSTRALIAN TEST MATCH RECORDS

BATTING RECORDS

BOWLING RECORDS

WICKET-KEEPING RECORDS

FIELDING RECORDS

TEAM RECORDS

APPEARANCES

CAPTAINCY

TEST SERIES

AUSTRALIAN LIMITED-OVERS INTERNATIONAL RECORDS

BATTING RECORDS

BOWLING RECORDS

WICKET-KEEPING RECORDS

FIELDING RECORDS

TEAM RECORDS

AUSTRALIAN FIRST-CLASS RECORDS

BATTING RECORDS

HIGHEST INDIVIDUAL SCORES

452*	D. G. Bradman	New South Wales v Queensland at Sydney	1929-30
437	W. H. Ponsford	Victoria v Queensland at Melbourne	1927-28
429	W. H. Ponsford	Victoria v Tasmania at Melbourne	1922-23
383	C. W. Gregory	New South Wales v Queensland at Brisbane	1906-07
369	D. G. Bradman	South Australia v Tasmania at Adelaide	1935-36
365*	C. Hill	South Australia v New South Wales at Adelaide	1900-01
364	L. Hutton	England v Australia at The Oval	1938
359	R. B. Simpson	New South Wales v Queensland at Brisbane	1963-64
357	D. G. Bradman	South Australia v Victoria at Melbourne	1935-36
356	B. A. Richards	South Australia v Western Australia at Perth	1970-71
355*	G. R. Marsh	Western Australia v South Australia at Perth	1989-90
352	W. H. Ponsford	Victoria v New South Wales at Melbourne	1926-27
345	C. G. Macartney	Australians v Nottinghamshire at Nottingham	1921
340*	D. G. Bradman	New South Wales v Victoria at Sydney	1928-29
336	W. H. Ponsford	Victoria v South Australia at Melbourne	1927-28
334	D. G. Bradman	Australia v England at Leeds	1930
334*	M. A. Taylor	Australia v Pakistan at Preshawar	1998-99
329*	M. E. K. Hussey	North Hamptonshire v Essex at North Hampton	2001
325*	H. S. T. L. Hendry	Victoria v New Zealanders at Melbourne	1925-26
325	C. L. Badcock	South Australia v Victoria at Adelaide	1935-36
324*	D. M. Jones	Victoria v South Australia at Melbourne	1994-95
321	W. L. Murdoch	New South Wales v Victoria at Sydney	1881-82
315*	A. F. Kippax	New South Wales v Queensland at Sydney	1927-28
311	R. B. Simpson	Australia v England at Manchester	1964
310*	M. E. K. Hussey	North Hamptonshire v Glouchester at Bristol	2002
307	M. C. Cowdrey	MCC v South Australia at Adelaide	1962-63
307	R. M. Cowper	Australia v England at Melbourne	1965-66
306*	D. W. Hookes	South Australia v Tasmania at Adelaide	1986-87
305*	F. E. Woolley	MCC v Tasmania at Hobart (TCA)	1911-12
304	D. G. Bradman	Australia v England at Leeds	1934
303*	W. W. Armstrong	Australians v Somerset at Bath	1905
300*	V. T. Trumper	Australians v Sussex at Hove	1899

HUNDRED ON FIRST-CLASS DEBUT
FOR AUSTRALIAN TEAMS

223

121	C. S. Gordon	Victoria v New South Wales at Melbourne	1869-70
128*	J. P. O'Halloran	Victoria v South Australia at Melbourne	1896-97
166	L. W. Pye	New South Wales v Queensland at Brisbane (Ex)	1896-97
135*	H. G. S. Morton	Queensland v Victoria at Melbourne	1904-05
123	W. M. McPetrie	Victoria v Tasmania at Melbourne	1904-05
104	A. G. Moyes	South Australia v Western Australia at Adelaide	1912-13
102	N. L. Gooden	South Australia v Western Australia at Adelaide	1912-13
108*	F. W. Hyett	Victoria v Tasmania at Melbourne	1914-15
207	N. F. Callaway	New South Wales v Queensland at Sydney	1914-15
145	J. Bogle	New South Wales v Victoria at Sydney	1918-19
143	E. E. B. Forssberg	New South Wales v Queensland at Sydney	1920-21
130	D. A. Mullarkey	New South Wales v Queensland at Brisbane (Ex)	1923-24
105	S. E. Wootton	Victoria v Tasmania at Hobart (TCA)	1923-24
127	H. O. Rock	New South Wales v South Australia at Sydney	1924-25
136*	L. T. Gun	South Australia v New South Wales at Adelaide	1924-25
118	D. G. Bradman	New South Wales v South Australia at Adelaide	1927-28
100	R. N. Ellis	Victoria v Tasmania at Hobart (TCA)	1927-28
137	B. W. Hone	South Australia v Victoria at Adelaide	1928-29
129	R. M. Levy	Queensland v Victoria at Brisbane (Ex)	1928-29
117	A. H. Allsopp	New South Wales v MCC at Sydney	1929-30
115	O. W. Bill	New South Wales v Tasmania at Sydney	1929-30
128	L. R. Leabeater	New South Wales v Tasmania at Sydney	1929-30
118	F. E. Fontaine	Victoria v Tasmania at Hobart (TCA)	1930-31
119	R. J. Lawson	Victoria v Tasmania at Hobart (TCA)	1930-31
102	R. N. Nutt	New South Wales v South Australia at Adelaide	1931-32
135	J. C. Francis	Victoria v Tasmania at Launceston	1932-33
108	H. H. E. Grangel	Victoria v Tasmania at Melbourne	1935-36
121	R. A. Hamence	South Australia v Tasmania at Adelaide	1935-36
181	K. R. Miller	Victoria v Tasmania at Melbourne	1937-38
113	A. E. O. Barras	Western Australia v Victoria at Perth	1938-39
148	A. R. Morris	New South Wales v Queensland at Sydney	1940-41
164	M. R. Thomas	Tasmania v Australian Services at Hobart (TCA)	1945-46
232*	S. J. E. Loxton	Victoria v Queensland at Melbourne	1946-47
118	E. W. Lukeman	New South Wales v South Australia at Adelaide	1946-47
112	E. A. D. Kerr	Victoria v Tasmania at Launceston	1946-47
122	J. L. Chambers	Victoria v Tasmania at Melbourne	1949-50
164	L. E. Favell	South Australia v New South Wales at Adelaide	1951-52
202	J. Hallebone	Victoria v Tasmania at Melbourne	1951-52
121	R. E. Briggs	New South Wales v Western Australia at Perth	1952-53
103*	B. K. Shepherd	Western Australia v Queensland at Perth	1955-56
102	R. B. Lyons	Queensland v Victoria at Brisbane	1955-56
102*	H. W. Pinkus	Tasmania v South Australia at Hobart (TCA)	1956-57
180	N. G. Marks	New South Wales v South Australia at Sydney	1958-59
129	D. Chadwick	Western Australia v Queensland at Brisbane	1963-64
100	J. F. C. Loxton	Queensland v Western Australia at Perth	1966-67
107	M. J. Lucas	Queensland v New South Wales at Brisbane	1968-69
104	R. W. Marsh	Western Australia v West Indians at Perth	1968-69
122	G. J. Gilmour	New South Wales v South Australia at Sydney	1971-72
140	M. F. Kent	Queensland v New South Wales at Brisbane	1974-75
119	K. J. Hughes	Western Australia v New South Wales at Perth	1975-76
106	J. M. Wiener	Victoria v Queensland at Brisbane	1977-78
107	M. D. Taylor	Victoria v Queensland at Melbourne	1977-78
112	C. E. Penter	Western Australia v New South Wales at Sydney	1979-80
100	D. M. Wellham	New South Wales v Victoria at Melbourne	1980-81
126	M. D. Haysman	South Australia v Queensland at Adelaide	1982-83
130	S. P. O'Donnell	Victoria v South Australia at Melbourne	1983-84
165	W. J. S. Seabrook	New South Wales v Victoria at Melbourne	1984-85

118	E. J. Harris	Tasmania v South Australia at Adelaide	1985-86
111	W. N. Phillips	Victoria v West Indians at Melbourne	1988-89
114	M. G. Bevan	South Australia v Western Australia at Perth	1989-90
155	G. I. Foley	Queensland v Pakistanis at Brisbane	1989-90
118	M. P. Lavender	Western Australia v Victoria at St Kilda	1990-91
149	M. L. Hayden	Queensland v South Australia at Brisbane	1991-92
133*	R. J. Davison	New South Wales v Tasmania at Sydney	1993-94

Note: A. R. Morris scored a century (111) in the second innings of his debut match, thus becoming the first player in world cricket to achieve such a feat.

HUNDRED IN EACH INNINGS OF A MATCH
FOR AUSTRALIAN TEAMS

C. J. Eady	116	112*	Tasmania v Victoria at Hobart (TCA)	1894-95
V. T. Trumper	109	119	Australians v Essex at Leyton	1902
J. R. M. Mackay	105	102*	New South Wales v South Australia at Sydney	1905-06
D. R. A. Gehrs	148*	100*	South Australia v Western Australia at Fremantle	1905-06
M. A. Noble	176	123	New South Wales v Victoria at Sydney	1907-08
V. S. Ransford	182	110	Victoria v New South Wales at Sydney	1908-09
W. Bardsley	136	130	Australia v England at The Oval	1909
A. Kenny	164	100*	Victoria v Queensland at Brisbane	1909-10
C. G. Macartney	119	126	New South Wales v South Africans at Sydney	1910-11
C. G. Macartney	142	121	Australians v Sussex at Hove	1912
R. S. Stephens	108	181	Victoria v Tasmania at Launceston	1913-14
J. M. Gregory	122	102	AIF Team v New South Wales at Sydney	1919-20
W. W. Armstrong	157*	245	Victoria v South Australia at Melbourne	1920-21
F. A. O'Keefe	177	141	The Rest v Australian XI at Sydney	1921-22
W. H. Ponsford	110	110*	Victoria v New South Wales at Sydney	1923-24
V. Y. Richardson	100	125	South Australia v New South Wales at Sydney	1924-25
A. F. Kippax	127	131	New South Wales v Queensland at Brisbane (Ex)	1926-27
L. P. D. O'Connor	103	143*	Queensland v New South Wales at Sydney	1926-27
A. Jackson	131	122	New South Wales v South Australia at Sydney	1927-28
D. G. Bradman	131	133*	New South Wales v Queensland at Brisbane (Ex)	1928-29
B. A. Onyons	105	127	Victoria v Queensland at Brisbane (Ex)	1928-29
D. G. Bradman	124	225	W. M. Woodfull's XI v J. Ryder's XI at Sydney	1929-30
A. F. Kippax	158	102*	Australians v Sussex at Hove	1930
S. J. McCabe	106	103*	New South Wales v Victoria at Sydney	1931-32
A. R. Lonergan	115	100	South Australia v Victoria at Melbourne	1933-34
K. E. Rigg	100	167*	Victoria v New South Wales at Melbourne	1936-37
D. G. Bradman	107	113	South Australia v Queensland at Brisbane	1937-38
A. L. Hassett	122	122	Victoria v New South Wales at Sydney	1939-40
C. L. Badcock	120	102	South Australia v Victoria at Melbourne	1940-41
R. A. Hamence	130	103*	South Australia v Victoria at Melbourne	1940-41
A. R. Morris	148	111	New South Wales v Queensland at Sydney	1940-41
A. L. Hassett	187	124*	Australian Services v Prince's XI at Delhi	1945-46
A. R. Morris	122	124*	Australia v England at Adelaide	1946-47
R. A. Hamence	132	101*	South Australia v New South Wales at Adelaide	1946-47
D. G. Bradman	132	127*	Australia v India at Melbourne	1947-48
J. Moroney	118	101*	Australia v South Africa at Johannesburg	1949-50
A. R. Edwards	103	105	Western Australia v Queensland at Perth	1950-51
K. R. Miller	100	101	A. L. Hassett's XI v A. R. Morris's XI at Melbourne	1953-54
J. W. Burke	138	125*	Australians v Somerset at Taunton	1956
L. E. Favell	112	114	South Australia v New South Wales at Sydney	1956-57
C. J. Pinch	110	100	South Australia v Western Australia at Perth	1956-57
C. J. Pinch	102	102	South Australia v Victoria at Melbourne	1957-58
G. B. Stevens	164	111	South Australia v New South Wales at Sydney	1957-58

L. E. Favell	104	145	South Australia v Western Australia at Adelaide	1958-59
S. C. Trimble	113	136*	Queensland v Victoria at Brisbane	1963-64
R. B. Simpson	153	115	Australia v Pakistan at Karachi	1964-65
R. B. Simpson	121	142*	New South Wales v South Australia at Sydney	1964-65
P. C. Kelly	119	108*	Western Australia v MCC at Perth	1965-66
K. G. Cunningham	107	101*	South Australia v Western Australia at Adelaide	1966-67
K. D. Walters	242	103	Australia v West Indies at Sydney	1968-69
G. S. Chappell	129	156*	South Australia v Queensland at Brisbane	1969-70
I. M. Chappell	145	106	Australians v World XI at Brisbane	1971-72
A. J. Sieler	157	105	Victoria v Queensland at Brisbane	1973-74
G. S. Chappell	180	101	Queensland v Victoria at Brisbane	1973-74
I. M. Chappell	141*	130	South Australia v Victoria at Adelaide	1973-74
I. M. Chappell	145	121	Australia v New Zealand at Wellington	1973-74
G. S. Chappell	247*	133	Australia v New Zealand at Wellington	1973-74
R. B. McCosker	138	136*	New South Wales v Western Australia at Sydney	1974-75
R. B. McCosker	111	115	Australians v Sussex at Hove	1975
G. S. Chappell	123	109*	Australia v West Indies at Brisbane	1975-76
D. W. Hookes	185	105	South Australia v Queensland at Adelaide	1976-77
D. W. Hookes	135	156	South Australia v New South Wales at Adelaide	1976-77
G. N. Yallop	105	114*	Victoria v New South Wales at Sydney	1977-78
A. R. Border	150*	153	Australia v Pakistan at Lahore	1979-80
R. B. McCosker	123*	118*	New South Wales v Victoria at Sydney	1981-82
R. B. Kerr	158	101	Queensland v Western Australia at Perth	1981-82
D. W. Hookes	137	107	South Australia v Victoria at Adelaide	1982-83
G. N. Yallop	113	145*	Victoria v Western Australia at Melbourne	1983-84
S. B. Smith	105	116	Australians v Guyana at Georgetown	1983-84
A. R. Border	140	114*	Australia v New Zealand at Christchurch	1985-86
K. C. Wessels	135	105*	Australians v South Africans at Port Elizabeth	1986-87
D. C. Boon	108	143	Tasmania v Queensland at Launceston	1987-88
M. A. Taylor	107	152*	New South Wales v Western Australia at Perth	1988-89
T. M. Moody	162	159	Western Australia v South Australia at Perth	1988-89
D. M. Jones	116	121*	Australia v Pakistan at Adelaide	1989-90
J. Cox	175	102	Tasmania v New South Wales at Hobart (Bel)	1989-90
M. A. Taylor	127	100	New South Wales v Queensland at Sydney	1989-90
S. M. Small	115	126	New South Wales v Wellington at North Sydney	1990-91
S. G. Law	142*	105	Queensland v Western Australia at Perth	1990-91
D. R. Martyn	132*	112	Western Australia v Queensland at Brisbane	1992-93
R. T. Ponting	107	100*	Tasmania v Western Australia at Hobart (Bel)	1992-93
D. C. Boon	108	106	Australians v Worcestershire at Worcester	1993
M. L. Hayden	165	116	Queensland v South Australia at Adelaide	1993-94
P. C. Nobes	140	106	South Australia v Queensland at Adelaide	1993-94
M. L. Hayden	126	155	Queensland v Victoria at Brisbane	1993-94
D. M. Jones	145	152*	Victoria v South Australia at Melbourne	1993-94
D. F. Hills	114	126	Tasmania v South Australia at Adelaide	1993-94
M. L. Love	187	116	Queensland v Tasmania at Brisbane	1994-95
S. G. Law	102	138	Queensland v Tasmania at Hobart (Bel)	1994-95
R. T. Ponting	118*	100*	Tasmania v Queensland at Brisbane	1995-96
M. T. G. Elliott	104*	135	Victoria v Western Australia at Perth	1995-96
R. T. Ponting	126	145*	Tasmania v Queensland at Hobart (Bel)	1996-97
J. Cox	143	125	Tasmania v New South Wales at Sydney	1996-97
S. R. Waugh	108	116	Australia v England at Manchester	1997
A. Symonds	163	100*	Queensland v South Australia at Adelaide	1997-98
D. S. Lehmann	103	100†	Australians v Rawalpindi Cricket Assn at Rawalpindi	1998-99
M. T. G. Elliott	108	103*	Victoria v New South Wales at Melbourne	1998-99
G. S. Blewett	169*	213*	Australian XI v England XI at Hobart (Bel)	1998-99
D. S. Lehmann	101*	113	South Australia v Tasmania at Hobart (Bel)	1999-00
J. Cox	106	128*	Tasmania v New South Wales at Hobart (Bel)	2000-01
R. T. Ponting	102	102*	Australians v BCCI President's XI at Delhi	2000-01
B. J. Hodge	140	110*	Victoria v South Australia at Adelaide	2001-02
R. T. Ponting	126	154	Tasmania v New South Wales at Sydney	2001-02
C. J. L. Rogers	101*	102*	Western Australia v South Australia at Perth	2001-02

† *Retired hurt.*

HUNDRED IN EACH INNINGS OF A MATCH
AGAINST AUSTRALIAN TEAMS

A. C. Maclaren....	142	100	A. E. Stoddart's XI v New South Wales at Sydney	1897-98
W. Rhodes.......	119	109	MCC v New South Wales at Sydney	1911-12
A. Sandham......	137	104	MCC v New South Wales at Sydney	1924-25
H. Sutcliffe	176	127	England v Australia at Melbourne	1924-25
C. C. R. Dacre ...	127*	101*	Auckland v Victoria at Auckland	1924-25
W. R. Hammond ..	119*	177	England v Australia at Adelaide	1928-29
W. R. Hammond ..	104	136	MCC v South Australia at Adelaide	1936-37
D. C. S. Compton..	147	103*	England v Australia at Adelaide	1946-47
V. S. Hazare......	116	145	India v Australia at Adelaide	1947-48
H. J. Keith	111	113*	South Africans v Victoria at Melbourne	1952-53
M. C. Cowdrey ...	110	103	MCC v New South Wales at Sydney	1954-55
C. L. Walcott	126	110	West Indies v Australia at Port-of-Spain	1954-55
C. L. Walcott	155	110	West Indies v Australia at Kingston	1954-55
P. B. H. May......	140	114	MCC v Australian XI at Sydney	1958-59
R. B. Kanhai	117	115	West Indies v Australia at Adelaide	1960-61
M. C. Cowdrey ...	149	121	Kent v Australians at Canterbury	1961
P. E. Richardson ..	111	115	Kent v Australians at Canterbury	1964
B. F. Butcher	115	172	West Indians v Combined XI at Perth	1968-69
R. C. Fredericks ..	158	118	Guyana v Australians at Georgetown	1972-73
G. M. Turner	101	110*	New Zealand v Australia at Christchurch	1973-74
I. V. A. Richards ..	160	107*	West Indians v Tasmania at Hobart (TCA)	1975-76
Mudassar Nazar...	103	123	Pakistanis v Victoria at Melbourne	1983-84
P. N. Kirsten	173	105*	South Africans v Australians at Cape Town	1986-87
A. J. Lamb	154	105	England XI v Australian XI at Hobart (Bel)	1990-91
Asif Mujtaba	102*	125*	Pakistanis v Queensland at Brisbane	1992-93
Basit Ali.........	137	101*	Pakistanis v South Australia at Adelaide	1995-96

MOST HUNDREDS IN CONSECUTIVE INNINGS
FOR AUSTRALIAN TEAMS

Six

D. G. Bradman	118	dnb	D. G. Bradman's XI v K. E. Rigg's XI at Melbourne ...	1938-39
	143	dnb	South Australia v New South Wales at Adelaide	1938-39
	225	dnb	South Australia v Queensland at Adelaide	1938-39
	107	dnb	South Australia v Victoria at Melbourne	1938-39
	186	dnb	South Australia v Queensland at Brisbane	1938-39
	135*	dnb	South Australia v New South Wales at Sydney	1938-39

Four

C. G. Macartney	105	dnb	Australians v Hampshire at Southampton	1921
	193	dnb	Australians v Northamptonshire at Northampton	1921
	345	dnb	Australians v Nottinghamshire at Nottingham	1921
	115	30	Australia v England at Leeds	1921
D. G. Bradman	dnb	135	New South Wales v South Africans at Sydney	1931-32
	226	dnb	Australia v South Africa at Brisbane	1931-32
	219	dnb	New South Wales v South Africans at Sydney	1931-32
	112	dnb	Australia v South Africa at Sydney	1931-32
D. G. Bradman	150	dnb	Australians v Gentlemen of England at Lord's	1948
	143	dnb	Australians v South of England at Hastings	1948
	153	dnb	Australians v H. G. D. Leveson Gower's XI at Scarborough	1948
	123	10	D. G. Bradman's XI v A. L. Hassett's XI at Melbourne .	1948-49
D. W. Hookes	185	105	South Australia v Queensland at Adelaide	1976-77
	135	156	South Australia v New South Wales at Adelaide	1976-77
A. R. Border	106	dnb	Australians v Somerset at Taunton	1985
	135	dnb	Australians v Worcestershire at Worcester	1985
	125	dnb	Australians v MCC at Lord's	1985
	100	dnb	Australians v Derbyshire at Derby	1985

M. G. Bevan	20	104	New South Wales v South Australia at Adelaide	1990-91
	153*	dnb	New South Wales v Victoria at Sydney	1990-91
	121	dnb	New South Wales v Queensland at Sydney	1990-91
	136	3	New South Wales v Tasmania at Hobart (Bel)	1990-91

MOST HUNDREDS IN A CAREER
(30 or more)

	100s	I	400+	300+	200+
D. G. Bradman	117	338	1	6	37
M. E. Waugh	80	550	0	0	5
G. S. Chappell	74	542	0	0	4
A. R. Border	70	625	0	0	3
D. C. Boon	68	585	0	0	3
R. N. Harvey	67	461	0	0	7
S. R. Waugh	67	486	0	0	4
K. C. Wessels	66	539	0	0	4
T. M. Moody	64	501	0	0	4
R. B. Simpson	60	436	0	2	10
D. S. Lehmann	60	350	0	0	8
I. M. Chappell	59	448	0	0	3
A. L. Hassett	59	322	0	0	8
D. M. Jones	55	415	0	1	8
M. L. Hayden	55	362	0	0	5
J. L. Langer	55	372	0	0	8
M. G. Bevan	55	341	0	0	3
S. G. Law	54	416	0	0	2
W. Bardsley	53	376	0	0	7
W. M. Lawry	50	417	0	0	4
C. G. Macartney	49	360	0	1	3
W. M. Woodfull	49	245	0	0	7
W. H. Ponsford	47	235	2	2	9
A. R. Morris	46	250	0	0	4
C. Hill	45	416	0	1	3
W. W. Armstrong	45	406	0	1	1
N. C. O'Neill	45	306	0	0	2
K. D. Walters	45	426	0	0	4
J. Cox	44	353	0	0	3
A. F. Kippax	43	256	0	1	6
V. T. Trumper	42	401	0	1	7
K. R. Miller	41	326	0	0	7
M. A. Taylor	41	435	0	1	1
G. S. Blewett	40	340	0	0	5
W. A. Brown	39	284	0	0	5
R. T. Ponting	39	240	0	0	2
P. J. P. Burge	38	354	0	0	5
M. A. Noble	37	377	0	0	7
G. M. Wood	35	375	0	0	0
J. D. Siddons	35	280	0	0	3
L. Livingston	34	384	0	0	4
M. T. G. Elliott	34	242	0	0	2
D. R. Martyn	34	260	0	0	1
F. A. Tarrant	33	541	0	0	4
G. R. Marsh	33	323	0	1	2
M. J. Slater	33	360	0	0	3
H. L. Collins	32	258	0	0	3
I. R. Redpath	32	391	0	0	2
D. W. Hookes	32	304	0	1	1
W. E. Alley	31	682	0	0	3
G. N. Yallop	30	283	0	0	3

MOST RUNS IN AN AUSTRALIAN SEASON

	Season	M	I	NO	R	HS	100s	50s	Avge
D. G. Bradman (New South Wales) ..	1928-29	13	24	6	1,690	340*	7	5	93.88
R. N. Harvey (Victoria)	1952-53	16	27	1	1,659	205	5	8	63.80
D. G. Bradman (New South Wales) ..	1929-30	11	16	2	1,586	452*	5	4	113.28
W. R. Hammond (MCC)...........	1928-29	13	18	1	1,553	251	7	1	91.35
D. G. Bradman (South Australia)....	1936-37	12	19	1	1,552	270	6	2	86.22
G. S. Chappell (Queensland)	1975-76	15	26	8	1,547	182*	6	7	85.94
R. B. Simpson (Western Australia) ..	1960-61	15	26	4	1,541	221*	4	9	64.21
B. A. Richards (South Australia)	1970-71	10	16	2	1,538	356	6	3	109.85
G. Boycott (MCC)	1970-71	13	22	6	1,535	173	6	7	95.93
G. A. Faulkner (South Africans)	1910-11	14	27	1	1,534	204	3	13	59.00
R. B. Simpson (New South Wales) ..	1963-64	14	25	2	1,524	359	4	4	66.26
E. J. Barlow (South Africans).......	1963-64	14	25	4	1,523	209	6	4	66.21
G. S. Chappell (Queensland)	1980-81	14	22	2	1,502	204	5	6	75.10

1,000 RUNS IN A SEASON

12 Times: D. G. Bradman 1928-29 (1,690), 1929-30 (1,586), 1930-31 (1,422), 1931-32 (1,403), 1932-33 (1,171), 1933-34 (1,171), 1935-36 (1,173), 1936-37 (1,552), 1937-38 (1,437), 1939-40 (1,475), 1946-47 (1,032), 1947-48 (1,296).

6 Times: I. M. Chappell 1965-66 (1,019), 1968-69 (1,476), 1970-71 (1,210), 1971-72 (1,140), 1973-74 (1,074), 1975-76 (1,310).

5 Times: G. S. Chappell 1973-74 (1,288), 1974-75 (1,484), 1975-76 (1,547), 1979-80 (1,066), 1980-81 (1,502); A. R. Border 1978-79 (1,220), 1982-83 (1,081), 1985-86 (1,247), 1986-87 (1,002), 1987-88 (1,164); D. S. Lehmann 1989-90 (1,142), 1993-94 (1,087), 1994-95 (1,104), 1995-96 (1,237), 1999-00 (1,142); G. S. Blewett 1993-94 (1,036), 1995-96 (1,173), 1998-99 (1,187), 2000-01 (1,162), 2001-02 (1,025).

4 Times: R. B. Simpson 1960-61 (1,541), 1962-63 (1,337), 1963-64 (1,524), 1967-68 (1,082); W. M. Lawry 1960-61 (1,042), 1963-64 (1,340), 1965-66 (1,445), 1968-69 (1,140); M. T. G. Elliott 1994-95 (1,029), 1995-96 (1,233), 1998-99 (1,014), 1999-00 (1,028); M. L. Hayden 1991-92 (1,028), 1992-93 (1,249), 1993-94 (1,136), 2001-02 (1,243); J. L. Langer 1993-94 (1,198), 1997-98 (1,075), 1999-00 (1,108), 2001-02 (1,030).

3 Times: A. R. Morris 1946-47 (1,234), 1948-49 (1,069), 1950-51 (1,332); D. W. Hookes 1982-83 (1,424), 1985-86 (1,001), 1987-88 (1,149); J. D. Siddons 1987-88 (1,077), 1990-91 (1,034), 1992-93 (1,190).

MOST RUNS ON AN AUSTRALIAN OVERSEAS TOUR

		Season	M	I	NO	R	HS	100s	50s	Avge
D. G. Bradman.....	England	1930	27	36	6	2,960	334	10	5	98.66
V. T. Trumper	England	1902	36	53	0	2,570	128	11	11	48.49
D. G. Bradman.....	England	1938	20	26	5	2,429	278	13	5	115.66
D. G. Bradman.....	England	1948	23	31	4	2,428	187	11	8	89.92
W. Bardsley.......	England	1912	36	52	6	2,365	184*	8	9	51.41
C. G. Macartney....	England	1921	31	41	2	2,317	345	8	6	59.41
C. G. Macartney....	England	1912	33	49	1	2,187	208	6	8	45.56
S. J. McCabe	England	1934	26	37	7	2,078	240	8	7	69.26
W. Bardsley.......	England	1909	33	49	4	2,072	219	6	7	46.04
M. A. Noble	England	1905	31	46	2	2,053	267	6	13	46.66
R. N. Harvey	England	1953	25	35	4	2,040	202*	10	5	65.80
D. G. Bradman.....	England	1934	22	27	3	2,020	304	7	6	84.16
W. M. Lawry	England	1961	23	39	6	2,019	165	9	7	61.18
W. Bardsley.......	England	1921	30	41	4	2,005	209	8	10	54.18

Most in countries other than England:

R. N. Harvey	South Africa	1949-50	19	25	5	1,526	178	8	4	76.30
A. R. Border	India	1979-80	15	28	3	1,423	178	5	4	56.92
G. S. Chappell ...	West Indies	1972-73	10	17	1	1,109	154	4	6	69.31

		Season	M	I	NO	R	HS	100s	50s	Avge
W. M. Woodfull .	New Zealand	1927-28	6	9	3	781	284	3	2	130.16
A. R. Border	Pakistan	1979-80	5	9	3	674	178	3	1	112.33
W. Bardsley....	North America	1913-14	5	6	2	437	142*	3	0	109.25
M. J. Slater......	Sri Lanka	1999-00	5	8	1	370	119	1	3	52.86
S. R. Waugh.....	Zimbabwe	1999-00	2	3	1	339	161	2	0	169.50

LEADING BATSMEN IN EACH AUSTRALIAN SEASON

(Qualification for top of averages: 8 completed innings)

Season	Leading Scorer	Runs	Avge	Top of Averages	Runs	Avge
1850-51	T. F. Hamilton (Vic)	45	22.50	n/a		
1851-52	T. F. Hamilton (Vic)	84	42.00	n/a		
1853-54	G. Cavenagh (Vic)	45	22.50	n/a		
1854-55	no games played					
1855-56	{ J. J. McKone (NSW)	18	18.00	n/a		
	{ R. Driver (NSW)	18	9.00	n/a		
1856-57	G. H. B. Gilbert (NSW)	33	16.50	n/a		
1857-58	T. W. Wills (Vic)..........	94	23.50	n/a		
1858-59	O. W. Lewis (NSW)	53	26.50	n/a		
1859-60	T. W. Wills (Vic)	24	12.00	n/a		
1860-61	J. M. Bryant (Vic)	32	16.00	n/a		
1861-62	W. Caffyn (England)	88	88.00	n/a		
1862-63	D. D'Arcy (NSW)	51	51.00	n/a		
1863-64	T. Lockyer (England)	84	84.00	n/a		
1864-65	no games played					
1865-66	E. J. Gregory (NSW)	61	30.50	n/a		
1866-67	S. Cosstick (Vic)	29	14.50	n/a		
1867-68	R. W. Wardill (Vic)	155	155.00	n/a		
1868-69	J. Phillips (Vic)	133	44.33	n/a		
1869-70	C. S. Gordon (Vic)	143	71.50	n/a		
1870-71	A. R. Loughnan (Vic)	71	23.67	n/a		
1871-72	N. Thompson (NSW)	46	23.00	n/a		
1872-73	J. L. A. Arthur (Tas)	86	28.67	n/a		
1873-74	no games played					
1874-75	C. Bannerman (NSW)	113	113.00	n/a		
1875-76	D. W. Gregory (NSW)	116	38.67	n/a		
1876-77	C. Bannerman (NSW)	243	48.60	n/a		
1877-78	N. Thompson (NSW)	101	33.67	n/a		
1878-79	G. Ulyett (England)	306	34.00	G. Ulyett (England)	306	34.00
1879-80	A. C. Bannerman (NSW) ...	103	25.75	n/a		
1880-81	T. P. Horan (Vic)	318	35.33	H. H. Massie (NSW)	299	37.38
1881-82	W. L. Murdoch (NSW)	679	61.73	W. L. Murdoch (NSW)	679	61.73
1882-83	A. C. Bannerman (NSW) ...	434	54.25	A. C. Bannerman (NSW) ..	434	54.25
1883-84	W. L. Murdoch (NSW)	567	113.40	n/a		
1884-85	W. Barnes (England)	520	43.33	W. Barnes (England)	520	43.33
1885-86	J. McIlwraith (Vic)	315	78.75	n/a		
1886-87	A. Shrewsbury (England) ...	721	48.07	A. Shrewsbury (England) .	721	48.07
1887-88	H. Moses (NSW)	815	62.69	H. Moses (NSW)	815	62.69
1888-89	G. H. S. Trott (Vic)	507	39.00	G. H. S. Trott (Vic)	507	39.00
1889-90	G. Giffen (SAust)	254	63.50	n/a		
1890-91	G. Giffen (SAust)	275	91.67	n/a		
1891-92	J. J. Lyons (SAust)	557	55.70	J. J. Lyons (SAust)	557	55.70
1892-93	G. Giffen (SAust)	468	58.50	G. Giffen (SAust)	468	58.50
1893-94	G. Giffen (SAust)	526	75.14	G. Giffen (SAust)	526	75.14
1894-95	A. Ward (England)	916	41.64	A. E. Stoddart (England) ..	870	51.18
1895-96	H. Donnan (SAust)	626	69.56	H. Donnan (NSW)	626	69.56
1896-97	J. J. Lyons (SAust)	404	57.71	G. H. S. Trott (Vic)	323	40.38
1897-98	C. Hill (SAust)	1,196	66.44	C. Hill (SAust)	1,196	66.44
1898-99	V. T. Trumper (NSW)	873	62.36	C. Hill (SAust)	841	64.69
1899-00	V. T. Trumper (NSW)	721	72.10	V. T. Trumper (NSW)	721	72.10

Season	Leading Scorer	Runs	Avge	Top of Averages	Runs	Avge
1900-01	C. Hill (SAust)	620	103.33	n/a		
1901-02	C. Hill (SAust)	1,035	51.75	A.C. MacLaren (England) .	929	58.06
1902-03	R. A. Duff (NSW)	786	87.33	R. A. Duff (NSW)	786	87.33
1903-04	V. T. Trumper (NSW)	990	55.00	M. A. Noble (NSW)	961	56.33
1904-05	W. W. Armstrong (Vic) ...	460	57.50	W. W. Armstrong (Vic) ...	460	57.50
1905-06	J. R. M. Mackay (NSW) ...	902	112.75	J. R. M. Mackay (NSW) ...	902	112.75
1906-07	A. J. Y. Hopkins (NSW) ...	617	56.09	A. J. Y. Hopkins (NSW) ...	617	56.09
1907-08	J. Hardstaff sr (MCC)	1,360	52.30	F. A. Tarrant (Vic)	762	76.20
1908-09	V. S. Ransford (Vic)	825	103.13	V. S. Ransford (Vic)	825	103.13
1909-10	H. H. L. Kortlang (Vic)	656	131.20	C. McKenzie (Vic)	377	47.13
1910-11	G. A. Faulkner (SAf)	1,534	59.00	V. T. Trumper (NSW) ...	1,246	69.22
1911-12	W. Rhodes (MCC)	1,098	54.90	R. B. Minnett (NSW)	882	63.00
1912-13	V. T. Trumper (NSW)	843	84.30	V. T. Trumper (NSW)	843	84.30
1913-14	C. G. Macartney (NSW) ...	892	111.50	C. G. Macartney (NSW) ...	892	111.50
1914-15	J. Ryder (Vic)	445	74.17	C. E. Pellew (SAust)	287	35.88
1915-16	no games played					
1916-17	no games played					
1917-18	no games played					
1918-19	W. W. Armstrong (Vic)	249	83.00	n/a		
1919-20	R. L. Park (Vic)	648	72.00	R. L. Park (Vic)	648	72.00
1920-21	E. H. Hendren (MCC)	1,178	62.00	W. W. Armstrong (Vic) ...	1,069	89.08
1921-22	F. A. O'Keefe (Vic)	708	118.00	H. S. B. Love (NSW)	424	43.00
1922-23	A. P. F. Chapman (MCC) ...	782	65.17	A. J. Richardson (SAust) ...	758	75.80
1923-24	W. H. Ponsford (Vic)	777	111.00	F. C. Thompson (Qld)	397	49.63
1924-25	H. Sutcliffe (MCC)	1,250	69.44	A. F. Kippax (NSW)	853	77.55
1925-26	A. J. Richardson (SAust) ...	904	50.22	C. G. Macartney (NSW) ...	795	88.33
1926-27	W. H. Ponsford (Vic)	1,229	122.90	W. H. Ponsford (Vic)	1,229	122.90
1927-28	W. H. Ponsford (Vic)	1,217	152.12	W. H. Ponsford (Vic)	1,217	152.12
1928-29	D. G. Bradman (NSW)	1,690	93.88	D. G. Bradman (NSW)	1,690	93.88
1929-30	D. G. Bradman (NSW)	1,586	113.28	D. G. Bradman (NSW)	1,586	113.28
1930-31	D. G. Bradman (NSW)	1,422	79.00	D. G. Bradman (NSW)	1,422	79.00
1931-32	D. G. Bradman (NSW)	1,403	116.91	D. G. Bradman (NSW)	1,403	116.91
1932-33	H. Sutcliffe (MCC)	1,318	73.22	H. Sutcliffe (MCC)	1,318	73.22
1933-34	D. G. Bradman (NSW)	1,192	132.44	D. G. Bradman (NSW)	1,192	132.44
1934-35	J. H. W. Fingleton (NSW) ...	880	58.67	L. S. Darling (Vic)	634	70.44
1935-36	D. G. Bradman (SAust)	1,173	130.33	D. G. Bradman (SAust)	1,173	130.33
1936-37	D. G. Bradman (SAust)	1,552	86.22	D. G. Bradman (SAust)	1,552	86.22
1937-38	D. G. Bradman (SAust)	1,437	89.81	D. G. Bradman (SAust)	1,437	89.81
1938-39	W. A. Brown (Qld)	1,057	105.70	W. A. Brown (Qld)	1,057	105.70
1939-40	D. G. Bradman (SAust)	1,475	122.91	D. G. Bradman (SAust)	1,475	122.91
1940-41	S. G. Barnes (NSW)	1,050	75.00	S. G. Barnes (NSW)	1,050	75.00
1941-42	V. N. Raymer (Qld)	130	130.00	n/a		
1942-43	no games played					
1943-44	no games played					
1944-45	no games played					
1945-46	S. G. Barnes (NSW)	794	88.22	S. G. Barnes (NSW)	794	88.22
1946-47	D. C. S. Compton (MCC) ...	1,432	65.09	D. G. Bradman (SAust)	1,032	79.38
1947-48	D. G. Bradman (SAust)	1,296	129.60	D. G. Bradman (SAust)	1,296	129.60
1948-49	A. R. Morris (NSW)	1,069	66.81	J. Moroney (NSW)	897	81.55
1949-50	A. R. C. McLean (SAust) ...	660	50.77	A. R. C. McLean (SAust) ..	660	50.77
1950-51	A. L. Hassett (Vic)	1,423	64.68	K. R. Miller (NSW)	1,332	78.35
1951-52	A. L. Hassett (Vic)	855	61.07	A. L. Hassett (Vic)	855	61.07
1952-53	R. N. Harvey (Vic)	1,659	63.80	R. N. Harvey (Vic)	1,659	63.80
1953-54	C. C. McDonald (Vic)	857	57.13	K. D. Mackay (Qld)	723	72.30
1954-55	R. N. Harvey (Vic)	1,009	45.86	D. C. S. Compton (MCC) ..	799	57.07
1955-56	J. W. Burke (NSW)	979	61.19	K. R. Miller (NSW)	638	70.89
1956-57	C. J. Pinch (SAust)	840	52.50	R. N. Harvey (Vic)	836	104.50
1957-58	N. C. O'Neill (NSW)	1,005	83.75	N. C. O'Neill (NSW)	1,005	83.75
1958-59	P. B. H. May (MCC)	1,197	57.00	C. C. McDonald (Vic) ...	990	61.87
1959-60	R. B. Simpson (WAust)	902	300.66	R. G. Flockton (NSW)	617	77.12
1960-61	R. B. Simpson (WAust)	1,541	64.21	B. C. Booth (NSW)	981	65.40

Season	Leading Scorer	Runs	Avge	Top of Averages	Runs	Avge
1961-62	R. B. Simpson (NSW)	704	46.93	B. K. Shepherd (WAust)	808	62.15
1962-63	K. F. Barrington (MCC)	1,451	85.35	K. F. Barrington (MCC)	1,451	85.35
1963-64	R. B. Simpson (NSW)	1,524	66.26	B. C. Booth (NSW)	1,180	90.76
1964-65	S. C. Trimble (Qld)	984	57.87	W. M. Lawry (Vic)	848	84.80
1965-66	W. M. Lawry (Vic)	1,445	72.25	R. M. Cowper (Vic)	1,418	74.63
1966-67	L. E. Favell (SAust)	847	49.82	N. C. O'Neill (NSW)	815	67.91
1967-68	R. B. Simpson (NSW)	1,082	56.94	A. P. Sheahan (Vic)	973	64.86
1968-69	I. M. Chappell (SAust)	1,476	82.00	I. M. Chappell (SAust)	1,476	82.00
1969-70	G. S. Chappell (SAust)	856	65.84	J. A. Steele (NSW)	677	67.70
1970-71	B. A. Richards (SAust)	1,538	109.85	B. A. Richards (SAust)	1,538	109.85
1971-72	I. M. Chappell (SAust)	1,140	60.00	K. D. Walters (NSW)	895	68.84
1972-73	A. P. Sheahan (Vic)	1,002	83.50	A. P. Sheahan (Vic)	1,002	83.50
1973-74	G. S. Chappell (Qld)	1,288	85.86	G. S. Chappell (Qld)	1,288	85.86
1974-75	G. S. Chappell (Qld)	1,484	61.83	G. S. Chappell (Qld)	1,484	61.83
1975-76	G. S. Chappell (Qld)	1,547	85.94	G. S. Chappell (Qld)	1,547	85.94
1976-77	D. W. Hookes (SAust)	861	71.75	R. D. Robinson (Vic)	828	82.80
1977-78	A. D. Ogilvie (Qld)	1,215	50.62	G. M. Wood (WAust)	678	56.50
1978-79	A. R. Border (NSW)	1,220	55.45	J. K. Moss (Vic)	881	67.77
1979-80	G. S. Chappell (Qld)	1,066	71.06	G. S. Chappell (Qld)	1,066	71.06
1980-81	G. S. Chappell (Qld)	1,502	75.10	G. S. Chappell (Qld)	1,502	75.10
1981-82	K. C. Wessels (Qld)	1,094	60.77	H. A. Gomes (West Indians)	712	89.00
1982-83	D. W. Hookes (SAust)	1,424	64.72	G. N. Yallop (Vic)	1,418	67.52
1983-84	G. N. Yallop (Vic)	1,132	113.20	G. N. Yallop (Vic)	1,132	113.20
1984-85	K. C. Wessels (Qld)	1,020	53.68	G. Shipperd (WAust)	823	68.58
1985-86	A. R. Border (Qld)	1,247	73.35	A. R. Border (Qld)	1,247	73.35
1986-87	G. R. Marsh (WAust)	1,200	48.00	M. R. J. Veletta (WAust)	971	74.69
1987-88	D. C. Boon (Tas)	1,287	67.74	M. D. Crowe (NZ)	715	89.38
1988-89	M. A. Taylor (NSW)	1,241	49.64	I. V. A. Richards (WI)	683	68.30
1989-90	M. A. Taylor (NSW)	1,403	70.15	M. E. Waugh (NSW)	1,009	77.62
1990-91	S. G. Law (Qld)	1,204	75.25	S. G. Law (Qld)	1,204	75.25
1991-92	D. M. Jones (Vic)	1,248	96.00	D. M. Jones (Vic)	1,248	96.00
1992-93	M. L. Hayden (Qld)	1,249	52.04	J. D. Siddons (SAust)	1,190	66.11
1993-94	M. G. Bevan (NSW)	1,312	77.18	M. L. Hayden (Qld)	1,136	126.22
1994-95	D. M. Jones (Vic)	1,251	69.50	D. M. Jones (Vic)	1,251	69.50
1995-96	D. S. Lehmann (SAust)	1,237	56.22	M. T. G. Elliott (Vic)	1,233	68.50
1996-97	J. Cox (Tas)	1,349	67.45	J. L. Langer (WAust)	771	77.10
1997-98	D. F. Hills (Tas)	1,220	55.45	T. M. Moody (WAust)	702	78.00
1998-99	G. S. Blewett (SAust)	1,187	118.70	G. S. Blewett (SAust)	1,187	118.70
1999-00	D. S. Lehmann (SAust)	1,142	63.44	R. T. Ponting (Tas)	582	72.75
2000-01	S. M. Katich (WAust)	1,282	71.22	R. T. Ponting (Tas)	726	80.67
2001-02	M. L. Hayden (Qld)	1,243	82.87	N. J. Astle (New Zealanders)	554	110.80

HIGHEST BATTING AVERAGE IN AN AUSTRALIAN SEASON
(Minimum 500 runs)

	Season	M	I	NO	R	HS	100s	50s	Avge
R. B. Simpson (Western Australia)	1959-60	5	6	3	902	236*	3	3	300.66
W. H. Ponsford (Victoria)	1922-23	3	4	0	616	429	2	1	154.00
D. G. Bradman (South Australia)	1938-39	7	7	1	919	225	6	0	153.17
C. Hill (South Australia)	1909-10	3	4	0	609	205	3	0	152.25
W. H. Ponsford (Victoria)	1927-28	6	8	0	1,217	437	4	1	152.13
D. G. Bradman (New South Wales)	1933-34	7	11	2	1,192	253	5	3	132.44
H. H. L. Kortlang (Victoria)	1909-10	5	9	4	656	197	2	3	131.20
D. G. Bradman (South Australia)	1935-36	8	9	0	1,173	369	4	1	130.33
D. G. Bradman (South Australia)	1947-48	9	12	2	1,296	201	8	1	129.60
W. M. Woodfull (Victoria)	1927-28	5	7	2	645	191*	2	1	129.00
M. L. Hayden (Queensland)	1993-94	6	12	3	1,136	173*	7	1	126.22
D. G. Bradman (South Australia)	1939-80	9	15	3	1,475	267	5	4	122.92
W. H. Ponsford (Victoria)	1926-27	6	10	0	1,229	352	6	2	122.90

	Season	M	I	NO	R	HS	100s	50s	Avge
G. S. Blewett (South Australia)	1998-99	7	12	2	1,187	213*	6	1	118.70
F. A. O'Keefe (Victoria)	1921-22	4	6	0	708	180	3	2	118.00
D. G. Bradman (New South Wales)	1931-32	10	13	1	1,403	299*	7	0	116.92
W. L. Murdoch (New South Wales)	1883-84	4	6	1	567	279*	2	1	113.40
D. G. Bradman (New South Wales)	1929-30	11	16	2	1,586	452*	5	4	113.29
G. N. Yallop (Victoria)	1983-84	8	11	1	1,132	268	5	2	113.20
J. R. M. Mackay (New South Wales)	1905-06	6	9	1	902	203	5	2	112.75
M. D. Crowe (New Zealanders)	1985-86	4	7	2	562	242*	2	1	112.40
C. G. Macartney (New South Wales)	1913-14	7	9	1	892	201	5	2	111.50
W. H. Ponsford (Victoria)	1923-24	5	8	1	777	248	4	1	111.00
B. A. Richards (South Australia)	1970-71	10	16	2	1,538	356	6	3	109.86
C. L. Badcock (South Australia)	1938-39	7	8	3	540	271*	2	1	108.00
C. G. Macartney (New South Wales)	1912-13	4	7	1	646	154	2	4	107.67
M. G. Bevan (Victoria)	1998-99	6	10	4	636	202*	3	1	106.00
W. A. Brown (Queensland)	1938-39	7	11	1	1,057	215	3	6	105.70
R. N. Harvey (Victoria)	1956-57	6	10	2	836	209	4	3	104.50
C. Hill (South Australia)	1900-01	4	7	1	620	365*	1	2	103.33
V. S. Ransford (Victoria)	1908-09	6	10	2	825	182	4	2	103.13
J. Ryder (Victoria)	1921-22	4	8	2	609	242	1	4	101.50

AUSTRALIANS WITH 10,000 RUNS IN FIRST-CLASS CRICKET

	Career	M	I	NO	R	HS	100s	50s	Avge
D. G. Bradman	1927-28 – 1948-49	234	338	43	28,067	452*	117	69	95.14
A. R. Border	1976-77 – 1995-96	385	625	97	27,131	205	70	142	51.38
K. C. Wessels	1973-74 – 1999-00	316	539	50	24,738	254	66	132	50.59
G. S. Chappell	1966-67 – 1983-84	322	542	72	24,535	247*	74	111	52.20
M. E. Waugh	1985-86 – 2001-02	324	521	64	24,074	229*	76	118	52.68
D. C. Boon	1978-79 – 1999	350	585	53	23,413	227	68	114	44.01
K. J. Greives	1945-46 – 1964	490	746	79	22,454	224	29	136	33.66
R. N. Harvey	1946-47 – 1962-63	306	461	35	21,699	231*	67	94	50.93
R. B. Simpson	1952-53 – 1977-78	257	436	62	21,029	359	60	100	56.22
T. M. Moody	1985-86 – 2000-01	300	501	47	21,001	272	64	94	46.26
S. R. Waugh	1984-85 – 2001-02	299	464	77	20,335	216*	64	86	52.55
I. M. Chappell	1961-62 – 1979-80	263	448	41	19,680	209	59	96	48.35
W. E. Alley	1945-46 – 1968	400	682	67	19,612	221*	31	92	31.88
D. M. Jones	1981-82 – 1997-98	245	415	45	19,188	324*	55	88	51.86
W. M. Lawry	1955-56 – 1971-72	250	417	49	18,734	266	50	100	50.90
D. S. Lehmann	1987-88 – 2002	205	350	23	18,447	255	60	82	56.41
S. G. Law	1988-89 – 2002	249	416	45	18,225	263	54	88	49.12
F. A. Tarrant	1898-99 – 1936-37	329	541	48	17,952	250*	33	93	36.41
M. A. Taylor	1985-86 – 1998-99	253	435	20	17,415	334*	41	97	41.96
M. L. Hayden	1991-92 – 2001-02	209	362	36	17,362	235*	55	74	53.26
C. Hill	1892-93 – 1924-25	252	416	21	17,213	365*	45	82	43.57
W. Bardsley	1903-04 – 1926-27	250	376	35	17,025	264	53	74	49.92
J. L. Langer	1991-92 – 2001-02	212	372	40	17,012	274*	55	63	51.24
W. L. Murdoch	1875-76 – 1904	391	679	48	16,953	321	19	85	26.86
V. T. Trumper	1894-95 – 1913-14	255	401	21	16,939	300*	42	87	44.57
A. L. Hassett	1932-33 – 1953-54	216	322	32	16,890	232	59	76	58.24
K. D. Walters	1962-63 – 1980-81	259	426	57	16,180	253	45	81	43.84
W. W. Armstrong	1898-99 – 1921-22	269	406	61	16,158	303*	45	57	46.83
M. G. Bevan	1989-90 – 2002	204	341	61	15,862	203*	55	69	56.65
V. E. Jackson	1936-37 – 1958	354	605	53	15,698	170	21	72	28.43
S. M. J. Woods	1886 – 1910	401	690	35	15,345	215	19	62	23.42
L. Livingston	1941-42 – 1964	236	384	45	15,269	210	34	78	45.04
E. S. Gregory	1889-90 – 1912	368	587	55	15,192	201	25	65	28.55
C. G. Macartney	1905-06 – 1935-36	249	360	32	15,019	345	49	53	45.78
I. R. Redpath	1961-62 – 1975-76	226	391	34	14,993	261	32	84	41.99
J. Cox	1987-98 – 2002	201	353	26	14,955	245	44	64	45.73
P. J. P. Burge	1952-53 – 1966-67	233	354	46	14,640	283	38	66	47.53

	Career	M	I	NO	R	HS	100s	50s	Avge
G. S. Blewett	1991-92 – 2001-02	190	340	25	14,633	268	40	70	46.45
K. R. Miller	1937-38 – 1959	226	326	36	14,183	281*	41	63	48.90
M. J. Slater	1991-92 – 2001-02	203	360	19	14,036	221	33	68	41.16
M. A. Noble	1893-94 – 1919-20	248	377	34	13,975	284	37	65	40.74
N. C. O'Neill	1955-56 – 1967-68	188	306	34	13,859	284	45	64	50.95
W. A. Brown	1932-33 – 1949-50	189	284	15	13,838	265*	39	65	51.44
W. H. Ponsford	1920-21 – 1934-35	162	235	23	13,819	437	47	42	65.18
W. M. Woodfull	1921-22 – 1934-35	174	245	39	13,388	284	49	58	64.99
G. M. Wood	1976-77 – 1991-92	227	375	42	13,353	186*	35	61	40.09
A. F. Kippax	1918-19 – 1935-36	175	256	33	12,762	315*	43	45	57.22
K. J. Hughes	1975-76 – 1990-91	216	368	20	12,711	213	26	69	36.52
D. W. Hookes	1975-76 – 1991-92	178	304	16	12,671	306*	32	65	43.39
A. R. Morris	1940-41 – 1963-64	162	250	15	12,614	290	46	46	53.67
C. L. McCool	1939-40 – 1960	251	412	34	12,420	172	18	66	32.85
L. E. Favell	1951-52 – 1969-70	202	347	9	12,379	190	27	68	36.62
S. J. McCabe	1928-29 – 1941-42	182	262	20	11,951	240	29	68	49.38
R. J. Inverarity	1962-63 – 1984-85	223	377	49	11,777	187	26	60	35.90
G. R. Marsh	1977-78 – 1993-94	184	323	25	11,760	355*	33	46	39.46
G. Giffen	1877-78 – 1903-04	251	421	23	11,758	271	18	51	29.54
R. Benaud	1948-49 – 1967-68	259	365	44	11,719	187	23	61	36.50
G. N. Yallop	1972-73 – 1986-87	164	283	30	11,615	268	30	57	45.90
J. D. Siddons	1984-85 – 1999-00	160	280	22	11,587	245	35	53	44.91
C. C. McDonald	1947-48 – 1962-63	192	307	26	11,376	229	24	57	40.48
B. C. Booth	1954-55 – 1968-69	183	283	35	11,265	214*	26	60	45.42
R. T. Ponting	1992-93 – 2001-02	143	240	35	11,218	233	39	48	54.72
R. W. Marsh	1968-69 – 1983-84	258	396	41	11,067	236	12	54	31.17
M. T. G. Elliott	1992-93 – 2001-02	131	242	19	11,016	203	34	51	49.40
D. R. Martyn	1990-91 – 2001-02	153	260	38	10,945	203*	34	55	49.30
K. D. Mackay	1946-47 – 1962-63	201	294	46	10,823	223	23	58	43.64
V. Y. Richardson	1918-19 – 1937-38	184	297	12	10,727	231	27	46	37.63
A. E. Trott	1892-93 – 1911	375	602	53	10,696	164	8	43	19.48
J. Darling	1893-94 – 1907-08	202	333	25	10,635	210	19	55	34.52
R. M. Cowper	1959-60 – 1969-70	147	228	31	10,595	307	26	58	53.78
J. Ryder	1912-13 – 1935-36	177	274	37	10,499	295	24	55	44.29
S. C. Trimble	1959-60 – 1975-76	144	262	16	10,282	252*	26	48	41.79
G. E. Tribe	1945-46 – 1959	308	454	82	10,177	136*	7	48	27.34
G. M. Ritchie	1980-81 – 1991-92	159	255	26	10,171	213*	24	54	44.03
K. R. Stackpole	1959-60 – 1973-74	167	279	22	10,100	207	22	50	39.29

HIGHEST PARTNERSHIPS FOR EACH WICKET

First wicket

456 W. H. Ponsford and R. E. Mayne, Victoria v Queensland at Melbourne 1923-24
431 M. R. J. Veletta and G. R. Marsh, Western Australia v South Australia at Perth 1989-90
388 K. C. Wessels and R. B. Kerr, Queensland v Victoria at St Kilda 1982-83
382 W. M. Lawry and R. B. Simpson, Australia v West Indies at Bridgetown 1964-65
375 W. M. Woodfull and W. H. Ponsford, Victoria v New South Wales at Melbourne 1926-27
374 G. R. Marsh and M. R. J. Veletta, Western Australia v Tamil Nadu at Perth 1988-89
353 M. T. G. Elliott and J. L. Arnberger, Victoria v Tasmania at Richmond 1999-00
337 C. C. McDonald and K. D. Meuleman, Victoria v South Australia at Adelaide 1949-50
331 B. A. Courtice and R. B. Kerr, Queensland v Tasmania at Brisbane 1984-85
329 G. R. Marsh and M. A. Taylor, Australia v England at Nottingham 1989
328 C. Milburn and D. Chadwick, Western Australia v Queensland at Brisbane 1968-69
323 J. B. Hobbs and W. Rhodes, England v Australia at Melbourne 1911-12
323 M. L. Hayden and M. T. G. Elliott, Australian XI v West Indians at Hobart (Bel) 1996-97
319 J. Dyson and R. B. McCosker, New South Wales v Western Australia at Sydney 1980-81
314 A. C. MacLaren and T. W. Hayward, A. C. MacLaren's XI v NSW at Sydney 1901-02
313 A. J. Richardson and L. T. Gun, South Australia v Western Australia at Adelaide 1925-26

310 G. R. Marsh and M. R. J. Veletta, Western Australia v Tasmania at Hobart (Bel) 1988-89
308 R. B. Simpson and G. Thomas, New South Wales v Western Australia at Sydney 1963-64
301 K. R. Stackpole and G. D. Watson, Australians v Hampshire at Southampton 1972

Second wicket

451 W. H. Ponsford and D. G. Bradman, Australia v England at The Oval 1934
386 G. S. Blewett and D. S. Lehmann, South Australia v Tasmania at Hobart (Bel) 2001-02
382 L. Hutton and M. Leyland, England v Australia at The Oval 1938
378 L. A. Marks and K. D. Walters, New South Wales v South Australia at Adelaide 1964-65
374 R. B. Simpson and R. M. Cowper, Australians v N.E. Transvaal at Pretoria 1966-67
368 W. Rhodes and C. A. G. Russell, MCC v South Australia at Adelaide 1920-21
368* M. L. Hayden and M. L. Love, Queensland v Tasmania at Hobart (Bel) 1995-96
365 M. L. Hayden and M. L. Love, Queensland v Tasmania at Brisbane 1995-96
358 C. McKenzie and H. H. L. Kortlang, Victoria v Western Australia at Perth 1909-10
351 G. A. Gooch and D. I. Gower, England v Australia at The Oval 1985
345* G. S. Blewett and C. J. Richards, Australian XI v England XI at Hobart (Bel) 1998-99
334 A. Jackson and D. G. Bradman, New South Wales v South Australia at Adelaide 1930-31
331 R. T. Robinson and D. I. Gower, England v Australia at Birmingham 1985
323 I. D. Craig and R. N. Harvey, New South Wales v Queensland at Sydney 1960-61
314 W. H. Ponsford and H. S. T. L. Hendry, Victoria v Queensland at Melbourne 1927-28
311* W. N. Phillips and D. M. Jones, Victoria v South Australia at Melbourne 1993-94
308 B. A. Richards and I. M. Chappell, South Australia v Western Australia at Perth 1970-71
306 C. L. Badcock and W. J. Horrocks, Combined XI v MCC at Perth 1936-37
304 W. Bardsley and M. A. Noble, New South Wales v Victoria at Sydney 1908-09
302 W. N. Phillips and D. M. Jones, Victoria v South Australia at Melbourne 1991-92
301 A. R. Morris and D. G. Bradman, Australia v England at Leeds 1948

Third wicket

390* J. M. Wiener and J. K. Moss, Victoria v Western Australia at St Kilda 1981-82
389 W. H. Ponsford and S. J. McCabe, Australians v MCC at Lord's 1934
363 D. G. Bradman and A. F. Kippax, New South Wales v Queensland at Sydney 1933-34
362 W. Bardsley and C. G. Macartney, Australians v Essex at Leyton 1912
356 D. G. Bradman and R. A. Hamence, South Australia v Tasmania at Adelaide 1935-36
355 W. Bardsley and V. S. Ransford, Australians v Essex at Leyton 1909
349 D. M. Jones and T. M. Moody, Australians v Warwickshire at Birmingham 1989
345 W. Bardsley and J. M. Taylor, New South Wales v South Australia at Adelaide 1920-21
341 E. J. Barlow and R. G. Pollock, South Africa v Australia at Adelaide 1963-64
330 G. M. Wood and G. R. Marsh, Western Australia v New South Wales at Sydney 1983-84
326 M. L. Love and S. G. Law, Queensland v Tasmania at Brisbane 1994-95
320 W. W. Armstrong and M. A. Noble, Australians v Somerset at Bath 1905
318 G. A. Faulkner and A. W. Nourse, South Africans v New South Wales at Sydney 1910-11
315 C. J. Badcock and A. L. Hassett, Australians v Leicestershire at Leicester 1938
312† M. L. Love, B. P. Nash and A. Symonds, Queensland v South Australia at Adelaide .. 2001-02
310 A. Shrewsbury and W. Gunn, Non Smokers v Smokers at East Melbourne 1886-87
308 R. B. Richardson and I. V. A. Richards, West Indies v Australia at St John's 1983-84
304 K. C. Wessels and G. M. Ritchie, Queensland v Tasmania at Devonport 1981-82
303 M. T. G. Elliott and L. D. Harper, Victoria v New South Wales at North Sydney 1997-98
300 I. M. Chappell and G. S. Chappell, Australians v Barbados at Bridgetown 1972-73

  † *Retired hurt*

Fourth wicket

462* D. W. Hookes and W. B. Phillips, South Australia v Tasmania at Adelaide 1986-87
424 I. S. Lee and S. O. Quin, Victoria v Tasmania at Melbourne 1933-34
388 W. H. Ponsford and D. G. Bradman, Australia v England at Leeds 1934
377 K. R. Miller and J. H. de Courcy, Australians v Comb. Services at Kingston-on-Thames .. 1953
336 W. M. Lawry and K. D. Walters, Australia v West Indies at Sydney 1968-69
333 E. H. Hendren and W. R. Hammond, MCC v New South Wales at Sydney 1928-29
325 N. C. O'Neill and B. C. Booth, New South Wales v Victoria at Sydney 1957-58
321 D. R. Martyn and M. W. Goodwin, Western Australia v Tasmania at Perth 2001-02
318 J. A. Brayshaw and D. S. Lehmann, South Australia v Western Australia at Adelaide . 1993-94
315 M. A. Noble and E. S. Gregory, New South Wales v Victoria at Sydney 1907-08

306* Javed Miandad and Younis Ahmed, Glamorgan v Australians at Neath 1985
301 L. P. J. O'Brien and L. S. Darling, Victoria v Queensland at Brisbane 1932-33

Fifth wicket

464* M. E. Waugh and S. R. Waugh, New South Wales v Western Australia at Perth 1990-91
405 S. G. Barnes and D. G. Bradman, Australia v England at Sydney 1946-47
397 W. Bardsley and C. Kelleway, New South Wales v South Australia at Sydney 1920-21
385 S. R. Waugh and G. S. Blewett, Australia v South Africa at Johannesburg 1996-97
377* G. P. Thorpe and M. R. Ramprakash, England XI v South Australia at Adelaide 1998-99
374 V. V. S. Laxman and R. S. Dravid, India v Australia at Kolkata 2000-01
344 M. C. Cowdrey and T. W. Graveney, MCC v South Australia at Adelaide 1962-63
344 B. C. Lara, †P. T. Collins and J. C. Adams, West Indies v Australia at Kingston 1998-99
343 R. I. Maddocks and J. Hallebone, Victoria v Tasmania at Melbourne 1951-52
336 W. H. Ponsford and H. S. B. Love, Victoria v Tasmania at Melbourne 1922-23
327 J. L. Langer and R. T. Ponting, Australia v Pakistan at Perth 1999-00
322* A. R. Border and S. R. Waugh, Australia v England at Leeds 1993
319 R. T. Ponting and R. J. Tucker, Tasmania v Westralia Australia at Hobart (Bel) 1994-95
316* L. D. Harper and G. B. Gardiner, Victoria v South Australia at Carlton 1997-98
301* C. E. Pellew and C. B. Willis, AIF Team v Worcestershire at Worcester 1919
301* R. B. Simpson and K. D. Meuleman, Western Australia v New South Wales at Perth . . . 1959-60

Sixth wicket

428 M. A. Noble and W. W. Armstrong, Australians v Sussex at Hove 1902
365 R. D. Jacobs and B. C. Lara, West Indians v Australia A at Hobart (Bel) 2000-01
346 J. H. W. Fingleton and D. G. Bradman, Australia v England at Melbourne 1936-37
332 N. G. Marks and N. C. O'Neill, New South Wales v South Australia at Sydney 1958-59
323 E. H. Hendren and J. W. H. T. Douglas, MCC v Victoria at Melbourne 1920-21
317 D. R. Martyn and A. C. Gilchrist, Australia v South Africa at Johannesburg 2001-02
298* D. B. Vengsarkar and R. J. Shastri, India v Australia at Bombay 1986-87
290 M. T. G. Elliott and D. S. Berry, Victoria v New South Wales at Sydney 1996-97
289 S. J. E. Loxton and D. T. Ring, Victoria v Queensland at Melbourne 1946-47
279 A. L. Hassett and E. A. Williams, Australian Services v Prince's XI at Delhi 1945-46
277 O. G. Smith and A. P. Binns, Jamaica v Australians at Kingston 1954-55
271 S. R. Waugh and G. R. J. Matthews, New South Wales v Tasmania at Hobart (Bel) . . 1989-90
269 V. T. Trumper and C. Hill, Australians v New Zealanders at Wellington 1904-05
262 A. Kenny and H. H. L. Kortlang, Victoria v Queensland at Brisbane 1909-10
260* D. M. Jones and S. R. Waugh, Australia v Sri Lanka at Hobart (Bel) 1989-90
260 D. S. Lehmann and T. J. Nielsen, South Australia v Queensland at Adelaide 1996-97
258 V. T. Trumper and F. A. Iredale, New South Wales v Tasmania at Sydney 1898-99
255 G. S. Sobers and B. N. Jarman, South Australia v Western Australia at Perth 1963-64
254 G. N. Yallop and R. D. Robinson, Victoria v Western Australia at Melbourne 1976-77
253 A. F. Kippax and J. G. Morgan, New South Wales v Queensland at Sydney 1927-28

Seventh wicket

347 D. S. Atkinson and C. C. Depeiza, West Indies v Australia at Bridgetown 1954-55
335 C. W. Andrews and E. C. Bensted, Queensland v New South Wales at Sydney 1934-35
273* W. W. Armstrong and J. Darling, Australians v Gentlemen of England at Lord's 1905
268 A. H. Kardar and Imtiaz Ahmed, North Zone v Australian Services at Lahore 1945-46
255 G. Thomas and R. Benaud, New South Wales v Victoria at Melbourne 1961-62
244 W. R. Patrick and C. F. W. Allcott, New Zealanders v New South Wales at Sydney . . 1925-26
232 W. Bruce and H. Trumble, Australians v Oxford and Cambridge Univ. at Portsmouth . . 1893
229 K. J. Schneider and W. A. S. Oldfield, Australians v Canterbury at Christchurch 1927-28
221 D. T. Lindsay and P. L. van der Merwe, South Africa v Australia at Johannesburg . . . 1966-67
217 K. D. Walters and G. J. Gilmour, Australia v New Zealand at Christchurch 1976-77
208 C. G. Macartney and A. J. Y. Hopkins, New South Wales v Queensland at Sydney . . . 1906-07
204 G. Shipperd and T. J. Zoehrer, Western Australia v New South Wales at Perth 1982-83
203* B. F. Davison and P. I. Faulkner, Tasmania v Western Australia at Perth 1983-84
202 S. J. E. Loxton and B. A. Barnett, Commonwealth XI v Bombay at Bombay 1953-54
200 Kapil Dev and C. S. Pandit, Indians v Queensland at Brisbane 1991-92

Eighth wicket

433 V. T. Trumper and A. Sims, Australians v Canterbury at Christchurch 1913-14
270 V. T. Trumper and E. P. Barbour, New South Wales v Victoria at Sydney 1912-13
253 N. J. Astle and A. C. Parore, New Zealand v Australia at Perth 2001-02
243 M. J. Hartigan and C. Hill, Australia v England at Adelaide 1907-08
242* T. J. Zoehrer and K. H. MacLeay, Western Australia v New South Wales at Perth . . . 1990-91
236 R. A. Duff and A. J. Y. Hopkins, New South Wales v Lord Hawke's XI at Sydney . . . 1902-03
218 C. G. Macartney and J. D. Scott, New South Wales v Queensland at Sydney 1913-14
215 W. W. Armstrong and R. L. Park, Victoria v South Australia at Melbourne 1919-20
204 W. A. S. Oldfield and C. O. Nicholls, New South Wales v Victoria at Sydney 1927-28

Ninth wicket

232 C. Hill and E. Walkley, South Australia v New South Wales at Adelaide 1900-01
226 C. Kelleway and W. A. S. Oldfield, New South Wales v Victoria at Melbourne 1925-26
225 W. W. Armstrong and E. A. C. Windsor, Australian XI v The Rest at Sydney 1907-08
221 E. F. Waddy and W. P. Howell, New South Wales v South Australia at Adelaide 1904-05
201 E. E. B. Forssberg and H. S. B. Love, New South Wales v Queensland at Sydney 1920-21

Tenth wicket

307 A. F. Kippax and J. E. H. Hooker, New South Wales v Victoria at Melbourne 1928-29
211 M. Ellis and T. J. Hastings, Victoria v South Australia at Melbourne 1902-03
169 R. B. Minnett and C. G. McKew, New South Wales v Victoria at Sydney 1911-12
154 F. R. Buttsworth and J. P. Lanigan, Western Australia v Victoria at Perth 1921-22
147 C. G. Macartney and S. C. Everett, Australian XI v Tasmania at Hobart (TCA) 1925-26
145 G. A. Rotherham and J. H. Naumann, Cambridge Univ. v AIF Team at Cambridge . . 1919
138* B. E. McNamara and P. J. S. Alley, New South Wales v Tasmania at Hobart (Bel) . . . 1996-97
136 J. P. O'Halloran and A. E. Johns, Victoria v South Australia at Melbourne 1896-97
135 W. A. S. Oldfield and A. A. Mailey, New South Wales v South Australia at Adelaide . 1923-24
132 R. W. McLeod and C. H. Ross, Victoria v South Australia at Adelaide 1899-00
130 R. E. Foster and W. Rhodes, England v Australia at Sydney 1903-04
127 J. M. Taylor and A. A. Mailey, Australia v England at Sydney 1924-25
124 W. A. S. Oldfield and A. A. Mailey, Australians v Warwickshire at Birmingham 1921
124 J. G. Bracewell and S. L. Boock, New Zealand v Australia at Sydney 1985-86
122 W. G. Ward and N. Dodds, Tasmania v Victoria at Hobart (TCA) 1898-99
120 R. A. Duff and W. W. Armstrong, Australia v England at Melbourne 1901-02
120 A. J. Y. Hopkins and W. H. McIntyre, New South Wales v Queensland at Sydney . . . 1906-07
120 S. L. Saunders and P. M. Clough, Tasmania v Western Australia at Perth 1981-82
119* W. H. Ponsford and A. J. Richardson, Australians v MCC at Lord's 1926
118 A. Hurwood and P. M. Hornibrook, Australians v Sussex at Hove 1930
118 D. S. Berry and M. W. H. Inness, Victoria v New South Wales at Melbourne 1997-98
116 R. E. Soule and G. D. Campbell, Tasmania v Queensland at Brisbane 1988-89
114 D. J. Saker and S. J. Jurgensen, Tasmania v Queensland at Hobart (Bel) 2001-02
112 J. J. Kelly and F. J. Laver, Australians v Gloucestershire at Bristol 1905
112 C. Kelleway and H. Carter, New South Wales v South Australia at Adelaide 1920-21
112* E. E. Hemmings and R. D. Jackman, England XI v South Australia at Adelaide 1982-83
111 M. A. Noble and W. P. Howell, New South Wales v Victoria at Sydney 1896-97
109 A. L. Newell and W. P. Howell, New South Wales v A. E. Stoddart's XI at Sydney . . 1897-98
105 L. W. Pye and A. J. Bowden, New South Wales v Queensland at Sydney 1899-00
105* W. T. Walmsley and J. E. Freeman, Queensland v NSW at Brisbane 1957-58
104 K. C. James and H. B. Massey, Wellington v Australians at Wellington 1927-28
104 L. Michael and E. I. Pynor, South Australia v Victoria at Adelaide 1949-50
103 P. A. McAlister and F. A. Tarrant, Victoria v New Zealanders at Melbourne 1898-99
103 A. J. Stewart and A. R. Caddick, England v Australia at Birmingham 2001
101 G. Giffen and J. P. F. Travers, South Australia v Victoria at Adelaide 1902-03
101 W. W. Armstrong and F. G. Trueman, Victoria v South Australia at Melbourne 1918-19
100 G. E. Palmer and W. H. Cooper, Victoria v New South Wales at Sydney 1881-82
100* D. Tallon and G. Noblet, D. G. Bradman's XI v A. L. Hassett's XI at Melbourne 1948-49

BOWLING RECORDS

TEN WICKETS IN AN INNINGS

10/43	E. Barratt	The Bowlers v Australians at The Oval	1878
10/66	G. Giffen	Australian XI v The Rest at Sydney	1883-84
10/28	W.P. Howell	Australians v Surrey at The Oval	1899
10/66	A. A. Mailey	Australians v Gloucestershire at Cheltenham	1921
10/37	C. V. Grimmett	Australians v Yorkshire at Sheffield	1930
10/36	T. W. Wall	South Australia v New South Wales at Sydney	1932-33
10/53	J. C. Laker	England v Australia at Manchester	1956
10/88	J. C. Laker	Surrey v Australians at The Oval	1956
10/61	P. J. Allan	Queensland v Victoria at Melbourne	1965-66
10/44	I. J. Brayshaw	Western Australia v Victoria at Perth	1967-68

BEST BOWLING IN AN INNINGS ON FIRST-CLASS DEBUT

9/55	J. Quilty	South Australia v Victoria at Adelaide	1881-82
9/67	H. P. Hay	South Australia v Lord Hawke's XI at Unley	1902-03
8/31	W. Brown	Tasmania v Victoria at Hobart (LRG)	1857-58
8/35	R. Wilson	Queensland v Auckland at Auckland	1896-97
8/36	J. L. Bevan	South Australia v Tasmania at Adelaide	1877-78
8/81	H. V. Hordern	New South Wales v Queensland at Sydney	1905-06
8/111	M. Pierce	New South Wales v South Australia at Adelaide	1892-93

BEST BOWLING IN A MATCH ON FIRST-CLASS DEBUT

15/73	W. Brown	Tasmania v Victoria at Hobart (LRG)	1857-58
14/59	J. L. Bevan	South Australia v Tasmania at Adelaide	1877-78
13/61	T. W. Antill	Victoria v Tasmania at Launceston	1850-51
13/265	M. Pierce	New South Wales v South Australia at Adelaide	1892-93
11/48	S. Cosstick	Victoria v New South Wales at Sydney	1860-61
11/80	J. E. Barrett	Victoria v South Australia at Melbourne	1884-85
11/97	R. Wilson	Queensland v Auckland at Auckland	1896-97
11/103	M. A. Polzin	Queensland v South Australia at Brisbane	1986-87
11/126	D. J. Noonan	New South Wales v Canterbury at Christchurch	1895-96
10/34	G. Elliott	Victoria v New South Wales at Melbourne	1855-56
10/36	J. J. McKone	New South Wales v Victoria at Melbourne	1855-56
10/46	F. D. Stephenson	Tasmania v Victoria at Melbourne	1981-82
10/97	J. Quilty	South Australia v Victoria at Adelaide	1881-82
10/141	R. B. C. Rees	South Australia v Victoria at Melbourne	1903-04
10/145	L. O'B. Fleetwood-Smith	Victoria v Tasmania at Hobart (TCA)	1931-32
10/226	A. C. Facy	Tasmania v Victoria at Hobart (TCA)	1908-09

MOST WICKETS IN A MATCH FOR AUSTRALIAN TEAMS

17/50	C. T. B. Turner	Australians v England XI at Hastings	1888
17/54	W. P. Howell	Australians v Western Province at Cape Town	1902-03
17/201	G. Giffen	South Australia v Victoria at Adelaide	1885-86
16/65	G. Giffen	Australians v Lancashire at Manchester	1886
16/79	C. T. B. Turner	New South Wales v A. Shrewsbury's XI at Sydney	1887-88
16/101	G. Giffen	Australians v Derbyshire at Derby	1886
16/137	R. A. L. Massie	Australia v England at Lord's	1972
16/166	G. Giffen	South Australia v Victoria at Adelaide	1891-92
16/186	G. Giffen	South Australia v New South Wales at Adelaide	1894-95
16/201	G. Giffen	Australians v Derbyshire at Derby	1886
16/289	C. V. Grimmett	South Australia v Queensland at Adelaide	1934-35

HAT-TRICKS

G. H. B. Gilbert	New South Wales v Victoria at Melbourne	1857-58
F. R. Spofforth	Australians v MCC at Lord's	1878
J. Robertson	Middlesex v Australians at Lord's	1878
F. R. Spofforth	Australians v Players of England at The Oval	1878
F. R. Spofforth	Australia v England at Melbourne	1878-79
G. Ulyett (4 in 4)	Lord Hawke's XI v New South Wales at Sydney	1878-79
W. A. Humphreys	Sussex v Australians at Hove	1880
G. E. Palmer	Australians v Sussex at Hove	1882
W. Bates	England v Australia at Melbourne	1882-83
W. A. Humphreys	Sussex v Australians at Hove	1884
G. Giffen	Australians v Lancashire at Manchester	1884
F. R. Spofforth	Australians v South of England at The Oval	1884
C. T. B. Turner	New South Wales v Victoria at Melbourne	1886-87
G. Giffen	South Australia v G. F. Vernon's XI at Adelaide	1887-88
J. Briggs	England v Australia at Sydney	1891-92
H. Trumble	Australians v Gloucestershire at Cheltenham	1896
G. Giffen	Australians v Wembley Park XI at Wembley Park	1896
A. D. Pougher	MCC v Australians at Lord's	1896
T. R. McKibbin	Australians v Lancashire at Liverpool	1896
M. A. Noble	New South Wales v Tasmania at Sydney	1898-99
J. T. Hearne	England v Australia at Leeds	1899
H. Trumble	Australia v England at Melbourne	1901-02
A. J. Y. Hopkins	Australians v Cambridge University at Cambridge	1902
W. P. Howell (4 in 5)	Australians v Western Province at Cape Town	1902-03
W. W. Armstrong	Victoria v New South Wales at Melbourne	1902-03
T. H. Howard (4 in 5)	New South Wales v Queensland at Sydney	1902-03
H. Hay	South Australia v Lord Hawke's XI at Unley	1902-03
A. J. Y. Hopkins	New South Wales v South Australia at Sydney	1903-04
H. Trumble	Australia v England at Melbourne	1903-04
W. P. Howell	Australians v New Zealand XI at Wellington	1904-05
G. A. Wilson	Worcestershire v Australians at Worcester	1905
T. J. Matthews	Victoria v Tasmania at Launceston	1908-09
J. A. Newman	Hampshire v Australians at Southampton	1909
T. J. Matthews (1st inns)	Australia v South Africa at Manchester	1912
T. J. Matthews (2nd inns)	Australia v South Africa at Manchester	1912
T. J. Matthews	Australians v Philadelphia at Philadelphia	1912-13
J. N. Crawford	South Australia v Western Australia at Adelaide	1912-13
C. Kelleway	New South Wales v Queensland at Brisbane	1913-14
J. Horsley	Derbyshire v AIF Team at Derby	1919
J. W. H. T. Douglas	MCC v New South Wales at Sydney	1920-21
A. P. Freeman	MCC v South Australia at Adelaide	1922-23
H. Ironmonger	Victoria v MCC at Melbourne	1924-25
H. I. Ebeling	Victoria v Queensland at Melbourne	1928-29
J. E. H. Hooker (4 in 4)	New South Wales v Victoria at Sydney	1928-29
C. V. Grimmett	South Australia v Queensland at Brisbane (Ex)	1928-29
F. L. Morton	Victoria v Tasmania at Melbourne	1931-32
H. J. Enthoven	Middlesex v Australians at Lord's	1934
R. K. Oxenham	Australians v All Ceylon at Colombo (PSS)	1935-36
M. G. Waite	South Australia v MCC at Adelaide	1935-36
B. Dooland	South Australia v Victoria at Melbourne	1945-46
C. R. Rangachari	Indians v Tasmania at Hobart (TCA)	1947-48
A. K. Walker	New South Wales v Queensland at Sydney	1948-49
H. J. Tayfield	South Africans v Victoria at Melbourne	1952-53
J. C. Treanor	New South Wales v Queensland at Brisbane	1954-55
L. F. Kline	Australia v South Africa at Cape Town	1957-58
G. F. Rorke	New South Wales v Queensland at Sydney	1958-59
L. R. Gibbs	West Indies v Australia at Adelaide	1960-61
A. K. Davidson	New South Wales v Western Australia at Perth	1962-63
D. Robins (4 in 4)	South Australia v New South Wales at Adelaide	1965-66
R. F. Surti	Queensland v Western Australia at Perth	1968-69

R. A. Woolmer	MCC v Australians at Lord's	1975
W. Prior	South Australia v New South Wales at Adelaide	1975-76
A. T. Sincock	South Australia v Indians at Adelaide	1977-78
L. S. Pascoe	New South Wales v South Australia at Adelaide	1980-81
P. M. Clough	Tasmania v New South Wales at Hobart (TCA)	1982-83
J. R. Thomson	Queensland v Western Australia at Brisbane	1984-85
D. R. Gilbert	New South Wales v Victoria at Sydney	1984-85
G. S. Le Roux	South Africans v Australian XI at Johannesburg	1985-86
C. E. B. Rice	South Africans v Australian XI at Johannesburg	1985-86
J. N. Maguire	Australians v Eastern Province at Port Elizabeth	1986-87
C. A. Walsh	West Indies v Australia at Brisbane	1988-89
M. G. Hughes	Australia v West Indies at Perth	1988-89
W. K. M. Benjamin	Leicestershire v Australians at Leicester	1989
W. J. Holdsworth	Australians v Derbyshire at Derby	1993
D. W. Fleming	Australia v Pakistan at Rawalpindi	1994-95
S. K. Warne	Australia v England at Melbourne	1994-95
S. C. G. MacGill	New South Wales v New Zealanders at Newcastle	1997-98
D. Gough	England v Australia at Sydney	1998-99
M. S. Kasprowicz	Queensland v Victoria at Brisbane	1998-99
M. W. H. Inness	Victoria v New South Wales at Melbourne	1999-00
G. D. McGrath	Australia v West Indies at Perth	2000-01
Harbhajan Singh	India v Australia at Kolkata	2000-01

MOST WICKETS IN AN AUSTRALIAN SEASON

	Season	M	B	Mdns	R	W	BB	5Wi	10Wm	Avge
C. T. B. Turner (NSW)	1887-88	12	4,267	473	1,441	106	8/39	13	5	13.59
G. Giffen (SAust)	1894-95	11	4,787	196	2,097	93	8/77	12	4	22.54
C. V. Grimmett (SAust) ...	1929-30	11	3,795	51	1,943	82	7/136	9	3	23.69
R. Benaud (NSW)	1958-59	13	4,467	142	1,579	82	7/32	6	1	19.25
A. A. Mailey (NSW)	1920-21	10	2,993	45	1,825	81	9/121	8	3	22.53
M. W. Tate (MCC)	1924-25	14	4,018	93	1,464	77	7/74	7	2	19.01
C. V. Grimmett (SAust) ...	1931-32	12	4,096	166	1,535	77	7/83	7	1	19.93
E. Jones (SAust)	1897-98	11	3,529	121	1,653	76	7/80	9	3	21.75
R. M. Hogg (SAust)	1978-79	14	3,483	97	1,249	76	6/74	6	2	16.43
C. V. Grimmett (SAust) ...	1930-31	11	3,524	99	1,417	74	7/87	7	1	19.14
C. V. Grimmett (SAust) ...	1939-40	9	3,543	57	1,654	73	6/118	10	3	22.65
C. V. Grimmett (SAust) ...	1928-29	10	5,152	135	2,432	71	6/109	5	0	34.25
C. T. B. Turner (NSW)	1886-87	7	2,145	273	538	70	8/32	8	3	7.68
W. J. Whitty (SAust)	1910-11	11	2,957	109	1,419	70	6/17	4	0	20.27
H. J. Tayfield (SAf)	1952-53	14	4,836	123	1,954	70	7/71	5	1	27.91
D. K. Lillee (WAust)	1976-77	11	2,832	59	1,368	70	6/26	8	4	19.54
C. R. Miller (Tas)	1997-98	12	3,896	172	1,749	70	7/49	5	2	24.99

50 WICKETS IN AN AUSTRALIAN SEASON

10 Times: C. V. Grimmett 59 (1924-25), 59 (1925-26), 71 (1928-29), 82 (1929-30), 74 (1930-31), 77 (1931-32), 55 (1932-33), 66 (1933-34), 58 (1934-35), 73 (1939-40).

6 Times: D. K. Lillee 56 (1972-73), 62 (1973-74), 62 (1975-76), 70 (1976-77), 69 (1980-81), 59 (1983-84).

5 Times: L. O'B. Fleetwood-Smith 50 (1932-33), 53 (1933-34), 63 (1934-35), 53 (1936-37), 64 (1937-38); A. A. Mallett 54 (1971-72), 62 (1972-73), 57 (1974-75), 56 (1975-76), 53 (1979-80); W. J. O'Reilly 62 (1932-33), 51 (1936-37), 64 (1937-38), 55 (1939-40), 55 (1940-41).

4 Times: C. J. McDermott 58 (1986-87), 54 (1989-90), 67 (1990-91), 60 (1991-92).

3 Times: G. D. McKenzie 51 (1962-63), 55 (1967-68), 60 (1968-69); A. A. Mailey 81 (1920-21), 55 (1922-23), 59 (1924-25); C. D. Matthews 57 (1986-87), 57 (1987-88), 53 (1991-92); J. R. Thomson 62 (1974-75), 62 (1975-76), 57 (1977-78); M. S. Kasprowicz 51 (1992-93), 64 (1995-96), 51 (2001-02).

MOST WICKETS ON AN AUSTRALIAN OVERSEAS TOUR

			M	O	Mdns	R	W	BB	5W/i	10W/m	Avge
C.T.B. Turner	England	1888	36	2,427.2	1,127	3,307	283	9/15	31	12	11.69
F.R. Spofforth	England	1884	31	1,538.2	646	2,564	201	8/62	24	11	12.75
J.J. Ferris	England	1888	37	2,080.1	937	2,934	199	8/41	17	3	14.74
J.J. Ferris	England	1890	30	1,545.2	628	2,657	186	7/16	15	5	14.28
C.T.B. Turner	England	1890	31	1,500.1	652	2,526	178	7/23	16	4	14.19
F.R. Spofforth	England	1882	30	1,470	646	2,079	157	9/51	16	6	13.24
G. Giffen	England	1886	35	1,673.2	710	2,674	154	9/60	13	5	17.36
C.T.B. Turner	England	1893	26	1,079	413	2,018	148	8/95	16	5	13.64
H. Trumble	England	1896	30	1,140.1	380	2,340	148	7/67	11	5	15.81
C.V. Grimmett	England	1930	26	1,015.1	262	2,427	144	10/37	15	5	16.85
H. Trumble	England	1899	32	1,246.3	432	2,618	142	8/35	10	3	18.44
E.A. McDonald	England	1921	26	809.2	158	2,284	138	8/41	9	3	16.55
H. Trumble	England	1902	29	912	292	1,921	137	9/39	13	7	14.02
E. Jones	England	1899	28	1,163.2	331	2,849	135	7/31	10	4	21.10
A.A. Mailey	England	1921	28	800	103	2,595	133	10/66	7	1	19.51
G.E. Palmer	England	1884	30	1,214.3	446	2,099	130	7/74	13	5	16.14
A.A. Mailey	England	1926	27	816	162	2,437	126	9/86	12	4	19.34
H.F. Boyle	England	1882	27	1,101.2	488	1,523	125	7/32	13	3	12.18
T.W. Garrett	England	1886	34	1,654.1	778	2,221	123	6/22	5	1	18.06
J.V. Saunders	England	1902	25	710	160	2,085	123	6/9	10	3	16.95
W.W. Armstrong	England	1905	30	990.4	298	2,221	122	8/50	9	2	18.20
E. Jones	England	1896	29	846.3	282	1,940	121	8/39	7	1	16.03
A. Cotter	England	1905	28	735.1	121	2,429	119	7/15	9	2	20.41
T.W. Garrett	England	1882	30	1,167.3	474	1,694	118	7/49	10	1	14.36
G. Giffen	England	1893	29	906.4	257	2,247	118	8/98	12	2	19.04
G. Giffen	England	1896	32	865.2	219	2,257	117	8/30	7	1	19.29
W.P. Howell	England	1899	32	1,119.4	426	2,381	117	10/28	6	2	20.35
J.M. Gregory	England	1921	27	655.4	126	1,924	116	7/52	8	2	16.39
F.J. Laver	England	1905	27	848.1	245	2,092	115	8/75	8	3	18.19
W.W. Armstrong	England	1909	29	857	263	1,852	113	6/35	9	0	16.39
C.V. Grimmett	England	1926	24	857.3	257	1,908	112	7/67	7	1	17.04
W.J. Whitty	England	1912	30	866.3	281	1,971	109	7/40	5	1	18.08
W.J. O'Reilly	England	1934	19	870	320	1,858	109	9/38	7	3	17.04
C.V. Grimmett	England	1934	21	985.4	308	2,159	109	7/109	9	1	19.80
H. Trumble	England	1893	29	834.1	274	1,794	108	7/31	9	3	16.61
L. O'B. Fleetwood-Smith	England	1934	20	713.5	160	2,036	106	7/40	12	3	19.20
W.J. O'Reilly	England	1938	20	709.4	213	1,726	104	8/104	9	2	16.59
W.A. Johnston	England	1948	21	850.1	278	1,675	102	7/81	6	2	16.42
G.E. Palmer	England	1886	33	1,393	552	2,306	101	7/84	6	1	22.83
T.R. McKibbin	England	1896	22	647.1	198	1,441	101	7/11	7	3	14.27
G.E. Palmer	England	1882	21	1,032.3	440	1,535	100	8/84	7	1	15.35
W.W. Armstrong	England	1921	30	733.1	271	1,444	100	7/55	8	1	14.44

Most in countries other than England:

R. Benaud	SAf	1957-58	18	743.6	187	2,057	106	7/46	11	2	19.40
R.K. Oxenham	India	1935-36	11	303.3	89	555	75	7/13	8	4	7.40
W.W. Armstrong	NZ	1913-14	8	312	81	789	52	7/17	7	1	15.17
S.W. Austin	NZ	1893-94	7	1,747	85	612	52	8/14	6	1	11.77
P.I. Philpott	WI	1964-65	9	449	99	1,207	49	6/86	2	0	24.63
R.J. Bright	Pak	1979-80	5	230.2	72	558	29	7/87	4	2	19.24
J.N. Crawford	NAmer	1913-14	5	116.2	21	359	33	6/40	3	0	10.88
C.J. McDermott	SL	1992-93	5	182	43	514	16	4/53	0	0	32.13
C.R. Miller	SL	1999-00	5	122.3	25	363	16	6/57	1	0	22.69
D.R. Gilbert	Zim	1985-86	2	68	14	215	15	7/43	2	1	14.33

LEADING BOWLERS IN EACH AUSTRALIAN SEASON

(Qualification for top of averages: 20 wickets)

Season	Leading Wicket-Taker	W	Avge	Top of Averages	W	Avge
1850-51	T. W. Antill (Vic)	13	4.00	n/a		
1851-52	W. Henty (Tas)	10	10.00	n/a		
1852-53	no games played					
1853-54	R. M. McDowall (Tas)	8	6.25	n/a		
1854-55	no games played					
1855-56	J. J. McKone (NSW)	10	3.60	n/a		
	G. Elliott (Vic)	10	3.20	n/a		
1856-57	T. W. Wills (Vic)	10	6.50	n/a		
1857-58	T. W. Wills (Vic)	26	5.03	T. W. Wills (Vic)	26	5.03
1858-59	T. W. Wills (Vic)	11	4.45	n/a		
1859-60	T. W. Wills (Vic)	9	4.33	n/a		
	G. D. Richardson (NSW)	9	6.00	n/a		
1860-61	S. Cosstick (Vic)	11	4.36	n/a		
1861-62	G. Bennett (The World)	14	8.21	n/a		
1862-63	C. Lawrence (NSW)	14	5.21	n/a		
1863-64	E. M. Grace (Anderson's XI)	9	7.67	n/a		
1864-65	no games played					
1865-66	S. Cosstick (NSW)	8	13.63	n/a		
	J. Conway (Vic)	8	15.25	n/a		
1866-67	D. W. Gregory (NSW)	7	9.57	n/a		
1867-68	T. W. Wills (Vic)	9	16.56	n/a		
1868-69	S. Cosstick (Vic)	23	5.42	S. Cosstick (Vic)	23	5.42
1869-70	S. Cosstick (Vic)	10	7.70	n/a		
1870-71	C. A. Reid (Vic)	16	9.50	n/a		
1871-72	F. E. Allan (Vic)	13	4.62	n/a		
1872-73	S. Cosstick (Vic)	23	6.52	S. Cosstick (Vic)	23	6.52
1873-74	no games played					
1874-75	J. Coates (NSW)	15	10.67	n/a		
1875-76	E. Evans (NSW)	21	5.62	E. Evans (NSW)	21	5.62
1876-77	A. Shaw (Lillywhite's XI)	17	11.76	n/a		
1877-78	E. Evans (NSW)	18	10.72	n/a		
1878-79	T. Emmett (Eng)	44	11.84	T. Emmett (Eng)	44	11.84
1879-80	W. H. Cooper (Vic)	12	10.75	n/a		
1880-81	E. Evans (NSW)	32	11.25	E. Evans (NSW)	32	11.25
1881-82	G. E. Palmer (Vic)	47	21.55	W. Bates (Eng)	30	17.33
1882-83	G. E. Palmer (Vic)	51	11.53	H. F. Boyle (Vic)	24	11.00
1883-84	G. E. Palmer (Vic)	29	17.51	G. E. Palmer (Vic)	29	17.51
1884-85	R. Peel (England)	35	19.22	W. Barnes (England)	26	13.23
1885-86	F. R. Spofforth (NSW)	18	15.22	n/a		
1886-87	C. T. B. Turner (NSW)	70	7.68	C. T. B. Turner (NSW)	70	7.68
1887-88	C. T. B. Turner (NSW)	106	13.59	W. Attewell (Eng)	55	10.72
1888-89	J. J. Ferris (NSW)	36	15.83	G. Giffen (SAust)	22	12.95
1889-90	H. Trumble (Vic)	29	14.21	H. Trumble (Vic)	29	14.21
1890-91	J. Phillips (Vic)	25	10.00	J. Phillips (Vic)	25	10.00
1891-92	G. Giffen (SAust)	50	17.30	W. Attewell (Eng)	44	13.02
1892-93	G. Giffen (SAust)	33	23.00	H. Trumble (Vic)	22	13.55
1893-94	C. T. B. Turner (NSW)	30	12.30	C. T. B. Turner (NSW)	30	12.30
1894-95	G. Giffen (SAust)	93	22.54	T. R. McKibbin (NSW)	44	16.66
1895-96	T. R. McKibbin (NSW)	46	23.87	E. Jones (SAust)	31	17.67
1896-97	T. R. McKibbin (NSW)	44	14.89	T. R. McKibbin (NSW)	44	14.89
1897-98	E. Jones (SAust)	76	21.75	W. Roche (Vic)	33	20.73
1898-99	E. Jones (SAust)	45	27.53	C. E. McLeod (Vic)	36	17.86
1899-00	M. A. Noble (NSW)	37	20.65	M. A. Noble (NSW)	37	20.65
1900-01	J. V. Saunders (Vic)	29	17.14	J. V. Saunders (Vic)	29	17.14
	J. P. F. Travers (SAust)	29	20.76			
1901-02	L. C. Braund (Eng)	62	28.69	S. F. Barnes (Eng)	41	16.49

Season	Leading Wicket-Taker	W	Avge	Top of Averages	W	Avge
1902-03	J. V. Saunders (Vic)	32	20.81	L. W. Pye (NSW)	23	19.30
1903-04	W. Rhodes (MCC)	65	16.23	A. Cotter (NSW)	30	13.47
1904-05	F. B. Collins (Vic)	27	23.37	F. B. Collins (Vic)	27	23.37
1905-06	G. L. Garnsey (NSW)	36	21.03	J. D. A. O'Connor (NSW)	32	21.70
1906-07	G. L. Garnsey (NSW)	32	21.94	M. A. Noble (NSW)	24	13.92
1907-08	{ J. V. Saunders (Vic) { J. N. Crawford (MCC)	66 66	24.04 25.19	S. F. Barnes (Eng)	54	21.94
1908-09	J. D. A. O'Connor (SAust)	40	23.00	A. H. Christian (WAust)	25	17.28
1909-10	J. V. Saunders (Vic)	49	17.33	J. D. Scott (NSW)	25	12.56
1910-11	W. J. Whitty (SAust)	70	20.27	H. V. Hordern (NSW)	58	14.83
1911-12	F. R. Foster (MCC)	62	20.19	F. R. Foster (MCC)	62	20.19
1912-13	R. J. A. Massie (NSW)	59	18.66	A. A. Mailey (NSW)	21	16.05
1913-14	C. Kelleway (NSW)	45	12.69	C. Kelleway (NSW)	45	12.69
1914-15	H. Ironmonger (Vic)	36	17.53	H. Ironmonger (Vic)	36	17.53
1915-16	no games played					
1916-17	no games played					
1917-18	no games played					
1918-19	E. A. McDonald (Vic)	25	15.72	E. A. McDonald (Vic)	25	15.72
1919-20	H. S. T. L. Hendry (NSW)	29	18.14	H. S. T. L. Hendry (NSW)	29	18.14
1920-21	A. A. Mailey (NSW)	81	22.53	J. M. Gregory (NSW)	43	22.37
1921-22	E. A. McDonald (Vic)	28	21.50	P. H. Wallace (Vic)	20	17.85
1922-23	A. A. Mailey (NSW)	55	21.64	A. E. Liddicut (Vic)	20	21.05
1923-24	{ A. E. V. Hartkopf (Vic) { N. L. Williams (SAust)	26 26	24.58 26.88	A. E. V. Hartkopf (Vic)	26	24.58
1924-25	M. W. Tate (MCC)	77	19.01	R. K. Oxenham (Qld)	22	14.50
1925-26	C. V. Grimmett (SAust)	59	30.41	C. G. Macartney (NSW)	24	18.88
1926-27	N. L. Williams (SAust)	35	32.03	D. D. Blackie (Vic)	33	24.64
1927-28	C. V. Grimmett (SAust)	42	27.40	D. D. Blackie (Vic)	31	22.23
1928-29	C. V. Grimmett (SAust)	71	34.25	J. C. White (MCC)	65	22.63
1929-30	C. V. Grimmett (SAust)	82	23.69	E. L. A'Beckett (Vic)	27	15.22
1930-31	C. V. Grimmett (SAust)	74	19.14	H. Ironmonger (Vic)	68	14.29
1931-32	C. V. Grimmett (SAust)	77	19.93	L. O'B. Fleetwood-Smith (Vic)	37	16.27
1932-33	W. J. O'Reilly (NSW)	62	19.95	C. J. Hill (NSW)	22	15.27
1933-34	C. V. Grimmett (SAust)	66	21.83	S. A. J. Smith (Vic)	20	17.90
1934-35	L. O'B. Fleetwood-Smith (Vic)	63	20.34	H. C. Chilvers (NSW)	46	18.63
1935-36	F. A. Ward (SAust)	50	20.94	T. W. Wall (SAust)	22	17.09
1936-37	{ L. O'B. Fleetwood-Smith (Vic) { F. A. Ward (SAust)	53 53	20.25 28.41	J. G. Lush (NSW)	27	17.89
1937-38	{ W. J. O'Reilly (NSW) { L. O'B. Fleetwood-Smith (Vic)	64 64	12.25 22.43	W. J. O'Reilly (NSW)	64	12.25
1938-39	L. O'B. Fleetwood-Smith (Vic)	30	19.01	C. V. Grimmett (SAust)	27	20.85
1939-40	C. V. Grimmett (SAust)	73	22.65	W. J. O'Reilly (NSW)	55	15.13
1940-41	W. J. O'Reilly (NSW)	55	12.43	W. J. O'Reilly (NSW)	55	12.43
1941-42	W. J. O'Reilly (NSW)	9	13.78	n/a		
1942-43	no games played					
1943-44	no games played					
1944-45	no games played					
1945-46	G. E. Tribe (Vic)	40	19.03	W. J. O'Reilly (NSW)	33	14.36
1946-47	D. V. P. Wright (MCC)	51	33.31	R. R. Lindwall (NSW)	39	22.08
1947-48	M. H. Mankad (Ind)	61	26.14	G. Noblet (SAust)	40	19.43
1948-49	I. W. G. Johnson (Vic)	43	24.12	A. K. Walker (NSW)	39	15.31
1949-50	J. B. Iverson (Vic)	46	16.52	J. B. Iverson (Vic)	46	16.52
1950-51	A. E. Bedser (MCC)	51	19.80	R. H. Price (WAust)	24	18.42
1951-52	W. A. Johnston (Vic)	54	20.63	R. R. Lindwall (NSW)	42	17.33
1952-53	H. J. Tayfield (SAf)	70	27.91	G. Noblet (SAust)	55	17.84
1953-54	I. W. G. Johnson (Vic)	45	22.76	R. R. Lindwall (Qld)	22	20.14
1954-55	F. H. Tyson (MCC)	51	19.64	W. P. A. Crawford (NSW)	34	16.03
1955-56	R. Benaud (NSW)	44	21.61	W. P. A. Crawford (NSW)	35	19.80
1956-57	L. F. Kline (Vic)	39	28.21	I. W. Meckiff (Vic)	27	23.67
1957-58	I. W. Quick (Vic)	32	27.25	N. C. O'Neill (NSW)	26	20.42
1958-59	R. Benaud (NSW)	82	19.25	J. C. Laker (MCC)	38	17.23

Season	Leading Wicket-Taker	W	Avge	Top of Averages	W	Avge
1959-60	J. W. Martin (NSW)	45	23.64	R. A. Gaunt (WAust)	24	16.75
1960-61	A. K. Davidson (NSW)	47	20.87	A. K. Davidson (NSW)	47	20.87
1961-62	R. Benaud (NSW)	47	17.97	A. K. Davidson (NSW)	42	13.61
1962-63	I. W. Meckiff (Vic)	58	19.86	I. W. Meckiff (Vic)	58	19.86
1963-64	R. H. D. Sellers (SAust)	54	26.57	P. I. Philpott (NSW)	30	25.73
1964-65	N. J. N. Hawke (SAust)	41	26.29	D. E. Hoare (WAust)	29	22.86
1965-66	N. J. N. Hawke (SAust)	49	25.73	O. J. Morgan (Qld)	25	19.20
1966-67	G. A. R. Lock (WAust)	51	21.29	R. C. Bitmead (Vic)	33	19.66
1967-68	A. N. Connolly (Vic)	60	20.18	L. C. Mayne (WAust)	20	15.10
1968-69	G. D. McKenzie (WAust)	60	27.66	P. J. Allan (Qld)	46	16.37
1969-70	A. L. Thomson (Vic)	55	18.74	A. L. Thomson (Vic)	55	18.74
1970-71	A. L. Thomson (Vic)	51	30.09	J. R. Hammond (SAust)	34	20.26
1971-72	A. A. Mallett (SAust)	54	19.64	A. A. Mallett (SAust)	54	19.64
1972-73	A. A. Mallett (SAust)	62	19.09	G. D. Watson (WAust)	20	18.40
1973-74	G. Dymock (Qld)	51	19.88	R. J. Bright (Vic)	32	19.66
1974-75 {	J. R. Thomson (Qld)	62	19.37	J. R. Thomson (Qld)	62	19.37
	D. K. Lillee (WAust)	62	25.14			
1975-76 {	J. R. Thomson (Qld)	62	23.75	W. Prior (SAust)	43	19.67
	D. K. Lillee (WAust)	62	24.03			
1976-77	D. K. Lillee (WAust)	70	19.54	J. R. Thomson (Qld)	27	14.00
1977-78	D. K. Lillee (WAust)	57	21.86	I. J. Brayshaw (WAust)	35	18.03
1978-79	R. M. Hogg (SAust)	76	16.43	P. H. Carlson (Qld)	31	15.90
1979-80	A. A. Mallett (SAust)	53	28.30	J. Garner (WI)	32	20.03
1980-81	D. K. Lillee (WAust)	69	21.18	L. S. Pascoe (NSW)	63	19.52
1981-82	B. Yardley (WAust)	49	22.55	J. Garner (WI)	23	16.17
1982-83	G. F. Lawson (NSW)	65	21.04	C. G. Rackemann (Qld)	35	15.80
1983-84	D. K. Lillee (WAust)	59	25.64	C. G. Rackemann (Qld)	28	18.68
1984-85	R. G. Holland (NSW)	59	25.80	Imran Khan (Pak)	28	19.14
1985-86	R. G. Holland (NSW)	48	32.40	R. J. Hadlee (NZ)	37	14.51
1986-87	C. J. McDermott (Qld)	58	22.34	G. C. Small (England)	33	18.97
1987-88	C. D. Matthews (WAust)	57	22.40	G. F. Lawson (NSW)	42	18.86
1988-89	M. R. Whitney (NSW)	58	23.62	T. M. Alderman (WAust)	48	20.94
1989-90	C. G. Rackemann (Qld)	50	21.48	C. D. Matthews (WAust)	42	19.19
1990-91	C. J. McDermott (Qld)	67	19.46	A. I. C. Dodemaide (Vic)	20	12.25
1991-92	C. J. McDermott (Qld)	62	20.80	D. A. Freedman (NSW)	28	18.59
1992-93	W. J. Holdsworth (NSW)	53	25.96	C. E. L. Ambrose (WI)	38	18.13
1993-94	S. K. Warne (Vic)	63	19.92	S. K. Warne (Vic)	63	19.92
1994-95	C. G. Rackemann (Qld)	52	23.60	S. K. Warne (Vic)	40	20.35
1995-96	M. S. Kasprowicz (Qld)	64	20.47	A. M. Stuart (NSW)	25	13.40
1996-97	M. S. Kasprowicz (Qld)	48	25.54	J. C. Scuderi (SAust)	23	17.34
1997-98	C. R. Miller (Tas)	70	24.99	D. W. Fleming (Vic)	39	18.08
1998-99	D. J. Saker (Vic)	45	23.31	A. C. Dale (Qld)	31	17.10
1999-00	A. J. Bichel (Qld)	60	20.12	M. S. Kasprowicz (Qld)	49	14.41
2000-01 {	A. J. Bichel (Qld)	49	23.35	J. H. Dawes (Qld)	49	20.47
	J. H. Dawes (Qld)	49	20.47			
2001-02	M. S. Kasprowicz (Qld)	51	24.29	M. W. H. Inness (Vic)	31	19.26

BEST BOWLING AVERAGE IN AN AUSTRALIAN SEASON
(Minimum 30 wickets)

		M	B	Mdns	R	W	BB	5Wi	10W/m	Avge
C. T. B. Turner (NSW)	1886-87	7	2,145	273	538	70	8/32	8	3	7.68
W. Attewell (Eng)	1887-88	9	3,086	425	590	54	7/15	4	2	10.92
E. Evans (NSW)	1880-81	4	1,749	251	360	32	5/34	5	1	11.25
G. E. Palmer (Vic)	1882-83	7	1,772	201	588	51	7/65	5	2	11.53
T. Emmett (Eng)	1878-79	5	1,933	255	521	44	8/47	6	2	11.84
G. A. Lohmann (Eng)	1887-88	8	2,667	364	755	63	7/43	7	2	11.98
W. J. O'Reilly (NSW)	1937-38	11	2,487	91	784	64	9/41	6	2	12.25
C. T. B. Turner (NSW)	1893-94	3	940	35	369	30	6/51	5	2	12.30

		M	B	Mdns	R	W	BB	5W/i	10W/m	Avge
W. J. O'Reilly (NSW)	1940-41	8	1,838	48	684	55	6/60	5	0	12.43
C. Kelleway (NSW)	1913-14	7	1,498	76	571	45	7/35	3	1	12.69
W. Attewell (Eng)	1891-92	8	2,858	241	573	44	6/34	4	1	13.02
J. Briggs (Eng))	1891-92	8	1,212	71	420	32	6/49	4	1	13.13
A. Cotter (NSW)	1903-04	5	740	18	404	30	6/40	2	0	13.47
C. T. B. Turner (NSW)	1887-88	12	4,267	473	1,441	106	8/39	12	5	13.59
A. K. Davidson (NSW)	1961-62	9	1,696	52	572	42	7/31	2	0	13.61
H. Ironmonger (Vic)	1930-31	10	3,037	112	972	68	8/31	7	4	14.29
W. J. O'Reilly (NSW)	1945-46	6	1,257	20	474	33	6/43	1	0	14.36
M. S. Kasprowicz (Qld)	1999-00	8	1,485	69	706	49	5/32	4	1	14.41
R. J. Hadlee (NZ)	1985-86	5	1,449	65	537	37	9/52	5	2	14.51
J. Briggs (Eng)	1887-88	8	2,263	215	436	30	6/40	2	1	14.53
J. J. Ferris (NSW)	1886-87	7	1,967	224	689	47	5/28	3	0	14.66
H. V. Hordern (NSW)	1910-11	8	1,448	29	860	58	7/31	6	2	14.83
T. R. McKibbin (NSW)	1896-97	4	1,381	46	655	44	8/74	5	2	14.89

AUSTRALIANS WITH 400 WICKETS IN FIRST-CLASS CAREER

		M	R	W	BB	5W/i	10W/m	Avge
A. E. Trott	1892-93 – 1911	375	35,317	1,674	10/42	131	41	21.09
F. A. Tarrant	1898-99 – 1936-37	329	26,391	1,506	10/90	133	38	17.52
C. V. Grimmett	1911-12 – 1940-41	248	31,740	1,424	10/37	127	33	22.28
E. A. McDonald	1909-10 – 1935	281	28,966	1,395	8/41	119	31	20.76
G. E. Tribe	1945-46 – 1959	308	28,321	1,378	9/43	93	23	20.55
G. D. McKenzie	1959-60 – 1975	383	32,868	1,219	8/71	49	5	26.96
J. E. Walsh	1936-37 – 1956	296	29,226	1,190	9/101	98	26	24.56
S. M. J. Woods	1886 – 1910	401	21,653	1,040	10/69	77	21	20.82
G. Giffen	1877-78 – 1903-04	251	21,782	1,023	10/66	95	30	21.29
B. Dooland	1945-46 – 1957-58	214	22,332	1,016	8/20	84	23	21.98
C. T. B. Turner	1882-83 – 1909-10	155	14,147	993	9/15	102	35	14.24
V. E. Jackson	1936-37 – 1958	354	23,874	965	8/43	43	6	24.73
T. M. Alderman	1974-75 – 1992-93	245	22,701	956	8/46	53	8	23.74
R. Benaud	1948-49 – 1967-68	259	23,370	945	7/18	56	9	24.73
H. Trumble	1887-88 – 1903-04	344	17,134	929	9/39	69	25	18.44
D. K. Lillee	1969-70 – 1988	198	20,696	882	8/29	50	13	23.46
F. R. Spofforth	1874-75 – 1897	155	12,759	853	9/18	84	32	14.95
W. W. Armstrong	1898-99 – 1921-22	269	16,406	832	8/47	50	5	19.71
J. J. Ferris	1886-87 – 1897-98	198	14,260	813	8/41	63	11	17.53
S. K. Warne	1990-91 – 2001-02	192	21,350	803	8/71	38	5	26.59
R. R. Lindwall	1941-42 – 1961-62	228	16,956	794	7/20	34	2	21.35
A. A. Mailey	1912-13 – 1930-31	158	18,778	779	10/66	61	16	24.10
W. J. O'Reilly	1927-28 – 1945-46	135	12,850	774	9/38	63	17	16.60
W. E. Alley	1945-46 – 1968	400	17,421	768	8/65	30	1	22.68
J. A. Cuffe	1902-03 – 1914	221	18,798	738	9/38	33	7	25.47
A. A. Mallett	1967-68 – 1980-81	183	18,208	693	8/59	33	5	26.27
C. J. McDermott	1983-84 – 1995-96	174	19,025	677	8/44	37	4	28.10
A. N. Connolly	1959-60 – 1970-71	201	17,974	676	9/67	25	4	26.58
J. R. Thomson	1972-73 – 1985-86	187	17,864	675	7/27	28	3	26.46
A. K. Davidson	1949-50 – 1962-63	193	14,048	672	7/31	33	2	20.90
G. F. Lawson	1977-78 – 1991-92	191	16,564	666	8/112	28	2	24.87
E. Jones	1892-93 – 1907-08	144	14,638	641	8/39	47	9	22.83
G. D. McGrath	1992-93 – 2001-02	143	13,308	639	8/38	36	7	20.83
M. A. Noble	1893-94 – 1919-20	248	14,445	625	8/48	33	7	23.11
M. S. Kasprowicz	1989-90 – 2001-02	161	16,890	624	7/36	34	3	27.07
I. W. G. Johnson	1935-36 – 1956-57	189	14,423	619	7/42	27	4	23.30
C. G. Rackemann	1979-80 – 1995-96	167	16,629	616	8/84	22	3	26.99
C. L. McCool	1939-40 – 1960	251	16,542	602	8/74	34	2	27.47
L. O. Fleetwood-Smith	1931-32 – 1939-40	112	13,519	597	9/36	57	18	22.64
G. E. Palmer	1878-79 – 1896-97	133	10,520	594	8/48	54	16	17.71
M. G. Hughes	1981-82 – 1994-95	165	17,249	593	8/87	21	3	29.09
W. A. Johnston	1945-46 – 1954-55	142	12,936	554	8/52	29	6	23.35

		M	R	W	BB	5Wi	10W/m	Avge
J. V. Saunders	1899-00 – 1913-14	107	12,064	553	8/106	48	9	21.81
P. R. Reiffel	1987-88 – 2001-02	167	14,392	545	6/57	16	2	26.41
A. I. C. Dodemaide	1983-84 – 1997-98	184	17,096	534	6/58	17	0	32.01
W. P. Howell	1894-95 – 1905-06	141	11,157	520	10/28	30	5	21.45
G. R. J. Matthews	1982-83 – 1997-98	190	16,413	516	8/52	22	5	31.81
J. S. Manning	1951-52 – 1960	146	11,662	513	8/43	25	4	22.73
J. M. Gregory	1919 – 1928-29	129	10,580	504	9/32	33	8	20.99
M. H. N. Walker	1968-69 – 1981-82	135	13,209	499	8/143	21	0	26.47
K. R. Miller	1937-38 – 1959	226	11,087	497	7/12	16	1	22.30
W. J. Whitty	1907-08 – 1925-26	119	11,488	491	8/27	26	4	23.39
K. J. O'Keeffe	1968-69 – 1979-80	169	13,382	476	7/38	24	5	28.11
R. J. Bright	1972-73 – 1987-88	184	15,114	471	7/87	24	2	32.08
H. Ironmonger	1909-10 – 1935-36	96	9,980	464	8/31	36	10	21.50
N. J. N. Hawke	1959-60 – 1970-71	145	12,088	458	8/61	23	5	26.39
D. T. Ring	1938-39 – 1953	129	12,847	451	7/88	21	2	28.48
J. Angel	1991-92 – 2001-02	108	10,920	449	6/52	15	1	24.32
C. R. Miller	1985-86 – 2001-02	126	13,814	446	7/49	16	3	30.97
T. W. Garrett	1876-77 – 1897-98	160	8,353	445	7/38	29	5	18.77
J. W. Martin	1956-57 – 1967-68	135	13,872	445	8/97	17	1	31.17
A. Cotter	1901-02 – 1913-14	113	10,730	442	7/15	31	4	24.27
T. B. A. May	1984-85 – 1995-96	142	15,721	439	7/93	19	2	35.81
B. P. Julian	1989-90 – 2000-01	138	13,295	435	7/39	21	2	30.56
J. W. Gleeson	1966-67 – 1974-75	116	10,729	430	7/52	22	2	24.95
G. Dymock	1971-72 – 1981-82	126	11,438	425	6/67	13	1	26.91
W. E. Midwinter	1874-75 – 1886-87	160	7,298	419	7/27	27	3	17.41
C. G. Macartney	1905-06 – 1935-36	249	8,781	419	7/58	17	1	20.95
M. R. Whitney	1980-81 – 1994-95	118	11,023	412	7/27	19	1	26.75
A. J. Bichel	1992-93 – 2002	96	9,864	406	9/93	21	4	24.30
F. J. Laver	1891-92 – 1913-14	163	9,989	404	8/31	19	5	24.72

MOST BALLS BOWLED IN AN INNINGS

Balls	M	R	W		
571	36	155	3	T. R. Veivers, Australia v England at Manchester	1964
522	12	309	5	G. Giffen, South Australia v A. E. Stoddart's XI at Adelaide	1894-95
522	11	298	1	L. O'B. Fleetwood-Smith, Australia v England at The Oval	1938
512	0	362	4	A. A. Mailey, New South Wales v Victoria at Melbourne	1926-27
510	26	178	5	W. J. O'Reilly, Australia v England at The Oval	1938
501	35	150	6	G. Giffen, South Australia v New South Wales at Adelaide	1890-91

MOST BALLS BOWLED IN A MATCH

Balls	M	R	W		
848	14	394	10	C. V. Grimmett, South Australia v New South Wales at Sydney	1925-26
749	37	256	13	J. C. White, England v Australia at Adelaide	1928-29
748	22	255	10	D. D. Blackie, Victoria v South Australia at Adelaide	1926-27
736	16	267	9	C. V. Grimmett, South Australia v Victoria at Adelaide	1924-25
725	58	152	11	R. W. McLeod, Victoria v New South Wales at Melbourne	1892-93
712	19	228	11	M. W. Tate, England v Australia at Sydney	1924-25
708	42	239	8	G. Giffen, Australia v England at Sydney	1894-95

MOST RUNS CONCEDED IN A MATCH

Runs			
394	(4/192, 6/202)	C. V. Grimmett, South Australia v New South Wales at Sydney	1925-26
362	(4/362)	A. A. Mailey, New South Wales v Victoria at Melbourne	1926-27
345	(3/190, 0/155)	J. D. Scott, South Australia v New South Wales at Sydney	1925-26
326	(6/134, 5/192)	N. L. Williams, South Australia v Victoria at Adelaide	1928-29
322	(5/309, 0/13)	G. Giffen, South Australia v A. E. Stoddart's XI at Adelaide	1894-95
308	(4/129, 3/179)	A. A. Mailey, Australia v England at Sydney	1924-25
302	(5/160, 5/142)	A. A. Mailey, Australia v England at Adelaide	1920-21

ALL-ROUND RECORDS

100 RUNS IN AN INNINGS AND TEN WICKETS IN A MATCH

R. G. Barlow	101	10/48	North of England v Australians at Nottingham	1884
G. Giffen	166	14/125	South Australia v Victoria at Adelaide	1887-88
G. Giffen	135	13/159	South Australia v Victoria at Melbourne	1888-89
G. Giffen	237	12/192	South Australia v Victoria at Melbourne	1890-91
G. Giffen	271	16/165	South Australia v Victoria at Adelaide	1891-92
G. Giffen	120	12/150	South Australia v New South Wales at Sydney	1891-92
G. Giffen	181	11/235	South Australia v Victoria at Adelaide	1892-93
W. W. Armstrong	126*	10/52	Australians v New Zealanders at Christchurch	1904-05
P. H. Carlson	102*	10/73	Queensland v New South Wales at Brisbane	1978-79
J. C. Scuderi	110	10/165	South Australia v New South Wales at Adelaide	1991-92

500 RUNS AND 50 WICKETS IN AN AUSTRALIAN SEASON

		M	R	Avge	W	Avge
G. Giffen (South Australia)	1891-92	6	509	50.90	50	17.30
G. Giffen (South Australia)	1894-95	11	902	50.11	93	22.55
L. C. Braund (MCC)	1907-08	16	783	35.59	50	32.88
J. N. Crawford (MCC)	1907-08	16	610	26.52	66	25.20
F. R. Foster (MCC)	1911-12	13	641	35.61	62	20.19
M. H. Mankad (Indians)	1947-48	13	889	38.65	61	26.15
G. S. Sobers (South Australia)	1962-63	10	1,001	52.68	51	26.56
G. S. Sobers (South Australia)	1963-64	9	1,128	80.57	51	28.25
G. R. J. Matthews (NSW)	1991-92	12	603	40.20	52	21.46
G. R. J. Matthews (NSW)	1992-93	13	625	36.76	51	28.92

10,000 RUNS AND 500 WICKETS IN A CAREER

	M	R	Avge	W	Avge
W. E. Alley	400	19,612	31.88	768	22.68
W. W. Armstrong	269	16,158	46.83	832	19.71
R. Benaud	259	11,719	36.50	945	23.74
G. Giffen	251	11,758	29.54	1,023	21.29
V. E. Jackson	354	15,698	28.43	965	24.73
C. L. McCool	251	12,420	32.85	602	27.47
M. A. Noble	248	13,975	40.74	625	23.11
F. A. Tarrant	326	17,857	36.37	1,489	17.66
G. E. Tribe	308	10,177	27.34	1,378	20.55
A. E. Trott	375	10,696	19.48	1,674	21.09

WICKET-KEEPING RECORDS

MOST DISMISSALS IN AN INNINGS

8	(all ct)	A. T. W. Grout, Queensland v Western Australia at Brisbane	1959-60
8	(6ct, 2st)	T. J. Zoehrer, Australians v Surrey at The Oval	1993
8	(7ct, 1st)	D. S. Berry, Victoria v South Australia at Melbourne	1996-97
7	(3ct, 4st)	D. Tallon, Queensland v Victoria at Brisbane	1938-39
7	(all ct)	R. A. Saggers, New South Wales v Combined XI at Brisbane	1940-41
7	(6ct, 1st)	H. B. Taber, New South Wales v South Australia at Adelaide	1968-69
7	(all ct)	J. A. Maclean, Queensland v Victoria at Melbourne	1977-78
7	(6ct, 1st)	R. B. Phillips, Queensland v New Zealanders at Brisbane	1982-83
7	(all ct)	J. M. Holyman, Tasmania v Western Australia at Hobart (Bel)	1990-91
7	(all ct)	A. C. Gilchrist, Western Australia v South Australia at Perth	1995-96
7	(all ct)	R. D. Jacobs, West Indies v Australia at Melbourne	2000-01

MOST DISMISSALS IN A MATCH

12	(9ct, 3st)	D. Tallon, Queensland v New South Wales at Sydney	1938-39
12	(9ct, 3st)	H. B. Taber, New South Wales v South Australia at Adelaide	1968-69
11	(all ct)	R. W. Marsh, Western Australia v Victoria at Perth	1975-76
11	(all ct)	T. J. Nielsen, South Australia v Western Australia at Perth	1990-91
11	(10ct, 1st)	I. A. Healy, Australians v N. Transvaal at Verwoerdburg	1993-94
11	(all ct)	D. S. Berry, Victoria v Pakistanis at Melbourne	1995-96
11	(10ct, 1st)	W. A. Seccombe, Queensland v Western Australia at Brisbane	1995-96
11	(10ct, 1st)	D. S. Berry, Victoria v South Australia at Melbourne	1996-97
10	(all ct)	A. C. Gilchrist, Australia v New Zealand at Hamilton	1999-00
10	(9ct, 1st)	R. A. Saggers, New South Wales v Combined XI at Brisbane	1940-41
10	(7ct, 3st)	B. N. Jarman, South Australia v New South Wales at Adelaide	1961-62
10	(9ct, 1st)	R. C. Jordan, Victoria v South Australia at Melbourne	1970-71
10	(all ct)	R. W. Marsh, Western Australia v South Australia at Perth	1976-77
10	(all ct)	S. J. Rixon, Australian XI v South Africa at Johannesburg	1985-86
10	(all ct)	S. J. Rixon, Australian XI v South Africa at Johannesburg	1986-87
10	(7ct, 3st)	A. C. Gilchrist, Young Australia v TCCB XI at Birmingham	1995
10	(all ct)	P. J. Roach, Victoria v South Australia at Melbourne	1995-96
10	(all ct)	A. C. Gilchrist, Western Australia v Victoria at Perth	1997-98
10	(all ct)	A. C. Gilchrist, Australia v New Zealand at Hamilton	1999-00

MOST DISMISSALS IN AN AUSTRALIAN SEASON

Total	Ct	St	M		
67	63	4	15	R. W. Marsh (Western Australia)	1975-76
67	64	3	13	W. A. Seccombe (Queensland)	1999-00
64	58	6	14	R. W. Marsh (Western Australia)	1974-75
62	58	4	12	A. C. Gilchrist (Western Australia)	1995-96
62	60	2	12	A. C. Gilchrist (Western Australia)	1996-97
61	59	2	14	R. W. Marsh (Western Australia)	1980-81
61	61	0	13	R. W. Marsh (Western Australia)	1982-83
59	54	5	13	R. W. Marsh (Western Australia)	1983-84
59	57	2	9	W. A. Seccombe (Queensland)	1995-96
58	57	1	11	W. A. Seccombe (Queensland)	2000-01
57	53	4	13	K. J. Wright (Western Australia)	1978-79
56	55	1	12	R. B. Phillips (Queensland)	1984-85
55	55	0	11	A. C. Gilchrist (Western Australia)	1994-95
54	52	2	13	P. A. Emery (New South Wales)	1992-93
54	52	2	11	D. S. Berry (Victoria)	1999-00
53	53	0	11	R. W. Marsh (Western Australia)	1976-77

AUSTRALIANS WITH 300 DISMISSALS IN A CAREER

	Career	M	Ct	St	Total
R. W. Marsh	1968-69 – 1983-84	241	788	66	854
I. A. Healy	1986-87 – 1999-00	231	698	69	767
W. A. S. Oldfield	1919 – 1937-38	238	396	262	658
A. T. W. Grout	1946-47 – 1965-55	178	471	114	585
B. N. Jarman	1955-56 – 1968-69	186	426	129	555
D. S. Berry	1989-90 – 2001-02	138	500	45	545
A. C. Gilchrist	1992-93 – 2001-02	118	474	28	502
S. J. Rixon	1974-75 – 1987-88	150	395	64	459
T. J. Zoehrer	1980-81 – 1993-94	144	411	38	449
J. M. Blackham	1874-75 – 1894-95	250	259	181	440
D. Tallon	1933-34 – 1953-54	150	302	131	433
W. A. Seccombe	1992-93 – 2001-02	85	385	16	401
H. B. Taber	1964-65 – 1973-74	125	341	50	391
P. A. Emery	1987-88 – 1998-99	121	337	47	384

	Career	M	Ct	St	Total
J. A. Maclean	1968-69 – 1978-79	106	352	29	381
G. R. A. Langley	1945-46 – 1956-57	120	291	77	368
B. A. Barnett	1929-30 – 1961	173	216	142	358
J. J. Kelly	1894-95 – 1906-07	180	243	112	355
R. D. Robinson	1971-72 – 1981-82	97	289	40	329
C. W. Walker	1928-29 – 1940-41	109	171	149	320
T. J. Nielsen	1990-91 – 1998-99	101	284	32	315

FIELDING RECORDS

MOST CATCHES IN AN INNINGS

6   J. F. Sheppard   Queensland v New South Wales at Brisbane 1914-15

Note: There are 13 instances of 5 catches in an innings.

MOST CATCHES IN A MATCH

7	J. A. Atkinson	Tasmania v Victoria at Melbourne	1928-29
7	E. W. Freeman	South Australia v Western Australia at Adelaide	1971-72
7	G. S. Chappell	Australia v England at Perth	1974-75
7	M. A. Taylor	New South Wales v Victoria at Melbourne	1995-96

Note: There are 15 instances of 6 catches in a match.

MOST CATCHES IN AN AUSTRALIAN SEASON

Ct	M		
27	14	I. M. Chappell (South Australia)	1968-69
26	13	G. B. Hole (South Australia)	1952-53
26	13	M. A. Taylor (New South Wales)	1997-98
25	16	L. C. Braund (MCC)	1907-08
25	14	M. A. Taylor (New South Wales)	1991-92
24	11	L. C. Braund (A. C. MacLaren's XI)	1901-02
24	12	J. M. Gregory (New South Wales)	1920-21
24	15	R. B. Simpson (Western Australia)	1960-61
24	11	R. B. Simpson (New South Wales)	1967-68
24	14	I. M. Chappell (South Australia)	1974-75
24	14	G. S. Chappell (Queensland)	1974-75
24	14	G. S. Chappell (Queensland)	1980-81
24	13	S. R. Waugh (New South Wales)	1986-87
24	13	M. R. J. Veletta (Western Australia)	1987-88
24	11	M. A. Taylor (New South Wales)	1995-96

AUSTRALIANS WITH 200 CATCHES IN A CAREER

	Career	M	Ct
K. J. Grieves	1945-46 – 1964	490	610
A. E. Trott	1892-93 – 1911	375	452
M. E. Waugh	1985-86 – 2001-02	344	413
R. B. Simpson	1952-53 – 1977-78	257	383
A. R. Border	1976-77 – 1995-96	385	379
G. S. Chappell	1966-67 – 1983-84	322	376
M. A. Taylor	1985-86 – 1998-99	253	350
H. Trumble	1887-88 – 1903-04	213	328
I. M. Chappell	1961-62 – 1979-80	263	312
F. A. Tarrant	1898-99 – 1936-37	329	304
T. M. Moody	1985-86 – 2000-01	300	294

	Career	M	Ct
W. E. Alley	1945-46 – 1968	400	293
D. C. Boon	1978-79 – 1999	350	283
S. G. Law	1988-89 – 2002	249	283
S. M. J. Woods	1886 – 1910	401	279
W. W. Armstrong	1898-99 – 1921-22	269	274
K. C. Wessels	1973-74 – 1999-00	316	268
C. L. McCool	1939-40 – 1960	251	262
R. Benaud	1948-49 – 1967-68	259	255
V. E. Jackson	1936-37 – 1958	354	250
R. J. Inverarity	1962-63 – 1984-85	223	250
S. R. Waugh	1984-85 – 2001-02	315	248
G. E. Tribe	1945-46 – 1959	308	242
R. N. Harvey	1946-47 – 1962-63	306	228
V. Y. Richardson	1918-19 – 1937-38	184	213
I. R. Redpath	1961-62 – 1975-76	226	211
J. E. Walsh	1936-37 – 1956	296	209
J. D. Siddons	1984-85 – 1999-00	160	206
G. D. McKenzie	1959-60 – 1975	383	201

TEAM RECORDS

HIGHEST INNINGS TOTALS

1,107	Victoria v New South Wales at Melbourne	1926-27
1,059	Victoria v Tasmania at Melbourne	1922-23
918	New South Wales v South Australia at Sydney	1900-01
7-903 dec.	England v Australia at The Oval	1938
843	Australians v Oxford and Cambridge Universities at Portsmouth	1893
839	New South Wales v Tasmania at Melbourne	1898-99
7-821 dec.	South Australia v Queensland at Adelaide	1939-40
815	New South Wales v Victoria at Sydney	1908-09
807	New South Wales v South Australia at Adelaide	1899-00
805	New South Wales v Victoria at Melbourne	1905-06
803	Non Smokers v Smokers at East Melbourne	1886-87
802	New South Wales v South Australia at Sydney	1920-21
793	Victoria v Queensland at Melbourne	1927-28
786	New South Wales v South Australia at Adelaide	1922-23
775	New South Wales v Victoria at Sydney	1881-82
7-774 dec.	Australians v Gloucestershire at Bristol	1948
770	New South Wales v South Australia at Adelaide	1920-21
769	A. C. MacLaren's XI v New South Wales at Sydney	1901-02
763	New South Wales v Queensland at Brisbane	1906-07
8-761 dec.	New South Wales v Queensland at Sydney	1929-30
8-758 dec.	Australia v West Indies at Kingston	1954-55
8-752 dec.	New South Wales v Otago at Dunedin	1923-24
7-734 dec.	MCC v New South Wales at Sydney	1928-29
6-729 dec.	Australia v England at Lord's	1930
724	Victoria v South Australia at Melbourne	1920-21
721	Australians v Essex at Southend	1948
713	New South Wales v South Australia at Adelaide	1908-09
6-713 dec.	New South Wales v Victoria at Sydney	1928-29
5-708 dec.	Australians v Cambridge University at Cambridge	1921
7-708 dec.	Australians v Hampshire at Southampton	1938
708	New South Wales v Victoria at Sydney	1925-26
705	New South Wales v Victoria at Melbourne	1925-26
701	Australia v England at The Oval	1934

HIGHEST FOURTH-INNINGS TOTALS

To Win

6-506	South Australia v Queensland at Adelaide	1991-92
6-446	New South Wales v South Australia at Adelaide	1926-27
7-435	Victoria v New South Wales at Melbourne	1931-32
7-409	Victoria v South Australia at Adelaide	1924-25
8-409	The Rest v New South Wales at Sydney	1933-34
3-404	Australia v England at Leeds	1948
6-402	Tasmania v Western Australia at Perth	1995-96
4-401	New South Wales v Queensland at Brisbane (Ex)	1928-29
3-401	Tasmania v Victoria at Hobart (Bel)	1997-98
7-392	Western Australia v South Australia at Perth	1992-93
8-391	Victoria v New South Wales at Melbourne	1996-97
4-387	New South Wales v Victoria at Sydney	1918-19
7-387	Victoria v Queensland at Melbourne	1965-66
7-386	South Australia v New Zealanders at Adelaide	1987-88
3-376	Australian XI v England XI at Hobart (Bel)	1998-99
6-373	Queensland v Tasmania at Albion	2000-01
9-371	Derbyshire v Australians at Derby	1997
6-370	Western Australia v New South Wales at Perth	1977-78
5-370	Queensland v South Australia at Brisbane	1984-85
6-369	Victoria v South Australia at Adelaide	1883-84
6-369	Australia v Pakistan at Hobart (Bel)	1999-00
4-367	Western Australia v Tasmania at Hobart (Bel)	1997-98
6-366	Tasmania v South Australia at Adelaide	1993-94

To Tie

9-402 (set 403)	D.G. Bradman's XI v A.L. Hassett's XI at Melbourne	1948-49

To Draw

9-529 (set 579)	Combined XI v South Africans at Perth	1963-64
3-430 (set 447)	New South Wales v South Australia at Sydney	1931-32
9-422 (set 499)	MCC v Victoria at Melbourne	1907-08
9-388 (set 419)	South Australia v Victoria at Melbourne	1977-78
6-385 (set 473)	South Australia v Victoria at Adelaide	1987-88
8-384 (set 435)	Australian XI v West Indians at Perth	1960-61
7-383 (set 461)	Victoria v Queensland at Melbourne	1984-85
7-381 (set 439)	Australia v New Zealand at Perth	2001-02
9-375 (set 389)	New South Wales v MCC at Sydney	1907-08
9-373 (set 387)	Western Australia v Tasmania at Perth	2000-01
5-358 (set 401)	South Australia v New South Wales at Adelaide	1948-49
7-358 (set 419)	Queensland v Western Australia at Perth	1974-75

To Lose

572 (set 593)	New South Wales v South Australia at Sydney	1907-08
518 (set 753)	Victoria v Queensland at Brisbane (Ex)	1926-27
472 (set 552)	New South Wales v Australian XI at Sydney	1905-06
466 (set 553)	New South Wales v West Indians at Sydney	1930-31
456 (set 507)	Queensland v Victoria at Melbourne	1928-29
445 (set 493)	India v Australia at Adelaide	1977-78
442 (set 487)	South Africans v New South Wales at Sydney	1910-11
430 (set 461)	Somerset v Young Australia at Taunton	1995
425 (set 547)	A.L. Hassett's XI v A.R. Morris's XI at Melbourne	1953-54
417 (set 463)	England v Australia at Melbourne	1976-77

LOWEST INNINGS TOTALS

15	Victoria v MCC at Melbourne	1903-04
17	Gloucestershire v Australians at Cheltenham	1896
18	Tasmania v Victoria at Melbourne	1868-69
18	Australians v MCC at Lord's	1896
19	MCC v Australians at Lord's	1878
23	South Australia v Victoria at East Melbourne	1882-83
23	Australians v Yorkshire at Leeds	1902
25	Tasmania v Victoria at Hobart (LRG)	1857-58
26	England XI v Australians at Birmingham	1884
27	Lord Sheffield's XI v Australians at Sheffield Park	1890
27	South Australia v New South Wales at Sydney	1955-56
28	Victoria v New South Wales at Melbourne	1855-56
28	England XI v Australians at Stoke-on-Trent	1888
28	Lancashire v Australians at Liverpool	1896
28	Leicestershire v Australians at Leicester	1899

HIGHEST MATCH AGGREGATES

R	W	Avge		
1,929	39	49.46	New South Wales v South Australia at Sydney	1925-26
1,911	34	56.20	New South Wales v Victoria at Sydney	1908-09
1,801	40	45.02	A. L. Hassett's XI v A. R. Morris's XI at Melbourne	1953-54
1,764	39	45.23	Australia v West Indies at Adelaide	1968-69
1,753	40	43.82	Australia v England at Adelaide	1920-21
1,752	34	51.52	New South Wales v Queensland at Sydney	1926-27
1,744	30	58.13	New South Wales v South Africans at Sydney	1910-11
1,739	40	43.47	New South Wales v A. E. Stoddart's XI at Sydney	1897-98
1,723	31	55.58	England v Australia at Leeds	1948
1,716	40	42.90	New South Wales v South Australia at Sydney	1907-08
1,704	39	43.69	J. Ryder's XI v W. M. Woodfull's XI at Sydney	1929-30

LOWEST MATCH AGGREGATE

(For a completed match)

R	W	Avge		
105	31	3.38	MCC v Australians at Lord's	1878

LARGEST VICTORIES

Largest Victories by Innings and Runs Margin

Inns and 666	Victoria v Tasmania at Melbourne	1922-23
Inns and 656	Victoria v New South Wales at Melbourne	1926-27
Inns and 605	New South Wales v South Australia at Sydney	1900-01
Inns and 579	England v Australia at The Oval	1938
Inns and 572	New South Wales v South Australia at Adelaide	1908-09
Inns and 517	Australians v Nottinghamshire at Nottingham	1921

Largest Victories by Runs Margin

685 runs	New South Wales v Queensland at Sydney	1929-30
675 runs	England v Australia at Brisbane (Ex)	1928-29
638 runs	New South Wales v South Australia at Adelaide	1920-21
571 runs	Victoria v South Australia at Melbourne	1926-27
562 runs	Australia v England at The Oval	1934
550 runs	Victoria v Tasmania at Launceston	1913-14
541 runs	New South Wales v South Australia at Sydney	1925-26
530 runs	Australia v South Africa at Melbourne	1910-11

NARROW VICTORIES

Victory by One Wicket

New South Wales def Victoria at Sydney (*Last Wkt*: 16)	1877-78
Nottinghamshire def Australians at Nottingham (*Last Wkt*: 2)	1880
Canterbury def Tasmania at Christchurch (*Last Wkt*: 8)	1883-84
Australians def Liverpool and Districts at Liverpool (*Last Wkt*: 4)	1884
Australians def Middlesex at Lord's (*Last Wkt*: 8)	1886
Victoria def New South Wales at Sydney (*Last Wkt*: 10)	1900-01
England def Australia at The Oval (*Last Wkt*: 15)	1902
Australians def England XI at Bournemouth (*Last Wkt*: 1)	1905
England def Australia at Melbourne (*Last Wkt*: 54)	1907-08
Australians def Sussex at Hove (*Last Wkt*: 22)	1909
AIF Team def Yorkshire at Sheffield (*Last Wkt*: 54)	1919
South Australia def New South Wales at Adelaide (*Last Wkt*: 5)	1927-28
Queensland def South Australia at Brisbane (Ex) (*Last Wkt*: 3)	1928-29
J. Ryder's XI def W. M. Woodfull's XI at Sydney (*Last Wkt*: 8)	1929-30
South Australia def West Indians at Adelaide (*Last Wkt*: 22)	1930-31
Tasmania def Victoria at Hobart (TCA) (*Last Wkt*: 11)	1935-36
Australians def Madras Presidency at Madras (*Last Wkt*: 77)	1935-36
New South Wales def Queensland at Brisbane (*Last Wkt*: 6)	1936-37
New South Wales def Qld and Victorian XI at Brisbane (*Last Wkt*: 10)	1940-41
New South Wales def Queensland at Sydney (*Last Wkt*: 17)	1949-50
Western Australia def West Indians at Perth (*Last Wkt*: 48)	1951-52
Australia def West Indies at Melbourne (*Last Wkt*: 38)	1951-52
Western Australia def South Australia at Adelaide (*Last Wkt*: 36)	1961-62
Queensland def Victoria at Melbourne (*Last Wkt*: 11)	1968-69
Queensland def Western Australia at Perth (*Last Wkt*: 2)	1968-69
Victoria def New South Wales at Melbourne (*Last Wkt*: 4)	1969-70
South Australia def New South Wales at Sydney (*Last Wkt*: 51)	1971-72
South Australia def Victoria at Adelaide (*Last Wkt*: 12)	1977-78
Victoria def New South Wales at Melbourne (*Last Wkt*: 6)	1979-80
England XI def Western Australia at Perth (*Last Wkt*: 5)	1982-83
New South Wales def Queensland at Sydney (*Last Wkt*: 14)	1984-85
New South Wales def Victoria at Sydney (*Last Wkt*: 2)	1986-87
Victoria def New South Wales at Melbourne (*Last Wkt*: 2)	1993-94
Pakistan def Australia at Karachi (*Last Wkt*: 57)	1994-95
Victoria def Tasmania at Melbourne (*Last Wkt*: 17)	1996-97
Derbyshire def Australians at Derby (*Last Wkt*: 11)	1997
England XI def Queensland at Cairns (*Last Wkt*: 36)	1998-99
West Indies def Australia at Bridgetown (*Last Wkt*: 9)	1998-99

Victory by Five Runs or Less

1	West Indies def Australia at Adelaide	1992-93
2	New South Wales def Queensland at Sydney	1903-04
2	Tasmania def Victoria at Launceston	1911-12
2	Philadelphia def Australians at Mannheim	1912-13
2	Western Australia def Victoria at Perth	1998-99
2	South Australia def Western Australia at Adelaide	1999-00
3	Australia def England at Manchester	1902
3	England def Australia at Melbourne	1982-83
3	Victoria def Queensland at Melbourne	1993-94
5	Western Australia def New South Wales at Fremantle	1906-07
5	Surrey def Australians at The Oval	1909
5	South Africa def Australia at Sydney	1993-94

OTHER VICTORIES

Victory after Following On

A. Shaw's XI (146 and 198) def Victoria (251 and 75) at Melbourne 1881-82
A. Shaw's XI (201 and 264) def Australian XI (294 and 114) at Melbourne 1886-87
Victoria (137 and 178) def New South Wales (240 and 63) at Sydney 1888-89
South Australia (212 and 330) def New South Wales (337 and 148) at Adelaide 1892-93
Kent (127 and 198) def Australians (229 and 60) at Canterbury 1893
Australians (196 and 319) def Cambridge University (290 and 108) at Cambridge 1893
England (325 and 437) def Australia (586 and 166) at Sydney 1894-95
South Australia (304 and 454) def Lord Hawke's XI (553 and 108) at Unley 1902-03
New South Wales (108 and 450) def Queensland (307 and 224) at Brisbane 1965-66
England (174 and 356) def Australia (9 for 401 dec. and 111) at Leeds 1981
India (171 and 7 for 657 dec.) def Australia (445 and 212) at Kolkata 2000-01

TIED MATCHES

Gloucestershire tied with Australians at Bristol 1930
MCC tied with Victoria at Melbourne 1932-33
A. L. Hassett's XI tied with D. G. Bradman's XI at Melbourne 1948-49
Victoria tied with New South Wales at St Kilda 1956-57
West Indies tied with Australia at Brisbane 1960-61
South Australia tied with Queensland at Adelaide 1976-77
New Zealanders tied with Victoria at Melbourne 1982-83
Australia tied with India at Madras 1986-87

MATCHES COMPLETED IN ONE DAY

Australians (41 and 1-12) def MCC (33 and 19) at Lord's . . . . May 27, 1878
Australia (76 and 6-33) def England XI (82 and 26) at Birmingham . . . . May 26, 1884
New South Wales (185 and 1-14) def Auckland (93 and 102) at Auckland . . . . Jan 20, 1894

MOST RUNS BY ONE SIDE IN A MATCH

R	W	Avge		
1,235	20	61.75	New South Wales v South Australia at Sydney	1925-26
1,107	10	110.70	Victoria v New South Wales at Melbourne	1926-27
1,074	20	53.70	New South Wales v South Australia at Adelaide	1920-21
1,059	10	105.90	Victoria v Tasmania at Melbourne	1922-23
1,034	20	51.70	Victoria v South Australia at Melbourne	1920-21
1,028	20	51.50	Australia v England at The Oval	1934
1,013	18	56.27	Australia v West Indies at Sydney	1968-69

LONGEST MATCHES

Eight days
Australia v England at Melbourne 1928-29
Seven days
Australia v England at Sydney 1911-12
Australia v England at Sydney 1924-25
Australia v England at Melbourne 1924-25
Australia v England at Adelaide 1924-25
Australia v England at Melbourne 1928-29
Australia v England at Adelaide . , ... 1928-29

MISCELLANEOUS

FIRST-CLASS TEAMS IN AUSTRALIA

	First Game	M	W	L	D	T
Tasmania	Feb 11 1851	405	61	180	164	0
Victoria	Feb 11 1851	973	374	290	306	3
New South Wales	Mar 26 1856	943	415	269	258	1
English Teams	Mar 1 1862	463	189	120	153	1
Combined Teams/Australian XIs	Dec 26 1872	143	41	44	58	0
Australia	Mar 15 1877	324	172	85	66	1
South Australia	Nov 10 1877	835	240	354	240	1
Western Australia	Mar 17 1893	578	177	178	224	0
Queensland	Apr 3 1893	711	186	267	257	1
New Zealanders	Feb 17 1899	80	11	32	36	1
South Africans	Nov 5 1910	79	20	27	32	0
West Indians	Nov 21 1930	133	43	51	38	1
Indians	Oct 17 1947	61	13	29	19	0
Pakistanis	Nov 27 1964	62	12	24	26	0
World XI	Nov 5 1971	12	5	2	5	0
Sri Lankans	Feb 10 1983	17	1	7	9	0
Zimbweans	Dec 18 1994	2	0	1	1	0
Others		46	14	14	16	2

TOURING TEAMS IN AUSTRALIA

		Captain	First-Class					All Matches				
			M	W	L	D	T	M	W	L	D	T
1861-62	H. H. Stephenson's Team	H. H. Stephenson	1	0	1	0	0	14	6	3	5	0
1863-64	G. Parr's Team	G. Parr	1	0	1	0	0	14	7	2	5	0
1873-74	W. G. Grace's Team	W. G. Grace	0	0	0	0	0	15	10	3	2	0
1876-77	J. Lillywhite's Team	J. Lillywhite	3	1	1	1	0	15	5	4	6	0
1878-79	Lord Harris's Team	Lord Harris	5	2	3	0	0	13	5	3	5	0
1881-82	A. Shaw's Team	A. Shaw	7	3	2	2	0	18	8	3	7	0
1882-83	Hon I. F. W. Bligh's Team	Hon I. F. W. Bligh	7	4	3	0	0	17	9	3	5	0
1884-85	A. Shaw's Team	A. Shrewsbury	8	6	2	0	0	33	16	2	15	0
1886-87	A. Shaw's Team	A. Shrewsbury	10	6	2	2	0	30	12	2	16	0
1887-88	G. F. Vernon's Team	G. F. Vernon	8	6	1	1	0	26	11	1	14	0
	A. Shrewsbury's Team	A. Shrewsbury	7	5	2	0	0	22	14	2	6	0
	Combined England	W. W. Read	1	1	0	0	0	1	1	0	0	0
1891-92	Lord Sheffield's Team	W. G. Grace	8	6	2	0	0	27	12	2	13	0
1894-95	A. E. Stoddart's Team	A. E. Stoddart	12	8	4	0	0	23	9	4	10	0
1897-98	A. E. Stoddart's Team	A. E. Stoddart	12	4	5	3	0	22	6	5	11	0
1898-99	New Zealanders	L. T. Cobcroft	2	0	2	0	0	4	1	2	1	0
1901-02	A. C. MacLaren's Team	A. C. MacLaren	11	5	6	0	0	22	8	6	8	0
1902-03	Lord Hawke's Team	P. F. Warner	3	0	2	1	0	3	0	2	1	0
1903-04	MCC	P. F. Warner	14	9	2	3	0	20	10	2	8	0
1907-08	MCC	A. O. Jones	18	7	4	7	0	19	7	4	8	0
1910-11	South Africans	P. W. Sherwell	15	6	7	2	0	22	12	7	3	0
1911-12	MCC	J. W. H. T. Douglas	14	11	1	2	0	18	12	1	5	0
1913-14	New Zealanders	D. Reese	4	1	2	1	0	9	5	2	2	0
1920-21	MCC	J. W. H. T. Douglas	13	5	6	2	0	22	9	6	7	0
1922-23	MCC	A. C. MacLaren	7	0	3	4	0	8	0	3	5	0
1924-25	MCC	A. E. R. Gilligan	17	7	6	4	0	23	8	6	9	0
1925-26	New Zealanders	W. R. Patrick	4	0	1	3	0	9	3	1	5	0
1927-28	New Zealanders	T. C. Lowry	1	0	1	0	0	1	0	1	0	0
1928-29	MCC	A. P. F. Chapman	17	8	1	8	0	24	10	1	13	0
1929-30	MCC	A. H. H. Gilligan	5	2	2	1	0	5	2	2	1	0
1930-31	West Indians	G. C. Grant	14	4	8	2	0	16	5	8	3	0

			First-Class					All Matches				
		Captain	M	W	L	D	T	M	W	L	D	T
1931-32	South Africans	H. B. Cameron	16	4	6	6	0	18	6	6	6	0
1932-33	MCC	D. R. Jardine	17	10	1	5	1	22	10	1	10	1
1935-36	MCC	E. R. T. Holmes	6	3	1	2	0	6	3	1	2	0
1936-37	MCC	G. O. B. Allen	17	5	5	7	0	25	7	5	13	0
1937-38	New Zealanders	M. L. Page	3	0	3	0	0	3	0	3	0	0
1946-47	MCC	W. R. Hammond	17	1	3	13	0	25	4	3	18	0
1947-48	Indians	L. Amarnath	14	2	7	5	0	20	5	7	8	0
1950-51	MCC	F. R. Brown	16	5	4	7	0	25	7	4	14	0
1951-52	West Indians	J. D. C. Goddard	13	4	8	1	0	15	5	8	2	0
1952-53	South Africans	J. E. Cheetham	16	4	3	9	0	23	7	3	13	0
1953-54	New Zealanders	B. Sutcliffe	3	2	0	1	0	3	2	0	1	0
1954-55	MCC	L. Hutton	17	8	2	7	0	23	13	2	8	0
1958-59	MCC	P. B. H. May	17	4	4	9	0	20	7	4	9	0
1960-61	West Indians	F. M. M. Worrell	14	4	5	4	1	22	10	5	5	2
1961-62	New Zealanders	J. R. Reid	3	0	2	1	0	3	0	2	1	0
1962-63	MCC	E. R. Dexter	15	4	3	8	0	26	12	3	11	0
1963-64	South Africans	T. L. Goddard	14	5	3	6	0	28	16	4	8	0
1964-65	Pakistanis	Hanif Mohammad	4	0	0	4	0	4	0	0	4	0
1965-66	MCC	M. J. K. Smith	15	5	2	8	0	23	13	2	8	0
1967-68	New Zealanders	B. W. Sinclair	4	0	2	2	0	7	2	2	3	0
	Indians	Nawab of Pataudi jr	9	0	6	3	0	15	4	6	5	0
1968-69	West Indians	G. S. Sobers	15	4	5	6	0	23	9	5	9	0
1969-70	New Zealanders	G. T. Dowling	3	0	3	0	0	8	3	0	5	0
1970-71	MCC	R. Illingworth	15	3	1	11	0	25	10	2	13	0
	New Zealanders	G. T. Dowling	1	0	0	1	0	2	0	1	1	0
1971-72	World XI	G. S. Sobers	12	5	2	5	0	16	5	3	8	0
	New Zealanders	G. T. Dowling	0	0	0	0	2	1	1	0	0	0
1972-73	Pakistanis	Intikhab Alam	8	2	5	1	0	13	5	6	2	0
	New Zealanders	B. E. Congdon	1	0	0	1	0	3	2	0	1	0
1973-74	New Zealanders	B. E. Congdon	9	2	5	2	0	13	5	6	2	0
1974-75	MCC	M. H. Denness	15	5	5	5	0	23	8	9	6	0
	New Zealanders	B. E. Congdon	0	0	0	0	0	3	3	0	0	0
1975-76	West Indians	C. H. Lloyd	13	3	6	4	0	21	8	7	6	0
1976-77	Pakistanis	Mushtaq Mohammad	5	1	2	2	0	5	1	2	2	0
	MCC	A. W. Greig	2	0	1	1	0	2	0	1	1	0
1977-78	Indians	B. S. Bedi	11	6	5	0	0	20	12	6	2	0
1978-79	England XI	J. M. Brearley	13	8	2	3	0	26	17	4	5	0
	Pakistanis	Mushtaq Mohammad	4	1	1	2	0	5	2	1	2	0
1979-80	England XI	J. M. Brearley	8	3	3	2	0	21	13	5	3	0
	West Indians	C. H. Lloyd	7	5	1	1	0	20	10	7	3	0
1980-81	New Zealanders	G. P. Howarth	7	1	2	4	0	29	14	9	6	0
	Indians	S. M. Gavaskar	8	2	2	4	0	25	8	11	6	0
1981-82	Pakistanis	Javed Miandad	8	2	2	4	0	21	8	8	5	0
	West Indians	C. H. Lloyd	7	4	1	2	0	24	16	5	3	0
1982-83	England XI	R. G. D. Willis	11	4	3	4	0	23	10	9	4	0
	New Zealanders	G. P. Howarth	2	0	0	1	1	22	13	7	1	1
	Sri Lankans	L. R. D. Mendis	2	0	0	2	0	5	1	1	3	0
1983-84	Pakistanis	Imran Khan	11	3	3	5	0	24	7	11	6	0
	West Indians	C. H. Lloyd	0	0	0	0	0	13	10	2	0	1
1984-85	West Indians	C. H. Lloyd	11	4	2	5	0	33	24	4	5	0
	Sri Lankans	L. R. D. Mendis	1	1	0	0	0	22	11	11	0	0
	England XI	D. I. Gower	0	0	0	0	0	3	0	3	0	0
	Indians	S. M. Gavaskar	0	0	0	0	0	5	5	0	0	0
	Pakistanis	Javed Miandad	0	0	0	0	0	5	3	2	0	0
	New Zealanders	G. P. Howarth	0	0	0	0	0	4	1	2	1	0
1985-86	New Zealanders	J. V. Coney	6	2	1	3	0	19	5	7	7	0
	Indians	Kapil Dev	5	1	0	4	0	19	8	7	4	0
1986-87	England XI	M. W. Gatting	11	5	3	3	0	30	19	7	4	0
	Pakistanis	Imran Khan	0	0	0	0	0	4	2	2	0	0
	West Indians	I. V. A. Richards	1	0	0	1	0	13	4	8	1	0

			First-Class					All Matches			
		Captain	M	W	L	D	T	M	W	L	D	T
1987-88	New Zealanders	J. J. Crowe	6	1	2	3	0	19	8	8	3	0
	Sri Lankans	R. S. Madugalle	3	0	1	2	0	18	6	9	3	0
	England XI	M. W. Gatting	1	0	0	1	0	2	0	1	1	0
1988-89	West Indians	I. V. A. Richards	11	4	2	5	0	23	11	7	5	0
	Tamil Nadu	S. Vasudevan	1	0	1	0	0	3	0	3	0	0
	Pakistanis	Imran Khan	1	0	0	1	0	14	6	7	1	0
	New Zealanders	J. G. Wright	0	0	0	0	0	1	0	1	0	0
	Worcestershire	P. A. Neale	0	0	0	0	0	2	0	2	0	0
1989-90	New Zealanders	J. G. Wright	3	0	0	3	0	4	0	1	3	0
	Sri Lankans	A. Ranatunga	6	0	2	4	0	17	5	9	3	0
	Pakistanis	Imran Khan	6	0	3	3	0	27	6	14	7	0
	Lancashire	D. P. Hughes	0	0	0	0	0	8	3	5	0	0
1990-91	England XI	G. A. Gooch	11	1	5	5	0	28	8	14	6	0
	Wellington	E. B. McSweeney	1	0	1	0	0	4	1	1	2	0
	New Zealanders	M. D. Crowe	0	0	0	0	0	11	4	7	0	0
	Lancashire	G. Fowler	0	0	0	0	0	6	4	2	0	0
1991-92	New Zealanders	M. D. Crowe	0	0	0	0	0	6	4	2	0	0
	Indians	M. Azharuddin	7	1	5	1	0	29	7	19	2	1
	West Indians	R. B. Richardson	1	0	0	1	0	22	12	8	1	1
	Pakistanis	Imran Khan	2	0	0	2	0	14	5	6	3	0
	South Africans	K. C. Wessels	0	0	0	0	0	12	7	3	2	0
	Zimbabweans	D. L. Houghton	0	0	0	0	0	6	1	5	0	0
	Sri Lankans	P. A. de Silva	0	0	0	0	0	7	2	4	1	0
	England XI	G. A. Gooch	0	0	0	0	0	9	6	2	1	0
1992-93	West Indians	R. B. Richardson	8	3	1	4	0	22	13	5	4	0
	Pakistanis	Javed Miandad	1	1	0	0	0	12	5	6	0	1
	England A	M. D. Moxon	4	0	2	2	0	11	4	4	3	0
1993-94	New Zealanders	M. D. Crowe	7	2	3	2	0	16	5	9	2	0
	South Africans	K. C. Wessels	5	1	2	2	0	17	6	9	2	0
	Indians	S. R. Tendulkar	0	0	0	0	0	3	0	3	0	0
1994-95	England XI	M. A. Atherton	11	3	4	4	0	24	9	11	4	0
	Zimbabweans	A. Flower	2	0	1	1	0	19	8	10	1	0
1995-96	Western Province	E. O. Simons	2	0	2	0	0	5	1	3	1	0
	Pakistanis	Rameez Raja	6	1	3	2	0	7	2	3	2	0
	Sri Lankans	A. Ranatunga	5	0	4	1	0	17	5	11	1	0
	West Indians	R. B. Richardson	2	0	0	2	0	14	4	8	2	0
1996-97	England A	A. J. Hollioake	3	2	0	1	0	6	3	1	2	0
	West Indians	C. A. Walsh	8	4	4	0	0	25	12	13	0	0
	Pakistanis	Wasim Akram	1	0	1	0	0	10	6	4	0	0
1997-98	Transvaal	K. R. Rutherford	0	0	0	0	0	7	1	6	0	0
	New Zealanders	S. P. Fleming	6	0	5	1	0	21	5	13	2	1
	South Africans	W. J. Cronje	6	0	1	5	0	20	11	4	5	0
1998-99	England XI	A. J. Stewart	10	2	4	4	0	27	10	13	4	0
	Sri Lankans	A. Ranatunga	0	0	0	0	0	15	5	10	0	0
1999-00	Pakistanis	Wasim Akram	5	1	4	0	0	21	6	15	0	0
	Indians	S. R. Tendulkar	6	1	4	1	0	15	2	12	1	0
2000	South Africans	S. M. Pollock	0	0	0	0	0	3	1	1	0	1
2000-01	South Africans	S. M. Pollock	0	0	0	0	0	3	1	1	0	1
	West Indians	J. C. Adams	8	0	7	1	0	18	2	14	2	0
	Zimbabweans	H. H. Streak	0	0	0	0	0	9	1	8	0	0
2001-02	New Zealanders	S. P. Fleming	5	0	1	4	0	18	6	8	4	0
	South Africans	S. M. Pollock	5	0	3	2	0	14	9	3	2	0
	Pakistanis	Waqar Younis	0	0	0	0	0	4	3	1	0	0

AUSTRALIANS ON TOUR

		Country	Captain	First-Class					All Matches				
				M	W	L	D	T	M	W	L	D	T
1868	Aboriginals	England	C. Lawrence	0	0	0	0	0	47	14	14	19	0
1877-78	Australians	New Zealand	D. W. Gregory	0	0	0	0	0	7	5	1	1	0
1878	Australians	England	D. W. Gregory	15	7	4	4	0	37	18	7	12	0
1878-79	Australians	North America	D. W. Gregory	1	0	0	1	0	6	4	0	2	0
1880	Australians	England	W. L. Murdoch	9	4	2	3	0	37	21	4	12	0
1880-81	Australians	New Zealand	W. L. Murdoch	0	0	0	0	0	10	6	1	3	0
1882	Australians	England	W. L. Murdoch	33	18	4	11	0	38	23	4	11	0
1882-83	Australians	North America	W. L. Murdoch	0	0	0	0	0	2	2	0	0	0
1883-84	Tasmania	New Zealand	J. G. Davies	4	0	3	1	0	7	2	3	2	0
1884	Australians	England	W. L. Murdoch	31	17	7	7	0	32	18	7	7	0
1886	Australians	England	H. J. H. Scott	37	9	7	21	0	39	9	8	22	0
1886-87	Australians	New Zealand	H. J. H. Scott	0	0	0	0	0	5	2	0	3	0
1888	Australians	England	P. S. McDonnell	37	17	13	7	0	40	19	14	7	0
1889-90	NSW	New Zealand	J. Davis	5	4	0	1	0	7	6	0	1	0
1890	Australians	England	W. L. Murdoch	34	10	16	8	0	38	13	16	9	0
1893	Australians	England	J. M. Blackham	31	14	10	7	0	36	18	10	8	0
1893-94	Australians	North America	J. M. Blackham	2	1	1	0	0	6	4	1	1	0
	NSW	New Zealand	J. Davis	7	4	1	2	0	8	4	1	3	0
1895-96	NSW	New Zealand	L. T. Cobcroft	5	3	1	1	0	5	3	1	1	0
1896	Australians	England	G. H. S. Trott	34	20	6	8	0	34	20	6	8	0
1896-97	Australians	North America	G. H. S. Trott	3	2	1	0	0	6	4	1	1	0
	Australians	New Zealand	G. H. S. Trott	0	0	0	0	0	5	3	0	2	0
	Queensland	New Zealand	O. C. Hitchcock	5	3	1	1	0	8	4	1	3	0
1899	Australians	England	J. Darling	35	16	3	16	0	35	16	3	16	0
1902	Australians	England	J. Darling	37	21	2	14	0	39	23	2	14	0
1902-03	Australians	South Africa	J. Darling	4	3	0	1	0	6	3	0	3	0
1904-05	Australians	New Zealand	M. A. Noble	4	3	0	1	0	6	4	0	2	0
1905	Australians	England	J. Darling	35	15	3	17	0	38	16	3	19	0
1909	Australians	England	M. A. Noble	37	11	4	22	0	39	13	4	22	0
1909-10	Australians	New Zealand	W. W. Armstrong	6	5	0	1	0	9	7	0	2	0
1912	Australians	England	E. S. Gregory	36	9	8	19	0	37	9	8	20	0
1912-13	Australians	North America	E. S. Gregory	2	1	1	0	0	7	5	1	1	0
1913-14	NSW	Ceylon	E. F. Waddy	0	0	0	0	0	9	8	1	0	0
	Australians	North America	A. Diamond	5	4	0	1	0	53	49	1	3	0
	Australians	New Zealand	A. Sims	8	6	0	2	0	16	8	0	8	0
1919	AIF Team	England	H. L. Collins	28	12	4	12	0	32	13	4	15	0
1919-20	AIF Team	South Africa	H. L. Collins	8	6	0	2	0	10	8	0	2	0
1920-21	Australians	New Zealand	V. S. Ransford	9	6	0	3	0	15	12	0	3	0
1921	Australians	England	W. W. Armstrong	34	21	2	11	0	39	23	2	14	0
1921-22	Australians	South Africa	H. L. Collins	6	4	0	2	0	6	4	0	2	0
1923-24	NSW	New Zealand	C. G. Macartney	6	5	0	1	0	12	8	0	4	0
1924-25	Victoria	New Zealand	R. E. Mayne	6	1	1	4	0	12	4	1	7	0
1926	Australians	England	H. L. Collins	33	9	1	23	0	40	12	1	27	0
1927-28	Australians	New Zealand	V. Y. Richardson	6	4	0	2	0	13	6	0	7	0
1930	Australians	England	W. M. Woodfull	31	11	1	18	1	33	12	1	19	1
1932-33	Australians	North America	V. Y. Richardson	0	0	0	0	0	51	46	1	4	0
1934	Australians	England	W. M. Woodfull	30	13	1	16	0	34	15	1	18	0
1935-36	Australians	Ceylon	J. Ryder	1	1	0	0	0	1	1	0	0	0
	Australians	India	J. Ryder	16	9	3	4	0	22	10	3	9	0
	Australians	South Africa	V. Y. Richardson	16	13	0	3	0	16	13	0	3	0
1938	Australians	England	D. G. Bradman	29	15	2	12	0	35	20	2	13	0
1945	Aus. Services	England	A. L. Hassett	6	3	2	1	0	48	24	9	15	0
1945-46	Australians	India	A. L. Hassett	8	1	2	5	0	9	1	2	6	0
	Australians	Ceylon	A. L. Hassett	1	1	0	0	0	1	1	0	0	0
	Australians	New Zealand	W. A. Brown	5	5	0	0	0	5	5	0	0	0
1948	Australians	England	D. G. Bradman	31	23	0	8	0	34	25	0	9	0
1949-50	Australians	South Africa	A. L. Hassett	21	14	0	7	0	25	18	0	7	0
	Australians	New Zealand	W. A. Brown	5	3	0	2	0	14	9	0	5	0

	Country	Captain	First-Class					All Matches				
			M	W	L	D	T	M	W	L	D	T
1953	Australians	England	A.L. Hassett	33	16	1	16	0	35	16	1	18	0
1954-55	Australians	West Indies	I.W.G. Johnson	9	5	0	4	0	11	5	0	6	0
1956	Australians	England	I.W.G. Johnson	31	9	3	19	0	35	12	3	20	0
1956-57	Australians	Pakistan	I.W.G. Johnson	1	0	1	0	0	1	0	1	0	0
	Australians	India	I.W.G. Johnson	3	2	0	1	0	3	2	0	1	0
	Australians	New Zealand	I.D. Craig	7	5	0	2	0	12	7	0	5	0
1957-58	Australians	South Africa	I.D. Craig	20	11	0	9	0	22	11	0	11	0
1959-60	Australians	Pakistan	R. Benaud	4	3	0	1	0	4	3	0	1	0
	Australians	India	R. Benaud	7	2	1	4	0	7	2	1	4	0
	Australians	New Zealand	I.D. Craig	6	2	0	4	0	9	4	0	5	0
1961	Australians	England	R. Benaud	32	13	1	18	0	37	14	2	21	0
1964	Australians	England	R.B. Simpson	30	11	3	16	0	36	14	4	18	0
1964-65	Australians	India	R.B. Simpson	3	1	1	1	0	3	1	1	1	0
	Australians	Pakistan	R.B. Simpson	1	0	0	1	0	1	0	0	1	0
	Australians	West Indies	R.B. Simpson	11	3	2	6	0	16	4	3	9	0
1966-67	Australians	South Africa	R.B. Simpson	17	7	5	5	0	24	11	6	7	0
	Australians	New Zealand	L.E. Favell	9	1	2	6	0	10	2	2	6	0
1968	Australians	England	W.M. Lawry	25	8	3	14	0	29	10	3	16	0
1969-70	Australians	Ceylon	W.M. Lawry	1	0	0	1	0	4	1	0	3	0
	Australians	India	W.M. Lawry	10	5	1	4	0	10	5	1	4	0
	Australians	South Africa	W.M. Lawry	12	4	4	4	0	12	4	4	4	0
	Australians	New Zealand	S.C. Trimble	8	2	0	6	0	8	2	0	6	0
1972	Australians	England	I.M. Chappell	26	11	5	10	0	37	14	10	13	0
1972-73	Australians	West Indies	I.M. Chappell	12	7	0	5	0	15	10	0	5	0
1973-74	Australians	New Zealand	I.M. Chappell	7	2	1	4	0	11	6	1	4	0
1974-75	Australians	North America	I.M. Chappell	0	0	0	0	0	5	2	1	2	0
1975	Australians	England	I.M. Chappell	15	8	2	5	0	21	12	4	5	0
1976-77	Australians	New Zealand	G.S. Chappell	6	5	0	1	0	8	5	2	1	0
1977	Australians	England	G.S. Chappell	22	5	4	13	0	31	8	8	15	0
1977-78	Australians	West Indies	R.B. Simpson	11	5	3	3	0	13	6	4	3	0
1979	Australians	England	K.J. Hughes	0	0	0	0	0	6	2	3	1	0
1979-80	Australians	India	K.J. Hughes	11	0	3	8	0	11	0	3	8	0
	Australians	Pakistan	G.S. Chappell	5	0	1	4	0	5	0	1	4	0
1980	Australians	England	G.S. Chappell	5	1	2	2	0	8	1	4	3	0
1980-81	Australians	Sri Lanka	K.J. Hughes	1	0	0	1	0	4	2	1	1	0
1981	Australians	England	K.J. Hughes	17	3	3	11	0	26	7	7	12	0
1981-82	Australians	New Zealand	G.S. Chappell	5	1	1	3	0	11	4	4	3	0
1982-83	Australians	Pakistan	K.J. Hughes	6	0	3	3	0	9	0	5	4	0
	Australians	Zimbabwe	D.M. Wellham	2	1	0	0	0	8	7	1	0	0
	Australians	Sri Lanka	G.S. Chappell	2	1	0	1	0	6	1	2	3	0
1983	Australians	England	K.J. Hughes	0	0	0	0	0	9	3	5	1	0
1983-84	Australians	West Indies	K.J. Hughes	10	1	3	6	0	15	2	6	7	0
1984-85	Australians	India	K.J. Hughes	0	0	0	0	0	6	4	0	2	0
	NSW	New Zealand	D.M. Wellham	0	0	0	0	0	1	1	0	0	0
	Australians	Sharjah	A.R. Border	0	0	0	0	0	2	1	1	0	0
1985	Australians	England	A.R. Border	20	4	3	13	0	29	9	5	15	0
1985-86	Australians	Zimbabwe	R.B. Kerr	2	1	0	1	0	9	3	5	1	0
	Australians	South Africa	K.J. Hughes	10	2	2	6	0	25	10	9	6	0
	Australians	New Zealand	A.R. Border	5	1	1	3	0	11	5	3	3	0
	Australians	Sharjah	R.J. Bright	0	0	0	0	0	1	0	1	0	0
1985-86	NSW	Zimbabwe	G.C. Dyer	2	1	0	1	0	8	5	2	1	0
1986-87	Australians	India	A.R. Border	7	0	0	6	1	13	2	3	7	1
	NSW	New Zealand	D.M. Wellham	0	0	0	0	0	2	1	1	0	0
	Australians	South Africa	K.J. Hughes	12	2	3	7	0	25	8	9	8	0
	SAust	New Zealand	D.W. Hookes	0	0	0	0	0	4	4	0	0	0
	Australians	Sharjah	A.R. Border	0	0	0	0	0	3	0	3	0	0
1987-88	NSW	Zimbabwe	D.M. Wellham	2	0	0	2	0	8	5	1	2	0
	Australians	India	A.R. Border	0	0	0	0	0	7	6	1	0	0
	Australians	Pakistan	A.R. Border	0	0	0	0	0	1	1	0	0	0
	Victoria	New Zealand	D.F. Whatmore	0	0	0	0	0	2	0	2	0	0

		Country	Captain	First-Class					All Matches				
				M	W	L	D	T	M	W	L	D	T
	Queensland	New Zealand	R. B. Kerr	0	0	0	0	0	3	3	0	0	0
1988	Aboriginals	England	J. MacGuire	0	0	0	0	0	27	15	11	1	0
1988-89	Australians	Pakistan	A. R. Border	6	0	1	5	0	7	0	2	5	0
1989	Australians	England	A. R. Border	20	12	1	7	0	31	20	3	7	1
1989-90	WAust	India	G. M. Wood	1	0	0	1	0	4	1	2	1	0
	Australians	India	A. R. Border	0	0	0	0	0	5	2	3	0	0
	Australians	New Zealand	A. R. Border	1	0	1	0	0	6	5	0	1	0
	Australians	Sharjah	A. R. Border	0	0	0	0	0	4	3	1	0	0
1990-91	Australians	West Indies	A. R. Border	10	2	2	6	0	19	10	3	6	0
1991	Victoria	England	S. P. O'Donnell	1	0	0	1	0	4	1	1	2	0
1991-92	Australians	Zimbabwe	M. A. Taylor	2	2	0	0	0	6	5	1	0	0
	Australians	New Zealand	A. R. Border	0	0	0	0	0	2	1	1	0	0
1992-93	Australians	Sri Lanka	A. R. Border	5	1	0	4	0	8	2	2	4	0
	Australians	New Zealand	A. R. Border	4	2	1	1	0	10	5	4	1	0
1993	Australians	England	A. R. Border	21	10	2	9	0	30	18	3	9	0
1993-94	Australians	South Africa	A. R. Border	6	3	1	2	0	16	7	5	4	0
	NSW	New Zealand	P. A. Emery	0	0	0	0	0	1	1	0	0	0
	Australians	Sharjah	M. A. Taylor	0	0	0	0	0	3	2	1	0	0
1994-95	Australians	Sri Lanka	M. A. Taylor	0	0	0	0	0	3	1	2	0	0
	Australians	Pakistan	M. A. Taylor	4	0	1	3	0	10	5	2	3	0
	Australians	New Zealand	M. A. Taylor	0	0	0	0	0	4	3	1	0	0
	Cricket Academy	New Zealand	N. W. Ashley	1	1	0	0	0	6	6	0	0	0
	Australians	West Indies	M. A. Taylor	7	3	1	3	0	16	8	5	3	0
1995	Young Australia	England	S. G. Law	8	5	1	2	0	16	11	3	2	0
	NSW	England	M. A. Taylor	1	0	0	1	0	2	1	0	1	0
1995-96	Tasmania	Zimbabwe	D. C. Boon	2	0	0	2	0	5	3	0	2	0
	Australians	India	M. A. Taylor	0	0	0	0	0	6	5	1	0	0
	Australians	Pakistan	M. A. Taylor	0	0	0	0	0	1	0	1	0	0
1996-97	Australians	Sri Lanka	I. A. Healy	0	0	0	0	0	6	4	2	0	0
	Australians	India	M. A. Taylor	2	0	1	1	0	7	0	6	1	0
	Australians	South Africa	M. A. Taylor	6	5	1	0	0	17	13	4	0	0
1997	Australians	England	M. A. Taylor	16	6	3	6	1	27	11	7	7	2
1997-98	Australians	New Zealand	S. R. Waugh	0	0	0	0	0	4	2	2	0	0
	Australians	India	M. A. Taylor	6	1	2	3	0	6	1	2	3	0
	Australians	Sharjah	S. R. Waugh	0	0	0	0	0	5	4	1	0	0
1998	Australians	Scotland	M. J. Di Venuto	2	0	0	2	0	5	2	0	3	0
	Australians	Ireland	M. J. Di Venuto	1	1	0	0	0	6	5	0	1	0
1998-99	Australians	Pakistan	M. A. Taylor	5	2	0	3	0	9	6	0	3	0
	Australians	Bangladesh	M. A. Taylor	0	0	0	0	0	1	0	1	0	0
	Australians	West Indies	S. R. Waugh	7	4	2	1	0	14	7	5	1	1
	Cricket Academy	Zimbabwe	B. J. Hodge	2	2	0	0	0	7	5	2	0	0
1999	Australians	England	S. R. Waugh	0	0	0	0	0	10	7	2	0	1
1999-00	Australians	North America	A. C. Gilchrist	0	0	0	0	0	5	4	1	0	0
	Australians	Sri Lanka	S. R. Waugh	5	2	1	2	0	10	6	2	2	0
	Australians	Zimbabwe	S. R. Waugh	2	2	0	0	0	5	5	0	0	0
	Australians	New Zealand	S. R. Waugh	5	4	1	0	0	11	8	1	2	0
	Australians	South Africa	S. R. Waugh	0	0	0	0	0	3	2	1	0	0
2000-01	Australians	Kenya	S. R. Waugh	0	0	0	0	0	2	1	1	0	0
	Australians	India	S. R. Waugh	6	1	2	3	0	12	4	5	3	0
2001	Australians	England	S. R. Waugh	11	8	2	1	0	20	13	4	2	1
2001-02	Australians	South Africa	S. R. Waugh	6	3	2	1	0	13	8	2	2	1

FIRST-CLASS GROUNDS

	First Game	Last Game	Games
N.T.C.A. Ground, Launceston, Tasmania	1850-51	1995-96	81
Emerald Hill Cricket Ground, Emerald Hill, Victoria	*1851-52		1
Melbourne Cricket Ground (MCG), Victoria	1855-56	2001-02	598
The Domain, Sydney, New South Wales	*1856-57	1868-69	6
Lower Domain Ground, Hobart, Tasmania	*1857-58		1
Albert Ground, Redfern, New South Wales	*1870-71	1876-77	5
Adelaide Oval, South Australia	1877-78	2001-02	528
Sydney Cricket Ground (SCG), New South Wales	1877-78	2001-02	604
East Melbourne Cricket Ground, Victoria	*1880-81		4
Tasmanian Cricket Association Ground, Hobart, Tasmania	1906-07	1986-87	86
Exhibition Ground, Brisbane, Queensland	**1892-93	1930-31	28
Brisbane Cricket Ground (The Gabba), Queensland	1897-98	2001-02	408
Western Australian Cricket Association Ground, Perth, WAust	1898-99	2001-02	367
Unley Oval, South Australia	1902-03		1
Fremantle Oval, Western Australia	**1905-06	1909-10	5
South Melbourne Cricket Ground (Lakeside Oval), Victoria	*1907-08	1931-32	2
Fitzroy Cricket Ground (Brunswick Street Oval), Victoria	*1925-26		1
Richmond Cricket Ground (Punt Road Oval), Victoria	1932-33	2001-02	6
Carlton Recreation Ground (Princes Park), Victoria	1945-46	1997-98	7
St Kilda Cricket Ground (Junction Oval), Victoria	1945-46	1992-93	28
Kardinia Park, Geelong, Victoria	**1961-62	1981-92	6
Sydney Cricket Ground No 2, New South Wales	*1966-67		1
Devonport Oval, Tasmania	1977-78	1997-98	27
Manuka Oval, Canberra, Australian Capital Territory	1978-79	1998-99	5
Oakes Oval, Lismore, New South Wales	1979-80	1991-92	2
No 1 Sports Ground, Newcastle, New South Wales	1981-82	1997-98	16
Salter Oval, Bundaberg, Queensland	1982-83		1
Showgrounds Oval, Wangaratta, Victoria	1986-87	1996-97	2
Endeavour Park, Townsville, Queensland	1986-87		1
Bellerive Oval, Tasmania	1987-88	2001-02	81
Sale Oval, Victoria	1989-90		1
Lavington Sports Ground, Albury, New South Wales	1989-90	1990-91	2
North Sydney Oval, New South Wales	1990-91	2000-01	3
Eastern Oval, Ballarat, Victoria	1990-91		1
Carrara Sports Ground, Queensland	**1990-91		1
Queen Elizabeth Oval, Bendigo, Victoria	1991-92	1994-95	2
Henzell Park, Caloundra, Queensland	1992-93		1
Southern Cross Reserve, Toowoomba, Queensland	1994-95		1
Newtown Oval, Maryborough, Queensland	1994-95		1
Hurstville Oval, New South Wales	1995-96		1
Harrup Park, Mackay, Queensland	1995-96		1
Bankstown Memorial Oval, New South Wales	1996-97		1
Cazaly's Australian Football Park, Cairns, Queensland	1997-98	1998-99	2
Allan Border Field, Albion, Queensland	1999-00	2000-01	6

* Denotes the ground no longer exists; ** Denotes that the ground is no longer used for cricket.

AUSTRALIAN TEST MATCH RECORDS

BATTING RECORDS

HIGHEST INDIVIDUAL INNINGS

334	D. G. Bradman	v England at Leeds	1930
334*	M. A. Taylor	v Pakistan at Preshawar	1998-99
311	R. B. Simpson	v England at Manchester	1964
307	R. M. Cowper	v England at Melbourne	1965-66
304	D. G. Bradman	v England at Leeds	1934
299*	D. G. Bradman	v South Africa at Adelaide	1931-32
270	D. G. Bradman	v England at Melbourne	1936-37
268	G. N. Yallop	v Pakistan at Melbourne	1983-84
266	W. H. Ponsford	v England at The Oval	1934
254	D. G. Bradman	v England at Lord's	1930
250	K. D. Walters	v New Zealand at Christchurch	1976-77
247*	G. S. Chappell	v New Zealand at Wellington	1973-74
244	D. G. Bradman	v England at The Oval	1934
242	K. D. Walters	v West Indies at Sydney	1968-69
235	G. S. Chappell	v Pakistan at Faisalabad	1979-80
234	D. G. Bradman	v England at Sydney	1946-47
234	S. G. Barnes	v England at Sydney	1946-47
232	D. G. Bradman	v England at The Oval	1930
232	S. J. McCabe	v England at Nottingham	1938
226	D. G. Bradman	v South Africa at Brisbane	1931-32
225	R. B. Simpson	v England at Adelaide	1965-66
223	D. G. Bradman	v West Indies at Brisbane (Ex)	1930-31
223	J. L. Langer	v India at Sydney	1999-00
219	M. A. Taylor	v England at Nottingham	1989
219	M. J. Slater	v Sri Lanka at Perth	1995-96
216	D. M. Jones	v West Indies at Adelaide	1988-89
214*	V. T. Trumper	v South Africa at Adelaide	1910-11
214	G. S. Blewett	v South Africa at Johannesburg (WS)	1996-97
213	K. J. Hughes	v India at Adelaide	1980-81
212	D. G. Bradman	v England at Adelaide	1936-37
211	W. L. Murdoch	v England at The Oval	1884
210	W. M. Lawry	v West Indies at Bridgetown	1964-65
210	D. M. Jones	v India at Chennai (Chepauk)	1986-87
207	K. R. Stackpole	v England at Brisbane	1970-71
206*	W. A. Brown	v England at Lord's	1938
206	A. R. Morris	v England at Adelaide	1950-51
205	R. N. Harvey	v West Indies at Melbourne	1952-53
205	W. M. Lawry	v West Indies at Melbourne	1968-69
205	A. R. Border	v New Zealand at Adelaide	1987-88
204	R. N. Harvey	v West Indies at Kingston	1954-55
204	G. S. Chappell	v India at Sydney	1980-81
204*	A. C. Gilchrist	v South Africa at Johannesburg (WS)	2001-02
203	H. L. Collins	v South Africa at Johannesburg (OW)	1921-22
203	M. L. Hayden	v India at Chennai	2000-01
201	E. S. Gregory	v England at Sydney	1894-95
201*	J. Ryder	v England at Adelaide	1924-25
201	D. G. Bradman	v India at Adelaide	1947-48
201	R. B. Simpson	v West Indies at Bridgetown	1964-65
201	G. S. Chappell	v Pakistan at Brisbane	1981-82
200	D. C. Boon	v New Zealand at Perth	1989-90
200*	A. R. Border	v England at Leeds	1993
200	S. R. Waugh	v West Indies at Kingston	1994-95

HUNDRED ON DEBUT

†C. Bannerman (165*)	v England at Melbourne	1876-77
H. Graham (107)	v England at Lord's	1893
R. A. Duff (104)	v England at Melbourne	1901-02
M. J. Hartigan (116)	v England at Adelaide	1907-08
H. L. Collins (104)	v England at Sydney	1920-21
W. H. Ponsford (110)	v England at Sydney	1924-25
A. Jackson (164)	v England at Adelaide	1928-29
J. W. Burke (101*)	v England at Adelaide	1950-51
K. D. Walters (155)	v England at Brisbane	1965-66
G. S. Chappell (108)	v England at Perth	1970-71
G. J. Cosier (109)	v West Indies at Melbourne	1975-76
D. M. Wellham (103)	v England at The Oval	1981
K. C. Wessels (162)	v England at Brisbane	1982-83
W. B. Phillips (159)	v Pakistan at Perth	1983-84
M. E. Waugh (138)	v England at Adelaide	1990-91
G. S. Blewett (102*)	v England at Adelaide	1994-95

† *Retired hurt*

HUNDRED IN EACH INNINGS OF A MATCH

	1st	*2nd*		
W. Bardsley	136	130	v England at The Oval	1909
A. R. Morris	122	124*	v England at Adelaide	1946-47
D. G. Bradman	132	127*	v India at Melbourne	1947-48
J. Moroney	118	101*	v South Africa at Johannesburg (EP)	1949-50
R. B. Simpson	153	115	v Pakistan at Karachi	1964-65
K. D. Walters	242	103	v West Indies at Sydney	1968-69
I. M. Chappell	145	121	v New Zealand at Wellington	1973-74
G. S. Chappell	247*	133	v New Zealand at Wellington	1973-74
G. S. Chappell	123	109*	v West Indies at Brisbane	1975-76
A. R. Border	150*	153	v Pakistan at Lahore	1979-80
A. R. Border	140	114*	v New Zealand at Christchurch	1985-86
D. M. Jones	116	121*	v Pakistan at Adelaide	1989-90
S. R. Waugh	108	116	v England at Manchester	1997

MOST RUNS IN A SERIES

	T	I	NO	R	HS	100s	Avge	Series
D. G. Bradman	5	7	0	974	334	4	139.14	1930 v England in England
M. A. Taylor	6	11	1	839	219	2	83.90	1989 v England in England
R. N. Harvey	5	9	0	834	205	4	92.66	1952-53 v South Africa in Australia
D. G. Bradman	5	9	0	810	270	3	90.00	1936-37 v England in Australia
D. G. Bradman	5	5	1	806	299*	4	201.50	1931-32 v South Africa in Australia
D. G. Bradman	5	8	0	758	304	2	94.75	1934 v England in England
D. G. Bradman	5	6	2	715	201	4	178.75	1947-48 v India in Australia
G. S. Chappell	6	11	5	702	182*	3	117.00	1975-76 v West Indies in Australia
K. D. Walters	4	6	0	699	242	4	116.50	1968-69 v West Indies in Australia
A. R. Morris	5	9	1	696	196	3	87.00	1948 v England in England
D. G. Bradman	5	8	1	680	234	2	97.14	1946-47 v England in Australia
W. M. Lawry	5	8	0	667	205	3	83.38	1968-69 v West Indies in Australia
V. T. Trumper	5	9	2	661	214*	2	94.43	1910-11 v South Africa in Australia
R. N. Harvey	5	8	3	660	178	4	132.00	1949-50 v South Africa in S. Africa
R. N. Harvey	5	7	1	650	204	3	108.33	1954-55 v West Indies in West Indies
K. R. Stackpole	7	12	0	627	207	2	52.25	1970-71 v England in Australia
M. J. Slater	5	10	0	623	176	3	62.30	1994-95 v England in Australia
G. S. Chappell	6	11	0	608	144	2	55.27	1974-75 v England in Australia
A. R. Border	6	11	2	597	196	2	66.33	1985 v England in England
K. J. Hughes	6	12	2	594	100	1	59.40	1979-80 v India in India

	T	I	NO	R	HS	100s	Avge	Series
W. M. Lawry	5	7	0	592	166	3	84.57	1965-66 v England in Australia
I. R. Redpath ...	6	11	0	575	103	3	52.27	1975-76 v West Indies in Australia
V. T. Trumper ...	5	10	1	574	185*	2	63.77	1903-04 v England in Australia
W. Bardsley	5	9	0	573	132	1	63.67	1910-11 v South Africa in Australia
W. H. Ponsford ..	4	7	1	569	266	2	94.83	1934 v England in England
D. M. Jones	6	9	1	566	157	2	70.75	1989 v England in England
H. L. Collins	5	9	0	557	162	2	61.89	1920-21 v England in Australia
D. C. Boon	5	9	2	556	135	3	79.43	1991-92 v India in Australia
M. T. G. Elliott ..	6	10	0	556	199	2	55.60	1997 v England in England
D. C. Boon	6	10	2	555	164*	2	69.38	1993 v England in England
G. N. Yallop	5	6	0	554	268	2	92.33	1983-84 v Pakistan in Australia
M. E. Waugh	6	10	1	550	137	1	61.11	1993 v England in England
M. L. Hayden ...	3	6	1	549	203	2	109.80	2000-01 v India in India
I. M. Chappell ...	5	8	0	548	165	2	68.50	1968-69 v West Indies in Australia
I. M. Chappell ...	5	9	2	542	109	2	77.43	1972-73 v West Indies in West Indies
J. M. Taylor	5	10	0	541	108	1	54.10	1924-25 v England in Australia
R. B. Simpson ...	5	10	0	539	176	2	53.90	1977-78 v India in Australia
J. Darling	5	8	0	537	178	3	67.13	1897-98 v England in Australia
A. R. Border	6	12	3	533	123*	2	59.22	1981 v England in England
B. C. Booth	4	7	1	531	169	2	88.50	1963-64 v South Africa in Australia
D. C. Boon	5	9	2	530	121	1	75.71	1990-91 v India in Australia
N. C. O'Neill ...	5	10	0	522	181	1	52.20	1960-61 v West Indies in Australia
C. Hill	5	10	0	521	99	0	52.10	1901-02 v England in Australia
A. R. Border	6	12	0	521	162	1	43.42	1979-80 v India in India
A. R. Border	5	10	3	521	100*	1	74.43	1983-84 v West Indies in West Indies
C. C. McDonald ..	5	9	1	519	170	2	64.88	1958-59 v England in Australia
M. A. Taylor	3	5	1	513	334*	1	128.25	1998-99 v Pakistan in Pakistan
W. A. Brown	4	8	1	512	206*	1	73.14	1938 v England in England
D. M. Jones	5	10	1	511	184*	2	56.78	1986-87 v England in Australia
D. G. Bradman ...	5	9	2	508	173*	2	72.57	1948 v England in England
S. R. Waugh	6	8	4	506	177*	2	126.50	1989 v England in England
K. C. Wessels ...	5	9	0	505	173	1	56.11	1984-85 v West Indies in Australia
A. R. Morris	5	8	1	503	155	1	71.86	1946-47 v England in Australia

Most runs in a series against opponents not mentioned above:

S. R. Waugh	3	3	2	362	170	2	362.00	1995-96 v Sri Lanka in Australia
G. S. Chappell ..	3	6	1	449	247*	2	89.30	1973-74 v New Zealand in N. Zealand
S. R. Waugh	1	1	1	151	151*	1	–	1999-00 v Zimbabwe in Zimbabwe

MOST RUNS IN A CALENDAR YEAR

	M	I	NO	R	HS	100s	Avge	Year
M. L. Hayden	14	25	3	1,391	203	5	63.23	2001
R. B. Simpson	14	26	3	1,381	311	3	60.04	1964
D. C. Boon	16	25	5	1,241	164*	4	62.05	1993
M. A. Taylor	11	20	1	1,219	219	4	64.16	1989
K. J. Hughes	15	28	4	1,163	130*	2	48.45	1979
M. A. Taylor	12	22	3	1,112	334*	3	58.53	1998
M. A. Taylor	15	23	2	1,106	170	4	52.67	1993
A. R. Border	11	20	2	1,099	196	4	64.65	1985
D. M. Jones	11	18	3	1,099	216	4	73.27	1989
A. R. Border	14	27	3	1,073	162	3	44.70	1979
G. S. Blewett	15	25	0	1,067	214	2	42.68	1997
C. Hill	12	21	2	1,060	142	2	55.79	1902
W. M. Lawry	14	27	2	1,056	157	2	42.24	1964
M. J. Slater	14	25	2	1,051	169	3	45.70	1999
M. E. Waugh	12	22	6	1,034	153	4	64.63	1998
D. G. Bradman	8	13	4	1,025	201	5	113.89	1948
A. R. Border	11	19	3	1,000	140	5	62.50	1986

MOST RUNS IN A CAREER

		M	I	NO	R	HS	100s	Avge
1	A. R. Border	156	265	44	11,174	205	27	50.56
2	S. R. Waugh	148	233	41	9,600	200	27	50.00
3	M. A. Taylor	104	186	13	7,525	334*	19	43.50
4	D. C. Boon	107	190	20	7,422	200	21	43.66
5	G. S. Chappell	88	151	19	7,110	247*	24	53.86
6	M. E. Waugh	125	205	17	7,949	153*	20	42.28
7	D. G. Bradman	52	80	10	6,996	334	29	99.94
8	R. N. Harvey	79	137	10	6,149	205	21	48.42
9	K. D. Walters	75	125	14	5,357	250	15	48.26
10	I. M. Chappell	76	136	10	5,345	196	14	42.42
11	M. J. Slater	74	131	7	5,312	219	14	42.84
12	W. M. Lawry	68	123	12	5,234	210	13	47.15
13	R. B. Simpson	62	111	7	4,869	311	10	46.82
14	I. R. Redpath	67	120	11	4,737	171	8	43.46
15	K. J. Hughes	70	124	6	4,415	213	9	37.42
16	I. A. Healy	119	182	23	4,356	161*	4	27.40
17	R. W. Marsh	97	150	13	3,633	132	3	26.52
18	D. M. Jones	52	89	11	3,631	216	11	46.55
19	A. R. Morris	46	79	3	3,533	206	12	46.49
20	J. L. Langer	51	85	5	3,516	223	12	43.95
21	R. T. Ponting	56	89	12	3,505	197	10	45.52
22	C. Hill	49	89	2	3,412	191	7	39.22
23	G. M. Wood	59	112	6	3,374	172	9	31.83
24	V. T. Trumper	48	89	8	3,163	214*	8	39.05
25	C. C. McDonald	47	83	4	3,107	170	5	39.33
26	A. L. Hassett	43	69	3	3,073	198*	10	46.56
27	K. R. Miller	55	87	7	2,958	147	7	36.98
28	W. W. Armstrong	50	84	10	2,863	159*	6	38.69
29	G. R. Marsh	50	93	7	2,854	138	4	33.19
30	K. R. Stackpole	44	80	5	2,807	207	7	37.43
31	N. C. O'Neill	42	69	8	2,779	181	6	45.56
32	G. N. Yallop	39	70	3	2,756	268	8	41.13
33	S. J. McCabe	39	62	5	2,748	232	6	48.21
34	G. S. Blewett	46	79	4	2,552	214	4	34.03
35	W. Bardsley	41	66	5	2,469	193*	6	40.48
36	M. L. Hayden	30	52	4	2,354	203	8	49.04
37	W. M. Woodfull	35	54	4	2,300	161	7	46.00
38	P. J. P. Burge	42	68	8	2,290	181	4	38.17
39	E. S. Gregory	58	100	7	2,282	201	4	24.54
40	R. Benaud	63	97	7	2,201	122	3	24.46
41	A. C. Gilchrist	31	44	8	2,160	204*	6	60.00
42	C. G. Macartney	35	55	4	2,131	170	7	41.78
43	W. H. Ponsford	29	48	4	2,122	266	7	48.23
44	S. K. Warne	101	139	13	2,091	99	0	16.60
45	R. M. Cowper	27	46	2	2,061	307	5	46.84
46	M. A. Noble	42	73	7	1,997	133	1	30.26
47	G. R. J. Matthews	33	53	8	1,849	130	4	41.09
48	B. C. Booth	29	48	6	1,773	169	5	42.21
49	K. C. Wessels	24	42	1	1,761	179	4	42.95
50	G. M. Ritchie	30	53	5	1,690	146	3	35.21

HIGHEST CAREER AVERAGES

	T	I	NO	R	HS	100s	Avge
A. E. Trott	3	5	3	205	85*	0	102.50
D. G. Bradman	52	80	10	6,996	334	29	99.94
S. G. Barnes	13	19	2	1,072	234	3	63.06
J. K. Moss	1	2	1	60	38*	0	60.00

	T	I	NO	R	HS	100s	Avge
A. C. Gilchrist	31	44	8	2,160	204*	6	60.00
C. Bannerman	3	6	2	239	165†	1	59.75
G. S. Chappell	88	151	19	7,110	247*	24	53.86
J. Ryder	20	32	5	1,394	201*	3	51.63
A. G. Fairfax	10	12	4	410	65	0	51.25
R. G. Gregory	2	3	0	153	80	0	51.00
A. R. Border	156	265	44	11,174	205	27	50.56
S. R. Waugh	148	233	41	9,600	200	27	50.00
M. L. Hayden	30	52	4	2,354	203	8	49.04
R. N. Harvey	79	137	10	6,149	205	21	48.42
K. D. Walters	75	125	14	5,357	250	15	48.26
W. H. Ponsford	29	48	4	2,122	266	7	48.23
S. J. McCabe	39	62	5	2,748	232	6	48.21
A. Jackson	8	11	1	474	164	1	47.40
W. M. Lawry	68	123	12	5,234	210	13	47.15

† *Bannerman retired hurt*

MOST HUNDREDS

	T	I	100s	Eng	SAf	WI	NZ	Ind	Pak	SL	Zim
D. G. Bradman	52	80	29	19	4	2	0	4	0	0	0
A. R. Border	156	265	27	8	0	3	5	4	6	1	0
S. R. Waugh	148	233	27	9	2	6	2	2	2	3	1
G. S. Chappell	88	151	24	9	0	5	3	1	6	0	0
R. N. Harvey	79	137	21	6	8	3	0	4	0	0	0
D. C. Boon	107	190	21	7	0	3	3	6	1	1	0
M. E. Waugh	125	205	20	6	4	4	1	1	3	1	0
M. A. Taylor	104	186	19	6	2	1	2	2	4	2	0
K. D. Walters	75	125	15	4	0	6	3	1	1	0	0
I. M. Chappell	76	136	14	4	0	5	2	2	1	0	0
M. J. Slater	74	131	14	7	0	1	2	0	3	1	0
W. M. Lawry	68	123	13	7	1	4	0	1	0	0	0
A. R. Morris	46	79	12	8	2	1	0	1	0	0	0
J. L. Langer	51	85	12	2	2	1	3	1	3	0	0
D. M. Jones	52	89	11	3	0	1	0	2	2	3	0
A. L. Hassett	43	69	10	4	3	2	0	1	0	0	0
R. B. Simpson	62	111	10	2	1	1	0	4	2	0	0
R. T. Ponting	56	89	10	2	2	1	1	2	1	1	0

CARRYING BAT THROUGH AN INNINGS

(Figures in brackets show side's total)

J. E. Barrett	67*	(176)	v England at Lord's	1890
W. W. Armstrong	159*	(309)	v South Africa at Johannesburg (OW)	1902-03
W. Bardsley	193*	(383)	v England at Lord's	1926
W. M. Woodfull	30*	(66)†	v England at Brisbane (Ex)	1928-29
W. M. Woodfull	73*	(193)†	v England at Adelaide	1932-33
W. A. Brown	206*	(422)	v England at Lord's	1938
W. M. Lawry	49*	(107)	v India at Delhi	1969-70
W. M. Lawry	60*	(116)†	v England at Sydney	1970-71
I. R. Redpath	159*	(346)	v New Zealand at Auckland	1973-74
D. C. Boon	58*	(103)	v New Zealand at Auckland	1985-86
M. A. Taylor	169*	(350)	v South Africa at Adelaide	1997-98

† *Denotes one or more batsmen absent or retired.*

HIGHEST PARTNERSHIP FOR EACH WICKET

382 for 1st	W. M. Lawry (210)/R. B. Simpson (201)	v West Indies at Bridgetown	1964-65
451 for 2nd	W. H. Ponsford (266)/D. G. Bradman (244)	v England at The Oval	1934
295 for 3rd	C. C. McDonald (127)/R. N. Harvey (204)	v West Indies at Kingston	1954-55
388 for 4th	W. H. Ponsford (181)/D. G. Bradman (304)	v England at Leeds	1934
405 for 5th	S. G. Barnes(234)/D. G. Bradman (234)	v England at Sydney	1946-47
346 for 6th	J. H. W. Fingleton (136) /D. G. Bradman (270)	v England at Melbourne	1936-37
217 for 7th	K. D. Walters (250)/G. J. Gilmour (101)	v New Zealand at Christchurch	1976-77
243 for 8th	M. J. Hartigan (116) /C. Hill (160)	v England at Adelaide	1907-08
154 for 9th	E. S. Gregory (201)/J. M. Blackham (74)	v England at Sydney	1894-95
127 for 10th	J. M. Taylor (108)/A. A. Mailey (46*)	v England at Sydney	1924-25

PARTNERSHIP RECORDS

451 for 2nd	W. H. Ponsford (266)/D. G. Bradman (244)	v England at The Oval	1934
405 for 5th	S. G. Barnes (234)/D. G. Bradman (234)	v England at Sydney	1946-47
388 for 4th	W. H. Ponsford (181)/D. G. Bradman (304)	v England at Leeds	1934
385 for 5th	G. S. Blewett (214)/S. R. Waugh (160)	v SAf at Johannesburg (WS)	1996-97
382 for 1st	W. M. Lawry (210)/R. B. Simpson (201)	v West Indies at Bridgetown	1964-65
346 for 6th	J. H. W. Fingleton (136)/D. G. Bradman (270)	v England at Melbourne	1936-37
336 for 4th	W. M. Lawry (151)/K. D. Walters (242)	v West Indies at Sydney	1968-69
332* for 5th	A. R. Border (200*)/S. R. Waugh (157*)	v England at Leeds	1993
329 for 1st	G. R. Marsh (138)/M. A. Taylor (219)	v England at Nottingham	1989
327 for 5th	J. L. Langer (144)/R. T. Ponting (197)	v Pakistan at Perth	1999-00
317 for 6th	D. R. Martyn (133)/A. C. Gilchrist (204*)	v SAf at Johannesburg (WS)	2001-02
301 for 2nd	A. R. Morris (182)/D. G. Bradman (173*)	v England at Leeds	1948
298 for 2nd	W. M. Lawry (205)/I. M. Chappell (165)	v West Indies at Melbourne	1968-69
295 for 3rd	C. C. McDonald (127)/R. N. Harvey (204)	v West Indies at Kingston	1954-55
281 for 5th	S. R. Waugh (199)/R. T. Ponting (104)	v West Indies at Bridgetown	1998-99
279 for 2nd	M. A. Taylor (334*)/J. L. Langer (116)	v Pakistan at Peshawar	1998-99
277 for 2nd	R. B. McCosker (127)/I. M. Chappell (192)	v England at The Oval	1975
276 for 3rd	D. G. Bradman (187)/A. L. Hassett (128)	v England at Brisbane	1946-47
275 for 2nd	C. C. McDonald (154)/A. L. Hassett (163)	v South Africa at Adelaide	1952-53
274 for 2nd	W. M. Woodfull (161)/D. G. Bradman (167)	v South Africa at Melbourne	1931-32
269 for 1st	M. J. Slater (169)/G. S. Blewett (89)	v Pakistan at Brisbane	1999-00
268 for 5th	M. T. G. Elliott (199)/R. T. Ponting (127)	v England at Leeds	1997
264 for 3rd	I. M. Chappell (145)/G. S. Chappell (247*)	v New Zealand at Wellington	1973-74
260* for 6th	D. M. Jones (118*)/S. R. Waugh (134*)	v Sri Lanka at Hobart	1989-90
260 for 1st	M. A. Taylor (111)/M. J. Slater (152)	v England at Lord's	1993
259 for 2nd	W. B. Phillips (159)/G. N. Yallop (141)	v Pakistan at Perth	1983-84
251 for 4th	G. M. Wood (126)/C. S. Serjeant (124)	v West Indies at Georgetown	1977-78

BOWLING RECORDS

MOST WICKETS IN AN INNINGS

9/121	A. A. Mailey	v England at Melbourne	1920-21
8/31	F. Laver	v England at Manchester	1909
8/38	G. D. McGrath	v England at Lord's	1997
8/43	A. E. Trott	v England at Adelaide	1894-95
8/53	R. A. L. Massie	v England at Lord's	1972
8/59	A. A. Mallett	v Pakistan at Adelaide	1972-73
8/65	H. Trumble	v England at The Oval	1902
8/71	G. D. McKenzie	v West Indies at Melbourne	1968-69
8/71	S. K. Warne	v England at Brisbane	1994-95
8/84	R. A. L. Massie	v England at Lord's	1972
8/87	M. G. Hughes	v West Indies at Perth	1988-89

8/97	C. J. McDermott	v England at Perth	1990-91
8/112	G. F. Lawson	v West Indies at Adelaide	1984-85
8/141	C. J. McDermott	v England at Manchester	1985
8/143	M. H. N. Walker	v England at Melbourne	1974-75

MOST WICKETS IN AN INNINGS ON DEBUT

8/43	A. E. Trott	v England at Adelaide	1894-95
8/53	R. A. L. Massie	v England at Lord's	1972
8/84	R. A. L. Massie	v England at Lord's	1972
7/55	T. K. Kendall	v England at Melbourne	1876-77
6/15	C. T. B. Turner	v England at Sydney	1886-87
6/37	C. V. Grimmett	v England at Sydney	1924-25
6/49	M. A. Noble	v England at Melbourne	1897-98
6/58	A. I. C. Dodemaide	v New Zealand at Melbourne	1987-88
6/74	R. M. Hogg	v England at Brisbane	1978-79
6/78	P. L. Taylor	v England at Sydney	1986-87
6/102	F. A. Ward	v England at Brisbane	1936-37
6/120	W. H. Cooper	v England at Melbourne	1881-82

MOST WICKETS IN A MATCH

16/137	R. A. L. Massie	v England at Lord's	1972
14/90	F. R. Spofforth	v England at The Oval	1882
14/199	C. V. Grimmett	v South Africa at Adelaide	1931-32
13/77	M. A. Noble	v England at Melbourne	1901-02
13/110	F. R. Spofforth	v England at Melbourne	1878-79
13/148	B. A. Reid	v England at Melbourne	1990-91
13/173	C. V. Grimmett	v South Africa at Durban (Kingsmead)	1935-36
13/217	M. G. Hughes	v West Indies at Perth	1988-89
13/236	A. A. Mailey	v England at Melbourne	1920-21
12/87	C. T. B. Turner	v England at Sydney	1887-88

MOST WICKETS IN A MATCH ON DEBUT

16/137	R. A. L. Massie	v England at Lord's	1972
11/82	C. V. Grimmett	v England at Sydney	1924-25
9/103	J. J. Ferris	v England at Sydney	1886-87
9/130	T. M. Alderman	v England at Nottingham	1981
9/162	J. V. Saunders	v England at Melbourne	1901-02
9/200	W. H. Cooper	v England at Melbourne	1881-82
8/52	A. E. Trott	v England at Adelaide	1894-95
8/68	C. T. B. Turner	v England at Sydney	1886-87
8/99	L. C. Mayne	v West Indies at Kingston	1964-65
8/105	H. V. Hordern	v South Africa at Melbourne	1910-11

HAT-TRICKS

F. R. Spofforth	v England at Melbourne	1878-79
H. Trumble	v England at Melbourne	1901-02
H. Trumble	v England at Melbourne	1903-04
T. J. Matthews*	v South Africa at Manchester	1912
T. J. Matthews†	v South Africa at Manchester	1912
L. F. Kline	v South Africa at Cape Town	1957-58
M. G. Hughes	v West Indies at Perth	1988-89
D. W. Fleming	v Pakistan at Rawalpindi	1994-95
S. K. Warne	v England at Melbourne	1994-95
G. D. McGrath	v West Indies at Perth	2000-01

* 1st Innings, † 2nd Innings

MOST WICKETS IN A SERIES

	T	O	Mdns	R	W	BB	5 W/i	10 W/m	Avge	
C. V. Grimmett	5	346.1	140	642	44	7/40	5	3	14.59	1935-36 v SAf in South Africa
T. M. Alderman	6	325	76	893	42	6/135	4	0	21.26	1981 v England in England
R. M. Hogg	6	217.4	60	527	41	6/74	5	2	12.85	1978-79 v England in Australia
T. M. Alderman	6	269.2	68	712	41	6/128	6	1	17.37	1989 v England in England
D. K. Lillee	6	311.4	81	870	39	7/89	2	1	22.31	1981 v England in England
W. J. Whitty	5	232.3	55	632	37	6/17	2	0	17.08	1910-11 v SAf in Australia
A. A. Mailey	5	244.1	27	946	36	9/121	4	2	26.28	1920-21 v England in Australia
G. D. McGrath	5	249.5	67	701	36	8/38	2	0	19.47	1997 v England in England
G. Giffen	5	343.2	111	820	34	6/155	3	0	24.12	1894-95 v England in Australia
G. F. Lawson	5	230.4	51	687	34	6/47	4	1	20.21	1982-83 v England in Australia
S. K. Warne	4	439.5	178	877	34	5/82	1	0	25.79	1993 v England in England
C. V. Grimmett	5	239.2	61	593	33	7/87	2	1	17.97	1930-31 v WI in Australia
C. V. Grimmett	5	306	108	557	33	7/83	3	1	16.88	1931-32 v SAf in Australia
A. K. Davidson	4	173.7	25	612	33	6/53	5	1	18.55	1960-61 v WI in Australia
J. R. Thomson	5	175.1	34	592	33	6/46	2	0	17.94	1974-75 v England in Australia
M. A. Noble	5	230	68	608	32	7/17	4	1	19.00	1901-02 v England in Australia
H. V. Hordern	5	277.3	43	780	32	7/90	4	2	24.38	1911-12 v England in Australia
C. J. McDermott	5	232.5	56	675	32	6/38	4	0	21.09	1994-95 v England in Australia
G. D. McGrath	5	194.2	56	542	32	7/76	4	0	16.94	2001 v England in England
J. V. Saunders	5	267.1	52	716	31	5/28	3	0	23.10	1907-08 v England in Australia
H. Ironmonger	4	221.5	112	296	31	6/18	3	1	9.55	1931-32 v SAf in Australia
R. Benaud	5	233.2	65	584	31	5/83	2	0	18.84	1958-59 v England in Australia
D. K. Lillee	5	249.5	83	548	31	6/66	3	1	17.68	1972 v England in England
C. J. McDermott	5	264.2	75	670	31	5/54	3	1	21.61	1991-92 v India in Australia
M. G. Hughes	6	296.2	78	845	31	5/92	1	0	27.26	1993 v England in England
S. K. Warne	5	195.2	41	580	31	7/165	3	1	18.71	2001 v England in England
R. Benaud	5	242.1	56	658	30	5/49	4	0	21.93	1957-58 v SAf in South Africa
G. D. McKenzie	5	206.1	27	758	30	8/71	1	0	25.27	1968-69 v WI in Australia
C. J. McDermott	5	234.2	21	901	30	8/141	2	0	30.03	1985 v England in England
G. D. McGrath	4	199.4	59	508	30	5/28	4	1	16.93	1998-99 v WI in West Indies

Most wickets in a series against opponents not mentioned above:

	T	O	Mdns	R	W	BB	5 W/i	10 W/m	Avge	
G. F. Lawson	5	188.3	40	580	24	5/49	2	0	24.17	1983-84 v Pakistan in Australia
A. K. Davidson	3	154.5	35	438	21	5/40	1	0	20.86	1995-96 v SL in Australia
S. K. Warne	3	170.4	36	476	19	5/88	1	0	25.05	1997-98 v NZ in Australia
G. D. McGrath	1	54	19	90	6	3/44	0	0	15.00	1999-00 v Zim in Zimbabwe
S. K. Warne	1	53.1	13	137	6	3/68	0	0	22.83	1999-00 v Zim in Zimbabwe

MOST WICKETS IN A CAREER

		T	Balls	Mdns	R	W	BB	5W/i	10W/m	Avge
1	S. K. Warne	101	28,345	1,359	11,935	450	8/71	21	5	26.52
2	G. D. McGrath	84	20,149	992	8,524	389	8/38	23	3	21.91
3	D. K. Lillee	70	18,467	652	8,493	355	7/83	23	7	23.92
4	C. J. McDermott	71	16,586	581	8,332	291	8/97	14	2	28.63
5	R. Benaud	63	19,108	805	6,704	248	7/72	16	1	27.03
6	G. D. McKenzie	61	17,684	547	7,328	246	8/71	16	3	29.79
7	R. R. Lindwall	61	13,650	419	5,251	228	7/38	12	0	23.03
8	C. V. Grimmett	37	14,513	736	5,231	216	7/40	21	7	24.22
9	M. G. Hughes	53	12,285	499	6,017	212	8/87	7	1	28.38
10	J. R. Thomson	51	10,535	300	5,602	200	6/46	8	0	28.01
11	A. K. Davidson	44	11,587	431	3,819	186	7/93	14	2	20.53
12	G. F. Lawson	46	11,118	386	5,501	180	8/112	11	2	30.56
13 {	K. R. Miller	55	10,389	337	3,906	170	7/60	7	1	22.98
	T. M. Alderman	41	10,181	432	4,616	170	6/47	14	1	27.15
15	W. A. Johnston	40	11,048	372	3,826	160	6/44	7	0	23.91
16	W. J. O'Reilly	27	10,024	585	3,254	144	7/54	11	3	22.60

		T	Balls	Mdns	R	W	BB	5W/i	10W/m	Avge
17	H. Trumble	32	8,099	452	3,072	141	8/65	9	3	21.79
18	M.H.N. Walker	34	10,094	380	3,792	138	8/143	6	0	27.48
19	A.A. Mallett	39	9,990	419	3,940	132	8/59	6	1	29.85
20	B. Yardley	33	8,909	379	3,986	126	7/98	6	1	31.63
21	R.M. Hogg	38	7,633	230	3,503	123	6/74	6	2	28.48
	J.N. Gillespie	33	6,301	285	3,205	123	7/37	6	0	21.91
23	M.A. Noble	42	7,159	361	3,025	121	7/17	9	2	25.00
24	B.A. Reid	27	6,244	245	2,784	113	7/51	5	2	24.64
25	I.W.G. Johnson	45	8,780	330	3,182	109	7/44	3	0	29.19
26	P.R. Reiffel	35	6,403	279	2,804	104	6/71	5	0	26.96
27	G. Giffen	31	6,391	434	2,791	103	7/117	7	1	27.10
28	A.N. Connolly	30	7,818	289	2,981	102	6/47	4	0	29.23
29	C.T.B. Turner	17	5,179	457	1,670	101	7/43	11	2	16.53
30	A.A. Mailey	21	6,119	115	3,358	99	9/121	6	2	33.92
31	F.R. Spofforth	18	4,185	416	1,731	94	7/44	7	4	18.41
32	J.W. Gleeson	30	8,857	378	3,367	93	5/61	3	0	36.20
33	N.J.N. Hawke	27	6,974	238	2,677	91	7/105	6	1	29.42
34	A. Cotter	21	4,639	86	2,549	89	7/148	7	0	28.64
	S.R. Waugh	148	7,193	309	3,197	89	5/28	3	0	35.92
36	W.W. Armstrong ...	50	8,022	407	2,923	87	6/35	3	0	33.60
37	J.M. Gregory	24	5,582	138	2,648	85	7/69	4	0	31.15
38	B. Lee	21	3,905	140	2,254	84	5/47	4	0	26.83
39	S.C.G. MacGill	17	4,139	153	2,051	82	7/50	4	1	25.01
40	J.V. Saunders	14	3,565	116	1,796	79	7/34	6	0	22.73
41	G.E. Palmer	17	4,517	452	1,678	78	7/65	6	2	21.51
	G. Dymock	21	5,545	179	2,116	78	7/67	5	1	27.13
42	T.B.A. May	24	6,577	322	2,606	75	5/9	3	0	34.75
	D.W. Fleming	20	4,129	153	1,942	75	5/30	3	0	25.89
45	H. Ironmonger	14	4,695	328	1,330	74	7/23	4	2	17.97
46	B. Simpson	62	6,881	253	3,001	71	5/57	2	0	42.27
47	C.R. Miller	18	4,091	163	1,805	69	5/32	3	1	26.16
48	J.D. Higgs	22	4,752	176	2,057	66	7/143	2	0	31.17
49	W.J. Whitty	14	3,357	163	1,373	65	6/17	3	0	21.12
50	E. Jones	19	3,754	161	1,857	64	7/88	3	1	29.02
	L.S. Pascoe	14	3,403	112	1,668	64	5/59	1	0	26.06
52	G.R.J. Matthews ...	33	6,271	256	2,942	61	5/103	2	1	48.23
	M.E. Waugh	125	4,739	166	2,358	59	5/40	1	0	39.97
54	T.W. Wall	18	4,812	154	2,010	56	5/14	3	0	35.89
55	G.J. Gilmour	15	2,661	93	1,406	54	6/85	3	0	26.04
56	K.J. O'Keeffe	24	5,384	189	2,018	53	5/101	1	0	38.08
	R.J. Bright	25	5,541	298	2,180	53	7/87	4	1	41.13
58	C. Kelleway	26	4,363	146	1,683	52	5/33	1	0	32.37
59	K.D. Mackay	37	5,792	267	1,721	50	6/42	2	0	34.42

LOWEST CAREER AVERAGES

	T	Balls	Mdns	R	W	BB	5W/i	10W/m	Avge
J. Benaud	3	24	1	12	2	2/12	0	0	6.00
W.H. Moule	1	51	4	23	3	3/23	0	0	7.67
P.C. Charlton	2	45	1	24	3	3/18	0	0	8.00
M.J. Slater	74	25	1	10	1	1/4	0	0	10.00
L.J. Johnson	1	282	10	74	6	3/8	0	0	12.33
L.J. Nash	2	311	12	126	10	4/18	0	0	12.60
M.F. Malone	1	342	24	77	6	5/63	1	0	12.83
T.P. Horan	15	373	45	143	11	6/40	1	0	13.00
J.P.F. Travers	1	48	2	14	1	1/14	0	0	14.00
J.H. Hodges	2	136	9	84	6	2/7	0	0	14.00
J.J. Ferris	8	2,030	224	684	48	5/26	4	0	14.25
A.E. Trott	5	948	54	390	26	8/43	2	0	15.00
J.W. Rutherford	1	36	2	15	1	1/11	0	0	15.00

WICKET-KEEPING RECORDS

MOST DISMISSALS IN AN INNINGS

6	(all ct)	A. T. W. Grout	v South Africa at Johannesburg	1957-58
6	(all ct)	R. W. Marsh	v England at Brisbane	1982-83
6	(all ct)	I. A. Healy	v England at Birmingham	1997

Note: There are 41 instances of 5 dismissals in an innings.

MOST DISMISSALS IN A MATCH

10	(all ct)	A. C. Gilchrist	v New Zealand at Hamilton	1999-00
9	(8ct, 1st)	G. R. A. Langley	v England at Lord's	1956
9	(all ct)	R. W. Marsh	v England at Brisbane	1982-83
9	(all ct)	I. A. Healy	v England at Brisbane	1994-95

Note: There are 13 instances of eight dismissals in a match.

MOST DISMISSALS IN A SERIES

28	(all ct)	R. W. Marsh	v England in Australia	1982-83
27	(25ct, 2st)	I. A. Healy	v England in England	1997
26	(all ct)	R. W. Marsh	v West Indies in Australia	1975-76
26	(21ct, 5st)	I. A. Healy	v England in England	1993
26	(24ct, 2st)	A. C. Gilchrist	v England in England	2001
25	(23ct, 2st)	I. A. Healy	v England in Australia	1994-95
24	(all ct)	I. A. Healy	v England in Australia	1990-91
23	(20ct, 3st)	A. T. W. Grout	v West Indies in Australia	1960-61
23	(21ct, 2st)	R. W. Marsh	v England in England	1972
23	(all ct)	R. W. Marsh	v England in England	1981
23	(19ct, 4st)	I. A. Healy	v West Indies in Australia	1992-93
22	(all ct)	S. J. Rixon	v India in Australia	1977-78
21	(13ct, 8st)	R. A. Saggers	v South Africa in South Africa	1949-50
21	(16ct, 5st)	G. R. A. Langley	v West Indies in Australia	1951-52
21	(20ct, 1st)	A. T. W. Grout	v England in England	1961
21	(all ct)	R. W. Marsh	v Pakistan in Australia	1983-84
21	(19ct, 2st)	A. C. Gilchrist	v West Indies in Australia	2000-01
20	(16ct, 4st)	D. Tallon	v England in Australia	1946-47
20	(16ct, 4st)	G. R. A. Langley	v West Indies in West Indies	1954-55
20	(17ct, 3st)	A. T. W. Grout	v England in Australia	1958-59
20	(19ct, 1st)	H. B. Taber	v South Africa in South Africa	1966-67

MOST DISMISSALS IN A CAREER

		M	Ct	St	Total
1	I. A. Healy	119	366	29	395
2	R. W. Marsh	97	343	12	355
3	A. T. W. Grout	51	163	24	187
4	A. C. Gilchrist	31	122	10	132
5	W. A. S. Oldfield	54	78	52	130
6	G. R. A. Langley	26	83	15	98
7	H. Carter	28	44	21	65
8	J. J. Kelly	36	43	20	63
9	J. M. Blackham	35	36	24	60
10	H. B. Taber	16	56	4	60
11	D. Tallon	21	50	8	58
12	B. N. Jarman	19	50	4	54
13	S. J. Rixon	13	42	5	47
14	W. B. Phillips	27	43	0	43
15	K. J. Wright	10	31	4	35

		M	Ct	St	Total
16	R. A. Saggers	6	16	8	24
	G. C. Dyer	6	22	2	24
18	T. J. Zoehrer	10	18	1	19
19	L. V. Maddocks	7	18	1	19
20	A. H. Jarvis	11	9	9	18
21	J. A. Maclean	4	18	0	18
	R. D. Woolley	2	7	0	7
23	W. Carkeek	6	6	0	6
	P. A. Emery	1	5	1	6
25	B. A. Barnett	4	3	2	5
26	H. S. B. Love	1	3	0	3
27	W. L. Murdoch	18	1	1	2
	F. J. Burton	2	1	1	2

FIELDING RECORDS

MOST CATCHES IN AN INNINGS

5   V. Y. Richardson . . . . v South Africa at Durban 1935-36

Note: There are 17 instances of four catches in an innings.

MOST CATCHES IN A MATCH

7	G. S. Chappell	v England at Perth	1974-75
6	J. M. Gregory	v England at Sydney	1920-21
6	V. Y. Richardson	v South Africa at Durban	1935-36
6	R. N. Harvey	v England at Sydney	1962-63
6	I. M. Chappell	v New Zealand at Adelaide	1973-74
6	D. F. Whatmore	v India at Kanpur	1979-80
6	M. E. Waugh	v India at Chennai (Chepauk)	2000-01

Note: There are 11 instances of five catches in a match.

MOST CATCHES IN A SERIES

15	J. M. Gregory	v England in Australia	1920-21
14	G. S. Chappell	v England in Australia	1974-75
13	R. B. Simpson	v South Africa in South Africa	1957-58
13	R. B. Simpson	v West Indies in Australia	1960-61
12	D. F. Whatmore	v India in India	1979-80
12	A. R. Border	v England in England	1981
11	R. B. Simpson	v West Indies in West Indies	1964-65
11	I. M. Chappell	v England in Australia	1974-75
11	I. R. Redpath	v England in Australia	1974-75
11	A. R. Border	v England in England	1985
11	M. A. Taylor	v England in England	1993
11	M. E. Waugh	v India in India	2000-01
11	R. T. Ponting	v South Africa in Australia	2001-02

Note: There are 14 instances of 10 catches in a series.

MOST CATCHES IN A CAREER

1	M. E. Waugh	173 in 125 matches
2	M. A. Taylor	157 in 104 matches
3	A. R. Border	156 in 156 matches
4	G. S. Chappell	122 in 88 matches
5	R. B. Simpson	110 in 62 matches

6	I. M. Chappell	105 in 76 matches
7	S. R. Waugh	102 in 148 matches
8	D. C. Boon	99 in 107 matches
9 {	I. R. Redpath	83 in 67 matches
	S. K. Warne	83 in 101 matches

TEAM RECORDS

HIGHEST INNINGS TOTALS

8-758 dec.	v West Indies at Kingston	1954-55
6-729 dec.	v England at Lord's	1930
701	v England at The Oval	1934
695	v England at The Oval	1930
674	v India at Adelaide	1947-48
668	v West Indies at Bridgetown	1954-55
8-659 dec.	v England at Sydney	1946-47
8-656 dec.	v England at Manchester	1964
4-653 dec.	v England at Leeds	1993
7-652 dec.	v South Africa at Johannesburg (WS)	2001-02
6-650 dec.	v West Indies at Bridgetown	1964-65
645	v England at Brisbane	1946-47
7-641 dec.	v England at The Oval	2001
4-632 dec.	v England at Lord's	1993
8-628 dec.	v South Africa at Johannesburg (WS)	1996-97
619	v West Indies at Sydney	1968-69
617	v Pakistan at Faisalabad	1979-80
5-617 dec.	v Sri Lanka at Perth	1995-96
6-607 dec.	v New Zealand at Brisbane	1993-94
604	v England at Melbourne	1936-37
6-602 dec.	v England at Nottingham	1989
8-601 dec.	v England at Brisbane	1954-55
7-601 dec.	v England at Leeds	1989
600	v England at Melbourne	1924-25
9-600 dec.	v West Indies at Port-of-Spain	1954-55

HIGHEST FOURTH-INNINGS TOTALS

To Win

3-404	v England at Leeds	1948
6-369	v Pakistan at Hobart (Bellerive)	1999-00
7-362	v West Indies at Georgetown	1977-78
8-342	v India at Perth	1977-78
5-336	v South Africa at Durban (Kingsmead)	1949-50

To Tie

232	(set 233)	v West Indies at Brisbane	1960-61

To Draw

7-381	(set 439)	v New Zealand at Perth	2001-02
7-344	(set 448)	v England at Sydney	1994-95
9-339	(set 359)	v West Indies at Adelaide	1968-69
3-329	(set 483)	v England at Lord's	1975
3-328	(set 468)	v England at Adelaide	1970-71

To Lose

402	(set 505)	v England at Manchester	1981
339	(set 377)	v South Africa at Adelaide	1910-11
336	(set 348)	v England at Adelaide	1928-29
335	(set 428)	v England at Nottingham	1930
333	(set 427)	v England at Melbourne	1894-95

LOWEST INNINGS TOTALS

36	v England at Birmingham	1902
42	v England at Sydney	1887-88
44	v England at The Oval	1896
53	v England at Lord's	1896
58	v England at Brisbane	1936-37
60	v England at Lord's	1888
63	v England at The Oval	1882
65	v England at The Oval	1912
66	v England at Brisbane	1928-29
68	v England at The Oval	1886
70	v England at Manchester	1888
74	v England at Birmingham	1909
75	v South Africa at Durban (Kingsmead)	1949-50
76	v West Indies at Perth	1984-85
78	v England at Lord's	1968
80	v England at The Oval	1888
80	v England at Sydney	1936-37
80	v Pakistan at Karachi	1956-57
81	v England at Manchester	1888
82	v England at Sydney	1887-88
82	v West Indies at Adelaide	1951-52
83	v England at Sydney	1882-83
83	v India at Melbourne	1980-81
84	v England at Sydney	1886-87
84	v England at Manchester	1956
86	v England at Manchester	1902
90	v West Indies at Port-of-Spain	1977-78
91	v England at The Oval	1893
92	v England at The Oval	1890
94	v West Indies at Port-of-Spain	1977-78
97	v England at Sydney	1886-87
97	v West Indies at Bridgetown	1983-84
100	v England at The Oval	1888
100	v England at Adelaide	1891-92

Lowest completed innings totals for opponents not mentioned above:

103	v New Zealand at Auckland	1985-86
188	v Sri Lanka at Kandy	1999-00
422	v Zimbabwe at Harare	1999-00

LARGEST VICTORIES

Largest Victories by Innings and Runs Margin

Innings and 360	v South Africa at Johannesburg (WS)	2001-02
Innings and 332	v England at Brisbane	1946-47
Innings and 259	v South Africa at Port Elizabeth	1949-50
Innings and 226	v India at Brisbane	1947-48
Innings and 222	v New Zealand at Hobart	1993-94
Innings and 217	v West Indies at Brisbane (Ex)	1930-31
Innings and 200	v England at Melbourne	1936-37

Largest Victories by Runs Margin

562 runs	v England at The Oval	1934
530 runs	v South Africa at Melbourne	1910-11
409 runs	v England at Lord's	1948
382 runs	v England at Adelaide	1894-95
382 runs	v West Indies at Sydney	1968-69
377 runs	v England at Sydney	1920-21

365 runs	v England at Melbourne	1936-37
352 runs	v West Indies at Melbourne	2000-01
348 runs	v Pakistan at Melbourne	1976-77
329 runs	v England at Perth	1994-95

NARROW VICTORIES

Victory by One Wicket

v West Indies at Melbourne (*Last Wkt:* 38 – D. T. Ring 32* and W. A. Johnston 7*) 1951-52

Victory by 20 Runs or Less

3	v England at Manchester	1902
6	v England at Sydney	1884-85
7	v England at The Oval	1882
11	v England at Adelaide	1924-25
16	v India at Brisbane	1977-78
16	v Sri Lanka at Colombo (SSC)	1992-93

HEAVIEST DEFEATS

Heaviest Defeat by an Innings and Runs Margin

Innings and 579	by England at The Oval	1938
Innings and 230	by England at Adelaide	1891-92
Innings and 225	by England at Melbourne	1911-12
Innings and 219	by India at Calcutta	1997-98
Innings and 217	by England at The Oval	1886

Heaviest Defeat by Runs Margin

675 runs	by England at Brisbane (Ex)	1928-29
408 runs	by West Indies at Adelaide	1979-80
343 runs	by West Indies at Bridgetown	1990-91
338 runs	by England at Adelaide	1932-33
323 runs	by South Africa at Port Elizabeth	1969-70
322 runs	by England at Brisbane	1936-37
307 runs	by South Africa at Johannesburg (WS)	1969-70
299 runs	by England at Sydney	1970-71
289 runs	by England at The Oval	1926
285 runs	by West Indies at Melbourne	1988-89

NARROW DEFEATS

Defeat by One Wicket

England at The Oval (*Last Wkt:* 15 – G. H. Hirst 58* and W. Rhodes 6*)	1902
England at Melbourne (*Last Wkt:* 39 – S. F. Barnes 38* and A. Fielder 18*)	1907-08
Pakistan at Karachi (*Last Wkt:* 57 – Inzamam-ul-Haq 58* and Mushtaq Ahmed 20*)	1994-95
West Indies at Bridgetown (*Last Wkt:* 9 – B. C. Lara 153* and C. A. Walsh 0*)	1998-99

Defeat by 20 Runs or Less

1	by West Indies at Adelaide	1992-93
3	by England at Melbourne	1982-83
5	by South Africa at Sydney	1993-94
10	by England at Sydney	1894-95
12	by England at Adelaide	1928-29
12	by England at Melbourne	1998-99
13	by England at Sydney	1886-87
18	by England at Leeds	1981
19	by England at The Oval	1997

APPEARANCES

MOST TEST APPEARANCES

	T	Eng	SAf	WI	NZ	Ind	Pak	SL	Zim
A. R. Border	156	47	6	31	23	20	22	7	–
S. R. Waugh	148	41	16	28	23	14	17	8	1
M. E. Waugh	125	29	18	28	14	14	12	9	1
I. A. Healy	119	33	12	28	11	9	14	11	1
D. C. Boon	107	31	6	22	17	11	11	9	–
M. A. Taylor	104	33	11	20	11	9	12	8	–
S. K. Warne	101	23	18	16	15	11	9	8	1
R. W. Marsh	97	43	–	17	14	3	20	–	–
G. S. Chappell	88	36	–	17	14	3	17	1	–
G. D. McGrath	84	18	14	18	9	7	11	6	1

YOUNGEST AUSTRALIAN PLAYERS ON DEBUT

Years	Days			
17	239	I. D. Craig	v South Africa at Sydney	1952-53
18	232	T. W. Garrett	v England at Melbourne	1876-77
19	54	A. Cotter	v England at Sydney	1903-04
19	96	C. Hill	v England at Lord's	1896
19	100	G. R. Hazlitt	v England at Sydney	1907-08
19	104	R. G. Archer	v South Africa at Melbourne	1952-53
19	107	R. N. Harvey	v India at Adelaide	1947-48
19	149	A. Jackson	v England at Adelaide	1928-29
19	173	J. T. Cottam	v England at Sydney	1886-87
19	252	J. J. Ferris	v England at Sydney	1886-87
19	252	C. J. McDermott	v West Indies at Melbourne	1984-85
19	331	S. J. McCabe	v England at Nottingham	1930
19	354	K. D. Walters	v England at Brisbane	1965-66
19	363	G. D. McKenzie	v England at Lord's	1961

OLDEST AUSTRALIAN PLAYERS ON DEBUT

Years	Days			
46	253	D. D. Blackie	v England at Sydney	1928-29
46	237	H. Ironmonger	v England at Brisbane (Ex)	1928-29
38	328	N. Thompson	v England at Melbourne	1876-77
38	35	R. G. Holland	v West Indies at Brisbane	1984-85
37	290	E. J. Gregory	v England at Melbourne	1876-77
37	184	H. S. B. Love	v England at Brisbane	1932-33
37	163	J. Harry	v England at Adelaide	1894-95
37	154	R. K. Oxenham	v England at Melbourne	1928-29
36	148	A. J. Richardson	v England at Sydney	1924-25
35	127	J. B. Iverson	v England at Brisbane	1950-51
35	81	K. H. Eastwood	v England at Sydney	1970-71
35	67	J. W. Wilson	v India at Bombay	1956-57
35	4	A. E. V. Hartkopf	v England at Melbourne	1924-25
35	3	T. V. Hohns	v West Indies at Sydney	1988-89

CAPTAINCY

CAPTAINS

		T	W	L	D	T	% Won
1	D. W. Gregory	3	2	1	0	0	66.66
2	W. L. Murdoch	16	5	7	4	0	31.25
3	T. P. Horan	2	0	2	0	0	0.00
4	H. H. Massie	1	1	0	0	0	100.00
5	J. M. Blackham	8	3	3	2	0	37.50
6	H. J. H. Scott	3	0	3	0	0	0.00
7	P. S. McDonnell	6	1	5	0	0	16.66
8	G. Giffen	4	2	2	0	0	50.00
9	G. H. S. Trott	8	5	3	0	0	62.50
10	J. Darling	21	7	4	10	0	33.33
11	H. Trumble	2	2	0	0	0	100.00
12	M. A. Noble	15	8	5	2	0	53.33
13	C. Hill	10	5	5	0	0	50.00
14	E. S. Gregory	6	2	1	3	0	33.33
15	W. W. Armstrong	10	8	0	2	0	80.00
16	H. L. Collins	11	5	2	4	0	45.45
17	W. Bardsley	2	0	0	2	0	0.00
18	J. Ryder	5	1	4	0	0	20.00
19	W. M. Woodfull	25	14	7	4	0	56.00
20	V. Y. Richardson	5	4	0	1	0	80.00
21	D. G. Bradman	24	15	3	6	0	62.50
22	W. A. Brown	1	1	0	0	0	100.00
23	A. L. Hassett	24	14	4	6	0	58.33
24	A. R. Morris	2	0	2	0	0	0.00
25	I. W. G. Johnson	17	7	5	5	0	41.17
26	R. R. Lindwall	1	0	0	1	0	0.00
27	I. D. Craig	5	3	0	2	0	60.00
28	R. Benaud	28	12	4	11	1	42.85
29	R. N. Harvey	1	1	0	0	0	100.00
30	R. B. Simpson	39	12	12	15	0	30.76
31	B. C. Booth	2	0	1	1	0	0.00
32	W. M. Lawry	26	9	8	9	0	34.61
33	B. N. Jarman	1	0	0	1	0	0.00
34	I. M. Chappell	30	15	5	10	0	50.00
35	G. S. Chappell	48	21	13	14	0	43.75
36	G. N. Yallop	7	1	6	0	0	14.28
37	K. J. Hughes	28	4	13	11	0	14.28
38	A. R. Border	93	32	22	38	1	34.40
39	M. A. Taylor	50	26	13	11	0	52.00
40	S. R. Waugh	37	26	6	5	0	70.27
41	A. C. Gilchrist	2	1	1	0	0	50.00

MOST CONSECUTIVE TESTS AS CAPTAIN

93	A. R. Border	December 1984 to March 1994
50	M. A. Taylor	September 1994 to January 1999
30	I. M. Chappell	February 1972 to August 1975
25	W. M. Woodfull	June 1930 to August 1934
21	W. M. Lawry	August 1968 to January 1971
21	S. R. Waugh	March 1999 to December 2000
19	R. Benaud	December 1958 to June 1961
19	R. B. Simpson	January 1964 to May 1965
17	G. S. Chappell	November 1975 to August 1977
16	G. S. Chappell	December 1979 to February 1981
15	I. W. G. Johnson	December 1954 to October 1956

TEST SERIES

Note: The Third Test at the Melbourne Cricket Ground from December 31, 1970–January 5, 1971 has been sanctioned by the Australian Cricket Board as an official Test match. The Australian Cricket Board in consultation with the MCC tour management declared the Test as a 'DRAW'. This decision was determined as the two teams had been officially announced, including the 12th men and the toss having been made. The Umpires were walking out to the ground when rain began to fall and thus preventing any further play in the match.

Opponent	Date of First Test	Tests	Won	Lost	Drawn	Tied
England............	Mar, 15, 1877	302	121	94	87	0
South Africa........	Oct, 11, 1902	71	39	15	17	0
West Indies........	Dec, 12, 1930	95	42	31	21	1
New Zealand........	Mar, 29, 1946	41	18	7	16	0
India	Nov, 28, 1947	60	29	13	17	1
Pakistan............	Oct, 11, 1956	46	18	11	17	0
Sri Lanka..........	Apr, 22, 1983	13	7	1	5	0
Zimbabwe..........	Oct 14, 1999	1	1	0	0	0
Total		629	275	172	180	2

AUSTRALIAN TEST MATCHES

Venue	Opponent	Result for Australia	Captain	Test/Opp
1876-77 in Australia				
Melbourne	England	Won by 45 runs	D. W. Gregory	1/1
Melbourne	England	Lost by four wickets	D. W. Gregory	2/2
1878-79 in Australia				
Melbourne	England	Won by ten wickets	D. W. Gregory	3/3
1880 in England				
The Oval	England	Lost by five wickets	W. L. Murdoch	4/4
1881-82 in Australia				
Melbourne	England	Drawn	W. L. Murdoch	5/5
Sydney	England	Won by five wickets	W. L. Murdoch	6/6
Sydney	England	Won by six wickets	W. L. Murdoch	7/7
Melbourne	England	Drawn	W. L. Murdoch	8/8
1882 in England				
The Oval	England	Won by seven runs	W. L. Murdoch	9/9
1882-83 in Australia				
Melbourne	England	Won by nine wickets	W. L. Murdoch	10/10
Melbourne	England	Lost by an innings and 27 runs	W. L. Murdoch	11/11
Sydney	England	Lost by 69 runs	W. L. Murdoch	12/12
Sydney	England	Won by four wickets	W. L. Murdoch	13/13
1884 in England				
Manchester	England	Drawn	W. L. Murdoch	14/14
Lord's	England	Lost by an innings and five runs	W. L. Murdoch	15/15
The Oval	England	Drawn	W. L. Murdoch	16/16
1884-85 in Australia				
Adelaide	England	Lost by eight wickets	W. L. Murdoch	17/17
Melbourne	England	Lost by ten wickets	T. P. Horan	18/18
Sydney	England	Won by six runs	H. H. Massie	19/19
Sydney	England	Won by eight wickets	J. M. Blackham	20/20
Melbourne	England	Lost by an innings and 98 runs	T. P. Horan	21/21

Venue	Opponent	Result for Australia	Captain	Test/Opp
1886 in England				
Manchester	England	Lost by four wickets	H. J. H. Scott	22/22
Lord's	England	Lost by an innings and 106 runs	H. J. H. Scott	23/23
The Oval	England	Lost by an innings and 217 runs	H. J. H. Scott	24/24
1886-87 in Australia				
Sydney	England	Lost by 13 runs	P. S. McDonnell	25/25
Sydney	England	Lost by 71 runs	P. S. McDonnell	26/26
1887-88 in Australia				
Sydney	England	Lost by 126 runs	P. S. McDonnell	27/27
1888 in England				
Lord's	England	Won by 61 runs	P. S. McDonnell	28/28
The Oval	England	Lost by an innings and 137 runs	P. S. McDonnell	29/29
Manchester	England	Lost by an innings and 21 runs	P. S. McDonnell	30/30
1890 in England				
Lord's	England	Lost by seven wickets	W. L. Murdoch	31/31
The Oval	England	Lost by two wickets	W. L. Murdoch	32/32
1891-92 in Australia				
Melbourne	England	Won by 54 runs	J. M. Blackham	33/33
Sydney	England	Won by 72 runs	J. M. Blackham	34/34
Adelaide	England	Lost by an innings and 230 runs	J. M. Blackham	35/35
1893 in England				
Lord's	England	Drawn	J. M. Blackham	36/36
The Oval	England	Lost by an innings and 43 runs	J. M. Blackham	37/37
Manchester	England	Drawn	J. M. Blackham	38/38
1894-95 in Australia				
Sydney	England	Lost by ten runs	J. M. Blackham	39/39
Melbourne	England	Lost by 94 runs	G. Giffen	40/40
Adelaide	England	Won by 382 runs	G. Giffen	41/41
Sydney	England	Won by an innings and 147 runs	G. Giffen	42/42
Melbourne	England	Lost by six wickets	G. Giffen	43/43
1896 in England				
Lord's	England	Lost by six wickets	G. H. S. Trott	44/44
Manchester	England	Won by three wickets	G. H. S. Trott	45/45
The Oval	England	Lost by 66 runs	G. H. S. Trott	46/46
1897-98 in Australia				
Sydney	England	Lost by nine wickets	G. H. S. Trott	47/47
Melbourne	England	Won by an innings and 55 runs	G. H. S. Trott	48/48
Adelaide	England	Won by an innings and 13 runs	G. H. S. Trott	49/49
Melbourne	England	Won by eight wickets	G. H. S. Trott	50/50
Sydney	England	Won by six wickets	G. H. S. Trott	51/51
1899 in England				
Nottingham	England	Drawn	J. Darling	52/52
Lord's	England	Won by ten wickets	J. Darling	53/53
Leeds	England	Drawn	J. Darling	54/54
Manchester	England	Drawn	J. Darling	55/55
The Oval	England	Drawn	J. Darling	56/56
1901-02 in Australia				
Sydney	England	Lost by an innings and 124 runs	J. Darling	57/57
Melbourne	England	Won by 229 runs	J. Darling	58/58
Adelaide	England	Won by four wickets	J. Darling	59/59
Sydney	England	Won by seven wickets	H. Trumble	60/60
Melbourne	England	Won by 32 runs	H. Trumble	61/61

Venue	Opponent	Result for Australia	Captain	Test/Opp
1902 in England				
Birmingham	England	Drawn	J. Darling	62/62
Lord's	England	Drawn	J. Darling	63/63
Sheffield	England	Won by 143 runs	J. Darling	64/64
Manchester	England	Won by three runs	J. Darling	65/65
The Oval	England	Lost by one wicket	J. Darling	66/66
1902-03 in South Africa				
Johannesburg (OW)	South Africa	Drawn	J. Darling	67/1
Johannesburg (OW)	South Africa	Won by 159 runs	J. Darling	68/2
Cape Town	South Africa	Won by ten wickets	J. Darling	69/3
1903-04 in Australia				
Sydney	England	Lost by five wickets	M. A. Noble	70/67
Melbourne	England	Lost by 185 runs	M. A. Noble	71/68
Adelaide	England	Won by 216 runs	M. A. Noble	72/69
Sydney	England	Lost by 157 runs	M. A. Noble	73/70
Melbourne	England	Won by 218 runs	M. A. Noble	74/71
1905 in England				
Nottingham	England	Lost by 213 runs	J. Darling	75/72
Lord's	England	Drawn	J. Darling	76/73
Leeds	England	Drawn	J. Darling	77/74
Manchester	England	Lost by an innings and 80 runs	J. Darling	78/75
The Oval	England	Drawn	J. Darling	79/76
1907-08 in Australia				
Sydney	England	Won by two wickets	M. A. Noble	80/77
Melbourne	England	Lost by one wicket	M. A. Noble	81/78
Adelaide	England	Won by 245 runs	M. A. Noble	82/79
Melbourne	England	Won by 308 runs	M. A. Noble	83/80
Sydney	England	Won by 49 runs	M. A. Noble	84/81
1909 in England				
Birmingham	England	Lost by ten wickets	M. A. Noble	85/82
Lord's	England	Won by nine wickets	M. A. Noble	86/83
Leeds	England	Won by 126 runs	M. A. Noble	87/84
Manchester	England	Drawn	M. A. Noble	88/85
The Oval	England	Drawn	M. A. Noble	89/86
1910-11 in Australia				
Sydney	South Africa	Won by an innings and 114 runs	C. Hill	90/4
Melbourne	South Africa	Won by 89 runs	C. Hill	91/5
Adelaide	South Africa	Lost by 38 runs	C. Hill	92/6
Melbourne	South Africa	Won by 530 runs	C. Hill	93/7
Sydney	South Africa	Won by seven wickets	C. Hill	94/8
1911-12 in Australia				
Sydney	England	Won by 146 runs	C. Hill	95/87
Melbourne	England	Lost by eight wickets	C. Hill	96/88
Adelaide	England	Lost by seven wickets	C. Hill	97/89
Melbourne	England	Lost by an innings and 225 runs	C. Hill	98/90
Sydney	England	Lost by 70 runs	C. Hill	99/91
1912 in England				
Manchester	South Africa	Won by an innings and 88 runs	E. S. Gregory	100/9
Lord's	England	Drawn	E. S. Gregory	101/92
Lord's	South Africa	Won by ten wickets	E. S. Gregory	102/10
Manchester	England	Drawn	E. S. Gregory	103/93
Nottingham	South Africa	Drawn	E. S. Gregory	104/11
The Oval	England	Lost by 244 runs	E. S. Gregory	105/94

Venue	Opponent	Result for Australia	Captain	Test/Opp
1920-21 in Australia				
Sydney	England	Won by 377 runs	W. W. Armstrong	106/95
Melbourne	England	Won by an innings and 91 runs	W. W. Armstrong	107/96
Adelaide	England	Won by 119 runs	W. W. Armstrong	108/97
Melbourne	England	Won by eight wickets	W. W. Armstrong	109/98
Sydney	England	Won by nine wickets	W. W. Armstrong	110/99
1921 in England				
Nottingham	England	Won by ten wickets	W. W. Armstrong	111/100
Lord's	England	Won by eight wickets	W. W. Armstrong	112/101
Leeds	England	Won by 219 runs	W. W. Armstrong	113/102
Manchester	England	Drawn	W. W. Armstrong	114/103
The Oval	England	Drawn	W. W. Armstrong	115/104
1921-22 in South Africa				
Durban (Lord's)	South Africa	Drawn	H. L. Collins	116/12
Johannesburg (OW)	South Africa	Drawn	H. L. Collins	117/13
Cape Town	South Africa	Won by ten wickets	H. L. Collins	118/14
1924-25 in Australia				
Sydney	England	Won by 193 runs	H. L. Collins	119/105
Melbourne	England	Won by 81 runs	H. L. Collins	120/106
Adelaide	England	Won by 11 runs	H. L. Collins	121/107
Melbourne	England	Lost by an innings and 29 runs	H. L. Collins	122/108
Sydney	England	Won by 307 runs	H. L. Collins	123/109
1926 in England				
Nottingham	England	Drawn	H. L. Collins	124/110
Lord's	England	Drawn	H. L. Collins	125/111
Leeds	England	Drawn	W. Bardsley	126/112
Manchester	England	Drawn	W. Bardsley	127/113
The Oval	England	Lost by 289 runs	H. L. Collins	128/114
1928-29 in Australia				
Brisbane (Ex)	England	Lost by 675 runs	J. Ryder	129/115
Sydney	England	Lost by eight wickets	J. Ryder	130/116
Melbourne	England	Lost by three wickets	J. Ryder	131/117
Adelaide	England	Lost by 12 runs	J. Ryder	132/118
Melbourne	England	Won by five wickets	J. Ryder	133/119
1930 in England				
Nottingham	England	Lost by 93 runs	W. M. Woodfull	134/120
Lord's	England	Won by seven wickets	W. M. Woodfull	135/121
Leeds	England	Drawn	W. M. Woodfull	136/122
Manchester	England	Drawn	W. M. Woodfull	137/123
The Oval	England	Won by an innings and 39 runs	W. M. Woodfull	138/124
1930-31 in Australia				
Adelaide	West Indies	Won by ten wickets	W. M. Woodfull	139/1
Sydney	West Indies	Won by an innings and 172 runs	W. M. Woodfull	140/2
Brisbane (Ex)	West Indies	Won by an innings and 217 runs	W. M. Woodfull	141/3
Melbourne	West Indies	Won by an innings and 122 runs	W. M. Woodfull	142/4
Sydney	West Indies	Lost by 30 runs	W. M. Woodfull	143/5
1931-32 in Australia				
Brisbane	South Africa	Won by an innings and 163 runs	W. M. Woodfull	144/15
Sydney	South Africa	Won by an innings and 155 runs	W. M. Woodfull	145/16
Melbourne	South Africa	Won by 169 runs	W. M. Woodfull	146/17
Adelaide	South Africa	Won by ten wickets	W. M. Woodfull	147/18
Melbourne	South Africa	Won by an innings and 72 runs	W. M. Woodfull	148/19

Venue	Opponent	Result for Australia	Captain	Test/Opp
1932-33 in Australia				
Sydney	England	Lost by ten wickets	W. M. Woodfull	149/125
Melbourne	England	Won by 111 runs	W. M. Woodfull	150/126
Adelaide	England	Lost by 338 runs	W. M. Woodfull	151/127
Brisbane	England	Lost by six wickets	W. M. Woodfull	152/128
Sydney	England	Lost by eight wickets	W. M. Woodfull	153/129
1934 in England				
Nottingham	England	Won by 238 runs	W. M. Woodfull	154/130
Lord's	England	Lost by an innings and 38 runs	W. M. Woodfull	155/131
Manchester	England	Drawn	W. M. Woodfull	156/132
Leeds	England	Drawn	W. M. Woodfull	157/133
The Oval	England	Won by 562 runs	W. M. Woodfull	158/134
1935-36 in South Africa				
Durban (Kingsmead)	South Africa	Won by nine wickets	V. Y. Richardson	159/20
Johannesburg (OW)	South Africa	Drawn	V. Y. Richardson	160/21
Cape Town	South Africa	Won by an innings and 78 runs	V. Y. Richardson	161/22
Johannesburg (OW)	South Africa	Won by an innings and 184 runs	V. Y. Richardson	162/23
Durban (Kingsmead)	South Africa	Won by an innings and six runs	V. Y. Richardson	163/24
1936-37 in Australia				
Brisbane	England	Lost by 322 runs	D. G. Bradman	164/135
Sydney	England	Lost by an innings and 22 runs	D. G. Bradman	165/136
Melbourne	England	Won by 365 runs	D. G. Bradman	166/137
Adelaide	England	Won by 148 runs	D. G. Bradman	167/138
Melbourne	England	Won by an innings and 200 runs	D. G. Bradman	168/139
1938 in England				
Nottingham	England	Drawn	D. G. Bradman	169/140
Lord's	England	Drawn	D. G. Bradman	170/141
Leeds	England	Won by five wickets	D. G. Bradman	171/142
The Oval	England	Lost by an innings and 579 runs	D. G. Bradman	172/143
1945-46 in New Zealand				
Wellington	New Zealand	Won by an innings and 103 runs	W. A. Brown	173/1
1946-47 in Australia				
Brisbane	England	Won by an innings and 332 runs	D. G. Bradman	174/144
Sydney	England	Won by an innings and 33 runs	D. G. Bradman	175/145
Melbourne	England	Drawn	D. G. Bradman	176/146
Adelaide	England	Drawn	D. G. Bradman	177/147
Sydney	England	Won by five wickets	D. G. Bradman	178/148
1947-48 in Australia				
Brisbane	India	Won by an innings and 226 runs	D. G. Bradman	179/1
Sydney	India	Drawn	D. G. Bradman	180/2
Melbourne	India	Won by 233 runs	D. G. Bradman	181/3
Adelaide	India	Won by an innings and 16 runs	D. G. Bradman	182/4
Melbourne	India	Won by an innings and 177 runs	D. G. Bradman	183/5
1948 in England				
Nottingham	England	Won by eight wickets	D. G. Bradman	184/149
Lord's	England	Won by 409 runs	D. G. Bradman	185/150
Manchester	England	Drawn	D. G. Bradman	186/151
Leeds	England	Won by seven wickets	D. G. Bradman	187/152
The Oval	England	Won by an innings and 149 runs	D. G. Bradman	188/153
1949-50 in South Africa				
Johannesburg (EP)	South Africa	Won by an innings and 85 runs	A. L. Hassett	189/25
Cape Town	South Africa	Won by eight wickets	A. L. Hassett	190/26
Durban (Kingsmead)	South Africa	Won by five wickets	A. L. Hassett	191/27
Johannesburg (EP)	South Africa	Drawn	A. L. Hassett	192/28
Port Elizabeth	South Africa	Won by an innings and 259 runs	A. L. Hassett	193/29

Venue	Opponent	Result for Australia	Captain	Test/Opp
1950-51 in Australia				
Brisbane	England	Won by 70 runs	A. L. Hassett	194/154
Melbourne	England	Won by 28 runs	A. L. Hassett	195/155
Sydney	England	Won by an innings and 13 runs	A. L. Hassett	196/156
Adelaide	England	Won by 274 runs	A. L. Hassett	197/157
Melbourne	England	Lost by eight wickets	A. L. Hassett	198/158
1951-52 in Australia				
Brisbane	West Indies	Won by three wickets	A. L. Hassett	199/6
Sydney	West Indies	Won by seven wickets	A. L. Hassett	200/7
Adelaide	West Indies	Lost by six wickets	A. R. Morris	201/8
Melbourne	West Indies	Won by one wicket	A. L. Hassett	202/9
Sydney	West Indies	Won by 202 runs	A. L. Hassett	203/10
1952-53 in Australia				
Brisbane	South Africa	Won by 96 runs	A. L. Hassett	204/30
Melbourne	South Africa	Lost by 82 runs	A. L. Hassett	205/31
Sydney	South Africa	Won by an innings and 38 runs	A. L. Hassett	206/32
Adelaide	South Africa	Drawn	A. L. Hassett	207/33
Melbourne	South Africa	Lost by six wickets	A. L. Hassett	208/34
1953 in England				
Nottingham	England	Drawn	A. L. Hassett	209/159
Lord's	England	Drawn	A. L. Hassett	210/160
Manchester	England	Drawn	A. L. Hassett	211/161
Leeds	England	Drawn	A. L. Hassett	212/162
The Oval	England	Lost by eight wickets	A. L. Hassett	213/163
1954-55 in Australia				
Brisbane	England	Won by an innings and 154 runs	I. W. G. Johnson	214/164
Sydney	England	Lost by 38 runs	A. R. Morris	215/165
Melbourne	England	Lost by 128 runs	I. W. G. Johnson	216/166
Adelaide	England	Lost by five wickets	I. W. G. Johnson	217/167
Sydney	England	Drawn	I. W. G. Johnson	218/168
1954-55 in West Indies				
Kingston	West Indies	Won by nine wickets	I. W. G. Johnson	219/11
Port-of-Spain	West Indies	Drawn	I. W. G. Johnson	220/12
Georgetown	West Indies	Won by eight wickets	I. W. G. Johnson	221/13
Bridgetown	West Indies	Drawn	I. W. G. Johnson	222/14
Kingston	West Indies	Won by an innings and 82 runs	I. W. G. Johnson	223/15
1956 in England				
Nottingham	England	Drawn	I. W. G. Johnson	224/169
Lord's	England	Won by 185 runs	I. W. G. Johnson	225/170
Leeds	England	Lost by an innings and 42 runs	I. W. G. Johnson	226/171
Manchester	England	Lost by an innings and 170 runs	I. W. G. Johnson	227/172
The Oval	England	Drawn	I. W. G. Johnson	228/173
1956-57 in Pakistan				
Karachi	Pakistan	Lost by nine wickets	I. W. G. Johnson	229/1
1956-57 in India				
Madras (Corp)	India	Won by an innings and five runs	I. W. G. Johnson	230/6
Bombay (BS)	India	Drawn	R. R. Lindwall	231/7
Calcutta	India	Won by 94 runs	I. W. G. Johnson	232/8
1957-58 in South Africa				
Johannesburg (WS)	South Africa	Drawn	I. D. Craig	233/35
Cape Town	South Africa	Won by an innings and 141 runs	I. D. Craig	234/36
Durban (Kingsmead)	South Africa	Drawn	I. D. Craig	235/37
Johannesburg (WS)	South Africa	Won by ten wickets	I. D. Craig	236/38
Port Elizabeth	South Africa	Won by eight wickets	I. D. Craig	237/39

Venue	Opponent	Result for Australia	Captain	Test/Opp
1958-59 in Australia				
Brisbane	England	Won by eight wickets	R. Benaud	238/174
Melbourne	England	Won by eight wickets	R. Benaud	239/175
Sydney	England	Drawn	R. Benaud	240/176
Adelaide	England	Won by ten wickets	R. Benaud	241/177
Melbourne	England	Won by nine wickets	R. Benaud	242/178
1959-60 in Pakistan				
Dacca	Pakistan	Won by eight wickets	R. Benaud	243/2
Lahore	Pakistan	Won by seven wickets	R. Benaud	244/3
Karachi	Pakistan	Drawn	R. Benaud	245/4
1959-60 in India				
Delhi	India	Won by an innings and 127 runs	R. Benaud	246/9
Kanpur	India	Lost by 119 runs	R. Benaud	247/10
Bombay (BS)	India	Drawn	R. Benaud	248/11
Madras (Corp)	India	Won by an innings and 55 runs	R. Benaud	249/12
Calcutta	India	Drawn	R. Benaud	250/13
1960-61 in Australia				
Brisbane	West Indies	Tied	R. Benaud	251/16
Melbourne	West Indies	Won by seven wickets	R. Benaud	252/17
Sydney	West Indies	Lost by 222 runs	R. Benaud	253/18
Adelaide	West Indies	Drawn	R. Benaud	254/19
Melbourne	West Indies	Won by two wickets	R. Benaud	255/20
1961 in England				
Birmingham	England	Drawn	R. Benaud	256/179
Lord's	England	Won by five wickets	R. N. Harvey	257/180
Leeds	England	Lost by eight wickets	R. Benaud	258/181
Manchester	England	Won by 54 runs	R. Benaud	259/182
The Oval	England	Drawn	R. Benaud	260/183
1962-63 in Australia				
Brisbane	England	Drawn	R. Benaud	261/184
Melbourne	England	Lost by seven wickets	R. Benaud	262/185
Sydney	England	Won by eight wickets	R. Benaud	263/186
Adelaide	England	Drawn	R. Benaud	264/187
Sydney	England	Drawn	R. Benaud	265/188
1963-64 in Australia				
Brisbane	South Africa	Drawn	R. Benaud	266/40
Melbourne	South Africa	Won by eight wickets	R. B. Simpson	267/41
Sydney	South Africa	Drawn	R. B. Simpson	268/42
Adelaide	South Africa	Lost by ten wickets	R. B. Simpson	269/43
Sydney	South Africa	Drawn	R. B. Simpson	270/44
1964 in England				
Nottingham	England	Drawn	R. B. Simpson	271/189
Lord's	England	Drawn	R. B. Simpson	272/190
Leeds	England	Won by seven wickets	R. B. Simpson	273/191
Manchester	England	Drawn	R. B. Simpson	274/192
The Oval	England	Drawn	R. B. Simpson	275/193
1964-65 in India				
Madras (Corp)	India	Won by 139 runs	R. B. Simpson	276/14
Bombay (BS)	India	Lost by two wickets	R. B. Simpson	277/15
Calcutta	India	Drawn	R. B. Simpson	278/16
1964-65 in Pakistan				
Karachi	Pakistan	Drawn	R. B. Simpson	279/5

Venue	Opponent	Result for Australia	Captain	Test/Opp
1964-65 in Australia				
Melbourne	Pakistan	Drawn	R. B. Simpson	280/6
1964-65 in West Indies				
Kingston	West Indies	Lost by 179 runs	R. B. Simpson	281/21
Port-of-Spain	West Indies	Drawn	R. B. Simpson	282/22
Georgetown	West Indies	Lost by 212 runs	R. B. Simpson	283/23
Bridgetown	West Indies	Drawn	R. B. Simpson	284/24
Port-of-Spain	West Indies	Won by ten wickets	R. B. Simpson	285/25
1965-66 in Australia				
Brisbane	England	Drawn	B. C. Booth	286/194
Melbourne	England	Drawn	R. B. Simpson	287/195
Sydney	England	Lost by an innings and 93 runs	B. C. Booth	288/196
Adelaide	England	Won by an innings and nine runs	R. B. Simpson	289/197
Melbourne	England	Drawn	R. B. Simpson	290/198
1966-67 in South Africa				
Johannesburg (WS)	South Africa	Lost by 233 runs	R. B. Simpson	291/45
Cape Town	South Africa	Won by six wickets	R. B. Simpson	292/46
Durban (Kingsmead)	South Africa	Lost by eight wickets	R. B. Simpson	293/47
Johannesburg (WS)	South Africa	Drawn	R. B. Simpson	294/48
Port Elizabeth	South Africa	Lost by seven wickets	R. B. Simpson	295/49
1967-68 in Australia				
Adelaide	India	Won by 146 runs	R. B. Simpson	296/17
Melbourne	India	Won by an innings and four runs	R. B. Simpson	297/18
Brisbane	India	Won by 39 runs	W. M. Lawry	298/19
Sydney	India	Won by 144 runs	W. M. Lawry	299/20
1968 in England				
Manchester	England	Won by 159 runs	W. M. Lawry	300/199
Lord's	England	Drawn	W. M. Lawry	301/200
Birmingham	England	Drawn	W. M. Lawry	302/201
Leeds	England	Drawn	B. N. Jarman	303/202
The Oval	England	Lost by 226 runs	W. M. Lawry	304/203
1968-69 in Australia				
Brisbane	West Indies	Lost by 125 runs	W. M. Lawry	305/26
Melbourne	West Indies	Won by an innings and 30 runs	W. M. Lawry	306/27
Sydney	West Indies	Won by ten wickets	W. M. Lawry	307/28
Adelaide	West Indies	Drawn	W. M. Lawry	308/29
Sydney	West Indies	Won by 382 runs	W. M. Lawry	309/30
1969-70 in India				
Bombay (BS)	India	Won by eight wickets	W. M. Lawry	310/21
Kanpur	India	Drawn	W. M. Lawry	311/22
Delhi	India	Lost by seven wickets	W. M. Lawry	312/23
Calcutta	India	Won by ten wickets	W. M. Lawry	313/24
Madras (Chepauk)	India	Won by 77 runs	W. M. Lawry	314/25
1969-70 in South Africa				
Cape Town	South Africa	Lost by 170 runs	W. M. Lawry	315/50
Durban (Kingsmead)	South Africa	Lost by an innings and 129 runs	W. M. Lawry	316/51
Johannesburg (WS)	South Africa	Lost by 307 runs	W. M. Lawry	317/52
Port Elizabeth	South Africa	Lost by 323 runs	W. M. Lawry	318/53
1970-71 in Australia				
Brisbane	England	Drawn	W. M. Lawry	319/204
Perth	England	Drawn	W. M. Lawry	320/205
Melbourne	England	Drawn	W. M. Lawry	321/206
Sydney	England	Lost by 299 runs	W. M. Lawry	322/207
Melbourne	England	Drawn	W. M. Lawry	323/208
Adelaide	England	Drawn	W. M. Lawry	324/209
Sydney	England	Lost by 62 runs	I. M. Chappell	325/210

Venue	Opponent	Result for Australia	Captain	Test/Opp
1972 in England				
Manchester	England	Lost by 89 runs	I. M. Chappell	326/211
Lord's	England	Won by eight wickets	I. M. Chappell	327/212
Nottingham	England	Drawn	I. M. Chappell	328/213
Leeds	England	Lost by nine wickets	I. M. Chappell	329/214
The Oval	England	Won by five wickets	I. M. Chappell	330/215
1972-73 in Australia				
Adelaide	Pakistan	Won by an innings and 114 runs	I. M. Chappell	331/7
Melbourne	Pakistan	Won by 92 runs	I. M. Chappell	332/8
Sydney	Pakistan	Won by 52 runs	I. M. Chappell	333/9
1972-73 in West Indies				
Kingston	West Indies	Drawn	I. M. Chappell	334/31
Bridgetown	West Indies	Drawn	I. M. Chappell	335/32
Port-of-Spain	West Indies	Won by 44 runs	I. M. Chappell	336/33
Georgetown	West Indies	Won by ten wickets	I. M. Chappell	337/34
Port-of-Spain	West Indies	Drawn	I. M. Chappell	338/35
1973-74 in Australia				
Melbourne	New Zealand	Won by an innings and 25 runs	I. M. Chappell	339/2
Sydney	New Zealand	Drawn	I. M. Chappell	340/3
Adelaide	New Zealand	Won by an innings and 57 runs	I. M. Chappell	341/4
1973-74 in New Zealand				
Wellington	New Zealand	Drawn	I. M. Chappell	342/5
Christchurch	New Zealand	Lost by five wickets	I. M. Chappell	343/6
Auckland	New Zealand	Won by 297 runs	I. M. Chappell	344/7
1974-75 in Australia				
Brisbane	England	Won by 166 runs	I. M. Chappell	345/216
Perth	England	Won by nine wickets	I. M. Chappell	346/217
Melbourne	England	Drawn	I. M. Chappell	347/218
Sydney	England	Won by 171 runs	I. M. Chappell	348/219
Adelaide	England	Won by 163 runs	I. M. Chappell	349/220
Melbourne	England	Lost by an innings and four runs	I. M. Chappell	350/221
1975 in England				
Birmingham	England	Won by an innings and 85 runs	I. M. Chappell	351/222
Lord's	England	Drawn	I. M. Chappell	352/223
Leeds	England	Drawn	I. M. Chappell	353/224
The Oval	England	Drawn	I. M. Chappell	354/225
1975-76 in Australia				
Brisbane	West Indies	Won by eight wickets	G. S. Chappell	355/36
Perth	West Indies	Lost by an innings and 87 runs	G. S. Chappell	356/37
Melbourne	West Indies	Won by eight wickets	G. S. Chappell	357/38
Sydney	West Indies	Won by seven wickets	G. S. Chappell	358/39
Adelaide	West Indies	Won by 190 runs	G. S. Chappell	359/40
Melbourne	West Indies	Won by 165 runs	G. S. Chappell	360/41
1976-77 in Australia				
Adelaide	Pakistan	Drawn	G. S. Chappell	361/10
Melbourne	Pakistan	Won by 348 runs	G. S. Chappell	362/11
Sydney	Pakistan	Lost by eight wickets	G. S. Chappell	363/12
1976-77 in New Zealand				
Christchurch	New Zealand	Drawn	G. S. Chappell	364/8
Auckland	New Zealand	Won by ten wickets	G. S. Chappell	365/9
1976-77 in Australia				
Melbourne	England	Won by 45 runs	G. S. Chappell	366/226

Venue	Opponent	Result for Australia	Captain	Test/Opp
1977 in England				
Lord's	England	Drawn	G. S. Chappell	367/227
Manchester	England	Lost by nine wickets	G. S. Chappell	368/228
Nottingham	England	Lost by seven wickets	G. S. Chappell	369/229
Leeds	England	Lost by an innings and 85 runs	G. S. Chappell	370/230
The Oval	England	Drawn	G. S. Chappell	371/231
1977-78 in Australia				
Brisbane	India	Won by 16 runs	R. B. Simpson	372/26
Perth	India	Won by two wickets	R. B. Simpson	373/27
Melbourne	India	Lost by 222 runs	R. B. Simpson	374/28
Sydney	India	Lost by an innings and two runs	R. B. Simpson	375/29
Adelaide	India	Won by 47 runs	R. B. Simpson	376/30
1977-78 in West Indies				
Port-of-Spain	West Indies	Lost by an innings and 106 runs	R. B. Simpson	377/42
Bridgetown	West Indies	Lost by nine wickets	R. B. Simpson	378/43
Georgetown	West Indies	Won by three wickets	R. B. Simpson	379/44
Port-of-Spain	West Indies	Lost by 198 runs	R. B. Simpson	380/45
Kingston	West Indies	Drawn	R. B. Simpson	381/46
1978-79 in Australia				
Brisbane	England	Lost by seven wickets	G. N. Yallop	382/232
Perth	England	Lost by 166 runs	G. N. Yallop	383/233
Melbourne	England	Won by 103 runs	G. N. Yallop	384/234
Sydney	England	Lost by 93 runs	G. N. Yallop	385/235
Adelaide	England	Lost by 205 runs	G. N. Yallop	386/236
Sydney	England	Lost by nine wickets	G. N. Yallop	387/237
Melbourne	Pakistan	Lost by 71 runs	G. N. Yallop	388/13
Perth	Pakistan	Won by seven wickets	K. J. Hughes	389/14
1979-80 in India				
Madras (Chepauk)	India	Drawn	K. J. Hughes	390/31
Bangalore	India	Drawn	K. J. Hughes	391/32
Kanpur	India	Lost by 153 runs	K. J. Hughes	392/33
Delhi	India	Drawn	K. J. Hughes	393/34
Calcutta	India	Drawn	K. J. Hughes	394/35
Bombay (WS)	India	Lost by an innings and 100 runs	K. J. Hughes	395/36
1979-80 in Australia				
Brisbane	West Indies	Drawn	G. S. Chappell	396/47
Perth	England	Won by 138 runs	G. S. Chappell	397/238
Melbourne	West Indies	Lost by ten wickets	G. S. Chappell	398/48
Sydney	England	Won by six wickets	G. S. Chappell	399/239
Adelaide	West Indies	Lost by 408 runs	G. S. Chappell	400/49
Melbourne	England	Won by eight wickets	G. S. Chappell	401/240
1979-80 in Pakistan				
Karachi	Pakistan	Lost by seven wickets	G. S. Chappell	402/15
Faisalabad	Pakistan	Drawn	G. S. Chappell	403/16
Lahore	Pakistan	Drawn	G. S. Chappell	404/17
1980 in England				
Lord's	England	Drawn	G. S. Chappell	405/241
1980-81 in Australia				
Brisbane	New Zealand	Won by ten wickets	G. S. Chappell	406/10
Perth	New Zealand	Won by eight wickets	G. S. Chappell	407/11
Melbourne	New Zealand	Drawn	G. S. Chappell	408/12
Sydney	India	Won by an innings and four runs	G. S. Chappell	409/37
Adelaide	India	Drawn	G. S. Chappell	410/38
Melbourne	India	Lost by 59 runs	G. S. Chappell	411/39

Venue	Opponent	Result for Australia	Captain	Test/Opp
1981 in England				
Nottingham	England	Won by four wickets	K.J. Hughes	412/242
Lord's	England	Drawn	K.J. Hughes	413/243
Leeds	England	Lost by 18 runs	K.J. Hughes	414/244
Birmingham	England	Lost by 29 runs	K.J. Hughes	415/245
Manchester	England	Lost by 103 runs	K.J. Hughes	416/246
The Oval	England	Drawn	K.J. Hughes	417/247
1981-82 in Australia				
Perth	Pakistan	Won by 286 runs	G.S. Chappell	418/18
Brisbane	Pakistan	Won by ten wickets	G.S. Chappell	419/19
Melbourne	Pakistan	Lost by an innings and 82 runs	G.S. Chappell	420/20
Melbourne	West Indies	Won by 58 runs	G.S. Chappell	421/50
Sydney	West Indies	Drawn	G.S. Chappell	422/51
Adelaide	West Indies	Lost by five wickets	G.S. Chappell	423/52
1981-82 in New Zealand				
Wellington	New Zealand	Drawn	G.S. Chappell	424/13
Auckland	New Zealand	Lost by five wickets	G.S. Chappell	425/14
Christchurch	New Zealand	Won by eight wickets	G.S. Chappell	426/15
1982-83 in Pakistan				
Karachi	Pakistan	Lost by nine wickets	K.J. Hughes	427/21
Faisalabad	Pakistan	Lost by an innings and three runs	K.J. Hughes	428/22
Lahore	Pakistan	Lost by nine wickets	K.J. Hughes	429/23
1982-83 in Australia				
Perth	England	Drawn	G.S. Chappell	430/248
Brisbane	England	Won by seven wickets	G.S. Chappell	431/249
Adelaide	England	Won by eight wickets	G.S. Chappell	432/250
Melbourne	England	Lost by three runs	G.S. Chappell	433/251
Sydney	England	Drawn	G.S. Chappell	434/252
1982-83 in Sri Lanka				
Kandy	Sri Lanka	Won by an innings and 38 runs	G.S. Chappell	435/1
1983-84 in Australia				
Perth	Pakistan	Won by an innings and nine runs	K.J. Hughes	436/24
Brisbane	Pakistan	Drawn	K.J. Hughes	437/25
Adelaide	Pakistan	Drawn	K.J. Hughes	438/26
Melbourne	Pakistan	Drawn	K.J. Hughes	439/27
Sydney	Pakistan	Won by ten wickets	K.J. Hughes	440/28
1983-84 in West Indies				
Georgetown	West Indies	Drawn	K.J. Hughes	441/53
Port-of-Spain	West Indies	Drawn	K.J. Hughes	442/54
Bridgetown	West Indies	Lost by ten wickets	K.J. Hughes	443/55
St John's	West Indies	Lost by an innings and 36 runs	K.J. Hughes	444/56
Kingston	West Indies	Lost by ten wickets	K.J. Hughes	445/57
1984-85 in Australia				
Perth	West Indies	Lost by an innings and 112 runs	K.J. Hughes	446/58
Brisbane	West Indies	Lost by eight wickets	K.J. Hughes	447/59
Adelaide	West Indies	Lost by 191 runs	A.R. Border	448/60
Melbourne	West Indies	Drawn	A.R. Border	449/61
Sydney	West Indies	Won by an innings and 55 runs	A.R. Border	450/62
1985 in England				
Leeds	England	Lost by five wickets	A.R. Border	451/253
Lord's	England	Won by four wickets	A.R. Border	452/254
Nottingham	England	Drawn	A.R. Border	453/255
Manchester	England	Drawn	A.R. Border	454/256
Birmingham	England	Lost by an innings and 118 runs	A.R. Border	455/257
The Oval	England	Lost by an innings and 94 runs	A.R. Border	456/258

Venue	Opponent	Result for Australia	Captain	Test/Opp
1985-86 in Australia				
Brisbane	New Zealand	Lost by an innings and 41 runs	A. R. Border	457/16
Sydney	New Zealand	Won by four wickets	A. R. Border	458/17
Perth	New Zealand	Lost by six wickets	A. R. Border	459/18
Adelaide	India	Drawn	A. R. Border	460/40
Melbourne	India	Drawn	A. R. Border	461/41
Sydney	India	Drawn	A. R. Border	462/42
1985-86 in New Zealand				
Wellington	New Zealand	Drawn	A. R. Border	463/19
Christchurch	New Zealand	Drawn	A. R. Border	464/20
Auckland	New Zealand	Lost by eight wickets	A. R. Border	465/21
1986-87 in India				
Madras (Chepauk)	India	Tied	A. R. Border	466/43
Delhi	India	Drawn	A. R. Border	467/44
Bombay (WS)	India	Drawn	A. R. Border	468/45
1986-87 in Australia				
Brisbane	England	Lost by seven wickets	A. R. Border	469/259
Perth	England	Drawn	A. R. Border	470/260
Adelaide	England	Drawn	A. R. Border	471/261
Melbourne	England	Lost by an innings and 14 runs	A. R. Border	472/262
Sydney	England	Won by 55 runs	A. R. Border	473/263
1987-88 in Australia				
Brisbane	New Zealand	Won by nine wickets	A. R. Border	474/22
Adelaide	New Zealand	Drawn	A. R. Border	475/23
Melbourne	New Zealand	Drawn	A. R. Border	476/24
Sydney	England	Drawn	A. R. Border	477/264
Perth	Sri Lanka	Won by an innings and 108 runs	A. R. Border	478/2
1988-89 in Pakistan				
Karachi	Pakistan	Lost by an innings and 188 runs	A. R. Border	479/29
Faisalabad	Pakistan	Drawn	A. R. Border	480/30
Lahore	Pakistan	Drawn	A. R. Border	481/31
1988-89 in Australia				
Brisbane	West Indies	Lost by eight wickets	A. R. Border	482/63
Perth	West Indies	Lost by 169 runs	A. R. Border	483/64
Melbourne	West Indies	Lost by 285 runs	A. R. Border	484/65
Sydney	West Indies	Won by seven wickets	A. R. Border	485/66
Adelaide	West Indies	Drawn	A. R. Border	486/67
1989 in England				
Leeds	England	Won by 210 runs	A. R. Border	487/265
Lord's	England	Won by six wickets	A. R. Border	488/266
Birmingham	England	Drawn	A. R. Border	489/267
Manchester	England	Won by nine wickets	A. R. Border	490/268
Nottingham	England	Won by an innings and 180 runs	A. R. Border	491/269
The Oval	England	Drawn	A. R. Border	492/270
1989-90 in Australia				
Perth	New Zealand	Drawn	A. R. Border	493/25
Brisbane	Sri Lanka	Drawn	A. R. Border	494/3
Hobart	Sri Lanka	Won by 173 runs	A. R. Border	495/4
Melbourne	Pakistan	Won by 92 runs	A. R. Border	496/32
Adelaide	Pakistan	Drawn	A. R. Border	497/33
Sydney	Pakistan	Drawn	A. R. Border	498/34
1989-90 in New Zealand				
Wellington	New Zealand	Lost by nine wickets	A. R. Border	499/26

Venue	Opponent	Result for Australia	Captain	Test/Opp
1990-91 in Australia				
Brisbane	England	Won by ten wickets	A. R. Border	500/271
Melbourne	England	Won by eight wickets	A. R. Border	501/272
Sydney	England	Drawn	A. R. Border	502/273
Adelaide	England	Drawn	A. R. Border	503/274
Perth	England	Won by nine wickets	A. R. Border	504/275
1990-91 in West Indies				
Kingston	West Indies	Drawn	A. R. Border	505/68
Georgetown	West Indies	Lost by ten wickets	A. R. Border	506/69
Port-of-Spain	West Indies	Drawn	A. R. Border	507/70
Bridgetown	West Indies	Lost by 343 runs	A. R. Border	508/71
St John's	West Indies	Won by 157 runs	A. R. Border	509/72
1991-92 in Australia				
Brisbane	India	Won by ten wickets	A. R. Border	510/46
Melbourne	India	Won by eight wickets	A. R. Border	511/47
Sydney	India	Drawn	A. R. Border	512/48
Adelaide	India	Won by 38 runs	A. R. Border	513/49
Perth	India	Won by 300 runs	A. R. Border	514/50
1992-93 in Sri Lanka				
Colombo (SSC)	Sri Lanka	Won by 16 runs	A. R. Border	515/5
Colombo (PIS)	Sri Lanka	Drawn	A. R. Border	516/6
Moratuwa	Sri Lanka	Drawn	A. R. Border	517/7
1992-93 in Australia				
Brisbane	West Indies	Drawn	A. R. Border	518/73
Melbourne	West Indies	Won by 139 runs	A. R. Border	519/74
Sydney	West Indies	Drawn	A. R. Border	520/75
Adelaide	West Indies	Lost by one run	A. R. Border	521/76
Perth	West Indies	Lost by an innings and 25 runs	A. R. Border	522/77
1992-93 in New Zealand				
Christchurch	New Zealand	Won by an innings and 60 runs	A. R. Border	523/27
Wellington	New Zealand	Drawn	A. R. Border	524/28
Auckland	New Zealand	Lost by five wickets	A. R. Border	525/29
1993 in England				
Manchester	England	Won by 179 runs	A. R. Border	526/276
Lord's	England	Won by an innings and 62 runs	A. R. Border	527/277
Nottingham	England	Drawn	A. R. Border	528/278
Leeds	England	Won by an innings and 148 runs	A. R. Border	529/279
Birmingham	England	Won by eight wickets	A. R. Border	530/280
The Oval	England	Lost by 161 runs	A. R. Border	531/281
1993-94 in Australia				
Perth	New Zealand	Drawn	A. R. Border	532/30
Hobart	New Zealand	Won by an innings and 222 runs	A. R. Border	533/31
Brisbane	New Zealand	Won by an innings and 96 runs	A. R. Border	534/32
Melbourne	South Africa	Drawn	A. R. Border	535/54
Sydney	South Africa	Lost by five runs	A. R. Border	536/55
Adelaide	South Africa	Won by 191 runs	A. R. Border	537/56
1993-94 in South Africa				
Johannesburg (WS)	South Africa	Lost by 197 runs	A. R. Border	538/57
Cape Town	South Africa	Won by nine wickets	A. R. Border	539/58
Durban (Kingsmead)	South Africa	Drawn	A. R. Border	540/59
1994-95 in Pakistan				
Karachi	Pakistan	Lost by one wicket	M. A. Taylor	541/35
Rawalpindi	Pakistan	Drawn	M. A. Taylor	542/36
Lahore	Pakistan	Drawn	M. A. Taylor	543/37

Venue	Opponent	Result for Australia	Captain	Test/Opp
1994-95 in Australia				
Brisbane	England	Won by 184 runs	M. A. Taylor	544/282
Melbourne	England	Won by 295 runs	M. A. Taylor	545/283
Sydney	England	Drawn	M. A. Taylor	546/284
Adelaide	England	Lost by 106 runs	M. A. Taylor	547/285
Perth	England	Won by 329 runs	M. A. Taylor	548/286
1994-95 in West Indies				
Bridgetown	West Indies	Won by ten wickets	M. A. Taylor	549/78
St John's	West Indies	Drawn	M. A. Taylor	550/79
Port-of-Spain	West Indies	Lost by nine wickets	M. A. Taylor	551/80
Kingston	West Indies	Won by an innings and 53 runs	M. A. Taylor	552/81
1995-96 in Australia				
Brisbane	Pakistan	Won by an innings and 126 runs	M. A. Taylor	553/38
Hobart	Pakistan	Won by 155 runs	M. A. Taylor	554/39
Sydney	Pakistan	Lost by 74 runs	M. A. Taylor	555/40
Perth	Sri Lanka	Won by an innings and 36 runs	M. A. Taylor	556/8
Melbourne	Sri Lanka	Won by ten wickets	M. A. Taylor	557/9
Adelaide	Sri Lanka	Won by 148 runs	M. A. Taylor	558/10
1996-97 in India				
Delhi	India	Lost by seven wickets	M. A. Taylor	559/51
1996-97 in Australia				
Brisbane	West Indies	Won by 123 runs	M. A. Taylor	560/82
Sydney	West Indies	Won by 124 runs	M. A. Taylor	561/83
Melbourne	West Indies	Lost by six wickets	M. A. Taylor	562/84
Adelaide	West Indies	Won by an innings and 183 runs	M. A. Taylor	563/85
Perth	West Indies	Lost by ten wickets	M. A. Taylor	564/86
1996-97 in South Africa				
Johannesburg (WS)	South Africa	Won by an innings and 196 runs	M. A. Taylor	565/60
Port Elizabeth	South Africa	Won by two wickets	M. A. Taylor	566/61
Centurion	South Africa	Lost by eight wickets	M. A. Taylor	567/62
1997 in England				
Birmingham	England	Lost by nine wickets	M. A. Taylor	568/287
Lord's	England	Drawn	M. A. Taylor	569/288
Manchester	England	Won by 268 runs	M. A. Taylor	570/289
Leeds	England	Won by an innings and 61 runs	M. A. Taylor	571/290
Nottingham	England	Won by 264 runs	M. A. Taylor	572/291
The Oval	England	Lost by 19 runs	M. A. Taylor	573/292
1997-98 in Australia				
Brisbane	New Zealand	Won by 186 runs	M. A. Taylor	574/33
Perth	New Zealand	Won by an innings and 70 runs	M. A. Taylor	575/34
Hobart	New Zealand	Drawn	M. A. Taylor	576/35
Melbourne	South Africa	Drawn	M. A. Taylor	577/63
Sydney	South Africa	Won by an innings and 21 runs	M. A. Taylor	578/64
Adelaide	South Africa	Drawn	M. A. Taylor	579/65
1997-98 in India				
Chennai (Chepauk)	India	Lost by 179 runs	M. A. Taylor	580/52
Calcutta	India	Lost by an innings and 219 runs	M. A. Taylor	581/53
Bangalore	India	Won by eight wickets	M. A. Taylor	582/54
1998-99 in Pakistan				
Rawalpindi	Pakistan	Won by an innings and 99 runs	M. A. Taylor	583/40
Peshawar	Pakistan	Drawn	M. A. Taylor	584/41
Karachi	Pakistan	Drawn	M. A. Taylor	585/42

Venue	Opponent	Result for Australia	Captain	Test/Opp
1998-99 in Australia				
Brisbane	England	Drawn	M. A. Taylor	586/293
Perth	England	Won by seven wickets	M. A. Taylor	587/294
Adelaide	England	Won by 205 runs	M. A. Taylor	588/295
Melbourne	England	Lost by 12 runs	M. A. Taylor	589/296
Sydney	England	Won by 98 runs	M. A. Taylor	590/297
1998-99 in West Indies				
Port-of-Spain	West Indies	Won by 312 runs	S. R. Waugh	591/87
Kingston	West Indies	Lost by ten wickets	S. R. Waugh	592/88
Bridgetown	West Indies	Lost by one wicket	S. R. Waugh	593/89
St John's	West Indies	Won by 176 runs	S. R. Waugh	594/90
1999-00 in Sri Lanka				
Kandy	Sri Lanka	Lost by six wickets	S. R. Waugh	595/11
Galle	Sri Lanka	Drawn	S. R. Waugh	596/12
Colombo (SSC)	Sri Lanka	Drawn	S. R. Waugh	597/13
1999-00 in Zimbabwe				
Harare	Zimbabwe	Won by ten wickets	S. R. Waugh	598/1
1999-00 in Australia				
Brisbane	Pakistan	Won by ten wickets	S. R. Waugh	599/44
Hobart (Bel)	Pakistan	Won by four wickets	S. R. Waugh	600/45
Perth	Pakistan	Won by an innings and 20 runs	S. R. Waugh	601/46
Adelaide	India	Won by 285 runs	S. R. Waugh	602/55
Melbourne	India	Won by 180 runs	S. R. Waugh	603/56
Sydney	India	Won by an innings and 141 runs	S. R. Waugh	604/57
1999-00 in New Zealand				
Auckland	New Zealand	Won by 62 runs	S. R. Waugh	605/36
Wellington	New Zealand	Won by six wickets	S. R. Waugh	606/37
Hamilton	New Zealand	Won by six wickets	S. R. Waugh	607/38
2000-01 in Australia				
Brisbane	West Indies	Won by an innings and 126 runs	S. R. Waugh	608/91
Perth	West Indies	Won by an innings and 27 runs	S. R. Waugh	609/92
Adelaide	West Indies	Won by five wickets	A. C. Gilchrist	610/93
Melbourne	West Indies	Won by 352 runs	S. R. Waugh	611/94
Sydney	West Indies	Won by six wickets	S. R. Waugh	612/95
2000-01 in India				
Mumbai (WS)	India	Won by ten wickets	S. R. Waugh	613/58
Kolkata	India	Lost by 171 runs	S. R. Waugh	614/59
Chennai (Chepauk)	India	Lost by two wickets	S. R. Waugh	615/60
2001 in England				
Birmingham	England	Won by an innings and 126 runs	S. R. Waugh	616/298
Lord's	England	Won by eight wickets	S. R. Waugh	617/299
Nottingham	England	Won by seven wickets	S. R. Waugh	618/300
Leeds	England	Lost by six wickets	A. C. Gilchrist	619/301
The Oval	England	Won by an innings and 25 runs	S. R. Waugh	620/302
2001-02 in Australia				
Brisbane	New Zealand	Drawn	S. R. Waugh	621/39
Hobart (Bel)	New Zealand	Drawn	S. R. Waugh	622/40
Perth	New Zealand	Drawn	S. R. Waugh	623/41
Adelaide	South Africa	Won by 246 runs	S. R. Waugh	624/66
Melbourne	South Africa	Won by nine wickets	S. R. Waugh	625/67
Sydney	South Africa	Won by ten wickets	S. R. Waugh	626/68

Venue	Opponent	Result for Australia	Captain	Test/Opp
2001-02 in South Africa				
Johannesburg (WS)	South Africa	Won by an innings and 360 runs	S. R. Waugh	627/69
Cape Town	South Africa	Won by four wickets	S. R. Waugh	628/70
Durban (Kingsmead)	South Africa	Lost by five wickets	S. R. Waugh	629/71

SERIES RESULTS FOR AUSTRALIA

Season	Opponent	Venue	Tests	Won	Lost	Drawn	Tied	Result of series
1876-77	England	Australia	2	1	1	0	0	Drawn 1-1
1878-79	England	Australia	1	1	0	0	0	Won 1-0
1880	England	England	1	0	1	0	0	Lost 1-0
1881-82	England	Australia	4	2	0	2	0	Won 2-0
1882	England	England	1	1	0	0	0	Won 1-0
1882-83	England	Australia	4	2	2	0	0	Drawn 2-2
1884	England	England	3	0	1	2	0	Lost 1-0
1884-85	England	Australia	5	2	3	0	0	Lost 3-2
1886	England	England	3	0	3	0	0	Lost 3-0
1886-87	England	Australia	2	0	2	0	0	Lost 2-0
1887-88	England	Australia	1	0	1	0	0	Lost 1-0
1888	England	England	3	1	2	0	0	Lost 2-1
1890	England	England	2	0	2	0	0	Lost 2-0
1891-92	England	Australia	3	2	1	0	0	Won 2-1
1893	England	England	3	0	1	2	0	Lost 1-0
1894-95	England	Australia	5	2	3	0	0	Lost 3-2
1896	England	England	3	1	2	0	0	Lost 2-1
1897-98	England	Australia	5	4	1	0	0	Won 4-1
1899	England	England	5	1	0	4	0	Won 1-0
1901-02	England	Australia	5	4	1	0	0	Won 4-1
1902	England	England	5	2	1	2	0	Won 2-1
1902-03	South Africa	South Africa	3	2	0	1	0	Won 2-0
1903-04	England	Australia	5	2	3	0	0	Lost 3-2
1905	England	England	5	0	2	3	0	Lost 2-0
1907-08	England	Australia	5	4	1	0	0	Won 4-1
1909	England	England	5	2	1	2	0	Won 2-1
1910-11	South Africa	Australia	5	4	1	0	0	Won 4-1
1911-12	England	Australia	5	1	4	0	0	Lost 4-1
1912	South Africa	England	3	2	0	1	0	Won 2-0
1912	England	England	3	0	1	2	0	Lost 1-0
1920-21	England	Australia	5	5	0	0	0	Won 5-0
1921	England	England	5	3	0	2	0	Won 3-0
1921-22	South Africa	South Africa	3	1	0	2	0	Won 1-0
1924-25	England	Australia	5	4	1	0	0	Won 4-1
1926	England	England	5	0	1	4	0	Lost 1-0
1928-29	England	Australia	5	1	4	0	0	Lost 4-1
1930	England	England	5	2	1	2	0	Won 2-1
1930-31	West Indies	Australia	5	4	1	0	0	Won 4-1
1931-32	South Africa	Australia	5	5	0	0	0	Won 5-0
1932-33	England	Australia	5	1	4	0	0	Lost 4-1
1934	England	England	5	2	1	2	0	Won 2-1
1935-36	South Africa	South Africa	5	4	0	1	0	Won 4-0
1936-37	England	Australia	5	3	2	0	0	Won 3-2
1938	England	England	4	1	1	2	0	Drawn 1-1
1945-46	New Zealand	New Zealand	1	1	0	0	0	Won 1-0
1946-47	England	Australia	5	3	0	2	0	Won 3-0
1947-48	India	Australia	5	4	0	1	0	Won 4-0
1948	England	England	5	4	0	1	0	Won 4-0
1949-50	South Africa	South Africa	5	4	0	1	0	Won 4-0
1950-51	England	Australia	5	4	1	0	0	Won 4-1

Season	Opponent	Venue	Tests	Won	Lost	Drawn	Tied	Result of series	
1951-52	West Indies	Australia	5	4	1	0	0	Won	4-1
1952-53	South Africa	Australia	5	2	2	1	0	Drawn	2-2
1953	England	England	5	0	1	4	0	Lost	1-0
1954-55	England	Australia	5	1	3	1	0	Lost	3-1
	West Indies	West Indies	5	3	0	2	0	Won	3-0
1956	England	England	5	1	2	2	0	Lost	2-1
1956-57	Pakistan	Pakistan	1	0	1	0	0	Lost	1-0
	India	India	3	2	0	1	0	Won	2-0
1957-58	South Africa	South Africa	5	3	0	2	0	Won	3-0
1958-59	England	Australia	5	4	0	1	0	Won	4-0
1959-60	Pakistan	Pakistan	3	2	0	1	0	Won	2-0
	India	India	5	2	1	2	0	Won	2-1
1960-61	West Indies	Australia	5	2	1	1	1	Won	2-1
1961	England	England	5	2	1	2	0	Won	2-1
1962-63	England	Australia	5	1	1	3	0	Drawn	1-1
1963-64	South Africa	Australia	5	1	1	3	0	Drawn	1-1
1964	England	England	5	1	0	4	0	Won	1-0
1964-65	India	India	3	1	1	1	0	Drawn	1-1
	Pakistan	Pakistan	1	0	0	1	0	Drawn	0-0
	Pakistan	Australia	1	0	0	1	0	Drawn	0-0
	West Indies	West Indies	5	1	2	2	0	Lost	2-1
1965-66	England	Australia	5	1	1	3	0	Drawn	1-1
1966-67	South Africa	South Africa	5	1	3	1	0	Lost	3-1
1967-68	India	Australia	4	4	0	0	0	Won	4-0
1968	England	England	5	1	1	3	0	Drawn	1-1
1968-69	West Indies	Australia	5	3	1	1	0	Won	3-1
1969-70	India	India	5	3	1	1	0	Won	3-1
	South Africa	South Africa	4	0	4	0	0	Lost	4-0
1970-71	England	Australia	7	0	2	5	0	Lost	2-0
1972	England	England	5	2	2	1	0	Drawn	2-2
1972-73	Pakistan	Australia	3	3	0	0	0	Won	3-0
	West Indies	West Indies	5	2	0	3	0	Won	2-0
1973-74	New Zealand	Australia	3	2	0	1	0	Won	2-0
	New Zealand	New Zealand	3	1	1	1	0	Drawn	1-1
1974-75	England	Australia	6	4	1	1	0	Won	4-1
1975	England	England	4	1	0	3	0	Won	1-0
1975-76	West Indies	Australia	6	5	1	0	0	Won	5-1
1976-77	Pakistan	Australia	3	1	1	1	0	Drawn	1-1
	New Zealand	New Zealand	2	1	0	1	0	Won	1-0
	England	Australia	1	1	0	0	0	Won	1-0
1977	England	England	5	0	3	2	0	Lost	3-0
1977-78	India	Australia	5	3	2	0	0	Won	3-2
	West Indies	West Indies	5	1	3	1	0	Lost	3-1
1978-79	England	Australia	6	1	5	0	0	Lost	5-1
	Pakistan	Australia	2	1	1	0	0	Drawn	1-1
1979-80	India	India	6	0	2	4	0	Lost	2-0
	West Indies	Australia	3	0	2	1	0	Lost	2-0
	England	Australia	3	3	0	0	0	Won	3-0
	Pakistan	Pakistan	3	0	1	2	0	Lost	1-0
1980	England	England	1	0	0	1	0	Drawn	0-0
1980-81	New Zealand	Australia	3	2	0	1	0	Won	2-0
	India	Australia	3	1	1	1	0	Drawn	1-1
1981	England	England	6	1	3	2	0	Lost	3-1
1981-82	Pakistan	Australia	3	2	1	0	0	Won	2-1
	West Indies	Australia	3	1	1	1	0	Drawn	1-1
	New Zealand	New Zealand	3	1	1	1	0	Drawn	1-1
1982-83	Pakistan	Pakistan	3	0	3	0	0	Lost	3-0
	England	Australia	5	2	1	2	0	Won	2-1
	Sri Lanka	Sri Lanka	1	1	0	0	0	Won	1-0
1983-84	Pakistan	Australia	5	2	0	3	0	Won	2-0
	West Indies	West Indies	5	0	3	2	0	Lost	3-0

Season	Opponent	Venue	Tests	Won	Lost	Drawn	Tied	Result of series
1984-85	West Indies	Australia	5	1	3	1	0	Lost 3-1
1985	England	England	6	1	3	2	0	Lost 3-1
1985-86	New Zealand	Australia	3	1	2	0	0	Lost 2-1
	India	Australia	3	0	0	3	0	Drawn 0-0
	New Zealand	New Zealand	3	0	1	2	0	Lost 1-0
1986-87	India	India	3	0	0	2	1	Drawn 0-0
	England	Australia	5	1	2	2	0	Lost 2-1
1987-88	New Zealand	Australia	3	1	0	2	0	Won 1-0
	England	Australia	1	0	0	1	0	Drawn 0-0
	Sri Lanka	Australia	1	1	0	0	0	Won 1-0
1988-89	Pakistan	Pakistan	3	0	1	2	0	Lost 1-0
	West Indies	Australia	5	1	3	1	0	Lost 3-1
1989	England	England	6	4	0	2	0	Won 4-0
1989-90	New Zealand	Australia	1	0	0	1	0	Drawn 0-0
	Sri Lanka	Australia	2	1	0	1	0	Won 1-0
	Pakistan	Australia	3	1	0	2	0	Won 1-0
	New Zealand	New Zealand	1	0	1	0	0	Lost 1-0
1990-91	England	Australia	5	3	0	2	0	Won 3-0
	West Indies	West Indies	5	1	2	2	0	Lost 2-1
1991-92	India	Australia	5	4	0	1	0	Won 4-0
	Sri Lanka	Sri Lanka	3	1	0	2	0	Won 1-0
1992-93	West Indies	Australia	5	1	2	2	0	Lost 2-1
	New Zealand	New Zealand	3	1	1	1	0	Drawn 1-1
1993	England	England	6	4	1	1	0	Won 4-1
1993-94	New Zealand	Australia	3	2	0	1	0	Won 2-0
	South Africa	Australia	3	1	1	1	0	Drawn 1-1
	South Africa	South Africa	3	1	1	1	0	Drawn 1-1
1994-95	Pakistan	Pakistan	3	0	1	2	0	Lost 1-0
	England	Australia	5	3	1	1	0	Won 3-1
	West Indies	West Indies	4	2	1	1	0	Won 2-1
1995-96	Pakistan	Australia	3	2	1	0	0	Won 2-1
	Sri Lanka	Australia	3	3	0	0	0	Won 3-0
1996-97	India	India	1	1	0	0	0	Lost 1-0
	West Indies	Australia	5	3	2	0	0	Won 3-2
	South Africa	South Africa	3	2	1	0	0	Won 2-1
1997	England	England	6	3	2	1	0	Won 3-2
1997-98	New Zealand	Australia	3	2	0	1	0	Won 2-0
	South Africa	Australia	3	1	0	2	0	Won 1-0
	India	India	3	1	2	0	0	Lost 2-1
1998-99	Pakistan	Pakistan	3	1	0	2	0	Won 1-0
	England	Australia	5	3	1	1	0	Won 3-1
	West Indies	West Indies	4	2	2	0	0	Drawn 2-2
1999-00	Sri Lanka	Sri Lanka	3	0	1	2	0	Lost 1-0
	Zimbabwe	Zimbabwe	1	1	0	0	0	Won 1-0
	Pakistan	Australia	3	3	0	0	0	Won 3-0
	India	Australia	3	3	0	0	0	Won 3-0
	New Zealand	New Zealand	3	3	0	0	0	Won 3-0
2000-01	West Indies	Australia	5	5	0	0	0	Won 5-0
	India	India	3	1	2	0	0	Lost 1-2
2001	England	England	5	4	1	0	0	Won 4-1
2001-02	New Zealand	Australia	3	0	0	3	0	Drawn 0-0
	South Africa	Australia	3	3	0	0	0	Won 3-0
	South Africa	South Africa	3	2	1	0	0	Won 2-1

Tests in Australia			324	172	85	66	1	
Tests abroad			305	103	87	114	1	
Total			629	275	172	180	2	

AUSTRALIAN LIMITED-OVERS INTERNATIONAL RECORDS

AUSTRALIAN LIMITED-OVERS INTERNATIONAL MATCHES

Date	Venue	Opponent	Result for Australia	Captain	Team/Opp
1970-71 in Australia					
Jan 5	Melbourne	England	Won by five wickets	W. M. Lawry	1/1
1972 in England					
Aug 24	Manchester	England	Lost by six wickets	I. M. Chappell	2/2
Aug 26	Lord's	England	Won by five wickets	I. M. Chappell	3/3
Aug 28	Birmingham	England	Lost by two wickets	I. M. Chappell	4/4
1973-74 in New Zealand					
Mar 30	Dunedin	New Zealand	Won by seven wickets	I. M. Chappell	5/1
Mar 31	Christchurch	New Zealand	Won by 31 runs	I. M. Chappell	6/2
1974-75 in Australia					
Jan 1	Melbourne	England	Lost by three wickets	I. M. Chappell	7/5
1975 World Cup in England					
Jun 7	Leeds	Pakistan	Won by 73 runs	I. M. Chappell	8/1
Jun 11	The Oval	Sri Lanka	Won by 52 runs	I. M. Chappell	9/1
Jun 14	The Oval	West Indies	Lost by seven wickets	I. M. Chappell	10/1
Jun 18	Leeds	England	Won by four wickets	I. M. Chappell	11/6
Jun 21	Lord's	West Indies	Lost by 17 runs	I. M. Chappell	12/2
1975-76 in Australia					
Dec 20	Adelaide	West Indies	Won by five wickets	G. S. Chappell	13/3
1977 in England					
Jun 2	Manchester	England	Lost by two wickets	G. S. Chappell	14/7
Jun 4	Birmingham	England	Lost by 99 runs	G. S. Chappell	15/8
Jun 6	The Oval	England	Won by two wickets	G. S. Chappell	16/9
1977-78 in West Indies					
Feb 22	St John's	West Indies	Lost on run-rate	R. B. Simpson	17/4
Apr 12	Castries	West Indies	Won by two wickets	R. B. Simpson	18/5
1978-79 in Australia					
Jan 13	Sydney	England	No result	G. N. Yallop	19/10
Jan 24	Melbourne	England	Lost by seven wickets	G. N. Yallop	20/11
Feb 4	Melbourne	England	Won by four wickets	G. N. Yallop	21/12
Feb 7	Melbourne	England	Won by six wickets	G. N. Yallop	22/13
1979 World Cup in England					
Jun 9	Lord's	England	Lost by six wickets	K. J. Hughes	23/14
Jun 13–14	Nottingham	Pakistan	Lost by 89 runs	K. J. Hughes	24/2
Jun 16	Birmingham	Canada	Won by seven wickets	K. J. Hughes	25/1
1979-80 World Series Cup in Australia					
Nov 27	Sydney	West Indies	Won by five wickets	G. S. Chappell	26/6
Dec 8	Melbourne	England	Lost by three wickets	G. S. Chappell	27/15
Dec 9	Melbourne	West Indies	Lost by 80 runs	G. S. Chappell	28/7
Dec 11	Sydney	England	Lost by 72 runs	G. S. Chappell	29/16
Dec 21	Sydney	West Indies	Won by seven runs	G. S. Chappell	30/8
Dec 26	Sydney	England	Lost by four wickets	G. S. Chappell	31/17
Jan 14	Sydney	England	Lost by two wickets	G. S. Chappell	32/18
Jan 18	Sydney	West Indies	Won by nine runs	G. S. Chappell	33/9
1980 in England					
Aug 20	The Oval	England	Lost by 23 runs	G. S. Chappell	34/19
Aug 22	Birmingham	England	Lost by 47 runs	G. S. Chappell	35/20

Date	Venue	Opponent	Result for Australia	Captain	Team/Opp
1980-81 World Series Cup in Australia					
Nov 23	Adelaide	New Zealand	Lost by three wickets	G. S. Chappell	36/3
Nov 25	Sydney	New Zealand	Won by 94 runs	G. S. Chappell	37/4
Dec 6	Melbourne	India	Lost by 66 runs	G. S. Chappell	38/1
Dec 7	Melbourne	New Zealand	Won by four wickets	G. S. Chappell	39/5
Dec 18	Sydney	India	Won by nine wickets	G. S. Chappell	40/2
Jan 8	Sydney	India	Won by nine wickets	G. S. Chappell	41/3
Jan 11	Melbourne	India	Won by seven wickets	G. S. Chappell	42/4
Jan 13	Sydney	New Zealand	Lost by one run	G. S. Chappell	43/6
Jan 15	Sydney	India	Won by 27 runs	G. S. Chappell	44/5
Jan 21	Sydney	New Zealand	No result	G. S. Chappell	45/7
Jan 29	Sydney	New Zealand	Won by 78 runs	G. S. Chappell	46/8
Jan 31	Melbourne	New Zealand	Won by seven wickets	G. S. Chappell	47/9
Feb 1	Melbourne	New Zealand	Won by six runs	G. S. Chappell	48/10
Feb 3	Sydney	New Zealand	Won by six wickets	G. S. Chappell	49/11
1981 in England					
Jun 4	Lord's	England	Lost by six wickets	K. J. Hughes	50/21
Jun 6	Birmingham	England	Won by two runs	K. J. Hughes	51/22
Jun 8	Leeds	England	Won by 71 runs	K. J. Hughes	52/23
1981-82 World Series Cup in Australia					
Nov 21	Melbourne	Pakistan	Lost by four wickets	G. S. Chappell	53/3
Nov 24	Sydney	West Indies	Won by seven wickets	G. S. Chappell	54/10
Dec 6	Adelaide	Pakistan	Won by 38 runs	G. S. Chappell	55/4
Dec 17	Sydney	Pakistan	Lost by six wickets	G. S. Chappell	56/5
Dec 20	Perth	West Indies	Lost by eight wickets	G. S. Chappell	57/11
Jan 20	Melbourne	Pakistan	Lost by 25 runs	G. S. Chappell	58/6
Jan 10	Melbourne	West Indies	Lost by five wickets	G. S. Chappell	59/12
Jan 14	Sydney	Pakistan	Won by 76 runs	G. S. Chappell	60/7
Jan 17	Brisbane	West Indies	Lost by five wickets	G. S. Chappell	61/13
Jan 19	Sydney	West Indies	Won on run-rate	G. S. Chappell	62/14
Jan 23	Melbourne	West Indies	Lost by 86 runs	G. S. Chappell	63/15
Jan 24	Melbourne	West Indies	Lost by 128 runs	G. S. Chappell	64/16
Jan 26	Sydney	West Indies	Won by 46 runs	G. S. Chappell	65/17
Jan 27	Sydney	West Indies	Lost by 18 runs	G. S. Chappell	66/18
1981-82 in New Zealand					
Feb 13	Auckland	New Zealand	Lost by 46 runs	G. S. Chappell	67/12
Feb 17	Dunedin	New Zealand	Won by six wickets	G. S. Chappell	68/13
Feb 9	Wellington	New Zealand	Won by eight wickets	G. S. Chappell	69/14
1982-83 in Pakistan					
Sep 20	Hyderabad	Pakistan	Lost by 59 runs	K. J. Hughes	70/8
Oct 8	Lahore	Pakistan	Lost by 28 runs	K. J. Hughes	71/9
Oct 22	Karachi	Pakistan	No result	K. J. Hughes	72/10
1982-83 World Series Cup in Australia					
Jan 9	Melbourne	New Zealand	Won by eight wickets	K. J. Hughes	73/15
Jan 11	Sydney	England	Won by 31 runs	K. J. Hughes	74/24
Jan 16	Brisbane	England	Won by seven wickets	K. J. Hughes	75/25
Jan 18	Sydney	New Zealand	Lost by 47 runs	K. J. Hughes	76/16
Jan 22	Melbourne	New Zealand	Lost by 58 runs	K. J. Hughes	77/17
Jan 23	Melbourne	England	Won by five wickets	K. J. Hughes	78/26
Jan 26	Sydney	England	Lost by 98 runs	K. J. Hughes	79/27
Jan 30	Adelaide	England	Lost by 14 runs	K. J. Hughes	80/28
Jan 31	Adelaide	New Zealand	Lost by 46 runs	K. J. Hughes	81/18
Feb 6	Perth	New Zealand	Won by 27 runs	K. J. Hughes	82/19
Feb 9	Sydney	New Zealand	Won by six wickets	K. J. Hughes	83/20
Feb 13	Melbourne	New Zealand	Won by 149 runs	K. J. Hughes	84/21
1982-83 in Australia					
Mar 17	Sydney	New Zealand	Lost by 14 runs	K. J. Hughes	85/22

Date	Venue	Opponent	Result for Australia	Captain	Team/Opp
1982-83 in Sri Lanka					
Apr 13	Colombo (PSS)	Sri Lanka	Lost by two wickets	G. S. Chappell	86/2
Apr 16	Colombo (PSS)	Sri Lanka	Lost by four wickets	G. S. Chappell	87/3
Apr 20	Colombo (SSC)	Sri Lanka	No result	G. S. Chappell	88/4
Apr 30	Colombo (SSC)	Sri Lanka	No result	G. S. Chappell	89/5
1983 World Cup in England					
Jun 9	Nottingham	Zimbabwe	Lost by 13 runs	K. J. Hughes	90/1
Jun 11–12	Leeds	West Indies	Lost by 101 runs	K. J. Hughes	91/19
Jun 13	Nottingham	India	Won by 162 runs	K. J. Hughes	92/6
Jun 16	Southampton	Zimbabwe	Won by 32 runs	K. J. Hughes	93/2
Jun 18	Lord's	West Indies	Lost by seven wickets	K. J. Hughes	94/20
Jun 20	Chelmsford	India	Lost by 118 runs	D. W. Hookes	95/7
1983-84 World Series Cup in Australia					
Jan 8	Melbourne	West Indies	Lost by 27 runs	K. J. Hughes	96/21
Jan 10	Sydney	Pakistan	Won by 34 runs	K. J. Hughes	97/11
Jan 15	Brisbane	Pakistan	No result	K. J. Hughes	98/12
Jan 17	Sydney	West Indies	Lost by 28 runs	K. J. Hughes	99/22
Jan 21	Melbourne	Pakistan	Won by 45 runs	K. J. Hughes	100/13
Jan 22	Melbourne	West Indies	Lost by 26 runs	K. J. Hughes	101/23
Jan 25	Sydney	Pakistan	Won by 87 runs	K. J. Hughes	102/14
Jan 29	Adelaide	West Indies	Lost by six wickets	K. J. Hughes	103/24
Jan 30	Adelaide	Pakistan	Won by 70 runs	K. J. Hughes	104/15
Feb 5	Perth	West Indies	Won by 14 runs	K. J. Hughes	105/25
Feb 8	Sydney	West Indies	Lost by nine wickets	K. J. Hughes	106/26
Feb 11	Melbourne	West Indies	Tied	K. J. Hughes	107/27
Feb 12	Melbourne	West Indies	Lost by six wickets	K. J. Hughes	108/28
1983-84 in West Indies					
Feb 29	Berbice	West Indies	Lost by eight wickets	K. J. Hughes	109/29
Mar 14	Port-of-Spain	West Indies	Won by four wickets	K. J. Hughes	110/30
Apr 19	Castries	West Indies	Lost by seven wickets	K. J. Hughes	111/31
Apr 26	Kingston	West Indies	Lost by nine wickets	K. J. Hughes	112/32
1984-85 in India					
Sep 28	New Delhi	India	Won by 48 runs	K. J. Hughes	113/8
Oct 1	Trivandrum	India	No result	K. J. Hughes	114/9
Oct 3	Jamshedpur	India	No result	K. J. Hughes	115/10
Oct 5	Ahmedabad	India	Won by seven wickets	K. J. Hughes	116/11
Oct 6	Indore	India	Won by six wickets	K. J. Hughes	117/12
1984-85 World Series Cup in Australia					
Jan 6	Melbourne	West Indies	Lost by seven wickets	A. R. Border	118/33
Jan 8	Sydney	Sri Lanka	Won by six wickets	A. R. Border	119/6
Jan 13	Brisbane	West Indies	Lost by five wickets	A. R. Border	120/34
Jan 15	Sydney	West Indies	Lost by five wickets	A. R. Border	121/35
Jan 19	Melbourne	Sri Lanka	Lost by four wickets	A. R. Border	122/7
Jan 20	Melbourne	West Indies	Lost by 65 runs	A. R. Border	123/36
Jan 23	Sydney	Sri Lanka	Won by three wickets	A. R. Border	124/8
Jan 27	Adelaide	West Indies	Lost by six wickets	A. R. Border	125/37
Jan 28	Adelaide	Sri Lanka	Won by 232 runs	A. R. Border	126/9
Feb 3	Perth	Sri Lanka	Won by nine wickets	A. R. Border	127/10
Feb 6	Sydney	West Indies	Won by 26 runs	A. R. Border	128/38
Feb 10	Melbourne	West Indies	Lost by four wickets	A. R. Border	129/39
Feb 12	Sydney	West Indies	Lost by seven wickets	A. R. Border	130/40
1984-85 World Championship in Australia					
Feb 17	Melbourne	England	Won by seven wickets	A. R. Border	131/29
Feb 24	Melbourne	Pakistan	Lost by 62 runs	A. R. Border	132/16
Mar 3	Melbourne	India	Lost by eight wickets	A. R. Border	133/13

Date	Venue	Opponent	Result for Australia	Captain	Team/Opp
1984-85 in United Arab Emirates					
Mar 24	Sharjah	England	Won by two wickets	A. R. Border	134/30
Mar 29	Sharjah	India	Lost by three wickets	A. R. Border	135/14
1985 in England					
May 30	Manchester	England	Won by three wickets	A. R. Border	136/31
Jun 1	Birmingham	England	Won by four wickets	A. R. Border	137/32
Jun 3	Lord's	England	Lost by eight wickets	A. R. Border	138/33
1985-86 World Series Cup in Australia					
Jan 9	Melbourne	New Zealand	No result	A. R. Border	139/23
Jan 12	Brisbane	India	Won by four wickets	A. R. Border	140/15
Jan 14	Sydney	New Zealand	Won by four wickets	A. R. Border	141/24
Jan 16	Melbourne	India	Lost by eight wickets	A. R. Border	142/16
Jan 19	Perth	New Zealand	Won by four wickets	A. R. Border	143/25
Jan 21	Sydney	India	Won by 100 runs	A. R. Border	144/17
Jan 26	Adelaide	India	Won by 36 runs	A. R. Border	145/18
Jan 27	Adelaide	New Zealand	Lost by 206 runs	A. R. Border	146/26
Jan 29	Sydney	New Zealand	Won by 99 runs	A. R. Border	147/27
Jan 31	Melbourne	India	Lost by six wickets	A. R. Border	148/19
Feb 5	Sydney	India	Won by 11 runs	A. R. Border	149/20
Feb 9	Melbourne	India	Won by seven wickets	A. R. Border	150/21
1985-86 in New Zealand					
Mar 19	Dunedin	New Zealand	Lost by 30 runs	A. R. Border	151/28
Mar 22	Christchurch	New Zealand	Lost by 53 runs	A. R. Border	152/29
Mar 26	Wellington	New Zealand	Won by three wickets	A. R. Border	153/30
Mar 29	Auckland	New Zealand	Won by 44 runs	A. R. Border	154/31
1985-86 in United Arab Emirates					
Apr 11	Sharjah	Pakistan	Lost by eight wickets	R. J. Bright	155/17
1986-87 in India					
Sep 7	Jaipur	India	Lost by seven wickets	A. R. Border	156/22
Sep 9	Srinagar	India	Won by three wickets	A. R. Border	157/23
Sep 24	Hyderabad	India	No result	A. R. Border	158/24
Oct 2	Delhi	India	Lost by three wickets	A. R. Border	159/25
Oct 5	Ahmedabad	India	Lost by 52 runs	A. R. Border	160/26
Oct 7	Rajkot	India	Won by seven wickets	A. R. Border	161/27
1986-87 World Challenge in Australia					
Jan 1	Perth	England	Lost by 37 runs	A. R. Border	162/34
Jan 2	Perth	Pakistan	Lost by one wicket	A. R. Border	163/18
Jan 4	Perth	West Indies	Lost by 164 runs	A. R. Border	164/41
1986-87 World Series Cup in Australia					
Jan 18	Brisbane	England	Won by 11 runs	A. R. Border	165/35
Jan 20	Melbourne	West Indies	Lost by seven wickets	A. R. Border	166/42
Jan 22	Sydney	England	Lost by three wickets	A. R. Border	167/36
Jan 25	Adelaide	West Indies	Lost by 16 runs	A. R. Border	168/43
Jan 26	Adelaide	England	Won by 33 runs	A. R. Border	169/37
Jan 28	Sydney	West Indies	Won by 36 runs	A. R. Border	170/44
Feb 1	Melbourne	England	Won by 109 runs	A. R. Border	171/38
Feb 6	Sydney	West Indies	Won by two wickets	A. R. Border	172/45
Feb 8	Melbourne	England	Lost by six wickets	A. R. Border	173/39
Feb 11	Sydney	England	Lost by eight runs	A. R. Border	174/40
1986-87 in United Arab Emirates					
Apr 3	Sharjah	Pakistan	Lost by six wickets	A. R. Border	175/19
Apr 6	Sharjah	India	Lost by seven wickets	G. R. Marsh	176/28
Apr 9	Sharjah	England	Lost by 11 runs	A. R. Border	177/41

Date	Venue	Opponent	Result for Australia	Captain	Team/Opp
1987-88 World Cup in India and Pakistan					
Oct 9	Madras	India	Won by one run	A. R. Border	178/29
Oct 13	Madras	Zimbabwe	Won by 96 runs	A. R. Border	179/3
Oct 19	Indore	New Zealand	Won by three runs	A. R. Border	180/32
Oct 22	New Delhi	India	Lost by 56 runs	A. R. Border	181/30
Oct 27	Chandigarh	New Zealand	Won by 17 runs	A. R. Border	182/33
Oct 30	Cuttack	Zimbabwe	Won by 70 runs	A. R. Border	183/4
Nov 4	Lahore	Pakistan	Won by 18 runs	A. R. Border	184/20
Nov 8	Calcutta	England	Won by seven runs	A. R. Border	185/42
1987-88 World Series Cup in Australia					
Jan 2	Perth	Sri Lanka	Won by 81 runs	A. R. Border	186/11
Jan 3	Perth	New Zealand	Lost by one run	A. R. Border	187/34
Jan 7	Melbourne	New Zealand	Won by six runs	A. R. Border	188/35
Jan 10	Adelaide	Sri Lanka	Won by 81 runs	A. R. Border	189/12
Jan 14	Melbourne	Sri Lanka	Won by 38 runs	A. R. Border	190/13
Jan 17	Brisbane	New Zealand	Won by five wickets	A. R. Border	191/36
Jan 19	Sydney	Sri Lanka	Won by three wickets	A. R. Border	192/14
Jan 20	Sydney	New Zealand	Won by 78 runs	A. R. Border	193/37
Jan 22	Melbourne	New Zealand	Won by eight wickets	A. R. Border	194/38
Jan 24	Sydney	New Zealand	Won by six wickets	A. R. Border	195/39
1987-88 in Australia					
Feb 4	Melbourne	England	Won by 22 runs	A. R. Border	196/43
1988-89 in Pakistan					
Oct 14	Lahore	Pakistan	Lost on fewer wickets	A. R. Border	197/21
1988-89 World Series in Australia					
Dec 11	Adelaide	Pakistan	Won by nine wickets	A. R. Border	198/22
Dec 13	Sydney	West Indies	Lost by one run	A. R. Border	199/46
Dec 15	Melbourne	West Indies	Lost by 34 runs	A. R. Border	200/47
Jan 2	Perth	Pakistan	Lost by 38 runs	A. R. Border	201/23
Jan 5	Melbourne	West Indies	Won by eight runs	A. R. Border	202/48
Jan 8	Brisbane	Pakistan	Won by five wickets	A. R. Border	203/24
Jan 10	Melbourne	Pakistan	Won on run-rate	A. R. Border	204/25
Jan 12	Sydney	West Indies	Won by 61 runs	A. R. Border	205/49
Jan 14	Melbourne	West Indies	Won by two runs	A. R. Border	206/50
Jan 16	Sydney	West Indies	Lost by 92 runs	A. R. Border	207/51
Jan 18	Sydney	West Indies	Lost on run-rate	A. R. Border	208/52
1989 in England					
May 25	Manchester	England	Lost by 95 runs	A. R. Border	209/44
May 27	Nottingham	England	Tied	A. R. Border	210/45
May 29	Lord's	England	Won by six wickets	A. R. Border	211/46
1989-90 in India					
Oct 19	Hyderabad	England	Lost by seven wickets	A. R. Border	212/47
Oct 21	Madras	West Indies	Won by 99 runs	A. R. Border	213/53
Oct 23	Bombay	Pakistan	Lost by 66 runs	A. R. Border	214/26
Oct 25	Goa	Sri Lanka	Won by 28 runs	A. R. Border	215/15
Oct 27	Bangalore	India	Lost by three wickets	A. R. Border	216/31
1989-90 World Series in Australia					
Dec 26	Melbourne	Sri Lanka	Won by 30 runs	A. R. Border	217/16
Dec 30	Perth	Sri Lanka	Won by nine wickets	A. R. Border	218/17
Jan 3	Melbourne	Pakistan	Won by seven wickets	A. R. Border	219/27
Jan 4	Melbourne	Sri Lanka	Won by 73 runs	A. R. Border	220/18
Feb 11	Brisbane	Pakistan	Won by 67 runs	A. R. Border	221/28
Feb 13	Sydney	Pakistan	Lost by five wickets	A. R. Border	222/29
Feb 18	Adelaide	Sri Lanka	Won by seven wickets	A. R. Border	223/19

Date	Venue	Opponent	Result for Australia	Captain	Team/Opp
Feb 20	Sydney	Pakistan	Lost by two runs	A. R. Border	224/30
Feb 23	Melbourne	Pakistan	Won by seven wickets	A. R. Border	225/31
Feb 25	Sydney	Pakistan	Won by 69 runs	A. R. Border	226/32

1989-90 in New Zealand

Mar 3	Christchurch	India	Won by 18 runs	A. R. Border	227/32
Mar 4	Christchurch	New Zealand	Won by 150 runs	A. R. Border	228/40
Mar 8	Hamilton	India	Won by seven wickets	A. R. Border	229/33
Mar 10	Auckland	New Zealand	Won on run-rate	G. R. Marsh	230/41
Mar 11	Auckland	New Zealand	Won by eight wickets	A. R. Border	231/42

1989-90 in United Arab Emirates

Apr 26	Sharjah	New Zealand	Won by 63 runs	A. R. Border	232/43
Apr 30	Sharjah	Bangladesh	Won by seven wickets	A. R. Border	233/1
May 2	Sharjah	Sri Lanka	Won by 114 runs	A. R. Border	234/20
May 4	Sharjah	Pakistan	Lost by 36 runs	A. R. Border	235/33

1990-91 World Series in Australia

Nov 29	Sydney	New Zealand	Won by 61 runs	A. R. Border	236/44
Dec 2	Adelaide	New Zealand	Won by six wickets	A. R. Border	237/45
Dec 9	Perth	England	Won by six wickets	A. R. Border	238/48
Dec 11	Melbourne	New Zealand	Won by 39 runs	A. R. Border	239/46
Dec 16	Brisbane	England	Won by 37 runs	A. R. Border	240/49
Dec 18	Hobart	New Zealand	Lost by one run	A. R. Border	241/47
Jan 1	Sydney	England	Won by 68 runs	A. R. Border	242/50
Jan 10	Melbourne	England	Won by three runs	A. R. Border	243/51
Jan 13	Sydney	New Zealand	Won by six wickets	G. R. Marsh	244/48
Jan 15	Melbourne	New Zealand	Won by seven wickets	G. R. Marsh	245/49

1990-91 in West Indies

Feb 26	Kingston	West Indies	Won by 35 runs	A. R. Border	246/54
Mar 9	Port-of-Spain	West Indies	Won by 45 runs	A. R. Border	247/55
Mar 10	Port-of-Spain	West Indies	Lost on run-rate	A. R. Border	248/56
Mar 13	Bridgetown	West Indies	Won by 46 runs	A. R. Border	249/57
Mar 20	Georgetown	West Indies	Won by six wickets	A. R. Border	250/58

1991-92 World Series in Australia

Dec 8	Perth	India	Lost by 107 runs	A. R. Border	251/34
Dec 10	Hobart	India	Won by eight wickets	A. R. Border	252/35
Dec 12	Melbourne	West Indies	Won by nine runs	A. R. Border	253/59
Dec 15	Adelaide	India	Won by six wickets	A. R. Border	254/36
Dec 18	Sydney	West Indies	Won by 51 runs	A. R. Border	255/60
Jan 9	Melbourne	West Indies	No result	A. R. Border	256/61
Jan 12	Brisbane	West Indies	Lost by 12 runs	A. R. Border	257/62
Jan 14	Sydney	India	Won by nine wickets	A. R. Border	258/37
Jan 18	Melbourne	India	Won by 88 runs	A. R. Border	259/38
Jan 20	Sydney	India	Won by six runs	A. R. Border	260/39

1991-92 World Cup in Australia and New Zealand

Feb 22	Auckland	New Zealand	Lost by 37 runs	A. R. Border	261/50
Feb 26	Sydney	South Africa	Lost by nine wickets	A. R. Border	262/1
Mar 1	Brisbane	India	Won by one run	A. R. Border	263/40
Mar 5	Sydney	England	Lost by eight wickets	A. R. Border	264/52
Mar 7	Adelaide	Sri Lanka	Won by seven wickets	A. R. Border	265/21
Mar 11	Perth	Pakistan	Lost by 48 runs	A. R. Border	266/34
Mar 14	Hobart	Zimbabwe	Won by 128 runs	A. R. Border	267/5
Mar 18	Melbourne	West Indies	Won by 57 runs	A. R. Border	268/63

Date	Venue	Opponent	Result for Australia	Captain	Team/Opp
1992-93 in Sri Lanka					
Aug 15	Colombo (PSS)	Sri Lanka	Lost by four wickets	A. R. Border	269/22
Sep 4	Colombo (PIS)	Sri Lanka	Lost on run-rate	A. R. Border	270/23
Sep 5	Colombo (PIS)	Sri Lanka	Won by five wickets	A. R. Border	271/24
1992-93 World Series in Australia					
Dec 6	Perth	West Indies	Lost by nine wickets	A. R. Border	272/64
Dec 8	Sydney	West Indies	Won by 14 runs	M. A. Taylor	273/65
Dec 10	Hobart	Pakistan	Tied	M. A. Taylor	274/35
Dec 13	Adelaide	Pakistan	Won by eight wickets	M. A. Taylor	275/36
Dec 15	Melbourne	West Indies	Won by four runs	M. A. Taylor	276/66
Jan 10	Brisbane	West Indies	Lost by seven runs	A. R. Border	277/67
Jan 12	Melbourne	Pakistan	Won by 32 runs	A. R. Border	278/37
Jan 14	Sydney	Pakistan	Won by 23 runs	A. R. Border	279/38
Jan 16	Sydney	West Indies	Lost by 25 runs	A. R. Border	280/69
Jan 18	Melbourne	West Indies	Lost by four wickets	A. R. Border	281/69
1992-93 in New Zealand					
Mar 19	Dunedin	New Zealand	Won by 129 runs	A. R. Border	282/51
Mar 21–22	Christchurch	New Zealand	Won by one wicket	M. A. Taylor	283/52
Mar 24	Wellington	New Zealand	Lost by 88 runs	A. R. Border	284/53
Mar 27	Hamilton	New Zealand	Lost by three wickets	M. A. Taylor	285/54
Mar 28	Auckland	New Zealand	Won by three runs	A. R. Border	286/55
1993 in England					
May 19	Manchester	England	Won by four runs	A. R. Border	287/53
May 21	Birmingham	England	Won by six wickets	A. R. Border	288/54
May 23	Lord's	England	Won by 19 runs	M. A. Taylor	289/55
1993-94 World Series in Australia					
Dec 9	Melbourne	South Africa	Lost by seven wickets	A. R. Border	290/2
Dec 12	Adelaide	New Zealand	Won by eight wickets	A. R. Border	291/56
Dec 14	Sydney	South Africa	Won by 103 runs	A. R. Border	292/3
Dec 16	Melbourne	New Zealand	Won by three runs	A. R. Border	293/57
Jan 9	Brisbane	South Africa	Won by 48 runs	A. R. Border	294/4
Jan 11	Sydney	New Zealand	Lost by 13 runs	A. R. Border	295/58
Jan 16	Perth	South Africa	Lost by 82 runs	M. A. Taylor	296/5
Jan 19	Melbourne	New Zealand	Won by 51 runs	A. R. Border	297/59
Jan 21	Melbourne	South Africa	Lost by 28 runs	A. R. Border	298/6
Jan 23	Sydney	South Africa	Won by 69 runs	A. R. Border	299/7
Jan 25	Sydney	South Africa	Won by 35 runs	A. R. Border	300/8
1993-94 in South Africa					
Feb 19	Johannesburg	South Africa	Lost by five runs	A. R. Border	301/9
Feb 20	Pretoria	South Africa	Lost by 56 runs	A. R. Border	302/10
Feb 22	Port Elizabeth	South Africa	Won by 88 runs	A. R. Border	303/11
Feb 24	Durban	South Africa	Lost by seven wickets	A. R. Border	304/12
Apr 2	East London	South Africa	Won by seven wickets	A. R. Border	305/13
Apr 4	Port Elizabeth	South Africa	Lost by 26 runs	A. R. Border	306/14
Apr 6	Cape Town	South Africa	Won by 36 runs	A. R. Border	307/15
Apr 8	Bloemfontein	South Africa	Won by one run	A. R. Border	308/16
1993-94 in United Arab Emirates					
Apr 14	Sharjah	Sri Lanka	Won by nine wickets	M. A. Taylor	309/25
Apr 16	Sharjah	New Zealand	Won by seven wickets	M. A. Taylor	310/60
Apr 19	Sharjah	India	Lost by seven wickets	M. A. Taylor	311/41

Date	Venue	Opponent	Result for Australia	Captain	Team/Opp
1994-95 in Sri Lanka					
Sep 7	Colombo (SSC)	Pakistan	Won by 28 runs	M. A. Taylor	312/39
Sep 9	Colombo (PIS)	India	Lost by 31 runs	M. A. Taylor	313/42
Sep 13	Colombo (SSC)	Sri Lanka	Lost on run-rate	M. A. Taylor	314/26
1994-95 in Pakistan					
Oct 12	Lahore	South Africa	Won by six wickets	M. A. Taylor	315/17
Oct 14	Multan	Pakistan	Won by seven wickets	M. A. Taylor	316/40
Oct 18	Faisalabad	South Africa	Won by 22 runs	M. A. Taylor	317/18
Oct 22	Rawalpindi	Pakistan	Lost by nine wickets	M. A. Taylor	318/41
Oct 24	Peshawar	South Africa	Won by three wickets	M. A. Taylor	319/19
Oct 30	Lahore	Pakistan	Won by 64 runs	M. A. Taylor	320/42
1994-95 World Series in Australia					
Dec 2	Perth	Zimbabwe	Won by two wickets	M. A. Taylor	321/6
Dec 6	Sydney	England	Won by 28 runs	M. A. Taylor	322/56
Dec 8	Hobart	Zimbabwe	Won by 85 runs	M. A. Taylor	323/7
Jan 10	Melbourne	England	Lost by 37 runs	M. A. Taylor	324/57
1994-95 in New Zealand					
Feb 15	Wellington	South Africa	Won by three wickets	M. A. Taylor	325/20
Feb 19	Auckland	New Zealand	Won by 27 runs	M. A. Taylor	326/61
Feb 22	Dunedin	India	Lost by five wickets	M. A. Taylor	327/43
Feb 26	Auckland	New Zealand	Won by six wickets	M. A. Taylor	326/62
1994-95 in West Indies					
Mar 8	Bridgetown	West Indies	Lost by six runs	M. A. Taylor	329/70
Mar 11	Port-of-Spain	West Indies	Won by 26 runs	M. A. Taylor	330/71
Mar 12	Port-of-Spain	West Indies	Lost by 133 runs	M. A. Taylor	331/72
Mar 15	Kingstown	West Indies	Lost on run-rate	M. A. Taylor	332/73
Mar 18	Georgetown	West Indies	Lost by five wickets	M. A. Taylor	333/74
1995-96 World Series in Australia					
Dec 17	Adelaide	West Indies	Won by 121 runs	M. A. Taylor	334/75
Dec 19	Melbourne	West Indies	Won by 24 runs	M. A. Taylor	335/76
Dec 21	Sydney	Sri Lanka	Won by five wickets	M. A. Taylor	336/27
Jan 1	Sydney	West Indies	Won by one wicket	M. A. Taylor	337/77
Jan 7	Brisbane	West Indies	Lost by 14 runs	M. A. Taylor	338/78
Jan 9	Melbourne	Sri Lanka	Lost by three wickets	M. A. Taylor	339/28
Jan 12	Perth	Sri Lanka	Won by 83 runs	M. A. Taylor	340/29
Jan 16	Melbourne	Sri Lanka	Lost by three wickets	M. A. Taylor	341/30
Jan 18	Melbourne	Sri Lanka	Won by 18 runs	M. A. Taylor	342/31
Jan 20	Sydney	Sri Lanka	Won on run-rate	M. A. Taylor	343/32
1995-96 World Cup in India, Pakistan and Sri Lanka					
Feb 23	Vishakhapatnam	Kenya	Won by 97 runs	M. A. Taylor	344/1
Feb 27	Bombay	India	Won by 16 runs	M. A. Taylor	345/44
Mar 1	Nagpur	Zimbabwe	Won by eight wickets	M. A. Taylor	346/8
Mar 4	Jaipur	West Indies	Lost by four wickets	M. A. Taylor	347/79
Mar 11	Chennai	New Zealand	Won by six wickets	M. A. Taylor	348/63
Mar 14	Chandigarh	West Indies	Won by five runs	M. A. Taylor	349/80
Mar 17	Lahore	Sri Lanka	Lost by seven wickets	M. A. Taylor	350/33
1996-97 in Sri Lanka					
Aug 26	Colombo (PIS)	Zimbabwe	Won by 125 runs	I. A. Healy	351/9
Aug 30	Colombo (PIS)	Sri Lanka	Lost by four wickets	I. A. Healy	352/34
Sep 6	Colombo (SSC)	India	Won by three wickets	I. A. Healy	353/45
Sep 7	Colombo (SSC)	Sri Lanka	Lost by 50 runs	I. A. Healy	354/35
1996-97 in India					
Oct 19	Indore	South Africa	Lost by seven wickets	M. A. Taylor	355/21
Oct 21	Bangalore	India	Lost by two wickets	M. A. Taylor	356/46
Oct 25	Faridabad	South Africa	Lost by two wickets	M. A. Taylor	357/22

Date		Venue	Opponent	Result for Australia	Captain	Team/Opp
Nov	1	Guwahati	South Africa	Lost by eight wickets	M. A. Taylor	358/23
Nov	3	Chandigarh	India	Lost by five runs	M. A. Taylor	359/47
1996-97 Carlton & United Series in Australia						
Dec	6	Melbourne	West Indies	Won by five wickets	M. A. Taylor	360/81
Dec	8	Sydney	West Indies	Won by eight wickets	M. A. Taylor	361/82
Dec	15	Adelaide	Pakistan	Lost by 12 runs	M. A. Taylor	362/43
Jan	1	Sydney	Pakistan	Lost by four wickets	M. A. Taylor	363/44
Jan	5	Brisbane	West Indies	Lost by seven wickets	M. A. Taylor	364/83
Jan	7	Hobart	Pakistan	Lost by 29 runs	M. A. Taylor	365/45
Jan	12	Perth	West Indies	Lost by four wickets	M. A. Taylor	366/84
Jan	16	Melbourne	Pakistan	Won by three wickets	M. A. Taylor	367/46
1996-97 in South Africa						
Mar	29	East London	South Africa	Lost by six wickets	M. A. Taylor	368/24
Mar	31	Port Elizabeth	South Africa	Won by seven wickets	M. A. Taylor	369/25
Apr	3	Cape Town	South Africa	Lost by 46 runs	I. A. Healy	370/26
Apr	5	Durban	South Africa	Won by 15 runs	I. A. Healy	371/27
Apr	8	Johannesburg	South Africa	Won by eight runs	I. A. Healy	372/28
Apr	10	Centurion	South Africa	Won by five wickets	I. A. Healy	373/29
Apr	13	Bloemfontein	South Africa	Lost by 109 runs	S. R. Waugh	374/30
1997 in England						
May	22	Leeds	England	Lost by six wickets	M. A. Taylor	375/58
May	24	The Oval	England	Lost by six wickets	M. A. Taylor	376/59
May	25	Lord's	England	Lost by six wickets	S. R. Waugh	377/60
1997-98 Carlton & United Series in Australia						
Dec	4	Sydney	South Africa	Lost by 67 runs	S. R. Waugh	378/31
Dec	7	Adelaide	New Zealand	Won by three wickets	S. R. Waugh	379/64
Dec	9	Melbourne	South Africa	Lost by 45 runs	S. R. Waugh	380/32
Dec	17	Melbourne	New Zealand	Won by six wickets	S. R. Waugh	381/65
Jan	11	Brisbane	South Africa	Lost by five wickets	S. R. Waugh	382/33
Jan	14	Sydney	New Zealand	Won by 131 runs	S. K. Warne	383/66
Jan	18	Perth	South Africa	Lost by seven wickets	S. R. Waugh	384/34
Jan	21	Melbourne	New Zealand	Lost by four wickets	S. R. Waugh	385/67
Jan	23	Melbourne	South Africa	Lost by six runs	S. R. Waugh	386/35
Jan	26	Sydney	South Africa	Won by seven wickets	S. R. Waugh	387/36
Jan	27	Sydney	South Africa	Won by 14 runs	S. R. Waugh	388/37
1997-98 in New Zealand						
Feb	8	Christchurch	New Zealand	Won by seven wickets	S. R. Waugh	389/68
Feb	10	Wellington	New Zealand	Won by 66 runs	S. R. Waugh	390/69
Feb	12	Napier	New Zealand	Lost by seven wickets	S. R. Waugh	391/70
Feb	14	Auckland	New Zealand	Lost by 30 runs	S. R. Waugh	392/71
1997-98 in India						
Apr	1	Kochi	India	Lost by 41 runs	S. R. Waugh	393/48
Apr	3	Ahmedabad	Zimbabwe	Won by 13 runs	S. R. Waugh	394/10
Apr	7	Kanpur	India	Lost by six wickets	S. R. Waugh	395/49
Apr	11	Delhi	Zimbabwe	Won by 16 runs	S. R. Waugh	396/11
Apr	14	Delhi	India	Won by four wickets	S. R. Waugh	397/50
1997-98 in United Arab Emirates						
Apr	18	Sharjah	New Zealand	Won by six wickets	S. R. Waugh	398/72
Apr	19	Sharjah	India	Won by 58 runs	S. R. Waugh	399/51
Apr	21	Sharjah	New Zealand	Won by five wickets	S. R. Waugh	400/73
Apr	22	Sharjah	India	Won on run-rate	S. R. Waugh	401/52
Apr	24	Sharjah	India	Lost by six wickets	S. R. Waugh	402/53
1998-99 in Bangladesh						
Oct	28	Dhaka	India	Lost by 44 runs	S. R. Waugh	403/54

Date	Venue	Opponent	Result for Australia	Captain	Team/Opp
1998-99 in Pakistan					
Nov 6	Karachi	Pakistan	Won by 86 runs	S.R. Waugh	404/47
Nov 8	Peshawar	Pakistan	Won by five wickets	S.R. Waugh	405/48
Nov 10	Lahore	Pakistan	Won by six wickets	S.R. Waugh	406/49
1998-99 Carlton & United Series in Australia					
Jan 10	Brisbane	England	Won on run-rate	S.K. Warne	407/61
Jan 13	Sydney	Sri Lanka	Won by eight wickets	S.K. Warne	408/36
Jan 15	Melbourne	England	Won by nine wickets	S.K. Warne	409/62
Jan 17	Sydney	England	Lost by seven runs	S.K. Warne	410/63
Jan 21	Hobart	Sri Lanka	Lost by three wickets	S.K. Warne	411/37
Jan 24	Adelaide	Sri Lanka	Won by 80 runs	S.K. Warne	412/38
Jan 26	Adelaide	England	Won by 16 runs	S.K. Warne	413/64
Jan 31	Perth	Sri Lanka	Won by 45 runs	S.K. Warne	414/39
Feb 5	Sydney	England	Won by four wickets	S.K. Warne	415/65
Feb 7	Melbourne	Sri Lanka	Won by 43 runs	S.K. Warne	416/40
Feb 10	Sydney	England	Won by ten wickets	S.K. Warne	417/66
Feb 13	Melbourne	England	Won by 162 runs	S.K. Warne	418/67
1998-99 in West Indies					
Apr 11	Kingstown	West Indies	Lost by 44 runs	S.R. Waugh	419/85
Apr 14	St George's	West Indies	Won by 46 runs	S.R. Waugh	420/86
Apr 17	Port-of-Spain	West Indies	Lost by five wickets	S.R. Waugh	421/87
Apr 18	Port-of-Spain	West Indies	Won by 20 runs	S.R. Waugh	422/88
Apr 21	Georgetown	West Indies	Match tied	S.R. Waugh	423/89
Apr 24	Bridgetown	West Indies	Won by four wickets	S.R. Waugh	424/90
Apr 25	Bridgetown	West Indies	Lost on run-rate	S.R. Waugh	425/91
1999 World Cup in England					
May 16	Worcester	Scotland	Won by six wickets	S.R. Waugh	426/1
May 20	Cardiff	New Zealand	Lost by five wickets	S.R. Waugh	427/74
May 23	Leeds	Pakistan	Lost by ten runs	S.R. Waugh	428/50
May 27	Chester-le-Street	Bangladesh	Won by seven wickets	S.R. Waugh	429/2
May 30	Manchester	West Indies	Won by six wickets	S.R. Waugh	430/92
Jun 4	The Oval	India	Won by 77 runs	S.R. Waugh	431/55
Jun 9	Lord's	Zimbabwe	Won by 44 runs	S.R. Waugh	432/12
Jun 13	Leeds	South Africa	Won by five wickets	S.R. Waugh	433/38
Jun 17	Birmingham	South Africa	Match tied	S.R. Waugh	434/39
Jun 20	Lord's	Pakistan	Won by eight wickets	S.R. Waugh	435/51
1999-2000 in Sri Lanka					
Aug 22	Galle	Sri Lanka	Won on run rate	S.R. Waugh	436/41
Aug 23	Galle	India	Won on run rate	S.R. Waugh	437/56
Aug 26	Colombo (PIS)	Sri Lanka	Won by 27 runs	S.R. Waugh	438/42
Aug 28	Colombo (SSC)	India	Won by 41 runs	S.R. Waugh	439/57
Aug 31	Colombo (PIS)	Sri Lanka	Lost by eight wickets	S.R. Waugh	440/43
1999-2000 in Zimbabwe					
Oct 21	Bulawayo	Zimbabwe	Won by 83 runs	S.R. Waugh	441/13
Oct 23	Harare	Zimbabwe	Won by nine wickets	S.R. Waugh	442/14
Oct 24	Harare	Zimbabwe	Won by nine wickets	S.R. Waugh	443/15
1999-2000 Carlton & United Series in Australia					
Jan 9	Brisbane	Pakistan	Lost by 45 runs	S.R. Waugh	444/52
Jan 12	Melbourne	India	Won by 28 runs	S.R. Waugh	445/58
Jan 14	Sydney	India	Won by five wickets	S.R. Waugh	446/59
Jan 16	Melbourne	Pakistan	Won by six wickets	S.R. Waugh	447/53
Jan 19	Sydney	Pakistan	Won by 81 runs	S.R. Waugh	448/54
Jan 23	Melbourne	Pakistan	Won by 15 runs	S.R. Waugh	449/55
Jan 26	Adelaide	India	Won by 152 runs	S.R. Waugh	450/60
Jan 30	Perth	India	Won by four wickets	S.R. Waugh	451/61
Feb 2	Melbourne	Pakistan	Won by six wickets	S.R. Waugh	452/56
Feb 4	Sydney	Pakistan	Won by 152 runs	S.R. Waugh	453/57

Date	Venue	Opponent	Result for Australia	Captain	Team/Opp
1999-2000 in New Zealand					
Feb 17	Wellington	New Zealand	No result	S. R. Waugh	454/75
Feb 19	Auckland	New Zealand	Won by five wickets	S. R. Waugh	455/76
Feb 23	Dunedin	New Zealand	Won by 50 runs	S. R. Waugh	456/77
Feb 26	Christchurch	New Zealand	Won by 48 runs	S. R. Waugh	457/78
Mar 1	Napier	New Zealand	Won by five wickets	S. R. Waugh	458/79
Mar 3	Auckland	New Zealand	Lost by seven wickets	S. R. Waugh	459/80
1999-2000 in South Africa					
Apr 12	Durban	South Africa	Lost by six wickets	S. R. Waugh	460/40
Apr 14	Cape Town	South Africa	Won by five wickets	S. R. Waugh	461/41
Apr 16	Johannesburg	South Africa	Lost by four wickets	S. R. Waugh	462/42
2000 Super Challenge in Australia					
Aug 12	Melbourne (CS)	South Africa	Won by 94 runs	S. R. Waugh	463/43
Aug 14	Melbourne (CS)	South Africa	Match tied	S. R. Waugh	464/44
Aug 16	Melbourne (CS)	South Africa	Lost by eight runs	S. R. Waugh	465/45
2000-01 in Kenya					
Oct 7	Nairobi	India	Lost by 20 runs	S. R. Waugh	466/62
2000-01 in Australia					
Jan 11	Melbourne	West Indies	Won by 74 runs	S. R. Waugh	467/93
Jan 14	Brisbane	West Indies	Won by nine wickets	A. C. Gilchrist	468/94
Jan 17	Sydney	West Indies	Won on run rate	A. C. Gilchrist	469/95
Jan 21	Melbourne	Zimbabwe	Won by eight wickets	A. C. Gilchrist	470/16
Jan 26	Adelaide	West Indies	Won by ten wickets	S. R. Waugh	471/96
Jan 28	Sydney	Zimbabwe	Won by 86 runs	S. R. Waugh	472/17
Jan 30	Hobart	Zimbabwe	Won by six wickets	S. R. Waugh	473/18
Feb 4	Perth	Zimbabwe	Won by one run	S. R. Waugh	474/19
Feb 7	Sydney	West Indies	Won by 134 runs	S. R. Waugh	475/97
Feb 9	Melbourne	West Indies	Won by 39 runs	S. R. Waugh	476/98
2000-01 in India					
Mar 23	Bangalore	India	Lost by 60 runs	S. R. Waugh	477/63
Mar 28	Pune	India	Won by eight wickets	S. R. Waugh	478/64
Mar 31	Indore	India	Lost by 118 runs	S. R. Waugh	479/65
Apr 3	Visakhapatnam	India	Won by 93 runs	S. R. Waugh	480/66
Apr 6	Goa	India	Won by four wickets	S. R. Waugh	481/67
2001 in England					
Jun 9	Cardiff	Pakistan	Won by seven wickets	S. R. Waugh	482/58
Jun 10	Bristol	England	Won by five wickets	S. R. Waugh	483/68
Jun 14	Manchester	England	Won on run rate	S. R. Waugh	484/69
Jun 19	Nottingham	Pakistan	Lost by 36 runs	S. R. Waugh	485/59
Jun 21	The Oval	England	Won by eight wickets	S. R. Waugh	486/70
Jun 23	Lord's	Pakistan	Won by nine wickets	S. R. Waugh	487/60
2001-02 in Australia					
Jan 11	Melbourne	New Zealand	Lost by 23 runs	S. R. Waugh	488/81
Jan 13	Melbourne	South Africa	Lost by four wickets	S. R. Waugh	489/46
Jan 17	Sydney	New Zealand	Lost by 23 runs	S. R. Waugh	490/82
Jan 20	Brisbane	South Africa	Won by 27 runs	S. R. Waugh	491/47
Jan 22	Sydney	South Africa	Won by eight wickets	S. R. Waugh	492/48
Jan 26	Adelaide	New Zealand	Lost by 77 runs	S. R. Waugh	493/83
Jan 29	Melbourne	New Zealand	Won by two wickets	S. R. Waugh	494/84
Feb 3	Perth	South Africa	Lost by 33 runs	S. R. Waugh	495/49
2001-02 in South Africa					
Mar 23	Johannes. (WS)	South Africa	Won by 19 runs	R. T. Ponting	496/50
Mar 24	Centurion	South Africa	Won by 45 runs	R. T. Ponting	497/51
Mar 27	Potchefstroom	South Africa	Tied	R. T. Ponting	498/52
Mar 30	Bloemfontein	South Africa	Won by 37 runs	R. T. Ponting	499/53

Date	Venue	Opponent	Result for Australia	Captain	Team/Opp
Apr 4	Durban (KM)	South Africa	Won by eight wickets	R. T. Ponting	500/54
Apr 6	Port Elizabeth	South Africa	Won by three wickets	R. T. Ponting	501/55
Apr 9	Cape Town	South Africa	Lost on run rate	R. T. Ponting	502/56

2001-02 in Australia

Jun 12	Melbourne DS	Pakistan	Won by seven wickets	R. T. Ponting	503/61
Jun 15	Melbourne DS	Pakistan	Lost by two wickets	R. T. Ponting	504/62
Jun 19	Brisbane	Pakistan	Lost by 91 runs	R. T. Ponting	505/63

SUMMARY OF AUSTRALIAN LIMITED-OVERS INTERNATIONALS

	M	W	L	NR	T	% Won
England	70	38	30	1	1	54.29
New Zealand	84	56	25	3	0	66.67
Pakistan	63	34	26	2	1	53.97
Sri Lanka	43	28	13	2	0	65.12
West Indies	98	43	52	1	2	43.88
Canada	1	1	0	0	0	100.00
India	67	39	25	3	0	58.21
Zimbabwe	19	18	1	0	0	94.74
South Africa	56	29	24	0	3	51.79
Bangladesh	2	2	0	0	0	100.00
Kenya	1	1	0	0	0	100.00
Scotland	1	1	0	0	0	100.00
Total	505	290	196	12	7	56.97

CAPTAINS

	M	W	L	NR	T	% Won
W. M. Lawry	1	1	0	0	0	100.00
I. M. Chappell	11	6	5	0	0	54.54
G. S. Chappell	49	21	25	3	0	42.85
R. B. Simpson	2	1	1	0	0	50.00
G. N. Yallop	4	2	1	1	0	50.00
K. J. Hughes	49	21	23	4	1	42.85
D. W. Hookes	1	0	1	0	0	0.00
A. R. Border	178	107	67	3	1	60.11
R. J. Bright	1	0	1	0	0	0.00
G. R. Marsh	4	3	1	0	0	75.00
M. A. Taylor	67	37	29	0	1	55.22
I. A. Healy	8	5	3	0	0	62.50
S. R. Waugh	106	67	35	1	3	63.21
S. K. Warne	11	10	1	0	0	90.91
A. C. Gilchrist	3	3	0	0	0	100.00
R. T. Ponting	10	6	3	0	1	60.00

MOST APPEARANCES

	M	Eng	NZ	Pak	SL	WI	Can	Ind	Zim	SAf	Ban	Kya	Sco
S. R. Waugh	325	30	60	43	24	50	–	53	14	47	2	1	1
A. R. Border	273	43	52	34	23	61	1	38	5	15	1	–	–
M. E. Waugh	244	21	39	29	23	47	–	27	13	42	1	1	1
D. C. Boon	181	21	39	19	16	32	–	29	5	19	1	–	–
S. K. Warne	181	14	26	19	17	27	–	18	12	45	1	1	1
M. G. Bevan	178	11	23	25	18	24	–	26	13	35	1	1	1
I. A. Healy	168	16	23	25	20	39	–	15	5	23	1	1	–
D. M. Jones	164	20	27	21	17	41	–	21	3	13	1	–	–
G. D. McGrath	156	14	18	22	15	18	–	19	10	37	1	1	1
R. T. Ponting	141	9	16	17	15	21	–	22	12	26	1	1	1

BATTING RECORDS

CENTURY-MAKERS

M. G. Bevan (6)	103	v South Africa at Centurion	1996-97
	108*	v England at The Oval	1997
	101*	v India at Sharjah	1997-98
	107	v New Zealand at Napier	1999-00
	106	v South Africa at Melbourne CS	2000-01
	102*	v New Zealand at Melbourne	2001-02
D. C. Boon (5)	111	v India at Jaipur	1986-87
	122	v Sri Lanka at Adelaide	1987-88
	102*	v India at Hobart	1991-92
	100	v New Zealand at Auckland	1991-92
	100	v West Indies at Melbourne	1991-92
A. R. Border (3)	105*	v India at Sydney	1980-81
	118*	v Sri Lanka at Adelaide	1984-85
	127*	v West Indies at Sydney	1984-85
G. S. Chappell (3)	125*	v England at The Oval	1977
	138*	v New Zealand at Sydney	1980-81
	108	v New Zealand at Auckland	1981-82
T. M. Chappell	110	v India at Nottingham	1983
A. C. Gilchrist (7)	100	v South Africa at Sydney	1997-98
	118	v New Zealand at Christchurch	1997-98
	103	v Pakistan at Lahore	1998-99
	131	v Sri Lanka at Sydney	1998-99
	154	v Sri Lanka at Melbourne	1998-99
	128	v New Zealand at Christchurch	1999-00
	105	v South Africa at Durban	2001-02
D. M. Jones (7)	104	v England at Perth	1986-87
	121	v Pakistan at Perth	1986-87
	101	v England at Brisbane	1986-87
	107	v New Zealand at Christchurch	1989-90
	102*	v New Zealand at Auckland	1989-90
	117*	v Sri Lanka at Sharjah	1989-90
	145	v England at Brisbane	1990-91
M. L. Hayden	111	v India at Visakhapatnam	2000-01
B. M. Laird	117*	v West Indies at Sydney	1981-82
S. G. Law	110	v Zimbabwe at Hobart	1994-95
D. S. Lehmann (2)	103*	v Pakistan at Karachi	1998-99
	110*	v West Indies at St George's	1998-99
G. R. Marsh (9)	125	v India at Sydney	1985-86
	104	v India at Jaipur	1986-87
	110	v India at Chennai	1987-88
	126*	v New Zealand at Chandigarh	1987-88
	101	v New Zealand at Sydney	1987-88
	125*	v Pakistan at Melbourne	1988-89
	111*	v England at Lord's	1989
	113	v West Indies at Bridgetown	1990-91
	106*	v West Indies at Georgetown	1990-91
D. R. Martyn (3)	116*	v New Zealand at Auckland	1999-00
	144*	v Zimbabwe at Perth	2000-01
	104*	v South Africa at Brisbane	2001-02
R. T. Ponting (9)	123	v Sri Lanka at Melbourne	1995-96
	102	v West Indies at Jaipur	1995-96
	100	v New Zealand at Melbourne	1997-98
	145	v Zimbabwe at Delhi	1997-98
	124*	v Pakistan at Lahore	1998-99
	115	v India at Melbourne	1999-00
	101	v India at Visakhapatnam	2000-01
	102	v England at Bristol	2001
	129	v South Africa at Bloemfontein	2001-02

S.B. Smith (2)	117	v New Zealand at Melbourne	1982-83
	106	v Pakistan at Sydney	1983-84
M.A. Taylor	105	v India at Bangalore	1996-97
A. Turner	101	v Sri Lanka at The Oval	1975
M.E. Waugh (18)	108	v New Zealand at Hamilton	1992-93
	113	v England at Birmingham	1993
	107	v South Africa at Sydney	1993-94
	121*	v South Africa at Rawalpindi	1994-95
	130	v Sri Lanka at Perth	1995-96
	130	v Kenya at Vishakhapatnam	1995-96
	126	v India at Mumbai	1995-96
	110	v New Zealand at Chennai	1995-96
	102	v West Indies at Brisbane	1996-97
	115*	v South Africa at Port Elizabeth	1996-97
	104	v New Zealand at Adelaide	1996-97
	104	v Zimbabwe at Lord's	1999
	106	v Zimbabwe at Bulawayo	1999-00
	116	v India at Adelaide	1999-00
	112*	v West Indies at Brisbane	2000-01
	102*	v Zimbabwe at Hobart	2000-01
	173	v West Indies at Melbourne	2000-01
	133*	v India at Pune	2000-01
S.R. Waugh (3)	102*	v Sri Lanka at Melbourne	1995-96
	120*	v South Africa at Birmingham	1999
	114*	v South Africa at Melbourne CS	2000-01
K.C. Wessels	107	v India at New Delhi	1984-85
G.M. Wood (3)	108	v England at Leeds	1981
	104*	v West Indies at Adelaide	1984-85
	114*	v England at Lord's	1985

HIGHEST PARTNERSHIPS FOR EACH WICKET

212 for 1st	G.R. Marsh and D.C. Boon	v India at Jaipur	1986-87
219 for 2nd {	M.E. Waugh and R.T. Ponting	v Zimbabwe at Delhi	1997-98
	M.L. Hayden and R.T. Ponting	v India at Visakhapatnam	2000-01
224* for 3rd	D.M. Jones and A.R. Border	v Sri Lanka at Adelaide	1984-85
222 for 4th	M.G. Bevan and S.R. Waugh	v South Africa at Melbourne (CS)	2000
172* for 5th	D.S. Lehmann and M.G. Bevan	v West Indies at Kingston	1998-99
112 for 6th	M.E. Waugh and S.P. O'Donnell	v England at Sydney	1990-91
102* for 7th	S.R. Waugh and G.C. Dyer	v India at Delhi	1986-87
119 for 8th	P.R. Reiffel and S.K. Warne	v South Africa at Port Elizabeth	1993-94
77 for 9th	M.G. Bevan and S.K. Warne	v West Indies at Port-of-Spain	1998-9
45 for 10th	T.J. Laughlin and M.H.N. Walker	v England at Sydney	1979-80
45* for 10th	M.G. Bevan and A.C. Dale	v South Africa at East London	1996-97

MOST RUNS IN A CAREER

	M	I	NO	R	HS	100s	Avge	S-R
M.E. Waugh	244	236	20	8,500	173	18	39.35	76.54
S.R. Waugh	325	288	58	7,569	120*	3	32.91	76.54
A.R. Border	273	252	39	6,524	127*	3	30.63	71.14
D.M. Jones	164	161	25	6,068	145	7	44.62	72.49
D.C. Boon	181	177	16	5,964	122	5	37.04	64.95
M.G. Bevan	178	156	53	5,751	108*	6	55.83	75.09
R.T. Ponting	141	141	16	5,110	145	9	40.88	75.61
G.R. Marsh	117	115	6	4,357	126*	9	39.97	55.37
A.C. Gilchrist	136	131	5	4,214	154	7	33.96	89.71
M.A. Taylor	113	110	1	3,514	105	1	32.24	59.42

	M	I	NO	R	HS	100s	Avge	Stk/Rt
G. S. Chappell	74	72	14	2,331	138*	3	40.19	74.62
G. M. Wood	83	77	11	2,219	114*	3	33.62	59.43
D. R. Martyn	97	83	27	2,202	144*	3	39.32	78.76
D. S. Lehmann	78	71	14	2,047	110*	2	35.91	81.98
K. J. Hughes	97	88	6	1,968	98	0	24.00	66.98
I. A. Healy	168	120	36	1,764	56	0	21.00	83.64
K. C. Wessels	54	51	3	1,740	107	1	36.25	62.08
D. S. Lehmann	69	62	11	1,727	110*	2	33.86	81.27
D. R. Martyn	79	65	23	1,681	144*	2	40.02	82.69
S. P. O'Donnell	87	64	15	1,242	74*	0	25.35	80.54
S. G. Law	54	51	5	1,237	110	1	26.89	74.74
R. W. Marsh	92	76	15	1,225	66	0	20.08	80.06

BOWLING RECORDS

BEST ANALYSES

T. M. Alderman (2)	5/17	v New Zealand at Wellington	1981-82
	5/32	v India at Christchurch	1989-90
A. J. Bichel	5/19	v South Africa at Sydney	2001-02
G. S. Chappell (2)	5/20	v England at Birmingham	1977
	5/15	v India at Sydney	1980-81
G. J. Cosier	5/18	v England at Birmingham	1977
A. I. C. Dodemaide	5/21	v Sri Lanka at Perth	1989-90
D. W. Fleming	5/36	v India at Mumbai	1995-96
D. R. Gilbert	5/46	v New Zealand at Sydney	1985-86
G. J. Gilmour (2)	6/14	v England at Leeds	1975
	5/48	v West Indies at Lord's	1975
A. G. Hurst	5/21	v Canada at Birmingham	1979
B. Lee	5/27	v India at Adelaide	1999-00
S. Lee	5/33	v Sri Lanka at Melbourne	1998-99
D. K. Lillee	5/34	v Pakistan at Leeds	1975
K. H. MacLeay	6/39	v India at Nottingham	1983
C. J. McDermott	5/44	v Pakistan at Lahore	1987-88
G. D. McGrath (4)	5/52	v Pakistan at Lahore	1994-95
	5/40	v Sri Lanka at Adelaide	1998-99
	5/14	v West Indies at Manchester	1999
	5/49	v Pakistan at Sydney	1999-00
S. P. O'Donnell	5/13	v New Zealand at Christchurch	1989-90
L. S. Pascoe	5/30	v New Zealand at Sydney	1980-81
C. G. Rackemann	5/16	v Pakistan at Adelaide	1983-84
B. A. Reid	5/53	v India at Adelaide	1985-86
A. M. Stuart	5/26	v Pakistan at Melbourne	1996-97
S. K. Warne	5/23	v West Indies at Sydney	1996-97
M. E. Waugh	5/24	v West Indies at Melbourne	1992-93

HAT-TRICKS

B. A. Reid	v New Zealand at Sydney	1985-86
A. M. Stuart	v Pakistan at Melbourne	1996-97

MOST WICKETS IN A CAREER

	M	Balls	Mdns	R	W	BB	5W/i	Avge
S. K. Warne	181	10,017	102	7,137	278	5/33	1	25.67
G. D. McGrath	156	8,383	174	5,523	236	5/14	4	23.40
C. J. McDermott	138	7,460	99	5,020	203	5/44	1	24.73
S. R. Waugh	325	8,883	54	6,764	195	4/33	0	34.69
D. W. Fleming	88	4,619	62	3,402	134	5/36	1	25.39
S. P. O'Donnell	87	4,350	49	3,102	108	5/13	1	28.72
P. R. Reiffel	92	4,732	84	3,095	106	4/13	0	29.20
D. K. Lillee	63	3,593	80	2,145	103	5/34	1	20.83
P. L. Taylor	83	3,937	32	2,740	97	4/38	0	28.25
T. M. Alderman	65	3,371	75	2,056	88	5/17	2	23.36
G. F. Lawson	79	4,259	94	2,592	88	4/26	0	29.45
R. M. Hogg	71	3,677	57	2,418	85	4/29	0	28.45
M. E. Waugh	244	3,687	10	2,938	85	5/24	1	34.56
C. G. Rackemann	52	2,791	51	1,833	82	5/16	1	22.35
A. R. Border	273	2,661	11	2,071	73	3/20	0	28.37
G. S. Chappell	74	3,108	41	2,096	72	5/15	2	29.11
B. Lee	39	2,069	22	1,702	69	5/27	1	24.67
B. A. Reid	61	3,250	53	2,201	63	5/53	1	34.94
G. R. J. Matthews	59	2,808	21	1,999	57	3/27	0	35.07
J. R. Thomson	50	2,696	37	1,942	55	4/67	0	35.31
L. S. Pascoe	29	1,568	21	1,066	53	5/30	1	20.11
J. N. Gillespie	37	2,031	26	1,494	51	4/26	0	29.29

WICKET-KEEPING RECORDS

MOST DISMISSALS IN AN INNINGS

6	(all ct)	A. C. Gilchrist v South Africa at Cape Town	1999-00
5	(all ct)	R. W. Marsh v England at Leeds	1981
5	(4ct, 1st)	A. C. Gilchrist v Pakistan at Melbourne DS	2001-02

Note: There are 23 instances of four dismissals in an innings.

MOST DISMISSALS IN A CAREER

	M	Ct	St	Total
I. A. Healy	168	194	39	233
A. C. Gilchrist	131	187	32	219
R. W. Marsh	92	120	4	124
W. B. Phillips	48	42	7	49
G. C. Dyer	23	24	4	28

FIELDING RECORDS

MOST CATCHES IN AN INNINGS

4   M. A. Taylor   v West Indies at Sydney 1992-93

Note: There are 18 instances of three catches in an innings.

MOST CATCHES IN A CAREER

A. R. Border	127 in 273 matches	M. G. Bevan	57 in 178 matches
S. R. Waugh	111 in 325 matches	M. A. Taylor	56 in 113 matches
M. E. Waugh	108 in 244 matches	D. M. Jones	54 in 164 matches
S. K. Warne	74 in 181 matches	R. T. Ponting	47 in 141 matches

TEAM RECORDS

HIGHEST INNINGS TOTALS

Batting first

6-349	v New Zealand at Christchurch	1999-00
6-338	v West Indies at Melbourne	2000-01
4-338	v India at Visakhapatnam	2000-01
7-337	v Pakistan at Sydney	1999-00
3-332	v Sri Lanka at Sharjah	1989-90
5-329	v India at Adelaide	1999-00
5-328	v Sri Lanka at The Oval	1975
8-324	v Pakistan at Karachi	1998-99
2-323	v Sri Lanka at Adelaide	1984-85
9-320	v India at Nottingham	1983
8-310	v Sri Lanka at Melbourne	1998-99
4-310	v New Zealand at Napier	1999-00
7-304	v Kenya at Visakhapatnam	1995-96
4-303	v Zimbabwe at Lord's	1999
6-303	v Zimbabwe at Bulawayo	1999-00
8-302	v New Zealand at Melbourne	1982-83
5-302	v Zimbabwe at Perth	2000-01
5-300	v Pakistan at Brisbane	1989-90

Batting Second

7-330	v South Africa at Port Elizabeth	2001-02
4-316	v Pakistan at Lahore	1998-99
4-289	v New Zealand at Madras	1995-96
5-287	v South Africa at Centurion	1996-97
284	v India at Chandigarh	1996-97
4-282	v Zimbabwe at Hobart	2000-01
4-280	v England at Birmingham	1993
4-279	v England at Lord's	1989
6-275	v England at Sydney	1998-99
274	v West Indies at Lord's	1975
5-273	v England at Birmingham	1980
5-272	v South Africa at Leeds	1999
5-272	v England at Bristol	2001
2-271	v South Africa at Durban	2001-02

AUSTRALIAN LIMITED-OVERS TEAMS

In July 2002 the national selectors chose two 14-man teams for overseas limited-overs tournaments as part of the lead-up to the World Cup in South Africa.

The Australian side was scheduled to play Pakistan and Kenya in a series in Nairobi from August 27 to September 7, and then travel to Sri Lanka for the ICC Champions Trophy from September 12 to September 29. The squad was: Ricky Ponting (captain), Adam Gilchrist (vice-captain), Michael Bevan, Andy Bichel, Jason Gillespie, Nathan Hauritz, Matthew Hayden, Brett Lee, Darren Lehmann, Jimmy Maher, Damien Martyn, Glenn McGrath, Shane Warne and Shane Watson.

The Australia A team was scheduled to play seven matches against South Africa A between September 4 and September 18. The squad was: Justin Langer (captain), Simon Katich (vice-captain), Greg Blewett, Nathan Bracken, Ryan Campbell, Stuart Clark, Michael Clarke, Ian Harvey, Mark Higgs, Brad Hogg, Mike Hussey, Andrew Symonds, Brad Williams and Damien Wright. – GEORGE THOMAS

SIX IN SIX

Not all promising young cricketers in Australia are named Watson, but 12 year-old Dean certainly emulated Shane, of Tasmania, as a player to watch. On 3 February, 2002, playing for the south-western Sydney suburb of Wetherill Park against Liverpool Catholic, Dean took six wickets in six balls. The Liverpool team seemed comfortably placed at three for 90 when Watson returned to the bowling crease for a second spell. Normally a medium-pacer who bowls first change, he had been given the new ball and had taken one for two from six overs. After a dot ball, the next five balls each produced a wicket, followed by another dismissal from the first ball of his next over to complete his double hat-trick, four of whose victims were clean bowled. Watson's complete analysis was 7.1-4-2-7 which will read well on the resume he prepares to gain admission to nearby Westfield Sports High School, winners of this year's Alan Davidson Shield competition for NSW secondary schools. – WARWICK FRANKS

FORTUNE ALMOST FAVOURS THE GOOD

At the beginning of the 2001-02 season, the Manly second grade side, under its captain, Dick Fry, took a decision that a no-sledging policy would be strictly observed and enforced. The team, whose moral stature had been enormously enhanced by its adherence to the policy, almost pulled off an amazing victory in the final against Northern District. In reply to Northern District's grafting and modest first innings of 239, Manly's normally reliable batting could only muster 145. When the Northern District second innings closed for 175 at 2.45 p.m. on the third day, the target of 270 in 35 overs appeared fanciful at best. Despite losing four for 58, the middle order prospered so dramatically that Manly raced to 256 from only 32.3 overs. Former state player Craig Glassock who has been seriously affected by chronic fatigue syndrome, showed his mettle with 62 made out of 108 in 44 minutes while he was at the wicket, a piece of concentrated flair which followed his 261 against Sutherland a week earlier in the semi-final. – WARWICK FRANKS

PART FOUR: AUSTRALIAN CRICKET IN 2001-02

THE NEW ZEALANDERS IN AUSTRALIA, 2001-02

By WARWICK FRANKS

As the Trans-Tasman Trophy series drew near, the fact of an Australian victory seemed comfortably assured and the only question worth discussing was the extent of the win. The home side appeared to be in excellent form after another comprehensive Ashes win in England, and it was nearly nine years since New Zealand had won a Test against the Australians. Yet only a month later the tourists were within a whisker of taking the trophy home after a remarkable performance in the Perth Test. Along the way, they garnered real admiration for their sturdy refusal to buckle and the way in which they harnessed and used the resources at their disposal. Admittedly, the rain which cut into the Brisbane Test allowed two enterprising captains to give both sides a late chance at victory which the visitors nearly seized, while the Hobart drenching probably protected New Zealand from defeat. Nevertheless, over the full five days of the Perth Test they held the whip hand, Adam Gilchrist's late charge notwithstanding.

They had arrived in Australia unexpectedly early after the events of September 11 caused the cancellation of their tour of Pakistan. Three practice matches were arranged against modest opposition but while some of the batsmen progressed well enough, the visiting bowlers found themselves chronically unable to take wickets quickly or consistently. Worse still, Daniel Vettori, who was only just returning after a 13-month absence from Test cricket caused by a stress fracture, strained ligaments in his ankle in the Canberra match and seemed destined to miss the first two Tests. Even though the off-spinner Paul Wiseman was sent as an immediate replacement, neither he nor Glen Sulzberger looked like deviating from the straight and narrow on Australian pitches.

In fact, the spectre of injury hovered over the team for much of the tour, causing the team management real problems in organising their bowling attack. Chris Cairns arrived still tentative following knee surgery, while the chronic back injury of Dion Nash flared again during the First Test, the same match in which Shayne O'Connor injured his knee while bowling. Shane Bond was thus a supplement to the fast bowling ranks and despite his modest returns he looked to have enough pace and enthusiasm to be an important member of future New Zealand attacks. Daryl Tuffey suffered a hamstring strain in the Hobart Test, so that Chris Drum was asked to cover for the last Test.

The patchwork attack was held together partly by Cairns, who had moments of real fire but other periods when he appeared to smoulder as his line and length became ragged. More importantly, there was the presence of Vettori, who was miraculously fit for each of the Tests and stood up well to prolonged spells at the bowling crease. He is that thing of wonder and beauty, an attacking left-arm spinner with the ability to make the ball bite and turn, and possessed of teasingly seductive powers of flight—powers which allowed him to make a number of Australian batsmen look vulnerably tentative. His bowling was an indispensable factor in his side's confident showing in the Perth Test.

In contrast, the batting achievements were more uniformly spread, apart from frailty in the opening partnerships. In Brisbane, it was four hours of resistance from Nathan Astle that kept his side in the game and signalled a series of consistent achievement. The second innings of six for 274 was a well-orchestrated team effort and came from 57 overs in a real run-chase as opposed to the contrived confection which is often seen in one-day cricket. In Hobart, Stephen Fleming showed that defence could be both composed and graceful, and in Perth Lou Vincent announced his arrival on the Test scene with a century of real enterprise and followed it up with a rippling fifty in the second innings. In this game, Fleming showed his mettle over the long haul, while Astle and Adam Parore reduced the Australian bowling to unaccustomed raggedness and bewilderment in their magnificent eighth-wicket partnership of 253. Along the way, Cairns and Craig McMillan weighed in with useful runs in their contrasting styles. The character and discipline of the batting were such that, between them, Australia's traditional strike weapons of Glenn McGrath and Shane Warne took just 11 wickets at 68.82. The batsmen withdrew completely from that zone of danger and uncertainty outside the off stump which McGrath exploits to perfection, so that he was forced to attack the stumps more directly and less effectively, while their footwork and patience nullified the frustration-inducing persistence of Warne.

Fleming's captaincy was an important ingredient in the team's progress. Calm, intelligent and tactically astute, he exuded both charm and dignity in the tribulations of the early part of the tour, while his easy authority subsequently lifted the team into unexpected zones of achievement.

In fairness to Australia, it should again be stressed that they would have gone to Perth two Tests up if the weather had held in both Brisbane and Hobart. Although Damien Martyn and Steve Waugh found their run banks low in funds, the batting was generally potent and productive, with 351 being the lowest total. Justin Langer and Matthew Hayden compiled double-century opening stands in successive innings in Brisbane and Hobart, while Ricky Ponting's century in the latter game was the creation of a batsman at the height of his powers. Adam Gilchrist more than compensated for the side's mid-innings frailty with several wondrous exhibitions of batting bravura, while Shane Warne made a belated claim for all-rounder status with an average of 50.25. Jason Gillespie returned from injury to bowl with both fire and precision while Brett Lee's bowling began to reveal more than just exhilarating speed.

Both captains deserve warm praise for their enterprising approach. On the last day in Brisbane, each threw down and then responded to the challenge of trying to snatch victory for his side, while the Perth Test produced 1,522 runs and a final afternoon on which both teams were still striving for a result. It was one of those refreshing reminders of how far Test cricket has come in enterprise and entertainment from the dreariness which infected too much of the 1950s and 1960s.

NEW ZEALAND TOURING PARTY

S.P. Fleming (Wellington) (*captain*), N.J. Astle (Canterbury), M.D. Bell (Wellington), C.L. Cairns (Canterbury), C.J. Drum (Auckland), C.S. Martin (Canterbury), C.D. McMillan (Canterbury) (*vice-captain*), D.C. Nash (Auckland), S.B. O'Connor (Otago), A.C. Parore (Auckland), M.H. Richardson (Otago), M.S. Sinclair (Central Districts), G.P. Sulzberger (Central Districts), D.R. Tuffey (Northern Districts), D.L. Vettori (Northern Districts), P.W. Wiseman (Otago).

D.L. Vettori returned home injured during the tour and was replaced by P.W. Wiseman; S.E. Bond was called as a replacement for the injured O'Connor. C.J. Drum was called into the touring party to cover for the injured Tuffey.

For the limited-overs internationals: A.R. Adams (Auckland), S.E. Bond (Canterbury), C.Z. Harris (Canterbury), J.E.C. Franklin (Wellington), B.B. McCullum (Otago), S.B. Styris (Northern Districts) and L. Vincent (Auckland) replaced M.D. Bell, C.S. Martin, S.B. O'Connor, M.S. Sinclair, G.P. Sulzberger and P.W. Wiseman.

K.C. Mills withdrew from the squad before it left New Zealand and was replaced by J.E.C. Franklin.

Manager: J.J. Crowe (Auckland). *Coach:* D.C. Aberhart (Canterbury).
Physiotherapist: D. Shackle. *Cricket Analyst:* Z. Hitchcock.

NEW ZEALAND TOUR RESULTS

Test matches – Played 3: Drawn 3.
First-class matches – Played 5: Lost 1, Drawn 4.
Losses – South Australia.
Draws – Australia and Queensland.
Limited-overs internationals – Played 10: Won 4, Lost 6. *Wins* – Australia (3), South Africa (1).
   Losses – Australia (1), South Africa (5).
Other non-first-class matches – Played 6: Won 2, Lost 1, Drawn 3. *Wins* – Prime Minister's XI,
   Australian Country XI. *Loss:* Australia A; *Draws* – Queensland Academy of Sport (2), ACT
   President's XI.

NEW ZEALANDERS V PRIME MINISTER'S X1

Back row: B. Climas (*referee*), P. Chapman (*umpire*), D.C. Aberhart (*coach*), J.J. Crowe (*manager*), M.S. Sinclair, M.H. Richardson, S.E. Bond, D.R. Tuffey, L. Vincent, C.J. Drum, M.D. Bell. *Front Row:* N.J. Astle, A.C. Parore, S.P. Fleming (*captain*), Rt Hon. John Howard (Prime Minister), C.D. McMillan, D.L. Vettori, C.L. Cairns.

TEST MATCH AVERAGES

AUSTRALIA – BATTING

	M	I	NO	R	HS	100s	50s	Avge	Ct/St
R.T. Ponting	3	5	2	251	157*	1	0	83.67	3
J.L. Langer	3	5	1	320	123	2	1	80.00	1
A.C. Gilchrist	3	5	1	260	118	1	1	65.00	6/1
M.L. Hayden	3	5	0	297	136	1	2	59.40	0
S.K. Warne	3	4	0	201	99	0	2	50.25	4
B. Lee	3	3	0	119	61	0	1	39.67	0
M.E. Waugh	3	4	0	140	86	0	1	35.00	2
D.R. Martyn	3	4	0	94	60	0	1	23.50	1
J.N. Gillespie	3	3	2	21	20*	0	0	21.00	1
S.R. Waugh.........	3	4	0	78	67	0	1	19.50	3
G.D. McGrath	3	1	1	0	0*	0	0	–	1

* Denotes not out.

BOWLING

	O	M	R	W	BB	5Wi	10Wm	Avge
B. Lee	100.5	19	352	14	5/67	1	0	25.14
J.N. Gillespie	111.4	27	316	11	3/45	0	0	28.73
M.E. Waugh	14	2	64	1	1/30	0	0	64.00
G.D. McGrath	117	37	327	5	2/46	0	0	65.40
S.K. Warne.........	124.2	19	430	6	3/89	0	0	71.67
D.R. Martyn..........	10	0	44	0	–	0	0	–
R.T. Ponting..........	7	3	9	0	–	0	0	–

NEW ZEALAND – BATTING

	M	I	NO	R	HS	100s	50s	Avge	Ct
N.J. Astle..........	3	5	1	322	156*	1	1	80.50	0
L. Vincent	1	2	0	158	104	1	1	79.00	1
A.C. Parore	3	5	3	150	110	1	0	75.00	6
S.P. Fleming	3	5	0	237	105	1	2	47.40	1
C.D. McMillan	3	5	1	146	55	0	1	36.50	2
C.L. Cairns	3	5	0	174	61	0	1	34.80	0
M.H. Richardson	3	5	0	152	57	0	1	30.40	3
M.S. Sinclair........	3	5	0	80	29	0	0	16.00	2
D.L. Vettori........	3	4	2	18	10*	0	0	9.00	5
M.D. Bell	2	3	0	15	6	0	0	5.00	0
S.E. Bond	2	2	0	8	8	0	0	4.00	2
D.J. Nash..........	1	1	1	25	25*	0	0	–	0
D.R. Tuffey	1	0	0	0	0	0	0	–	0
C.S. Martin	1	0	0	0	0	0	0	–	0
S.B. O'Connor	1	0	0	0	0	0	0	–	0

* Denotes not out.

BOWLING

	O	M	R	W	BB	5Wi	10Wm	Avge
D.L. Vettori.........	131.2	23	440	13	6/87	2	0	33.85
C.D. McMillan.........	34	3	178	4	3/65	0	0	44.50
C.L. Cairns............	108	19	455	10	5/146	1	0	45.50
N.J. Astle	45	13	108	2	1/30	0	0	54.00
S.E. Bond.............	67	5	289	3	1/74	0	0	96.33
C.S. Martin...........	35	4	139	1	1/88	0	0	139.00
S.B. O'Connor	17.2	4	67	0	–	0	0	–
D.R. Tuffey	15	1	74	0	–	0	0	–
D.J. Nash	30	6	93	0	–	0	0	–

NEW ZEALAND TOUR AVERAGES
FIRST-CLASS MATCHES

BATTING

	M	I	NO	R	HS	100s	50s	Avge	Ct/St
N.J. Astle	4	7	2	554	223	2	1	110.80	0
L. Vincent	2	4	0	232	104	1	2	58.00	1
A.C. Parore	5	9	3	276	110	1	0	46.00	11/1
S.P. Fleming	4	7	0	306	105	1	3	43.71	2
C.L. Cairns	4	7	1	244	61	0	1	40.67	0
C.D. McMillan	5	9	1	272	55	0	2	34.00	3
D.R. Tuffey	2	2	0	66	56	0	1	33.00	0
G.P. Sulzberger	2	3	0	76	41	0	0	25.33	2
M.S. Sinclair	5	9	0	200	80	0	1	22.22	4
M.H. Richardson	5	9	0	187	57	0	1	20.78	5
M.D. Bell	4	7	0	49	29	0	0	7.00	1
D.L. Vettori	4	6	2	23	10*	0	0	5.75	6
S.E. Bond	3	4	0	12	8	0	0	3.00	4
C.S. Martin	3	3	3	4	4*	0	0	–	3
D.J. Nash	1	1	1	25	25*	0	0	–	0
S.B. O'Connor	2	1	1	11	11*	0	0	–	1

* Denotes not out.

BOWLING

	O	M	R	W	BB	5W/i	10W/m	Avge
D.L. Vettori	189.5	38	580	22	6/80	3	0	26.36
C.L. Cairns	140	24	565	15	5/71	2	0	37.67
C.D. McMillan	49.3	5	242	6	3/65	0	0	40.33
D.R. Tuffey	43	8	166	4	3/71	0	0	41.50
N.J. Astle	45	13	108	2	1/30	0	0	54.00
S.E. Bond	97	13	367	6	2/35	0	0	61.17
S.B. O'Connor	53.2	17	128	2	1/18	0	0	64.00
G.P. Sulzberger	57	7	259	4	2/75	0	0	64.75
C.S. Martin	93	14	360	3	1/59	0	0	120.00
D.J. Nash	30	6	93	0	–	0	0	–
L. Vincent	1	0	2	0	–	0	0	–

Note: Matches in this section that were not first-class are signified by a dagger.

†QUEENSLAND ACADEMY OF SPORT v NEW ZEALANDERS

At Allan Border Field, Albion, October 16, 17 (no play), 18, 19, 2001. Drawn. Toss: Queensland Academy of Sport.

The visitors' modest first innings depended heavily on their captain's determination and fluency. Fleming (253 minutes, 216 balls, 24 fours, one six) overcame a persevering attack in which Damian MacKenzie bowled with both enthusiasm and effect. After a blank second day owing to rain, the young Queensland side made a steady reply marked by the contrasting approaches of Daniel Payne (186 minutes, 133 balls, five fours, one six) and all-rounder James Hopes (111 minutes, 85 balls, 14 fours). The New Zealanders' second innings looked like being a meagre affair until Fleming (152 minutes, 139 balls, 10 fours) and Adam Parore (154 minutes, 158 balls, 16 fours, one six) put the situation into perspective with a sixth-wicket partnership of 158. A third declaration left Payne time to complete his second fifty of the match.

Close of play: First day, New Zealanders (1) 8-297 (Fleming 133, Tuffey 12; Second day, no play; Third day, New Zealanders (2) 1-25 (Bell 4, Sinclair 16).

New Zealanders

M.H. Richardson c Hartley b O'Leary	40	– c Hartley b Johnson 0
M.D. Bell lbw b Johnson	8	– c Hartley b Hauritz 22
M.S. Sinclair b MacKenzie	17	– b Hopes 57
*S.P. Fleming not out	133	– (6) c Simpson b Hopes 68
N.J. Astle c Hartley b MacKenzie	0	– (4) c Simpson b MacKenzie 7
C.D. McMillan c O'Leary b Hopes	33	– (5) b Hauritz 15
†A.C. Parore lbw b MacKenzie	22	– not out 100
D.J. Nash c Hartley b MacKenzie	0	– not out 10
D.L. Vettori c Carseldine b Johnson	15	
D.R. Tuffey not out	12	
B 5, l-b 8, n-b 4	17	B 3, l-b 7, w 1, n-b 6 17

(97 overs, 352 mins) (8 wkts dec) 297 (90.2 overs, 302 mins) (6 wkts dec) 296
Fall: 36 69 77 83 142 201 203 247 Fall: 0 54 79 108 110 268

S.B. O'Connor and C.S. Martin did not bat.

Bowling: *First Innings*—Johnson 22–7–78–2; Hopes 29–10–74–1; MacKenzie 21–7–52–4; O'Leary 11–3–36–1; Hauritz 14–0–44–0. *Second Innings*—Johnson 17–4–51–1; MacKenzie 14–3–63–1; Hauritz 38–8–110–2; Hopes 13–6–25–2; Carseldine 8–1–31–0; Philipson 0.2–0–6–0.

Queensland Academy of Sport

C.P. Simpson lbw b Tuffey	5	– (2) run out (McMillan) 14
D.M. Payne b Martin	57	– (1) c Sinclair b Martin 51
B.P. Nash b Fleming b Nash	29	– not out 29
L.A. Carseldine c Vettori b O'Connor	4	– not out 16
J.R. Hopes c Parore b Tuffey	75	
C.A. Philipson c Richardson b Vettori	31	
†C.D. Hartley c Astle b Nash	16	
N.M. Hauritz not out	17	
D.R. MacKenzie not out	17	
L-b 4, n-b 12	16	N-b 4 4

(70 overs, 289 mins) (7 wkts dec) 267 (33 overs, 121 mins) (2 wkts) 114
Fall: 6 59 66 174 190 233 233 Fall: 47 82

*J.L. Cassell, M.G. Johnson and S.J. O'Leary did not bat.

Bowling: *First Innings*—Tuffey 17–1–72–2; O'Connor 16–1–62–1; Nash 15–5–36–2; Martin 9–1–33–1; Vettori 13–1–60–1. *Second Innings*—Tuffey 6–1–26–0; O'Connor 6–2–15–0; Nash 4–0–18–0; Vettori 10–2–31–0; Martin 5–0–24–1.

Umpires: T.P. Laycock and N.S. McNamara.

†ACT PRESIDENT'S XI v NEW ZEALANDERS

At Manuka Oval, Canberra, October 21, 22, 23, 2001. Drawn. Toss: ACT President's XI.

With the First Test 17 days away, Daniel Vettori's apparently serious injury to his right ankle marred a high-scoring game at Manuka against an Australian Capital Territory President's XI strengthened by the inclusion of four of New South Wales' senior squad: Corey Richards, Matthew Phelps, Grant Lambert and Jamie Heath. Attempting to stop a straight drive from Phelps in the opening session, Vettori fell awkwardly and suffered ligament and tendon damage. In his first game after knee surgery, Chris Cairns bowled 25 undemanding overs as the local side's first innings was marked by the sustained application of nuggety 24-year-old local Jack Smith (430 minutes, 351 balls, 24 fours, two sixes), although he did gallop past his century with a six and two fours off successive balls from off-spinner Glen Sulzberger. Lambert (180 minutes, 145 balls, 15 fours, one six) played with freedom and flair as the local team batted into middle of the second day. The visitors' innings was dominated by another pair of contrasting innings, in this case from the laborious Matthew Bell (325 minutes, 324 balls, 13 fours) and the attractively fluent Mathew Sinclair (232 minutes, 203 balls, 22 fours).

Close of play: First day, ACT President's XI (1) 3-280 (Smith 145, Lambert 18); Second day, New Zealanders (1) 1-133 (Bell 44, Sinclair 51).

ACT President's XI

C.J. Richards c Bell b Cairns	1				
J.K. Smith lbw b Sulzberger	156	–	(1) not out	24	
M.J. Phelps c Parore b O'Connor	51				
D.S. Hazell c Parore b O'Connor	56				
G.M. Lambert c O'Connor b Sulzberger	101				
S.L. Maxwell not out	51				
M.T. Clark c Bell b O'Connor	4				
†D.G. Dawson not out	6	–	(2) not out	10	
B 1, l-b 8, n-b 4	13		B 4, n-b 1	5	

(141 overs, 510 mins)	(6 wkts dec) 439	(12 overs, 45 mins) (0 wkt) 39

Fall: 2 87 212 360 405 424

*J.D. Robson, H.R. Axelby, J.M. Heath and E. Kellar did not bat.

Bowling: *First Innings*—Cairns 25–5–115–1; O'Connor 32–10–89–3; Martin 27–7–74–0; Vettori 2–0–6–0; Sulzberger 48–11–134–2; Astle 7–2–12–0. *Second Innings*—Cairns 4–1–15–0; O'Connor 4–1–14–0; Sinclair 2–0–5–0; Martin 2–1–1–0.

New Zealanders

M.H. Richardson c Dawson b Lambert	31	S.B. O'Connor not out	9
M.D. Bell retired hurt	107		
M.S. Sinclair c Heath b Clark	145	L-b 2, n-b 14	16
N.J. Astle lbw b Lambert	23		
L. Vincent b Heath	4	(127 overs, 469 mins) (4 wkts dec) 340	
G.P. Sulzberger not out	5	Fall: 65 267 321 327	

*S.P. Fleming, C.L. Cairns, †A.C. Parore, D.L. Vettori and C.S. Martin did not bat.

Bowling: Heath 32–8–90–1; Kellar 19–7–44–0; Lambert 33–4–89–2; Clark 24–8–52–1; Axelby 12–4–33–0; Robson 5–0–26–0; Smith 2–1–4–0.

Umpires: D. Harris and W.F. Ruse.

†QUEENSLAND ACADEMY OF SPORT v NEW ZEALANDERS

At Allan Border Field, Albion, October 26, 27, 28, 2001. Drawn. Toss: Queensland Academy of Sport.

After rain permitted only 12 overs on the first day, the New Zealand bowling was so severely treated by the Queensland Academy captain, Jerry Cassell (292 minutes, 243 balls, 20 fours, three sixes) and Lee Carseldine (266 minutes, 188 balls, 35 fours, two sixes) that their fourth-wicket partnership of 205 came only in 146 minutes from 231 balls. The sobering facts for the visitors were that this exhibition came from batsmen who have been unable to maintain regular places in Queensland's senior side and that this took to 12 for 955 the aggregate conceded by their bowlers in the three practice matches. The slackening tension of the last day was reflected in the statistics of the three century-makers: Lou Vincent (269 minutes, 261 balls, 19 fours) was restrained and careful, Craig McMillan (170 minutes, 141 balls, 10 fours, five sixes) found conditions to his liking, while Chris Cairns (118 minutes, 81 balls, 11 fours, seven sixes) made hay from the fodder offered to him late in the day. He reached his century in 87 minutes from 67 balls, his sixth-wicket partnership of 221 with McMillan occupying 118 minutes and coming from 184 balls.

Close of play: First day, Queensland Academy of Sport (1) 2-20 (Cassell 9, Sippel 4); Second day, New Zealanders (1) 2-44 (Vincent 25, Fleming 0).

Queensland Academy of Sport

D.M. Betts lbw b Cairns	0	†C.D. Hartley c Fleming b Nash	7
*J.L. Cassell c and b Astle	163	S.J. O'Leary not out	17
M.N. Lunn c Richardson b Tuffey	6	B 4, l-b 7, w 2, n-b 12	25
M. Sippel b McMillan	58		
L.A. Carseldine not out	200	(101 overs, 412 mins) (6 wkts dec)	477
C.A. Philipson c Wiseman b McMillan	1	Fall: 0 13 130 335 348 386	

M.A. Anderson, M.J. Petrie, B.O. Williams and M.T. George did not bat.

Bowling: Cairns 25–5–130–1; Tuffey 24–4–106–1; Nash 21–1–81–1; McMillan 15–2–55–2; Sulzberger 4–0–43–0; Wiseman 6–0–36–0; Astle 6–2–15–1.

New Zealanders

M.H. Richardson c Hartley b Petrie	7	†A.C. Parore not out	12
M.D. Bell c Hartley b George	12	D.J. Nash c Hartley b Williams	0
L. Vincent c Hartley b George	136	G.P. Sulzberger not out	1
*S.P. Fleming lbw b Williams	47	B 1, l-b 3, w 2, n-b 7	13
N.J. Astle c Sippel b Carseldine	35		
C.D. McMillan retired	116	(121 overs, 444 mins) (8 wkts)	498
C.L. Cairns retired	119	Fall: 9 33 147 203 262 483 485 486	

D.R. Tuffey and P.J. Wiseman did not bat.

Bowling: Williams 26–4–124–2; Petrie 13.5–4–37–1; George 20–1–85–2; O'Leary 9–0–60–0; Anderson 28–4–126–0; Carseldine 22.1–5–57–1; Sippel 1–0–5–0; Lunn 1–1–0–0.

Umpires: A.J. McQuillan and L.D. Musch.

QUEENSLAND v NEW ZEALANDERS

At Brisbane Cricket Ground, Brisbane, November 1, 2, 3, 4, 2001. Drawn. Toss: New Zealanders. First-class debut: M.G Johnson.

A double-century from Nathan Astle was the highlight of this Test-eve clash on a batting-friendly Gabba wicket. Astle's 223 (424 minutes, 380 balls, 27 fours, two sixes) was the second-highest by a New Zealand tourist in Australia, behind Martin Crowe's 242 against South Australia in 1985-86. Although he was dropped twice in the slips by Jimmy Maher, Astle deserved full credit for helping revive his team from a precarious three for 34. Chris Cairns' explosive cameo included one six off Mike Kasprowicz into the Brisbane Lions' social club. On his first-class debut, Mitchell Johnson was no-balled nine times for over-stepping, and took one wicket, that of Mark Richardson, with a delivery which replays showed could also have been called. Cairns bowled effectively, while Matthew Hayden's 97 (230 minutes, 166 balls, eight fours, two sixes) was a sign of things to come. Mathew Sinclair's solid knock (201 minutes, 176 balls, eight fours) in the second innings mixed luck with good management, and Cairns caused a cyclonic disturbance as he smashed four sixes from the 13 balls he faced. Andrew Symonds (32 minutes, 26 balls, seven fours, one six) answered in similar coin in Queensland's improbable run-chase.

Close of play: First day, New Zealanders (1) 6-332 (Astle 160, Parore 6); Second day, Queensland (1) 1-140 (Hayden, 56, Love 33); Third day, New Zealanders (2) 3-53 (Sinclair 17, McMillan 20).

Attendance: 2,250.

New Zealanders

M. H. Richardson c Noffke b Johnson	11	– c Seccombe b Kasprowicz 0
M. D. Bell lbw b Bichel	1	– lbw b Bichel 4
M. S. Sinclair c Seccombe b Noffke	16	– c Love b Johnson 80
*S. P. Fleming c Law b Perren	69	– c Seccombe b Bichel 0
N. J. Astle c Hayden b Symonds	223	– (8) not out 9
C. D. McMillan run out (Symonds/Seccombe)	0	– (5) c Law b Kasprowicz 43
C. L. Cairns c Perren b Bichel	39	– not out 31
†A. C. Parore b Symonds	30	– (6) c (sub) N. M. Hauritz b Symonds 24
G. P. Sulzberger c Perren b Johnson	0	
S. B. O'Connor not out	11	
C. S. Martin not out	4	
B 3, l-b 14, w 2, n-b 21	40	L-b 4, n-b 18 22

(136 overs, 522 mins) (9 wkts dec) 444   (53.5 overs, 223 mins) (6 wkts dec) 213
Fall: 10 29 34 209 214 310 420 421 427   Fall: 0 9 9 104 167 185

Bowling: First Innings—Bichel 23–5–65–2; Johnson 26–8–64–2; Noffke 27–10–78–1; Kasprowicz 22–0–118–0; Symonds 24–2–87–2; Perren 14–7–15–1. *Second Innings*—Kasprowicz 13–2–39–2; Bichel 12–2–43–2; Noffke 8–2–32–0; Johnson 13–4–42–1; Law 1–1–0–0; Symonds 6.5–0–53–1.

Queensland

M. L. Hayden c Bell b Martin	97	
J. P. Maher st Parore b Sulzberger	47	– (1) b Martin 62
M. L. Love c Parore b Cairns	39	– (2) lbw b Sulzberger 42
C. T. Perren c McMillan b Cairns	34	– (3) not out 47
A. Symonds c (sub) L. Vincent b O'Connor	48	– (4) c O'Connor b Sulzberger 47
*S. G. Law c Sulzberger b Cairns	36	– not out 0
†W. A. Seccombe c Parore b Cairns	1	– (5) c (sub) L. Vincent b O'Connor . 0
A. J. Bichel run out (Sinclair)	14	
A. A. Noffke lbw b McMillan	13	
M. S. Kasprowicz c Fleming b Cairns	0	
M. G. Johnson not out	6	
B 1, l-b 7, n-b 4	12	L-b 2, n-b 2 4

(110.3 overs, 430 mins) 347   (42 overs, 177 mins) (4 wkts) 202
Fall: 64 162 191 271 271 286 312 339 339 347   Fall: 78 119 182 188

Bowling: First Innings—Cairns 22–5–71–5; O'Connor 27–11–43–1; Martin 22–5–66–1; Sulzberger 33–4–122–1; McMillan 6.3–0–37–1. *Second Innings*—Cairns 10–0–39–0; O'Connor 9–2–18–1; Sulzberger 11–0–75–2; Martin 10–0–59–1; McMillan 2–0–9–0.

Umpires: B. N. J. Oxenford and P. D. Parker.
TV Umpire: J. F. Torpey.

AUSTRALIA v NEW ZEALAND

First Test Match

At Brisbane Cricket Ground, Brisbane, November 8, 9, 10, 11, 12, 2001. Drawn. Toss: New Zealand.

Once in a while human ingenuity overcomes the ravages of the elements. The First Test of this compressed series was a case in point. The uncharitable Brisbane weather washed away over a third of the scheduled playing time, yet on a memorable, marathon final day the captains retrieved the contest from the flood-drains by boldly reconstituting a win-or-lose countdown. That the match still finished as a draw was cause for satisfaction rather than regret. New Zealand's gamble, after all, had been from the underdog's stance, while Australia had maintained mastery from the start of the match until the final frantic hour.

Steve Waugh's team, having won 20 of their last 23 Tests, with never a draw, were seen as a school of confident, voracious sharks when the next prey, New Zealand, floated into view like a shoal of innocent hoki. Few sides have entered a Test match 15-to-1 outsiders. After Stephen Fleming put Australia in, the fifth ball sparked discord. Justin Langer was patently leg-before, but given not out by a subsequently repentant umpire Daryl Harper, and not until over four hours later was the first-wicket stand broken. The Matthew Hayden/Langer alliance of 224 was the highest in any Test by a pair of left-handed openers and also passed the Australian first-wicket record against New Zealand, part-held by the ousted Michael Slater, who was now playing for New South Wales in Melbourne. Hayden, 71 at lunch, with Australia 103, had lobbed a six off the first ball from Daniel Vettori (whose ankle injury had seemed certain to keep him out of the tour), and the Queensland giant handled the seamers more easily than did Langer. At 83, Hayden was almost caught by a leaping Craig McMillan at short cover, but with further regal strokeplay and awesome power he sailed to his fourth Test hundred, his first on his home ground, grinning broadly as he did so and crossing himself. After tea came another Hayden six, off Nathan Astle, before he top-edged a pull to end a commanding innings (251 minutes, 195 balls, 20 fours, two sixes).

New Zealand's front-line attack had failed, but after Chris Cairns bounced Ricky Ponting to his downfall at square cover, the back-up seamers sent shockwaves through Australia. Astle had a shuffling and scoreless Mark Waugh leg-before, and his brother Steve, with only a grade innings behind him in 11 weeks, fell to McMillan, edging a hesitant drive. McMillan indulged in frenzied celebration as Damien Martyn, like Ponting, cut fatally to deep point, and Langer (317 minutes, 231 balls, 13 fours), like his opening partner, topped a pull not long after completing his ninth Test century.

Rain blighted the second day, only 29 overs being possible. Shane Warne was soon out, but Brett Lee supported Adam Gilchrist, who yet again toyed with the bowling. The New Zealanders fell on the defensive while seeming to believe that Gilchrist had a weakness to the short ball. He went on merrily, brutally pulling the long-hops. At times Lee looked like an adventurous No. 4. His uppercut six to third man raised the 400 and the century stand, and the pair broke the Australian eighth-wicket record against New Zealand (set by Kerry O'Keeffe and Gary Gilmour at Auckland in 1976-77). Lee's fifty came off 69 balls, and after Gilchrist hit Astle for six and tea was taken, down came the rain. Shayne O'Connor's knee injury was the tourists' latest problem.

The next ball was not bowled until the following day, Saturday, federal election day. When the tarpaulin and hessian were dragged off, the pitch looked ominously juicy, and sawdust was needed for the bowlers' footholds. Lee (132 minutes, 93 balls, nine fours, one six) soon went, given out caught off a pad flap, but at lunch Gilchrist was 98. Practicality rather than sentimentality permitted him the opportunity to bat on, and soon he reached his third Test century for the year. There were a number of verbal retorts from McMillan as his bowling was dispatched to all parts of the Gabba, and the carnage ended only when substitute Lou Vincent dived spectacularly to catch Gilchrist (242 minutes, 158 balls, 17 fours, one six), giving Cairns a well-earned fifth wicket.

Mark Richardson and Matthew Bell fought for 29 without loss before more rain brought down the curtain after less than 20 overs for the day. Everything now rested on the follow-on. A hostile field setting and sharp bowling, especially by Jason Gillespie, tested New Zealand nerve and technique, and there was little surprise when four wickets toppled for 55, including Fleming first ball to a lifting cutter. Lee, who repeatedly beat the bat – especially Astle's – ended a one-hour encampment by Mathew Sinclair that yielded only three runs, and had not Martyn put down two catches New Zealand's plight of four for 115 at lunch would have been much worse. McMillan made a defiant 45 before touching a Lee outswinger, and Astle reached a gritty fifty in almost three hours before rain yet again intervened.

The ground was almost deserted when the final day's play began at 9.30 a.m., but by 6.20 p.m. a total of 459 runs (the most runs in a day in a Test for 47 years) had been hit, and the result was in doubt until the final over. New Zealand nudged towards the crucial follow-on target, losing the doughty Astle (230 minutes, 161 balls, seven fours) and cavalier Cairns (94 minutes, 70 balls, eight fours) in consecutive overs, after which the run flow almost dried up. When the eighth wicket fell (Adam Parore giving Steve Waugh his 100th Test catch, a low, one-handed chance at gully, and Lee his fifth wicket of the innings) 16 runs were still needed. Vettori, dropped next ball by Warne, wide to his left at slip, went on to help Dion Nash reach salvation. Nash's precious 25 came at the expense of further damage to abdominal muscles, which shortly afterwards obliged him to return home. The instant the follow-on was negated, Fleming declared, 199 in arrears. The hoki were nibbling impudently at the sharks' tail fins.

Australia now banged up 84 at a run a ball, Gilchrist and Hayden losing their wickets sacrificially, and the target set New Zealand was 284 in a minimum of 57 overs. By tea they were 55 after 13 overs for the loss of Bell. While Sinclair could only hit the ball to fieldsmen, left-hander Richardson struck a 54-ball fifty, latterly with a runner. Both were then dismissed by Warne, setting the stage for a vigorous and imaginative century stand by Fleming and Astle that scattered the field into defensive positions.

One of the biggest upsets in Test history was looming. Astle finally swished across the line and spooned Warne to mid-off, but this merely ushered Cairns in, and Australia's apprehension swelled as the floodlights were switched on, never before, surely, seen as such a boon. Off 12 overs 92 runs were needed. For a time it was mainly singles to the far-flung field off McGrath and Warne. Fleming (116 minutes, 73 balls, six fours) was then narrowly run out. But danger man Cairns pounded Warne up into the Northern Stand, was dropped at cover, and repeated his monumental blow off Warne. Meanwhile, McMillan had pulled McGrath for six, and emulated Cairns in a Warne over that cost 17 runs. Now only 21 were needed off 18 balls. With indulgent interpretation of a wide, McGrath managed an over from which only a single came, McMillan flailing impotently well inside the line of five deliveries and looking embarrassed at the end of it. Lee replaced Warne for the penultimate over – there was little choice – and Cairns (56 minutes, 38 balls, two sixes) could only emulate McMillan, swishing at where he wished the ball had been. Another attempt at a six ended as a catch just inside the long-on rope. With 15 needed off McGrath and eight men patrolling the boundary, only five singles could be found.

For the first time in over two years Australia had played a drawn match. But it was an exceptional draw which reflected credit on two enterprising captains (and their advisers) and served as a reminder of five-day cricket's unique propensity to thrill. – DAVID FRITH.

Man of the Match: B. Lee.   *Attendance:* 36,752.

Close of play: First day, Australia (1) 6-294 (Gilchrist 13, Warne 18); Second day, Australia (1) 7-435 (Gilchrist 88, Lee 60); Third day, New Zealand (1) 0-29 (Richardson 10, Bell 6); Fourth day, New Zealand (1) 5-186 (Astle 51, Cairns 25).

Australia

J.L. Langer c Vettori b McMillan	104	– (4) not out	18
M.L. Hayden c Richardson b Cairns	136	– run out (sub) L. Vincent/Cairns	13
R.T. Ponting c Vettori b Cairns	5	– not out	32
M.E. Waugh lbw b Astle	0		
*S.R. Waugh c Parore b McMillan	3		
D.R. Martyn c Vettori b McMillan	4		
†A.C. Gilchrist c (sub) L. Vincent b Cairns	118	(1) b Cairns	20
S.K. Warne c Sinclair b Cairns	22		
B. Lee c Parore b Cairns	61		
J.N. Gillespie not out	20		
L-b 4, w 1, n-b 8	13	N-b 1	1

(131 overs, 550 mins)   (9 wkts dec) 486   (14 overs, 57 mins)   (2 wkts dec) 84
Fall: 224 233 235 256 260 263 302 437 486   Fall: 30 39

G.D. McGrath did not bat.

Bowling: *First Innings*—Cairns 37–8–146–5; Nash 30–6–93–0; O'Connor 17.2–4–67–0; Vettori 13.4–0–65–0; Astle 19–7–46–1; McMillan 14–1–65–3. *Second Innings*—Cairns 5–1–29–1; McMillan 7–0–47–0; Vettori 2–0–8–0.

New Zealand

M.H. Richardson lbw b Gillespie	26	– lbw b Warne	57
M.D. Bell c Ponting b Gillespie	6	– lbw b McGrath	5
M.S. Sinclair c Ponting b Lee	3	– st Gilchrist b Warne	23
*S.P. Fleming c Gilchrist b Gillespie	0	– run out (S.R. Waugh)	57
N.J. Astle c Gilchrist b Lee	66	– c Gillespie b Warne	49
C.D. McMillan c Warne b Lee	45	– (7) not out	23
C.L. Cairns c S.R. Waugh b Lee	61	– (6) c Ponting b Lee	43
†A.C. Parore c S.R. Waugh b Lee	11	– not out	3
D.J. Nash not out	25		
D.L. Vettori not out	3		
S.B. O'Connor			
L-b 15, n-b 26	41	B 1, l-b 9, w 1, n-b 3	14

(88.4 overs, 405 mins)   (8 wkts dec) 287   (57 overs, 250 mins)   (6 wkts) 274
Fall: 36 51 51 55 147 242 243 271   Fall: 33 89 90 190 213 264

Bowling: *First Innings*—McGrath 26–6–80–0; Gillespie 18.4–6–56–3; Lee 23–6–67–5; Warne 18–2–61–0; Ponting 3–0–8–0. *Second Innings*—Lee 10–0–53–1; Gillespie 8–0–48–0; McGrath 20–4–66–1; Warne 18–2–89–3; M.E. Waugh 1–0–8–0.

Umpires: S.A. Bucknor (West Indies) and D.J. Harper.
TV Umpire: P.D. Parker.
Referee: J.L. Hendriks (West Indies).

SOUTH AUSTRALIA v NEW ZEALANDERS

At Adelaide Oval, Adelaide, November 16, 17, 18, 19, 2001. South Australia won by 17 runs. Toss: South Australia.

In a match dominated by spin bowling on a dark and dusty pitch, a nine-wicket haul by veteran leg-spinner Peter McIntyre brought South Australia a narrow win with three overs to spare. Set 196 to win in just over two sessions, the visitors had no consistent answer to the experienced leg-spinner. Earlier Greg Blewett (222 minutes, 164 balls, 16 fours) had scored an enterprising century, his third for the summer, while Lou Vincent (235 minutes, 190 balls, eight fours) top-scored against a side which included several of his former colleagues from South Australian junior teams. Daryl Tuffey (94 minutes, 74 balls, six fours, two sixes) injected some vigour into an otherwise lacklustre New

Zealand first innings which rain delays extended to the best part of two days. After Blewett (134 minutes, 103 balls, six fours) and Darren Lehmann (112 minutes, 82 balls, four fours) had added a comfortable century stand for the third wicket, Daniel Vettori dominated the rest of the South Australian second innings. Fast bowler Shayne O'Connor flew home at the end of the match because of an injured knee.

Close of play: First day, South Australia (1) 8-281 (Manou 23, Rofe 1); Second day, New Zealanders (1) 3-110 (McMillan 49, Vincent 26); Third day, South Australia (2) 3-110 (Higgins 6).

Attendance: 7,822.

South Australia

S. A. Deitz lbw b Tuffey	4	–	(2) b Bond	8
D. A. Fitzgerald c Sulzberger b Vettori	50	–	(1) b Bond	0
G. S. Blewett c Parore b Sulzberger	106	–	c Martin b Vettori	61
*D. S. Lehmann c Bond b Vettori	0	–	c and b Vettori	51
B. H. Higgins c Sinclair b Tuffey	11	–	c Martin b Tuffey	11
B. E. Young c Parore b Vettori	37	–	c Parore b McMillan	15
M. J. Smith run out (Sinclair)	10	–	c Sinclair b Vettori	15
†G. A. Manou c Richardson b Bond	34	–	c Bond b Vettori	17
P. E. McIntyre c Richardson b Tuffey	15	–	not out	9
P. C. Rofe not out	5	–	lbw b Vettori	0
M. A. Harrity not out	1	–	c Martin b Vettori	10
B 3, l-b 9, w 1, n-b 12	25		B 6, l-b 3, n-b 6	15

(94 overs, 384 mins)	(9 wkts dec) 297	(69.3 overs, 279 mins) 212

Fall: 19 131 137 170 195 233 235 275 292

Fall: 0 21 122 130 144 170 172 194 194 212

Bowling: *First Innings*—Tuffey 18-5–71–3; Martin 20–4–70–0; Bond 17–5–43–1; Vettori 30–8–60–3; Sulzberger 8-1–39–1; Vincent 1–0–2–0. *Second Innings*—Bond 13–3–35–2; Martin 6–1–26–0; Tuffey 10-2–21–1; Vettori 28.3–7–80–6; Sulzberger 5–2–23–0; McMillan 7–2–18–1.

New Zealanders

M. H. Richardson lbw b McIntyre	16	–	c Manou b McIntyre	8
M. D. Bell run out	0	–	run out (Fitzgerald)	29
M. S. Sinclair c Manou b McIntyre	10	–	b McIntyre	14
*C. D. McMillan b Smith	51	–	c Deitz b McIntyre	32
L. Vincent b Harrity	74	–	lbw b McIntyre	0
†A. C. Parore c Lehmann b Young	48	–	c Blewett b McIntyre	24
G. P. Sulzberger b Lehmann	35	–	c Manou b Smith	41
D. L. Vettori b Harrity	5	–	lbw b McIntyre	0
D. R. Tuffey c Deitz b Lehmann	56	–	b Smith	10
S. E. Bond lbw b McIntyre	1	–	run out (Smith)	3
C. S. Martin not out	0	–	not out	0
B 5, l-b 4, w 2, n-b 7	18		B 3, l-b 8, n-b 6	17

(115.2 overs, 448 mins)	314	(66.1 overs, 269 mins) 178

Fall: 6 24 40 120 205 225 233 301 308 314

Fall: 26 46 73 74 95 150 150 174 175 178

Bowling: *First Innings*—Harrity 11–4–22–2; Rofe 21–10–29–0; Smith 19–5–38–1; Young 33–5–99–1; McIntyre 29–5–101–3; Lehmann 2.2–0–16–2. *Second Innings*—Harrity 4–0–12–0; Rofe 10–2–19–0; McIntyre 29.1–7–75–6; Smith 12–3–31–2; Young 11–1–30–0.

Umpires: K. D. Perrin and S. J. A. Taufel.
TV Umpire: S. D. Fry.

AUSTRALIA v NEW ZEALAND

Second Test Match

At Bellerive Oval, Hobart, November 22, 23, 24, 25, 26, 2001. Drawn. Toss: New Zealand. Test debut: S. E. Bond.

The Hobart Test fell victim to one of Hobart's wettest springs in recent memory. After a frenetic first day, when Australia scored 411 runs for the loss of six wickets, rain intervened to allow only another 390 runs over the last four days. Despite the disappointing outcome, there was much to appreciate. Justin Langer continued to enjoy a remarkable renaissance, scoring his third century in as many Tests since his recall at The Oval three months previously. Dropped by Matthew Bell in the gully off Daryl Tuffey's first ball in a Test on Australian soil, Langer proceeded to make a mockery of Stephen Fleming's decision to send Australia in, and reached his fifty in the tenth over of the morning. Twice he took three fours off an over in an exhilarating first three-quarters of an hour, and soon the rarity of a century before lunch on the first day of a Test looked possible. Langer's opening partner, Matthew Hayden, made his third run after Langer had reached 60 in the first over after the drinks break. Thereafter, however, Langer became more circumspect, and by the time he reached three figures in the early afternoon, over two and a half hours had elapsed, and Hayden had moved on to 63. In making his tenth Test century, Langer became Western Australia's most prolific Test century-maker.

Relishing the happy chemistry that clearly existed between them, the two left-handers powered to a formidable 223 (one less than in Brisbane) before they were parted, Langer (198 minutes, 153 balls, 20 fours) hitting Chris Cairns to cover. This allowed the home crowd to feast on the talents of Ricky Ponting, who showed no sign of the nerves that might have afflicted one whose previous Test scores before his home crowd had been four, nought and nought. Adding to the pressure on him was a repeat of the Brisbane middle-order collapse, which saw Australia slump to five for 267. Hayden (212 minutes, 141 balls, 11 fours, one six), who had earlier lifted Daniel Vettori for the long-on boundary, was caught there trying again, Mark Waugh played over an arm ball, Steve Waugh shouldered arms to a delivery that appeared to strike him rather high, and Damien Martyn became Vettori's third wicket when trapped in front, first ball. Vettori's 22-over spell also claimed Adam Gilchrist after a short but characteristic counter-offensive, and it was left to Shane Warne to partner Ponting to the day's end. Warne did not merely survive, but flourished to the extent of adding 75 with his more illustrious partner in just over an hour before the close of play. The crowd of just under 5,000 had by then witnessed a team scoring over 400 in a day's play in Australia for the first time since Australia scored three for 428 against West Indies in 1931. For New Zealand, Vettori provided the most menace in an otherwise pedestrian attack, although newcomer Shane Bond demonstrated impressive spirit and raw pace.

Next morning Ponting duly completed the hundred that the crowd demanded, while Warne (135 minutes, 107 balls, 11 fours) had time to move to his first Test half-century for two years before his first incursion by the weather. When play resumed in the late afternoon, Brett Lee (59 minutes, 55 balls, five fours, two sixes) took advantage of Australia's strong position to unleash some powerful shots, including sixes off Bond and Vettori. Ponting (309 minutes, 218 balls, 20 fours, one six) carried on in similar vein, and his hit over the fence off Bond took him to 3,000 Test runs in his 49th match.

Declaring overnight, Australia took the field on the third morning, but were again frustrated by the weather. Only 35 overs were possible, one more than the previous day, and in that time New Zealand lost Matthew Bell and Mathew Sinclair for 71 runs. Bell struggled for 32 balls before getting off the mark, and, having scored six and five at Brisbane, maintained the pattern here by making just four before bottom-edging Warne via his pad to Gilchrist. Minutes after bad light had forced the players off in mid-afternoon a spectacular thunderstorm engulfed the ground and, with surface water flooding the field, no more play was possible.

Despite a prompt start, rain on the fourth day allowed no more than 50 overs of play. Mark Richardson departed early, a hint of bat contaminating his leg-before decision, and Nathan Astle was picked up at slip off Mark Waugh. Craig McMillan joined Fleming, and the two batted patiently to take their team through to the final rain break at 3.30 p.m. Particularly obvious was their tactic of not playing Glenn McGrath unless absolutely necessary, frustrating his penchant for taking wickets with balls pitched well outside the off stump. In the meantime Ponting conceded a rare five with a boundary overthrow that took the fifth-wicket partnership to a record against Australia, beating the lowly 92 set by McMillan and Astle in the Brisbane Test just days before. McGrath thus had to wait to the final day before taking his first wickets of the match, claiming Fleming (251 minutes, 184 balls, seven fours) with the first ball of the morning after lengthy consideration by Steve Bucknor. Like Fleming, McMillan (209 minutes, 167 balls, six fours, one five) shouldered arms once too often, losing his off stump to Jason Gillespie. Fewer than 20 overs were possible before the final deluge consigned the match to a forlorn conclusion just before midday.

This was the first international match played in front of spectators enjoying the luxury of the new Southern Stand. With a capacity of nearly 6,000, the stand was well received by those who patronised it, if not by the local residents, many of whom had provided fierce opposition to the development. Some teething problems were evident on the first morning, when an overheated fan in the public bar caused the fire alarm to intrude loudly upon the cricket. More serious for umpire Steve Davis was the continuing construction at the opposite end of the oval. Leaving the ground after a function on the second evening, and unaware of the open gate just metres to his left, Davis severely damaged his right knee in scaling the temporary fencing in order to reach his taxi, and spent the rest of the match in hospital. Local first-class umpire John Smeaton was elevated from his position as third umpire to stand with Steve Bucknor for the last three days. – RIC FINLAY.

Man of the Match: R.T. Ponting.   *Attendance:* 16,471.

Close of play: First day, Australia (1) 6-411 (Ponting 92, Warne 31); Second day, Australia (1) 8-558; Third day, New Zealand (1) 2-71 (Richardson 25, Fleming 16); Fourth day, New Zealand (1) 4-197 (Fleming 71, McMillan 51).

Australia

J.L. Langer c Vettori b Cairns	123	S.K. Warne b Astle		70
M.L. Hayden c Bond b Vettori	91	B. Lee c McMillan b Vettori		41
R.T. Ponting not out	157			
M.E. Waugh b Vettori	12	B 3, l-b 5, w 2, n-b 15		25
*S.R. Waugh lbw b Bond	0			—
D.R. Martyn lbw b Vettori	0	(124 overs, 508 mins)	(8 wkts dec)	558
†A.C. Gilchrist b Vettori	39	Fall: 223 238 253 266 267 336 481 558		

J.N. Gillespie and G.D. McGrath did not bat.

Bowling: Cairns 28–3–122–1; Tuffey 15–1–74–0; Bond 28–0–135–1; Vettori 36–5–138–5; McMillan 8–0–51–0; Astle 9–0–30–1.

New Zealand

M.H. Richardson lbw b Gillespie	30	†A.C. Parore not out	10
M.D. Bell c Gilchrist b Warne	4	D.L. Vettori not out	10
M.S. Sinclair b Gillespie	23		
*S.P. Fleming lbw b McGrath	71	L-b 1, n-b 8	9
N.J. Astle c Warne b M.E. Waugh	11		
C.D. McMillan b Gillespie	55	(105.2 overs, 442 mins) (7 wkts)	243
C.L. Cairns c Gilchrist b McGrath	20	Fall: 11 53 76 100 197 219 223	

D.R. Tuffey and S.E. Bond did not bat.

Bowling: McGrath 27–12–46–2; Gillespie 28–14–45–3; Warne 24.2–3–70–1; Lee 19–5–51–0; M.E. Waugh 7–1–30–1.

Umpires: S. A. Bucknor (West Indies) and S.J. Davis. J. H. Smeaton replaced S.J. Davis after Day Two.
TV Umpire: J. H. Smeaton. B. W. Jackman replaced J. H. Smeaton after Day Two.
Referee: L. Hendriks (West Indies).

AUSTRALIA v NEW ZEALAND

Third Test Match

At WACA Ground, Perth, November 30, December 1, 2, 3, 4, 2001. Drawn. Toss: New Zealand. Test debut: L. Vincent.

New Zealand, generally outplayed in the first two Tests, rebounded magnificently in an enthralling contest that produced record-breaking performances and 1,522 runs. Each side glimpsed victory on the final day before the match ended in a draw and left the three-Test series fittingly tied at 0-0 after Australia had entered the series with a succession of 23 Tests without a draw.

New Zealand gambled by promoting New Zealand-born but Adelaide-reared middle-order batsman Lou Vincent to open in his first Test in place of the unconvincing Matthew Bell and picking medium-pacer Chris Martin to replace the injured Daryl Tuffey. Stephen Fleming's decision to bat was looking unsound when he joined Vincent at the end of the seventh over with New Zealand on two for 19. Glenn McGrath, who had taken an early wicket, suffered from back spasms soon after and had to leave the field, and the New Zealand pair grew in confidence against the remaining Australian bowlers. They brought up their century in 131 minutes, then added another 50 in 42 minutes. Vincent, sound against the new ball, revealed nimble footwork and a solid forward defence against the spin of Shane Warne. Five minutes after he became the sixth New Zealander to score a Test century on debut, Vincent (273 minutes, 207 balls, 15 fours, one six) departed in controversial circumstances, driving at Warne and being given out by umpire Darrell Hair, brilliantly caught, left-handed, by a diving Mark Waugh at slip. Television replays showed that the ball had merely spun sharply and had not hit the bat. Fleming's innings (316 minutes, 223 balls, 13 fours), only his third century in 63 Tests, ended when Jason Gillespie and Brett Lee struck with the second new ball late on the first day. Australia took four for 17 in the space of 20 deliveries and reclaimed the advantage. On Saturday, however, Nathan Astle (408 minutes, 276 balls, 22 fours, one six), cover-driving and cutting strongly, and Adam Parore (308 minutes, 243 balls, 14 fours, one six) dominated the Australian attack. Having started cautiously, they accelerated into complete domination of the attack, batting together until the middle of the final session in an eighth-wicket stand of 253 (scored off 75 overs) that has been bettered only once in Test history (313 by Wasim Akram and Saqlain Mushtaq, for Pakistan v Zimbabwe at Sheikhupura in 1996-97). It was the first time four New Zealand batsmen had scored centuries in the same Test innings.

In the final 70 minutes before stumps on the second day, Australia lost Matthew Hayden and Ricky Ponting. The following day they were six for 192 after Justin Langer (222 minutes, 157 balls, seven fours, one six) gloved a pull at Chris Cairns and walked, umpire Ian Robinson failing to notice that the bowler's front foot was several centimetres over the popping crease. When Adam Gilchrist went for a duck Australia looked in grave danger of being forced to follow on but Damien Martyn (168 minutes, 127 balls, seven fours) and Warne added 78 for the seventh wicket. Then Warne (213 minutes, 157 balls, ten fours), balancing attack and defence capably, made the most of lives on ten and 51 before he swung wildly at Daniel Vettori and skied a catch to deep mid-wicket, missing the chance of his initial first-class hundred. Vettori had troubled all the batsmen in conditions that favoured batting, and fully deserved his six wickets.

With a first-innings lead of 183, New Zealand chased quick runs on the fourth day. Vincent (88 minutes, 54 balls, seven fours) again shone with his forthright strokeplay, and several others sacrificed their wickets as Steve Waugh set defensive fields. In a bid to restrict the scoring, Lee sent down six successive short-pitched balls in the 65th over to Craig McMillan, who ducked under them all. When Lee bowled Shane Bond for the second time in the match and directed him to the pavilion, Fleming closed the innings, thus giving New Zealand the rare achievement of not being dismissed once in the series. Lee's achievement was not so rare: match referee Jackie Hendriks found him guilty of misconduct and fined him $8,250.

Set 440 to win off a minimum of 107 overs, Australia lost Langer and Ponting before stumps and started the final day needing 371. New Zealand's hopes bloomed when Mark Waugh (169 minutes, 158 balls, 11 fours, one six) tried to cut a ball from McMillan off the middle stump, missed and was bowled, leaving Australia four for 195. Shortly afterwards Steve Waugh, on 13, attempted a big cut at Vettori, appeared to get a thick edge and was snapped up by wicket-keeper Parore. The New Zealanders' dance of celebration was cut short when they realised umpire Robinson had turned down the appeal. After Martyn was yorked by Vettori, Waugh (226 minutes, 154 balls, seven fours) and Gilchrist concentrated on holding New Zealand at bay, Gilchrist scoring a solitary single from the first 22 balls he faced. Belatedly, in the final session Gilchrist unleashed a tremendous onslaught on Vettori and Cairns, racing from 17 to 60 in the space of 18 balls to give Australia a glimmer of victory. But a scorching back-foot drive by Gilchrist deflected off Vettori's fingers onto the stumps at the non-striker's end to run out Waugh and leave Australia vulnerable at six for 339. After Warne was run out, Gilchrist (130 minutes, 109 balls, 12 fours, two sixes) and Gillespie held firm for the final 40 minutes to thwart New Zealand's final bid for victory. – KEN CASELLAS.

Man of the Match: D.L. Vettori. *Man of the Series:* J.L. Langer. *Attendance:* 41,853.

Close of play: First day, New Zealand (1) 7-293 (Astle 28, Parore 5); Second day, Australia (1) 2-75 (Langer 34, M.E. Waugh 5); Third day, Australia 351 all out; Fourth day, Australia (2) 2-69 (Hayden 31, M.E. Waugh 8).

New Zealand

M.H. Richardson b Gillespie	9	– run out (S.R. Waugh)	30
L. Vincent c M.E. Waugh b Warne	104	– c M.E. Waugh b Lee	54
M.S. Sinclair lbw b McGrath	2	– c Gilchrist b McGrath	29
*S.P. Fleming lbw b Lee	105	– (5) b Warne	4
N.J. Astle not out	156	– (6) c Langer b Gillespie	40
C.D. McMillan lbw b Gillespie	4	– (7) c Warne b Gillespie	19
D.L. Vettori c Martyn b Gillespie	2	– (9) c S.R. Waugh b Lee	3
C.L. Cairns c Gilchrist b Lee	8	– (4) c Warne b Lee	42
†A.C. Parore c McGrath b Lee	110	– (8) not out	16
S.E. Bond b Lee	0	– b Lee	8
B 4, l-b 15, w 2, n-b 13	34	B 1, l-b 6, n-b 4	11

(162.5 overs, 683 mins)　　(9 wkts dec) 534　　(71.0 overs, 315 mins) (9 wkts dec) 256
Fall: 12 19 218 264 269 272 281　　　　　　Fall: 77 90 128 151 199 208 241
　　　534 534　　　　　　　　　　　　　　　　　246 256

C.S. Martin did not bat.

Bowling: *First Innings*—McGrath 27–11–72–1; Gillespie 40–7–112–3; Lee 32.5–5–125–4; Warne 43–9–135–1; Martyn 10–0–44–0; M.E. Waugh 6–1–26–0; Ponting 4–3–1–0. *Second Innings*—McGrath 17–4–63–1; Gillespie 17–0–55–2; Lee 16–3–56–4; Warne 21–3–75–1.

Australia

J.L. Langer c Parore b Cairns	75	– c Vettori b Bond	0
M.L. Hayden c Vincent b Bond	0	– c Sinclair b Vettori	57
R.T. Ponting c Parore b Martin	31	– b Cairns	26
M.E. Waugh c Bond b Vettori	42	– b McMillan	86
*S.R. Waugh c Parore b Vettori	8	– run out (Vettori)	67
D.R. Martyn c Fleming b Cairns	60	– b Vettori	30
†A.C. Gilchrist c Richardson b Vettori	0	– not out	83
S.K. Warne c Richardson b Vettori	99	– run out (Cairns/Sinclair)	10
B. Lee c McMillan b Vettori	17		
J.N. Gillespie c Parore b Vettori	0	– (9) not out	1
G.D. McGrath not out	0		
L-b 2, w 1, n-b 16	19	L-b 3, w 2, n-b 16	21

(103.4 overs, 446 mins)　　　　　351　　(110 overs, 445 mins)　　(7 wkts) 381
Fall: 3 61 122 137 191 192 270 342 346 351　　Fall: 1 52 130 195 244 339 355

Bowling: *First Innings*—Cairns 23–5–86–2; Bond 18–2–74–1; Martin 23–4–88–1; Vettori 34.4–7–87–6; Astle 5–1–14–0. *Second Innings*—Bond 21–3–80–1; Martin 12–0–51–0; Vettori 45–11–142–2; Cairns 15–2–72–1; Astle 12–5–18–0; McMillan 5–2–15–1.

Umpires: I.D. Robinson (Zimbabwe) and D.B. Hair.
TV Umpire: D.J. Harper.
Referee: J.L. Hendriks (West Indies).

†PRIME MINISTER'S XI v NEW ZEALANDERS

At Manuka Oval, Canberra, December 6, 2001. New Zealanders won by four wickets. Toss: Prime Minister's XI.

The tourists completed the first leg of their stint in Australia with a comfortable win, victory coming with 12 balls to spare by courtesy of a six from top-scorer Nathan Astle. In his only appearance of the tour, reinforcement Chris Drum bowled an opening eight-over spell of 4/8 which jarred the progress of an innings which had seen 60 runs come from the first 12 overs. Greg Blewett made a quick 41 (two fours, two sixes), but the Australian Capital Territory's Jack Smith guided the innings towards a reasonable total with an enterprising unbeaten 48 (five fours). The New Zealanders' reply took off only when Chris Cairns joined Astle in a brisk fifth-wicket partnership of 77 from 76 balls. Young Victorian leg-spinner Cameron White bowled a tidy and competent spell. More than 7,000 spectators continued the tradition of strong Canberra support for this annual fixture.

Prime Minister's XI

†B.J. Haddin b Drum	35	(36)
C. Dann c Vincent b Drum	18	(51)
M.L. Love b Drum	1	(14)
S.R. Watson lbw b Drum	10	(19)
M.J. Clarke lbw b McMillan	20	(41)
*G.S. Blewett b Drum	41	(56)
J.K. Smith not out	48	(65)

B.E. Young c Vincent b McMillan	15	(14)
C.L. White not out	15	(13)
L-b 5, w 8, n-b 1	14	
(50 overs, 206 mins) (7 wkts)	217	
Fall: 60 62 67 74 111 156 179		

D.G. Wright and S.R. Clark did not bat.

Bowling: Bond 7–0–40–0; Tuffey 8–0–39–0; Astle 10–3–30–0; Drum 10–1–34–5; McMillan 10–1–37–2; Sulzberger 5–0–32–0.

New Zealanders

†L. Vincent lbw b Clark	0	(5)
M.H. Richardson c Clarke b Watson	40	(62)
M.S. Sinclair b Wright	11	(17)
*C.D. McMillan c Dann b White	15	(31)
C.L. Cairns c Dann b White	35	(38)
N.J. Astle not out	85	(93)

M.D. Bell c Haddin b Clark	0	(3)
G.P. Sulzberger not out	23	(40)
L-b 8, w 4, n-b 1	13	
(48 overs, 208 mins) (6 wkts)	222	
Fall: 0 23 64 74 151 151		

D.R. Tuffey, S.E. Bond and C.J. Drum did not bat.

Bowling: Clark 10–2–36–2; Wright 9–0–51–1; Watson 10–0–31–1; White 10–0–44–2; Young 9–1–52–0.

Umpires: P.D. Chapman and R.G. Patterson.

†AUSTRALIA A v NEW ZEALANDERS

At Brisbane Cricket Ground, Brisbane, January 8, 2002. Day/night game. Australia A won by 60 runs. Toss: New Zealanders.

Darren Lehmann responded to the captaincy by top-scoring and taking a key late-order wicket as New Zealand were well beaten in a star-studded exhibition match. In the debilitating 37-degree heat, Shane Bond had to be taken to hospital suffering from heat exhaustion after four expensive overs, while Dion Nash suffered a sore calf muscle after bowling just three overs. The contrasting approaches of Ryan Campbell and Jimmy Maher laid the foundation for a steadily accelerating team effort, which was capped by Lehmann's energetic and inventive innings. Needing to score at almost six an over, the New Zealanders were best served by top-scorer Craig McMillan and Chris Cairns, who hit powerfully but too briefly. Returning from a shoulder injury, Jason Gillespie bowled an impressive spell, while Stuart MacGill recovered from a mauling to take three useful wickets. In the trying conditions during daylight, fielding positions square of the wicket under the shade of the grandstand were prized, while water carriers ran bottles onto the ground after every second over.

Man of the Match: D.S. Lehmann. *Attendance:* 15,302.

Australia A

J.P. Maher c (sub) A.R. Adams b Vettori	42	(63)		S.R. Watson not out	18	(16)
†R.J. Campbell run out (Vincent/Parore)	46	(49)				
G.S. Blewett run out (Vincent)	42	(51)		L-b 2, w 7	9	
S.M. Katich c Fleming b McMillan	47	(50)				
*D.S. Lehmann run out (Styris)	50	(49)		(50 overs, 203 mins) (5 wkts)	282	
M.E.K. Hussey not out	28	(22)		Fall: 88 100 160 207 248		

S.C.G. MacGill, J.N. Gillespie, N.W. Bracken and S.R. Clark did not bat.

Bowling: Cairns 10–0–54–0; Bond 4–0–21–0; Nash 3–0–20–0; Styris 10–0–60–0; Vettori 10–0–57–1; Harris 10–0–38–0; McMillan 3–0–30–1.

New Zealanders

L. Vincent lbw b Gillespie	11	(18)		†A.C. Parore lbw b MacGill	0	(2)
M.H. Richardson c Campbell b Clark	11	(13)		D.L. Vettori c Campbell b Clark	14	(11)
*S.P. Fleming c Campbell b Bracken	25	(44)		S.E. Bond not out	3	(2)
C.D. McMillan c and b MacGill	67	(84)				
C.L. Cairns c Gillespie b Watson	32	(30)		L-b 5, w 13, n-b 1	19	
S.B. Styris c Bracken b MacGill	19	(40)				
C.Z. Harris lbw b Lehmann	16	(20)		(45.3 overs, 190 mins)	222	
D.J. Nash b Maher b Clark	5	(10)		Fall: 17 26 94 137 166 192 199 200 206 222		

Bowling: Gillespie 6–0–17–1; Clark 9.3–0–45–3; Bracken 7–0–27–1; MacGill 10–0–71–3; Watson 5–0–30–1; Lehmann 8–0–27–1.

Umpires: R.L. Parry and J.H. Smeaton.

†AUSTRALIAN COUNTRY XI v NEW ZEALANDERS

At Bradman Oval, Bowral, January 23, 2002. New Zealanders won by 249 runs. Toss: New Zealanders.

Against a representative team chosen from the players at the recently held country championships, the New Zealanders had a run-feast. The 20-year-old Brendon McCullum and Stephen Fleming each took just 35 balls to reach fifty against a hapless attack, while Dion Nash showed what big shoulders could produce on a small ground. In reply, the Australian Country XI lasted just 40 overs and were beyond hope when the score slipped to six for 50, although the tail worked conscientiously to lift the total to modest respectability. The innings included a rare appearance at the bowling crease by Mark Richardson, who had begun his career as a left-arm spinner.

New Zealanders

B.B. McCullum c Haworth b Tonkin	96	(81)		A.R. Adams b Klemm	1	(3)
M.H. Richardson c May b Tonkin	44	(59)		S.B. Styris not out	17	(7)
*S.P. Fleming c Haworth b Males	76	(53)		B 1, l-b 2, w 3, n-b 3	9	
C.D. McMillan b Barber	28	(23)				
D.J. Nash not out	72	(49)		(50 overs, 243 mins) (6 wkts)	392	
L. Vincent c Burns b Klemm	49	(28)		Fall: 135 160 229 263 350 371		

†A.C. Parore, J.E.C. Franklin and S.E. Bond did not bat.

Bowling: Klemm 6–0–56–2; Ambrose 8–0–56–0; Hughes 10–0–89–0; Tonkin 10–1–74–2; Males 6–0–60–1; Barber 10–0–54–1.

Australian Country XI

L. G. Burns run out	4	(17)	B. Ambrose lbw b Richardson	16	(30)
D. R. Else c Parore b Franklin	4	(16)	D. Hughes not out	16	(30)
B. K. D. May c and b Adams	16	(40)	B. Klemm run out	12	(8)
G. A. Grimmond run out	5	(19)			
C. J. Haworth c Vincent b Bond	13	(23)	B 2, l-b 1, w 2, n-b 7	12	
P. A. Barber lbw b Nash	27	(34)		—	
C. Tonkin lbw b Bond	0	(2)	(40 overs, 154 mins)	143	
C. J. Males b Richardson	18	(27)	Fall: 9 14 25 50 50 50 91 97 123 143		

Bowling: Nash 10–3–18–1; Franklin 6–0–17–1; Bond 4–1–15–2; Adams 6–0–19–1; Fleming 6–0–37–0; Richardson 8–1–34–2.

Umpires: B. Whiteman and D. Goodger.

New Zealand's matches v Australia and South Africa in the VB Series (January 11–February 8) may be found in that section.

REACHING A TEST CENTURY WITH A SIX

There have been 59 instances of batsmen reaching their century with a hit over the boundary in 126 years of Test cricket. The first to achieve this was England's Stanley Jackson, who hit Australia's George Giffen over the boundary line (then worth only four runs) to reach his hundred in the Oval Test of August 1893.

Australia's Joe Darling became the first batsman to reach his 100 with a six, which in those days involved hitting the ball right out of the ground and not merely over the boundary, which became the definition of a six after 1910. Darling achieved the feat in the Adelaide Test of January 1898 off the bowling of England's Johnny Briggs. It was the first six ever scored in Test cricket without the aid of overthrows.

Twenty-five years elapsed before South Africa's captain Herbie Taylor reached his century with a six off England's Alex Kennedy at Durban in February 1923.

So far 47 batsmen have reached their Test century with a six 59 times, two achieving it four times each, one three times and four twice. Ken Barrington of England and India's Sachin Tendulkar have done so four times. Barrington, not exactly a six symbol, achieved this off Australia's Bob Simpson at Adelaide in 1962-63, off South Africa's Michael "Kelly" Seymour at Johannesburg in 1964-65, off Australia's Tom Veivers at Melbourne in 1965-66 and off West Indian Lance Gibbs at Port-of-Spain in 1967-68. The Indian prodigy has performed this feat off the West Indian Courtney Walsh at Nagpur in 1994-95, off England's Min Patel at Birmingham in 1996, off New Zealander Daniel Vettori at Wellington in 1998-99 and off Australia's Colin Miller at Chennai in 2000-01.

Sri Lankan Aravinda de Silva achieved it three times: off Pakistan's Imran Khan at Faisalabad in 1985-86, off India's Anil Kumble at Colombo in 1993-94 and off Pakistan's Mushtaq Ahmed also at Colombo the next summer. Four cricketers – England's Ian Botham (1979 and 1981), Imran Khan (1982-83 and 1986-87), West Indian Desmond Haynes (1988-89 and 1992-93) and another West Indian Ridley Jacobs (2000-01 and 2001-02) – have twice reached their tons with a six. Haynes reached his 1992-93 century with two successive sixes off Pakistan's Asif Mujtaba in the Bridgetown Test. So far, the above are Jacobs' only Test centuries.

Some odd instances are provided by West Indian Collis King, who brought up his 100 with a six off the last ball of the Christchurch Test against New Zealand in 1979-80, and Pakistan's Ijaz Faqih, who reached both his 50 and 100 with sixes off India's Maninder Singh in the Ahmedabad Test of 1986-87.

The latest member in the "Century with a Six Club" is Pakistan's Imran Nazir, who hit New Zealander Chris Harris for a six to reach his 100 in the Lahore Test of May 2002.

Nine Australians have reached a test century with a six, as shown on page 348.
– KERSI MEHER-HOMJI and RAJESH KUMAR

THE SOUTH AFRICANS IN AUSTRALIA, 2001-02

By WARWICK FRANKS

This tour was the one that the Australian cricket public had been anticipating. South Africa's recent Test record had been impressively consistent and in the previous 12 months, they had won series against New Zealand and Sri Lanka at home and against West Indies in the Caribbean. They had won six of the 11 Tests and lost only the last of the games in the West Indies when the series was already secure. Here, at last, was a side which might give the Australians a run for their money and produce a closely fought contest for the Mandela Trophy. Despite the Australians' outstanding form and results over a long period, the sterling performance of the New Zealanders, particularly in the final match at Perth, confirmed the feeling that this could be a real Test occasion.

The famous conductor Sir Thomas Beecham once said that as long as the orchestra begins together and ends together, the audience doesn't give a damn what happens in the middle. Test cricket is more unforgiving, and while the first three days in Adelaide and the last day and a half in Sydney were sturdily contested, in between the South Africans lost the series comprehensively. The fourth day at Adelaide was an important signpost: Shaun Pollock's captaincy seemed bereft of ideas or purpose as the Australians strolled towards a second-innings declaration. The collapse of the South African batting on the last day meant that they went to Melbourne robbed of that vital confidence which is indispensable to sporting success. Pollock's unenviable task was further complicated by the sense of tension which eddied around the team. For example, his uncle, Graeme Pollock, saw no conflict of interest in providing brutally frank assessments of the team's performance through the media. Then there was the messy selection of Justin Ontong for the last Test where, after UCBSA administrators intervened to alter the composition of the team, they tried to defend their action in terms of form instead of political imperative. The captain's own form was not commanding enough to provide a spark of inspiration, so that he was left with the perspiration of honest effort.

Unlike the redoubtable New Zealanders, the South African batsmen seemed overawed by the task confronting them and conveyed a sense of timidity and tentativeness in their approach. Each of the specialists played one or two innings of substance but only Jacques Kallis conveyed a sense that he had an organised campaign plan and the skilled determination to put it into practice. Nevertheless, it was symptomatic of the summer that in Melbourne he should have run himself out while trying to complete a well-merited century. After a partnership of 87 in Adelaide, the opening stands of Gary Kirsten and Herschelle Gibbs produced little, although Kirsten finished the series with an innings of prolonged defiance at Sydney. Neil McKenzie gave glimpses of quality, while Boeta Dippenaar survived a series of blinding catches and basic batting errors to show his attractive promise in his last innings. The young left-hander Jacques Rudolph batted with enough pluck and style on several occasions to mark him as a possibility for the future but, unfortunately, it was he who suffered during the selection shambles before the

Sydney Test. Lance Klusener's decline as an all-rounder was distressingly absolute, although Mark Boucher's batting continued to be as useful as his keeping was reliable.

Nor did the bowling live up to expectations. While Allan Donald battled an injured foot, it seemed as though the years were dulling the edge of his extreme pace and it was no surprise to find that he did not last the series in South Africa. If sheer willpower produced wickets, then Nantie Hayward would have taken plenty, but he lacked that finesse which had made Donald such a great bowler. Claude Henderson, who deputised for the injured Nicky Boje, had a good opening day at Adelaide but thereafter was too lacking in subtlety to cause much concern. Boje, on the other hand, looked a much better attacking proposition when he arrived for the Sydney Test.

The Australian team continued on its confidently assured way. Matthew Hayden, Justin Langer and Damien Martyn, the three recycled batsmen, scored Australia's seven centuries between them. Hayden and Langer added two more double-century stands to bolster their case as a great Australian opening partnership, a case which depends not only on brute numbers but on the verve and authority of their approach. In both Melbourne and Sydney, they had the visitors in survival mode before the end of the first day. Martyn returned to dwell in that sphere of batting maturity which he reached in England. When three of the batsmen scored over 1,000 runs between them it did not matter that the other specialist batsmen were only sporadically successful. The fact that one of these was Steve Waugh contributed to that manufactured sense of unease which is discussed in Notes by the Editor.

Glenn McGrath and Shane Warne returned to their accustomed bowling roles of relentless attackers and were back among the wickets, relishing the fact that in contrast to the New Zealanders, these opponents lacked both a plan and the self-disciplined skill to combat them. It was also a reminder to other cricketing nations of Australia's reserves that at Sydney Stuart MacGill played his first Test for 12 months and immediately became a crucial component of Australia's success by bowling 65.2 overs and taking seven wickets in the match.

A decade after its return to Test cricket in the post-apartheid era, South African cricket is facing major challenges. A number of the generation which served it so well during that time have left the game and on the evidence of this tour that process may be about to accelerate. Klusener and Donald seemed to have run their course, while Kirsten's time could well be approaching. Under first Kepler Wessels and then Hansie Cronje, success of the last ten years has been built on fierce determination and an ability to apply relentless pressure over long periods. While the batsmen gathered runs prudently and the bowlers ground away relentlessly at the opposition, it was only in the field that the side looked exuberantly aggressive. Sadly, that approach now seemed shop-worn and stale, and much of the South African cricket in this series seemed unadventurously rigid, one-dimensional and one-paced. None of this is to underestimate the trauma of Cronje's disgrace and the pall that it cast over his country's cricketing psyche. Nor is it to be unmindful of the complex and sensitive task of ensuring that cricket plays a vibrant and constructive role in the transformation of South African society. What it does entail is the hope that administrative wisdom off the field combines with performance on it in order to maintain and develop the game's place in the Republic and also maintain it in the wider world of cricket.

SOUTH AFRICAN TOURING PARTY

S. M. Pollock (KwaZulu-Natal) (*captain*), M. V. Boucher (*vice-captain*), D. P. Dippenaar (Free State), A. A. Donald (Free State), S. Elworthy (Northerns), H. H. Gibbs (Western Province), N. Hayward (Eastern Province), C. W. Henderson (Boland), J. H. Kallis (Western Province), G. Kirsten (Western Province), L. Klusener (KwaZulu-Natal), N. D. McKenzie (Gautung), M. L. Ntini (Border), J. L. Ontong (Boland) and J. A. Rudolph (Northerns).

Note: N. Boje (Free State) was originally selected in the squad but withdrew with an injury and was replaced by C. W. Henderson.

For the limited-overs internationals: J. M. Kemp (Easterns), C. K. Langeveldt (Boland) and J. N. Rhodes (KwaZulu-Natal) replaced N. Hayward, C. W. Henderson and J. A. Rudolph.

Manager: G. Raja. *Coach:* G. X. Ford. *Assistant coach:* C. J. P. Van Zyl. *Physiotherapist:* C. Smith.

SOUTH AFRICAN TOUR RESULTS

Test matches – Played 3: Lost 3.
First-class matches – Played 5: Lost 3, Drawn 2.
    Losses – Australia (3).
    Draws – Western Australia, New South Wales.
Limited-overs internationals – Played 10: Won 7, Lost 3. *Wins* – Australia (2), New Zealand (5).
    Losses – Australia (2), New Zealand (1).
Other non-first-class matches – Played 2: Won 1, Lost 1. *Win* – ACB Chairman's XI. *Loss:*
    Australia A.

TEST MATCH AVERAGES

AUSTRALIA – BATTING

	M	I	NO	R	HS	100s	50s	Avge	Ct/St
D. R. Martyn	3	4	2	299	124*	2	1	149.50	1
M. L. Hayden........	3	6	2	429	138	3	0	107.25	2
J. L. Langer	3	6	1	365	126	2	1	73.00	2
S. R. Waugh.........	3	4	0	141	90	0	1	35.25	0
M. E. Waugh	3	4	0	129	74	0	1	32.25	4
R. T. Ponting	3	5	1	115	54	0	1	28.75	11
B. Lee	3	3	0	64	32	0	0	21.33	1
S. K. Warne........	3	4	0	85	41	0	0	21.25	2
S. C. G. MacGill......	1	1	0	20	20	0	0	20.00	1
A. C. Gilchrist	3	4	1	93	34	0	0	31.00	9/1
A. J. Bichel	1	1	0	5	5	0	0	5.00	2
J. N. Gillespie	1	1	0	3	3	0	0	3.00	0
G. D. McGrath.......	3	3	1	6	5	0	0	3.00	1

* *Denotes not out.*

SOUTH AFRICAN TOURING PARTY, 2001-2002

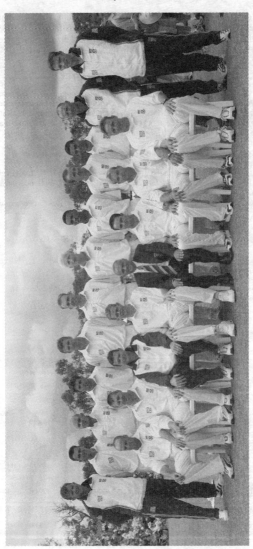

Back row: C.J.P. Van Zyl (*assistant coach*), J.A. Rudolph, H.H. Gibbs, N.D. McKenzie, S. Elworthy, C.W. Henderson, N. Hayward, M.L. Nini, D.P. Dippenaar, J.L. Ontong, C. Smith (*physiotherapist*), A. Grey (*fitness adviser*). *Front row*: G. Kirsten, L. Klusener, G.X. Ford (*coach*), S.M. Pollock (*captain*), G. Raja (*manager*), M.V. Boucher (*vice-captain*), J.H. Kallis, A.A. Donald.

BOWLING

	O	M	R	W	BB	5W/i	Avge
D.R. Martyn	5	2	4	1	1/3	0	4.00
A.J. Bichel	32	6	96	4	3/44	0	24.00
S.C.G. MacGill	65.2	19	174	7	4/123	0	24.86
G.D. McGrath	139	43	350	14	3/13	0	25.00
S.K. Warne	173.3	35	473	17	5/113	1	27.82
B. Lee	105	27	314	9	3/77	0	34.89
J.N. Gillespie	34	11	80	2	2/23	0	40.00
M.E. Waugh	17	2	42	1	1/19	0	42.00
R.T. Ponting	1	0	11	0	–	0	–

SOUTH AFRICA – BATTING

	M	I	NO	R	HS	100s	50s	Avge	Ct
J.H. Kallis	3	6	1	245	99	0	2	49.00	4
G. Kirsten	3	6	0	245	153	1	0	40.83	1
N.D. McKenzie	3	6	0	224	87	0	2	37.33	6
S.M. Pollock	3	6	2	128	61*	0	1	32.00	2
M.V. Boucher	3	6	0	169	64	0	1	28.17	7
H.H. Gibbs	3	6	0	164	78	0	1	27.33	0
H.H. Dippenaar	3	6	0	130	74	0	1	21.67	0
J.L. Ontong	1	2	0	41	32	0	0	20.50	0
M. Hayward	2	4	2	26	14	0	0	13.00	0
L. Klusener	2	4	0	47	22	0	0	11.75	1
C.W. Henderson	3	6	0	65	30	0	0	10.83	2
M. Ntini	1	2	0	13	9	0	0	6.50	1
N. Boje	1	2	0	8	7	0	0	4.00	0
A.A. Donald	2	4	1	11	7	0	0	3.67	1

* Denotes not out.

BOWLING

	O	M	R	W	BB	5W/i	Avge
N. Boje	27.3	6	78	4	4/63	0	19.50
S.M. Pollock	112	27	312	8	3/84	0	39.00
L. Klusener	25	5	82	2	2/44	0	41.00
M. Hayward	67	6	249	5	3/108	0	49.80
A.A. Donald	65	11	238	4	3/103	0	59.50
C.W. Henderson	120.1	11	480	8	4/116	0	60.00
J.H. Kallis	70	7	266	4	3/45	0	66.50
M. Ntini	27	10	77	0	–	0	–
J.L. Ontong	2	0	10	0	–	0	–

SOUTH AFRICAN TOUR AVERAGES

FIRST-CLASS MATCHES

BATTING

	M	I	NO	R	HS	100s	50s	Avge	Ct
J.H. Kallis	4	8	1	386	120	1	2	55.14	4
N.D. McKenzie	4	8	0	373	114	1	2	46.63	6
M.V. Boucher	5	9	1	372	134	1	1	46.50	10
G. Kirsten	5	10	0	454	153	1	2	45.40	3
S.M. Pollock	4	8	3	217	61*	0	2	43.40	3
H.H. Gibbs	5	9	0	386	145	1	2	42.89	2
H.H. Dippenaar	4	8	1	276	115	1	1	39.43	0
J.A. Rudolph	2	4	0	151	59	0	2	37.75	1
S. Elworthy	2	2	0	60	31	0	0	30.00	0
L. Klusener	4	8	0	105	50	0	1	13.13	1
M. Hayward	2	4	2	26	14	0	0	13.00	0
C.W. Henderson	5	8	0	102	30	0	0	12.75	2
J.L. Ontong	2	4	0	41	32	0	0	10.25	0
A.A. Donald	4	6	3	21	8*	0	0	7.00	1
M. Ntini	2	3	0	13	9	0	0	4.33	1
N. Boje	1	2	0	8	7	0	0	4.00	0

* Denotes not out.

BOWLING

	O	M	R	W	BB	5W/i	Avge
N. Boje	27.3	6	78	4	4/63	0	19.50
L. Klusener	72	19	237	7	2/33	0	33.86
S.M. Pollock	137	33	373	9	3/84	0	41.44
M. Hayward	67	6	249	5	3/108	0	49.80
S. Elworthy	56	15	177	3	3/57	0	59.00
C.W. Henderson	206.1	33	748	11	4/116	0	68.00
J.H. Kallis	90	12	326	4	3/45	0	81.50
A.A. Donald	115	20	429	5	3/103	0	85.80
M. Ntini	59	18	185	2	2/108	0	92.50
J.L. Ontong	14	1	68	0	–	0	–
J.A. Rudolph	2	0	6	0	–	0	–

Note: Matches in this section that were not first-class are signified by a dagger.

†ACB CHAIRMAN'S XI v SOUTH AFRICANS

At Lilac Hill Park, Caversham, December 5, 2001. South Africans won by 48 runs. Toss: South Africans.

The traditional tour opener at Lilac Hill, the first without the late Barry Shepherd who had pioneered the match, again involved a couple of guest celebrities in former champions Dean Jones and Bruce Reid plus several current internationals. The South Africans scored at five an over, Neil McKenzie (12 fours, one six) playing a polished innings and joining Lance Klusener (seven fours, one six) in a stabilising 98 for the fifth wicket from 108 balls. Reid, 38 and now Western Australia's fast-bowling coach, shared the new ball with Andy Bichel who, looking to impress immediately, took two early wickets and snared a third in his second spell. The South Africans had some firepower of their own, with their five front-line pace men all playing. Apart from Michael Hussey (five fours, one six) and the warmly welcomed 40-year-old Jones (five fours), the Chairman's side struggled. Allan Donald settled concerns about his fitness with a lively performance which accounted for both openers, while Herschelle Gibbs took four catches.

South Africans

G. Kirsten c Slater b Bichel	7	(14)	S. Elworthy c Campbell b Angel	1	(6)
H.H. Gibbs c Cary b Angel	39	(36)	C.W. Henderson not out	21	(21)
J.A. Rudolph c Hussey b Bichel	4	(9)	M. Ntini not out	8	(12)
N.D. McKenzie c and b Cary	76	(84)			
H.H. Dippenaar c Bichel b Williams	0	(10)	L-b 2, w 9	11	
L. Klusener c Williams b North	64	(74)			
†M.V. Boucher c Katich b Bichel	26	(33)	(50 overs, 203 mins) (9 wkts) 257		
*S.M. Pollock c Katich b North	0	(1)	Fall: 13 30 74 89 187 213 213 220 233		

A.A. Donald and M. Hayward did not bat.

Bowling: Bichel 8–0–28–3; Reid 5–0–26–0; Angel 8–1–56–2; Williams 5–2–25–1; Hogg 8–1–34–0; Cary 8–0–47–1; North 7–0–36–2; Jones 1–0–3–0.

ACB Chairman's XI

M.J. Slater c Gibbs b Donald	14	(20)	A.J. Bichel c Boucher b Elworthy	5	(5)
†R.J. Campbell c Boucher b Donald	29	(19)	B.A. Williams c Klusener b Henderson	12	(5)
*S.M. Katich c Gibbs b Elworthy	5	(23)	J. Angel not out	0	(2)
M.W. Goodwin c Henderson b Elworthy	13	(32)			
M.E.K. Hussey c Pollock b Klusener	56	(77)	L-b 3, w 8, n-b 1	12	
M.J. North c Gibbs b Henderson	20	(33)			
D.M. Jones c Gibbs b Klusener	38	(41)	(44.1 overs, 194 mins) 209		
G.B. Hogg c Boucher b Elworthy	5	(9)	Fall: 40 49 68 71 125 187 188 196 209 209		

B.A. Reid and S.R. Cary did not bat.

Bowling: Pollock 6–0–27–0; Donald 8–0–42–2; Elworthy 7.1–0–27–4; Hayward 6–1–21–0; Ntini 6–0–38–0; Henderson 8–1–36–2; Klusener 3–0–15–2.

Umpires: B. Bennett and J. Brookes.

WESTERN AUSTRALIA v SOUTH AFRICANS

At WACA Ground, Perth, December 7, 8, 9, 10, 2001. Drawn. Toss: South Africans.

In a high-scoring draw on a bouncy pitch, Western Australia amassed both the highest score of the season and the largest total by a state side against a touring South African team, as the potency of the visitors' attack came into question. Acting captain Mark Boucher (184 minutes, 150 balls, 21 fours) was in sparkling touch as he rallied the visitors from six for 197 on the first day. While others fell victim to extravagant strokes without first assessing the pitch's extra bounce, youngster Jacques Rudolph (109 minutes, 74 balls, 11 fours) showed both polish and good sense. Matthew Nicholson claimed five wickets in his most impressive performance since his knee arthroscopy 12 months previously. Taking advantage of some loose pace bowling, 21-year-old Scott Meuleman (264 minutes, 199 balls, 18 fours and one top-edged six) became the third generation of his family to score a century for Western Australia. As the bowling wilted, Nicholson streaked to his own maiden first-class century (192 mins, 139 balls, 13 fours, three sixes), joining Brad Hogg (194 minutes, 158 balls, 11 fours) in a punishing seventh-wicket partnership of 175. Allan Donald limped from the field with a bruised and cut big toe, having inexplicably bowled in new boots. Herschelle Gibbs did not bat in the second innings because of a groin strain, and a blow on the toe while he was batting prevented Nicholson from bowling on the last day. Centuries from Jacques Kallis (228 minutes, 173 balls, 15 fours, three sixes) and Neil McKenzie (159 minutes, 152 balls, 12 fours, two sixes) allowed Boucher to express his satisfaction with the match from a batting point of view, although he conceded that "maybe we bowled a little longer than we expected to".

Close of play: First day, Western Australia (1) 0-2 (Hussey 2, Meuleman 0); Second day, Western Australia (1) 3-303 (Goodwin 41, North 49); Third day, South Africans (2) 0-40 (Kirsten 28, Rudolph 12).

Attendance: 6,322.

South Africans

G. Kirsten c Katich b Karppinen	31	– c and b Hogg	59
H. H. Gibbs c Campbell b Ntini	2		
J. A. Rudolph c Campbell b Nicholson	59	– (2) c Campbell b Swan	12
J. H. Kallis c Campbell b Karppinen	21	– (3) c Campbell b Hogg	120
N. D. McKenzie b Swan	35	– (4) c Goodwin b Karppinen	114
L. Klusener b Karppinen	8	– (5) lbw b Hogg	50
*†M. V. Boucher c Katich b Karppinen	134	– (6) not out	25
S. Elworthy c North b Nicholson	29		
C. W. Henderson c Campbell b Nicholson	24		
A. A. Donald not out	8		
M. Ntini c North b Nicholson	0		
B 4, l-b 10, w 2	16	B 5, w 1, n-b 4	10

(86.3 overs, 361 mins)   367   (98.5 overs, 379 mins)   (5 wkts) 390
Fall: 16 46 125 125 149 197 275 359 367 367   Fall: 40 117 278 324 390

Bowling: *First Innings*—Nicholson 20.3–5–68–5; Karppinen 26–6–110–4; Swan 13–2–64–1; Oldroyd 13–1–71–0; Hogg 10–2–21–0; North 4–0–19–0. *Second Innings*—Swan 22–6–69–1; Karppinen 22–6–85–1; Oldroyd 19–3–64–0; Hogg 24.5–4–119–3; North 7–0–33–0; Hussey 4–0–15–0.

Western Australia

M. E. K. Hussey c Kirsten b Ntini	21	M. J. Nicholson not out	101
S. W. Meuleman c Boucher b Henderson	109	S. J. Karppinen b Klusener	0
*S. M. Katich c Boucher b Ntini	66	B. J. Oldroyd not out	19
M. W. Goodwin run out (Henderson)	61	B 9, l-b 19, n-b 6	34
M. J. North b Donald	71		
†R. J. Campbell c Boucher b Henderson	28	(166 overs, 680 mins) (8 wkts dec) 600
G. B. Hogg b Klusener	90	Fall: 81 202 212 349 349 391 566 566

G. G. Swan did not bat.

Bowling: Donald 25–1–100–1; Elworthy 30–6–88–0; Ntini 32–8–108–2; Kallis 20–5–60–0; Henderson 40–11–120–2; Klusener 19–3–96–2.

Umpires: I. H. Lock and R. J. U. Woolridge.
TV Umpire: B. Bennett.

AUSTRALIA v SOUTH AFRICA

First Test Match

At Adelaide Oval, Adelaide, December 14, 15, 16, 17, 18, 2001. Australia won by 246 runs. Toss: Australia.

Much was expected from this game as the contenders for the position of leading Test nation met for the first time in nearly four years. The sense of anticipation surrounding the event was leavened by a pinch of farce when Stuart MacGill's selection was followed by a public admonition from the chairman of the selectors that the leg-spinner look to his behaviour, following which he spent five days honing his skills in the art of carrying drinks. South Africa, on the other hand, suffered the handicap of entering the game without the services of Allan Donald because of an injured foot.

A short ceremony before play began marked the 100th joint Test appearance of the brothers Waugh, following which the home side celebrated first use of a benign pitch with another purposeful start from the openers. Despite being dropped twice, Ricky Ponting (119 minutes, 86 balls, four fours) was at his most insouciant. Justin Langer continued to demonstrate the way in which he has overlaid solidity with enterprise as he drove, cut and pulled with a power and certainty exemplified by the sweetly on-driven six with which he reached his century (232 minutes, 171 balls, 15 fours and one six). After tea, greater attention to the first principles of bowling throttled the progress of the innings, only 69 runs coming for the loss of three wickets in the final session. Claude Henderson, in particular, caused problems by extracting surprising turn and bounce with his slow left-armers. Langer was so shackled that his final 12 runs took 100 minutes and 75 balls.

Next day, Damien Martyn once again emphasised the cultured maturity of his batting as the visitors tried vainly for the quick wickets which would have opened the game up to them. In particular, he gave a master class in off-side play, being equally at home with strokes behind or forward of the wicket. Despite being dropped in the gully by Shaun Pollock when he was on 95, Martyn's undefeated innings (294 minutes, 210 balls, nine fours) effectively laid the ghosts of the criticism directed at him after his previous innings against South Africa, at Sydney in 1993-94. He was well supported to his maiden Test century in Australia by Shane Warne and Brett Lee, who both offered determined essays at batsmanship. Nantie Hayward bowled with explosive enthusiasm, while Henderson lifted himself for the occasion with an exhibition of thoughtful spin bowling. Too much of the rest of the bowling looked merely honest, while five dropped catches were too many gifts to press on the home side.

South Africa's reply began with a business-like stand between Herschelle Gibbs and Gary Kirsten, which was augmented on the third morning by 90 minutes of resistance by night watchman Henderson. Periodically, Gibbs (261 minutes, 187 balls, nine fours) revealed an off-side stroke of real authority, but at six for 214, the innings looked to be on sinking foundations. At this point, however, Neil McKenzie (218 minutes, 168 balls, 16 fours) and Mark Boucher (206 minutes, 149 balls, eight fours), both playing their initial Test innings against Australia, mixed stern defence with appropriate aggression in a seventh-wicket partnership of 141. The innings ultimately crumbled, Warne being rewarded for some long spells of nagging leg-stump attack which were mixed with some vintage examples of the leg-spinner's art. His achievement was framed by the fact that it was the first five-wicket haul by an Australian leg-spinner in a Test at Adelaide since Richie Benaud had taken 5/96 in West Indies' first innings in 1960-61. Lee brought no credit to himself with a gormless display of short-pitched bowling against the tail-enders which escaped official censure from umpire Taufel. Unfortunately, Lee's tactics were given mealy-mouthed and spurious justifications by other members of the team. Three of the 11 no-balls bowled by the Australians during the innings would have produced wickets had they been legal deliveries.

Pollock's captaincy on the fourth day had a curiously desultory quality; it was as if he had decided that there was little point in resisting the inevitable declaration, so that the batsmen were placed under no real pressure. The effect was to let the tide of the match ebb away from the visitors after three days of sturdy contest. Matthew Hayden (261 minutes, 207 balls, 12 fours, four sixes) and Mark Waugh (194 minutes, 134 balls, nine fours), joined in a third-wicket stand of 181 during which they had the luxury of milking easy runs from a long and innocuous spell from Henderson, while the seriously under-bowled Makhaya Ntini languished in the outfield. Hayden's innings did, however, resonate with the assurance and power which has stamped his batting as being authentically Test class.

A declaration late in the day set the visitors 375 for victory, and Steve Waugh signalled his aggressive intentions by bringing Warne into the attack for the fourth over of the innings, with four men stalking the bat. Mark Waugh dropped Kirsten at slip from Warne's first ball, but Ponting at silly point made no mistake from the last ball of the day which left the Proteas at a parlous two for 17. On the final day, bad soon became worse as the innings became a melancholy procession of batsmen who seemed to lack the ability or the willingness to resist the Australian bowling on a pitch whose behaviour remained predictable. The honourable exception was Jacques Kallis (234 minutes, 174 balls, seven fours) who pegged out his claim to occupy the crease and then defended it unflinchingly. The ultimate comment on the feebleness of the batting was that Ntini resisted capably for 71 minutes which produced a ninth-wicket partnership of 39, the highest of the innings. Glenn McGrath bowled with his customary mathematical aggression, while Jason Gillespie took two vital middle-order wickets. Warne spun his wiles unceasingly for 25 consecutive overs, while the captain indulged Lee with the opportunity to filch the last two wickets, which flattered considerably the worth of his bowling during the match. The South Africans were left to contemplate the fact that being competitive for only 60 per cent of a Test match was a seriously flawed effort which was unlikely to produce insomnia in the Australian camp. – WARWICK FRANKS.

Close of play: First day, Australia (1) 6-272 (Martyn 37, Warne 7); Second day, South Africa (1) 2-101 (Gibbs 42, Henderson 3); Third day, Australia (2) 0-3 (Langer 0, Hayden 3); Fourth day, South Africa (2) 2-17 (Dippenaar 0).

Man of the Match: S.K. Warne.   *Attendance:* 77,555.

Australia

J.L. Langer c Pollock b Henderson	116	– c Boucher b Pollock	1
M.L. Hayden c Ntini b Klusener	31	– b Kallis	131
R.T. Ponting run out (Dippenaar/Boucher)	54	– lbw b Kallis	25
M.E. Waugh c Boucher b Hayward	2	– c Boucher b Henderson	74
*S.R. Waugh c McKenzie b Henderson	8	– (6) c Pollock b Henderson	13
D.R. Martyn not out	124	– (7) not out	6
†A.C. Gilchrist c Kallis b Henderson	7	– (5) c McKenzie b Kallis	22
S.K. Warne b Klusener	41	– b Henderson	6
B. Lee c McKenzie b Hayward	32		
J.N. Gillespie c Boucher b Henderson	3		
G.D. McGrath b Hayward	5		
L-b 6, n-b 10	16	B 8, l-b 16, n-b 7	31

(141 overs, 574 mins)   439   (78.1 overs, 324 mins) (7 wkts dec) 309

Fall: 80 182 199 211 238 248 332 409 434 439   Fall: 8 66 247 273 291 303 309

Bowling: *First Innings*—Pollock 28–8–64–0; Hayward 31–5–108–3; Ntini 19–7–64–0; Kallis 16–1–37–0; Klusener 14–4–44–2; Henderson 33–4–116–4. *Second Innings*—Pollock 12–4–38–1; Hayward 10–0–32–0; Henderson 29.1–1–130–3; Kallis 15–2–45–3; Ntini 8–3–13–0; Klusener 4–0–27–0.

South Africa

H. H. Gibbs st Gilchrist b Warne	78	– c Langer b McGrath	9
G. Kirsten lbw b McGrath	47	– c Ponting b Warne	7
H. H. Dippenaar c Ponting b McGrath	4	– c Warne b McGrath	0
C. W. Henderson run out (McGrath/Lee)	30	– (9) c Ponting b Warne	3
J. H. Kallis lbw b McGrath	5	– (4) not out	65
N. D. McKenzie lbw b Martyn	87	– (5) lbw b McGrath	0
L. Klusener b Warne	22	– (6) c Warne b Gillespie	18
†M. V. Boucher c Langer b Warne	64	– (7) c Gilchrist b Gillespie	0
*S. M. Pollock c Gilchrist b Warne	0	– (8) c Ponting b Warne	1
M. Ntini c Ponting b Warne	9	– b Lee	4
M. Hayward not out	0	– c Gilchrist b Lee	12
B 8, l-b 9, n-b 11	28	B 4, l-b 1, w 1, n-b 3	9

(121.4 overs, 512 mins)	374	(67 overs, 280 mins)	128

Fall: 87 93 155 178 178 214 355 356
365 374

Fall: 12 17 21 21 54 58 67 74
113 128

Bowling: *First Innings*—McGrath 33–10–94–3; Gillespie 23–7–57–0; Warne 39.4–9–113–5; M.E. Waugh 3–0–9–0; Lee 19–2–81–0; Martyn 4–2–3–1. *Second Innings*—McGrath 14–8–13–3; Gillespie 11–4–23–2; Warne 29–7–57–3; Lee 12–3–29–2; Martyn 1–0–1–0.

Umpires: S. Venkataraghavan (India) and S.J.A. Taufel.
TV Umpire: S. J. Davis.
Referee: R. S. Madugalle (Sri Lanka).

NEW SOUTH WALES v SOUTH AFRICANS

At Sydney Cricket Ground, Sydney, December 20, 21, 22, 23, 2001. Drawn. Toss: South Africans.

New South Wales fielded a second-string team, eight of their most senior players being injured, unavailable, or simply resting. Herschelle Gibbs (229 minutes, 205 balls, 25 fours, one six) cut loose in the opening two sessions of playing, dominating a second-wicket partnership of 164 with Jacques Rudolph (147 minutes, 123 balls, eight fours). Stuart MacGill bowled 31 consecutive overs on the opening day, his three quick wickets around tea including Gibbs neatly caught one-handed at cover by Mark Higgs. Boeta Dippenaar (188 minutes, 179 balls, 23 fours) then regained form with an array of powerful strokes. Acting captain Michael Bevan's masterful 183 not out (373 minutes, 276 balls, 26 fours, three sixes) lifted his average at the Sydney Cricket Ground over the past two seasons to over 100. Had he known that Shaun Pollock was interested only in match practice, rather than a result, Bevan might have batted on and helped himself to a double-century rather than declaring with his team well in arrears. Gibbs (108 minutes, 84 balls, 16 fours) was again flamboyant, while Gary Kirsten (203 minutes, 172 balls, 10 fours) moved with more restraint. Pollock did not declare until mid-afternoon on the final day, setting New South Wales a token target of 383 at almost ten an over. Allan Donald aggravated a foot injury while bowling just four expensive overs on the last day and other concerns came from the fact that, between them, Justin Ontong and Lance Klusener lasted a total of 25 balls in collecting their four ducks.

Close of play: First day, South Africans (1) 6-375 (Dippenaar 78, Pollock 14); Second day, New South Wales (1) 3-170 (Bevan 60, Bradstreet 11); Third day, South Africans (2) 1-112 (Kirsten 34, Rudolph 2).

Attendance: 8,386.

South Africans

G. Kirsten st Haddin b MacGill	31	– c Clarke b MacGill	88
H. H. Gibbs c Higgs b MacGill	145	– lbw b MacGill	75
J. A. Rudolph b Bradstreet	52	– c Haddin b MacGill	28
H. H. Dippenaar c and b Heath	115	– (6) not out	31
J.L. Ontong c Haddin b MacGill	0	c Haddin b MacGill	0
L. Klusener b MacGill	0	(4) b Higgs	0
†M. V. Boucher lbw b MacGill	44		
*S.M. Pollock c Haddin b Heath	53	– (7) not out	36
S. Elworthy c MacGill b Heath	31		
C. W. Henderson c MacGill b Higgs	13		
A. A. Donald not out	2		
B 3, l-b 4, n-b 5	12	B 7, l-b 4	11

(128.1 overs, 458 mins) 498   (80 overs, 283 mins) (5 wkts dec) 269

Fall: 67 231 235 235 239 344 445 460 487 498   Fall: 109 190 200 200 201

Bowling: *First Innings*—Nash 19–5–67–0; Heath 23–8–72–3; Bradstreet 18–2–123–1; Higgs 21.1–3–71–1; MacGill 40–7–132–5; Bevan 4–0–21–0; Clarke 3–0–5–0. *Second Innings*—Nash 14–4–48–0; Heath 10–0–39–0; Bradstreet 11–5–47–0; MacGill 33–8–89–4; Higgs 12–0–35–1.

New South Wales

G.J. Mail lbw b Elworthy	54	b Klusener	54
B.P. Van Deinsen c Gibbs b Pollock	1	c Kirsten b Klusener	61
C.J. Richards c Gibbs b Elworthy	37	not out	12
*M.G. Bevan not out	183		
S.D. Bradstreet b Henderson	15		
M.J. Clarke c Pollock b Elworthy	37	(4) not out	5
M.A. Higgs c Rudolph b Klusener	23		
†B.J. Haddin not out	20		
B 4, l-b 4, n-b 7	15	N-b 3	3

(123 overs, 472 mins) (6 wkts dec) 385   (41 overs, 147 mins) (2 wkts) 135

Fall: 2 54 149 179 252 359   Fall: 101 130

D. A. Nash, S. C. G. MacGill and J. M. Heath did not bat.

Bowling: *First Innings*—Donald 21–8–64–0; Pollock 20–4–53–1; Klusener 15–8–26–1; Elworthy 21–9–57–3; Henderson 40–11–130–1; Ontong 6–0–47–0. *Second Innings*—Donald 4–0–27–0; Pollock 5–2–8–0; Elworthy 5–0–32–0; Klusener 13–3–33–2; Henderson 6–0–18–0; Ontong 6–1–11–0; Rudolph 2–0–6–0.

Umpires: D. M. Brandon and R. L. Parry.
TV Umpire: D. B. Hair.

AUSTRALIA v SOUTH AFRICA

Second Test Match

At Melbourne Cricket Ground, Melbourne, December 26, 27, 28, 29, 2001. Australia won by nine wickets. Toss: Australia.

The South Africans were not merely beaten in this Test, but beaten into submission, capitulating on the fourth day so abjectly as to call their whole recent record into question. Their grim, austere, rather regimented cricket was made to appear brittle by the confident ebullience of Steve Waugh's men, for whom victory retained the Mandela Trophy.

Nominally, the South Africans took their strongest XI into the match, but its composition was based on deeds recalled rather than deeds recently recorded: Donald's first Test appearance since April was in spite of having taken only one wicket on tour; and Lance Klusener's continued tenure followed a pair against New South Wales. The

Australians lacked the injured Jason Gillespie, but Queensland's Andy Bichel fitted into the ensemble so snugly with four wickets, two catches and a run-out that disruption was minimal. Western Australia's Brad Williams had his first taste of international cricket, acting as 12th man.

Only 40 overs were bowled on the first day in the gloomy weather for which Melbourne's Boxing Day has developed a reputation. The conditions tried the patience of a crowd of 61,000 and the application of the South African batsmen sent in. Herschelle Gibbs, Gary Kirsten and Boeta Dippenaar were found wanting, the last a little unlucky to be caught at gully by Matthew Hayden diving full-length to his right. Neil McKenzie (232 minutes, 163 balls, eight fours) showed impressive poise again on the second day, adding 72 in 173 balls with Jacques Kallis and 67 in 110 balls with Mark Boucher, but none was able to master an attack against whom even survival was a struggle. Kallis, dropped twice and troubled by the short ball when he propped on the front foot, needed almost three hours for his 38, then was adjudged caught at the wicket from a ball he clearly missed. The veterans Klusener and Donald had an especially miserable time, the former shovelling back a return catch to Bichel from his first ball, the latter arriving and departing in the span of a menacing over from Brett Lee.

Though Shaun Pollock and Nantie Hayward gave South Africa's innings an affirmative finish with a last-wicket stand of 44 in 53 minutes, they were later ineffectual with the ball while Hayden and Justin Langer were even more positive in commencing Australia's reply. Donald was also costly as Australia's first 50 materialised in 49 minutes, and the openers proceeded without difficulty on the third day to their third double-century partnership in eight starts, only for Langer (233 minutes, 176 balls, seven fours) to be out next ball. Hayden's flawless innings (290 minutes, 211 balls, 17 fours) climaxed a 12-month period in which he finally repaid the faith of supporters and selectors. Bob Simpson's 37-year-old Australian record of 1,381 runs in a calendar year (1964) at an average of 60.04 was overhauled; Hayden finished the game having amassed 1,391 at 63.22 in 14 Tests in 2001. Australia passed the South African score for the loss of three wickets in enervating heat: ideal conditions for their captain to run himself back into form after a strangely unproductive summer.

Steve Waugh was below his best – Dippenaar, twice caught on his heels when bat-pad chances looped towards him, let Donald down badly at short leg – but still quick to dispose of the loose deliveries offered. He even essayed a rare hook during his stay (174 minutes, 156 balls, 12 fours), although the innings' most dramatic feature was its conclusion. Beaten by Gibbs' direct hit after an impetuous call from Damien Martyn, Waugh did not see umpire Darrell Hair's raised finger, and was composing himself for a third-umpire arbitration when informed of his dismissal. His reluctance to move off – he remained at the wicket almost 20 seconds – appeared to involve a query about consulting the replay, contradicting his public statements a month earlier that Australia would "lead the way" in respecting umpire's decisions. The replay did raise some questions about the dismissal – one bail apparently having been slightly disturbed by Boucher before the ball struck the stumps – but match referee Ranjan Madugalle was moved to dock Waugh half his match fee. Australia's captain complained after the match of having "basically been crucified in the papers", and of official restriction on his scope for comment and appeal. It was also Waugh's tenth Test innings to end in the nineties: an unwanted record. South Africa regained some heart, and Donald, Pollock and Hayward some rhythm, thereafter. When Glenn McGrath fell in the first over of the fourth day, Australia had lost their last five wickets for only 25 in 73 deliveries.

But the visiting batsmen, with the exception of Kallis, gave a puny display, despite the excellence of the pitch and the sapping temperatures. Australia also fielded brilliantly even by their stellar standards: Hayden at short leg caught Dippenaar off a full-blooded punch, Mark Waugh took two slick catches at slip that belied their difficulty, and Martyn executed two run-outs. The latter, involving a smart gather by Adam Gilchrist on the half volley as the flat return rocketed in from the point boundary, caught Kallis a foot or two short of a century as he tried to commandeer the strike with last man Hayward at the crease. It ended a brave innings (287 minutes, 180 balls, eight fours) and more than seven and a half hours' batting for the match: a feat splendid in its defiance and disappointing in its loneliness. – GIDEON HAIGH.

Close of play: First day, South Africa (1) 3-89 (Kallis 22, McKenzie 14); Second day, Australia (1) 0-126 (Langer 67, Hayden 55); Third day, Australia (1) 9-487 (Gilchrist 30, McGrath 0).

Man of the Match: M.L. Hayden.   *Attendance:* 153,025.

South Africa

H.H. Gibbs c Ponting b McGrath	14	– c Gilchrist b Lee	21
G. Kirsten b McGrath	10	– c Ponting b Lee	10
H.H. Dippenaar c Hayden b Lee	26	– c Hayden b Warne	23
J.H. Kallis c Gilchrist b Bichel	38	– run out (Martyn/Gilchrist)	99
N.D. McKenzie lbw b Lee	67	– c Gilchrist b Warne	12
L. Klusener c and b Bichel	0	– lbw b McGrath	7
†M.V. Boucher c Bichel b M.E. Waugh	43	– c M.E. Waugh b Warne	0
*S.M. Pollock not out	42	– run out (Martyn)	18
C.W. Henderson run out (Bichel)	5	– c M.E. Waugh b McGrath	16
A.A. Donald c Ponting b Lee	0	– b Bichel	7
M. Hayward c M.E. Waugh b Bichel	14	– not out	0
B 1, l-b 10, n-b 7	18	B 4, n-b 2	6

(103.5 overs, 277 mins)   277   (75.1 overs, 331 mins)   219
Fall: 24 36 59 131 131 198 220 225   Fall: 24 37 74 107 120 121 157
   233 277   192 215 219

Bowling: *First Innings*—McGrath 26–8–70–2; Lee 31–10–77–3; Bichel 19.5–6–44–3; Warne 19–3–56–0; M.E. Waugh 8–1–19–1. *Second Innings*—McGrath 21–6–43–2; Lee 18–5–52–2; Warne 24–3–68–3; Bichel 12.1–0–52–1.

Australia

J.L. Langer c Klusener b Donald	85	– c Henderson b Pollock	7
M.L. Hayden c Donald b Henderson	138	– not out	3
R.T. Ponting b Kallis b Hayward	22	– not out	0
M.E. Waugh b Donald	34		
*S.R. Waugh run out (Gibbs)	90		
D.R. Martyn c Kallis b Pollock	52		
†A.C. Gilchrist not out	30		
S.K. Warne c Kirsten b Donald	1		
B. Lee c McKenzie b Hayward	3		
A.J. Bichel c Boucher b Pollock	5		
G.D. McGrath lbw b Pollock	0		
L-b 17, w 1, n-b 9	27		

(139 overs, 563 mins)   487   (3 overs, 14 mins)   (1 wkt)   10
Fall: 202 267 267 348 429 462 463 470 475 487   Fall: 7

Bowling: *First Innings*—Donald 29–5–103–3; Pollock 31–3–84–3; Hayward 26–1–109–2; Kallis 17–3–55–0; Henderson 29–3–108–1; Klusener 7–1–11–0. *Second Innings*—Donald 2–0–4–0; Pollock 1–0–6–1.

Umpires: E.A. Nicholls (West Indies) and D.B. Hair.
TV Umpire: R.L. Parry.
Referee: R.S. Madugalle (Sri Lanka).

AUSTRALIA v SOUTH AFRICA

Third Test Match

At Sydney Cricket Ground, Sydney, January 2, 3, 4, 5, 2002. Australia won by ten wickets. Toss: Australia. Test debut: J.L. Ontong.

It may have crossed a few South African minds before this match that miracles do occasionally happen at Sydney. Eight years earlier the South Africans had won a Test here against all odds, bowling out the Australians for 111 on the final day to win by five runs. Similar fortune seemed necessary now if South Africa were to overcome a home side which had been so plainly superior in the previous two Tests.

A controversial South African team selection caused a stir before play began. The selectors had chosen a young white player, Jacques Rudolph, to fill a vacancy in the original side, but they were overruled by the United Cricket Board of South Africa's president, Percy Sonn, who insisted that a 21-year-old coloured batsman, Justin Ontong, play instead. Sonn was applying an established policy – that extra non-white players should be included in the team where possible – but the matter touched raw nerves, especially in the South African camp. Much sympathy was felt for Ontong, who had been thrust into an awkward position and could not have enjoyed the resulting media attention.

For the first time in 12 months, Stuart MacGill came into the Australian side as a second leg-spinner, replacing Andy Bichel, so it was predictable that, having won the toss, Steve Waugh would choose to bat on a pitch likely to take spin later. After a testing morning session during which they had to keep Allan Donald and Shaun Pollock at bay, Matthew Hayden and Justin Langer went to lunch with the score at 93, and were still together at tea, by which time the total had accelerated to 215. Boeta Dippenaar gave Hayden more time at the crease when he dropped an uncomplicated catch at square leg when the batsman, then on 68, had misdirected a sweep from Claude Henderson. When Hayden (240 minutes, 198 balls, 14 fours, one six) was out soon after tea, the pair had reached their fourth double-century opening stand in the six home Tests of the season, a performance unmatched by any opening pair in history. Indeed, they were only the third pair of batsmen from any country (and the first from Australia) to have four double-century Test partnerships for any wicket. Yet it was not just the quantity of runs they scored which must have dispirited the South Africans, but also the ease with which they appeared to score them, as if they had wholly mastered the attack.

Hayden's dismissal was followed by four more before stumps. Ricky Ponting was run out sprinting for a single called by Langer and failing to beat Ontong's sharp return, and Langer (276 minutes, 211 balls, 19 fours, one six) himself went a few minutes later to a neat bat-pad catch. Mark and Steve Waugh began to build a partnership, but neither was to last until stumps: Steve was bowled by a ball which Pollock angled between bat and pads, and Mark, who had had very little strike, was out caught behind in the last over, swishing loosely outside the off stump. Having toiled all day in oppressive heat, the South Africans could have felt relieved that the stumps score was no worse than five for 308. Any such relief soon disappeared in the continued sapping heat of the second day as the Australians built relentlessly on their overnight total. The not-out batsman, Damien Martyn, had been unfairly labelled as Australia's most conspicuous failure in the batting debacle on this ground against South Africa eight years earlier. Now, however, he proceeded to play a stylish and sometimes brilliant innings (225 minutes, 166 balls, 13 fours) which, having started deliberately, grew into assured confidence and culminated in audaciously effective reverse sweeping of the spinners. Solid support almost to the end of the tail enabled Australia to add another 246 runs by tea and produce another unbeatable total. Nicky Boje was the most effective bowler, and although he profited from the late-order's long handle, he did extract enough turn to be treated with respect.

So far, almost everything had gone Australia's way. By stumps nothing had changed: in just under two and a half hours' batting the South Africans had lost their top four for 93. Next morning the innings fell apart entirely, beginning with Neil McKenzie's dismissal to the third ball of the day, bowled by a Shane Warne leg-break to which he did not offer a stroke. By lunch, the innings was over, the South Africans having lost six wickets for 61 runs to finish 400 runs behind. Much interest centred on how the leg-spinners, Warne and MacGill, compared but, in fact, they shared honours, each taking three wickets.

Following on, the South Africans rallied strongly and batted with refreshing combativeness and skill. Hoping to continue and drive home his hold over the batsmen, Warne was used to open the bowling with Glenn McGrath. Brett Lee claimed an early success, bowling Herschelle Gibbs with a high-speed delivery, but after that the South Africans gave no more ground, Gary Kirsten having been presented with the rare gift of Mark Waugh spilling a straightforward chance at second slip when he was only 12. Kirsten and Boeta Dippenaar (146 minutes, 116 balls, 14 fours) scored 149 purposeful runs between them before Dippenaar fell to MacGill, after which Jacques Kallis continued the resistance. On the fourth day, when the South Africans reached four for 350, just 50 behind, they may even have wondered whether they might yet set Australia a challenging fourth-innings target. Kirsten (437 minutes, 359 balls, 20 fours) returned to run-making with one of his epics of resistance which saw him march on deliberately, receiving able support from both McKenzie and an admirably composed Ontong. His dismissal began a crumbling of five for 47, before Pollock (87 minutes, 83 balls, five fours, three sixes) made a final defiant assault, dominating a last-wicket partnership of 49 with Allan Donald. By late afternoon, however, the Australian bowlers – of whom MacGill and Warne bowled 87.5 overs for seven wickets – had worn the South Africans down, but not before South Africa had made their highest total of the series. Hitting eight fours and a six between them, Hayden and Langer knocked off the winning runs in 44 minutes, ensuring victory with a day to spare and in the process taking their partnership runs for the summer past 1,000. – PHILIP DERRIMAN.

Close of play: First day, Australia (1) 5-308 (Martyn 1); Second day, South Africa (1) 4-93 (McKenzie 20, Ontong 8); Third day, South Africa (2) 2-209 (Kirsten 82, Kallis 32).

Man of the Match: M.L. Hayden and J.L. Langer. *Man of the Series:* M.L. Hayden. *Attendance:* 120,281.

Australia

J.L. Langer c McKenzie b Boje	126	– not out	30
M.L. Hayden c Kallis b Pollock	105	– not out	21
R.T. Ponting run out (Ontong/Boucher)	14		
M.E. Waugh c Boucher b Donald	19		
*S.R. Waugh b Pollock	30		
D.R. Martyn c McKenzie b Boje	117		
†A.C. Gilchrist c Boucher b Kallis	34		
S.K. Warne b Pollock	37		
B. Lee b Boje	29		
S.C.G. MacGill c Henderson b Boje	20		
G.D. McGrath not out	1		
B 4, l-b 4, w 1, n-b 9	22	L-b 2, n-b 1	3

(144.2 overs, 554 mins)	554	(10.1 overs, 44 mins)	(0 wkt) 54

Fall: 219 247 253 302 308 356 439 502 542 554

Fall:

Bowling: *First Innings*—Donald 31–6–119–1; Pollock 37–11–109–3; Kallis 22–1–129–1; Henderson 27–3–112–0; Boje 25.2–6–63–4; Ontong 2–0–10–0. *Second Innings*—Donald 3–0–12–0; Pollock 3–1–11–0; Boje 2.1–0–15–0; Henderson 2–0–14–0.

South Africa

H.H. Gibbs c M.E. Waugh b MacGill	32	– b Lee	10
G. Kirsten c Ponting b McGrath	18	– b MacGill	153
H.H. Dippenaar b McGrath	3	– c Ponting b MacGill	74
J.H. Kallis c Gilchrist b MacGill	4	– c Gilchrist b Warne	34
N.D. McKenzie b Warne	20	– c MacGill b Lee	38
J.L. Ontong lbw b Warne	9	– lbw b Warne	32
†M.V. Boucher c Ponting b Warne	35	– c Gilchrist b McGrath	27
*S.M. Pollock c Martyn b McGrath	6	– not out	61
N. Boje run out (Langer/McGrath)	7	– b MacGill	1
C.W. Henderson c McGrath b MacGill	9	– b MacGill	2
A.A. Donald not out	2	– c Lee b Warne	2
L-b 8, n-b 1	9	B 8, l-b 7, n-b 3	18

(62.2 overs, 241 mins)	154	(141.5 overs, 525 mins)	452
Fall: 37 43 56 77 93 98 111		Fall: 17 166 211 282 356 372	
121 148 154		392 393 403 452	

Bowling: *First Innings*1`McGrath 17–6–35–3; Lee 6–2–13–0; MacGill 20.2–6–51–3; Warne 19–5–47–3. *Second Innings*—McGrath 28–5–95–1; Warne 42.5–8–132–3; Lee 19–5–62–2; MacGill 45–13–123–4; M.E. Waugh 6–1–14–0; Ponting 1–0–11–0.

Umpires: D.R. Shepherd (England) and D.J. Harper.
TV Umpire: S.J.A. Taufel.
Referee: R.S. Madugalle (Sri Lanka).

†AUSTRALIA A v SOUTH AFRICANS

At Adelaide Oval, Adelaide, January 10, 2002. Day/night game. Australia A won by five wickets. Toss: South Africans.

In preparation for the ensuing VB Series, the tourists played an engrossing contest with Australia A, the match going into the 100th over before the Australians won by just five balls to spare. In 40-degree heat, South Africa recovered from a poor start with veteran Jonty Rhodes at his improvising and impish best being joined by Shaun Pollock in a busy sixth-wicket partnership of 94 from 117 balls. The standard of the rest of the batting can be gauged by the fact that the left-arm spinners Darren Lehmann and Simon Katich took four wickets between them in six overs. Jimmy Maher managed Australia's reply calmly, surviving an appeal for obstructing the field at 92 when he bumped into Makhaya Ntini at the bowler's end while running through for a sharp single. Lehmann, with a valuable knock in the middle order, also continued to remind the selectors of his value as a limited-overs player.

Man of the Match: J.P. Maher. *Attendance:* 11,485.

South Africans

H.H. Gibbs c Campbell b Bracken	22	(53)	N. Boje not out	9	(6)
G. Kirsten c Clark b Bracken	4	(5)	C.K. Langeveldt st Campbell b Katich	5	(7)
J.H. Kallis run out (Hussey)	1	(2)	M. Ntini not out	2	(1)
N.D. McKenzie c Maher b Gillespie	4	(10)			
J.N. Rhodes c Clark b Lehmann	69	(97)	L-b 8, w 8	16	
†M.V. Boucher c Higgs b MacGill	14	(26)			
*S.M. Pollock c and b Katich	56	(76)	(50 overs, 210 mins)	(9 wkts)	215
L. Klusener lbw b Katich	13	(16)	Fall: 11 16 30 43 79 173 197 198 213		

Bowling: Gillespie 10–2–28–1; Bracken 8–1–28–2; Clark 6–0–29–0; Higgs 10–0–47–0; MacGill 10–1–42–1; Lehmann 2–0–12–1; Katich 4–0–21–3.

Australia A

J.P. Maher c Langeveldt b Ntini	94 (120)	†R.J. Campbell not out	20 (16)
G.S. Blewett b Langeveldt	5 (19)		
S.M. Katich c Ntini b Kallis	18 (51)	B 1, l-b 5, w 5	12
*D.S. Lehmann lbw b Kallis	41 (57)		—
M.E.K. Hussey not out	25 (28)	(49.1 overs, 224 mins) (5 wkts)	219
M.A. Higgs run out (Pollock)	4 (4)	Fall: 21 76 148 174 182	

J.N. Gillespie, N.W. Bracken, S.R. Clark and S.C.G. MacGill did not bat.

Bowling: Pollock 10–1–34–0; Langeveldt 8–0–35–1; Kallis 9.1–1–45–2; Ntini 10–1–37–1; Klusener 7–0–33–0; Boje 5–0–28–0.

Umpires: P.D. Parker and R.G. Patterson.

South Africa's matches v Australia and New Zealand in the VB Series (January 11–February 8) may be found in that section.

AUSTRALIANS REACHING A TEST CENTURY WITH A SIX

Batsman	Bowler	Against	Venue	Season
J. Darling	J. Briggs	England	Adelaide	1897-98
J. Benaud	Intikhab Alam	Pakistan	Melbourne	1972-73
K.R. Stackpole	M.L.C. Foster	West Indies	Kingston	1972-73
K.D. Walters	R.G.D. Willis	England	Perth	1974-75
I.C. Davis	Salim Altaf	Pakistan	Adelaide	1976-77
R.B. McCosker	R.G.D. Willis	England	Nottingham	1977
G.R.J. Matthews	V.R. Brown	New Zealand	Brisbane	1985-86
J.L. Langer	C.W. Henderson	South Africa	Adelaide	2001-02
R.T. Ponting	P.R. Adams	South Africa	Cape Town	2001-02

John Benaud reached his hundred with a six after he was told that he had been dropped from the next Test in Sydney. Walters' six is remembered as the most exciting, as he reached his century in a session off the last ball of the day by hooking English fast bowler Bob Willis into the Perth crowd. "The time I hit that six was the most perfect moment in my life," Walters recalled, and added tongue-in-cheek: "In that session it appeared as if bowlers were aiming at the middle of my bat and hitting it; they were that accurate!" – KERSI MEHER-HOMJI and RAJESH KUMAR

THE PAKISTANIS IN AUSTRALIA, 2001-02

By WARWICK FRANKS

Least said, soonest mended. Even the *Star Wars* pretension of numbering the contest could not hide the fact that the aggregate attendance for the three games of just over 40,000 was an eloquent comment on the underwhelming impact of this contrived entertainment. The law of diminishing returns for winter cricket seemed to have set in almost immediately, as this total was less than half the aggregate for the grandiloquently titled Super Challenge against South Africa two years earlier. Sweeping vistas of icily empty seats emphasised the forlorn atmosphere. Attempts to inject synthetic life into the proceedings fell largely flat and the widely expressed view was that the Australian Cricket Board should not repeat the experiment.

The Australians went into the series with reasonable expectations of success. They were only a few weeks on from having dealt with South Africa to the tune of 5-1, while 12 months previously they had crushed Pakistan in the final of the triangular tournament in England. Initially, all went to expectation with Australia coasting to victory in a first encounter in which they required only 32.5 overs to send the crowd home in time for the late news. Pakistan's batting showed the vein of frailty which often undermines it, while with nothing to defend their bowlers looked flat and friendly. In contrast, the Australian attack looked purposeful, and Adam Gilchrist made his usual ebullient contribution with both the gloves and the bat.

The second match signalled a change in the drift of the series. This time, Wasim Akram opened up the Australian batting and the rest of the Pakistan attack kept up the pressure to choke the development of the innings. A steady Australian bowling performance was met by Pakistan batting whose determination overcame a poor start. The visitors seemed to flower with the move to Brisbane's slightly warmer atmosphere for the last match and they gave an expansive batting display, topped off by Akram's reminder that even at 36 years of age he is still capable of an explosive impact on the course of a match. Shoaib Akhtar's devastating pace shredded the Australian innings, whose only bright spot was a sensible hand from the young Shane Watson.

This was the series that we had been told was a vital component of Australia's preparation for the World Cup in South Africa. As such, it contributed nothing to the development or the refinement of the squad and, as the lights were turned out and the Milo was warmed, it drifted back into the void from whence it had come. Needless to say, the matches had not caused even a nano-blip on the sporting radar screens of any of the football codes and their followers.

PAKISTANIS TOURING PARTY

Waqar Younis (*captain*), Inzamam-ul-Haq (*vice-captain*), Azhar Mahmood, Imran Nazir, Mohammad Sami, Rashid Latif, Saeed Anwar, Shahid Afridi, Shoaib Malik, Shoaib Akhtar, Wasim Akram, Younis Khan, Yousuf Youhana.

Misbah-ul-Haq withdrew from the touring party prior to departing Pakistan.

Manager: Yawar Saeed. *Coach:* Mudassar Nazar.

PAKISTANIS TOUR RESULTS

Limited-overs internationals – Played 3: Won 2, Lost 1. *Win* – Australia (2). *Loss* – Australia (1).
Other non-first-class matches – Played 1: Won 1. *Win* – Queensland Invitational XI.

AUSTRALIA – BATTING

	M	I	NO	R	HS	100s	50s	Avge	C/S	S-R
S.R. Watson	3	2	1	52	44*	0	0	52.00	0	49.06
D.R. Martyn	3	3	1	84	56	0	1	42.00	2	64.12
D.S. Lehmann	3	3	1	59	31	0	0	29.50	0	62.77
A.C. Gilchrist	3	3	0	76	56	0	1	25.33	7/1	93.83
M.L. Hayden	2	2	0	50	45	0	0	25.00	1	61.73
M.G. Bevan	3	2	0	40	30	0	0	20.00	0	60.61
S.K. Warne	3	2	0	32	31	0	0	16.00	2	52.46
J.P. Maher	1	1	0	12	12	0	0	12.00	0	48.00
R.T. Ponting	3	3	0	27	14	0	0	9.00	1	54.00
A.J. Bichel	3	2	0	7	7	0	0	3.50	0	35.00
G.D. McGrath	3	2	0	4	3	0	0	2.00	0	36.36
B. Lee	1	1	1	3	3*	0	0	–	0	50.00
J.N. Gillespie	2	1	0	0	0	0	0	0.00	0	0.00

* Denotes not out.

BOWLING

	O	M	R	W	BB	5Wi	Avge
D.S. Lehmann	13.3	0	47	4	2/23	0	11.75
A.J. Bichel	28	2	105	5	3/30	0	21.00
B. Lee	10	0	44	2	2/44	0	22.00
S.K. Warne	30	2	118	5	2/42	0	23.60
J.N. Gillespie	19	1	77	1	1/43	0	77.00
G.D. McGrath	25.5	8	86	1	1/22	0	86.00
S.R. Watson	18	1	93	1	1/38	0	93.00
D.R. Martyn	4.3	0	19	0	–	0	–

PAKISTAN – BATTING

	M	I	NO	R	HS	100s	50s	Avge	C/S	S-R
Imran Nazir	3	3	1	111	66	0	1	55.50	1	74.00
Yousuf Youhana	3	3	1	109	61*	0	1	54.50	0	61.24
Younis Khan	3	3	1	74	56*	0	1	37.00	0	66.67
Wasim Akram	3	3	1	72	49*	0	0	36.00	1	104.35
Shoaib Malik	1	1	0	27	27	0	0	27.00	1	48.21
Inzamam-ul-Haq	3	3	0	70	33	0	0	23.33	0	57.85
Saeed Anwar	2	2	0	26	26	0	0	13.00	1	50.88
Rashid Latif	3	3	0	29	16	0	0	9.67	7	50.00
Shahid Afridi	3	3	0	18	14	0	0	6.00	1	66.67
Azhar Mahmood	3	3	0	11	6	0	0	3.67	0	21.57
Waqar Younis	3	2	2	17	9*	0	0	–	0	73.91
Mohammad Sami	1	0	0	0	0	0	0	–	0	–
Shoaib Akhtar	2	0	0	0	0	0	0	–	1	–

* Denotes not out.

BOWLING

	O	M	R	W	BB	5W/i	Avge
Shoaib Akhtar	16	1	55	7	5/25	1	7.86
Shahid Afridi	25.3	3	78	6	3/28	0	13.00
Wasim Akram	21	2	69	4	3/18	0	17.25
Mohammad Sami	9	0	53	2	2/53	0	26.50
Azhar Mahmood	22	0	106	1	1/51	0	106.00
Waqar Younis	23	1	107	1	1/41	0	107.00
Shoaib Malik	2	0	16	0	–	0	–

Note: Matches in this section were not first-class.

QUEENSLAND INVITATIONAL XI v PAKISTANIS

At Allan Border Field, Albion, June 8, 2002. Pakistanis won by 15 runs. Toss: Queensland Invitational XI.

This was a 40-over per side practice match in which the local side named 12 players but fielded and batted 11. Shahid Afridi enlivened the opening stages with a run-a-ball innings, while teenage pace bowler Nathan Rimmington bowled impressively. The sensible batting of Nathan Hauritz gave his side a chance but Wasim Akram was too formidable a proposition.

Pakistanis

Imran Nazir c Seccombe b Edmondson	8	(17)
Shahid Afridi c Betts b Hopes	52	(52)
Azhar Mahmood c Betts b Petrie	21	(28)
Saeed Anwar c Simpson b Rimmington	31	(55)
Yousuf Youhana c Petrie b Hauritz	3	(10)
Younis Khan lbw b Petrie	1	(9)
Shoaib Malik c Hopes b Rimmington	3	(8)
†Rashid Latif not out	25	(36)
Wasim Akram b Rimmington	2	(10)
Shoaib Akhtar not out	25	(19)
B 1, l-b 4, w 13, n-b 5	23	
(40 overs, 161 mins) (8 wkts)	194	

Fall: 23 79 92 106 109 126 134 151

*Waqar Younis did not bat.

Bowling: Edmondson 8–1–60–1; Mohammad Sami 7–0–30–0; Petrie 8–0–34–2; Hopes 4–0–25–1; Hauritz 8–1–24–1; Rimmington 5–0–16–3.

Queensland Invitational XI

C.P. Simpson b Wasim Akram	9	(18)
D.M. Betts run out (Imran Nazir)	18	(30)
J.R. Hopes c Azhar Mahmood b Wasim Akram	1	(6)
*†W.A. Seccombe b Shoaib Akhtar	12	(22)
M. Sippel c Azhar Mahmood b Waqar Younis	23	(27)
D.M. Payne b Shoaib Akhtar	0	(1)
N.M. Hauritz st Rashid Latif b Shahid Afridi	61	(77)
M.G. Johnson c Imran Khan b Shahid Afridi	33	(54)
Mohammad Sami b Wasim Akram	0	(2)
M.J. Petrie not out	2	(3)
B.M. Edmondson b Wasim Akram	0	(1)
B 6, l-b 7, w 3, n-b 4	20	
(39.3 overs, 171 mins)	179	

Fall: 19 24 45 47 47 84 172 177 179

N.J. Rimmington did not bat.

Bowling: Wasim Akram 7.3–1–24–4; Waqar Younis 7–0–33–1; Shoaib Akhtar 6–2–27–2; Azhar Mahmood 8–1–31–0; Shoaib Malik 5–0–32–0; Shahid Afridi 6–0–19–2.

Umpires: D.B. Hair and B.N.J. Oxenford.

AUSTRALIA v PAKISTAN

At Colonial Stadium, Melbourne, June 12, 2002. Day/night game. Australia won by seven wickets. Toss: Australia.

The much-vaunted speed contest between Shoaib Akhtar and Brett Lee failed to eventuate because of a hip injury to the former, while the Australians preferred the greater precision of Andy Bichel in their attack. He joined with Glenn McGrath in exploiting the early moisture in a drop-in pitch which offered plenty of early bounce and movement. After the rapid departure of Shahid Afridi, at one for six, Imran Nazir sustained a severe blow on the forearm from McGrath serious enough for him to make a precautionary trip to hospital. From there, the innings never caught fire, a series of modest contributions snuffed out by Bichel's accuracy and the safe work of Adam Gilchrist behind the stumps. Nazir returned for the 35th over after the fall of the sixth wicket and shrugged off the earlier injury with a number of cracking drives. Darren Lehmann underlined his versatility in this form of the game with two handy wickets, while Shane Warne bowled with restraining accuracy. In contrast to the tentativeness of the visitors, Gilchrist (nine fours) and Matthew Hayden took only 97 balls to take the score past 100. With a Wagnerian accompaniment of thunder, lightning and rain lashing down on the stadium's closed roof, Gilchrist unleashed a series of slashing cuts and explosive pull shots that made light of the still-lively pitch. Hayden's composed and sensible innings was cut short by Shoaib Malik's athletic catch at square leg. In the closing stages, Lehmann joined Damien Martyn in a measured stroll to the required total. The match concluded at 9.04 p.m. in an atmosphere of considerable anti-climax which echoed the sparse attendance.

Man of the Match: A.C. Gilchrist.　　*Attendance:* 11,861.

Pakistan

Imran Nazir not out	39	(53)	†Rashid Latif c Gilchrist b Lehmann	11	(29)	
Shahid Afridi c Warne b McGrath	1	(9)	Wasim Akram c Hayden b Watson	13	(18)	
Yousuf Youhana c Gilchrist b Warne	19	(38)	*Waqar Younis not out	9	(9)	
Inzamam-ul-Haq c Gilchrist b Bichel	33	(42)	L-b 2, w 4, n-b 1	7		
Younis Khan c Gilchrist b Bichel	16	(30)		—		
Azhar Mahmood c Martyn b Bichel	1	(17)	(50 overs, 211 mins)　(8 wkts)	176		
Shoaib Malik st Gilchrist b Lehmann	27	(56)	Fall: 3 55 71 75 78 104 124 153			

Mohammad Sami did not bat.

Bowling: McGrath 7–2–22–1; Gillespie 9–1–34–0; Bichel 10–1–30–3; Warne 10–1–27–1; Watson 9–0–38–1; Lehmann 5–0–23–2.

Australia

†A.C. Gilchrist c Shahid Afridi			D.R. Martyn not out	18	(30)
b Mohammad Sami	56	(47)	D.S. Lehmann not out	28	(35)
M.L. Hayden c Shoaib Malik			L-b 4, w 3, n-b 10	17	
b Mohammad Sami	45	(65)			
*R.T. Ponting c Rashid Latif			(32.5 overs, 154 mins)　(3 wkts)	177	
b Shahid Afridi	13	(26)	Fall: 101 121 127		

M.G. Bevan, S.R. Watson, S.K. Warne, A.J. Bichel, J.N. Gillespie and G.D. McGrath did not bat.

Bowling: Wasim Akram 6–1–24–0; Waqar Younis 5–0–31–0; Mohammad Sami 9–0–53–2; Azhar Mahmood 5–0–29–0; Shahid Afridi 5.5–0–20–1; Shoaib Malik 2–0–16–0.

Umpires: D.J. Harper and R.B. Tiffin.
TV Umpire: S.J. Davis.

AUSTRALIA v PAKISTAN

At Docklands Stadium, Melbourne, June 15, 2002. Day/night game. Pakistan won by two wickets. Toss: Australia.

Despite the low scoring, the closeness of the contest kept a modicum of interest in it on a pitch with enough pace, bounce and turn to encourage the bowlers to believe that they might be more than bit players in the theatre of limited-overs cricket. The speed contest between Brett Lee and Shoaib Akhtar failed to reach supersonic proportions, although the Pakistani pace man did reach 151.9 km/h with one delivery. Wasim Akram's decisive opening over saw Gilchrist immediately caught behind from a lethal outswinger and the Australian captain on his way to balls later. The wicket of Jimmy Maher in Akram's fifth over meant that the home side were constantly struggling to get on even terms. Damien Martyn (three fours, one six) batted with considerable composure, joining with Darren Lehmann in the only moderately substantial partnership of the innings. Martyn, however, had profited from a closely examined refusal of a catch claimed by Waqar Younis at mid-on from a botched pull shot when he was only seven. Shoaib Akhtar and Shahid Afridi combined their contrasting bowling styles to take the last five wickets for only 29 runs. Pakistan's opening was similarly dismal after a needless run-out had seen Saeed Anwar depart to the third ball of the innings. Brett Lee worked up to genuine speed. The middle order did not prosper and it was left to Younis Khan (four fours) to play a thoughtfully conventional innings during which the later batsmen gave him enough support to see his coolness rewarded with a narrow victory.

Man of the Match: Younis Khan.   *Attendance:* 16,981.

Australia

†A.C. Gilchrist c Rashid Latif			
b Wasim Akram	..	0	(1)
J.P. Maher c Rashid Latif			
b Wasim Akram	..	12	(25)
*R.T. Ponting c and b Wasim Akram	.	0	(2)
D.R. Martyn c Imran Nazir			
b Shahid Afridi	..	56	(87)
D.S. Lehmann c Rashid Latif	....		
b Azhar Mahmood	..	31	(58)
M.G. Bevan c Rashid Latif			
b Shoaib Akhtar	..	30	(52)
S.R. Watson lbw b Shahid Afridi	...	8	(28)
S.K. Warne lbw b Shahid Afridi	....	1	(7)
A.J. Bichel b Shoaib Akhtar	....	7	(16)
B. Lee not out	....	3	(6)
G.D. McGrath run out			
(Inzamam-ul-Haq/Afridi)	..	1	(1)
L-b 5, w 5, n-b 8	....	18	
(45.4 overs, 221 mins)		167	
Fall: 0 0 23 89 121 138 143 163			
164 167			

Bowling: Wasim Akram 8–1–18–3; Waqar Younis 10–1–35–0; Azhar Mahmood 10–0–51–1; Shoaib Akhtar 8–0–30–2; Shahid Afridi 9.4–1–28–3.

Pakistan

Imran Nazir lbw b Lee	....	6	(24)
Saeed Anwar run out (Watson)	......	0	(0)
Azhar Mahmood c Gilchrist b Lee	...	4	(22)
Yousuf Youhana c Martyn b Warne	..	29	(56)
Inzamam-ul-Haq b Bichel	....	24	(49)
Younis Khan not out	....	56	(76)
†Rashid Latif b Warne	....	16	(26)
Shahid Afridi c Ponting b Lehmann	.	3	(7)
Wasim Akram run out (Ponting)	....	10	(19)
*Waqar Younis not out	....	8	(14)
B 1, l-b 4, w 7	....	12	
(48.5 overs, 232 mins)	(8 wkts)	168	
Fall: 0 18 21 65 85 120 131 150			

Shoaib Akhtar did not bat.

Bowling: McGrath 8.5–3–16–0; Lee 10–0–44–2; Watson 4–1–9–0; Bichel 10–1–28–1; Warne 10–0–49–2; Lehmann 6–0–17–1.

Umpires: D.B. Hair and R.B. Tiffin.
TV Umpire: S.J.A. Taufel.

AUSTRALIA v PAKISTAN

At Brisbane Cricket Ground, Brisbane, June 19, 2002. Day/night game. Pakistan won by 91 runs. Toss: Pakistan.

As this match went on, so did Pakistan's domination of it become complete. The wise maturity of Wasim Akram and the youthful exuberance of Shoaib Akhtar ultimately proved irresistible in providing their side with their largest limited-overs win in runs against Australia. The contrasting styles of Saeed Anwar and Imran Nazir (six fours, two sixes), got the visitors away to a sound start, their stand of 94 taking 19.2 overs. For the next 20 overs, however, it seemed as though the chance of a substantial total was being frittered away through a combination of indolent batting and amateurish running between the wickets. The only check to Australia's success seemed to be the retirement of Darren Lehmann, who was struck in the face when he was bowling. The complexion of the game was changed by a riveting eighth-wicket partnership of 88 from 65 balls between Yousuf Youhana and Wasim Akram (three fours, two sixes), the latter joining Mohammed Azharuddin in a world-record-equalling 334th limited-overs international appearance. They brought the innings to a dizzy conclusion with a calculated assault on McGrath in the last over of the innings which produced 23 runs including two straight-driven sixes from Akram. The all-rounder was immediately back into the fray as, having made an early breakthrough with Hayden's wicket, his accuracy stopped Adam Gilchrist from launching his customary initial assault on the bowling. A 23-ball burst from Akhtar then split the innings at the seams. The two Shanes, Warne and Watson, batted sensibly but unavailingly for 15 overs, before Akhtar returned to join Shahid Afridi in mopping up the innings.

Man of the Match: Shoaib Akhtar.   *Attendance:* 11,612.

Pakistan

Imran Nazir c Warne b Lehmann	....	66	(73)	Shahid Afridi run out (Ponting/Warne)	14	(11)
Saeed Anwar lbw b Warne	....	26	(51)	Wasim Akram not out	 49	(32)
Yousuf Youhana not out	....	61	(84)			
Inzamam-ul-Haq lbw b Warne	......	13	(30)	L-b 4, w 11, n-b 2 17		
Younis Khan c Gilchrist b Gillespie	..	2	(5)			
†Rashid Latif c Gilchrist b Bichel	....	2	(3)	(50 overs, 219 mins) (7 wkts) 256		
Azhar Mahmood run out (Bichel)	....	6	(12)	Fall: 94 108 133 136 139 153 168		

Shoaib Akhtar and *Waqar Younis did not bat.

Bowling: McGrath 10-3-48-0; Gillespie 10-0-43-1; Bichel 8-0-47-1; Watson 5-0-46-0; Warne 10-1-42-2; Lehmann 2.3-0-7-1; Martyn 4.3-0-19-0.

Australia

†A.C. Gilchrist run out				A.J. Bichel c Shoaib Akhtar		
(Yousuf Youhana)	20	(33)		b Shahid Afridi ..	0	(4)
M.L. Hayden lbw b Wasim Akram	...	5	(16)	J.N. Gillespie lbw b Shoaib Akhtar ..	0	(1)
*R.T. Ponting b Shoaib Akhtar	......	14	(22)	G.D. McGrath c Rashid Latif		
D.R. Martyn c Saeed Anwar				lbw b Waqar Younis ..	3	(10)
b Shoaib Akhtar		10	(14)	B 9, l-b 7, w 5, n-b 7	28	
D.S. Lehmann b Shoaib Akhtar	.....	0	(1)			
M.G. Bevan c Rashid Latif				(40 overs, 203 mins)	165	
b Shoaib Akhtar	..	10	(14)	Fall: 17 44 44 52 65 83 140 142		
S.R. Watson not out	....	44	(78)	142 165		
S.K. Warne b Shahid Afridi	....	31	(54)			

Bowling: Wasim Akram 7-0-27-1; Waqar Younis 8-0-41-1; Shoaib Akhtar 8-1-25-5; Azhar Mahmood 7-0-26-0; Shahid Afridi 10-2-30-2.

Umpires: S.J.A. Taufel and R.B. Tiffin.
TV Umpire: D.B. Hair.
Series Referee: C.H. Lloyd (West Indies).

VB SERIES, 2001-02

By KEN PIESSE

Australia's failure to make the finals of the triangular limited-overs series, known for the first time in 2001-02 as the VB Series, was overshadowed by the bonus points controversy which once again stained the game after New Zealand and South Africa deliberately under-performed in the final qualifying weekend in Perth. The root of the problem was nothing as nefarious as match-fixing, but rather the working of an incentive system adopted from Australia's ING Cup which awarded bonus points to teams that won by large margins.

Aiming for their eighth limited-overs title in nine years, the Australians, who had been slow to establish themselves after early losses, were denied a place in the finals by the new rules, which captain Steve Waugh claimed conspired against his team. Fresh from being hailed as one of the great leaders of world cricket, New Zealand's Stephen Fleming was accused of unfairly manipulating the system when he handed the South Africans an all-important bonus point in the second-last qualifying match, guaranteeing the Proteas a place in the finals. Fleming said his only thought behind the batting go-slow was for his team and how best they could survive after they had peaked at the start of the tournament only to hit a trough of poor form.

Just 36 hours later, South Africa's Shaun Pollock triggered more outrage when his team refused to go all out for a win, instead centring their innings around a lesser target which denied Australia the bonus point they needed to qualify ahead of New Zealand. Pollock insisted that his team had initially tried to win and that the South Africans' aim was simply to set up a final series against opponents they had beaten in 14 of their previous 16 encounters. Given a choice and with a winner-take-all purse of $50,000 at stake, why would you want to win the final qualifier if it meant walking into another showdown with the world champions?

Waugh called for an urgent review so such distasteful events could be avoided at the 2002-03 World Cup, but Fleming said he would exploit the rules again if similar circumstances arose. Ruthless it may be, but others would certainly have done the same. Fleming's justification was to see the Black Caps into the finals. While Australians around the country voiced their protests, some New Zealand fans called it their revenge after the infamous underarm incident 21 years before, which had triggered so much condemnation on both sides of the Tasman.

The International Cricket Council said it did not condone teams pulling up in the home straight. However, it ruled out an investigation, saying the events were merely "unfortunate". ICC chairman Malcolm Gray said the manipulation of matches was an embarrassment to the game and particularly damning given the recent match-fixing furore. "The more you introduce artificial rules to a competition, the more chance there is to have contrived, unusual or even silly results," he said.

Geoff Prenter, ING's sponsorship manager and creator of the bonus points system, said it worked best in a six-team competition. He said the system that rewarded teams for winning a match inside 40 overs rather than 50 had enlivened the Australian domestic limited-overs competition since its introduction in 2000-01. It was at Prenter's suggestion, too, that fast bowlers were again permitted to bowl one bouncer per over without fear of being no-balled. While scores fell, it meant a far more even battle between batsman and bowler, especially on the bouncier wickets in Melbourne and Perth.

It was a pity that controversy about the tournament's playing conditions briefly overshadowed the spectacular cricket that had been played. From a rousing Chris Cairns onslaught one Saturday night in Brisbane to the miracle of the MCG and Michael Bevan's once-in-a-lifetime century, there were some dazzling moments. The New Zealanders unearthed an exciting new express bowler in Christchurch policeman and part-time cricketer Shane Bond, whose 21 wickets gave him the Player of the Series award. Jonty Rhodes and Mark Boucher were consistent match-winners in South Africa's lower middle order, hitting boldly and running like whippets.

A big-hitting Pollock created a new Australian limited-overs international high when he clubbed 27 runs from an over from New Zealand left-armer James Franklin in Perth. Two days later it was Allan Donald's turn to feel the heat as his ninth over went for 27, including 26 to Brett Lee, whose thumping straight hits threatened the safety of those camped under the sun tarpaulin at the front of the Farley Stand.

South Africa were the leading qualifiers with 18 points, from New Zealand and Australia, each with 17, New Zealand qualifying ahead of the Australians given their 3-1 record in head-to-head clashes. Their run-rate, however, was marginally inferior to Australia's. In the disappointingly lacklustre final series, New Zealand caved in, South Africa winning by eight wickets in Melbourne and by six in Sydney.

The Australian Cricket Board said Australia's failure to make the finals for only the third time in the competition's 23 years did not affect the series finances, which after a succession of Australia-wide sell-outs had already well exceeded budget. Even without the Australians in the finals, the overall summer takings were a record $15.1 million and the international match attendances 890,000 – more than 70,000 above 1997-98, when South Africa and New Zealand last toured. A record Brisbane limited-overs international crowd of 35,761 cemented the Gabba's standing as one of the premier stadiums in the country.

In front of a succession of vibrant crowds, who in the first match in Melbourne behaved so badly that the scheduling of future limited-overs matches at the MCG was questioned, the Australians lost their first three games and never recovered. The Waugh twins batted from memory and Shane Warne's leg-breaks were treated with relative disdain. Steve Waugh passed 50 only once, and after an indifferent Test summer was under increasing pressure to justify his place. After the series, and a spectacularly successful career as Australia's limited-overs captain, he was told that he would not be selected in the limited-overs squad for South Africa. Given his standing as arguably the most respected Australian cricketer since Don Bradman, it was a huge story. Suddenly the bonus points issue didn't seem quite as important.

AUSTRALIA – BATTING

	M	I	NO	R	HS	100s	50s	Avge	C/S	S-R
M.G. Bevan	7	6	1	251	102*	1	1	50.20	3	74.48
R.J. Campbell......	1	1	0	38	38	0	0	38.00	2/1	73.08
D.R. Martyn	8	8	2	226	104*	1	0	37.67	2	63.13
R.T. Ponting	8	8	0	254	80	0	2	31.75	3	77.44
S.R. Waugh	8	7	1	187	62	0	1	31.17	3	69.00
J.N. Gillespie	5	3	2	29	15	0	0	29.00	0	60.42
M.E. Waugh........	7	7	1	126	55*	0	1	21.00	3	70.79
B. Lee	5	5	1	79	51*	0	1	19.75	0	101.28
A.J. Bichel	6	3	1	37	17	0	0	18.50	3	75.51
A.C. Gilchrist.......	7	6	0	97	31	0	0	16.17	14/1	97.98
S.K. Warne........	8	6	0	72	29	0	0	12.00	2	56.69
M.L. Hayden	2	2	0	20	10	0	0	10.00	1	38.46
I.J. Harvey	3	3	0	23	12	0	0	7.67	1	48.94
G.D. McGrath	7	3	1	14	7	0	0	7.00	0	50.00
A. Symonds	4	3	0	14	11	0	0	4.67	4	66.67
D.S. Lehmann	1	1	1	49	49*	0	0	–	0	106.52
B.A. Williams	1	1	1	13	13*	0	0	–	0	59.09

Denotes not out.

BOWLING

	O	M	R	W	BB	5W/i	Avge
D.S. Lehmann	5	0	28	2	2/28	0	14.00
G.D. McGrath	69.4	10	226	14	4/30	0	16.14
D.R. Martyn............	3	0	20	1	1/20	0	20.00
M.E. Waugh............	11	0	46	2	2/38	0	23.00
A.J. Bichel	46.3	2	206	8	5/19	1	25.75
B. Lee	45.3	4	223	8	3/43	0	27.88
J.N. Gillespie	49	6	183	6	2/28	0	30.50
I.J. Harvey	30	1	134	4	2/40	0	33.50
A. Symonds	27	0	126	3	3/48	0	42.00
S.K. Warne.............	75	4	324	6	2/65	0	54.00
S.R. Waugh	10	0	59	0	–	0	–
B.A. Williams	10	2	31	0	–	0	–
M.G. Bevan	4	0	27	0	–	0	–

NEW ZEALAND – BATTING

	M	I	NO	R	HS	100s	50s	Avge	C/S	S-R
C.L. Cairns........	9	9	2	314	102*	1	2	44.86	2	93.18
C.Z. Harris	10	10	4	240	63*	0	1	40.00	6	63.49
S.P. Fleming.......	9	9	0	309	85	0	3	34.33	5	65.61
C.D. McMillan.....	10	10	0	275	73	0	1	27.50	2	76.18
L. Vincent	10	10	0	225	55	0	1	22.50	5	58.14
N.J. Astle	6	6	0	122	95	0	1	20.33	4	62.89
A.C. Parore	10	9	3	109	36*	0	0	18.17	16	64.12
B.B. McCullum	4	4	0	71	37	0	0	17.75	1	55.04
S.B. Styris	4	4	0	64	23	0	0	16.00	1	64.00
D.L. Vettori	10	8	3	61	30	0	0	12.20	0	49.96
D.J. Nash	4	3	0	45	24	0	0	15.00	1	78.95
M.H. Richardson ...	4	4	0	42	26	0	0	10.50	1	43.30
A.R. Adams	4	4	1	37	13*	0	0	12.33	1	115.63
S.E. Bond.........	9	4	2	32	17*	0	0	16.00	2	76.19
J.E.C. Franklin.....	7	5	1	18	9*	0	0	4.50	3	45.00

Denotes not out.

BOWLING

	O	M	R	W	BB	5W/i	Avge
S.E. Bond	82.2	10	344	21	5/25	1	16.38
D.J. Nash	28	1	124	6	3/37	0	20.67
C.L. Cairns	70	5	319	12	3/42	0	26.58
A.R. Adams	36	0	174	4	2/33	0	43.50
C.Z. Harris	82.3	0	371	8	3/37	0	46.38
J.E.C. Franklin	54	0	289	6	2/41	0	48.17
D.L. Vettori	83.1	1	368	7	2/36	0	52.57
S.B. Styris	13	0	74	0	–	0	–
C.D. McMillan	7	0	39	0	–	0	–
N.J. Astle	10	0	51	0	–	0	–

SOUTH AFRICA – BATTING

	M	I	NO	R	HS	100s	50s	Avge	C/S	S-R
J.N. Rhodes	10	9	3	345	107*	1	2	57.50	4	73.25
J.H. Kallis	8	8	2	322	104*	1	2	53.67	5	70.61
M.V. Boucher	10	9	3	246	58	0	3	41.00	12	102.07
H.H. Dippenaar	6	6	1	185	79*	0	1	37.00	3	61.46
H.H. Gibbs	10	10	0	293	89	0	1	29.30	6	69.10
G. Kirsten	10	10	0	265	97	0	1	26.50	4	63.25
S.M. Pollock	10	7	3	111	69*	0	1	27.75	4	130.59
N.D. McKenzie	6	6	0	150	68	0	1	25.00	1	63.56
L. Klusener	7	5	1	64	25*	0	0	16.00	4	98.46
S. Elworthy	3	3	1	29	18	0	0	14.50	0	61.70
N. Boje	8	2	1	14	13*	0	0	14.00	1	33.33
J.M. Kemp	3	2	1	11	10*	0	0	11.00	1	68.75
J.L. Ontong	2	1	0	4	4	0	0	4.00	4	44.44
C.K. Langeveldt	1	1	0	3	3	0	0	3.00	0	60.00
M. Ntini	9	2	1	2	2*	0	0	2.00	2	18.18
A.A. Donald	7	0	0	–	–	0	0		4	

Denotes not out.

BOWLING

	O	M	R	W	BB	5W/i	Avge
M. Ntini	81.2	7	338	14	5/31	1	24.14
A.A. Donald	65	5	301	12	3/29	0	25.08
S.M. Pollock	87.1	8	333	13	3/25	0	25.62
N. Boje	58	0	205	8	4/31	0	25.63
L. Klusener	44.4	0	238	9	2/27	0	26.44
J.H. Kallis	63.5	2	287	10	3/23	0	28.70
S. Elworthy	20	1	100	3	2/53	0	33.33
J.M. Kemp	19	0	99	2	2/50	0	49.50
J.L. Ontong	7	0	34	0	–	0	–
C.K. Langeveldt	5	-0	31	0	–	0	–

AUSTRALIA v NEW ZEALAND

At Melbourne Cricket Ground, Melbourne, January 11, 2002. Day/night game. New Zealand won by 23 runs. Toss: Australia. New Zealand 4 pts. Limited-overs international debuts: S.E. Bond, M.H. Richardson, B.A. Williams.

Without the injured Nathan Astle, their leading limited-overs batsman, New Zealand were a patched-up combination for the start of the VB Series. Sent in on a bouncy pitch used for the low-scoring Victoria versus New South Wales ING Cup match six days before, the New Zealanders were down and almost out at seven for 94 after a pace onslaught from Glenn McGrath, Brad Williams and Brett Lee. Steve Waugh set Test-type fields throughout, especially for Lee, who had the luxury of four slips and a gully as he netted three wickets in his first five high-speed overs, during which one of his deliveries was timed at 154.1 km/h. If the early batsmen were intimidated, Chris Harris at number seven showed more fight in a 70-run eighth-wicket stand with Daniel Vettori as, in the ABC radio box, debutant commentator Paul Reiffel noted that no New Zealand team ever rolled over and died. Unbeaten for two years at World Series level, the Australians started as if they had a party to attend, Shane Bond conceding 31 runs from his first three overs to Adam Gilchrist and Ricky Ponting as the run-rate rollicked along at six an over. In mid-innings there was an unseemly crowd disturbance and an eight-minute delay after a half-full plastic bottle landed near Mark Richardson at third man. More debris was thrown onto the ground and police made dozens of arrests and evicted many more. Seeking a bonus point, the Australians became careless and their innings faltered. Some brave off-side hitting by Williams was followed by the news that his thumb had been broken by a ball from Bond. With his teasing slow-medium deliveries Harris bottled up the scoring, and Bond and Chris Cairns cashed in at the other end, taking six wickets between them. The game finished acrimoniously when umpire Bob Parry gave Glenn McGrath out caught behind. So furious was McGrath's reaction that he received a one-match suspension from referee Hanumant Singh, and a further two-match suspended sentence was left hanging over his head should he transgress again during the tournament.

Man of the Match: C. Z. Harris.   *Attendance:* 46,687.

New Zealand

L. Vincent c S. R. Waugh b Lee	17	(37)	†A. C. Parore run out (Martyn/Lee)	3	(5)
M. H. Richardson c Gilchrist b McGrath	8	(14)	D. L. Vettori run out (Warne/Gilchrist)	30	(50)
*S. P. Fleming c M. E. Waugh b McGrath	1	(11)	J. E. C. Franklin not out	9	(22)
C. D. McMillan c Gilchrist b Lee	17	(28)	L-b 6, w 6, n-b 6	18	
C. L. Cairns c Ponting b Lee	10	(8)			
S. B. Styris c and b Harvey	23	(39)	(50 overs, 215 mins) (8 wkts)	199	
C. Z. Harris not out	63	(92)	Fall: 20 22 41 54 67 89 94 166		

S. E. Bond did not bat.

Bowling: McGrath 10-1-47-2; Williams 10-2-31-0; Lee 10-1-43-3; Harvey 10-1-35-1; Warne 10-0-37-0.

Australia

†A. C. Gilchrist c and b Cairns	23	(18)	B. Lee b Cairns	0	(5)
M. E. Waugh c Parore b Bond	1	(3)	B. A. Williams not out	13	(22)
R. T. Ponting c Franklin b Bond	45	(54)	G. D. McGrath c Parore b Vettori	7	(12)
M. G. Bevan c Franklin b Bond	27	(46)	B 1, w 3, n-b 9	13	
*S. R. Waugh run out (Vincent/Parore)	15	(28)			
D. R. Martyn lbw b Vettori	24	(49)	(42.0 overs)	176	
I. J. Harvey b Cairns	5	(12)	Fall: 5 63 98 104 135 142 150 151		
S. K. Warne b Harris	3	(12)	168 176		

Bowling: Bond 10-1-53-3; Franklin 5-0-27-0; Cairns 10-1-42-3; Vettori 10-1-36-2; Harris 7-0-17-1.

Umpires: D. B. Hair and R. L. Parry.
TV Umpire: R. G. Patterson.

AUSTRALIA v SOUTH AFRICA

At Melbourne Cricket Ground, Melbourne, January 13, 2002. Day/night game. South Africa won by four wickets. Toss: Australia. South Africa 4 pts.

The tournament favourites suffered their second defeat in a row as South Africa extended to five their unbeaten record in limited-overs internationals against the Australians at the MCG. In another low-scoring game in front of a bigger, but far better behaved, Melbourne crowd, the Australians again failed to bat out 50 overs and dropped key catches. While Steve Waugh top-scored with 62 he could easily have been given out caught behind at ten, umpire Steve Davis ruling against the most confident of appeals. After a modest Test series, Shaun Pollock returned to his best bowling form, dismissing Adam Gilchrist with the first ball of the match, while Jacques Kallis dismissed Waugh, Andrew Symonds (second ball) and Damien Martyn. It was the first time in four years under Waugh's captaincy that the Australians had failed to make 200 in consecutive innings. After reaching 50 in the ninth over in a free-flowing opening, the South Africans were always in control. Shane Warne exerted some pressure on the middle order before Symonds conceded 19 runs from two overs. Waugh had little option but to continue with him, given Ian Harvey's relegation to 12th man duties and Mark Waugh's absence under the team's controversial rotation policy. Jonty Rhodes' coolness under pressure and his judicious shot selection ensured victory with nine balls to spare.

Man of the Match: S. M. Pollock.   *Attendance:* 62,136.

Australia

†A.C. Gilchrist c Donald b Pollock	..	0	(1)	B. Lee c Rhodes b Donald 0 (4)
M.L. Hayden c Klusener b Pollock	...	10	(18)	A.J. Bichel lbw b Pollock 17 (15)
R.T. Ponting run out (Rhodes)	......	51	(75)	J.N. Gillespie not out 1 (3)
M.G. Bevan run out (Ntini)	....	10	(32)	L-b 6, w 6 12
*S.R. Waugh b Kallis	....	62	(86)	—
D.R. Martyn c McKenzie b Kallis	...	31	(46)	(48.5 overs, 212 mins) 198
A. Symonds c Gibbs b Kallis	....	0	(2)	Fall: 0 39 64 106 164 164 170 171
S.K. Warne c Pollock b Klusener	....	4	(11)	196 198

Bowling: Pollock 9–1–25–3; Donald 10–0–54–1; Kallis 9.5–1–30–3; Ntini 10–0–31–0; Klusener 7–0–33–1; Boje 3–0–19–0.

South Africa

H.H. Gibbs c Gilchrist b Gillespie	...	38	(51)	†M.V. Boucher c Symonds b Lee ... 11 (15)
G. Kirsten c Gilchrist b Bichel	....	22	(26)	*S.M. Pollock not out 5 (4)
J.H. Kallis c Gilchrist b Gillespie	....	6	(22)	B 2, l-b 12, w 4, n-b 4 22
N.D. McKenzie c Symonds b Warne	..	34	(59)	—
J.N. Rhodes not out	....	43	(101)	(48.3 overs, 221 mins) (6 wkts) 199
L. Klusener c Gilchrist b Lee	....	18	(17)	Fall: 51 66 71 136 169 187

N. Boje, A. A. Donald and M. Ntini did not bat.

Bowling: Lee 9.3–1–42–2; Gillespie 10–3–28–2; Bichel 10–1–45–1; Warne 10–1–19–1; Symonds 7–0–41–0; Bevan 2–0–10–0.

Umpires: S.J. Davis and S.J.A. Taufel.
TV Umpire: R.L. Parry.

NEW ZEALAND v SOUTH AFRICA

At Bellerive Oval, Hobart, January 15, 2002. South Africa won by 26 runs. Toss: South Africa. South Africa 4 pts.

The momentum swung South Africa's way in the final overs of their innings thanks to wicket-keeper Mark Boucher. After being given not out by umpire Daryl Harper despite apparently scooping a full toss straight back to Chris Cairns in the 49th over, Boucher scored 19 off the final over, bowled by Shane Bond, including a six that struck the windows of the AGC Pavilion beyond mid-wicket. Another vibrant start, this time 82 from the first 15 overs by Herschelle Gibbs and Gary Kirsten, set up an imposing target of 257 which was built around Kirsten's unflustered contribution. The fielding highlight was the outfield catch by Craig McMillan at fine leg to dismiss Boeta Dippenaar, when he ran 15 metres at top pace, dived and took the ball two-handed just centimetres off the ground. Needing five an over, the New Zealanders played bravely, Stephen Fleming top-scoring with 85 after calling for an arm-guard when shaken by the bounce generated by Makhaya Ntini. McMillan gave him competent support but the loss of seven wickets for 50 slowly accumulated runs put the match beyond reach, although Bond hit two late sixes to deny South Africa a bonus point and gain some revenge for the pasting he had taken earlier.

Man of the Match: G. Kirsten.   *Attendance:* 5,963.

South Africa

H. H. Gibbs c Fleming b Vettori	36	(46)	*S. M. Pollock run out (Styris)	0	(1)
G. Kirsten run out (Harris)	97	(118)	J. M. Kemp not out	10	(12)
H. H. Dippenaar c McMillan b Bond	37	(55)			
J. N. Rhodes c Harris b Cairns	13	(14)	L-b 3, w 1, n-b 3 7		
N. D. McKenzie c Fleming b Franklin	22	(27)			
L. Klusener b Vettori	5	(11)	(50 overs, 204 mins) (7 wkts) 257		
†M. V. Boucher not out	30	(19)	Fall: 82 157 178 194 215 217 217		

A. A. Donald and M. Ntini did not bat.

Bowling: Bond 10–0–64–1; Franklin 8–0–42–1; Cairns 10–0–54–1; Vettori 10–0–37–2; Harris 10–0–43–0; Styris 2–0–14–0.

New Zealand

L. Vincent c Pollock b Ntini	23	(45)	D. L. Vettori c Kirsten b Donald	0	(2)
M. H. Richardson c Klusener b Donald	8	(10)	J. E. C. Franklin c Boucher b Donald	2	(7)
*S. P. Fleming c Dippenaar b Klusener	85	(112)	S. E. Bond not out	17	(12)
C. D. McMillan c Gibbs b Kemp	36	(46)			
C. L. Cairns b Ntini	11	(16)	B 3, l-b 8, w 5, n-b 1 17		
S. B. Styris c Boucher b Klusener	9	(6)			
C. Z. Harris c Dippenaar b Kemp	2	(11)	(50 overs) (9 wkts) 231		
†A. C. Parore not out	21	(32)	Fall: 10 71 152 170 181 183 192 196 202		

Bowling: Pollock 10–1–38–0; Donald 10–1–40–3; Ntini 10–0–36–2; Kemp 10–0–50–2; Klusener 10–0–56–2.

Umpires: S. J. Davis and D. J. Harper.
TV Umpire: J. H. Smeaton.

AUSTRALIA v NEW ZEALAND

At Sydney Cricket Ground, Sydney, January 17, 2002. Day/night game. New Zealand won by 23 runs. Toss: New Zealand. New Zealand 4 pts. Limited-overs international debuts: R.J. Campbell, B.B. McCullum.

The Australians were unbackable favourites to win, especially with Stephen Fleming's last-minute withdrawal after being struck on the elbow during the pre-game warm-up. The Australians named 29-year-old Western Australian Ryan Campbell for his debut, allowing Adam Gilchrist to fly home to Perth and spend time with his wife and their newborn son. Former New Zealand Under-19s captain Brendon McCullum was named for his debut game. Glenn McGrath made a timely return, consistently beating the bat and moving the ball off the seam. Dean Jones, called in to the New Zealand camp as an adviser, had recommended that the New Zealand batsmen remain patient against McGrath and bat aggressively against the rest. While Shane Warne took a wicket in his first over, he also conceded nine runs, and 65 in all in a wayward display. Chris Harris once again top-scored, his resourceful improvisation allowing the New Zealanders to set an imposing target after their slow start. After Australia had drawn a one-over penalty because of their slow over-rate, Campbell made a good start to his international career, but Steve Waugh was out to an acrobatic two-handed catch at gully by Harris. The last six Australian wickets tumbled for 38 after Chris Cairns, in his first game as acting captain, removed Michael Bevan. A fingertip deflection then caught Damien Martyn backing up too far at the bowler's end, and Harris continued to put his stamp on the match by completing the rout. It was the first time in four years Australia had lost three limited-overs internationals in a row.

Man of the Match: C.Z. Harris.   *Attendance:* 39,602.

New Zealand

M.H. Richardson st Campbell b Warne	26	(71)	†A.C. Parore c M.E. Waugh b Warne	18	(11)
B.B. McCullum run out (Lee)	5	(15)	D.L. Vettori c Campbell b Lee	2	(7)
L. Vincent c Ponting b Harvey	24	(45)	J.E.C. Franklin run out (Lee)	5	(6)
C.D. McMillan c Campbell b Martyn	39	(45)	B 2, l-b 18, w 3	23	
*C.L. Cairns c S.R. Waugh b Gillespie	31	(29)		
S.B. Styris c Bevan b Harvey	20	(28)	(50 overs, 213 mins) (9 wkts)	235	
C.Z. Harris not out	42	(43)	Fall: 13 54 74 135 137 182 210 216 235	

S.E. Bond did not bat.

Bowling: McGrath 10–2–22–0; Gillespie 10–0–28–1; Harvey 10–0–40–2; Lee 8–1–40–1; Warne 9–0–65–2; Martyn 3–0–20–1.

Australia

M.E. Waugh run out (Vincent)	0	(7)	B. Lee lbw b Franklin	1	(4)
†R.J. Campbell c Harris b Vettori	38	(52)	J.N. Gillespie not out	13	(18)
R.T. Ponting c Parore b Bond	11	(17)	G.D. McGrath c Vincent b Harris	1	(3)
M.G. Bevan c Styris b Cairns	66	(98)	L-b 7, w 18, n-b 4	29	
*S.R. Waugh c Harris b Bond	9	(17)		
D.R. Martyn c Harris (Cairns)	24	(42)	(47.2 overs, 208 mins)	212	
I.J. Harvey c Vincent b Harris	6	(15)	Fall: 1 29 98 118 174 178 181	
S.K. Warne c Richardson b Harris	14	(15)	188 203 212	

Bowling: Bond 8–1–28–2; Franklin 9–0–46–1; Cairns 9–2–32–1; Vettori 10–0–45–1; Harris 8.2–0–37–3; Styris 3–0–17–0.

Umpires: R.L. Parry and S.J.A. Taufel.
TV Umpire: D.B. Hair.

NEW ZEALAND v SOUTH AFRICA

At Brisbane Cricket Ground, Brisbane, January 19, 2002. Day/night game. New Zealand won by four wickets. Toss: South Africa. New Zealand 4 pts.

Chris Cairns inspired one of the great limited-overs escapes with an unbeaten century from 99 balls as New Zealand accelerated to an astonishing four-wicket victory. Set 242 on the truest batting wicket of the tournament, the New Zealanders were five for 98 and seemingly out of contention before Cairns' remarkable rescue mission. Armed with his extra-long, multi-gripped bat known as "The Monster", he wrested the match from South Africa's grip with some ferocious hitting. A steadying sixth-wicket partnership of 62 from 82 balls prepared the way for the final assault in which Adam Parore fed him the strike during an unfinished stand of 84 from 73 balls, Cairns maintained his composure, ultimately smashing nine fours and three sixes. He finished the game with a thumping drive past extra cover to Shaun Pollock's first delivery of the 50th over, and raised his bat in response to the applause of a record crowd at the Gabba for a game not involving Australia. Earlier, the South Africans had begun and finished badly, Herschelle Gibbs being bowled by the first ball of the match, and then losing their last five wickets for 10 runs in 24 balls. In between, a century partnership for the second wicket between Gary Kirsten and Jacques Kallis and a sprightly 73 for the fifth wicket between Jonty Rhodes and Mark Boucher provided some substance for the innings. Shane Bond again impressed with his best figures in a limited-overs international.

Man of the Match: C.L. Cairns.   *Attendance:* 17,457.

South Africa

H.H. Gibbs b Franklin	0	(1)
G. Kirsten c and b Harris	43	(63)
J.H. Kallis c Vincent b Bond	65	(68)
J.N. Rhodes c Harris b Cairns	44	(54)
H.H. Dippenaar run out (Bond)	7	(14)
†M.V. Boucher c Franklin b Bond	51	(57)
*S.M. Pollock c Parore b Franklin	15	(16)
J.M. Kemp c Parore b Cairns	1	(4)
J.L. Ontong c McMillan b Bond	4	(9)
S. Elworthy c Cairns b Bond	0	(1)
M. Ntini not out	2	(5)
L-b 6, w 2, n-b 1	9	
(48.3 overs, 192 mins)	241	

Fall: 0 115 115 131 204 231 234
      236 237 241

Bowling: Franklin 8–0–41–2; Bond 9.3–0–37–4; Cairns 10–0–44–2; Vettori 10–0–58–0; Harris 10–0–45–1; McMillan 1–0–10–0.

New Zealand

M.H. Richardson c Ontong b Pollock	0	(2)
B.B. McCullum c Kallis b Ntini	37	(64)
L. Vincent c Boucher b Pollock	9	(22)
*S.P. Fleming c Ontong b Kallis	23	(22)
C.D. McMillan c Pollock b Kallis	6	(14)
C.L. Cairns not out	102	(99)
C.Z. Harris lbw b Elworthy	24	(42)
†A.C. Parore not out	21	(32)
L-b 8, w 8, n-b 6	22	
(49.1 overs, 203 mins) (6 wkts)	244	

Fall: 0 31 71 73 98 160

D.L. Vettori, J.E.C. Franklin and S.E. Bond did not bat.

Bowling: Pollock 9.1–2–29–2; Elworthy 10–0–47–1; Ntini 8–0–46–1; Kallis 10–0–57–2; Ontong 5–0–26–0; Kemp 7–0–31–0.

Umpires: S.J. Davis and D.B. Hair.
TV Umpire: P.D. Parker.

AUSTRALIA v SOUTH AFRICA

At Brisbane Cricket Ground, Brisbane, January 20, 2002. Day/night game. Australia won by 27 runs. Toss: Australia. Australia 4 pts.

Two hours of exhilarating batting from Ricky Ponting and Damien Martyn ensured Australia's first win of the tournament. By adding 171 for the third wicket in front of the biggest Gabba cricket crowd since the stadium was redeveloped two years earlier, the pair lifted Australia to almost five runs an over, an imposing target even on the best limited-overs wicket of the summer. Martyn was elevated to number four in place of Michael Bevan who was rested, his third limited-overs international century coming from117 balls. The driving of both batsmen was powerful and stylish, while their agile running between the wickets put constant pressure on the field. Glenn McGrath defied the batting-friendly conditions to take two wickets in his first seven-over spell for just 20 runs. While Neil McKenzie showed his best form since the Tests, others squandered starts or needlessly forfeited their wickets as the run-rate target ballooned. Andrew Symonds' sharp return catch from Mark Boucher was one of the best of the season. From a relatively comfortable four for 150 in the 35th over the Proteas lost their last six for 64 and were bundled out in the 49th over.

Man of the Match: D.R. Martyn.   *Attendance:* 35,761.

Australia

M.E. Waugh c Boucher b Elworthy	..	15	(30)	*S.R. Waugh not out 22 (19)	
M.L. Hayden c Kirsten b Elworthy	...	10	(34)	W 2, n-b 5 7	
R.T. Ponting c Gibbs b Klusener	.....	80	(95)		
D.R. Martyn not out		104	(121)	(50 overs, 196 mins) (4 wkts) 241	
A. Symonds c Rhodes b Boje	....	3	(6)	Fall: 25 29 200 205	

†A.C. Gilchrist, S.K. Warne, A.J. Bichel, J.N. Gillespie and G.D. McGrath did not bat.

Bowling: Pollock 10–1–28–0; Elworthy 10–1–53–2; Langeveldt 5–0–31–0; Kallis 7–0–38–0; Klusener 8–0–43–1; Boje 10–0–43–1.

South Africa

H.H. Gibbs c Bichel b McGrath	.....	18	(22)	N. Boje b McGrath 1 (6)	
G. Kirsten c Gilchrist b McGrath	....	22	(40)	S. Elworthy not out 11 (11)	
J.H. Kallis lbw b Gillespie	....	37	(55)	C.K. Langeveldt b McGrath 3 (5)	
N.D. McKenzie c Gilchrist b Gillespie		68	(85)		
J.N. Rhodes c Gilchrist b Symonds	...	2	(9)	L-b 1, w 6, n-b 1 8	
†M.V. Boucher c and b Symonds	....	10	(17)		
*S.M. Pollock c Hayden b Symonds	..	18	(26)	(48.4 overs, 202 mins) 214	
L. Klusener b Bichel	....	16	(17)	Fall: 34 49 126 135 153 175 191 199 204 214	

Bowling: McGrath 9.4–0–30–4; Gillespie 10–1–60–2; Bichel 9–1–27–1; Warne 10–1–48–0; Symonds 10–0–48–3.

Umpires: D.J. Harper and S.J.A. Taufel.
TV Umpire: P.D. Parker.

AUSTRALIA v SOUTH AFRICA

At Sydney Cricket Ground, Sydney, January 22, 2002. Day/night game. Australia won by eight wickets. Toss: South Africa. Australia 5 pts.

Even the loss of 41 minutes to rain early in the South African innings could not produce a post-dinner session of more than 10.4 overs. The absence of South Africa's best player, Jacques Kallis, with an ankle injury proved crucial in humid conditions. Six of the South Africans were out without scoring, equalling Pakistan's record, against

England at Edgbaston in 1987 and against West Indies at Cape Town in 1992-93, only Gary Kirsten having both the technique and the toughness to survive for long. In contrast, the effervescence of Mark Waugh and Ricky Ponting enabled Australia to scamper to victory in the 19th over. Enjoying the steepling bounce, Andy Bichel returned his best figures for Australia, while Glenn McGrath's three wickets included Herschelle Gibbs to the second ball of the match. He also sent Steve Elworthy to hospital after the retreating tailender was hit on the side of the helmet by a bouncer. Shaun Pollock later said that he should not have elected to bat first, admitting that he had misread the conditions. After the match Steve Waugh found himself embroiled in controversy and accused of callousness. When Pollock was asked in his media conference about Elworthy's condition, Waugh had murmured to an ACB staffer: "And I bet they didn't find a brain either." The quip was overheard and reported by the South African press.

Man of the Match: A.J. Bichel.   *Attendance:* 39,127.

South Africa

H.H. Gibbs c Gilchrist b McGrath	...	0	(2)	N. Boje not out	13	(36)
G. Kirsten lbw b Warne		44	(77)	S. Elworthy c S.R. Waugh b McGrath	18	(35)
H.H. Dippenaar c Warne b McGrath		0	(6)	M. Ntini c and b Bichel	0	(6)
N.D. McKenzie b Bichel		18	(47)			
J.N. Rhodes c Gilchrist b Bichel		0	(7)	L-b 3, w 9	12	
†M.V. Boucher lbw b Bichel		1	(11)			
*S.M. Pollock lbw b Bichel		0	(2)	(38.3 overs, 161 mins)	106	
L. Klusener lbw b Gillespie		0	(2)	Fall: 1 5 42 44 49 49 50 79 103 106		

Bowling: McGrath 10–1–29–3; Gillespie 9–1–27–1; Symonds 4–0–7–0; Bichel 6.3–1–19–5; Warne 6–1–13–1; M.E. Waugh 3–0–8–0.

Australia

M.E. Waugh not out		55	(62)	L-b 1, w 1, n-b 3	5	
†A.C. Gilchrist b Pollock		8	(13)			
R.T. Ponting b Klusener		33	(37)	(18.4 overs, 78 mins) (2 wkts)	107	
D.R. Martyn not out		6	(3)	Fall: 24 101		

*S.R. Waugh, M.G. Bevan, A. Symonds, S.K. Warne, A.J. Bichel, J.N. Gillespie and G.D. McGrath did not bat.

Bowling: Pollock 7–0–36–1; Ntini 7–2–36–0; Klusener 2.4–0–28–1; Boje 2–0–6–0.

Umpires: D.B. Hair and D.J. Harper.
TV Umpire: S.J.A. Taufel.

AUSTRALIA v NEW ZEALAND

At Adelaide Oval, Adelaide, January 26, 2002. Day/night game. New Zealand won by 77 runs. Toss: New Zealand. New Zealand 5 pts.

Another withering burst from Shane Bond enabled tournament pacesetters New Zealand to win their fourth match out of five and their third game in a row against the Australians. They fully earned the bonus point from their comfortable victory. Having recovered from a broken bone in his wrist, Nathan Astle made an immediate impact, his quickfire 95 at the head of the order allowing him to surpass Martin Crowe as New Zealand's most prolific limited-overs international batsman. His second-wicket partnership of 128 with Lou Vincent followed Brendon McCullum's departure to the first ball of the game. Chris Cairns' three sixes and a four in 23 balls saw the New Zealanders score 52 runs from the final six overs. Then, in one of the best spells of the summer, during which one of his deliveries was clocked at 151 km/h, Bond dismissed Adam Gilchrist, Ricky Ponting and Damien Martyn on his way to figures of three for eight from his first three overs. Complete humiliation was averted by Steve Waugh and Michael Bevan but in the end the Australians were lucky to make even 165. Bond's 5/25 underlined his status as the find of the season. For a player who had only returned to cricket 12 months earlier after a year working full-time in the police force it was a stunning performance, especially as he had only made it to Australia as a reinforcement for the injured Dion Nash.

Man of the Match: S.E. Bond.   *Attendance:* 28,011.

New Zealand

B.B. McCullum c Gilchrist b McGrath	0	(3)
N.J. Astle b McGrath	95	(135)
L. Vincent c Symonds b M.E. Waugh	55	(83)
C.D. McMillan c and b M.E. Waugh	8	(16)
*S.P. Fleming st Gilchrist b Warne	13	(19)
C.L. Cairns not out	39	(23)
C.Z. Harris not out	19	(21)
L-b 8, w 5	13	
(50 overs, 203 mins) (5 wkts)	242	
Fall: 0 128 152 176 197		

†A.C. Parore, D.J. Nash, D.L. Vettori and S.E. Bond did not bat.

Bowling: McGrath 10–3–36–2; Gillespie 10–1–40–0; Warne 10–1–33–1; Bichel 6–0–57–0; Symonds 6–0–30–0; M.E. Waugh 8–0–38–2.

Australia

†A.C. Gilchrist b Bond	21	(19)
M.E. Waugh c and b Nash	0	(5)
R.T. Ponting c Parore b Bond	0	(2)
D.R. Martyn c Vincent b Bond	2	(15)
*S.R. Waugh c Fleming b Vettori	30	(58)
M.G. Bevan c Bond b Harris	45	(62)
A. Symonds c McCullum b Harris	11	(13)
S.K. Warne c Parore b Cairns	22	(32)
A.J. Bichel c Astle b Bond	7	(29)
J.N. Gillespie b Bond	15	(27)
G.D. McGrath not out	6	(13)
L-b 1, w 2, n-b 3	6	
(45.2 overs, 189 mins)	165	
Fall: 7 8 25 26 97 106 114 139		
154 165		

Bowling: Nash 8–1–31–1; Bond 9.2–2–25–5; Cairns 6–0–19–1; Vettori 10–0–44–1; Astle 2–0–10–0; Harris 10–0–35–2.

Umpires: S.J. Davis and S.J.A. Taufel.
TV Umpire: D.J. Harper.

NEW ZEALAND v SOUTH AFRICA

At Adelaide Oval, Adelaide, January 27, 2002. Day/night game. South Africa won by 93 runs. Toss: South Africa. South Africa 5 pts.

New Zealand saw their runaway lead in the series reduced to just four points as South Africa convincingly ended a three-match losing streak. After Herschelle Gibbs had made a solid 89, an 86-run partnership from just 45 balls between Jonty Rhodes and Mark Boucher allowed the Proteas to set a target in excess of five runs an over. Boucher's 50 came from only 27 balls with three fours and two sixes, the fastest fifty in the competition since New Zealander Lance Cairns' 21-ball half-century against the Australians at the MCG 20 years previously. From their last ten overs, South Africa scored an astonishing 111 runs in the batting blitz of the summer. Despite losing Nathan Astle to the first ball of the innings, sensible batting took the New Zealand total past the 100 in the 29th over for the loss of only two wickets. Nicky Boje then slowed the scoring and cut down the dangerous middle order on a pitch which was increasingly friendly to his spin. The bonus point allowed South Africa to move into second position on the table with 13 points, four behind New Zealand and four ahead of Australia.

Man of the Match: M.V. Boucher.   *Attendance:* 10,889.

South Africa

H. H. Gibbs b Cairns	89 (132)		*S. M. Pollock not out	4 (2)
G. Kirsten c Parore b Bond	0 (8)			
J. H. Kallis c Parore b Cairns	30 (57)		B 2, l-b 6, w 5	13
N. D. McKenzie c Parore b Vettori	5 (15)			
J. N. Rhodes c Fleming b Franklin	55 (54)		(50 overs, 188 mins)	(5 wkts) 253
†M. V. Boucher not out	57 (32)		Fall: 9 74 93 156 242	

J. L. Ontong, N. Boje, M. Ntini and A. A. Donald did not bat.

Bowling: Franklin 10–0–39–1; Bond 10–0–47–1; Cairns 10–0–69–2; Vettori 10–0–34–1; Harris 10–0–56–0.

New Zealand

B. B. McCullum lbw b Kallis	29 (47)		D. L. Vettori c Ontong b Boje	0 (2)
N. J. Astle c Boucher b Pollock	0 (1)		J. E. C. Franklin lbw b Donald	2 (4)
L. Vincent c Donald b Pollock	20 (41)		S. E. Bond c Donald b Ntini	9 (13)
*S. P. Fleming c Gibbs b Donald	43 (80)		B 3, l-b 7, w 4, n-b 2	16
C. D. McMillan c Ontong b Boje	16 (34)			
C. L. Cairns c Rhodes b Boje	9 (20)		(45.2 overs, 192 mins)	160
C. Z. Harris not out	9 (22)		Fall: 1 37 59 102 130 134 145	
†A. C. Parore b Boje	7 (9)		145 148 160	

Bowling: Pollock 8–0–24–2; Ntini 9.2–1–32–1; Kallis 6–0–18–1; Donald 10–0–37–2; Boje 10–0–31–4; Ontong 2–0–8–0.

Umpires: D. J. Harper and R. L. Parry.
TV Umpire: S. J. Davis.

AUSTRALIA v NEW ZEALAND

At Melbourne Cricket Ground, Melbourne, January 29, 2002. Day/night game. Australia won by two wickets. Toss: New Zealand. Australia 4 pts.

Michael Bevan produced one of the consummate innings of his illustrious limited-overs international career to lead a memorable Australian revival against tournament leaders New Zealand after the visitors had made all the running. Shane Warne's first over cost 19 runs, and at one point the inventive Craig McMillan faced up to him with an impudent, ever-so-open stance and glanced the delivery for three. Such was Australia's need for variety that for the first time in ten months Steve Waugh used himself as a bowler. Coming into the match with a back strain, Chris Cairns had played as a specialist batsman, but the New Zealand attack, led by the irresistible Shane Bond, was undaunted. Damien Martyn took 15 balls to score a run and was so hamstrung by Stephen Fleming's inventive field placings – five men being spread in zig-zag fashion between gully and short cover – that he soon offered a gully catch from the bowling of Andre Adams, another young New Zealander to be blooded against the Australians. At six for 82 in the 22nd over, Warne joined Bevan in adding 58 in 15 overs before Warne was out hooking. With 11 overs left, 88 were still needed, but when the 40th over from Harris produced 14, Fleming for the first time showed genuine concern. On the wide-open expanses, he was unable to get the fleet-footed Bevan off strike, Bevan consistently taking on the outfielders and running a string of twos. With Brett Lee unleashing his trademark drives and scoring at a run a ball, the Australians crept to within 22 of victory before Lee's dismissal in the 48th over, the pair having added 81 from 66 balls. Just 16 runs were needed from two overs. Fleming took minutes to rearrange his field, and the game went well over time. Entrusted with the second-last over, Adams was struck for four twos in a row and another two from his sixth delivery as Bevan reached his epic century, from just 93 balls. Fleming had no option but to bring the field up, but two Andy Bichel square cuts ended the match to allow Australia an apparently improbable victory with three balls to spare. Fleming's report on a charge of dissent and Daniel Vettori's whiplash and mild concussion after he fell while attempting a catch at third man further darkened New Zealand's night.

Man of the Match: M.G. Bevan.   *Attendance:* 40,065.

New Zealand

L. Vincent c Gilchrist b McGrath	....	5	(14)	†A.C. Parore lbw b McGrath	1 (3)
N.J. Astle c Warne b Lee		11	(15)	A.R. Adams not out	13 (6)
*S.P. Fleming run out				D.L. Vettori not out	0 (0)
(SR Waugh/Warne)	..	50	(94)		
C.D. McMillan c Ponting b Harvey	..	34	(34)	L-b 4, w 4, n-b 3	11
C.L. Cairns c Bevan b Warne		55	(63)		
C.Z. Harris run out (Warne/Harvey)	..	41	(54)	(50 overs, 206 mins) (8 wkts)	245
D.J. Nash run out (Harvey)		24	(20)	Fall: 7 19 73 143 178 226 228 235	

S.E. Bond did not bat.

Bowling: McGrath 10–0–41–2; Lee 8–0–32–1; Bichel 6–0–20–0; Warne 10–0–56–1; Harvey 10–0–59–1; S.R. Waugh 6–0–33–0.

Australia

M.E. Waugh c Adams b Nash		21	(36)	S.K. Warne c Bond b Adams	29 (54)
†A.C. Gilchrist b Bond		14	(8)	B. Lee c Astle b Bond	27 (29)
R.T. Ponting c Astle b Bond		8	(17)	A.J. Bichel not out	13 (5)
D.R. Martyn c Harris b Adams		6	(28)	W 3, n-b 6	9
*S.R. Waugh c Parore b Nash		7	(11)		
M.G. Bevan not out		102	(95)	(49.3 overs, 233 mins) (8 wkts)	248
I.J. Harvey c Parore b Bond		12	(20)	Fall: 24 40 51 53 65 82 143 224	

G.D. McGrath did not bat.

Bowling: Nash 9–0–50–2; Bond 9.3–2–38–4; Adams 10–0–52–2; Vettori 10–0–36–0; Harris 8–0–50–0; Astle 3–0–22–0.

Umpires: D.B. Hair and S.J.A. Taufel.
TV Umpire: R.G. Patterson.

NEW ZEALAND v SOUTH AFRICA

At WACA Ground, Perth, February 1, 2002. Day/night game. South Africa won by 67 runs. Toss: New Zealand. South Africa 5 pts.

Having lost four for 35 in the first 12 overs, South Africa made a remarkable recovery on a whitish WACA pitch and fast outfield which offered full value for the shot-makers. Jonty Rhodes, with an unbeaten 107 from 135 balls, was pivotal in the revival. The absence of injured bowlers Chris Cairns and Shane Bond proved costly as Rhodes, Mark Boucher and Shaun Pollock knocked 105 runs off the last ten overs. During Pollock's onslaught he took a record 27 runs (2, 6, 6, 6, 6, 1) from the 50th over, delivered by James Franklin. Previously Rod Marsh and Ian Botham had jointly held the Australian limited-overs international record with 26 from an over. Pollock hit five sixes, all in a 50-metre arc between mid-wicket and long-on. To ensure a bonus point and guarantee their place in the finals, the South Africans had to restrict New Zealand to 216 or less. Stephen Fleming insisted the New Zealanders were going for the win, but after Craig McMillan, Scott Styris and Chris Harris all fell between the 26th and 29th overs, the run chase was called off, Fleming deciding it would be better to give South Africa the bonus point and hope that the South Africans could deny Australia maximum points on the Sunday. It was a hollow finish to a game which had been played at such rollicking pace earlier in the day.

Man of the Match: J.N. Rhodes.   *Attendance:* 15,196.

South Africa

H.H. Gibbs c Fleming b Nash	8	(21)	*S.M. Pollock not out 69 (34)
G. Kirsten c Vincent b Franklin	0	(8)	
J.H. Kallis b Nash	11	(30)	L-b 5, w 4, n-b 5 14
N.D. McKenzie b Nash	3	(3)	—
J.N. Rhodes not out	107	(135)	(50 overs, 208 mins) (5 wkts) 270
†M.V. Boucher c Astle b Harris	58	(74)	Fall: 10 14 23 35 173

N. Boje, J.M. Kemp, A.A. Donald and M. Ntini did not bat.

Bowling: Franklin 10–0–65–1; Nash 10–0–37–3; Adams 10–0–57–0; Styris 8–0–43–0; Vettori 4–0–21–0; McMillan 3–0–15–0; Harris 5–0–27–1.

New Zealand

L. Vincent c Boucher b Donald	22	(43)	D.J. Nash c Gibbs b Donald 12 (24)
N.J. Astle c Kallis b Ntini	0	(3)	†A.C. Parore not out 36 (67)
A.R. Adams c Boucher b Ntini	10	(11)	D.L. Vettori not out 20 (39)
*S.P. Fleming c Boucher b Kallis	27	(37)	L-b 9, w 5, n-b 4 18
C.D. McMillan c Kirsten b Pollock	46	(41)	
S.B. Styris c Kemp b Pollock	12	(27)	(50 overs, 216 mins) (8 wkts) 203
C.Z. Harris lbw b Boje	0	(11)	Fall: 4 22 61 72 129 130 130 156

J.E.C. Franklin did not bat.

Bowling: Pollock 10–1–55–2; Ntini 10–1–23–2; Kallis 10–1–44–1; Donald 10–2–35–2; Kemp 2–0–18–0; Boje 8–0–19–1.

Umpires: D.B. Hair and D.J. Harper.
TV Umpire: R.L. Parry.

AUSTRALIA v SOUTH AFRICA

At WACA Ground, Perth, February 3, 2002. Australia won by 33 runs. Toss: South Africa. Australia 4 pts.

The Australians won the game, but failed to qualify for the finals after a Jacques Kallis century denied them the bonus point they needed. Stacking their side with batsmen, the Australians made a healthy and consistently compiled 283 with seven contributions in excess of 20. Allan Donald received the roughest treatment of his career as Brett Lee launched a violent display of straight hitting. After Darren Lehmann had chipped a single from the opening ball of the 48th over, Lee hit three sixes over mid-off and two fours as Donald's ninth over went for 27, equalling the record Shaun Pollock had set in the previous match. With more than 100 required from the last ten overs, Pollock decided to concentrate on achieving the 227 needed to deny Australia the bonus point, the South Africans easily reaching this more modest target in the 48th over. Although hundreds of disgruntled spectators left the ground in the final hour, the specious attempts to inject synthetic life into the competition still had not prevented the two most consistent teams from contesting the finals.

Man of the Match: J.H. Kallis.   *Attendance:* 25,287.

Australia

†A.C. Gilchrist b Ntini	31	(40)	S.K. Warne b Pollock	0	(3)
M.E. Waugh c Kallis b Donald	34	(35)	B. Lee not out	51	(36)
R.T. Ponting run out (Gibbs)	26	(31)			
D.R. Martyn c Boucher b Boje	29	(54)	B 1, l-b 12, w 6, n-b 1	20	
*S.R. Waugh b Boje	42	(52)			
M.G. Bevan c Pollock b Ntini	1	(4)	(50 overs, 218 mins) (7 wkts)	283	
D.S. Lehmann not out	49	(46)	Fall: 47 76 117 150 157 194 195		

A.J. Bichel and G.D. McGrath did not bat.

Bowling: Pollock 9–0–44–1; Ntini 10–1–58–2; Kallis 9–0–52–0; Donald 9–2–62–1; Boje 10–0–38–2; Klusener 3–0–16–0.

South Africa

H.H. Gibbs c Bevan b Bichel	34	(51)	L. Klusener not out	25	(18)
G. Kirsten c Martyn b Lee	10	(29)			
J.H. Kallis not out	104	(120)	L-b 1, w 6, n-b 5	12	
H.H. Dippenaar c Gilchrist b McGrath	33	(48)			
J.N. Rhodes c Martyn b Lehmann	20	(29)	(50 overs, 221 mins) (5 wkts)	250	
†M.V. Boucher c Bichel b Lehmann	12	(10)	Fall: 30 66 129 172 198		

N. Boje, *S.M. Pollock, A.A. Donald and M. Ntini did not bat.

Bowling: McGrath 10–3–21–1; Lee 10–1–66–1; Bichel 9–0–38–1; Warne 10–0–53–0; Bevan 2–0–17–0; S.R. Waugh 4–0–26–0; Lehmann 5–0–28–2.

Umpires: S.J. Davis and R.L. Parry.
TV Umpire: D.B. Hair.

QUALIFYING TABLE

	Played	Won	Lost	Bonus Points	Points	Net Run-rate
South Africa	8	4	4	2	18	–0.0401
New Zealand	8	4	4	1	17	–0.1040
Australia	8	4	4	1	17	0.1864

Net run-rate was calculated by subtracting runs conceded per over from runs scored per over. New Zealand advanced to the final as they had defeated Australia 3-1 in the preliminary games.

FIRST FINAL

NEW ZEALAND v SOUTH AFRICA

At Melbourne Cricket Ground, Melbourne, February 6, 2002. Day/night game. South Africa won by eight wickets. Toss: New Zealand.

The New Zealanders were heartened by the return of Shane Bond and Chris Cairns and on winning the toss looked to set a target of 200-plus, knowing that only two teams in the previous 12 MCG internationals had been able to make 200 on the drop-in wicket. After the loss of two wickets by the eighth over, a century stand between Stephen Fleming and Craig McMillan provided promising momentum. However, after Fleming skied a drive and McMillan, who batted superbly, tried to steal a run to Herschelle Gibbs on the leg side and was run out, the innings disintegrated, the last eight wickets falling while a paltry 63 runs were cobbled together. Makhaya Ntini bowled with sustained accuracy at a hostile pace and, having dismissed the openers, ran through the bottom order. Shaun Pollock contained the runs by positioning his outfielders 15 metres in from the fence. Defending their second-lowest score of the tournament, New Zealand's only chance was for Bond to take early wickets, but Gary Kirsten and Gibbs played carefully against him, and with Dion Nash re-injuring an abdominal muscle and Cairns well short of his best, Bond lacked support. Even the normally frugal Chris Harris could not change the fortunes, his seventh over costing 15 as Boeta Dippenaar and Jacques Kallis joined in an unfinished third-wicket partnership of 139 to guide the South Africans to a 1-0 lead with 29 balls to spare.

Man of the Match: M. Ntini.   *Attendance:* 20,721.

New Zealand

L. Vincent c Rhodes b Ntini	7	(15)	A. R. Adams c Klusener b Ntini	13	(9)
N. J. Astle c Kallis b Ntini	9	(21)	D. L. Vettori not out	6	(12)
*S. P. Fleming c Kallis b Klusener	50	(79)	S. E. Bond run out (Rhodes)	1	(6)
C. D. McMillan run out (Gibbs)	73	(99)	L-b 5, w 6	11	
C. L. Cairns c Kirsten b Klusener	0	(4)			
C. Z. Harris c Boucher b Pollock	9	(19)	(47.5 overs, 206 mins)	190	
D. J. Nash c Donald b Ntini	9	(13)	Fall: 15 18 127 128 155 158 168		
†A. C. Parore c Boucher b Ntini	2	(10)	168 187 190		

Bowling: Pollock 9–0–30–1; Ntini 10–0–31–5; Donald 8–0–44–0; Kallis 6.5–0–25–0; Klusener 7–0–27–2; Boje 7–0–28–0.

South Africa

H. H. Gibbs c Parore b Cairns	24	(47)	L-b 1, w 1, n-b 2	4	
G. Kirsten run out (McMillan)	25	(39)			
J. H. Kallis not out	59	(80)	(45.1 overs, 172 mins)	(2 wkts) 191	
H. H. Dippenaar not out	79	(107)	Fall: 51 52		

J. N. Rhodes, †M. V. Boucher, L. Klusener, N. Boje, *S. M. Pollock, A. A. Donald and M. Ntini did not bat.

Bowling: Bond 8–2–21–0; Nash 1–0–6–0; Adams 8–0–32–0; Vettori 5–0–32–0; Cairns 8–1–27–1; McMillan 3–0–14–0; Harris 9.1–0–44–0; Astle 3–0–14–0.

Umpires: D. J. Harper and S. J. A. Taufel.
TV Umpire: R. L. Parry.

SECOND FINAL

NEW ZEALAND v SOUTH AFRICA

At Sydney Cricket Ground, Sydney, February 8, 2002. Day/night game. South Africa won on run-rate. Toss: New Zealand.

Prolonged rains in Sydney had forced the ground staff to enclose the pitch in a huge tent for days so that it could be ready in time. Even then the game was reduced to 46 overs a side after a violent late-afternoon storm with hailstones the size of gobstoppers interrupted play for 91 minutes with New Zealand at five for 75. Other than Lou Vincent, who continued to impress as a frontline stroke-maker, and Chris Cairns, who top-scored in an uncharacteristically measured display, the Kiwis played too many death-or-glory shots. In his Australian farewell Allan Donald came on in the 13th over and took a valuable 3/29. The South African target was reduced to 172 under the Duckworth/Lewis method. While Shane Bond took an early wicket and Andre Adams stepped up a class, the early run-rate was more than five an over, with Herschelle Gibbs particularly aggressive. Fittingly, Jonty Rhodes and Mark Boucher, two of the stars of the tournament, finished the game in the 39th over.

Man of the Match: J.N. Rhodes. *Player of the Series:* S.E. Bond. *Attendance:* 30,809.

New Zealand

L. Vincent c Ntini b Kallis	43 (42)	D.L. Vettori lbw b Donald	3 (10)
N.J. Astle c Klusener b Pollock	7 (19)	J.E.C. Franklin lbw b Donald	0 (1)
A.R. Adams c Boucher b Ntini	1 (6)	S.E. Bond not out	5 (11)
*S.P. Fleming c Dippenaar b Donald	17 (17)	B 2, l-b 1, w 8	11
C.D. McMillan c Ntini b Kallis	0 (4)		—
C.L. Cairns c Boje b Kallis	57 (73)	(41.1 overs, 177 mins)	175
C.Z. Harris lbw b Klusener	31 (63)	Fall: 15 17 68 68 72 147 147 157	
†A.C. Parore c Gibbs b Klusener	0 (1)	157 175	

Bowling: Pollock 6–2–24–1; Ntini 7–2–45–1; Donald 8–0–29–3; Kallis 5.1–0–23–3; Boje 8–0–21–0; Klusener 7–0–30–2.

South Africa

H.H. Gibbs b Adams	46 (51)	†M.V. Boucher not out	16 (6)
G. Kirsten c Parore b Bond	2 (11)	L-b 1, w 6, n-b 2	9
J.H. Kallis c Parore b Adams	10 (24)		—
H.H. Dippenaar c Parore b Cairns	29 (71)	(38.1 overs, 149 mins) (4 wkts)	173
J.N. Rhodes not out	61 (68)	Fall: 50 65 68 141	

L. Klusener, *S.M. Pollock, N. Boje, A.A. Donald and M. Ntini did not bat.

Bowling: Bond 8–2–31–1; Franklin 4–0–29–0; Vettori 4.1–0–25–0; Adams 8–0–33–2; Cairns 7–1–32–1; Astle 2–0–5–0; Harris 5–0–17–0.

Umpires: S.J. Davis and S.J.A. Taufel.
TV Umpire: D.J. Harper.
Series Referee: Hanumant Singh (India).

WINNING A TEST WITH A SIX

Up to February 2002, only 18 batsmen had hit a six to win a Test in 126 years of Test cricket. Then, in the space of just 14 days in March, the feat was achieved three times.

Harbhajan Singh, recognised more as an off-spinner, started this epidemic. He won the thrilling Delhi Test for India against Zimbabwe on March 5 by hitting Heath Streak for a six. He is only the second Indian, after Kapil Dev, to join the "Winning Six Club". Kapil smashed England's Phil Edmonds for a six to win the 1986 Lord's Test.

Harbhajan allowed Indian spectators to witness this feat for the first time. Auckland has seen it most times, thrice. Exactly a week after Harbhajan's "sky-writing", Australia's Ricky Ponting hammered a six on March 12 not only to win the Cape Town Test against South Africa but to reach his century as well. Ponting is the only cricketer to both reach his Test century and win a Test with a six. The bowler was Paul Adams. Six days later, on March 18, the South African captain Mark Boucher returned the compliment by hitting Mark Waugh for a six to win the Durban Test against Australia.

Only two players have hit a six to win a Test on two separate occasions: England's Wally Hammond in 1932-33 and 1934-35 and New Zealand's Richard Hadlee in 1981-82 and 1982-83.

The pioneering member of this "club" was Englishman Eddie Paynter. During the first innings of the Brisbane Test against Australia in February 1933, he was hospitalised for acute tonsillitis. But hearing on the radio that England were in trouble, he left the hospital bed to play a heroic four-hour knock of 83. In the second innings, he hit Stan McCabe for a six which won the Test and regained the Ashes for England.

A full list of 21 batsmen winning a Test by hitting a six 23 times is given on page 388.
– KERSI MEHER-HOMJI and RAJESH KUMAR

WORLD SERIES CRICKET RECORDS

Benson & Hedges World Series Cup

Season	Winners	Runners-Up	Third Team	Fourth Team
1979-80	West Indies	England	Australia	–
1980-81	Australia	New Zealand	India	–
1981-82	West Indies	Australia	Pakistan	–
1982-83	Australia	New Zealand	England	–
1983-84	West Indies	Australia	Pakistan	–
1984-85	West Indies	Australia	Sri Lanka	–
1985-86	Australia	India	New Zealand	–
1986-87	England	Australia	West Indies	–
1987-88	Australia	New Zealand	Sri Lanka	–
1988-89	West Indies	Australia	Pakistan	–

Benson & Hedges World Series

1989-90	Australia	Pakistan	Sri Lanka	–
1990-91	Australia	New Zealand	England	–
1991-92	Australia	India	West Indies	–
1992-93	West Indies	Australia	Pakistan	–
1993-94	Australia	South Africa	New Zealand	–
1994-95	Australia	Australia A	England	Zimbabwe
1995-96	Australia	Sri Lanka	West Indies	–

Carlton & United Series

1996-97	Pakistan	West Indies	Australia	–
1997-98	Australia	South Africa	New Zealand	–
1998-99	Australia	England	Sri Lanka	–
1999-00	Australia	Pakistan	India	–

Carlton Series

2000-01	Australia	West Indies	Zimbabwe	–

VB Series

2001-02	South Africa	New Zealand	Australia	–

RESULTS

	M	W	L	NR	T
Australia A	8	3	5	0	0
Australia	245	153	86	4	2
England	55	24	31	0	0
India	40	12	27	0	1
New Zealand	81	31	48	2	0
Pakistan	66	23	41	1	1
Sri Lanka	46	10	36	0	0
South Africa	31	18	13	0	0
West Indies	114	67	44	1	2
Zimbabwe	14	2	12	0	0
Total	350				

HIGHEST INDIVIDUAL SCORES

173	M.E. Waugh	Australia v West Indies at Melbourne	2000-01
158	D.I. Gower	England v New Zealand at Brisbane	1982-83
154	A.C. Gilchrist	Australia v Sri Lanka at Melbourne	1998-99
153*	I.V.A. Richards	West Indies v Australia at Melbourne	1979-80
145	D.M. Jones	Australia v England at Brisbane	1990-91
144*	D.R. Martyn	Australia v Zimbabwe at Perth	2000-01
141	S.C. Ganguly	India v Pakistan at Adelaide	1999-00
138*	G.S. Chappell	Australia v New Zealand at Sydney	1980-81
131	A.C. Gilchrist	Australia v Sri Lanka at Sydney	1998-99
130	M.E. Waugh	Australia v Sri Lanka at Perth	1995-96

* Denotes not out.

MOST RUNS

	M	I	NO	R	HS	100s	50s	Avge	S-R
A.R. Border (Aust)...	160	148	22	3,899	127*	3	23	30.94	69.67
M.E. Waugh (Aust)..	116	110	9	3,730	173	8	22	36.93	73.56
D.M. Jones (Aust)....	93	90	16	3,456	145	2	28	46.70	70.26
D.C. Boon (Aust)....	94	91	9	3,016	122	2	20	36.78	63.31
S.R. Waugh (Aust)...	142	126	31	2,801	102*	1	14	29.48	70.77
D.L. Haynes (WI)....	83	83	8	2,782	123*	4	21	37.09	59.42
I.V.A. Richards (WI) .	65	60	5	2,563	153*	3	22	46.60	85.26
R.T. Ponting (Aust) .	66	66	6	2,405	123	3	17	40.08	76.79
M.G. Bevan (Aust)...	72	64	24	2,369	105	1	16	59.23	74.08
G.R. Marsh (Aust) ...	65	64	3	2,197	125*	3	12	36.02	54.35

* Denotes not out.

HIGHEST PARTNERSHIPS FOR EACH WICKET

206	for 1st	A.C. Gilchrist and M.E Waugh	Australia v West Indies at Brisbane ..	2000-01
205	for 2nd	D.L. Haynes and I.V.A. Richards	West Indies v Australia at Melbourne	1979-80
224*	for 3rd	D.M. Jones and A.R. Border	Australia v Sri Lanka at Adelaide ...	1984-85
187	for 4th	S.V. Carlisle and G.W. Flower	Zimbabwe v Australia at Perth	2000-01
159	for 5th	R.T. Ponting and M.G. Bevan	Australia v Sri Lanka at Melbourne ..	1995-96
124	for 6th	C.D. McMillan and C.Z. Harris	New Zealand v South Africa at Adelaide	1997-98
95*	for 7th	S.R. Waugh and I.A. Healy	Australia v England at Melbourne ...	1990-91
88*	for 8th	D.S. Lehmann and B. Lee	Australia v South Africa at Perth	2001-02
63	for 9th	R.J. Hadlee and G.B. Troup	New Zealand v England at Brisbane .	1982-83
		M.D. Marshall and J. Garner	West Indies v Australia at Sydney ..	1984-85
45	for 10th	T.J. Laughlin and M.H.N. Walker	Australia v England at Sydney	1979-80

* Denotes unbroken partnership.

HIGHEST INNINGS TOTALS

Batting first

6-338 Australia defeated West Indies at Melbourne	2000-01
7-337 Australia defeated Pakistan at Sydney	1999-00
329 Australia defeated India at Adelaide	1999-00
2-323 Australia defeated Sri Lanka at Adelaide	1984-85
3-315 Pakistan defeated Sri Lanka at Adelaide	1989-90
8-310 Australia defeated Sri Lanka at Melbourne	1998-99
6-309 West Indies defeated Sri Lanka at Perth	1984-85
8-302 Australia defeated New Zealand at Melbourne	1982-83
3-302 England lost to Sri Lanka at Adelaide	1998-99
5-302 Australia defeated to Zimbabwe at Perth	2000-01
5-300 Australia defeated Pakistan at Brisbane	1989-90
6-300 South Africa defeated New Zealand at Brisbane	1997-98

Batting second

9-303 Sri Lanka defeated England at Adelaide	1998-99
6-301 Zimbabwe lost to Australia at Perth	2000-01
299 West Indies lost to Australia at Melbourne	2000-01
9-298 New Zealand lost to South Africa at Brisbane	1997-98
6-297 New Zealand defeated England at Adelaide	1982-83
8-288 Sri Lanka lost to Pakistan at Adelaide	1989-90
3-284 West Indies defeated Australia at Brisbane	1996-97
4-282 Australia defeated Zimbabwe at Hobart	2000-01
6-275 Australia defeated England at Sydney	1998-99
6-273 West Indies defeated Australia at Melbourne	1984-85

LOWEST INNINGS TOTALS

Batting first

63	India lost to Australia at Sydney	1980-81
71	Pakistan lost to West Indies at Brisbane	1992-93
100	India lost to Australia in Sydney	1999-00
102	Sri Lanka lost to West Indies at Brisbane	1995-96
106	South Africa lost to Australia at Sydney	2001-02

Batting second

69	South Africa lost to Australia	1993-94
70	Australia lost to New Zealand at Adelaide	1985-86
81	Pakistan lost to West Indies at Sydney	1992-93
87	West Indies lost to Australia at Sydney	1992-93
91	Sri Lanka lost to Australia at Adelaide	1984-85
91	West Indies lost to Zimbabwe at Sydney	2000-01

BEST ANALYSES

5/15	G. S. Chappell	Australia v India at Sydney	1980-81
5/15	R. J. Shastri	India v Australia at Perth	1991-92
5/16	C. G. Rackemann	Australia v Pakistan at Adelaide	1983-84
5/17	C. E. L. Ambrose	West Indies v Australia at Melbourne	1988-89
5/19	A. J. Bichel	Australia v South Africa at Sydney	2001-02
5/21	A. I. C. Dodemaide	Australia v Sri Lanka at Perth	1987-88
5/22	A. M. E. Roberts	West Indies v England at Adelaide	1979-80
5/24	M. E. Waugh	Australia v West Indies at Melbourne	1992-93
5/24	L. Klusener	South Africa v Australia at Melbourne	1997-98
5/25	I. R. Bishop	West Indies v Pakistan at Brisbane	1992-93

MOST WICKETS

	M	O	Mdns	R	W	BB	5W/i	Avge
S. K. Warne (Australia)	77	717	40	3,016	126	5/33	1	23.94
G. D. McGrath (Australia)	67	611.4	74	2,361	125	5/40	2	18.89
C. J. McDermott (Australia)	82	728	67	2,805	122	4/25	0	22.99
S. R. Waugh (Australia)	142	648.5	27	2,775	86	4/33	0	32.27
M. A. Holding (West Indies)	49	459.4	44	1,602	74	5/26	1	21.65
P. L Taylor (Australia)	54	465.1	23	1,878	71	4/38	0	26.45
J. Garner (West Indies)	48	435.5	62	1,381	70	5/31	1	19.73
M. D. Marshall (West Indies)	56	497	50	1,748	69	4/18	0	25.33
S. P. O'Donnell (Australia)	52	432	26	1,826	69	4/19	0	26.46
D. K. Lillee (Australia)	40	358.2	55	1,248	68	4/12	0	18.35

MOST CATCHES

A. R. Border (Aust)	83 in 160 matches	M. G. Bevan (Aust) 31 in 72 matches
S. R. Waugh (Aust)	55 in 142 matches	D. M. Jones (Aust) 29 in 93 matches
M. E. Waugh (Aust)	48 in 116 matches	P. L. Taylor (Aust) 28 in 54 matches
S. K. Warne (Aust)	39 in 77 matches	I. V. A. Richards (WI) 28 in 65 matches
M. A. Taylor (Aust)	32 in 53 matches	D. R. Martyn (Aust) 26 in 51 matches

MOST DISMISSALS

124	(108ct, 16st)	... I.A. Healy (Aust)	30	(27ct, 3st)	.... D.J. Richardson (SAf)
94	(83ct, 11st)	.... A.C. Gilchrist (Aust)	29	(26ct, 3st)	.... W.B. Phillips (Aust)
79	(78ct, 1st)	..... R.W. Marsh (Aust)	25	(21ct, 4st)	.... J.R. Murray (WI)
69	(60ct, 9st)	.... P.J.L. Dujon (WI)	25	(19ct, 6st)	.... R.S. Kaluwitharana (SL)
31	(24ct, 7st)	..... Moin Khan (Pak)	25	(23ct, 2st)	.... A.C. Parore (NZ)

MOST APPEARANCES

	M	Aust	Aust A	Eng	Ind	NZ	Pak	SL	SAf	WI	Zim
A.R. Border (Aust)	..160	–	–	19	18	35	22	6	13	47	–
S.R. Waugh (Aust)	..142	–	3	12	17	27	23	14	16	27	3
M.E. Waugh (Aust)	..116	–	4	13	7	17	16	13	16	27	5
D.C. Boon (Aust)	 94	–	4	6	13	21	9	7	10	22	2
D.M. Jones (Aust)	 93	–	–	10	8	15	14	5	11	30	–
I.A. Healy (Aust)	 86	–	3	6	6	10	18	6	10	25	2
D.L. Haynes (WI)	... 83	49	–	8	4	–	18	–	4	–	–
C.J. McDermott (Aust)	82	–	4	1	13	13	8	6	11	25	1
S.K. Warne (Aust)	... 77	–	3	9	1	12	7	11	16	13	5
M.G. Bevan (Aust)	.. 72	3	1	7	4	8	10	10	10	14	5

MOST RUNS, 2001-02

	M	I	NO	R	HS	100s	50s	Avge	S-R
J.N. Rhodes (SAf)....	10	9	3	345	107*	1	2	57.50	73.25
J.H. Kallis (SAf).....	8	8	2	322	104*	1	2	53.67	70.61
C.L. Cairns (NZ)....	9	9	2	314	102*	1	2	44.86	93.18
S.P. Fleming (NZ) ...	9	9	0	309	85	0	3	34.33	65.61
H.H. Gibbs (SAf)	10	10	0	293	89	0	1	29.30	69.10
C.D. McMillan (NZ) .	10	10	0	275	73	0	1	27.50	76.18
G. Kirsten (SAf)	10	10	0	265	97	0	1	26.50	63.25
R.T. Ponting (Aust) ..	8	8	0	254	80	0	2	31.75	77.44
M.V. Boucher (SAf)..	10	9	3	246	58	0	3	41.00	102.07
C.Z. Harris (NZ).....	10	10	4	240	63*	0	1	40.00	63.49

* Denotes not out.

MOST WICKETS, 2001-02

	M	O	Mdns	R	W	BB	Avge
S.E. Bond (NZ)	9	82.2	10	344	21	5/25	16.38
G.D. McGrath (Aust)	7	69.4	10	226	14	4/30	16.14
M. Ntini (SAf)	9	81.2	7	338	14	5/31	24.14
S.M. Pollock (SAf)	10	87.1	8	333	13	3/25	25.62
A.A. Donald (SAf)	7	65	5	301	12	3/29	25.08
C.L. Cairns (NZ)	9	70	5	319	12	3/42	26.58
J.H. Kallis (SAf)	8	63.5	2	287	10	3/23	28.70
L. Klusener (SAf)	7	44.4	0	238	9	2/27	26.44
A.J. Bichel (Aust)	6	46.3	2	206	8	5/19	25.75
N. Boje (SAf)	8	58	0	205	8	4/31	25.63
B. Lee (Aust)	5	45.3	4	223	8	3/43	27.88
C.Z. Harris (NZ)	10	82.3	0	371	8	3/37	46.38

AUSTRALIAN FIRST-CLASS SEASON, 2001-02

FEATURES OF 2001-02

Highest Individual Scores

246	D.S. Lehmann	South Australia v Tasmania at Hobart (Bel).
223	N.J. Astle	New Zealanders v Queensland at Brisbane.
209	J.P. Maher	Queensland v South Australia at Brisbane.
203*	M.G. Bevan	New South Wales v Western Australia at Sydney.
202†	M.L. Love	Queensland v South Australia at Adelaide.
200*	M.J. North	Tasmania v Victoria at Melbourne.
198	J.P. Maher	Queensland v New South Wales at Sydney
189	D.R. Martyn	Western Australia v Tasmania at Perth.
184	M.L. Love	Queensland v New South Wales at Sydney.
183*	M.G. Bevan	New South Wales v South Africans at Sydney.

* Denotes not out. † Denotes retired hurt.

Leading Run-Makers

	M	I	NO	R	HS	100s	50s	Avge
1. M.L. Hayden (Qld/Aust)	10	17	2	1,243	147	6	4	82.87
2. J.P. Maher (Qld)	10	19	1	1,194	209	3	6	66.33
3. M.L. Love (Qld)	12	22	3	1,189	202†	2	6	62.58
4. J.L. Langer (WAust/Aust)	10	18	3	1,030	133	5	3	68.67
5. G.S. Blewett (SAust)	11	21	3	1,025	169*	5	3	56.94
6. M.G. Bevan (NSW)	8	14	2	868	203*	4	3	72.33
7. B.J. Hodge (Vic)	10	18	3	858	140	4	2	57.20
8. D.S. Lehmann (SAust)	8	14	0	823	246	4	1	58.79
9. M.T.G. Elliott (Vic)	10	20	2	780	135*	1	6	43.33
10. R.T. Ponting (Tas/Aust)	8	14	3	733	157*	3	2	66.64

* Denotes not out. † Denotes retired hurt.

Leading Batting Averages

(Qualification: 500 Runs)

	M	I	NO	R	HS	100s	50s	Avge
1. N.J. Astle (New Zealanders)	4	7	2	554	223	2	1	110.80
2. M.L. Hayden (Qld/Aust)	10	17	2	1,243	147	6	4	82.87
3. M.G. Bevan (NSW)	8	14	2	868	203*	4	3	72.33
4. J.L. Langer (WAust/Aust)	10	18	3	1,030	133	5	3	68.67
5. D.R. Martyn (WAust/Aust)	8	11	2	616	189	3	2	68.44
6. R.T. Ponting (Tas/Aust)	8	14	3	733	157*	3	2	66.64
7. J.P. Maher (Qld)	10	19	1	1,194	209	3	6	66.33
8. G.B. Hogg (WAust)	7	11	3	525	90	0	6	65.63
9. M.L. Love (Qld)	12	22	3	1,189	202†	2	6	62.58
10. B.A. Johnson (SAust)	7	14	3	653	138*	3	2	59.36
11. D.S. Lehmann (SAust)	8	14	0	823	246	4	1	58.79
12. B.J. Hodge (Vic)	10	18	3	858	140	4	2	57.20
13. G.S. Blewett (SAust)	11	21	3	1,025	169*	5	3	56.94
14. S.G. Clingeleffer (Tas)	11	15	4	517	141*	2	1	47.00
15. M.E. Waugh (NSW/Aust)	8	11	0	500	168	1	3	45.45
16. M.J. North (WAust)	9	15	1	633	200*	3	1	45.21
17. M.T.G. Elliott (Vic)	10	20	2	780	135*	1	6	43.33
18. R.J. Campbell (WAust)	9	15	1	576	121	1	4	41.14
19. G.J. Mail (NSW)	8	14	1	528	150*	1	5	40.62
20. M.G. Dighton (Tas)	10	15	0	594	126	2	3	39.60

* Denotes not out.

Notable Partnerships

First Wicket
224   J.L. Langer/M.L. Hayden, Australia v New Zealand at Brisbane.
223   J.L. Langer/M.L. Hayden, Australia v New Zealand at Hobart (Bel).
219   J.L. Langer/M.L. Hayden, Australia v South Africa at Sydney.
205   D.F. Hills/J. Cox, Tasmania v New South Wales at Sydney.
202   J.L. Langer/M.L. Hayden, Australia v South Africa at Melbourne.

Second Wicket
386   G.S. Blewett/D.S. Lehmann, South Australia v Tasmania at Hobart (Bel).
294   J.P. Maher/M.L. Love, Queensland v New South Wales at Sydney.
193   J.L. Langer/S.M. Katich, Western Australia v Tasmania at Perth.
179   J.P. Maher/M.L. Love, Queensland v Western Australia at Perth.
177   B.P. Nash/M.L. Love, Queensland v Tasmania at Brisbane.

Third Wicket
312   M.L. Love/B.P. Nash/A. Symonds, Queensland v South Australia at Adelaide.
217   G.S. Blewett/D.S. Lehmann, South Australia v Victoria at Adelaide.
201   G.S. Blewett/D.S. Lehmann, South Australia v Queensland at Brisbane.
199   L. Vincent/S.P. Fleming, New Zealand v Australia at Perth.
197   M.G. Dighton/M.J. Di Venuto, Tasmania v Victoria at Melbourne.

Fourth Wicket
321   D.R. Martyn/A.C. Gilchrist, Western Australia v Tasmania at Perth.
184   M.G. Dighton/D.J. Marsh, Tasmania v Victoria at Hobart (Bel).
181   M.G. Bevan/M.A. Higgs, New South Wales v Western Australia at Sydney.
175   S.P. Fleming/N.J. Astle, New Zelanders v Queensland at Brisbane.
150   J. Cox/D.J. Marsh, Tasmania v South Australia at Adelaide.

Fifth Wicket
155   A. Symonds/S.G. Law, Queensland v Tasmania at Brisbane.
154   R.J. Campbell/C.J.L. Rogers, Western Australia v New South Wales at Perth.
144   M.J. North/C.J.L. Rogers, Western Australia v South Australia at Perth.
111   M.J. Di Venuto/S.P. Kremerskothen, Tasmania v Queensland at Brisbane.
110   B.H. Higgins/C.J. Davies, South Australia v Queensland at Brisbane.

Sixth Wicket
199   J. Moss/D.S. Berry, Victoria v New South Wales at Sydney.
175   M.J. Clark/B.J. Haddin, New South Wales v Queensland at Sydney.
174*   C.J.L. Rogers/G.B. Hogg, Western Australia v South Australia at Perth.
155   S. Young/S.G. Clingeleffer, Tasmania v South Australia at Hobart (Bel).
154   A.C. Gilchrist/M.J. North, Western Australia v Queensland at Brisbane.

Seventh Wicket
175   G.B. Hogg/M.J. Nicholson, Western Australia v South Africans at Perth.
145   R.T. Ponting/S.K. Warne, Australia v New Zealand at Hobart (Bel).
141   N.D. McKenzie/M.V. Boucher, South Africa v Australia at Adelaide.
135   B.E. Young/G.A. Manou, South Australia v New South Wales at Adelaide.
123   S.G. Clingeleffer/D.G. Wright, Tasmania v South Australia at Adelaide.

Eighth Wicket
253   N.J. Astle/A.C. Parore, New Zealand v Australia at Perth.
135   A.C. Gilchrist/B. Lee, Australia v New Zealand at Brisbane.
86   C.L. White/P.R. Reiffel, Victoria v South Australia at Melbourne.
85   M.J. North/M.J. Nicholson, Western Australia v Victoria at Melbourne.
84   M.V. Boucher/C.W. Henderson, South Africans v Western Australia at Perth.

Ninth Wicket
105   A.A. Noffke/N.M. Hauritz, Queensland v Victoria at Richmond.
110   M.J. Nicholson/J. Angel, Western Australia v Queensland at Perth.
75   P.R. Reiffel/M.L. Lewis, Victoria v South Australia at Melbourne.
69*   D.S. Berry/D.W. Fleming, Victoria v Tasmania at Melbourne.
67   D.G. Wright/S.B. Tubb, Tasmania v Western Australia at Hobart (Bel).

Tenth Wicket

114	D. J. Saker/S. J. Jurgensen, Tasmania v Queensland at Hobart (Bel).
71	B. A. Johnson/M. A. Harrity, South Australia v Victoria at Melbourne.
54*	M. J. Phelps/S. R. Clark, New South Wales v Queensland at Sydney.
52	A. A. Noffke/J. H. Dawes, Queensland v Tasmania at Brisbane.
49	S. M. Pollock/A. A. Donald, South Africa v Australia at Sydney.

    * *Denotes unbroken partnership.*

Highest Innings Totals

8-600 dec.	Western Australia v South Africans at Perth.
7-594 dec.	Western Australia v Tasmania at Hobart (Bel).
5-589 dec.	South Australia v Tasmania at Hobart (Bel).
578	Western Australia v New South Wales at Sydney.
8-558 dec.	Australia v New Zealand at Hobart (Bel).
554	Australia v South Africa at Sydney.
6-553 dec.	South Australia v Queensland at Brisbane.
9-534 dec.	New Zealand v Australia at Perth.
4-528 dec.	Queensland v New South Wales at Sydney.
527-9 dec.	Tasmania v Victoria at Hobart (Bel).

Highest Fourth-Innings Totals

7-381	Australia v New Zealand at Perth.
9-311	New South Wales v Western Australia at Perth.
294	Tasmania v Queensland at Brisbane.
8-277	South Australia v Western Australia at Perth.
6-274	New Zealand v Australia at Brisbane.
247	New South Wales v South Australia at Adelaide.
6-240	Victoria v Queensland at Richmond.
4-202	Queensland v New Zealanders at Brisbane.
9-202	New South Wales v Queensland at Sydney.
192	South Australia v New South Wales at Sydney.

Lowest Innings Totals

98	Victoria v Western Australia at Melbourne.
100	Tasmania v Queensland at Brisbane.
101	Queensland v Tasmania at Hobart (Bel).
107	Queensland v Victoria at Brisbane.
109	New South Wales v Victoria at Sydney.
120	Queensland v New South Wales at Sydney.
122	Victoria v Queensland at Brisbane.
128	South Africa v Australia at Adelaide.
130	Queensland v Tasmania at Hobart (Bel).
132	Queensland v Tasmania at Brisbane.
132	South Australia v Queensland at Adelaide.

Best Innings Analyses

8/50	J. N. Gillespie	South Australia v New South Wales at Sydney.
7/19	M. W. H. Inness	Victoria v New South Wales at Sydney.
7/52	P. C. Rofe	South Australia v New South Wales at Adelaide.
7/98	M. J. Smith	South Australia v Queensland at Brisbane.
6/32	S. R. Watson	Tasmania v Queensland at Hobart.
6/46	W. N. Carr	Victoria v Queensland at Brisbane.
6/52	J. Angel	Western Australia v Victoria at Melbourne.
6/60	P. C. Rofe	South Australia v New South Wales
6/65	S. J. Jurgensen	Tasmania v Queensland at Brisbane.
6/75	P. E. McIntyre	South Australia v New Zealanders at Adelaide.

Leading Wicket-Takers

		M	O	Mdns	R	W	BB	5W/i	10W/m	Avge
1.	M. S. Kasprowicz (Qld)	10	378.5	87	1239	51	5/44	2	0	24.29
2.	S. R. Clark (NSW)	9	387	108	1047	45	5/42	4	0	23.27
3.	J. Angel (WAust)	10	412	124	1074	44	6/52	1	0	24.41
4.	P. C. Rofe (SAust)	11	441.4	152	1060	41	7/52	3	1	25.85
5.	A. A. Noffke (Qld)	11	380.4	97	1110	39	5/31	2	0	28.46
6.	D. J. Saker (Tas)	11	366.3	103	1003	38	5/53	1	0	26.39
7.	S. J. Jurgensen (Tas)	9	290	85	710	36	6/65	4	2	19.72
8.	M. J. Nicholson (WAust)	9	299.4	62	936	33	5/68	1	0	28.36
9.	B. A. Williams (WAust)	7	279	72	906	32	4/34	0	0	28.31
10.	M. W. H. Inness (Vic)	7	214.5	61	597	31	7/19	1	1	19.26

Leading Bowling Averages

(Qualification: 20 wickets)

		M	O	Mdns	R	W	BB	5W/i	10W/m	Avge
1.	M. W. H. Inness (Vic)	7	214.5	61	597	31	7/19	1	1	19.26
2.	S. J. Jurgensen (Tas)	9	290	85	710	36	6/65	4	2	19.72
3.	S. R. Clark (NSW)	9	387	108	1047	45	5/42	4	0	23.27
4.	S. R. Watson (Tas)	7	126.4	20	514	22	6/32	2	1	23.36
5.	M. S. Kasprowicz (Qld)	10	378.5	87	1239	51	5/44	2	0	24.29
6.	J. Angel (WAust)	10	412	124	1074	44	6/52	1	0	24.41
7.	J. N. Gillespie (SAust/Aust)	6	243.4	60	689	28	8/50	1	1	24.61
8.	P. C. Rofe (SAust)	11	441.4	152	1060	41	7/52	3	1	25.85
9.	B. Lee (NSW/Aust)	7	228.5	51	763	29	5/56	2	0	26.31
10.	D. L. Vettori (New Zealanders)	4	189.5	38	580	22	6/80	3	0	26.36
11.	D. J. Saker (Tas)	11	366.3	103	1003	38	5/53	1	0	26.39
12.	A. Symonds (Qld)	10	226.5	61	588	22	4/45	0	0	26.73
13.	B. A. Williams (WAust)	7	279	72	906	32	4/34	0	0	28.31
14.	M. J. Nicholson (WAust)	9	299.4	62	936	33	5/68	1	0	28.36
15.	A. A. Noffke (Qld)	11	380.4	97	1110	39	5/31	2	0	28.46
16.	M. J. Smith (SAust)	8	273.2	54	917	29	7/98	1	0	31.62
17.	N. W. Bracken (NSW)	8	248.5	55	763	24	4/10	0	0	31.79
18.	G. D. McGrath (NSW/Aust)	8	340.5	107	880	24	3/13	0	0	36.67
19.	S. K. Warne (Vic/Aust)	8	373	63	1156	29	5/113	1	0	39.86
20.	D. G. Wright (Tas)	11	346.3	114	932	23	3/15	0	0	40.52

Most Catches in an Innings

4	D. R. Martyn	Western Australia v Tasmania at Perth.
4	J. P. Maher	Queensland v Western Australia at Perth.
4	B. A. Johnson	South Australia v Queensland at Adelaide
4	J. P. Maher	Queensland v New South Wales at Sydney.
4	D. J. Marsh	Tasmania v New South Wales at Hobart (Bel).

Most Catches in a Match

6	D. R. Martyn	Western Australia v Tasmania at Perth.
6	J. P. Maher	Queensland v Western Australia at Perth.
6	D. J. Marsh	Tasmania v New South Wales at Hobart (Bel).
5	R. T. Ponting	Australia v South Africa at Adelaide.
5	D. J. Marsh	Tasmania v South Australia at Adelaide.

Most Dismissals in an Innings

7	(7ct)	W. A Seccombe	Queensland v New South Wales at Brisbane.
5	(5ct)	N. S. Pilon	New South Wales v Victoria at Sydney.
5	(5ct)	R. J. Campbell	Western Australia v South Australia at Adelaide.
5	(5ct)	S. G. Clingeleffer	Tasmania v Queensland at Hobart (Bel).
5	(5ct)	W. A. Seccombe	Queensland v Tasmania at Brisbane.

Most Dismissals in a Match

9	(9ct)	N. S. Pilon	New South Wales v South Australia at Sydney.
9	(9ct)	S. G. Clingeleffer	Tasmania v Queensland at Hobart (Bel).
9	(9ct)	W. A. Seccombe	Queensland v Tasmania at Brisbane.
8	(8ct)	R. J. Campbell	Western Australia v South Australia at Adelaide.
7	(7ct)	W. A. Seccombe	Queensland v New South Wales at Brisbane.
7	(5ct, 2st)	D. S. Berry	Victoria v Western Australia at Melbourne.
7	(7ct)	D. S. Berry	Victoria v Queensland at Brisbane.

FIRST-CLASS AVERAGES, 2001-02

BATTING

* Denotes not out. † Denotes left-handed batsman.

	M	I	NO	R	HS	100s	50s	Avge	Ct/St
N. T. Adcock (SAust)	3	5	0	83	46	0	0	16.60	1
† J. Angel (WAust)	10	15	4	180	61	0	1	16.36	1
J. L. Arnberger (Vic)	8	16	2	401	70*	0	2	28.64	4
N. J. Astle (New Zealanders)	4	7	2	554	223	2	1	110.80	0
M. D. Bell (New Zealanders)	4	7	0	49	29	0	0	7.00	1
D. S. Berry (Vic)	10	16	3	382	148	1	1	29.38	32/3
† M. G. Bevan (NSW)	8	14	2	868	203*	4	3	72.33	4
A. J. Bichel (Qld/Aust)	5	5	1	69	23	0	0	17.25	5
G. S. Blewett (SAust)	11	21	3	1025	169*	5	3	56.94	8
† N. Boje (South Africans)	1	2	0	8	7	0	0	4.00	0
S. E. Bond (New Zealanders)	3	4	0	12	8	0	0	3.00	4
M. V. Boucher (South Africans)	5	9	1	372	134	1	1	46.50	10
N. W. Bracken (NSW)	8	14	5	145	38	0	0	16.11	4
S. D. Bradstreet (NSW)	1	1	0	15	15	0	0	15.00	0
S. A. Brant (Qld)	3	3	2	35	19*	0	0	35.00	3
C. L. Cairns (New Zealanders)	4	7	1	244	61	0	1	40.67	0
R. J. Campbell (WAust)	9	15	1	576	121	1	4	41.14	36
W. N. Carr (Vic)	3	3	1	4	4	0	0	2.00	0
† L. A. Carseldine (Qld)	4	8	3	192	39	0	0	38.40	4
S. R. Cary (WAust)	3	4	3	25	10*	0	0	25.00	1
J. L. Cassell (Qld)	5	9	0	211	86	0	1	23.44	3
A. M. Clark (NSW)	2	2	1	18	12	0	0	18.00	1
M. W. Clark (WAust)	5	5	4	11	6	0	0	11.00	2
S. R. Clark (NSW)	9	15	5	145	31*	0	0	14.50	1
M. J. Clarke (NSW)	9	18	1	663	132	2	2	39.00	7
† S. G. Clingeleffer (Tas)	11	15	4	517	141*	2	1	47.00	36
J. Cox (Tas)	11	18	1	660	174	2	3	38.82	3
†A. C. Dale (Qld)	1	0	0	0	0	0	0	–	1
C. J. Davies (SAust)	5	9	1	306	119*	1	1	38.25	3
J. H. Dawes (Qld)	8	10	3	46	26	0	0	6.57	1
† S. A. Deitz (SAust)	4	8	0	178	86	0	1	22.25	6
D. M. Dempsey (SAust)	3	5	0	38	21	0	0	7.60	5
G. J. Denton (Tas)	2	3	0	8	8	0	0	2.67	0
† M. J. Di Venuto (Tas)	5	8	1	273	83	0	2	39.00	9

	M	I	NO	R	HS	100s	50s	Avge	Ct/St
M. G. Dighton (Tas)	10	15	0	594	126	2	3	39.60	4
H. H. Dippenaar (South Africans)	4	8	1	276	115	1	1	39.43	0
X. J. Doherty (Tas)	2	2	1	10	6	0	0	10.00	0
A. A. Donald (South Africans)	4	6	3	21	8*	0	0	7.00	1
A. G. Downton (Tas)	2	2	1	0	0*	0	0	0.00	0
† M. T. G. Elliott (Vic)	10	20	2	780	135*	1	6	43.33	15
S. Elworthy (South Africans)	2	2	0	60	31	0	0	30.00	1
D. A. Fitzgerald (SAust)	8	15	0	426	139	1	1	28.40	6
D. W. Fleming (Vic)	5	6	2	92	39*	0	0	23.00	1
† S. P. Fleming (New Zealanders)	4	7	0	306	105	1	3	43.71	2
H. H. Gibbs (South Africans)	5	9	0	386	145	1	2	42.89	2
† A. C. Gilchrist (WAust/Aust)	8	12	2	477	118	1	2	47.70	22/2
J. N. Gillespie (SAust/Aust)	6	8	4	91	32*	0	0	22.75	1
M. W. Goodwin (WAust)	8	13	0	474	141	1	2	36.46	3
B. J. Haddin (NSW)	10	18	2	515	102	1	3	32.19	27/1
R. J. Harris (SAust)	2	2	0	0	0	0	0	0.00	0
M. A. Harrity (SAust)	10	14	5	59	19	0	0	6.56	4
I. J. Harvey (Vic)	7	11	2	432	87	0	4	48.00	1
K. M. Harvey (WAust)	5	8	2	134	59	0	1	22.33	3
N. M. Hauritz (Qld)	7	9	1	102	41	0	0	12.75	5
† M. L. Hayden (Qld/Aust)	10	17	2	1243	147	6	4	82.87	6
M. Hayward (South Africans)	2	4	2	26	14	0	0	13.00	0
J. M. Heath (NSW)	1	0	0	0	0	0	0	–	1
C. W. Henderson (South Africans)	5	8	0	102	30	0	0	12.75	2
† I. S. L. Hewett (Vic)	1	1	0	3	3	0	0	3.00	0
† B. H. Higgins (SAust)	10	18	2	467	80	0	5	29.19	3
† M. A. Higgs (NSW)	10	18	3	490	80	0	4	32.67	4
† D. F. Hills (Tas)	4	8	0	186	136	1	0	23.25	0
B. J. Hodge (Vic)	10	18	3	858	140	4	2	57.20	4
† G. B. Hogg (WAust)	7	11	3	525	90	0	6	65.63	4
J. R. Hopes (Qld)	3	5	0	40	14	0	0	8.00	0
† M. E. K. Hussey (WAust)	11	19	1	621	100	1	4	34.50	16
† M. W. H. Inness (Vic)	7	9	5	11	8*	0	0	2.75	3
† P. A. Jaques (NSW)	1	2	0	23	23	0	0	11.50	1
N. Jewell (Vic)	2	4	0	49	26	0	0	12.25	0
† B. A. Johnson (SAust)	7	14	3	653	138*	3	2	59.36	9
† M. G. Johnson (Qld)	2	2	2	18	12*	0	0	–	0
S. J. Jurgensen (Tas)	9	10	4	119	56	0	1	19.83	1
J. H. Kallis (South Africans)	4	8	1	386	120	1	2	55.14	4
S. J. Karppinen (WAust)	1	1	0	0	0	0	0	0.00	0
M. S. Kasprowicz (Qld)	10	11	2	26	13	0	0	2.89	4
† S. M. Katich (WAust)	11	18	0	651	131	1	4	36.17	8
† G. Kirsten (South Africans)	5	10	0	454	153	1	2	45.40	3
M. Klinger (Vic)	7	11	2	251	58	0	2	27.89	1
† L. Klusener (South Africans)	4	8	0	105	50	0	1	13.13	1
† S. P. Kremerskothen (Tas)	7	9	2	228	55	0	1	32.57	9
G. M. Lambert (NSW)	2	4	1	88	45*	0	0	29.33	0
† J. L. Langer (WAust/Aust)	10	18	3	1030	133	5	3	68.67	7
S. G. Law (Qld)	10	16	3	316	70	0	2	24.31	8
B. Lee (NSW/Aust)	7	8	0	191	61	0	1	23.88	2
S. Lee (NSW)	6	10	0	170	41	0	0	17.00	10
† D. S. Lehmann (SAust)	8	14	0	823	246	4	1	58.79	3
M. L. Lewis (Vic)	7	11	2	130	54*	0	1	14.44	2
M. L. Love (Qld)	12	23	3	1189	202*	2	6	62.58	10
S. C. G. MacGill (NSW/Aust)	8	11	2	177	53	0	1	19.67	5
D. R. MacKenzie (Qld)	1	2	0	21	17	0	0	10.50	0
† J. P. Maher (Qld)	10	19	1	1194	209	3	6	66.33	14
G. J. Mail (NSW)	8	14	1	528	150*	1	5	40.62	7
G. A. Manou (SAust)	10	16	1	312	62	0	1	20.80	33/2
D. J. Marsh (Tas)	11	17	2	433	97	0	2	28.87	20

	M	I	NO	R	HS	100s	50s	Avge	Ct/St
C. S. Martin (New Zealanders)	3	3	3	4	4*	0	0	–	3
D. R. Martyn (WAust/Aust)	8	11	2	616	189	3	2	68.44	9
† S. R. Mason (Tas)	7	10	1	187	41	0	0	20.78	3
A. B. McDonald (Vic)	2	4	1	43	26	0	0	14.33	3
B. E. McGain (Vic)	2	2	0	3	3	0	0	1.50	2
G. D. McGrath (NSW/Aust)	8	7	3	46	26	0	0	11.50	3
P. E. McIntyre (SAust)	6	12	2	121	40	0	0	12.10	0
N. D. McKenzie (South Africans)	4	8	0	373	114	1	2	46.63	6
C. D. McMillan (New Zealanders)	5	9	1	272	55	0	2	34.00	3
S. W. Meuleman (WAust)	8	13	0	307	109	1	1	23.62	3
C. R. Miller (Vic)	4	5	1	35	17	0	0	8.75	0
J. Moss (Vic)	5	9	0	378	109	1	3	42.00	4
† M. P. Mott (Vic)	9	16	0	378	87	0	2	23.63	6
† B. P. Nash (Qld)	5	10	1	395	157	1	2	43.89	3
D. A. Nash (NSW)	9	14	0	127	27	0	0	9.07	1
D. J. Nash (New Zealanders)	1	1	1	25	25*	0	0	–	0
M. J. Nicholson (WAust)	9	14	3	334	101*	1	1	30.36	4
A. A. Noffke (Qld)	11	13	3	275	73	0	1	27.50	4
† M. J. North (NSW)	9	15	1	633	200*	3	1	45.21	11
M. Ntini (South Africans)	2	3	0	13	9	0	0	4.33	1
† A. W. O'Brien (NSW)	1	1	0	6	6	0	0	6.00	0
† S. B. O'Connor (New Zealanders)	2	1	1	11	11*	0	0	–	1
† B. J. Oldroyd (WAust)	3	5	2	28	19*	0	0	9.33	0
J. L. Ontong (South Africans)	2	4	0	41	32	0	0	10.25	0
A. C. Parore (New Zealanders)	5	9	3	276	110	1	0	46.00	11/1
D. M. Payne (Qld)	2	4	0	82	35	0	0	20.50	3
C. T. Perren (Qld)	8	14	3	173	47*	0	0	15.73	11
M. J. Phelps (NSW)	2	4	1	243	84	0	3	81.00	2
N. S. Pilon (NSW)	1	2	0	16	16	0	0	8.00	9
S. M. Pollock (South Africans)	4	8	3	217	61*	0	2	43.40	3
R. T. Ponting (Tas/Aust)	8	14	3	733	157*	3	2	66.64	15
P. R. Reiffel (Vic)	4	6	2	122	75	0	1	30.50	3
C. J. Richards (NSW)	5	10	1	276	74	0	1	30.67	1
† M. H. Richardson (New Zealanders)	5	9	0	187	57	0	1	20.78	5
P. C. Rofe (SAust)	11	15	7	57	9	0	0	7.13	3
† C. J. L. Rogers (WAust)	4	7	2	411	102*	2	2	82.20	5
† J. A. Rudolph (South Africans)	2	4	0	151	59	0	2	37.75	1
† G. C. Rummans (NSW)	2	4	0	138	60	0	2	34.50	0
D. J. Saker (Tas)	11	12	6	199	66*	0	1	33.17	2
W. A. Seccombe (Qld)	12	18	3	171	49	0	0	11.40	52
M. S. Sinclair (New Zealanders)	5	9	0	200	80	0	2	22.22	4
M. J. Slater (NSW)	7	13	1	314	58*	0	2	26.17	2
M. J. Smith (SAust)	8	15	2	270	46	0	0	20.77	9
† G. P. Sulzberger (New Zealanders)	2	3	0	76	41	0	0	25.33	2
G. G. Swan (WAust)	3	1	0	0	0	0	0	0.00	0
A. Symonds (Qld)	10	17	2	405	91	0	2	27.00	9
B. J. Thomas (Tas)	1	2	0	25	21	0	0	12.50	0
S. B. Tubb (Tas)	3	3	0	39	33	0	0	13.00	1
D. R. Tuffey (New Zealanders)	2	2	0	66	56	0	1	33.00	0
D. A. Turner (NSW)	2	4	0	51	39	0	0	12.75	0
B. P. Van Deinsen (NSW)	4	8	0	182	61	0	2	22.75	6
J. M. Vaughan (SAust)	3	5	1	82	69	0	1	20.50	1
† D. L. Vettori (New Zealanders)	4	6	2	23	10*	0	0	5.75	6
L. Vincent (New Zealanders)	2	4	0	232	104	1	2	58.00	1
S. K. Warne (Vic/Aust)	8	11	1	296	99	0	2	29.60	8
S. R. Watson (Tas)	7	11	1	292	58*	0	3	29.20	3
M. E. Waugh (NSW/Aust)	8	11	0	500	168	1	3	45.45	6
S. R. Waugh (Aust)	6	8	0	219	90	0	2	27.38	3
C. L. White (Vic)	5	8	0	144	91	0	1	18.00	4
B. A. Williams (WAust)	7	6	0	67	20	0	0	11.17	2

	M	I	NO	R	HS	100s	50s	Avge	Ct/St
V.M. Williams (NSW)	1	2	0	4	4	0	0	2.00	0
P. Wilson (SAust)	1	2	1	2	2	0	0	2.00	0
D.G. Wright (Tas)	11	15	3	409	63	0	4	34.08	6
B.E. Young (SAust)	9	16	0	406	122	1	0	25.38	5
† S. Young (Tas)	5	8	0	259	84	0	3	32.38	1

BOWLING

† Denotes left-arm bowler.

	O	M	R	W	BB	5W/i	10W/m	Avge
N.T. Adcock (SAust)	29.2	3	90	2	1/19	0	0	45.00
J. Angel (WAust)	412	124	1074	44	6/52	1	0	24.41
N.J. Astle (New Zealanders)	45	13	108	2	1/30	0	0	54.00
M.G. Bevan (NSW)	20	0	94	0	–	0	0	–
A.J. Bichel (Qld/Aust)	166	40	508	19	4/54	0	0	26.74
G.S. Blewett (SAust)	70	13	176	7	3/15	0	0	25.14
N. Boje (South Africans)	27.3	6	78	4	4/63	0	0	19.50
S.E. Bond (New Zealanders)	97	13	367	6	2/35	0	0	61.17
† N.W. Bracken (NSW)	248.5	55	763	24	4/10	0	0	31.79
S.D. Bradstreet (NSW)	29	7	170	1	1/123	0	0	170.00
† S.A. Brant (Qld)	56	16	126	7	3/23	0	0	18.00
C.L. Cairns (New Zealanders)	140	24	565	15	5/71	2	0	37.67
W.N. Carr (Vic)	94.2	28	276	16	6/46	1	0	17.25
† L.A. Carseldine (Qld)	4	1	11	0	–	0	0	–
S.R. Cary (WAust)	106	27	280	3	1/34	0	0	93.33
J.L. Cassell (Qld)	1	0	4	0	–	0	0	–
A.M. Clark (NSW)	43	4	151	4	4/130	0	0	37.75
† M.W. Clark (WAust)	128	45	324	7	3/49	0	0	46.29
S.R. Clark (NSW)	387	108	1047	45	5/42	4	0	23.27
† M.J. Clarke (NSW)	18	1	51	2	2/25	0	0	25.50
A.C. Dale (Qld)	38	13	97	5	3/51	0	0	19.40
J.H. Dawes (Qld)	238.4	64	706	19	3/4	0	0	37.16
G.J. Denton (Tas)	78.3	12	271	6	3/67	0	0	45.17
M.J. Di Venuto (Tas)	1	0	5	0	–	0	0	–
X.J. Doherty (Tas)	74.5	17	197	5	2/23	0	0	39.40
A.A. Donald (South Africans)	115	20	429	5	3/103	0	0	85.80
† A.G. Downton (Tas)	41	8	194	2	2/94	0	0	97.00
S. Elworthy (South Africans)	56	15	177	3	3/57	0	0	59.00
D.W. Fleming (Vic)	124.2	39	391	13	3/34	0	0	30.08
J.N. Gillespie (SAust/Aust)	243.4	60	689	28	8/50	1	1	24.61
R.J. Harris (SAust)	35.4	10	99	2	2/26	0	0	49.50
† M.A. Harrity (SAust)	335.2	67	1106	27	5/65	1	0	40.96
I.J. Harvey (Vic)	207.4	49	623	17	3/53	0	0	36.65
K.M. Harvey (WAust)	117.4	31	338	9	4/43	0	0	37.56
N.M. Hauritz (Qld)	178	37	484	16	4/119	0	0	30.25
M. Hayward (South Africans)	67	6	249	5	3/108	0	0	49.80
J.M. Heath (NSW)	33	8	111	3	3/72	0	0	37.00
C.W. Henderson (South Africans)	206.1	33	748	11	4/116	0	0	68.00
† I.S.L. Hewett (Vic)	33	9	102	3	3/63	0	0	34.00
† B.H. Higgins (SAust)	24.2	7	80	1	1/49	0	0	80.00
M.A. Higgs (NSW)	131.5	17	469	6	2/99	0	0	78.17
B.J. Hodge (Vic)	62.3	14	181	2	1/0	0	0	90.50
G.B. Hogg (WAust)	182.5	42	575	17	3/95	0	0	33.82
J.R. Hopes (Qld)	98.4	28	299	3	2/50	0	0	99.67
M.E.K. Hussey (WAust)	7	1	21	0	–	0	0	–
† M.W.H. Inness (Vic)	214.5	61	597	31	7/19	1	1	19.26
† N. Jewell (Vic)	3	1	6	0	–	0	0	–
B.A. Johnson (SAust)	42	5	173	3	2/26	0	0	57.67
† M.G. Johnson (Qld)	71	17	216	6	2/64	0	0	36.00

	O	M	R	W	BB	5W/i	10W/m	Avge
S. J. Jurgensen (Tas)	290	85	710	36	6/65	4	2	19.72
J. H. Kallis (South Africans)	90	12	326	4	3/45	0	0	81.50
S. J. Karppinen (WAust)	48	12	195	5	4/110	0	0	39.00
M. S. Kasprowicz (Qld)	378.5	87	1239	51	5/44	2	0	24.29
S. M. Katich (WAust)	43.3	4	199	5	2/51	0	0	39.80
L. Klusener (South Africans)	72	19	237	7	2/33	0	0	33.86
S. P. Kremerskothen (Tas)	48.5	9	169	6	2/29	0	0	28.17
G. M. Lambert (NSW)	36	4	165	4	3/86	0	0	41.25
S. G. Law (Qld)	20	3	74	1	1/54	0	0	74.00
B. Lee (NSW/Aust)	228.5	51	763	29	5/56	2	0	26.31
S. Lee (NSW)	76.5	8	313	5	2/32	0	0	62.60
D. S. Lehmann (SAust)	66.5	11	178	7	3/42	0	0	25.43
M. L. Lewis (Vic)	184.4	43	621	16	4/64	0	0	38.81
S. C. G. MacGill (NSW/Aust)	328.1	70	1124	27	5/132	1	0	41.63
D. R. MacKenzie (Qld)	13.3	1	45	3	3/45	0	0	15.00
G. J. Mail (NW)	1	0	9	0	–	0	0	–
D. J. Marsh (Tas)	155	31	473	8	4/70	0	0	59.13
C. S. Martin (New Zealanders)	93	14	360	3	1/59	0	0	120.00
D. R. Martyn (WAust/Aust)	15	2	48	1	1/3	0	0	48.00
A. B. McDonald (Vic)	9.4	2	20	2	1/6	0	0	10.00
B. E. McGain (Vic)	53.3	10	202	6	3/46	0	0	33.67
G. D. McGrath (NSW/Aust)	340.5	107	880	24	3/13	0	0	36.67
P. E. McIntyre (SAust)	225.4	42	741	18	6/75	1	0	41.17
C. D. McMillan (New Zealanders) ..	49.3	5	242	6	3/65	0	0	40.33
S. W. Meuleman (WAust)	1	0	1	0	–	0	0	–
C. R. Miller (Vic)	132.1	26	435	6	2/98	0	0	72.50
J. Moss (Vic)	74	22	153	7	3/35	0	0	21.86
M. P. Mott (Vic)	7	4	15	0	–	0	0	–
D. A. Nash (NSW)	259	60	909	21	4/59	0	0	43.29
D. J. Nash (New Zealanders)	30	6	93	0	–	0	0	–
M. J. Nicholson (WAust)	299.4	62	936	33	5/68	1	0	28.36
A. A. Noffke (Qld)	380.4	97	1110	39	5/31	2	0	28.46
M. J. North (WAust)	92	17	304	3	1/11	0	0	101.33
M. Ntini (South Africans)	59	18	185	2	2/108	0	0	92.50
A. W. O'Brien (NSW)	33	3	134	1	1/134	0	0	134.00
† S. B. O'Connor (New Zealanders) ...	53.2	17	128	2	1/18	0	0	64.00
B. J. Oldroyd (WAust)	91	21	276	1	1/25	0	0	276.00
J. L. Ontong (South Africans)	14	1	68	0	–	0	0	–
C. T. Perren (Qld)	14	7	15	1	1/15	0	0	15.00
S. M. Pollock (South Africans)	137	33	373	9	3/84	0	0	41.44
R. T. Ponting (Tas/Aust)	12	3	45	1	1/25	0	0	45.00
P. R. Reiffel (Vic)	100.3	24	280	10	4/71	0	0	28.00
P. C. Rofe (SAust)	441.4	152	1060	41	7/52	3	1	25.85
† J. A. Rudolph (South Africans)	2	0	6	0	–	0	0	–
† G. C. Rummans (NSW)	1	0	6	0	–	0	0	–
D. J. Saker (Tas)	366.3	103	1003	38	5/53	1	0	26.39
M. J. Slater (Vic)	1	0	15	0	–	0	0	–
M. J. Smith (SAust)	273.2	54	917	29	7/98	1	0	31.62
G. P. Sulzberger (New Zealanders) ..	57	7	259	4	2/75	0	0	64.75
G. G. Swan (WAust)	88	17	352	4	2/60	0	0	88.00
A. Symonds (Qld)	226.5	61	588	22	4/45	0	0	26.73
B. J. Thomas (Tas)	8	1	52	1	1/52	0	0	52.00
S. B. Tubb (Tas)	28	9	80	5	3/57	0	0	16.00
D. R. Tuffey (New Zealanders)	43	8	166	4	3/71	0	0	41.50
D. A. Turner (NSW)	46.1	8	168	0	–	0	0	–
B. P. Van Deinsen (NSW)	34	12	109	3	3/42	0	0	36.33
D. L. Vettori (New Zealanders)	189.5	38	580	22	6/80	3	0	26.36
L. Vincent (New Zealanders)	1	0	2	0	–	0	0	–
S. K. Warne (Vic/Aust)	373	63	1156	29	5/113	1	0	39.86
S. R. Watson (Tas)	126.4	20	514	22	6/32	2	1	23.36

	O	M	R	W	BB	5W/i	10W/m	Avge
M. E. Waugh (NSW/Aust)	31	4	106	2	1/19	0	0	53.00
C. L. White (Vic)	103	15	405	7	3/97	0	0	57.86
B. A. Williams (WAust)	279	72	906	32	4/34	0	0	28.31
P. Wilson (SAust)	51	9	151	3	2/98	0	0	50.33
D. G. Wright (Tas)	346.3	114	932	23	3/15	0	0	40.52
B. E. Young (SAust)	299.2	61	864	14	3/21	0	0	61.71
S. Young (Tas)	58	17	156	1	1/13	0	0	156.00

INDIVIDUAL SCORES OF 100 AND OVER

There were 84 three-figure innings in 41 first-class matches in 2001-02, 22 more than in 2000-01 when 38 matches were played. Of these, six were double-hundreds compared with four in 2000-01. This list includes 57 hundreds hit in the Pura Cup, the same as in the previous two seasons.

*Denotes not out. † Denotes retired hurt.

M. L. Hayden (6)
143   Qld v WAust, Brisbane.
147   Qld v Vic, Richmond.
136   Aust v New Zealand, Brisbane.
131   Aust v South Africa, Adelaide.
138   Aust v South Africa, Melbourne.
105   Aust v South Africa, Sydney.

G. S. Blewett (5)
169*   SAust v Vic, Adelaide.
163   SAust v Tas, Hobart (Bel).
106   SAust v New Zealanders, Adelaide.
109   SAust v Qld, Brisbane.
112*   SAust v WAust, Perth.

J. L. Langer (5)
133   WAust v Tas, Perth.
104   Aust v New Zealand, Brisbane.
123   Aust v New Zealand, Hobart (Bel).
116   Aust v South Africa, Adelaide.
126   Aust v South Africa, Sydney.

M. G. Bevan (4)
102   NSW v Tas, Sydney.
128   NSW v Vic, Richmond.
203*   NSW v WAust, Sydney.
183*   NSW v South Africans, Sydney.

B. J. Hodge (4)
140   Vic v SAust, Adelaide.
110*   Vic v SAust, Adelaide.
109   Vic v Tas, Melbourne.
131   Vic v WAust, Melbourne.

D. S. Lehmann (4)
103   SAust v Vic, Adelaide.
246   SAust v Tas, Hobart (Bel).
143   SAust v NSW, Adelaide.
129   SAust v Qld, Brisbane.

B. A. Johnson (3)
121*   SAust v WAust, Adelaide.
138*   SAust v Vic, Melbourne.
138   SAust v Tas, Adelaide.

J. P. Maher (3)
174   Qld v WAust, Perth.
209   Qld v SAust, Brisbane.
198   Qld v NSW, Sydney.

D. R. Martyn (3)
189   WAust v Tas, Perth.
117   Aust v South Africa, Sydney.
131   Aust v South Africa, Adelaide.

M. J. North (3)
106   WAust v Qld, Perth.
200*   WAust v Vic, Melbourne.
111   WAust v SAust, Perth.
169*   SAust v Vic, Adelaide.

R. T. Ponting (3)
126   Tas v NSW, Sydney.
154   Tas v NSW, Sydney.
157*   Aust v New Zealand, Hobart (Bel).

N. J. Astle (2)
223   New Zealanders v Qld, Brisbane.
156*   New Zealand v Aust, Perth.

M. J. Clarke (2)
111   NSW v Vic, Richmond.
132   NSW v SAust, Adelaide.

S. G. Clingeleffer (2)
141*   Tas v SAust, Hobart (Bel).
112   Tas v Vic, Hobart (Bel).

J. Cox (2)
107   Tas v NSW, Sydney.
174   Tas v SAust, Adelaide.

M. G. Dighton (2)
126   Tas v Vic, Hobart (Bel).
124   Tas v Vic, Melbourne.

M. L. Love (2)
†202* Qld v SAust, Adelaide.
184   Qld v NSW, Sydney.

C. J. L. Rogers (2)
101*   WAust v SAust, Perth.
102*   WAust v SAust, Perth.

The following each played one three-figure innings:

D.S. Berry, 148, Vic v NSW, Sydney; M.V. Boucher, 134, South Africans v WAust, Perth.
R.J. Campbell, 121, WAust v NSW, Perth.
C.J. Davies, 119, SAust v Qld, Brisbane; H.H. Dippenaar, 115, South Africans v NSW, Sydney.
M.T.G. Elliott, 135*, Vic v Tas, Hobart (Bel).
D.A. Fitzgerald, 139, SAust v Qld, Adelaide; S.P. Fleming, 105, New Zealand v Aust, Perth.
H.H. Gibbs, 145, South Africans v NSW, Sydney; A.C. Gilchrist, 118, Aust v New Zealand,
    Brisbane; M.W. Goodwin, 141, WAust v Tas, Perth.
B.J. Haddin, 102, NSW v Qld, Sydney; D.F. Hills, 136, Tas v NSW, Sydney; M.E.K. Hussey, 100,
    WAust v NSW, Sydney.
J.H. Kallis, 120, South Africans v WAust, Perth; S.M. Katich, 131, WAust v NSW, Sydney; G.
    Kirsten, 153, South Africa v Aust, Sydney.
G.J. Mail, 150*, NSW v SAust, Sydney; N.D. McKenzie, 114*, South Africans v WAust, Perth; S.
    W. Meuleman, 109, WAust v South Africans, Perth; J. Moss, 109, Vic v NSW, Sydney.
B.P. Nash, 157, Qld v SAust, Adelaide; M.J. Nicholson, 101*, WAust v South Africans, Perth.
A.C. Parore 110, New Zealand v Aust, Perth.
L. Vincent, 104, New Zealand v Aust, Perth.
M.E. Waugh, 168, NSW v Tas, Sydney.
B.E. Young, 122, SAust v NSW, Adelaide.

TEN OR MORE WICKETS IN A MATCH

S.J. Jurgensen (2)
11/123   Tas v NSW, Hobart (Bel).
11/172   Tas v Qld, Brisbane.

J.N. Gillespie (1)
10/162   SAust v NSW, Sydney.

M.W.H. Inness (1)
11/186   Vic v NSW, Sydney.

P.C. Rofe (1)
13/112   SAust v NSW, Sydney.

S.R. Watson (1)
11/78   Tas v Qld, Hobart (Bel).

FIVE OR MORE WICKETS IN AN INNINGS

S.R. Clark (4)
5/64   NSW v Tas, Sydney.
5/47   NSW v Vic, Richmond.
5/75   NSW v Vic, Sydney.
5/42   NSW v Qld, Sydney.

S.J. Jurgensen (4)
5/38   Tas v NSW, Hobart (Bel).
6/65   Tas v NSW, Hobart (Bel).
5/68   Tas v Qld, Brisbane.
6/104   Tas v Qld, Brisbane.

P.C. Rofe (3)
5/30   SAust v WAust, Adelaide.
6/60   SAust v NSW, Adelaide.
7/52   SAust v NSW, Adelaide.

D.L. Vettori (3)
6/80   New Zealanders v SAust, Adelaide.
5/138   New Zealand v Aust, Hobart.
6/87   New Zealand v Aust, Perth.

C.L. Cairns (2)
5/71   New Zealanders v Qld, Brisbane.
5/146   New Zealand v Aust, Brisbane.

M.S. Kasprowicz (2)
5/44   Qld v NSW, Brisbane.
5/60   Qld v Tas, Brisbane.

B. Lee (2)
5/56   NSW v SAust, Sydney.
5/67   Aust v New Zealand, Brisbane.

A.A. Noffke (2)
5/103   Qld v WAust, Perth.
5/31   Qld v SAust, Adelaide.

S.R. Watson (2)
6/32 Tas v Qld, Hobart (Bel).
5/46 Tas v Qld, Hobart (Bel).

The following each took five wickets or more in an innings on one occasion:

J. Angel, 6/52, WAust v Vic, Perth.
W.N. Carr, 6/46, Vic v Qld, Brisbane.
J.N. Gillespie, 8/50, SAust v NSW, Sydney.

M. A. Harrity, 5/65, SAust v Tas, Hobart (Bel).

M. W. H. Inness, 7/19, Vic v NSW, Sydney.

S. C. G. MacGill, 5/132, NSW v South Africans, Sydney; P. E. McIntyre, 6/75, SAust v New Zealanders, Adelaide.

M. J. Nicholson, 5/68, WAust v South Africans, Perth.

D. J. Saker, 5/53, Tas v SAust, Adelaide; M. J. Smith, 7/98, SAust v Qld, Brisbane.

S. K. Warne, 5/113, Aust v South Africa, Adelaide.

BATSMEN WINNING A TEST WITH A SIX

Batsman (score)	Team v Opponent	Bowler	Venue	Season
E. R. Paynter (14*)	England v Australia	S. J. McCabe	Brisbane	1932-33
W. R. Hammond (75*)	England v Australia	P. K. Lee	Sydney	1932-33
W. R. Hammond (29*)	England v West Indies	E. A. Martindale	Bridgetown	1934-35
L. Hutton (32*)	England v South Africa	N. B. F. Mann	Leeds	1947
W. Watson (27*)	England v West Indies	E. D. Weekes	Georgetown	1953-54
H. R. Lance (28*)	South Africa v Australia	I. M. Chappell	Port Elizabeth	1966-67
Javed Miandad (25*)	Pakistan v New Zealand	P. J. Petherick	Lahore	1976-77
A. Turner (20*)	Australia v New Zealand	E. J. Chatfield	Auckland	1976-77
Zaheer Abbas (34*)	Pakistan v India	G. R. Viswanath	Lahore	1978-79
R. J. Hadlee (6*)	New Zealand v Australia	B. Yardley	Auckland	1981-82
Mohsin Khan (14*)	Pakistan v Australia	K. J. Hughes	Karachi	1982-83
P. J. Dujon (17*)	West Indies v India	M. Amarnath	Kingston	1982-83
R. J. Hadlee (17*)	New Zealand v Sri Lanka	J. R. Ratnayeke	Wellington	1982-83
Kapil Dev (23*)	India v England	P. H. Edmonds	Lord's	1986
A. L. Logie (6*)	West Indies v India	M. Venkataramana	Kingston	1988-89
I. V. A. Richards (73*)	West Indies v England	R. K. Illingworth	Birmingham	1991
S. T. Jayasuriya (6*)	Sri Lanka v England	P. C. R. Tufnell	Colombo	1992-93
Rashid Latif (13*)	Pakistan v New Zealand	S. A. Thomson	Auckland	1993-94
I. A. Healy (10*)	Australia v South Africa	W. J. Cronje	Port Elizabeth	1996-97
C. L. Hooper (6*)	West Indies v Sri Lanka	M. Muralitharan	St John's	1996-97
Harbhajan Singh (14*)	India v Zimbabwe	H. H. Streak	Delhi	2001-02
R. T. Ponting (100*)	Australia v South Africa	P. R. Adams	Cape Town	2001-02
M. V. Boucher (8*)	South Africa v Australia	M. E. Waugh	Durban	2001-02

– KERSI MEHER-HOMJI and RAJESH KUMAR

PURA CUP, 2001-02

By WARWICK FRANKS

Queensland won their third successive Pura Cup. How accomplished and expected it all seemed, when even a decade ago such a headline would have looked like a postscript to *Brave New World*. All the old jokes about Queensland's chances of winning a trophy, like all the sniggering southern condescension, are now dated curiosities and have gone to join the autocratic administrators who once strutted the stage of their banana empire at the Gabba. The likes of Leo O'Connor, Ron Oxenham and Cecil Thompson who gave their considerable all in those lean early years of Sheffield Shield endeavour must rest content that their state is now the acknowledged power in Australian domestic cricket.

Despite a less prosperous second half to the season, Queensland never looked like losing the competition lead, just as they never looked like losing the final. Perhaps the most satisfying aspect of all of their recent successes is that each time justice was not only done, but was seen to be done, as they have been clearly the outstanding team both over the long haul of the season and in the crucible of the final. Astutely led by Stuart Law, the team exuded a purpose and self-belief which are the hallmarks of all successful teams. This season, they had the two most prolific batsmen of the competition in Martin Love and Jimmy Maher. Not only did they both pass 1,000 runs for the season, but they made the runs with a style and conviction which added to their already considerable reputations. Love combined elegance and rigour, and his ability to perform on the big occasion was underlined by another ninety in the final which took his average past 55 for the six finals in which he has appeared. Maher so grew in confidence and command at the crease that it was no surprise that he was recalled to the Australian limited-overs side. Apart from Matthew Hayden's productive contributions at the beginning of the season, the rest of the batting was patchy, although Brendan Nash did enough, particularly in the final, to suggest that he had a real future. It was significant, though, that when the chips were down in the final, the experience of both Andrew Symonds and Law allowed them to transcend the scratchiness of their form with match-defining innings. The attack was led by the maturity of Michael Kasprowicz and balanced by the continued youthful vigour of Ashley Noffke, with sufficient support to make batting against the Queenslanders never a comfortable proposition. Needless to say, the keeping of Wade Seccombe met the exacting standard of excellence which he has struck during his career.

The Tasmanians had another season of split fortunes, and seemed to have reached their nadir when Queensland gave them a two-day thrashing at the Gabba, leaving the islanders with just four points from five matches. They then won four of their last five matches outright, beginning with their own two-day riposte to Queensland, at Hobart, and continued to play with a purpose and an aggression which evaporated briefly, but fatally, in one miserable session on the second day of the final. The youthful hue of the side, harnessed by the wisdom and example of Jamie Cox, promised well for the future, with such players as wicket-keeper Sean Clingeleffer already being mentioned for future advancement. During the season, the selectors also served notice that they were interested only in players who were both able and willing to be part of a team effort in putting side before self.

Western Australia rose from fifth to third place, and an ability to convert more than three of their matches into outright wins might have taken them further. Jo Angel, Brad Williams and Matthew Nicholson continued the long tradition of pace bowling in the west, although the batting was limited in achievement, Simon Katich's quiet season costing him his ACB contract.

The South Australians climbed two steps out of the cellar and had the satisfaction of beating Queensland in style at the Gabba. There is still concern as to when the new generation of substantial players will appear, although an important partial answer came with the arrival of Paul Rofe, a fast bowler whose appetite for work never dulled the edges of either his accuracy or his penetration.

Victoria had a doleful decline from second to fifth spot, needing to reach the sixth match before they registered a point. Further into the nether regions, New South Wales dropped to the bottom of the competition for the third time in four seasons, scoring their last point from their third match, in early November. All the old assumptions about the innate strength of cricket in these two states now no longer even offer a rag of comfort and both states need to address a crisis which has already arrived. Both of them have allowed such bloated and unwieldy metropolitan competitions to spawn and develop that more than one state selector has asserted that grade and district form is a totally unreliable guide to performance at higher levels. If the parochialism of narrow club interest, combined with a Micawber-like belief that something will turn up, continues any further, both states can expect to continue to occupy the bottom rungs of the Pura Cup ladder.

The bowling aggregates were still dominated by the quick bowlers to the extent that not one of the 16 bowlers who took more than 20 wickets was a spinner, even Stuart MacGill being strangely ineffective. Yet a welcome feature of the season was the appearance of several young spin bowlers of promise. Victoria's Cameron White did not have a prolific season but continued to work at the complexities of his art, while a number of critics were impressed with Xavier Doherty, Tasmania's new slow left-armer, who has an obvious grasp of the attacking potential of flight and spin. The notion of a Queensland spinner seemed to have become an oxymoron but the off-breaks of Nathan Hauritz were nurtured and supported to the point where he became an important member of the attack, and made a satisfactory step up into the Australian limited-overs side. He, too, is an artful bowler to watch, avoiding the English tendency to confuse darts bowled at the batsman's leg stump with genuine off-spin bowling.

The season saw much cricket that was skilful and stimulating. Darren Lehmann's 246 at Hobart rose towards the sublime in his thrilling domination of an attack, while Charlie Puckett, whose obituary appears in this issue, would have seen a kindred spirit in Tasmania's Shane Jurgensen, who finished the season with a series of sustained spells of accuracy and venom. Late in the season, there was an engrossing match at Melbourne in which Western Australia trailed the home side by 275 runs on the first innings, yet swooped on victory by 37 runs late on the last day, thanks to an undefeated double-century by Marcus North and self-belief by his side's bowlers. Cricket does not come much more absorbing than this game, yet it was watched by few spectators, apart from the devotees of the Matthew Mott Appreciation Society.

Unfortunately, coverage of the final went the same way, apart from the two states directly involved. In what Melbourne lawyer and cricket devotee J. Neville Turner termed "a perversion of values", the light of the climax of the domestic season was hidden under a media bushel. Fugitive items, occasional news updates and sporadic broadcasts were all that was offered to most cricket followers at the high point of the domestic year. Pura Cup cricket needs and deserves better: that is the challenge for the ACB and the state associations.

2001-02 POINTS TABLE

	Played	Won	Lost	Drawn	1st-inns Points	Points	Quotient
Queensland	10	8	2	0	6	36	1.178
Tasmania	10	7	3	0	6	30	1.227
Western Australia	10	7	3	0	8	26	1.094
South Australia	10	4	6	0	2	18	0.893
Victoria	10	2	8	0	4	16	0.950
New South Wales	10	2	8	0	0	12	0.776

Outright win = 6 pts; lead on first innings in a drawn or lost game = 2 pts.

Quotient = runs per wicket scored divided by runs per wicket conceded.

Under Australian Cricket Board playing conditions, a penalty of one run for a no-ball and a wide shall be scored. This penalty shall stand in addition to any other runs which are scored or awarded.

PURA CUP FINAL, 2001-02

QUEENSLAND v TASMANIA

At Brisbane Cricket Ground, Brisbane, March 22, 23, 24, 25, 26, 2002. Queensland won by 235 runs. Toss: Tasmania.

Any Tasmanian hopes that a third time in the final might prove lucky came crashing to earth between tea and stumps on the second day. Losing a calamitous eight wickets for 68 in that session undid all the good work of the bowlers and gave Queensland an unexpected cache of runs which they used as a deposit on which to build an unassailable 530-run lead.

In contrast, the Tasmanians had made good headway until mid-afternoon on the first day when they had Queensland at an unconvincing three for 85. Even at that stage, though, there had been the ill-omen of Daniel Marsh limping from the field during the first session after injuring his knee while making a second attempt to catch Daniel Payne at first slip. The sense that the wheel of fortune was spinning against them was compounded when umpire Steve Davis turned down a stentorian appeal for leg before wicket to the first ball faced by Andrew Symonds and another of similar conviction when the batsman was only three. The advent of the Queensland captain soon after brought together two players who had both experienced wretched seasons: Symonds had lost his spot in the national limited-overs side and had cobbled together just 187 Pura Cup runs at 17.00, while Law had battled a broken finger and had made an unconvincing 196 runs at 19.60. They spent the rest of the day laying their batting ghosts to rest as they demonstrated the value of the combination of temperament, experience and self-discipline. Symonds (210 minutes, 157 balls, seven fours, one six) was more restrained than usual, showing real discretion in picking the ball to hit, while Law (211 minutes, 165 balls, seven fours) mixed obduracy with the occasional dismissive stroke in their partnership of 155.

David Saker's breaking of the partnership in the opening over of the second morning heralded a complete crumbling of the Queensland innings. Six wickets fell for 49 runs as Shane Jurgensen and Gerard Denton docked the tail efficiently and seemed to have put the Tasmanians firmly back into the contest. During the afternoon session, they made unspectacular progress to two for 73, Queensland having lost young left-arm pace man Scott Brant with a side strain after he had bowled only four overs. From there, Michael Kasprowicz led an assault on the batting, demonstrating that combination of finesse and fire that make him such a formidable proposition, particularly in Brisbane. He was given excellent support by both Ashley Noffke, who repeated his bowling success of the previous season's final, and Symonds. Four catches by keeper Wade Seccombe and several more in the arc between first slip and gully were evidence of the way in which too many of the batsmen were reluctant to get behind the line.

The Queenslanders knew that to ensure the inevitable result from there was just a matter of sensible occupation of the crease. Brendan Nash (273 minutes, 216 balls, eight fours) and Martin Love (228 minutes, 190 balls, eight fours) set the policy in motion with a second-wicket partnership of 177 during which they avoided risk while ensuring that the scoreboard kept moving. Even at this stage, the Tasmanian bowlers prevented a total rout as Jurgensen in particular showed his ability to bowl for long spells without blunting his attacking potential. In gaining his fourth successive return of five wickets in an innings, he also achieved the best match figures by a bowler in the history of Sheffield Shield/Pura Cup finals. A further scrape of icing was added to the Queensland cake when Noffke (117 minutes, 87 balls, three fours) batted sensibly, finally being joined by Joe Dawes in a last-wicket partnership of 52.

None of the miracles needed for Tasmania to win eventuated. Instead of the several big centuries which would have been a minimum requirement, Michael Di Venuto (178 minutes, 147 balls, five fours, one six) did best with 65, joining Scott Kremerskothen (140 minutes, 107 balls, one four) in a fifth-wicket partnership of 111 which took the match into a fifth day. Kasprowicz and Symonds combined efficiently to snuff out any threatening signs of resistance to ensure that Queensland achieved their third successive victory in a Pura Cup final.

Man of the Match: A. Symonds. *Attendance:* 7,768.

Close of play: First day, Queensland (1) 4-253 (Symonds 91, Law 62); Second day, Queensland (2) 0-25 (Payne 21, Nash 3); Third day, Queensland (2) 6-279 (Law 1); Fourth day, Tasmania (2) 4-190 (Di Venuto 42, Kremerskothen 26).

Queensland

B.P. Nash c Clingeleffer b Jurgensen	12	–	(2) c Di Venuto b Marsh	96
D.M. Payne c (sub) Tubb b Denton	17	–	(1) c Dighton b Saker	29
M.L. Love lbw b Jurgensen	34	–	c Wright b Kremerskothen	93
L.A. Carseldine c Kremerskothen b Jurgensen	29	–	c Kremerskothen b Jurgensen	12
A. Symonds b Jurgensen	91	–	lbw b Jurgensen	32
*S.G. Law c Wright b Saker	69	–	c Marsh b Jurgensen	15
†W.A. Seccombe c Di Venuto b Jurgensen	1	–	c Clingeleffer b Jurgensen	5
A.A. Noffke c Clingeleffer b Denton	14	–	not out	47
M.S. Kasprowicz c Clingeleffer b Denton	2	–	c Clingeleffer b Jurgensen	2
S.A. Brant not out	16	–	c (sub) Doherty b Jurgensen	0
J.H. Dawes c Di Venuto b Wright	7	–	c Clingeleffer b Kremerskothen	26
L-b 9, n-b 1	10		L-b 7, w 4	11

(114 overs, 455 mins)   302
Fall: 29 48 85 98 253 261 263
    274 279 302

(124.5 overs, 485 mins)   368
Fall: 46 223 225 270 273 279
    310 312 316 368

Bowling: *First Innings*—Saker 29–8–68–1; Jurgensen 35–12–68–5; Denton 22–7–67–3; Wright 21–6–60–1; Kremerskothen 7–0–30–0. *Second Innings*—Saker 17–6–36–1; Jurgensen 34–6–104–6; Denton 27–4–97–0; Wright 17–6–39–0; Marsh 16–5–39–1; Kremerskothen 13.5–1–46–2.

Tasmania

S.R. Mason lbw b Symonds	17	–	(2) c Seccombe b Kasprowicz	39
*J. Cox c Payne b Kasprowicz	14	–	(1) c Payne b Kasprowicz	19
M.G. Dighton c Love b Kasprowicz	29	–	c Kasprowicz b Symonds	38
M.J. Di Venuto c Seccombe b Kasprowicz	11	–	c Carseldine b Symonds	65
D.J. Marsh lbw b Symonds	27	–	c Seccombe b Symonds	2
S.P. Kremerskothen c (sub) Perren b Kasprowicz	10	–	c (sub) Anderson b Symonds	41
†S.G. Clingeleffer c Carseldine b Noffke	5	–	c Seccombe b Noffke	12
D.G. Wright c Seccombe b Noffke	12	–	not out	27
D.J. Saker c Seccombe b Noffke	2	–	c Seccombe b Noffke	5
G.J. Denton c Seccombe b Kasprowicz	0	–	c Seccombe b Kasprowicz	0
S.J. Jurgensen not out	0	–	c Carseldine b Kasprowicz	8
B 4, l-b 4, w 3, n-b 3	14		L-b 7, W 9, n-b 22	38

(56.2 overs, 239 mins)   141
Fall: 25 63 78 89 119 119 131
    136 141 141

(99.5 overs, 411 mins)   294
Fall: 54 110 115 122 233 234
    252 270 276 294

Bowling: *First Innings*—Kasprowicz 20–7–60–5; Brant 4–1–10–0; Dawes 14–5–28–0; Noffke 10.2–3–15–3; Symonds 8–1–20–2. *Second Innings*—Kasprowicz 27.5–5–103–4; Dawes 22–5–66–0; Noffke 24–3–62–2; Symonds 22–8–45–4; Carseldine 4–1–11–0.

Umpires: S.J. Davis and S.J.A. Taufel.
TV Umpire: P.D. Parker.

STATISTICS, 2001-02

	M	For Runs	For Wickets	For Avge	Against Runs	Against Wickets	Against Avge
New South Wales	10	5,208	175	29.76	5,367	140	38.34
Queensland	11	5,134	155	33.12	4,927	180	27.37
South Australia	10	5,125	161	31.83	5,595	157	35.64
Tasmania	11	5,118	145	35.30	4,915	159	30.91
Victoria	10	4,667	150	31.11	4,715	144	32.74
Western Australia	10	5,421	148	36.63	5,154	154	33.47

OVERS BOWLED AND RUNS SCORED, 2001-02

	Overs bowled per hour	Runs scored/ 100 balls
New South Wales	15.22	55.81
Queensland	15.48	53.21
South Australia	15.45	52.49
Tasmania	15.52	49.67
Victoria	14.93	47.36
Western Australia	16.41	53.11

LEADING BATTING AVERAGES, 2001-02

(Qualification: 500 runs)

	M	I	NO	R	HS	100s	50s	Avge
J.P. Maher (Qld)	9	17	1	1,085	209	3	5	67.81
M.L. Love (Qld)	11	20	3	1,108	202*	2	6	65.18
D.S. Lehmann (SAust)	7	12	0	772	246	4	0	64.33
B.A. Johnson (SAust)	7	14	3	653	138*	3	2	59.36
B.J. Hodge (Vic)	10	18	3	858	140	4	2	57.20
M.G. Bevan (NSW)	7	13	1	685	203*	3	3	57.08
G.S. Blewett (SAust)	10	19	3	858	169*	4	2	53.63
S.G. Clingeleffer (Tas)	11	15	4	517	141*	2	1	47.00
M.T.G. Elliott (Vic)	10	20	2	780	135*	1	6	43.33
M.J. North (WAust)	8	14	1	562	200*	3	0	43.23

* Denotes not out.

LEADING BOWLING AVERAGES, 2001-02

(Qualification: 15 wickets)

	M	O	Mdns	R	W	BB	5W/i	10W/m	Avge
M.W.H. Inness (Vic)	7	214.5	61	597	31	7/19	1	1	19.26
S.J. Jurgensen (Tas)	9	290	85	710	36	6/65	4	2	19.72
M.S. Kasprowicz (Qld)	9	343.5	85	1,082	49	5/44	2	0	22.08
S.R. Clark (NSW)	9	387	108	1,047	45	5/42	4	0	23.27
S.R. Watson (Tas)	7	126.4	20	514	22	6/32	2	1	23.36
J. Angel (WAust)	10	412	124	1,074	44	6/52	1	0	24.41
P.C. Rofe (SAust)	10	410.4	140	1,012	41	7/52	3	1	24.68
A.A. Noffke (Qld)	10	345.4	85	1,000	38	5/31	2	0	26.32
D.J. Saker (Tas)	7	366.3	103	1,003	38	5/53	1	0	26.39
B.A. Williams (WAust)	7	279	72	906	32	4/34	0	0	28.31

MOST CATCHES, 2001-02

	M	Ct
D.J Marsh (Tas)	11	20
M.E.K. Hussey (WAust)	10	16
M.T.G. Elliott (Vic)	10	15
J.P. Maher (Qld)	9	14
S. Lee (NSW)	6	10

MOST DISMISSALS, 2001-02

	M	Ct	St	Total
W. A. Seccombe (Qld)	11	49	0	49
S. G. Clingeleffer (Tas)	11	36	0	36
D. S. Berry (Vic)	10	32	3	35
G. A. Manou (SAust)	9	30	2	32
R. J. Campbell (WAust)	8	30	0	30
B. J. Haddin (NSW)	9	23	0	23
N. S. Pilon (NSW)	1	9	0	9
A. C. Gilchrist (WAust)	2	7	0	7

AUSTRALIAN DOMESTIC FIRST-CLASS COMPETITION WINNERS

Sheffield Shield

Season	Winner	Season	Winner
1892-93		1937-38	New South Wales
1893-94	South Australia	1938-39	South Australia
1894-95	Victoria	1939-40	New South Wales
1895-96	New South Wales	1940-41	–
1896-97	New South Wales	1941-42	–
1897-98	Victoria	1942-43	–
1898-99	Victoria	1943-44	–
1899-00	New South Wales	1944-45	–
1900-01	Victoria	1945-46	–
1901-02	New South Wales	1946-47	Victoria
1902-03	New South Wales	1947-48	Western Australia
1903-04	New South Wales	1949-50	New South Wales
1904-05	New South Wales	1950-51	Victoria
1905-06	New South Wales	1951-52	New South Wales
1906-07	New South Wales	1952-53	South Australia
1907-08	Victoria	1953-54	New South Wales
1908-09	New South Wales	1954-55	New South Wales
1909-10	South Australia	1955-56	New South Wales
1910-11	New South Wales	1956-57	New South Wales
1911-12	New South Wales	1957-58	New South Wales
1912-13	South Australia	1958-59	New South Wales
1913-14	New South Wales	1959-60	New South Wales
1914-15	Victoria	1960-61	New South Wales
1915-16	–	1961-62	New South Wales
1916-17	–	1962-63	Victoria
1917-18	–	1963-64	South Australia
1918-19	–	1963-64	South Australia
1919-20	New South Wales	1964-65	New South Wales
1920-21	New South Wales	1965-66	New South Wales
1921-22	Victoria	1966-67	Victoria
1922-23	New South Wales	1967-68	Western Australia
1923-24	Victoria	1968-69	South Australia
1924-25	Victoria	1969-70	Victoria
1925-26	New South Wales	1970-71	South Australia
1926-27	South Australia	1971-72	Western Australia
1927-28	Victoria	1972-73	Western Australia
1928-29	New South Wales	1973-74	Victoria
1929-30	Victoria	1974-75	Western Australia
1930-31	Victoria	1975-76	South Australia
1931-32	New South Wales	1976-77	Western Australia
1932-33	New South Wales	1977-78	Western Australia
1933-34	Victoria	1978-79	Victoria
1934-35	Victoria	1979-80	Victoria
1935-36	South Australia	1980-81	Western Australia
1936-37	Victoria	1981-82	South Australia
		1982-83	New South Wales

1983-84	Western Australia	1994-95	Queensland
1984-85	New South Wales	1995-96	South Australia
1985-86	New South Wales	1996-97	Queensland
1986-87	Western Australia	1997-98	Western Australia
1987-88	Western Australia	1998-99	Western Australia
1988-89	Western Australia	**Pura Milk Cup**	
1989-90	New South Wales	1999-00	Queensland
1990-91	Victoria		
1991-92	Western Australia	**Pura Cup**	
1992-93	New South Wales	2000-01	Queensland
1993-94	New South Wales	2001-02	Queensland

Note: The Sheffield Shield was not played during World Wars I and II.

FINALS

1982-83	Western Australia lost to New South Wales at Perth by 54 runs.
1983-84	Western Australia defeated Queensland at Perth by four wickets.
1984-85	New South Wales defeated Queensland at Sydney by one wicket.
1985-86	New South Wales drew with Queensland at Sydney.
1986-87	Western Australia drew with Victoria at Perth.
1987-88	Western Australia defeated Queensland at Perth by five wickets.
1988-89	Western Australia drew with South Australia at Perth.
1989-90	New South Wales defeated Queensland at Sydney by 345 runs.
1990-91	Victoria defeated New South Wales at Melbourne by eight wickets.
1991-92	Western Australia defeated New South Wales at Perth by 44 runs.
1992-93	New South Wales defeated Queensland at Sydney by eight wickets.
1993-94	New South Wales defeated Tasmania at Sydney by an innings and 61 runs.
1994-95	Queensland defeated South Australia at Brisbane by an innings and 101 runs.
1995-96	South Australia drew with Western Australia at Adelaide.
1996-97	Western Australia lost to Queensland at Perth by 160 runs.
1997-98	Western Australia defeated Tasmania at Perth by seven wickets.
1998-99	Queensland lost to Western Australia at Brisbane by an innings and 131 runs.
1999-00	Queensland drew with Victoria at Brisbane.
2000-01	Queensland defeated Victoria at Brisbane by four wickets.
2001-02	Queensland defeated Tasmania at Brisbane by 235 runs.

Note: Since 1982-83 the winner of the season's competition has been decided by the two top teams at the end of the competition playing a final at the top of the table's choice of venue.

MATCH RESULTS, 1892-93 TO 2001-02

Opponent	Played	Won	Lost	Drawn	Tied
South Australia	679	192	300	186	1
New South Wales	688	294	191	202	1
Victoria	681	251	197	232	1
Queensland	571	160	197	213	1
Western Australia	457	158	129	170	0
Tasmania	228	41	82	105	0
Total	1,652	1,096	1,096	554	2

PLACINGS

	1st	2nd	3rd	4th	5th	6th	Seasons
South Australia	13	21	32	11	19	4	100
New South Wales	42	22	19	9	5	3	100
Victoria	25	33	21	7	7	7	100
Queensland	5	14	15	23	12	1	70
Western Australia	15	7	11	14	8	0	55
Tasmania	0	3	2	6	4	10	25
Total	100	100	100	70	55	25	100

LAST TEN YEARS' PLACINGS

	92-93	93-94	94-95	95-96	96-97	97-98	98-99	99-00	00-01	01-02
South Australia ...	5	4	2	1	6	6	4	4	6	4
New South Wales .	1	1	5	5	3	4	6	6	3	6
Victoria	6	5	3	6	5	5	3	2	2	5
Queensland	2	6	1	3	1	3	2	1	1	1
Western Australia .	4	3	4	2	2	1	1	3	5	3
Tasmania	3	2	6	4	4	2	5	5	4	2

MOST RUNS IN A SEASON

		M	I	NO	R	HS	100s	50s	Avge
G.N. Yallop (Vic)..............	1982-83	10	18	0	1,254	246	4	5	69.66
M.G. Bevan (NSW)............	1993-94	11	20	5	1,240	203*	5	7	82.67
W.H. Ponsford (Vic)	1927-28	5	8	0	1,217	437	4	1	152.12
D.M. Jones (Vic)	1994-95	10	19	3	1,216	324*	4	3	76.00
G.S. Blewett (SAust)	2000-01	9	18	1	1,162	260*	3	6	68.35
J. Cox (Tas)................	1996-97	10	20	1	1,149	143	4	7	60.47
B.A. Richards (SAust)	1970-71	8	13	2	1,145	356	4	3	104.09
S.M. Katich (WAust)	2000-01	10	19	3	1,145	228*	6	2	71.56
J.L. Langer (WAust)	1993-94	10	18	2	1,137	233	1	6	71.06
M.L. Hayden (Qld)............	1993-94	6	12	3	1,136	173*	7	1	126.22
D.F. Hills (Tas)...............	1997-98	11	21	1	1,132	265	4	2	56.60
J.D. Siddons (SAust)	1992-93	10	19	2	1,116	197	4	6	65.65
M.T.G. Elliott (Vic)...........	1995-96	9	17	2	1,116	203	5	3	74.40
D.M. Wellham (NSW).........	1982-83	11	20	5	1,109	136*	2	10	73.93
M.L. Love (Qld)..............	2001-02	11	20	3	1,108	202*	6	2	65.18
D.S. Lehmann (SAust)..........	1994-95	11	20	1	1,104	202*	3	6	58.11
D.S. Lehmann (SAust)..........	1995-96	11	21	1	1,099	161	4	6	54.95
R.B. McCosker (NSW)	1982-83	11	21	3	1,096	124	3	9	60.88
W.H. Ponsford (Vic)	1926-27	5	8	0	1,091	352	5	2	136.37
S.G. Law (Qld)...............	1990-91	10	18	4	1,087	142*	3	8	77.64
J.P. Maher (Qld).............	2001-02	9	17	1	1,085	209	5	3	67.81
J. Cox (Tas)................	2000-01	10	19	3	1,070	160	5	3	66.88
D.S. Lehmann (SAust)	1993-94	10	17	0	1,065	200	4	4	62.65
D.G. Bradman (SAust)..........	1939-40	6	10	2	1,062	267	3	4	132.75
A.D. Ogilvie (Qld)	1977-78	9	18	2	1,060	194	6	2	66.25
T.M. Moody (WAust)	1988-89	11	18	1	1,038	202	4	3	61.06
M.T.G. Elliott (Vic)...........	1999-00	10	19	4	1,028	183*	4	4	68.53
K.C. Wessels (Qld)	1981-82	9	15	0	1,015	220	5	2	67.66
D.F. Hills (Tas)..............	1993-94	11	21	1	1,015	185*	3	7	50.75
D.W. Hookes (SAust)	1987-88	10	18	1	1,014	132	3	7	59.65
G.M. Wood (WAust)	1987-88	11	16	3	1,014	186*	3	5	78.00
G.S. Chappell (Qld)	1973-74	7	13	2	1,013	180	4	4	92.09
J. Dyson (NSW)	1983-84	10	18	3	1,006	241	3	3	67.07
N.C. O'Neill (NSW)	1957-58	8	14	2	1,005	233	4	3	83.75
M.J. Slater (NSW)	1992-92	9	17	1	1,005	143	3	6	62.81

* Denotes not out.

MOST RUNS IN A CAREER

	M	I	NO	R	HS	100s	50s	Avge
D.S. Lehmann (SAust/Vic) ..	119	215	13	10,936	255	37	43	54.14
J.D. Siddons (Vic/SAust)....	146	259	21	10,643	245	30	50	44.72
D.M. Jones (Vic)	110	194	16	9,622	324*	31	40	54.06
J. Cox (Tas)...............	134	244	16	9,601	245	29	41	42.11
D.W. Hookes (SAust)	120	205	9	9,364	306*	26	44	47.78
R.J. Inverarity (WAust/SAust)	159	275	32	9,341	187	22	46	38.44
D.G. Bradman (NSW/SAust).	62	96	15	8,926	452*	36	20	110.19

	M	I	NO	R	HS	100s	50s	Avge
T. M. Moody (WAust)	132	228	22	8,853	272	20	46	42.98
G. S. Chappell (SAust/Qld) ..	101	173	20	8,762	194	27	44	57.27
S. C. Trimble (Qld)	123	230	13	8,647	252*	22	40	39.85
A. R. Border (NSW/Qld)	108	181	19	8,497	200	19	47	52.45
L. E. Favell (SAust).........	121	220	4	8,269	164	20	43	38.28
D. C. Boon (Tas)	119	203	7	8,029	227	20	43	40.96
S. G. Law (Qld)	123	202	24	7,812	216	22	40	43.89
I. M. Chappell (SAust)	89	157	13	7,665	205*	22	45	53.22
A. M. J. Hilditch (NSW/SAust)	109	192	11	7,613	230	18	41	42.06
M. G. Bevan (SAust/NSW) ..	91	162	31	7,549	203*	29	32	57.63
G. S. Blewett (SAust)	83	157	9	7,365	268	20	35	49.76
M. L. Hayden (Qld).	82	149	17	7,323	234	24	30	55.48
M. R. J. Veletta (WAust).....	114	198	20	7,306	262	18	40	41.04
P. J. P. Burge (Qld)	83	138	12	7,084	283	22	31	56.22
G. R. Marsh (WAust)	100	175	12	7,009	355*	21	28	43.00

    * *Denotes not out.*

HIGHEST PARTNERSHIPS FOR EACH WICKET

431 for 1st	M. R. J. Veletta and G. R. Marsh		
	Western Australia v South Australia at Perth	1989-90
386 for 2nd	G. S. Blewett and D. S. Lehmann		
	South Australia v Tasmania at Hobart (Bel).	2001-02
390* for 3rd	J. M. Weiner and J. K. Moss		
	Victoria v Western Australia at St. Kilda	1981-82
462* for 4th	D. W. Hookes and W. B. Phillips		
	South Australia v Tasmania at Adelaide	1986-87
464* for 5th	M. E. Waugh and S. R. Waugh		
	New South Wales v Western Australia at Perth	1990-91
332 for 6th	N. G. Marks and G. Thomas		
	New South Wales v South Australia at Sydney	1958-59
335 for 7th	C. W. Andrews and E. C. Bensted		
	Queensland v New South Wales at Sydney	1934-35
270 for 8th	V. T. Trumper and E. P. Barbour		
	New South Wales v Victoria at Sydney	1912-13
232 for 9th	C. Hill and E. A. Walkley		
	South Australia v New South Wales at Adelaide	1900-01
307 for 10th	A. F. Kippax and J. E. H. Hooker		
	New South Wales v Victoria at Melbourne	1928-29

    * *Denotes unbroken partnership.*

MOST WICKETS IN A SEASON

		M	Balls	Mdns	R	W	BB	5W/i	10W/m	Avge
C. R. Miller (Tas)	1997-98	11	3,590	159	1,642	67	7/49	5	0	24.51
L. O. Fleetwood-Smith (Vic)	1934-35	6	2,164	25	1,137	60	8/113	8	0	18.95
P. R. Reiffel (Vic)	1999-00	11	2552	118	982	59	5/65	1	0	16.64
C. D. Matthews (WAust) ...	1987-88	11	2,553	81	1,215	56	8/101	3	0	21.70
J. Garner (SAust)	1982-83	8	2,419	131	976	55	7/78	4	0	17.74
C. J. McDermott (Qld)	1989-90	10	1,392	100	1,375	54	8/44	4	0	25.46
A. J. Bichel (Qld)	1999-00	11	2421	124	989	53	6/45	2	1	18.66
W. J. O'Reilly (NSW)	1939-40	6	1,766	48	705	52	8/23	6	0	13.55
G. R. A. Lock (WAust)	1966-67	8	2,392	104	1,086	51	6/85	3	0	21.29
B. A. Williams (WAust)	1999-00	10	2194	94	1,151	50	6/74	5	0	23.02

MOST WICKETS IN A CAREER

	M	Balls	Mdns	R	W	BB	5W/i	10W/m	Avge
C. V. Grimmett (Vic/SAust)	79	28,465	446	12,976	513	9/180	48	13	25.29
J. Angel (WAust)	94	20.176	942	9,343	387	6/52	12	0	24.14
T. M. Alderman (WAust)	97	19,288	778	9,299	384	7/28	17	3	24.21
C. G. Rackemann (Qld)	102	22,400	920	10,079	383	7/43	12	1	26.32
G. F. Lawson (NSW)	103	21,391	873	8,742	367	6/31	12	0	23.82
G. R. J. Matthews (NSW)	116	26,764	1,376	10,518	363	8/52	19	4	28.98
J. R. Thomson (NSW-Qld)	84	16,939	429	8,591	355	7/27	18	3	24.20
A. A. Mallett (SAust)	77	20,906	673	8,173	344	7/57	19	2	23.76
D. K. Lillee (WAust/Tas)	75	17,814	475	8,086	338	7/36	18	4	23.92
P. R. Reiffel (Vic)	86	19,137	843	8,242	318	6/57	7	2	25.92
M. S. Kasprowicz (Qld)	74	16,055	680	7,768	316	6/47	20	2	24.58
C. D. Matthews (WAust/Tas)	79	17,663	614	8,912	307	8/101	18	0	29.03
C. R. Miller (SAust/Vic/Tas)	84	20,285	820	9,738	304	7/49	11	2	32.03
C. J. McDermott (Qld)	67	14,974	541	7,605	303	8/44	22	2	25.10
G. A. R. Lock (WAust)	63	20,107	544	7,210	302	7/53	16	2	23.87
A. N. Connolly (Vic)	71	18,033	365	7,745	297	9/67	12	4	26.00
B. P. Julian (WAust)	87	16,143	612	8,573	292	7/39	15	2	29.36
A. I. C. Dodemaide (Vic)	94	19,892	822	8,884	281	6/67	12	0	31.62
J. W. Martin (NSW/SAust)	77	17,078	242	8,703	273	8/97	12	0	31.87
T. B. A. May (SAust)	80	22,575	931	9,943	270	7/93	15	2	36.83
M. G. Hughes (Vic)	76	16,762	582	8,169	267	7/81	10	2	30.60
R. Benaud (NSW)	73	17,811	471	7,174	266	7/32	11	3	26.96
G. Dymock (Qld)	75	17,110	449	7,223	266	6/79	8	0	27.15
D. Tazelaar (Qld)	73	15,371	623	7,050	257	6/48	9	1	27.43
P. R. Sleep (SAust)	127	19,467	671	9,893	254	8/133	7	0	38.94
R. J. Bright (Vic)	101	22,789	1,013	8,833	252	6/61	10	0	35.05
M. R. Whitney (NSW)	77	14,983	562	7,314	251	7/75	10	0	29.14

MOST CATCHES IN A CAREER

R. J. Inverarity (WAust/SAust) ..... 189 in 159 matches
J. D. Siddons (Vic/SAust) .... 189 in 146 matches
M. R. J. Veletta (WAust) .... 138 in 114 matches
D. W. Hookes (SAust) .... 123 in 120 matches
M. A. Taylor (NSW) .... 120 in 85 matches
A. R. Border (NSW/Qld) .... 117 in 108 matches
I. M. Chappell (SAust) .... 114 in 89 matches
T. M. Moody (WAust) .... 114 in 132 matches
D. F. Whatmore (Vic) .... 109 in 85 matches
S. G. Law (Qld) .... 109 in 123 matches
G. S. Chappell (SAust/Qld) .... 103 in 101 matches
G. R. J. Matthews (NSW) .... 102 in 116 matches
M. T. G. Elliott (Vic) .... 102 in 74 matches

MOST DISMISSALS IN A CAREER

	M	Ct	St	Total
D. S. Berry (SAust/Vic)	124	447	41	488
W. A. Seccombe (Qld)	74	352	10	362
T. J. Zoehrer (WAust)	107	331	28	359
R. W. Marsh (WAust)	81	311	33	344
P. A. Emery (NSW)	109	298	41	339
J. A. Maclean (Qld)	86	289	24	313
T. J. Nielsen (SAust)	92	255	29	284
A. T. W. Grout (Qld)	84	213	63	276
S. J. Rixon (NSW)	94	218	43	261
M. N. Atkinson (Tas)	84	236	25	261
A. C. Gilchrist (NSW/WAust)	50	243	8	251
B. N. Jarman (SAust)	77	193	57	250

MOST APPEARANCES

159	R. J. Inverarity (WAust/SAust)	1962-63 – 1984-85
146	J. D. Siddons (Vic/SAust)	1984-85 – 1999-00
134	J. Cox (Tas)	1987-88 – 2001-02
132	T. M. Moody (WAust)	1985-86 – 2000-01
127	P. R. Sleep (SAust)	1976-77 – 1992-93
124	D. S. Berry (SAust/Vic)	1989-90 – 2001-02
123	S. C. Trimble (Qld)	1959-60 – 1975-76
123	S. G. Law (Qld)	1988-89 – 2001-02
121	L. E. Favell (SAust)	1951-52 – 1969-70
120	D. W. Hookes (SAust)	1975-76 – 1991-92
119	D. C. Boon (Tas)	1978-79 – 1998-99
119	D. S. Lehmann (SAust/Vic)	1987-88 – 2001-02
116	G. R. J. Matthews (NSW)	1982-83 – 1997-98
114	M. R. J. Veletta (WAust)	1983-84 – 1994-95
110	D. M. Wellham (NSW/Tas/Qld)	1980-81 – 1993-94
110	D. M. Jones (Vic)	1981-82 – 1997-98
109	G. M. Wood (WAust)	1977-78 – 1991-92
109	A. M. J. Hilditch (NSW/SAust)	1976-77 – 1991-92
109	P. A. Emery	1989-90 – 1998-99
108	A. R. Border (NSW/Qld)	1976-77 – 1995-96
107	H. N. Dansie (SAust)	1949-50 – 1966-67
107	T. J. Zoehrer (WAust)	1980-81 – 1993-94
105	T. V. Hohns (Qld)	1972-73 – 1990-91
104	S. Young (Tas)	1991-92 – 2001-02
103	G. F. Lawson (NSW)	1977-78 – 1991-92
102	C. G. Rackemann (Qld)	1979-80 – 1995-96
101	G. S. Chappell (SAust/Qld)	1966-67 – 1983-84
101	R. J. Bright (Vic)	1972-73 – 1987-88
100	K. D. Mackay (Qld)	1946-47 – 1963-64
100	G. R. Marsh (WAust)	1977-78 – 1993-94
100	T. J. Barsby (Qld)	1984-85 – 1996-97
100	D. F. Hills (Tas)	1991-92 – 2001-02

PLAYED FOR THREE OR MORE STATES

			Batting				Bowling		
			M	R	Avge	W	Avge	Ct
G. D. Watson	Vic	(1964-65 – 1970-71)	34	1,555	32.40	53	26.57	20
	WAust	(1971-72 – 1974-75)	22	997	31.16	54	24.37	25
	NSW	(1976–77)	4	122	20.33	8	22.50	1
	Total		60	2,674	31.09	115	25.25	46
G. J. Cosier	Vic	(1971-72 & 1980-81)	4	133	22.17	2	43.00	2
	SAust	(1974-75 – 1976-77)	20	1,059	29.42	34	22.18	17
	Qld	(1977-78 – 1979-80)	22	1,295	35.97	16	36.75	22
	Total		46	2,487	31.88	52	27.46	41
T. M. Chappell	SAust	(1972-73 – 1975-76)	14	473	18.92	1	60.00	6
	WAust	(1976–77)	4	160	40.00	–	–	2
	NSW	(1979-80 – 1984-85)	45	2,320	32.68	51	21.06	29
	Total		63	2,953	29.53	52	21.90	37
R. J. McCurdy	SAust	(1980-81)	5	45	4.50	17	34.82	3
	Vic	(1981-82 – 1983-84)	20	239	12.58	67	34.19	7
	SAust	(1984-85)	8	128	12.80	36	29.47	5
	Total		33	412	10.56	120	32.87	15
D. M. Wellham	NSW	(1980-81 – 1986-87)	59	3,812	44.33	0	–	28
	Tas	(1988-89 – 1989-90)	30	1,600	41.03	0	–	12
	Qld	(1991-92 – 1993-94)	21	1,327	39.03	0	–	13
	Total		110	6,739	42.38	0	–	53

				Batting			Bowling	
			M	R	Avge	W	Avge	Ct
C.R. Miller	Vic	(1985-86 – 2001-02)	10	88	7.33	27	42.46	2
	SAust	(1988-89 – 1991-92)	20	274	13.05	67	28.96	6
	Tas	(1992-93 – 1999-00)	54	783	15.35	210	31.70	17
	Total		84	1,145	13.63	304	32.03	25
G.J. Rowell	NSW	(1989-90 – 1990-91)	3	77	25.67	11	26.09	1
	Qld	(1991-92 – 1997-98)	34	400	10.81	116	29.80	18
	Tas	(1998-99)	6	12	4.00	18	25.50	3
	Total		43	489	11.37	145	28.99	22

NEW SOUTH WALES

Chief Executive: D. R. Gilbert.

President: A. K. Davidson AM MBE

Cricket Coach: S. J. Rixon

Captain: S. Lee.

Shane Lee

A season that was hoped to end years of first-class famine and extend the previous summer's limited-overs feast came and went with limited-overs champagne but an unfilled Pura Cup. It started well, even without Steve Waugh. The Australian captain was unavailable for New South Wales' first five games, engaging belatedly only in club cricket before the First Test owing to deep vein thrombosis, a disturbing condition detected after he sustained a double tear of his left calf muscle during the triumphant tour of England.

Even when Test spearheads Glenn McGrath and Brett Lee and ageless batting artist Mark Waugh were required for international duty, New South Wales were equal to the task of winning away, and winning well, claiming their Pura Cup match against Victoria by seven wickets at Richmond. Drawing their first home match with Tasmania and then overwhelming South Australia by 290 runs at the Sydney Cricket Ground as well as winning their first three ING Cup limited-over matches, New South Wales revelled in the rarefied atmosphere of leading both interstate competitions by mid-November. Then came New South Wales' usual pre-Christmas spasm, and they lost three of their next four Pura Cup games outright and had to bat marvellously in their second innings at the Sydney Cricket Ground to avoid a bad loss to the Western Australians, thanks essentially to Michael Bevan's unconquered 203, during which the left-hander overtook Alan Kippax's long-standing New South Wales first-class record aggregate of 8,005 runs.

Bevan was to make an unbeaten 183 soon after against the touring South Africans, following which his services were lost for long periods due to Australia's limited-overs commitments. Bevan has been the mainstay of New South Wales's batting for more than a decade and the question persists why the nursery of so many great Australian batsmen has failed to produce a new generation of prolific run-scorers. If it is asking too much for another set of Waugh twins, why cannot the state's system generate batsmen such as Sid Carroll, Warren Saunders, Bobby Madden and Trevor Bayliss, a quartet never to represent Australia, but splendid run-makers for New South Wales? In Michael Clarke, the former outstanding Australian youth batsman from Western Suburbs club, New South Wales have a batsman of special quality. A lovely stroke-maker and brilliant outfielder, he was perhaps unfortunate not to be included in the Australian team for the end-of-season tour of South Africa as a grounding at least for the next World Cup.

One of the selectors' most significant actions was to drop rangy opening batsman Greg Mail, a player of durability and commendable attitude, who had gradually established himself in first-class ranks in 2000-01. New South Wales' plan had been to build innings around the rock-like Mail and the strategy appeared to be working when he made an unbeaten 150 against South Australia in October, which paved the way for an overwhelming win at the Sydney Cricket Ground. Yet, six games later, in which time Mail made four half-centuries, the selectors omitted him from the team to play Western Australia in Perth. For this match, always a testing affair, the selectors chose limited-overs international wicket-keeper Brad Haddin to fill his limited-overs role and open the innings. As it eventuated, Haddin's unexpected partner was newly promoted all-rounder Grant Lambert, following a back injury sustained early in the game by specialist opener Brett Van Deinsen. The situation was made the more frustrating for all concerned by the return to Sydney of Corey Richards, who had just hit a Man-of-the-Match 151 in the ING Cup at the WACA Ground two days previously. After that performance, Richards should have remained in Perth and been included in the Pura Cup team, especially as the New South Wales batsmen, with the exception of Bevan and Clarke, were by then performing poorly.

As has been the case for too many years, New South Wales' failings revolved around their batsmen. A veritable army of young players has come and gone over the last decade without responding adequately to the challenge. All-rounder Mark Higgs is one of those gifted batsman who fell by the wayside. The selectors persisted with him until the last Pura Cup match in Hobart.

The most significant decline and meteoric return was by Michael Slater. Having played the first four Tests in England before his omission for the Oval Test in August 2001, the flamboyant right-hander hit one half-century in six first-class games for New South Wales and then, hindered by a severe ankle sprain from a net mishap, was dropped from both the team's limited-overs and first-class programs.

Slater might well have remained on the outer but for the strangest set of circumstances. Within days, all-rounder Shane Lee, captaining the team for the second season, aggravated a right knee injury for which he had undergone surgery, Stuart MacGill and Bevan were required for Australia's tour of South Africa, and Graeme Rummans, the impressive young captain of the New South Wales Second XI, was suspended for the remainder of the season for taking the banned drug probenecid, a masking agent recommended by his family doctor as treatment for a persistent boil on his shoulder. Slater was welcomed back to first-class cricket, celebrating the state captaincy for the first time in a roll of drums and fanfare of trumpets, but innings of 50 and seven while batting at number three were inadequate to save his team from defeat in three days in Hobart. At the end of the season, the national selectors removed Slater from their 25-member contracted squad. But the captaincy served as an incentive and may lead to a change of fortunes for the dashing opener.

As the season progressed and his knee injury became a greater hindrance, Shane Lee's stature as a limited-overs international waned. By early December the state selectors were concerned at his failure to be the first-change pace man required, at least for games at the SCG. The injury deteriorated to the point where Lee was chosen as a specialist batsman for the last half of the season. Almost as disturbing were the injuries and the efforts of left-arm pace man Nathan Bracken. He returned from the Ashes tour to England after only two games, his excellent start marred by a shoulder injury. Surgery led to Bracken missing the first two ING Cup games of the season, but he immediately began taking wickets to present himself as a Test candidate. An ING Cup hat-trick against Victoria at the Melbourne Cricket Ground was proof enough of Bracken's talents, but his Pura Cup efforts left much to be desired. Likewise, the performances of fast bowler Don Nash, left-arm spinner Higgs and off-spinner Anthony Clark all deteriorated, and all suffered the indignity of omission from the team.

Amid New South Wales' first-class staggers and stumbles in the Pura Cup, pace man Stuart Clark stood supreme. For long better known as the Sutherland club new-ball partner of Glenn McGrath, Clark at last blossomed into the accurate, penetrative representative bowler predicted some years ago. It was due essentially to Clark, Bracken and leg-spinner MacGill that New South Wales won eight of their 11 ING Cup games.

Younger players who showed they had much to offer in the seasons ahead were wicket-keeper Nathan Pilon, the subject of conjecture of an interstate transfer, all-rounder Dominic Thornely, and the batsmen Clarke, Haddin and Rummans, with Corey

NEW SOUTH WALES PURA CUP TEAM, 2001-02

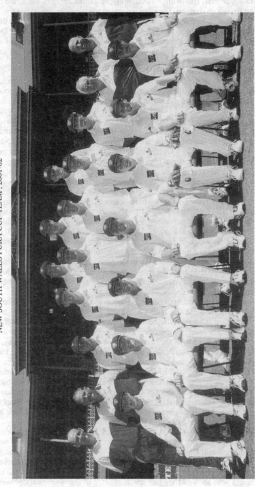

Back row: A. W. O'Brien, B. P. Van Deinsen, A.M. Clark. Middle row: D. Kerr (room attendant), S.J. Rixon (coach), D. A. Nash, J.M. Heath, S. R. Clark, N. W. Bracken, G.J. Mail, S.D. Bradstreet, M. Seres (room attendant), P. Farhart (physiotherapist). Front row: M.J. Clarke, S.C. G. MacGill, M. G. Bevan, S. Lee (captain), B.J. Haddin, C.J. Richards, M.A. Higgs.

Richards and Matthew Phelps hinting that at last they are about to justify the selectors' long-held confidence in them.

Chairman of selectors John Benaud announced his intention to resign after another five-year term on the state panel and former Test opening batsman Steve Smith and senior selector Dion Bourne will head the new selection panel. Coach Steve Rixon has signed a new contract for his third year with Cricket New South Wales. Soon after the season ended, the organisation announced that Simon Katich would leave Perth to play for New South Wales from 2002-03. He will be a welcome addition to the ranks. With the representative futures of Steve and Mark Waugh uncertain, the new season looms as a fascinating one for followers of New South Wales. – PHIL WILKINS.

NEW SOUTH WALES RESULTS, 2001-02

All first-class matches – Played 11: Won 2, Lost 4, Drawn 5.
Pura Cup – Played 10: Won 2, Lost 4, Drawn 4.
ING Cup matches – Played 11: Won 8, Lost 3.
Competition placings – Pura Cup, 6th; ING Cup, 1st.

PURA CUP AVERAGES, 2001-02

BATTING

	M	I	NO	R	HS	100s	50s	Avge	Ct
M.J. Phelps	2	4	1	243	84	0	3	81.00	2
M.E. Waugh	2	3	0	231	168	1	1	77.00	0
M.G. Bevan.	7	13	1	685	203*	3	3	57.08	4
M.J. Clarke	8	16	0	621	132	2	2	38.81	6
G.J. Mail	7	12	1	420	150*	1	3	38.18	7
G.C. Rummans	2	4	0	138	60	0	2	34.50	0
M.A. Higgs	9	17	3	467	80	0	4	33.36	3
B.J. Haddin	9	17	1	495	102	1	3	30.94	23
G.M. Lambert	2	4	1	88	45*	0	0	29.33	0
C.J. Richards.	4	8	0	227	74	0	1	28.38	1
M.J. Slater.	7	13	1	314	58*	0	2	26.17	2
G.D. McGrath	2	3	1	40	26	0	0	20.00	1
B.P. Van Deinsen	3	6	0	120	60	0	1	20.00	6
S.C.G. MacGill.	6	10	2	157	53	0	1	19.63	2
A.M. Clark	2	2	1	18	12	0	0	18.00	1
S. Lee.	6	10	0	170	41	0	0	17.00	10
N.W. Bracken	8	14	5	145	38	0	0	16.11	1
S.R. Clark	9	15	5	145	31*	0	0	14.50	1
D.A. Turner.	2	4	0	51	39	0	0	12.75	0
P.A. Jaques	1	2	0	23	23	0	0	11.50	1
D.A. Nash	8	14	0	127	27	0	0	9.07	1
N.S. Pilon	1	2	0	16	16	0	0	8.00	9
A.W. O'Brien	1	1	0	6	6	0	0	6.00	0
B. Lee	1	2	0	8	8	0	0	4.00	1
V.M. Williams	1	2	0	4	4	0	0	2.00	0

* *Denotes not out.*

BOWLING

	O	M	R	W	BB	5W/i	Avge
B. Lee	23	5	97	6	5/56	1	16.17
M. J. Clarke.	15	1	46	2	2/25	0	23.00
S. R. Clark.	387	108	1047	45	5/42	4	23.27
N. W. Bracken	248.5	55	763	24	4/10	0	31.79
B. P. Van Deinsen.	34	12	109	3	3/42	0	36.33
A. M. Clark	43	4	151	4	4/130	0	37.75
D. A. Nash	226	51	794	21	4/59	0	37.81
G. D. McGrath	84.5	27	203	5	3/25	0	40.60
G. M. Lambert	36	4	165	4	3/86	0	41.25
S. Lee	76.5	8	313	5	2/32	0	62.60
S. C. G. MacGill	189.5	36	729	11	4/54	0	66.27
M. A. Higgs	98.4	14	363	4	2/99	0	90.75
A. W. O'Brien.	33	3	134	1	1/134	0	134.00
M. G. Bevan	16	0	73	0	–	0	–
G. J. Mail.	1	0	9	0	–	0	–
G. C. Rummans	1	0	6	0	–	0	–
M. J. Slater	1	0	15	0	–	0	–
D. A. Turner	46.1	8	168	0	–	0	–

NEW SOUTH WALES v TASMANIA

At Sydney Cricket Ground, Sydney, October 17, 18, 19, 20, 2001. Drawn. Toss: New South Wales. Tasmania 2 pts.

In what has become a tradition, Jamie Cox (221 minutes, 187 balls, 14 fours) and Dene Hills (331 minutes, 242 balls, 19 fours) forged a massive opening partnership of 205 for a Tasmanian first-wicket record against New South Wales at the Sydney Cricket Ground, after being put in on a cream-grassed strip. It was not until Stuart Clark claimed three wickets in eight balls with the second new ball, and sent Scott Kremerskothen to hospital with a blow under the helmet visor, that the decision to bowl first proved justified. In his first season as captain, Ricky Ponting (236 minutes, 174 balls, 20 fours; then in the second innings 218 minutes, 166 balls, 27 fours, one six) began with twin centuries. Although Michael Bevan (219 minutes, 175 balls, 17 fours) and Mark Waugh (290 minutes, 211 balls, 23 fours, one six) responded with their own centuries, pace man David Saker and the increasingly valuable all-rounder Shane Watson troubled New South Wales sufficiently to maintain their side's superiority. The first-innings welter of runs put an outright decision beyond reach and Tasmania batted throughout the last day.

Man of the Match: R. T. Ponting.   *Attendance:* 3,390.

Close of play: First day, Tasmania (1) 4-328 (Ponting 75, Young 0); Second day, New South Wales (1) 2-168 (Bevan 80, Waugh 10); Third day, Tasmania (2) 0-30 (Hills 13, Cox 16).

Tasmania

D.F. Hills c (sub) Bradstreet b S.R. Clark	136	– lbw b McGrath	32
J. Cox c Higgs b S.R. Clark	107	– c Mail b Nash	80
*R.T. Ponting run out (Mail)	126	– c Lee b Nash	154
S.R. Watson b S.R. Clark	0	– not out	58
S.P. Kremerskothen retired hurt	0		
D.J. Marsh c Mail b S.R. Clark	0	– (5) not out	11
S. Young c Haddin b S.R. Clark	3		
†S.G. Clingeleffer c McGrath b MacGill	40		
D.G. Wright lbw b McGrath	50		
D.J. Saker not out	23		
A.G. Downton lbw b Lee	0		
B 7, l-b 8, w 1, n-b 3	19	B 9, l-b 8, w 1, n-b 3	21

(135.2 overs, 533 mins)　　　(9 wkts dec) 504　　(104 overs, 395 mins)　　(3 wkts) 356
Fall: 205 318 318 324 338 416 452 503 504　　Fall: 77 204 329

Bowling: *First Innings*—McGrath 32–8–106–1; Nash 22–4–111–0; S.R. Clark 32–12–64–5; MacGill 33–4–140–1; Lee 11.2–1–49–1; Higgs 5–1–19–0. *Second Innings*—McGrath 22–11–35–1; S.R. Clark 19–7–52–0; MacGill 23–5–88–0; Nash 18–4–62–2; Bevan 5–0–16–0; Lee 7–2–25–0; Higgs 9–1–46–0; Slater 1–0–15–0.

New South Wales

M.J. Slater c Ponting b Wright	19	S.C.G. MacGill c Watson b Downton	34
G.J. Mail lbw b Saker	52	S.R. Clark not out	31
M.G. Bevan c Clingeleffer b Downton	102	G.D. McGrath lbw b Saker	12
M.E. Waugh c Wright b Watson	168		
M.A. Higgs b Saker	37	B 3, l-b 4, w 1, n-b 9	17
*S. Lee b Saker	17		
†B.J. Haddin lbw b Watson	0	(128.5 overs, 492 mins)	489
D.A. Nash c Clingeleffer b Watson	0	Fall: 26 139 220 333 359 360 360 431 462 489	

Bowling: Wright 31–6–103–1; Saker 27.5–6–115–4; Downton 19–3–94–2; Marsh 14–1–35–0; Watson 19–3–88–3; Young 18–6–47–0.

Umpires: D.M. Brandon and D.B. Hair.

NEW SOUTH WALES v SOUTH AUSTRALIA

At Sydney Cricket Ground, Sydney, October 26, 27, 28, 29, 2001. New South Wales won by 290 runs. Toss: South Australia. New South Wales 6 pts.

South Australia failed to capitalise on an important toss, their bowlers thwarted on a moist pitch by the professional resourcefulness of Michael Bevan, whose 135-minute innings provided the margin for an important lead. On a pitch renowned for its conduciveness to spin, Jason Gillespie's return of 8/50 was the finest by a pace bowler at the ground since Tim Wall's 10 for 36, also for South Australia, in 1932-33. But the New South Wales pace attack carried sharper bayonets, Brett Lee, having recovered from a side strain, Glenn McGrath, Nathan Bracken and Shane Lee slicing through the South Australian first innings after tea when eight wickets fell for 109. Twenty wickets fell for 346 runs on an eventful first day, before Greg Mail batted through the second innings for his second first-class century (407 minutes, 310 balls, 18 fours), making victory remote for the visitors against the all-international attack. Only Jeff Vaughan (190 minutes, 147 balls, 11 fours) batted for long enough to build a substantial innings. While McGrath lacked match-conditioning after the Ashes tour, Lee and Bracken generated considerable hostility to complete an impressive victory just after tea on the third day.

Man of the Match: G.J. Mail.　*Attendance:* 4,985.

Close of play: First day, New South Wales (2) 0-16 (Slater 15, Mail 1); Second day, New South Wales (2) 9-415 (Mail 142, McGrath 14).

New South Wales

G. J. Mail lbw b Gillespie	9	– (2) not out	150
M. J. Slater lbw b Gillespie	1	– (1) c Manou b Rofe	49
M. G. Bevan b Gillespie	55	– c Manou b Rofe	11
M. E. Waugh b Gillespie	12	– run out (Gillespie/Manou)	51
M. A. Higgs b Gillespie	0	– c Rofe b Lehmann	53
*S. Lee c Dempsey b Harrity	30	– c Blewett b Gillespie	6
†N. S. Pilon b McIntyre	0	– run out (Gillespie)	16
B. Lee c Manou b Gillespie	8	– b Harrity	0
S. C. G. MacGill c Harrity b Gillespie	27	– c Dempsey b Lehmann	53
N. W. Bracken c Manou b Gillespie	38	– c Deitz b Lehmann	8
G. D. McGrath not out	2	– lbw b Gillespie	26
B 4, l-b 1, n-b 1	6	B 7, n-b 6	13

(42.4 overs, 181 mins)   188   (105.3 overs, 407 mins)   436
Fall: 7 18 40 44 101 104 119   Fall: 68 92 164 262 288 307 309
      124 185 188   377 392 436

Bowling: *First Innings*—Gillespie 16.4–3–50–8; Harrity 8–0–41–1; Rofe 9–1–49–0; McIntyre 9–0–43–1. *Second Innings*—Gillespie 26.3–3–112–2; Harrity 22.4–92–1; McIntyre 26–3–108–0; Rofe 17–3–75–2; Lehmann 14–2–42–3.

South Australia

J. M. Vaughan c Pilon b McGrath	0	– (2) c Pilon b S. Lee	69
S. A. Deitz b Bracken	11	– (1) c Pilon b B. Lee	6
G. S. Blewett c S. Lee b B. Lee	0	– c Mail b B. Lee	6
*D. S. Lehmann c Pilon b Bracken	49	– c Pilon b B. Lee	0
D. M. Dempsey run out (S Lee)	21	– c Pilon b Bracken	6
B. H. Higgins c Pilon b S. Lee	10	– c Pilon b B. Lee	41
†G. A. Manou lbw b McGrath	0	– b B. Lee	30
J. N. Gillespie c B. Lee b McGrath	23	– lbw b Bracken	5
P. E. McIntyre run out (Pilon)	12	– c Mail b Bracken	16
P. C. Rofe c Pilon b S. Lee	1	– not out	6
M. A. Harrity not out	3	– b Bracken	0
L-b 2, n-b 10	12	L-b 4, w 1, n-b 2	7

(42.5 overs, 192 mins)   142   (54.2 overs, 221 mins)   192
Fall: 0 6 41 81 103 103 105   Fall: 9 15 15 25 124 156 165
      118 120 142   177 188 192

Bowling: *First Innings*—McGrath 16.5–4–25–3; B. Lee 8–3–41–1; Bracken 11–1–42–2; S. Lee 7–0–32–2. *Second Innings*—McGrath 14–4–37–0; B. Lee 15–2–56–5; Bracken 6.2–4–10–4; S. Lee 7–0–38–1; MacGill 12–3–47–0.

Umpires: N. S. Fowler and S. J. A. Taufel.

At Richmond Cricket Ground, Richmond, November 8, 9, 10, 11, 2001. NEW SOUTH WALES defeated VICTORIA by seven wickets.

At Brisbane Cricket Ground, Brisbane, November 25, 26, 27, 2001. NEW SOUTH WALES lost to QUEENSLAND by eight wickets.

NEW SOUTH WALES v WESTERN AUSTRALIA

At Sydney Cricket Ground, Sydney, December 14, 15, 16, 17, 2001. Drawn. Toss: New South Wales. Western Australia 2 pts. First-class debut: A. W. O'Brien.

New South Wales began without four Test players, and on the morning of the game lost their captain Shane Lee with a knee strain, an injury which troubled him for the remainder of the season. Western Australia selected an all-pace attack, a decision which initially appeared inspired as Kade Harvey's probing medium-pacers and the sheer speed of Brad Williams saw the home side dismissed by tea on the first day. Michael Hussey (306 minutes, 262 balls, 12 fours) and Simon Katich (235 minutes, 192 balls, 10 fours, three sixes) built on the 127-run opening stand by Hussey and Scott Meuleman to establish a 363-run lead. The visitors were then hampered by the lack of variety in their attack as New South Wales staged ten hours of resistance to save the game, Michael Bevan (562 minutes, 453 balls, 28 fours) profiting from an early dropped catch to post his third double-century and equal-highest score in an innings of intense concentration. He shared painstaking century partnerships with Greg Mail (252 minutes, 216 balls, seven fours) and Brad Haddin (252 minutes, 193 balls, 13 fours). On 184 Bevan became the leading run scorer for New South Wales in first-class cricket when he passed Alan Kippax's total of 8,005 runs.

Man of the Match: M.G. Bevan. *Attendance:* 2,527.

Close of play: First day, Western Australia (1) 2-147 (Hussey 55, Katich 8); Second day, Western Australia (1) 6-511 (Rogers 36, Hogg 57); Third day, New South Wales (2) 3-188 (Bevan 78, Higgs 0).

New South Wales

M.J. Slater c Hogg b Nicholson	40	– (2) c North b Williams	24
G.J. Mail c North b Williams	0	– (1) c Meuleman b North	59
*M.G. Bevan c Campbell b Harvey	26	– not out	203
M.J. Clarke c Campbell b Angel	43	– lbw b Hogg	17
M.A. Higgs c Hussey b Williams	3	– c Katich b Hogg	80
†B.J. Haddin b Angel	50	– not out	52
A.W. O'Brien c Harvey b Williams	6		
D.A. Nash c Campbell b Harvey	15		
A.M. Clark not out	6		
S.R. Clark c Rogers b Harvey	15		
N.W. Bracken c Katich b Harvey	2		
L-b 2, w 1, n-b 6	9	B 1, l-b 4, w 1, n-b 11	17
(52.4 overs, 219 mins)	215	(167 overs, 622 mins) (4 wkts)	452

Fall: 3 66 70 86 162 175 183 191 213 215

Fall: 35 135 186 367

Bowling: *First Innings*—Williams 15–3–71–3; Angel 20–7–68–2; Harvey 10.4–0–43–4; Nicholson 7–0–31–1. *Second Innings*—Williams 32–13–73–1; Angel 24–9–45–0; Hogg 28–6–102–2; Nicholson 32–10–61–0; Harvey 20–4–63–0; North 25–4–81–1; Katich 3–0–15–0; Hussey 2–0–6–0; Meuleman 1–0–1–0.

Western Australia

M.E.K. Hussey b Bracken	100	M.J. Nicholson not out	14
S.W. Meuleman c Haddin b S.R. Clark	60	J. Angel c Bevan b A.M. Clark	10
K.M. Harvey c Higgs b S.R. Clark	5	B.A. Williams b S.R. Clark	19
*S.M. Katich lbw b O'Brien	131	B 19, l-b 15, w 1, n-b 7	42
M.J. North c Bevan b A.M. Clark	26		
†R.J. Campbell c Clarke b A.M. Clark	57	(154.4 overs, 569 mins)	578
C.J.L. Rogers c Haddin b S.R. Clark	53	Fall: 127 133 282 343 365 424 520	
G.B. Hogg c and b A.M. Clark	61	532 553 578	

Bowling: Bracken 22–4–51–1; S.R. Clark 38.4–10–125–4; Nash 18–3–69–0; A.M. Clark 36–3–130–4; O'Brien 33–3–134–1; Clarke 4–0–17–0; Mail 1–0–9–0; Higgs 2–0–9–0.

Umpires: J.I. Cameron and D.B. Hair.

At Adelaide Oval, Adelaide, January 16, 17, 18, 19, 2002. NEW SOUTH WALES lost to SOUTH AUSTRALIA by 67 runs.

NEW SOUTH WALES v VICTORIA

At Sydney Cricket Ground, Sydney, January 25, 26, 27, 2002. Victoria won by ten
wickets. Toss: New South Wales. Victoria 6 pts. First-class debut: B. E. McGain; D. A.
Turner.

New South Wales' gradual batting disintegration of the previous two months, which
led to the controversial omission of Michael Slater from this match, continued. Stuart
MacGill must have regretted his decision to bat first on a moist pitch when Victoria
dismissed New South Wales in less than three hours. The left-arm fast-medium seamers
of Mathew Inness were too much for the technique and temperament of the New South
Wales batsmen. Victoria wobbled to five for 50 before Jon Moss, formerly of New
South Wales (268 minutes, 235 balls, 19 fours), hit his maiden century, sharing a cool
and confident 199-run partnership in just under four hours with Darren Berry (310
minutes, 258 balls, 19 fours, one six). Berry's innings was particularly gratifying, as it
came in the match in which he passed Dean Jones' previous record of 110 appearances
for Victoria in domestic first-class competition matches. Stuart Clark and Don Nash both
bowled with vigour and accuracy. Ian Hewett and Inness took wickets regularly when
New South Wales batted again, Inness's outswingers and off-cutters yielding 11/86 for
the game in a comprehensive three-day victory for Victoria.

Man of the Match: M. W. H. Inness.   *Attendance:* 1,819.

Close of play: First day, Victoria (1) 5-147 (Moss 59, Berry 49); Second day, New
South Wales (2) 2-82 (Mail 26, Turner 0).

New South Wales

B. P. Van Deinsen c Berry b Inness	2	– (2) c Hodge b Hewett	8
G. J. Mail c Berry b Inness	4	– (1) b Hewett	26
C. J. Richards c Berry b Moss	18	– (5) lbw b McGain	38
M. J. Clarke run out (Hewett)	11	– (5) c Lewis b McGain	42
G. C. Rummans c Berry b Lewis	11	– (6) b Inness	60
M. A. Higgs not out	40	– (7) lbw b Inness	52
†B. J. Haddin c Elliott b Inness	7	– (8) b Inness	41
D. A. Turner c Elliott b Inness	5	– (4) run out (Hewett)	2
D. A. Nash c Hodge b Inness	0	– c Moss b Inness	5
*S. C. G. MacGill c McGain b Inness	0	– (11) not out	2
S. R. Clark c Mott b Inness	2	– (10) b Hewett	3
B 1, l-b 9, w 1, n-b 4	15	B 7, l-b 16, w 3, n-b 2	28
	109		**307**

(42.1 overs, 173 mins)   109   (90.2 overs, 352 mins)   307
Fall: 5 6 17 41 50 81 89   Fall: 14 74 82 100 161 252 259
      89 91 109   269 293 307

Bowling: *First Innings*—Inness 12.1–5–19–7; Hewett 13–3–39–0; Lewis 8–3–20–1; Hodge 1–0–1–0;
Moss 7–1–20–1; McGain 1–1–0–0. *Second Innings*—Inness 18.2–3–67–4; Hewett 20–6–63–3; Moss
16–4–39–0; Lewis 11–3–41–0; McGain 20–5–64–2; Hodge 5–3–10–0.

Victoria

*M. T. G. Elliott c Clarke b Clark	21	– (2) not out	35
J. L. Arnberger c Van Deinsen b Clark	5	– (1) not out	23
M. P. Mott c Richards b Clark	8		
B. J. Hodge c Van Deinsen b Nash	1		
M. Klinger b Nash	0		
J. Moss b Nash	109		
†D. S. Berry c Haddin b Higgs	148		
I. S. L. Hewett lbw b Nash	3		
M. L. Lewis not out	54		
B. E. McGain b Clark	3		
M. W. H. Inness lbw b Clark	0		
B 1, l-b 5	6	N-b 1	1

(117.4 overs, 428 mins)   358   (22.5 overs, 71 mins)   (0 wkt)   59
Fall: 15 29 30 30 50 249 253 314 356 358   Fall:

Bowling: *First Innings*—Clark 32.4–10–75–5; Nash 26.3–12–59–4; Van Deinsen 12.3–7–22–0; MacGill 23–3–111–0; Turner 13–0–66–0; Higgs 10–3–19–1. *Second Innings*—Clark 5–2–14–0; Van Deinsen 7–2–14–0; Turner 6.5–1–25–0; MacGill 4–1–6–0.

Umpires: J. E. Cameron and N. S. D. Fowler.
TV Umpire: T. J. Keel.

At WACA Ground, Perth, February 15,16,17,18, 2002. NEW SOUTH WALES drew with WESTERN AUSTRALIA.

NEW SOUTH WALES v QUEENSLAND

At Sydney Cricket Ground, Sydney, March 1, 2, 3, 4, 2002. Drawn. Toss: Queensland. Queensland 2 pts.

Dropped at seven, Jimmy Maher (445 minutes, 365 balls, 27 fours) revealed both his maturity and a refined technique in an innings of substance and style. After a 134-run opening stand with Brendan Nash, he shared a 294-run partnership with Martin Love (364 minutes, 295 balls, 23 fours), a second-wicket record for Queensland against New South Wales. After Stuart Law declared at tea on the second day, Matthew Phelps (233 minutes, 210 balls, 11 fours) and Corey Richards (228 minutes, 176 balls, 10 fours) gave New South Wales a welcome start of 166 in 228 minutes, whereupon five wickets fell for 22. But two of New South Wales' batting hopes of the future, Brad Haddin (186 minutes, 155 balls, 14 fours) and Michael Clarke (211 minutes, 180 balls, 12 fours), put on a 175-run stand at almost a run a minute. Off-spinner Nathan Hauritz intervened to claim both wickets in successive overs, giving him his first four-wicket haul in an innings and a first-innings lead for his team. In an astonishing last day's developments, New South Wales dismissed Queensland for 120 in the second innings, Stuart Clark waving a spirited flag for his team. Both teams made a brave attempt for outright victory, New South Wales recovering from seven for 102 while Phelps (112 minutes, 74 balls, four fours) played another intelligent hand, Clark joining him in a rousing last-wicket stand of 54 in 31 minutes. After rain interruptions earlier in the day, play finished at 8.01 p.m. with the home side four runs short of its target.

Man of the Match: J. P. Maher.   *Attendance:* 2,387.

Close of play: First day, Queensland (1) 1-325 (Maher 151, Love 101); Second day, New South Wales (1) 0-95 (Phelps 48, Richards 42); Third day, New South Wales (1) 8-398 (Turner 25, Bracken 7).

Queensland

J.P. Maher c Phelps b Clark	198	– (2) b Nash	14
B.P. Nash c Lee b Nash	60	– (1) c Phelps b Clark	4
M.L. Love c Haddin b Clark	184	– lbw b Clark	42
A. Symonds lbw b Clark	13	– (5) c Lee b Clark	3
L.A. Carseldine not out	30	– (4) c (sub) G.M. Lambert b Nash	25
*S.G. Law not out	23	– c Haddin b Clark	4
†W.A. Seccombe (did not bat)		– (11) not out	1
A.A. Noffke (did not bat)		– (7) b Nash	4
N.M. Hauritz (did not bat)		– (8) b Bracken	18
M.S. Kasprowicz (did not bat)		– (9) b Clark	1
J.H. Dawes (did not bat)		– (10) lbw b Bracken	3
B 6, l-b 9, w 2, n-b 3	20	L-b 1	1

(152.2 overs, 575 mins)	(4 wkts dec) 528	(36.2 overs, 155 mins) 120
Fall: 134 428 462 482		Fall: 4 38 69 87 93 97 97 107 117 120

Bowling: *First Innings*—Clark 32–3–106–3; Bracken 28–4–101–0; Nash 25–4–73–1; Turner 26.2–7–77–0; Higgs 29–4–106–0; Bevan 7–0–24–0; Clarke 1–0–4–0; Lee 4–1–22–0. *Second Innings*—Clark 17–1–42–5; Nash 11–2–45–3; Bracken 8.2–1–32–2.

New South Wales

M.J. Phelps c Noffke b Hauritz	84	– (7) not out	65
C.J. Richards c Love b Kasprowicz	74	– (1) c Love b Dawes	13
M.G. Bevan c Hauritz b Kasprowicz	0	– c Maher b Kasprowicz	0
M.J. Clarke c Nash b Hauritz	76	– lbw b Kasprowicz	20
M.A. Higgs c Law b Hauritz	5	– (6) c Maher b Noffke	8
*S. Lee run out (Noffke)	3	– (5) b Noffke	41
†B.J. Haddin c Kasprowicz b Hauritz	102	– (2) c Maher b Kasprowicz	3
D.A. Turner c Love b Dawes	39	– run out (Noffke)	5
D.A. Nash lbw b Symonds	2	– (10) c Seccombe b Dawes	3
N.W. Bracken not out	32	– (9) b Dawes	16
S.R. Clark c Maher b Dawes	5	– not out	23
L-b 12, n-b 8	20	L-b 5	5

(144.5 overs, 516 mins)	442	(46 overs, 199 mins) (9 wkts) 202
Fall: 166 168 170 179 188 363 366 388 436 442		Fall: 5 5 35 53 70 95 102 138 148

Bowling: *First Innings*—Kasprowicz 26–9–88–2; Dawes 26.5–5–90–2; Hauritz 41–8–119–4; Noffke 25–11–69–0; Symonds 21–7–44–1; Law 5–1–20–0. *Second Innings*—Kasprowicz 15–3–72–3; Dawes 15–0–66–3; Noffke 8–3–28–2; Hauritz 8–0–31–0.

Umpires: D.B. Hair and S.J.A. Taufel.
TV Umpire: J.I. Cameron.

At Bellerive Oval, Hobart, March 13, 14, 15, 2002. NEW SOUTH WALES lost to TASMANIA by ten wickets.

AUSTRALIAN DOMESTIC FIRST-CLASS RESULTS TABLE

Opponent	M	W	L	D	T
South Australia	195	107	52	36	0
Victoria	201	73	62	65	1
Queensland	144	57	36	51	0
Western Australia	102	40	30	32	0
Tasmania	46	17	11	18	0
Total	688	294	191	202	1

AUSTRALIAN DOMESTIC FIRST-CLASS RECORDS

Highest score for:	452*	D.G. Bradman v Queensland at Sydney	1929-30
Highest score against:	365*	C. Hill (South Australia) at Adelaide	1900-01
Best bowling for:	9/41	W.J. O'Reilly v South Australia at Adelaide	1937-38
Best bowling against:	10/36	T.W. Wall (South Australia) at Sydney	1932-33
Highest total for:	918	v South Australia at Sydney	1900-01
Highest total against:	1,107	by Victoria at Melbourne	1926-27
Lowest total for:	56	v Western Australia at Perth	1998-99
Lowest total against:	27	by South Australia at Sydney	1955-56

* Denotes not out.

MOST RUNS

	M	I	NO	R	HS	100s	50s	Avge
M.G. Bevan	85	150	29	7,211	203*	28	30	59.60
M.E. Waugh	74	124	13	6,172	229*	23	24	55.60
A.F. Kippax	61	95	9	6,096	315*	23	14	70.88
M.A. Taylor	85	147	3	6,090	199	15	34	42.29
J. Dyson	82	150	16	5,648	241	11	29	42.15
K.D. Walters	91	159	16	5,602	253	17	24	39.17
G.R.J. Matthews	116	177	27	5,567	184	8	28	37.11
S.R. Waugh	70	119	13	5,390	216*	17	21	50.85
R.B. McCosker	70	124	15	5,280	168	17	26	48.44
B.C. Booth	81	128	14	4,943	177	10	25	43.36

* Denotes not out.

HIGHEST PARTNERSHIP FOR EACH WICKET

319	for 1st	R.B. McCosker and J. Dyson v Western Australia at Sydney	1980-81
378	for 2nd	L.A. Marks and K.D. Walters v South Australia at Adelaide	1964-65
363	for 3rd	D.G. Bradman and A.F. Kippax v Queensland at Sydney	1933-34
325	for 4th	N.C. O'Neill and B.C. Booth v Victoria at Sydney	1957-58
464*	for 5th	M.E. Waugh and S.R. Waugh v Western Australia at Perth	1990-91
332	for 6th	N.G. Marks and G. Thomas v South Australia at Sydney	1958-59
255	for 7th	G. Thomas and R. Benaud v Victoria at Melbourne	1961-62
270	for 8th	E.P. Barbour and V.T. Trumper v Victoria at Sydney	1912-13
226	for 9th	C. Kelleway and W.A.S. Oldfield v Victoria at Melbourne	1925-26
307	for 10th	A.F. Kippax and J.E.H. Hooker v Victoria at Melbourne	1928-29

* Denotes unbroken partnership.

MOST WICKETS

	M	Balls	Mdns	R	W	BB	5W/i	10W/m	Avge
G.F. Lawson	103	21,391	873	8,742	367	6/31	12	0	23.82
G.R.J. Matthews	116	26,764	1,376	10,518	363	8/52	19	4	28.98
R. Benaud	73	17,811	471	7,174	266	7/32	11	3	26.96
J.W. Martin	70	16,034	239	7,949	263	8/97	12	0	30.22
M.R. Whitney	77	14,983	562	7,314	251	7/75	10	0	29.14
A.K. Davidson	62	13,423	270	5,195	246	7/31	10	0	21.12
W.J. O'Reilly	33	10,748	362	3,472	203	9/41	18	7	17.10
R.G. Holland	60	15,435	806	6,250	193	9/83	7	1	32.38
K.J. O'Keeffe	58	11,964	315	5,064	187	6/49	11	1	27.08
L.S. Pascoe	49	9,566	279	4,895	183	8/41	8	2	26.75

MOST DISMISSALS

	M	Ct	St	Total
P. A. Emery	109	298	41	339
S. J. Rixon	94	218	43	261
H. B. Taber	64	179	32	211
W. A. S. Oldfield	51	109	70	179
D. A. Ford	56	107	51	107

MOST CATCHES

M. A. Taylor	120 in 85 matches	R. B. McCosker	91 in 70 matches
G. R. J. Matthews	102 in 116 matches	M. E. Waugh	85 in 74 matches
R. Benaud	92 in 73 matches	J. W. Martin	78 in 70 matches

MOST APPEARANCES

116	G. R. J. Matthews	1982-83 – 1997-98	85	M. A. Taylor	1985-86 – 1998-99
109	P. A. Emery	1987-88 – 1998-99	85	M. G. Bevan	1990-91 – 2001-02
103	G. F. Lawson	1977-78 – 1991-92	82	J. Dyson	1975-76 – 1988-89
94	S. J. Rixon	1974-75 – 1987-88	81	B. C. Booth	1954-55 – 1968-69
91	K. D. Walters	1962-63 – 1980-81	77	M. R. Whitney	1980-81 – 1993-94

QUEENSLAND

Chief Executive: G.J. Dixon

President: J.N. McKnoulty

Cricket Coach: B. King

Captain: S.G. Law

Stuart Law

Queensland were given the task of "raising the Bullbar" by coach Bennett King when they entered the 2001-02 first-class season chasing their third consecutive title. King and captain Stuart Law knew that it would be difficult to win another championship as they tried to mould the next wave of Queensland talent into the top ranks. But they had not expected the injury woes which beset the side from the first month, forcing them to endure one of the toughest seasons of their decorated decade.

That Queensland won the final, with a methodical 235-run victory over Tasmania, was testament as much to the younger players as it was to the established hands. Queensland had four players unavailable for the final because of international duty in South Africa, while bowling backbone Adam Dale was still recovering from the shoulder injury that limited him to just one Pura Cup appearance.

Queensland fielded 21 players, including three captains, during their defence, surpassed only by New South Wales with 25 players. Brendan Nash, however, typified the emerging talent when he scored a valuable 96 in the final to ensure that Queensland moved beyond the reach of Tasmania. Nash's performance was among the most satisfying for King, who left Queensland after the final to take up the head coaching position at the Australian Cricket Academy. He was pleased that the next generation, including Australian limited-overs off-spinner Nathan Hauritz, was showing Queensland fans that their treasured run of success would not have to end when the experienced players retired.

Yet it was the top players who still played the most important roles, matching a simple theory that King held about domestic cricket. He reasoned that a team would probably qualify for the final if it had two batsmen averaging better than 50 and one bowler taking more than 40 wickets. Queensland filled those criteria, with Maher and Love becoming the twin pillars of Queensland's batting while Mike Kasprowicz again proved his class with the ball. Kasprowicz was the competition's leading wicket-taker with 49 at 22.08, gaining the most support from Ashley Noffke (38 at 26.32). Love rattled up 1,108 runs at 65.18 to claim the Pura Cup batting aggregate ahead of Maher, who scored 1,085 at 67.81 despite missing the last two matches on national duty. With Test regular Hayden hitting 420 runs in just three matches, Queensland again finished on top of the points table with five outright wins and three first-innings victories.

Queensland did, however, hit some speed bumps during the title defence, especially when the stalwart Dale was forced to undergo surgery on his bowling shoulder and national commitments allowed Andy Bichel just three matches. Teenager Mitchell Johnson, labelled a "once in a lifetime" talent by Dennis Lillee, joined the injury list after just one Pura Cup appearance, enabling another teenager, Scott Brant from Zimbabwe, to make his first-class debut late in the season.

The season ended with a surprise when Law announced he would step down from the captaincy after leading Queensland to its fifth title in eight seasons. Only Richie Benaud

QUEENSLAND PURA CUP TEAM, 2001-02

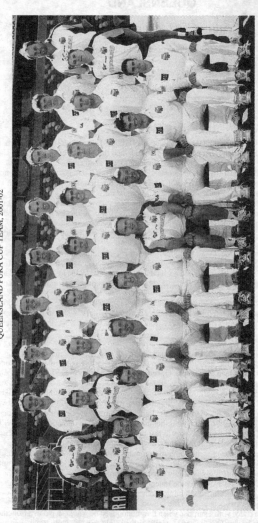

Back row: T. G. Oliver (*assistant coach*), D. R. McKenzie, A. A. Noffke, S. A. Muller, J. L. Cassell, M. A. Anderson, N. M. Hauritz, J. R. Hopes, R. S. Done (*QAS coach*). *Middle row*: T. Wilson (*conditioner*), J. Sterned (*technical officer*), W. A. Seccombe, S. J. O'Leary, L. A. Carseldine, M. G. Johnson, S. A. Brant, C. T. Perren, S. Partridge (*physiotherapist*). *Front row*: C. D. Hartley, A. C. Dale, M. L. Love, M. S. Kasprowicz, S. G. Law (*captain*), B. A. King (*coach*), A. Symonds, J. F. Dawes, B. P. Nash. *Absent*: M. L. Hayden, J. P. Maher, A. J. Bichel.

could match Law's captaincy record of five championships, but Law felt it was time to prolong his career by playing without the leadership responsibility. He had endured one of his most disappointing seasons, scoring just 280 runs at an average of 23.33 and missing two matches with a broken knuckle. He had agreed to drop to No. 6 in the order, against his personal wishes but in accordance with King, who wanted to expose Queensland's younger batsmen to a more demanding role.

The Queenslanders also gained satisfaction from their individual deeds, with eight players representing Australia at some level in the 12 months following the 2000-01 championship. With Hayden now a fixture at the top level and the likes of new state captain Maher and Bichel receiving more exposure, the development of the younger players could not be more timely. – MICHAEL CRUTCHER.

QUEENSLAND RESULTS, 2001-02

All first-class matches – Played 12: Won 6, Lost 2, Drawn 4.
Pura Cup matches – Played 11: Won 6, Lost 2, Drawn 3.
ING Cup matches – Played 11: Won 7, Lost 4.
Competition placings – Pura Cup, 1st; ING Cup, 2nd.

PURA CUP AVERAGES, 2001-02

BATTING

	M	I	NO	R	HS	100s	50s	Avge	Ct
M.L. Hayden	3	5	0	420	147	2	1	84.00	3
J.P. Maher	9	17	1	1,085	209	3	5	67.81	14
M.L. Love	11	20	3	1,108	202*	2	6	65.18	9
B.P. Nash	5	10	1	395	157	1	2	43.89	3
L.A. Carseldine	4	8	3	192	39	0	0	38.40	4
S.A. Brant	3	3	2	35	19*	0	0	35.00	3
A.A. Noffke	10	12	3	262	73	0	1	29.11	3
A.J. Bichel	3	3	1	50	23	0	0	25.00	3
A. Symonds	9	15	2	310	91	0	2	23.85	9
J.L. Cassell	5	9	0	211	86	0	1	23.44	3
S.G. Law	9	14	2	280	70	0	2	23.33	6
D.M. Payne	2	4	0	82	35	0	0	20.50	3
W.A. Seccombe	11	16	3	170	49	0	0	13.08	49
N.M. Hauritz	7	9	1	102	41	0	0	12.75	5
D.R. MacKenzie	1	2	0	21	17	0	0	10.50	4
C.T. Perren	7	12	2	92	37	0	0	9.20	9
J.R. Hopes	3	5	0	40	14	0	0	8.00	1
J.H. Dawes	8	10	3	46	26	0	0	6.57	1
M.S. Kasprowicz	9	10	2	26	13	0	0	3.25	4
A.C. Dale	1	0	0	0	–	0	0	–	1
M.G. Johnson	1	1	1	12	12*	0	0	–	0

* Denotes not out.

BOWLING

	O	M	R	W	BB	5W/i	Avge
D.R. MacKenzie	13.3	1	45	3	3/45	0	15.00
S.A. Brant	56	16	126	7	3/23	0	18.00
A.C. Dale	38	13	97	5	3/51	0	19.40
M.S. Kasprowicz	343.5	85	1,082	49	5/44	2	22.08
A. Symonds	196	59	448	19	4/45	0	23.58
A.A. Noffke	345.4	85	1,000	38	5/31	2	26.32
A.J. Bichel	99	27	304	11	4/54	0	27.64
N.M. Hauritz	178	37	484	16	4/119	0	30.25
M.G. Johnson	32	5	110	3	2/66	0	36.67
J.H. Dawes	238.4	64	706	19	3/4	0	37.16
S.G. Law	19	2	74	1	1/54	0	74.00
J.R. Hopes	98.4	28	299	3	2/50	0	99.67
L.A. Carseldine	4	1	11	0	–	0	–
J.L. Cassell	1	0	4	0	–	0	–

QUEENSLAND v WESTERN AUSTRALIA

At Brisbane Cricket Ground, Brisbane, October 17 (no play), 18, 19, 20, 2001.
Queensland won by six wickets. Toss: Western Australia. Queensland 6 pts.

After a dry Brisbane winter, the rain arrived on the opening day of Queensland's first-class season, preventing any play. On a sunny second day Justin Langer (220 minutes, 185 balls, 12 fours) gave his side a composed start before Adam Gilchrist (139 minutes, 112 balls, 11 fours, four sixes) tucked into Queensland's top-line bowling attack, dominating a rattling sixth-wicket partnership of 154 with Marcus Noffke (111 minutes, 100 balls, eight fours). Western Australia's total looked solid until another Test batsman, Matthew Hayden, set up Queensland's victory. Hayden (288 minutes, 215 balls, 18 fours, two sixes) became Queensland's leading first-class century-maker with his 23rd hundred as he shared successive century partnerships with Jimmy Maher (147 minutes, 134 balls, seven fours) and Martin Love (169 minutes, 136 balls, five fours) before the Queensland bowlers clicked into gear, dismissing Western Australia for 207 in the second innings. With his team needing 165 runs from 33 overs to take outright points, Andrew Symonds (65 minutes, 43 balls, six fours, three sixes) sealed victory with an exhilarating innings in which his first 50 runs came from 27 balls, faster than anyone else in the either the first-class or the limited-overs season.

Man of the Match: M.L. Hayden.   *Attendance:* 1,864.

Close of play: First day, No play; Second day, Queensland (1) 0-41 (Hayden 12, Maher 29); Third day, Western Australia (2) 0-16 (Langer 9, Hussey 5).

Western Australia

J.L. Langer b Dale	96	– c Hayden b Dale	27
M.E.K. Hussey c Seccombe b Dale	0	– c and b Noffke	66
S.M. Katich b Kasprowicz	25	– c Law b Dale	1
D.R. Martyn run out (Bichel/Seccombe/K'wicz)	22	– c Hayden b Dale	12
M.W. Goodwin c Love b Kasprowicz	24	– run out (Noffke)	28
*†A.C. Gilchrist c Dale b Bichel	98	– c Seccombe b Noffke	7
M.J. North c and b Kasprowicz	47	– c Hayden b Bichel	11
M.J. Nicholson c Perren b Bichel	5	– c Symonds b Kasprowicz	25
J. Angel not out	10	– c Seccombe b Kasprowicz	0
S.R. Cary not out	2	– not out	10
G.G. Swan (did not bat)		– c Seccombe b Kasprowicz	0
L-b 9, n-b 22	31	B 2, l-b 1, w 1, n-b 16	20

(95 overs, 375 mins)   (8 wkts dec) 360   (88.4 overs, 347 mins)   207
Fall: 10 69 98 174 184   Fall: 22 48 120 127 139 155
   338 344 358   158 188 207 207

Bowling: *First Innings*—Bichel 23–4–98–2; Dale 21–9–46–2; Kasprowicz 20–3–89–3; Noffke 18–2–76–0; Symonds 13–1–42–0. *Second Innings*—Bichel 22–8–52–1; Dale 17–4–51–3; Kasprowicz 17.4–6–38–3; Noffke 17–6–47–2; Symonds 15–7–16–0.

Queensland

M.L. Hayden c Hussey b Katich	143	– (2) c Martyn b Cary 24
J.P. Maher c Langer b Nicholson	73	– (1) c North b Nicholson 8
M.L. Love b Angel	78	– b Katich 25
C.T. Perren c Langer b Angel	7	– (5) c Gilchrist b Katich 5
A. Symonds lbw b Angel	15	– (4) not out 75
*S.G. Law c Gilchrist b Nicholson	35	– not out 27
†W.A. Seccombe not out	29	
A.J. Bichel not out	12	
L-b 4, n-b 7	11	L-b 1, n-b 1 2

(113 overs, 437 mins)   (6 wkts dec) 403   (27.3 overs, 111 mins)   (4 wkts) 166
Fall: 112 288 305 310 333 368   Fall: 14 49 81 97

M.S. Kasprowicz, A.C. Dale and A.A. Noffke did not bat

Bowling: *First Innings*—Nicholson 24–5–90–2; Swan 19–1–88–0; Angel 25–7–70–3; Cary 29–3–76–0; Katich 13–0–61–1; North 3–0–14–0. *Second Innings*—Angel 7–1–25–0; Nicholson 7–0–48–1; Cary 7–0–41–1; Katich 6.3–0–51–2.

Umpires: P.D. Parker and J.F. Torpey.

At Richmond Cricket Ground, Richmond, October 24, 25, 26, 27, 2001. QUEENSLAND drew with VICTORIA.

At WACA Ground, Perth, November 8, 9, 10, 11, 2001. QUEENSLAND drew with WESTERN AUSTRALIA.

QUEENSLAND v NEW SOUTH WALES

At Brisbane Cricket Ground, Brisbane, November 25, 26, 27, 2001. Queensland won by eight wickets. Toss: Queensland. Queensland 6 pts.

New South Wales' batsmen did not enjoy the green Gabba wicket after they were invited to bat. The Queensland bowlers routed them for 146, with Andrew Symonds playing an important role with his medium pace. He claimed three quick wickets, including Michael Bevan caught off a wide warm-up delivery. Michael Kasprowicz mopped up the innings with four wickets from his last 17 balls. A storm halted the Queensland reply but their batsmen were in just as much trouble as an excellent spell by Stuart Clark left them at three for 44. Stuart Law then played one of his best knocks of the season, crafting a patient 70 (170 minutes, 134 balls, six fours, two sixes) and joining with Wade Seccombe (147 minutes, 108 balls, four fours) in a vital sixth-wicket partnership of 109. When Symonds took another three wickets in the second innings, Queensland were on the way to outright points, despite another long vigil by Greg Mail (176 minutes, 146 balls, six fours) which took his combined innings time in the match to 381 minutes. Jimmy Maher (127 minutes, 108 balls, seven fours) and Martin Love (118 minutes, 86 balls, nine fours) then batted entertainingly to secure a comfortable home win inside three days.

Man of the Match: A. Symonds.   *Attendance:* 3,089.

Close of play: First day, Queensland (1) 4-109 (Perren 37, Law 12); Second day, New South Wales (2) 7-180 (Nash 5, MacGill 5).

New South Wales

M.J. Slater c Seccombe b Kasprowicz	15	–	(2) lbw b Noffke	41
G.J. Mail lbw b Kasprowicz	42	–	(1) lbw b Symonds	56
M.G. Bevan c Hauritz b Symonds	3	–	lbw b Noffke	9
M.J. Clarke c Seccombe b Symonds	0	–	c Cassell b Symonds	36
M.A. Higgs c Seccombe b Symonds	18	–	c Law b Symonds	4
*S. Lee c Seccombe b Noffke	17	–	c Cassell b Kasprowicz	7
†B.J. Haddin lbw b Kasprowicz	24	–	lbw b Kasprowicz	0
D.A. Nash c Seccombe b Dawes	10	–	c Symonds b Kasprowicz	27
S.C.G. MacGill c Seccombe b Kasprowicz	2	–	not out	16
N.W. Bracken not out	2	–	c Hauritz b Noffke	0
S.R. Clark c Seccombe b Kasprowicz	0	–	c Perren b Kasprowicz	7
L-b 5, w 1, n-b 7	13		L-b 15, w 2, n-b 2	19

(52.5 overs, 214 mins) 146   (62.4 overs, 257 mins) 222
Fall: 17 38 38 72 98 124 141   Fall: 73 88 142 148 169 169 173
   143 146 146   206 207 222

Bowling: *First Innings*—Kasprowicz 12.5–3–44–5; Dawes 14–4–34–1; Noffke 14–3–33–1; Symonds 12–3–30–3. *Second Innings*—Kasprowicz 20.4–4–87–4; Noffke 19–5–48–3; Dawes 15–1–53–0; Symonds 8–2–19–3.

Queensland

J.P. Maher b S.R. Clark	10	–	c MacGill b S.R. Clark	61
J.L. Cassell lbw b S.R. Clark	12	–	c MacGill b S.R. Clark	0
M.L. Love c Lee b S.R. Clark	12	–	not out	65
C.T. Perren c Haddin b Bracken	37	–	not out	4
A. Symonds run out (Nash/Bevan)	23			
*S.G. Law b Bracken	70			
†W.A. Seccombe c Haddin b Bracken	49			
A.A. Noffke c Lee b S.R. Clark	6			
N.M. Hauritz b Nash	10			
M.S. Kasprowicz c Haddin b Nash	0			
J.H. Dawes not out	2			
L-b 5, w 1, n-b 1	5		L-b 3	3

(73.2 overs, 307 mins) 236   (34.3 overs, 133 mins)   (2 wkts) 133
Fall: 18 23 44 90 109 218 219 234 234 236   Fall: 2 123

Bowling: *First Innings*—Bracken 18–3–71–3; S.R. Clark 22.2–6–61–4; Nash 16–4–49–2; Lee 10–2–31–0; MacGill 7–2–21–0. *Second Innings*—Bracken 6–1–20–0; S.R. Clark 11–3–34–2; Nash 4–0–19–0; Lee 6–0–29–0; MacGill 7.3–2–28–0.

Umpires: A.J. McQuillan and P.D. Parker.

QUEENSLAND v TASMANIA

At Brisbane Cricket Ground, Brisbane, December 13, 14, 2001. Queensland won by ten wickets. Toss: Queensland. Queensland 6 pts.

Someone had to be blamed for the day-and-a-half of batting inadequacy in this remarkable match. In the end, both captains said the batsmen, and not the Gabba wicket, were to blame for the shortest domestic four-day match in Australian cricket history. The Queensland pace men shared the wickets, with Andy Bichel charging in after carrying the drinks in three consecutive Tests and Joe Dawes seeming to mesmerise the Tasmanians. Shane Jurgensen derived some pleasure from his return to his home state, taking the wickets of Martin Love and Clinton Perren with successive balls and ending with his best first-class figures to date. In the context of the match, Jimmy Maher's innings (131 minutes, 91 balls, six fours) was a triumph of survival. Tasmania were not helped by Michael Di Venuto's retirement because of food poisoning in their second innings, but they should still have been able to set Queensland more than 51 runs to win, Michael Kasprowicz and Dawes both being efficiently destructive. Queensland reached their second-innings target without losing a wicket, completing the match in 569 minutes – 31 minutes less than the previous shortest game, when Western Australia defeated Victoria at the MCG in 1975-76.

Man of the Match: A.J. Bichel.   *Attendance:* 1,065.

Close of play: First day, Tasmania (2) 0-6 (Hills 3, Cox 3).

Tasmania

D.F. Hills c Maher b Bichel	5	– lbw b Kasprowicz	3
*J. Cox b Dawes	20	– c Maher b Bichel	21
M.G. Dighton c Symonds b Bichel	4	– c Hauritz b Kasprowicz	0
M.J. Di Venuto c Law b Dawes	28	– (8) retired hurt	4
S.R. Watson b Symonds	1	– (4) c Seccombe b Kasprowicz	0
D.J. Marsh lbw b Bichel	9	– (5) c Maher b Symonds	15
†S.G. Clingeleffer c and b Bichel	0	– c Bichel b Dawes	19
S. Young c Perren b Kasprowicz	8	– (6) c Seccombe b Kasprowicz	1
D.G. Wright c Seccombe b Dawes	18	– c Seccombe b Dawes	1
D.J. Saker not out	1	– not out	5
S.J. Jurgensen c Perren b Kasprowicz	0	– c Seccombe b Dawes	10
L-b 3, n-b 3	6	L-b 3	3

(45.4 overs, 100 mins) 100   (34.5 overs, 151 mins) (9 wkts dec) 82
Fall: 7 13 55 60 62 68 74 99 99 100   Fall: 9 11 11 27 28 58 66 66 82

Bowling: *First Innings*—Bichel 14-3-54-4; Kasprowicz 15.4-6-34-2; Dawes 9-7-4-3; Symonds 6-4-4-1; Hauritz 1-0-1-0. *Second Innings*—Bichel 12-6-21-1; Kasprowicz 9-3-22-4; Dawes 9.5-5-28-3; Symonds 4-1-8-1.

Queensland

J.P. Maher c Marsh b Saker	35	– not out	13
B.P. Nash c Watson b Wright	19	– not out	35
M.L. Love b Jurgensen	10		
C.T. Perren c Di Venuto b Jurgensen	0		
A. Symonds lbw b Saker	8		
*S.G. Law c Clingeleffer b Young	14		
†W.A. Seccombe c Clingeleffer b Watson	5		
A.J. Bichel c Saker b Jurgensen	23		
N.M. Hauritz c Clingeleffer b Jurgensen	4		
M.S. Kasprowicz not out	5		
J.H. Dawes b Watson	0		
L-b 8, n-b 1	9	B 2, l-b 1	3

(44.5 overs, 186 mins) 132   (11.4 overs, 48 mins) (0 wkt) 51
Fall: 37 52 52 67 86 94 112 118 129 132

Bowling: *First Innings*—Wright 13-3-33-1; Saker 11-1-43-2; Jurgensen 10-5-16-4; Young 7-3-13-1; Watson 3.5-0-19-2. *Second Innings*—Wright 4-0-17-0; Jurgensen 5.4-1-18-0; Watson 2-0-13-0.

Umpires: B.N.J. Oxenford and J.F. Torpey.
TV Umpire: L.D. Musch.

At Bellerive Oval, Hobart, January 17,18, 2002. Tasmania won by an innings and 50 runs. Toss: Queensland. Tasmania 6 pts.

QUEENSLAND v SOUTH AUSTRALIA

At Brisbane Cricket Ground, Brisbane, January 25, 26, 27, 28, 2002. South Australia won by nine wickets. Toss: Queensland. South Australia 6 pts.

Queensland suffered a rare slip at their Gabba fortress as South Australia's twin batting pillars Darren Lehmann and Greg Blewett ran amok after being invited to bat. Lehmann (202 minutes, 173 balls, 17 fours), on the verge of a recall to the Australian limited-overs team, was at his expansive best and Blewett (253 minutes, 214 balls, 14 fours) compiled a classy century. With Chris Davies (240 minutes, 201 balls, 12 fours, two sixes) stroking an excellent maiden century, the South Australians batted Queensland out of the match. The home side were soon in more trouble when Martin Love was taken to hospital after being struck by a bouncer. When he returned with the score at six for 107 to finish a gallant innings (206 minutes, 171 balls, six fours), Queensland were already resigned to following on. Jimmy Maher's heroic double century (483 minutes, 360 balls, 20 fours) was almost enough to save the match, particularly when 300 was passed with only four wickets down. All-rounder Mike Smith, however, then took four quick wickets without conceding a run, giving his side time to complete an impressive victory.

Man of the Match: M.J. Smith.   *Attendance:* 3,003.

Close of play: First day, South Australia (1) 4-349 (Higgins 15, Davies 15); Second day, Queensland (1) 6-107 (Hayden 38); Third day, Queensland (2) 1-164 (Maher 90, Love 28).

South Australia

D.A. Fitzgerald c Seccombe b Noffke	39	– (2) run out (Hopes)	10
B.A. Johnson c Law b Noffke	25	– (1) not out	26
G.S. Blewett c Law b Hauritz	109	– not out	14
*D.S. Lehmann c Seccombe b Dawes	129		
B.H. Higgins c Love b Law	54		
C.J. Davies not out	119		
N.T. Adcock c and b Hauritz	19		
M.J. Smith not out	40		
B 1, 1-b 2, n-b 16	19	W 1	1

(157 overs, 562 mins)	(6 wkts dec) 553	(9.4 overs, 42 mins) (1 wkt) 51
Fall: 33 95 296 323 433 478		Fall: 18

†G.A. Manou, P.C. Rofe and M.A. Harrity did not bat.

Bowling: *First Innings*—Kasprowicz 25–4–78–0; Dawes 28–6–100–1; Noffke 29–4–121–2; Hopes 24–6–81–0; Hauritz 37–7–116–2; Law 14–1–54–1. *Second Innings*—Dawes 5–0–32–0; Hopes 4.4–0–19–0.

Queensland

J.P. Maher c (sub) Williams b Harrity	6	– c Manou b Smith	209
M.L. Hayden c Manou b Blewett	63	– c Lehmann b Rofe	43
M.L. Love c Manou b Harrity	84	– b Smith	41
J.L. Cassell lbw b Rofe	0	– c Manou b Smith	20
*S.G. Law c Manou b Harrity	11	– c Manou b Smith	1
J.R. Hopes b Smith	11	– c Blewett b Smith	14
†W.A. Seccombe b Smith	5	– lbw b Blewett	6
A.A. Noffke lbw b Blewett	14	– lbw b Smith	20
N.M. Hauritz c Johnson b Adcock	10	– lbw b Smith	3
M.S. Kasprowicz b Rofe	3	– c Johnson b Smith	0
J.H. Dawes not out	0	– not out	0
B 5, l-b 14, n-b 6	25	B 5, l-b 4, n-b 4	13

(84 overs, 331 mins)	232	(128.2 overs, 507 mins)	370
Fall: 9 34 51 81 87 107 171		Fall: 85 198 270 279 307 318	
218 228 232		362 367 367 370	

Bowling: *First Innings*—Rofe 19–4–41–2; Harrity 18–2–61–3; Smith 14–1–40–2; Blewett 17–6–26–2; Johnson 6–0–24–0; Adcock 7–1–19–1; Lehmann 3–2–2–0. *Second Innings*—Rofe 33–9–65–2; Harrity 26–5–89–0; Smith 31.2–9–98–7; Adcock 7–1–18–0; Blewett 16–3–39–1; Johnson 3–0–18–0; Lehmann 10–1–23–0; Higgins 2–0–11–0.

Umpires: P.D. Parker and J.F. Torpey.

At Adelaide Oval, Adelaide, February 13, 14, 15, 16, 2002. QUEENSLAND defeated SOUTH AUSTRALIA by 106 runs.

At Sydney Cricket Ground, Sydney, March 1, 2, 3, 4, 2002. QUEENSLAND drew with NEW SOUTH WALES.

QUEENSLAND v VICTORIA

At Brisbane Cricket Ground, Brisbane, March 13, 14, 15, 2002. Queensland won by five wickets. Toss: Queensland. Queensland 6 pts and Victoria 2 pts. First-class debut: D.M. Payne.

Queenslanders look forward with relish to Victoria's chronically unsuccessful visits to the Gabba. The chuckling continued when the Victorians were skittled for 148 against a Queensland team led by Martin Love in the absence of the injured Stuart Law. Love was well served by teenage pace man Scott Brant, who took three wickets and two catches in his first match at the Gabba. In their turn, the Victorians had something to cheer about when they reduced Queensland to six for 22. With young right-arm pace man Will Carr taking 6/46, Victoria claimed first-innings points on the second day, but their lead of 41 was not enough on a difficult wicket. In less than four hours, they were back in their Gabba rut after scoring just 122. Queensland needed 164 runs to secure another home Pura Cup final and Love (123 minutes, 105 balls, seven fours) set his side on the way with a mature innings which was well supported by the obduracy of Daniel Payne (169 minutes, 117 balls, three fours). The match was completed by lunch on the third day.

Man of the Match: S.A. Brant. *Attendance:* 1,425.

Close of play: First day, Queensland (1) 6-64 (Carseldine 36, Noffke 9); Second day, Queensland (2) 1-66 (Payne 16, Love 34).

Victoria

*M. T. G. Elliott c Seccombe b Brant	9	– (2) lbw b Brant 4
M. P. Mott c Brant b Kasprowicz	34	– (1) c Payne b Brant 7
B. J. Hodge c Symonds b Brant	2	– b Kasprowicz 1
J. Moss c Seccombe b Kasprowicz	10	– c Dawes b Brant 38
N. Jewell b Symonds	26	– c Perren b Kasprowicz 4
A. B. McDonald c Kasprowicz b Noffke	26	– c Symonds b Kasprowicz 7
C. L. White c Nash b Dawes	13	– c Seccombe b Noffke 7
†D. S. Berry c Brant b Dawes	0	– c Perren b Noffke 41
M. L. Lewis b Brant	11	– c Seccombe b Noffke 8
M. W. H. Inness c Brant b Noffke	0	– not out 0
W. N. Carr not out	0	– c Perren b Noffke 0
L-b 5, n-b 12	17	L-b 3, n-b 2 5

(58.2 overs, 243 mins)	148	(52.5 overs, 218 mins)	122

Fall: 15 18 38 92 92 123 123 146 148 148

Fall: 9 12 12 35 45 57 87 119 122 122

Bowling: *First Innings*—Kasprowicz 20–2–64–2; Brant 10–2–23–3; Dawes 13–3–26–2; Noffke 9.2–3–21–2; Symonds 6–2–9–1. *Second Innings*—Kasprowicz 16–3–37–3; Brant 12–2–31–3; Dawes 11–4–22–0; Noffke 13.5–5–29–4.

Queensland

B. P. Nash c McDonald b Carr	1	– (2) c Elliott b Lewis 11
D. M. Payne b Inness	1	– (1) c and b White 35
*M. L. Love c Berry b Dawes	5	– c Berry b McDonald 61
L. A. Carseldine c Berry b Inness	39	– c Berry b Hodge 21
A. Symonds c Mott b Carr	0	– c Berry b Inness 18
C. T. Perren b Carr	2	– not out 9
†W. A. Seccombe c Berry b Inness	1	– not out 0
A. A. Noffke c White b Inness	9	
M. S. Kasprowicz c Moss b Carr	13	
S. A. Brant not out	19	
J. H. Dawes c Berry b Carr	7	
B 1, w 5, n-b 4	10	B 1, l-b 1, n-b 7 9

(49.2 overs, 211 mins)	107	(54.4 overs, 225 mins)	(5 wkts)	164

Fall: 1 1 3 15 15 21 22 64 80 84 107

Fall: 17 116 120 149 163

Bowling: *First Innings*—Inness 17–6–31–4; Carr 15.2–4–46–6; Lewis 7–1–18–0; Moss 6–2–7–0; White 4–0–4–0. *Second Innings*—Inness 17–8–29–1; Carr 11–2–29–0; Lewis 12–1–54–1; Moss 2–1–5–0; McDonald 6.4–1–14–1; White 5–0–31–1; Hodge 1–1–0–1.

Umpires: B. N. J. Oxenford and P. D. Parker.
TV Umpire: L. D. Musch.

FINAL

At Brisbane Cricket Ground, Brisbane, March 23, 24, 25, 26, 27, 2001. QUEENSLAND defeated TASMANIA by 235 runs. For details see section on Pura Cup, 2001-02.

AUSTRALIAN DOMESTIC FIRST-CLASS RESULTS TABLE

Opponent	M	W	L	D	T
New South Wales	144	36	57	51	0
South Australia	139	42	50	45	1
Victoria	138	41	48	49	0
Western Australia	104	24	35	45	0
Tasmania	46	16	7	23	0
Total	571	160	197	213	1

AUSTRALIAN DOMESTIC FIRST-CLASS RECORDS

Highest score for:	283*	P.J.P. Burge v New South Wales at Brisbane	1963-64
Highest score against:	452*	D.G. Bradman (New South Wales) at Sydney	1929-30
Best bowling for:	10/61	P.J. Allan v Victoria at Melbourne	1965-66
Best bowling against:	9/67	A.N. Connolly (Victoria) at Brisbane	1964-65
Highest total for:	687	v New South Wales at Brisbane	1930-31
Highest total against:	7-821 dec	by South Australia at Adelaide	1939-40
Lowest total for:	49	v Victoria at Melbourne	1936-37
Lowest total against:	54	by Western Australia at Brisbane	1972-73

* Denotes not out.

MOST RUNS

	M	I	NO	R	HS	100s	50s	Avge
S.C. Trimble	123	230	13	8,647	252*	22	40	39.84
S.G. Law	123	202	24	7,812	216	22	40	43.89
M.L. Hayden	82	149	17	7,323	234	24	30	55.48
P.J.P. Burge	83	138	12	7,084	283	22	31	56.22
A.R. Border	87	143	19	6,779	196	15	37	54.67
K.D. Mackay	100	162	22	6,341	223	14	32	45.29
M.L. Love	83	142	11	6,201	228	15	27	47.34
G.M. Ritchie	94	154	14	6,096	213*	14	34	43.54
T.J. Barsby	100	181	7	6,052	165	13	28	34.78
J.P. Maher	90	159	18	5,761	209	28	10	40.86

* Denotes not out.

HIGHEST PARTNERSHIP FOR EACH WICKET

388	for 1st	K.C. Wessels and R.B. Kerr v Victoria at St Kilda	1982-83
368*	for 2nd	M.L. Hayden and M.L. Love v Tasmania at Hobart (Bel)	1995-96
326	for 3rd	M.L. Love and S.G. Law v Tasmania at Brisbane	1994-95
295	for 4th	P.J.P. Burge and T.R. Veivers v South Australia at Brisbane	1962-63
231	for 5th	K.D. Mackay and R.G. Archer v Victoria at Brisbane	1953-54
		A.R. Border and G.S. Trimble v Victoria at Brisbane	1987-88
211	for 6th	T.R. Veivers and J.D. Bratchford v South Australia at Brisbane	1959-60
335	for 7th	W.C. Andrews and E.C. Bensted v New South Wales at Sydney	1934-35
146	for 8th	T.V. Hohns and G. Dymock v Victoria at Melbourne	1978-79
152*	for 9th	A.T.W. Grout and W.T. Walmsley v New South Wales at Sydney	1956-57
105*	for 10th	W.T. Walmsley and J.E. Freeman v New South Wales at Brisbane	1957-58

MOST WICKETS

	M	Balls	Mdns	R	W	BB	5W/i	10W/m	Avge
C.G. Rackemann	102	22,400	920	10,079	383	7/43	12	1	26.32
J.R. Thomson	77	15,166	404	7,927	328	7/27	17	3	24.17
M.S. Kasprowicz	74	16,065	680	7,768	316	6/47	20	2	24.58
C.J. McDermott	67	14,974	541	7,605	303	8/44	22	2	25.10
G. Dymock	75	17,110	449	7,032	266	6/79	6	0	26.44
D. Tazelaar	73	15,371	623	7,050	257	6/49	9	1	27.43
A.J. Bichel	51	11,350	494	5,412	244	6/45	13	2	22.18
T.V. Hohns	105	16,664	680	7,330	188	6/56	8	1	38.99
P.J. Allan	47	9,840	153	4,603	182	10/61	11	3	25.29
J.N. Maguire	64	12,945	438	5,893	178	6/62	7	1	33.11

MOST DISMISSALS

	M	Ct	St	Total
W. A. Seccombe	74	352	10	362
J. A. Maclean	86	289	24	313
A. T. W. Grout	84	213	63	276
R. B. Phillips	68	214	12	226
D. Tallon	67	145	61	206

MOST CATCHES

S. G. Law	109 in 123 matches	G. M. Ritchie	74 in 94 matches
J. P. Maher	100 in 90 matches	T. J. Barsby	73 in 100 matches
A. R. Border	99 in 87 matches	S. C. Trimble	72 in 123 matches
M. L. Love	93 in 83 matches	P. J. P. Burge	70 in 83 matches
M. L. Hayden	75 in 82 matches	R. B. Kerr	69 in 79 matches

MOST APPEARANCES

123	S. C. Trimble	1959-60 – 1975-76	100	T. J. Barsby	1984-85 – 1996-97
123	S. G. Law	1988-89 – 2001-02	94	G. M. Ritchie	1980-81 – 1991-92
105	T. V. Hohns	1972-73 – 1990-91	90	J. P. Maher	1993-94 – 2001-02
102	C. G. Rackemann	1979-80 – 1995-96	87	A. R. Border	1980-81 – 1995-96
100	K. D. Mackay	1946-47 – 1963-64	86	J. A. Maclean	1968-69 – 1978-79

SOUTH AUSTRALIA

Chief Executive: M. Deare

President: Hon. I. M. McLachlan AO

Cricket Coach: G. S. Chappell

Captain: D. S. Lehmann

Darren Lehmann

South Australia's last Sheffield Shield success in 1995-96 was one to savour. The drama on the last afternoon of the season and the nail-biting climax of a 59-ball countdown until Peter McIntyre and Shane George saw their side home in front of a crowd that swelled to around 10,000 was one of the Adelaide Oval's most treasured cricketing moments. It is only six years ago now but of the victorious 13 in the team photograph, only five – current skipper Darren Lehmann, Greg Blewett, Jason Gillespie, Mark Harrity and Ben Johnson – remain at the first-class level. Captain at the time Jamie Siddons, Tim May, James Brayshaw, Paul Nobes, George, Darren Webber and Tim Nielsen have all retired and McIntyre quit at the end of last season. That is a major loss of talent.

South Australia's cricketing successes have generally come at steady intervals. Six years ago the side won because they were a well-balanced side: three dominant batsmen in Lehmann, Blewett and Siddons; solid 800-run 40-average men like Brayshaw and Nobes; good young developing bats in Webber and Johnson; a fine wicket-keeper-batsman in Nielsen; an exciting new-ball attack with the second-year development of Gillespie and the strong support of Harrity and George; plus the wily spin combination of May and McIntyre.

After defeating Queensland by nine wickets at the end of January 2002 the South Australians sat in second place in the Pura Cup table but the latter part of the summer proved disappointing and the year ended up as one of promise rather than fulfilment. The problem compared to 1995-96 is one of balance. Then there were three class batsmen, now there are two in the mature Lehmann and Blewett. The side has not picked up the regular 800-run, 40-average men, although David Fitzgerald more than threatened that class in 1999-00 and Johnson's return to form last summer has put his career back on track. Gillespie is rarely available, so the supporting pace bowlers need to work hard for at least half their games on a traditionally unresponsive Adelaide Oval pitch; McIntyre and Brad Young have their moments but throughout their careers have bought their wickets at more than 40 runs apiece. Graham Manou, brilliant young keeper though he is, is yet to prove as regular a run-getter as Nielsen. Yet the feeling is that the state is not that far away from a quality side which will enable the silverware to be brought home.

Let us look at the positives. Lehmann continued to lead from the front and it was pleasing that his 772 runs at 64.33 with four centuries helped to win his Australian recall, while Blewett made four centuries and scored over 800 runs. At Hobart in November, Lehmann's explosive 246 and Blewett's century combined in a South Australian second-wicket record stand of 385 to provide the springboard for an amazing victory. Johnson equalled Bill Lawry's Australian record of carrying his bat through an innings in two successive matches, against Western Australia and Victoria, and, in his third century of the season against Tasmania at the Adelaide Oval, he came within a wicket of achieving it on a third occasion. His season's total of 653 runs at 59.36 was full of merit.

SOUTH AUSTRALIA PURA CUP TEAM, 2001-02

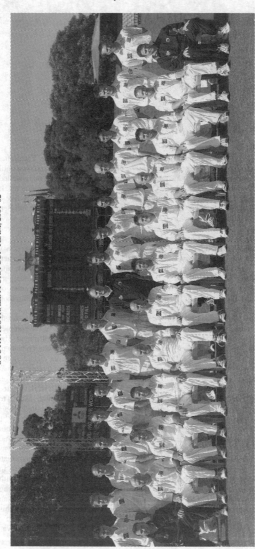

Back row: C.J. Ferguson, A.J. Borgas, M.C. Miller, L.J. Williams, D.M. Dempsey, M. Weeks, P. Wilson, P.C. Rofe, G.S. Chappell (*coach*), N.A. Harrity, N.T. Adcock, M.J. Smith, J.M. Vaughan, B.A.S. Johnson, B.E. Young. *Front row*: T.M. Neilsen (*assistant coach*), S.A. Deitz, R.J. Harris, G.A. Manou, P.E. McIntyre, D.S. Lehmann (*captain*), G.S. Blewett (*vice-captain*), D.J. Harris, C.J. Davies, D.A. Fitzgerald, B.H. Higgins, R. Hunt (*physiotherapist*).

Among the bowlers, Gillespie achieved a career-best of 8/50 in the first innings of the match against New South Wales at the Sydney Cricket Ground but he was only available for two games. The outstanding success of the summer was fast-medium Paul Rofe, who turned 21 during his brilliant match-winning performance of 13/112 against New South Wales in January. Rofe bowled sustained spells of penetrating accuracy, as his figures of 410.4 overs, 140 maidens, 1,012 runs, 41 wickets attest. In the match against Tasmania when South Australia were a bowler short, Rofe delivered 20-13-24-3 to create such pressure that Harrity was able to capitalise and dismiss the batsmen from the other end in achieving his own career-best figures of 5/65. It seems astonishing that Rofe was overlooked for an ACB contract at season's end. Mike Smith also performed strongly throughout the season to capture 26 wickets at 32.62 with a brilliant performance of 7/98 against Queensland in Brisbane, as well as batting responsibly.

The promise in a few other players was obvious. Chris Davies finally broke through for a maiden first-class century and Ben Higgins made a number of gritty half-centuries, including a fine match-saving performance against Shane Warne and Colin Miller in the first home game of the season. Young also made a fine century against New South Wales in Adelaide but the middle-order batsmen need to push their averages up around 40 to give the bowlers larger targets to bowl at. One of the problems for the side was its long tail, and keeper Manou lost his place to Shane Deitz for the last game of the year in an attempt to strengthen this aspect of the line-up.

Harrity had a frustrating year after some good early form, and the spinners generally lacked penetration, with McIntyre's best performance of the year coming in the tour match against the New Zealanders. Nevertheless, McIntyre's retirement at the end of the year following his loss of contract is a blow to the South Australians, as his accurate leg-spin has won a number of matches on final-day Les Burdett Adelaide Oval wickets.

The low point of the year was undoubtedly the home game against Queensland in February when South Australia lost seven wickets for 34 runs on the final afternoon to allow other states to take over as championship contenders. – BERNARD WHIMPRESS.

SOUTH AUSTRALIA RESULTS, 2001-02

All first-class matches – Played 11: Won 4, Lost 5, Drawn 2.
Pura Cup matches – Played 10: Won 3, Lost 5, Drawn 2.
ING Cup matches – Played 10: Won 6, Lost 4
Competition placings – Pura Cup, 4th; ING Cup, 3rd.

PURA CUP AVERAGES, 2001-02

BATTING

	M	I	NO	R	HS	100s	50s	Avge	Ct/St
D.S. Lehmann	7	12	0	772	246	4	0	64.33	2
B.A. Johnson	7	14	3	653	138*	3	2	59.36	9
G.S. Blewett	10	19	3	858	169*	4	2	53.63	7
C.J. Davies	5	9	1	306	119*	1	1	38.25	3
J.N. Gillespie	2	4	2	67	32*	0	0	33.50	0
B.H. Higgins	9	16	2	446	80	0	5	31.86	3
D.A. Fitzgerald	7	13	0	376	139	1	0	28.92	6
S.A. Deitz	3	6	0	166	86	0	1	27.67	4
B.E. Young	8	14	0	354	122	1	0	25.29	5
M.J. Smith	7	13	2	245	46	0	0	22.27	9
J.M. Vaughan	3	5	1	82	69	0	1	20.50	1
G.A. Manou	9	14	1	261	62	0	1	20.08	30/2
N.T. Adcock	3	5	0	83	46	0	0	16.60	1
P.E. McIntyre	5	10	1	97	40	0	0	10.78	0
D.M. Dempsey	3	5	0	38	21	0	0	7.60	5
P.C. Rofe	10	13	6	52	9	0	0	7.43	3
M.A. Harrity	9	12	4	48	19	0	0	6.00	4
P. Wilson	1	2	1	2	2	0	0	2.00	0
R.J. Harris	2	2	0	0	0	0	0	0.00	0

* Denotes not out.

BOWLING

	O	M	R	W	BB	5W/i	Avge
J.N. Gillespie	98	22	293	15	8/50	1	19.53
P.C. Rofe	410.4	140	1,012	41	7/52	3	24.68
G.S. Blewett	70	13	176	7	3/15	0	25.14
D.S. Lehmann	64.3	11	162	5	3/42	0	32.40
M.J. Smith	242.2	46	848	26	7/98	1	32.62
M.A. Harrity	320.2	63	1,072	25	5/65	1	42.88
N.T. Adcock	29.2	3	90	2	1/19	0	45.00
R.J. Harris	35.4	10	99	2	2/26	0	49.50
P. Wilson	51	9	151	3	2/98	0	50.33
B.E. Young	255.2	55	735	13	3/21	0	56.54
B.A. Johnson	42	5	173	3	2/26	0	57.67
P.E. McIntyre	167.3	30	565	9	2/56	0	62.78
B.H. Higgins	24.2	7	80	1	1/49	0	80.00

SOUTH AUSTRALIA v VICTORIA

At Adelaide Oval, Adelaide, October 17, 18, 19, 20, 2001. Drawn. Toss: South Australia. South Australia 2 pts. First-class debut: D.M. Dempsey.

This match was played at a pedestrian pace but provided a gritty finish on the last afternoon with the home team defying the spin-bowling wiles of Shane Warne and Colin Miller. Brad Hodge (409 minutes, 323 balls, 16 fours) continued his fine form from the previous season as the visitors batted until after lunch on the second day. At two for 311, with Greg Blewett and Darren Lehmann (244 minutes, 199 balls, 11 fours) in control, South Australia seemed to be cruising to easy first-innings points. However, Ian Harvey had both Lehmann and Ben Higgins caught by substitute fielder Jonathan Moss, and trapped former Victorian Darren Dempsey in front to capture Victoria's seventh hat-trick and the first at Adelaide Oval since Len Pascoe in 1980-81. Blewett remained serene in his unconquered century (392 minutes, 291 balls, 23 fours, one six) and the home side stuttered to first-innings points. Victoria were in no hurry in their second innings and Hodge brought up his second century of the match (289 minutes, 229 balls, eight fours, one six) before Paul Reiffel set a victory target of 209 in just under four hours. Fleming broke through the top order but Lehmann, the inexperienced Ben Higgins (142 minutes, 124 balls, six fours) and Jason Gillespie stood firm.

Close of play: First day, Victoria (1) 4-228 (Hodge 100, Harvey 29); Second day, South Australia (1) 2-139 (Blewett 78, Lehmann 17); Third day, Victoria (2) 1-88 (Arnberger 40, Hodge 43).

Man of the Match: B.J. Hodge.   *Attendance:* 2,410.

Victoria

M.T.G. Elliott run out (Lehmann)	42	– (8) b Gillespie	1
J.L. Arnberger c Higgins b Rofe	17	– (1) c Fitzgerald b Rofe	43
M.P. Mott c Manou b Rofe	2	– (2) c Manou b Harrity	4
B.J. Hodge c Blewett b Young	140	– (3) not out	110
M. Klinger c Manou b Harrity	35	– (4) c and b Lehmann	10
I.J. Harvey c Fitzgerald b Young	62	– (5) c Dempsey b Lehmann	23
†D.S. Berry c Blewett b Harrity	5	– (6) lbw b Gillespie	0
S.K. Warne b Gillespie	4	– (7) c Manou b Gillespie	2
*P.R. Reiffel c Manou b Young	13	– not out	11
D.W. Fleming c Dempsey b Gillespie	7		
C.R. Miller not out	3		
L-b 3, w 1	4	B 4, l-b 1, w 1, n-b 1	7

(132.5 overs, 506 mins) 334   (79 overs, 303 mins)   (7 wkts dec) 211
Fall: 45 47 92 175 279 287 296 319 324 334   Fall: 4 100 135 174 174 178 188

Bowling: *First Innings*—Gillespie 34.5–8–95–2; Harrity 27–6–94–2; Rofe 28–12–46–2; Young 32–10–70–3; Lehmann 6–1–11–0; Higgins 5–1–15–0. *Second Innings*—Gillespie 20–8–36–3; Harrity 15–2–53–1; Rofe 19–8–38–1; Young 4.3–0–19–0; Lehmann 20.3–3–60–2.

South Australia

D.A. Fitzgerald c Berry b Warne	34	– c Arnberger b Fleming	11
S.A. Deitz c Berry b Miller	5	– st Berry b Miller	15
G.S. Blewett not out	169	– c Reiffel b Fleming	4
*D.S. Lehmann c (sub) Moss b Harvey	103	– c Mott b Fleming	39
B.H. Higgins c (sub) Moss b Harvey	0	– (6) not out	58
D.M. Dempsey lbw b Harvey	0	– (5) lbw b Warne	10
B.E. Young c Mott b Fleming	0		
†G.A. Manou b Fleming	4		
J.N. Gillespie not out	7	– (7) not out	32
B 4, l-b 8, n-b 3	15	B 3, l-b 6, n-b 1	10

(113.1 overs, 442 mins)   (7 wkts dec) 337   (56 overs, 228 mins)   (5 wkts) 179
Fall: 23 94 311 311 311 312 320   Fall: 24 34 36 49 124

P.C. Rofe and M.A. Harrity did not bat.

Bowling: *First Innings*—Fleming 20–7–80–2; Reiffel 17–6–38–0; Miller 28–5–81–1; Harvey 23–6–65–3; Warne 23.1–4–61–1; Hodge 2–2–0–0. *Second Innings*—Fleming 16–7–37–3; Reiffel 3–0–18–0; Miller 19–3–41–1; Warne 18–1–74–1.

Umpires: S.J. Davis and D.J. Harper.

At Sydney Cricket Ground, Sydney, October 26, 27, 28, 29, 2001. SOUTH AUSTRALIA lost to NEW SOUTH WALES by 290 runs.

At Bellerive Oval, Hobart, November 8, 9, 10, 11, 2001. SOUTH AUSTRALIA defeated TASMANIA by an innings and 40 runs.

SOUTH AUSTRALIA v WESTERN AUSTRALIA

At Adelaide Oval, Adelaide, November 25, 26, 27, 28, 2001. Western Australia won by 76 runs. Toss: Western Australia. Western Australia 6 pts.

Uncharacteristic swing for the new-ball bowlers produced a surprisingly low-scoring game in which just 796 runs were scored in four completed innings. Rangy 20-year-old medium-fast bowler Paul Rofe got the home side off to a fine start with the first five-wicket haul of his career. Brad Hogg (192 minutes, 146 balls, five fours) led stout resistance which saw the second half of the Western Australian order more than double the total. The South Australians were unable to take advantage of Rofe's work and Greg Blewett and Darren Lehmann had poor matches. Ben Johnson, called up as a reserve opener, carried his bat (339 minutes, 243 balls, 14 fours) but after his 132-run fourth-wicket partnership with Chris Davies (181 minutes, 157 balls, six fours) there was little resistance to visiting pace men Matthew Nicholson and Jo Angel. A peculiar feature of the innings was that eight batsmen recorded a mere five runs between them. Rofe led a bowling comeback with another display of sustained accuracy but Nicholson destroyed South Australia's victory hopes by removing Blewett and Lehmann in his first two overs late on the third day. Wicket-keeper Graham Manou and all-rounder Mike Smith added 68 in 14 overs for the seventh wicket but the innings wound up quickly after their departure.

Close of play: First day, South Australia (1) 0-6 (Young 1, Johnson 4); Second day, Western Australia (2) 0-23 (Mueleman 14, Hussey 7); Third day, South Australia (2) 4-52 (Young 30, Smith 1).

Man of the Match: M. J. Nicholson. *Attendance:* 2,864.

Western Australia

M. E. K. Hussey c Manou b Johnson	40	– (2) c Johnson b Rofe	11
S. W. Meuleman c Young b Rofe	0	– (1) lbw b Rofe	23
*S. M. Katich c Smith b Johnson	42	– c Young b Smith	38
M. W. Goodwin c Davies b Harrity	12	– c Davies b Young	33
M. J. North c Manou b Rofe	5	– c Manou b Smith	0
†R. J. Campbell c Smith b Rofe	21	– c Manou b Rofe	22
G. B. Hogg not out	56	– b Harrity	26
M. J. Nicholson b McIntyre	15	– c Manou b McIntyre	15
J. Angel b Rofe	14	– lbw b Harrity	8
B. J. Oldroyd b Rofe	0	– (11) not out	0
B. A. Williams b Harrity	11	– (10) c Rofe b McIntyre	20
L-b 2, n-b 9	11	L-b 7, w 1, n-b 5	13

(90.1 overs, 360 mins) 227   (84.3 overs, 327 mins) 209
Fall: 0 86 92 106 108 127 184   Fall: 32 37 95 95 113 143 179
216 216 227   181 205 209

Bowling: *First Innings*—Harrity 25.1–6–71–2; Rofe 23–11–30–5; Smith 22–5–61–0; Johnson 5–0–26–2; McIntyre 15–2–37–1. *Second Innings*—Harrity 18–3–42–2; Rofe 19–10–31–3; Young 23–6–45–1; McIntyre 14.3–2–56–2; Smith 10–4–28–2.

South Australia

B. E. Young c Campbell b Williams	2	– (2) b Angel		30
B. A. Johnson not out	121	– (1) c Nicholson b Williams		13
G. S. Blewett c Campbell b Williams	0	– lbw b Nicholson		0
*D. S. Lehmann c Campbell b Nicholson	12	– c Campbell b Nicholson		2
C. J. Davies run out ((S)Harvey, KM)	52	– c Goodwin b Oldroyd		5
B. H. Higgins c Campbell b Nicholson	0	– (7) c North b Williams		8
M. J. Smith b Nicholson	1	– (6) c Campbell b Nicholson		31
†G. A. Manou c Campbell b Nicholson	0	– c Campbell b Hogg		43
P. E. McIntyre b Angel	2	– not out		11
P. C. Rofe c North b Angel	0	– lbw b Hogg		9
M. A. Harrity lbw b Angel	0	– lbw b Nicholson		1
B 4, l-b 5, w 1, n-b 6	16	L-b 1		1

(82.5 overs, 339 mins) 206　　(58.1 overs, 234 mins) 154
Fall: 7 8 31 163 163 173 173　　　　Fall: 24 30 32 45 52 61 129
185 192 206　　　　　　　　　　　　134 153 154

Bowling: *First Innings*—Williams 8–3–17–2; Nicholson 23–6–58–4; Oldroyd 21–5–50–0; Angel 20.5–4–48–3; Hogg 9–2–24–0; North 1–1–0–0. *Second Innings*—Williams 9–3–30–2; Angel 14–5–34–1; Nicholson 16.1–3–60–4; Oldroyd 12–5–25–1; Hogg 7–4–4–2.

Umpires: P.M. Angley and D.J. Harper.
TV Umpire: C.D. Fry.

At Melbourne Cricket Ground, Melbourne, December 13, 14, 15, 2001. SOUTH AUSTRALIA lost to VICTORIA by nine wickets.

SOUTH AUSTRALIA v NEW SOUTH WALES

At Adelaide Oval, Adelaide, January 16, 17, 18, 19, 2002. South Australia won by 67 runs. Toss: South Australia. South Australia 6 pts.

Paul Rofe turned 21 on the first day, and as the match unfolded all his birthdays seemed to come at once. South Australia began by dawdling to two for 9 from 16 overs in the first 70 minutes. However, a fighting career-highest score by Ben Higgins (171 minutes, 127 balls, 12 fours), and century partnerships between Higgins and Brad Young (282 minutes, 219 balls, 11 fours, one six) and between Young and Graham Manou (133 minutes, 92 balls, six fours, one six) gave the innings substance. New South Wales' reply was built around Michael Clarke's distinguished century (276 minutes, 204 balls, 23 fours) in the middle order, his main support coming from breezy half-centuries by Brett Van Deinsen (112 minutes, 82 balls, 11 fours, one six) and Brad Haddin (89 minutes, 61 balls, six fours, one six). Rofe ran through the tail with the second new ball to give South Australia first-innings points. Fortune favoured Darren Lehmann on the third afternoon when he was dropped four times on the way to a blazing 143 (184 minutes, 130 balls, 22 fours, one six) which was virtually half his team's total. New South Wales, chasing 315 for victory, fell once more to Rofe, who operated in Glenn McGrath style with superb line and lift. He broke the back of the New South Wales innings during the morning, and finished off the tail after Mark Higgs (137 minutes, 112 balls, 10 fours, one six) and Haddin had added a quick 104 runs in the middle session. Rofe took 13/112 for the game, a brilliant performance by a pace bowler on the placid Adelaide Oval pitch.

Close of play: First day, South Australia (1) 6-291 Young 102, Manou 37); Second day, New South Wales (1) 6-275 (Clarke 94, Nash 6); Third day, New South Wales (2) 0-10 (Mail 1, Van Deinsen 9).

Man of the Match: P.C. Rofe.　　*Attendance:* 3,056.

South Australia

D. A. Fitzgerald c Van Deinsen b S. R. Clark	7	–	(2) c Haddin b S. R. Clark	26
B. A. Johnson c Slater b S. R. Clark	1	–	(1) b Bracken	8
G. S. Blewett c Slater b Bracken	38	–	b Van Deinsen	28
*D. S. Lehmann c Haddin b Bracken	11	–	c Mail b Van Deinsen	143
B. H. Higgins b MacGill	80	–	c Haddin b Bracken	23
B. E. Young c Nash b Bracken	122	–	c Van Deinsen b Nash	28
M. J. Smith c Mail b MacGill	9	–	not out	19
†G. A. Manou c Van Deinsen b Bracken	62	–	c Mail b Nash	0
P. E. McIntyre c Van Deinsen b S. R. Clark	6	–	c Haddin b Van Deinsen	0
P. C. Rofe not out	8	–	b Nash	1
M. A. Harrity not out	6	–	b S. R. Clark	2
B 6, l-b 3	9		B 3, l-b 6	9

(112.1 overs, 457 mins)   (9 wkts dec) **359**   (68 overs, 285 mins) **287**
Fall: 6 9 34 77 179 197   Fall: 8 55 95 159 263 264 264
   332 345 345   265 266 287

Bowling: *First Innings*—Nash 21–7–49–0; S. R. Clark 33–5–100–3; Bracken 27.1–6–79–4; MacGill 23–4–101–2; Higgs 8–1–21–0. *Second Innings*—Bracken 8–1–43–2; Nash 13–4–52–3; S. R. Clark 15–4–49–2; MacGill 13–1–62–0; Van Deinsen 9–2–42–3; Higgs 10–2–30–0.

New South Wales

G. J. Mail c Manou b Rofe	11	–	c Smith b Rofe	10
B. P. Van Deinsen b McIntyre	60	–	c Manou b Rofe	23
M. J. Slater lbw b Rofe	10	–	c Manou b Rofe	0
M. J. Clarke c Smith b Rofe	132	–	c Fitzgerald b Young	30
C. J. Richards b Smith	0	–	lbw b McIntyre	27
M. A. Higgs b Harrity	23	–	c Manou b Rofe	67
†B. J. Haddin c Harrity b McIntyre	55	–	c Manou b Rofe	47
D. A. Nash c and b Rofe	18	–	c Fitzgerald b Rofe	4
*S. C. G. MacGill c Higgins b Rofe	0	–	c and b Smith	9
S. R. Clark c Blewett b Rofe	7	–	c Blewett b Rofe	20
N. W. Bracken not out	0	–	not out	0
B 4, l-b 3, w 2, n-b 7	16		B 2, l-b 4, w 1, n-b 3	10

(90.4 overs, 369 mins) **332**   (76 overs, 304 mins) **247**
Fall: 40 76 91 98 151 261 310   Fall: 26 34 43 96 96 200 212
   310 331 332   227 227 247

Bowling: *First Innings*—Harrity 15–3–68–1; Rofe 20.4–5–60–6; McIntyre 24–3–89–2; Smith 23–5–82–1; Young 8–2–26–0. *Second Innings*—Harrity 10–4–19–0; Rofe 20–6–52–7; Young 15–4–41–1; McIntyre 18–4–69–1; Smith 13–3–60–1.

Umpires: S. D. Fry and K. D. Perrin.

At Brisbane Cricket Ground, Brisbane, January 25, 26, 27, 28, 2002. SOUTH AUSTRALIA defeated QUEENSLAND by nine wickets.

SOUTH AUSTRALIA v QUEENSLAND

At Adelaide Oval, Adelaide, February 13, 14, 15, 16, 2002. Queensland won by 106 runs. Toss: Queensland. Queensland 6 pts. First-class debut: S. A. Brant.

South Australia, hoping to stage a home-ground final Pura Cup final, made a brilliant start when Mark Harrity dismissed Jerry Cassell with the first ball of the match, but after that it was a long, hot struggle. The centrepiece of the Queensland innings was the punishing third-wicket partnership of 296 between Martin Love (521 minutes, 412 balls, 21 fours) and Brendan Nash (334 minutes, 279 balls, 15 fours, two sixes) which was truncated by Love being forced to retire hurt with a groin injury. It was his third double-century in first-class cricket and Nash's first century and their partnership was a record for any Queensland wicket against South Australia. In reply, a second-wicket stand of 176 between David Fitzgerald (422 minutes, 343 balls, 18 fours) and Greg Blewett (231 minutes, 203 balls, eight fours) put South Australia in a strong position before a middle-order collapse. At the end of the third day, with South Australia still at the crease, a draw seemed the likely result. Jimmy Maher thought otherwise, and Queensland's second-innings thrash enabled him to set a target of 239 off 60 overs. South Australia were never in the hunt, and the collapse of eight wickets for 34 to some spirited bowling by pace man Ashley Noffke and tight off-spin by Nathan Hauritz and Andrew Symonds gave the Queenslanders victory with two overs to spare.

Close of play: First day, Queensland (1) 2-257 (Love 120, Nash 59); Second day, South Australia (1) 1-133 (Fitzgerald 59, Blewett 17); Third day, South Australia (2) 8-373 (Manou 43, Rofe 4).

Man of the Match: M.L. Love. *Attendance:* 1,960.

Queensland

J.L. Cassell lbw b Harrity	0	– st Manou b Blewett	43
*J.P. Maher c Johnson b Rofe	66	– c Smith b Blewett	52
M.L. Love retired hurt	202	– (4) b Young	0
B.P. Nash c Johnson b Blewett	157	– (5) c Manou b Young	0
A. Symonds c Johnson b Young	21	– (3) run out (Rofe/Blewett)	0
L.A. Carseldine not out	21	– not out	15
†W.A. Seccombe c Johnson b Smith	20	– b Blewett	0
N.M. Hauritz	–	st Manou b Young	6
A.A. Noffke	–	not out	6
B 1, l-b 9, w 1, n-b 5	16	B 2, l-b 3	5

(151.5 overs, 576 mins)	(5 wkts dec) 503	(22 overs, 105 mins)	(7 wkts dec) 127

Fall: 0 138 450 462 503

Fall: 92 93 93 93 113 113 120

S.A. Brant and J.H. Dawes did not bat.

Bowling: *First Innings*—Harrity 24–3–89–1; Rofe 26–9–67–1; Smith 23.5–3–79–1; Blewett 18–3–46–1; McIntyre 30–8–83–0; Young 28–2–118–1; Johnson 2–0–11–0. *Second Innings*—Harrity 4–0–23–0; Rofe 6–0–39–0; Smith 3–0–24–0; Blewett 5–0–15–3; Young 4–1–21–3.

South Australia

D.A. Fitzgerald c Seccombe b Noffke	139	– (2) b Noffke	2
B.A. Johnson b Dawes	52	– (1) c Seccombe b Symonds	49
*G.S. Blewett c Carseldine b Hauritz	71	– b Noffke	13
B.H. Higgins c Symonds b Hauritz	9	– (6) lbw b Hauritz	14
C.J. Davies lbw b Dawes	10	– (4) c Seccombe b Noffke	32
B.E. Young c Seccombe b Noffke	8	– (7) b Hauritz	0
M.J. Smith lbw b Brant	11	– (8) lbw b Noffke	0
†G.A. Manou lbw b Noffke	44	– (5) c (sub) Perren b Symonds	11
P.E. McIntyre c Nash b Hauritz	2	– c Seccombe b Noffke	0
P.C. Rofe b Noffke	6	– not out	5
M.A. Harrity not out	16	– lbw b Hauritz	0
B 8, l-b 5, n-b 11	24	B 4, l-b 1, n-b 1	6

(145.3 overs, 548 mins)	392	(58 overs, 231 mins)	132

Fall: 83 259 276 297 308 322 326 354 375 392

Fall: 15 39 98 110 114 116 120 122 132 132

Bowling: *First Innings*—Dawes 28–8–84–2; Brant 23–10–41–1; Noffke 38.3–12–112–4; Hauritz 37–10–83–3; Symonds 19–6–59–0. *Second Innings*—Noffke 18–7–31–5; Brant 7–1–21–0; Hauritz 10–3–22–3; Dawes 8–3–16–0; Symonds 15–4–37–2.

Umpires: J.S. Booth and D.J. Harper.

SOUTH AUSTRALIA v TASMANIA

At Adelaide Oval, Adelaide, March 1, 2, 3, 4, 2002. Tasmania won by an innings and 32 runs. Toss: South Australia. Tasmania 6 pts.

All states had the opportunity of making the Pura Cup final and South Australia were in a better position than most. But they blew away most of their chances with a middle-order collapse on the first day. After a steady opening partnership of 69 they slumped to seven for 119 before Graham Manou and Peter McIntyre joined in an eighth-wicket stand of 65, McIntyre's innings being the second-highest of his 14-season career. Jamie Cox and Michael Dighton, who added 137 for the second wicket, effectively batted South Australia out of the match. The Tasmanians ground on for 170.1 overs, with Cox's controlled innings (486 minutes, 399 balls, 17 fours) providing a solid platform and Dighton, Daniel Marsh, Sean Clingeleffer and Damien Wright contributing half-centuries. With David Fitzgerald and Greg Blewett back in the pavilion before stumps the odds were against anything but a Tasmanian victory, and on the last day Ben Johnson's three herculean effort of the season (418 minutes, 340 balls, 12 fours) was a lone effort. David Saker bowled with persistence and penetration throughout the match and 21-year-old quickish left-arm wrist-spinner Shannon Tubb created havoc in the closing stages.

Close of play: First day, Tasmania (1) 1-26 (Cox 21, Dighton 4); Second day, Tasmania (1) 3-291 (Cox 144, Marsh 63); Third day, South Australia (2) 2-66 (Johnson 34, Higgins 7).

Man of the Match: J. Cox.   *Attendance:* 2,678.

South Australia

D. A. Fitzgerald c Marsh b Saker	31	– (2) c Clingeleffer b Saker	0
B. A. Johnson c Kremerskothen b Wright	50	– (1) c and b Tubb	138
*G. S. Blewett c Kremerskothen b Jurgensen	5	– c Marsh b Wright	21
B. H. Higgins c Di Venuto b Jurgensen	4	– c Marsh b Saker	7
C. J. Davies b Marsh	19	– c Marsh b Saker	3
B. E. Young b Wright	0	– b Kremerskothen	21
M. J. Smith lbw b Saker	7	– c Clingeleffer b Tubb	31
†G. A. Manou run out (Mason/Jurgensen)	33	– b Tubb	0
P. E. McIntyre c Marsh b Kremerskothen	40	– c Clingeleffer b Saker	8
P. C. Rofe not out	8	– not out	4
M. A. Harrity c Di Venuto b Saker	0	– lbw b Saker	1
L-b 1, n-b 2	3	B 3, l-b 3, n-b 2	8

(84.3 overs, 316 mins)   **200**   (115 overs, 426 mins)   **242**
Fall: 69 74 86 98 98 117 119   Fall: 4 41 75 79 140 204 208
184 196 200   235 241 242

Bowling: *First Innings*—Wright 22–8–47–2; Saker 21.3–5–63–3; Jurgensen 18–1–42–2; Marsh 17–7–22–1; Tubb 2–0–12–0; Kremerskothen 4–1–13–1. *Second Innings*—Wright 18.3–6–43–1; Saker 31–13–53–5; Jurgensen 23.3–8–47–0; Marsh 14–6–21–0; Tubb 18–5–57–3; Kremerskothen 10–5–15–1.

Tasmania

S. R. Mason lbw b Harrity	1	D. G. Wright lbw b Smith	55
*J. Cox c Harrity b McIntyre	174	S. B. Tubb c Johnson b Smith	1
M. G. Dighton c Davies b Smith	76		
M. J. Di Venuto c Smith b Young	5	B 1, l-b 2, n-b 4	7
D. J. Marsh lbw b McIntyre	63		
S. P. Kremerskothen b Harrity	26	(170.1 overs, 629 mins) (8 wkts dec)	474
†S. G. Clingeleffer not out	66	Fall: 10 147 152 302 349 349 472 474	

D. J. Saker and S. J. Jurgensen did not bat.

Bowling: Harrity 24–7–76–2; Rofe 34–11–76–0; Smith 25.1–4–83–3; Blewett 14–1–50–0; Young 33–5–90–1; Johnson 7–3–11–0; McIntyre 31–8–80–2; Higgins 2–1–5–0.

Umpires: S. J. Davis and S. D. Fry.

At WACA Ground, Perth, March 13, 14, 15, 16, 2002. SOUTH AUSTRALIA drew with WESTERN AUSTRALIA. Toss: South Australia. Western Australia 2 pts.

AUSTRALIAN DOMESTIC FIRST-CLASS RESULTS TABLE

Opponent	M	W	L	D	T
New South Wales	195	52	107	36	0
Victoria	196	46	98	52	0
Queensland	139	50	43	45	1
Western Australia	104	28	44	32	0
Tasmania	45	16	8	21	0
Total	679	192	300	186	1

AUSTRALIAN DOMESTIC FIRST-CLASS RECORDS

Highest score for:	365*	C. Hill v New South Wales at Adelaide	1900-91
Highest score against:	355*	G. R. Marsh (Western Australia) at Perth	1989-90
Best bowling for:	10/35	T. W. Wall v New South Wales at Sydney	1932-33
Best bowling against:	9/40	E. L. McCormick (Victoria) at Adelaide	1936-37
Highest total for:	7-821dec	Queensland at Adelaide	1939-40
Highest total against:	918	by New South Wales at Sydney	1900-01
Lowest total for:	27	v New South Wales at Sydney	1955-56
Lowest total against:	41	by Western Australia at Adelaide	1990-91

* Denotes not out.

MOST RUNS

	M	I	NO	R	HS	100s	50s	Avge
D. W. Hookes	120	205	9	9,364	306*	26	44	47.78
D. S. Lehmann	91	167	9	8,923	255	31	33	56.47
L. E. Favell	121	220	4	8,269	164	20	43	38.28
I. M. Chappell	89	157	13	7,665	205*	22	45	53.23
G. S. Blewett	83	157	9	7,365	268	20	35	49.76
H. N. Dansie	107	196	6	6,692	185	17	32	35.22
A. M. J. Hilditch	91	161	11	6,504	230	17	32	43.36
C. Hill	68	126	6	6,270	365*	18	27	52.25
P. R. Sleep	127	211	37	6,106	146*	12	29	35.09
V. Y. Richardson	77	146	7	6,027	203	18	27	43.36
J. D. Siddons	82	150	10	5,940	197	17	26	42.43

* Denotes not out.

HIGHEST PARTNERSHIP FOR EACH WICKET

281	for 1st	L. E. Favell and J. P. Causby v New South Wales at Adelaide	....	1967-68
386	for 2nd	G. S. Blewett and D. S. Lehmann v Tasmania at Hobart (Bel)	....	2001-02
286	for 3rd	G. S. Blewett and D. S. Lehmann v Tasmania at Adelaide	....	1993-94
462*	for 4th	D. W. Hookes and W. B. Phillips v Tasmania at Adelaide	....	1986-87
281	for 5th	C. L. Badcock and M. G. Waite v Queensland at Adelaide	....	1939-40
260	for 6th	D. S. Lehmann and T. J. Nielsen v Queensland at Adelaide	....	1996-97
198	for 7th	G. A. Bishop and T. B. A. May v Tasmania at Adelaide	....	1990-91
174	for 8th	D. F. G. O'Connor and A. K. Zesers v Victoria at Adelaide	....	1984-85
232	for 9th	C. Hill and E. A. Walkley v New South Wales at Adelaide	....	1900-01
104	for 10th	L. Michael and E. I. Pynor v Victoria at Adelaide	....	1949-50

MOST WICKETS

	M	Balls	Mdns	R	W	BB	5W/i	10W/m	Avge
C. V. Grimmett	78	28,144	445	12,878	504	9/180	47	13	25.55
A. A. Mallett	77	20.988	673	8,171	344	7/57	19	2	23.75
T. B. A. May	80	22,575	931	9,943	270	7/93	15	2	36.82
P. R. Sleep	127	19,482	671	9,883	252	8/133	7	0	39.22
P. E. McIntyre	61	17,419	576	8,974	215	6/64	8	2	41.74
E. Jones	39	12,145	501	5,516	208	8/157	19	3	26.52
T. J. Jenner	65	13,559	245	6,312	207	7/127	8	1	30.49
G. Giffen	38	11,682	402	5,676	192	9/147	18	7	29.56
G. Noblet	38	11,156	273	3,396	190	7/29	10	2	17.87
G. R. Attenborough	50	11,137	280	5,371	172	7/90	8	2	31.23

MOST DISMISSALS

	M	Ct	St	Total
T. J. Nielsen	92	255	29	284
B. N. Jarman	77	193	57	250
C. W. Walker	57	103	87	190
G. R. A. Langley	46	111	24	135
K. J. Wright	36	102	9	111

MOST CATCHES

D. W. Hookes	128 in 120 matches	V. Y. Richardson .... 99 in 77 matches
I. M. Chappell	113 in 89 matches	P. R. Sleep .... 84 in 127 matches
J. D. Siddons	113 in 82 matches	G. A. Bishop .... 60 in 84 matches

MOST APPEARANCES

127	P. R. Sleep .... 1976-77 – 1992-93	91 A. M. J Hilditch ... 1982-83 – 1991-92
121	L. E. Favell .... 1951-52 – 1969-70	91 D. S. Lehmann .... 1987-88 – 2001-02
120	D. W. Hookes ...... 1975-76 – 1991-92	89 I. M. Chappell .... 1961-62 – 1979-80
107	H. N. Dansie ...... 1949-50 – 1966-67	84 G. A. Bishop ..... 1982-83 – 1992-93
92	T. J. Nielsen ...... 1990-91 – 1998-99	83 G. S. Blewett ..... 1991-92 – 2001-02

TASMANIA

Chief Executive: D. A. Johnston

Chairman: G. Gillies

Cricket Coach: G. Shipperd

Captain: R. T. Ponting

Ricky Ponting

For the third time in the past nine seasons Tasmania were runners-up in the final. Yet in their despair after a 235-run loss to Queensland at the Gabba, they can take some consolation from rival captain Stuart Law. After leading the rampaging Queenslanders to their third successive title, Law reflected: "Tassie might feel pretty down at the moment, but they should remember we lost six of them before we won our first in '94-95. If you learn from your losses and become stronger like we've had to, then I think you won't be too far away from winning one."

What Tasmania must do to win their first title is get early points on the board to enhance their chances of hosting the final. It will be the first major challenge for new coach Brian McFadyen, whose appointment ended Greg Shipperd's 11 seasons at the helm. The importance of starting well is rammed home by the statistic that only four of Tasmania's 25 wins in the past ten seasons have been before Christmas.

Unlike Tasmania's two previous bids for glory, this one was not fuelled by their much-vaunted batsmen, but by their oft-maligned bowlers. Indeed, not one batsman topped 700 runs. The pick of them was Jamie Cox, most of whose 660 runs came in the second half of the season. Along the way, Cox passed David Boon as Tasmania's games record-holder to add to the record he already held of being the state's highest run-scorer. He and Dene Hills, the most successful opening pair in Australian domestic first-class history, looked set to go on their merry way after piling on 203 against New South Wales at the SCG in the opening round. Sadly, Hills' tendency to flirt with the short ball outside the off stump cost him dearly and he was dropped after failing in the next three games. The attrition rate did nothing to help the team's cause. Michael Di Venuto and Scott Kremerskothen suffered serious leg and facial injuries respectively before and during that opening match, while Gerard Denton did not return from chronic back problems until late in the summer.

Two tall men who did measure up in an under-achieving batting line-up were former Western Australian Michael Dighton and wicket-keeper Sean Clingeleffer. Dighton, a powerful driver off the front foot, overcame a horror start against the rising ball around off stump to finish with 594 runs and two centuries. Heir apparent to Adam Gilchrist, the 21-year-old Clingeleffer continued his rapid improvement with the bat as well as the gloves by scoring 517 with two centuries and claiming 36 catches.

The shortcomings of the batting were largely made up by the strike-rate of the bowlers, particularly the odd couple of barrel-chested veteran David Saker and lanky journeyman Shane Jurgensen. Their best work was done later in the season. At the halfway mark a berth in the final for Tasmania seemed remote. After five rounds they were languishing on the bottom of the ladder with only four points. It was bad enough being humiliated by South Australia by an innings and 40 runs at Bellerive after a swashbuckling 246 by Darren Lehmann but even worse was to follow. When

TASMANIA PURA CUP TEAM, 2001-02

Back row: D.J. Ramshaw (assistant coach), A. W. Polkinghorne, G. T. Cunningham, S.J. Jurgensen, M.G. Dighton, D.J. Saker, S.G. Clingeleffer, G. Shipperd (coach). Front row: D.G. Wright, S. Mason, D.J. Marsh, S.B. Tubb, S.P. Kremerskothen, M.J. Di Venuto, S. R. Watson.

Queensland gored Tasmania by ten wickets just before lunch on the second day on a Gabba green-top, back home the public and media were howling for blood.

The selectors responded by dumping Shaun Young, Hills and Di Venuto and Tasmania avenged that debacle in the return game at Bellerive by routing Queensland by an innings and 50 runs in a touch under two days. The destroyer was all-rounder Shane Watson, who made his old state pay a high price for ignoring his talents. He cut a swathe through the Queenslanders, taking 11/78 with some of the fastest bowling ever seen at the ground and providing Clingeleffer with five of his record nine catches for the match. That and subsequent performances with ball and bat clinched Watson a surprise berth on the Australian tour of South Africa. To remove any doubts that the Queensland massacre may have been an aberration, Tasmania then trounced Western Australia and South Australia by an innings and New South Wales by ten wickets to charge into the final.

It was very much a bowler-led recovery on a Bellerive wicket which went from benign to pace-friendly after the $18 million grandstand redevelopment cut out the howling wind off the Derwent and enabled it to retain moisture for longer. Saker showed that age did not weary him by taking the most wickets and winning the Tasmanian Player of the Year award. He bowled with a lot of grunt and stamina off a shortish run, and troubled batsmen with his ability to move the ball away. The affable Jurgensen, from Queensland via Western Australia, was a late-flowering revelation. Overlooked for the first two rounds, he claimed match figures of 11/103, including a hat-trick, in the home win over the Blues in the last round and a record 11/172 off a marathon 69 overs in the final. Damien Wright, whose recurrence of a thigh injury in the final thrust an even greater load onto Saker and Jurgensen, did a good if not always economical job as the third seamer with 23 wickets at 40.52. Wright was also a valuable contributor with the bat down the order, almost attaining all-rounder status by scoring 409 runs at 34.08 with four fifties. Providing an effective alternative to this staple diet of pace were left-arm orthodox spinner Xavier Doherty and chinaman bowler Shannon Tubb. Doherty was a member of Australia's Under-19s World Cup-winning side along with fellow Tasmanian George Bailey.

A key component in the charter of the states is to produce players to represent their country and in that regard Tasmania has done its job well. Before the start of the season Ricky Ponting was promoted to state captain and celebrated it by hitting a century in each innings of the first match. Ponting was later appointed captain of the Australian limited-overs team, and Watson played under him. – DAVID STOCKDALE.

TASMANIA RESULTS, 2001-02

All first-class matches – Played 11: Won 4, Lost 3, Drawn 4.
Pura Cup matches – Played 11: Won 4, Lost 3, Drawn 4.
ING Cup matches – Played 10: Won 1, Lost 8, No result 1.
Competition placings – Pura Cup, 2nd; ING Cup, 6th.

PURA CUP AVERAGES, 2001-02

BATTING

	M	I	NO	R	HS	100s	50s	Avge	Ct
R. T. Ponting	2	4	0	367	154	2	1	91.75	1
S. G. Clingeleffer	11	15	4	517	141*	2	1	47.00	36
M. G. Dighton	10	15	0	594	126	2	3	39.60	4
M. J. Di Venuto	5	8	1	273	83	0	2	39.00	9
J. Cox	11	18	1	660	174	2	3	38.82	3
D. G. Wright	11	15	3	409	63	0	4	34.08	6
D. J. Saker	11	12	6	199	66*	0	1	33.17	2
S. P. Kremerskothen . .	7	9	2	228	55	0	1	32.57	9
S. Young	5	8	0	259	84	0	3	32.38	1
S. R. Watson	7	11	1	292	58*	0	3	29.20	3
D. J. Marsh	11	17	2	433	97	0	2	28.87	20
D. F. Hills	4	8	0	186	136	1	0	23.25	0
S. R. Mason	7	10	1	187	41	0	0	20.78	3
S. J. Jurgensen	9	10	4	119	56	0	1	19.83	1
S. B. Tubb	3	3	0	39	33	0	0	13.00	1
B. J. Thomas	1	2	0	25	21	0	0	12.50	0
X. J. Doherty	2	2	1	10	6	0	0	10.00	0
G. J. Denton	2	3	0	8	8	0	0	2.67	0
A. G. Downton	2	2	1	0	0*	0	0	0.00	0

* Denotes not out.

BOWLING

	O	M	R	W	BB	5W/i	10W/m	Avge
S. B. Tubb	28	9	80	5	3/57	0	0	16.00
S. J. Jurgensen	290	85	710	36	6/65	4	2	19.72
S. R. Watson	126.4	20	514	22	6/32	2	1	23.36
R. T. Ponting	4	0	25	1	1/25	0	0	25.00
D. J. Saker	366.3	103	1003	38	5/53	1	0	26.39
S. P. Kremerskothen	48.5	9	169	6	2/29	0	0	28.17
X. J. Doherty	74.5	17	197	5	2/23	0	0	39.40
D. G. Wright	346.3	114	932	23	3/15	0	0	40.52
G. J. Denton	78.3	12	271	6	3/67	0	0	45.17
B. J. Thomas	8	1	52	1	1/52	0	0	52.00
D. J. Marsh	155	31	473	8	4/70	0	0	59.13
A. G. Downton	41	8	194	2	2/94	0	0	97.00
S. Young	58	17	156	1	1/13	0	0	156.00
M. J. Di Venuto	1	0	5	0	–	0	0	

At Sydney Cricket Ground, Sydney, October 17, 18, 19, 20, 2001. TASMANIA drew with NEW SOUTH WALES.

At WACA Ground, Perth, October 26, 27, 28, 29, 2001. TASMANIA drew with WESTERN AUSTRALIA.

TASMANIA v SOUTH AUSTRALIA

At Bellerive Oval, Hobart, November 8, 9, 10, 11, 2001. South Australia won by an innings and 40 runs. Toss: South Australia. South Australia 6 pts. First-class debut: R. J. Harris.

Tasmania's first home game under the shadow of the imposing new Southern Stand was supposed to have been a celebration of Tasmanian cricket's progress. Instead, Darren Lehmann turned it into a humiliation. South Australia sent the home side in on a wicket with early life and the decision looked to be vindicated when the first five wickets tumbled for 122. The slump was arrested by a fighting sixth-wicket stand of 155 between Sean Clingeleffer (332 minutes, 268 balls, 12 fours, one six), who hit his maiden century, and Shaun Young (241 minutes, 208 balls, 12 fours). The wicket of opener David Fitzgerald and the retirement of Jeff Vaughan after being struck in the head by a wickedly lifting ball from David Saker buoyed Tasmania's hopes, but that was to be their last hurrah. Despite the seam and variable bounce in the wicket, Lehmann (295 minutes, 238 balls, 39 fours, four sixes) batted with absolute assurance as he dismantled the Tasmanian attack in a memorable innings which included hundreds in each of the first two sessions of the third day. His first century occupied 155 minutes and came from 116 balls, while his second hundred took a further 114 minutes and only 97 balls. He dominated a 386-run partnership for the second wicket with Greg Blewett (391 minutes, 279 balls, 20 fours, one six) which set a second-wicket record for South Australia, eclipsing the 308 added by Barry Richards and Ian Chappell against Western Australia at Perth in 1970-71. Facing a 207-run deficit, Tasmania capitulated to aggressive pace bowling by Mark Harrity and Paul Rofe who met resistance only from a feisty Shane Watson (130 minutes, 116 balls, nine fours).

Close of play: First day, Tasmania (1) 5-236 (Young 66, Clingeleffer 51); Second day, South Australia (1) 1-108 (Blewett 45, Lehmann 31); Third day, South Australia (1) 5-589 (Higgins 69, Manou 27).

Man of the Match: D.S. Lehmann.   *Attendance:* 872.

Tasmania

D.F. Hills c Vaughan b Harrity	0	– (8) b Blewett b Rofe		0
*J. Cox c Manou b Harrity	35	– (1) lbw b Harrity		0
M.G. Dighton c Dempsey b Harris	6	– (2) c Manou b Harrity		15
S.R. Watson c Fitzgerald b Harris	32	– (3) b Harrity		58
D.J. Marsh c Manou b Rofe	26	– (4) c (sub) S.A. Deitz b Harrity		31
S. Young lbw b Higgins	84	– (5) lbw b Young		10
†S.G. Clingeleffer not out	141	– (6) not out		28
B.J. Thomas c Fitzgerald b Young	21	– (7) lbw b Rofe		4
D.G. Wright not out	4	– c Harrity b Rofe		0
D.J. Saker (did not bat)		– lbw b Young		5
S.J. Jurgensen (did not bat)		– c (sub) b Harrity		7
B 9, l-b 10, w 4, n-b 10	33	B 5, l-b 2, w 2		9

(150 overs, 564 mins)	(7 wkts dec) 382	(73.1 overs, 281 mins)	167
Fall: 0 10 63 98 122		Fall: 0 35 110 115 123 128 128	
277 365		128 135 167	

Bowling: *First Innings*—Harrity 35–11–73–2; Harris 9.4–2–26–2; Rofe 44–14–94–1; Higgins 15.2–5–49–1; Young 35–8–97–1; Lehmann 11–2–24–0. *Second Innings*—Harrity 22.1–5–65–5; Rofe 20–13–24–3; Young 31–13–71–2.

South Australia

D.A. Fitzgerald lbw b Saker	31	B.E. Young b Thomas	21
J.M. Vaughan retired hurt	0	†G.A. Manou not out	27
G.S. Blewett c Watson b Saker	163	B 20, l-b 4, w 2, n-b 5	31
*D.S. Lehmann c Saker b Wright	246		
B.H. Higgins not out	69	(136 overs, 522 mins) (5 wkts dec) 589	
D.M. Dempsey c Clingeleffer b Wright	1	Fall: 63 449 469 473 549	

R.J. Harris, P.C. Rofe and M.A. Harrity did not bat.

Bowling: Wright 28–9–98–2; Saker 26–4–119–2; Watson 12–2–69–0; Jurgensen 25–7–82–0; Young 17–4–49–0; Thomas 8–1–52–1; Marsh 20–2–96–0.

Umpires: S.J. Davis and J.H. Smeaton.
TV Umpire: K.J. McGinness.

TASMANIA v VICTORIA

At Bellerive Oval, Hobart, November 30, December 1, 2, 3, 2001. Drawn. Toss: Tasmania. Tasmania 2 pts. First-class debut: X. J. Doherty.

Despite centuries to Michael Dighton and Sean Clingeleffer, the weather was the only victor in this game, which was plagued by continual stoppages for rain. Indeed, a highlight was the antics of a family of plovers, whose parents repeatedly dive-bombed a security guard when he returned their wandering chicks to the hill. Tasmania made the most of the wicket's early volatility by winning the toss and firing out the Victorians cheaply. David Saker and Damien Wright were ably supported by young left-arm spinner Xavier Doherty on his first-class debut. After running out Jason Arnberger, Doherty bowled with admirable control and flight. After a faltering start, Dighton (319 minutes, 235 balls, 18 fours, one six), Clingeleffer (303 minutes, 230 balls, 13 fours), Daniel Marsh (221 minutes, 167 balls, 16 fours) and Shaun Young (167 minutes, 139 balls, 10 fours) buried Victoria under a mountain of runs. Only Paul Reiffel resisted their onslaught. Matthew Elliott (458 minutes, 341 balls, 16 fours) was the only man to get any joy out of a rain-shortened final day, sharing an opening partnership which inched its way to 105 from 62 overs with Arnberger, on the way to an unbeaten century.

Close of play: First day, Tasmania (1) 3-139 (Dighton 63, Marsh 28); Second day, Tasmania (1) 6-435 (Clingeleffer 73, Wright 16); Third day, Victoria (2) 0-38 (Arnberger 19, Elliott 17).

Man of the Match: M. G. Dighton. *Attendance:* 976.

Victoria

M. T. G. Elliott c Clingeleffer b Jurgensen	29	– (2) not out	135
J. L. Arnberger run out (Doherty)	1	– (1) b Jurgensen	50
M. P. Mott c Marsh b Wright	30	– c Cox b Doherty	33
B. J. Hodge c Clingeleffer b Wright	8	– not out	59
M. Klinger lbw b Saker	1		
I. J. Harvey lbw b Saker	3		
C. L. White c Clingeleffer b Watson	20		
†D. S. Berry c Dighton b Wright	13		
*P. R. Reiffel not out	18		
D. W. Fleming c Mason b Doherty	11		
M. W. H. Inness c (sub) Polkinghorne b Doherty	0		
L-b 2, w 2, n-b 1	5	W 1, n-b 4	5

(53.5 overs, 220 mins) 139   (123 overs, 458 mins) (2 wkts) 282
Fall: 7 60 66 71 74 75 96 120 139 139   Fall: 105 186

Bowling: *First Innings*—Saker 15–6–30–2; Wright 18–6–53–3; Jurgensen 8–3–11–1; Doherty 8.5–1–23–2; Watson 4–0–20–1. *Second Innings*—Saker 21–9–40–0; Wright 25–10–70–0; Jurgensen 26–9–56–1; Watson 12–4–38–0; Doherty 28–7–55–1; Marsh 11–3–23–0.

Tasmania

S. R. Mason lbw b Reiffel	30	D. J. Saker not out	7
*J. Cox lbw b Fleming	2	X. J. Doherty c Arnberger b Harvey	6
M. G. Dighton b Reiffel	126	S. J. Jurgensen not out	5
S. R. Watson c Berry b Harvey	4		
D. J. Marsh c Hodge b Harvey	97	B 6, l-b 4, n-b 9	19
S. Young c Elliott b Hodge	70		
†S. G. Clingeleffer c and b Reiffel	112	(168 overs, 669 mins) (9 wkts dec)	527
D. G. Wright c Elliott b Reiffel	49	Fall: 9 63 85 269 277 396 502 509 516	

Bowling: Fleming 5.4–1–15–1; Inness 38–9–102–0; Reiffel 27.2–9–71–4; White 29–4–107–0; Harvey 47–13–136–3; Hodge 18–1–77–1; Mott 3–1–9–0.

Umpires: J. H. Smeaton and S. J. A. Taufel.

At Brisbane Cricket Ground, Brisbane, December 13,14, 2001. TASMANIA lost to QUEENSLAND by ten wickets.

TASMANIA v QUEENSLAND

At Bellerive Oval, Hobart, January 17, 18, 2002. Tasmania won by an innings and 50 runs. Toss: Queensland. Tasmania 6 pts. First-class debut: D. R. MacKenzie.

It was payback time for Tasmania after their blink-of-an-eye ten-wicket rout by Queensland at the Gabba the previous month. And, as irony would have it, the chief executioner was burly speedster Shane Watson, a former Queenslander. After being sent in, Tasmania crashed to nine for 167 against a depleted Queensland attack. Then the ungainly Shane Jurgensen (91 minutes, 72 balls, five fours) joined his fellow pace bowler David Saker (123 minutes, 91 balls, 12 fours), and they first held out and then hit out in a last-wicket partnership of 114. Buoyed by their deeds with the bat, Saker and Jurgensen shot out the openers before Watson ripped through the rest to finish with career-best figures from some frighteningly quick bowling, against which only Jerry Cassell and Ashley Noffke provided any fight. Forced to follow on, Queensland fared even worse and were dismissed before stumps on the second day, the irresistible Watson finishing with match figures of 11/78 and Sean Clingeleffer with a Tasmanian record of nine catches in the match. The match concluded at 6.40 pm on the second day after only 781 minutes of play.

Close of play: First day, Queensland (1) 0-5 (Maher 5, Love 0).
Man of the Match: S.R. Watson.   *Attendance:* 560.

Tasmania

S.R. Mason c Maher b Noffke	22	D.J. Saker not out 66
*J. Cox c Love b Dawes	12	S.B. Tubb c Noffke b Hauritz 5
M.G. Dighton c Seccombe b MacKenzie ...	21	S.J. Jurgensen c Love b MacKenzie 56
S.R. Watson c Perren b Dawes	4	
D.J. Marsh c Love b Hauritz	11	L-b 3, w 7, n-b 23 33
S.P. Kremerskothen c Seccombe b Noffke ..	42	
†S.G. Clingeleffer lbw b MacKenzie	5	(90.3 overs, 383 mins) 281
D.G. Wright c (sub) Nash b Hauritz	4	Fall: 19 50 56 72 103 128 139 153 167 281

Bowling: Dawes 20–8–57–2; Hopes 18–6–54–0; MacKenzie 13.3–1–45–3; Noffke 23–2–81–2; Hauritz 16–3–41–3.

Queensland

J.P. Maher c Kremerskothen b Saker	20	– c Clingeleffer b Watson	41
M.L. Love c Wright b Jurgensen	11	– (3) lbw b Jurgensen	3
J.L. Cassell c Clingeleffer b Watson	41	– (2) c Clingeleffer b Jurgensen	9
C.T. Perren b Wright	6	– c Clingeleffer b Wright	8
*S.G. Law c Clingeleffer b Watson	2	– c Clingeleffer b Watson	2
J.R. Hopes c Clingeleffer b Saker	0	– (9) b Wright	1
†W.A. Seccombe c Clingeleffer b Watson	0	– (6) c Clingeleffer b Watson	7
A.A. Noffke not out	34	– (7) b Wright	1
N.M. Hauritz c Mason b Watson	2	– (8) not out	8
D.R. MacKenzie b Watson	4	– b Watson	17
J.H. Dawes lbw b Watson	1	– c Marsh b Watson	0
B 2, l-b 5, n-b 2	9	L-b 1, w 1, n-b 2	4
(52.5 overs, 219 mins)	130	(42 overs, 179 mins)	101
Fall: 23 53 70 79 80 83 92 100 106 130		Fall: 23 27 42 57 68 69 73 75 101 101	

Bowling: *First Innings*—Wright 15–5–35–1; Saker 18–6–45–2; Jurgensen 8–4–11–1; Watson 11.5–1–32–6. *Second Innings*—Saker 7–0–14–0; Jurgensen 12–7–25–2; Wright 14–9–15–3; Watson 9–0–46–5.

Umpires: B.W. Jackman and P.V. Mulcahy.

TASMANIA v WESTERN AUSTRALIA

At Bellerive Oval, Hobart, January 25, 26, 27, 2002. Tasmania won by an innings and 76 runs. Toss: Western Australia. Tasmania 6 pts.

After being sent in, Tasmania finished with a healthy total, although Michael Dighton, Shane Watson and Scott Kremerskothen all failed to make the most of good starts. Captain Jamie Cox broke David Boon's Tasmanian record for the most first-class appearances, but falling leg-before without offering a shot was not the way to celebrate. Damien Wright (126 minutes, 111 balls, 10 fours, one six) added weight to his case for all-rounder status by hitting the top score of his career. After Tasmania's solid innings, and given Western Australia's accomplished batting line-up, the visiting side's loss of 20 wickets in 92.1 overs was hard to credit. Simon Katich's defiant first innings (160 minutes, 116 balls, 13 fours, one six) was the sole serious resistance to the accuracy and aggression of Tasmania's pace quartet. The weakness of the visitors' batting can be gauged by the fact that Katich's first innings was the only occupation of the crease by a Western Australian which lasted for more than two hours. Only a stubborn stand between Matthew Nicholson and Jo Angel took the match into a third day.

Close of play: First day, Tasmania (1) 8-306 (Wright 52, Tubb 5); Second day, Western Australia (2) 7-117 (Nicholson 8, Angel 26).

Man of the Match: D. G. Wright.   *Attendance:* 1,208.

Tasmania

S. R. Mason c Meuleman b Angel	26
*J. Cox lbw b Angel	4
M. G. Dighton run out (Campbell)	65
S. R. Watson c Campbell b Clark	49
D. J. Marsh lbw b Harvey	14
S. P. Kremerskothen c Harvey b Angel	55
†S. G. Clingeleffer lbw b Katich	22
D. G. Wright c Campbell b Angel	63
D. J. Saker b Clark	4
S. B. Tubb b Nicholson	33
S. J. Jurgensen not out	1
L-b 3, w 5, n-b 3	11
(113 overs, 424 mins)	347

Fall: 18 42 152 153 187 244 257 274 341 347

Bowling: Nicholson 24–7–75–1; Angel 25–7–79–4; Clark 22–7–70–2; Harvey 11–2–45–1; Oldroyd 26–7–66–0; Katich 5–2–9–1.

Western Australia

*J. L. Langer b Saker	10	– lbw b Jurgensen	1
M. E. K. Hussey c Clingeleffer b Jurgensen	33	– lbw b Saker	2
S. M. Katich c Dighton b Saker	68	– lbw b Saker	1
M. W. Goodwin lbw b Wright	0	– c Clingeleffer b Wright	37
S. W. Meuleman c Marsh b Wright	7	– c Kremerskothen b Watson	12
†R. J. Campbell run out (Mason/Clingeleffer)	0	– c Clingeleffer b Watson	8
K. M. Harvey run out (Tubb)	0	– c Marsh b Wright	8
M. J. Nicholson lbw b Tubb	3	– c Kremerskothen b Saker	13
J. Angel lbw b Tubb	4	– b Watson	27
B. J. Oldroyd c Wright b Saker	2	– b Watson	7
M. W. Clark not out	0	– not out	3
L-b 4, w 2, n-b 4	10	B 2, l-b 6, w 2, pen 5	15
(46.1 overs, 191 mins)	137	(46 overs, 186 mins)	134

Fall: 20 73 79 98 98 103 124 132 136 137

Fall: 5 6 15 59 68 77 77 122 131 134

Bowling: *First Innings*—Saker 14.1–2–48–3; Wright 15–8–35–2; Jurgensen 8–3–16–1; Watson 5–0–28–0; Tubb 4–2–6–2. *Second Innings*—Saker 9–3–21–3; Jurgensen 6–1–17–1; Wright 10–4–25–2; Watson 13–3–35–4; Tubb 4–2–5–0; Marsh 4–0–18–0.

Umpires: K. J. McGinness and J. H. Smeaton.
TV Umpire: D. G. Wright.

At Melbourne Cricket Ground, Melbourne, February 17, 18, 19, 20, 2002. TASMANIA drew with VICTORIA.

At Adelaide Oval, Adelaide, March 1,2,3,4, 2002. TASMANIA defeated SOUTH AUSTRALIA by an innings and 32 runs.

TASMANIA v NEW SOUTH WALES

At Bellerive Oval, Hobart, March 13, 14, 15, 2002. Tasmania won by ten wickets. Toss: New South Wales. Tasmania 6 pts. First-class debut: V. M. Williams.

Thanks to the superb bowling of Shane Jurgensen, who twice improved on his best first-class figures to take match figures of 11/103 including a hat-trick, Tasmania charged into their third domestic first-class final. New South Wales acting captain Michael Slater won the toss and elected to bat on a wicket which provided the pace men with seam and occasional variable bounce. The depleted New South Wales side appeared to have weathered the initial storm with a second-wicket stand of 77 between Matthew Phelps (203 minutes, 145 balls, seven fours) and Slater (81 minutes, 72 balls, 10 fours). After Slater was given out leg-before to David Saker, a decision he took with ill-disguised disgust, the innings collapsed, the last nine wickets falling for 67. In reply Tasmania batted strongly on an improving wicket. Jamie Cox (231 minutes, 142 balls, 12 fours) and Scott Mason opened with an enterprising stand of 106, which later batsmen headed by Michael Dighton (135 minutes,101 balls, 15 fours) steadily built on. New South Wales fared better the second time around, Phelps and Corey Richards giving them an 82-run start. Jurgensen then swept through the top and middle order and took Tasmania's second first-class hat-trick (Michael Clarke, Vaughan Williams and Brad Haddin). He emulated Peter Clough, who had performed the feat in 1982-83, on the same ground against the same opponents. Daniel Marsh's catch at first slip to remove Haddin gave him six for the match, a Tasmanian record, as the home side won with an hour still to go on the third day.

Close of play: First day, Tasmania (1) 1-126 (Cox, 58, Dighton 9); Second day, New South Wales (2) 0-65 (Phelps 29, Richards 34).

Man of the Match: S. J. Jurgensen. *Attendance:* 1,580.

New South Wales

M.J. Phelps c Marsh b Wright	53	– c Marsh b Saker	41
C.J. Richards lbw b Jurgensen	15	– c Marsh b Jurgensen	42
*M.J. Slater lbw b Saker	50	– c Marsh b Jurgensen	7
M.J. Clarke c Mason b Denton	7	– lbw b Jurgensen	20
P.A. Jaques lbw b Saker	0	– c Clingeleffer b Denton	23
V.M. Williams c Clingeleffer b Jurgensen	4	– lbw b Jurgensen	0
†B.J. Haddin b Jurgensen	12	– c Marsh b Jurgensen	0
G.M. Lambert c Marsh b Jurgensen	3	– not out	45
N.W. Bracken b Jurgensen	2	– c Di Venuto b Kremerskothen	22
D.A. Nash c Clingeleffer b Denton	4	– c Cox b Kremerskothen	6
S.R. Clark not out	0	– b Jurgensen	18
L-b 7, w 6, n-b 1	14	L-b 7, n-b 7	14

(56.3 overs, 231 mins)   164   (70.5 overs, 282 mins)   238
Fall: 20 97 114 115 134 148 148   Fall: 82 89 94 131 131 131 140
154 164 164   186 195 238

Bowling: *First Innings*—Saker 17–3–56–2; Wright 13–3–22–1; Jurgensen 14–5–38–5; Denton 12.3–0–41–2. *Second Innings*—Saker 20–3–71–1; Jurgensen 26.5–7–65–6; Denton 17–1–66–1; Kremerskothen 7–2–29–2.

Tasmania

S. R. Mason lbw b Clark	41	– (2) not out	0
*J. Cox c Jaques b Clark	72	– (1) not out	4
M. G. Dighton b Clarke	84		
M. J. Di Venuto lbw b Nash	39		
D. J. Marsh lbw b Lambert	29		
S. P. Kremerskothen c Haddin b Clarke	12		
†S. G. Clingeleffer lbw b Lambert	11		
D. G. Wright b Bracken	13		
D. J. Saker not out	40		
G. J. Denton b Lambert	8		
S. J. Jurgensen b Nash	19		
B 10, l-b 15, n-b 8	33		0

(111.3 overs, 467 mins) **401**   (0.1 overs, 1 mins)   (0 wkt) **4**

Fall: 106 188 245 259 282 303 312 343 357 401

Bowling: *First Innings*—Nash 23.3–2–81–2; Clark 32–7–99–2; Bracken 30–7–85–1; Lambert 16–2–86–3; Clarke 10–1–25–2. *Second Innings*—Clark 0.1–0–4–0.

Umpires: K. J. Jones and J. H. Smeaton.

FINAL

At Brisbane Cricket Ground, Brisbane, March 22, 23, 24, 25, 26, 2002. TASMANIA lost to QUEENSLAND by 235 runs. For details see section on Pura Cup Final 2001-02.

AUSTRALIAN DOMESTIC FIRST-CLASS RESULTS TABLE

Opponent	M	W	L	D	T
Western Australia	46	6	21	19	0
Victoria	45	9	12	24	0
South Australia	45	8	16	21	0
Queensland	46	7	16	23	0
New South Wales	46	11	17	18	0
Total	228	41	82	105	0

AUSTRALIAN DOMESTIC FIRST-CLASS RECORDS

Highest score for:	265	D. F. Hills v South Australia at Hobart (Bellerive)	1997-98
Highest score against:	306*	D. W. Hookes (South Australia) at Adelaide	1986-97
Best bowling for:	8/95	P. M. Clough v Western Australia at Perth	1983-84
Best bowling against:	8/41	L. S. Pascoe (New South Wales) at Hobart (TCA)	1981-82
Highest total for:	592	v South Australia at Adelaide	1987-88
Highest total against:	673	by South Australia at Adelaide	1987-88
Lowest total for:	76	v New South Wales at Hobart (Bellerive)	1991-92
Lowest total against:	83	by Victoria at Melbourne	1981-82

* *Denotes not out.*

MOST RUNS

	M	I	NO	R	HS	100s	50s	Avge
J. Cox	134	244	16	9,601	245	29	41	42.11
D. C. Boon	119	203	7	8,029	227	20	43	40.96
D. F. Hills	100	187	8	6,887	265	18	36	38.47
M. J. Di Venuto	85	149	6	5,798	189	9	42	40.55
S. Young	104	176	29	5,565	175*	10	35	37.86
R. T. Ponting	47	87	13	4,749	233	20	14	64.18

	M	I	NO	R	HS	100s	50s	Avge
R.T. Tucker	90	153	24	4,611	165	7	24	35.74
D.J. Buckingham	75	129	11	4,407	167	9	22	37.35
R.D. Woolley	68	114	13	4,120	144	7	25	40.79
B.F. Davison............	41	75	7	3,062	173	9	13	45.03

* Denotes not out.

HIGHEST PARTNERSHIP FOR EACH WICKET

297	for 1st	D.F. Hills and J. Cox v Victoria at Hobart (Bellerive)	1997-98
294	for 2nd	J. Cox and M.J. Di Venuto v New South Wales at Hobart (Bellerive)	1999-00
290	for 3rd	D.F. Hills and R.T. Ponting v South Australia at Adelaide	1993-94
258	for 4th	M.D. Taylor and D.J. Buckingham v South Australia at Adelaide	1987-88
319	for 5th	R.T. Ponting and R.J. Tucker v Western Australia at Hobart (Bellerive) ..	1994-95
213	for 6th	B.F. Davison and R.D. Woolley v South Australia at Adelaide	1980-81
203*	for 7th	B.F. Davison and P.I. Faulkner v Western Australia at Perth	1983-84
148	for 8th	B.F. Davison and P.I. Faulkner v South Australia at Adelaide	1983-84
118*	for 9th	B.F. Davison and P.I. Faulkner v Queensland at Brisbane	1983-84
120	for 10th	S.L. Saunders and P.M. Clough v Western Australia at Perth	1981-82

* Denotes unbroken partnership.

MOST WICKETS

	M	Balls	Mdns	R	W	BB	5W/i	10W/m	Avge
C.R. Miller	54	13,846	556	6,657	210	7/49	8	2	31.70
S. Young	104	16,393	745	7,884	201	5/26	5	1	39.22
M.W. Ridgway	44	9,433	347	5,160	153	6/29	6	0	33.73
C.D. Matthews	35	7,922	272	4,234	119	6/89	7	0	35.57
R.J. Tucker	90	9,139	316	4,561	112	4/56	0	0	40.72
D.R. Gilbert	36	7,345	247	3,513	110	7/127	5	0	31.94
D.J. Marsh	61	9,203	373	4,464	107	7/57	1	0	41.72
P.M. Clough	28	6,142	226	2,913	102	8/95	5	0	28.56
P.T. McPhee	25	5,669	225	2,803	89	6/36	4	1	31.49
R.L. Brown	29	5,146	128	3,197	75	7/80	2	1	42.63

MOST DISMISSALS

	M	Ct	St	Total
M.N. Atkinson	84	237	25	262
R.D. Woolley	43	97	13	110
R.E. Soule	51	103	4	107
S.G. Clingeleffer	21	57	4	61
J.M. Holyman	9	25	1	26

MOST CATCHES

D.C. Boon	93 in 119 matches	D.F. Hills	67 in 100 matches
D.J. Marsh	72 in 61 matches	S. Young	62 in 104 matches
M.J. Di Venuto	73 in 85 matches	J. Cox	61 in 134 matches

MOST APPEARANCES

134	J. Cox	1987-88 – 2001-02	84	M.N. Atkinson ...	1991-92 – 1999-00
119	D.C. Boon	1978-79 – 1998-99	85	M.J. Di Venuto ..	1991-92 – 2001-02
104	S. Young	1991-92 – 2001-02	75	D.J. Buckingham .	1983-84 – 1993-94
100	D.F. Hills	1991-92 – 2001-02	68	R.D. Woolley	1977-78 – 1987-88
90	R.J. Tucker	1988-89 – 1998-99	54	C.R. Miller	1992-93 – 1999-00

VICTORIA

Chief Executive Officer: K. W. Jacobs

President: R. F. Merriman

Cricket Coach: M. J. O'Sullivan

Captain: P. R. Reiffel

Paul Reiffel

Having been runners-up for the past two seasons, and gone close to defeating Queensland in the 2000-01 final, Victoria embarked on the 2001-02 season confident of going one better and winning the competition for the first time since 1990-91. Such expectations were quickly dashed as Victoria managed to win just two of their ten Pura Cup games, and only narrowly avoided finishing last.

The season could scarcely have got off to a worse start. The Ansett Airlines collapse forced the cancellation of the state's regular pre-season training camp in Western Australia, then, just days before the opening game, came the shock resignation of the coach, John Scholes, who had held the post for six years. Michael O'Sullivan, the newly appointed assistant coach, was hurriedly named as his replacement. Then Paul Reiffel, appointed Pura Cup captain for a third season but replaced as captain of the ING Cup side by Matthew Elliott, expressed disappointment at his unexpected exclusion from the limited-overs side.

By mid-December Victoria stood at the foot of the Pura Cup table, having gained no points from their first four matches. The first points eventually came in a nine-wicket victory over South Australia in Melbourne, highlighted by a fine innings of 91 by 18-year-old Cameron White. However, the next match resulted in a heavy defeat at the hands of Western Australia in Perth, and Reiffel, citing a loss of motivation, unexpectedly announced his immediate retirement from all cricket. Only two games earlier he had become the state's highest wicket-taker in all first-class cricket when he overhauled Alan Connolly's record of 330. The vice-captain, Elliott, was appointed captain for the remaining matches.

Victoria recorded their best performance of the season a week later, when they defeated New South Wales in Sydney by ten wickets. The stars were Mathew Inness, whose 11-wicket haul included first innings figures of 7/19, and Jonathon Moss and Darren Berry, who both scored centuries and put on 199 for the sixth wicket. There would be no more victories. The last two games were lost outright, the loss to Western Australia in Melbourne being particularly painful, as Victoria, after leading by 275 on the first innings and needing just 135 to win, were routed for 98. The final match, against Queensland in Brisbane, was lost when Victoria were dismissed for only 122 in their second innings after gaining a first innings lead of 41.

The batting was brittle. Among the batsmen to occupy the top five positions in the batting order, only Elliott and Hodge had good seasons. Elliott was consistently solid, although he was able to convert only one of his seven half-centuries into a hundred, a match-saving 135 not out against Tasmania in Hobart. Hodge was the state's leading batsman for the second year in a row and was named joint Pura Cup Player of the Year. He began brilliantly by making a century in each innings against South Australia in Adelaide, but reached 50 only once in the next six matches before another burst of heavy scoring brought 85, 109 and 131 in consecutive innings against Tasmania and Western Australia. The lean seasons of Jason Arnberger, Matthew Mott and Michael Klinger meant that Victoria could seldom compile substantial totals. Of the remaining batsmen, only all-rounders Ian Harvey, with four half-centuries, and Moss, who came into the side when Harvey was called up for national duties in January, were reliable run-scorers.

Victoria's pace attack, the side's strong point in recent years, was hampered by a never-ending run of injuries. Reiffel missed two games early on with back problems; Damien Fleming could play in only five games, breaking down in one after completing just five overs, and being restricted by injury in two others; Inness, after demolishing New South Wales, missed the next two games after breaking his toe in a freak training mishap; Ian Hewett, who played against New South Wales after Reiffel's retirement, was unable to play again due to back trouble; and Shane Harwood, who impressed with his pace and fire when introduced to the ING Cup side mid-season and was in strong contention for Pura Cup selection, was ruled out after breaking his ankle while bowling in a club match. Left-armer Inness, who captured 31 wickets at 19.25 in the process troubling many batsmen with his control of length and movement, was easily the leading wicket-taker. No one else took 20 wickets. Ian Harvey and Mick Lewis both proved expensive, although Lewis bowled better than his figures suggest. The many injuries did, however, provide an opportunity for 25-year-old fast bowler Will Carr, whose success was one of the few bright spots in Victoria's season. After taking just two wickets in three Second Eleven matches before Christmas, he impressed with his pace and ability to obtain lift and trouble good batsmen when called up for the last three Pura Cup matches.

Spin bowling remains a significant weakness for Victoria. With Shane Warne available for only two games, it was hoped that Colin Miller, with his mixture of medium pace and off-spin, would play a key role. However, his effectiveness declined so sharply that he was dropped after the first three matches and played only once more. As a result the mantle of the state's main spinner fell on teenage leg-spinner Cameron White. He met with limited success, as his five matches, played either side of leading Australia to victory in the Under-19s World Cup in New Zealand, yielded only seven wickets. He will attend the Australian Cricket Academy next season and it is to be hoped that the burden of high expectations will not affect his progress. Late in the season, Bryce McGain, a 29-year-old leg-spinner, bowled tidily.

No fault could be found with the wicket-keeping. When he was replaced as vice-captain before the start of the season, many thought Berry's place could be in jeopardy, but this proved not to be the case. He kept wicket superbly throughout, as well as rediscovering some of his best batting form.

Despite his lack of previous leadership experience, Elliott made a good fist of his elevation to the captaincy. Although Warne might be recalled to the captaincy in 2002-03, Elliott is likely to continue to lead the side during Warne's absences on national duty.

The poor showing led to much soul-searching at the end of the season, especially as to why Victoria, with the second-largest state population to draw from, have managed to win the Sheffield Shield/Pura Cup only once since 1980. Inevitably several changes took place. In May the injury-plagued Damien Fleming, still probably the best swing bowler in the country, was not offered a contract. Long-serving selectors Shaun Graf and Neil Buszard were replaced by ex-Test spinner Ray Bright and John MacWhirter, a former South Melbourne and Essendon batsman. Michael O'Sullivan was the only selector to keep his place, although Graf continued as cricket manager. Much interest then centred on the appointment of the coach. Although no criticism for the state's poor performance could be levelled at O'Sullivan, who was popular and well organised, the coaching position was widely advertised. Out of a large field of applicants from Australia and overseas, it was announced in June that Victoria's new coach would be David Hookes, the former South Australian Test batsman. The highly experienced Greg Shipperd, who had coached Tasmania since 1991, was named as his assistant. Although Hookes' appointment raised some eyebrows, especially in view of his heavy media commitments and lack of previous coaching experience, many felt that his flair and high profile would make him the ideal person to lead Victorian cricket out of the doldrums. – KEN WILLIAMS.

VICTORIA PURA CUP TEAM, 2001-02

Back row: S.A.J. Craig, J.L. Arnberger, B.E. McGain, D.W. Fleming, I.S.L. Hewett, N. Jewell, A.B. McDonald, W.N. Carr, B.C. Oliver, T.H. Welsford, A.D. McQuire. *Middle row:* D.J. Hussey, A. Kent, T.R. Birt, S.M. Harwood, C.L. White, M.P. Mott, M. Klinger, R.A. Bartlett, D.S. Berry, J. Moss, S.P. Dart. *Front row:* B. Harrop, L. Buchanan, B.J. Hodge, M.T.G. Elliott, M.J. O'Sullivan (*coach*), P.R. Reiffel (*captain*), C.R. Miller, J.M. Davison, M.L. Lewis, P.J. Roach.

VICTORIA RESULTS, 2001-02

All first-class matches – Played 10: Won 2, Lost 4, Drawn 4.
Pura Cup matches – Played 10: Won 2, Lost 4, Drawn 4.
ING Cup matches – Played 10: Won 3, Lost 6, No result 1.
Competition placings – Pura Cup, 5th; ING Cup, 5th.

PURA CUP AVERAGES, 2001-02

BATTING

	M	I	NO	R	HS	100s	50s	Avge	Ct/St
B. J. Hodge	10	18	3	858	140	4	2	57.20	4
I. J. Harvey.........	7	11	2	432	87	0	4	48.00	1
M. T. G. Elliott.......	10	20	2	780	135*	1	6	43.33	15
J. Moss.............	5	9	0	378	109	1	3	42.00	4
P. R. Reiffel.........	4	6	2	122	75	0	1	30.50	3
D. S. Berry...........	10	16	3	382	148	1	1	29.38	32/3
J. L. Arnberger.......	8	16	2	401	70*	0	2	28.64	4
M. Klinger...........	7	11	2	251	58	0	2	27.89	1
M. P. Mott	9	16	0	378	87	0	2	23.63	6
D. W. Fleming	5	6	2	92	39*	0	0	23.00	1
C. L. White	5	8	0	144	91	0	1	18.00	4
M. L. Lewis	7	11	2	130	54*	0	1	14.44	2
A. B. McDonald	2	4	1	43	26	0	0	14.33	3
N. Jewell	2	4	0	49	26	0	0	12.25	0
C. R. Miller	4	5	1	35	17	0	0	8.75	0
S. K. Warne	2	3	1	10	4*	0	0	5.00	2
I. S. L. Hewett	1	1	0	3	3	0	0	3.00	0
M. W. H. Inness	7	9	5	11	8*	0	0	2.75	3
W. N. Carr..........	3	3	1	4	4	0	0	2.00	0
B. E. McGain........	2	2	0	3	3	0	0	1.50	2

* Denotes not out.

BOWLING

	O	M	R	W	BB	5W/i	10W/m	Avge
A. B. McDonald	9.4	2	20	2	1/6	0	0	10.00
W. N. Carr.............	94.2	28	276	16	6/46	1	0	17.25
M. W. H. Inness	214.5	61	597	31	7/19	1	1	19.26
J. Moss	74	22	153	7	3/35	0	0	21.86
P. R. Reiffel...........	100.3	24	280	10	4/71	0	0	28.00
D. W. Fleming	124.2	39	391	13	3/34	0	0	30.08
B. E. McGain	53.3	10	202	6	3/46	0	0	33.67
I. S. L. Hewett	33	9	102	3	3/63	0	0	34.00
I. J. Harvey	207.4	49	623	17	3/53	0	0	36.65
M. L. Lewis	184.4	43	621	16	4/64	0	0	38.81
S. K. Warne	75.1	9	253	6	4/118	0	0	42.17
C. L. White	103	15	405	7	3/97	0	0	57.86
C. R. Miller............	132.1	26	435	6	2/98	0	0	72.50
B. J. Hodge	62.3	14	181	2	1/0	0	0	90.50
M. P. Mott	7	4	15	0	–	0	0	–
N. Jewell..............	3	1	6	0	–	0	0	–

At Adelaide Oval, Adelaide, October 17, 18, 19, 20, 2001. VICTORIA drew with SOUTH AUSTRALIA.

VICTORIA v QUEENSLAND

At Richmond Cricket Ground, Richmond, October 24, 25, 26, 27, 2001. Drawn. Toss: Queensland. Queensland 2 pts. First-class debut: N.M. Hauritz.

As in the previous two seasons, Victoria began their home season at the Richmond Cricket Ground. They were led for the first time in a first-class match by Matthew Elliott, after Paul Reiffel was ruled out with a recurrence of a back injury. On a wicket that provided little encouragement for bowlers early on, Queensland gained the early ascendancy as Matthew Hayden (381 minutes, 283 balls, 17 fours, three sixes, in his 50th first-class hundred) and Jimmy Maher (143 balls, ten fours) were untroubled during a run-a-minute opening stand. Ian Harvey and Shane Warne brought about a middle-order collapse in which five wickets fell for 11 runs, but Ashley Noffke and newcomer Nathan Hauritz defied the Victorian attack in a ninth-wicket stand of 105. After the third day was lost to rain, both captains made declarations. Victoria closed before the start of play, then Queensland closed their second innings after batting for an hour, setting the home side a tempting target of 312 from 95 overs. The early loss of Elliott was a setback, but Matthew Mott, Brad Hodge and Michael Klinger gave Victoria a chance of victory. However, after the loss of seven overs through rain, play was called off due to fading light at 6.46 p.m., with Victoria still 72 runs short. With daylight saving not commencing until the day after the match, the decision to start each day's play at 11.00 a.m., rather than 10.30 a.m., came in for criticism.

Man of the Match: M.L. Hayden.   *Attendance:* 2,475.

Close of play: First day, Queensland (1) 417 (Hayden 145, Noffke 4); Second day, Victoria (1) 3-160 (Hodge 39, Klinger 20); Third day, no play (rain).

Queensland

M.L. Hayden b Inness	147			
J.P. Maher c Inness b Miller	96	– (1) c and b Inness		9
M.L. Love lbw b Harvey	33	– (2) not out		34
C.T. Perren c Berry b Harvey	1	– (3) c Mott b Inness		2
A. Symonds lbw b Warne	1	– (4) not out		9
*S.G. Law lbw b Warne	3			
†W.A. Seccombe c Arnberger b Warne	1			
A.J. Bichel c Warne b Inness	15			
A.A. Noffke c Elliott b Warne	73			
N.M. Hauritz c Warne b Fleming	41			
M.S. Kasprowicz not out	0			
B 6	6			

(122.4 overs, 475 mins)	417	(15 overs, 59 mins) (2 wkts dec)	54
Fall: 176 250 252 253 259 261 299 312 417 417		Fall: 23 37	

Bowling: *First Innings*—Fleming 23.4–10–54–1; Inness 19–4–71–2; Miller 24–1–108–1; Harvey 20–8–50–2; Warne 34–4–118–4; Mott 1–0–6–0; Hodge 1–0–4–0. *Second Innings*—Fleming 4–1–14–0; Inness 7–1–19–2; Harvey 4–0–21–0.

Victoria

*M.T.G. Elliott c Seccombe b Bichel	56	– (2) c Seccombe b Bichel		4
J.L. Arnberger c Bichel b Hauritz	20	– (1) b Kasprowicz		33
M.P. Mott lbw b Symonds	20	– c Seccombe b Kasprowicz		87
B.J. Hodge not out	39	– b Bichel		33
M. Klinger not out	20	– not out		44
I.J. Harvey (did not bat)		– c Seccombe b Kasprowicz		9
†D.S. Berry (did not bat)		– c Seccombe b Kasprowicz		7
S.K. Warne (did not bat)		– not out		4
B 4, n-b 1	5	B 6, l-b 7, n-b 6		19

(70 overs, 244 mins)	(3 wkts dec) 160	(76.4 overs, 328 mins)	(6 wkts) 240
Fall: 52 84 112		Fall: 9 65 127 196 212 230	

D.W. Fleming, C.R. Miller and M.W.H. Inness did not bat.

Bowling: *First Innings*—Bichel 12–4–36–1; Kasprowicz 18–10–37–0; Noffke 12–5–25–0; Hauritz 16–4–35–1; Symonds 12–4–23–1. *Second Innings*—Bichel 16–2–43–2; Kasprowicz 20–2–53–4; Noffke 14.4–2–63–0; Symonds 14–3–32–0; Hauritz 12–2–36–0.

Umpires: R.L. Parry and R.G. Patterson.
TV Umpire: G.T.D. Morrow.

VICTORIA v NEW SOUTH WALES

At Richmond Cricket Ground, Richmond, November 8, 9, 10, 11, 2001. New South Wales won by seven wickets. Toss: Victoria. New South Wales 6 pts.

Despite the absence of their Test representatives, New South Wales comfortably defeated Victoria. After the early dismissal of Matthew Elliott, the home side struggled, and with Jason Arnberger taking three and a quarter hours to make 47, Victoria did not reach 150 until the 77th over. The tempo increased later as Ian Harvey (119 minutes, 93 balls, 14 fours) punished some loose deliveries. After Damien Fleming dismissed both New South Wales openers, the visitors gained the upper hand during an excellent third-wicket stand of 186 by Michael Bevan and Michael Clarke. Clarke (218 minutes, 189 balls, 16 fours) was the dominant partner, batting with confidence and power to make his second first-class hundred. Bevan (345 minutes, 260 balls, 15 fours, one six) was more sedate in compiling his 51st first-class century. With the trio of Nathan Bracken, Stuart Clark and Stuart MacGill once again troubling them, Victoria struggled in their second innings on a rain-interrupted third day and by the close were still ten runs in arrears with six wickets in hand. Despite some bright batting on the final day from Harvey and Elliott (who was forced to bat down the order after being off the field with a stomach disorder on the third day), Victoria were able to set the visitors only 115 to win. After losing three early wickets to Fleming, New South Wales hit off the runs in 100 minutes, with Michael Slater hitting freely to lead the way.

Man of the Match: M.J. Clarke. *Attendance:* 1,655.

Close of play: First day, Victoria (1) 6-221 (Harvey 55); Second day, New South Wales (1) 5-257 (Bevan 116, Haddin 15); Third day, Victoria (2) 4-69 (Harvey 12, Berry 10).

Victoria

*M. T. G. Elliott b S. R. Clark	2	– (7) c Haddin b S. R. Clark	50
J. L. Arnberger c Lee b MacGill	47	– (1) lbw b Bracken	9
M. P. Mott c Haddin b Bracken	35	– (2) c Lee b MacGill	9
B. J. Hodge c Haddin b Lee	44	– (3) c Haddin b S. R. Clark	26
M. Klinger c S. R. Clark b MacGill	27	– (4) c Haddin b S. R. Clark	0
I. J. Harvey c Clarke b Bracken	74	– (5) lbw b MacGill	48
†D. S. Berry c Haddin b MacGill	4	– (6) c Clarke b S. R. Clark	18
C. R. Miller c Clarke b Bracken	0	– lbw b S. R. Clark	0
D. W. Fleming c Lee b MacGill	11	– c Bevan b MacGill	17
M. L. Lewis b Bracken	1	– b MacGill	8
M. W. H. Inness not out	0	– not out	2
B 7	7	B 3, l-b 3	6

(109 overs, 413 mins)	259	(59.2 overs, 250 mins)	193

Fall: 3 68 100 150 194 221 240 254 258 259

Fall: 17 47 47 47 87 149 152 181 183 193

Bowling: *First Innings*—Bracken 33–12–76–4; S. R. Clark 24–9–46–1; A. M. Clark 3–1–5–0; Lee 18–2–54–1; MacGill 31–8–71–4. *Second Innings*—Bracken 12–3–42–1; S. R. Clark 24–7–47–5; MacGill 13.2–3–54–4; A. M. Clark 4–0–16–0; Lee 6–0–28–0.

New South Wales

M. J. Slater c Berry b Fleming	0	– not out	58
G. J. Mail c Berry b Fleming	1		
M. G. Bevan b Inness	128	– c Lewis b Fleming	10
M. J. Clarke lbw b Harvey	111	– c Berry b Fleming	0
M. A. Higgs c Klinger b Harvey	4	– not out	32
*S. Lee c (sub) C. L. White b Miller	3		
†B. J. Haddin lbw b Inness	33	– (2) b Fleming	15
A. M. Clark c Berry b Inness	12		
S. C. G. MacGill c (sub) P. C. Ayres b Inness	14		
S. R. Clark c Fleming b Harvey	8		
N. W. Bracken not out	15		
L-b 7, n-b 2	9	L-b 1, n-b 1	2

(98.4 overs, 382 mins)	338	(23.1 overs, 100 mins) (3 wkts)	117

Fall: 0 1 187 203 206 286 295 315 319 338

Fall: 19 41 41

Bowling: *First Innings*—Fleming 17–3–66–2; Inness 17–4–61–4; Lewis 12–2–72–0; Miller 25–8–60–1; Harvey 19.4–4–53–3; Hodge 8–1–19–0. *Second Innings*—Fleming 9–1–34–3; Inness 7–1–30–0; Miller 4.1–0–28–0; Harvey 3–0–24–0.

Umpires: R. L. Parry and R. G. Patterson.

At Bellerive Oval, Hobart, November 30, December 1, 2, 3, 2001. VICTORIA drew with TASMANIA.

VICTORIA v SOUTH AUSTRALIA

At Melbourne Cricket Ground, Melbourne, December 13, 14, 15, 2001. Victoria won by nine wickets. Toss: Victoria. Victoria 6 pts.

Victoria gained the upper hand in the opening session when Paul Reiffel, Mathew Inness and Michael Lewis broke through South Australia's top order. Ben Johnson played a lone hand, carrying his bat (259 minutes, 199 balls, 20 fours) and contributing 60.26 per cent of his team's total. He became the first player to carry his bat in consecutive first-class matches in Australia since Bill Lawry in 1971-72. Johnson's best support came from Mark Harrity, a noted No. 11, who survived for 55 minutes to help put on 71 for the last wicket, easily the highest stand of the innings. Victoria lost six wickets before gaining a first innings lead (and their first points of the season), with useful contributions from Michael Klinger and Ian Harvey. Brad Hodge was forced to bat at No. 6 after suffering a gash to the face on the first day when he missed a sharp slips catch from Johnson. A fine innings from Cameron White (148 minutes, 130 balls, 13 fours), marked by strong driving and pulling, ensured first innings points. He fell nine runs short of becoming, at 18 years and 118 days, the youngest Victorian to score a century in Sheffield Shield/Pura Cup cricket, ahead of Les Joslin (18 years and 341 days against Western Australia in 1966-67). Reiffel (124 minutes, 11 fours) also hit out strongly, adding 86 for the eighth wicket with White and 75 for the ninth with Lewis. South Australia fought hard in their second innings, with all the top-order batsmen getting a start, although Ben Higgins was the only player to reach 50. During this innings Darren Lehmann, who was handicapped by a back injury, became the leading scorer in the domestic first-class competition, moving past Jamie Siddons' tally of 10,643. Victoria cruised to victory with a day to spare, taking just two hours to hit off the 128 they needed.

Man of the Match: C.L. White. *Attendance:* 4,153.

Close of play: First day, Victoria (1) 3-103 (Klinger 8, Harvey 29); Second day, South Australia 2-74 (Blewett 23, Higgins 15).

South Australia

B. A. Johnson not out	138	– (2) lbw b Inness	22
J.M. Vaughan c Hodge b Reiffel	1	– (1) c Berry b Lewis	12
G.S. Blewett c Elliott b Inness	0	– c Elliott b Harvey	41
*D.S. Lehmann c Berry b Lewis	12	– (5) c Elliott b Lewis	26
B.H. Higgins lbw b Inness	11	– (4) c Inness b Harvey	58
N.T. Adcock c Harvey b Inness	0	– c White b Lewis	46
B.E. Young b White	25	– c Berry b Reiffel	44
M.J. Smith lbw b White	0	– c (sub) C. Brown b Harvey	40
†G.A. Manou b Lewis	0	– c Reiffel b Inness	7
P.C. Rofe b Lewis	2	– c Elliott b Lewis	1
M.A. Harrity lbw b Reiffel	19	– not out	0
B 4, l-b 8, n-b 9	21	B 2, l-b 2, n-b 2	6

(61.1 overs, 259 mins)	229	(91.1 overs, 370 mins)	303
Fall: 12 17 65 86 90 139 143		Fall: 35 35 111 159 182 242 271	
146 158 229		278 279 303	

Bowling: *First Innings*—Reiffel 13.1–4–29–2; Inness 12–4–26–3; Lewis 15–2–67–3; Harvey 14–1–59–0; White 7–1–36–2. *Second Innings*—Reiffel 13–4–37–1; Inness 21–6–58–2; Lewis 20–6–64–4; White 16–4–62–0; Harvey 19.1–3–72–3; Hodge 2–0–6–0.

Victoria

M.T.G. Elliott c Higgins b Smith	19	– (2) lbw b Adcock	45
J.L. Arnberger lbw b Smith	36	– (1) not out	70
M.P. Mott c Manou b Rofe	5		
M. Klinger lbw b Harrity	50		
I.J. Harvey c Young b Rofe	46	– (3) not out	11
B.J. Hodge b Harrity	16		
C.L. White c Smith b Rofe	91		
†D.S. Berry b Smith	19		
*P.R. Reiffel run out (Vaughan)	75		
M.L. Lewis not out	27		
M.W.H. Inness b Rofe	0		
B 2, l-b 4, n-b 15	21	L-b 1, n-b 2	3

(102.5 overs, 402 mins)	405	(32.2 overs, 121 mins) (1 wkt)	129
Fall: 51 63 66 134 174 198 241 327 402 405		Fall: 113	

Bowling: *First Innings*—Harrity 22–2–97–2; Rofe 29.5–8–101–4; Smith 23–1–118–3; Young 18–3–44–0; Adcock 3–1–8–0; Johnson 7–0–31–0. *Second Innings*—Harrity 5–0–19–0; Rofe 8–2–22–0; Smith 7–1–24–0; Johnson 4–0–17–0; Adcock 4.2–0–23–1; Young 4–0–23–0.

Umpires: G. T. D. Morrow and R. L. Parry.

At WACA Ground, Perth, January 18, 19, 20, 21, 2002. VICTORIA lost to WESTERN AUSTRALIA by ten wickets.

At Sydney Cricket Ground, Sydney, January 25, 26, 27, 2002. VICTORIA defeated NEW SOUTH WALES by ten wickets.

VICTORIA v TASMANIA

At Melbourne Cricket Ground, Melbourne, February 17, 18, 19, 20, 2002. Drawn. Toss: Victoria. Tasmania 2 pts. First-class debut: W. N. Carr, A. B. McDonald.

Rain on the final day ended any chance of an outright result. Batting first on a pitch that offered early encouragement for bowlers, Victoria struggled at first against accurate bowling from David Saker and Damien Wright. The rate of scoring increased during a fourth-wicket stand by Brad Hodge (212 minutes, 177 balls, 12 fours, one six) and Ian Harvey (181 minutes, 148 balls, 13 fours). Next day, Darren Berry and Damien Fleming enabled Victoria to score 114 in the first session and declare at lunch. Tasmania's reply centred on a third-wicket stand of 197 by Michael Dighton and Michael Di Venuto. Dighton (267 minutes, 226 balls, 17 fours, one six), who survived three chances, made his second century of the season against Victoria. When Wright was ninth out Tasmania still needed 16 runs for first innings points. It took half an hour for Xavier Doherty and Shane Jurgensen to score the necessary runs, Jurgensen surviving a chance from the bowling of Harvey. Victoria attempted to force the pace, but found progress difficult against Tasmania's accurate attack. Matthew Elliott and Brad Hodge (his third century of the season, 227 minutes, 203 balls, 12 fours, one six), put on 123 for the second wicket, and Victoria declared after lunch on the last day, setting Tasmania 250 to win from 55 overs. Carr worked up good pace to capture three wickets in his first four overs, but rain interrupted play soon after and the match petered out into a draw.

Man of the Match: M. G. Dighton. *Attendance:* 2,256.

Close of play: First day, Victoria (1) 6-257 (Harvey 65, Berry 13); Second day, Tasmania (1) 2-191 (Dighton 78, Di Venuto 68); Third day, Victoria (2) 1-120 (Elliott 60 Hodge 50).

Victoria

*M. T. G. Elliott c Kremerskothen b Wright	64	– (2) c Marsh b Saker	72
J. L. Arnberger b Jurgensen	19	– (1) b Wright	10
B. J. Hodge b Saker	85	– c and b Marsh	109
J. Moss c Clingeleffer b Saker	1	– run out (Dighton)	19
I. J. Harvey c Cox b Doherty	87		
A. B. McDonald b Saker	0	– (7) not out	10
C. L. White c Di Venuto b Saker	3	– (5) c Dighton b Marsh	8
†D. S. Berry not out	62	– (6) c Jurgensen b Marsh	7
M. L. Lewis c Kremerskothen b Doherty	4	– (8) c Di Venuto b Marsh	0
D. W. Fleming not out	39	– (9) not out	7
L-b 5, n-b 2	7	B 4, l-b 6	10

(133 overs, 468 mins)	(8 wkts dec) 371	(73 overs, 268 mins) (7 wkts dec) 252
Fall: 47 93 111 211 211 221 286 302		Fall: 19 142 178 206 213 239 239

W. N. Carr did not bat.

Bowling: *First Innings*—Saker 35–16–71–4; Wright 29–8–78–1; Jurgensen 22–5–65–1; Doherty 28–8–78–2; Kremerskothen 7–0–36–0; Marsh 12–2–38–0. *Second Innings*—Saker 19–6–40–1; Wright 18–5–57–1; Doherty 10–1–41–0; Marsh 17–1–70–4; Di Venuto 1–0–5–0; Jurgensen 8–1–29–0.

Tasmania

S.R. Mason c McDonald b Lewis	11	– (2) c McDonald b Carr	0
*J. Cox c (sub) M. Klinger b White	24	– (1) lbw b Carr	2
M.G. Dighton c Elliott b Carr	124	– c Elliott b Carr	4
M.J. Di Venuto b McDonald	83	– lbw b White	38
D.J. Marsh b Fleming	9	– not out	40
S.P. Kremerskothen c Berry b Lewis	21	– not out	21
†S.G. Clingeleffer lbw b Carr	1		
D.G. Wright c (sub) M. Klinger b White	48		
D.J. Saker c Moss b White	13		
X.J. Doherty not out	4		
S.J. Jurgensen not out	13		
B 11, l-b 10, n-b 2	23	L-b 1, n-b 4	5

(121.5 overs, 483 mins)	(9 wkts dec) 374	(32 overs, 133 mins)	(4 wkts) 110
Fall: 24 50 247 263 275 278 307 347 356		Fall: 3 4 12 83	

Bowling: *First Innings*—Fleming 21–6–64–1; Carr 22–8–55–2; Lewis 23–8–46–2; Harvey 22.5–5–63–0; White 23–2–97–3; Hodge 4–1–13–0; Moss 3–1–9–0; McDonald 3–1–6–1. *Second Innings*—Fleming 8–3–27–0; Carr 11–4–34–3; Lewis 7–1–30–0; White 6–1–18–1.

Umpires: G.T.D. Morrow and A.J. Soulsby.

VICTORIA v WESTERN AUSTRALIA

At Melbourne Cricket Ground, Melbourne, February 28, March 1, 2, 3, 2002. Western Australia won by 37 runs. Toss: Victoria. Victoria 2 and Western Australia 6 pts. First-class debut: N. Jewell.

A magnificent unbeaten double-century from Marcus North enabled Western Australia to achieve the greatest comeback in the history of Australian first-class cricket. Victoria's batsmen dominated the first day with Matthew Elliott (149 minutes, 101 balls, ten fours, two sixes) and Matthew Mott (220 minutes, 179 balls, nine fours) putting on 145 for the first wicket. Brad Hodge, after a slow start, cut and pulled confidently to reach his fourth hundred of the season (267 minutes, 237 balls, 18 fours) and received solid support from Jon Moss. A hard-hitting 56-ball innings from Ian Harvey enabled Victoria to declare at lunch on the second day. Western Australia soon slumped to four for 40, and although Ryan Campbell batted forcefully, they followed on 275 in arrears. After the loss of three early wickets the remaining batsmen fought hard throughout the rain-affected third day, aided by a slow pitch and a damp ball. Mike Hussey began the recovery, but the honours went to North, who was unbeaten with 127 at the close, by which stage the visitors had just cleared the arrears with four wickets in hand. On the final day an early Victorian victory appeared likely when Brad Hogg fell in the first over, but North (504 minutes, 378 balls, 18 fours, three sixes) was resolute, defending stoutly and punishing loose deliveries, adding 85 for the eighth wicket with Matthew Nicholson and an invaluable 47 in even time for the tenth wicket with Michael Clark. Set 136 to win, Victoria lost Mott second ball, but when Elliott and Moss added 45 for the second wicket, they appeared safely on the way to victory. However, both fell in successive overs, and Harvey was brilliantly thrown out by Brad Williams. When the injured Hodge was dismissed, the innings collapsed in the face of some hostile and accurate bowling, especially from Williams and Nicholson. This was only the third time in the history of the competition that a side had won after following on, the previous instances having been in 1892-93, when South Australia defeated New South Wales by 57 runs in the very first Shield match, and in 1965-66, when New South Wales defeated Queensland by 27 runs.

Man of the Match: M.J. North. *Attendance:* 4,414.

Close of play: First day, Victoria (1) 2-313 (Hodge 100, Moss 34); Second day, Western Australia (2) 2-16 (Hussey 9, Katich 0); Third day, Western Australia (2) 6-278 (North 127, Hogg 18).

Victoria

*M.T.G. Elliott c Campbell b Williams	88	– (2) c North b Angel	23
M.P. Mott c Rogers b Hogg	84	– (1) c Rogers b Williams	0
B.J. Hodge c Hussey b Nicholson	131	– (7) lbw b Nicholson	22
J. Moss run out (Nicholson)	59	– (3) c and b Williams	21
I.J. Harvey not out	61	– run out (Williams)	8
N. Jewell c Hussey b Hogg	5	– (4) c Campbell b Hogg	14
C.L. White lbw b Hogg	0	– (6) c Rogers b Williams	0
†D.S. Berry not out	10	– not out	3
B.E. McGain (did not bat)		– (10) lbw b Nicholson	0
M.L. Lewis (did not bat)		– (9) b Nicholson	0
W.N. Carr (did not bat)		– b Williams	4
L-b 9, n-b 1	10	B 2, n-b 1	3

(128 overs, 481 mins)	(6 wkts dec) 450	(34 overs, 148 mins)	98

Fall: 145 193 361 369 392 395

Fall: 0 45 45 53 56 90 92 93 93 98

Bowling: *First Innings*—Williams 26–3–92–1; Angel 29–6–87–0; Nicholson 27–3–94–1; Clark 10–0–42–0; Hogg 25–3–95–3; North 8–1–29–0; Katich 3–1–2–0. *Second Innings*—Williams 12–3–34–4; Nicholson 8–3–13–3; Angel 5–0–29–1; Katich 5–1–17–0; Hogg 4–1–3–1.

Western Australia

M.E.K. Hussey c Mott b Harvey	0	– (2) c Berry b Moss	61
S.W. Meuleman c Berry b Lewis	5	– (1) c Berry b Carr	0
*S.M. Katich c Berry b Carr	5	– (4) c Berry b Carr	11
M.J. North b Lewis	14	– (5) not out	200
†R.J. Campbell c McGain b Moss	63	– (6) c Moss b Carr	29
C.J.L. Rogers st Berry b McGain	26	– (7) b Harvey	15
G.B. Hogg c White b Lewis	30	– (8) c Elliott b Carr	18
M.J. Nicholson lbw b Moss	4	– (9) st Berry b Moss	49
J. Angel c Elliott b McGain	6	– (3) lbw b Harvey	3
B.A. Williams c Elliott b McGain	4	– b Moss	0
M.W. Clark not out	0	– b McGain	6
B 3, l-b 4, w 1, n-b 10	18	B 5, l-b 6, w 1, n-b 6	18

(51.4 overs, 213 mins)	175	(142.3 overs, 567 mins)	410

Fall: 5 10 18 40 117 128 146
161 170 175

Fall: 0 14 39 123 178 231 278
363 363 410

Bowling: *First Innings*—Carr 10–2–35–1; Harvey 8–2–18–1; Lewis 8.4–1–40–3; White 2–0–11–0; McGain 14–3–46–3; Moss 9–3–18–2. *Second Innings*—Carr 25–8–77–4; Harvey 27–7–62–2; Lewis 29–8–88–0; Moss 26–9–35–3; McGain 18.3–1–92–1; White 11–3–39–0; Jewell 3–1–6–0; Mott 3–3–0–0.

Umpires: R.L. Parry and R.G. Patterson.

At Brisbane Cricket Ground, Brisbane, March 13, 14, 15, 2002. VICTORIA lost to QUEENSLAND by five wickets.

AUSTRALIAN DOMESTIC FIRST-CLASS RESULTS TABLE

	M	W	L	D	T
New South Wales	201	62	73	65	1
South Australia	196	98	46	52	0
Queensland	138	48	41	49	0
Western Australia	101	31	28	42	0
Tasmania	45	12	9	24	0
Total	681	251	197	232	1

AUSTRALIAN DOMESTIC FIRST-CLASS RECORDS

Highest score for:	437	W. H. Ponsford v Queensland at Melbourne	1927-28
Highest score against:	357	D. G. Bradman (South Australia) at Melbourne	1935-36
Best bowling for:	9/40	E. L. McCormick v South Australia at Adelaide	1936-37
Best bowling against:	10/44	I. J. Brayshaw (Western Australia) at Perth	1967-68
Highest total for:	1,107	v New South Wales at Melbourne	1926-27
Highest total against:	815	by New South Wales at Sydney	1908-09
Lowest total for:	31	v New South Wales at Melbourne	1906-07
Lowest total against:	49	by Queensland at Melbourne	1936-37

MOST RUNS

	M	I	NO	R	HS	100s	50s	Avge
D. M. Jones	110	194	16	9,622	324*	31	40	54.06
M. T. G. Elliott	74	144	12	6,973	203	23	33	52.83
W. M. Lawry	85	139	14	6,615	266	17	41	52.92
G. N. Yallop	76	137	11	5,881	246	18	31	46.67
A. L. Hassett	58	97	10	5,535	229	18	27	63.62
W. H. Ponsford	43	70	5	5,413	437	21	14	83.28
D. F. Whatmore	85	150	7	5,235	170	10	31	36.61
I. R. Redpath	76	132	11	5,222	261	11	28	43.16
B. J. Hodge	78	145	14	5,057	140	13	24	38.60
W. W. Armstrong	59	106	7	4,997	250	17	17	50.47
J. D. Siddons	64	109	11	4,703	245	13	24	47.99

* Denotes not out.

HIGHEST PARTNERSHIP FOR EACH WICKET

375 for 1st	W. M. Woodfull and W. H. Ponsford v New South Wales at Melbourne	...	1926-27
314 for 2nd	W. H. Ponsford and H. S. T. L. Hendry v Queensland at Melbourne		1927-28
390* for 3rd	J. M. Wiener and J. K. Moss v Western Australia at St Kilda		1981-82
301 for 4th	L. P. J. O'Brien and L. S. Darling v Queensland at Brisbane		1932-33
316* for 5th	L. D. Harper and G. B. Gardener v South Australia at Carlton		1997-98
290 for 6th	M. T. G. Elliott and D. S. Berry v New South Wales at Sydney		1996-97
185 for 7th	P. A. Hibbert and R. J. Bright v New South Wales at Melbourne		1985-86
215 for 8th	R. L. Park and W. W. Armstrong v South Australia at Melbourne		1919-20
143 for 9th	G. R. Hazlitt and A. Kenny v South Australia at Melbourne		1910-11
211 for 10th	M. Ellis and T. J. Hastings v South Australia at Melbourne		1902-03

* Denotes unbroken partnership.

MOST WICKETS

	M	Balls	Mdns	R	W	BB	5W/i	10W/m	Avge
P.R. Reiffel	86	19,137	843	8,242	318	6/57	7	2	25.92
A.N. Connolly	71	17,973	365	7,745	297	9/67	12	4	26.08
A.I.C. Dodemaide	94	19,892	822	8,884	281	6/67	12	0	31.62
M.G. Hughes	76	16,762	582	8,169	267	7/81	10	2	30.60
R.J. Bright	101	22,899	1,013	8,821	252	6/61	10	0	35.00
L.O. Fleetwood-Smith ...	41	11,576	119	6,034	246	9/135	25	8	24.53
J.D. Higgs	75	14,961	376	7,202	240	8/66	12	2	30.01
D.W. Fleming	67	14,648	657	6,675	221	7/90	7	1	30.20
M.H.N. Walker	62	15,071	429	6,476	220	6/49	11	0	29.44
H. Ironmonger	44	14,594	432	5,290	215	7/13	16	4	24.60

MOST DISMISSALS

	M	Ct	St	Total
D.S. Berry	114	416	38	454
R.D. Robinson	68	213	26	239
R.C. Jordan	70	199	31	230
M.G.D. Dimattina	60	149	19	168
J.L. Ellis	49	111	45	156

MOST CATCHES

D.F. Whatmore	110 in 85 matches	J.D. Siddons	76 in 64 matches
M.T.G. Elliott	102 in 74 matches	W.W. Armstrong ...	68 in 59 matches
D.M. Jones	96 in 110 matches	G.N. Yallop	66 in 76 matches

MOST APPEARANCES

114	D.S. Berry	1990-91 – 2001-02	85	D.F. Whatmore ...	1975-76 – 1988-89
110	D.M. Jones	1981-82 – 1997-98	78	B.J. Hodge	1993-94 – 2001-02
101	R.J. Bright	1972-73 – 1987-88	76	G.N. Yallop	1972-73 – 1984-85
94	A.I.C. Dodemaide .	1983-84 – 1997-98	76	M.G. Hughes	1981-82 – 1994-95
86	P.R. Reiffel	1987-88 – 2000-01	76	I.R. Redpath	1961-62 – 1975-76
85	W.M. Lawry	1955-56 – 1971-72	75	J.D. Higgs	1970-71 – 1982-83

WESTERN AUSTRALIA

Chief Executive Officer: K. White

President: P. B. Rakich

Cricket Coach: M. R .J. Veletta

Captain: A. C. Gilchrist

Adam Gilchrist

Sadly, the record-breaking feats of Jo Angel were overshadowed during a summer of discontent which ended with stand-in captain and star batsman Simon Katich opting to pursue his career with New South Wales. The loss of the accomplished left-hander will be a serious blow to Western Australia. There was an undercurrent of unrest and tension during the summer, when Western Australia battled to come to terms with the retirement of Tom Moody and Brendon Julian and had to adjust to the stricter discipline imposed by Mike Veletta in his first year as coach after the more relaxed Wayne Clark had moved on to coach Yorkshire after six years at the helm in Perth.

Even though the loss of Moody and Julian left Western Australia in a rebuilding stage, particularly with Justin Langer, Adam Gilchrist and Damien Martyn absent for the bulk of the season on international duties, only three wins from ten matches in the Pura Cup was a disappointing result for the state which had been a trendsetter in Australia since the 1960s. Typifying a season of exhilarating highs and destabilising lows were Western Australia's remarkable Pura Cup victory over Victoria at the MCG after following on, and the dismal loss by an innings to Tasmania to record the state's first loss at Bellerive Oval.

There was considerable turmoil and a series of crises at the WACA in mid-February when it was revealed that Katich had threatened to resign several weeks earlier. Katich had been concerned over some selection decisions, particularly the dropping of Murray Goodwin, and had offered to stand down as captain. Goodwin, fast bowler Matthew Nicholson and spinner Brad Oldroyd all considered moving interstate after being dropped during the season, and there were reports of a brewing revolt by players, many of whom were disgruntled over selection policies and stern disciplinary measures. Katich played down all the talk of problems and declared that his move to Sydney was to reinvigorate his batting and to have greater opportunities with his left-arm wrist-spinners on a responsive SCG pitch. To end a tempestuous season, during which he scored only one first-class century and managed 585 runs at an average of 34.41 (after his 1,145 runs at 71.56 the previous summer), the man who had made his Test debut in 2001 lost his ACB contract. Reports in the latter stages of the season that Western Australia were attempting to lure Adam Dale, Paul Wilson and Damien Fleming to Perth also had a destabilising effect on the squad.

Western Australia, for many years a powerful force at home on fast, bouncy pitches, were no longer feared in Perth and managed only one home win, over lowly Victoria. Curator Richard Winter produced a succession of excellent pitches, but the Western Australian batsmen managed to score only six Pura Cup centuries at home, three of them in the last match. The tally of nine Pura Cup hundreds for the season fell well short of the Western Australian record of 18 in the glorious summer of 1997-98.

The bowlers, too, struggled, with only one, the tireless Angel, achieving a five-wicket haul. Angel's 6/52 off 25.3 overs against Victoria at the WACA was the outstanding

WESTERN AUSTRALIA PURA CUP TEAM, 2001-02

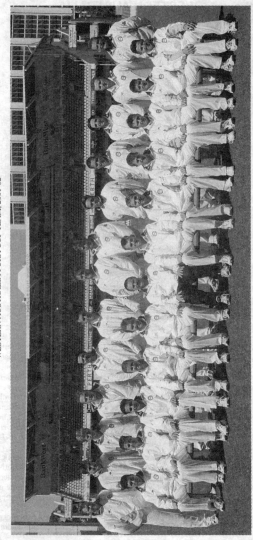

Back row: B. A. Williams, G. I. Cullen, A. C. Voges, G. G. Swan, B. J. Oldroyd, M. J. Thistle, M. J. Nicholson, S. R. Cary, S. J. Karppinen, M. J. North, P. C. Worthington, C. J. Rogers, N. Knight (*assistant coach*). *Front row*: R. J. Campbell, R. M. Baker, D. J. Wates, M. W. Goodwin, J. L. Langer, M. R. J. Valetta (*coach*), A. C. Gilchrist (*captain*), D. R. Martyn, S. M. Katich, K. M. Harvey, M. E. K. Hussey, G. B. Hogg.

bowling performance for the season. Angel had an exceptional season, moving past Terry Alderman as Western Australia's leading wicket-taker in the domestic four-day competition and becoming the leading wicket-taker from all states in the domestic limited-overs competition. His tally at the end of the summer stood at 387 Sheffield Shield/Pura Cup wickets, taking him into second place on the all-time Australian list behind Clarrie Grimmett. Angel received solid support from fast men Brad Williams (32 Pura Cup wickets at 28.31) and Matthew Nicholson (28 at 31.00), while Brad Hogg was the best spinner, taking 14 wickets after missing the first three Pura Cup matches and a later one when under suspension.

Of the 19 men used in Pura Cup matches, only one was a debutant: willowy left-arm fast-medium bowler Michael Clark, son of Wayne Clark, who showed promise of developing into a strong contributor for his state. Langer, Martyn and Gilchrist performed soundly during limited opportunities, but established batsmen Katich, Mike Hussey and Goodwin were inconsistent. Ryan Campbell missed the first two matches before excelling behind the stumps and showing a return to good form with the bat to finish the season. Young opener Scott Meuleman scored a century against the South Africans, but disappointing form in the Pura Cup led to his omission for the final match. The most heartening feature of the side's batting was the form of young left-handers Marcus North, whose 200 not out led the fightback against Victoria, and Chris Rogers, who hit twin unbeaten centuries in the last match.

While these youngsters were standing up, some of the old established parts of the WACA Ground came tumbling down. The 1931 Farley Stand and the Players' Stand were demolished, and as soon as the season ended, work began on a $12 million ground refurbishment program. The redesigned ground will have a capacity of 30,000, the members' stand moving from the Prindiville Stand to the Lillee–Marsh Stand. Seating will be on a higher rake to improve viewing, and steep grass banks will replace the concrete and plastic seating on the eastern and western boundaries. – KEN CASELLAS.

WESTERN AUSTRALIA RESULTS, 2001-02

All first-class matches – Played 11: Won 3, Lost 2, Drawn 7.
Pura Cup matches – Played 10: Won 3, Lost 2, Drawn 6.
ING Cup matches – Played 10: Won 5, Lost 5.
Competition placings – Pura Cup, 3rd; ING Cup, 4th.

PURA CUP AVERAGES, 2001-02

BATTING

	M	I	NO	R	HS	100s	50s	Avge	Ct
C.J.L. Rogers	4	7	2	411	102*	2	2	82.20	5
D.R. Martyn	2	3	0	223	189	1	0	74.33	7
G.B. Hogg	6	10	3	435	84	0	5	62.14	3
J.L. Langer	4	7	1	345	133	1	1	57.50	4
M.J. North	8	14	1	562	200*	3	0	43.23	9
R.J. Campbell	8	14	1	548	121	1	4	42.15	30
A.C. Gilchrist	2	3	0	124	98	0	1	41.33	7
M.E.K. Hussey	10	18	1	600	100	1	4	35.29	16
M.W. Goodwin	7	12	0	413	141	1	1	34.42	2
S.M. Katich	10	17	0	585	131	1	3	34.41	6
S.R. Cary	3	4	3	25	10*	0	0	25.00	1
K.M. Harvey	5	8	2	134	59	0	1	22.33	3
M.J. Nicholson	8	13	2	233	59*	0	1	21.18	6
S.W. Meuleman	7	12	0	198	60	0	1	16.50	3
J. Angel	10	15	4	180	61	0	1	16.36	1
B.A. Williams	7	6	0	67	20	0	0	11.17	2
M.W. Clark	5	5	4	11	6	0	0	11.00	2
B.J. Oldroyd	2	4	1	9	7	0	0	3.00	0
G.G. Swan	2	1	0	0	0	0	0	0.00	0

* Denotes not out.

BOWLING

	O	M	R	W	BB	5W/i	Avge
J. Angel	412	124	1074	44	6/52	1	24.41
B.A. Williams	279	72	906	32	4/34	0	28.31
M.J. Nicholson	279.1	57	868	28	4/58	0	31.00
G.B. Hogg	148	36	435	14	3/95	0	31.07
K.M. Harvey	117.4	31	338	9	4/43	0	37.56
S.M. Katich	43.3	4	199	5	2/51	0	39.80
M.W. Clark	128	45	324	7	3/49	0	46.29
M.J. North	81	17	252	3	1/11	0	84.00
S.R. Cary	106	27	280	3	1/34	0	93.33
G.G. Swan	53	9	219	2	2/60	0	109.50
B.J. Oldroyd	59	17	141	1	1/25	0	141.00
S.W. Meuleman	1	0	1	0	–	0	–
M.E.K. Hussey	3	1	6	0	–	0	–

At Brisbane Cricket Ground, Brisbane, October 17, 18, 19, 20, 2001. WESTERN AUSTRALIA lost to QUEENSLAND by six wickets.

WESTERN AUSTRALIA v TASMANIA

At WACA Ground, Perth, October 26, 27, 28, 29, 2001. Drawn. Toss: Western Australia. Western Australia 2 pts.

With Justin Langer, Damien Martyn and Murray Goodwin all scoring centuries, Western Australia amassed their highest total in 43 Sheffield Shield/Pura Cup matches between the two states. Tasmania, however, defied the home side's attack to hold out for a draw in a contest in which 1,168 runs were scored and only 24 wickets fell. Adam Gilchrist's decision to send the opposition in to bat was well and truly vindicated when Tasmania were struggling at five for 108, with Ricky Ponting out for a whirlwind 58 (68 minutes, 48 balls, nine fours and two hooked sixes off Brad Williams). At this point, the tail wagged consistently to treble the score and secure a competitive total for Tasmania. Langer's painstaking innings (322 minutes, 247 balls, 19 fours) laid the foundation for his side's massive total. Martyn played a majestic innings (320 minutes, 250 balls, 23 fours, one six) as he hit his tenth first-class century against Tasmania. He and the aggressive Goodwin (277 minutes, 217 balls, 19 fours, two sixes) added 321, a Western Australian record for the fourth wicket and their third-highest partnership for any wicket. Despite his unflattering figures Shane Watson earned praise for his express pace from Langer. Watson's victim was Goodwin, bowled when attempting a big hit after he had moved from 95 to 141 in the space of 18 deliveries. After a long vigil by Jamie Cox (241 minutes, 177 balls, 11 fours), the resolve of the Tasmanian tail thwarted the Western Australians for a second time on a final day when 224 runs were squeezed from 96 overs.

Close of play: First day, Tasmania (1) 8-316 (Wright 41, Saker 17); Second day, Western Australia (1) 2-226 (Katich 75, Martyn 4); Third day, Tasmania (2) 0-13 (Hills 5, Cox 8).

Man of the Match: D.R. Martyn. *Attendance:* 5,008.

Tasmania

D.F. Hills c Martyn b Williams	4	– c Martyn b Angel	6
J. Cox c Gilchrist b Swan	7	– c Gilchrist b Williams	63
*R.T. Ponting c Martyn b Angel	58	– run out (Williams)	29
S.R. Watson c Martyn b Swan	56	– lbw b Cary	30
M.G. Dighton c Gilchrist b Williams	2	– lbw b Angel	0
D.J. Marsh c Gilchrist b Angel	2	– c Martyn b Angel	47
S. Young lbw b Williams	67	– b Williams	16
†S.G. Clingeleffer c Martyn b Angel	47	– not out	8
D.G. Wright b Williams	51	– not out	14
D.J. Saker c Gilchrist b Angel	28		
A.G. Downton not out	0		
L-b 9, w 1, n-b 5	15	L-b 8, w 2, n-b 14	24

(105.1 overs, 389 mins) 337
Fall: 9 50 90 99 108 147 245 276 337 337

(106 overs, 414 mins) (7 wkts) 237
Fall: 22 71 139 140 148 209 215

Bowling: *First Innings*—Williams 29–5–104–4; Cary 24–6–69–0; Swan 16–3–60–2; Angel 22.1–6–53–4; North 14–5–42–0. *Second Innings*—Williams 30–13–65–2; Cary 24–13–34–1; Angel 29–12–51–3; Swan 18–5–71–0; Hussey 1–1–0–0; Katich 1–0–3–0; North 3–2–5–0.

Western Australia

J.L. Langer lbw b Saker	133	M.J. North c Clingeleffer b Marsh	1
M.E.K. Hussey c Marsh b Wright	9	J. Angel not out	6
S.M. Katich c Clingeleffer b Saker	79	B 5, l-b 8, w 1, n-b 3	17
D.R. Martyn c Wright b Marsh	189		
M.W. Goodwin b Watson	141	(170 overs, 658 mins) (7 wkts dec) 594
*†A.C. Gilchrist c Young b Ponting	19	Fall: 29 222 233 554 570 576 594

S.R. Cary, G.G. Swan and B.A. Williams did not bat.

Bowling: Wright 35–12–102–1; Saker 28–6–70–2; Watson 35–7–126–1; Downton 22–5–100–0; Marsh 30–4–111–2; Young 16–4–47–0; Ponting 4–0–25–1.

Umpires: D.J. Harper and I.H. Lock.

WESTERN AUSTRALIA v QUEENSLAND

At WACA Ground, Perth, November 8, 9, 10,11, 2001. Drawn. Toss: Queensland. Queensland 2 pts. First-class debut: J.R. Hopes.

Proof that Perth's once-feared lightning-fast pitches had become more friendly to batsmen was provided by tailenders Matthew Nicholson and Jo Angel, who added 110 for the ninth wicket and then struggled for success with the ball as Queensland amassed a big first-innings score. Western Australia were struggling when Ashley Noffke removed Mike Hussey and Simon Katich in his second over, but Marcus North (231 minutes, 191 balls, 17 fours) hit a polished maiden first-class century, followed by the important and batsman-like stand between Nicholson (184 minutes, 150 balls, three fours) and Angel (122 minutes, 112 balls, eight fours). Jimmy Maher and Jerry Cassell (223 minutes, 186 balls, nine fours) got the visitors away to a flying start, and with Maher and Martin Love (183 minutes, 151 balls, eight fours) in command, Queensland were coasting at one for 350 in the 105th over before Love was caught and bowled. The left-handed Maher (447 minutes, 319 balls, 23 fours) was within sight of a double-century when he played well forward and was adjudged leg-before in left-arm wrist-spinner Katich's first over. After gaining first-innings points, Queensland batted on with little initiative or aggression. Queensland captain Stuart Law experimented with innovative field placings when Western Australia batted again, frequently employing no slips, but two or three gullies, a short leg, a short cover and a silly mid-off. However, a result was never a real possibility, and the final day is best forgotten. Maher's six catches set a record for matches between the states.

Close of play: First day, Western Australia (1) 8-305 (Nicholson 6, Angel 0); Second day, Queensland (1) 0-157 (Maher 69, Cassell 80); Third day, Queensland (1) 7-474 (Seccombe 37, Noffke 33).

Man of the Match: J.P. Maher.   *Attendance:* 2,622.

Western Australia

M.E.K. Hussey c Symonds b Noffke	2	– c Maher b Hopes	35
S.W. Meuleman c Perren b Hopes	37	– c Seccombe b Noffke	15
*S.M. Katich c Cassell b Noffke	0	– c Maher b Kasprowicz	38
M.W. Goodwin c Symonds b Johnson	68	– c Symonds b Johnson	16
M.J. North c Seccombe b Noffke	106	– run out (Symonds)	15
†R.J. Campbell c Maher b Johnson	19	– not out	72
K.M. Harvey c Maher b Kasprowicz	31	– c Seccombe b Hopes	4
M.J. Nicholson not out	59	– b Kasprowicz	7
S.R. Cary c Maher b Noffke	6	– (10) not out	7
J. Angel c Seccombe b Noffke	61	– (9) c Seccombe b Kasprowicz	1
B.A. Williams c Maher b Kasprowicz	13		
L-b 14, w 1, n-b 15	30	B 2, l-b 2, n-b 6	10

(138.1 overs, 513 mins)	432	(80 overs, 325 mins) (8 wkts) 220
Fall: 5 5 80 167 197 285 293 303 413 432		Fall: 28 88 92 123 136 148 159 169

Bowling: *First Innings*—Kasprowicz 34.1–8–99–2; Noffke 36–5–103–5; Johnson 19–2–66–2; Hopes 30–9–95–1; Symonds 19–5–55–0. *Second Innings*—Kasprowicz 26–7–77–3; Johnson 13–3–44–1; Noffke 16–4–36–1; Hopes 22–7–50–2; Symonds 2–1–5–0; Cassell 1–0–4–0.

Queensland

J.P. Maher lbw b Katich	174	A.A. Noffke c Campbell b Nicholson	34
J.L. Cassell c Nicholson b Williams	86	M.S. Kasprowicz c Angel b Nicholson	0
M.L. Love c and b Cary	91	M.G. Johnson not out	12
C.T. Perren lbw b Nicholson	11		
A. Symonds c Nicholson b Williams	1	B 2, l-b 10, w 3, n-b 8	23
*S.G. Law b Williams	4		
†W.A. Seccombe c Campbell b Nicholson	40	(153.1 overs, 603 mins)	490
J.R. Hopes c Meuleman b Angel	14	Fall: 171 350 374 377 382 392 410 475 475 490

Bowling: Williams 29–5–103–3; Angel 30–7–108–1; Nicholson 33.1–6–97–4; Cary 22–5–60–1; Harvey 20–7–55–0; North 15–4–34–0; Katich 4–0–21–1.

Umpires: A.R. Craig and I.H. Lock.

At Adelaide Oval, Adelaide, November 25, 26, 27, 28, 2001. WESTERN AUSTRALIA defeated SOUTH AUSTRALIA by 73 runs.

At Sydney Cricket Ground, Sydney, December 14, 15, 16, 17, 2001. WESTERN AUSTRALIA drew with NEW SOUTH WALES.

WESTERN AUSTRALIA v VICTORIA

At WACA Ground, Perth, January 18, 19, 20, 21, 2002. Western Australia won by ten wickets. Toss: Victoria. Western Australia 6 pts. First-class debut: M.W. Clark.

A nine-wicket haul by Jo Angel was the highlight of Western Australia's easy victory in the 50th Sheffield Shield/Pura Cup match between the sides in Perth. Surprisingly, Victoria omitted experienced swing bowler Damien Fleming, who had taken 35 wickets at 23.71 against Western Australia at the WACA Ground. Debutant Michael Clark dismissed Jason Arnberger with his 11th delivery when the right-hander drove hard and edged a catch behind. Michael Klinger (189 minutes, 180 balls, five fours, one six) and Jon Moss (230 minutes, 160 balls, nine fours) saved Victoria from embarrassment in the first innings. Western Australia had middle-order batsmen Ryan Campbell (101 minutes, 73 balls, nine fours) and Brad Hogg (181 minutes, 135 balls, 11 fours) to thank for their substantial first-innings lead and for adding some vigour to an otherwise slow match. Kade Harvey (207 minutes, 155 balls, six fours, one six) played a restrained but important hand later in the innings. A sore left thigh forced Campbell to relinquish the wicket-keeping gloves early in Victoria's second innings but Mike Hussey relished his opportunity behind the stumps and snapped up four catches. The Victorian batting was lamentably inept, only Matthew Elliott (160 minutes, 115 balls, nine fours) and, for a second time, Moss (183 minutes, 139 balls, eight fours) looking convincing. Angel's 6/52 were his best innings figures in his 104 first-class matches.

Close of play: First day, Victoria (1) 6-226 (Moss 60, Reiffel 0); Second day, Western Australia (1) 6-241 (Hogg 38, Harvey 10); Third day, Victoria (2) 5-135 (Moss 30, Berry 24).

Man of the Match: J. Angel.   *Attendance:* 3,672.

Victoria

M.T.G. Elliott c Langer b Clark	30	– (2) c Hussey b Clark	51
J.L. Arnberger c Campbell b Clark	2	– (1) c Campbell b Angel	16
M.P. Mott c Campbell b Harvey	15	– c Katich b Nicholson	5
B.J. Hodge lbw b Hogg	32	– c Hussey b Nicholson	0
M. Klinger c Hussey b Harvey	58	– lbw b Angel	6
J. Moss c Hussey b Clark	70	– b Angel	51
†D.S. Berry c Katich b Nicholson	20	– c Nicholson b Angel	25
*P.R. Reiffel c Hussey b Angel	5	– c Hussey b Angel	0
C.R. Miller c Nicholson b Angel	17	– (10) c Hussey b Nicholson	8
M.L. Lewis c Campbell b Angel	8	– c Langer b Angel	9
M.W.H. Inness not out	1	– not out	8
B 5, l-b 4, w 1, n-b 4	14	B 1, l-b 3, w 1, n-b 1	6

(110.3 overs, 432 mins)   272   (73.3 overs, 300 mins)   185
Fall: 7 42 60 105 169 222 233 257   Fall: 26 41 52 96 137 137 163
     263 272   167 185

Bowling: *First Innings*—Angel 27.3–9–58–3; Clark 19–7–49–3; Nicholson 25–4–68–1; Harvey 20–5–53–2; Hogg 19–7–35–1. *Second Innings*—Angel 25.3–10–52–6; Clark 19–8–36–1; Nicholson 16–2–56–3; Hogg 6–2–14–0; Harvey 7–3–23–0.

Western Australia

M.E.K. Hussey b Lewis	18	– (2) not out	22
*J.L. Langer b Miller	34	– (1) not out	44
S.M. Katich c Berry b Inness	34		
M.W. Goodwin lbw b Moss	26		
S.W. Meuleman c Berry b Lewis	4		
†R.J. Campbell c Berry b Reiffel	61		
G.B. Hogg lbw b Miller	84		
K.M. Harvey c Arnberger b Reiffel	59		
M.J. Nicholson b Reiffel	14		
J. Angel c Berry b Inness	26		
M.W. Clark not out	2		
B 4, l-b 12, w 1, n-b 7	24	L-b 2, n-b 4	6

(123.2 overs, 519 mins)   386   (22.3 overs, 86 mins)   (0 wkt)   72
Fall: 55 64 119 123 157 214 313 342 366 386   Fall:

Bowling: *First Innings*—Reiffel 26–1–78–3; Inness 22.2–5–68–2; Miller 28–8–98–2; Lewis 23–6–58–2; Moss 5–1–20–1; Hodge 19–5–48–0. *Second Innings*—Lewis 9–1–23–0; Inness 7–5–16–0; Miller 4–1–19–0; Reiffel 1–0–9–0; Hodge 1.3–0–3–0.

Umpires: I.H. Lock and A.J. Craig.

At Bellerive Oval, Hobart, January 25,26,27, 2002. WESTERN AUSTRALIA lost to TASMANIA by an innings and 76 runs.

WESTERN AUSTRALIA v NEW SOUTH WALES

At WACA Ground, Perth, February 15, 16, 17,18, 2002. Drawn. Toss: New South Wales. Western Australia 2 pts. First-class debut: G.M. Lambert.

Shane Lee sent the home side in on a well-grassed pitch, but Western Australia amassed 500 against an array of nine bowlers. Among other selection surprises, Western Australia had dropped fast bowler Matthew Nicholson and New South Wales had not found room for Corey Richards, who had scored 151 against Western Australia in an ING Cup match earlier in the week. After good early efforts by Mike Hussey (215 minutes, 161 balls, 13 fours), Scott Meuleman and Simon Katich, Ryan Campbell (164 minutes, 133 balls, 17 fours), Chris Rogers (273 minutes, 201 balls, 12 fours) and Brad Hogg (107 minutes, 93 balls, nine fours) lifted the tempo and put the game out of New

South Wales' reach. A top-edged pull by the left-handed Rogers was caught at deep fine leg to deprive him of his maiden first-class century. Opening the batting on debut, Grant Lambert was out hit wicket when he went back and forced the ball to backward square leg before his back foot hit the stumps. Katich did not enforce the follow-on and eventually set New South Wales a victory target of 406 off a minimum of 106 overs. After a steady third-wicket partnership of 154 between Michael Bevan (206 minutes, 141 balls, nine fours, one six) and the accomplished Michael Clarke (199 minutes, 166 balls, 14 fours), wickets tumbled to leave New South Wales eight for 286 in the 89th over. But the defiant batting of Mark Higgs, Nathan Bracken and Stuart Clark foiled Western Australia's hopes of victory.

Close of play: First day, Western Australia (1) 4-333 (Campbell 108, Rogers 31); Second day, New South Wales (1) 3-121 (Bevan 49, Rummans 26); Third day, New South Wales (2) 0-26 (Lambert 8, Haddin 14).

Man of the Match: R.J. Campbell.　　*Attendance:* 4,386.

Western Australia

M.E.K. Hussey c and b Higgs	86	– (2) c Lee b Nash	60
S.W. Meuleman lbw b Lambert	35	– (1) c Haddin b Clark	0
*S.M. Katich c Haddin b Nash	52	– c Haddin b Clark	23
M.J. North run out (Clarke)	7	– (5) b Nash	9
†R.J. Campbell c Bracken b Higgs	121	– (4) b Nash	11
C.J.L. Rogers c Bevan b Clark	96	– c Clarke b Higgs	18
G.B. Hogg c (sub) Turner b Clark	62	– not out	17
K.M. Harvey not out	14	– not out	13
J. Angel not out	4		
B 8, l-b 15	23	L-b 3, w 1, n-b 3	7

(139.1 overs, 551 mins)　　　　(7 wkts dec) 500　　　(33.4 overs, 149 mins) (6 wkts dec) 158
Fall: 61 162 169 196 350 467 488　　　Fall: 0 49 79 103 119 142

B.A. Williams and M.W. Clark did not bat.

Bowling: *First Innings*—Clark 39.1–14–90–2; Bracken 28–5–68–0; Nash 17–4–66–1; Lambert 20–2–79–1; Van Deinsen 5.3–1–31–0; Higgs 24–2–99–2; Lee 0.3–0–5–0; Bevan 4–0–33–0; Rummans 1–0–6–0. *Second Innings*—Clark 10–2–39–2; Bracken 11–3–43–0; Nash 11–1–59–3; Higgs 1.4–0–14–1.

New South Wales

G.M. Lambert hit wicket b Williams	29	– c Clark b Williams	11
†B.J. Haddin c Campbell b Angel	13	– c Harvey b Angel	41
M.G. Bevan c Clark b Williams	66	– c Hogg b North	72
M.J. Clarke c Campbell b Angel	1	– lbw b Harvey	81
G.C. Rummans c Campbell b Angel	55	– (7) c Rogers b Angel	12
*S. Lee c Katich b Clark	18	– c Campbell b Williams	28
M.A. Higgs c Hussey b Williams	23	– (8) not out	18
B.P. Van Deinsen c Campbell b Angel	27	– (5) lbw b Harvey	0
D.A. Nash run out (Rogers/Angel)	9	– c Hussey b Williams	24
N.W. Bracken c and b Williams	0	– lbw b Hogg	8
S.R. Clark not out	6	– not out	0
B 1, l-b 5	6	B 12, l-b 1, n-b 3	16

(98 overs, 377 mins)　　　　253　　　(106 overs, 420 mins)　　(9 wkts) 311
Fall: 20 58 69 139 169 205 217　　　Fall: 46 56 210 215 216 255
　245 246 253　　　　　255 286 302

Bowling: *First Innings*—Williams 27–7–89–4; Angel 30–8–91–4; Clark 22–14–33–1; Harvey 12–6–20–0; Hogg 5–1–8–0; North 2–0–6–0. *Second Innings*—Williams 26–7–78–3; Angel 28–9–74–2; Clark 17–7–35–0; Harvey 17–4–36–2; Hogg 11–2–45–1; North 7–0–30–1.

Umpires: I.H. Lock and B. Bennett.
TV Umpire: A.R. Craig.

At Melbourne Cricket Ground, Melbourne, February 28, March 1, 2, 3, 2002. WESTERN AUSTRALIA defeated VICTORIA by 37 runs.

WESTERN AUSTRALIA v SOUTH AUSTRALIA

At WACA Ground, Perth, March 13, 14, 15, 16, 2002. Drawn. Toss: South Australia. Western Australia 2 pts.

Each side had a chance to reach the Pura Cup final until Tasmania's victory in Hobart late on the third day took much of the life out of this match. The South Australian selectors dropped Graham Manou, Mark Harrity, Peter McIntyre and Ben Higgins (bringing in Paul Wilson, Shane Deitz, Ryan Harris and Nathan Adcock) and Western Australia replaced Scott Meuleman with Murray Goodwin. Six of the eight Western Australians to bat in the first innings, including century-makers Marcus North (284 minutes, 227 balls, 18 fours) and Chris Rogers (223 minutes, 167 balls, 18 fours), were left-handers. The highlight of South Australia's reply was Deitz's solid knock (214 minutes, 157 balls, 10 fours). Opener David Fitzgerald retired hurt on four after he had been struck by a fierce Brad Williams lifter and received a fractured left cheekbone. He returned bravely late in the innings and scored another 22 runs. In the second innings Rogers became the fifth Western Australian to score a century in each innings (186 minutes, 148 balls, 14 fours) and he and Brad Hogg put on 174 in 43 overs before Katich declared to leave South Australia a victory target of 322. Greg Blewett batted through to the end (315 minutes, 231 balls, 16 fours) to thwart the home side. Jo Angel's seven wickets took his tally for Western Australia in Sheffield Shield/Pura Cup matches to 387, overtaking the record of Terry Alderman (384).

Close of play: First day, Western Australia (1) 4-272 (North 193, Rogers 52); Second day, South Australia (1) 5-229 (Deitz 53, Smith 2); Third day, Western Australia (2) 5-220 (Rogers 83, Hogg 43).

Man of the Match: C. J. L. Rogers.   *Attendance:* 3,664.

Western Australia

M. E. K. Hussey c Johnson b Rofe	39	– (2) c Adcock b Wilson	16
M. W. Goodwin c Young b Rofe	3	– (1) lbw b Smith	25
*S. M. Katich lbw b Smith	32	– c Deitz b Smith	5
M. J. North c Young b Smith	111	– c Deitz b Smith	10
†R. J. Campbell lbw b Wilson	34	– lbw b Smith	30
C. J. L. Rogers not out	101	– not out	102
G. B. Hogg c Deitz b Wilson	4	– not out	77
M. J. Nicholson c Smith b Johnson	10		
J. Angel not out	0		
B 4, l-b 7, n-b 1	12	L-b 7, w 1, n-b 3	11

(116.1 overs, 462 mins)   (7 wkts dec) 346   (78.5 overs, 300 mins) (5 wkts dec) 276
Fall: 8 61 107 155 299 306 343   Fall: 41 45 50 73 102

B. A. Williams and M. W. Clark did not bat.

Bowling: *First Innings*—Wilson 32–5–98–2; Rofe 24.1–9–62–2; Smith 25–6–82–2; R. J. Harris 18–4–53–0; Young 11–1–28–0; Johnson 6–2–12–1. *Second Innings*—Wilson 19–4–53–1; R. J. Harris 8–4–20–0; Rofe 11–5–40–0; Smith 22–4–69–4; Johnson 2–0–23–0; Adcock 8–0–22–0; Young 8.5–0–42–0.

South Australia

D.A. Fitzgerald c Campbell b Nicholson	26	– (7) c Katich b Hogg 20
B.A. Johnson b Angel	2	– (1) b Williams 8
*G.S. Blewett lbw b Angel	64	– not out 112
C.J. Davies c North b Hogg	42	– c Goodwin b Angel 24
N.T. Adcock c Campbell b Nicholson	18	– c Campbell b Nicholson 0
B.E. Young c Hussey b North	36	– c Hussey b Hogg 17
†S.A. Deitz c Hussey b Hogg	86	– (2) c Hogg b Angel 43
M.J. Smith c Campbell b Williams	10	– c Nicholson b Angel 46
R.J. Harris lbw b Williams	0	– c North b Angel 0
P. Wilson c North b Angel	2	– not out 0
P.C. Rofe not out	1	
B 4, l-b 5, w 1, n-b 4	14	B 2, l-b 3, w 1, n-b 1 7

(98.5 overs, 408 mins)	301	(83 overs, 329 mins) (8 wkts) 277

Fall: 4 85 127 139 214 255 255 262 293 301   Fall: 8 64 100 100 131 173 269 269

Bowling: *First Innings*—Williams 18–6–67–2; Angel 28–10–53–3; Nicholson 23.5–6–78–2; Clark 13–1–46–0; Hogg 13–2–37–2; North 3–0–11–1. *Second Innings*—Williams 18–1–83–1; Angel 22–7–49–4; Nicholson 13–2–39–1; Hogg 21–6–68–2; Clark 6–1–13–0; Katich 3–0–20–0.

Umpires: A.R. Craig and I.H. Lock.

AUSTRALIAN DOMESTIC FIRST-CLASS RESULTS TABLE

Opponent	M	W	L	D	T
New South Wales	102	30	40	32	0
South Australia	104	44	28	32	0
Queensland	104	35	24	45	0
Victoria	101	28	31	42	0
Tasmania	46	21	6	19	0
Total	457	158	129	170	0

AUSTRALIAN DOMESTIC FIRST-CLASS RECORDS

Highest score for:	355*	G.R. Marsh v South Australia at Perth	1989-90
Highest score against:	356	B.A. Richards (South Australia) at Perth	1970-71
Best bowling for:	10/44	I.J. Brayshaw v Victoria at Perth	1967-68
Best bowling against:	8/66	J.D. Higgs (Victoria) at Melbourne	1974-75
Highest total for:	654	v Victoria at Perth	1986-87
Highest total against:	4-601 dec	by New South Wales at Perth	1990-91
Lowest total for:	41	v South Australia at Adelaide	1989-90
Lowest total against:	52	by Queensland at Perth	1982-83

* *Denotes not out.*

MOST RUNS

	M	I	NO	R	HS	100s	50s	Avge
T.M. Moody	132	228	22	8,853	272	20	46	42.98
M.R.J. Veletta	114	198	20	7,306	262	18	40	41.04
G.R. Marsh	100	175	12	7,009	355*	21	28	43.00
G.M. Wood	109	174	25	6,904	186*	20	32	46.34
R.J. Inverarity	108	188	18	6,888	187	20	29	40.52
D.R. Martyn	92	162	16	6,639	203*	20	32	45.47
J.L. Langer	71	130	11	6,438	274*	20	22	54.10
M.E.K. Hussey	75	137	7	5,371	187	12	24	41.31
B.K. Shepherd	75	127	13	4,934	219	11	26	43.28
R.W. Marsh	86	139	9	4,412	168*	6	23	33.94

* *Denotes not out.*

HIGHEST PARTNERSHIP FOR EACH WICKET

431	for 1st	M.R.J. Veletta and G.R. Marsh v South Australia at Perth	1989-90
254	for 2nd	G.R. Marsh and M.R.J. Veletta v Queensland at Brisbane	1985-86
330	for 3rd	G.M. Wood and G.R. Marsh v New South Wales at Sydney	1983-84
321	for 4th	D.R. Martyn and M.W. Goodwin v Tasmania at Perth	2001-02
301*	for 5th	R.B. Simpson and K.D. Meuleman v New South Wales at Perth	1959-60
244	for 6th	J.T. Irvine and R. Edwards v New South Wales at Sydney	1968-69
204	for 7th	G. Shipperd and T.J. Zoehrer v New South Wales at Perth	1982-83
242*	for 8th	T.J. Zoehrer and K.H. MacLeay v New South Wales at Perth	1990-91
168*	for 9th	K.H. MacLeay and V.J. Marks v New South Wales at Perth	1986-87
91	for 10th	I.J. Brayshaw and J.B. Gannon v Queensland at Brisbane	1969-70

* Denotes unbroken partnership.

MOST WICKETS

	M	Balls	Mdns	R	W	BB	5W/i	10W/m	Avge
J. Angel	94	20,176	942	9,343	387	6/52	12	0	24.14
T.M. Alderman	97	20,482	778	9,299	384	7/28	17	3	24.22
D.K. Lillee	70	16,617	439	7,544	323	7/36	18	4	23.36
G.A.R. Lock	66	20,107	544	7,210	302	7/53	16	2	23.87
B.P. Julian	87	16,143	612	8,573	292	7/39	15	2	29.36
G.D. McKenzie	73	16,566	287	7,322	232	6/100	7	0	31.56
K.H. MacLeay	90	17,761	836	7,033	229	6/93	5	0	30.71
T.M. Moody	132	14,431	673	6,297	220	7/38	5	1	28.62
C.D. Matthews	44	9,741	342	4,678	188	8/101	11	0	24.88
B.A. Reid	49	11,520	496	4,980	181	6/54	7	1	27.51

MOST DISMISSALS

	M	Ct	St	Total
T.J. Zoehrer	107	331	28	359
R.W. Marsh	81	311	33	344
A.C. Gilchrist	50	243	8	251
B.L. Buggins	57	131	18	149
G.C. Becker	39	90	17	107

MOST CATCHES

R.J. Inverarity	138 in 108 matches	D.R. Martyn	87 in 92 matches
M.R.J. Veletta	138 in 114 matches	G.A.R. Lock	80 in 66 matches
T.M. Moody	114 in 132 matches	T.M. Alderman	80 in 97 matches
I.J. Brayshaw	95 in 91 matches	G.M. Wood	77 in 109 matches

MOST APPEARANCES

132	T.M. Moody	1985-86 – 2000-01	100	G.R. Marsh	1977-78 – 1993-94
114	M.R.J. Veletta	1983-84 – 1994-95	97	T.M. Alderman	1974-75 – 1992-93
109	G.M. Wood	1977-78 – 1991-92	94	J. Angel	1991-92 – 2001-02
108	R.J. Inverarity	1962-63 – 1978-79	92	D.R. Martyn	1990-91 – 2001-02
107	T.J. Zoehrer	1980-81 – 1993-94	91	I.J. Brayshaw	1960-61 – 1977-78

ING CUP, 2001-02

By KEN PIESSE

By winning back-to-back titles, New South Wales cemented their standing as Australia's premier limited-overs combination. Even without many leading players who were on international duty, New South Wales won seven of their ten qualifying games and were only a bonus point short of leading qualifier Queensland, who also won seven matches. Defending a modest score of just 204 in the final at the Gabba, New South Wales dismissed Queensland for 185 in a low-scoring final dominated by the medium-pacers and featuring brilliant fielding from both sides. Taking 4/47 from his ten overs in the final, Queensland off-spinner Nathan Hauritz capped his first full season of interstate cricket with selection in Australia's limited-overs squad which later toured South Africa.

The gifted Darren Lehmann clinched his second consecutive limited-overs Player of the Season award, and the third of his career, polling 22 votes to win on a countback from South Australian team-mate Greg Blewett. Queensland's polished number three Martin Love was third and his team-mate Andrew Symonds fourth. Lehmann scored 374 runs in eight games at a strike-rate of 82. His highest score was 101 from 95 balls against New South Wales at Coffs Harbour, a whirlwind innings which showed his mastery of placement and included 35 singles.

The season's highest run-maker, Western Australia's Mike Hussey (440 runs) was also one of the most popular players, especially after winning a $200,000 bonus for hitting an ING Cup bonus board on the full in the match against New South Wales at the WACA. Normally any bonus money is divided equally among squad members on a pro-rata games-played basis, but the Western Australian players had decided that if a player was able to hit the sign, he should take 40 per cent of the booty; Hussey's share was therefore a cool $80,000. Earlier, in the first game of the season at North Sydney, Victoria's Shane Warne, swinging into a full toss from Stuart MacGill, had just missed a bonus board at square leg. The fastest half-century of the season was shared between Tasmania's Michael Di Venuto and Symonds, who each reached fifty from just 33 balls. Symonds also had the best strike-rate of any of the specialist batsmen, his 300 runs coming at 110 per 100 balls.

For the second consecutive season, MacGill took most wickets in the competition – 21 at an imposing strike-rate of one every three overs. While he also conceded more than a run per ball, he twice took five wickets in an innings, a rare feat at limited-overs level, to keep his name before the national selectors. His team-mate Nathan Bracken claimed a hat-trick in heat-wave conditions against the Victorians in Melbourne. He collected 18 wickets, as did Western Australia's Brad Williams and Hauritz. Williams averaged a wicket every four overs and was included in Australia's limited-overs team for the first time. The most economical of the front-line bowlers was Victoria's Ian Harvey, who continued to vary his deliveries expertly, his slower top-spinner complementing his off-cutter and faster seam-up deliveries. With an economy rate of 3.08 and the competition's best bowling average of 14.50, together with his aggressive batting, he was also a front-line choice for Australia.

The bonus point system, which proved so controversial at VB Series level, was used again and saw all teams, mindful of overall run-rates, playing positively and enhancing the entertainment of the spectators.

The season's record-breaking game was at Bankstown in October. New South Wales scored a record total of four for 397, Brad Haddin racing to his century from 74 balls, equalling the record of Queensland's Stuart Law. In reply, Tasmania scored seven for 327, the first time a side batting second had scored 300. The most gripping game was between South Australia and Western Australia in Adelaide. Set 236 to win, Western Australia clinched the match with just two balls to spare when their No. 11, Brad Williams, belted a six.

2001-02 POINTS TABLE

	Played	Won	Lost	No Result	Bonus Points	Points	Net Run-rate
Queensland	10	7	3	0	3	31	0.45
New South Wales	10	7	3	0	2	30	0.16
South Australia	10	6	4	0	3	27	0.16
Western Australia	10	5	5	0	2	22	0.14
Victoria	10	3	6	1	1	15	–0.44
Tasmania	10	1	8	1	1	7	–0.61

Net run-rate was calculated by subtracting runs conceded per over from runs scored per over.

FINAL

QUEENSLAND v NEW SOUTH WALES

At Brisbane Cricket Ground, Brisbane, February 24, 2002. New South Wales won by 19 runs. Toss: Queensland.

A game which never rose to stratospheric heights nevertheless provided a fascinating spectacle. Queensland expectations were buoyant when Stuart Law won the toss and utilised his traditional Gabba pace attack on a pitch which was dry but sufficiently green to promise pace and bounce and offer encouragement to seam bowling. Corey Richards continued his resurgence in batting form and with Brad Haddin as his partner, took the game into the 19th over in a disciplined opening partnership of 82 from 109 balls. This good start was all but forgotten by the time New South Wales had slumped to five for 126 with the departure of Shane Lee. Haddin's 45, with its usual quota of glistening boundaries, ended by Law's superb 25-metre running catch at long-on, became the highest score of the innings. Mark Higgs and Matthew Phelps restored some order with their 35-run stand from 46 balls, and Dominic Thornely batted grittily at No. 9. Queensland's lesser-known bowlers, off-spinner Nathan Hauritz and medium-fast all-rounder James Hopes, who played despite a stress fracture in his foot, provided conspicuous performances, as did Ashley Noffke in his seven testing overs. The fear of failure gnawed at Queensland's batsmen. They lost Jimmy Maher to Haddin's diving leg-side catch from Nathan Bracken in the eighth over, and although Martin Love made the only half-century of the final, the early loss of Law and Andrew Symonds put the Queenslanders in a negative frame of mind from which they never recovered. The floodlights came on in mid-afternoon, and the lights went out for Clinton Perren and Lee Carseldine, both falling victim to Thornely's clever slow-medium deliveries. The crowning moment for New South Wales came when Shawn Bradstreet, whose medium-pacers have been frequently targeted by rivals, claimed 4/6 from 13 balls to end Queensland's innings with seven deliveries remaining.

Man of the Match: D.J. Thornely.   *Attendance:* 12,005.

New South Wales

C.J. Richards c Seccombe b Hopes ... 34	(61)	
†B.J. Haddin c Law b Noffke 45	(50)	
M.G. Bevan c Seccombe b Kasprowicz 8	(21)	
M.J. Clarke c Seccombe b Noffke 7	(9)	
*S. Lee c Law b Hauritz 14	(24)	
M.A. Higgs c and b Hauritz 22	(37)	
M.J. Phelps c Hopes b Hauritz 31	(44)	
S.D. Bradstreet c Perren b Hauritz ... 0	(2)	

D.J. Thornely not out 20	(34)	
D.A. Nash c Hauritz b Hopes 4	(8)	
N.W. Bracken b Hopes 8	(11)	
L-b 7, w 3, n-b 1 11		
	—	
(50 overs, 196 mins)	204	
Fall: 82 82 93 102 126 161 161		
181 189 204		

S.R. Clark did not bat.

Bowling: Kasprowicz 8–1–31–1; Dawes 10–1–42–0; Hopes 9–0–33–3; Noffke 7–1–24–2; Symonds 6–0–20–0; Hauritz 10–0–47–4.

Queensland

J.P. Maher c Haddin b Bracken 10	(23)	
M.L. Love c Haddin b Nash 53	(73)	
*S.G. Law b Thornely 10	(17)	
A. Symonds c Haddin b Clark 8	(18)	
C.T. Perren c Phelps b Thornely 36	(69)	
L.A. Carseldine c Richards b Thornely 29	(43)	
J.R. Hopes c Haddin b Bradstreet 19	(24)	
†W.A. Seccombe c Bracken		
b Bradstreet .. 4	(11)	

N.M. Hauritz c Richards b Bradstreet 3	(6)	
A.A. Noffke b Bradstreet 4	(8)	
M.S. Kasprowicz not out 1	(1)	
B 1, l-b 3, w 4 8		
	—	
(48.5 overs, 201 mins)	185	
Fall: 26 51 72 101 149 157 168		
173 184 185		

J.H. Dawes did not bat.

Bowling: Clark 9–1–27–1; Bracken 9–1–32–1; Thornely 8–0–36–3; Nash 8–1–31–1; Higgs 8–0–32–0; Bradstreet 6.5–0–23–4.

Umpires: D.B. Hair and D.J. Harper.
TV Umpire: P.D. Parker.

STATISTICS, 2001-02

		Batting			Bowling		
	M	Runs	Overs	Run-rate	Runs	Overs	Run-rate
Queensland	10	2,173	461	4.71	2,102	493.3	4.79
New South Wales	10	2,420	488.4	4.95	2,235	467.0	4.79
South Australia	10	2,071	486.3	4.26	2,007	490.4	4.09
Western Australia	10	2,330	498.1	4.68	2,126	468.5	4.53
Victoria	10	1,608	428.5	3.75	1,825	435.3	4.19
Tasmania	10	1,922	436.1	4.41	2,229	443.5	5.02

Note: Preliminary rounds only.

MOST RUNS, 2001-02

	M	I	NO	R	HS	100s	50s	Avge	S-R
M.E.K. Hussey (WAust).	10	10	2	440	103*	1	2	55.00	79.71
G.S. Blewett (SAust)....	10	10	0	436	80	0	4	43.60	75.04
M.T.G. Elliott (Vic).....	10	10	1	431	118*	1	3	47.89	73.42
M.L. Love (Qld)........	11	11	1	423	127*	2	2	42.30	77.90
J.P. Maher (Qld)........	11	11	1	391	71*	0	3	39.100	72.41
D.S. Lehmann (SAust)...	8	8	2	374	101	1	3	62.33	82.02
B.J. Haddin (NSW)	10	10	0	360	120	1	2	36.00	104.96
C.T. Perren (Qld).......	11	11	2	317	96	0	2	35.22	67.88
A. Symonds (Qld).......	10	10	0	300	91	0	2	30.00	110.29
S.M. Katich (WAust)....	10	10	0	293	118	1	1	29.30	61.43

Denotes not out.

MOST WICKETS, 2001-02

	M	O	Mdns	R	W	BB	5W/i	Avge
S.C.G. MacGill (NSW)	8	61.3	2	381	21	5/50	2	18.14
B.A. Williams (WAust)	8	69.2	4	295	18	4/44	0	16.39
N.W. Bracken (NSW)	9	81	5	394	18	5/38	1	21.89
N.M. Hauritz (Qld)	11	91.5	1	381	18	4/47	0	21.17
M.A. Harrity (SAust)	10	77.5	7	336	17	3/15	0	19.76
J.R. Hopes (Qld)	11	90	8	347	16	3/30	0	21.69
B.E. Young (SAust)	9	64.2	0	292	15	4/55	0	19.47
A.A. Noffke (Qld)	9	84.5	7	378	15	4/32	0	25.20
J. Angel (WAust)	9	80.3	5	333	14	5/16	1	23.79
D.G. Wright (Tas)	10	68	11	383	13	4/23	0	29.46
M.L. Lewis (Vic)	10	73	9	320	13	4/41	0	24.62

AUSTRALIAN DOMESTIC LIMITED-OVERS WINNERS

Australasian (V & G) Knock-Out Competition

Season	Winner	Runner-up	Season	Winner	Runner-up
1969-70	New Zealanders	Victoria	1970-71	Western Australia	Queensland

Australasian (Coca-Cola) Knock-Out Competition

1971-72	Victoria	South Australia	1972-73	New Zealanders	Queensland

Gillette Cup

1973-74	Western Australia	New Zealanders	1976-77	Western Australia	Victoria
1974-75	New Zealanders	Western Australia	1977-78	Western Australia	Tasmania
1975-76	Queensland	Western Australia	1978-79	Tasmania	Western Australia

McDonald's Cup

1979-80	Victoria	New South Wales	1984-85	New South Wales	South Australia
1980-81	Queensland	Western Australia	1985-86	Western Australia	Victoria
1981-82	Queensland	New South Wales	1986-87	South Australia	Tasmania
1982-83	Western Australia	New South Wales	1987-88	New South Wales	South Australia
1983-84	South Australia	Western Australia			

FAI Insurance Cup

1988-89	Queensland	Victoria	1990-91	Western Australia	New South Wales
1989-90	Western Australia	South Australia	1991-92	New South Wales	Western Australia

Mercantile Mutual Cup

1992-93	New South Wales	Victoria	1997-98	Queensland	New South Wales
1993-94	New South Wales	Western Australia	1998-99	Victoria	New South Wales
1994-95	Victoria	South Australia	1999-00	Western Australia	Queensland
1995-96	Queensland	Western Australia	2000-01	New South Wales	Western Australia
1996-97	Western Australia	Queensland			

ING Cup

2001-02	New South Wales	Queensland

MATCH RESULTS, 1969-70 TO 2001-02

	M	W	L	NR	T	Won Batting First	Won Batting Second
Australian Capital Territory .	18	3	15	0	0	16.67%	16.67%
New South Wales	130	77	51	1	1	53.25%	70.59%
New Zealanders	10	7	3	0	0	60.00%	80.00%
Queensland	128	72	52	4	0	53.85%	62.71%
South Australia	123	52	70	0	1	43.10%	42.19%
Tasmania	110	29	79	2	0	26.09%	27.42%
Victoria	126	53	67	5	1	40.28%	50.00%
Western Australia	146	93	48	4	1	66.67%	65.48%
Total	396					47.73%	52.40%

RESULTS AT EACH VENUE

	First Game	M	NR	T	Won Batting First	Won Batting Second
Melbourne (MCG)	1969-70	51	1	0	44.00%	56.00%
Perth	1969-70	79	3	1	44.00%	56.00%
Sydney	1969-70	45	1	0	38.64%	61.36%
Adelaide (Adelaide Oval) ..	1970-71	64	0	1	47.62%	52.38%
Brisbane (Gabba)	1970-71	65	2	0	41.27%	58.73%
Launceston	1970-71	6	0	0	66.67%	33.33%
Hobart (TCA)	1973-74	12	0	0	66.67%	33.33%
Melbourne (Waverley)	1979-80	1	0	0	100.00%	–
Melbourne (St Kilda)	1981-82	1	0	0	–	100.00%
Devonport	1984-85	4	0	0	75.00%	25.00%
Adelaide (Football Park) ...	1986-87	2	0	0	50.00%	50.00%
Hobart (Bellerive)	1988-89	27	1	0	57.69%	42.31%
North Sydney	1989-90	15	0	0	66.67%	33.33%
Melbourne (Carlton)	1992-93	2	0	0	50.00%	50.00%
Canberra	1997-98	10	0	0	70.00%	30.00%
Bendigo	1997-98	1	0	0	100.00%	–
Melbourne (Richmond)	1999-00	5	0	0	20.00%	80.00%
Brisbane (Albion)	1999-00	2	0	0	50.00%	50.00%
Sydney (Bankstown)	2000-01	3	0	0	66.67%	33.33%
Coffs Harbour	2001-02	1	0	0	100.00%	–

LAST TEN YEARS' PLACINGS

	92-93	93-94	94-95	95-96	96-97	97-98	98-99	99-00	00-01	01-02
Australia Capital Territory	–	–	–	–	–	6	6	6	–	–
New South Wales .	1	1	6	3	3	2	2	3	1	1
Queensland	4	4	4	1	2	1	3	2	4	2
South Australia ...	6	3	2	4	6	4	4	4	3	3
Tasmania	5	6	5	5	5	5	7	6	5	6
Victoria	2	5	1	6	4	7	1	5	6	5
Western Australia .	3	2	3	2	1	3	5	1	2	4

HIGHEST INNINGS SCORES

167	M. W. Goodwin	Western Australia v New South Wales at Perth	2000-01
164	R. B. McCosker	New South Wales v South Australia at Sydney	1981-82
159	S. G. Law	Queensland v Tasmania at Brisbane (Gabba)	1993-94
152*	M. L. Hayden	Queensland v Victoria at Melbourne (MCG)	1998-99
151	C. J. Richards	New South Wales v Western Australia at Perth	2001-02
146	J. L. Langer	Western Australia v South Australia at Perth	1999-00
142*	D. S. Lehmann	South Australia v Tasmania at Adelaide	1994-95
140*	P. C. Nobes	South Australia v Western Australia at Perth	1994-95
140	D. R. Martyn	Western Australia v Tasmania at Hobart (Bellerive)	1997-98
139*	D. M. Jones	Victoria v New South Wales at Sydney	1986-87

* Denotes not out.

FASTEST HALF-CENTURIES

Balls

21	D. W. Hookes	South Australia v Western Australia at Perth	1990-91
24	D. A. Nash	New South Wales v South Australia at North Sydney ..	2000-01
27	I. J. Harvey	Victoria v Tasmania at Hobart (Bellerive)	1998-99
28	D. S. Berry	Victoria v New South Wales at North Sydney	1997-98
30	M. G. Bevan	New South Wales v Victoria at Sydney	1992-93
31	R. W. Marsh	Western Australia v South Australia at Adelaide	1983-84
31	B. J. Hodge	Victoria v Tasmania at Hobart (Bellerive)	1998-99
31	M. A. Higgs	New South Wales v Queensland at Sydney	2001-02
32	S. G. Law	Queensland v Tasmania at Brisbane (Gabba)	1993-94
32	R. J. Campbell	Western Australia v Victoria at Perth	1996-97

FASTEST CENTURIES

Balls

74	S. G. Law	Queensland v Tasmania at Brisbane (Gabba)	1998-99
74	B. J. Haddin	New South Wales v Tasmania at Bankstown	2001-02
82	R. J. Campbell	Western Australia v Queensland at Perth	1999-00
83	D. S. Lehmann	South Australia v Victoria at Adelaide	2000-01
86	D. J. Marsh	Tasmania v New South Wales at Bankstown	2001-02
88	J. P. Maher	Queensland v Western Australia at Perth	1999-00
90	S. Lee	New South Wales v Queensland at Brisbane	1999-00
90	M. L. Hayden	Queensland v South Australia at Adelaide	1999-00
90	M. W. Goodwin	Western Australia v New South Wales at Perth	2000-01
90	R. T. Ponting	Tasmania v Western Australia at Perth	2001-02

MOST RUNS

	M	I	NO	R	HS	100s	Avge	S-R
D. S. Lehmann (SAust/Vic)	67	66	9	2,623	142*	6	46.02	85.89
J. P. Maher (Qld).........	61	61	9	2,426	128	4	46.65	75.88
M. L. Hayden (Qld)	51	51	9	2,231	152*	8	53.12	72.18
M. G. Bevan (SAust/NSW)	54	54	19	2,146	135*	1	61.31	74.26
D. M. Jones (Vic)	55	52	10	2,122	139*	4	50.52	74.07
J. L. Langer (WAust)	61	59	5	2,063	146	2	38.20	65.97
G. S. Blewett (SAust)	60	58	5	2,033	101*	1	38.36	65.69
T. M. Moody (WAust)	75	71	12	2,004	102*	2	33.97	72.22
S. G. Law (Qld)..........	71	65	6	1,916	159	5	32.47	89.37
D. R. Martyn (WAust)	51	48	7	1,879	140	3	45.83	74.39

*Denotes not out.

HIGHEST PARTNERSHIP FOR EACH WICKET

253 for 1st	R.B. McCosker and J. Dyson,	
	New South Wales v South Australia at Sydney	1981-82
260 for 2nd	M.L. Hayden and S.G. Law,	
	Queensland v Tasmania at Brisbane (Gabba)	1993-94
257 for 3rd	M.W. Goodwin and M.E. Hussey,	
	Western Australia v New South Wales at Perth	2000-01
180 for 4th	G.C. Rummans and S. Lee,	
	New South Wales v Queensland at Brisbane (Gabba)	1999-00
156 for 5th	K.J. Roberts and R. Chee Quee,	
	New South Wales v South Australia at Sydney	1995-96
173* for 6th	M.E. Hussey and G.B. Hogg,	
	Western Australia v Victoria at Melbourne (MCG)	1999-00
124 for 7th	G.T. Cunningham and C.M. Smart,	
	Australian Capital Territory v Victoria at Richmond	1999-00
106* for 8th	A.C. Gilchrist and B.P. Julian,	
	Western Australia v New South Wales at Sydney	1995-96
96* for 9th	S.M. Thompson and S.D. Bradsteeet,	
	New South Wales v Queensland at North Sydney	1998-99
54 for 10th	B.E. McNamara and G.R. Robertson,	
	New South Wales v South Australia at Adelaide	1996-97

Denotes unbroken partnership.

HIGHEST INNINGS TOTALS

Batting First

4-397 New South Wales v Tasmania at Bankstown	2001-02
6-325 South Australia defeated Tasmania at Hobart (TCA)	1986-87
5-325 Western Australia defeated New South Wales at Perth	2000-01
4-320 Queensland defeated Tasmania at Brisbane	1993-94
7-319 New South Wales defeated South Australia at North Sydney	1997-98
4-310 New South Wales defeated South Australia at Sydney	1981-82
5-310 New South Wales defeated Victoria at North Sydney	1991-92
6-310 Western Australia defeated Tasmania at Hobart (Bellerive)	1997-98
7-307 New South Wales defeated Tasmania at North Sydney	1993-94
7-307 South Australia defeated Victoria at Adelaide	1997-98
8-306 Queensland defeated Western Australia at Brisbane	2000-01
7-302 South Australia defeated Western Australia at Perth	1999-00
5-202 New South Wales defeated Western Australia at North Sydney	2000-01
6-301 Western Australia defeated Queensland at Perth	1999-00

Batting Second

7-327 Tasmania v New South Wales at Bankstown	2001-02
7-284 Western Australia defeated Victoria at Perth	1990-91
7-284 Queensland defeated Western Australia at Perth	1997-98
282 South Australia lost to New South Wales at North Sydney	1997-98
5-282 South Australia defeated Victoria at Adelaide	2000-01
6-281 South Australia defeated Western Australia at Perth	1994-95
4-280 Victoria defeated Queensland at Melbourne	1998-99
9-278 Queensland lost to New South Wales at Brisbane	2000-01
4-276 New South Wales defeated Western Australia at Perth	2000-01
5-275 South Australia defeated New South Wales at North Sydney	1994-95

MOST WICKETS

	M	B	Mdns	R	W	BB	5W/i	Avge
J. Angel (WAust)	62	3,117	47	2,053	73	5/16	1	28.12
T.M. Moody (WAust)	75	3,205	41	2,131	70	4/30	0	30.44
P. Wilson (SAust)	46	2,540	42	1,676	70	4/23	0	23.94
S.A. Prestwidge (Qld)	45	2,189	18	1,755	67	5/59	1	26.19
S.C.G. MacGill (NSW)	30	1,503	14	1,297	63	5/40	3	20.59
M.S. Kasprowicz (Qld)	52	2,651	28	1,928	62	4/21	0	31.10
I.J. Harvey (Vic)	53	2,191	19	1,652	63	5/34	1	26.22
K.M. Harvey (WAust)	50	2,072	22	1,689	61	4/8	0	26.22
B.P. Julian (WAust)	54	2,318	19	1,779	59	4/43	0	30.15
B.E. McNamara (NSW)	42	2,005	22	1,281	57	6/25	1	22.47

HAT-TRICKS

A.G. Hurst	Victoria v Western Australia at Perth	1978-79
R.M. Baker	Western Australia v Australian Capital Territory at Perth	1999-00
N.W. Bracken	New South Wales v Victoria at Melbourne	2001-02

BEST BOWLING ANALYSES

7/34	C.G. Rackemann	Queensland v South Australia at Adelaide	1988-89
6/18	J.R. Thomson	Queensland v South Australia at Brisbane	1978-79
6/25	B.E. McNamara	New South Wales v Tasmania at Sydney	1996-97
5/15	D.L. Boyd	Western Australia v Victoria at Perth	1982-83
5/16	J. Angel	Western Australia v Victoria at Perth	2001-02
5/20	G.D. Watson	Victoria v Western Australia at Melbourne	1969-70
5/22	H.J. Howarth	New Zealanders v New South Wales at Sydney	1969-70
5/23	R.J. McCurdy	South Australia v Western Australia at Adelaide	1984-85
5/23	J.P. Marquet	Tasmania v Queensland at Hobart (Bel)	1995-96
5/26	D.J. Hickey	Victoria v Western Australia at Melbourne	1985-86

MOST CATCHES IN A MATCH

5	B.E. Young	South Australia v Tasmania at Launceston	2001-02
4	J.W. Scholes	Victoria v New Zealanders at Melbourne	1971-72
4	I.M. Chappell	South Australia v New Zealanders at Adelaide	1972-73
4	M.A. Taylor	New South Wales v Queensland at Sydney	1998-99
4	J.D. Siddons	South Australia v A.C.T. at Canberra	1999-00

MOST CATCHES

J.D. Siddons (Vic/SAust) ... 31 in 62 matches	G.B. Hogg (WAust)	27 in 54 matches
A.R. Border (NSW/Qld) ... 30 in 49 matches	M.E.K. Hussey (WAust) ..	27 in 45 matches
S. Lee (NSW) .... 30 in 57 matches	T.M. Moody (WAust)	25 in 75 matches
S.G. Law (Qld) .... 30 in 71 matches	M.E. Waugh (NSW)	23 in 41 matches
D.M. Jones (Vic) .... 28 in 55 matches	B.E. Young (SAust)	25 in 36 matches

MOST DISMISSALS IN A MATCH

6	(all ct)	K.J. Wadsworth......	New Zealanders v New South Wales at Sydney ...	1969-70
6	(5ct, 1st)	B.J. Haddin	New South Wales v Western Australia at Perth ...	2001-02
6	(5ct, 1st)	R.J. Campbell	Western Australia v New South Wales at Perth ...	2000-01
6	(all ct)	R.J. Campbell	Western Australia v Tasmania at Perth	2000-01
5	(all ct)	R. Edwards.........	Western Australia v New Zealanders at Perth	1970-71
5	(all ct)	I.A. Healy	Queensland v Tasmania at Hobart (Bellerive)	1995-96

MOST DISMISSALS

	M	Ct	St	Total
D. S. Berry (S Aust/Vic)	63	77	24	101
P. A. Emery (NSW)	58	69	12	81
W. A. Seccombe (Qld)	49	69	12	81
A. C. Gilchrist (NSW/WAust)	34	56	6	62
T. J. Nielsen (SAust)	45	55	3	58
R. J. Campbell (WAust)	27	52	6	58
I. A. Healy (Qld)	29	47	7	54
R. W. Marsh (WAust)	33	50	1	51
M. N. Atkinson (Tas)	35	43	7	50
T. J. Zoehrer (WAust)	35	41	4	45

MOST APPEARANCES

75	T. M. Moody (W Aust)	1985-86 – 2000-01
73	D. S. Berry (SAust/Vic)	1989-90 – 2001-02
71	S. G. Law (Qld)	1988-89 – 2001-02
67	D. S. Lehmann (SAust/Vic)	1988-89 – 2001-02
64	S. Young (Tas)	1990-91 – 2001-02

NEW SOUTH WALES

The ING Cup was everything the Pura Cup failed to be for New South Wales. Having won last season's limited-overs trophy, then known as the Mercantile Mutual Cup, in the final at the WACA Ground in Perth, to win away again in Brisbane revealed a maturity and temperament within a pleasing balance of youth and age in New South Wales ranks which promised, yet again, far better things at first-class level.

It was in the ING Cup that left-arm pace man Nathan Bracken excelled, and while the national selectors refrained from calling him, his performances justified his retention on the Australian Cricket Board's 25-player contracted list and sustained his challenge for World Cup involvement. Bracken was responsible for only the third hat-trick in the domestic competition, against Victoria at the Melbourne Cricket Ground. Of greater influence, in terms of run-economy if not in a wicket-taking sense, Stuart Clark was a model of consistency with his sustained pace and variation. His contract from the Australian Cricket Board at season's end was a thoroughly warranted reward. Nation-wide, he was one of the outstanding players of the summer. Leg-spinner Stuart MacGill proved as indispensable in the ING Cup competition as he was in first-class cricket, having remarkable wicket-taking success, only to be deprived of the winners' champagne at the Gabba final by his inclusion in the Australian team for South Africa, a tour on which he missed selection for all three Tests and then the limited-overs leg of the tour. Sometimes success carries a rank odour.

While the search for batting consistency in this form of cricket often appears to be seeking the impossible, Michael Bevan, Michael Clarke, Brad Haddin and, later, Corey Richards, all made important contributions, with Mark Higgs and Graeme Rummans providing their own distinctive moments of flair and stability. There was no shortage of leaders in the ranks, four players captaining the team. Shane Lee started and ended the campaign, Bevan and MacGill continued it on various occasions and Steve Waugh stood in as leader twice.

The ING Cup's unique 12-man rotation system, extensions of fielding limitations during the 50-overs-a-side game, the batting and bowling bonus point for a dominant side winning within 40 overs or by a substantial percentage of runs – all were employed to player and spectator satisfaction. Whatever the fallibility of the bonus point incentive in the triangular international VB Series, there were no qualms in the ING Cup with its six-team format where the incentive system could not be so manipulated. Of perhaps greater significance was the one-bouncer-per-over law. It had a much-needed influence in providing the level playing field security against batsmen in the day-night game. Jason Gillespie took a wicket with his first bouncer of the ING Cup for South Australia and batsmen always remembered it. – PHIL WILKINS.

RESULTS, 2001-02

ING Cup matches – Played 11: Won 8, Lost 3.
Competition placing – 1st.

ING CUP AVERAGES, 2001-02

BATTING

	M	I	NO	R	HS	100s	50s	Avge	Ct/St	S-R
C.J. Richards	6	6	1	291	151	1	1	58.20	3	81.51
M.E. Waugh.	4	4	0	208	123	1	1	52.00	2	97.65
M.G. Bevan	9	9	2	284	68*	0	3	40.57	4	69.78
M.J. Clarke.	10	8	1	273	101*	1	2	39.00	3	71.09
B.J. Haddin	10	10	0	360	120	1	2	36.00	20/5	104.96
G.C. Rummans	6	6	1	177	73*	0	1	35.40	2	60.20
S. Lee	9	8	1	228	83	0	1	32.57	7	85.07
N.S. Pilon.	1	1	0	28	28	0	0	28.00	1	75.68
S.D. Bradstreet	9	7	3	107	46*	0	0	26.75	1	82.95
M.A. Higgs	10	9	1	158	63*	0	1	19.75	4	75.96
M.J. Phelps.	2	2	0	35	31	0	0	17.50	1	64.81
M.J. Slater	5	5	0	73	35	0	0	14.60	0	69.52
D.J. Thornely	5	3	1	26	20*	0	0	13.00	3	42.62
D.A. Nash	6	6	1	36	10	0	0	7.20	0	67.92
N.W. Bracken	9	4	1	20	9	0	0	6.67	2	57.14
S.C.G. MacGill . . .	8	2	0	3	3	0	0	1.50	0	60.00
B.P. Van Deinsen. .	1	1	0	0	0	0	0	0.00	1	0.00
A.W. O'Brien.	1	1	0	0	0	0	0	0.00	0	0.00
A.M. Clark	1	1	1	3	3*	0	0	–	0	23.08
S.R. Clark.	11	1	1	2	2*	0	0	–	1	40.00
G.M. Lambert	1	1	1	3	3*	0	0	–	0	100.00
B. Lee	3	1	1	44	44*	0	0	–	0	151.72
G.D. McGrath	3	0	0	0	0	0	0	–	0	–
S.R. Waugh	2	2	2	133	101*	1	0	–	0	90.48

* Denotes not out.

BOWLING

	O	M	R	W	BB	5W/I	Avge
G.M. Lambert	6	0	33	2	2/33	0	16.50
S.C.G. MacGill	61.3	2	381	21	5/50	2	18.14
M.J. Clarke.	11	0	64	3	3/57	0	21.33
N.W. Bracken	81	5	394	18	5/38	1	21.89
G.D. McGrath	21	2	98	3	2/36	0	32.67
S. Lee	31	1	131	4	2/39	0	32.75
S.D. Bradstreet.	39.5	1	224	6	4/23	0	37.33
M.A. Higgs	33	0	187	5	3/48	0	37.40
D.J. Thornely	38	1	191	5	3/36	0	38.20
D.A. Nash	41.1	5	201	5	3/31	0	40.20
S.R. Clark.	101.5	8	372	9	3/25	0	41.33
B. Lee	28	2	109	2	1/31	0	54.50
A.M. Clark.	1	0	3	0	–	0	–

NEW SOUTH WALES v VICTORIA

At Bankstown Memorial Oval, Bankstown, October 7, 2001. New South Wales won by 123 runs. Toss: New South Wales. New South Wales 5 pts.

Shane Lee was seen at his best in this game with a cavalier innings which included six fours and three sixes. His partnership of 63 with Michael Slater, after their team was in early difficulties at three for 55, laid the foundations for a ridiculously comfortable but unexpected victory. With Nathan Bracken recovering from a shoulder injury, Stuart Clark came into the team and immediately bowled so well and with such precision that he became an indispensable member of the squad. Nevertheless, batting last on one of the best pitches in Australia, the Victorians were abysmal, dismissed in 35.3 overs to provide New South Wales with a bonus point that hardly seemed possible halfway through the game.

Man of the Match: S. Lee. *Attendance:* 4,386.

New South Wales

M. E. Waugh c Hodge b Harvey	21	(23)		D. A. Nash st Berry b Harvey	10	(12)
†B. J. Haddin c Hewett b Lewis	21	(16)		S. C. G. MacGill run out (Elliott/Berry)	3	(4)
M. G. Bevan run out (Hodge/Berry)	7	(16)		S. R. Clark not out	2	(5)
M. J. Slater c Lewis b Warne	35	(63)				
*S. Lee c Warne b Harvey	83	(93)		B 4, l-b 4, w 5, n-b 4	17	
M. A. Higgs run out (Arnberger/Berry)	17	(23)				
M. J. Clarke c Berry b Lewis	11	(13)		(50 overs, 189 mins) (9 wkts)	256	
S. D. Bradstreet not out	29	(36)		Fall: 44 44 55 118 166 191 228 245 249		

G. D. McGrath did not bat.

Bowling: Fleming 9–0–51–0; Lewis 7–0–40–2; Harvey 10–0–38–3; Hewett 7–1–27–0; Oliver 5–0–25–0; Warne 10–1–49–1; Hodge 2–0–18–0.

Victoria

*M. T. G. Elliott c Haddin b Nash	4	(16)		S. K. Warne c Waugh b MacGill	25	(21)
J. L. Arnberger c Higgs b Nash	21	(23)		I. S. L. Hewett not out	3	(18)
B. J. Hodge c Lee b McGrath	8	(14)		D. W. Fleming run out (Slater)	0	(0)
M. Klinger c Haddin b Nash	4	(12)				
I. J. Harvey c Lee b Clark	24	(20)		W 2	2	
J. Moss run out (Bradstreet)	25	(40)				
B. C. Oliver b Clark	0	(2)		(35.3 overs, 148 mins)	133	
†D. S. Berry b MacGill	17	(47)		Fall: 18 31 38 38 69 69 95 126 133 133		

M. L. Lewis did not bat.

Bowling: McGrath 7–1–22–1; Nash 7–1–31–3; Lee 5–0–18–0; Clark 10–0–30–2; MacGill 6–0–32–2; Bradstreet 0.3–0–0–0.

Umpires: D. B. Hair and S. J. A. Taufel.
TV Umpire: D. M. Brandon.

NEW SOUTH WALES v TASMANIA

At Bankstown Memorial Oval, Bankstown, October 14, 2001. New South Wales won on run rate. Toss: New South Wales. New South Wales 4 pts.

So benign was the pitch that the former innings record in Australian domestic one-day cricket of 325 was broken by each of the teams. Rarely does a Mark Waugh century remain in the shadows, especially on his club home ground, but the 74-ball century of his opening partner, Brad Haddin was so dynamic that all else paled into insignificance. Haddin struck his four sixes and 17 fours with astonishing power, while Waugh (16 fours, two sixes) batted with customary elegance in their two-hour, 228-run opening partnership. They took only 28.4 overs to put their team on course for a new competition record score. In all, New South Wales' batsmen pulverised the bowling for ten sixes and 47 fours. In perfect conditions boundaries became mundane, and Michael Bevan's run-a-ball 68 scarcely warranted notice. Tasmania's batsmen were anything but overawed by the enormity of their task. Michael Di Venuto and Shane Watson began with a 92-run partnership in 12 overs before the unexpected advent of left-arm finger-spinner Michael Clarke as first change brought him both openers' wickets as well as that of Ricky Ponting in a 17-delivery burst. Daniel Marsh's ferocious innings, including nine fours and three sixes, offered late entertainment before a rainstorm reduced Tasmania's overs to 47 and a revised target of 363.

Man of the Match: B. J. Haddin. *Attendance:* 3,183.

New South Wales

†B.J. Haddin b Marquet	120 (84)	*S. Lee not out	42	(17)
M.E. Waugh b Marquet	123 (103)	L-b 6, w 4, n-b 3	13	
D.A. Nash c Young b Polkinghorne	0 (3)			
M.G. Bevan not out	68 (64)	(50 overs, 204 mins) (4 wkts)	397	
M.J. Slater c Watson b Saker	31 (33)	Fall: 228 231 257 324		

M.A. Higgs, M.J. Clarke, S.D. Bradstreet, S.C.G. MacGill, S.R. Clark and G.D. McGrath did not bat.

Bowling: Wright 10–0–79–0; Saker 7–0–61–1; Marquet 10–0–62–2; Watson 7–0–65–0; Young 7–0–60–0; Polkinghorne 9–0–64–1.

Tasmania

M.J. Di Venuto c Lee b Clarke	52 (35)	A.W. Polkinghorne st Haddin b MacGill 14		(9)
S.R. Watson c Bevan b Clarke	51 (46)	D.G. Wright not out	4	(2)
*R.T. Ponting c Lee b Clarke	7 (8)			
S. Young c Bradstreet b Clark	1 (6)	B 6, l-b 6, w 8	20	
J. Cox run out (Bradstreet/Haddin)	31 (41)		—	
D.J. Marsh not out	101 (86)	(47 overs, 186 mins) (7 wkts)	327	
G.T. Cunningham c Clarke b Lee	46 (49)	Fall: 92 102 103 119 176 271 300		

†S.G. Clingeleffer, D.J. Saker and J.P. Marquet did not bat.

Bowling: McGrath 5–0–40–0; Nash 4–0–36–0; Clarke 10–0–57–3; Clark 10–1–44–1; MacGill 5–0–44–1; Lee 8–0–40–1; Bradstreet 4–0–37–0; Higgs 1–0–17–0.

Umpires: N.S.D. Fowler and S.J.A. Taufel.
TV Umpire: S.A. Reed.

NEW SOUTH WALES v QUEENSLAND

At Sydney Cricket Ground, Sydney, November 18, 2001. New South Wales won on run rate. Toss: New South Wales. New South Wales 4 pts.

Put in to bat, Queensland posted what might have been a match-winning score after being precariously placed at six for 186 against a strong attack. An 88-run partnership from 74 balls by the feisty pair of Andrew Bichel and Wade Seccombe revived the game, which was held in a stiff wind and intermittent rain. New South Wales experienced their own early setbacks before Steve Waugh, enjoying a reprieve from a possible gloved catch at 11, struck his sixth century of the summer, sharing a stand of 114 for the third wicket with Michael Bevan. Waugh described his century as "scratchy", but Mark Higgs more than made up for Waugh's uncertainty. Higgs' flamboyant half-century, the fastest of the season, came in 31 balls and included a six and seven fours as the pair added 105 runs from only 72 balls. New South Wales reached their revised 250-run target with three balls remaining of the 44th and final over.

Man of the Match: M.A. Higgs.   *Attendance:* 4,917.

Queensland

M.L. Hayden c M.E. Waugh b McGrath	14 (39)	†W.A. Seccombe b McGrath	37	(44)
J.P. Maher b Bracken	57 (66)	A.J. Bichel not out	59	(42)
M.L. Love c and b Bracken	30 (45)	B 1, l-b 5, w 5, n-b 4	15	
A. Symonds c Haddin b MacGill	26 (19)		—	
C.T. Perren lbw b MacGill	22 (33)	(50 overs, 205 mins) (7 wkts)	274	
*S.G. Law c Bevan b MacGill	14 (16)	Fall: 54 113 113 157 166 186 274		

J.R. Hopes, M.S. Kasprowicz, A.A. Noffke and N.M. Hauritz did not bat.

Bowling: McGrath 9–1–36–2; B. Lee 8–0–44–0; Clark 6–0–27–0; Bracken 10–1–58–2; MacGill 10–1–56–3; Higgs 3–0–21–0; S. Lee 4–0–26–0.

New South Wales

M.E. Waugh b Kasprowicz	4	(6)	M.A. Higgs not out	63	(39)
†B.J. Haddin c Hauritz b Bichel	0	(3)			
M.G. Bevan c Seccombe b Hopes	56	(79)	B 3, l-b 6, w 9, n-b 1	19	
*S.R. Waugh not out	101	(120)		—	
M.J. Slater lbw b Bichel	2	(4)	(43.3 overs, 171 mins)	(5 wkts) 252	
S. Lee c Maher b Hauritz	7	(11)	Fall: 3 8 122 127 147		

B. Lee, S.C.G. MacGill, N.W. Bracken, S.R. Clark and G.D. McGrath did not bat.

Bowling: Bichel 8.3–0–38–2; Kasprowicz 9–0–50–1; Noffke 9–2–54–0; Hopes 9–0–50–1; Hauritz 4–0–29–1; Symonds 4–0–22–0.

Umpires: N.S.D. Fowler and T.J. Keel.
TV Umpire: D.M. Brandon.

At Brisbane Cricket Ground, Brisbane, November 30, 2001. Day/night game. NEW SOUTH WALES lost to QUEENSLAND by six wickets.

At Adelaide Oval, Adelaide, December 8, 2001. NEW SOUTH WALES defeated SOUTH AUSTRALIA by 135 runs.

At Melbourne Cricket Ground, Melbourne, January 6, 2002. NEW SOUTH WALES lost to VICTORIA by two wickets.

NEW SOUTH WALES v SOUTH AUSTRALIA

At International Sports Stadium, Coffs Harbour, January 12, 2002. South Australia won by 114 runs. Toss: New South Wales. South Australia 5 pts. Competition debut: D.J. Thornely, B.P. Van Deinsen.

South Australia gained an away win with a resounding victory on a day as intolerable as any of the season, first stiflingly hot and then made worse by a bristling wind. Darren Lehmann continued his exemplary batting to claim his fourth match award of the season. He became so dehydrated late in his innings that when he returned to the pavilion he was placed on a chair under a cold shower and given an intravenous saline drip by New South Wales' medical officer, Dr Harry Harinath. Having conceded 24 runs from his first two overs, Stuart MacGill returned to the attack and claimed five wickets as the South Australians lost seven for 59. Graeme Rummans was the only New South Wales batsman to stand his ground in an otherwise woeful performance, although Nathan Bracken joined him in adding 53 from 47 balls for the tenth wicket to give the innings a semblance of respectability.

Man of the Match: D.S. Lehmann.   *Attendance:* 4,900.

South Australia

D.A. Fitzgerald b Bracken	33	(70)	M.J. Smith not out	30	(18)
G.S. Blewett c Haddin b Clark	8	(9)	J.N. Gillespie b MacGill	2	(3)
C.J. Davies c Higgs b Bracken	1	(6)	P. Wilson st Haddin b MacGill	0	(1)
*D.S. Lehmann c Thornely b Higgs	101	(95)	B 2, l-b 3, w 3, n-b 5	13	
B.A. Johnson c Rummans b MacGill	51	(74)		—	
N.T. Adcock st Haddin b Higgs	3	(10)	(49.5 overs, 210 mins)	258	
B.E. Young lbw b MacGill	2	(3)	Fall: 16 17 78 199 208 211 212		
†G.A. Manou c Van Deinsen b MacGill	14	(15)	239 258 258		

M.A. Harrity did not bat.

Bowling: Clark 7–0–19–1; Bracken 7–0–30–2; Bradstreet 8–0–50–0; Nash 6–1–17–0; MacGill 6.5–0–53–5; Thornely 6–0–33–0; Higgs 9–0–51–2.

New South Wales

M.J. Clarke c Smith b Gillespie	.....	6	(23)	
†B.J. Haddin c Manou b Smith	......	15	(33)	
B.P. Van Deinsen lbw b Wilson	.....	0	(4)	
C.J. Richards c Manou b Gillespie	...	1	(6)	
G.C. Rummans not out	....	73	(107)	
M.A. Higgs b Smith	....	2	(8)	
D.J. Thornely c Smith b Harrity	.....	3	(23)	
S.D. Bradstreet c Manou b Gillespie	..	8	(20)	

D.A. Nash c Smith b Johnson	......	8	(14)
*S.C.G. MacGill c Harrity b Johnson	0	(1)
N.W. Bracken c Manou b Harrity	...	9	(15)
L-b 9, w 6, n-b 4	....	19
		—
(41.5 overs, 177 mins)		144
Fall: 19 20 32 37 41 56 73 91 91 144		

S.R. Clark did not bat.

Bowling: Gillespie 10–0–31–3; Wilson 8–2–16–1; Smith 8–0–18–2; Harrity 7.5–1–28–2; Johnson 5–0–25–2; Young 3–0–17–0.

Umpires: D.M. Brandon and S.A. Reed.
TV Umpire: R.D. Goodger.

WESTERN AUSTRALIA v NEW SOUTH WALES

At Sydney Cricket Ground, Sydney, February 3, 2002. New South Wales won by five wickets. Toss: Western Australia. New South Wales 4 pts.

A thrilling final home victory provided New South Wales with the momentum and belief that they could claim the competition again. A win to Western Australia would probably have eliminated New South Wales and played South Australia into the final against Queensland. Fresh from four centuries in six Tests, Justin Langer and Scott Meuleman dashed to a century stand in just 15.4 overs before Stuart MacGill's leg-spinners brought four wickets in as many overs. Despite Langer's second domestic limited-overs century and Mike Hussey's typically industrious knock, MacGill claimed the unique honour of capturing five wickets in successive matches. New South Wales lost two early wickets before Michael Clarke joined Brad Haddin in a match-reviving 78-run partnership, Clarke's cultured stroke-making yielding him his maiden limited-overs century. New South Wales were still five runs from victory as they began the last over, but Clarke and Corey Richards remained cool and brought up the winning run with a ball to spare.

Man of the Match: M.J. Clarke.   *Attendance:* 2,606.

Western Australia

*J.L. Langer c Higgs b Thornely	.....	107	(124)
S.W. Meuleman lbw b MacGill	.....	47	(59)
†R.J. Campbell b MacGill	..	2	(7)
S.M. Katich c Thornely b MacGill	...	6	(11)
R.M. Baker c Haddin b MacGill	.....	0	(3)
M.E.K. Hussey c Rummans b Bracken	63	(64)
G.B. Hogg b MacGill	....	1	(4)

K.M. Harvey not out	....	19	(27)
D.J. Wates b Bracken	....	0	(1)
L-b 9, w 5	....	14
		—
(50 overs, 207 mins)	(8 wkts)	259
Fall: 106 118 133 133 204 214 254 259		

S.R. Cary, J. Angel and M.W. Clark did not bat.

Bowling: Clark 10–1–38–0; Bracken 10–0–51–2; Higgs 2–0–18–0; Bradstreet 8–0–53–0; MacGill 10–1–50–5; Thornely 10–0–40–1.

New South Wales

M.J. Phelps c Hussey b Clark	4	(10)
†B.J. Haddin c Campbell b Hogg	61	(66)
G.C. Rummans c Campbell b Clark	6	(14)
M.J. Clarke not out	101	(132)
*S. Lee c Wates b Angel	45	(46)
M.A. Higgs st Campbell b Hogg	3	(4)

C.J. Richards not out	33	(27)
B 2, l-b 5	7	
(49.5 overs, 189 mins) (5 wkts)	260	
Fall: 7 25 103 202 214		

S.D. Bradstreet, D.J. Thornely, S.C.G. MacGill, N.W. Bracken and S.R. Clark did not bat.

Bowling: Cary 10–1–36–0; Clark 7–0–40–2; Angel 10–0–36–1; Hogg 10–0–60–2; Wates 5–0–27–0; Harvey 5.5–0–37–0; Katich 2–0–17–0.

Umpires: G.J. Lill and S.J. Taufel.

At Devonport Oval, Devonport, February 10, 2002. NEW SOUTH WALES defeated TASMANIA by seven wickets.

At WACA Ground, Perth, February 13, 2002. Day/night game. NEW SOUTH WALES defeated WESTERN AUSTRALIA by three runs.

FINAL

At Brisbane Cricket Ground, Brisbane, February 24, 2002. NEW SOUTH WALES defeated QUEENSLAND by 19 runs. For details, see section on ING Cup, 2001-02, page 476.

DOMESTIC LIMITED-OVERS RESULTS

	M	W	L	NR	T
Australian Capital Territory	3	3	0	0	0
New Zealanders	1	0	1	0	0
Queensland	29	18	11	0	0
South Australia	19	10	9	0	0
Tasmania	21	18	3	0	0
Victoria	27	14	12	1	0
Western Australia	30	14	15	0	1
Total	130	77	51	1	1

RECORDS

Highest score for:	164	R.B. McCosker v South Australia at Sydney	1981-82
Highest score against:	165	M.W. Goodwin (Western Australia) at Perth	2000-01
Best bowling for:	6/25	B.E. McNamara v Tasmania at Sydney	1996-97
Best bowling against:	5/22	H.J. Howarth (New Zealanders) at Sydney	1969-70
Highest total for:	4-397	v Tasmania at Bankstown	2001-02
Highest total against:	7-327	by Tasmania at Bankstown	2001-02
Lowest total for:	92	v Queensland at Brisbane	1972-73
Lowest total against:	80	by Tasmania at Devonport	1984-85

MOST RUNS

	M	I	NO	R	HS	100s	50s	Avge	S-R
M.G. Bevan	52	52	18	2,068	135*	1	18	60.82	74.52
S.R. Waugh	39	38	8	1,548	131	3	9	51.60	82.21
M.E. Waugh	45	44	4	1,477	123	3	9	36.93	80.58
S. Lee	57	51	6	1,405	115	2	7	31.22	87.65
M.A. Taylor	38	38	0	1,218	84	0	12	32.05	59.33
C.J. Richards	39	36	4	1,090	151	2	6	34.06	72.46

	M	I	NO	R	HS	100s	50s	Avge	S-R
M.J. Slater	39	39	0	910	96	0	7	23.33	67.31
R. Chee Quee	22	22	1	860	131	1	5	40.95	66.62
R.B. McCosker	21	21	2	847	164	2	5	44.58	63.99
J. Dyson	21	21	2	789	101	2	6	41.53	54.90

* *Denotes not out.*

HIGHEST PARTNERSHIP FOR EACH WICKET

253	for 1st	R.B. McCosker and J. Dyson, v South Australia at Sydney	1981-82
199	for 2nd	R. Chee Quee and M.G. Bevan, v Western Australia at Sydney	1993-94
240	for 3rd	S.R. Waugh and M.E. Waugh, v Victoria at North Sydney	1991-92
180	for 4th	G.C. Rummans and S. Lee, v Queensland at Brisbane	1999-00
156	for 5th	K.J. Roberts and R. Chee Quee, v South Australia at Sydney	1995-96
105	for 6th	M.G. Bevan and G.R.J. Matthews, v Western Australia at Perth	1990-91
116	for 7th	C.J. Richards and B.J. Haddin, v South Australia at North Sydney	2000-01
90	for 8th	B.E. McNamara and P.A. Emery, v Tasmania at Sydney	1992-93
96*	for 9th	S.M. Thompson and S.D. Bradstreet, v Victoria at North Sydney	1998-99
54	for 10th	B.E. McNamara and G.R. Robertson, v South Australia at Adelaide	1996-97

MOST WICKETS

	M	Balls	Mdns	R	W	BB	5W/i	Avge
S.C.G. MacGill	30	1,503	14	1,297	63	5/40	3	20.59
B.E. McNamara	42	2,005	22	1,281	57	6/25	1	22.47
S. Lee	57	2,155	13	1,695	54	4/59	0	31.39
G.R.J. Matthews	50	2,302	25	1,500	49	3/29	0	30.61
M.R. Whitney	36	1,926	36	1,188	41	4/30	0	28.98
G.F. Lawson	35	1,811	38	1,053	39	4/31	0	27.00
S.R. Clark	33	1,762	22	1,095	36	4/26	0	30.42
S.R. Waugh	39	1,092	18	845	34	4/32	0	24.85
N.W. Bracken	23	1,151	18	828	34	5/38	1	24.35
W.J. Holdsworth	27	1,295	17	891	30	5/28	1	29.70

MOST DISMISSALS

	M	Ct	St	Total
P.A. Emery	58	70	11	81
B.J. Haddin	26	39	15	54
S.J. Rixon	25	25	6	31
H.B. Taber	6	8	1	9
G.C. Dyer	10	4	2	6
M. Hendricks	9	3	3	6

MOST CATCHES

S. Lee	30 in 57 matches	S.R. Waugh	14 in 37 matches
M.E. Waugh	25 in 45 matches	M.A. Higgs	14 in 28 matches
M.A. Taylor	24 in 38 matches	M.G. Bevan	14 in 52 matches
G.R.J. Matthews	15 in 50 matches	C.J. Richards	13 in 29 matches
R. Chee Quee	14 in 22 matches	R.B. McCosker	11 in 21 matches

MOST APPEARANCES

58	P.A. Emery	1987-88 – 1998-99	42	B.E. McNamara . .	1989-90 – 1999-00
57	S. Lee	1992-93 – 2001-02	39	M.J. Slater	1992-93 – 2001-02
52	M.G. Bevan	1990-91 – 2001-02	39	S.R. Waugh	1984-85 – 2001-02
50	G.R.J. Matthews . .	1982-83 – 1997-98	39	C.J. Richards	1996-97 – 2001-02
45	M.E. Waugh	1985-86 – 2001-02	38	M.A. Taylor	1985-86 – 1998-99

QUEENSLAND

Queensland changed their training routine in an attempt to eliminate the inconsistency that had plagued their 2000-01 limited-overs campaign. Coach Bennett King introduced more centre-wicket practice sessions to simulate match conditions. That included a four-hour workout on the Gabba wicket after the limited-overs internationals in January. The positive results helped Queensland host the ING Cup final against New South Wales after a tense finish to the qualifying rounds.

Queensland won seven of their ten qualifying matches, dropping just one match at the Gabba when they were unable to haul in South Australia under lights. But Queensland's overall goal to win both the first-class and limited-overs championships fizzled during a disappointing run-chase in the final. Needing 205 for victory, the Queenslanders unravelled against a determined New South Wales side.

But Queensland received a high pass mark for their limited-overs summer, shaking off the wobbly form of the previous season. They chased down high scores and defended moderate totals as they benefited from the continued development of younger players such as off-spinner Nathan Hauritz and all-rounder James Hopes. The pair was central to the Queensland campaign, taking 18 and 16 wickets respectively against more seasoned players. Hauritz was rewarded with selection in the Australian limited-overs squad for the series in South Africa, where he continued his good form in the national side. Hopes proved he was a genuine all-rounder, hitting 213 runs in his 11 matches at a strike-rate of almost 80 to add some bite towards the end of the Queensland innings.

Martin Love and Jimmy Maher topped the run-scoring lists in the same way they dominated the first-class competition. Love scored 423 runs from 11 matches, including two excellent centuries, once again proving his worth in both forms of the game. Maher became Queensland's highest domestic limited-overs scorer with another 391 runs from 11 matches before shining alongside Hauritz in South Africa. Andrew Symonds was dumped from the national squad in January but he was again valuable for the Queenslanders with bat and ball, opening the season with a memorable 91 from 57 balls against Western Australia and contributing tight overs of off-spin and medium pace.

Despite the individual rewards, there was ultimately disappointment in losing the final. For King the 19-run loss was a sour finish to the season, especially as his batsmen had not carried out the team's game plan. But King appreciated the team's achievement in topping the points table and claiming three bonus points without the presence of limited-overs spearhead Adam Dale, whose need for shoulder surgery robbed the Quenslanders of one of their most valuable assets. – MICHAEL CRUTCHER.

RESULTS, 2001-02

ING Cup matches – Played 11: Won 7, Lost 4.
Competition placing – 2nd.

ING CUP AVERAGES, 2001-02

BATTING

	M	I	NO	R	HS	100s	50s	Avge	Ct/St	S-R
M.L. Love	11	11	1	423	127*	2	2	42.30	2	77.90
J.P. Maher	11	11	1	391	71*	0	3	39.10	10	72.41
C.T. Perren......	11	11	2	317	96	0	2	35.22	3	67.88
A. Symonds	10	10	0	300	91	0	2	30.00	4	110.29
J.R. Hopes	11	9	1	213	52*	0	1	26.63	4	78.60
B.P. Nash	7	6	1	124	63	0	1	24.80	3	59.62
A.A. Noffke......	9	4	2	48	22*	0	0	24.00	5	63.16
L.A. Carseldine	3	3	1	43	29	0	0	21.50	0	69.35
S.G. Law	7	6	0	86	25	0	0	14.33	6	63.24
M.L. Hayden	5	5	0	69	40	0	0	13.80	0	60.00
N.M. Hauritz	11	5	2	40	18*	0	0	13.33	6	52.63
M.S. Kasprowicz...	8	3	2	13	7	0	0	13.00	0	92.86
W.A. Seccombe....	11	8	1	83	37	0	0	11.86	19/1	70.34
D.R. MacKenzie ...	2	2	0	11	9	0	0	5.50	0	55.00
A.J. Bichel........	4	2	2	74	59*	0	1	–	0	115.63
J.H. Dawes	7	1	1	1	1*	0	0	–	0	10.00
S.A. Brant	1	0	0	0	0	0	0	–	1	–
S.A. Muller	2	1	0	0	0	0	0	0.00	1	0.00
M. Sippel	1	1	0	0	0	0	0	0.00	2	0.00

* Denotes not out.

BOWLING

	O	M	R	W	BB	5W/I	Avge
D.R. MacKenzie	13	0	50	3	2/21	0	16.67
J.H. Dawes	59	2	244	12	3/26	0	20.33
C.T. Perren..............	11	1	41	2	1/19	0	20.50
N.M. Hauritz	91.5	1	381	18	4/47	0	21.17
J.R. Hopes	90	8	347	16	3/30	0	21.69
A.A. Noffke.............	84.5	7	378	15	4/32	0	25.20
A.J. Bichel.............	35.3	1	135	5	2/28	0	27.00
S.A. Brant	8	1	33	1	1/33	0	33.00
M.S. Kasprowicz..........	65	2	303	6	3/36	0	50.50
A. Symonds	63	3	285	5	2/33	0	57.00
S.A. Muller	12	0	59	1	1/22	0	59.00

QUEENSLAND v WESTERN AUSTRALIA

At Brisbane Cricket Ground, Brisbane, October 21, 2001. Queensland won by seven wickets. Toss: Queensland. Queensland 5 pts.

Just 24 hours after thrashing Western Australia's bowlers in a Pura Cup match, Andrew Symonds unleashed another batting sideshow on them. Hitting 13 fours and two sixes, he helped Queensland make short work of the visitors. Andy Bichel had set the visitors on a wobbly start when he dismissed Test team-mate Adam Gilchrist cheaply. Although the Western Australians batted out their 50 overs, only Damien Martyn looked convincing but their total seemed testing when Matthew Hayden and Martin Love were out cheaply. Then Symonds joined the reliable Jimmy Maher in a hurried run-chase which brought 129 from 106 balls. Symonds would probably have posted the fastest century in the history of the competition if he had not clipped a catch to Brad Williams at third man.

Man of the Match: A. Symonds.   *Attendance:* 4,845.

Western Australia

*†A.C. Gilchrist c Hopes b Bichel	...	8	(6)	G.B. Hogg c Maher b Hauritz	......	9	(14)
D.R. Martyn b Hauritz	....	82	(130)	D.J. Wates not out	....	1	(1)
S.M. Katich c Seccombe b Hopes	....	10	(37)				
M.W. Goodwin c Law b Bichel	.....	28	(43)	W 4	....		4
M.E.K. Hussey b Hauritz	....	24	(38)				
J.L. Langer c Hauritz b Noffke	......	3	(6)	(50 overs, 183 mins)	(7 wkts)		189
K.M. Harvey not out	....	20	(25)	Fall: 10 50 113 145 156 164 188			

S.J. Karppinen, M.J. Nicholson and B.A. Williams did not bat.

Bowling: Bichel 9–0–28–2; Noffke 10–0–34–1; Kasprowicz 10–0–42–0; Hopes 6–1–27–1; Symonds 7–0–35–0; Hauritz 8–0–23–3.

Queensland

J.P. Maher not out	....	71	(81)				
M.L. Hayden run out (Katich)	....	0	(3)	L-b 2, w 1, n-b 1	....		4
M.L. Love c Gilchrist b Williams	....	2	(4)				—
A. Symonds c Williams b Harvey	....	91	(57)	(29.5 overs, 124 mins)	(3 wkts)		191
C.T. Perren not out	....	23	(35)	Fall: 1 10 139			

*S.G. Law, J.R. Hopes, †W.A. Seccombe, A.J. Bichel, M.S. Kasprowicz, N.M. Hauritz and A.A. Noffke did not bat.

Bowling: Williams 7–0–37–1; Karppinen 3–0–13–0; Nicholson 2–0–21–0; Wates 6–0–43–0; Harvey 7–1–46–1; Hogg 3.5–0–19–0; Katich 1–0–10–0.

Umpires: A.J. McQuillan and B.N.J. Oxenford.
TV Umpire: L.D. Musch.

At Richmond Cricket Ground, Richmond, October 28, 2001. QUEENSLAND defeated VICTORIA by one wicket.

At Sydney Cricket Ground, Sydney, November 18, 2001. QUEENSLAND lost to NEW SOUTH WALES on run rate.

QUEENSLAND v NEW SOUTH WALES

At Brisbane Cricket Ground, Brisbane, November 30, 2001. Day/night game. Queensland won by six wickets. Toss: New South Wales. Queensland 4 pts.

Brad Haddin helped New South Wales rebound from a Pura Cup loss three days earlier by tucking into Queensland's attack. His buccaneering 74 included 13 fours and two sixes, and did much to set up New South Wales' formidable total. Martin Love, however, again proved his worth as a limited-overs batsman with an unbeaten century (15 fours, one six) of real quality that drove the Queenslanders to a comfortable victory. Jimmy Maher became Queensland's leading domestic limited-overs run-scorer during his valuable innings, while James Hopes provided support to Love with an unbeaten half-century.

Man of the Match: M.L. Love. *Attendance:* 14,731.

New South Wales

M.J. Slater c Seccombe b Dawes	....	5	(4)	S.D. Bradstreet not out	....	20	(15)
†B.J. Haddin c and b Hopes	....	74	(55)	D.A. Nash not out	....	6	(5)
M.G. Bevan c Love b Symonds	....	26	(63)				
*S. Lee c Symonds b Noffke	....	21	(39)	L-b 3, w 12, n-b 2	....		17
M.J. Clarke c Hopes b Noffke	....	62	(79)				
M.A. Higgs c Noffke b Kasprowicz	..	22	(20)	(50 overs, 188 mins)	(7 wkts)		271
G.C. Rummans b Noffke	....	18	(22)	Fall: 7 109 125 155 197 242 253			

S.C.G. MacGill, N.W. Bracken and S.R. Clark did not bat.

Bowling: Noffke 10–0–56–3; Dawes 5–0–34–1; Kasprowicz 8–0–60–1; Hopes 10–0–40–1; Symonds 10–0–37–1; Hauritz 7–0–41–0.

Queensland

J.P. Maher c Lee b MacGill	47	(62)	J.R. Hopes not out	52	(50)
M.L. Love not out	127	(127)	L-b 9, w 8	17	
*S.G. Law c Clarke b Lee	25	(35)		—	
A. Symonds c and b Lee	4	(6)	(4 wkts) 272		
C.T. Perren lbw b MacGill	0	(3)	Fall: 114 181 194 197		

B.P. Nash, †W.A. Seccombe, A.A. Noffke, N.M. Hauritz, M.S. Kasprowicz and J.H. Dawes did not bat.

Bowling: Bracken 8–0–48–0; Clark 10–1–43–0; Nash 9.1–1–58–0; Bradstreet 2–0–13–0; MacGill 10–0–62–2; Lee 8–0–39–2.

Umpires: L. D. Musch and J.F. Torpey.

QUEENSLAND v TASMANIA

At Brisbane Cricket Ground, Brisbane, December 18, 2001. Day/night game. Queensland won by 97 runs. Toss: Queensland. Queensland 5 pts. Competition debut: S.J. Jurgensen.

Martin Love unleashed his second consecutive limited-overs century while Clinton Perren scored a timely 96 to help Queensland to another winning platform against Tasmania. Queensland needed a rescue mission after falling to three for 46 in the 12th over and the run-rate slipped further before Perren and Love ignited the innings in a fourth-wicket partnership of 173 from 163 balls. Perren was dropped on 46 by Shane Watson, who had an unhappy return to his home town. Tasmania were always going to struggle chasing 293 for victory, especially after the loss of Michael Di Venuto in the first over. With off-spinner Nathan Hauritz showing mature bowling form, Queensland reduced the match to a clinical, one-sided win.

Man of the Match: C.T. Perren.   *Attendance:* 5,369.

Queensland

M.L. Love c Dighton b Marsh	107	(124)	B.P. Nash not out	11	(10)
J.P. Maher c Cox b Saker	4	(10)	†W.A. Seccombe not out	15	(12)
*S.G. Law c Clingeleffer b Saker	6	(9)	L-b 4, w 11, n-b 1	16	
A. Symonds c and b Saker	9	(13)			
C.T. Perren b Marsh	96	(89)	(50 overs, 195 mins)	(6 wkts) 292	
J.R. Hopes c Young b Marsh	28	(34)	Fall: 12 34 46 219 263 263		

A.J. Bichel, A.A. Noffke, N.M. Hauritz and M.S. Kasprowicz did not bat.

Bowling: Wright 10–2–31–0; Saker 10–0–48–3; Jurgensen 4–0–21–0; Watson 5–0–39–0; Young 6–0–50–0; Polkinghorne 5–0–43–0; Marsh 10–0–56–3.

Tasmania

M.J. Di Venuto c Law b Bichel	0	(4)	A. W. Polkinghorne b Kasprowicz	7	(10)
M.G. Dighton c Noffke b Hopes	5	(18)	D.G. Wright c Law b Hauritz	17	(41)
*J. Cox c Symonds b Hopes	14	(25)	D.J. Saker not out	4	(6)
S. Young b Kasprowicz	29	(71)			
S.R. Watson c Maher b Hopes	1	(6)	L-b 12, w 12, n-b 5	29	
D.J. Marsh lbw b Hauritz	48	(56)			
G.T. Cunningham c Maher b Kasprowicz	11	(16)	(47.5 overs, 191 mins)	195	
†S.G. Clingeleffer c Maher b Noffke	30	(39)	Fall: 0 31 32 35 101 126 127 143 188 195		

S.J. Jurgensen did not bat.

Bowling: Bichel 10–1–30–1; Noffke 9.5–0–53–1; Hopes 9–1–30–3; Kasprowicz 10–1–36–3; Hauritz 9–0–34–2.

Umpires: G. N. Cubit and P. D. Parker.
TV Umpire: L. D. Musch.

At WACA Ground, Perth, January 4, 2002. Day/night game. QUEENSLAND lost to WESTERN AUSTRALIA by 42 runs.

At Bellerive Oval, Hobart, January 13, 2002. QUEENSLAND defeated TASMANIA won by 76 runs.

QUEENSLAND v VICTORIA

At Brisbane Cricket Ground, Brisbane, February 1, 2002. Day/night game. Queensland won by four runs. Toss: Queensland. Queensland 4 pts. Competition debut: D. R. MacKenzie; N. Jewell.

Andrew Symonds had a point to prove to the national selectors, who had dropped him from the Australian limited-overs squad. He stated his case with a typically brisk 61, combining with captain Jimmy Maher in a match-turning 106-run stand from 107 balls. Victoria were well on track for Queensland's 216 at one for 107 after 25 overs until Maher employed the dual spin attack of Symonds and Nathan Hauritz to slow the run-rate effectively. The match effectively ended in a mad scramble when Darren Berry was run out with eight balls remaining. Berry was clearly unhappy with the decision, and was later fined his match fee for showing dissent to the umpires. Victorian all-rounder Andrew McDonald had to hit a six off the final ball from James Hopes for victory, but his single left the Victorians short again at the Gabba.

Man of the Match: A. Symonds.   *Attendance:* 5,089.

Queensland

M. L. Hayden c Berry b Fleming	13	(32)
*J. P. Maher c McDonald b Inness	54	(74)
M. L. Love c Bartlett b Hewett	13	(27)
A. Symonds c Berry b Lewis	61	(63)
B. P. Nash c Hodge b Inness	13	(21)
C. T. Perren c Klinger b Hewett	24	(26)
J. R. Hopes c Elliott b Hewett	14	(18)
†W. A. Seccombe run out (Hodge)	3	(6)
N. M. Hauritz not out	2	(6)
D. R. MacKenzie run out (McDonald)	2	(4)
S. A. Muller b Fleming	0	(2)
L-b 10, w 7	17	
(46.3 overs, 201 mins)	216	

J. H. Dawes did not bat.

Fall: 16 35 141 162 185 203 211 212 215 216

Bowling: Fleming 8.3–2–25–2; Inness 10–2–36–2; Hewett 10–0–49–3; Lewis 10–1–49–1; Hodge 2–0–16–0; Moss 3–0–16–0; McDonald 3–0–15–0.

Victoria

*M. T. G. Elliott c Seccombe b Dawes	73	(110)
R. A. Bartlett c Symonds b Muller	5	(6)
B. J. Hodge b Symonds	38	(62)
M. Klinger c Seccombe b Hauritz	0	(14)
N. Jewell c Nash b Hauritz	31	(42)
J. Moss st Seccombe b Symonds	9	(14)
A. B. McDonald not out	19	(29)
†D. S. Berry run out (Hauritz)	17	(18)
I. S. L. Hewett c Seccombe b MacKenzie	0	(3)
D. W. Fleming not out	3	(4)
L-b 1, w 14, n-b 2	17	
(50 overs, 200 mins) (8 wkts)	212	

M. L. Lewis and M. W. H. Inness did not bat.

Fall: 13 107 113 156 171 172 203 203

Bowling: Muller 6–0–22–1; Dawes 9–0–44–1; Hopes 8–0–47–0; MacKenzie 7–0–29–1; Symonds 10–1–33–2; Hauritz 10–0–36–2.

Umpires: L. D. Musch and J. F. Torpey.

QUEENSLAND v SOUTH AUSTRALIA

At Brisbane Cricket Ground, Brisbane, February 8, 2002. Day/night game. South Australia won by 66 runs. Toss: South Australia. South Australia 5 pts.

Queensland began the match by dropping Greg Blewett in the second over, following which the home team's fortunes did not improve. Blewett batted steadily before falling to a fine outfield catch by Clinton Perren, but South Australia had already laid a solid foundation on a difficult day for the batsmen. The South Australians' moderate total looked tough for Queensland when Paul Rofe dismissed Matthew Hayden and Martin Love in the opening six overs. The Queenslanders then slid steadily to defeat in the face of some fine pace bowling by Mark Harrity.

Man of the Match: M. A. Harrity.   *Attendance:* 5,350.

South Australia

G.S. Blewett c Perren b MacKenzie . .	45	(62)	M.J. Smith b Dawes	9	(6)
D.A. Fitzgerald c Seccombe b Dawes .	22	(36)	†G. A. Manou not out	2	(2)
C.J. Davies c Perren b MacKenzie . . .	15	(31)	P. Wilson not out	2	(1)
*D.S. Lehmann c Nash b Hopes	13	(31)	L-b 4, w 4, n-b 3	11	
B.A. Johnson c Muller b Hauritz	44	(75)			
N.T. Adcock run out (Nash)	8	(21)	(50 overs, 192 mins) (8 wkts)	203	
B.E. Young c Maher b Dawes	32	(38)	Fall: 66 80 95 104 123 176 198 200		

P.C. Rofe and M. A. Harrity did not bat.

Bowling: Muller 6–0–37–0; Dawes 9–1–37–3; Hopes 10–3–19–1; MacKenzie 6–0–21–2; Symonds 10–0–46–0; Hauritz 9–0–39–1.

Queensland

*J.P. Maher c Lehmann b Harrity	24	(45)	N. M. Hauritz c Adcock b Smith	2	(29)
M.L. Hayden b Rofe	2	(7)	D.R. MacKenzie c Fitzgerald b Young	9	(16)
M.L. Love c Manou b Rofe	2	(8)	J.H. Dawes not out	1	(10)
A. Symonds b Rofe	18	(13)			
C.T. Perren c and b Harrity	24	(47)	L-b 10, w 11	21	
B.P. Nash c Manou b Smith	3	(20)			
J.R. Hopes b Blewett	30	(48)	(41.2 overs, 170 mins)	137	
†W. A. Seccombe c Smith b Harrity . .	1	(5)	Fall: 11 17 43 83 89 96 97 118 133 137		

S. A. Muller did not bat.

Bowling: Wilson 10–1–27–0; Rofe 7–1–44–3; Harrity 10–3–15–3; Smith 9–0–28–2; Blewett 3.2–0–8–1; Young 2–0–5–1.

Umpires: A.J. McQuillan and B. N. J. Oxenford.

At Adelaide Oval, Adelaide, February 17, 2002. QUEENSLAND defeated SOUTH AUSTRALIA by five wickets.

FINAL

At Brisbane Cricket Ground, Brisbane, February 24, 2002. QUEENSLAND lost to NEW SOUTH WALES. For details see section on ING Cup, 2001-02, page 475.

DOMESTIC LIMITED-OVERS RESULTS

	M	W	L	NR	T
Australian Capital Territory	3	3	0	0	0
New South Wales	29	11	18	0	0
New Zealanders	1	0	1	0	0
South Australia	22	17	5	0	0
Tasmania	24	16	7	1	0
Victoria	22	13	8	1	0
Western Australia	27	12	13	2	0
Total	128	72	52	4	0

RECORDS

Highest score for:	159	S.G. Law v Tasmania at Brisbane	1993-94
Highest score against:	131	S.R. Waugh (New South Wales) at Brisbane	1992-93
Best bowling for:	7/34	C.G. Rackemann v South Australia at Adelaide	1988-89
Best bowling against:	5/23	J.P. Marquet (Tasmania) at Hobart (Bellerive)	1995-96
Highest total for:	4-320	v Tasmania at Brisbane	1993-94
Highest total against:	6-301	by Western Australia at Perth	1999-00
Lowest total for:	62	v Western Australia at Perth	1976-77
Lowest total against:	77	by Western Australia at Perth	1976-77

* *Denotes not out.*

MOST RUNS

	M	I	NO	R	HS	100s	50s	Avge	S-R
J.P. Maher	61	61	9	2,426	128	4	15	46.65	75.88
M.L. Hayden........	51	51	9	2,231	152*	8	11	53.12	72.18
S.G. Law	71	65	6	1,916	159	5	5	32.47	89.37
M.L. Love	58	55	7	1,744	127*	3	9	36.33	75.66
T.J. Barsby	42	41	2	1,145	101	1	10	29.36	61.10
A.R. Border.........	43	40	8	1,049	97	0	9	32.78	72.60
A. Symonds	48	45	4	973	91	0	3	23.73	95.96
G.M. Ritchie........	27	24	4	825	114	1	5	41.25	74.93
G.S. Chappell	20	20	0	682	92	0	7	34.10	78.66
G.I. Foley	41	34	7	677	66	0	3	25.07	65.79

* *Denotes not out.*

HIGHEST PARTNERSHIP FOR EACH WICKET

250	for 1st	M.L. Hayden and J.P. Maher, v Australian Capital Territory at Canberra ..	1999-00
260	for 2nd	M.L. Hayden and S.G. Law, v Tasmania at Brisbane	1993-94
187	for 3rd	J.M. Thomas and S.G. Law, v Western Australia at Brisbane	1993-94
173	for 4th	M.L. Love and C.T. Perren, v Tasmania at Brisbane	2001-02
98	for 5th	G.M. Ritchie and G.S. Trimble, v South Australia at Brisbane	1984-85
86	for 6th	P.L. Taylor and I.A. Healy, v Tasmania at Brisbane	1990-91
91	for 7th	J.N. Langley and J.A. Maclean, v South Australia at Brisbane	1975-76
55*	for 8th	S.A. Prestwidge and A.J. Bichel, v New South Wales at Sydney	1997-98
62	for 9th	S.A. Prestwidge and M.S. Kasprowicz, v New South Wales at Brisbane ..	1997-98
33	for 10th	M.L. Love and C.G. Rackemann, v New South Wales at Brisbane	1993-94

* *Denotes unbroken partnership*

MOST WICKETS

	M	Balls	Mdns	R	W	BB	5W/i	Avge
S. A. Prestwidge	45	2,189	18	1,755	67	5/59	1	26.19
M. S. Kasprowicz	52	2,651	28	1,928	62	4/21	0	31.10
C. G. Rackemann	36	1,975	38	1,249	48	7/34	1	26.02
A. J. Bichel	43	2,188	27	1,584	45	4/45	0	35.20
G. Dymock	23	1,300	20	749	39	5/27	1	19.21
A. C. Dale	27	1,451	20	842	36	4/26	0	23.39
J. R. Thomson	25	1,273	19	821	35	6/19	1	23.46
C. J. McDermott	25	1,250	27	783	30	4/14	0	26.10
B. N. Creevey	25	1,123	13	893	28	3/26	0	31.89
G. S. Chappell	20	761	9	492	27	4/35	0	18.22
J. R. Hopes	16	798	11	536	27	5/29	1	19.85

MOST DISMISSALS

	M	Ct	St	Total
W. A. Seccombe	49	69	12	81
I. A. Healy	29	47	7	54
J. A. Maclean	19	32	1	33
R. B. Phillips	18	22	0	22
P. W. Anderson	6	4	0	4

MOST CATCHES

S. G. Law	31 in 71 matches	M. L. Love	19 in 58 matches
J. P. Maher	27 in 61 matches	M. L. Hayden	16 in 51 matches
A. R. Border	26 in 43 matches	A. J. Bichel	15 in 42 matches
A. Symonds	23 in 48 matches	G. I. Foley	12 in 41 matches
G. S. Chappell	20 in 27 matches	M. S. Kasprowicz	12 in 52 matches

MOST APPEARANCES

71	S. G. Law	1988-89 – 2001-02	49	W. A. Seccombe	1994-95 – 2001-02
61	J. P. Maher	1993-94 – 2001-02	48	A. Symonds	1993-94 – 2001-02
58	M. L. Love	1993-94 – 2001-02	45	S. A. Prestwidge	1992-93 – 2000-01
52	M. S. Kasprowicz	1989-90 – 2001-02	43	A. R. Border	1980-81 – 1995-96
51	M. L. Hayden	1992-93 – 2001-02	42	A. J. Bichel	1992-93 – 2001-02

SOUTH AUSTRALIA

South Australia were disappointed with third place in a season in which they defeated both finalists, New South Wales and Queensland. It was a strange year, given that the side lost its opening game against Western Australia, then won twice against Victoria at home and away, and lost two home games against Western Australia and New South Wales before finding its best form in January and February with four successive wins over Tasmania, New South Wales, Tasmania and Queensland, three of them away. A win in the final game against Queensland at home would have secured a place in the final, but instead the five-wicket defeat eliminated the side from the competition. The three home losses were probably the worst statistic, although the match against Western Australia in November, with its one-wicket/two-ball margin of defeat, could have gone South Australia's way.

Nevertheless there were a number of thrilling performances. A scintillating 69 off 59 balls to add to three for 16 with his left-arm darts gave skipper Darren Lehmann the Man of the Match performance in the first win over Victoria at Adelaide Oval, and Lehmann was again to the fore with a punishing half-century in the next game against the same opponents at Richmond. Greg Blewett made a fluent 73 in the fourth game against Western Australia. Lehmann won his third match award against Tasmania in Launceston with a score of 85 not out, and left-armers Mark Harrity and Brad Young bowled accurately and led the attack with three wickets apiece.

The best result of the year was the match at Coffs Harbour, where the South Australians inflicted a 114-run defeat on New South Wales and Lehmann claimed his fourth award with the only century for the season by a South Australian. The captain's Australian call-up obviously left the side less potent, although Blewett stepped into the breach with a top score of 65 and two wickets in the win over Tasmania in Adelaide, and Harrity's sustained accuracy in claiming three for 15 from ten overs in the win over Queensland at the Gabba left the side in a good position before the final home defeat.

Lehmann, with 374 runs at 62.33 and a strike rate of 82.02 from eight games, was the most effective batsman and he was strongly supported by Blewett with 436 runs at 43.60 and a strike rate of 75.04. However, there were no other consistent scorers. By contrast, the bowlers made more even contributions. Fast man Harrity and left-arm spinner Young proved more effective than in the longer form of the game with 17 wickets and 15 wickets respectively at under 20, while Mike Smith was consistent with 12 wickets at 19.25 and Paul Rofe's ten wickets was a substantial contribution from the young bowler. Jason Gillespie was only available for four matches but gathered seven wickets at under 20 apiece. – BERNARD WHIMPRESS.

RESULTS, 2001-02

ING Cup matches – Played 10: Won 6, Lost 4.
Competition placing – 3rd.

ING CUP AVERAGES, 2001-02

BATTING

	M	I	NO	R	HS	100s	50s	Avge	Ct/St	S-R
D. S. Lehmann	8	8	2	374	101	1	3	62.33	1	82.02
G. S. Blewett	10	10	0	436	80	0	4	43.60	2	75.04
D. A. Fitzgerald	8	8	0	204	62	0	1	25.50	2	60.53
B. A. Johnson	10	10	1	216	51	0	1	24.00	4	69.68
C. J. Davies	8	8	0	180	46	0	0	22.50	0	60.40
B. E. Young	9	9	0	200	56	0	1	22.22	10	73.80
B. H. Higgins	6	5	2	65	36	0	0	21.67	2	55.56
N. T. Adcock	6	5	0	102	45	0	0	20.40	1	64.15
M. J. Smith	7	7	3	69	30*	0	0	17.25	6	90.79
G. A. Manou	10	9	4	72	15	0	0	14.40	18/1	66.67
J. M. Vaughan	4	4	0	41	28	0	0	10.25	4	52.56
P. Wilson	6	5	3	19	8*	0	0	9.50	2	118.75
J. N. Gillespie	4	2	0	5	3	0	0	2.50	0	38.46
R. J. Harris	3	1	0	2	2	0	0	2.00	3	20.00
M. A. Harrity	10	1	0	0	0	0	0	0.00	5	0.00
P. C. Rofe	9	2	2	1	1*	0	0	–	0	12.35
B. A. Swain	1	0	0	0	0	0	0	–	0	–
M. D. King	1	0	0	0	0	0	0	–	0	–

* Denotes not out.

BOWLING

	O	M	R	W	BB	5W/I	Avge
M. J. Smith	62	4	231	12	3/32	0	19.25
B. E. Young	64.2	0	292	15	4/55	0	19.47
J. N. Gillespie	38.4	5	137	7	3/31	0	19.57
M. A. Harrity	77.5	7	336	17	3/15	0	19.76
G. S. Blewett	14.2	0	64	3	2/41	0	21.33
P. Wilson	54	3	187	8	3/35	0	23.38
D. S. Lehmann	20	0	100	4	3/16	0	25.00
B. A. Johnson	22	0	107	4	2/25	0	26.75
P. C. Rofe	80	7	349	10	3/44	0	34.90
R. J. Harris	19	1	72	2	1/20	0	36.00
M. D. King	6	0	43	0	–	0	–
B. A. Swain	6	1	24	0	–	0	–

At WACA Ground, Perth, October 12, 2001. SOUTH AUSTRALIA lost to WESTERN AUSTRALIA by 56 runs.

SOUTH AUSTRALIA v VICTORIA

At Adelaide Oval, Adelaide, October 21, 2001. South Australia won by seven wickets. Toss: Victoria. South Australia 5 pts.

South Australian captain Darren Lehmann led his side to an easy victory over Victoria, taking three late wickets and then plundering an unbeaten 69 (seven fours, one six) as his side won with more than 12 overs to spare. Victorian captain Matthew Elliott (seven fours) was the anchor-man for his side but no one could stay with him to build a partnership against a keen bowling and fielding unit. Openers David Fitzgerald and Greg Blewett gave the home side a solid start with 73 off 16 overs, and after Jeff Vaughan departed one run later a 66-run partnership in 17 overs between Fitzgerald and Lehmann allowed the South Australians to cruise to victory.

Man of the Match: D. S. Lehmann. *Attendance:* 2,887.

Victoria

J.L. Arnberger c Vaughan b Rofe	11	(26)
*M.T.G. Elliott c Harris b Lehmann	84	(107)
M. Klinger b Harrity	20	(30)
J. Moss c Harris b Rofe	2	(5)
I.J. Harvey c Vaughan b Harrity	13	(11)
M.P. Mott c Manou b Harris	10	(22)
B.C. Oliver b Johnson	3	(11)
†D.S. Berry b Lehmann	17	(27)

S.K. Warne b Lehmann	5	(17)
I.S.L. Hewett c Manou b Gillespie	7	(12)
D.W. Fleming not out	0	(0)
L-b 2, w 2	5	
	—	
(44.4 overs, 186 mins)	177	
Fall: 29 59 68 93 114 121 152		
164 177 177		

M.L. Lewis did not bat.

Bowling: Gillespie 8.4–3–27–1; Rofe 10–0–41–2; Harrity 7–0–40–2; Harris 7–0–21–1; Johnson 7–0–29–1; Lehmann 5–0–16–3.

South Australia

D.A. Fitzgerald b Oliver	62	(104)
G.S. Blewett c Oliver b Moss	35	(53)
J.M. Vaughan c Berry b Moss	0	(1)
*D.S. Lehmann not out	69	(59)
B.A. Johnson not out	9	(7)

B 1, w 2, n-b 1	4
	—
(37.1 overs, 153 mins) (3 wkts)	179
Fall: 73 74 140	

B.H. Higgins, N.T. Adcock, R.J. Harris, †G.A. Manou, J.N. Gillespie, P.C. Rofe and M.A. Harrity did not bat.

Bowling: Fleming 5–0–22–0; Hewett 9–0–46–0; Lewis 3–0–13–0; Oliver 6.1–0–35–1; Moss 5–0–23–2; Warne 7–2–15–0; Mott 2–0–24–0.

Umpires: P.M. Angley and K.D. Perrin.

At Richmond Cricket Ground, Richmond, November 4, 2001. SOUTH AUSTRALIA defeated VICTORIA by four wickets.

SOUTH AUSTRALIA v WESTERN AUSTRALIA

At Adelaide Oval, Adelaide, November 30, 2001. Day/night game. Western Australia won by one wicket. Toss: South Australia. Western Australia 4 pts. Competition debut: M.D. King.

Western Australia won a thrilling encounter when last batsman Brad Williams struck a ball from Brad Young over the mid-wicket fence with just two balls of the game remaining. Greg Blewett (12 fours) was the mainstay of South Australia's innings, and his 97-run second-wicket partnership with Chris Davies gave the innings its main substance. The Western Australian openers Chris Rogers and Ryan Campbell got their team away to a brisk start but the steady spin bowling of Brad Young caused middle-order wickets to fall at regular intervals. Mike Hussey and Stuart Karppinen, however, kept the visitors in the game with quick-fire contributions, setting up the opportunity for Williams' final blow.

Man of the Match: G.S. Blewett.   *Attendance:* 3,152.

South Australia

J.M. Vaughan c Campbell b Williams	9	(20)
G.S. Blewett b Harvey	73	(101)
C.J. Davies b Angel	40	(45)
*D.S. Lehmann c Goodwin b Harvey	25	(40)
B.A. Johnson c Karppinen b Hogg	37	(51)
B.E. Young run out (Williams)	13	(21)
†G.A. Manou c Hussey b Williams	14	(14)

B.H. Higgins not out	15	(10)
M.J. Smith not out	1	(2)
L-b 3, w 1, n-b 4	8	
	—	
(50 overs, 204 mins) (7 wkts)	235	
Fall: 24 121 134 167 193 216 221		

M.D. King, P.C. Rofe and M.A. Harrity did not bat.

Bowling: Williams 8–1–32–2; Karppinen 10–1–37–0; Nicholson 7–0–44–0; Angel 10–0–36–1; Harvey 10–0–45–2; Hogg 5–0–38–1.

Western Australia

C.J.L. Rogers c Manou b Harrity	 39	(53)	G.B. Hogg run out (Smith)	 7	(9)
†R.J. Campbell lbw b Harrity	 20	(22)	M.J. Nicholson not out	 5	(5)
*S.M. Katich st Manou b Lehmann	.. 38	(74)	B.A. Williams not out	 6	(2)
M.W. Goodwin c Blewett b Smith	... 20	(41)	B 1, l-b 2, w 6, n-b 4	 13	
M.E.K. Hussey c Vaughan b Young	.. 45	(50)			
S.J. Karppinen b Young	 22	(22)	(49.4 overs, 209 mins)	(9 wkts) 238	
K.M. Harvey c Smith b Young	 6	(9)	Fall: 49 62 109 139 174 184 205		
M.J. North lbw b Young	 17	(15)	223 231		

J. Angel did not bat.

Bowling: King 6–0–43–0; Rofe 10–1–23–0; Harrity 10–2–40–2; Smith 9–0–54–1; Young 9.4–0–55–4; Lehmann 5–0–20–1.

Umpires: J.S. Booth and P.J. Weeks.

SOUTH AUSTRALIA v NEW SOUTH WALES

At Adelaide Oval, Adelaide, December 8, 2001. New South Wales won by 135 runs. Toss: South Australia. South Australia 4 pts.

Paul Wilson, in his first match for the season, dismissed Michael Slater and Michael Bevan to the second and third balls of the match, then claimed Brad Haddin to have the visitors reeling at three for 16. A well-crafted innings by Michael Clarke (six fours, one six) helped New South Wales to recover somewhat to seven for 162 in the 42nd over before savage hitting by Brett Lee (two fours and three sixes) and Shawn Bradstreet in an unbeaten stand of 73 from 53 balls boosted the team to a strong total. South Australia also got off to a poor start with Stuart Clark capturing two early wickets, and when Brett Lee removed Greg Blewett in the middle of a fiery spell the South Australians were in trouble at three for 28. The dismissal of Darren Lehmann at five for 53 left the result beyond doubt.

Man of the Match: B. Lee.   *Attendance:* 2,263.

New South Wales

†B.J. Haddin c Young b Wilson	 10	(16)	S.D. Bradstreet not out	 46	(48)
M.J. Slater b Wilson	 0	(1)	B. Lee not out	 44	(29)
M.G. Bevan c Smith b Wilson	 0	(1)			
M.J. Clarke c and b Young	 62	(91)	L-b 10, w 3, n-b 3	 16	
*S. Lee c Young b Smith	 14	(35)			
M.A. Higgs c Manou b Harrity	 14	(33)	(50 overs, 201 mins)	(7 wkts) 238	
G.C. Rummans c Johnson b Young	.. 32	(48)	Fall: 3 3 16 67 104 123 165		

S.C.G. MacGill, N.W. Bracken and S.R. Clark did not bat.

Bowling: Wilson 10–0–35–3; Rofe 10–2–38–0; Smith 10–1–35–1; Harrity 6–0–44–1; Lehmann 6–0–43–0; Young 8–0–33–2.

South Australia

G.S. Blewett c Higgs b B. Lee	11	(29)	M.J. Smith lbw b S. Lee	5	(17)
J.M. Vaughan c Haddin b Clark	4	(9)	P. Wilson st Haddin b MacGill	8	(8)
C.J. Davies lbw b Clark	0	(7)	P.C. Rofe not out	0	(0)
*D.S. Lehmann c and b Clark	29	(38)			
B.A. Johnson c Haddin b Bracken	5	(15)	L-b 2, w 2, n-b 6	10	
B.H. Higgins b Bracken	12	(37)			
B.E. Young run out (B. Lee/Haddin)	12	(45)	(37.4 overs, 172 mins)	103	
†G.A. Manou c Clarke b MacGill	7	(27)	Fall: 7 12 28 37 53 68 84 94 99 103		

M.A. Harrity did not bat.

Bowling: B. Lee 10–0–31–1; Clark 10–1–25–3; Bracken 8–0–25–2; S. Lee 6–1–8–1; MacGill 3.4–0–12–2.

Umpires: S.D. Fry and D.J. Harper.
TV Umpire: M.R. Bartlett.

At NTCA Ground, Launceston, January 6, 2002. SOUTH AUSTRALIA defeated TASMANIA by 42 runs.

At International Sports Stadium, Coffs Harbour, January 12, 2002. SOUTH AUSTRALIA defeated NEW SOUTH WALES by 114 runs.

SOUTH AUSTRALIA v TASMANIA

At Adelaide Oval, Adelaide, February 1, 2002. Day/night game. South Australia won by 34 runs. Toss: South Australia. South Australia 4 pts. Competition debut: S.B. Tubb.

South Australia held the upper hand from the start of this match. Greg Blewett and David Fitzgerald set an example of firm driving and quick singles, and the run-rate remained steady at about five an over throughout the innings. Some fine work by the Tasmanians in the field was not enough to make up for their benign bowling. Needing a solid start, Tasmania lost three wickets in eight deliveries from Mike Smith. Michael Di Venuto and Daniel Marsh gave them some hope during a stand of 97 in 18 overs, and a desperate last-wicket flurry of 28 from 16 balls gave the innings a look of respectability, but the South Australian bowlers maintained their accuracy and penetration and the result was never really in doubt.

Man of the Match: G.S. Blewett.   *Attendance:* 3,624.

South Australia

*G.S. Blewett run out (Marsh)	65	(93)	M.J. Smith not out	5	(4)
D.A. Fitzgerald run out (Mason)	44	(57)	†G.A. Manou not out	3	(3)
C.J. Davies c Cox b Marsh	45	(60)			
B.A. Johnson st Clingeleffer b Marsh	31	(38)	B 2, l-b 5, w 2, n-b 4	13	
N.T. Adcock b Wright	40	(41)			
B.H. Higgins c Clingeleffer b Watson	0	(1)	(50 overs, 196 mins)	(7 wkts) 250	
B.E. Young run out (Watson)	4	(7)	Fall: 93 143 181 210 211 228 245		

P.C. Rofe, P. Wilson and M.A. Harrity did not bat.

Bowling: Saker 10–0–42–0; Wright 10–0–43–1; Watson 8–0–53–1; Jurgensen 7–0–32–0; Marsh 10–0–45–2; Tubb 5–0–28–0.

Tasmania

S. R. Mason c Manou b Rofe	16 (35)	†S. G. Clingeleffer not out	19 (14)
M. G. Dighton c Johnson b Smith	35 (64)	D. J. Saker b Wilson	3 (7)
S. R. Watson c Manou b Smith	5 (22)	S. B. Tubb b Wilson	13 (8)
M. J. Di Venuto c Manou b Blewett	44 (57)	B 1, l-b 4, w 3, n-b 5	13
*J. Cox c Wilson b Smith	0 (2)		
D. J. Marsh c Harrity b Young	51 (61)	(47 overs, 196 mins)	216
S. P. Kremerskothen run out (Smith)	12 (12)	Fall: 43 59 60 60 157 165 180	
D. G. Wright c Manou b Blewett	5 (6)	180 188 216	

S. J. Jurgensen did not bat.

Bowling: Wilson 9–0–30–2; Rofe 10–2–34–1; Smith 8–1–32–3; Harrity 6–0–33–0; Blewett 7–0–41–2; Young 7–0–41–1.

Umpires: P. M. Angley and M. R. Bartlett.

At Brisbane Cricket Ground, Brisbane, February 8, 2002. Day/night game. SOUTH AUSTRALIA defeated QUEENSLAND by 66 runs.

SOUTH AUSTRALIA v QUEENSLAND

At Adelaide Oval, Adelaide, February 17, 2002. Queensland won by five wickets. Toss: Queensland. Queensland 4 pts. Competition debut: S. A. Brant.

South Australia's prospects of staging their first limited-overs final since 1984 were destroyed following a disheartening loss to Queensland in the Pura Cup match the day before. They made a brisk start but lost wickets regularly as the scoring rate slowed before Brad Young's hard hitting (four fours, one six) put some respectability into the score. Queensland made a quick start before losing three wickets for 15, but a fourth-wicket stand of 97 between Martin Love (six fours, one six) and Clinton Perren (seven fours) restored the innings. Left-arm spinner Young gave the South Australians a chance when he dismissed Love and James Hopes within four balls but that was the final success, as Perren and Lee Carseldine guided their side to victory at a run a ball with plenty of overs to spare.

Man of the Match: C. T. Perren.   *Attendance:* 3,318.

South Australia

*G. S. Blewett c Noffke b Brant	21 (38)	M. J. Smith run out (Symonds/Seccombe)	15 (21)
D. A. Fitzgerald c Seccombe b Dawes	20 (22)	†G. A. Manou not out	6 (14)
C. J. Davies c Hauritz b Noffke	30 (55)	P. Wilson not out	1 (1)
B. H. Higgins c and b Symonds	36 (66)	L-b 1	1
B. A. Johnson c Seccombe b Hopes	2 (6)		
N. T. Adcock c Brant b Perren	6 (19)	(50 overs, 196 mins) (8 wkts)	194
B. E. Young b Hopes	56 (58)	Fall: 25 53 81 88 106 132 167 193	

P. C. Rofe and M. A. Harrity did not bat.

Bowling: Dawes 6–0–22–1; Brant 8–1–33–1; Noffke 9–2–27–1; Hopes 9–1–36–2; Perren 4–0–19–1; Hauritz 10–0–36–0; Symonds 4–1–20–1.

Queensland

*J. P. Maher c Blewett b Rofe	37 (39)	L. A. Carseldine not out	12 (15)
B. P. Nash c Manou b Wilson	9 (21)		
M. L. Love c and b Young	64 (79)	L-b 8, w 3	11
A. Symonds c Wilson b Smith	5 (6)		
C. T. Perren not out	57 (83)	(41 overs, 172 mins) (5 wkts)	195
J. R. Hopes lbw b Young	0 (3)	Fall: 41 51 56 153 153	

†W. A. Seccombe, A. A. Noffke, N. M. Hauritz, S. A. Brant and J. H. Dawes did not bat.

Bowling: Wilson 8–0–46–1; Rofe 10–1–30–1; Smith 9–0–38–1; Harrity 4–0–29–0; Young 6–0–29–2; Blewett 4–0–15–0.

Umpires: S.J. Davis and S.D. Fry.
TV Umpire: M.R. Bartlett.

DOMESTIC LIMITED-OVERS RESULTS

	M	W	L	NR	T
Australian Capital Territory	3	3	0	0	0
New South Wales	19	9	10	0	0
New Zealanders	2	0	2	0	0
Queensland	22	5	17	0	0
Tasmania	20	14	6	0	0
Victoria	26	10	15	0	1
Western Australia	31	11	20	0	0
Total	123	52	70	0	1

RECORDS

Highest score for:	142	D.S. Lehmann v Tasmania at Adelaide	1994-95
Highest score against:	164	R.B. McCosker (New South Wales) at Sydney	1981-82
Best bowling for:	5/23	R.J. McCurdy v Western Australia at Adelaide	1984-85
Best bowling against:	7/34	C.G. Rackemann (Queensland) at Adelaide	1988-89
Highest total for:	6-325	v Tasmania at Hobart (TCA)	1986-87
Highest total against:	7-310	by New South Wales at North Sydney	1997-98
Lowest total for:	87	v Western Australia at Perth	1989-90
Lowest total against:	119	by Queensland at Adelaide	1993-94

MOST RUNS

	M	I	NO	R	HS	100s	50s	Avge	S-R
D.S. Lehmann	56	56	8	2,431	142*	6	16	50.65	87.51
G.S. Blewett	60	58	5	2,033	101*	1	14	38.36	65.69
J.D. Siddons	42	40	4	1,169	102	1	8	32.47	78.77
D.W. Hookes	38	38	1	1,149	101	1	6	31.05	80.07
D.A. Fitzgerald	34	34	1	1,010	114	2	6	30.61	70.33
C.J. Davies	33	32	0	908	125	1	5	28.38	66.33
B.A. Johnson	43	42	7	870	83	0	3	24.86	69.71
P.R. Sleep	30	28	4	846	90	0	4	35.25	65.58
P.C. Nobes	27	27	4	745	140*	1	4	32.39	58.43
G.A. Bishop	26	25	1	708	119*	2	2	29.50	66.48

HIGHEST PARTNERSHIP FOR EACH WICKET

217* for 1st	D.S. Lehmann and P.C. Nobes, v Tasmania at Adelaide		1994-95
145 for 2nd	B.A. Richards and I.M. Chappell, v Queensland at Adelaide		1970-71
153 for 3rd	C.J. Davies and D.S. Lehmann, v Victoria at Adelaide		2000-01
125 for 4th	G.S. Chappell and K.G. Cunningham, v Western Australia at Perth		1972-73
133* for 5th	A.M.J. Hilditch and M.D. Haysman, v Queensland at Brisbane		1984-85
88 for 6th	P.R. Sleep and J.K. Pyke, v New South Wales at Sydney		1987-88
106* for 7th	J.K. Pyke and C.M. Killen, v Victoria at Adelaide		1987-88
64* for 8th	D.S. Lehmann and B.A. Swain, v Australian Capital Territory at Canberra		1999-00
61* for 9th	M. Hendrick and A.A. Mallett, v Western Australia at Perth		1974-75
32 for 10th	T.B.A. May and C.J. Owen, v Tasmania at Adelaide		1991-92

* Denotes unbroken partnership.

MOST WICKETS

	M	Balls	Mdns	R	W	BB	5W/i	Avge
P. Wilson	46	2,540	42	1,676	70	4/23	0	23.94
M.A. Harrity	33	1,700	20	1,256	52	5/42	1	24.15
G.S. Blewett	60	1,856	10	1,546	45	4/33	0	34.36
B.E. Young	36	1,515	6	1,252	38	4/24	0	32.95
J.N. Gillespie	19	1,102	19	748	34	4/46	0	22.00
J.C. Scuderi	37	1,759	13	1,357	32	3/36	0	42.41
S.P. George	20	1,049	7	881	29	4/33	0	30.28
B.N. Wigney	26	1,318	23	876	29	3/24	0	30.21
T.B.A. May	24	1,318	18	818	27	4/9	0	30.30
A.A. Mallett	15	881	9	589	23	3/43	0	25.61

MOST DISMISSALS

	M	Ct	St	Total
T.J. Nielsen	45	55	3	58
G.A. Manou	25	39	1	40
W.B. Phillips	13	18	0	18
K.J. Wright	14	15	3	18
D.S. Berry	4	5	2	7
D.B. Yagmich	2	5	1	6

MOST CATCHES

B.E. Young	27 in 36 matches	B.A. Johnston	19 in 43 matches
D.W. Hookes	22 in 38 matches	D.F.G. O'Connor	12 in 14 matches
J.D. Siddons	20 in 42 matches	D.A. Fitzgerald	11 in 34 matches
G.S. Blewett	21 in 60 matches	J.M. Vaughan	11 in 20 matches
D.S. Lehmann	16 in 56 matches		

MOST APPEARANCES

60	G.S. Blewett	1992-93 – 2001-02	37	J.C. Scuderi	1988-89 – 1998-99
56	D.S. Lehmann	1988-89 – 2001-02	36	B.E. Young	1996-97 – 2001-02
46	P. Wilson	1993-94 – 2001-02	34	D.A. Fitzgerald	1997-98 – 2001-02
43	B.A. Johnson	1994-95 – 2001-02	33	C.J. Davies	1997-98 – 2001-02
42	J.D. Siddons	1991-92 – 1999-00	33	M.A. Harrity	1995-96 – 2001-02
38	D.W. Hookes	1975-76 – 1991-92			

TASMANIA

Once again, in the short version of the game, Tasmania were a long way off the pace. They finished with one win, eight losses and a no-result washout which Victoria would have been at very short odds to win anyway. Tasmania have finished last or second-last in the limited-overs competition in nine of the past ten seasons.

In the first two matches Tasmania gave their supporters something to cheer. Chasing a record New South Wales total at Bankstown, they themselves set a competition record for a team batting second before falling short. In their next match, at Perth, Ricky Ponting made such short work of the target that Tasmania earned a bonus point; thereafter, however, nothing went right. The batsmen made too many attempts at big hits instead of working the ball into the gaps and turning the strike over, while the wayward line and length of the bowlers was illustrated by the fact that eight of them conceded more than five runs per over.

Tasmania turned over 23 players in a bid to get their mix right, and the preoccupation with picking all-rounders, too many of whom were not good enough in either department, underlined one of their major deficiencies. Shane Watson and Daniel Marsh were the leading run-getters with 243 apiece, Marsh with the creditable strike-rate of 82.94. Only one other, skipper Ricky Ponting (203 runs at a strike-rate of 103.05) topped 200 runs and that from only three games because of national duties. The experienced trio of Jamie Cox, Michael Di Venuto and Shaun Young contributed little, and the younger players were unable to compensate.

The most successful bowler was pace man Damien Wright, who took his 13 wickets at 3.83 per over besides making some occasional useful runs. David Saker gave solid support, but the other bowlers were simply not up to the challenges of interstate limited-overs cricket. Young and Scott Kremerskothen, after taking 27 wickets between them the previous season, struggled to break through, and Watson and Shane Jurgensen were unable to adapt their good first-class bowling form to the shorter game. – DAVID STOCKDALE.

RESULTS, 2001-02

ING Cup matches – Played 10: Won 1, Lost 8, No result 1.
Competition placing – 6th.

ING CUP AVERAGES, 2001-02

BATTING

	M	I	NO	R	HS	100s	50s	Avge	Ct/St	S-R
R. T. Ponting	3	3	0	203	102	1	1	67.67	0	103.05
D. J. Marsh	10	8	1	243	101*	1	1	34.71	0	82.94
S. P. Kremerskothen	5	5	2	103	43*	0	0	34.33	1	68.67
G. J. Bailey	1	1	0	33	33	0	0	33.00	0	63.46
S. R. Watson	9	8	0	243	96	0	3	30.38	2	62.63
M. J. Di Venuto	8	7	0	182	52	0	1	26.00	1	75.83
S. G. Clingeleffer	10	6	2	95	30	0	0	23.75	10/1	77.24
S. Young	7	6	1	108	43	0	0	21.60	2	48.00
J. Cox	9	8	2	125	48*	0	0	20.83	4	62.19
M. G. Dighton	6	5	0	98	52	0	1	19.60	3	66.67
D. G. Wright	10	7	2	89	40	0	0	17.80	3	75.42
G. T. Cunningham	8	7	0	112	46	0	0	16.00	3	71.34
D. F. Hills	2	2	0	29	29	0	0	14.50	0	44.62
S. B. Tubb	1	1	0	13	13	0	0	13.00	0	162.50
S. R. Mason	3	3	0	35	16	0	0	11.67	0	39.33
D. J. Saker	9	4	1	25	13	0	0	8.33	1	78.13
A. W. Polkinghorne	6	5	0	35	14	0	0	7.00	1	77.78
X. J. Doherty	2	1	0	3	3	0	0	3.00	1	33.33
B. J. Thomas	2	1	1	16	16*	0	0	–	1	114.29
S. J. Jurgensen	5	1	1	3	3*	0	0	–	0	33.33
G. J. Denton	1	0	0	0	0	0	0	–	0	–
M. D. Pascoe	1	0	0	0	0	0	0	–	0	–
J. P. Marquet	2	0	0	0	0	0	0	–	0	–

* Denotes not out.

BOWLING

	O	M	R	W	BB	5W/I	Avge
M. D. Pascoe	8	0	38	2	2/38	0	19.00
D. G. Wright	100	11	383	13	4/23	0	29.46
D. J. Marsh	49	0	233	7	3/56	0	33.29
D. J. Saker	83.3	2	383	11	3/48	0	34.82
J. P. Marquet	17.1	0	110	3	2/62	0	36.67
S. J. Jurgensen	33	2	156	3	2/41	0	52.00
G. J. Denton	10	0	53	1	1/53	0	53.00
S. R. Watson	62	0	381	6	2/46	0	63.50
X. J. Doherty	15	0	65	1	1/36	0	65.00
S. Young	53	1	269	3	1/32	0	89.67
A. W. Polkinghorne	39	0	237	2	1/39	0	118.50
S. P. Kremerskothen	4.2	0	38	0	–	0	–
S. B. Tubb	5	0	28	0	–	0	–
B. J. Thomas	10	1	59	0	–	0	–

At Bankstown Memorial Oval, Bankstown, October 14, 2001. TASMANIA lost to
NEW SOUTH WALES on run rate.

At WACA Ground, Perth, October 24, 2001. Day/night game. TASMANIA defeated
WESTERN AUSTRALIA by five wickets.

TASMANIA v WESTERN AUSTRALIA

At Bellerive Oval, Hobart, November 3, 2001. Western Australia won by five wickets. Toss: Tasmania. Western Australia 4 pts.

An unbeaten century by Mike Hussey exposed Tasmania's second-string bowlers and hoisted Western Australia to a comfortable win with 15 balls to spare. With the Western Australians under siege at three for 39 in the 14th, it looked as though the Tasmanians would christen their newly redeveloped ground with a win, but Hussey (11 fours) feasted on an attack which, apart from the persistent Damien Wright, wore its mediocrity like a badge. Justin Langer gave him solid support before Ryan Campbell and Hussey finished Tasmania off with a stand of 59 from the last 42 balls. Tasmania's total was anchored by Ricky Ponting's pyrotechnic innings which featured seven fours and four sixes, but left-arm wrist-spinner Brad Hogg denied him his century by bowling him and finishing with four wickets.

Man of the Match: M.E.K. Hussey.   *Attendance:* 2,279.

Tasmania

D.F. Hills run out (Goodwin/Gilchrist)	0	(6)	D.J. Marsh c and b Hogg	6	(6)
S.R. Watson c Oldroyd b Angel	15	(40)	G.T. Cunningham lbw b Hogg	9	(20)
*R.T. Ponting b Hogg	94	(94)	B.J. Thomas not out	16	(14)
S. Young c Gilchrist b Hogg	43	(68)	L-b 6, w 3, n-b 1	10	
A.W. Polkinghorne c Karppinen					
b Oldroyd	0	(2)	(50 overs, 202 mins) (7 wkts)	241	
J. Cox not out	48	(51)	Fall: 2 61 144 145 173 184 204		

†S.G. Clingeleffer, D.J. Saker and D.G. Wright did not bat.

Bowling: Williams 9–1–38–0; Karppinen 10–0–31–0; Angel 9–0–51–1; Oldroyd 8–0–43–1; Harvey 4–0–22–0; Hogg 10–0–50–4.

Western Australia

*†A.C. Gilchrist c Clingeleffer b Wright	20	(33)	R.J. Campbell not out	20	(21)
J.L. Langer c Wright b Watson	57	(96)			
S.M. Katich c Cunningham b Wright	7	(8)	B 4, l-b 3, w 6, n-b 1	14	
M.W. Goodwin lbw b Saker	1	(5)			
M.E.K. Hussey not out	103	(109)	(48.3 overs, 205 mins) (5 wkts)	245	
S.J. Karppinen b Watson	23	(20)	Fall: 26 34 39 137 186		

K.M. Harvey, G.B. Hogg, B.A. Williams, J. Angel and B.J. Oldroyd did not bat.

Bowling: Wright 10–2–22–2; Saker 9.3–1–44–1; Young 6–0–19–0; Thomas 3–0–19–0; Marsh 7–0–43–0; Polkinghorne 6–0–45–0; Watson 7–0–46–2.

Umpires: K.J. Jones and J.H. Smeaton.
TV Umpire: B.W. Jackman.

TASMANIA v VICTORIA

At Bellerive Oval, Hobart, December 9, 2001. No result. Toss: Victoria. Tasmania 2 pts and Victoria 2 pts. Competition debut: R.A. Bartlett, S.M. Harwood, C.L. White.

The only man singing in the rain in this soggy stalemate was Victorian captain Matthew Elliott (15 fours), who looked in easy command of an attack in which only David Saker demanded respect. After a sensible opening partnership of 85 in 17.3 overs with Robbie Bartlett who was appearing in only his second match for Victoria in eight years, Elliott and Brad Hodge rattled up a record second-wicket stand for Victoria against Tasmania of 129 off 23 overs before the rain arrived. The Tasmanians were thankful to collect a couple of points, given how tough it would have been to reach the revised run-rate target of 265 off 42 overs on a sodden outfield.

Attendance: 820.

Victoria

*M. T. G. Elliott not out	118	(129)			
R. A. Bartlett c Di Venuto b Saker	40	(51)	L-b 1, w 2, n-b 1		4
B. J. Hodge b Marquet	60	(68)			
I. J. Harvey run out (Watson)	0	(1)	(42.1 overs, 184 mins)	(3 wkts)	223
M. Klinger not out	1	(4)	Fall: 85 214 214		

S.P. Dart, J. Moss, S.M. Harwood, †D.S. Berry, I.S.L. Hewett, M.L. Lewis and C.L. White did not bat.

Bowling: Saker 8–0–28–1; Wright 10–1–50–0; Marquet 7.1–0–48–1; Marsh 2–0–9–0; Young 4–0–29–0; Watson 7–0–35–0; Polkinghorne 4–0–23–0.

Tasmania

M.J. Di Venuto, S.R. Watson, M.G. Dighton, S. Young, *J. Cox, D.J. Marsh, G.T. Cunningham, A.W. Polkinghorne, † S.G. Clingeleffer, D.G. Wright, D.J. Saker, J.P. Marquet.

Umpires: P. V. Mulcahy and J. H. Smeaton.
TV Umpire: B. W. Jackman.

At Brisbane Cricket Ground, Brisbane, December 18, 2001. Day/night game. TASMANIA lost to QUEENSLAND by 97 runs.

TASMANIA v SOUTH AUSTRALIA

At NTCA Ground, Launceston, January 6, 2002. South Australia won by 42 runs. Toss: South Australia. South Australia 4 pts. Competition debut: X.J. Doherty.

After clubbing 246 in the Pura Cup match at Bellerive two months earlier, Darren Lehmann returned to give Tasmania some more stick. He rescued the South Australians from early trouble, this time not so much bludgeoning the bowling as dissecting it, his innings including 46 singles gathered from all around the wicket. The pick of the bowlers was again Damien Wright who was both restraining and penetrative. Tasmania never really recovered from slumping to six for 85, after which Scott Kremerskothen was the only batsman to fly the flag as left-arm spinner Brad Young and pace man Mark Harrity made merry. Young was never out of the game, also making useful runs and taking five catches to claim the record for the most in an Australian domestic limited-overs innings.

Man of the Match: D.S. Lehmann.   *Attendance:* 2,201.

South Australia

G.S. Blewett b Saker	22	(20)	†G.A. Manou b Watson	3	(10)
D.A. Fitzgerald b Wright	14	(23)	M.J. Smith run out (Polkinghorne)	4	(8)
C.J. Davies c Polkinghorne b Wright	3	(12)	P. Wilson not out	8	(5)
*D.S. Lehmann not out	85	(116)	B 3, l-b 6, w 2	11	
B.A. Johnson c Clingeleffer b Saker	8	(11)			
N.T. Adcock b Young	45	(68)	(50 overs, 209 mins)	(8 wkts)	226
B.E. Young b Wright	23	(27)	Fall: 39 41 42 51 141 192 198 210		

P.C. Rofe and M.A. Harrity did not bat.

Bowling: Saker 10–0–46–2; Wright 10–2–32–3; Watson 10–0–55–1; Young 10–1–32–1; Doherty 5–0–29–0; Polkinghorne 5–0–23–0.

Tasmania

*J. Cox c Young b Rofe	4	(6)	A.W. Polkinghorne b Young	10	(18)	
M.J. Di Venuto c Manou b Smith	24	(28)	D.G. Wright c Young b Smith	17	(24)	
S. Young lbw b Wilson	3	(12)	D.J. Saker lbw b Young	5	(5)	
G.T. Cunningham c Young b Harrity	27	(47)				
D.J. Marsh c Young b Harrity	5	(19)	B 2, l-b 4, w 4, n-b 4	14		
S.R. Watson c Young b Harrity	10	(32)				
S.P. Kremerskothen not out	42	(73)	(48.4 overs, 200 mins)	184		
†S.G. Clingeleffer c Harrity b Young	23	(32)	Fall: 7 17 54 65 78 85 137 154 177 184			

X.J. Doherty did not bat.

Bowling: Wilson 9–0–33–1; Rofe 7–0–41–1; Smith 9–2–26–2; Harrity 10–1–31–3; Johnson 5–0–18–0; Young 8.4–0–29–3.

Umpires: B.W. Jackman and P.V. Mulcahy.

TASMANIA v QUEENSLAND

At Bellerive Oval, Hobart, January 13, 2002. Queensland won by 76 runs. Toss: Tasmania. Queensland 5 pts. Competition debut: M. Sippel.

It was hard to believe Tasmania's limited-overs form could get any worse, but it did, as chasing a gettable target, they disintegrated. To add insult to injury, Queensland secured the bonus point without Matthew Hayden, Andy Bichel, Stuart Law and Andrew Symonds, as pace men Ashley Noffke and Joe Dawes did the damage with the ball. The only Tasmanian batsman who could hold his head up was Shane Watson, who batted determinedly for 146 minutes, but those around him gave away their wickets with suicidal shots. Queensland's unspectacular innings was built around a rock-solid knock by opener Brendan Nash, supplemented by handy contributions all the way down the order culminating in an invaluable, unbroken ninth-wicket run-a-ball partnership from Noffke and Nathan Hauritz.

Man of the Match: A.A. Noffke.　　*Attendance:* 733.

Queensland

*J.P. Maher b Saker	31	(54)	L.A. Carseldine run out (Marsh)	2	(4)	
B.P. Nash c Cunningham b Wright	63	(92)	A.A. Noffke not out	21	(24)	
M.L. Love c Kremerskothen b Young	20	(30)	N.M. Hauritz not out	18	(20)	
C.T. Perren lbw b Jurgensen	1	(10)	B 2, l-b 4, w 3, n-b 1	10		
J.R. Hopes run out (Clingeleffer/Marsh)	26	(37)				
†W.A. Seccombe lbw b Marsh	11	(24)	(50 overs, 201 mins)　(8 wkts)	203		
M. Sippel c Wright b Watson	0	(8)	Fall: 62 105 111 143 151 160 161 163			

M.S. Kasprowicz and J.H. Dawes did not bat.

Bowling: Saker 10–1–27–1; Wright 10–2–43–1; Young 10–0–41–1; Jurgensen 7–1–26–1; Marsh 8–0–31–1; Watson 5–0–29–1.

Tasmania

M.G. Dighton c Maher b Hopes	1	(5)	S. Young b Dawes	4	(16)	
M.J. Di Venuto c Maher b Dawes	6	(15)	D.G. Wright not out	6	(8)	
*J. Cox c Hauritz b Noffke	15	(44)	D.J. Saker c Maher b Hauritz	13	(14)	
S.R. Watson c Sippel b Dawes	53	(107)				
S.P. Kremerskothen c Seccombe b Perren	4	(12)	L-b 4, w 5, n-b 6	15		
D.J. Marsh c Seccombe b Noffke	8	(18)				
†S.G. Clingeleffer c Sippel b Noffke	0	(10)	(41.5 overs, 182 mins)	127		
G.T. Cunningham c Seccombe b Noffke	2	(9)	Fall: 1 12 43 58 72 88 90 106 108 127			

S.J. Jurgensen did not bat.

Bowling: Dawes 10–0–26–3; Hopes 7–2–16–1; Kasprowicz 2–0–7–0; Noffke 10–1–32–4; Perren 7–1–22–1; Hauritz 5.5–1–20–1.

Umpires: K. J. McGinness and J. H. Smeaton.

At Adelaide Oval, Adelaide, February 1, 2002. Day/night game. TASMANIA lost to SOUTH AUSTRALIA by 34 runs.

TASMANIA v NEW SOUTH WALES

At Devonport Oval, Devonport, February 10, 2002. New South Wales won by seven wickets. Toss: Tasmania. New South Wales 4 pts. Competition debut: N. S. Pilon.

After Tasmania had made a challenging total, a New South Wales side boasting a galaxy of internationals reached the target with seven wickets and ten balls to spare. With national selectors Trevor Hohns and David Boon among the substantial crowd, Shane Watson provided them with more compelling evidence that he could be their next all-rounder by plundering seven fours in a fine innings. He received spirited support from Michael Dighton (five fours, two sixes), who was promoted to open in the absence of injured skipper Jamie Cox, and Scott Kremerskothen. New South Wales were given a steady start by Mark Waugh and Corey Richards, who hit three sixes, in an opening stand of 116 off 24.2 overs. Then the old masters Michael Bevan and Steve Waugh saw them comfortably home.

Man of the Match: S. R. Watson.   *Attendance:* 4,907.

Tasmania

S. R. Mason c S. Lee b B. Lee	5	(23)	D. G. Wright b Bracken	0	(1)
M. G. Dighton c and b Thornely	52	(54)	†S. G. Clingeleffer not out	1	(1)
S. R. Watson run out (S. Lee)	96	(124)			
M. J. Di Venuto c Pilon b MacGill	29	(43)	L-b 2, w 6, n-b 4	12	
S. P. Kremerskothen not out	43	(44)			
*D. J. Marsh c MacGill b Bracken	6	(9)	(50 overs, 219 mins)	(7 wkts) 249	
G. T. Cunningham b Bracken	5	(5)	Fall: 19 81 154 216 234 248 248		

D. J. Saker, G. J. Denton and S. J. Jurgensen did not bat.

Bowling: B. Lee 10–2–34–1; Clark 10–1–44–0; Bracken 10–0–49–3; MacGill 10–0–72–1; Thornely 10–1–48–1.

New South Wales

C. J. Richards c Cunningham b Denton	60	(79)			
M. E. Waugh c Clingeleffer b Watson	60	(81)	L-b 4, w 3, n-b 1	8	
†N. S. Pilon c Dighton b Marsh	28	(37)			
M. G. Bevan not out	62	(68)	(48.2 overs, 203 mins)	(3 wkts) 250	
*S. R. Waugh not out	32	(27)	Fall: 116 136 191		

M. J. Clarke, D. J. Thornely, S. Lee, B. Lee, S. R. Clark, S. C. G. MacGill and N. W. Bracken did not bat.

Bowling: Saker 10–0–50–0; Wright 10–0–38–0; Jurgensen 5–0–36–0; Denton 10–0–53–1; Watson 9–0–43–1; Marsh 4–0–20–1; Kremerskothen 0.2–0–6–0.

Umpires: B. W. Jackman and K. J. Jones.

At Melbourne Cricket Ground, Melbourne, February 16, 2002. TASMANIA defeated VICTORIA by 19 runs.

DOMESTIC LIMITED-OVERS RESULTS

	M	W	L	NR	T
Australian Capital Territory	3	2	1	0	0
New South Wales	21	3	18	0	0
New Zealanders	1	0	1	0	0
Queensland	24	7	16	1	0
South Australia	20	6	14	0	0
Victoria	18	6	11	1	0
Western Australia	23	5	18	0	0
Total.......................	110	29	79	2	0

RECORDS

Highest score for:	129*	M.J. Di Venuto v South Australia at Hobart (Bellerive) 1996-97
Highest score against:	159	S.G. Law (Queensland) at Brisbane 1993-94
Best bowling for:	5/23	J.P. Marquet v Queensland at Hobart (Bellerive) 1995-96
Best bowling against:	6/25	B.E. McNamara (New South Wales) at Sydney 1996-97
Highest total for:	7-327	v New South Wales at Bankstown................ 2001-02
Highest total against:	4-397	by New South Wales at Bankstown................ 2001-02
Lowest total for:	80	v New South Wales at Devonport 1984-85
Lowest total against:	133	by Western Australia at Hobart (TCA) 1978-79

* Denotes not out.

MOST RUNS

	M	I	NO	R	HS	100s	50s	Avge	S-R
D.C. Boon..........	55	52	4	1,725	116	1	16	35.94	66.22
J. Cox..............	62	60	4	1,537	99	0	12	27.45	64.44
S. Young	64	56	6	1,428	96	0	9	28.56	65.59
M.J. Di Venuto	57	55	7	1,443	129*	2	6	30.06	79.59
D.F. Hills..........	42	39	3	1,137	81	0	8	31.58	56.40
R.T. Ponting	30	30	4	930	102	1	6	35.77	78.09
D.J. Marsh..........	41	36	8	900	101*	1	4	32.14	73.65
R.J. Tucker	39	38	2	869	75	0	6	24.14	76.56
D.J. Buckingham	22	22	4	506	61	0	2	28.11	74.41
R.D. Woolley	22	20	2	454	80*	0	2	25.22	77.53

HIGHEST PARTNERSHIP FOR EACH WICKET

210	for 1st	J. Cox and D.C. Boon, v New South Wales at Hobart (Bellerive)	1998-99
137	for 2nd	M.J. Di Venuto and R.T. Ponting, v South Australia at Adelaide	2000-01
152	for 3rd	G.W. Goodman and J.H. Hampshire, v Queensland at Brisbane	1978-79
118	for 4th	S. Young and R.J. Tucker, v New South Wales at Hobart (Bellerive)	1994-95
127	for 5th	S. Young and D.F. Hills, v Western Australia at Perth	1998-99
95	for 6th	D.J. Marsh and G.T. Cunningham, v New South Wales at Bankstown	2001-02
96*	for 7th	T.W. Docking and J. Simmons, v Western Australia at Hobart (TCA)	1978-79
44	for 8th	S.G. Clingeleffer and D.G. Wright, v Victoria at Melbourne	2001-02
67	for 9th	G.T. Cunningham and D.J. Saker, v Western Australia at Perth	2000-01
28	for 10th	M.G. Farrell and M.W. Ridgway, v Western Australia at Hobart (Bellerive)	1996-97

* Denotes unbroken partnership.

MOST WICKETS

	M	Balls	Mdns	R	W	BB	5W/i	Avge
S. Young	64	2,642	39	1,864	43	3/16	0	43.35
D.G. Wright	27	1,498	27	913	37	4/23	0	24.68
R.J. Tucker	39	1,461	4	1,263	34	4/31	0	37.15
C.R. Miller	33	1,843	31	1,267	34	4/48	0	37.26
M.W. Ridgway	21	1,170	22	868	28	4/37	0	31.00
M.G. Farrell	28	1,224	3	885	27	4/51	0	32.78
P.J. Marquet	16	862	7	674	24	5/23	1	28.08
D.J. Marsh	41	1,135	2	916	22	3/47	0	41.64
D.J. Saker	16	867	6	641	19	3/48	0	33.74
S.P. Kremerskothen	23	422	1	443	15	3/33	0	29.53

MOST DISMISSALS

	M	Ct	St	Total
M.N. Atkinson	35	43	7	50
R.D. Woolley	22	16	1	17
S.G. Clingeleffer	20	21	2	23
R.E. Soule	11	9	0	9
B.R. Doolan	7	6	1	7

MOST CATCHES

S. Young	24 in 64 matches	D.J. Marsh	17 in 41 matches
M.J. Di Venuto	20 in 57 matches	D.C. Boon	15 in 55 matches
R.T. Ponting	18 in 30 matches	R.J. Tucker	13 in 39 matches
J. Cox	17 in 62 matches	D.F. Hills	10 in 42 matches

MOST APPEARANCES

64	S. Young	1990-91 – 2001-02	41	D.J. Marsh	1996-97 – 2001-02
62	J. Cox	1988-89 – 2001-02	39	R.J. Tucker	1987-88 – 1998-99
57	M.J. Di Venuto	1992-93 – 2001-02	35	M.N. Atkinson	1992-93 – 2000-01
55	D.C. Boon	1978-79 – 1998-99	33	C.R. Miller	1992-93 – 1999-00
42	D.F. Hills	1992-93 – 2001-02	30	R.T. Ponting	1992-93 – 2001-02

VICTORIA

Even before a ball was bowled, it seemed that Victoria's limited-overs season would be fraught with difficulty after a searing argument between deposed limited-overs captain Paul Reiffel and Victoria's selection chairman Shaun Graf on the eve of the opening game in October. The pair broke away from the main training group at the MCG and vented their frustrations for some minutes, an undignified and very public breakdown in communications. Despite new coach Mick O'Sullivan's assurances that both Reiffel and Colin Miller would come into selection contention, it never eventuated. Reiffel retired in January, Miller soon afterwards signed his own death warrant by saying publicly that the selectors did not know what they were doing, and the long-serving Graf was voted off the panel in April.

The 2000-01 wooden-spooners lost their first four games to forfeit well before Christmas any serious chance of making the ING Cup final. They seldom fielded the best possible side, instead selecting a stream of all-rounders who rarely lived up to the selectors' estimation. New captain Matthew Elliott led the weakest batting line-up in the competition, which failed to make even 225 in any of the ten games. With 431 runs, Elliott was by far the leading run-maker, and the only centurion with his 118 not out in the rained-out fixture against Tasmania in Hobart. New vice-captain Brad Hodge was the next best, with 227 runs at a mediocre average of 25. Elliott had four opening partners, the most effective being international all-rounder Ian Harvey, who made a flamboyant 72 from just 66 balls in a pinch-hitting role against Queensland at Richmond Cricket Ground. Young St Kilda batsman Nick Jewell showed promise in his two matches late in the season, and 21-year-old Michael Klinger, who played every match, gained valuable experience for the future.

For all their batting woes, the Victorians' bowling was only partially better, especially with the much-discussed non-selection of Reiffel and Miller, and Damien Fleming's limited availability. First-change specialist Mick Lewis was the leading wicket-taker with 13, at a strike-rate of a wicket every five or six overs. The only others to take ten or more wickets were Harvey (12) and Ian Hewett (ten). Inexperienced bowlers who were called upon included Shane Harwood, who moved the ball away from the right-handers at good pace before being injured, and his Melbourne team-mate, all-rounder Andrew McDonald, who was judged the state's Young Cricketer of the Year.

Fielding standards were consistently high, with Darren Berry's glovework remaining sharp and efficient. However, the one-wicket loss to a full-strength Queensland at the Richmond Cricket Ground came when, in the tense finish, a wide throw resulted in a missed run-out which would have given the Victorians an important early victory.
– KEN PIESSE.

RESULTS, 2001-02

ING Cup matches – Played 10: Won 3, Lost 6, No result 1.
Competition placing – 5th.

ING CUP AVERAGES, 2001-02

BATTING

	M	I	NO	R	HS	100s	50s	Avge	Ct/St	S-R
S.P. Dart.........	5	4	2	100	51*	0	1	50.00	2	62.11
M.T.G. Elliott	10	10	1	431	118*	1	3	47.89	2	73.42
N. Jewell..........	2	2	0	70	39	0	0	35.00	0	72.92
B.J. Hodge	9	9	0	227	61	0	2	25.22	4	72.52
M.L. Lewis........	10	4	3	25	15*	0	0	25.00	2	64.10
M. Klinger	10	10	1	211	55	0	2	23.44	2	60.46
J. Moss	9	8	1	162	64*	0	1	23.14	1	59.12
I.J. Harvey	8	8	0	170	72	0	1	21.25	4	89.01
J.L. Arnberger	3	3	0	55	23	0	0	18.33	0	63.22
D.S. Berry	10	8	2	85	17	0	0	14.17	16/3	54.84
I.S.L. Hewett	9	7	3	52	29*	0	0	13.00	2	64.12
R.A. Bartlett.......	5	5	0	57	40	0	0	11.40	2	52.29
A.B. McDonald	3	3	1	21	19*	0	0	10.50	1	56.76
M.P. Mott.........	1	1	0	10	10	0	0	10.00	0	45.45
S.A.J. Craig	2	2	0	17	11	0	0	8.50	1	73.91
S.K. Warne........	4	4	0	30	25	0	0	7.50	2	60.00
D.W. Fleming	7	5	2	12	9	0	0	4.00	0	54.05
B.C. Oliver........	2	2	0	3	3	0	0	1.50	1	23.08
C.L. White........	4	3	1	1	1*	0	0	0.50	0	16.67
S.M. Harwood	3	1	0	0	0	0	0	0.00	0	0.00
M.W.H. Inness	4	0	0	0	0	0	0	–	0	–

* Denotes not out.

BOWLING

	O	M	R	W	BB	5W/I	Avge
I.J. Harvey	56.2	6	174	12	3/19	0	14.50
S.M. Harwood	20	5	61	4	3/22	0	15.25
J. Moss	14.1	0	66	4	2/23	0	16.50
M.L. Lewis	73	9	320	13	4/41	0	24.62
I.S.L. Hewett	67	6	276	10	4/22	0	27.60
M.W.H. Inness	33	3	123	4	2/36	0	30.75
S.K. Warne...............	37	4	159	4	2/40	0	39.75
D.W. Fleming	61.3	4	251	6	2/25	0	41.83
B.C. Oliver..............	11.1	0	60	1	1/35	0	60.00
A.B. McDonald	11	0	75	1	1/44	0	75.00
C.L. White	16	0	89	1	1/37	0	89.00
B.J. Hodge	16.2	1	108	1	1/7	0	108.00
M.P. Mott	2	0	24	0	–	0	–

At Bankstown Memorial Oval, Bankstown, October 7, 2001. VICTORIA lost to NEW SOUTH WALES won by 123 runs.

At Adelaide Oval, Adelaide, October 21, 2001. VICTORIA lost to SOUTH AUSTRALIA by seven wickets.

VICTORIA v QUEENSLAND

At Richmond Cricket Ground, Richmond, October 28, 2001. Queensland won by one wicket. Toss: Queensland. Queensland 4 pts.

Having been humbled in their first two games, the Victorians, batting first on an excellent wicket, raced to two for 177 in the 35th over. Ian Harvey was elevated to open and responded with one of the season's fastest half-centuries, from 43 balls, while Brad Hodge was also in imposing touch. But Nathan Hauritz, varying his pace cleverly and bowling an immaculate length, took both their wickets and the Victorians lost momentum. After a run-a-ball opening stand between Matthew Hayden and Jimmy Maher, Queensland struggled against Harvey and Shane Warne. Eleven runs were needed at the start of the 48th over with Queensland's last pair at the wicket. Andy Bichel drove Mick Lewis to deep cover and Jon Moss, normally the surest of fieldsmen, overran the ball in his attempt to stop the second run. With the batsmen hesitating before deciding late to take Moss on, his throw flew wide of Darren Berry, allowing Bichel to make his ground. The winning runs came soon afterwards with six balls to spare.

Man of the Match: I.J. Harvey.   *Attendance:* 2,061.

Victoria

I.J. Harvey c Symons b Hauritz	72	(66)	S.K. Warne c Law b Noffke	0	(6)
*M.T.G. Elliott c Maher b Hopes	6	(19)	I.S.L. Hewett b Hopes	3	(7)
B.J. Hodge c Noffke b Hauritz	61	(77)	M.L. Lewis not out	3	(5)
M. Klinger c Noffke b Symons	39	(71)	L-b 6, w 4, n-b 2	12	
S.P. Dart run out (Hopes)	7	(15)			
S.A.J. Craig run out (Hopes/Symonds)	6	(10)	(50 overs, 201 mins) (9 wkts)	222	
J. Moss c Seccombe b Noffke	1	(4)	Fall: 36 122 177 192 197 198		
†D.S. Berry not out	12	(22)	207 210 217		

M.W.H. Inness did not bat.

Bowling: Bichel 8–0–39–0; Hopes 6–0–26–2; Noffke 10–1–41–2; Kasprowicz 8–0–34–0; Symonds 8–1–40–1; Hauritz 10–0–36–2.

Queensland

M.L. Hayden c and b Hewett	40	(34)	A.J. Bichel not out	15	(22)
J.P. Maher st Berry b Harvey	33	(46)	A.A. Noffke run out (Craig/Hewett)	1	(2)
M.L. Love c Harvey b Warne	0	(6)	M.S. Kasprowicz not out	5	(4)
A. Symonds c Klinger b Lewis	46	(47)			
C.T. Perren c Craig b Warne	34	(71)	B 3, l-b 3, w 6	12	
*S.G. Law c Elliott b Harvey	23	(37)			
J.R. Hopes b Harvey	4	(13)	(49 overs, 217 mins) (9 wkts)	223	
†W.A. Seccombe c Warne b Lewis	10	(12)	Fall: 66 67 89 136 182 190 191 207 212		

N.M. Hauritz did not bat.

Bowling: Lewis 10–1–57–2; Inness 3–1–15–0; Hewett 9–1–46–1; Moss 2–0–14–0; Warne 10–0–40–2; Harvey 10–3–19–3; Hodge 5–0–26–0.

Umpires: G.T.D. Morrow and A.J. Soulsby.
TV Umpire: D.L. Parry.

VICTORIA v SOUTH AUSTRALIA

At Richmond Cricket Ground, Richmond, November 4, 2001. South Australia won by four wickets. Toss: Victoria. South Australia 4 pts.

The fluctuating fortunes so often triggered by limited-overs cricket saw Victoria all but snatch victory from the jaws of defeat in the final overs. After Victoria's batting again failed to set a challenging target, South Australia were cruising on a friendly wicket at four for 200, Greg Blewett having led the way before falling to one of Darren Berry's signature leg-side stumpings. With ten runs needed from three overs and Darren Lehmann in charge, part-time off-spinner Brad Hodge was introduced and bowled the South Australian captain around his legs. Ian Harvey maintained the pressure in the 49th over, bowling Brad Young and so restricting the run flow that seven still were needed from the last. Graham Manou whacked Hodge's first ball almost into the traffic in Punt Road. His six tied the scores, before a single from the next ball gave the South Australians victory with four balls to spare.

Man of the Match: D.S. Lehmann.   *Attendance:* 3,576.

Victoria

*M. T. G. Elliott c Higgins b Rofe	....	23	(30)	†D. S. Berry not out 9 (7)
I. J. Harvey b Rofe	16	(21)		I. S. L. Hewett run out (Blewett/Lehmann) 0 (0)
B. J. Hodge c Higgins b Harrity	14	(18)		M. L. Lewis not out 1 (1)

*M. T. G. Elliott c Higgins b Rofe 23 (30)
I. J. Harvey b Rofe 16 (21)
B. J. Hodge c Higgins b Harrity 14 (18)
M. Klinger lbw b Johnson 55 (86)
S. P. Dart c Manou b Harris 32 (53)
S. K. Warne c Harrity b Young 0 (6)
J. Moss c Harris b Gillespie 37 (66)
S. A. J. Craig c Fitzgerald b Gillespie . 11 (13)

D. W. Fleming did not bat.

†D. S. Berry not out 9 (7)
I. S. L. Hewett run out (Blewett/Lehmann) 0 (0)
M. L. Lewis not out 1 (1)

B 1, l-b 7, w 2, n-b 1 11

(50 overs, 197 mins)　　　(9 wkts) 209
Fall: 29 44 57 118 119 170 195 203 203

Bowling: Gillespie 10–0–32–2; Rofe 10–0–48–2; Harrity 7–0–25–1; Young 10–0–39–1; Harris 6–1–20–1; Johnson 3–0–16–1; Lehmann 4–0–21–0.

South Australia

G. S. Blewett st Berry b Moss 76 (93)
D. A. Fitzgerald b Hewett 6 (16)
C. J. Davies run out (Dart/Berry) 46 (82)
*D. S. Lehmann b Hodge 51 (68)
B. A. Johnson c Dart b Warne 1 (3)
B. E. Young c and b Harvey 14 (27)

B. H. Higgins not out 2 (3)
†G. A. Manou not out 8 (4)

L-b 2, w 4 6

(49.2 overs, 204 mins)　　　(6 wkts) 210
Fall: 31 111 156 157 200 200

R. J. Harris, J. N. Gillespie, P. C. Rofe and M. A. Harrity did not bat.

Bowling: Fleming 10–0–44–0; Hewett 7–1–26–1; Warne 10–1–55–1; Lewis 7–1–33–0; Harvey 10–0–30–1; Moss 4–0–13–1; Hodge 1.2–1–7–1.

Umpires: R. L. Parry and J. D. Ward.
TV Umpire: R. G. Patterson.

At Bellerive Oval, Hobart, December 9, 2001. VICTORIA and TASMANIA – No result due to rain.

VICTORIA v WESTERN AUSTRALIA

At Melbourne Cricket Ground, Melbourne, December 23, 2001. Victoria won by ten runs. Toss: Western Australia. Victoria 4 pts. Competition debut: S. W. Meuleman.

The bounciest MCG drop-in wicket of the summer produced an entertaining and gripping contest. A fiery burst from Brad Williams against his old state lifted him into Australia's squad for the Boxing Day Test, his pace on the lively wicket forcing Ryan Campbell to stand back 25 metres. The Victorians were able to recover from three for 34 against the lesser bowlers, Matthew Elliott and youngsters Michael Klinger and Simon Dart scoring half-centuries and lifting the Victorians' run-rate above four an over. Left-armer Ian Hewett, running in faster than in previous summers, produced an irresistible burst, taking the first four wickets for just 22. Campbell and Scott Meuleman rebuilt the innings before further wickets fell. Last pair Campbell and Williams had added 16 to bring the visitors within reach when, with his first ball of the match, Jon Moss, a late inclusion to the side, had Campbell caught at the wicket.

Man of the Match: I. S. L. Hewett.　　*Attendance:* 2,937.

Victoria

*M.T.G. Elliott c Hussey b Nicholson	60	(98)	J. Moss lbw b Hogg	17	(26)
R.A. Bartlett c Nicholson b Williams .	8	(34)	C.L. White not out	1	(1)
B.J. Hodge c Campbell b Williams ...	0	(1)	L-b 9, w 10, n-b 2	21	
I.J. Harvey c Campbell b Williams ...	1	(8)			
M. Klinger b Hogg	51	(70)	(50 overs, 204 mins) (6 wkts)	210	
S.P. Dart not out	51	(64)	Fall: 32 32 34 111 161 208		

I.S.L. Hewett, †D.S. Berry, S.M. Harwood and M.L. Lewis did not bat.

Bowling: Williams 10–2–29–3; Karppinen 9–1–30–0; Angel 7–0–31–0; Nicholson 10–0–39–1; Harvey 6–0–35–0; Hogg 8–0–37–2.

Western Australia

C.J.L. Rogers c Berry b Hewett	17	(38)	K.M. Harvey lbw b Lewis	16	(20)
M.W. Goodwin c Berry b Hewett	9	(20)	M.J. Nicholson run out (Dart/White)	14	(13)
*S.M. Katich c Berry b Hewett	3	(10)	B.A. Williams not out	1	(1)
M.E.K. Hussey b Hewett	6	(17)	L-b 2, w 1, n-b 4	7	
†R.J. Campbell c Berry b Moss	77	(94)			
S.W. Meuleman c Harvey b Harwood	49	(73)	(48.1 overs, 204 mins)	200	
S.J. Karppinen lbw b Harvey	0	(4)	Fall: 17 25 38 39 129 131 133		
G.B. Hogg run out (Dart/Klinger)	1	(3)	158 184 200		

J. Angel did not bat.

Bowling: Harwood 10–2–39–1; Hewett 10–2–22–4; Lewis 10–1–40–1; White 9–0–52–0; Harvey 9–0–45–1; Moss 0.1–0–0–1.

Umpires: G.T.D. Morrow and R.G. Patterson.
TV Umpire: A.J. Soulsby.

VICTORIA v NEW SOUTH WALES

At Melbourne Cricket Ground, Melbourne, January 6, 2002. Victoria won by two wickets. Toss: Victoria. Victoria 5 pts. Competition debut: A.M. Clark, A.W. O'Brien.

The MCG wicket again helped the bowlers, who wound up the match an hour and a half early. In hot conditions, New South Wales were bowled out for 120, Shane Harwood taking three for 22 in ten spirited overs, despite having Mark Higgs and Don Nash dropped in the field. In the circumstances, Graeme Rummans' 30, which prevented a rout among the late order, was worth many more. After Stuart Clark effected a brilliant direct-hit run-out of Robbie Bartlett and Michael Bevan ran out Matthew Elliott from mid-wicket, the Victorian reply lacked conviction. When Nathan Bracken took only the third hat-trick in the competition's history – dismissing Cameron White, Darren Berry and Shane Harwood – Victoria were eight for 88. Riding his luck, however, Ian Hewett played a series of big off-side shots and the Victorians raced to victory in the 29th over, thanks to Hewett's fifth four, a thumping drive past extra cover.

Man of the Match: N.W. Bracken. *Attendance:* 2,717.

New South Wales

M.J. Clarke c Dart b Fleming	6	(10)	D.A. Nash c Bartlett b Fleming	8	(11)
†B.J. Haddin c Hodge b Hewett	8	(13)	A.M. Clark not out	3	(13)
*M.G. Bevan b Lewis	17	(26)	N.W. Bracken c Berry b Harvey	2	(7)
C.J. Richards run out (Dart)	12	(35)			
G.C. Rummans lbw b Harvey	30	(74)	L-b 1, w 19, n-b 3	23	
M.A. Higgs c Berry b Harwood	11	(36)			
S.D. Bradstreet c Berry b Harwood	0	(3)	(38.4 overs, 165 mins)	120	
A.W. O'Brien b Harwood	0	(7)	Fall: 15 17 57 59 91 91 94 109 116 120		

S.R. Clark did not bat.

Bowling: Fleming 9–1–32–2; Hewett 5–0–27–1; Lewis 7–2–20–1; Harwood 10–3–22–3; Harvey 7.4–1–18–2.

Victoria

*M.T.G. Elliott run out (Bevan)	18	(25)	†D.S. Berry c Haddin b Bracken	0	(1)
R.A. Bartlett run out (S.R. Clark)	1	(2)	S.M. Harwood b Bracken	0	(1)
B.J. Hodge c Haddin b Bracken	18	(26)	I.S.L. Hewett not out	29	(27)
M. Klinger c Haddin b Nash	23	(34)	L-b 3, w 1, n-b 1	5	
I.J. Harvey c Richards b Bracken	17	(25)			
S.P. Dart not out	10	(29)	(28.5 overs, 142 mins) (8 wkts)	121	
C.L. White b Bracken	0	(4)	Fall: 5 41 41 70 82 88 88 88		

Bowling: S.R. Clark 9.5–1–40–0; Nash 7–1–28–1; Bracken 9–3–38–5; Bradstreet 2–1–9–0; A.M. Clark 1–0–3–0.

D.W. Fleming and M.L. Lewis did not bat.

Umpires: R.L. Parry and R.G. Patterson.
TV Umpire: G.T.D. Morrow.

At WACA Ground, Perth, January 16, 2002. Day/night game. VICTORIA lost to WESTERN AUSTRALIA by 116 runs.

At Brisbane Cricket Ground, Brisbane, February 1, 2002. Day/night game. VICTORIA lost to QUEENSLAND by four runs.

VICTORIA v TASMANIA

At Melbourne Cricket Ground, Melbourne, February 16, 2002. Victoria won by 19 runs. Toss: Victoria. Victoria 4 pts. Competition debut: G.J. Bailey.

This bottom-of-the-ladder clash featured three of Australia's Under-19 World Cup team: Cameron White, George Bailey and Xavier Doherty, who were just home from their triumph in New Zealand. There were some notable performances, particularly from Jon Moss, who handled the conditions better than anybody else, and from Damien Wright, who on top of his valuable batting and bowling took an outstanding running catch to dismiss Matthew Elliott. Set 207 to win, Tasmania lost early wickets before Wright, debutant Bailey and Sean Clingeleffer mounted a revival, only for Ian Harvey, once again keeping his nerve at the death, to finish the game with his second wicket.

Man of the Match: D.G. Wright.   *Attendance:* 1,457.

Victoria

M. Klinger c Clingeleffer b Wright	14	(21)	†D.S. Berry c Dighton b Doherty	10	(22)
*M.T.G. Elliott c Wright b Jurgensen	10	(21)	D.W. Fleming c Cox b Jurgensen	9	(17)
B.J. Hodge b Wright	5	(10)	M.L. Lewis not out	15	(19)
I.J. Harvey c Doherty b Wright	27	(39)			
N. Jewell c Clingeleffer b Pascoe	39	(54)	L-b 7, w 3, n-b 1	11	
C.L. White lbw b Wright	0	(1)			
J. Moss not out	64	(92)	(50 overs, 192 mins) (9 wkts)	206	
A.B. McDonald c Clingeleffer b Pascoe	2	(5)	Fall: 16 24 34 74 74 130 136 157 177		

M.W.H. Inness did not bat.

Bowling: Jurgensen 10–1–41–2; Wright 10–2–23–4; Pascoe 8–0–38–2; Kremerskothen 4–0–32–0; Doherty 10–0–36–1; Marsh 8–0–29–0.

Tasmania

S.R. Mason c Berry b Harvey	14	(31)	D.G. Wright c Hodge b Harvey	40	(36)
M.G. Dighton lbw b Fleming	5	(6)	X.J. Doherty run out (Hodge/Harvey)	3	(9)
S.P. Kremerskothen c Berry b Inness	2	(9)	S.J. Jurgensen not out	3	(9)
M.J. Di Venuto run out (McDonald)	27	(58)			
*J. Cox c Berry b Lewis	11	(30)	L-b 4, w 5	9	
D.J. Marsh run out (Elliott)	18	(38)		—	
G.J. Bailey c Harvey b White	33	(52)	(49.4 overs, 207 mins)	187	
†S.G. Clingeleffer lbw b Lewis	22	(27)	Fall: 7 13 43 60 61 106 127 171 183 187		

M.D. Pascoe did not bat.

Bowling: Fleming 10–0–32–1; Inness 10–0–47–1; Harvey 9.4–2–24–2; Lewis 10–3–27–2; McDonald 3–0–16–0; White 7–0–37–1.

Umpires: R.G. Patterson and J.D. Ward.
TV Umpire: A.J. Soulsby.

DOMESTIC LIMITED-OVERS RESULTS

	M	W	L	NR	T
Australian Capital Territory	3	1	2	0	0
New South Wales	27	12	14	1	0
New Zealanders	2	1	1	0	0
Queensland	22	8	13	1	0
South Australia	26	15	10	0	1
Tasmania	18	11	6	1	0
Western Australia	28	5	21	2	0
Total	127	53	67	5	1

RECORDS

Highest score for:	139*	D.M. Jones v New South Wales at Sydney	1986-87
Highest score against:	150*	M.L. Hayden (Queensland) at Melbourne	1998-99
Best bowling for:	5/20	G.D. Watson v Western Australia at Melbourne	1969-70
Best bowling against:	5/15	D.L. Boyd (Western Australia) at Perth	1982-83
Highest total for:	5-282	v Western Australia at Perth	1990-91
Highest total against:	5-310	by New South Wales at North Sydney	1991-92
Lowest total for:	78	v Queensland at Brisbane	1989-90
Lowest total against:	59	by Western Australia at Melbourne	1969-70

* Denotes not out.

MOST RUNS

	M	I	NO	R	HS	100s	50s	Avge	S-R
D.M. Jones	55	52	10	2,122	139*	4	12	50.52	74.07
B.J. Hodge	56	54	5	1,739	118*	2	13	35.49	72.31
M.T.G. Elliott	52	56	4	1,587	118*	5	7	34.50	67.85
J.M. Wiener	20	20	2	1,003	108*	1	10	55.72	66.52
I.J. Harvey	53	48	3	892	72	0	5	19.82	81.09
G.M. Watts	19	19	0	590	85	0	6	31.05	51.39
G.N. Yallop	24	24	2	586	91	0	3	26.64	68.50
D.S. Berry	69	52	15	615	64*	0	1	16.62	64.26
M. Klinger	21	21	3	473	80*	0	3	26.28	62.24
G.R. Vimpani	19	19	0	467	92	0	2	24.58	63.54
A.I.C. Dodemaide	38	30	8	454	40	0	0	20.64	58.13

* Denotes not out.

HIGHEST PARTNERSHIP FOR EACH WICKET

194	for 1st	M.T.G. Elliott and G.R. Vimpani, v New South Wales at North Sydney ..	1999-00
129	for 2nd	M.T.G. Elliott and B.J. Hodge, v Tasmania at Hobart (Bellerive)........	2001-02
135	for 3rd	D.M. Jones and M.T.G. Elliott, v Tasmania at Hobart (Bellerive)	1995-96
127	for 4th	G.N. Yallop and J.K. Moss, v Western Australia at Perth	1978-79
124*	for 5th	B.J. Hodge and S.A.J. Craig, v Australian Capital Territory at Canberra ..	1998-99
92	for 6th	B.J. Hodge and P.R. Reiffel, v New South Wales at North Sydney	1997-98
98*	for 7th	T.J. Laughlin and R.J. Bright, v New South Wales at Sydney	1976-77
73*	for 8th	A.M. Smith and A.I.C. Dodemaide, v Queensland at Melbourne	1996-97
73	for 9th	R.C. Jordon and R.K. Rowan, v South Australia at Adelaide	1970-71
30	for 10th	D.W. Fleming and D.J. Saker, v Western Australia at Melbourne	1995-96

* Denotes unbroken partnership.

MOST WICKETS

	M	Balls	Mdns	R	W	BB	5W/i	Avge
I.J. Harvey	53	2,191	19	1,652	63	5/34	1	26.22
D.W. Fleming	46	2,433	43	1,584	48	3/25	0	33.00
P.R. Reiffel	40	1,844	35	1,201	37	4/14	0	32.46
A.I.C. Dodemaide	38	2,019	34	1,268	35	3/11	0	36.23
M.G. Hughes	30	1,523	26	1,147	33	4/34	0	34.76
S.K. Warne	20	1,037	15	754	29	5/35	1	26.00
D.J. Saker	27	1,344	32	869	27	4/35	0	32.19
M.L. Lewis	24	1,092	20	845	29	4/41	0	29.14
M.H.N. Walker	18	1,098	18	583	24	4/37	0	24.29
P.W. Jackson	14	754	14	502	22	4/26	0	22.82
S.F. Graf	15	815	14	537	22	4/15	0	24.41

MOST DISMISSALS

	M	Ct	St	Total
D.S. Berry	69	88	25	113
M.G.D. Dimattina	18	16	2	18
R.D. Robinson	17	11	4	15
P.G. Sacristani	4	8	0	8
N.M. Carlyon	3	6	1	7

MOST CATCHES

D.M. Jones	30 in 55 matches	J.D. Siddons	11 in 20 matches
B.J. Hodge	23 in 56 matches	M.G. Hughes	10 in 30 matches
M.T.G. Elliott	22 in 52 matches	D.W. Fleming	9 in 46 matches
I.J. Harvey	16 in 53 matches	S.K. Warne	9 in 20 matches
P.R. Reiffel	12 in 40 matches		

MOST APPEARANCES

69	D.S. Berry	...... 1990-91 – 2001-02		46	D.W. Fleming	.... 1988-89 – 2001-02
55	D.M. Jones	.... 1981-82 – 1997-98		40	P.R. Reiffel	...... 1987-88 – 2000-01
56	B.J. Hodge	.... 1993-94 – 2001-02		38	A.I.C. Dodemaide	1983-84 – 1997-98
53	I.J. Harvey	.... 1993-94 – 2001-02		30	M.G. Hughes	..... 1981-82 – 1994-95
52	M.T.G. Elliott	.... 1992-93 – 2001-02		27	D.J. Saker	.... 1994-95 – 1999-00

WESTERN AUSTRALIA

Left-hander Mike Hussey enhanced his growing reputation as one of the country's finest batsmen in limited-overs cricket, fast bowlers Brad Williams and Jo Angel excelled and Brad Hogg continued to be a livewire all-rounder. But, with international duties forcing Adam Gilchrist, Damien Martyn and Justin Langer to miss several matches, Western Australia's senior players lacked consistent support. It was no surprise that Western Australia, with five wins and five losses, failed to reach the final. Oddly, though, when Martyn scored 82 at the Gabba and 108 against Tasmania in Perth, and when Langer hit 107 in Sydney, Western Australia were beaten easily on each occasion.

A few years ago Hussey was considered unsuited to the hectic pace of limited-overs cricket. He is now an outstanding middle-order batsman, a brilliant fieldsman and capable change bowler in the abbreviated form of the game. After scoring 428 runs at 53.50 the previous season, Hussey maintained that standard in 2001-02, scoring 440 at 55.00. The highlights of his season were an unbeaten century against Tasmania in Hobart and his sweep for six at the WACA Ground which hit a sponsor's sign and earned him and his team-mates $200,000.

Williams, plagued by injury in the previous season when he appeared in only three limited-overs matches and took three wickets, was a firebrand enforcer in 2001-02, particularly at the WACA Ground where he took 12 wickets at 13.25 in four matches. While the lion-hearted Angel took 14 wickets at 23.71 and conceded only 4.13 runs an over, Matthew Nicholson managed only two expensive wickets from five matches. Left-armer Michael Clark played in the side's final three games and showed promise, but apart from left-arm wrist-spinner Hogg's 12 wickets at 25.67, the rest of the bowlers had disappointing results.

Hogg augmented the usefulness of his bowling by playing some valuable innings in the final few overs of several matches. Martyn began the season in fine touch, scoring 224 runs in the first three matches but Simon Katich was less prolific than in previous seasons, being dismissed for 20 or less seven times, with only his 70 against Queensland and 118 against Victoria (both at the WACA Ground in January) saving his reputation. Murray Goodwin had a poor season, eventually losing his spot, and Rob Baker under-achieved in his long-awaited return after illness. Apart from Hussey's $200,000 sweep, the most significant Western Australian hit of the season was Williams' towering last-over six that brought a thrilling victory over South Australia in Adelaide. – KEN CASELLAS.

RESULTS, 2001-02

ING Cup matches – Played 10: Won 5, Lost 5.
Competition placing – 4th.

ING CUP AVERAGES, 2001-02

BATTING

	M	I	NO	R	HS	100s	50s	Avge	Ct/St	S-R
D. R. Martyn	3	3	0	224	108	1	1	74.67	0	65.88
M. E. K. Hussey	10	10	2	440	103*	1	2	55.00	9	79.71
R. J. Campbell	6	6	1	181	77	0	1	36.20	9/1	88.73
K. M. Harvey	10	8	5	106	29	0	0	35.33	1	86.89
J. L. Langer	6	6	0	197	107	1	1	32.83	4	69.61
S. W. Meuleman	5	5	0	157	49	0	0	31.40	0	78.11
S. M. Katich	10	10	0	293	118	1	1	29.30	1	61.43
A. C. Gilchrist	4	4	0	117	84	0	1	29.25	5/1	106.36
G. B. Hogg	10	9	4	128	39*	0	0	25.60	2	81.53
C. J. L. Rogers	4	4	0	100	39	0	0	25.00	0	58.82
M. W. Goodwin	6	6	0	112	33	0	0	18.67	1	67.47
M. J. North	1	1	0	17	17	0	0	17.00	0	113.33
S. J. Karppinen	5	3	0	45	23	0	0	15.00	2	97.83
R. M. Baker	4	4	0	55	27	0	0	13.75	1	65.48
M. J. Nicholson	5	3	1	23	14	0	0	11.50	3	85.19
M. W. Clark	3	1	0	7	7	0	0	7.00	2	43.75
D. J. Wates	7	4	2	8	6	0	0	4.00	2	61.54
J. Angel	9	1	0	2	2	0	0	2.00	0	40.00
L. Ronchi	1	1	0	0	0	0	0	0.00	1	0.00
B. A. Williams	8	2	2	7	6*	0	0	–	1	233.33
B. J. Oldroyd	1	0	0	0	0	0	0	–	1	–
S. R. Cary	2	0	0	0	0	0	0	–	1	–

* Denotes not out.

BOWLING

	O	M	R	W	BB	5W/I	Avge
B. A. Williams	69.2	4	295	18	4/44	0	16.39
M. W. Clark	23	1	109	5	3/34	0	21.80
J. Angel	80.3	5	333	14	5/16	1	23.79
G. B. Hogg	57.1	0	307	12	4/50	0	25.58
S. R. Cary	18	1	61	2	2/25	0	30.50
B. J. Oldroyd	8	0	43	1	1/43	0	43.00
K. M. Harvey	63	6	319	6	2/45	0	53.17
D. J. Wates	52	5	271	5	3/32	0	54.20
M. J. Nicholson	31	0	167	2	1/30	0	83.50
S. M. Katich	3	0	27	0	–	0	–
S. J. Karppinen	37	2	142	0	–	0	–

WESTERN AUSTRALIA v SOUTH AUSTRALIA

At WACA Ground, Perth, October 12, 2001. Western Australia won by 56 runs. Toss: Western Australia. Western Australia 5 pts.

Adam Gilchrist and Damien Martyn got Western Australia's season away to a flying start with a sparkling opening stand of 107 from 112 balls. Gilchrist thumped the ball to all parts of the ground and hit 14 fours and two sixes. Justin Langer, Simon Katich, Murray Goodwin, Mike Hussey and Brad Hogg also made valuable contributions. South Australia lost swing bowler Brett Swain, who badly damaged his left shoulder when he landed heavily when diving to field a ball at deep fine leg and had to leave the field after he had sent down six overs. South Australia's batting never really looked likely to achieve the target despite a polished innings by Greg Blewett. Darren Wates struck a major blow when he removed Darren Lehmann for one, caught on the boundary. Brad Williams bowled with plenty of fire to finish with his best limited-overs figures.

Man of the Match: A.C. Gilchrist.   *Attendance:* 5,704.

Western Australia

D.R. Martyn c Manou b Harrity	34	(63)	G.B. Hogg not out 27 (28)
*†A.C. Gilchrist c Vaughan b Harrity	84	(67)	
J.L. Langer c and b Young	26	(44)	L-b 3, w 2, n-b 4 9
S.M. Katich c Johnson b Gillespie	20	(37)	
M.W. Goodwin c Johnson b Harrity	33	(30)	
M.E.K. Hussey not out	36	(37)	(50 overs, 210 mins) (5 wkts) 269
			Fall: 107 130 162 177 212

K.M. Harvey, M.J. Nicholson, D.J. Wates, J. Angel and B.A. Williams did not bat.

Bowling: Gillespie 10–2–47–1; Swain 6–1–24–0; Rofe 6–0–50–0; Harrity 10–0–51–3; Young 10–0–44–1; Harris 6–0–31–0; Johnson 2–0–19–0.

South Australia

G.S. Blewett c Hussey b Williams	80	(85)	J.N. Gillespie lbw b Hogg 3 (10)
D.A. Fitzgerald c Langer b Williams	3	(9)	P.C. Rofe not out 1 (8)
J.M. Vaughan c Gilchrist b Nicholson	28	(48)	M.A. Harrity st Gilchrist b Hogg ... 0 (2)
*D.S. Lehmann c Hussey b Wates	1	(8)	L-b 2, w 5, n-b 1 8
B.A. Johnson c Gilchrist b Williams	28	(32)	
B.E. Young c Katich b Hogg	44	(45)	(45.2 overs, 191 mins) 213
R.J. Harris c Nicholson b Williams	2	(11)	Fall: 11 76 82 140 147 162 194
†G.A. Manou b Harvey	15	(19)	212 213 213

B.A. Swain did not bat.

Bowling: Williams 10–0–44–4; Angel 10–2–41–0; Nicholson 7–0–30–1; Wates 6–0–45–1; Harvey 9–2–41–1; Hogg 3.2–0–10–3.

Umpires: A.R. Craig and I.H. Lock.

At Brisbane Cricket Ground, Brisbane, October 21, 2001. WESTERN AUSTRALIA lost to QUEENSLAND by seven wickets.

WESTERN AUSTRALIA v TASMANIA

At WACA Ground, Perth, October 24, 2001. Day/night game. Tasmania won by five wickets. Toss: Western Australia. Tasmania 5 pts.

Ricky Ponting stole the show with his power-packed century, but it was a superb spell of fast-medium bowling by Damien Wright that set Tasmania on the path to victory. Wright's opening over cost nine runs, but he conceded only 13 runs from his remaining nine overs – seven singles, a two and a straight drive for four by Damien Martyn. Wright employed three slips and a gully to Simon Katich, with a wide mid-on the only leg-side fieldsman. A frustrated Katich eventually chopped a ball from Wright onto his stumps. Martyn played a lone hand before he was dismissed in the penultimate over. The target of 196 never really challenged the Tasmanians, who coasted to victory with five wickets in hand and 65 balls to spare, Ponting racing to his century off 90 deliveries. Dropping four catches did not help the home side's cause.

Man of the Match: D.G. Wright.   *Attendance:* 3,508.

Western Australia

D.R. Martyn c Cox b Saker	108 (147)		G.B. Hogg not out	20	(25)
*†A.C. Gilchrist c Watson b Wright	5	(4)	K.M. Harvey not out	3	(5)
J.L. Langer c Clingeleffer b Saker	1	(5)			
S.M. Katich b Wright	5	(24)	L-b 3	3	
M.W. Goodwin c Thomas b Young	21	(27)			
M.E.K. Hussey c Clingeleffer			(50 overs, 198 mins) (6 wkts) 195		
b Polkinghorne	29	(59)	Fall: 21 23 42 72 148 189		

D.J. Wates, S.J. Karppinen, B.A. Williams and J. Angel did not bat.

Bowling: Wright 10–0–22–2; Saker 9–0–37–2; Thomas 7–1–40–0; Young 10–0–38–1; Polkinghorne 10–0–39–1; Watson 4–0–16–0.

Tasmania

D.F. Hills b Angel	29	(58)	J. Cox not out	2	(2)
S.R. Watson c Gilchrist b Williams	12	(11)			
*R.T. Ponting c Hussey b Harvey	102	(98)	L-b 4, w 2, n-b 1	7	
S. Young not out	28	(52)			
A.W. Polkinghorne b Williams	4	(6)	(39.1 overs, 159 mins) (5 wkts) 196		
G.T. Cunningham b Williams	12	(11)	Fall: 17 105 175 180 194		

D.J. Marsh, D.G. Wright, †S.G. Clingeleffer, D.J. Saker and B.J. Thomas did not bat.

Bowling: Williams 8–0–39–3; Wates 7–0–34–0; Angel 9–2–35–1; Hogg 5–0–26–0; Karppinen 5–0–31–0; Harvey 5.1–1–27–1.

Umpires: B. Bennett and R.J.U. Woolridge.
TV Umpire: R.J. Evans.

At Bellerive Oval, Hobart, November 3, 2001. WESTERN AUSTRALIA defeated TASMANIA by five wickets.

At Adelaide Oval, Adelaide, November 30, 2001. Day/night game. WESTERN AUSTRALIA defeated SOUTH AUSTRALIA by one wicket.

At Melbourne Cricket Ground, Melbourne, December 23, 2001. WESTERN AUSTRALIA lost to VICTORIA by 10 runs.

WESTERN AUSTRALIA v QUEENSLAND

At WACA Ground, Perth, January 4, 2002. Day/night game. Western Australia won by 42 runs. Toss: Western Australia. Western Australia 4 pts.

Darren Wates grasped his chance with both hands when he was called into the Western Australian side at the last minute to replace injured seamer Stuart Karppinen. Wates produced a wonderful spell of swing bowling which set his side on the path to an easy win. He removed Stuart Law, Jimmy Maher and Clinton Perren in rapid succession to have the Queenslanders in serious trouble at four for 51 in the 16th over. Andrew Symonds and James Hopes then produced a 66-run partnership before Jo Angel removed both of them. Earlier, enterprising batting by Scott Meuleman and Simon Katich had enabled Western Australia to set a challenging target. Outstanding running between wickets by openers Meuleman and Chris Rogers put the Queensland fieldsmen under pressure and led to three fives, the result of three overthrows that crossed the boundary.

Man of the Match: S.M. Katich.   *Attendance:* 8,548.

Western Australia

S. W. Meuleman c Seccombe b Hopes	43 (42)
C. J. L. Rogers c Seccombe b Dawes	16 (30)
*S. M. Katich c Symonds b Hauritz	70 (110)
R. M. Baker c Seccombe b Dawes	7 (15)
M. E. K. Hussey lbw b Noffke	28 (41)
†R. J. Campbell c Love b Dawes	20 (22)
M. J. Nicholson c Nash b Hauritz	4 (9)

G. B. Hogg not out	24 (28)
K. M. Harvey not out	12 (11)
L-b 3, w 7, n-b 3	13
(50 overs, 204 mins) (7 wkts)	237
Fall: 40 81 98 167 187 193 206	

D. J. Wates, B. A. Williams and J. Angel did not bat.

Bowling: Noffke 10–0–57–1; Dawes 10–0–39–3; Hopes 7–0–23–1; Kasprowicz 10–0–43–0; Symonds 4–0–32–0; Hauritz 9–0–40–2.

Queensland

M. L. Love c Campbell b Williams	5 (21)
J. P. Maher c Hogg b Wates	23 (42)
*S. G. Law c Nicholson b Wates	8 (22)
A. Symonds c Baker b Angel	32 (31)
C. T. Perren c Campbell b Wates	0 (1)
J. R. Hopes c Hussey b Angel	40 (44)
B. P. Nash run out (Katich)	25 (44)
†W. A. Seccombe run out (Harvey)	2 (4)

A. A. Noffke not out	22 (41)
N. M. Hauritz b Williams	15 (14)
M. S. Kasprowicz b Williams	7 (9)
L-b 7, w 4, n-b 5	16
(44.2 overs, 183 mins)	195
Fall: 9 26 47 51 117 123 125	
168 187 195	

Bowling: Williams 7.2–0–29–3; Wates 10–2–32–3; Nicholson 5–0–33–0; Harvey 6–0–35–0; Angel 10–1–33–2; Hogg 6–0–26–0.

J. H. Dawes did not bat.

Umpires: A. R. Craig and I. H. Lock.

WESTERN AUSTRALIA v VICTORIA

At WACA Ground, Perth, January 16, 2002. Day/night game. Western Australia won by 116 runs. Toss: Western Australia. Western Australia 5 pts. Competition debut: M. W. Clark, L. Ronchi; A. B. McDonald.

Veteran seamer Jo Angel returned his best figures in a domestic limited-overs match and Simon Katich hit his second century in the competition to help Western Australia to a crushing victory. After a circumspect beginning to the innings, Katich and fellow left-hander Mike Hussey pulverised the Victorian attack in a record partnership of 167 from 174 balls for the fourth wicket. The last four wickets, including those of Katich and Hussey, fell for two runs in the final seven deliveries of the innings, with Michael Lewis picking up three scalps in the 50th over. Michael Clark, a rangy left-armer, opened the attack on his interstate debut and took three valuable wickets before Sean Cary and Angel tore through the rest of an inept batting line-up.

Man of the Match: S. M. Katich.   *Attendance:* 5,788.

Western Australia

*J. L. Langer c Lewis b Inness	3 (8)
S. W. Meuleman c Berry b Fleming	17 (24)
S. M. Katich lbw b McDonald	118 (141)
R. M. Baker c Berry b Lewis	21 (35)
M. E. K. Hussey c Moss b Lewis	61 (88)
K. M. Harvey not out	1 (3)
G. B. Hogg b Lewis	0 (1)

†L. Ronchi b Lewis	0 (1)
D. J. Wates not out	1 (1)
L-b 5, w 6, n-b 1	12
(50 overs, 211 mins) (7 wkts)	234
Fall: 4 26 65 232 232 233 233	

S. R. Cary, M. W. Clark and J. Angel did not bat.

Bowling: Fleming 10–1–45–1; Inness 10–0–25–1; Hewett 10–1–33–0; Lewis 9–0–41–4; Hodge 6–0–41–0; McDonald 5–0–44–1.

Victoria

*M. T. G. Elliott c Langer b Clark	 35	(32)	
R. A. Bartlett c Cary b Clark	 3	(16)	
B. J. Hodge b Cary	 23	(38)	
M. Klinger c Hussey b Clark	 4	(7)	
J. L. Arnberger c Hussey b Angel	 23	(39)	
J. Moss c Ronchi b Angel	 7	(27)	
A. B. McDonald lbw b Cary	 0	(3)	
†D. S. Berry c Langer b Angel	 3	(11)	

I. S. L. Hewett not out	 10	(14)
D. W. Fleming c Langer b Angel	 0	(1)
M. L. Lewis c Wates b Angel	 6	(15)
L-b 1, w 3	 4	
(33.3 overs, 139 mins)	118	

M. W. H. Inness did not bat.

Fall: 20 46 51 89 91 93 98 104 104 118

Bowling: Wates 9–1–42–0; Clark 10–0–34–3; Cary 8–0–25–2; Angel 6.3–0–16–5.

Umpires: B. Bennett and I. H. Lock.

At Sydney Cricket Ground, Sydney, February 3, 2002. WESTERN AUSTRALIA lost to NEW SOUTH WALES by five wickets.

WESTERN AUSTRALIA v NEW SOUTH WALES

At WACA Ground, Perth, February 13, 2002. Day/night game. New South Wales won by three runs. Toss: New South Wales. New South Wales 4 pts. Competiton debut: G. M. Lambert.

Western Australia lost in a tight finish and thus failed to qualify for the final of the competition, but there were scenes of jubilation in their rooms after the defeat as the players celebrated Mike Hussey's big hit which earned a $200,000 cash jackpot. New South Wales' victory, set up by a dominating innings by opener Corey Richards (18 fours, two sixes), earned them the right to contest the final. He survived a dropped catch by Kade Harvey in the covers on 68, finally departing in the 46th over, caught at long-off as he attempted his third six. Jo Angel's three wickets took his tally to 73, making him the leading wicket-taker in the history of the competition, passing Tom Moody. Ryan Campbell got the home side away to a fast start, but the real excitement came in the 29th over when the left-handed Hussey swept a ball from Dominic Thornely in the medium-pacer's second over. The ball crashed into the sponsor's sign, the six taking Hussey to 35. During a subsequent break an announcement confirmed that he had earned the $200,000 jackpot. But he charged the first ball after drinks, missed with his vigorous swipe and was bowled.

Man of the Match: C. J. Richards. *Attendance:* 4,425.

New South Wales

C. J. Richards c Clark b Harvey	151	(147)
†B. J. Haddin c Harvey b Wates	 6	(8)
M. G. Bevan c Clark b Angel	 40	(71)
M. J. Clarke c Campbell b Williams	.. 18	(28)
*S. Lee c Campbell b Williams	 2	(3)
G. C. Rummans b Angel	 18	(30)
M. A. Higgs run out (Hogg)	 4	(4)
D. J. Thornely run out (Hussey)	 3	(3)

S. D. Bradstreet c (sub) M. J. North		
b Angel ..	4	(7)
G. M. Lambert not out	 3	(3)
N. W. Bracken not out	 1	(2)
B 4, l-b 7, w 4, n-b 2	 17	
(50 overs, 209 mins)	(9 wkts) 267	

S. R. Clark did not bat.

Fall: 19 112 156 158 246 255 256 263 264

Bowling: Williams 10–0–47–2; Wates 9–2–48–1; Clark 6–1–35–0; Harvey 10–2–31–1; Angel 9–0–54–3; Hogg 6–0–41–0.

Western Australia

†R. J. Campbell c Bevan b Higgs	42 (38)	D. J. Wates c Haddin b Lambert	6 (10)
C. J. L. Rogers c Haddin b Clark	28 (52)	J. Angel c Bevan b Lambert	2 (5)
*S. M. Katich c Haddin b Bradstreet	16 (25)	M. W. Clark c Haddin b Bradstreet	7 (16)
M. E. K. Hussey b Bracken	45 (54)	B 1, l-b 4, w 17	22
R. M. Baker c Haddin b Higgs	27 (35)		
S. W. Meuleman st Haddin b Higgs	1 (3)	(49.3 overs, 225 mins)	264
G. B. Hogg not out	39 (49)	Fall: 71 74 109 173 177 185 235	
K. M. Harvey run out (Lambert)	29 (23)	247 251 264	

B. A. Williams did not bat.

Bowling: Clark 10–1–35–1; Bracken 10–0–63–1; Higgs 10–0–48–3; Bradstreet 8.3–0–39–2; Lambert 6–0–33–2; Thornely 4–0–34–0; Clarke 1–0–7–0.

Umpires: A. R. Craig and I. H. Lock.
TV Umpire: B. Bennett.

DOMESTIC LIMITED-OVERS RESULTS

	M	W	L	NR	T
Australian Capital Territory	3	3	0	0	0
New South Wales	30	15	14	0	1
New Zealanders	3	2	1	0	0
Queensland	27	13	12	2	0
South Australia	31	20	11	0	0
Tasmania	23	18	5	0	0
Victoria	29	22	5	2	0
Total	146	93	48	4	1

RECORDS

Highest score for:	167	M. W. Goodwin v New South Wales at Perth	2000-01
Highest score against:	151	C. J. Richards (New South Wales) at Perth	2001-02
Best bowling for:	5/15	D. L. Boyd v Victoria at Perth	1982-83
Best bowling against:	5/23	R. J. McCurdy (South Australia) at Adelaide	1984-85
Highest total for:	5-325	v New South Wales at Perth	2000-01
Highest total against:	8-306	by Queensland at Brisbane	2000-01
Lowest total for:	59	v Victoria at Melbourne	1969-70
Lowest total against:	62	by Queensland at Perth	1976-77

MOST RUNS

	M	I	NO	R	HS	100s	50s	Avge	S-R
J. L. Langer	61	59	5	2,063	146	2	17	38.20	65.97
T. M. Moody	75	71	12	2,004	102*	2	14	33.97	72.22
D. R. Martyn	51	48	7	1,879	140	3	13	45.83	74.39
G. R. Marsh	38	37	7	1,596	110	3	12	53.20	62.30
M. E. Hussey	45	42	5	1,538	103*	2	11	41.57	77.05
S. M. Katich	38	37	3	1,178	118	2	8	34.65	71.31
M. R. J. Veletta	42	39	8	1,077	105*	1	8	34.74	62.18
R. J. Campbell	48	47	1	1,033	108	1	6	22.46	83.58
A. C. Gilchrist	34	31	3	972	115	1	7	34.71	87.73
G. M. Wood	42	38	3	851	108*	1	4	24.31	57.46

* Denotes not out.

HIGHEST PARTNERSHIP FOR EACH WICKET

171	for 1st	G.R. Marsh and M.W. McPhee, v Queensland at Perth	1990-91
188*	for 2nd	J.L. Langer and D.R. Martyn, v Victoria at Melbourne	1997-98
257	for 3rd	M.W. Goodwin and M.E. Hussey, v New South Wales at Perth	2000-01
110	for 4th	G.R. Marsh and M.R.J. Veletta, v New South Wales at Perth	1990-91
129	for 5th	J.L. Langer and W.S. Andrews, v Queensland at Brisbane	1992-93
173	for 6th	M.E. Hussey and G.B. Hogg, v Victoria at Melbourne	1999-00
111*	for 7th	R.W. Marsh and B. Yardley, v New South Wales at Sydney	1973-74
106*	for 8th	A.C. Gilchrist and B.P. Julian, v New South Wales at Sydney	1995-96
57	for 9th	D.R. Martyn and B.P. Julian, v Queensland at Brisbane	1997-98
36	for 10th	K.H. MacLeay and P.M. Clough, v New South Wales at Perth	1984-85

* Denotes unbroken partnership.

MOST WICKETS

	M	Balls	Mdns	R	W	BB	5W/i	Avge
J. Angel	62	3,117	47	2,053	73	5/16	1	28.12
T.M. Moody	75	3,205	41	2,131	70	4/30	0	30.40
K.M. Harvey	50	2,072	22	1,689	61	4/8	0	27.69
B.P. Julian	54	2,318	19	1,779	59	4/41	0	30.15
K.H. MacLeay	38	1,896	32	1,165	53	5/30	1	21.98
D.K. Lillee	26	1,505	32	766	48	4/21	0	15.96
T.M. Alderman	35	1,938	34	1,169	40	4/14	0	29.23
G.B. Hogg	54	1,180	4	1,023	38	4/50	0	26.92
J. Stewart	32	1,564	9	1,117	36	4/34	0	31.03
M.P. Atkinson	27	1,325	11	984	34	4/38	0	28.94

MOST DISMISSALS

	M	Ct	St	Total
A.C. Gilchrist	34	56	6	62
R.J. Campbell	27	52	6	58
R.W. Marsh	33	51	1	52
T.J. Zoehrer	35	41	4	45
M.J. Cox	5	10	0	10

MOST CATCHES

T.M. Moody	27 in 75 matches	M.R.J. Veletta	17 in 40 matches
G.B. Hogg	27 in 54 matches	B.P. Julian	16 in 54 matches
M.E. Hussey	27 in 45 matches	R.J. Inverarity	14 in 19 matches
J.L. Langer	24 in 61 matches	D.R. Martyn	14 in 51 matches
G.R. Marsh	20 in 38 matches		

MOST APPEARANCES

75	T.M. Moody	1985-86 – 2000-01	
62	J. Angel	1992-93 – 2001-02	
61	J.L. Langer	1991-92 – 2001-02	
54	B.J. Julian	1991-92 – 2000-01	
54	G.B. Hogg	1993-94 – 2001-02	
51	D.R. Martyn	1991-92 – 2001-02	
50	K.M. Harvey	1994-95 – 2001-02	
48	R.J. Campbell	1992-93 – 2001-02	
45	M.E.K. Hussey	1996-97 – 2001-02	

MINOR CRICKET IN AUSTRALIA, 2001-02

By KEN PIESSE

The ACB Cup again featured eight teams, including the Australian Capital Territory, the Queensland Academy of Sport and the Australian Cricket Academy. The competition was conducted on a differential basis and served a dual purpose: many first-class players were able to regain form in these matches, while a number of young players showed the potential for playing at the next level.

New South Wales sealed their competition win by defeating Tasmania in their final match, a victory which gave them four mostly comfortable wins from five matches. Their only drawn match was against Victoria when Paul Reiffel led stout second-innings resistance by the Victorian tail to avert outright defeat. Their season, however, had begun disastrously when, in the first innings of their first match, against the Australian Cricket Academy, they collapsed to be all out for 85 in less than two hours. Western Australia were a close second, also with four wins from five fixtures.

New South Wales had the highest run-maker in Brett Van Deinsen; his 438 runs included 239 compiled during a prolonged display of concentration against the Victorian Second XI at Melbourne's Junction Oval. Earlier, he had missed another century by only three runs against the Australian Cricket Academy in New South Wales' opening match of the season, followed by an entertaining 95 against the Queensland Academy of Sport at the Allan Border Field. Both Corey Richards and Graeme Rummans showed their first-class experience, the latter being in fine touch against South Australia with innings of 117 and 90 not out. The state also had two of the leading wicket-takers in all-rounders Shawn Bradstreet and Grant Lambert, who each took 17 economical wickets. Pace man Jamie Heath was also prominent with three for 76 and six for 57 against the Cricket Academy at Penrith's Howell Oval in late September, while Lambert took six for 52 against the Queensland Academy. Nathan Pilon's unbeaten 116 against South Australia included ten fours and nine sixes, four in the final two overs from leg-spinner Jamie Marsh, his fireworks coming in an unfinished last-wicket partnership of 114, to which Anthony Clark contributed 19. Pilon capped an accomplished season with the gloves with eight catches in the final match, against Tasmania, which took his season's tally to 26 catches and three stumpings from five games.

Runners-up Western Australia also had a rich reservoir of batting talent with Chris Rogers, the returning Robbie Baker, Adam Voges and left-hander Geoff Cullen each hitting centuries. Rogers was one of only four players to make 400 runs in the ACB Cup, starting with a patient 151 against the Australian Cricket Academy, during which the left-hander passed 1,000 runs in the ACB Cup, form that earned him a highly successful promotion into the state side. Voges (against the Queensland Academy of Sport) and Cullen (against Victoria) each made 144, Voges from 234 balls and Cullen from 207; both innings were full of robust strokes. Western Australia also had one of the leading wicket-takers in Matthew Healey, who claimed 17 at an average of 19.05. He began the season with eight wickets in the match against the Australian Cricket Academy, following up with first-innings figures of six for 50 against South Australia.

Victoria missed out on second place after being beaten by 56 runs by Western Australia in Perth. Broad-shouldered fast bowler Will Carr was their find of the season. He took six wickets in this game and 16 in three matches before being called into the Pura Cup team. Off-spinner Jon Davison produced the most startling analysis of the season: nine for 67 from 23.2 overs against South Australia at Adelaide Oval No. 2. After Andrew McDonald had dismissed South Australian opener Shane Deitz, Davison took the last nine wickets to fall as South Australia lost by an innings. Born in British Columbia, he is likely to take a front-line role in Canada's World Cup team in South Africa in 2002-03. New-ball pair Ian Hewett and Shane Harwood warmed up for representative action with 13 wickets between them against Tasmania at Camberwell. With 172 against the Australian Cricket Academy at the Albert Ground, Shawn Craig made his side's highest individual score, while another young player to make his mark was tall right-hander Nick Jewell, who was lifted from Premier League ranks without a contract into the Victorian Second XI, where he made 132 against South Australia at the beginning of the summer. By February, he was in the state team, playing in the last two matches at both Pura Cup and ING Cup level.

South Australia had a frustrating season, being unable to string together successive victories. Nathan Adcock had a season-best 170 not out when captaining South Australia against Western Australia at Adelaide Oval No. 2. With a consistent 401 runs at an average of 50.12, Shane Deitz also regained first-class honours, his 18 catches and one stumping prompting the selectors to try him with the gloves in South Australia's last Pura Cup match of the season. Team-mate Luke Williams also passed the 400 mark to increase his ACB Cup career aggregate to a record 1,376 in 17 matches. Fast bowler Paul Rofe played an early match in the competition, taking five for 81 and one for 36 against the Cricket Academy in October, before a highly successful season at first-class level. Chris Davies says that he is fortunate to be as healthy as he is. "I was diagnosed with cystic fibrosis at six months, so have lived with it all my life," he says. "But it's only a relatively small dose and it's manageable. I'm much healthier than the next person, who simply isn't able to do as much fitness work." By refusing to allow the condition to affect his life, Davies has been able to push himself to limits some doctors had thought impossible. In 2001-02, he forced his way back into the South Australian Pura Cup team with a monumental 233 not out (455 minutes, 366 balls, 20 fours, four sixes) in the ACB Cup against Australian Capital Territory at the Adelaide Oval. He was joined by Ryan Harris (100 not out) in a rousing unfinished sixth-wicket partnership of 183 in only 132 minutes. Dan Dempsey also batted skilfully, scoring centuries in the first and last matches of the season.

While Tasmania beat the Australian Capital Territory by an innings at Manuka Oval, they made a horrible botch of attempting to score just 96 to beat the Cricket Academy outright in the first match of the season, at Hobart's New Town Oval, sliding to a paltry eight for 67. Experienced all-rounder Brad Thomas took five for 29 and spinner Shannon Tubb six for 55 against Australian Capital Territory, a game in which left-handed opener Scott Mason made 144 (355 minutes, 294 balls, 14 fours). Earlier, Mason had contributed a convincing 88 to Tasmania's total of 366 against the Australian Cricket Academy, before things went awry on the last afternoon.

Queensland Academy of Sport began the season with a match which had to be abandoned when the Australian Cricket Academy team could not get a flight from Adelaide to Brisbane following the collapse of Ansett Airlines. They did record a handsome victory over the Australian Capital Territory in their last match, thanks to a commanding 230 not out by Lee Carseldine (355 minutes, 273 balls, 36 fours), who came to the wicket in the third over at two for 11 and was unbeaten when Queensland were all out for 345. Earlier in the season, although his side was outclassed by New South Wales, Brendan Nash conducted a solo feat of batting resistance. In the first innings he top-scored with 47 which he ground out in five minutes under three hours. After the visitors had declared at six for 548, Nash arrived at the crease to face the fourth ball of the second innings with the score already at two for 0; he then made a superb and undefeated 125 (271 minutes, 226 balls, 20 fours) out of his side's paltry 199.

The Australian Cricket Academy gave New South Wales a fright on the first morning of their match, a combined effort from the bowlers restricting the home side to just 85. Academy wicket-keeper Daniel Smith cracked 61 from 71 balls to complement Shaun Marsh's more sedate effort and produce a lead of 151. Xavier Doherty then gave a consummate display of the persistent and probing arts of the slow left-armer which helped to compensate for his batsmen's inability to reach the modest target of 174.

Doherty (three for 78 and four for 20) teamed with left-arm wrist spinner Beau Casson (five for 55 and one for 17) to almost snatch victory against the Tasmanians. Later in the season, there was a satisfying win over the Australian Capital Territory at Manuka Oval, when a steady performance with both bat and ball was topped off by a run-chase which saw the Academy post a victorious fourth-innings total of five for 336, the last 136 runs coming from a partnership between David Bandy (71 not out) and Daniel Smith (59) in the final match, against Victoria; despite the Academy's heavy loss, there were two contributions with the stamp of class on them. In the first innings, Tim Welsford made a fighting 94 (249 minutes, 204 balls, 10 fours) which carried on from the 89 which he had made against Western Australia two matches previosly. In the second innings, Luke Ronchi played with real verve in making 107 (176 minutes, 141 balls, 12 fours, three sixes).

Australian Capital Territory failed to win a match, despite several promising displays. Among the most prominent players was 24-year-old right-handed opener Jack Smith, who made 118 against the Australian Cricket Academy. Smith also notched a century representing an Australian Capital Territory Invitational XI against New Zealand at Manuka Oval in October. Fellow opener Dave Jeffrey also showed real capability with 59 and 100 against South Australia at the Adelaide Oval, while he contributed a solid 69 to an opening partnership of 161 with Smith in the second innings against the Cricket Academy.

AUSTRALIAN CRICKET BOARD CUP, 2001-02

POINTS TABLE, 2001-02

	Played	WO	WI	D	LI	LO	T	Points	Quotient
New South Wales Second XI	5	4	1	0	0	0	0	36.4	1.722
Western Australia Second XI	4	3	1	0	0	0	0	35.0	1.284
Victoria Second XI	5	3	0	0	1	1	0	25.2	1.291
South Australia Second XI	5	2	0	0	1	2	0	16.8	1.098
Tasmania Second XI	4	1	1	0	0	2	0	14.0	0.914
Queensland Academy of Sport	4	1	0	1	0	2	0	10.5	0.723
Australian Cricket Academy	7	1	0	1	1	4	0	10.0	0.766
Australian Capital Territory	4	0	0	0	0	4	0	0.0	0.518

Quotient = runs per wicket scored divided by runs per wicket conceded.

Points are determined by multiplying game points by 7 then dividing by the number of games played by each team. Allotted games for each team: 7 – ACA, 5 – NSW, SAust, Vic, 4 – ACT, Qld, Tas, SAust.

AUSTRALIAN CRICKET BOARD CUP AVERAGES, 2001-02

BATTING

(Qualification: 200 runs)

	M	I	NO	R	HS	100s	50s	Avge
C.J. Davies (SAust)	1	2	1	265	233*	1	0	265.00
L.A. Carseldine (Qld)	2	3	1	302	230*	1	0	151.00
S.A.J. Craig (Vic)	3	5	1	397	172	1	3	99.25
C.J. Richards (NSW)	3	4	0	353	189	1	2	88.25
N.T. Adcock (SAust)	3	5	1	312	170*	1	1	78.00
B.P. Nash (Qld)	2	4	1	226	125*	1	0	75.33
G.C. Rummans (NSW)	4	6	1	367	117	1	2	73.40
B.P. Van Deinsen (NSW)	4	6	0	438	239	1	2	73.00
S.R. Mason (Tas)	3	4	0	269	144	1	1	67.25
D.M. Dempsey (SAust)	4	7	1	385	139	2	1	64.17

* Denotes not out.

BOWLING

(Qualification: 10 wickets)

	M	O	Mdns	R	W	BB	5W/i	10W/m	Avge
S.M. Harwood (Vic)	2	52.3	14	144	13	6/41	1	0	11.08
S.D. Bradstreet (NSW) ..	3	99	34	191	17	4/21	0	0	11.24
M.D. King (SAust)	3	94	35	222	14	5/49	1	0	15.86
M.J. Thistle (ACA)	2	59	14	183	10	5/89	1	0	18.30
M.R. Healey (Tas)	4	125.1	39	324	17	6/50	1	0	19.05
D.A. Horsley (NSW)	3	96.4	32	192	10	6/46	1	0	19.20
B.M. Edmondson (QAS).	3	84	15	274	14	4/28	0	0	19.57
G.M. Lambert (NSW) ...	5	110.1	19	371	17	6/52	1	0	21.82
X.J. Doherty (ACA).....	4	104.5	25	306	14	6/68	1	0	21.85
I.S.L. Hewett (Vic)	3	80.2	25	221	10	5/47	1	0	22.10

Note: Games played in this competition were not first-class.

NEW SOUTH WALES SECOND XI v AUSTRALIAN CRICKET ACADEMY

At Howell Oval, Penrith, September 24, 25, 26, 2001. New South Wales Second XI won by 17 runs. Toss: New South Wales Second XI.

New South Wales Second XI

B.P. Van Deinsen b Magoffin	5	– (2) st Smith b Doherty	97
P.A. Jaques c Casson b Scott	4	– (1) st Smith b Casson	35
*G.C. Rummans run out (Doherty)	26	– c Smith b Casson	23
A.W. O'Brien lbw b Magoffin	0	– lbw b Magoffin	25
G.M. Lambert c Smith b Scott	2	– b Doherty	4
D.J. Thornely c Cosgrove b Magoffin	3	– c Smith b Magoffin	77
†N.S. Pilon c Ronchi b Cosgrove	10	– st Smith b Doherty	8
A.M. Clark run out	13	– c Ronchi b Doherty	2
S.P. Coombes c Smith b Cosgrove	0	– c Welsford b Doherty	3
M.A.W. Goldsmith c Magoffin b Cosgrove	1	– c Scott b Doherty	26
J.M. Heath not out	3	– not out	0
L-b 1, w 1, n-b 16	18	B 3, l-b 8, w 1, n-b 12	24

(25.4 overs, 117 mins)	85	(93.2 overs, 347 mins)
Fall: 12 16 16 27 30 64 64		Fall: 81 139 181 197 197 215
65 68 85		221 233 315 324

(93.2 overs, 347 mins) 324

D.A. Horsley did not bat.

Bowling: *First Innings*—Magoffin 10.4–1–47–3; Scott 7–0–20–2; Welsford 4–0–15–0; Cosgrove 4–2–2–3. *Second Innings*—Magoffin 24.2–5–72–2; Scott 12–2–52–0; Welsford 12–1–46–0; Casson 18–2–75–2; Doherty 27–6–68–6.

Australian Cricket Academy

S. W. Meuleman c Pilon b Heath	1	– (2) c Van Deinsen b Heath 10
D. M. Betts c Pilon b Lambert	27	– (1) c Pilon b Heath 26
S. E. Marsh lbw b Horsley	54	– c Clark b Heath 0
*R. J. Brewster lbw b Clark	23	– st Pilon b O'Brien 29
L. Ronchi c Pilon b Horsley	5	– c Pilon b Heath 10
T. H. Welsford c Jaques b Coombes	7	– c Clark b Lambert 0
M. J. Cosgrove c Pilon b Heath	11	– lbw b Goldsmith 22
†D. Smith b Lambert	61	– c Pilon b Heath 4
B. Casson c O'Brien b Thornely	11	– c Pilon b O'Brien 17
X. J. Doherty b Heath	15	– not out 14
S. J. Magoffin not out	2	– c Clark b Heath 16
B 2, l-b 6, n-b 11	19	B 1, l-b 3, n-b 3 8

(68.4 overs, 287 mins)	236	(50.3 overs, 207 mins) 156
Fall: 8 49 90 101 124 128 150 202		Fall: 15 15 60 77 81 85 124
224 236		128 156

A. R. Scott did not bat.

Bowling: *First Innings*—Heath 21.4–4–76–3; Horsley 14–6–30–2; Lambert 13–2–51–2; Goldsmith 6–3–28–0; Clark 6–0–23–1; Coombes 5–1–10–1; Thornely 3–0–10–1. *Second Innings*—Heath 15.3–1–57–6; Horsley 5–0–19–0; Clark 4–2–11–0; O'Brien 9–1–20–2; Lambert 9–5–16–1; Goldsmith 8–1–29–1.

Umpires: T. M. Donahoo and J. Evans.

SOUTH AUSTRALIA SECOND XI v AUSTRALIAN CRICKET ACADEMY

At Adelaide Oval No. 2, Adelaide, October 2, 3, 4, 5, 2001. South Australia Second XI won by nine wickets. Toss: Australian Cricket Academy.

Australian Cricket Academy

S. W. Meuleman c Deitz b Kelly	31	– (2) b King 0
D. M. Betts c Deitz b Kelly	16	– (1) c Kelly b King 1
S. E. Marsh c Deitz b Rofe	0	– lbw b Marsh 40
R. J. Brewster c Deitz b Rofe	8	– c Deitz b King 1
D. Smith c Deitz b King	41	– b King 0
*T. H. Welsford b Rofe	38	– b Marsh 42
M. J. Cosgrove c Higgins b Rofe	53	– c Harris b Rofe 24
†L. Ronchi c Deitz b King	9	– b Marsh 11
B. Casson not out	33	– lbw b Marsh 2
X. J. Doherty c Deitz b Rofe	29	– not out 8
S. J. Magoffin did not bat.		– run out (Deitz) 12
L-b 8, n-b 8	16	N-b 1 1

(86.1 overs, 347 mins)	(9 wkts dec)	274	(51.2 overs, 210 mins) 142
Fall: 46 47 53 59 116 196 210			Fall: 1 2 4 10 67 105 109 121
210 274			126 142

A. C. L. James did not bat.

Bowling: *First Innings*—Rofe 30.1–9–81–5; King 24–5–72–2; Kelly 12–1–50–2; Crook 14–3–49–0; Marsh 6–1–14–0. *Second Innings*—Rofe 15.2–5–36–1; King 15–7–38–4; Kelly 6–2–22–0; Marsh 15–4–46–4.

South Australia Second XI

L. Williams lbw b James	1	– (2) not out		75
†S. A. Deitz c Ronchi b Welsford	31	– (1) b Welsford		95
D. J. Harris c Ronchi b Magoffin	10	– not out		2
*J. M. Vaughan b Cosgrove	46			
D. M. Dempsey lbw b Doherty	100			
B. H. Higgins not out	14			
L-b 2, n-b 24	26	B 2, l-b 1, n-b 14		17

(57.5 overs, 243 mins) (5 wkts dec) 228   (40.3 overs, 161 mins) (1 wkt) 189
Fall: 3 33 59 159 228   Fall: 182

C. J. Borgas, A. R. Crook, J. I. Marsh, T. P. Kelly, M. D. King and P. C. Rofe did not bat.

Bowling: *First Innings*—Magoffin 16–4–41–1; James 13–1–61–1; Welsford 10–1–20–1; Doherty 8.5–0–48–1; Casson 5–0–33–0; Cosgrove 5–0–23–1. *Second Innings*—Magoffin 8–1–31–0; James 9–1–55–0; Welsford 11–1–44–1; Doherty 9–3–30–0; Casson 3.3–1–26–0.

Umpires: B. Crompton and R. A. Falk.

SOUTH AUSTRALIA SECOND XI v VICTORIA SECOND XI

At Adelaide Oval No. 2, Adelaide, October 8, 9, 10, 2001. Victoria Second XI won by an innings and 12 runs. Toss: Victoria Second XI.

South Australia Second XI

L. Williams c Roach b McDonald	18	– (2) lbw b Davison		56
†S. A. Deitz c Craig b McDonald	77	– (1) b McDonald		19
D. J. Harris c McDonald b Inness	20	– b Davison		13
*B. H. Higgins c Carr b Inness	1	– c Roach b Davison		0
D. M. Dempsey lbw b Carr	25	– not out		78
C. J. Borgas lbw b Craig	10	– lbw b Davison		0
M. J. Smith c Dart b Craig	0	– c Bartlett b Davison		3
C. J. Ferguson lbw b Inness	6	– c Kent b Davison		3
M. D. King c Jewell b McDonald	4	– c and b Davison		0
J. I. Marsh c Dart b Inness	0	– lbw b Davison		13
T. P. Kelly not out	0	– c Jewell b Davison		13
B 2, l-b 5, n-b 4	11	B 1, l-b 9, n-b 2		12

(88.2 overs, 336 mins) 172   (79.2 overs, 299 mins) 210
Fall: 34 89 91 130 149 151 167   Fall: 40 74 74 111 111 125 145
    167 172 172   145 170 210

S. M. Maraun did not bat.

Bowling: *First Innings*—Inness 20.2–9–27–4; Carr 17–4–46–1; McDonald 20–8–45–3; Davison 13–4–30–0; Bartlett 12–6–13–0; Craig 6–2–4–2. *Second Innings*—Inness 14–5–44–0; Bartlett 7–4–5–0; Carr 19–7–43–0; McDonald 16–3–41–1; Davison 23.2–8–67–9.

Victoria Second XI

P. Q. Harper b King	28	†P. J. Roach c Deitz b Maraun		15
R. A. Bartlett c Higgins b King	20	J. M. Davison b Smith		17
*M. P. Mott lbw b Maraun	17	M. W. H. Inness not out		20
S. P. Dart c Dempsey b King	32	B 8, l-b 8, n-b 8		24
N. Jewell c Dempsey b Marsh	132			
S. A. J. Craig c Higgins b King	59	(107.5 overs, 426 mins)		394
A. J. Kent c Williams b King	30	Fall: 47 55 77 156 288 312 313 329		
A. B. McDonald b Maraun	0	351 394		

W. N. Carr did not bat.

Bowling: Smith 22–3–91–1; King 29.5–15–49–5; Kelly 11–0–67–0; Maraun 22–6–81–3; Marsh 20–5–83–1; Higgins 3–1–7–0.

Umpires: D.J. Harper and C. D'Cruz.

SOUTH AUSTRALIA SECOND XI v AUSTRALIAN CAPITAL TERRITORY

At Adelaide Oval, Adelaide, October 29,30,31, November 1, 2001. South Australia Second XI won by eight wickets. Toss: South Australia Second XI.

South Australia Second XI

D.J. Harris c Dawson b Dennett	10	– (2) run out (Hazell)	3
L. Williams c Dawson b Kellar	38	– (1) not out	43
C.J. Davies not out	233	– c Heading b Axelby	32
*B.A. Johnson c Axelby b Dennett	10	– not out	1
N.T. Adcock c Dawson b Kellar	46		
M.J. Smith run out (Anderson/Dawson)	35		
R.J. Harris not out	100		
L-b 8, w 2, n-b 5	15		

(132 overs, 492 mins) (5 wkts dec) 487   (18.4 overs, 68 mins) (2 wkts) 79
Fall: 26 88 107 241 304   Fall: 10 78

†D.A. Reeves, A.R. Crook, M.D. King, J.I. Marsh and S.M. Maraun did not bat.

Bowling: *First Innings*—Dennett 29–5–124–2; Anderson 16–2–75–0; Kellar 33–7–72–2; Axelby 9–0–55–0; Elliott 27–3–93–0; Jeffrey 15–4–41–0; Smith 2–0–12–0; Heading 1–0–7–0. *Second Innings*—Dennett 3–0–11–0; Kellar 3–0–15–0; Axelby 6.4–0–18–1; Robson 6–0–35–0.

Australian Capital Territory

J.K. Smith c R.J. Harris b Maraun	6	– (2) lbw b Maraun	1
D.M. Jeffrey c and b Marsh	59	– (1) c R.J. Harris b Adcock	100
D.S. Hazell c Reeves b R.J. Harris	13	– c Smith b Crook	68
S.L. Maxwell c Williams b Adcock	62	– lbw b King	27
†D.G. Dawson c Johnson b Smith	49	– lbw b Adcock	39
G. Elliott lbw b Johnson	10	– c Williams b King	4
A.J. Heading b Smith	1	– lbw b Marsh	4
*J.D. Robson b Marsh	39	– c Reeves b Smith	19
H.R. Axelby b R.J. Harris	15	– (10) c King b Marsh	2
D. Anderson c Johnson b King	7	– (9) st Reeves b Marsh	2
E. Kellar not out	1	– not out	1
B 5, l-b 3, n-b 11	19	B 5, l-b 5, w 3, n-b 4	17

(125.1 overs, 456 mins) 281   (109.4 overs, 408 mins) 284
Fall: 6 23 142 158 168 169 225   Fall: 3 172 176 214 243 247 279
250 277 281   281 283 284

B.W. Dennett did not bat.

Bowling: *First Innings*—Maraun 17–4–44–1; R.J. Harris 23–10–43–2; Johnson 16–5–33–1; Smith 17–4–48–2; King 14.1–5–38–1; Marsh 23–9–42–2; Adcock 15–5–25–1. *Second Innings*—R.J. Harris 21–7–48–0; Maraun 10–4–27–1; Johnson 11–3–25–2; King 11–3–25–2; Marsh 27–10–82–3; Crook 8–1–18–1; Adcock 19.4–5–36–2; Smith 11–1–27–1.

Umpires: M.R. Bartlett and P.J. Weeks.

TASMANIA SECOND XI v AUSTRALIAN CRICKET ACADEMY

At New Town Oval, New Town, November 5, 6, 7, 8, 2001. Match drawn. Toss: Tasmania Second XI.

Australian Cricket Academy

T.R. Birt b Marquet	0	– (2) c Cunningham b Downton	31
D.M. Betts c Dighton b Downton	22	– (1) c McDermott b Marquet	0
S.E. Marsh c McDermott b Marquet	5	– lbw b Downton	48
*R.J. Brewster c McDermott b Pascoe	12	– lbw b Pascoe	43
L. Ronchi c Dighton b Pascoe	10	– b Marquet	26
T.H. Welsford c Cunningham b Marquet	13	– c Marquet b Colegrave	16
M.J. Cosgrove c McDermott b Pascoe	43	– lbw b Tubb	69
†D. Smith lbw b Pascoe	10	– st McDermott b Tubb	1
B. Casson c Bailey b Colegrave	18	– not out	6
X.J. Doherty c McDermott b Pascoe	0	– b Tubb	0
S.P. Crook not out	28	– c McDermott b Selby	1
B 12, l-b 8, n-b 6	26	B 13, l-b 7, n-b 13	33

(63.5 overs, 273 mins) 187 (82.3 overs, 322 mins) 274
Fall: 0 12 39 53 81 91 120 Fall: 2 84 107 163 172 222 235
    143 143 187   273 273 274

A.R. Scott did not bat.

Bowling: *First Innings*—Marquet 20–7–43–3; Jurgensen 10–5–16–0; Pascoe 17–3–50–5; Polkinghorne 4–1–8–0; Downton 12–1–48–1; Colegrave 0.5–0–2–1. *Second Innings*—Marquet 17–5–48–2; Pascoe 19–1–73–1; Colegrave 16–6–46–1; Downton 17–3–54–2; Tubb 11–2–33–3; Selby 2.3–2–0–1.

Tasmania Second XI

S.R. Mason lbw b Casson	88	– (2) c Ronchi b Welsford	15
M.R. Nutting c Casson b Welsford	44	– (1) c Ronchi b Doherty	4
*G.T. Cunningham c Smith b Doherty	47	– c Smith b Scott	0
J.G.J. Selby c Ronchi b Betts	0	– b Scott	7
G.J. Bailey st Smith b Casson	32	– lbw b Doherty	8
†S.T. McDermott c Welsford b Casson	71	– c Ronchi b Doherty	3
T.D. Paine st Smith b Casson	13	– (8) not out	7
S.B. Tubb st Smith b Casson	12	– (7) c Crook b Casson	15
A.G. Downton c Smith b Doherty	1	– b Doherty	3
M.D. Pascoe st Smith b Doherty	4	– not out	1
M.D. Colegrave not out	0		
B 1, l-b 5, w 17, n-b 31	54	L-b 2, w 1, n-b 1	4

(87.1 overs, 338 mins) 366 (27 overs, 108 mins) (8 wkts) 67
Fall: 94 185 186 216 294 347 350 352 366 366 Fall: 5 6 17 29 39 43 59 62

J.P. Marquet, A.W. Polkinghorne, S.J. Jurgensen, B.J. Thomas and M.G. Dighton did not bat.

Bowling: *First Innings*—Scott 10–0–53–0; Cosgrove 8–1–45–0; Welsford 15–2–64–1; Crook 6–0–47–0; Doherty 25–7–78–3; Betts 4–0–18–1; Casson 19.1–2–55–5. *Second Innings*—Scott 8–2–23–2; Doherty 13–4–20–4; Welsford 1–0–5–1; Casson 5–0–17–1.

Umpires: B.W. Jackman and B.L. Wedd.

QUEENSLAND ACADEMY OF SPORT v NEW SOUTH WALES SECOND XI

At Allan Border Field, Albion, November 12, 13, 14, 15, 2001. New South Wales Second XI won by an innings and 143 runs. Toss: Queensland Academy of Sport.

Queensland Academy of Sport

L. W. Kahler c Thornely b Krejza	39	– (2) c Pilon b Bradstreet			0
D. M. Payne b Horsley	16	– (1) c Pilon b Bradstreet			9
C. P. Simpson c Thornely b Bradstreet	12	– c Pilon b Bradstreet			0
*B. P. Nash c Pilon b Horsley	47	– not out			125
M. Sippel lbw b Bradstreet	26	– c Rummans b Lambert			17
C. A. Philipson c Van Deinsen b Horsley	1	– c Pilon b Bradstreet			31
C. D. Hartley c Pilon b Horsley	26	– lbw b Lambert			7
S. J. O'Leary lbw b Lambert	6	– lbw b Lambert			0
D. R. MacKenzie c Lambert b Horsley	19	– c Bradstreet b Lambert			6
M. A. Anderson not out	4	– b Lambert			0
B. M. Edmondson b Horsley	0	– lbw b Lambert			0
L-b 4, n-b 6	10	L-b 2, n-b 2			4

(88.4 overs, 354 mins)   206   (74.4 overs, 280 mins)   199
Fall: 24 63 82 137 140 149 165   Fall: 0 0 19 72 151 183 189
     201 202 206   197 197 199

M. T. George did not bat.

Bowling: *First Innings*—Heath 9–3–18–0; Horsley 26.4–10–46–6; Lambert 16–3–54–1; Bradstreet 21–9–29–2; Krejza 7–1–34–1; Rummans 4–2–4–0; Thornely 5–1–17–0. *Second Innings*—Horsley 17–8–28–0; Bradstreet 11–4–21–4; Krejza 8–2–31–0; Lambert 13.4–1–52–6; Rummans 7–1–16–0; O'Brien 16–4–39–0; Van Deinsen 2–0–10–0.

New South Wales Second XI

M. J. Phelps c Nash b Edmondson	56	G. M. Lambert not out 6
B. P. Van Deinsen c Sippel b Anderson	95	
*G. C. Rummans c Simpson b Edmondson	93	B 1, l-b 13, w 1, n-b 8 23
C. J. Richards c Nash b Edmondson	189	
D. J. Thornely c Simpson b Edmondson	44	(149 overs, 546 mins) (6 wkts dec) 548
A. W. O'Brien c Simpson b MacKenzie	42	Fall: 131 170 316 394 514 548

S. D. Bradstreet, †N. S. Pilon, J. J. Krejza, D. A. Horsley and J. M. Heath did not bat.

Bowling: MacKenzie 31–5–120–1; George 19–5–66–0; O'Leary 30–8–103–0; Edmondson 29–3–99–4; Anderson 34–6–130–1; Nash 6–3–16–0.

Umpires: T. P. Laycock and J. M. Rowe.

WESTERN AUSTRALIA SECOND XI v AUSTRALIAN CRICKET ACADEMY

At Richardson Park, South Perth, November 12, 13, 14, 15, 2001. Western Australia Second XI won by nine wickets. Toss: Australian Cricket Academy.

Australian Cricket Academy

T. R. Birt c Clark b Karppinen	12	– (2) c Voges b Healey	0
D. M. Betts c Walsh b Wates	12	– (1) c Rogers b Karppinen	58
S. E. Marsh c Baker b Healey	2		
R. J. Brewster c Walsh b Karppinen	40	– (3) c Rogers b Healey	0
*D. Smith c Cullen b Wates	21	– (4) c Rogers b Karppinen	6
M. J. Cosgrove lbw b Healey	15	– (5) c Simmons b Karppinen	0
T. H. Welsford c Walsh b Wates	0	– (6) c Rogers b Worthington	89
†L. Ronchi b Healey	2	– (7) c Simmons b Wates	28
B. Casson lbw b Healey	6	– (8) c Walsh b Healey	21
X. J. Doherty c Walsh b Worthington	35	– (9) c Baker b Karppinen	39
M. J. Thistle not out	20	– (10) not out	6
R. J. Slowey (did not bat)		– lbw b Healey	0
L-b 9, n-b 3	12	B 1, l-b 2, n-b 6	9

(77.4 overs, 295 mins)	177	(80.4 overs, 311 mins) 256
Fall: 22 27 41 64 83 90 99		Fall: 0 1 11 19 112 171 191
114 118 177		246 250 256

Bowling: *First Innings*—Clark 12–4–20–0; Wates 20–4–55–3; Healey 19–6–29–4; Karppinen 16–7–24–2; Voges 5–1–24–0; Worthington 5.4–0–16–1. *Second Innings*—Karppinen 19–7–42–4; Healey 14.4–4–50–4; Clark 16–3–46–0; Wates 13–4–46–1; Voges 4–0–28–0; Worthington 9–1–20–1; Jones 5–0–21–0.

Western Australia Second XI

B. D. Jones c Ronchi b Thistle	31	– (2) not out	10
C. J. Simmons lbw b Slowey	2	– (1) lbw b Thistle	0
G. I. Cullen c Ronchi b Slowey	0		
R. M. Baker c Ronchi b Thistle	29	– (3) not out	32
*C. J. L. Rogers c Doherty b Thistle	151		
P. C. Worthington c Welsford b Thistle	24		
A. C. Voges lbw b Welsford	44		
D. J. Wates c Ronchi b Welsford	15		
S. J. Karppinen lbw b Casson	12		
†M. J. Walsh b Thistle	50		
M. W. Clark not out	13		
L-b 6, n-b 13	19	L-b 1, n-b 1	2

(111.5 overs, 456 mins)	390	(10.3 overs, 39 mins)	(1 wkt) 44
Fall: 18 18 61 66 135 234 262 294 364 390		Fall: 0	

M. R. Healey did not bat.

Bowling: *First Innings*—Thistle 30.5–8–89–5; Slowey 27–7–92–2; Welsford 10–7–51–2; Doherty 22–5–62–0; Cosgrove 12–0–51–0; Casson 8–1–32–1; Betts 2–0–7–0. *Second Innings*—Thistle 5.3–2–29–1; Slowey 5–1–14–0.

Umpires: C. R. Allen and B. Bennett.

VICTORIA SECOND XI v NEW SOUTH WALES SECOND XI

At Junction Oval, St Kilda, November 19, 20, 21, 22, 2001. Drawn. Toss: Victoria Second XI,

New South Wales Second XI

C. J. Richards c Roach b McDonald	74	G. M. Lambert lbw b McDonald	0
B. P. Van Deinsen st Roach b Davison	239	S. D. Bradstreet not out	38
*G. C. Rummans b Carr	18	L-b 6, w 1, n-b 11	18
M. J. Phelps b Reiffel	35		
A. W. O'Brien not out	47	(147 overs, 566 mins) (6 wkts dec)	485
P. A. Jaques c Arnberger b McDonald	16	Fall: 177 273 378 382 411 411	

†N. S. Pilon, A. M. Clark, A. M. Stuart and D. A. Horsley did not bat.

Bowling: Carr 31–6–111–1; Hewett 34–12–95–0; Reiffel 14–5–28–1; Oliver 9–1–42–0; Davison 43–6–141–1; McDonald 16–5–62–3.

Victoria Second XI

R. A. Bartlett c Rummans b Stuart	1	– (2) c Van Deinsen b Bradstreet	113
J. L. Arnberger c Pilon b Bradstreet	36	– (1) c Bradstreet b Clark	16
S. P. Dart run out (Stuart)	24	– c Pilon b Stuart	40
J. Moss c and b Clark	63	– b Bradstreet	0
N. Jewell c Jaques b Clark	44	– b Phelps b Clark	18
A. B. McDonald c Van Deinsen b Horsley	40	– c Clark b Stuart	0
B. C. Oliver st Pilon b O'Brien	0	– lbw b Bradstreet	25
†P. J. Roach lbw b Bradstreet	14	– c Stuart b Bradstreet	35
*P. R. Reiffel not out	12	– not out	52
I. S. L. Hewett c Stuart b Horsley	1	– not out	25
J. M. Davison c Van Deinsen b Lambert	7		
B 1, l-b 3, n-b 3	7	B 8, l-b 7, n-b 13	28
(112.3 overs, 390 mins)	249	(116 overs, 451 mins) (8 wkts)	352

Fall: 5 46 80 154 192 197 229 231 239 249

Fall: 65 157 157 192 192 194 247 293

W. N. Carr did not bat.

Bowling: *First Innings*—Horsley 20–5–36–2; Stuart 16–5–37–1; Clark 28–5–76–2; O'Brien 37–11–67–1; Bradstreet 11–4–25–2; Lambert 0.3–0–4–1. *Second Innings*—Stuart 16–5–38–2; Lambert 8–1–25–0; Clark 30–2–107–2; Horsley 14–3–33–0; O'Brien 20–3–75–0; Bradstreet 20–11–28–4; Rummans 5–1–22–0; Van Deinsen 3–1–9–0.

Umpires: A. J. Barrow and T. M. Ward.

AUSTRALIAN CAPITAL TERRITORY v AUSTRALIAN CRICKET ACADEMY

At Manuka Oval, Canberra, November 18, 19, 20, 21, 2001. Australian Cricket Academy won by five wickets. Toss: Australian Capital Territory.

Australian Capital Territory

J. K. Smith b Thistle	0	– (2) lbw b Bandy	118
D. M. Jeffrey c Smith b Thistle	7	– (1) c Smith b Coombes	69
D. S. Hazell c Ronchi b Kelly	39	– c Betts b Brant	12
S. L. Maxwell c Brewster b Thistle	8	– lbw b Brant	35
†D. G. Dawson c Smith b Coombes	42	– b Shaw	16
*J. D. Robson run out	59	– b Kelly	26
A. J. Heading c Smith b Bandy	14	– c Brewster b Coombes	49
G. Elliott c Kelly b Coombes	10	– b Coombes	4
H. R. Axelby b Coombes	10	– lbw b Coombes	32
E. Kellar not out	8	– c Brewster b Coombes	15
B. W. Dennett lbw b Thistle	1	– not out	0
B 2, l-b 10, n-b 2	14	B 6, l-b 7, w 2, n-b 5	20
(69.4 overs, 251 mins)	212	(129.1 overs, 441 mins)	396

Fall: 0 16 24 84 118 170 181 194 207 212

Fall: 161 193 214 249 290 290 342 358 393 396

D. Anderson did not bat.

Bowling: *First Innings*—Thistle 13.4–2–37–4; Brant 12–5–40–0; Bandy 10–2–37–1; Betts 5–1–14–0; Kelly 8–2–18–1; Coombes 21–6–54–3. *Second Innings*—Thistle 9–2–28–0; Brant 21–9–42–2; Kelly 19–2–73–1; Bandy 19–7–49–1; Coombes 35.1–6–128–5; Betts 5–0–28–0; Phillips 2–2–0–0; Shaw 19–7–35–1.

Australian Cricket Academy

T.R. Birt c Dawson b Kellar	24	– (3) lbw b Axelby	4
L. Ronchi b Dennett	16	– b Elliott	62
S.J. Phillips c Dawson b Dennett	74	– (4) c Dennett b Axelby	38
*R.J. Brewster run out	42	– (5) c Dawson b Axelby	41
D.C. Bandy lbw b Smith	26	– (6) not out	71
D.M. Betts c Dawson b Robson	22	– (1) c Jeffrey b Axelby	28
†D. Smith lbw b Robson	16	– not out	59
M. Shaw b Jeffrey	6		
S.P. Coombes b Kellar	4		
S. Brant not out	6		
M.J. Thistle b Kellar	16		
L-b 14, w 1, n-b 9	24	B 2, l-b 11, n-b 20	33

(91 overs, 328 mins)	276	(99.4 overs, 363 mins) (5 wkts)	336

Fall: 42 55 139 194 195 233 246 246 253 276   Fall: 84 100 112 181 200

T.P. Kelly did not bat.

Bowling: *First Innings*—Anderson 9–0–47–0; Dennett 21–3–73–2; Kellar 16–6–37–3; Elliott 4–0–20–0; Axelby 15–6–37–0; Jeffrey 14–7–28–1; Smith 6–2–13–1; Robson 6–3–7–2. *Second Innings*—Kellar 18–6–47–0; Dennett 11–1–38–0; Anderson 6–0–50–0; Axelby 36–10–103–4; Elliott 14.4–3–45–1; Hazell 4–0–10–0; Smith 7–2–18–0; Jeffrey 3–1–12–0.

Umpires: G. Clifton and P.M. Kelso.

VICTORIA SECOND XI v TASMANIA SECOND XI

At Camberwell Sports Ground, Camberwell, November 26, 27, 28, 29, 2001. Victoria Second XI won by 205 runs. Toss: Victoria Second XI.

Victoria Second XI

P.Q. Harper c Dighton b Griffith	19	– (2) b Pascoe	16
S.P. Dart c McDermott b Polkinghorne	45	– (1) c McDermott b Pascoe	23
S.A.J. Craig c Cunningham b Polkinghorne	64	– lbw b Downton	60
J. Moss c Cunningham b Tubb	38	– c Paine b Tubb	23
A.B. McDonald c McDermott b Pascoe	23	– not out	41
A.J. Kent c McDermott b Pascoe	44	– c McDermott b Downton	1
D.J. Hussey lbw b Griffith	69	– not out	40
S.M. Harwood run out (Downton)	41		
†D.C. Brede run out (Selby)	2		
*I.S.L. Hewett c Downton b Pascoe	21		
M.L. Lewis not out	2		
B 2, l-b 9, w 1, n-b 8	20	B 2, l-b 6, w 1, n-b 2	11

(133.2 overs, 508 mins)	388	(58 overs, 204 mins) (5 wkts dec)	215

Fall: 49 78 131 171 213 290 335 342 386 388   Fall: 27 50 103 146 152

B.E. McGain did not bat.

Bowling: *First Innings*—Downton 27–8–61–0; Pascoe 32–5–84–3; Griffith 28–8–66–2; Thomas 8–1–30–0; Polkinghorne 13.2–2–50–2; Tubb 21–3–80–1; Selby 4–1–6–0. *Second Innings*—Pascoe 13–1–45–2; Downton 14–0–50–2; Tubb 20–3–64–1; Thomas 7–0–31–0; Griffith 4–0–17–0.

Tasmania Second XI

S.R. Mason c Hewett b McGain	22		
M.G. Dighton run out (Hussey)	81		
A.W. Polkinghorne c Brede b Lewis	35		
G.T. Cunningham c Brede b Harwood	12	– (3) c Harper b Harwood	60
*B.J. Thomas b Lewis	0	– (4) b Harwood	9
C.W.G. Bassano lbw b Hewett	23	– (5) b Harwood	2
J.G.J. Selby c Craig b Hewett	17	– lbw b McGain	39
†S.T. McDermott not out	4	– c Lewis b Hewett	11
S.B. Tubb lbw b Hewett	0	– c Brede b Harwood	0
A.G. Downton c Dart b Hewett	12	– not out	7
M.D. Pascoe c Brede b Hewett	0		
A.R. Griffith did not bat.		– c McDonald b Harwood	0
M.R. Nutting did not bat.		– (1) b Hewett	34
T. Little did not bat.		– (2) b McGain	12
T.D. Paine did not bat.		– (6) lbw b Harwood	0
B 4, l-b 1, n-b 7	12	L-b 2, n-b 4	6

(70.2 overs, 275 mins)	218	(80.3 overs, 307 mins) 180
Fall: 79 117 151 152 166 194 202		Fall: 22 76 110 115 137 137 171
202 214 218		171 180 180

Bowling: *First Innings*—Harwood 15–7–37–1; Hewett 18.2–6–47–5; McDonald 14–5–44–0; Lewis 15–2–48–2; McGain 8–1–37–1. *Second Innings*—Harwood 15.3–3–41–6; McDonald 12–6–25–0; Hewett 12–3–27–2; McGain 19–8–35–2; Lewis 13–5–29–0; Hussey 9–3–21–0.

Note: Mason, Dighton and Polkinghorne were called into the Tasmanian ING cup team and were substituted by Nutting, Little and Paine.

Umpires: G.R.J. Brindley and J.D. Ward.

SOUTH AUSTRALIA SECOND XI v WESTERN AUSTRALIA SECOND XI

At Adelaide Oval No. 2, Adelaide, December 3, 4, 5, 6, 2001. Drawn. Toss: Western Australia Second XI.

South Australia Second XI

D.A. Fitzgerald c Rogers b Healey	11	– (2) c Walsh b Clark	23
L. Williams c Walsh b Healey	27	– (1) c Voges b Howman	33
†S.A. Deitz c Glew b Baker	66	– c Voges b Healey	83
D.M. Dempsey st Walsh b Baker	21	– c Rogers b Clark	6
*N.T. Adcock c Rogers b Healey	59	– not out	170
W.D. Thomas c Glew b Baker	7	– lbw b Voges	11
D.J. Harris c Walsh b Healey	1	– c Rogers b Healey	31
J.I. Marsh c Baker b Healey	3		
P. Wilson c Walsh b Healey	16		
D.A. Ross b Howman	3		
N. Rowe not out	0	– (8) not out	22
N-b 3	3	B 6, l-b 5, w 1, n-b 7	19

(85.4 overs, 304 mins)	217	(140.5 overs, 525 mins)(6 wkts dec) 398
Fall: 20 50 110 131 143 144 169 204 217 217		Fall: 49 73 132 203 234 335

C. Parish did not bat.

Bowling: *First Innings*—Clark 16–5–41–0; Howman 14–4–29–1; Healey 22.4–7–50–6; Wates 9–2–21–0; Worthington 4–0–18–0; Baker 20–5–58–3. *Second Innings*—Healey 28.5–6–105–2; Wates 22–6–45–0; Clark 29–10–56–2; Howman 22.5–8–54–1; Baker 12–4–26–0; Voges 20–1–86–1; Worthington 6.1–0–15–0.

Western Australia Second XI

*C. J. L. Rogers c Deitz b Rowe	59	– c Adcock b Rowe		12
D. Waters c Deitz b Rowe	33	– c Marsh b Ross		12
G. I. Cullen c Deitz b Rowe	58	– c Marsh b Ross		12
R. M. Baker c Williams b Parish	10	– b Ross		5
S. A. Glew c Harris b Adcock	20	– not out		42
A. C. Voges c Fitzgerald b Thomas	144	– not out		27
D. J. Wates c Deitz b Rowe	9			
P. C. Worthington c Williams b Marsh	31			
†M. J. Walsh c Deitz b Thomas	10			
S. Howman c Williams b Marsh	33			
M. W. Clark not out	8			
B 1, l-b 12, w 2	15	B 4		4

(140.5 overs, 501 mins) 430   (25 overs, 83 mins) (4 wkts) 114
Fall: 92 98 126 179 183 201 259 293 400 430   Fall: 13 29 35 42

M. R. Healey did not bat.

Bowling: *First Innings*—Wilson 20–7–41–0; Rowe 32–10–82–4; Parish 26–7–97–1; Adcock 23–8–32–1; Ross 6–1–27–0; Marsh 26–6–106–2; Thomas 7.5–3–32–2. *Second Innings*—Wilson 5–2–18–0; Rowe 3–1–7–1; Ross 9–1–37–3; Marsh 5–1–33–0; Adcock 3–1–15–0.

Umpires: R. A. Falk and S. Knobben.

QUEENSLAND ACADEMY OF SPORT v WESTERN AUSTRALIA SECOND XI

At Allan Border Field, Albion, December 9, 10, 11, 12, 2001. Western Australia Second XI won by three wickets. Toss: Queensland Academy of Sport.

Queensland Academy of Sport

C. P. Simpson run out (Voges/Clark)	88	– lbw b Howman		17
D. M. Payne c Walsh b Wates	46	– b Glew		60
B. P. Nash c Clark b Voges	31	– c Walsh b Howman		23
L. A. Carseldine c Walsh b Clark	37	– b Wates		35
A. M. Rowe b Worthington	40	– c Waters b Glew		58
M. Sippel c Glew b Clark	0	– b Wates		11
*J. R. Hopes c Walsh b Clark	21	– c Rogers b Howman		25
†C. D. Hartley lbw b Howman	1	– not out		25
S. J. O'Leary c Cullen b Clark	14	– b Glew		1
D. R. MacKenzie b Wates	31	– c Rogers b Worthington		14
M. A. Anderson not out	2			
L-b 8, w 5, n-b 6	19	L-b 5, w 1, n-b 3		9

(130.5 overs, 471 mins) 330   (74 overs, 308 mins) (9 wkts dec) 278
Fall: 89 154 206 239 239 277 278   Fall: 47 104 108 159 171 229
282 320 330   247 263 278

B. M. Edmondson did not bat.

Bowling: *First Innings*—Clark 32–10–58–4; Wates 28.5–10–75–2; Healey 19–7–41–0; Howman 20–5–63–1; Voges 12–0–38–1; Worthington 19–4–47–1. *Second Innings*—Clark 17–5–44–0; Wates 18–2–62–2; Howman 22–3–91–3; Worthington 4–0–44–1; Glew 13–4–32–3.

Western Australia Second XI

*C.J.L. Rogers c Nash b Edmondson	87	– c Sippel b Edmondson	51
D. Waters lbw b Anderson	13	– c Simpson b Anderson	22
G.I. Cullen c Hartley b MacKenzie	5	– (4) c Carseldine b Hopes	49
R.M. Baker c Anderson b MacKenzie	116	– (3) run out (Carseldine)	61
S.A. Glew c Hartley b Hopes	13	– c Nash b Edmondson	45
A.C. Voges not out	73	– c Nash b Edmondson	18
D.J. Wates c Hartley b Hopes	4	– not out	5
P.C. Worthington not out	16	– c Rowe b Edmondson	7
†M.J. Walsh		– not out	8
L-b 2, w 2, n-b 3	7	B 4, l-b 5	9

(116.5 overs, 426 mins) (6 wkts dec) 334
Fall: 57 69 160 217 245 260

(59.3 overs, 226 mins) (7 wkts) 275
Fall: 70 101 170 210 249 255 264

S. Howman, M.W. Clark and M.R. Healey did not bat.

Bowling: *First Innings*—Hopes 31–13–49–2; Carseldine 15–5–45–0; MacKenzie 23–4–72–2; Edmondson 17–2–62–1; Anderson 18.5–5–67–1; O'Leary 12–2–37–0. *Second Innings*—MacKenzie 10–0–42–0; Hopes 17–1–71–1; Anderson 14–0–67–1; Edmondson 8.3–1–28–4; O'Leary 6–0–34–0; Carseldine 4–0–24–0.

Umpires: G.N. Cubit and J. Veivers.

VICTORIA SECOND XI v AUSTRALIAN CRICKET ACADEMY

At Junction Oval, St Kilda, December 17, 18, 19, 20, 2001. Victoria Second XI won by 160 runs. Toss: Victoria Second XI.

Victoria Second XI

R.A. Bartlett b Bandy	37	– c Brewster b Harrop	4
S.P. Dart c Bailey b Cosgrove	37	– lbw b Harrop	12
S.A.J. Craig c Brewster b Coombes	172	– (7) not out	42
J. Moss c Bandy b Magoffin	9	– b Magoffin	6
A.B. McDonald run out (Ronchi/Smith)	1	– (3) b Magoffin	3
A.J. Kent c Brewster b Coombes	14	– (5) lbw b Cosgrove	32
†P.J. Roach c Bailey b Magoffin	54	– (6) b Coombes	38
S.M. Harwood c Smith b Magoffin	18	– c Harrop b Coombes	45
*I.S.L. Hewett c Betts b Harrop	12	– not out	7
J.M. Davison c Welsford b Bandy	17		
B.E. McGain not out	6		
B 4, l-b 6, w 2, n-b 13	25	B 1, l-b 3, n-b 1	5

(114.2 overs, 432 mins) 402
Fall: 56 121 139 145 183 305 337 357 392 402

(59 overs, 222 mins) (7 wkts dec) 194
Fall: 12 21 27 29 89 109 185

W.N. Carr did not bat.

Bowling: *First Innings*—Magoffin 31–4–114–3; Harrop 27–6–110–1; Bandy 17.2–3–50–2; Coombes 23–3–57–2; Cosgrove 10–4–38–1; Betts 6–2–23–0. *Second Innings*—Magoffin 14–0–47–2; Harrop 6–1–23–2; Coombes 23–3–69–2; Bandy 8–1–25–0; Cosgrove 8–2–26–1.

Australian Cricket Academy

D.M. Betts c Hewett b Harwood	4	– (2) c Bartlett b McDonald	18
P.J. Dickson run out (Carr/Roach)	28	– (1) c Moss b Harwood	0
*T.H. Welsford run out (Moss/Roach)	94	– b Harwood	8
R.J. Brewster b Harwood	20	– c Dart b McDonald	25
L. Ronchi b Hewett	12	– c McGain b Moss	107
M.J. Cosgrove b Hewett	10	– lbw b McDonald	9
D.C. Bandy lbw b Hewett	0	– b McDonald	12
G.J. Bailey c Bartlett b Harwood	17	– not out	25
†D. Smith not out	11	– b Moss	0
S.J. Magoffin b Harwood	1	– c Hewett b Moss	0
B.D. Harrop c Craig b McGain	0	– c Hewett b Moss	0
B 3, l-b 9, n-b 14	26	L-b 7, W 1, n-b 1	9

(75.2 overs, 285 mins)	223	(64.1 overs, 235 mins)	213
Fall: 5 73 126 146 158 159 204 208		Fall: 0 26 46 71 85 132 211 211	
215 223		211 213	

S.P. Coombes did not bat.

Bowling: *First Innings*—Harwood 15–2–44–4; Hewett 10–2–28–3; McGain 14.2–5–28–1; Moss 9–1–29–0; Carr 12–2–46–0; Davison 15–4–36–0. *Second Innings*—Harwood 7–2–22–2; Carr 3–0–17–0; McDonald 16–4–48–4; Hewett 6–2–24–0; Davison 9–1–33–0; McGain 13–5–39–0; Kent 1–1–0–0; Moss 7.1–1–21–4; Bartlett 2–1–2–0.

Umpires: A.J. Soulsby and A.P. Ward.

AUSTRALIAN CAPITAL TERRITORY v TASMANIA SECOND XI

At Manuka Oval, Canberra, January 7, 8, 9, 10, 2002. Tasmania Second XI won by an innings and 22 runs. Toss: Australian Capital Territory.

Australian Capital Territory

D.M. Jeffrey c Hills b Hilfenhaus	25	– (2) lbw b Hilfenhaus	19
J.K. Smith lbw b Kremerskothen	62	– (1) c Tubb b Pascoe	0
D.S. Hazell lbw b Hilfenhaus	2	– (4) lbw b Tubb	32
†D.G. Dawson b Thomas	21	– (3) b Tubb	22
*S.L. Maxwell lbw b Thomas	25	– b Tubb	14
M.A. Hatton lbw b Thomas	20	– lbw b Tubb	32
A.J. Heading c McDermott b Downton	3	– c Cunningham b Tubb	49
H.R. Axelby b Thomas	0	– (9) c McDermott b Downton	9
E. Kellar b Pascoe	5	– (10) c Hills b Tubb	4
B.W. Dennett c Cunningham b Thomas	23	– (11) not out	0
T.L. Hill not out	18	– (8) lbw b Thomas	0
B 1, l-b 3, w 1, n-b 11	16	L-b 5, n-b 2	7

(86.5 overs, 325 mins)	220	(77 overs, 273 mins)	188
Fall: 42 58 115 121 165 168 168 171		Fall: 4 24 70 90 101 174 175 175	
182 220		188 188	

M.K. Rice did not bat.

Bowling: *First Innings*—Pascoe 13–5–37–1; Downton 20–6–36–1; Hilfenhaus 11–4–30–2; Tubb 14–4–42–0; Thomas 16.5–9–29–5; Kremerskothen 12–3–42–1. *Second Innings*—Pascoe 19–7–43–1; Hilfenhaus 6–1–20–1; Downton 10–5–25–1; Tubb 29–11–55–6; Thomas 11–3–24–1; Kremerskothen 2–0–16–0.

Tasmania Second XI

*D.F. Hills c Axelby b Jeffrey	70	
S.R. Mason lbw b Jeffrey	144	
G.T. Cunningham lbw b Dennett	38	
S.P. Kremerskothen c and b Dennett	0	
C.W.G. Bassano b Rice	35	
J.A. Dykes c Dawson b Kellar	34	
B.J. Thomas not out	53	
†S.T. McDermott run out (Dennett/Dawson)	13	

S.B. Tubb c Rice b Hatton	1
M.D. Pascoe st Dawson b Hatton	9
A.G. Downton lbw b Axelby	11
B 3, l-b 14, w 1, n-b 4	22

B.W. Hilfenhaus did not bat.

(150.4 overs, 545 mins)　　　430
Fall: 132 209 209 291 318 354 381
　　　399 417 430

Bowling: Kellar 34–15–72–1; Rice 17–3–66–1; Dennett 23–5–78–2; Axelby 24.4–5–59–1; Hatton 20–3–57–2; Hill 11–0–39–0; Jeffrey 19–10–30–2; Smith 2–0–12–0.

Umpires: D.B. Harris and W.F. Ruse.

NEW SOUTH WALES SECOND XI v SOUTH AUSTRALIA SECOND XI

At Hurstville Oval, Hurstville, January 7, 8, 9, 10, 2002. New South Wales Second XI won by eight wickets. Toss: New South Wales Second XI.

South Australia Second XI

D.A. Fitzgerald b Nash	58	– (2) c Pilon b Bradstreet	4
L. Williams c and b Clark	92	– (1) lbw b O'Brien	19
*J.M. Vaughan c O'Brien b Nash	35	– b Bradstreet	2
D.M. Dempsey c Richards b Heath	16	– lbw b Heath	139
N.T. Adcock b Nash	8	– lbw b Nash	29
M.C. Miller c Van Deinsen b Nash	72	– st Pilon b O'Brien	10
†S.A. Deitz c Pilon b Bradstreet	3	– b Bradstreet	27
M. Weekes lbw b Clark	26	– lbw b Bradstreet	2
B.A. Swain not out	17	– not out	23
J.I. Marsh c Richards b Nash	4	– c Rummans b Nash	0
P. Wilson b Nash	1	– b Nash	7
L-b 9, n-b 8	17	B 8, l-b 7, n-b 1	16

(125.4 overs, 489 mins)	349	(102.3 overs, 383 mins)	278
Fall: 119 187 207 217 219 232 308		Fall: 8 10 37 108 139 210 212	
328 344 349		255 260 278	

T.P. Kelly did not bat.

Bowling: *First Innings*—Nash 26.4–6–61–6; Heath 21–6–56–1; Bradstreet 21–5–42–1; Lambert 14–2–44–0; Clark 29–5–83–2; O'Brien 11–0–31–0; Thornely 3–0–23–0. *Second Innings*—Nash 20.3–5–59–3; Heath 20–4–48–1; Bradstreet 15–1–46–4; O'Brien 28–9–52–2; Clark 7–1–25–0; Lambert 7–2–28–0; Rummans 5–3–5–0.

New South Wales Second XI

C.J. Richards c Deitz b Wilson	65	– (2) st Deitz b Marsh	25
B.P. Van Deinsen c Deitz b Wilson	2	– (1) c Deitz b Swain	0
*G.C. Rummans c Wilson b Marsh	117	– not out	90
M.J. Phelps c Deitz b Kelly	82	– not out	31
D.J. Thornely c Williams b Marsh	1		
A.W. O'Brien c Deitz b Adcock	2		
S.D. Bradstreet c Dempsey b Marsh	10		
G.M. Lambert c Vaughan b Marsh	6		
†N.S. Pilon not out	116		
D.A. Nash c and b Swain	24		
A.M. Clark not out	19		
B 1, l-b 4, w 8, n-b 19	32	B 3, l-b 2, n-b 1	6

(108 overs, 424 mins) (9 wkts dec) 476 (26.3 overs, 104 mins) (2 wkts) 152
Fall: 8 109 246 247 250 271 289 317 362 Fall: 1 68

J.M. Heath did not bat.

Bowling: *First Innings*—Wilson 28–4–91–2; Swain 18–3–81–1; Kelly 14–2–41–1; Weekes 11–1–84–0; Adcock 13–2–52–1; Marsh 24–2–122–4. *Second Innings*—Wilson 7–2–35–0; Swain 4–0–25–1; Marsh 9–0–44–1; Kelly 4–0–23–0; Adcock 2.3–0–20–0.

Umpires: T.M. Donahoo and R. Furtner.

AUSTRALIAN CAPITAL TERRITORY v QUEENSLAND ACADEMY OF SPORT

At Manuka Oval, Canberra, January 14, 15, 16, 2002. Queensland Academy of Sport won by eight wickets. Toss: Queensland Academy of Sport.

Queensland Academy of Sport

D.M. Payne b Dennett	18	– (2) not out	21
D.M. Betts c Dawson b Dennett	4	– (1) lbw b Dennett	8
C.P. Simpson c Dawson b Dennett	1	– st Dawson b Kellar	18
*L.A. Carseldine not out	230		
A.M. Rowe c Smith b Kellar	13	– (4) not out	4
M. Sippel c Axelby b Dennett	44		
†C.D. Hartley c Hatton b Smith	0		
S.J. O'Leary lbw b Smith	0		
M.A. Anderson b Dennett	5		
S.J. Magoffin c Dawson b Kellar	15		
M.J. Petrie run out (Dawson)	13		
L-b 1, w 1	2	B 1, l-b 1, n-b 1	3

(93.3 overs, 353 mins) 345 (10.5 overs, 44 mins) (2 wkts) 54
Fall: 9 11 56 112 224 257 257 275 302 345 Fall: 8 38

B.M. Edmondson did not bat.

Bowling: *First Innings*—Dennett 22–2–93–5; Rice 13–0–65–0; Kellar 22.3–8–55–2; Axelby 8–0–30–0; Jeffrey 12–4–22–0; Hatton 7–0–25–0; Hill 4–0–26–0; Smith 5–0–28–2. *Second Innings*—Dennett 5.5–1–31–1; Kellar 5–2–21–1.

Australian Capital Territory

D. M. Jeffrey c Rowe b Edmondson	30	– (2) c Anderson b Magoffin	10
J. K. Smith lbw b Anderson	47	– (1) lbw b Anderson	63
†D. G. Dawson c Rowe b Carseldine	40	– c Hartley b Magoffin	0
D. S. Hazell c Carseldine b Anderson	0	– c Payne b Anderson	27
*S. L. Maxwell c Hartley b Carseldine	13	– c Rowe b Carseldine	21
M. A. Hatton b Edmondson	2	– c Petrie b Anderson	0
A. J. Heading c Payne b Edmondson	16	– c Anderson b Magoffin	24
T. L. Hill c Rowe b Magoffin	1	– b Magoffin	0
H. R. Axelby c Hartley b Edmondson	10	– not out	44
B. W. Dennett b Magoffin	9	– c Carseldine b Anderson	8
E. Kellar not out	0	– lbw b Edmondson	6
B 2, l-b 8, w 1, n-b 8	19	B 1, l-b 3, n-b 1	5

(101.3 overs, 363 mins)	187	(62 overs, 224 mins)	208

Fall: 83 93 98 130 137 152 160
170 187 187

Fall: 26 26 97 100 106 132 133
147 181 208

M. K. Rice did not bat.

Bowling: *First Innings*—Edmondson 18.3–8–46–4; Petrie 11–5–16–0; Magoffin 25–12–43–2; Carseldine 13–4–34–2; Anderson 25–17–25–2; O'Leary 8–2–11–0; Rowe 1–0–2–0. *Second Innings*—Magoffin 13–1–60–4; Petrie 7–2–13–0; Anderson 21–7–49–4; O'Leary 5–1–23–0; Edmondson 11–1–39–1; Carseldine 5–1–20–1.

Umpires: P. D. Chapman and W. F. Ruse.

TASMANIA SECOND XI v NEW SOUTH WALES SECOND XI

At Bellerive Oval, Hobart, February 3 ,4, 5, 6, 2002. New South Wales won by five wickets. Toss: Tasmania Second XI.

New South Wales Second XI

N. J. Catalano b Denton	14	– (2) c Paine b Pascoe	11
G. J. Mail b Downton	20	– (1) c Paine b Pascoe	9
*M. J. Phelps c Paine b Downton	29	– (7) not out	15
P. A. Jaques c Tubb b Pascoe	52	– (3) c Paine b Downton	2
V. M. Williams c Paine b Denton	74	– (6) not out	41
A. W. O'Brien c Paine b Pascoe	0	– (4) c Cunningham b Denton	9
†N. S. Pilon c Griffith b Thomas	60	– (5) c Thomas b Downton	3
D. A. Turner c Paine b Denton	6		
G. M. Lambert c Downton b Denton	21		
A. M. Clark c Paine b Denton	24		
A. C. Warren not out	0		
L-b 5, n-b 12	17	W 1, n-b 7	8

(102.1 overs, 419 mins)	317	(31.2 overs, 137 mins)	(5 wkts)	98

Fall: 17 50 70 145 145 245 258 269 314 317

Fall: 21 27 27 34 63

M. A. W. Goldsmith did not bat.

Bowling: *First Innings*—Denton 27.1–6–96–5; Pascoe 19–5–57–2; Griffith 16–7–42–0; Downton 23–7–55–2; Thomas 8–1–28–1; Tubb 6–1–31–0; Nutting 3–1–3–0. *Second Innings*—Pascoe 10.2–2–26–2; Downton 11–2–24–2; Denton 6–0–17–1; Griffith 3–0–23–0; Tubb 1–0–8–0.

Tasmania Second XI

M. R. Nutting c Catalano b Warren	6	– c Mail b Warren	53
*D. F. Hills c Pilon b Warren	9	– b Lambert	29
G. T. Cunningham c Clark b Lambert	18	– c Pilon b Lambert	0
C. W. G. Bassano c Pilon b Goldsmith	19	– c Pilon b Lambert	62
B. J. Thomas c Pilon b Goldsmith	2	– c Phelps b Turner	42
†T. D. Paine c Pilon b Goldsmith	0	– lbw b Clark	49
S. T. McDermott b Goldsmith	0	– lbw b Goldsmith	16
S. B. Tubb lbw b Lambert	5	– c Pilon b Goldsmith	0
G. J. Denton lbw b O'Brien	13	– lbw b Lambert	15
A. G. Downton c Pilon b Warren	9	– b Clark	20
A. R. Griffith not out	0	– not out	0
L-b 2, n-b 11	13	B 5, l-b 8, n-b 21	34

(36.4 overs, 164 mins) 94   (107.5 overs, 421 mins) 320
Fall: 10 33 37 50 58 58 63   Fall: 54 54 141 206 212 245 246
65 91 94   277 317 320

M. D. Pascoe did not bat.

Bowling: *First Innings*—Goldsmith 12–1–42–4; Warren 12–5–17–3; Lambert 9–1–22–2; O'Brien 3.4–1–11–1. *Second Innings*—Goldsmith 19–1–61–2; Warren 23–5–75–1; Lambert 20–2–75–4; O'Brien 13–5–25–0; Clark 13.5–4–33–2; Turner 19.4–38–1.

Umpires: P. W. Mann and B. L. Wedd.

WESTERN AUSTRALIA SECOND XI v VICTORIA SECOND XI

At Fletcher Park, Carlisle, February 4, 5, 6, 7, 2002. Western Australia Second XI won by 56 runs. Toss: Western Australia Second XI.

Western Australia Second XI

*C. J. L. Rogers c Jewell b Davison	41	– (2) c Kent b Carr	1
B. D. Jones c McDonald b Carr	1	– (1) b McDonald	31
G. I. Cullen c McDonald b Jewell	144	– c Carr b McDonald	18
A. C. Voges c Roach b Davison	11	– c Hussey b Davison	2
B. J. Lillis c McGain b Jewell	38	– lbw b Carr	12
†L. Ronchi c Harrop b Fleming	49	– c McDonald b Fleming	8
P. C. Worthington c Roach b Harrop	13	– c Roach b Carr	17
C. D. Thorp c McDonald b Carr	1	– lbw b Harrop	28
S. Howman c Jewell b Harrop	19	– c Roach b Carr	0
B. J. Oldroyd c Harrop b McGain	1	– (11) not out	4
M. R. Healey not out	0	– (10) c McDonald b Harrop	6
B 8, l-b 7, n-b 4	19	B 2, l-b 6	8

(107 overs, 400 mins) 337   (48.1 overs, 193 mins) 135
Fall: 5 73 99 223 269 307 308 334 335 337   Fall: 10 50 50 56 64 90 95 95 130 135

A. C. L. James did not bat.

Bowling: *First Innings*—Fleming 17–5–40–1; Carr 18–6–46–2; Harrop 17–5–34–2; McDonald 14–3–39–0; Welsford 7–1–23–0; Davison 10–6–27–2; McGain 16–3–70–1; Jewell 8–1–43–2. *Second Innings*—Fleming 13–5–34–1; Carr 13–4–50–4; Harrop 9.1–5–12–2; McDonald 11–5–30–2; Davison 2–1–1–1.

Victoria Second XI

T. H. Welsford lbw b Thorp	22	– (6) c Jones b James	0
A. D. McQuire c and b Howman	52	– (1) c Cullen b James	22
A. B. McDonald c Cullen b James	39	– b James	62
N. Jewell c Ronchi b James	8	– c Ronchi b Howman	6
D. J. Hussey c Voges b Thorp	13	– c Ronchi b Howman	9
A. J. Kent c Howman b Thorp	14	– (2) c Ronchi b Thorp	0
†P. J. Roach c Rogers b Thorp	46	– not out	18
*D. W. Fleming c Thorp b Healey	4	– c Worthington b Thorp	21
J. M. Davison c James b Howman	23	– c Rogers b James	0
B. E. McGain c Cullen b James	9	– c Cullen b James	4
B. D. Harrop not out	12		
W. N. Carr did not bat.		– c Howman b Thorp	9
L-b 7, w 2, n-b 3	12	L-b 5, W 1, n-b 5	11

(87.5 overs, 339 mins)	254	(50.1 overs, 210 mins)	162
Fall: 43 100 126 131 153 166 171		Fall: 1 42 82 105 106 111 136	
198 227 254		136 141 162	

Bowling: *First Innings*—James 14–2–40–3; Howman 20–4–62–2; Healey 14–5–30–1; Thorp 17.5–3–52–4; Worthington 10–2–26–0; Oldroyd 12–1–37–0. *Second Innings*—Thorp 13.1–3–22–3; Howman 9–3–29–2; Healey 7–4–19–0; James 16–4–57–5; Worthington 5–0–30–0.

Umpires: B. Bennett and J. Brookes.

SYDNEY GREGORY CUP

QUEENSLAND ACADEMY OF SPORT v
NEW SOUTH WALES COLTS

At Allan Border Field, Albion, October 29, 30, 31, November 1, 2001. New South Wales Colts won by an innings and 41 runs. Toss: Queensland Academy of Sport.

Queensland Academy of Sport

N.J. Kruger c Wotherspoon b Cameron	30	– c Catalano b Krejza	45
D.M. Betts c Jaques b Cameron	53	– c Coombes b Baker	2
C.P. Simpson c Catalano b Cameron	119	– c Wotherspoon b O'Brien	26
A.M. Rowe c Wotherspoon b Cameron	9	– c Wotherspoon b Krejza	16
C.A. Philipson c Smith b Daley	9	– lbw b O'Brien	0
A.P. Maynard c Stanton b Daley	9	– lbw b Krejza	12
*†C.D. Hartley c Smith b O'Brien	19	– b Cameron	1
D.R. MacKenzie b Baker	34	– c Cameron b Krezka	30
G.S. Chiesa not out	5	– c M.J. Catalano b Cameron	13
L.R. Davis b Baker	0	– not out	1
S.J. Magoffin c Smith b Baker	0	– c Smith b Cameron	0
L-b 5, n-b 18	23	B 2, l-b 2, w 1, n-b 14	19

(96.5 overs, 375 mins)	310
Fall: 79 90 140 170 185 262 283	
310 310 310	

(53.5 overs, 239 mins)	165
Fall: 6 52 81 82 101 103 123	
161 161 165	

J.J. Bird did not bat.

Bowling: *First Innings*—Daley 17–5–41–2; Baker 13.5–1–56–3; Coombes 10–2–47–0; Cameron 17–7–52–4; Krejza 9–0–54–0; O'Brien 26–9–52–1; Wotherspoon 4–2–3–0. *Second Innings*—Baker 7–1–19–1; Cameron 14.5–1–53–3; O'Brien 12–4–22–2; Daley 11–2–33–0; Krejza 9–1–34–4.

New South Wales Institute of Sport Colts

D.S. Wotherspoon c MacKenzie b Magoffin	7	J.J. Krejza not out	15
N.J. Catalano c Bird b MacKenzie	90	M.J. Baker not out	4
P.A. Jaques b Magoffin	52		
A.W. O'Brien c Simpson b Davis	137	B 1, l-b 8, w 2, n-b 9	20
S.J. Phillips lbw b MacKenzie	2		
*S.D. Stanton c Simpson b Magoffin	63	(146 overs, 551 mins) (7 wkts dec)	516
†D. Smith b MacKenzie	126	Fall: 11 150 168 178 291 476 509	

M.A. Cameron, S.P. Coombes and K.M. Daley did not bat.

Bowling: First Innings—MacKenzie 29–8–93–3; Magoffin 28–5–89–3; Bird 31–6–91–0; Chiesa 17–2–83–0; Rowe 2–0–11–0; Davis 28–2–115–1; Simpson 9–3–21–0; Maynard 2–1–4–0.

Umpires: G.N. Cubit and T.P. Laycock.

JOHNNY MULLAGH TROPHY

ATSIC CHAIRMAN'S XI v PRIME MINISTER'S XI

At Manuka Oval, Canberra, March 8, 2002. Prime Minister's XI won by eight wickets. Toss: Prime Minister's XI.

The Prime Minister's XI for this 40-over match included four of the Australian team which had just won the Under-19s World Cup in New Zealand, together with Victorian Barry Firebrace, who captained the Aboriginal and Torres Strait Islander youth team to England in 2001. The Chairman's team made heavy weather of good batting conditions, the innings being held together by a captain's knock of real authority from Matthew Bradley (ten fours, two sixes) who plays with Sutherland in the Sydney grade competition. His only support came from wicket-keeper Jacob Sarra in a bright eighth-wicket partnership of 55, and Ryan Bulger, who hit two big sixes at No. 11. Nathan Hauritz, Xavier Doherty and Cameron White bowled their differing varieties of spin to good effect. The Prime Minister's XI needed only 23.2 overs to race to the small target, Brad Haddin, Martin Love and Brad Hodge all batting exuberantly.

Man of the Match: M.S. Bradley.

ATSIC Chairman's XI

C. Dann c Love b M.J. Smith	3	(29)	†J. Sarra c and b White	19	(30)
P. Thomas b Christian	6	(38)	G. Martin lbw b Doherty	0	(3)
*M.S. Bradley not out	74	(90)	R.W. Bulger not out	14	(10)
D. Duroux c Love b Hauritz	4	(13)			
K.E. Vowles c Firebarce b Hauritz	5	(12)	B 2, l-b 4, w 9, n-b 1	16	
T. Dann c Hauritz b Doherty	0	(5)			
S. Gower c Love b Hauritz	0	(4)	(40 overs, 143 mins)	(9 wkts)	144
I. Redpath c M.J. Smith b White	3	(7)	Fall: 12 24 32 47 52 54 58 113 114		

T. Cullaro did not bat.

Bowling: Rofe 8–5–7–0; M.J. Smith 6–1–11–1; Christian 5–0–13–1; Hauritz 5–1–20–3; Doherty 8–0–28–2; White 7–1–42–2; Love 1–0–17–0.

Prime Minister's XI

C.J. Simmons c Sarra b Martin	6	(13)	L-b 1, w 8, n-b 5	14	
†B.J. Haddin b Gower	41	(42)			
*M.L. Love not out	48	(57)	(23.2 overs, 83 mins)	(2 wkts)	145
B.J. Hodge not out	36	(29)	Fall: 31 90		

B.P.C. Firebrace, J.K. Smith, C.L. White, X.J. Doherty, N.M. Hauritz, D.T. Christian, M.J. Smith and P.C. Rofe did not bat.

Bowling: Martin 5–3–21–1; Cullaro 4–0–30–0; Gower 4–0–35–1; Redpath 5–0–31–0; Bulger 3.2–0–22–0; Thomas 2–0–5–0.

Umpires: G.R. Clifton and A. Shelley.

AUSTRALIAN CRICKET BOARD CUP
LIMITED-OVERS SERIES, 2001-02

By WARWICK FRANKS

The limited-overs series of the ACB Cup was played in February as a round-robin in Canberra and was contested by five teams. The Queensland Academy of Sport and New South Wales both lost only one game, QAS comprehensively to New South Wales, who in turn suffered at the hands of Tasmania. The Australian Cricket Academy and Tasmania each won two of their matches, while the Australian Capital Territory went without a win. Victoria, South Australia and Western Australia did not participate.

The opening match, between QAS and the Australian Cricket Academy, was a closely fought affair in which both sides started well, only to lose wickets rapidly. Academy opener Duncan Betts made a poised 67 (99 balls), while Rowan Brewster made a quick-fire 65 not out (67 balls), but a decline from two for 141 to be all out for 217 was a waste of a good start. In similar vein, QAS opener Daniel Payne made a solid 55 (94 balls) and Clinton Perren an aggressive 63 (67 balls) but then the northerners only scraped home after having been two for 165. Tim Welsford took a creditable 4/49 but the Academy bowlers were wickedly wasteful in delivering 31 no-balls. Perren continued to be seen to advantage against Tasmania with 61 and, for good measure, five for 32.

Phil Jacques starred for New South Wales in a low-scoring match against QAS with 82 not out from only 73 balls. He was in even more spectacular form against the Australian Cricket Academy with 140 from 145 balls and finished off with 77 (110 balls) against Tasmania. His effort was in vain, though, as Chris Bassano played exuberantly for 73 (75 balls) to set up a comfortable Tasmanian victory.

The Australian Capital Territory were involved in the two highest-scoring games. QAS made seven for 257, thanks mainly to Lee Carseldine's 84 (87 balls), although Ben Southam's four for 29 from ten overs was a remarkable feat of containment and penetration. The ACT appeared to be cruising at two for 171, but slow left-armer Matthew Anderson recovered from a mauling to capture four quick wickets which turned the tide. Against the Australian Cricket Academy, the ACT made a highly satisfactory 242 and appeared to be well in control with the Australian Cricket Academy teetering at six for 119, off-spinner Heath Axelby having taken three important wickets. At this point, however, Daniel Smith (106 not out in 85 balls) and Welsford (38 not out in 45 balls) launched an electrifying attack on the bowling which produced a partnership of 125 that achieved victory with 4.1 overs to spare.

ROUND ONE

AUSTRALIAN CAPITAL TERRITORY v NEW SOUTH WALES SECOND XI

At Stirling Oval, Stirling, February 18, 2002. New South Wales Second XI won by 65 runs. Toss: New South Second XI. New South Wales Second XI eight for 215 (N.J. Catalano 38, M.J. Phelps 35, G.J. Mail 26, A.W. O'Brien 25, P.A. Jaques 24, V.M. Williams 21; D.M. Jeffrey 2/23, M.A. Hatton 2/39) defeated Australian Capital Territory 150 (J.K. Smith 41, D.G. Dawson 40; A.W. O'Brien 3/29, D. Bollinger 2/23, A.M. Clark 2/27, J.M. Heath 2/34).

AUSTRALIAN CRICKET ACADEMY v QUEENSLAND ACADEMY OF SPORT

At Boomanulla Oval, Narrabundah, February 18, 2002. Queensland Academy of Sport won by two wickets. Toss: Australian Cricket Academy. Australian Cricket Academy 217 (R.J. Brewster 68*, D.M. Betts 67, S.J. Phillips 25, C.J. Ferguson 22; M.A. Anderson 3/34, S.J. Magoffin 2/26, M.J. Petrie 2/48) lost to Queensland Academy of Sport eight for 218 (C.T. Perren 63, D.M. Payne 55, L.A. Carseldine 41; T.H. Welsford 4/49).

ROUND TWO

AUSTRALIAN CAPITAL TERRITORY v TASMANIA SECOND XI

At Chisholm Oval, Chisholm, February 19, 2002. Tasmania Second XI won by three runs. Toss: Tasmania Second XI. Tasmania Second XI six for 133 (S.B. Tubb 34, B.J. Thomas 33, M.R. Nutting 22; B.W. Dennett 2/16, A. Jones 2/18) defeated Australian Capital Territory 130 (H.R. Axelby 14, D.M. Jeffery 12; A.R. Griffith 3/24, C. Viney 2/13, L. Butterworth 2/25, A.W. Polkinghorne 2/29).

NEW SOUTH WALES SECOND XI v QUEENSLAND ACADEMY OF SPORT

At Boomanulla Oval, Narrabundah, February 19, 2002. New South Wales Second XI won by 61 runs. Toss: New South Wales Second XI. New South Wales Second XI seven for 195 (P.A. Jaques 82*, V.M. Williams 45, G.J. Mail 23, A.W. O'Brien 21; M.A. Anderson 2/22, S.J. Magoffin 2/26) defeated Queensland Academy of Sport 134 (C.P. Simpson 20, M.A. Anderson 20; D. Bollinger 4/15, A.W. O'Brien 2/16, A.M. Clark 2/41).

ROUND THREE

AUSTRALIAN CRICKET ACADEMY v NEW SOUTH WALES SECOND XI

At Kingston Oval, Kingston, February 20, 2002. New South Wales Second XI won by 63 runs. Toss: New South Wales Second XI. New South Wales Second XI five for 255 (P.A. Jaques 140, M.J. Phelps 42, A.W. O'Brien 26) defeated Australian Cricket

Academy 192 (L. Ronchi 64, S.J. Phillips 49, D.M. Betts 26; D.J. Thornely 3/30, D. Bollinger 2/24).

QUEENSLAND ACADEMY OF SPORT v TASMANIA SECOND XI

At Chisholm Oval, Chisholm, February 20, 2002. Queensland Academy of Sport won by 80 runs. Toss: Queensland Academy of Sport. Queensland Academy of Sport seven for 236 (C.T. Perren 61, D.M. Payne 58, A.M. Rowe 36, B. Shinnick 29; A.W. Polkinghorne 2/33, M.D. Pascoe 2/40) defeated Tasmania Second XI 156 (C.W.G. Bassano 37, M.R. Nutting 27, G.J. Bailey 26, G.T. Cunningham 22; C.T. Perren 5/32, S.J. Magoffin 2/24).

ROUND FOUR

AUSTRALIAN CAPITAL TERRITORY v QUEENSLAND ACADEMY OF SPORT

At Boomanulla Oval, Narrabundah, February 21, 2002. Queensland Academy of Sport won by 19 runs. Toss: Queensland Academy of Sport. Queensland Academy of Sport seven for 251 (L.A. Carseldine 84, B. Shinnick 32; B.S. Southam 4/29, E. Kellar 2/36) defeated Australian Capital Territory 232 (D.G. Dawson 69, M.J. Dawn 57, J.K. Smith 50, B.S. Southam 23; M.A. Anderson 4/63, M. Petrie 3/34).

AUSTRALIAN CRICKET ACADEMY v TASMANIA SECOND XI

At Stirling Oval, Stirling, February 21, 2002. Australian Cricket Academy won by 18 runs. Toss: Tasmania Second XI. Australian Cricket Academy nine for 230 (D.M. Betts 55, R.J. Brewster 41, D.C. Bandy 26, S.J. Phillips 23; S.B. Tubb 2/38) lost to Australian Cricket Academy 212 (G.J. Bailey 45, G.T. Cunningham 42, B.J. Thomas 32*; D.C. Bandy 3/39, S.P. Coombs 2/37, N.J. Rimmington 2/41).

ROUND FIVE

AUSTRALIAN CAPITAL TERRITORY v AUSTRALIAN CRICKET ACADEMY

At Kingston Oval, Kingston, February 22, 2002. Australian Cricket Academy won by four wickets. Toss: Australian Capital Territory. Australian Capital Territory 242 (S.L. Maxwell 53, M.J. Dawn 38, D.M. Jeffrey 37, J.K. Smith 30; D.C. Bandy 2/27, N.J. Rimmington 2/30, S.P. Coombes 2/30) lost to Australian Cricket Academy six for 244 (D. Smith 106*, S.J. Phillips 51, T.H. Welsford 38*; H.E. Axelby 3/39, E. Kellar 2/31).

NEW SOUTH WALES SECOND XI v TASMANIA SECOND XI

At Boomanulla Oval, Narrabundah, February 22, 2002. Tasmania Second XI won by six wickets. Toss: New South Wales Second XI. New South Wales Second XI nine for 200 (P.A. Jaques 77, D.S. Wotherspoon 36, J.N. Burke 22; S.B. Tubb 4/55, A.G. Downton 2/21) lost to Tasmania Second XI four for 203 (C.W.G. Bassano 73, A.W. Polkinghorne 43*, S.B. Tubb 37*, M.R. Nutting 28; A.W. O'Brien 2/39).

AUSTRALIAN CRICKET ACADEMY, 2001-02

By KEN PIESSE

After a decade nurturing and advancing the prospects of Australia's finest young cricketers, Academy head coach Rod Marsh left to fill a similar role with England's elite youngsters. Since 1991, Marsh had helped launch the international careers of almost 30 Australians, including the notable quartet of Shane Warne, Glenn McGrath, Ricky Ponting and Adam Gilchrist. He said the rewards had been considerable, watching young cricketers develop and flower to new levels of expertise. However, at 53, he felt it was time for new challenges and particularly exciting to assist another cricketing nation establish a similar program to reinforce its international performance and playing depth.

The Australian Cricket Board's James Sutherland said Marsh had for years been a key figure in elite cricket development and mentor to dozens of first-class players around the country. "Although in the ideal world Rod would have remained at the Academy, we accept his decision and wish him good luck in the new role," said Sutherland. "He leaves with our sincere thanks for his outstanding work."

Marsh regards the cricketers with the most simple and uncomplicated techniques as the most "coachable". He said it was easier to add the finesse if a player already had a solid base, not only in technique but physically and mentally as well. A key point in the Marsh method was to insist on the scholars training three and sometimes four times a day, six days a week. He said the consequent acceleration in the development of the players was considerable.

After a highly successful period as Queensland's coach, Marsh's successor, Bennett King, a former Queensland rugby league winger who has also worked with underprivileged children, had an immediate challenge to maintain the profile of the program, renowned for years as the best in the world. Appointed for an initial three-year period, King looked to work with the elite teenagers in specialised streams, using the most up-to-date training techniques and aids.

Marsh's departure coincided with significant changes in the Academy's structure. Rather than the annual selection of 13 or 14 full-time scholars, who lived in Adelaide for a six-month period before the start of the Academy's Australia-wide tour each September, the Australian Cricket Board looked to streamline the program and involve more players for shorter stints. Among those to benefit in the Academy's 15th year of operation in 2002 were members of Australia's victorious Under-19 World Cup squad, many of whom visited India for a ten-day training camp in April.

The 2001-02 scholars were: Duncan Betts (Queensland), Travis Birt (Victoria), Rowan Brewster (New South Wales), Mark Cosgrove (South Australia), Xavier Doherty (Tasmania), Brett Geeves (Tasmania), Mitchell Johnson (Queensland), Shaun Marsh (Western Australia), Scott Meuleman (Western Australia), Luke Ronchi (Western Australia), Daniel Smith (New

South Wales), Michael Thistle (Western Australia), Matthew Weeks (South Australia) and Tim Welsford (Victoria).

Once again several of the scholars played at state level. Meuleman made a maiden century against the visiting South Africans in Perth, having made his first-class debut late in 2000-01. Doherty and Johnson also played at Pura Cup level. A left-arm finger-spinner, Doherty took 6/68 from 27 overs against New South Wales Second XI at Howell Oval. He went on to play two matches against Victoria home and away, taking five wickets and impressing with his flight and drift. He also played two ING Cup matches.

Johnson originally hails from Townsville and despite an injury-interrupted summer is regarded by Dennis Lillee as a budding Test player. Just as Marsh was enamoured by Ponting's youthful skills and Terry Jenner by the big breaks of Warne years earlier, Lillee was sold on Johnson after just three deliveries during one of his elite pace bowling clinics in Brisbane three years ago. Having taken three wickets on his lively first-class debut against Western Australia in Perth, Johnson, 19, succumbed to a stress fracture in his back and missed the remainder of the summer.

Along with staff member Troy Cooley and scholarship coach Mathew Inness from Victoria, Lillee was again one of the mentors for the young fast bowlers, both the full-timers and the non-residential scholarship holders. Wayne Phillips and Marsh conducted the batting classes and Terry Jenner and Ashley Mallett the spin bowling.

Tim Welsford, a bowling all-rounder from Melbourne, said the full-timers benefited most from an increased work ethic. "We realised we could work our bodies harder and train three or four times a day when previously we'd trained only once. We could all see the benefits," he said. Welsford was one of the Academy's best players, his 94 batting at No. 3 against Victoria at the Albert Ground an example of his batting capabilities. The New Zealand-born wicket-keeper-batsman Luke Ronchi was another to excel, with 107 from 141 balls in the second innings.

The Academy's most memorable win came against Australian Capital Territory in Canberra. Set 333 to win, the Academy won with just five wickets down. Michael Thistle had earlier helped to set up the win with 4/37. He also took five wickets in an innings against a strong Western Australian side at Richardson Park. The best performance by one of the part-timers was by New South Wales' Steven Phillips, who made 74 and an ebullient 156 (16 fours, five sixes) against New South Wales Colts at Bankstown Oval.

AUSTRALIAN CRICKET ACADEMY, 2001-02

At Howell Oval, Penrith, September 24, 25, 26, 27, 2001. AUSTRALIAN CRICKET ACADEMY lost to NEW SOUTH WALES SECOND XI by 17 runs. For details see section on ACB Cup.

At Adelaide Oval No.2, Adelaide, October 2, 3, 4, 5, 2001. AUSTRALIAN CRICKET ACADEMY lost to SOUTH AUSTRALIA SECOND XI by nine wickets. For details see section on ACB Cup.

NEW ZEALAND CRICKET ACADEMY v
AUSTRALIAN CRICKET ACADEMY

At Bert Sutcliffe Oval, Lincoln, October 15, 16, 17, 2001. Drawn. Toss: Australian Cricket Academy.

Close of play: First day, Australian Cricket Academy (1) 7-87 (White 9, Doherty 2); Second day, New Zealand Cricket Academy (2) 6-160.

New Zealand Cricket Academy

*J.M. How run out (Bailey)	4	–	lbw b James	18
L.J. Woodcock c Doherty b James	16	–	run out (Bailey)	16
N.K.W. Horsley b Christian	5	–	c Cosgrove b Crook	0
S.L. Stewart not out	74	–	lbw b Doherty	39
J.P. McNamee lbw b James	0	–	lbw b White	0
C.L. Cairns lbw b Cosgrove	21	–	retired hurt	34
B.B. McCullum lbw b Cosgrove	4	–	c Doherty b Casson	80
†R.A. Young lbw b White	25	–	c Dickson b Doherty	0
N.L. McCullum c Ferguson b Casson	15	–	c Doherty b Crook	66
S.J.G. Whiteman run out (Crosthwaite)	12	–	not out	5
W.A. Cornelius c White b Casson	5	–	not out	2
B 3, l-b 9, w 11, n-b 4	27		B 8, l-b 9, w 10, n-b 3	30

(66 overs, 262 mins)	208	(72.2 overs, 299 mins) (8 wkts dec)	290
Fall: 20 27 29 29 67 71 123 158 185 208		Fall: 24 25 50 50 131 141 266 277	

T.P. Robin did not bat.

Bowling: *First Innings*—James 13–4–31–2; Christian 5–1–18–1; Cosgrove 9–1–26–2; Crook 5–1–24–0; White 10–3–25–1; Doherty 13–2–28–0; Casson 11–2–44–2. *Second Innings*—James 14–3–41–1; Christian 8–4–25–0; Crook 10–1–33–2; White 17–3–79–1; Cosgrove 4–1–25–0; Doherty 13–4–33–2; Casson 6.2–0–37–1.

Australian Cricket Academy

P.J. Dickson c Young b Cornelius	16	–	run out (Robin/N.L. McCullum)	57
C.J. Ferguson run out (B.B. McCullum)	15	–	c Young b Cornelius	14
C.J. Borgas b Cornelius	1	–	lbw b Cornelius	2
M.J. Cosgrove c B.B. McCullum b Cairns	11	–	c Woodcock b N.L. McCullum	11
G.J. Bailey c McNamee b Whiteman	23	–	b Whiteman	101
B. Casson c Young b Whiteman	1	–	c How b N.L. McCullum	50
*C.L. White b Cornelius	41	–	run out (Whiteman/Young)	8
†A.J. Crosthwaite b Cornelius	0	–	lbw b N.L. McCullum	2
X.J. Doherty c B.B. McCullum b Whiteman	36	–	not out	16
D.T. Christian b Cornelius	12	–	not out	9
A.C.L. James not out	2			
L-b 8, w 2, n-b 1	11		L-b 4, n-b 1	5

(55.2 overs, 231 mins)	169	(72 overs, 299 mins) (8 wkts)	275
Fall: 21 31 38 55 67 78 79 130 167 169		Fall: 41 49 86 86 162 199 218 259	

S.P. Crook did not bat.

Bowling: *First Innings*—Cornelius 15.2–2–55–2; Whiteman 20–4–59–3; Cairns 11–4–28–1; Robin 8–0–18–0; Woodcock 1–0–1–0. *Second Innings*—Cornelius 17–5–39–2; Whiteman 16–3–61–1; Robin 11–4–30–0; N.L. McCullum 19–4–92–3; Woodcock 9–2–49–0.

Umpires: G.A. Baxter and D.M. Quested.

NEW ZEALAND CRICKET ACADEMY v
AUSTRALIAN CRICKET ACADEMY

At Bert Sutcliffe Oval, Lincoln, October 19, 20, 21, 2001. Drawn. Toss: New Zealand Cricket Academy.

Close of Play: First day, Australian Cricket Academy (1) 9-304 (Crosthwaite 31, Rimmington 10); Second day, New Zealand Cricket Academy (1) 9-289 (Robin 1, Cornelius 18).

Australian Cricket Academy

P.J. Dickson c Woodcock b Bond	3	– c B.B. McCullum b Robin 49
C.J. Ferguson c N.L. McCullum b Bond	51	– (7) c and b N.L. McCullum 32
J.N. Burke c B.B. McCullum b Cornelius	52	– c Stewart b N.L. McCullum 30
M.J. Cosgrove c McNamee b Bond	30	– (2) c N.L. McCullum b Bond 0
G.J. Bailey lbw b Bond	0	– (6) c B.B. McCullum b N.L. McCullum ... 16
B. Casson c Horsley b Robin	32	– (4) not out 100
*C.L. White c McNamee b Bond	51	– (5) lbw b N.L. McCullum 22
X.J. Doherty c N.L. McCullum b Bond	2	– not out 5
†A.J. Crosthwaite not out	31	
D.T. Christian lbw b Bond	5	
N.J. Rimmington not out	10	
B 11, l-b 13, w 4, n-b 9	37	L-b 5, n-b 1 6

(78 overs, 322 mins)   (9 wkts dec) 304   (64 overs, 236 mins)   (6 wkts dec) 260
Fall: 5 99 140 140 170 223 256 260 270   Fall: 0 56 111 142 166 248

A.C.L. James did not bat.

Bowling: *First Innings*—Bond 23–10–55–7; Cornelius 16–6–38–1; Robin 14–2–59–1; Stewart 15–1–77–0; N.L. McCullum 9–0–49–0; Woodcock 1–0–2–0. *Second Innings*—Bond 9–1–30–1; Cornelius 11–2–43–0; N.L. McCullum 25–3–103–4; Woodcock 13–0–53–0; Robin 3–0–19–1; Horsley 1–0–4–0; How 2–0–2–0.

New Zealand Cricket Academy

*J.M. How c Cosgrove b White	25	– c Dickson b Christian 5
R.A. Young run out	89	
N.K.W. Horsley c Cosgrove b White	16	– c Christian b White 16
S.L. Stewart b Doherty	48	– (5) lbw b Rimmington 3
J.P. McNamee lbw b Doherty	3	– (4) c Ferguson b Rimmington 6
†B.B. McCullum b Doherty	53	– (2) b White 72
N.L. McCullum c Crosthwaite b Christian	25	– not out 9
L.J. Woodcock c Crosthwaite b Christian	1	– (6) not out 12
S.E. Bond b Christian	0	
T.P. Robin not out	1	
W.A. Cornelius not out	18	
L-b 2, w 1, n-b 8	11	L-b 2 2

(79 overs, 318 mins)   (9 wkts dec) 289   (28 overs, 128 mins)   (5 wkts) 125
Fall: 60 128 153 188 189 255 263 269 270   Fall: 43 95 98 105

Bowling: *First Innings*—James 13–1–45–0; White 15–6–47–2; Rimmington 11–2–41–0; Christian 11–4–43–4; Cosgrove 7–2–16–0; Doherty 13–2–57–2; Burke 3–0–14–0, Casson 6–0–24–0. *Second Innings*—James 5–1–39–0; Christian 6–0–42–1; Rimmington 7–0–25–2; White 7–4–6–2; Doherty 3–0–11–0.

Umpires: G.A. Baxter and B.F. Bowden.

NEW ZEALAND CRICKET ACADEMY v
AUSTRALIA CRICKET ACADEMY

At Bert Sutcliffe Oval, Lincoln, October 23, 2001. Australian Cricket Academy won by 151 runs. Toss: Australian Cricket Academy.

Australian Cricket Academy

P.J. Dickson c How b Woodcock	.... 36 (46)	M.J. Cosgrove not out	.... 19 (11)
C.J. Ferguson st Young b Woodcock	. 61 (67)		
J.N. Burke b Woodcock	.... 14 (34)	L-b 5, w 8, n-b 3	 16
B. Casson c B.B. McCullum b Stewart	36 (41)		
*C.L. White b Cornelius	.... 75 (68)	(50 overs, 212 mins)　　(5 wkts) 302	
G.J. Bailey not out	.... 45 (36)	Fall: 88 109 128 187 276	

X.J. Doherty, †A.J. Crosthwaite, S.P. Crook, D.T. Christian and N.J. Rimmington did not bat.

Bowling: Cornelius 10–0–78–1; Franklin 10–0–56–0; Robin 10–0–53–0; Woodcock 10–1–26–3; N. L. McCullum 6–0–49–0; Stewart 4–0–35–1.

New Zealand Cricket Academy

J.M. How c Crosthwaite b Rimmington	5 (12)	L.J. Woodcock c Cosgrove b Burke	. 3 (9)
B.B. McCullum c Crook b Cosgrove	.. 20 (22)	W.A. Cornelius c Bailey b Doherty	.. 7 (13)
N.K.W. Horsley c Crosthwaite b Cosgrove	.. 0 (4)	T.P. Robin not out	.... 1 (4)
S.L. Stewart c Cosgrove b Burke	.... 68 (71)	L-b 6, w 6, n-b 1	 13
J.P. McNamee st Crosthwaite b White	23 (31)		
J.E.C. Franklin b White	.... 6 (8)	(31.1. overs, 138 mins)　　　　151	
*N.L. McCullum c Crosthwaite b Crook	1 (3)	Fall: 10 14 34 90 101 102 117	
†R.A. Young run out	.... 4 (11)	143 144 151	

Bowling: Rimmington 8–1–38–1; Cosgrove 7–2–30–2; White 6–0–29–2; Crook 6–0–37–1; Doherty 2.1–0–7–1; Burke 2–0–4–2.

Umpires: R.D. Anderson and M.P. George.

NEW ZEALAND CRICKET ACADEMY v
AUSTRALIAN CRICKET ACADEMY

At Bert Sutcliffe Oval, Lincoln, October 24, 2001. Australian Cricket Academy won by 9 runs. Toss: Australian Cricket Academy.

Australian Cricket Academy

C.J. Ferguson c N.L. McCullum b Franklin	... 1 (10)	X.J. Doherty run out (Cornelius/Young)	1 (2)
P.J. Dickson run out (B.B. McCullum)	2 (11)	D.T. Christian b Robin	.... 4 (10)
J.N. Burke b Cornelius	.... 14 (11)	†A.J. Crosthwaite not out	.... 22 (19)
C.J. Borgas c Young b Robin	.... 74 (93)	S.P. Crook not out	.... 6 (8)
*C.L. White c Stewart b Cornelius	... 0 (8)	L-b 12, w 4	 16
G.J. Bailey c Stewart b Woodcock	... 32 (46)	(41 overs, 171 mins)　　(9 wkts) 209	
M.J. Cosgrove c N.L. McCullum b Redmond	.. 36 (28)	Fall: 5 18 20 26 74 147 153 173 174	

A.C.L. James did not bat.

Bowling: Franklin 6–0–19–1; Cornelius 9–0–27–2; Robin 8–0–41–2; Woodcock 8–0–32–1; N.L. McCullum 7–0–44–0; Redmond 3–0–34–1.

New Zealand Cricket Academy

J.M. How lbw b Doherty	43 (78)	J.E.C. Franklin not out	18 (12)
B.B. McCullum st Crosthwaite		C.J. Cornelius b Christian	2 (5)
b Doherty	41 (58)	†R.A. Young run out	19 (8)
N.K.W. Horsley run out	4 (11)	T.P. Robin not out	3 (2)
S.L. Stewart run out	18 (29)	B 2, l-b 7, w 12	21
J.P. McNamee c Bailey b James	30 (36)		
A.J. Redmond b Burke	0 (5)	(41 overs, 180 mins) (9 wkts) 200	
*N.L. McCullum run out	1 (2)	Fall: 86 97 100 129 142 150 155 163 196	

L.J. Woodcock did not bat.

Bowling: James 8–0–44–1; Cosgrove 5–0–17–0; Doherty 9–2–22–2; White 6–0–35–0; Christian 8–0–36–1; Burke 4–0–23–1; Crook 1–0–14–0.

Umpires: R.D. Anderson and M.P. George.

NEW ZEALAND CRICKET ACADEMY v AUSTRALIAN CRICKET ACADEMY

At Bert Sutcliffe Oval, Lincoln, October 26, 2001. Australian Cricket Academy won by 48 runs. Toss: Australian Cricket Academy.

Australian Cricket Academy

C.J. Ferguson c B.B. McCullum b Mills	2 (7)	M.J. Cosgrove run out	
J.N. Burke b Franklin	95 (106)	(B.B. McCullum)	31 (26)
C.J. Borgas c Franklin b Mills	5 (18)	X.J. Doherty not out	0 (1)
B. Casson b Redmond	82 (92)	B 2, l-b 6, w 8, n-b 6	22
*C.L. White not out	57 (47)		
G.J. Bailey c N.L. McCullum		(50 overs, 220 mins) (6 wkts) 294	
b Cornelius	0 (10)	Fall: 9 26 190 198 217 290	

D.T. Christian, †A.J. Crosthwaite, S.P. Crook and N.J. Rimmington did not bat.

Bowling: Franklin 10–1–45–1; Mills 10–1–42–2; Cornelius 10–1–61–1; Woodcock 3–0–33–0; N.L. McCullum 10–0–58–0.

New Zealand Cricket Academy

J.M. How c Crosthwaite b Rimmington	1 (9)	J.E.C. Franklin obstructing the field	8 (10)
*†B.B. McCullum st Crosthwaite		C.J. Cornelius c Bailey b White	3 (3)
b White	80 (88)	R.A. Young not out	0 (0)
N.K.W. Horsley c Casson b Doherty	26 (61)		
S.L. Stewart st Crosthwaite b White	59 (60)	L-b 2, w 9, n-b 1	12
A.J. Redmond run out	29 (31)		
J.P. McNamee lbw b White	0 (3)	(47.3 overs, 216 mins)	246
N.L. McCullum st Crosthwaite b White	15 (10)	Fall:12 99 147 192 195 221 222	
K.D. Mills c Ferguson b White	13 (11)	237 244 246	

L.J. Woodcock did not bat.

Bowling: Rimmington 10–0–51–1; Cosgrove 6–1–41–0; Christian 9–1–34–0; White 9.3–0–43–6; Doherty 10–0–53–1; Casson 3–0–20–0.

Umpires: G.A. Baxter and D.M. Quested.

NEW ZEALAND CRICKET ACADEMY v
AUSTRALIAN CRICKET ACADEMY

At Bert Sutcliffe Oval, Lincoln, October 27, 2001. New Cricket Academy won by 133 runs. Toss: New Zealand Cricket Academy.

New Zealand Cricket Academy

J. M. How c Bailey b Cosgrove	23	(19)	K. D. Mills b James	24	(19)
*B. B. McCullum c Borgas b Cosgrove	67	(42)	I. J. Woodcock not out	9	(21)
N. K. W. Horsley c Crook b Doherty	15	(15)	W. A. Cornelius lbw b James	1	(2)
S. L. Stewart c Bailey b Doherty	16	(41)			
†R. A. Young run out (Bailey)	7	(16)	L-b 3, w 8, n-b 2	13	
J. P. McNamee c Crosthwaite b Christian	49	(64)			
J. E. C. Franklin c Crook b Burke	12	(24)	(46.4 overs, 194 mins)	244	
N. L. McCullum run out (Christian)	8	(18)	Fall: 62 96 110 128 135 170 192 227 242 244		

T. P. Robin did not bat.

Bowling: Crook 10–0–80–0; Cosgrove 8–0–55–2; Doherty 10–1–31–2; Burke 10–1–30–1; Christian 5–0–21–1; James 3.4–0–24–2.

Australian Cricket Academy

P. J. Dickson c Young b Cornelius	12	(17)	†A. J. Crosthwaite b Cornelius	0	(7)
J. N. Burke b Cornelius	8	(14)	D. T. Christian b Woodcock	5	(13)
C. J. Borgas c Woodcock b Cornelius	18	(12)	S. P. Crook c N. L. McCullum		
B. Casson not out	32	(64)	b Woodcock	11	(18)
*C. L. White b Cornelius	1	(5)	L-b 3, w 16, n-b 2	21	
G. J. Bailey b Cornelius	3	(12)			
M. J. Cosgrove c How b Mills	0	(3)	(27.2 overs, 129 mins)	111	
X. J. Doherty lbw b Mills	0	(1)	Fall: 17 28 45 47 52 54 54 70 80 111		

A. C. L. James did not bat.

Bowling: Franklin 5–0–29–0; Cornelius 10–2–32–6; Mills 6–2–16–2; Woodcock 3.2–0–15–2; Robin 3–0–16–0.

Umpires: G. A. Baxter and D. M. Quested.

At New Town Oval, New Town, November 5, 6, 7, 8, 2001. AUSTRALIAN CRICKET ACADEMY drew with TASMANIA SECOND XI. For details see section on ACB Cup.

At Richardson Park, Perth, November 12, 13, 14, 15, 2001. AUSTRALIAN CRICKET ACADEMY lost to WESTERN AUSTRALIA SECOND XI. For details see section on ACB Cup.

At Manuka Oval, Canberra, November 18, 19, 20, 21, 2001. AUSTRALIAN CRICKET ACADEMY defeated AUSTRALIAN CAPITAL TERRITORY by five wickets. For details see section on ACB Cup.

At Henley Oval, Adelaide, December 3, 4, 5, 2001. AUSTRALIAN CRICKET ACADEMY lost to ECB NATIONAL ACADEMY by an innings and 31 runs. For details see section on Minor cricket.

At Junction Oval, St Kilda, December 17, 18, 19, 20, 2001. AUSTRALIAN CRICKET ACADEMY lost to VICTORIA SECOND XI by 160 runs. For details see section on ACB Cup.

At Boomanulla Oval, Boomanulla, February 18, 2002. AUSTRALIAN CRICKET ACADEMY lost to QUEENSLAND ACADEMY OF SPORT by two wickets. For details see section on ACB Cup.

At Kingston Oval, Kingston, February 20, 2002. AUSTRALIAN CRICKET ACADEMY lost to NEW SOUTH WALES SECOND XI by 63 runs. For details see section on ACB Cup.

At Stirling Oval, Stirling, February 21, 2002. AUSTRALIAN CRICKET ACADEMY defeated TASMANIA SECOND XI by 18 runs. For details see section on ACB Cup.

At Kingston Oval, Kingston, February 22, 2002. AUSTRALIAN CRICKET ACADEMY defeated AUSTRALIAN CAPITAL TERRITORY won by four wickets. For details see section on ACB Cup.

NEW SOUTH WALES INSTITUTE OF SPORTS COLTS v AUSTRALIAN CRICKET ACADEMY

At David Phillips South Oval, Daceyville, February 25, 2002. Australian Cricket Academy won on run rate. Toss: New South Wales Institute of Sport.

New South Wales Institute of Sports Colts

J.N. Burke c James b Cosgrove	44 (54)	P.M. Wooden not out	20 (40)
*N.J. Catalano b James	30 (50)	†J. Allsopp st Ronchi b Casson	3 (11)
D.S. Wotherspoon run out	20 (32)	A.C. Bird not out	16 (16)
S.J. Phillips lbw b Cosgrove	0 (3)		
K.K.J. Luiters c Welsford b Cosgrove	8 (18)	L-b 7, w 8	15
S.D. Stanton b Casson	18 (34)		
J.J. Krejka c and b Coombes	3 (6)	(50 overs, 180 mins) (9 wkts)	194
M.J. Baker c Ronchi b Casson	17 (36)	Fall: 75 79 83 98 121 129 145 162 168	

K.M. Daley did not bat.

Bowling: Petrie 7–1–23–0; Rimmington 8–0–44–0; Cosgrove 10–0–40–3; James 5–0–20–1; Coombes 10–0–41–1; Casson 10–2–19–3.

Australian Cricket Academy

D. Smith c Allsopp b Baker	25 (21)	B. Casson not out	1 (2)
D.M. Betts c Wooden b Phillips	27 (42)		
T.R. Birt c Phillips b Burke	22 (29)	L-b 1, w 5	6
R.J. Brewster c Allsopp b Krejza	16 (23)		
†L. Ronchi c Phillips b Krejza	26 (14)	(25 overs, 113 mins) (5 wkts)	152
M.J. Cosgrove not out	29 (18)	Fall: 40 58 90 95 147	

*T.H. Welsford, N.J. Rimmington, S.P. Coombes, A.C.L. James and M.J. Petrie did not bat.

Bowling: Daley 5–0–24–0; Bird 2–0–8–0; Baker 6–0–30–1; Phillips 4–0–22–1; Burke 4–0–25–1; Krejza 4–0–42–2.

Umpires: D. Goodger and A. Kelleher.

At David Phillips South Oval, February 26, 2002. AUSTRALIAN CRICKET ACADEMY lost to ECB CRICKET ACADEMY by 34 runs. For details see section on Minor Cricket.

NEW SOUTH WALES INSTITUTE OF SPORT COLTS v AUSTRALIAN CRICKET ACADEMY

At David Phillips North Oval, Daceyville, February 28, 2002. New South Wales Institute of Colts won by one run. Toss: New South Wales Institute of Colts.

New South Wales Institute of Sports Colts

A. Jeffrey c Smith b Welsford	8	(24)
P. A. Jaques b Cosgrove	93	(82)
P. Maraziotis lbw b Coombes	25	(38)
S. Spoljaric not out	24	(30)
M. Schenke not out	10	(16)

L-b 3, w 10, n-b 2 15

(33 overs, 127 mins)   (3 wkts) 175
Fall: 47 125 144

*†N. S. Pilon, M. W. B. Faraday, D. T. Christian, L. A. Zammit, C. P. Eve, A. Fleming and K. Connor did not bat.

Bowling: Rimmington 5–0–23–0; Petrie 4–0–20–0; Casson 7–0–30–0; Welsford 5–0–27–1; Coombes 7–1–40–1; Cosgrove 5–0–32–1.

Australian Cricket Academy

D. Smith b Fleming	8	(16)	
D. M. Betts lbw b Eve	21	(26)	
T. R. Birt b Eve	1	(8)	
R. J. Brewster st Pilon b Connor	53	(49)	
†L. Ronchi c Pilon b Zammit	19	(24)	
*T. H. Welsford b Connor	9	(21)	
M. J. Cosgrove c Jeffrey b Connor	17	(15)	
B. Casson lbw b Zammit	0	(2)	

N. J. Rimmington run out	9	(10)
A. C. L. James not out	7	(16)
M. J. Petrie c Schenke b Spoljaric	12	(14)

L-b 1, w 14, n-b 3 18

(33 overs, 140 mins)   174
Fall: 20 22 53 109 115 133 135
139 150 174

Bowling: Eve 7–0–28–2; Fleming 6–0–31–1; Christian 3–0–35–0; Connor 7–0–33–3; Zammit 7–0–23–2; Spoljaric 3–0–23–1.

NEW SOUTH WALES INSTITUTE OF SPORT COLTS v AUSTRALIAN CRICKET ACADEMY

At Memorial Oval, Bankstown, March 11, 12, 13, 14, 2002. New South Wales Institute of Sport won by 35 runs. Toss: New South Wales Institute of Sport Colts.

New South Wales Institute of Sport Colts

*N. J. Catalano c Smith b Scott	0	– (2) not out	201
A. Jeffrey c Stanton b Coombes	16	– (1) c Smith b Coombes	10
A. W. O'Brien c Ferguson b Cosgrove	25	– c Smith b Geeves	99
D. S. Wotherspoon c Phillips b Scott	37	– c Stanton b Petrie	101
J. N. Burke c Brewster b Coombes	99	– c Ferguson b Petrie	1
J. J. Krejza b Scott	0	– c Birt b Coombes	13
A. C. Bird st Smith b Petrie	33	– b Petrie	7
L. A. Zammit run out (Smith)	9		
†J. Allsopp not out	16		
K. M. Daley b Coombes	3		
D. Bollinger run out (Phillips)	0		

L-b 3, n-b 1	4

L-b 1, n-b 2 3

(84.2 overs, 323 mins)   242
Fall: 2 39 51 117 117 180 196 229 240 242

(98.2 overs, 373 mins) (6 wkts dec) 435
Fall: 37 197 380 388 411 435

K. O'Connor did not bat.

Bowling: *First Innings*—Scott 19–6–44–3; Geeves 16.2–4–47–0; Petrie 20–4–118–1; Coombes 18–3–49–3; Cosgrove 11–1–51–1. *Second Innings*—Petrie 22.2–5–64–3; Coombes 27–4–127–2; Geeves 16–1–74–1; Scott 8–0–28–0; Cosgrove 11–2–56–0; Phillips 2–1–12–0; Betts 1–0–13–0; Brewster 1–0–4–0; Ferguson 5–0–24–0; Smith 5–0–32–0.

Australian Cricket Academy

D. M. Betts c Allsopp b Bollinger	21	– (2) c Allsopp b Bollinger	31
C. J. Ferguson c Zammit b Bird	21	– (1) Bollinger	23
S. J. Phillips c Zammit b Bollinger	74	– c O'Brien b Krejza	156
*R. J. Brewster c Jeffrey b Daley	9	– c Krejza b Daley	40
S. D. Stanton c Bird b Zammit	39	– c Allsopp b Daley	1
†D. Smith b Bird	6	– c Allsopp b Bollinger	78
M. J. Cosgrove b Krejza	54	– c Zammit b Bollinger	4
T. R. Birt c O'Brien b Krejza	24	– c Wotherspoon b Krejza	23
B. A. Geeves lbw b Krejza	3	– c Allsopp b Krejza	0
M. J. Petrie c O'Brien b Krejza	6	– run out (Daley)	4
S. P. Coombes not out	7	– not out	2
L-b 1	1	B 4, l-b 8, w 1, n-b 2	15

(63.5 overs, 260 mins)	265	(99.0 overs, 384 mins)	377

Fall: 37 63 113 136 169 190 246
249 252 265

Fall: 55 60 141 149 328 339
359 363 374 377

A. Scott did not bat.

Bowling: *First Innings*—Daley 9–3–34–1; Bird 15–2–54–2; Zammit 15–4–46–1; Bollinger 12–2–63–2; Krejza 9.5–2–56–4; Connor 3–0–11–0. *Second Innings*—Daley 22–3–62–2; Bird 1–0–8–0; Bollinger 25–5–78–4; Connor 15–2–78–0; Zammit 11–3–52–0; O'Brien 11–4–31–0; Krejza 11–1–36–3; Burke 3–0–20–0.

Umpires: T.J. Keel and G.J. Gill.

MADRAS RUBBER FACTORY XI v AUSTRALIAN CRICKET ACADEMY At ICL Gurunanais, Chennai, Australian Cricket Academy won by two wickets. MRF XI eight for 261 (J. Harish 88, M. A. Satish 60; A. A. Noffke 3/38) lost to Australian Cricket Academy seven for 262 (A. A. Noffke 56, J. N. Burke 50, C. L. White 48, C. J. Simmons 43, G. J. Bailey 43).

COMBINED XI v AUSTRALIAN CRICKET ACADEMY

At MA Chidambaram Stadium, Chepauk, Chennai, April 8, 9, 10, 2002. Australian Cricket Academy won by six wickets. Toss: Australian Cricket Academy.

Close of Play: First day, Australian Cricket Academy (1) 4-130 (North 56); Second day, Conbined XI (2) 6-171 (Vasudevadas 58, Nair 27).

Combined XI

P. Satish b Noffke	0	– (6) c Simmons b White	3
N. V. Ojha c Harris b White	39	– c Symonds b Cassell	1
J. Harish c Burke b White	66	– c Doherty b Cassell	33
S. V. Saravanan b White	0	– b Noffke	9
K. Vasudevadas c Burke b Doherty	19	– run out (North)	105
*Tanveer Jabbar c Cassell b White	7	– (7) c Casson b Doherty	11
S. R. Nair c Symonds b Doherty	5	– (8) b Simmons	38
†K. K. D. Karthik st Clingeleffer b Casson	28	– (1) c Bailey b Noffke	19
D. Dhandapani c Symonds b Doherty	19	– not out	28
T. Kumaran not out	3	– b Simmons	27
Y. A. Golwalkar c North b Casson	0	–	
K. S. Veeranan (did not bat)		– b Simmons	0
B 9, l-b 6, n-b 6	21	B 5, l-b 2, n-b 4	11

(61.3 overs)	207	(69 overs)	285

Fall: 0 104 104 129 144 149 152
204 206 207

Fall: 2 43 54 80 83 100 201
247 285 285

R. Jesuraj did not bat.

Bowling: *First Innings*—Noffke 12–3–28–1; Cassell 9–4–30–0; Harris 4–1–17–0; Symonds 4–0–25–0; White 19–6–58–4; Casson 4.3–0–11–2; Doherty 9–2–23–3. *Second Innings*—Noffke 18–6–57–2; Cassell 11–4–39–2; White 11–1–61–1; Doherty 7–0–32–1; Symonds 3–0–11–0; Casson 9–1–41–0; Simmons 10–1–37–3.

Australian Cricket Academy

J. N. Burke c Karthik b Kumaran	17	– st Ojha b Nair	44
C. J. Simmons b Kumaran	0	– c Satish b Golwalkar	69
M. J. North c Kumaran b Dhandapani	152		
*A. Symonds c Veeranan b Satish	16	– not out	31
C. L. White c and b Golwalkar	41		
G. J. Bailey c Ojha b Kumaran	0	– (5) c Harish b Golwalkar	1
†S. G. Clingeleffer c Vasudevadas b Dhandapani	21	– (6) not out	7
B. Casson lbw b Dhandapani	45		
R. J. Harris lbw b Nair	1	– (3) c Saravanan b Nair	1
X. J. Doherty not out	8		
R. J. Cassell c Harish b Dhandapani	5		
B 5, l-b 10, n-b 9	24	B 1, l-b 7, n-b 3	11
(76.4 overs)	330	(33 overs) (4 wkts)	164

Fall: 5 22 41 130 155 196 300 303 324 330

Fall: 109 121 121 140

A. A. Noffke did not bat.

Bowling: *First Innings*—Kumaran 11–5–14–3; Veeranan 5–1–30–0; Nair 20–1–84–1; Satish 9–1–43–1; Saravanan 2–0–20–0; Dhandapani 18.4–3–65–4; Golwalkar 5–1–41–1; Jesuraj 6–3–18–0. *Second Innings*—Veeranan 4–2–9–0; Satish 4.0–12–0; Jesuraj 5–1–26–0; Saravanan 3–0–17–0; Dhandapani 1–0–14–0; Nair 8–2–42–2; Golwalkar 7–0–28–2; Vasudevadas 1–0–8–0.

Umpires: V. Gururajan and S. Balaji.

COMBINED XI v AUSTRALIAN CRICKET ACADEMY

At MA Chidambaram Stadium, Chepauk, Chennai, April 12, 2002. Australian Cricket Academy won by seven wickets. Toss: Combined XI.

Combined XI

A. R. Kapoor c Ojha b Cassell	13	(15)
S. Mahesh c Satish b Harris	9	(10)
S. R. Nair c Doherty b Cassell	5	(12)
*Tanveer Jabbar b Burke	11	(16)
J. Harish c Clingeleffer b Doherty	34	(48)
†K. K. D. Karthik c Cassell b Satish	125	(113)
K. Vasudevadas lbw b Doherty	12	(19)
M. R. Shrinivas b White	22	(30)
D. Dhandapani not out	33	(30)
Tanseer Jabbar not out	3	(7)
L-b 5, w 4	9	
(50 overs) (8 wkts)	276	

Fall: 22 27 28 48 110 132 178 259

R. Jesuraj and Y. A. Golwalkar did not bat.

Bowling: Cassell 8–0–46–2; Harris 8–0–42–1; Doherty 10–2–50–2; Burke 10–0–44–1; White 6–0–47–1; Casson 5–0–21–0; Satish 2–0–12–1; Simmons 1–0–9–0.

Australian Cricket Academy

J. N. Burke c Jesuraj b Mahesh	24	(23)
C. J. Simmons c Nair	82	(71)
N. V. Ojha c White b Shrinivas	56	(57)
C. L. White not out	79	(78)
P. Satish not out	26	(27)
L-b 4, w 3, n-b 6	13	
(41.4 overs) (3 wkts)	280	

Fall: not available

G. J. Bailey, *†S. G. Clingeleffer, B. Casson, R. J. Harris, X. J. Doherty and R. J. Cassell did not bat.

Bowling: Shrinivas 6–0–45–1; Mahesh 9–0–51–1; Kapoor 8–0–61–0; Jesuraj 1–0–15–0; Nair 8–0–52–1; Tanveer Jabbar 7–1–32–0; Golwalkar 2.4–0–20–0.

Umpires: V. Gururajan and P. Satish.

ENGLAND CRICKET BOARD NATIONAL ACADEMY IN AUSTRALIA, 2001-02

By WARWICK FRANKS

The tour was conducted in two parts, with three matches played in late November and early December, and another eight matches after the side returned in late January. It was particularly significant because it was the first English Cricket Board National Academy tour under the charge of Rod Marsh, and early signs of his approach could be seen in the vigour and purpose with which the team approached its cricket. The results were highly satisfactory for the Academy side, with eight wins, two losses, and a drawn game in which the tourists were only three runs short of victory.

The batting looked both stylish and effective, with Ian Bell, Robert Key, Mark Wagh and Matthew Wood contributing six of the seven centuries. In four of the five longer games, the side passed 350, and reached 601 against the Australian Academy. The bowling, on the other hand, was less effective, with too much of the attack occupying that narrow band of the bowling spectrum between the honest trier and the modestly competent. An important exception was fast bowler Stephen Harmison, who looked penetrative, if expensive at times.

ECB NATIONAL ACADEMY TOURING PARTY

I. R. Bell (Warwickshire), S. J. Harmison (Durham), A. Flintoff (Lancashire), S. P. Jones (Glamorgan), D. A. Kenway (Hampshire), R. W. T. Key (Kent), S. P. Kirby (Yorkshire), N. Peng (Durham), C. P. Schofield (Lancashire), O. A. Shah (Middlesex), A. J. Strauss (Middlesex), G. P. Swann (Northamptonshire), C. T. Tremlett (Hampshire), A. J. Tudor (Surrey), M. A. Wagh (Warwickshire), M. A. Wallace (Glamorgan), M. J. Wood (Yorkshire). R. J. Sidebottom (Yorkshire) flew out to strengthen the squad in February.

Director: R. W. Marsh. *Assistant Coach:* J. Abrahams. *Manager:* N. E. F. Laughton. *Physiotherapist:* K. A. Russell. *Physiologist:* R. Smith.

TOUR AVERAGES

BATTING

	M	I	NO	R	HS	100s	50s	Avge	Ct/St
C. P. Schofield	8	7	4	231	49	0	0	77.00	4
N. Peng	4	5	1	216	75	0	2	54.00	0
R. W. T. Key	10	14	3	543	177	1	3	49.36	6
I. R. Bell	9	13	1	575	117	2	3	47.92	5
M. J. Wood	10	14	1	613	112	2	4	47.15	3
M. A. Wagh	10	13	2	475	164	1	3	43.18	6
O. A. Shah	3	3	0	120	74	0	1	40.00	2
M. A. Wallace	11	9	2	238	62	0	1	34.00	21/5
A. J. Strauss	10	13	0	431	113	1	3	33.15	6
G. P. Swann	8	8	0	238	77	0	2	29.75	4
A. J. Tudor	6	6	1	134	70	0	1	26.80	2
D. A. Kenway	8	11	2	206	60	1	0	22.89	4/1
S. P. Kirby	7	3	2	13	13	0	0	13.00	2
R. J. Sidebottom	5	2	1	13	13	0	0	13.00	2
A. Flintoff	1	1	0	8	8	0	0	8.00	1
C. T. Tremlett	6	5	0	25	23	0	0	5.00	1
S. J. Harmison	7	4	2	2	1*	0	0	1.00	3
S. P. Jones	6	1	0	1	1	0	0	1.00	0

BOWLING

	O	M	R	W	BB	5W/i	10W/m	Avge
R.J. Sidebottom	76.2	20	208	15	4/23	0	0	13.87
S.J. Harmison	114.7	12	493	21	4/61	0	0	23.48
C.P. Schofield	88.4	11	387	15	5/72	1	0	25.80
I.R. Bell	80.7	11	340	13	5/22	1	0	26.15
S.P. Jones	56.5	14	189	7	6/48	1	0	27.00
A. Flintoff	5	0	27	1	1/27	0	0	27.00
M.A. Wagh	128.1	21	436	15	3/42	0	0	29.07
M.J. Wood	25.1	1	92	3	2/40	0	0	30.67
C.T. Tremlett	104.5	18	308	10	3/31	0	0	30.80
S.P. Kirby	120.4	12	539	17	4/29	0	0	31.71
G.P. Swann	104.5	11	438	13	3/41	0	0	37.54
A.J. Tudor	92.2	12	378	10	3/35	0	0	37.80
O.A. Shah	5	0	37	0	–	0	0	–

Note: Not all games in this section were first-class.

TASMANIA v ECB NATIONAL ACADEMY

At Adelaide Park 25, Adelaide, November 22, 2001. ECB National Academy won by 73 runs. Toss ECB National Academy.

ECB National Academy

A.J. Strauss c McDermott b Downton	21
N. Peng lbw b Polkinghorne	50
O.A. Shah c Polkinghorne b Tubb	74
A. Flintoff b Griffith	8
*I.R. Bell c Pickering b Downton	55
M.J. Wood run out	2
M.A. Wagh b Griffith	15
D. Kenway not out	36
C.P. Schofield not out	9
B 1, l-b 8, w 14, n-b 1	24
(Overs 50) (7 wkts)	294

Fall: 47 83 94 211 223 238 255

†M.A. Wallace, S.J. Harmison and C.T. Tremlett did not bat.

Bowling: Downton 9–0–50–2; Pascoe 5–1–35–0; Griffith 10–1–47–2; Polkinghorne 7–1–46–1; Tubb 9–0–52–1; Pickering 10–0–55–0.

Tasmania

S.R. Mason b Flintoff	37
*M.G. Dighton b Tremlett	17
G.T. Cunningham c Flintoff b Bell	27
G.J. Bailey lbw b Bell	0
B.J. Thomas b Wagh	19
A.W. Polkinghorne b Schofield	27
S.B. Tubb st Wallace b Schofield	7
†S.T. McDermott c Strauss b Wagh	20
M.D. Pascoe b Wagh	2
A.G. Downton run out	36
K.S. Pickering not out	8
L-b 3, w 18	21
(44.5 overs)	221

Fall: 38 89 90 96 142 150 155 160 200 221

Bowling: Harmison 7–0–46–0; Tremlett 8.5–1–31–1; Flintoff 5–0–27–1; Schofield 10–3–46–2; Bell 4–0–26–2; Wagh 10–0–42–3.

Umpires: J.S. Booth and R.A. Falk.

SOUTH AUSTRALIA SECOND XI v ECB NATIONAL ACADEMY

At Adelaide Oval No. 2, Adelaide, November 28, 2001. ECB National Academy won by 70 runs. Toss: South Australia Second XI.

ECB National Academy

D. A. Kenway b King	5	
R. W. T. Key run out	4	
M. A. Wagh b King	8	
O. A. Shah c Vaughan b Rowe	35	
A. J. Strauss c Vaugha b Adcock	56	
N. Peng c Deitz b Parrish	39	
I. R. Bell run out	0	
G. P. Swann c Williams b Parrish	16	

C. P. Schofield not out	30
*†M. A. Wallace b King	36
S. J. Harmison b King	0
L-B 3, w 7 n-b 2	11
(48.3 overs)	240

S. P. Kirby did not bat.

Fall: 7 10 31 84 143 143 168 177 237 240

Bowling: King 9.3–1–49–4; Southam 5–0–24–0; Rowe 9–0–41–1; Adcock 10–0–44–1; Marsh 2–0–23–0; Parrish 10–0–39–2; Thomas 3–0–17–0.

South Australian Second XI

L. Williams c Wallace b Harmison	14	
*J. M. Vaughan c and b Bell	18	
D. J. Harris c Wallace b Bell	4	
W. D. Thomas b Harmison	32	
N. T. Adcock c (sub) M. J. Wood b Bell	19	
†S. A. Deitz b Bell	0	
J. D. Borgas c Schofield b Bell	0	
J. T. Southam not out	50	

J. I. Marsh c and b Swann	4
N. Rowe c Wagh b Swann	7
M. D. King b Swann	0
B 1, l-b 1, w 16, n-b 4	22
(41 overs)	170

C. Parrish did not bat.

Fall: 38 51 52 81 81 81 141 149 159 170

Bowling: Harmison 10–1–42–2; Harmison 7–0–29–0; Bell 10–2–22–5; Schofield 5–0–21–0; Shah 3–0–13–0; Swann 6–0–41–3.

Umpires: J. S. Booth and G. Duperouzel.

AUSTRALIAN CRICKET ACADEMY v ECB NATIONAL ACADEMY

At Henley Oval, Henley, December 3, 4, 5, 2001. ECB National Academy won by an innings and 31 runs. Toss: Australian Cricket Academy.

Close of play: First day, ECB National Academy (1) 4-374 (Bell 49, Kenway 13); Second day Australian Cricket Academy (1) 4-217 (Welsford 27, Smith 14).

ECB National Cricket Academy

A. J. Strauss run out (sub T. J. Cooley)	113	
M. J. Wood c Phillips b Thistle	3	
R. W. T. Key c Thistle b Smith	177	
O. A. Shah b Tueon	11	
I. R. Bell run out (Betts)	104	
D. A. Kenway c Betts b Coombes	60	
G. P. Swann c Ronchi b Bandy	77	

C. P. Schofield run out (Sainsbury)	35
*†M. A. Wallace not out	4
B 1, l-b 4, w 8, n-b 4	17
(143.4 overs) (8 wkts dec)	601

S. J. Harmison, S. P. Kirby and C. T. Tremlett did not bat.

Fall: 21 241 279 325 474 483 592 601

Bowling: Thistle 10–1–34–1; Scott 22–4–120–0; Tueon 20–2–90–1; Bandy 15–3–68–1; Coombes 52–7–183–1; Betts 3–1–20–0; Phillips 2–0–13–0; Smith 18–2–61–1; Brewster 1.4–0–7–0.

Australian Cricket Academy

D. M. Betts st Wallace b Scholfield	79	– run out (Harrison) 11
A. J. Sainsbury c Kenway b Harrison	11	– lbw b Tremlett 14
S. J. Phillips lbw b Kirby	37	– c Schofield b Swann 10
*R. J. Brewster c Schofield b Swann	34	– c Key b Swann 30
T. H. Welsford c Wallace b Kirby	91	– c Bell b Tremlett 6
D. Smith c Key b Kirby	17	– c Wallace b Harrison 67
D. C. Bandy c Kenway b Kirby	58	– c Harrison b Bell 10
†L. Ronchi c Shah b Harrison	22	– c Shah b Harrison 14
M. J. Thistle b Harrison	5	– c Shah b Bell 1
D. Tueon not out	7	– b Harrison 4
A. R. Scott c Wood b Harrison	3	– not out 1
B 4, l-b 4, w 2, n-b 12	22	B 5, l-b 4, w 1, n-b 6 16

(90.2 overs)	386

Fall: 37 110 166 178 228 333 372
372 380 386

(41.3 overs)	184

Fall: 26 30 72 75 102 136 164
178 182 184

S. P. Coombes did not bat.

Bowling: *First Innings*—Harrison 17.2–1–78–4; Kirby 21–2–100–4; Tremlett 9–3–16–0; Bell 10–0–56–0; Bell 10–0–56–0; Scholfield 19–2–68–1; Swann 14–2–60–1. *Second Innings*—Harrison 10–1–42–3; Tremlett 8–1–27–2; Bell 5.3–1–28–2; Kirby 8–1–23–0; Swann 8–1–31–2; Shah 2–0–24–0.

Umpires: A. Willoughby and G. Duperouzel.

VICTORIA SECOND XI v ECB NATIONAL ACADEMY

At Melbourne Cricket Ground, Melbourne, January 21, 22, 23, 24, 2002. ECB National Academy won by 29 runs. Toss: Victoria Second XI.

Close of play: First day, ECB National Academy (1) 3-103 (Key 29, Wagh 1); Second day, Victoria Second XI (1) 4-83 (Jewell 14, Kent 0); Third day, ECB National Academy (2) 7-319 (Schofield 27, Wallace 19).

ECB National Academy

A. J. Strauss c Roach b Fleming	8	– c Roach b Fleming 5
M. J. Wood c Jewell b Fleming	7	– lbw b Davison 88
R. W. T. Key c Roach b Fleming	29	– c Roach b Robertson 7
I. R. Bell c McDonald b Fleming	48	– lbw b McGain 117
M. A. Wagh not out	74	– c Roach b Davison 11
D. A. Kenway c Roach b McDonald	7	– lbw b Harrop 6
G. P. Swann b Harrop	1	– c Jewell b Harrop 34
C. P. Schofield st Roach b McGain	49	– not out 48
*†M. A. Wallace lbw b Jewell	7	– not out 36
C. T. Tremlett lbw b Robertson	0	
S. P. Kirby c Jewell b Fleming	0	
B 5, l-b 4, w 8	17	B 1, l-b 2, w 1, n-b 2 6

(83.2 overs, 319 mins)	247

Fall: 14 15 101 106 119 126 211 233 242 247

(87.3 overs, 324 mins) (7 wkts dec)	358

Fall: 8 15 204 225 232 238 281

S. J. Harmison did not bat.

Bowling: *First Innings*—Fleming 20.2–9–36–5; Robertson 16–3–47–1; McDonald 21–7–41–1; Harrop 11–1–71–1; Davison 8–3–24–0; McGain 5–1–15–1; Jewell 2–0–4–1. *Second Innings*—Fleming 9–0–35–1; Robertson 13.3–1–57–1; Harrop 14–1–82–2; McDonald 3–0–9–0; Welsford 5–0–27–0; McGain 12–3–37–1; Davison 18–2–71–2; Jewell 9–1–24–0; Hussey 3–0–13–0; Kent 1–1–0–0.

Victoria

R.A. Bartlett c Wallace b Harmison	0	– (5) c and b Wagh	10
T.H. Welsford c Wallace b Tremlett	13	– (1) c Wallace b Harmison	17
A.B. McDonald c Bell b Kirby	29	–	
D.J. Hussey lbw b Kirby	1	– c Wallace b Harmison	112
N. Jewell c Swann b Harmison	19	– (3) c Strauss b Wagh	118
A.J. Kent c Kenway b Tremlett	0	– c Schofield b Tremlett	39
†P.J. Roach lbw b Schofield	58	– c Wallace b Harmison	30
J.M. Davison c Tremlett b Harmison	3	– (9) c Harmison b Kirby	1
*D.W. Fleming c Bell b Harmison	24	– (10) not out	10
B.E. McGain lbw b Schofield	10	–	
B.D. Harrop not out	1	–	
P.J. Dickson (did not bat)		– (2) c Wallace b Kirby	2
M.P. Simpson (did not bat)		– (8) c Wallace b Kirby	8
A.P.S. Robertson (did not bat)		– (11) c Kenway b Harmison	0
B 1, l-b 7, w 13, n-b 23	44	L-b 2, w 16, n-b 9	27

(47 overs, 211 mins)	202	(84.1 overs, 340 mins) 374
Fall: 18 40 50 81 90 93 110		Fall: 16 34 264 270 282 343 360
142 187 202		364 364 374

This match commenced with a Victorian team of 12. During its course, A.B. McDonald and B.E. McGain were selected for a Pura Cup match and were replaced by P.J. Dickson and M.P. Simpson.

Bowling: *First Innings*—Harmison 14–3–61–4; Tremlett 17–3–42–2; Kirby 11–0–71–2; Bell 2–0–5–0; Schofield 3–0–15–2. *Second Innings*—Harmison 19.1–1–79–4; Kirby 13–0–69–3; Tremlett 17–1–62–1; Bell 5–0–20–0; Swann 7–0–52–0; Schofield 5–0–30–0; Wagh 18–4–60–2.

Umpires: A.J. Barrow and A.P. Ward.

AUSTRALIAN CAPITAL TERRITORY v ECB NATIONAL ACADEMY

At Manuka Oval, Canberra, January 27, 28, 29, 30, 2002. Drawn. Toss: Australian Capital Territory.

Close of play: First day, Australian Capital Territory (1) 5-327 (Hazell 59); Second day, Australian Capital Territory (2) 2-179.

Australian Capital Territory

J.K. Smith c Wallace b Harmison	0	– (2) c Wallace b Harmison	62
†D.G. Dawson c Strauss b Bell	17	– (1) st Wallace b Wagh	105
D.S. Hazell c Key b Wagh	199	– retired hurt	1
S.A. Holcombe c Wagh b Harmison	6	– c Key b Tremlett	46
S.L. Maxwell lbw b Harmison	97	– lbw b Tudor	9
C.D. Hanna c Wallace b Wagh	6	– lbw b Wagh	1
A. Lade lbw b Kirby	2	– run out	17
*M.A. Hatton not out	51	– b Tremlett	22
T.L. Hill lbw b Wagh	0	– st Wallace b Wagh	5
B.W. Dennett c and b Kirby	5	– b Tremlett	0
E. Kellar (did not bat)		– not out	0
B 9, l-b 5, w 6, n-b 23	43	B 4, l-b 9, w 7, n-b 11	31

(126.4 overs, 486 mins)	(9 wkts) 426	(90.1 overs, 330 mins) (9 wkts dec) 299
Fall: 5 49 91 285 323 328		Fall: 114 191 219 250 255 287
410 414 426		299 299 299

D. Anderson did not bat.

Bowling: *First Innings*—Harmison 24–4–82–3; Tudor 14–4–30–0; Jones 3.2–1–3–0; Kirby 20.4–2–109–2; Bell 12–4–3–46–1; Tremlett 17–3–44–0; Wagh 29–6–78–3; Wood 6–0–20–0. *Second Innings*—Harmison 10–1–37–1; Kirby 5–1–32–0; Tudor 16–2–61–1; Tremlett 16–5–31–3; Wagh 37.1–7–106–3; Wood 6–1–19–0.

ECB National Academy

A. J. Strauss lbw b Hill	48	– c Hatton b Smith	32
M. J. Wood lbw b Hill	107	– c Dawson b Dennett	9
M. A. Wagh b Dennett	164	– c and b Hatton	73
D. A. Kenway b Dennett	18	– lbw b Smith	0
*†M. A. Wallace c Dawson b Kellar	67	–	
R. W. T. Key c Dawson b Kellar	0	– (5) not out	72
I. R. Bell c Dawson b Kellar	3	– (6) c Maxwell b Kellar	60
A. J. Tudor c Dawson b Dennett	0	– (7) not out	3
C. T. Tremlett c Dawson b Kellar	23		
S. J. Harmison b Dennett	1		
S. P. Kirby not out	0		
B 3, l-b 5, w 1, n-b 19	28	B 3, l-b 6, w 1, n-b 5	15

(109.3 overs, 409 mins)	459

(55 overs, 214 mins)	(5 wkts)	264

Fall: 111 191 244 404 404 416 417 437 459 459

Fall: 21 58 58 150 256

S. P. Jones did not bat.

Bowling: *First Innings*—Dennett 23.3–3–98–4; Kellar 23–6–75–4; Anderson 9–0–61–0; Hill 25–4–95–2; Hatton 10–2–43–0; Lade 15–0–54–0; Smith 4–0–25–0. *Second Innings*—Dennett 13–1–80–1; Kellar 14–3–45–1; Anderson 6–0–28–0; Smith 7–0–36–2; Hatton 11–1–49–1; Lade 4–0–17–0.

Umpires: A. L. Shelley and G. R. Vines.

AUSTRALIAN CAPITAL TERRITORY v ECB NATIONAL ACADEMY

At Manuka Oval, Canberra, February 2, 2002. Australian Capital Territory won on run rate. Toss: Australian Capital Territory.

Australian Capital Territory

J. K. Smith run out (Strauss/Tudor)	20	*M. A. Hatton c Harmison b Wood	18
D. M. Jeffrey c Kenway b Tudor	2	H. R. Axelby st Kenway b Bell	19
†D. G. Dawson b Strauss b Tremlett	15	A. D. Jones not out	6
S. A. Holcombe c Bell b Wagh	16	B 7, l-b 7, w 15, n-b 3	32
S. L. Maxwell b Wagh	27		
C. D. Hanna not out	79	(50 overs, 191 mins) (8 wkts)	253
A. J. Heading c Wagh b Wood	19	Fall: 10 44 45 101 104 149 207 247	

B. W. Dennett and E. Kellar did not bat.

Bowling: Tudor 10–0–50–1; Tremlett 10–1–45–1; Harmison 3–0–20–0; Bell 7–0–47–1; Wagh 10–1–38–2; Wood 10–0–40–2.

ECB National Academy

†D. A. Kenway c Dawson b Kellar	15	A. J. Tudor c Hatton b Jones	0
*R. W. T. Key b Dennett	17	C. T. Tremlett b Axelby	0
M. A. Wagh c Dawson b Kellar	0	S. J. Harmison not out	1
I. R. Bell c Dawson b Axelby	49		
M. A. Wallace run out (Axelby)	45	L-b 6, w 3, n-b 1	10
A. J. Strauss c Heading b Jones	14		
M. J. Wood c Heading b Jones	13	(28.5 overs, 124 mins)	165
S. P. Jones b Axelby	1	Fall: 35 35 37 130 143 163 163 164 164 165	

Bowling: Kellar 7–2–27–2; Jones 5–0–29–3; Dennett 3–0–10–1; Jeffrey 3–0–27–0; Smith 4–0–33–0; Hatton 3–0–20–0; Axelby 3.5–0–13–3.

Umpires: G. R. Clifton and D. B. Day.

SOUTH AUSTRALIA SECOND XI v ECB NATIONAL ACADEMY

At Pembroke School Oval, Kensington, February 11, 12, 13, 14, 2002. South Australia
Second XI won by seven wickets. Toss ECB National Academy.

ECB National Academy

*M. J. Wood c Dempsey b Marsh	94	– c Dempsey b Marsh	31
R. W. T. Key lbw b Swain	2	– c R. J. Harris b Marsh	31
M. A. Wagh b Wilson	2	– c Deitz b Marsh	0
I. R. Bell b Wilson	0	– b R. J. Harris	10
D. A. Kenway c Wilson b R. J. Harris	22	– c and b Marsh	2
N. Peng c Deitz b R. J. Harris	26	– c unknown b R. J. Harris	75
†M. A. Wallace c Deitz b Thomas	20	– c Deitz b Wilson	2
A. J. Tudor c Marsh b Adcock	35	– lbw b Wilson	70
G. P. Swann c Dempsey b Marsh	6	– c Adcock b Wilson	36
C. T. Tremlett c Adcock b Marsh	1	– b Swain	1
S. J. Harmison not out	0		
R. J. Sidebottom (did not bat).		– not out	0
L-b 2, n-b 4	6	B 4, l-b 3, n-b 3	10

(75.2 overs, 295 mins)   214
Fall: 4 9 11 58 102 153 189
    202 214 214

(83.2 overs, 324 mins)   268
Fall: 61 68 69 79 83 88 208
    261 268 268

Bowling: *First Innings*—Wilson 17–3–34–2; Swain 16–3–38–1; R.J. Harris 14–2–39–2; Thomas
12–4–49–1; Adcock 8–2–24–1; Marsh 8.2–2–28–3. *Second Innings*—Wilson 18–6–38–3; Swain
9.2–1–32–1; Marsh 26–5–99–4; R.J. Harris 18–6–41–2; Adcock 7–0–36–0; Thomas 5–1–15–0.

South Australia Second XI

L. Williams c Kenway b Tudor	25	– (2) b Tudor	13
†S. A. Deitz c Wallace b Tudor	18	– (1) c Wallace b Swann	43
D. J. Harris c Key b Swann	58	– (4) c (sub C. P. Schofield) b Wood	45
*J. M. Vaughan lbw b Sidebottom	0		
D. M. Dempsey c Tudor b Swann	64		
M. C. Miller b Wagh	18	– (5) not out	16
N. T. Adcock c Wallace b Sidebottom	67	– (3) not out	64
R. J. Harris b Wagh	1		
B. A. Swain c Wallace b Sidebottom	30		
P. Wilson c Wallace b Tudor	0		
J. I. Marsh not out	0		
L-b 8, n-b 2, w 3	13	B 6, l-b 1, n-b 1	8

(85.2 overs, 335 mins)   294
Fall: 33 64 65 147 191 211 219 291 294 294

(32.1 overs, 143 mins)   (3 wkts) 189
Fall: 26 82 169

O. C. Thomas did not bat.

Bowling: *First Innings*—Harmison 0.4–0–6–0; Tudor 14.2–3–61–3; Sidebottom 17.2–6–34–3;
Tremlett 2–0–10–0; Bell 11–4–21–0; Swann 27–4–111–2; Wagh 13–3–43–2. *Second Innings*—
Sidebottom 8–3–24–0; Tudor 4–0–30–1; Bell 2–0–18–0; Swann 8–0–51–1; Wagh 7–0–46–0; Wood
3.1–0–13–1.

Umpires: C. Hollard and L. G. Donisthorpe.

NEW SOUTH WALES INVITATIONAL XI v ECB NATIONAL ACADEMY

At David Phillips North Oval, Daceyville, February 25, 2002. ECB National Academy won on run rate. Toss: New South Wales Invitational XI.

New South Wales Invitational XI

*†N. S. Pilon lbw b Kirby	19	C. P. Eve st Wallace b Schofield	1
A. Jeffrey b Kirby	50	A. L. Fleming lbw b Swann	1
P. Maraziotis b Kirby	0	K. Connor not out	1
S. Spoljaric c Wallace b Kirby	6		
M. Schenke c Wagh b Schofield	6	L-b 8, w 12, n-b 3	23
M. W. B. Faraday st Wallace b Schofield	0		
D. T. Christian c Wood b Swann	24	(44.5 overs, 165 mins)	151
L. A. Zammit c Wagh b Schofield	20	Fall: 65 65 92 100 103 108 148 149 149 151	

Bowling: Tudor 5–1–16–0; Jones 5–1–18–0; Kirby 10–2–29–4; Sidebottom 7–0–28–0; Schofield 10–1–35–4; Swann 7.5–0–17–2.

ECB National Academy

*A. J. Strauss st Pilon b Connor	63
M. J. Wood not out	61
R. W. T. Key not out	0
L-b 4, w 4	8
(26 overs, 95 mins) (1 wkt)	132
Fall: 128	

M. A. Wagh, †M. A. Wallace, G. P. Swann, C. P. Schofield, R. J. Sidebottom, S. P. Kirby, S. P. Jones and A. J. Tudor did not bat.

Bowling: Eve 6–2–24–0; Fleming 4–1–17–0; Zammit 8–1–47–0; Christian 5–0–27–0; Connor 2–1–9–1; Spoljaric 1–0–4–0.

Umpires: J. A. Evans and W. D. Hendricks.

AUSTRALIAN CRICKET ACADEMY v ECB NATIONAL ACADEMY

At David Phillips South Oval, Daceyville, February 26, 2002. ECB National Academy won by 34 runs. Toss: ECB National Academy.

ECB National Academy

*A. J. Strauss c Petrie b Rimmington	1	G. P. Swann c and b Petrie	3
M. J. Wood c Petrie b James	69	C. P. Schofield not out	11
R. W. T. Key c Ronchi b Rimmington	0	B 1, w 14, n-b 3	18
M. A. Wagh c Coombes b Cosgrove	15		
I. R. Bell c James b Rimmington	82	(50 overs, 191 mins) (6 wkts)	234
D. A. Kenway not out	35	Fall: not available	

†M. A. Wallace, R. J. Sidebottom, S. P. Jones and A. J. Tudor did not bat.

Bowling: Petrie 10–0–50–1; Rimmington 10–0–44–3; Cosgrove 8–0–28–1; Casson 10–0–40–0; Coombes 7–0–35–0; James 5–0–36–1.

Australian Cricket Academy

D. Smith run out	34
D. M. Betts b Tudor	0
T. R. Birt lbw b Bell	17
R. J. Brewster b Sidebottom	61
†L. Ronchi c Tudor b Swann	50
*T. H. Welsford b Jones	13
M. J. Cosgrove c Jones b Tudor	0
B. Casson b Tudor	0
N. J. Rimmington b Sidebottom	4
S. P. Coombes not out	2
A. C. L. James lbw b Sidebottom	0
L-b 5, w 12, n-b 2	19
(39 overs, 158 mins)	200
Fall: not available	

M. J. Petrie did not bat.

Bowling: Tudor 8–0–35–3; Jones 7–1–34–1; Bell 5–1–25–1; Sidebottom 7–0–21–3; Schofield 4–0–31–0; Seann 5–0–3–1; Wagh 3–0–19–0.

Umpires: L. G. Donisthorpe and C. Hollard.

NEW SOUTH WALES INSTITUTE OF SPORT COLTS v ECB NATIONAL ACADEMY

At David Phillips South Oval, Daceyville, February 28, 2002. ECB National Academy won by six wickets. Toss: ECB National Academy.

New South Wales Institute of Sport Colts

J. N. Burke c Kirby b Sidebottom	15
*N. J. Catalano c Wallace b Sidebottom	30
D. S. Wotherspoon c Strauss b Sidebottom	6
S. J. Phillips b Kirby	2
K. J. J. Luiters b Sidebottom	26
S. D. Stanton b Bell	6
J. J. Krejza run out (Peng)	25
M. J. Baker not out	4
K. M. Daley not out	0
L-b 5, w 1, n-b 1	7
(37 overs, 143 mins) (7 wkts)	121
Fall: 34 41 44 60 71 112 118	

†J. Allsopp, P. M. Wooden and D. Bollinger did not bat.

Bowling: Kirby 8–2–15–1; Jones 7–0–29–0; Sidebottom 8–2–23–4; Bell 7–0–26–1; Swann 6–0–19–0; Wagh 1–0–4–0.

ECB National Academy

*A. J. Strauss lbw b Daley	15
M. J. Wood c Phillips b Baker	3
R. W. T. Key c Baker b Bollinger	38
M. A. Wagh lbw b Krejza	5
I. R. Bell not out	29
N. Peng not out	26
L-b 1, w 4, n-b 2	7
(34.2 overs, 138 mins) (4 wkts)	123
Fall: 8 46 63 66	

†M. A. Wallace, G. P. Swann, C. P. Schofield, R. J. Sidebottom, S. P. Jones and S. P. Kirby did not bat.

Bowling: Daley 8–1–26–1; Baker 7–1–25–1; Wooden 3–0–17–0; Bollinger 8–0–19–1; Krejza 7–1–26–1; Luiters 1.2–0–9–0.

Umpires: D. Goodger and J. A. Evans.

WESTERN AUSTRALIA SECOND XI v ECB NATIONAL ACADEMY

At Abbett Park, Scarborough, March 10, 11, 12, 13, 2002. ECB National Academy won by 112 runs. Toss: ECB National Academy.

Close of play: First day, ECB National Academy (1) 7-309 (Swann 28, Schofield 11); Second day, Western Australia Second XI (1) 7-249 (Ronchi 73, Thorp 18); Third day, Western Australian Second XI (2) 0-71 (Jones 27, Simmons 26).

ECB National Academy

A.J. Strauss c Ronchi b Thorp	3	– b Jacques	52
M.J. Wood c Ronchi b Johnston	14	– run out (Jones/Ronchi)	112
R.W.T. Key c Ronchi b Robinson	78	– not out	87
M.A. Wagh c Jones b Robinson	98	– not out	10
*I.R. Bell c Harvey b Robinson	18		
†M.A. Wallace c Bandy b Thorp	26		
A.J. Tudor c Bandy b Johnston	26		
G.P. Swann run out (Thorp)	65		
C.P. Schofield b Johnston	49		
R.J. Sidebottom c Ronchi b Jones	13		
S.P. Kirby not out	13		
B 4, n-b 6	10	B 1, l-b 1, n-b 11	13

(132 overs, 494 mins)	413	(61 overs, 223 mins) (2 wkts dec)	274

Fall: 4 35 157 201 222 258 292 385 387 413   Fall: 108 251

S.P. Jones did not bat.

Bowling: *First Innings*—James 13-3-55-0; Thorp 30-12-72-2; Johnston 18-5-49-3; Jacques 9-1-23-0; Casson 24-5-83-0; Bandy 7-2-16-0; Robinson 20-2-82-3; Jones 11-3-29-1. *Second Innings*—James 5-2-21-0; Thorp 9-1-26-0; Johnston 9-1-49-0; Jacques 8-0-32-1; Casson 12-1-59-0; Jones 13-0-52-0; Robinson 5-0-33-0.

Western Australia Second XI

C.J. Simmons c Key b Schofield	85	– (2) b Sidebottom	49
B.D. Jones run out (Jones/Wallace)	7	– (1) c Strauss b Schofield	64
G.I. Cullen c Swann b Jones	26	– b Sidebottom	10
*K.M. Harvey lbw b Jones	19	– b Tudor	0
D.C. Bandy c Wallace b Jones	2	– c Sidebottom b Schofield	56
†L. Ronchi b Jones	83	– c Wallace b Sidebottom	45
B. Casson b Jones	1	– c Wood b Schofield	35
W. Robinson lbw b Sidebottom	8	– b Schofield	2
C.D. Thorp not out	28	– c Sidebottom b Schofield	8
M.W. Johnston b Sidebottom	1	– c and b Swann	0
A.C.L. James b Jones	0		
S.W.T. Jacques (did not bat)		– not out	7
B 7, l-b 1, n-b 9	19	B 7, l-b 1, n-b 12	20

(74.3 overs, 312 mins)	279	(75.4 overs, 299 mins)	296

Fall: 32 106 144 146 146 147 187   Fall: 87 103 105 162 226 249 252
    265 278 279   260 272 296

Bowling: *First Innings*—Tudor 9-0-62-0; Kirby 8-1-23-0; Sidebottom 18-7-45-2; Swann 4-1-22-0; Jones 19.3-7-48-6; Schofield 16-2-69-1. *Second Innings*—Tudor 12-2-33-1; Kirby 9-1-39-0; Jones 15-4-57-0; Schofield 16.4-3-72-5; Swann 12-3-54-1; Sidebottom 11-2-33-3.

Umpires: J.K. Brookes and. T. Rann.

AUSTRALIAN UNDER-19s, 2001-02

By KEN PIESSE

A bonus for the best players in the Commonwealth Bank national Under-19s championships in Newcastle was selection in Australia's 14-man squad which contested the Under-19s World Cup in New Zealand in January and February. In defeating Queensland in the final by 22 runs, New South Wales won their tenth national championship. Tasmania were third, ensuring their place in Division 1 in 2002-03. Victoria were fourth, Western Australia fifth, South Australia sixth, Northern Territory seventh and Australian Capital Territory eighth. In a tournament where the quality of pitches did not always match the quality of the hospitality, low scores were the norm, teams batting first generally having the better of the conditions. The wickets outside the Newcastle Sportsground were particularly low and dusty.

The Victorian wicket-keeper, 17-year-old Adam Crosthwaite, was player of the championships with the highest aggregate of 296 runs, plus nine catches and one stumping. He was named in the World Cup squad despite not being among the initial 25 squad members leading into the carnival. Unlike most of his team-mates, who play at first-grade standard, he had been playing for the second XI at his club team Richmond, and was still eligible to play at Under-17s level.

New South Wales were unbeaten for the tournament and had the best-balanced team. Daniel Christian was a dominating presence in the final, scoring 68 and taking the last wicket, while Brad Rowarth was equally important with 37 and 3/43. Rowarth also made some significant earlier contributions, with 86 against Victoria in round one and a carefree 82 from 54 balls, including eight fours and five sixes, against Western Australia. The captain, Jarrad Burke, played some audacious knocks, scoring strongly square of the wicket. In the semi-final against South Australia, Jason Krejza made 200 not out in a nine-hour marathon, having batted at number 10 earlier in the tournament. Left-hander Brett Eriksson's opening-day century against Victoria was a superb knock and he supplemented his batting with handy leg-breaks.

As the tournament's only unbeaten side and leading qualifier, New South Wales had the luxury of being able to bat for more than an hour into the second day of the final, ensuring that Queensland would not only have to chase 243, but also score at more than three an over. In reply Queensland's Aaron Maynard and Greg Moller shared a third-wicket stand of 65 but once they were separated only some belligerent lower-order hitting from Scott Brant kept the side within touch. The last two wickets added 65 before Luke Davis was run out and Brant bowled, ensuring New South Wales their first title since 1998-99.

New South Wales had comfortably defeated the Queenslanders in an earlier meeting, the left-handed Burke motoring to 104. In that game Brant and Davis shared a face-saving 62-run stand for the last wicket after Queensland had slumped to nine for 105 chasing 232. The closest New South

Wales came to defeat was in the very first game against the Victorians. Chasing 311 for victory, the Victorians recovered from four for 38 overnight to make 267. Despite a deteriorating wicket on the second day, Crosthwaite with 74 was in irresistible touch, his straight driving down the ground a feature. He received excellent support from Aaron Connaughton, Leigh Murphy and Paul Boraston.

The Victorians, in particular, struggled to adapt to the slower and lower Newcastle pitches. They were happiest playing on the Sportsground wickets which provided more bounce for their pace men. Robert Cassell was the outstanding strike bowler for the carnival with 14 wickets at 12.50, demonstrating that he had fully recovered from back and knee injuries which in the previous two seasons had seen him spend more time recuperating than playing. In New Zealand, where he bowled mainly into the wind, his fastest deliveries were timed at over 130 km/h. Mark Simpson, who captained the side, took 12 wickets at 13.33 including a best of 6/29 against South Australia. Cameron White did not play because of his selection for the Prime Minister's XI. He did, however, captain the Australian Under-19s World Cup team.

Tasmania's Clinton Viney returned the best figures of the carnival with 6/20 against Western Australia. Team-mate Xavier Doherty claimed 5/33 from 28.1 overs against Northern Territory. The leading wicket-takers for the carnival were the Northern Territory's 17-year-old wrist-spinner Ryan LeLoux and Western Australia's chinaman bowler Beau Casson. Each claimed 18 wickets in five matches, LeLoux averaging a wicket every 24 balls. A third of his overs were maidens. With more than 120 overs, Casson bowled the longest spells of the carnival.

Northern Territory's Ken Skewes, who had only just turned 17, was among the leading run-makers with 257 including 174 not out against Tasmania. Along with LeLoux and another highly promising youngster, South Australia's Callum Ferguson, he also appeared in the Under-17s titles in Melbourne in the new year.

The most assured batsman of the carnival was Western Australia's Shaun Marsh, who averaged almost 40 over the five games. A first-class debutant in 2000-01, he appeared in particularly fine form in a fiercely contested game against Victoria only to be unluckily given out leg-before for 25. He was one of five Western Australian players to be adjudged leg-before in a team score of eight for 228, highlighted by Aaron Heal's match-winning 100 not out. Craig Simmons scored 108 and was eighth out in a team score of 245 in a drawn encounter with Queensland.

South Australia's Tom Plant carried his bat in making 63 not out in five hours in a low-scoring game against Tasmania at Miller Field. In reply to Tasmania's 127, South Australia made 132. Plant also batted through the innings for 160 not out until a declaration at six for 326 against Australian Capital Territory.

Australian Capital Territory's Daniel Callaghan made 114 not out in the wooden-spoon play-off against Northern Territory. Team-mate Michael Shaw was the leading wicket-taker with 11, including six in one game.

This season several of the best-performed players were rewarded with representative selection, including for the first time Scott Brant, George Bailey and Xavier Doherty. Harare-born Brant was promoted into Queensland's Pura Cup team after injuries to key new-ball bowlers. Having lived in Australia for only three years, Brant was ineligible for the World Cup on residential grounds, but he played for the winning team in the final of the Pura Cup. Bailey, a well-organised right-handed batsman, debuted successfully for Tasmania in the ING Cup, while Doherty played impressively in four matches for Tasmania, including two at Pura Cup level.

Team coaches were Greg Irvine (Australian Capital Territory), David Freedman (New South Wales), Graham House (Northern Territory), Mark McLatchey (Queensland), Peter Muggleton (South Australia), Alister de Winter (Tasmania), Neil Buszard (Victoria) and Doug Harris (Western Australia).

ROUND ONE

Group A

At Cahill Oval, Belmont, December 3, 4, 2001. New South Wales won on first innings. Toss: New South Wales. New South Wales 310 (B. A. Eriksson 104*, B. Roworth 76, J. N. Burke 64, M. W. B. Faraday 34; R. J. Cassell 4/29, S. M. Jones 3/81, B. T. Anderton 2/46); Victoria 267 (A. J. Crosthwaite 74, A. Connaughton 51, P. M. Boraston 44, L. Murphy 37; A. L. Fleming 3/25, B. A. Eriksson 3/55, J. J. Krejza 2/68.

At Harker Oval, New Lambton, December 3, 4, 2001. Drawn. Toss: Queensland. Western Australia 245 (C. J. Simmons 108, S. E. Marsh 41, A. Heal 33*; N. J. Rimmington 5/50); Queensland six for 187 (C. J. McCabe 53*, N. J. Kruger 42; B. Casson 4/58).

Group B

At No. 2 Sports Ground, Newcastle, December 3, 4, 2001. South Australia won on first innings. Toss: South Australia. South Australia six for 326 declared (T. C. Plant 160*, C. J. Borgas 61; D. Callaghan 3/39, D. D'Cruz 3/88) and two for 65; Australian Capital Territory 182 (S. A. Holcombe 86, W. J. P. Baker 33; M. J. Cosgrove 3/27, B. J. Pahl 3/28, T. P. Kelly 2/21).

At No. 1 Sports Ground, Newcastle, December 3, 4, 2001. Tasmania won on first innings. Toss: Tasmania. Tasmania 130 (T. D. Paine 34, L. Butterworth 30; L. Mauger 2/17, M. Keith 2/20); Australian Capital Territory 384 (K. J. Skewes 174*, L. Mauger 93; B. W. Hilfenhaus 2/47, L. Butterworth 2/65).

ROUND TWO

Group A

At Lorn Park, Maitland, December 5, 6, 2001. New South Wales won on first innings. Toss: Queensland. New South Wales 272 (J. N. Burke 104, M. W. B. Faraday 48; A. P. Maynard 3/28, S. A. Brant 3/31); Queensland 167 (S. A. Brant 39, L. R. Davis 33*; A. L. Fleming 3/26, J. J. Krejza 3/42) and four for 154 (N. J. Kruger 41, A. P. Maynard 33, M. C. Bragg 32*; J. N. Burke 2/28).

At No. 1 Sports Ground, Newcastle, December 5, 6, 2001. Western Australia won on first innings. Toss: Western Australia. Victoria 211 (A.J. Crosthwaite 70, P.J. Dickson 68, M.G. Simpson 30; B. Casson 4/55, A.C.L. James 2/49, T. Crook 2/59); Western Australia eight for 228 (A. Heal 100*, B. Casson 37; S.M. Jones 2/35, B.T. Anderton 2/42, R.J. Cassell 2/54).

Group B

At Miller Field, Belmont, December 5, 6, 2001. South Australia won on first innings. Toss: South Australia. Tasmania 127 (D. Anderson 28, B. Coombs 23*; M.R. Burr 4/44, C. Duval 2/13, S.W. Tait 2/15) and six for 74 (G.J. Bailey 27, X.J. Doherty 24; T.P. Kelly 3/24); South Australia 132 (T.C. Plant 63*; C.J. Borgas 35; B.W. Hilfenhaus 3/44, C. Viney 2/7, L. Butterworth 2/35, X.J. Doherty 2/39).

At University Oval, Callaghan, December 5, 6, 2001. Northern Territory won on first innings. Toss: Northern Territory. Australian Capital Territory 109 (J. Haywood 21, R. Humphreys 21; M. Keith 4/15, R. LeLoux 3/18, L. Mauger 2/33); Northern Territory six for 345 (Z.T. Pacey 120, M.M. Brown 87, S. McNally 48, R. LeLoux 45).

ROUND THREE

Group A

At No. 1 Sports Ground, Newcastle, December 9, 2001. Queensland won by four wickets. Toss: Victoria. Victoria 148 (A.J. Crosthwaite 45*, G.J. Kellar 26, P. Petricola 26; C.L. McCabe 2/21, J.P. Loader 2/22, S.A. Brant 2/24); Queensland six for 152 (A.P. Maynard 57; S.M. Jones 2/26).

At No. 2 Sports Ground, Newcastle, December 9, 2001. New South Wales won by 38 runs. Toss: New South Wales seven for 273 (B. Roworth 82, M.W.B. Faraday 43, J.N. Burke 37; B. Casson 3/44, R.J. Slowey 2/22); Western Australia nine for 235 (C.J. Simmons 82, S.E. Marsh 64; J.J. Krejza 3/46, J.N. Burke 2/37, A.C. Bird 2/38).

Group B

At Cahill Oval, Belmont, December 9, 2001. Tasmania won by 94 runs. Toss: Australian Capital Territory. Tasmania 163 (G.J. Bailey 34, L. Butterworth 34*; J. Haywood 3/12, M.E.L. Shaw 2/24, D.C. Pascoe 2/51); Australian Capital Territory 69 (W.J.P. Baker 31; X.J. Doherty 3/3, B. Coombs 2/7, C. Viney 2/17).

At Wallsend Oval, Wallsend, December 9, 2001. South Australia won by 71 runs. Toss: Northern Territory. South Australia 153 (Extras 33, C.J. Ferguson 31; R. LeLoux 4/28, L. Mauger 2/17); Northern Territory 82 (S. McNally 23, L. Mauger 21; M.J. Cosgrove 3/13, C. Duval 3/21).

All Round Three games scheduled for December 8, 9, 2001 were abandoned due to rain and were re-scheduled as limited-overs games for December 9.

QUALIFYING FINALS

At University Oval, Callaghan, December 11, 12, 2001. New South Wales won on first innings. Toss: New South Wales. New South Wales nine for 401 declared (J.J. Krejza 200*, S.G. Karam 73; T.P. Kelly 3/64, C. Duval 2/40, M.J. Cosgrove 2/86); South Australia 136 (M.J. Cosgrove 34, C.J. Borgas 24; A.C. Bird 4/38, B.A. Eriksson 3/43, A.L. Fleming 2/21).

At No. 2 Sports Ground, Newcastle, December 11, 12, 2001. Drawn. Toss: Queensland. Queensland eight for 415 declared (J.C. Nielsen 112, C.A. Philipson 94, G.D. Moller 75, C.J. McCabe 56; J. Allenby 2/16, T. Crook 2/80, B. Casson 2/110).

At Lorn Park, Maitland, December 11, 12, 2001. Tasmania won on first innings. Toss: Northern Territory. Northern Territory 177 (S. Chatto 40, S. McNally 36; X.J. Doherty 5/33, S. Paske 3/18); Tasmania 357 (G.J. Bailey 110, D. Anderson 102; R. LeLoux 4/63).

At Miller Field, Belmont, December 11, 12, 2001. Victoria won on first innings. Toss: Victoria. Victoria nine for 290 declared (A. Connaughton 68, S.F. Hill 62, L. Murphy 51, S.M. Jones 34; D. Callaghan 3/38, D. D'Cruz 3/58) and four for 51); Australian Capital Territory 67 (J. Haywood 21; M.G. Simpson 3/7, R.J. Cassell 3/20, S.M. Jones 2/11).

CONSOLATION FINALS

AUSTRALIAN CAPITAL TERRITORY v NORTHERN TERRITORY

At Harker Oval, New Lambton, December 13, 14, 2001. Northern Territory won on first innings. Toss: Northern Territory.
Close of Play: First day, Australian Capital Territory 9-233 (Callaghan 114).

Australian Capital Territory

*†S.A. Halcombe b Bayly	7	D. Callaghan not out	114
W.J.P. Baker c LeLoux b Mauger	14	R. Humphreys c Bayly b Ingall	28
D.C. Pascoe run out	12	D. D'Cruz c Brown b Ingall	0
C. Hamill lbw b Mauger	16	B 17, l-b 5	22
M.E.L. Shaw c McNally b LeLoux	10		—
J. Haywood c Pacey b LeLoux	2	(89.3 overs, 320 mins) (9 wkts dec)	233
D.A. King c Chatto b LeLoux	8	Fall: 12 32 53 66 66 79 84 225 233	

D.J. Reynolds and M.K. Rice did not bat.

Bowling: Bayly 10–1–28–1; Hartley 10–1–16–0; Skewes 12–3–39–0; Mauger 24–10–53–2; LeLoux 17–6–31–3; Ingall 9.3–2–21–2; Richards 3–0–14–0; McNally 3–0–8–0; Chatto 1–0–1–0.

Northern Territory

J.G. McKay st Holcombe b Shaw	8	R. LeLoux b Shaw	0
D.W. Richards c and b Shaw	40	N.M. Ingall not out	31
*S. McNally c Baker b Pascoe	31	C. Hartley not out	10
S. Chatto c and b Shaw	8		
K.J. Skewes b Shaw	48	B 1, l-b 7, w 2, n-b 1	11
†M.M. Brown c Holcombe b Hamill	14		
Z.T. Pacey lbw b D'Cruz	32	(111 overs, 394 mins) (9 wkts)	234
L. Mauger c D'Cruz b Shaw	1	Fall: 32 78 86 101 150 161 163 165 219	

T. Bayly did not bat.

Bowling: D'Cruz 17–3–46–1; Rice 12–4–25–0; Reynolds 6–1–13–0; Pascoe 27–12–46–1; Callaghan 8–3–13–0; Shaw 31–16–45–6; Humphreys 6–3–19–0; Haywood 2–0–8–0; Hamill 2–0–11–1.

Umpires: K.J. McGinniss and R. Raynor.

SOUTH AUSTRALIA v VICTORIA

At No. 2 Sports Ground, Newcastle, December 13, 14, 2001. Victoria won on first innings. Toss: Victoria.

Close of Play: First day, Victoria 4-93 (Petricola 16, Crosthwaite 17).

South Australia

J. Carson c Connaughton b Simpson	16	C. Duval lbw b Simpson 0
T.C. Plant c Jones b Cassell	4	B.J. Pahl not out 15
C.J. Ferguson c Connaughton b Cassell	4	S.W. Tait b Cassell 1
*C.J. Borgas c and b Simpson	23	
S. Smith c Kellar b Simpson	5	B 5, l-b 2, n-b 2 9
M.J. Cosgrove c Crosthwaite b Simpson	91	
†M. Wake c Crosthwaite b Cassell	1	(64.3 overs, 263 mins) 175
M.R. Burr c Kellar b Simpson	6	Fall: 7 13 39 50 71 89 139 139 162 175

T.P. Kelly did not bat.

Bowling: Cassell 15.3–2–43–4; Anderton 15–5–45–0; Simpson 16–6–29–6; Boraston 9–2–30–0; Petricola 8–1–19–0; Connaughton 1–0–2–0.

Victoria

P.J. Dicson lbw b Pahl	11	S.F. Hill not out 26
G.J. Kellar c Burr b Kelly	22	L. Murphy lbw b Tait 4
*M.G. Simpson lbw b Pahl	4	B 4, l-b 17, n-b 4 25
A. Connaughton c Duval b Tait	7	
P. Petricola c Ferguson b Pahl	54	(58.3 overs, 242 mins) (7 wkts) 252
†A.J. Crosthwaite c Borgas b Ferguson	99	Fall: 27 47 47 58 177 239 252

P.M. Boraston, R.J. Cassell, S.M. Jones and B.T. Anderton did not bat.

Bowling: Kelly 13–5–33–1; Pahl 11–1–49–3; Burr 11–4–38–0; Tait 6.3–2–20–2; Duval 10–1–46–0; Cosgrove 4–0–20–0; Carson 1–0–15–0; Ferguson 2–0–10–1.

Umpires: J.S. Booth and T.P. Laycock.

TASMANIA v WESTERN AUSTRALIA

At Cahill Oval, Belmont, December 13, 14, 2001. Tasmania won on first innings. Toss: Western Australia.

Close of Play: First day, Tasmania 1-24 (Aird 4).

Western Australia

C.J. Simmons lbw b Hilfenhaus	20	T. Crook c Paine b Viney 0
J. Allenby c Aird b Viney	6	A.C.L. James lbw b Viney 17
*S.E. Marsh b Little b Butterworth	17	R.J. Slowey not out 16
B. Casson c Paine b Viney	19	
S. Walters c Coombs b Viney	2	B 2, l-b 8, w 3, n-b 1 14
M. Swart c Knight b Butterworth	10	
†D. Weston c Paine b Viney	1	(91.2 overs, 250 mins) 123
A. Heal c Aird b Coombs	1	Fall: 24 49 49 55 74 84 85 86 91 123

A. Crawford did not bat.

Bowling: Hilfenhaus 16–7–30–1; Paske 20–5–25–0; Butterworth 20–8–24–2; Viney 19.2–7–20–6; Bailey 3–1–3–0; Coombs 12–7–3–0; Bennett 1–0–3–0.

Tasmania

N. Aird c Weston b Crook	5	C. Viney c Weston b Slowey	0
*D. Anderson lbw b Casson	18	B. Coombs c Simmons b Casson	0
T.D. Paine c Crook b Slowey	52	B.H. Hilfenhaus not out	2
*G.J. Bailey c Simmons b Casson	15	B 2, l-b 3, n-b 4	9
M. Knight c Weston b Casson	19		
T. Little not out	15	(70 overs, 372 mins) (8 wkts)	141
L. Butterworth c Allenby b Casson	6	Fall: 18 39 68 117 117 129 130 137	

M. Bennett and S. Paske did not bat.

Bowling: James 10–3–19–0; Crawford 8–3–14–0; Crook 11–3–21–1; Casson 31–8–71–5; Heal 1–0–6–0; Slowey 8–5–5–2; Allenby 1–1–0–0.

Umpires: G.R. Clifton and S.A. Reed.

CHAMPIONSHIP FINAL

NEW SOUTH WALES v QUEENSLAND

At No. 1 Sports Ground, Newcastle, December 13, 14, 2001. New South Wales won on first innings. Toss: New South Wales.
Close of Play: First day, New South Wales 8-210 (Christian 56, Allsopp 12).

New South Wales

R.J.G. Lockyear c Bragg b Brant	14	G. Geise lbw b Loader	22
J.J. Krejza c Nielsen b McCabe	29	†J.B. Allsopp c Nielsen b Summers	28
*J.N. Burke c Nielsen b Rimmington	1	A.C. Bird not out	1
M.W.B. Faraday b Rimmington	0		
S.G. Karam c Bragg b Loader	29	L-b 8, w 2, n-b 1	11
B.A. Eriksson c Bragg b Loader	2		
B. Roworth c Philipson b Maynard	37	(123 overs, 432 mins)	242
D.T. Christian lbw b Summers	68	Fall: 29 41 41 57 69 82 131 173 241 242	

A.L. Fleming did not bat.

Bowling: Brant 28–9–52–1; Loader 22–10–39–3; Rimmington 14–4–46–2; Summers 5–1–9–2; McCabe 16–5–28–1; Davis 24–12–30–0; Maynard 10–3–25–1; Philipson 4–2–5–0.

Queensland

N.J. Kruger c Karam b Bird	9	N.J. Rimmington c Christian b Bird	4
A.P. Maynard c Burke b Roworth	42	S.A. Brant b Christian	49
*C.A. Philipson c Allsopp b Fleming	8	C. Summers not out	3
G.D. Moller run out	35		
J.C. Nielsen c Eriksson b Roworth	0	B 1, l-b 1, w 1, n-b 1	4
C.J. McCabe c Allsopp b Roworth	16		
†M.C. Bragg b Roworth	19	(65.1 overs, 237 mins)	220
L.R. Davis run out	31	Fall: 13 28 93 93 98 126 142 155 196 220	

J.P. Loader did not bat.

Bowling: Bird 16–1–66–2; Fleming 15–2–54–1; Christian 2.1–0–7–1; Krejza 7–1–19–0; Roworth 10–2–43–4; Eriksson 4–2–6–0; Burke 11–3–23–0.

Umpires: A.R. Craig and J. Ward.

UNDER-19s CRICKET CHAMPIONSHIPS RECORDS

CHAMPIONSHIP WINNERS

Series	Venue	Winner	Player of the Year
1969-70	Melbourne	Victoria	no award
1970-71	Sydney	Victoria	no award
1971-72	Adelaide	Victoria	R. Wallace (Qld)
1972-73	Canberra	New Zealand	G.C. Hughes (NSW)
1973-74	Melbourne	South Australia	D.W. Hookes (SAust)
1974-75	Brisbane	Victoria	D. Brown (Qld)
1975-76	Perth	New South Wales	D.M. Wellham (NSW)
1976-77	Hobart	New Zealand	J.J. Crowe (NZ)
1977-78	Christchurch	New South Wales	P.S. Clifford (NSW)
1978-79	Sydney	Western Australia	R.J. Thomas (NZ)
1979-80	Adelaide	Western Australia/Victoria	M.D. Crowe (NZ)
1980-81	Brisbane	Victoria	D. Knox (NSW)
1981-82	Canberra	Victoria	M.R.J. Veletta (WAust)
1982-83	Perth	Victoria	I.A. Healy (Qld)
1983-84	Melbourne	South Australia	S.R. Waugh (NSW)
1984-85	Hobart	Victoria	J.K. Pyke (ACT)
1985-86	Sydney	Queensland/New South Wales	J.C. Scuderi (Qld)
1986-87	Adelaide	New South Wales	G.R. Parker (Vic)
1987-88	Brisbane	Western Australia	R.C. Kelly (WAust)
1988-89	Canberra	New South Wales	M.G. Bevan (ACT)
1989-90	Melbourne	New South Wales	J.E.R. Gallian (NSW)
1990-91	Sydney	South Australia	A.C. Gilchrist (NSW)
1991-92	Perth	Western Australia	A.D. McQuire (NSW)
1992-93	Brisbane	Victoria	J. Bray (NSW)
1993-94	Melbourne	Western Australia	J.L. Cassell (Qld)
1994-95	Sydney	Queensland/New South Wales	B.A. Clemow (NSW)
1995-96	Adelaide	Victoria	P.A. Sutherland (NSW)
1996-97	Canberra	New South Wales	D.J. McLauchlan (NSW)
1997-98	Melbourne	South Australia	G.A. Manou (SAust)
1998-99	Adelaide	New South Wales	M. Klinger (Vic)
1999-00	Perth	Victoria/Queensland	L. Buchanan (Vic)
2000-01	Hobart	Queensland	B. Casson (WAust)
2001-02	Newcastle	New South Wales	A.J. Crosthwaite (Vic)

LAST TEN YEARS' PLACINGS

	92-93	93-94	94-95	95-96	96-97	97-98	98-99	99-00	00-01	01-02
Australian Capital Territory	5	7	8	7	6	7	6	7	7	8
New South Wales	2	3	1	2	1	2	1	3	4	1
Northern Territory	7	8	7	8	8	8	8	8	8	7
Queensland	3	5	1	3	5	3	2	1	1	2
South Australia	6	4	6	5	3	1	4	5	5	6
Tasmania	8	6	5	6	7	6	7	4	6	3
Victoria	1	2	3	1	2	5	3	1	2	4
Western Australia	4	1	4	4	4	4	5	6	3	5

HIGHEST INDIVIDUAL SCORES

244	G.H. Armstrong, Australian Capital Territory v Queensland at Brisbane	1987-88
242	R.J. Davison, New South Wales v Northern Territory at Brisbane	1987-88
222*	M.P. Mott, Queensland v Northern Territory at Perth	1991-92
215*	G.S. Milliken, New South Wales v Tasmania at Perth	1982-83
214	D.A. Tuckwell, Queensland v Northern Territory at Sydney	1985-86
206*	M.L. Love, Queensland v South Australia at Brisbane	1992-93
205*	B. Zacny, ACT v Northern Territory at Melbourne	1997-98
202*	G.S. Blewett, South Australia v Northern Territory at Melbourne	1989-90
201	R. Bowden, Northern Territory v Australian Capital Territory at Sydney	1990-91
200	J.J. Krejza, New South Wales v South Australia at Newcastle	2001-02

HIGHEST PARTNERSHIP FOR EACH WICKET

318 for 1st	V.W. Williams and D.S. Wotherspoon, NSW v South Australia at Canberra .	1996-97
224 for 2nd	J. Allenby and S.E. Marsh, Western Australia v Northern Territory at Hobart .	2000-01
339 for 3rd	M. Armstrong and S.P. Heaney, ACT v Northern Territory at Perth	1999-00
240 for 4th	A.I.C. Dodemaide and A. Grant, Victoria v South Australia at Perth	1982-83
231 for 5th {	D.M. Wellham and M. Cox, NSW v Australian Capital Territory at Perth .	1975-76
	M.L. Love and A. Walduck, Queensland v Tasmania at Perth	1991-92
185 for 6th	K.K. Beazleigh and P. Holland, New South Wales v Victoria at Melbourne .	1991-92
251 for 7th	C. Mason and K.M. Harvey, Western Australia v Queensland at Melbourne .	1993-94
144 for 8th	A.J. Heading and A.C.L. James, ACT v Northern Territory at Hobart	2000-01
117 for 9th	B.A. Birrell and A. McDonald, South Australia v Tasmania at Sydney ...	1994-95
98* for 10th	S. Bannerman and J. Cooper, ACT v South Australia at Melbourne	1989-90

BEST BOWLING IN AN INNINGS

9/11	D.J. McLauchlan, New South Wales v South Australia at Canberra	1996-97
9/70	M.C. Dolman, South Australia v Western Australia at Sydney	1978-79
8/13	C. Simpson, Queensland v Northern Territory at Melbourne	1997-98
8/25	M. Reidy-Crofts, Western Australia v ACT at Adelaide	1979-80
8/31	S. Hill, Western Australia v New Zealand at Sydney	1978-79
8/41	M.L. Clews, ACT v South Australia at Melbourne	1969-70
8/46	I. Woolf, Victoria v South Australia at Adelaide	1971-72
8/49	R.J. Thomas, New Zealand v ACT at Sydney	1978-79
8/58	P. Walker, ACT v Tasmania at Adelaide	1971-72
8/78	M. White, ACT v South Australia at Sydney	1978-79
8/84	S.P. Davis, Victoria v Tasmania at Christchurch	1977-78

BEST BOWLING IN A MATCH

14/15	D.J. McLauchlan, New South Wales v South Australia at Canberra	1996-97
13/18	C. Simpson, Queensland v Northern Territory at Melbourne	1997-98
10/43	D.W. Fleming, Victoria v Northern Territory at Canberra	1988-89
10/59	A.J. De Winter, Tasmania v Western Australia at Sydney	1985-86

HAT-TRICKS

D.A. Johnston, South Australia v Tasmania at Canberra	1972-73
R. Bucholz, Queensland v Victoria at Adelaide	1979-80
H.V. Hammelman, Queensland v South Australia at Perth	1982-83
A.J. De Winter, Tasmania v Western Australia at Sydney	1985-86
M.G. Bevan, ACT v New South Wales at Adelaide	1986-87
I. Connell, Tasmania v ACT at Brisbane	1992-93
J. Southam, Northern Territory v South Australia at Adelaide	1995-96
S.G. Busbridge, South Australia v ACT at Canberra	1996-97
P.D. Waite, Western Australia v Queensland at Canberra	1996-97
D.R. Mackenzie, Queensland v South Australia at Adelaide	1998-99

UNDER-19's CRICKET CHAMPIONSHIP, 2001-02

POINTS TABLE

Group A	P	WO	W1	D	L1	LO	T	Points	Quotient
New South Wales	3	0	3	0	0	0	0	18	1.270
Queensland	3	0	1	1	1	0	0	9	1.145
Western Australia	3	0	1	1	1	0	0	9	0.899
Victoria	3	0	0	0	3	0	0	0	0.726
Group B									
South Australia	3	0	3	0	0	0	0	18	1.869
Northern Territory	3	0	2	0	1	0	0	12	2.387
Tasmania	3	0	1	0	2	0	0	6	0.704
Australian Capital Territory	3	0	0	0	3	0	0	0	0.320

Quotient = runs per wicket scored divided by runs per wicket conceded.

FINAL PLACINGS

1st	New South Wales
2nd	Queensland
3rd	Tasmania
4th	Victoria
5th	Western Australia
6th	South Australia
7th	Northern Territory
8th	Australian Capital Territory

HIGHEST INDIVIDUAL SCORE

200*	J.J. Krejza	New South Wales v South Australia at University Oval
174*	K.J. Skewes........	Northern Territory v Tasmania at No. 1 Sports Ground
160*	T.C. Plant	South Australia v Australian Capital Territory at No. 2 Sports Ground
120	Z.T. Pacey........	Northern Territory v Australian Capital Territory at University Oval
121	D. Callaghan	Australian Capital Territory v Northern Territory at Harker Oval
122	J.C. Nielsen.......	Queensland v Western Australia at No. 2 Sports Ground
123	G.J. Bailey........	Tasmania v Northern Territory at Lorn Park
108	C.J. Simmons	Western Australia v Queensland at Harker Oval
104*	B.A. Eriksson	New South Wales v Victoria at Cahill Oval
104	J.N. Burke	New South Wales v Queensland at Lorn Park
105	D. Anderson	Tasmania v Northern Territory at Lorn Park
106	A. Heal..........	Western Australia v Victoria at No. 1 Sports Ground

MOST RUNS

	M	I	NO	R	HS	100s	50s	Avge
A.J. Crosthwaite (Vic)	5	5	1	296	99	0	3	74.00
K.J. Skewes (N.T) ...	5	5	2	257	174*	1	0	85.66
T.C. Plant (SAust) ...	5	6	2	257	160*	1	1	64.25
J.J. Krejza (NSW)....	5	4	1	249	200*	1	0	83.00
J.N. Burke (NSW) ...	5	5	0	211	104	1	1	42.20
C.J. Simmons (WAust)	5	5	0	210	108	1	1	42.00
B. Roworth (NSW) ...	5	5	0	207	82	2	0	41.40
G.J. Bailey (Tas).....	5	6	0	202	110	1	0	33.66
S.E. Marsh (WAust)..	5	5	0	189	64	0	1	37.80
Z.T. Pacey (N.T).....	5	5	0	168	120	1	0	33.60

MOST WICKETS

	M	O	Mdns	R	W	BB	5W/i	10W/M	Avge
R. LeLoux (N.T)	5	72.2	23	167	18	4/27	0	0	9.27
B. Casson (WAust)	5	120.1	29	338	18	5/71	1	0	18.77
R. Cassell (Vic)	5	78	18	175	14	4/29	0	0	12.50
M.G. Simpson (Vic)	5	57	18	160	12	6/29	1	0	13.33
C. Viney (Tas)	5	62.4	18	136	12	6/20	1	0	11.33
T.P. Kelly (SAust)	5	71.1	22	172	11	3/24	0	0	15.63
M.E.L. Shaw (ACT)	5	83	30	173	11	6/45	1	0	15.72
X.J. Doherty (Tas)	3	68.1	30	75	10	5/33	1	0	7.50
D. D'Cruz (ACT)	5	86.5	15	291	10	3/58	0	0	29.10
A.L. Fleming (NSW)	4	47.5	7	146	9	3/25	0	0	16.22

BEST BOWLING IN AN INNINGS

6/20	C. Viney.	Tasmania v Western Australia at Cahill Oval
6/29	M.G. Simpson.	Victoria v South Australia at No. 2 Sports Ground
6/45	M.E.L. Shaw.	Australian Capital Territory v Northern Territory at Harker Oval
5/33	X.J. Doeherty	Tasmania v Northern Territory at Lorn Park
5/50	N.J. Rimmington. . .	Queensland v Western Australia at Harker Oval
5/71	B. Casson.	Western Australia v Tasmania at Cahill Oval

HIGHEST TOTALS

8d-415 Queensland v Western Australia at No. 2 Sports Ground
9d-401 New South Wales v South Australia at University Oval
   384 Northern Territory v Tasmania at No. 1 Sports Ground
   357 Tasmania v Northern Territory at Lorn Park
6-345 Northern Territory v Australian Capital Territory at University Oval

LOWEST TOTALS

 67 Australian Capital Territory v Victoria at Miller Field
 69 Australian Capital Territory v Tasmania at Cahill Oval
 82 Northern Territory v South Australia at Wallsend Oval
109 Australian Capital Territory v Northern Territory at University Oval
123 Western Australia v Tasmania at Cahill Oval

AUSTRALIAN UNDER-17s, 2001-02

By KEN PIESSE

In making their eighth final in ten years and winning their tenth title since the Under-17s championships were instigated in 1986-87, New South Wales maintained their presence as pace-setters in unearthing and developing the finest teenage players in the country. They were unbeaten in their first four matches before comfortably winning the R.J. Parish Trophy in the final against South Australia at the Melbourne Cricket Ground despite the fact that none of the boys, or coach David Patterson, had seen the ground before. For Patterson it was his third title in six years. Queensland finished third, Victoria fourth, Northern Territory fifth, Western Australia sixth, Tasmania seventh and Australian Capital Territory eighth.

In the final, New South Wales recovered to make 307 after the loss of openers Jed Sawkins and Ben Crawley for ducks. South Australia started promisingly enough to reach two for 70 only to be bowled out for 167, James Harford making 36 and captain Callum Ferguson 35. For New South Wales, spinners Shane Wallace took 3/49 and Vilen Sithloo 2/58.

New South Wales were the most balanced team, with significant contributions coming from six or seven players including captain Steven O'Keeffe, Sam Hinton, wicket-keeper Scott Jamieson and bowlers Joel Tuccia, Preeth John and leg-spinner Sithloo. Tim Sparke made 111 against Queensland. The team's finest moments in the qualifying games came in the closely fought match with Victoria. Replying to 243, New South Wales recovered from four for 17 before passing the Victorians with the last pair at the crease. O'Keeffe with 70 and Hinton 97 played critical roles.

Runners-up South Australia had the most prolific batsman in 17-year-old Ferguson who, in addition to scoring 135 in the first match against New South Wales, amassed a competition-high 258 not out in a one-sided semi-final against Queensland. South Australia batted for 186 overs in scoring five for 431 declared. With less than 40 overs possible in reply, Queensland had no chance, South Australia qualifying for the final because of their superior form in the opening three games. Particularly assured off the front foot and with an unflappable temperament, Ferguson's aggregate of 574 runs in five matches was also a new competition record. In the last three championships, Ferguson has amassed a record 1,078 runs. He also took six wickets at 18.50 and was judged the Kookaburra Player of the Championship.

Northern Territory boasted the other 100-plus averaging batsman in Ken Skewes, who made 415 runs in five matches at an average of 138.33. Leg-spinner Ryan LeLoux claimed ten wickets. Like Ferguson and Skewes, he also played in the Under-19s national carnival. Northern Territory had prolific openers in Michael Barry and captain Dwaine Richards, who amassed two century stands. Skewes, with 70 and four wickets and Richards, 52, also shone in the gripping consolation final against Queensland, when in reply to Northern Territory's 248, Queensland finished with eight for 248. Peter

Brown's 87 not out in a high-scoring game against Western Australia was also noteworthy.

After making four finals in five years in the late 1990s, Queensland finished in mid-list for the third consecutive year. Andrew Hicks with 123 in the consolation final against Northern Territory was his team's only centurion.

Victoria had the leading wicket-taker for the carnival in Peter Siddle from Morwell, who claimed 20 wickets, including 11/47 against South Australia. He bowled at good pace and consistently moved the ball away from the right-handers. The last Victorian to take 11 wickets in an Under-17s match was John Scholes in 1964-65. Wicket-keeper Peter Nevill claimed 19 catches and three stumpings, including eight dismissals against South Australia. The leading batsman was opener Tom Evans, who made two half-centuries on his way to a 215-run aggregate.

Western Australia created a new record score by amassing three for 342 from 74 overs having been set 341 runs to win by Northern Territory. They won with 12 overs to spare thanks to captain Theo Doropolous, who made 151 from 154 balls, and Matt Johnstone, who made 78, the pair adding a rare double-century stand for the second wicket, before Ryan Phillimore made an unbeaten century from just 74 balls and Rhys May a quick-fire 70 not out. Johnstone had a prolific fortnight, also making 167 against Tasmania and 84 against Australian Capital Territory.

Tasmania finished seventh, but played some fine cricket, wicket-keeper-captain Tim Paine to the forefront with 105 against Northern Territory. At 16 the youngest-ever state-contracted player, the gifted Tasmanian also claimed ten catches and three stumpings and played several matches at ACB Cup level. He was also part of Australia's training squad for the Under-19s World Cup. His vice-captain, left-hander Dane Anderson, scored 111 against Western Australia and 90 against Australian Capital Territory. Team-mate Shane Stewart took 4/15 in this match, and Jarrod Hughes took 5/30 against Northern Territory.

Australian Capital Territory had one of the top three bowlers in leg-spinner Sam Gaskin, who claimed 12 wickets, including 6/76 against Victoria. He bowled more overs than anyone else in the tournament. Matt Lucas's 102 not out at number eight helped Australian Capital Territory to a fighting draw against Western Australia. At one stage they were seven for 41 before recovering to eight for 242.

The wickets were generally hard and very flat, those at Melbourne Grammar, the Albert Ground and Princes Park No. 1 being particularly praised. Once again the medium-pacers were restricted to no more than six overs in a row with a good rest between spells and no more than 16 overs per day. All teams stayed at St Mary's College at Melbourne University. The championship's committee chairman was Ian Crawford from Prahran and the patron, Bob Parish, also from Prahran. The team coaches were: Andrew Dawson (Australian Capital Territory), David Patterson (New South Wales), Greg Aldam (Northern Territory), Terry Oliver (Queensland), Dean Sayers

(South Australia), Luke McCormack (Tasmania), Cameron Matthews (Victoria) and Jamie Snadden (Western Australia).

In early April, an 18-man development squad chosen by the Australian Cricket Academy's Troy Cooley and ACB youth selector Brian Taber trained at the Australian Cricket Academy for a week: Dane Anderson (Tasmania), Michael Barry (Northern Territory), Theo Doropoulos (Western Australia), Callum Ferguson (South Australia), Sam Gaskin (Australian Capital Territory), Andrew Hicks (Queensland), Sam Hinton (New South Wales), Preeth John (New South Wales), Matt Johnstone (Western Australia), Ryan LeLoux (Northern Territory), Shane Mott (New South Wales), Peter Nevill (Victoria), Tim Paine (Tasmania), Peter Siddle (Victoria), Ken Skewes (Northern Territory), Vilen Sithloo (New South Wales), Matthew Turich (Queensland) and Simon Wiesse (South Australia).

ROUND ONE

Group A

At Bill Lawry Oval, Northcote, January 4, 5, 2002. New South Wales won on first innings. Toss: New South Wales. New South Wales nine for 321 declared (T. Sparke 91, P. Forrest 55, S. Wallace 48*, V. Sithloo 34; S.C. Wiese 4/44, C.B. Bailey 3/61) defeated South Australia 253 (C.J. Ferguson 135, M. Crook 35, J.H.T. Harford 31; P. John 4/27, V. Sithloo 3/67).

At University Ground, Parkville, January 4, 5, 2002. Queensland won on first innings. Toss: Victoria. Queensland seven for 291 declared (R. Mackay 83, R.J. Neyland 58*, Z.E. Turner 43, C. La'Porte 37; L. Kentish 2/31, L. Blake 2/44) defeated Victoria 207 (T. Evans 46, N. Allan 46, P.M. Neville 42; C.J. Bilewicz 4/25, M.G.D. Turich 3/36).

Group B

At Albert Cricket Ground, Melbourne, January 4, 5, 2002. Northern Territory won on first innings. Toss: Australian Capital Territory. Australian Capital Territory 145 (P. O'Callaghan 49; R. LeLoux 3/40, K.J. Skewes 2/14, S. Mitchell 2/29); Northern Territory seven for 428 (K.J. Skewes 147*, D.W. Richards 96, M. Barry 84, R. Hodgson 32; S. Rice 2/62, A. Pascoe 2/62, S. Gaskin 2/129).

At Princes Park Oval, Carlton, January 4, 5, 2002. Western Australia won on first innings. Toss: Western Australia. Western Australia three for 342 declared (M. Johnstone 167, P. Edwards 43, R. May 43*, T, Doropolous 40) and two for 121 (P. Edwards 57*, L. Pomersbach 37; J. Willcox 2/13) defeated Tasmania 250 (D. Anderson 111, J. Willcox 45, T.D. Paine 33, B.L. Burgess 31; L. Pomersbach 3/63, B. Mathers 2/25, C.R. Verco 2/28).

ROUND TWO

Group A

At Stewart Oval, Altona Meadows, January 6, 7, 2002. Drawn. Toss: South Australia. South Australia 179 (J.H.T. Harford 66; P. Siddle 5/16) and 178 (C.J. Ferguson 64, S. Hum 45; P. Siddle 6/31) drew with Victoria 179 (A. Hardy 56, M. Harrison 46; D.J. Franco 3/34, C.B. Bailey 3/48).

At Melbourne Grammar Oval, South Yarra, January 6, 7, 2002. New South Wales won on first innings. Toss: Queensland. Queensland 265 (M.G.D. Turich 85, C. LaPorte 77*; J. Tuccia 4/19, V. Sithloo 2/61) lost to New South Wales four for 269 (T. Sparke 111, L.J. Reynolds 53, B. Crawley 50; C.C. Ditchmen 3/68).

Group B

At AG Gillon Oval, Brunswick, January 6, 7, 2002. Drawn. Toss: Tasmania. Tasmania 290 (D. Anderson 90, B.L. Gurgess 45, W. Ripper 44; S. Rice 2/39, D. Goodsell 2/45, S. Gaskin 2/47) drew with Australian Capital Territory nine for 194 (D. Goodsell 66, R. Maddox 41; S. Stewart 3/27, N. Cashion 2/38).

At Preston City Oval, Preston, January 6, 7, 2002. Western Australia won on first innings. Toss: Northern Territory. Northern Territory 340 (P. Brown 87*, K.J. Skewes 83, R. LeLoux 49, R. Hodgson 41; B. Mathers 2/38, T. Houston 2/38, S. Barnes-Siddall 2/45) lost to Western Australia three for 432 (T. Doropolous 151, R. Phillimore 100*, M. Johnstone 78, R. May 70*; R. Hodgson 2/62).

ROUND THREE

Group A

At Alf Mills Oval, Dandenong, January 9, 10, 2002. South Australia won on first innings. Toss: South Australia. Queensland 147 (Z.E. Turner 29, P.J. Hagenbach 28; C.J. Ferguson 4/28, L. Oswald-Jacobs 3/20, G.D. Putland 2/25) lost to South Australia 174 (C.J. Ferguson 63, L. Oswald-Jacobs 29, P. Allegretto 27; C.C. Ditchmen 2/1, C.J. Bilewicz 2/14, R.J. Neyland 2/16, J. Robinson 2/38).

At Marles Playing Field, Bulleen, January 9, 10, 2002. New South Wales won on first innings. Toss: New South Wales. Victoria 243 (P.M. Nevill 49, K. Tenace 37, M. Harrison 36, A. Mato 36, N. Allan 32; J. Tuccia 5/50, P. John 2/44) lost to New South Wales nine for 246 (S.J. Hinton 97, S. O'Keeffe 70; P. Siddle 5/45, L. Blake 2/60).

Group B

At St Kevins College Oval, Toorak, January 9, 10, 2002. Drawn. Toss: Australian Capital Territory. Western Australia 295 (M. Johnstone 84, R. Phillimore 66; D. Goodsell 3/28, R.G. Bissell 3/60) drew with Australian Capital Territory eight for 242 (M. Lucas 102*, D. Goodsell 78; T. Doropolous 3/20, T. Houston 2/2).

At Essendon Grammar Oval, Essendon, January 9, 10, 2002. Tasmania won on first innings. Toss: Tasmania. Tasmania 289 (T.D. Paine 105, W. Ripper 49; L. LeRoux 4/93, A. Dilley 3/48, S. Cantwell 2/25) defeated Northern Territory 262 (T.C. Clements 68, R. LeLoux 47, S. Regan 37; J. Hughes 5/30, L. Powell 2/91).

QUALIFYING FINALS

At Dunshea Oval, Bulleen, January 12, 13, 2002. New South Wales won on first innings. Toss: New South Wales. New South Wales 165 (S.J. Hinton 67, B. Crawley 32; D.N. Porter 3/27, M. Johnstone 2/3, C.R. Verco 2/13) and seven for 81 (S.J. Hinton 31; B. Mathers 3/18, R. May 2/17) defeated Western Australia 139 (P. Edwards 45; V. Sithloo 5/40, S. Mott 3/34, P. John 2/15).

At Marles Playing Field, Bulleen, January 12, 13, 2002. Drawn. Toss: Queensland. South Australia five for 431 declared (C.J. Ferguson 258*, J.H.T. Harford 57, C.H.

Harper 40, P. Allegretto 37) drew with Queensland five for 166 (N. Reardon 62, R. J. Neyland 38, R. Mackay 34*; C. B. Bailey 2/4, S. C. Wiese 2/61).

At Melbourne Grammar Oval, South Yarra, January 12, 13, 2002. Victoria won on first innings. Toss: Victoria. Victoria 249 (T. Evans 86, A. Mato 49; S. Gaskin 6/76) defeated Australian Capital Territory 202 (W. Hay 57; T. M. O'Brien 5/61. P. Siddle 2/34, N. Allan 2/56).

At Scotch College Oval, Hawthorn, January 12, 13, 2002. Northern Territory won on first innings. Toss: Tasmania. Tasmania 194 (S. Stewart 24, A. Jackett 23; S. Mitchell 3/21, P. A. W. Cook 2/37) and two for 36 lost to Northern Territory 395 (K. J. Skewes 115, M. Barry, 98, D. W. Richards 55, R. LeRoux 50; J. Lambert 5/47, S. Stewart 2/49).

CONSOLATION FINALS

AUSTRALIAN CAPITAL TERRITORY v TASMANIA

At Richmond Cricket Ground, Richmond, January 14, 15, 2002. Tasmania won on first innings. Toss: Tasmania. Tasmania 136 (T. D. Paine 55; A. Pascoe 3/34, S. Gaskin 2/30) and three for 98 (D. Anderson 38; A. Pascoe 2/30) defeated Australian Capital Territory 79 (D. Poidevin 38; S. Stewart 4/15, B. L. Burgess 3/14, G. S. Kerr 2/18).

NORTHERN TERRITORY v QUEENSLAND

At Junction Oval, St Kilda, January 14, 15, 2002. Drawn. Toss: Queensland. Queensland 248 (A. J. Hicks 123; K. J. Skewes 4/32, R. LeLoux 2/35) drew with Northern Territory eight for 248 (K. J. Skewes 70*, D. W. Richards 52, R. LeLoux 45; R. J. Neyland 3/48).

VICTORIA v WESTERN AUSTRALIA

At Toorak Park, Toorak, January 14, 15, 2002. Victoria won on first innings. Toss: Western Australia. Western Australia 230 (B. Spark 72*, T. Doropolous 44; K. Tenace 3/31, S. Anderson 2/43, A. Hardy 2/54) lost to Victoria seven for 234 (T. Evans 60, A. Hardy 43, L. Kentish 32; T. Houston 3/39, C. R. Verco 2/26).

CHAMPIONSHIP FINAL

NEW SOUTH WALES v SOUTH AUSTRALIA

At Melbourne Cricket Ground, Melbourne, January 14, 15, 2002. New South Wales won on first innings. Toss: New South Wales.

New South Wales

J. Sawkins b Ferguson	0	
B. Crawley c Harper b Eckermann	0	
*L. J. Reynolds c Harford b Ferguson	44	
T. Sparke c Crook b Oswald-Jacobs	8	
P. Forrest c Crook b Oswald-Jacobs	47	
S. J. Hinton c Bailey b Oswald-Jacobs	47	
B. Maher c and b Franco	62	
†S. Jamieson c Hum b Franco	65	
P. John did not bat.		

V. Sithloo not out	15
S. Wallace c Crook b Wiese	2
S. Mott c Hum b Oswald-Jacobs	6
B 3, l-b 5, n-b 3	11
(96 overs)	307

Fall: 0 8 25 82 152 169 262 287 292 307

Bowling: Oswald–Jacobs 16–1–40–4; Franco 16–3–50–2; Wiese 16–3–44–1; Ferguson 11–3–40–1; Eckermann 16–6–33–1; Harper 1–0–6–0; Harford 4–1–27–0; Bailey 16–0–59–0.

South Australia

C.H. Harper run out (Wallace)	0	C.B. Bailey c Sawkins b Wallace 0
S. Smith b Forrest	13	S.C. Wiese run out 0
*C.J. Ferguson b Sithloo	35	P. Eckermann not out 0
J.H.T. Harford b Wallace	36	
L. Oswald-Jacobs run out	26	L-b 3, w 1, n-b 6 10
P. Allegretto c Mott b Sithloo	10	
S. Hum run out	16	(Overs 72.2) 167
†M. Crook c Jamieson b Wallace	21	Fall: 0 47 70 103 130 132 167 167 167 167

D.J. Franco did not bat.

Bowling: Wallace 21.2–1–49–3; Sithloo 14–4–58–2; Forrest 8–3–16–1; Maher 2–0–13–0; Mott 10–2–19–0; John 6–2–9–0.

Umpires: J.K. Brookes and B.N.J. Oxenford

UNDER-17s CRICKET CHAMPIONSHIPS RECORDS

UNDER-17s CHAMPIONSHIPS

Series	Venue	Winner	Player of the Year
1986-87	Melbourne	New South Wales	M. Galbraith (Vic)
1987-88	Launceston	New South Wales	J.C. Young (NSW)
1988-89	Sydney	South Australia	M.J.P. Minagall (SA)
1989-90	Adelaide	Victoria	T.F. Corbett (Vic)
1990-91	Brisbane	New South Wales	J.P. Maher (Qld)
1991-92	Canberra	New South Wales	B.J. Hodge (Vic)
1992-93	Hobart	New South Wales	B.A. Clemow (NSW)
1993-94	Adelaide	New South Wales	M.D. Pascoe (Qld)
1994-95	Perth	New South Wales	D.J. Thornely (NSW)
1995-96	Melbourne/Geelong	Queensland	M.J. North (WAust)
1996-97	Brisbane	New South Wales	L. Williams (SAust)
1997-98	Hobart	Victoria	A. Kent (Vic)
1998-99	Sydney	New South Wales	E. Cowan (NSW)
1999-00	Brisbane	Victoria	P. Boraston (SAust)
2000-01	Brisbane	South Australia	C.J. Borgas (SAust)
2001-02	Melbourne	New South Wales	C.J. Ferguson (SAust)

LAST TEN YEARS' PLACINGS

	92-93	93-94	94-95	95-96	96-97	97-98	98-99	99-00	00-01	01-02
Australian Capital Territory	7	4	6	7	7	7	5	7	7	8
New South Wales	1	1	1	6	1	6	1	2	2	1
Northern Territory	8	8	8	8	8	4	7	8	8	5
Queensland	4	3	1	1	2	8	2	4	4	3
South Australia	2	6	4	2	4	5	8	3	1	2
Tasmania	5	7	5	5	6	3	6	6	5	7
Victoria	6	2	3	3	5	1	4	1	3	4
Western Australia	3	5	7	4	3	2	3	5	6	6

UNDER-17s CRICKET CHAMPIONSHIP, 2001-02

POINTS TABLE

Group A	P	WO	W1	D	L1	LO	T	Points	Quotient
New South Wales	3	0	3	0	0	0	0	18	1.498
South Australia	3	0	1	1	1	0	0	9	0.879
Queensland	3	0	1	0	2	0	0	6	0.957
Victoria	3	0	0	1	2	0	0	3	0.846
Group B									
Western Australia	3	0	2	1	0	0	0	12	2.225
Northern Territory	3	0	1	0	2	0	0	6	1.013
Tasmania	3	0	1	1	1	0	0	6	0.722
Australian Capital Territory	3	0	0	2	1	0	0	0	0.574

Quotient = runs per wicket scored divided by runs per wicket conceded.

FINAL PLACINGS

1st	New South Wales
2nd	South Australia
3rd	Queensland
4th	Victoria
5th	Northern Territory
6th	Western Australia
7th	Tasmania
8th	Australian Capital Territory

HIGHEST INDIVIDUAL SCORE

258*	C.J. Ferguson ...	South Australia v Queensland at Marles Playing Field
167	M. Johnstone	Western Australia v Tasmania at Princess Park Oval No. 1
151	T. Doropolous ...	Western Australia v Northern Territory at Preston City Oval
147	K.J. Skewes	Northern Territory v Australian Capital Territory at Albert Cricket Gnd
135	C.J. Ferguson ...	South Australia v New South Wales at Bill Lawry Oval
123	A.J. Hicks	Queensland v Northern Territory at Junction Oval
115	K.J. Skewes	Northern Territory v Tasmania at Scotch College Oval
111	D. Anderson	Tasmania v Western Australia at Princess Park Oval No. 1
111	T. Sparke	New South Wales v Queensland at Melbourne Grammar Oval
105	T.D. Paine	Tasmania v Northern Territory at Essendon Grammar Oval
102*	M. Lucas	Australian Capital Territory v Western Australia at St Kevins College Oval
100*	R Phillimore	Western Australia v Northern Territory at Preston City Oval

MOST RUNS

	M	I	NO	R	HS	100s	50s	Avge
C.J. Ferguson (SAust)	5	6	1	574	258*	2	2	114.80
K.J. Skewes (N.T) ...	5	5	2	415	147*	2	2	138.33
M. Johnstone (WAust)	5	5	0	357	167	2	1	71.40
D. Anderson (Tas)....	5	6	0	262	111	1	1	43.66
S.J. Hinton (NSW) ...	5	6	1	256	97	2	0	51.20
M. Barry (N.T)	5	5	0	250	98	2	0	50.00
T. Doropolous (WAust)	5	5	0	245	151	1	0	49.00
T.D. Paine (Tas)	5	6	0	242	105	1	1	40.33
D.W. Richards (N.T) .	5	5	0	231	96	0	3	46.20
T. Sparke (NSW).....	5	6	0	229	111	1	1	38.16

MOST WICKETS

	M	O	Mdns	R	W	BB	5W/i	10W/M	Avge
P. Siddle (Vic)	5	95.2	31	206	20	6/31	3	1	10.30
V. Sithloo (WAust)	5	91	25	241	12	5/40	1	0	20.08
S. Gaskin (ACT)	5	120.5	15	401	12	6/76	1	0	33.41
S. Stewart (Tas)	5	86	27	202	11	4/15	0	0	18.36
B. Mathers (WAust)	5	88	26	193	10	3/18	0	0	19.30
J. Tuccia (NSW)	3	47.4	11	104	9	5/50	1	0	11.55
P. John (NSW)	5	65.2	14	147	9	4/27	0	0	16.33

BEST BOWLING

6/31	P. Siddle	Victoria v South Australia at Stewart Oval
6/76	S. Gaskin	Australian Capital Territory v Victoria at Melbourne Grammar Oval
5/16	P. Siddle	Victoria v South Australia at Stewart Oval
5/30	J. Hughes	Northern Territory v Tasmania at Essendon Grammar Oval
5/40	V. Sithloo	Western Australia v New South Wales at Dunshea Oval
5/45	P. Siddle	Victoria v South Australia at Marles Playing Field
5/47	J. Lambert	Tasmania v Northern Territory at Scotch College Oval
5/50	J. Tuccia	New South Wales v Victoria at Marles Playing Field
5/61	T. M. O'Brien . . .	Victoria v Australian Capital Territory at Melbourne Grammar Oval

HIGHEST TOTALS

3-432	Western Australia v Northern Territory at Preston City Oval
5d-431	Queensland v South Australia at Marles Playing Field
7-428	Northern Territory v Australian Capital Territory at Albert Cricket Ground
395	Northern Territory v Tasmania at Scotch College Oval
3d-342	Western Australia v Tasmania at Princess Park Oval No. 1

LOWEST TOTAL

79	Australian Capital Territory v Tasmania at Richmond Cricket Ground
139	Western Australia v New South Wales at Dunshea Oval
136	Tasmania v Australian Capital Territory at Richmond Cricket Ground
145	Australian Capital Territory v Northern Territory at Albert Cricket Ground
147	Queensland v South Australia at Alf Mills Oval

AUSTRALIAN CAPITAL TERRITORY
FIRST-GRADE CRICKET, 2001-02

By ADAM MOREHOUSE

The 2001-02 first-grade season was one of the closest in many years, with the semi-finalists not decided until the last regular round of competition. For the second year in succession, Weston Creek beat Queanbeyan in the final.

Weston Creek overcame the loss of Australian Capital Territory players Cade Brown and Anthony McQuire to win their second premiership. They were led by top ACT batsman Jack Smith, with 658 runs at an average of 34. To overcome the loss of Brown and McQuire, the club recruited well, securing the services of Adelaide batsman Christian Hanna and Melbourne spinner Mark Oliver. Ben Southam was the pick of the Weston Creek bowlers with 40 wickets while veteran Dean "Warrior" Lovett took 25.

Queanbeyan were again defeated by Weston Creek in the final but the team did very well just to get there. After being in second-last place at the halfway mark of the season, they recovered to win their last four matches and scrape into the semi-finals, where they then upset minor premiers Western District. Exciting Comets player Adam Heading led the batting with 792 runs and finished second in the aggregates for the competition. Fast-medium bowler Michael Stachow led the wicket-takers for the club with 40.

Western District were the form team, with four outright victories during the season. Unfortunately, they stumbled in the semi-finals to Queanbeyan. Their good form was based upon their two strike bowlers, pace man Ben Keens with 59 wickets and former Tasmanian off-spinner Mark Hatton with 52. Swee-Tin Pang led the batting with 586 runs. North Canberra–Gungahlin made the semi-finals for the first time in ten seasons in a much improved performance. Captained by Comets off-spinner Heath Axelby, who took 46 wickets, the bowling was the key for the club, but the inconsistent batting ultimately cost the side a grand-final spot.

Tuggeranong Valley missed the semi-finals for the first time for some seasons. In a relatively inexperienced side, the best performances came from Dave Jeffrey with 559 runs and Evan Kellar with 25 wickets. Eastlake had an up-and-down season, losing outright four times. Their batting was their strength, with five players passing 350 runs. The highest individual innings of the season was by Eastlake's Michael Dawn, whose unbeaten 200 against Queanbeyan was only the sixth double-century in ACT grade cricket.

Ginninderra–West Belconnen improved on previous seasons and challenged for a semi-final spot late into the final rounds. The star of the competition was Ginninderra–West Belconnen's young wicket-keeper David Dawson, who was the leading scorer for the competition with 950 runs at an average of 63. Three players passed 30 wickets for Ginninderra–West Belconnen during the season and the team could challenge again for the finals next season. The inexperienced ANU struggled again, winning only once and collecting the wooden spoon for the third season in a row. No player passed 300 runs for the side, and Daniel Pascoe was the leading wicket-taker with 26.

Queanbeyan won the Konica Cup limited-overs competition, defeating North Albury in the final. It was the third season in a row that an Albury side had lost the final of the Konica Cup. In their first season in the competition and with little experience on turf wickets, the Canberra City & Suburban side reached the semi-finals, defeating more experienced sides including last season's victors, Tuggeranong Valley.

AUSTRALIAN CAPITAL TERRITORY

FIRST-GRADE TABLE, 2001-02

	M	WO	W1	D	L1	LO	T	Points
Western District	11	4	5	0	2	0	66	1.3356
Weston Creek	11	1	6	0	4	0	46	1.3100
North Canberra–Gungahlin	11	0	7	0	4	0	42	1.0549
Queanbeyan	11	0	6	0	4	1	40	0.9396
Tuggeranong Valley	11	1	4	0	6	0	34	1.1273
Ginninderra–West Belconnen	11	1	4	0	5	1	34	0.9547
Eastlake	11	1	3	0	3	4	28	0.8096
Australian National University	11	0	1	0	8	2	6	0.6639

AUSTRALIAN CAPITAL TERRITORY
FIRST-GRADE AVERAGES, 2001-02

BATTING

(Qualification: 400 runs)

	M	I	NO	R	HS	100s	50s	Avge
D.G. Dawson (Ginninderra–W. Belconnen)	14	18	3	950	130	2	7	63.33
A.J. Heading (Queanbeyan)	18	20	2	792	125	2	4	44.00
D.M. Jeffrey (Tuggeranong Valley)	15	15	1	559	111	2	1	39.92
P.W. Coleborne (Queanbeyan)	17	17	4	473	109	1	2	36.38
S.L. Maxwell (Weston Creek)	17	20	4	557	80	0	4	34.81
J.K. Smith (Weston Creek)	16	20	1	658	94	0	7	34.63
M.J. Kavanagh (Eastlake)	16	19	2	586	95	0	5	34.47
C.W. Grebert (Eastlake)	15	19	1	609	78	0	5	33.83
P.B. Radford (Ginninderra–W. Belconnen)	13	17	2	505	122*	1	3	33.66
S.T. Pang (Weston District)	15	20	1	586	93	0	5	30.84
S.E. Frost (Queanbeyan)	19	21	1	595	99	0	6	29.75

Denotes not out.

BOWLING

(Qualification: 25 wickets)

	M	O	Mdns	R	W	BB	5W/i	10W/m	Avge
B.M. Keens (Weston District)	17	297.3	81	718	59	7/25	2	0	12.16
M.A. Hatton (Weston District)	14	264.4	76	678	52	7/26	3	1	13.03
B.A. Mikkelsen									
(North Canberra–Gungahlin)	8	170	36	410	31	4/16	0	0	13.22
B.S. Southam (Weston Creek)	16	232.5	49	572	40	5/42	1	0	14.30
E. Kellar (Tuggeranong Valley)	12	202	58	407	25	5/26	1	0	16.28
H.R. Axelby									
(North Canberra–Gungahlin)	17	336	96	779	46	5/42	1	0	16.93
R.F. Humphreys									
(Ginninderra–W. Belconnen)	13	147.2	23	481	27	4/18	0	0	17.81
M. Stachow (Queanbeyan)	19	257.1	58	749	40	6/33	1	0	18.72
L.J. Bulkeley									
(Ginninderra–W. Belconnen)	14	222.5	42	598	30	5/33	2	0	19.93
D.D. D'Cruz									
(Ginninderra–W. Belconnen)	14	212.3	42	626	31	5/35	1	0	20.19
R. Mongan (Eastlake)	12	153.5	24	512	25	4/32	0	0	20.48

AUSTRALIAN CAPITAL TERRITORY SEMI-FINALS, 2001-02

WESTON CREEK v NORTH CANBERRA–GUNGAHLIN

At Boomanulla Oval, Narrabundah, March 16, 17, 18, 2002. Toss: Weston Creek. Weston Creek won by 62 runs. Weston Creek 171 (E. A.Mackenzie 27, M. W.Oliver 25, J.K.Smith 23, B. S.Southam 23; S. Cluff 3/37, H.R. Axelby 3/47, D.R. Womble 3/51) and 283(C. D. Hanna 63, B. S. Southam 55, S. Stokes 51; D.R. Womble 4/99) defeated North Canberra–Gungahlin 131 (D. E. Lovett 5/45, B. S. Southam 4/52) and 261 (B.S. Borgelt 69, D. Wilson 57; B.S. Southam 4/67).

QUEANBEYAN v WESTERN DISTRICT

At Manuka Oval, Canberra, March 16, 17, 18, 2002. Toss: Queanbeyan. Queanbeyan won on first innings. Queanbeyan 330 (A.J. Heading 117, P. W. Coleborne 109; A.D. Jones 4/75, M. A. Hatton 3/57) defeated Western District 259 (D. King 62, D.J. Richards 46; M. Stachow 3/79).

AUSTRALIAN CAPITAL TERRITORY FINAL, 2001-02

WESTON CREEK v QUEANBEYAN

At Manuka Oval, Canberra, March 23, 24, 25, 2002. Weston Creek won on first innings. Toss: Weston Creek.

In a repeat of the previous season's grand final, Weston Creek took on Queanbeyan. Winning the toss and batting first under partly cloudy skies, Weston Creek struggled early, giving four chances to Queanbeyan in the first hour. Jack Smith steadied the side before the introduction of the spinners sparked a middle-order collapse. The gritty batting of Peter Seberry enabled the side to survive the day, and on the second morning Weston Creek batted on to reach 278, Seberry making 81 with the support of the lower order. After the loss of an early wicket, Queanbeyan moved into a strong position with a century partnership between Michael O'Rourke and Peter Coleborne. Having reached two for 178, the middle order collapsed against Smith's part-time medium pace, the next five wickets falling for the addition of only 34 runs, including that of O'Rourke who had kept his side in the match with a well-played century. The Queanbeyan tail wagged on the final morning, eking out valuable runs, and the match was finally decided when a direct throw by Ewan Mackenzie ran out Herdegan. Weston Creek batted a second time before stumps were drawn early.

Close of Play: First day; Weston Creek (1) 7-233 (Seberry 52, Hay 14); Second day; Queanbeyan (1) 8-238 (Stachow 10).

Weston Creek

A.G. Rhynehart c M.F. Frost b Herdegan	3	– (2) not out	82
J.K. Smith c Collier b S.E. Frost	63	– (1) c Mansfield b Herdegan	7
*S.L. Maxwell lbw b Harvey	32	– c and b M.J. Frost	57
C.D. Hanna lbw b S.E. Frost	39	– c Heading b M.J. Frost	17
B.S. Southam c Heading b Collier	7	– not out	5
P.R. Seberry lbw b O'Rourke	81		
S. Stokes c Collier b Harvey	13		
E.A. Mackenzie b O'Rourke	0		
†A. Hay run out (O'Rourke)	17		
M.W. Oliver lbw b O'Rourke	10		
D.E. Lovett not out	0		
B1, l-b 10, w 1, n-b1	13	B 4, l-b 3, n-b 1	8

(120.5 overs, 427 mins) 278   (46 overs, 144 mins) (3 wkts) 176
Fall: 10 62 128 145 149 187 198 247 277 278   Fall: 13 111 160

Bowling: *First Innings*—Harvey 28–6–76–2; Herdegan 18–10–29–1; Stachow 22–5–73–0; O'Rourke 16.5–9–13–3; Collier 18–5–39–1; S.E. Frost 18–5–37–2. *Second Innings*—Harvey 5–9–26–0; Herdegan 5–0–23–1; Stachow 3–3–0–0; O'Rourke 3–1–13–0; Collier 7–2–26–0; S.E. Frost 6–2–17–0; M.J. Frost 10–5–19–2; Fahey 2–0–14–0; Coleborne 3–0–14–0; Mansfield 3–0–17–0.

Queanbeyan

*S.E. Frost c (sub) T. Purcell b Southam	11	M. Stachow not out	25
M.P. O'Rourke c Hay b Smith	107	S. Harvey c Hay b Southam	4
P.W. Coleborne c Hanna b Smith	45	J. Herdegan run out (Mackenzie)	5
†A.J. Heading c Hanna b Smith	24		
D. Mansfield b Lovett	26	B 6, l-b 4, n-b 1	11
M.J. Frost lbw b Smith	0		
R. Collier c Maxwell b Smith	4	(95 overs, 314 mins)	263
S. Fahey c Oliver b Mackenzie	1	Fall: 25 132 178 199 199 211 212 238 249 263	

Bowling: Southam 15–3–47–2; Lovett 15–2–44–1; Stokes 9–3–25–0; Hanna 11–3–16–0; Oliver 15–2–52–1; Mackenzie 19–6–46–1; Smith 11–5–23–4.

Umpires: P.D. Chapman and D.B. Harris.

NEWCASTLE FIRST-GRADE CRICKET, 2001-02

By JACK BROWN

The competition quickly split into two groups as the top seven teams left the bottom five trailing in their wake. In the previous season's final Hamilton–Wickham suffered the mortification of a wash-out after scoring 411 and then reducing Merewether to five for 48 after 16 overs on the second day. This season, however, they completed a comfortable win over the same team. They also completed a treble of first-grade titles, securing the Tom Locker Trophy for limited-overs cricket and winning the state-wide NRMA Cup after a victory over the Wollongong team Balgownie.

Hamilton–Wickham's success was based on an impressive depth of performance, in which the batting order's valuable contributions combined with a versatile battery of bowlers. They amassed a record Newcastle cricket innings total with their nine for 578 from 100 overs against Wallsend. In a tribute to the run-soaked Wallsend pitch, the home side replied with 329. The Hamilton–Wickham batting strength was further underlined when Steve Mudford (168 not out) and Steve Cowen (111 not out) joined in an unfinished second-wicket partnership of 292 against Southern Lakes, the fourth-highest partnership recorded in the Newcastle competition. Cowen's maiden first-grade century was a potent demonstration of the development in his batting which made him such a valuable member of the side.

Merewether were minor premiers in each of the top four grades and finished 14 points clear of Hamilton–Wickham in first grade. The depth of their playing resources was underlined by their victory in the club championship for the second successive season. Their leading batsman, Jamie Brazier, scored more than 600 runs for the third successive season, during which time he has made in excess of 2,000 runs at an average of 52. Consistent opening bowler Duncan McIlveen topped the district averages and took his total of wickets for the past five seasons to 198.

The other semi-finalists, Waratah–Mayfield and Lambton, maintained their consistent form of last season. Waratah's wicket-keeper, Luke Piper, not only effected most dismissals behind the stumps (31), but also weighed in with 422 valuable runs. Brad Bannister, Lambton's accurate medium-fast bowler, topped both the district averages and aggregates, his skill and attitude being rewarded with both the players' and umpires' awards.

Charlestown, who had been consistent semi-finalists in recent seasons, dropped back to fifth spot. Despite the recent retirement of some of his fellow club stalwarts, Mark Curry celebrated his 20th season in first grade with another two centuries, which took him past 9,000 first-grade runs. In addition, 38 more wickets with his slow left-armers lifted his tally to 327. Charlestown's new opening bowler, Steve Threadgold, also had a fine season, leaving the club ruminating on what they might have achieved with more batting consistency.

Despite his team's lowly position, Jason Vero of Cardiff had a productive summer, particularly before Christmas when his fluent batting produced three centuries and a new club record aggregate. The best bowling performances for the season also came from the less fashionable clubs: the lively Jason Lawson of Belmont took 8/43, while Newcastle City's Darren Whittingham returned 8/50 with his medium-pacers. Waratah's Murray Christie retired from the Newcastle representative side after 13 seasons, including the last three as captain.

NEWCASTLE FIRST-GRADE TABLE, 2001-02

	M	WO	W1	D	L1	LO	Points
Merewether	13	3	7	2	1	0	57
Waratah–Mayfield	13	1	7	2	3	0	43
Hamilton–Wickham	13	0	9	3	1	0	43
Lambton	13	1	6	3	3	0	41
Charlestown	13	1	6	2	4	0	40
Belmont	13	0	7	2	4	0	36
Stockton	13	1	4	4	4	0	36
Newcastle City	13	0	4	1	6	2	24
Cardiff–Boolaroo	13	0	2	4	5	2	21
University	13	0	2	2	8	1	20
Southern Lakes	13	0	1	2	10	0	18
Wallsend	13	0	2	1	8	2	18

NEWCASTLE FIRST-GRADE AVERAGES, 2001-02

BATTING

(Qualification: 400 runs)

	I	NO	R	HS	100s	50s	Avge
S. Moore (Merewether)	10	3	454	146	2	1	64.86
S. Cowen (Hamilton–Wickham)	11	3	517	111*	1	4	64.63
J. Brazier (Merewether)	12	1	626	128	2	3	56.91
S. Mudford (Hamilton–Wickham)	10	2	419	168*	2	0	52.38
J. Vero (Cardiff–Boolaroo)	14	0	724	164	3	2	51.71
R. Soper (Hamilton–Wickham)	8	0	411	109	1	2	51.38
J. Price (Hamilton–Wickham)	9	0	420	177	1	2	46.66
G. Grimmond (Lambton)	12	2	447	104	1	2	44.70
J. Whitehead (Stockton)	11	1	433	116	1	1	43.30
G. Geise (Wallsend)	14	2	466	101	1	3	38.83

BOWLING

(Qualification: 25 wickets)

	O	M	R	W	BB	5W/i	10W/m	Avge
D. McIlveen (Merewether)	219	60	519	36	5/25	1	0	14.42
B. Bannister (Lambton)	230	69	567	39	7/40	4	0	14.54
M. Curry (Charlestown)	241	78	579	38	7/39	1	0	15.24
H. Khan (Stockton)	132	26	408	25	4/12	0	0	16.32
D. Keast (Belmont)	224	54	643	39	6/49	4	0	16.48
S. Threadgold (Charlestown)	251	66	650	37	6/73	2	0	17.57
S. Finlay (Waratah–Mayfield)	239	70	576	32	7/35	2	0	18.00
T. Disney (Charlestown)	200	63	501	26	5/104	1	0	19.27
T. Mason (Stockton)	225	44	666	33	5/48	2	0	20.18
D. Whittingham (Newcastle City)	251	49	699	33	8/50	1	0	21.18

NEWCASTLE FIRST-GRADE SEMI-FINALS, 2001-02

MEREWETHER v LAMBTON

At No. 1 Sports Ground, Newcastle, March 16, 17, 2002. Merewether won on first innings. Merewether 339 (P. Stanbridge 89, S. Moore 47, N. Crittenden 42; G. Sutton 4/72, B. Bannister 3/98) defeated Lambton 293 (T. Bush 143, M. Cooper 48; D. McIlveen 4/69, C. White 3/63).

WARATAH–MAYFIELD v HAMILTON–WICKHAM

At Cahill Oval, Belmont, March 16, 17, 2002. Hamilton–Wickham won on first innings. Waratah–Mayfield 252 (A. Weekes 78, L. Piper 51; R. Soper 3/26, D. Herbert 3/40) lost to Hamilton–Wickham five for 253 (T. Campbell 94, D. Herbert 80*).

NEWCASTLE FIRST-GRADE FINAL, 2001-02

MEREWETHER v HAMILTON–WICKHAM

At No. 1 Sports Ground, Newcastle, March 23, 24, 2002. Hamilton–Wickham won on first innings. Toss: Hamilton–Wickham.

The result must have made Hamilton–Wickham look more kindly on the weather gods, as a fine weekend removed any possibility of a repeat of the previous year's disaster when rain robbed the side of certain victory. This time, all the old adages emphasising that sporting success is built on teamwork were underlined by Hamilton–Wickham's collective triumph over the more fancied Merewether side.

After early wickets fell cheaply, Steve Cowen and Rhys Soper put together a determined third-wicket partnership of 105, punctuating sound defence with judicious strokeplay. Three quick wickets left the innings finely balanced at five for 144 but the lower order was resolute and scored valuable runs while using up important time at the crease. After tea, wicket-keeper Michael Jordan, in particular, was a decisive influence in important partnerships for the ninth and tenth wickets with youngsters Andrew Maher and Sam Webber. Duncan McIlveen was called upon to bowl a third of the overs in the innings and as usual responded to the challenge with persistence and skill.

Merewether were three for 41 at stumps on the first day and Phil Stanbridge greeted the new morning with three handsome boundaries, but after his dismissal Merewether never recovered. Rhys Soper was their chief tormentor, bowling with vigour and aggression, and the innings stumbled to seven for 84. Nightwatchman Tim O'Neill and Mitch Irwin brought a modicum of relief with a sensible partnership of 77 before Soper dismissed them both and snuffed out Merewether's resistance. Jordan complemented his batting with a skilful display behind the stumps which netted him four catches. In a closer contest, bowlers on both sides may have rued their inattention to detail which resulted in a large number of no-balls.

Close of Play: First day, Merewether (1) 3-41.

Hamilton–Wickham

J. Price b McIlveen	0		†M. Jordan not out	29
S. Mudford c Stone b N. Crittenden	2		A. Maher c White b O'Neill	18
S. Cowen lbw b Stanbridge	79		S. Webber b Stanbridge	23
R. Soper c Gurr b McIlveen	54			
*T. Campbell c Stone b McIlveen	15		L-b 8, w 2, n-b 11	21
D. Herbert c Stanbridge b McIlveen	0			———
T. Crittenden c O'Neill b N. Crittenden	19		(80.5 overs)	268
T. Mitchell c Stone b Irwin	8		Fall: 0 16 121 144 144 169 184 200 232 268	

Bowling: McIlveen 26–4–100–4; N. Crittenden 17–2–62–2; Stanbridge 11.5–3–25–2; White 9–1–31–0; Moore 1–0–4–0; Irwin 11–2–30–1; O'Neill 5–2–8–1.

Merewether

M. Gurr c Jordan b Herbert	2		M. Irwin c Campbell b Soper	34
N. Crittenden b Maher	16		D. McIlveen b Webber	5
S. Moore lbw b Soper	8		†L. Stone not out	1
P. Stanbridge c Jordan b Soper	14			
T. O'Neill c Jordan b Soper	55		B 1, l-b 1, n-b 18	20
J. Brazier c Maher b Soper	9			———
T. Goodwin c Jordan b Soper	0		(58.5 overs)	170
*C. White c Cowen b Soper	6		Fall: 3 25 33 55 69 69 84 161 169 170	

Bowling: Herbert 15–1–39–1; T. Crittenden 10–2–21–0; Soper 19–2–63–7; Maher 9–1–28–1; Webber 5.5–0–17–1.

Umpires: K. Bourke and M. Jones.

SYDNEY FIRST-GRADE CRICKET

By PHIL WILKINS

Fairfield–Liverpool emerged as the vibrant new force of Sydney cricket after the most controversial season in the competition's history. A dramatic final month featured two protests over pitches, a reallocation of points which changed the outcome of the minor premiership, a mid-match change of venue for a semi-final, and the suspension of a state player.

While all the off-field turmoil generated media interest and temporarily overshadowed on-field deeds, it could not detract from Fairfield–Liverpool's first premiership in any senior grade. Led by a strong bowling attack and the massive contributions of New South Wales all-rounder Grant Lambert, the Lions became the first of the three clubs admitted to the competition in 1985-86 to win the top grade title. Fairfield–Liverpool's consistent form throughout the season and finals earned a deserved reward. But the reallocation of points from their crucial last-round game possibly went some way to denying the competition's newest club a fairytale finale to its first season.

The competition was reduced to 19 clubs in the off-season after Randwick and Petersham decided to merge. The new entity took the premiership by storm and appeared to have finished top after a last-round first innings home win over Fairfield–Liverpool. However, the clubs swapped positions on the ladder after SCA Committee of Management upheld Fairfield–Liverpool's protest over the preparation of the pitch for the second day, awarding the points to them.

On the same night as the appeal, Fairfield–Liverpool's fast bowler Don Nash was suspended for one match and missed the opening weekend of the finals after he was found guilty of improper and disorderly conduct by the SCA Judiciary Committee. The punishment was imposed following an incident in which Nash made physical contact with Randwick–Petersham's Richard Chee Quee after having him caught behind. During the course of the same final-round fixture at Coogee, Nash recorded the competition's season-best bowling figures of nine for 63.

Randwick–Petersham failed to progress beyond the opening weekend of the finals when they lost away to the strong UTS–Balmain side, who then became embroiled in another major controversy. The scheduled second day of their home semi-final against North Sydney at Drummoyne Oval was washed out with the visitors five for 101 chasing 155. An attempt to conclude the match on a third day on Easter Monday was also unsuccessful as the pitch remained unplayable, and the SCA Committee of Management sought to have the game completed on the Tuesday and Wednesday, again without success. The match was drawn, which would have put UTS–Balmain through to the final as the higher placed side, but North Sydney protested over the preparation and protection of the pitch. While the SCA found no evidence that UTS–Balmain were directly responsible for wilful damage to the playing surface, it determined that "the interests of the game of cricket would be best served" by rescheduling the second day to the Friday of that week, and moving it to Bankstown Oval because Drummoyne was unavailable.

One Sydney paper reported that some UTS–Balmain players favoured a boycott of the game because they thought their participation would effectively condone what they considered an unfair change of venue, but the match was concluded on the date set down for the first day of the final. North Sydney completed a first innings victory and the final started the next day. After all the hubbub over pitches in recent weeks, security guards were hired to watch over the grounds hosting the five senior grade finals on the nights before and during the games.

The turbulent last month apart, the competition struggled for exposure unless one of the senior representative players made a rare appearance. Two such instances generated enormous media interest. Australian captain Steve Waugh made his first appearance of the domestic season in a grade game for Bankstown after recovering from deep vein thrombosis. Michael Slater also generated headlines in an ill-fated return to grade cricket with University of NSW after he was dropped from the state team. Pakistan fast bowler Shoaib Akhtar also created interest in a short stint with Mosman. Opening batsmen were spared the frightening prospect of facing the fearsome new-ball partnership of Akhtar and Brett Lee, as Lee's first-class commitments prevented them from turning out together for Mosman.

While defending premiers St George dropped to sixth, Fairfield–Liverpool improved from tenth. Much of their success was due to Lambert, who finally broke into the New South Wales team. The fast-medium bowler took a competition-leading 64 wickets at 17.68 and was the tenth-highest run-scorer with 789 at 46.41. None of his team-mates averaged more than 31 with the bat, though four of them finished with over 500 runs. He received strong bowling support from Nash, who took 32 wickets at just 11.37, and another state squad member, spinner Anthony Clark, who claimed 33 at 24.66. Lambert was runner-up in the O'Reilly Medal for Player of the Year to the resurgent Chee Quee, who accrued a competition-topping haul of 1,003 runs at 45.59. Bankstown's Paul Maraziotis was next-best with 969 at 74.53, a performance which earned him a state contract. Lambert finished just one wicket ahead of Randwick–Petersham pace man Adam Warren, the only other bowler to snare more than 60 victims.

Generally good weather saw the number of draws decline from 23 in 2000-01 to just seven. Penrith won the Sydney first-grade limited-overs title with a five-wicket win over Mosman. With Blacktown promoted from Shires, the competition will be back to 20 clubs in 2002-03, when with luck the focus will once again fall on events on the field.

SYDNEY FIRST-GRADE TABLE, 2001-02

	M	WO	W1	D	L1	LO	T	Points	Quotient
Fairfield–Liverpool	18	2	9	0	6	0	1	89	1.3236
Mosman	18	2	11	0	5	0	0	88	1.1887
UTS–Balmain	18	2	9	2	4	0	1	83	1.3518
Randwick–Petersham ..	18	0	13	0	3	2	0	82	1.2603
North Sydney	18	2	9	0	6	1	0	80	1.0494
St George	18	0	12	0	5	1	0	78	1.2319
Bankstown	18	1	9	2	5	1	0	74	1.1488
Penrith	18	0	11	0	6	1	0	72	1.2389
Western Suburbs	18	2	7	0	8	0	1	71	1.0956
Sutherland	18	2	6	0	8	2	0	62	0.9281
Northern District	18	0	8	1	8	0	1	57	1.1145
Sydney University	18	1	6	0	11	0	0	52	0.8421
University of NSW	18	0	7	0	10	1	0	48	0.7949
Campbelltown–Camden	18	0	7	1	9	1	0	48	0.7645
Hawkesbury	18	1	5	0	11	1	0	46	0.6501
Eastern Suburbs	18	0	6	1	11	0	0	42	0.9104
Gordon	18	1	4	2	10	1	0	36	0.7982
Manly–Warringah	18	0	5	3	10	0	0	34	1.1269
Parramatta	18	1	1	2	9	5	0	22	0.6214

SYDNEY FIRST-GRADE AVERAGES, 2001-02

BATTING

(Qualification: 500 runs)

	M	I	NO	Runs	HS	100s	50s	Avge
P. Maraziotis (Bankstown)...........	17	18	5	969	137	4	4	74.53
D.J. Thornely (Northern District)	17	18	6	873	130*	2	6	72.75
G.C. Rummans (St George).........	14	14	3	715	160	3	4	65.00
M.N. Atkinson (UTS–Balmain)......	13	13	5	513	119*	2	3	64.12
P.G. Toole (Randwick–Petersham) ...	19	23	6	862	100	1	7	50.70
M. Schenke (UTS–Balmain)	16	18	1	837	139	4	2	49.23
V.M. Williams (Bankstown)	18	20	2	858	128	3	3	47.66
G.M. Lambert (Fairfield–Liverpool)..	20	22	5	789	118*	2	4	46.41
R. Chee Quee (Randwick–Petersham).	20	24	2	1,003	113	3	6	45.59
M.J. Phelps (Manly–Warringah)	16	18	3	666	196	1	4	44.40

BOWLING

(Qualification: 30 wickets)

	M	O	Mdns	R	W	BB	5W/i	10W/m	Avge
D.A. Nash (Fairfield–Liverpool)	9	117.5	24	364	32	9-63	2	0	11.37
W.D. Buttigieg (UTS–Balmain)	20	222.1	48	766	51	6-44	3	0	15.01
D.A. Turner (Penrith)	9	197	46	496	33	7-29	2	1	15.03
W.J. Adlam (Mosman)	20	267.1	50	764	47	5-16	2	0	16.25
M.A. Gordon (Parramatta)	13	204.2	50	558	34	6-46	1	0	16.41
J.M. Heath (Manly–Warringah)	15	239.2	60	670	39	5-23	1	0	17.17
G..Sullivan (North Sydney)	16	214.4	36	717	41	5-27	2	1	17.48
D.T. Johnston (Mosman)	20	231	42	738	42	5-45	2	0	17.57
R.R.T. Burton (UTS–Balmain)	20	265	71	688	39	5-26	2	0	17.64
G.M. Lambert (Fairfield–Liverpoool)	20	387.2	75	1,132	64	6-49	3	0	17.68

SYDNEY FIRST-GRADE QUALIFYING FINALS, 2001-02

UTS–BALMAIN v RANDWICK–PETERSHAM

At Drummoyne Oval, Drummoyne, March 23, 24, 2002. UTS–Balmain won on first innings. UTS–Balmain 280 (M. Schenke 75, N.D. Maxwell 46, N.W. Bracken 45, S.G. Karam 38; A.C. Warren 5/84) defeated Randwick–Petersham 220 (R. Chee Quee 80, D.W. Parmenter 55, G.R. Doig 40; W.D. Buttigieg 3/43, R.R.T. Burton 2/9, N.W. Bracken 2/57).

FAIRFIELD–LIVERPOOL v ST GEORGE

At Rosedale Oval, Warwick Farm, March 23, 24, 2002. Fairfield–Liverpool won on first innings. St George 195 (N.J.Catalano 43, P.J. Ryan 34, B.P. Van Deinsen 30; A.M. Clark 4/52, D. Bollinger 3/40, G.M. Lambert 3/67) and seven for 109 declared (N.J. Catalano 46, S.M. Thompson 23; G.M. Lambert 4/48) lost to Fairfield–Liverpool 199 (D. Kelley 50, B.J. Rohrer 41, G.M. Lambert 32; S.C.G. MacGill 4/85, B.P. Van Deinsen 3/43, J.A. Turner 2/23) and one for 48 (C. Karantz 30*).

NORTH SYDNEY v MOSMAN

At Allan Border Oval, Mosman, March 23, 24, 2002. North Sydney 225 (N.B. Taylor 70, D.S. Wotherspoon 69; D.T. Johnston 3/21, W.J. Adlam 3/56) defeated Mosman 220 (C.B. Guthrie 35, C.J. Hughes 31, D.T. Johnston 31; J.C. Peterson 5/39, M.J. Baker 3/52).

SYDNEY FIRST-GRADE SEMI-FINALS, 2001-02

FAIRFIELD–LIVERPOOL v MOSMAN

At Rosedale Oval, Warwick Farm, March 30, 31, 2002. Fairfield–Liverpool won on first innings. Fairfield–Liverpool 351 (M. Liddell 111, C. Karantz 88, J.J. Krejza 44, S.M. Pope 43; W.J. Adlam 4/95, C.J. Hughes 3/32) defeated Mosman 107 (C.J. Hughes 43, L. Hodgson 18, D.A. Nash 4/27, A.M. Clark 3/21).

UTS–BALMAIN v NORTH SYDNEY

At Drummoyne Oval, Drummoyne, March 30, 31, April 1 (no play) and Bankstown Memorial Oval on April 5, 2002. North Sydney won on first innings. UTS–Balmain 151 (G.R. Robertson 36, M. Schenke 34, B.P. Schutz 33; M.G. Burton 4/40, G.Sullivan 2/31, J.C. Peterson 2/32, M.J. Baker 2/44) and one for 216 (M. Schenke 116*, G.J. Hayne 93*) lost to North Sydney 282 (N.B. Taylor 105, R.C.Aitken 85; R.R.T. Burton 5/70, G.R. Robertson 2/41, N.W. Bracken 2/65) on the first innings.

SYDNEY FIRST-GRADE FINAL, 2001-02

FAIRFIELD–LIVERPOOL v NORTH SYDNEY

At Bankstown Oval, Bankstown, April 6, 7, 8, 2002. Fairfield–Liverpool won on first innings. Toss: Fairfield–Liverpool.

A wonderful recovery from a parlous position on the first morning provided Fairfield–Liverpool with the foundation which ultimately secured the south-western Sydney club their maiden first-grade title in surprisingly comfortable fashion. The minor premiers' prospects of securing the Belvidere Cup looked bleak as they crashed to four for 29 in the 18th over after choosing to bat first. North Sydney opening bowler Matthew Burton enhanced his team's chances of winning their first premiership since 1931-32 by taking 3/4 from his first 8.1 overs in conditions which offered the bowlers some early assistance. Fairfield–Liverpool's comeback was almost inevitably initiated by Grant Lambert, who added 81 in 95 minutes for the fifth wicket with Ben Rohrer. At seven for 143, the Lions were back in trouble, but a club record eighth-wicket stand of 168 in 194 minutes between Dean Magee and Jason Krejza, who each struck 15 fours, tilted the game in their side's favour.

North Sydney failed to build any substantial partnerships in reply. They were reasonably placed at one for 51 at lunch on the second day and at four for 154 just after tea before they lost three cheap wickets. Lambert had earlier gnawed through the top half of the order while his state squad colleague Don Nash picked up two wickets and forced Jim Petersen to retire hurt after he was cut above the left eye attempting a hook. New South Wales Colt Darren Wotherspoon defied the Lions' attack for just over three hours.

Leading by 137 on first innings, Fairfield–Liverpool proceeded to bat their foes out of the game when they returned to the crease shortly before stumps on the second day. An unbroken second-wicket stand of 152 in 151 minutes between Mark Liddell and outstanding state Under-19s all-rounder Krejza, who was promoted to No. 3, prompted North Sydney to concede at lunch on the third and final day.

Man of the Match (Benaud Medal): G. M. Lambert.

Close of play: First day, Fairfield–Liverpool 7-291 (Krejza 71, Magee 77); Second day, Fairfield–Liverpool 0-8 (Karantz 2, Liddell 6)

Fairfield–Liverpool

M. Liddell c Wotherspoon b Baker		5	– (2) not out		73
C. Karantz c Taylor b Burton		5	– (1) b Baker		10
G. M. Lambert lbw b Sullivan		65			
D. Kelley b Burton		3			
A. M. Clark b Burton		1			
B. J. Rohrer c Wotherspoon b Bird		38			
*†S. M. Pope c Burton b Bird		9			
J. J. Krejza c Taylor b Sullivan		97	– (3) not out		84
D.J.T. Magee run out		81			
D. A. Nash c Wotherspoon b Burton		1			
D. Bollinger not out		22			
B 3, l-b 9, w 4, n-b 1		17	W 1		1

(110.4 overs, 457 mins)	344	(49 overs, 175 mins) (1 wkt)	168

Fall: 10 15 25 29 110 120 143 311 314 344   Fall: 16

Bowling: First Innings—Baker 24–4–89–1; Burton 32–10–66–4; Bird 14–1–61–2; Sullivan 20.4–6–54–2; Aitken 12–5–25–0; Peterson 8–1–37–0. Second Innings—Baker 11–4–33–1; Burton 13–4–27–0; Aitken 11–0–47–0; Sullivan 8–0–37–0; Posniak 6–2–24–0.

North Sydney

M.E. Posniak lbw b Lambert	29	M.G. Burton c Pope b Lambert	0
N. Munro c Clark b Lambert	10	A.C. Bird c Krejza b Bollinger	24
*†N.B. Taylor c Liddell b Nash	31	G. Sullivan not out	0
A.M. Dignan b Rohrer b Lambert	1		
D.S. Wotherspoon c Lambert b Clark	56	B 1, l-b 10, n-b 16	27
R.C. Aitken b Kelley b Nash	26		
J.C. Peterson retired hurt	0	(57.4 overs, 262 mins) (9 wkts dec)	207
M.J. Baker c Pope b Lambert	3	Fall: 32 53 66 117 154 168 168 195 207	

Bowling: Nash 17–2–71–2; Lambert 20–4–52–5; Clark 11–2–27–1; Bollinger 8.4–0–46–1; Krejza 1–1–0–0.

Umpires: D.B. Hair and S.J.A. Taufel.

BRISBANE FIRST-GRADE CRICKET

By STEPHEN GRAY

The 2001-02 season was notable for the emergence of a distinct generation gap emerging in virtually all of the first-grade teams. For the handful of thirty-somethings regularly pulling on the whites in first-grade, there are hordes of Generation X-ers ready to mix it with them. In lower grades, the imbalance is less marked, with most clubs still retaining those die-hard cricketing Peter Pans who are the lifeblood of a club. While Queensland's current first-class powerhouse busily generates titles and propels increasing numbers of players to the next level of representation, the first-grade premiership churns along with a mix of past, present and future. Sandgate–Redcliffe won the First-grade premiership with a side full of experience, while Northern Suburbs won the limited-overs competition with a team brimming with youth.

A further case in point is the examination of the bowling returns, which show the rewards shared between up-and-comers and seasoned performers. The leading wicket-takers were Sandgate–Redcliffe left-arm medium-pacer Paul Pink and Wynnum–Manly's veteran Scott Prestwidge, each claiming 37. An unfashionable type, Pink has been a rock for the Sandgate–Redcliffe in recent seasons with both bat and ball and shapes as a key player as they rebuild in 2002-03. Pink, who took 7/65 during the season and 7/96 in the semi-finals, was one of three Sandgate–Redcliffe bowlers who produced noteworthy bowling returns. Teenage right-arm quick Nathan Rimmington took six wickets in an innings three times, with his best figures of 6/7 including a hat-trick, while left-arm spinner Matthew Anderson had his team's best haul of 7/46.

Others to excel included Valley team-mates Lee Carseldine (8/37) and Chris Lanagan, whose final season with Ashgrove included a career-best 8/33, and Wynnum–Manly quick Boyd Williams, who took five or more wickets four times to bowl himself into the Queensland Second XI. The bowling average went to Wests veteran captain Greg Rowell, who took 27 wickets at 11.92. Rowell also received the personal reward of winning the Peter Burge Medal for the best and fairest first-grade player, presented by Burge's widow Joan at the annual trophy night.

Batting high points came from Souths left-hander Michael Sippel, who finished with 675 runs, including three centuries, to be the leading run-scorer. No double-centuries were recorded, with Gold Coast's Andrew Symonds hitting the highest score of 182.

The limited-overs final pitted defending champions Valley against Northern Suburbs at Allan Border Field, with young left-arm pace bowler Scott Brant's 3/34 off 10 overs for Norths catching the eye of the state selection panel. Norths (208) won their first trophy in more than a decade in a thrilling finish against Valley (seven for 206), who were unable to get the required ten off the final over bowled by James Hopes.

The women's competition continued to be fine-tuned, with numbers increasing to allow a two-grade competition to be conducted. Wests went one better than their male club counterparts, winning the first-grade premiership by defeating Wynnum–Manly, while Sandgate–Redcliffe beat Wynnum to take out the second-grade title.

Season's end saw another thirty-something calling it quits, with Sandgate's former Queensland all-rounder Brendan Creevey confirming his retirement to concentrate on his teaching career, having now reached the level of deputy principal at his Catholic primary school in Brisbane's north.

BRISBANE FIRST-GRADE TABLE, 2001-02

	M	WO	Wl	D	Ll	LO	Points
Sandgate–Redcliffe	11	2	4	3	2	0	152.93
Western Suburbs	11	1	6	1	2	1	150.56
Valley	11	1	5	2	3	0	145.03
Wynnum–Manly	11	1	5	2	2	1	142.19
South Brisbane	11	0	6	1	4	0	137.48
University of Queensland	11	0	6	2	3	0	135.36
Sunshine Coast	11	0	4	2	5	0	109.93
Redlands	11	0	4	3	3	1	107.93
Northern Suburbs	11	1	2	4	4	0	103.22
Gold Coast	11	0	3	3	3	2	93.61
Beenleigh–Logan	11	1	0	2	7	1	69.98
Toombul	11	0	1	1	8	1	61.67

BRISBANE FIRST-GRADE AVERAGES, 2001-02

BATTING

(Qualification: 400 runs)

	M	I	NO	R	HS	100s	Avge
M. Sippel (South Brisbane)............	11	13	1	675	141*	3	56.25
C. A. Torrisi (University of Queensland) .	11	13	3	505	161*	2	50.50
G. A. Fitness (Sandgate–Redcliffe)......	11	11	2	410	109*	1	45.55
A. Maynard (Sunshine Coast)..........	10	13	1	546	104	1	45.50
M. N. Lunn (South Brisbane)	11	14	2	539	110	1	44.91
N. J. Kruger (Valley)	10	11	0	493	139	1	44.82
D. M. Payne (Redlands)...............	11	15	2	540	132	1	41.53
M. R. Hayward (Redlands)	11	13	1	468	156	1	39.00
M. Goggin (Sandgate–Redcliffe)	11	12	0	466	100	1	38.83
T. Sawyer (South Brisbane)	10	15	3	459	102	1	38.25

BOWLING

(Qualification: 25 wickets)

	M	O	Mdns	R	W	Avge
G. J. Rowell (Western Suburbs)	9	175	68	322	27	11.92
N. J. Rimmington (Sandgate–Redcliffe)	8	108	22	380	27	13.10
C. J. Lanagan (Valley)	8	148	43	361	26	13.88
M. A. Anderson (Sandgate–Redcliffe)	10	217	79	466	30	15.53
M. Shackle (University of Queensland)	8	162.5	47	410	26	15.76
S. A. Prestwidge (Wynnum–Manly)	11	196	42	591	37	15.97
B. O. Williams (Wynnum–Manly)	9	188	46	626	32	19.56
P. D. Pink (Sandgate–Redcliffe)	11	263	60	816	37	22.05
D. R. Turner (Valley)	11	218	57	715	32	22.34

BRISBANE FIRST-GRADE SEMI-FINALS, 2001-02

WESTERN SUBURBS v VALLEY

At Graceville No.1 Oval, Graceville, March 9, 10, 2002. Western Suburbs won on first innings. Valley nine for 276 declared (J. Potts 67, T. Dudgeon 53, J. Dellit 31; G. Schossow 4/62 lost to Western Suburbs eight for 277 (A. Nye 98, M. Lane 47, D. Tuckwell 42; J. Dawes 3/55).

SANDGATE–REDCLIFFE v WYNNUM–MANLY

At Albury Oval, Deagon, March 9, 10, 2002. Drawn. Sandgate–Redcliffe advanced as minor premiers. Wynnum–Manly nine for 305 (S.J. O'Leary 66, S.A Prestwidge 44, I. Duncan 37; P. Pink 7/96) Sandgate–Redcliffe seven for 300 (G.A.J. Fitness 109, G. Batticciotto 40; S.A. Prestwidge 4/65, B. Williams 3/48).

BRISBANE FIRST-GRADE FINAL, 2001-02

SANDGATE–REDCLIFFE v WESTERN SUBURBS

At Allan Border Field, Albion, March 16, 17, 23, 24. Toss: Western Suburbs. Sandgate–Redcliffe won on first innings.

Having dominated Brisbane cricket for the past five years, Sandgate–Redcliffe were not to be denied one more chance of glory, despite sentiment being firmly with the season's surprise packets Western Suburbs. Playing in their first final since winning the premiership in 1987-88, Wests rode into the decider on the back of their inspirational captain, Greg Rowell, who juggled his playing demands with a burgeoning law career.

The final began dourly, with Wests batting first and reaching a competitive total thanks to two of their young guns, Aaron Nye and Steve Paulsen. In his first season since switching from Norths, Nye scored 98 in the semi-final and again fell two runs short of a century in the final. Steve Paulsen also finished just short of a century after hooking a catch to the fine-leg boundary.

Sandgate made a methodical start to their chase, with captain Chris Maclean and former Australian Under-19s batsman Glen Batticciotto whittling away their opponent's lead by the close of day two. If the first two days had been solid rather than spectacular, the second half of the match was a revelation. After Wests mounted an early sortie to have their opponents five down for 234, Gavin Fitness delivered a match-changing counterattack. The veteran keeper, fresh from a century in the semi-final, smashed 85 off 96 balls, including 11 fours and two sixes, to snatch any momentum from Wests. With Paul Pink then providing the finish, Sandgate–Redcliffe gained a lead of 45.

Batting a second time, the crumbling Wests looked in danger of succumbing on the last day until the pugnacious Dean Tuckwell, the only survivor from the 1987-88 premiership team, did his best to turn the clock back. Coming to the crease at four for 79, the 35-year-old right-hander blasted 98 off just 62 balls, clouting seven fours and clearing the Allan Border Field fence on five occasions. With Paulsen again among the runs, Wests declared to give themselves the sniff of a result late on the final day. However, Sandgate–Redcliffe openers Andrew Francey and Batticciotto weathered the storm and ensured the Cup made its fourth visit in five years to the Sandgate–Redcliffe clubhouse at Deagon.

Close of Play: First day, Western Suburbs (1) 5-188 (Paulsen 42, Nye 54); Second day, Sandgate–Redcliffe (1) 1-113 (Francy 17, McLean 52); Third day, Western Suburbs (2) 3-71.

Western Suburbs

A. Bailey c Paterson b Anderson	9	– c Goggin b Pink	9
B. Beavan c Batticcotto b Rimmington	13	– c Hughes b Anderson	30
R. Lupton lbw b Pink	13	– c Pink b Anderson	27
A. Nye run out	98	– c Goggin b Rimmington	6
M. Lane b Rimmington	29	– (7) not out	56
D. Tuckwell c Paterson b Batticcotto	19	– run out	98
S. Paulsen c Pink b Creevey	99	– (5) c Francey b Anderson	44
†C. McLeod st Fitness b Anderson	15		
*G.J. Rowell not out	17	– (8) not out	23
S.J. Magoffin c Goggin b Rimmington	1		
G. Schossow c Fitness b Batticcotto	2		
L-b 7, w 1, n-b 7	15	B 1, l-b 6, n-b 2	9

(149.1 overs) 330 (43 overs) (6 wkts dec) 302
Fall: 20 36 36 97 119 284 304 311 324 330 Fall: 11 59 74 79 137 277

Bowling: *First Innings*—Creevey 32–13–58–1; Pink 27–10–56–1; Rimmington 33–11–81–3; Anderson 46–16–96–2; Batticcotto 11.1–4–32–2. *Second Innings*—Creevey 16–0–115–0; Pink 5–1–18–1; Rimmington 9–0–75–1; Anderson 13–0–87–3.

Sandgate–Redcliffe

A. Francey b Rowell	44	– (2) not out	86
G. Batticcotto c Tuckwell b Nye	37	– (1) c Tuckwell b Schossow	36
*C. McLean c McLeod b Magoffin	52	– c Schossow b Lane	32
M. Goggin c Magoffin b Paulsen	24	– not out	12
G. Hughes c Lupton b Magoffin	13		
†G.A.J. Fitness c Lane b Rowell	85		
M. Paterson c Lane b Paulsen	39		
P. Pink not out	43		
B.N. Creevey c Nye b Rowell	1		
M.A. Anderson c Lane b Paulsen	3		
N.J. Rimmington b Lane	16		
B 3, l-b 3, w 1, n-b 11	18	L-b 1, w 4	5

(121.5 overs) 375 (54 overs) (2 wkts) 171
Fall: 45 115 163 170 234 298 317 320 337 375 Fall: 74 151

Bowling: *First Innings*—Magoffin 26–5–78–2; Rowell 37–12–81–3; Schossow 15–1–83–0; Nye 19–4–41–1; Paulsen 14–1–60–3; Lane 5.5–3–7–1; Beavan 1–0–2–0; Lupton 4–1–17–0. *Second Innings*—Magoffin 10–2–30–0; Rowell 7–2–23–0; Schossow 6–0–34–1; Nye 9–1–25–0; Paulsen 9–2–19–0; Lane 11–2–39–1; Bailey 2–2–0–0.

Umpires: A.J. McQuillan and J.P. Torpey

ADELAIDE A-GRADE CRICKET

By LAWRIE COLLIVER

Kensington made the most of their opportunities to take out the 2001-02 premiership. The Browns were struggling approaching the finals but a narrow win over West Torrens in the second-last round and a massive win over eventual runners-up Sturt in the last round were just enough to clinch fourth spot by less than a point from Glenelg, who had been in the top four all season. Steady rather than strong in bowling, it was their batting that made Kensington the best team during the finals. Their 519 in the final was the highest score in that fixture since 1991-92. Jason Morgan made 244 in that innings and led the competition aggregates, while skipper Dean Waugh and the dependable Barry Steele (389 runs at 35.36 and 25 wickets at 23.64) were the foundations for premiers' success.

Sturt, after suffering three consecutive semi-final losses, made the final, but the bowlers who had performed so well throughout the season let them down. Some might attribute this to the Price Memorial pitch, which was very welcoming to the bowlers in its first season after being relaid. Oliver Thomas and Shaun Tait had fabulous seasons, and Tim Haysman (549 runs at 34.31 and 20 wickets at 17.55) won the Bradman Medal. Matthew King also continued to develop, taking 25 wickets at 18.52 and gaining a place in the ING Cup team.

University finished top in the minor round after improving from sixth last season. Skipper Nathan Adcock (389 runs at 48.62) was dominant and veteran Nick Mosey (370 runs at 37.00) made important runs, but it was the Blacks' bowling that won them most matches. Paul Wilson took 24 wickets at a minimal 10.88 and Mike Smith (20 at 10.50) was also potent when not on state duties. Tea Tree Gully continued their steady improvement to make their first finals appearance since 1997-98. Left-hander Wes Thomas and Ben Cameron continued their exciting development with the bat, and as usual Peter McIntyre bowled plenty of overs. For the second year in a row, Gary Wright made a stack of runs.

Glenelg again narrowly missed the finals, but the fault could not be sheeted home to the bowlers. Neil and Daniel Rowe were well supported by all-rounder Ben Hook (344 runs at 28.66 and 24 wickets at 15.04) but the batting was not up to scratch, with only Toby Koch averaging over 40. Adelaide missed the finals for the second season in a row despite their depth of batting talent. Luke Williams continued to be ignored for a state berth, while his brother Sam (351 runs at 39.00) was useful, and Chris Davies (387 at 77.40) and Ben Johnson (330 at 55.00) both made an impact when available. Lachlan Stevens moved to Adelaide from Queensland and made 117 against Prospect in round 11.

Northern Districts used 21 players and relied heavily on Ryan Harris (243 runs at 34.71 and 23 wickets at 21.08). Mark Cosgrove's average (37.38 from 299 runs) was inflated by a final-round 113 against lowly West Torrens. Left-arm quick Steven Busbridge (21 wickets at 29.48) did well and managed an injury-free season. Prospect dropped seven places and, unlike in 2000-01, could not get away with weak batting. Jeff Vaughan made 204 against Port Adelaide but appeared to lose confidence after being hit in the head by a ball from David Saker at Bellerive Oval early in the season. Apart from the left-arm swingers of Mike Harden (33 at 16.21) the Pirates had little going for them.

Southern Districts improved from second-last mainly due to the efforts of Shane Deitz. His weight of runs earned him a Pura Cup recall for the final match of the season. Skipper Jason Riley (408 runs at 40.80) performed well, but it was the bowling that served the Stingrays best. Experienced seamer Andrew Watherston, off-spinner Dwayne Ross and medium-pacer Brett Bevan (24 wickets at 13.42) were all able to put their team in winning positions at various times. West Torrens and Woodville finished tenth and eleventh respectively again, after Woodville declined the Eagles' merger proposal. Both teams are in the western suburbs where junior numbers are lacking. For the Eagles, Ben Higgins (346 runs at 69.20) was the only player to average over 30, while for Woodville, Mick Miller batted well but was unable to bowl because of a shoulder ailment and Andrew Eime (32 wickets at 25.25) toiled away for 264 overs, the second-highest in the competition

East Torrens continued their fall from grace, although the experienced Graeme Yates maintained his high standard with the bat. In the bowling only youngster Chad Parrish (23 at 25.74) really showed any improvement. Port Adelaide finished bottom for the fourth season in a row, having notched only five wins in that period. Their team was full of imports: captain Andrew Sainsbury (386 runs at 35.09) and Rohan Brewster came over from New South Wales, while Zimbabwe's Dougie Hondo, Stuart Matsikenyeri and Guy Croxford also played in the first eleven.

The competition needs a number of changes if it is to improve. It should repeal the compulsory closure rule which was introduced ten seasons ago, and it needs a merger of two clubs or the removal of one club in order to eliminate the bye, which is a real scourge, particularly for the those teams having a bye near the Christmas break.

ADELAIDE A-GRADE TABLE, 2001-02

	M	WO	W	D	T	L	LO	Match Points	Bonus Points	O/rate Points	Total Points
University	12	2	5	2	0	3	0	130	63.71	0.75	192.96
Sturt	12	1	6	2	0	3	0	125	64.63	–	189.63
Tea Tree Gully	12	0	7	1	0	4	0	112.5	65.49	–	177.99
Kensington	12	0	7	1	0	4	0	112.5	64.07	–	176.57
Glenelg	12	0	7	1	0	4	0	112.5	63.40	–	175.90
Adelaide	12	0	6	2	0	4	0	105	55.64	–	160.64
Northern Districts ..	12	0	6	1	0	5	0	97.5	57.50	0.25	154.75
Prospect	12	0	6	0	0	4	2	90	60.02	–	150.02
Southern Districts ..	12	0	5	1	0	6	0	82.50	63.17	–	145.67
West Torrens	12	0	4	0	0	8	0	60	62.43	–	122.43
Woodville	12	0	3	2	0	7	0	60	53.73	–	113.73
East Torrens	12	0	3	1	0	8	0	52.5	49.04	–	101.54
Port Adelaide	12	0	2	2	0	7	1	45	49.66	0.75	93.91

ADELAIDE A-GRADE AVERAGES, 2001-02

BATTING

(Qualification: 400 runs)

	M	I	NO	R	HS	100s	50s	Avge
S. A. Deitz (Southern Districts)	11	15	4	627	124	1	4	57.00
L. Williams (Adelaide)	11	11	3	453	103*	2	2	56.62
M. C. Miller (Woodville)	8	9	1	449	106	1	3	56.12
W. D. Thomas (Tea Tree Gully)	13	14	2	594	98	0	5	49.50
D. P. Waugh (Kensington)	13	14	1	618	156	2	3	47.53
J. B. Morgan (Kensington)	13	16	0	739	244	1	6	46.18
G. J. Wright (Tea Tree Gully).......	13	14	0	634	162	2	3	45.28
T. K. Koch (Glenelg).............	10	12	1	493	122	1	5	44.81
B. P. Cameron (Tea Tree Gully)......	13	14	2	491	153	1	2	40.91
G. C. Yates (East Torrens)	11	15	4	441	118*	2	2	40.09

* Denotes not out.

BOWLING

(Qualification: 25 wickets)

	M	O	Mdns	R	W	BB	5Wi	10W/m	Avge
S. W. Tait (Sturt)	10	157.5	33	442	31	5/56	1	0	14.29
M. J. Harden (Prospect)	11	186.1	39	535	33	5/27	3	0	16.21
A. Watherston (Southern Districts) ..	12	152.2	34	495	29	4/17	0	0	17.06
D. A. Ross (Southern Districts)	12	286	95	663	36	5/37	2	0	18.41
P. E. McIntyre (Tea Tree Gully)	13	214.5	68	500	27	5/95	1	0	18.51
M. D. King (Sturt)	11	183.2	48	463	25	4/40	0	0	18.52
N. M. Rowe (Glenelg)	12	248.5	69	585	30	5/31	1	0	19.50
M. Munn (Woodville)	7	201.3	44	559	28	6/70	3	0	19.96
D. L. Rowe (Glenelg)	12	198.5	57	554	27	5/26	1	0	20.51
O. C. Thomas (Sturt)	14	235.4	49	774	35	5/36	2	0	22.11

ADELAIDE A-GRADE SEMI-FINALS, 2001-02

STURT v TEA TREE GULLY

At Adelaide Oval No. 2, Adelaide, March 16, 17, 2002. Sturt won on first innings. Sturt 304 (J. R. Orchard 68, C. J. Borgas 58; T. G. R. Borlace 4/49) defeated Tea Tree Gully 179 (W. D. Thomas 45; S. W. Tait 4/34).

UNIVERSITY v KENSINGTON

At Adelaide Oval, Adelaide, March 16, 17, 2002. Kensington won on first innings. Kensington 252 (J. B. Morgan 52, D. P. Waugh 58, B. H. Steele 53) defeated University 192 (N. J. Mosey 54, C. J. Slattery 46; B. H. Steele 5/50).

ADELAIDE A-GRADE FINAL, 2001-02

KENSINGTON v STURT

At Adelaide Oval, Adelaide, March 23, 24, 25, 2002. Kensington won on first innings. Toss: Kensington.

Kensington won their second flag in three seasons, making the highest score in a final since Salisbury's 520 in 1991-92. Jason Morgan was the hero of the match, and indeed the finals, for the Browns, with his nine-hour innings the backbone of the mammoth score. After losing Critchley in Thomas's second over, and Greg Blewett, driving lazily to cover point, inside two hours, Kensington never gave Sturt another glimpse. John Lee joined Morgan and the pair took Kensington to virtual control of the match, adding 147 and looking to be set for more until Lee tickled one to the keeper after tea. Dean Waugh joined Morgan, and the opener brought up his century from 219 balls. Waugh showed little sympathy for the Sturt bowling in his near run-a-ball innings, the pair adding a quick 83 for the fourth wicket. Waugh went in the final hour of the first day to a top-edged pull, then Morgan brought up his 150, and Kensington finished the day still with 50 overs to bat before the compulsory closure.

Sunday's pre-lunch session proved luckless for Sturt, as Morgan and Darren Dempsey ground on to a double-century partnership. Dempsey, who had struggled in the season with an average of 25 to date, made the best of a scratchy start and saw Morgan to his double-century off 390 deliveries. Half an hour after lunch, Morgan and Dempsey fell within an over of each other, Morgan driving to cover and Dempsey edging a drive to the keeper. Morgan batted 526 minutes, faced 428 balls and hit 27 fours and a six, making the highest score in a final since Jack Murray's 248 for East Torrens v Sturt in 1923-24. Sturt's bowlers soldiered on and took some late wickets as Kensington became the first side in a final to bat through to 150 overs and a compulsory closure since the rule was introduced ten seasons ago.

Sturt's only hope for the flag was to bat out 150 overs for a draw, as they had finished above Kensington in the minor round. After Tamblyn was trapped in front in the eighth over, the only real resistance of the innings came as skipper James Orchard added 68 with Tim Haysman. Orchard played aggressively, facing just 42 balls before Blewett began his steady demolition of the innings with a sharp in-ducking yorker. Cameron Borgas became the third leg-before victim, and just as Jason Borgas and Haysman looked as if they would survive the day, the opener got an apparent tickle down the leg side to the very last ball of the day, making his disappointment at the decision clear to all. Unfortunately for Sturt the final day dawned clear, and 55 minutes was all it took for Blewett and Barry Steele to do the mopping up. Veteran James Pyke, playing his last game, made a duck as the Blues crashed quickly to allow for a Browns lunch-time celebration.

David Hookes Medallist: J.B. Morgan.

Close of Play: First day, Kensington 4-321 (Morgan 168, Dempsey 9), Second day, Sturt 4-137 (J.D. Borgas 13).

Kensington

C.M. Critchley c Ferguson b Thomas	1
J.B. Morgan c J.D. Borgas b Haysman	244
G.S. Blewett c Tamblyn b King	16
J.D. Lee c Ferguson b Burr	68
*D.P. Waugh c Ferguson b King	41
D.M. Dempsey c Ferguson b Tait	96
J.B. Creek not out	16

B.H. Steele b Tait	0
†J.B. Palmer c Orchard b Haysman	0
J. Panelli c Burr b Thomas	15
B 4, l-b 11, w 3, n-b 4	22

(150 overs, 566 mins)   (9 wkts dec) 519

Fall: 2 49 196 279 486 487 489 490 519

B. Johnswood did not bat.

Bowling: Thomas 35–9–139–2; Tait 26–3–100–2; King 27–7–74–2; Haysman 24–6–76–2; Burr 34–7–86–1; J.D. Borgas 3–0–23–0; Pyke 1–0–6–0.

Sturt

T. Tamblyn lbw b Johnswood	9
T.P. Haysman c Palmer b Blewett	57
*J.R. Orchard lbw b Blewett	40
C.J. Borgas lbw b Panelli	10
J.D. Borgas b Steele	23
J.K. Pyke c Palmer b Blewett	0
M.R. Burr c Waugh b Blewett	1
†T.C. Ferguson c Waugh b Steele	4

M.D. King c Steele b Blewett	0
O.C. Thomas not out	5
S.W. Tait c Critchley b Blewett	0
L-b 7, w 1, n-b 2	10

(61.5 overs, 219 mins) 159

Fall: 25 93 108 137 143 147 151 154 158 159

Bowling: Steele 22–5–71–2; Johnswood 8–0–25–1; Blewett 19.5–9–28–6; Lee 5–0–22–0; Panelli 7–3–6–1.

Umpires: S.D. Fry and K.D. Perrin.

TASMANIAN CRICKET ASSOCIATION FIRST-GRADE CRICKET

By COLIN CHUNG

As usual with TCA grade cricket, the weather played a telling role in the outcome of many games. In a season of fluctuating fortunes, a number of clubs trailed on the first innings but bounced back to win outright. The early struggles of the Tasmanian team also resulted in a number of clubs benefiting, with senior players like Shaun Young and Dene Hills – of North Hobart and University respectively – spending much of the second half of the season with their club sides. The return of Young was central to North Hobart making the finals, although a knee operation stopped him from playing in them.

One of the highlights of the season was the development of 20-year-old Nathan Webb, who had captained the Tasmanian Under-19s side for two seasons. An Australian Cricket Academy graduate who had promised so much but failed to deliver, the right-hander's game was transformed after a change of clubs from Kingborough to Lindisfarne. Having never passed 50 in four seasons in first grade, Webb finally unleashed his talents with a season-high 174 against North Hobart in round four.

Webb's was one of 18 centuries made during a strange season which also included 125 ducks, 209 instances of batsmen not passing four and only 422 innings reaching double figures out of 900 innings completed. For the second season in a row, no batsman reached 500 runs. The outstanding batsman was Kingborough's Tim Scott, who topped both the aggregates and the averages, scoring 480 runs (with two centuries) at 53.33. Lindisfarne's Mark Nutting enjoyed a good season for the second year running, scoring 440 runs at 29.33. Only three other batsmen passed 400.

Predictably, bowlers enjoyed plenty of success, especially early in the season. Heading the aggregates was University's veteran pace man Josh Marquet, who took 47 at an average of 14.70. Clarence's Mark Colegrave was next with 44 at 14.34. The outstanding bowler, however, was Lindisfarne's Shane Jurgensen. He finished with 31 wickets at the incredible average of 7.32 despite playing only half the season before being elevated into the state side, where his efforts with the ball were paramount in Tasmania reaching the Pura Cup final. As an extreme example of the dominance of bowlers, South Hobart–Sandy Bay medium-pacer Paul Stewart took advantage of the helpful Kingborough wicket to send down nine consecutive maidens against North Hobart before a run was finally scored off his 59th ball. He finished with figures of 18–12–19–3.

Controversy again dogged the finals. Defending champions Lindisfarne were livid at being asked to play Kingborough at New Town, where the well-grassed pitch and overcast conditions meant the toss of the coin was crucial. Predictably Kingborough asked Lindisfarne to bat first, and wickets fell with such monotonous regularity that the game was over in the first session of day two. North Hobart advanced to the final at the expense of Clarence, who could at least be satisfied with their improvement after finishing last the previous season. The final was an accurate reflection of the season, with bowlers dominating and no batsman managing to pass 50 in the four completed innings. North Hobart emerged victorious with their sixth first-grade premiership in 11 seasons, completing the double with the Statewide Kookaburra Cup limited-overs title.

South Hobart–Sandy Bay's Adam Polkinghorne asserted his domination of club cricket by winning his second consecutive TCA Medal with another fine all-round effort which yielded him 425 runs at 38.64 and 33 wickets at 11.27.

TASMANIAN CRICKET ASSOCIATION
FIRST-GRADE LADDER, 2001-02

	M	WO	WI	D	LI	LO	Points	Quotient
Lindisfarne	10	2	4	1	3	0	99.55	1.270
North Hobart	10	2	3	2	3	0	98.87	1.523
Clarence	10	1	4	2	3	0	95.08	1.125
Kingborough	10	0	7	1	2	0	94.43	1.143
South Hobart-Sandy Bay	10	2	1	2	3	2	85.27	1.005
University	10	1	3	1	5	0	79.05	0.996
New Town	10	0	3	2	4	1	72.01	0.892
Glenorchy	10	0	1	1	3	5	54.33	0.449

TASMANIAN CRICKET ASSOCIATION
FIRST-GRADE AVERAGES, 2001-02

BATTING

(Qualification: 300 runs)

	I	NO	R	HS	100s	50s	Avge
T.I. Scott (Kingborough)	10	1	480	127	2	2	53.33
S.R. Mason (New Town)	9	2	369	173*	1	0	52.71
S. Young (North Hobart)	7	0	325	100	1	3	46.43
B.L. Harris (Clarence)	9	1	346	129	1	2	43.25
A.W. Polkinghorne (Sth Hobart-Sandy Bay)	11	0	425	130	1	1	38.64
G.T. Cunningham (New Town)	11	1	356	143	1	1	35.60
N.G. Webb (Lindisfarne)	15	3	426	174	1	1	35.50
R.A. Allanby (Lindisfarne)	13	1	401	161	1	1	33.42
A.J. Dykes (Clarence)	13	1	390	133	1	1	32.50
T.A. Pinnington (North Hobart)	10	0	312	105	1	2	31.20

BOWLING

(Qualification: 20 wickets)

	O	M	R	W	BB	5WI	10W/m	Avge
S.J. Jurgensen (Lindisfarne)	122.3	45	227	31	8/15	4	1	7.32
G.J. Denton (Kingborough)	103.2	24	203	23	8/53	2	0	8.83
A.W. Polkinghorne (Sth Hobart-Sandy Bay)	164.4	40	372	33	6/34	2	0	11.27
M.R. Harry (North Hobart)	116	33	261	21	5/5	2	0	12.45
S.K. Fingas (New Town)	111.3	30	261	20	5/21	2	0	13.05
A.R. Griffith (North Hobart)	176.4	43	448	34	6/47	3	0	13.18
M.J. Parbs (South Hobart-Sandy Bay)	178.2	51	477	35	5/31	1	0	13.63
R.A. Allanby (Lindisfarne)	218.1	74	472	33	8/30	3	1	14.30
M.D. Colegrave (Clarence)	283.2	73	631	44	7/35	2	1	14.34
J.P. Marquet (University)	272.3	71	691	47	7/37	4	1	14.70

TASMANIAN CRICKET ASSOCIATION
FIRST-GRADE SEMI-FINALS, 2001-02

LINDISFARNE v KINGBOROUGH

At New Town Oval, New Town, March 16, 17, 2002. Kingborough won by seven wickets on the first innings. Toss: Kingborough. Lindisfarne 109 (S.P. Heaney 42; R.W. Hodgson 5/38, J.T. Knott 3/27); Kingborough three for 112 (P.G. Di Venuto 51*, S.H. Clark 47*).

NORTH HOBART v CLARENCE

At Anzac Park, Lindisfarne, March 16, 17, 2002. North Hobart won by 67 runs on the first innings. Toss: Clarence. North Hobart 232 (M.D. Pascoe 40, A.R. Griffith 35, D.G.A. Mizzen 32, P.W. Collins 30; M.D. Colegrave 3/84); Clarence 165 (B.G. Costello 46, D.J. Hurd 43; A.R. Griffith 5/60, M.R. Harry 4/47).

TASMANIAN CRICKET ASSOCIATION
FIRST-GRADE FINAL, 2001-02

NORTH HOBART v KINGBOROUGH

At Bellerive Oval, Hobart, March 22, 23, 24, 2002. North Hobart won by 86 runs. Toss: North Hobart.

North Hobart won the toss and elected to bat. Todd Pinnington and Geoff Valentine, playing against his former club, justified the decision with a brisk 86-run opening stand before Valentine was dismissed. His partner followed shortly afterwards, bowled by young pace man Luke Swards with a ball that appeared to keep ominously low. The second session was dominated by the Kingborough bowlers, who cut a swathe through the batting line-up, capturing the last eight wickets for the addition of only 64 runs. Only Ben Donaldson showed any fight as the normally reliable middle to lower order crumbled. Swards finished with career-best figures of 6/81.

Kingborough openers Steve Stubbings and Stuark Clark comfortably put on 37 before Clark was dismissed, whereupon the floodgates opened with the last six batsmen going for 67 runs. Fringe Tasmanian pace man Adam Griffith showed excellent stamina and accuracy, bowling 17.5 consecutive overs on day two.

With a first innings lead of 29 and plenty of time, North Hobart's batsmen again failed to come to terms with the wicket and the accuracy of Robert Hodgson. Five batsmen managed to get a start but North Hobart ended the second day with an overall lead of 175 with two wickets in hand and the stage set for a thrilling last day. Kingborough's hopes of wrapping the innings up quickly were frustrated by some resistance by Paul Guinane and Matthew Pascoe, who carried the lead past 200, eventually setting the Knights a tough 209 for victory. Hodgson was the star, finishing with match figures of 10/103.

Griffith and Pascoe all but ended the contest by reducing Kingborough to five for 46. At this point, Tim Scott, the competition's leading run-scorer, decided to take the attack to the bowlers, clubbing 24 from as many balls, including a towering six off Griffith which disappeared over the grandstand. His dismissal foreshadowed the end, although some resistance late in the order ensured that North Hobart did not start celebrating its sixth first-grade premiership in 11 seasons until well into the final session. Griffith finished with match figures of 9/89.

Man of the Match: A. Griffith.
Close of Play: First day, Kingborough 4-83 (Di Venuto 26, Scott 6); Second day, North Hobart 8-146 (Guinane 8, Pascoe 2).

North Hobart

G. M. Valentine c Monaghan b Swards	35	– (2) lbw Hodgson	21
†T. A. Pinnington b Swards	47	– (1) c Knott b Hodgson	5
C. B. Donaldson b Swards	43	– b Hodgson	23
*M. R. Harry lbw b Swards	7	– lbw b Hodgson	32
P. B. Guinane lbw b Swards	0	– (7) c Monaghan b Knott	16
D. G. A. Mizzen b Swards	2	– c Monaghan b Knott	25
A. R. Griffith c Clark b Hodgson	0	– (9) c Scott b Hodgson	0
M. D. Pascoe lbw b Hodgson	6	– (10) c Clark b Knott	14
P. Collins not out	11	– (5) c Pascoe b Burbury	16
D. G. Templeman c Di Venuto b Hodgson	2	– (8) c Monaghan b Hodgson	2
L. B. O'Shea c Monaghan b Hodgson	4	– not out	6
B 7, l-b 4, n-b 12	23	B 8, l-b 8, n-b 3	19

(51.5 overs, 221 mins)	180	(58.5 overs, 245 mins)	179
Fall: 86 91 116 116 138 142 161		Fall: 12 39 54 81 132 132 144
161 167 180		144 171 179

Bowling: *First Innings*—Hodgson 17.5–2–61–4; Knott 6–3–13–0; De Venuto 7–2–14–0; Swards 21–2–81–6. *Second Innings*—Hodgson 21–6–42–6; Knott 13.5–4–42–3; Burbury 11–1–40–1; Swards 12–2–38–0; Di Venuto 1–0–1–0.

Kingborough

S. D. Stubbings lbw b Griffith	16	– (2) c Pinnington b Griffith	5
S. H. Clark lbw b Griffith	23	– (1) lbw b Pascoe	17
S. A. Verrier b Harry	3	– c Pascoe b Griffith	0
T. A. Burbury c Valentine b Pascoe	3	– c Pinnington b Pascoe	5
*P. G. Di Venuto c Guinane b Pascoe	36	– lbw b Pascoe	5
T. I. Scott c Pinnington b Griffith	6	– b Pascoe	24
†E. J. Monaghan c Guinane b Griffith	0	– (11) not out	2
D. Collins c Pinnington b Griffith	5	– (7) b O'Shea	11
J. T. Knott not out	31	– (8) b O'Shea	1
B. Ribbon lbw b O'Shea	2	– (9) b Griffith	21
L. Swards c Pinnington b Griffith	0	– (10) lbw b O'Shea	17
B 16, l-b 5, w 3, n-b 2	26	B 5, l-b 6, n-b 3	14

(68.5 overs, 287 mins)	151	(55.3 overs, 229)	122
Fall: 37 42 48 58 84 113 114 127 146 151		Fall: 10 14 23 33 46 67 69 88 120 122

Bowling: *First Innings*—Griffith 30.5–11–50–6; Pascoe 24–9–60–2; Harry 8–4–10–1; O'Shea 6–1–10–1. *Second Innings*—Pascoe 15–6–28–4; Griffith 15.3–3–39–3; Harry 12–4–22–0; O'Shea 13–5–22–3.

Umpires: B. W. Jackman and K. J. McGuinness

VICTORIAN PREMIER CRICKET, 2001-02

By KEN WILLIAMS

After finishing the home-and-away programme in fifth place, Fitzroy–Doncaster convincingly defeated Melbourne University, the minor premiers, in the final to win their first premiership since 1993-94. The evenness of the competition was reflected in the qualifying finals, in which the fourth, fifth and sixth-placed teams, St Kilda, Fitzroy–Doncaster and Essendon, defeated their higher-placed opponents. This meant that Melbourne and Carlton, despite finishing second and third on the ladder, failed to reach the semi-finals. Despite a somewhat cool and damp summer, batsmen generally did well, and the season's average of 25.01 runs per wicket was the highest for four seasons.

Fitzroy–Doncaster's success was well deserved as they were easily the strongest batting side. Skipper Brendan Joyce and David Plumpton were the season's leading run-scorers and were well supported by Robbie Bartlett, who top-scored in each of the finals to finish with 851 runs at 47.27, while Chris Reidy and Lloyd Mash also exceeded 500 runs. The club's aggregate of 5,279 runs for the season set a new record. Their attack was unremarkable, with only the new-ball pair of Chris Street (35) and James Renkin (32) capturing 20 or more wickets. Excellent fielding was an important factor in their success. The premiership was a particular triumph for coach Simon Helmot, who had rejoined the club after four years at Hawthorn–Waverley, during which time he coached them to a premiership and three other finals appearances.

Runners-up Melbourne University were stronger in bowling than batting. The experienced Ashley Robertson moved past James Sutherland's club record of 345 wickets. He was well supported by fellow pace men Brett Harrop (31 wickets) and skipper Dan Lowery. Brendan Joseland was easily their leading batsman, with no one else reaching 400 runs.

The beaten semi-finalists, St Kilda and Essendon, who had played off for the 2000-01 flag, were the only sides from that season's top six to appear in these finals. Defending premiers St Kilda headed the table for much of the season but fell away towards the end. Captain Tim O'Sullivan topped the batting averages with 602 runs at 40.13. The absence through injury of Shawn Craig for the second half of the season weakened the batting and Nick Jewell (457) was the only other batsman to exceed 400 runs. The strong pace attack was headed by Justin Murch and Adrian Jones (32 wickets). Justin Gale, who took 5/38 and scored a century in the team's qualifying final win over Carlton, topped the averages with 24 wickets at 15.04.

Essendon were a strong batting side, headed by 22-year-old right-hander, Ben Fletcher, who scored four centuries. Others to score heavily were the consistent Craig Berger (741 runs) and opening batsmen Ricky Marcy (593) and Justin Baker (526). Opening bowlers Jody Hutchinson (43 wickets) and Stuart Clark (38) also did well.

Melbourne lost the qualifying final to the eventual premiers. As usual, they were strong in batting and Warren Ayres' four centuries included the season's highest score, 218 against North Melbourne. He has now made 30 hundreds, a total exceeded by only Jack Ryder (37) and Peter McAlister (31). In making 109 against Footscray–Victoria University he achieved the remarkable feat of having scored hundreds against each of the other 17 clubs. Other batsman to score heavily were Andrew McDonald (598 runs), Andrew Kent (552) and Brad Hodge (446). The bowling averages were headed by newcomer Robert Cassell (20 wickets at 16.90), a member of Australia's winning Under-19s World Cup side.

The remaining finalist, Carlton, owed much to the seam and swing bowling of Craig Sheedy, the only bowler to take 50 wickets. He was supported by Andrew Dickinson (39 wickets) while David Sokulsky topped the batting averages with 656 runs at 43.73, closely followed by the consistent Paul Hetherington (666 runs).

Geelong, one of the early favourites, narrowly missed the finals after a mid-season slump. Skipper Jason Bakker headed the competition's bowling averages and was also the club's leading run-scorer. The absence through injury of their leading batsman, Clinton Peake, for the later part of the season was keenly felt. Camberwell Magpies were well served by all-rounders Damien Shanahan and Aaron Kellett, while Matthew Elliott topped the competition's batting averages for the second year in a row.

For Footscray–Victoria University, who improved from 16th to ninth, Dale McDonald scored 622 runs at 41.46 and Colin Miller toiled hard to capture 33 wickets. Hawthorn–Monash University (formerly Hawthorn–Waverley) slipped from fourth to tenth, thereby missing the finals for the first time since the introduction of the final six in 1997-98. As usual they were well served by their captain and wicket-keeper Peter Roach, who scored 630 runs. Prahran, well placed mid-season, slumped to 11th after failing to win any of their last six matches. Leg-spinner Bryce McGain, the new captain, netted 48 wickets at 18.89, to make him the competition's second-highest wicket-taker, while Jonathan Moss topped both the batting and bowling averages for the second year in a row. Former ACT batsman Anthony McQuire (631 runs) also impressed.

Among the lower clubs, Richmond, premiers in 1999-00, could manage no higher than 12th despite effective bowling by medium-pacer Matthew Albers. Ian Hewett led the batting averages with 393 runs at 49.12 and Gavan Holland was the competition's leading wicket-keeper with 39 dismissals. North Melbourne slipped from sixth to 13th despite good contributions from their captain Liam Pickering (569 runs) and opening bowlers Shannon Waters (38 wickets) and newcomer Emmett Bronca (31). For Northcote, who failed to win a game after Christmas, Michael Allen scored 615 runs including three centuries. Dandenong, for whom fast bowler Will Carr captured 38 wickets, slipped from eight to 15th, while 16th-placed Ringwood's best was former state leg-spinner Craig Howard (35 wickets). South Melbourne came second-last, despite solid batting by the experienced Michael Hansen (614 runs) and Grant Gardiner (571). Although finishing last for the second year in a row,

Frankston Peninsula had several well-performed players. Matthew Mott scored 216 not out against South Melbourne, Justin Mathers made 708 runs, and opening bowlers Cameron Wallace and Darren Groves each took over 30 wickets.

Three players who each played over 200 games retired at the end of the season: Ian Wrigglesworth, the 1996-97 Ryder Medallist, who scored 6,169 runs and took 331 wickets in a career spanning five clubs, most recently Dandenong; Essendon's highly respected captain David Tate, 4,303 runs and 158 wickets; and Richmond's wicket-keeper Gavan Holland, whose career tally of 498 dismissals is exceeded by only Rob Templeton and David Cowper.

The Ryder Medal was won by Warren Ayres, who was previously successful in 1994-95. He joins Keith Stackpole, Warren Whiteside (both three times) and John Grant (twice) as the only players to win the medal more than once. In a tight poll, Ayres received 34 votes, to finish ahead of David Sokulsky (30) and Damien Shanahan (29). The following players made up the Premier Cricket Team of the Season: Warren Ayres (Melbourne), Will Carr (Dandenong), Ben Fletcher (Essendon), Brendan Joseland (Melbourne University), Brendan Joyce (Fitzroy–Doncaster), Dale McDonald (Footscray–Victoria University), Bryce McGain (Prahran) (captain), Jonathan Moss (Prahran), David Plumpton (Fitzroy–Doncaster), Peter Roach (Hawthorn–Monash University), Ashley Robertson (Melbourne University) and Craig Sheedy (Carlton).

VICTORIAN PREMIER CRICKET FIRST XI TABLE, 2001-02

	M	WO	W1	W2	D	LO	L2	L1	T	A	Pts	Quot.
Melbourne University	16	0	7	5	0	2	2	0	0	1	72	1.452
Melbourne	16	1	5	5	0	2	2	0	1	1	70	-0.650
Carlton	17	0	4	7	1	3	1	0	1	0	66	1.158
St.Kilda	17	1	3	6	0	2	2	0	3	0	64	1.308
Fitzroy–Doncaster	17	0	7	3	0	0	3	1	3	0	63	1.408
Essendon	16	0	6	4	0	2	3	0	1	1	60	1.056
Geelong	16	1	2	6	0	5	1	0	1	1	58	1.184
Camberwell Magpies	16	0	7	1	0	1	6	0	1	1	48	1.008
Footscray-Vic University	16	0	3	5	0	4	2	0	2	1	48	0.886
Hawthorn–Monash Uni.	17	0	3	5	0	6	3	0	0	0	48	0.851
Prahran	16	0	3	4	0	5	3	0	1	1	42	1.214
Richmond	16	0	3	4	0	5	3	0	1	1	42	1.126
North Melbourne	17	1	2	1	1	4	6	1	1	0	31	0.752
Northcote	16	0	4	1	1	3	6	0	1	1	30	0.763
Dandenong	16	0	2	3	1	6	4	0	0	1	30	0.720
Ringwood	17	0	2	2	0	7	6	0	0	0	24	0.669
South Melbourne	17	0	2	2	0	5	6	0	2	0	24	0.644
Frankston Peninsula	17	0	3	1	0	6	6	0	1	0	24	-0.041

VICTORIAN PREMIER CRICKET FIRST XI AVERAGES, 2001-02

BATTING

(Qualification: 250 runs)

	M	I	NO	R	HS	100s	50s	Avge
M. T. G. Elliott (Camberwell Magpies)	7	7	1	483	170*	2	2	80.50
B. R. Fletcher (Essendon)	17	19	5	904	132*	4	2	64.57
B. J. Hodge (Melbourne)	8	8	1	446	144	1	3	63.71
D. R. Plumpton (Fitzroy–Doncaster) . .	20	19	3	957	170	3	5	59.81
B. A. Joyce (Fitzroy–Doncaster)	20	20	3	958	95	0	9	56.35
M. P. Mott (Frankston Peninsula)	12	12	2	550	216*	1	2	55.00
W. G. Ayres (Melbourne)	17	17	0	924	218	4	3	54.35
J. Moss (Prahran)	10	11	2	469	127	2	2	52.11
B. R. Joseland (Melbourne University)	19	20	3	885	108*	2	6	52.06
H. P. Birrell (Melbourne University) . .	5	5	0	258	155	1	0	51.60

* Denotes not out.

BOWLING

(Qualification: 20 wickets)

	M	O	Mdns	R	W	BB	5W/i	10W/m	Avge
J. R. Bakker (Geelong)	14	161	40	369	29	5/32	1	0	12.72
A. P. S. Robertson (Melbourne University)	17	250	65	540	42	4/26	0	0	12.86
C. J. Wallace (Frankston Peninsula) . .	17	189.5	53	506	34	4/22	0	0	14.88
J. Moss (Prahran)	10	157.3	43	404	27	5/48	1	0	14.96
J. Gale (St Kilda)	13	142.5	33	361	24	6/61	2	0	15.04
C. I. Sheedy (Carlton)	18	288.3	80	804	53	8/72	2	1	15.17
M. R. Albers (Richmond)	16	284.3	100	679	43	6/29	3	0	15.79
D. Groves (Frankston Peninsula)	17	217.2	57	574	35	6/67	2	1	16.40
S. Pietersz (Camberwell Magpies) . . .	14	202.2	48	509	31	4/19	0	0	16.42
D. Fanning (Geelong)	16	124.1	36	352	21	4/44	0	0	16.76

VICTORIAN PREMIER CRICKET
FIRST XI SEMI-FINALS, 2001-02

ST KILDA v MELBOURNE UNIVERSITY

At St Kilda Cricket Ground, St Kilda. March 23, 24, 2002. Melbourne University won
on first innings. Melbourne University seven declared for 271 (B.R. Joseland 81,
M. D. Hotton 67; A.P. Jones 2/49) defeated St Kilda 181 (T.B.D O'Sullivan 46, M.
Klinger 45; B.D. Harrop 4/40, T.J. Grant 3/42).

FITZROY–DONCASTER v ESSENDON

At Schramms Reserve, Doncaster, March 23, 24, 2002. Fitzroy–Doncaster won on first
innings. Fitzroy–Doncaster 412 (R. A. Bartlett 115, B. A. Joyce 74, C.S. Reidy 66,
L. R. Mash 55, D. R. Plumpton 45;; M. W. H. Inness 3/63) defeated Essendon 342
(B.R Fletcher 109, D. A. Tate 63, J. T. Baker 57, M. W. H. Inness 44; C. B. D. Street
3/61).

VICTORIAN PREMIER CRICKET FIRST XI FINAL, 2001-02

FITZROY–DONCASTER v MELBOURNE UNIVERSITY

At Albert Ground, Melbourne, March 30, 31, 2002. Fitzroy–Doncaster won on first innings. Toss: Melbourne University.

The two clubs had met once in a final: in 1928-29 when University defeated Fitzroy to win their first VCA premiership. University went into this match without their most experienced batsman, Geoff Allardice, who had not recovered from a serious calf injury sustained in the qualifying final.

University chose to bat on a pitch that provided early encouragement for bowlers but generally played well. Coming on after nine overs, left-arm fast-medium bowler Jarrod Travaglia gained movement through the air and off the seam, dismissing Brett Murphy, Huw Birrell and Michael Hotton in his first three overs. University were six for 85 soon after lunch, but Brendan Joseland (260 minutes, nine fours) and Dan Lowery brought about a partial recovery in a patient seventh-wicket stand that added 72 in 140 minutes. When they both fell quickly it ended any chance University had of setting Fitzroy–Doncaster a challenging target. Travaglia finished with career-best figures. Remarkably, he had captured just 13 wickets previously in the season and this was his first five-wicket haul in 55 first eleven matches.

University faced a difficult task in defending their moderate total against Fitzroy–Doncaster's powerful batting. After Ashley Robertson bowled Chris Reidy in his second over, Robbie Bartlett and Brendan Joyce settled into a long partnership. Bartlett played positive strokes all round the wicket, at one stage hitting fast bowler Brett Harrop for three fours in an over. University's slim chances of victory faded when Robertson, their key bowler, broke down with a hamstring strain during his sixth over. Bartlett (170 minutes, 11 fours) and Joyce added 111 for the second wicket. With 78 needed for a first-innings win, David Plumpton joined Joyce and immediately attacked the bowling. Plumpton was in sparkling form, batting only a little over an hour and a half and hitting ten fours. By contrast, Joyce, the only survivor from Fitzroy–Doncaster's last premiership side in 1993-94, batted nearly four and a half hours for his ninth half-century of the season. Each had scored 898 runs for the season before this match and during their innings each passed the previous club record of 915, set by Gary Watts in 1995-96.

University made Fitzroy–Doncaster fight hard for their runs, with tight bowling and excellent ground fielding, but as soon as Fitzroy–Doncaster gained a first-innings lead, Lowery, recognising his side's hopeless position, conceded the game, even though well over a day's play remained. Jarrod Travaglia was awarded the inaugural VCA Medal as Player of the Final.

Player of the Final: J. Travaglia.

Close of play: First day, Fitzroy–Doncaster (1) 0-1 (Bartlett 1, Reidy 0).

Melbourne University

B. F. Murphy c Plumpton b Travaglia	10	B. D. Harrop run out (McNees)	4
M. D. Horton c Sacristani b Travaglia	6	A. P. S. Robertson not out	13
H. P. Birrell lbw b Travaglia	6	†P. A. Percy b Travaglia	11
B. R. Joseland c Travaglia b Renkin	73		
T. W. H. Irvine lbw b Street	0	B 2, l-b 9, w 1, n-b 5	17
J. E. Lusk c Sacristani b Renkin	10		
T. J. Grant b Street	9	(95.4 overs, 361 mins)	191
*D. W. Lowery c Plumpton b Travaglia	32	Fall: 20 26 29 30 51 85 157 166 170 191	

Bowling: Street 26–4–55–3; Renkin 16–4–43–2; Travaglia 17.4–7–32–5; McNees 6–1–17–0; Williams 13–4–23–0; Bartlett 17–13–10–0.

Fitzroy–Doncaster

R. A. Bartlett c Irvine b Lowery	73	L-b 2, n-b 1	3
C. S. Reidy b Robertson	0		
*B. A. Joyce not out	60	(67.5 overs, 276 mins)	(2 wkts) 195
D. R. Plumpton not out	59	Fall: 3 114	

L. R. Mash, †R. J. Sacristani, A. R. Williams, J. P. Renkin, D. A. McNees, C. B. D. Street and J. L. Travaglia did not bat.

Bowling: Robertson 6.3–2–10–1; Harrop 20–2–68–0; Lowery 16–3–45–1; Joseland 15.3–8–32–0; Grant 9.5–2–38–0.

Umpires: G. T. D. Morrow and R. L. Parry.

PERTH FIRST-GRADE CRICKET, 2001-02

By KEN CASELLAS

The once overflowing well that produced quality fast bowlers of the calibre of Graham McKenzie, Dennis Lillee, Terry Alderman and Bruce Reid, to name just a few, has dried up, and in recent years a dearth of fast bowlers has been haunting Western Australian cricket. Finally, the Western Australian Cricket Association has confronted the problem and taken steps to overcome it. After another disappointing season in which Western Australia failed to qualify for either of the interstate finals, the WACA launched the Dennis Lillee Fast Bowling Academy to boost the state's fast bowling stocks. Lillee and former Western Australian coach Daryl Foster will design individual programs for all academy members. Thirty-one young pace bowlers from across the state have been identified and will undergo specialised tuition in the hope of developing their talents to continue the great tradition of Western Australian fast bowling.

The lack of fast bowling talent in the state is illustrated by the fact that in the past few years five pace bowlers from the east of Australia – Steve Nikitaras, Matthew Nicholson, Shane Jurgensen, Stuart Karppinen and Brad Williams – have headed west to play first-class cricket. And the WACA was so concerned at its plight that, at the end of the 2001-02 season, it spoke with Queensland's Adam Dale, Victoria's Damien Fleming and South Australia's Paul Wilson about playing in Perth. Eventually, Wilson agreed to make the move.

Only a few promising fast bowlers are emerging from club ranks in Perth. Three of the most successful in first-grade ranks in 2001-02 are in the veteran class. Subiaco–Floreat's Gavin Swan (31 years old) took 45 wickets at 17.91, Willetton's Sean Cary (31) took 54 at 12.99 and Bayswater–Morley's Peter Rogers finished with 52 at 13.08. South Perth's 24-year-old swing bowler Darren Wates continued to shine at club level and finished the season with 45 wickets at 18.82. The best of the younger brigade of new-ball bowlers included Michael Clark (35 wickets at 15.94), Stephen Jacques (40 at 15.20), Sam Howman (42 at 15.64), Chas Keogh (37 at 23.21), Gavin Wates (37 at 22.27), Wes Robinson (38 at 16.82) and Callum Thorp (50 at 16.38). High hopes are held for Michael Thistle, a member of the Australian Cricket Academy last summer, Andrew James and Joe Barnes.

The most successful of the slow bowlers were left-arm orthodox spinner Brad Oldroyd (39 wickets at 23.36), veteran leg-spinner Scott Moody (39 at 20.82), experienced off-spinner Roshan Jurangapathy (38 at 18.03) and young left-arm wrist-spinner Beau Casson (30 at 14.57), who also scored 368 runs at 92.00. Another left-arm wrist-spinner, Melville's Adam Voges, took nine wickets at 29.88 during a season in which he concentrated, with great success, on his right-handed batting. He topped the first-grade aggregates with 836 runs, including five centuries, at 76.00. He was the deserving winner of the Olly Cooley Medal as the best player in the first-grade competition, and he also scored 144 for the Western Australia Second XI against South Australia.

Others to score in excess of 600 first-grade runs were Perth's Luke Ronchi (706 at 41.52), Gosnells' Ben Hutton (664 at 55.33), South Perth's Chris Rogers (664 at 60.36), Melville's Scott Meuleman (641 at 53.42), Subiaco–Floreat's Kosta Kapinkoff (620 at 36.47), Midland–Guildford's Mark Lavender (618 at 47.54) and Subiaco–Floreat's Murray Goodwin (607 at 50.58). Members of the Western Australian Pura Cup side scored freely from limited opportunities in club cricket. The exception was Adam Gilchrist, who made five runs in his two appearances for Perth.

Subiaco–Floreat consolidated their position as Perth's leading club when they won their second successive first-grade premiership and also took the titles in the third grade, Under-15s and Under-13s competitions. The first-grade premiership was a triumph for captain Gavin Swan and coach Noel Knight, the Western Australian assistant coach. Knight had coached Subiaco–Floreat to victory the previous season and had been coach of two previous premiers, Scarborough (1995) and Bayswater–Morley (1999). The finals were not plain sailing for Subiaco–Floreat. A sensational display by medium-fast opening bowler Gavin Wates, who took 8/14, enabled South Perth to rout Subiaco–Floreat for 77 in an elimination final. South Perth replied with 119 to advance to the semi-finals. Despite the designation of the match, Subiaco–Floreat were not eliminated because they had finished on top of the table after the 13 rounds of qualifying matches. They then scrambled to a 22-run win over Bayswater–Morley in a semi-final and trailed by 53 runs on the first innings in the final.

PERTH FIRST-GRADE TABLE, 2001-02

	M	WO	W1	D	L1	LO	T	Points
Subiaco–Floreat	13	2	8	0	3	0	0	177.46
Melville	13	1	9	0	3	0	0	173.20
Bayswate–Morley	13	0	10	1	2	0	0	164.86
Scarborough	13	3	5	1	4	0	0	161.26
Wanneroo	13	1	7	2	3	0	0	146.06
South Perth	13	0	8	0	5	0	0	144.19
University	13	0	6	0	7	0	0	118.48
Joondalup	13	1	4	0	6	2	0	118.45
Claremon–Nedlands ...	13	1	4	1	7	0	0	116.63
Midlands–Guildford ...	13	1	3	2	7	0	0	104.27
Willetton	13	0	4	3	5	1	0	102.46
Fremantle	13	0	4	0	6	3	0	96.78
Gosnells	13	0	4	3	6	0	0	96.42
Mount Lawley	13	0	4	3	6	0	0	95.99
Perth	13	0	3	1	7	2	0	86.48
Rockingham–Mandurah	13	0	2	1	8	2	0	73.02

PERTH FIRST-GRADE AVERAGES, 2001-02

BATTING

(Qualification: 300 runs)

	I	NO	R	HS	100s	50s	Avge
B. Casson (Scarborough)	9	5	368	122*	1	2	92.00
A.C. Voges (Melville)	15	4	836	170*	5	1	76.00
R.J. Campbell (Subiaco–Floreat).	8	2	451	180*	2	1	75.17
M.J. North (Bayswater–Morley)	11	3	547	136	2	3	68.38
M.E.K. Hussey (Wanneroo)	8	1	442	148	2	2	63.14
C.J.L. Rogers (South Perth).	12	1	664	158	3	2	60.36
B. Hutton (Gosnells).	14	2	664	145*	1	4	55.33
S.W. Meuleman (Melville)	14	2	641	175*	2	2	53.42
M.W. Goodman (Subiaco–Floreat) . . .	13	1	607	123	2	3	50.58
M. Atkinson (Mount Lawley).	15	3	587	106*	3	1	48.91

* Denotes not out.

BOWLING

(Qualification: 25 wickets)

	O	Mdns	R	W	BB	5W/i	10W/m	Avge
J. Barnes (Claremont–Nedlands)	138.2	30	420	33	7/46	3	0	12.72
S.R. Cary (Willetton)	325	99	699	54	6/43	4	0	12.99
P.J. Rogers (Bayswater–Morley)	321.3	107	680	52	6/28	3	0	13.08
B. Casson (Scarborough)	148	39	437	30	5/40	1	0	14.57
B.R. Williams (Bayswater–Morley)	124.2	34	377	25	6/20	1	0	15.08
S. Jacques (Joondalup)	221.4	60	608	40	8/28	2	1	15.20
K.M. Harvey (Scarborough)	179	59	405	26	6/37	1	0	15.58
S.G. Howman (Subiaco–Floreat)	282	87	657	42	6/35	2	0	15.64
M.W. Clark (Subiaco–Floreat)	251	95	558	35	5/41	1	0	15.94
C.D. Thorp (Willetton)	340.3	92	819	50	6/41	3	0	16.38

PERTH FIRST-GRADE ELIMINATION FINALS, 2001-02

SCARBOROUGH v BAYSWATER–MORLEY

At Hillcrest, March 16, 17, 2002. Bayswater–Morley won on first innings. Scarborough 207 (R.M. Baker 124; P.J. Rogers 4/32, B.R. Williams 3/52) lost to Bayswater–Morley eight for 211 (N. Pishos 45, D. Weston 43, M.J. North 40; D.C. Bandy 4/40).

MELVILLE v WANNEROO

At Tompkins Reserve, Alfred Cove, March 16, 17, 2002. Melville won on first innings. Melville 205 (A.D. Mascarenhas 55, A.C. Vogues 45; I. Purcell 3/24) defeated Wanneroo 169 (M.E.K. Hussey 50, C.D. Thorp 48; C. Keogh 4/76).

SUBIACO–FLOREAT v SOUTH PERTH

At Floreat Park Oval, Floreat, March 16, 17, 2002. South Perth won on first innings. Subiaco–Floreat 77 (S.A. Glew 36; G.A. Wates 8/14) and two for 38 lost to South Perth 119 (S.M. Gibson 44; P. Henryon 4/25, S. Moody 4/35).

PERTH FIRST-GRADE SEMI-FINALS, 2001-02

MELVILLE v SOUTH PERTH

At Fletcher East, Carlisle, March 23, 24, 2002. South Perth won on first innings. South Perth seven declared for 266 (C.J.L. Rogers 90*, K.W. Daye 55, G.A. Wates 40; A.D. Mascarenhas 2/66) defeated Melville 184 (J.D. Meuleman 40; B.J. Oldroyd 6/69).

SUBIACO–FLOREAT v BAYSWATER–MORLEY

At WACA Ground, Perth, March 23, 24, 2002. Subiaco–Floreat won on first innings. Subiaco–Floreat 164 (M.W. Goodwin 77, M.P. Simpson 41; B.R. Williams 4/35, P.J. Rogers 4/47) defeated Bayswater–Morley 142 (C.G. Mason 52, M.J. North 43; S.G. Howman 3/22, M.W. Clark 3/33).

PERTH FIRST-GRADE FINAL, 2001-02

SUBIACO–FLOREAT v SOUTH PERTH

At WACA Ground, Perth, March 29, 30, 31, April 1, 2002. Subiaco–Floreat won by 66 runs. Toss: South Perth.

Darren Wates, elder brother of Gavin, gave a fine display of swing bowling and helped South Perth dismiss Subiaco–Floreat for a moderate first-innings score. Kosta Kapinkoff, with a defiant three-hour innings, and Scott Moody rescued the side from disaster after coming together at a perilous seven for 83. Gavin Wates and Chris Rogers made good starts, but South Perth also slumped badly, and were seven for 105 before Christian Moir (138 balls) and Gareth Cooks put on 122 for the eighth wicket to give South Perth a handy first-innings lead. Subiaco–Floreat then asserted their authority. Openers Rob Campbell and David Bolton put on 126 before Murray Goodwin (165 balls) hammered a stylish century, and the side were able to set South Perth a target in the hope of dismissing them and winning outright. Subiaco–Floreat's pace trio of Gavin Swan, Michael Clark and Sam Howman then made early breakthroughs before Moody's leg-spin completed the task. Only Darren Wates (who hit 13 boundaries off 67 balls) and Shaun Gibson showed the required spirit of defiance.

Man of the Match: G.G. Swan.

Close of play: First day, South Perth (1) 1-49 (Wates 35, Daye 11). Second day, Subiaco–Floreat (1) 0-96 (Campbell 42, Bolton 45). Third day, South Perth (2) 1-12 (Daye 4).

Subiaco–Floreat

D. J. Bolton c Higgins b Cooks	12	– (2) c Brown b G. A. Wates	70
R. J. Campbell c Gibson b Cooks	0	– (1) c D. J. Wates b G. A. Wates	50
M. W. Goodwin b D. J. Wates	24	– b Oldroyd	106
S. A. Glew run out (Higgins)	9	– c Moir b Gibson	21
K. Kapinkoff not out	79	– c Moir b Rogers	22
C. J. Cann c Moir b D. J. Wates	5	– c Gardiner b Oldroyd	32
†M. P. Simpson lbw b Higgins	2	– c Daye b Gibson	6
S. G. Howman c Moir b D. J. Wates	0	– (9) not out	8
S. A. Moody c Moir b D. J. Wates	27	– (10) not out	3
M. W. Clark c and b Oldroyd	5	– (8) c Daye b Gibson	2
*G. G. Swan c and b D. J. Wates	6		
L-b 7, w 3, n-b 9	19	B 1, l-b 8, w 2, n-b 4	15

(73 overs, 289 mins) 188 (110 overs, 478 mins) (8 wkts dec) 335
Fall: 12 46 46 63 71 82 83 157 177 188 Fall: 126 143 192 246 314 321 322 324

Bowling: *First Innings*—D. J. Wates 22–7–54–5; G. A. Wates 16–5–29–0; Cooks 12–2–43–2; Higgins 8–3–15–1; Oldroyd 15–2–40–1. *Second Innings*—D. J. Wates 31–8–84–0; G. A. Wates 19–7–40–2; Higgins 6–2–20–0; Oldroyd 34–2–117–2; Cooks 5–3–12–0; Gibson 8–1–29–3; Rogers 7–0–24–1.

South Perth

H. F. Brown lbw b Swan	0	– lbw b Swan	8
K. W. Daye lbw b Swan	13	– c Simpson b Clark	4
G. A. Wates c Simpson b Swan	46	– c Glew b Swan	10
C. J. L. Rogers c Simpson b Howman	30	– c Simpson b Howman	15
*D. J. Wates lbw b Howman	11	– lbw b Moody	66
S. M. Gibson c Simpson b Clark	0	– c Swan b Moody	57
B. S. Gardiner lbw b Clark	1	– (8) lbw b Clark	13
†C. A. Moir lbw b Howman	72	– (7) c Bolton b Moody	2
G. Cooks c Simpson b Swan	48	– c Howman b Moody	20
B. J. Oldroyd c Kapinkoff b Swan	14	– c Goodwin b Moody	10
C. S. Higgins not out	0	– not out	5
B 1, l-b 5	6	B 1, l-b 4, n-b 1	6

(82.5 overs, 301 mins) 241 (73.3 overs, 263 mins) 216
Fall: 0 62 63 94 95 97 105 Fall: 12 12 28 78 127 140 181
227 241 241 182 195 216

Bowling: *First Innings*—Swan 23.5–5–70–5; Clark 22–7–57–2; Howman 20–4–61–3; Campbell 1–0–5–0; Moody 14–3–40–0; Bolton 2–0–2–0. *Second Innings*—Swan 22–10–59–2; Clark 20–9–43–2; Howman 10–1–43–1; Campbell 3–0–14–0; Moody 18.3–5–52–5.

Umpires: A. R. Craig and I. H. Lock.

NATIONAL COUNTRY CRICKET
CHAMPIONSHIPS, 2001-02

By WARWICK TORRENS

Going into the championships with nine new players, three of whom were replacements after the initial team had been selected, Queensland pulled off a surprise by winning the 18th series of National Country Cricket Championships quite comfortably. David Else of Toowoomba, who had been the Queensland wicket-keeper in 1998-99, his only previous championships, returned to the team as captain and opening batsman. He handled all positions with great skill and was voted Player of the Series as well as being selected in the Australian Country XI to play the New Zealanders at Bowral. His team-mate Brian May headed the competition aggregates with 336 runs at 84.00, and Else was second with 282 at 40.28.

The success of the youthful Queensland team brought disappointment to other participants. Victoria had high hopes in a home series and began well by defeating Western Australia, only to lose to New South Wales in the second highest scoring game of the series. In the fourth round the Victorians found the youthful Australian Capital Territory too strong and dropped out of contention. They gained some consolation in the final round when they defeated Queensland narrowly to retain the Heinz Cup, the trophy the two teams fight for each year.

Runners-up New South Wales began by losing to Australian Capital Territory in a close game but then began to perform well, only to lose to Queensland in the fourth round. In the final round they required an outright victory to have any chance of retaining the title they had won the previous season at Albany. Niggling injuries were beginning to take their toll, and although New South Wales outplayed South Australia there was insufficient time for an outright victory. Daniel Hughes took most wickets in the competition with 17 at 15.76.

Australian Capital Territory adopted a selection policy of including a large number of young players, a policy that worked well. Though finishing in fourth place they managed to defeat New South Wales and Victoria and tie with Queensland in the limited-overs match. They were disappointed to lose to the two teams to finish below them on the points table. They brought only 12 players, with only former New South Wales Colt Michael O'Rourke, the captain, having previous championships experience. Their overall performances promise well for future success.

South Australia and Western Australia each had their moments, the former winning one match, the latter two. The low point of the championships was South Australia's performance in their opening match against Queensland, when they were dismissed twice. Queensland were left to score 88 runs for victory in half an hour, and managed 45 before time ended the game. In this match Queensland's Brett Ambrose captured a total of nine wickets (and 15 for the competition at 15.53), passing the previous record of eight, a figure that had been achieved on six occasions and was to be achieved again by South Australian opening bowler Ben Klemm (who took 16 wickets in the competition) in the second round. For South Australia in the same match Dan Stratford top-scored in each innings (making 21 and 36), a feat achieved only once previously, by Lew Schulte for Queensland in 1989-90.

For the first time the championships were held in and around Warrnambool on Victoria's western coast. As well as gaining three selections in the Australian Country team, Queensland also provided the two reserves: 19-year-old Nathan Stains was the batting reserve and 20-year-old Cameron Glass the bowling reserve.

Player of the Series: D. R. Else (Queensland)
Don Bradman Batting Trophy: B. K. D. May (Queensland)
Bill O'Reilly Bowling Trophy: D. Hughes (New South Wales)
Fieldsman of the Series: S. A. Baker (Queensland)

ROUND ONE

At Reid Oval, Albert Park, Warrnambool, January 7, 8, 2002. Australian Capital Territory won on first innings. Australian Capital Territory 248 (C. D. Hanna 102, C. J. Males 44; D. Hughes 3/52) and three for 40; New South Wales 240 (G. A. Grimmond 136; A. D. Jones 3/47).

At Recreation Reserve, Merrivale, January 7, 8, 2002. Queensland won on first innings. South Australia 64 (B. W. Ambrose 5/24, C. R. Glass 4/24) and 166 (B. W. Ambrose 4/52, P. J. Reimers 3/20); Queensland four for 143 declared and four for 45 (S. J. Merkel 3/19).

At Davidson Oval, Warrnambool, January 7, 8, 2002. Victoria won on first innings. Western Australia nine for 289 declared (L. G. Burns 133, C. G. R. Tonkin 52; P. A. Barber 4/54); Victoria seven for 306 (B. J. Glenn 102*, D. K. Taylor 88; P. M. Tomasi 3/113).

ROUND TWO

At Recreation Reserve, Dennington, January 9, 10, 2002. South Australia won on first innings. Australian Capital Territory 211 (S. A. Holcombe 58; B. Klemm 4/52) and six for 61 (B. Klemm 4/28); South Australia 250 (S. J. Merkel 63, R. A. Johnson 49, C. W. Reimann 46; A. D. Jones 6/77).

At Walter Oval, Albert Park, Warrnambool, January 9, 10, 2002. New South Wales won on first innings. Victoria eight for 304 (P. A. Barber 131, B. J. Glenn 51; D. Hughes 3/51); New South Wales seven for 325 (B. Nott 69*, R. Starr 67, S. G. Moore 45; D. G. Ablitt 4/69).

At Avery's Paddock, Southcombe Park, Port Fairy, January 9, 10, 2002. Queensland won on first innings. Queensland eight for 270 (B. K. D. May 132*; J. M. Partington 3/72, C. Phelps 3/91); Western Australia 131 (S. B. Connor 6/18) and three for 94.

ROUND THREE

At Recreation Reserve, Allansford, January 11, 2002. Match tied. Queensland six for 251 (N. J. Stains 69*, C. M. Murree 67; C. J. Males 4/36); Australian Capital Territory

251 (A.J. Brettell 61, S.A. Holcombe 53, M.J. Dawn 49; B.W. Ambrose 3/46, P.J. Reimers 4/55).

At Recreation Reserve, Merrivale, January 11, 2002. New South Wales won by 78 runs. New South Wales eight for 263 (C.J. Haworth 106, H.J. Muller 49*, S.G. Moore 46; J.M. Partington 3/56); Western Australia 185 (G.J. Dehring 84, L Hardie 63; D. Hughes 4/30, M. Chicken 3/26).

At Avery's Paddock, Southcombe Park, Port Fairy, January 11, 2002. Victoria won by six wickets. South Australia seven for 229 (T. Wilton 92; D.G. Ablitt 3/40); Victoria four for 232 (D. Thatcher 65, K.J. Burdett 60, H. Behrens 59*).

ROUND FOUR

At Recreation Reserve, Allansford, January 13, 14, 2002. Australian Capital Territory won on first innings. Australian Capital Territory 259 (P.W. Colebourne 78, M.P. O'Rourke 55, D.J. Richards 46; S.A. Rea 3/39, T.D. Wrigglesworth 3/66) and one for 85 (M.J. Dawn 53*); Victoria 204 (T.D. Wrigglesworth 66, C.J. Bambury 40; C.J. Males 4/46, P.T. Grant 4/52).

At Recreation Reserve, Dennington, January 13, 14, 2002. Queensland won on first innings. Queensland six for 352 (D.R. Else 113, B.K.D. May 68, C.M. Murree 57; D. Hughes 4/111) and one for 70; New South Wales 246 (C.J. Haworth 57, G.A. Grimmond 56, H.J. Muller 40*; C.R. Glass 6/114, C.M. Murree 3/20).

At Walter Oval, Albert Park, Warrnambool, January 13, 14, 2002. Western Australia won on first innings. Western Australia nine for 334 (C.G.R. Tonkin 142, L. Hardie 91; B. Klemm 4/58, R.A. Johnson 3/71) and four for 120 (L.G. Burns 49*, L. Hardie 40); South Australia 131 (G.D. Fiebig 49; M. Carmody 6/78).

ROUND FIVE

At Recreation Reserve, Merrivale, January 15, 16, 2002. Western Australia won on first innings. Australian Capital Territory 174 (A.J. Brettell 65; P.M. Tomasi 4/33, M. Carmody 3/34); Western Australia eight for 254 (P.M. Tomasi 46, G.J. Dehring 45, J.M. Partington 43; C.J. Males 3/42).

At Davidson Oval, Warrnambool, January 15, 16, 2002. New South Wales won on first innings. South Australia 153 (G.D. Fiebig 45; M. Chicken 5/66); New South Wales four for 297 (S.J. Mace 110, S.G. Moore 81, G.A. Grimmond 60; B. Klemm 3/62).

At Reid Oval, Albert Park, Warrnambool, January 15, 16, 2002. Victoria won on first innings. Victoria 256 (D.K. Taylor 54, P.A. Barber 48, K.J. Burdett 42; D.P. Richardson 4/97, B.W. Ambrose 3/82); Queensland 250 (D.R. Else 85, B.K.D. May 49; T.D. Wrigglesworth 4/46, C.J. Bambury 3/36).

POINTS TABLE, 2001-02

	Played	Won	Lost	Tied	Points
Queensland	5	3	1	1	48.20
New South Wales	5	3	2	0	40.48
Victoria	5	3	2	0	39.80
Australian Capital Territory	5	2	2	1	37.18
Western Australia	5	2	3	0	34.72
South Australia	5	1	4	0	26.04

CHAMPIONSHIP WINNERS

Season	Venue	Winner
1984-85	Beenleigh, Qld	New South Wales
1985-86	Riverland, SAust	New South Wales
1986-87	Dubbo, NSW	Australian Capital Territory
1987-88	Canberra, ACT	Queensland
1988-89	Bunbury, WAust	New South Wales
1989-90	Bendigo, Vic	New South Wales
1990-91	Townsville, Qld	Victoria
1991-92	Riverland, SAust	New South Wales
1992-93	Newcastle, NSW	New South Wales
1993-94	Canberra, ACT	Australian Capital Territory
1994-95	Albany, WAust	Queensland
1995-96	Sale–Maffra, Vic	New South Wales
1996-97	Toowoomba, Qld	Queensland
1997-98	Mount Gambier, SAust	Western Australia
1998-99	Barooga, NSW	Queensland
1999-00	Canberra, ACT	Queensland
2000-01	Albany, WAust	New South Wales
2001-02	Warrnambool, Vic	Queensland

CHAMPIONSHIP AVERAGES, 2001-02

BATTING

	M	I	NO	R	HS	100s	50s	Avge
B. K. D. May (Qld)	5	6	2	336	132*	1	1	84.00
C. J. Haworth (NSW)	5	5	1	221	106	1	1	55.25
L. G. Burns (WAust)	4	6	1	276	133	1	0	55.20
G. A. Grimmond (NSW)...........	5	5	0	268	136	1	2	53.60
N. J. Stains (Qld).................	5	6	2	213	69*	0	1	53.25
P. A. Barber (Vic)	5	5	0	237	131	1	0	47.40
C. G. R. Tonkin (WAust)	5	5	0	211	142	1	1	42.20
S. G. Moore (NSW)................	5	5	0	206	81	0	1	41.20
D. R. Else (Qld)...................	5	7	0	282	113	1	1	40.28
L. Hardie (WAust)	4	6	0	226	91	0	2	37.66
A. J. Brettell (ACT)................	5	6	0	212	65	0	2	35.33

* Denotes not out.

BOWLING

	M	O	Mdns	R	W	BB	5W/i	10W/m	Avge
M. Chicken (NSW)	3	53.1	16	139	10	5/66	1	0	13.90
B. W. Ambrose (Qld)	4	109.4	34	233	15	5/25	1	0	15.53
D. Hughes (NSW)	5	101	34	268	17	4/30	0	0	15.76
C. J. Males (ACT)	5	107	41	229	14	4/36	0	0	16.35
T. D. Wrigglesworth (Vic)..........	4	69	15	191	10	4/46	0	0	19.10
P. M. Tomasi (WAust)	4	67	21	195	10	4/33	0	0	19.50
A. D. Jones (ACT)	4	81.5	17	221	11	6/77	1	0	20.09
B. Klemm (SAust)	5	107.2	25	337	16	4/28	0	0	21.06
M. Carmody (WAust)	5	84	17	232	11	6/78	1	0	21.09
D. P. Richardson (Qld)	4	93.5	32	227	10	4/97	0	0	22.70

SCHOOLS' CRICKET, 2001-02

By Dr GREG McKIE

After struggling to justify its existence for several years, the Australian Schools' Cricket Council held a "do-or-die" meeting in the Australian Cricket Board's offices in December 2001. The President (Jim Thompson OAM) opened the meeting by providing a brief summary of the history of ASCC. Started in the mid-1960s, ASCC's primary function was to provide overseas tours for schoolboy cricketers. This role later expanded into running the Australian Under-16s and Under-19s national competitions, hosting overseas national youth team tours and running the Australian Champion School Team Competition.

The ACB took over the running of the Under-16s (now Under-17s) and the Under-19s competitions in 1981, as they wished these competitions to be open, and not just restricted to schoolboys. The transition to ACB control was smooth, as the majority of ASCC personnel were closely aligned with state associations and they carried on their organisational tasks as if nothing had changed. The Champion School Team Competition was called the Gillette Cup between 1988 and 1996 and was then part-sponsored by the ACB for a further two years. It has been in abeyance since then because of the lack of a national sponsor. The ASCC have hired a professional "sponsor-seeker" to find a sponsor, but to no avail.

The meeting reflected on the success of this competition. Although the competing teams were only school teams and the competition ran for only ten years, a surprising number of top-flight cricketers played in these matches. A total of 23 first-class players appeared, including the late Ben Hollioake (who played Test cricket for England) and Australian international level players such as Shane Lee, Wade Seccombe, Nathan Hauritz and Michael Di Venuto. Naturally, the demise of this competition was regretted.

After these introductions, Ross Turner (ACB General Manager, Game Development) then outlined how the ACB's Game Development Strategic Plan had been created and the importance of cricket in schools for the future of the game. The ACB realised they need a body which could provide them with advice and information regarding school cricket. The question for discussion then was whether ASCC was to be this body or whether something more suitable should be created.

State-by-state, the situation within schools was then explained by the various delegates. The Australian Capital Territory has a college, a primary and a women's competition which work closely with the senior association. All competitions are fully representative of all three school streams (government, private non-Catholic, and Catholic). Plans are in hand to create an indigenous team which would compete as an equal entity within the existing structure. No primary school cricket is played in the Northern Territory, yet they still manage to play an interstate exchange with Queensland. Effectively, any youngsters learning cricket in the Northern Territory do so through their club. The secondary school cricket set-up is based around Darwin and Alice Springs. The winners of each section play off to gain the title of "Champion School Cricket Team".

New South Wales continues to run a weekly schoolboys competition and a champion school knockout competition. All school systems are eligible to compete in the knockout competition. A week-long interstate cricket exchange with Queensland continues at the senior school level. Queensland runs state-wide competitions at Under-15s and Under-19s levels. As well as these, it still runs a Champion School Cricket Team competition.

The SACA runs South Australia schools' cricket and they continue to stage the Champion School Cricket Team competition, which is open to all school systems. Because of the college situation, Tasmanian government schools do not play any schools cricket beyond Year 10 level. The private schools continue to play their roster games and the game is still strong in these schools.

The Victoria Schools' Cricket Association has now been absorbed by the VCA. Existing competitions will be maintained, but they will now be fitted into VCA under-age competitions so that players are not put in the position of having to choose whether to represent their school or to play in a competition which is part of the "cricket pathway". The interstate game against South Australia was cancelled for the second year in a row because of clashes with VCA fixtures. South Australia had the same problem. Western Australian schools' cricket continues to be run by the senior association. The inter-school knockout competition continues to thrive but the game is still healthy only within the private school system.

In summary, in the majority of states or territories the school competitions are now run by state associations. This arrangement has advantages from the funding viewpoint, but it means that school competitions are sometimes fitted around existing state competitions, which is not always to the benefit of the game in schools. A shortage of teachers able and willing to run the game has always been part of the problem, but the inevitable clashes of fixtures with senior associations mean that the better class of school cricketers will probably choose the match which leads to higher honours. Schools cannot offer such attractions.

The ACB's attitude is that Australian cricket must have both a vibrant school and viable club cricket system. To help both of these entities, stronger links need to be made between schools and clubs. This has been tried in Victoria with some success, but further progress is necessary. One way to force the issue is to compel senior teams to field an equivalent number of junior sides. Where this has happened, clubs have had to create junior sides. If they could not do that, the logical way to go was to approach the local school and offer to run a Friday night or Saturday morning side for them. Both organisations obviously benefit from such an arrangement.

At the end of the meeting, the concept of reviving a national schools' carnival was strongly endorsed by all delegates. The proviso was that such a carnival did not interfere with the ACB's overall game development plan. ASCC saw its role as "providing input, opportunity and resources for the furthering of cricket as a part of the educational system and in partnership with the ACB". ASCC resolved also to provide resources to the ACB to "assist in the dissemination of information and ideas from the educational community".

The ACB seemed to agree with these objectives, as they require continuing information on what is happening in schools as part of their national game development strategy. The meeting felt that School Sport Australia was not fully representative of cricket in Australian schools and that a body such as ASCC was more in tune with what was happening at state and national level.

At the end of the meeting a series of suggestions was made in an attempt to revive the game in schools. The northern states warmed to the idea of an interchange with Asian school teams in either Malaysia or Indonesia. As Northern Territory teams have been competing for several years in Papua New Guinea, this concept has already been tested and found to work. All states noted that with the demise of the Gillette Cup, the number of teams entering state-wide competitions has declined. The Australian Champion School Cricket Team Competition certainly persuaded schools to play cricket, many schools having their first contact of inter-school sport at this level. The number of schools competing at the elimination level throughout Australia in the last year of the competition (1998) was well over 1,300. Some of these schools have stopped playing inter-school sport, which has implications for the future of the game at the national level and for the health of the game at school level.

The meeting was positive in the sense that ASCC will continue to exist. Against this however is the realisation that the people running ASCC are not getting any younger (most of them are long retired) and that there has simply not been an influx of younger teachers into school cricket administration. Without extra personnel, ASCC is doomed to collapse unless it can justify its existence by running some sort of national competition. Without sponsorship, this seems unlikely.

WOMEN'S CRICKET, 2001-02

By ERICA SAINSBURY

AUSTRALIAN WOMEN'S NATIONAL CRICKET LEAGUE, 2001-02

New South Wales underlined their continuing dominance of senior women's cricket in Australia with their sixth consecutive national title, in the process extending their unbeaten finals record to 14 games. Ably led by former vice-captain Julie Hayes following the transfer of Australian captain Belinda Clark to Victoria, New South Wales also became the first team in the six-year history of the competition to achieve a perfect record of ten victories from ten games.

Lisa Sthalekar (347 runs at 38.55 and 11 wickets at 20.54) replaced Clark at the top of the batting order, and enjoyed a highly profitable partnership with Lisa Keightley (339 runs at 33.90). Martha Winch (245 at 35.00) made a welcome return to the New South Wales team, and veteran opening bowler Bronwyn Calver set a new national league record in taking 18 wickets (at 16.44), well supported by Emma Twining (14 at 14.71). For Victoria, the addition of Clark (433 runs at 43.30) signalled an upturn in fortune as she led them from last place in the previous season to a finals berth; Melanie Jones (321 runs at 40.12) was another of the tournament's leading batters. South Australian captain Karen Rolton was again named Player of the Season for her all-round performance of 509 runs (at 63.62 and a strike-rate of 91.38, with two centuries) and ten wickets at 20.10, but hers was too much a lone hand, and South Australia finished third. Queensland slipped two places to fourth, but several young players showed great promise, including 18-year-old Belinda Matheson (10 wickets at 21.90, including the season's best figures of 5/19 off ten overs) and 21-year-old Melissa Bulow (265 runs at 33.12, including a century). Western Australia's experienced internationals Zoe Goss and Avril Fahey suffered loss of form and the side failed to win a match. Several other young players made their mark, including Australian Capital Territory Under-19s captain Kris Britt (196 runs at 24.50), who elected to play for South Australia in the absence of a senior Australian Capital Territory side, and Alex Blackwell from New South Wales, who along with Matheson and Bulow were selected in the Australian Youth team that defeated New Zealand A in Melbourne in February.

PRELIMINARY GAMES

At Thomas Dalton Park, Wollongong, November 3, 2001. New South Wales won by 42 runs. Toss: New South Wales. New South Wales eight for 183 (B.L. Calver 53, M.A.J. Goszko 49; L. Ebsary 3/29, K.L. Rolton 2/28, N. Maidment 2/39); South Australia 141 (K.L. Rolton 49, K. Britt 36; E. Twining 3/16, B.L. Calver 3/25).

At Allan Border Field, Albion, November 3, 2001. Victoria won by five wickets. Toss: Queensland. Queensland eight for 192 (M. Bulow 61, B. Matheson 47; C.L. Fitzpatrick 2/34, B. White 2/35); Victoria five for 193 (S. Edwards 64, B.J. Clark 62; B. Buckley 3/32).

At Thomas Dalton Park, Wollongong, November 4, 2001. New South Wales won by 129 runs. Toss: New South Wales. New South Wales three for 230 (M.A.J. Goszko 85, M.A. Winch 65*; E. Sampson 2/41); South Australia 101 (K. Britt 33; S. Andrews 2/7, T.A. McGregor 2/16).

At Allan Border Field, Albion, November 4, 2001. Victoria won by 42 runs. Toss: Victoria. Victoria nine for 235 (B.J. Clark 116, M. Jones 46; C. Kross 5/28, B. Matheson 2/19); Queensland eight for 193 (C. Kross 38*, R. Lee 34*; B. White 2/29, N. Wood 2/30, S. Young 2/37).

At Abblett Park, Scarborough, November 24, 2001. South Australia won by 68 runs. Toss: Western Australia. South Australia eight for 229 (K.L. Rolton 147; N. Morrison 2/36, J. Burnett 2/43); Western Australia 161 (H. Taylor 35; E. Sampson 3/30, H. Booth 2/17).

At Abblett Park, Scarborough, November 25, 2001. South Australia won by seven wickets. Toss: Western Australia. Western Australia eight for 207 (E.P Campbell 51); South Australia three for 208 (K.L. Rolton 82, K. Britt 78).

At Drummoyne Oval, Drummoyne, December 1, 2001. New South Wales won by six wickets. Toss: Queensland. Queensland eight for 183 (J.C. Price 66; T.A. McGregor 2/29, L.C. Sthalekar 2/34); New South Wales four for 185 (L.C. Sthalekar 80*, M.A. Winch 32).

At Drummoyne Oval, Drummoyne, December 2, 2001. New South Wales won by six wickets. Toss: Queensland. Queensland 122 (S.A. Cooper 30; B.L. Calver 3/21, E. Twining 2/24, L.C. Sthalekar 2/28); New South Wales four for 123 (L.M. Keightley 45).

At Central Reserve, Glen Waverley, December 8, 2001. Victoria won by seven wickets. Toss: Victoria. Western Australia 123 (E.P. Campbell 34, D. Holden 33*; N. Wood 2/15, S. Young 2/17, C.R. Smith 2/30); Victoria three for 124 (M. Jones 40*, K. Applebee 32*; N. Morrison 2/25).

At Central Reserve, Glen Waverley, December 9, 2001. Victoria won by six wickets. Toss: Victoria. Western Australia 175 (A. Gray 60; C.L. Fitzpatrick 2/23, S. Young 2/28, K. Applebee 2/32); Victoria four for 176 (B.J. Clark 62, L.C. Broadfoot 52; Z.J. Goss 2/22).

At Adelaide Oval, Adelaide, December 22, 2001. Victoria won by 77 runs. Toss: South Australia. Victoria eight for 219 (B.J. Clark 84, M. Jones 64; K.L. Rolton 4/27); South Australia nine for 142 (L. Ebsary 51, N. Maidment 44; K. Winterton 3/10).

At Adelaide Oval, Adelaide, December 23, 2001. South Australia won by 27 runs. Toss: South Australia. South Australia 156 (K.L. Rolton 65; S. Young 3/32, C.R. Smith 2/10); Victoria 129 (K. Britt 3/17, B. Noack 3/37, H. Booth 2/11).

At WACA Ground, Perth, December 29, 2001. New South Wales won by eight wickets. Toss: Western Australia. Western Australia six for 209 (Z.J. Goss 59, H. Taylor 41; B.L. Calver 3/44); New South Wales two for 210 (L.M. Keightley 67, L.C. Sthalekar 66; J. Burnett 2/37).

At WACA Ground, Perth, December 30, 2001. New South Wales won by 105 runs. Toss: New South Wales. New South Wales four for 237 (L.M. Keightley 72, L.C. Sthalekar 60, M.A.J. Goszko 43); Western Australia 132 (including five run-outs).

At Adelaide Oval No. 2, Adelaide, January 12, 2002. South Australia won by one wicket. Toss: Queensland. Queensland six for 194 (T.E. Brown 58*, S.A. Cooper 42; B. Noack 2/39); South Australia nine for 195 (K.L. Rolton 106; L. Shields 2/35, B. Buckley 2/42).

At Adelaide Oval No. 2, Adelaide, January 13, 2002. Queensland won by 81 runs. Toss: Queensland. Queensland eight for 192 (J.C. Price 58; B. Noack 3/27); South Australia 111 (B. Matheson 5/19, C. Kross 2/19).

At Melbourne University, Melbourne, January 19, 2002. New South Wales won by runs. Toss: New South Wales. New South Wales nine for 122 (S. Cunneen 44; C.L. Fitzpatrick 3/24, J. Dean 2/16, K. Winterton 2/29); Victoria eight for 116 (B.J. Clark 40; L.C. Sthalekar 2/14, E. Twining 2/19, B.L. Calver 2/27).

At Allan Border Field, Albion, January 19, 2002. Queensland won by 88 runs. Toss: Queensland. Queensland six for 256 (M. Bulow 106, B. Matheson 30; K. Tyrrell 2/44, J. Burnett 2/49); Western Australia 168 (A. Gray 52; M.L. White 3/34, R. Lee 2/14, K. Pike 2/22).

At Melbourne University, Melbourne, January 20, 2002. New South Wales won by six wickets. Toss: Victoria. Victoria 118 (K. Applebee 35; J. Hayes 2/9, E. Twining 2/22); New South Wales four for 119 (M.A. Winch 34; S. Young 2/17).

At Allan Border Field, Albion, January 20, 2002. Queensland won by three wickets. Toss: Western Australia. Western Australia 136 (T.E. Brown 2/18); Queensland seven for 138 (B. Matheson 37; Z.J. Goss 2/28).

POINTS TABLE, 2001-02

	Played	Won	Lost	Points	Net run-rate
New South Wales	8	8	0	48	0.944
Victoria	8	5	3	30	0.341
South Australia	8	4	4	24	−0.541
Queensland	8	3	5	18	0.192
Western Australia	8	0	8	0	−0.974

Net run-rate was calculated by subtracting runs conceded per over from runs scored per over.

FIRST FINAL

NEW SOUTH WALES v VICTORIA

At Memorial Oval, Bankstown, February 2, 2002. New South Wales won by seven wickets. Toss: New South Wales

Heavy overnight rain delayed the start of play by 80 minutes, but nothing could slow the momentum of the New South Wales machine as they systematically dismantled the Victorian challenge to their supremacy. Sent in on a pitch of variable bounce, Victoria survived the first hour with the loss of only Sarah Edwards' wicket to Emma Twining, whose opening spell of six overs yielded only three runs, but the dismissal of Belinda Clark precipitated a disastrous period in which Victoria scored only 27 runs for the loss of three wickets in 17 overs. Louise Broadfoot steadied the innings, and with support from the lower order managed to double the total in the final 16 overs. New South Wales began their chase cautiously in response to tight bowling by Cathryn Fitzpatrick and Clea Smith, but solid contributions from all top-order batters saw them home with eight overs to spare. The highlight for the small but vocal crowd came when the helmetless Martha Winch hooked three Fitzpatrick bouncers to the boundary to seal the victory.

Victoria

*B. J. Clark b Calver	18	(56)	J. Dean b Calver	13	(16)
S. Edwards c Hayes b Twining	13	(29)	K. Winterton run out (Sthalekar/Calver)	0	(2)
M. Jones c Winch b Hayes	8	(28)	S. Young not out	1	(1)
K. Applebee c Cunneen b Calver	0	(7)		
L. C. Broadfoot c Coleman b Twining	41	(88)	L-b 8, w 6	14
C. L. Fitzpatrick lbw b Sthalekar	5	(24)		
S. R. Theodore b McGregor	9	(31)	(50 overs, 168 mins)	133
†A. Aparo run out (Twining/Sthalekar)	11	(25)	Fall: 21 40 40 40 53 74 110 124 131 133

C. I. Smith did not bat.

Bowling: Twining 10–5–20–2; McGregor 10–1–33–1; Calver 9–4–23–3; Hayes 9–3–18–1; Sthalekar 8–1–16–1; Nelson 4–0–15–0.

New South Wales

L. M. Keightley c Broadfoot b Applebee	20	(69)	
L. C. Sthalekar c Fitzpatrick b Broadfoot	31	(81)	B 4, l-b 5, w 8, n-b 1	18
M. A. J. Goszko not out	28	(41)	
M. A. Winch c Broadfoot b Dean	29	(40)	(42 overs, 136 mins) (3 wkts) 134
S. Cunneen not out	8	(22)	Fall: 61 65 111

*J. Hayes, A. Blackwell, T. A. McGregor, B. L. Calver, E. Twining, †L. Coleman and D. Nelson did not bat.

Bowling: Fitzpatrick 10–3–29–0; Smith 8–2–28–0; Dean 10–1–28–1; Winterton 4–2–8–0; Young 3–1–9–0; Applebee 3–1–14–1; Broadfoot 4–1–9–1.

Umpires: R. Furtner and W. Hendricks.

SECOND FINAL

NEW SOUTH WALES v VICTORIA

At Memorial Oval, Bankstown, February 3, 2002. New South Wales won by four wickets. Toss: New South Wales

Under an overcast sky, the visitors were again invited to bat, and the initial stages of the innings resembled those of the previous day, as opener Sarah Edwards struggled to rotate the strike, and Belinda Clark scored freely. Another middle-order collapse brought together the experienced campaigners Melanie Jones, striving to regain her Australian team place, and Cathryn Fitzpatrick. Jones was fluid in her stroke-making, while Fitzpatrick played a critical supporting role as the pair revived the Victorian cause through judicious choice of shots and aggressive running. A cameo by the punishing Stephanie Theodore further boosted the score, but the momentum was lost after Jones' dismissal, with the final three Victorians surrendering their wickets to a combination of wild running and pinpoint accuracy by the New South Wales fielders. Lisa Sthalekar underlined her position as the premier spin bowler in the competition as she applied the brakes to the Victorian scoring, and Therese McGregor was instrumental in five of the nine wickets with three of her own and two run-outs. The New South Wales reply was built on a succession of partnerships, anchored by Player of the Finals Lisa Sthalekar until she was run out by a direct hit from Shannon Young in the 42nd over. The required rate crept to a run a ball, and on the loss of captain Julie Hayes with 41 runs to go, the relatively inexperienced Shannon Cunneen was joined by 17-year-old Alex Blackwell. Young and Fitzpatrick kept pressure on the two young Blues, who used a combination of aggressive hitting and improvisation to bring the target within reach. When Cunneen tempted fate once too often, three runs were needed from three balls. The normally imperturbable Fitzpatrick let fly a leg-side full toss, the batters scrambled a run, and amid the chaos of a run-out appeal, the square-leg umpire's arm was extended in a call of no ball. The target was suddenly just one run from three balls, and McGregor had no difficulty in coolly pushing the antepenultimate delivery for a single.

Victoria

*B.J. Clark c Blackwell b McGregor	34 (49)	J. Dean run out (McGregor)	0 (0)
S. Edwards c Keightley b Sthalekar	5 (46)	K. Winterton run out (McGregor)	0 (0)
M. Jones b McGregor	77 (100)	S. Young not out	1 (3)
K. Applebee b Sthalekar	1 (7)		
L.C. Broadfoot c Keightley b McGregor	9 (12)	B 2, l-b 5, w 4	11
C.L. Fitzpatrick c Twining b Andrews	29 (63)		
S.R. Theodore not out	19 (18)	(50 overs, 170 mins) (9 wkts)	186
†A. Aparo run out (Twining)	0 (2)	Fall: 39 43 47 56 146 180 183 183 184	

C.I. Smith did not bat.

Bowling: Twining 10–3–30–0; Calver 10–1–49–0; Hayes 6–1–23–0; Sthalekar 10–1–22–2; McGregor 10–1–40–3; Andrews 4–0–16–1.

New South Wales

L.C. Sthalekar run out (Young)	68 (128)	A. Blackwell not out	12 (19)
L.M. Keightley c Theodore b Dean	35 (35)	T.A. McGregor not out	1 (1)
M.A.J. Goszko c Broadfoot b Dean	15 (48)	L-b 2, w 17, n-b 2	21
M.A. Winch c Theodore b Applebee	7 (16)		
S. Cunneen run out (Jones)	28 (48)	(49.4 overs, 170 mins) (6 wkts)	187
*J. Hayes c Theodore b Young	0 (3)	Fall: 49 95 112 146 146 184	

B.L. Calver, E. Twining, †L. Coleman and S. Andrews did not bat.

Bowling: Smith 10–1–47–0; Fitzpatrick 9.4–1–38–0; Dean 10–1–23–2; Young 6–0–24–1; Broadfoot 5–0–22–0; Winterton 5–1–15–0; Applebee 4–1–16–1.

Umpires: R. Furtner and W. Hendricks.

NEW ZEALAND A IN AUSTRALIA, 2001-02

NEW ZEALAND A TOURING PARTY

E.A. Travers (*captain*), A.L. Mason (*vice-captain*), V.J. Brown, N.J. Browne, A.M. Corbin, M.F. Fahey, P.B. Flannery, F.S. King, B.H. McNeill, L.E. Milliken, K.L. Pulford, N. Scripps, N.M. Thessman.

In keeping with the desire for development of the game at the tier below full international level, the Australia Youth team and the New Zealand A side engaged in a series of matches in Australia. Australia Youth were led by international representative Lisa Sthalekar, and achieved a 3-1 series victory over the visitors, who included six members of the senior New Zealand team.

VICTORIA XI v NEW ZEALAND A

At Geelong Cricket Ground, Geelong, February 6, 2002. New Zealand A won by seven wickets. Toss: New Zealand A. Victorian XI 90 (B.H. McNeill 3/17, V.J. Brown 3/26); New Zealand A three for 91 (J. Hunter 3/18).

VICTORIA XI v NEW ZEALAND A

At Geelong Cricket Ground, Geelong, February 7, 2002. New Zealand A won by 25 runs. Toss: New Zealand A. New Zealand A 159 (M.F. Fahey 57, B.H. McNeill 38; J. Hunter 3/21, K. Winterton 3/27, B. White 2/36); Victorian XI 134 (S. Edwards 76*; N. Scripps 3/23, L.E. Milliken 2/18).

AUSTRALIA YOUTH v NEW ZEALAND A

At Camberwell Sports Ground, Camberwell, February 10, 2002. Australia Youth won by four wickets. Toss: Australia Youth. New Zealand A 116 (K.L. Pulford 46, A.L. Mason 31; T.E. Brown 4/20, B. Matheson 3/35, C.R. Smith 2/14); Australia Youth six for 117 (A. Blackwell 32; L.E. Milliken 2/28).

AUSTRALIA YOUTH v NEW ZEALAND A

At Camberwell Sports Ground, Camberwell, February 11, 2002. Australia Youth won by 26 runs. Toss: Australia Youth. Australia Youth 144 (K. Britt 32; N.J. Browne 2/8, A.L. Mason 2/20); New Zealand A 118 (N.M. Thessman 37, A.M. Corbin 30; L.C. Sthalekar 2/4, B. Matheson 2/17).

AUSTRALIA YOUTH v NEW ZEALAND A

At Caulfield Park, Caulfield, February 13, 2002. Australia Youth won by 15 runs. Toss: Australia Youth. Australia Youth 119 (F.S. King 3/28, A.L. Mason 2/18, A.M. Corbin 2/19, B.H. McNeill 2/21); New Zealand A seven for 104 (L.C. Sthalekar 2/13, B. Matheson 2/29).

AUSTRALIA YOUTH v NEW ZEALAND A

At E.E. Gunn Reserve, Ormond, February 14, 2002. New Zealand A won by 32 runs. Toss: New Zealand A. New Zealand A nine for 172 (F.S. King 34; T.E. Brown 4/30, C.R. Smith 2/24); Australia Youth 140 (N.J. Browne 3/32, F.S. King 2/18, B.H. McNeill 2/19).

NEW ZEALANDERS IN AUSTRALIA, 2001-02

NEW ZEALANDERS TOURING PARTY

E.C. Drumm (Auckland) (*captain*), K.A. Ramel (*vice-captain*), N.J. Browne (Rose Bowl tour only), S.K. Burke (Queensland series only), A.M. Corbin, P.A. Flannery, F.E. Fraser (Queensland series only), F.S. King (Rose Bowl tour only), A.L. Mason, E.T. McDonald (Queensland series only), A.M. O'Leary, N. Payne, R.J. Pullar, R.J. Rolls, H.M. Tiffen, E.A. Travers (Queensland series only), H.M. Watson.

New Zealand toured Australia twice in the 2001-02 season, the first time as a rapidly organised replacement for their cancelled tour of India, and the second time as part of the originally scheduled home-and-away Rose Bowl series. During the pre-Christmas tour, New Zealand easily disposed of Queensland in a three-match series, but the Rose Bowl tour saw them pitted against arch-rivals Australia for the first time since the 2000 World Cup final. The 5-1 result in favour of Australia was a fair reflection of the difference in standards as New Zealand struggled to find replacements for retired stalwarts Debbie Hockley, Catherine Campbell, Clare Nicholson and Katrina Keenan. Australia recalled Melanie Jones and Clea Smith, while New South Wales left-arm seamer Emma Twining was rewarded for several seasons' consistency with a debut selection.

QUEENSLAND v NEW ZEALANDERS

At Allan Border Field, Albion, December 17, 2001. New Zealand won by 73 runs. Toss: New Zealand. New Zealand nine for 198 (A.M. O'Leary 51; C. Kross 3/39, B. Buckley 2/25, B. Matheson 2/32); Queensland eight for 125 (B. Matheson 38; A.M. Corbin 2/27, H.M. Tiffen 2/28).

QUEENSLAND v NEW ZEALANDERS

At Brisbane Cricket Ground, Brisbane, December 19, 2001. New Zealand won by 94 runs. Toss: New Zealand. New Zealand eight for 245 (E.C. Drumm 75, N. Payne 52, H.M. Tiffen 49; S.A. Cooper 2/37, M.L. White 2/38, C. Kross 2/39); Queensland 151 (J.C. Price 64, K. Matthews 34; A.M. Corbin 4/29, K.A. Ramel 2/41).

QUEENSLAND v NEW ZEALANDERS

At Brisbane Cricket Ground, Brisbane, December 20, 2001. New Zealand won by six wickets. Toss: Queensland. Queensland seven for 140 (M. Bulow 37, J.C. Price 32*; E.T. McDonald 3/27); New Zealand four for 142 (R.J. Rolls 54, H.M. Tiffen 36*; B. Buckley 2/22).

AUSTRALIA YOUTH v NEW ZEALANDERS

At Greaves Reserve, Dandenong, February 16, 2002. New Zealand won by 21 runs. Toss: New Zealand batted first by agreement. New Zealand 128 (C.R. Smith 3/21, S. Andrews 2/13, K. Britt 2/30); Australia Youth 107 (L. Coleman 35; A.L. Mason 2/24, K.A. Ramel 2/28).

SOUTH AUSTRALIA v NEW ZEALANDERS

At Park 25, Adelaide, February 18, 2002. New Zealand won by 148 runs. Toss: New Zealand batted first by agreement. New Zealand 242 (E.C. Drumm 78, K.A. Ramel 38, R.J. Rolls 30; B. Noack 3/35, E. Sampson 2/51); South Australia 94 (C. Ward 32*; A.L. Mason 4/19).

AUSTRALIANS IN NEW ZEALAND, 2001-02

AUSTRALIAN TOURING PARTY

B.J. Clark (Vic) (*captain*), K.L. Rolton (SAust) (*vice-captain*), S.A. Cooper (Qld), C.L. Fitzpatrick (Vic), M.A.J. Goszko (NSW), J. Hayes (NSW), M. Jones (Vic), L.M. Keightley (NSW), T.A. McGregor (NSW), J.C. Price (Qld), C.R. Smith (Vic), L.C. Sthalekar (NSW), E. Twining (NSWs).

Coach: S. Jenkin. *Assistant Coach:* C. Matthews. *Physiotherapist:* L. Ross. Manager: C. Connolly. *Fitness Adviser:* S. Bailey. *Scorer–statistician:* E.J. Sainsbury.

CANTERBURY XI v AUSTRALIANS

At Hagley Oval, Christchurch, February 27, 2002. Australia won by 184 runs. Toss: Australia batted first by agreement. Australia eight for 263 (L. M. Keightley 53, S. A. Cooper 53, J. Hayes 35; R. Steele 3/52, S. K. Burke 2/41); Canterbury XI 79 (E. Twining 4/10, T. A. McGregor 4/28).

CANTERBURY XI v AUSTRALIANS

At Hagley Oval, Christchurch, February 28, 2002. Australia won by 89 runs. Toss: Australia batted first by agreement. Australia 243 (K.L. Rolton 72, J.C. Price 65; Z. McWilliams 2/7, L.C. Sthalekar 2/35); Canterbury XI nine for 154 (L.C. Sthalekar 33; J. Hayes 2/23). (T.A. McGregor and L.C. Sthalekar of Australia played with Canterbury XI in this match.)

ROSE BOWL MATCHES

For this inaugural home-and-away Rose Bowl series, a points system was introduced which discriminated between a home win (two points) and an away win (three points), and which additionally incorporated provision for bonus points (one point when a team scored at least 25 per cent faster than the other). The series and the points system proved successful, and similar series are expected in the future.

POINTS TABLE

	Played	Home win	Away win	Loss	Bonus	Points
Australia	6	3	2	1	2	14
New Zealand	6	1	0	5	0	2

AUSTRALIA v NEW ZEALAND

First Limited-Overs International

At Adelaide Oval, Adelaide, February 20, 2002. Australia won by 53 runs. Toss: New Zealand.

Expectations were high for this replay of the 2000 World Cup final, but as a contest it never reached great heights. Australia maintained the upper hand throughout, largely as a result of the solidity of their middle order and the tightness of their attack. A brisk start, with the run-rate maintained at four runs per over for the first 20 overs, set a strong base, and although the middle of the innings was a fraction slower, wickets in hand at 40 overs allowed the team to pass 200 comfortably. Melanie Jones made a welcome return to the side to top-score, sharing a productive partnership with Lisa Sthalekar. The fiery pace of Cathryn Fitzpatrick perfectly complemented the nagging slow-medium of Julie Hayes as they cut through the top and middle order of New Zealand, with only Rebecca Rolls showing any confidence against them. Emma Twining made a sound debut, although going without a wicket, and the Australians captured a bonus point.

Australia

*B. J. Clark b Tiffen	27	(48)	C. L. Fitzpatrick not out	23	(19)
L. M. Keightley lbw b Browne	3	(11)	J. Hayes not out	0	(0)
K. L. Rolton b Tiffen	33	(42)			
M. A. J. Goszko c Flannery b Corbin	10	(34)	B 2, l-b 4, w14, n-b 2	22	
M. Jones c and b Ramel	40	(82)			
L. C. Sthalekar c Pullar b Browne	33	(41)	(50 overs, 170 mins)	(7 wkts) 204	
†J. C. Price c Ramel b Tiffen	13	(25)	Fall: 13 70 73 93 158 165 200		

T. A. McGregor and E. Twining did not bat.

Bowling: Pullar 10–1–34–0; Browne 10–0–29–2; Ramel 6–0–46–1; Tiffen 8–2–32–3; Mason 10–1–32–0; Corbin 6–1–25–1.

New Zealand

A. M. O'Leary c Price c Fitzpatrick	2	(12)	R. J. Pullar not out	27	(38)
†R. J. Rolls lbw b Rolton	61	(67)	A. M. Corbin c Rolton b Sthalekar	9	(19)
*E. C. Drumm b McGregor	3	(13)	N. J. Browne b Fitzpatrick	0	(2)
H. M. Tiffen lbw b Hayes	2	(37)			
K. A. Ramel run out (Jones)	3	(6)	L-b 5, w 10	15	
P. B. Flannery run out (Clark)	21	(52)			
H. M. Watson c Sthalekar b Hayes	3	(23)	(46.4 overs, 158 mins)	151	
A. L. Mason c Sthalekar b Rolton	5	(11)	Fall: 3 13 60 79 81 92 101 125 146 151		

Bowling: Fitzpatrick 7.4–3–13–2; McGregor 7–2–30–1; Twining 8–0–32–0; Hayes 10–3–20–2; Rolton 8–0–27–2; Sthalekar 6–0–24–1.

Umpires: S. J. Davis and D. J. Harper.

AUSTRALIA v NEW ZEALAND

Second Limited-Overs International

At Adelaide Oval, Adelaide, February 21, 2002. Day/night game. Australia won by three wickets. Toss: New Zealand.

A rare day/night game produced a closer contest. Cathryn Fitzpatrick began with a stunning burst: starting with four consecutive maidens, she then removed both Rebecca Rolls and Emily Drumm in the space of six balls. The medium pace of Therese McGregor, Karen Rolton and Julie Hayes again applied pressure to the middle order, and a steady loss of wickets prevented the development of any scoring momentum. Fitzpatrick returned with the old ball to clean up the tail with a combination of pace and guile. Australia made relatively heavy weather of their reply, particularly to the New Zealand spinners Aimee Mason and Anna Corbin, who kept the batters tied to their crease, but judicious batting by Melanie Jones and Julia Price brought the target within reach.

New Zealand

A. M. O'Leary lbw b McGregor	8	(39)	H. M. Watson c Sthalekar b Fitzpatrick	8	(7)
†R. J. Rolls c Jones b Fitzpatrick	13	(24)	A. M. Corbin run out (Cooper/Price)	7	(9)
*E. C. Drumm lbw b Fitzpatrick	1	(5)	N. J. Browne not out	1	(1)
H. M. Tiffen b Hayes	40	(80)			
K. A. Ramel c Fitzpatrick b Sthalekar	25	(58)	L-b 8, w 1	9	
P. B. Flannery run out (Clark/Price)	11	(9)			
R. J. Pullar c Clark b Fitzpatrick	24	(40)	(49.4 overs, 169 mins)	163	
A. L. Mason c McGregor b Rolton	16	(26)	Fall: 21 23 23 75 94 124 134 151 162 163		

Bowling: Fitzpatrick 10–4–15–4; McGregor 10–3–32–1; Rolton 8.4–4–24–1; Sthalekar 5–0–34–1; Twining 9–0–25–0; Hayes 7–2–25–1.

Australia

L.M. Keightley st Rolls b Mason	....	23	(41)	C.L. Fitzpatrick run out (O'Leary)	... 0	(3)
*B.J. Clark c Rolls b Tiffen	....	19	(33)	J. Hayes not out	 9	(18)
K.L. Rolton c and b Mason	....	32	(34)			
M. Jones c Rolls b Corbin	....	32	(68)	L-b 3, w 9	 12	
S.A. Cooper c Corbin b Mason	......	1	(17)			
L.C. Sthalekar c Pullar b Corbin	.....	12	(29)	(47.3 overs, 159 mins)	(7 wkts) 166	
†J.C. Price not out	....	26	(42)	Fall: 39 61 81 87 121 141 141		

T.A. McGregor and E. Twining did not bat.

Bowling: Pullar 10–1–33–0; Browne 6–0–26–0; Tiffen 9–1–36–1; Mason 10–2–29–3; Coring 10–1–28–2; Ramel 2.3–0–11–0.

Umpires: S.J. Davis and D.J. Harper.

AUSTRALIA v NEW ZEALAND

Third Limited-Overs International

At Melbourne Cricket Ground, Melbourne, February 23, 2002. Australia won by 57 runs. Toss: Australia.

On only the fourth occasion of a women's match on the MCG, Australia took a commanding lead in the series, with a win and second bonus point for the tournament. The small but vocal crowd was entertained by the first half-century opening partnership of the series by Belinda Clark and Lisa Keightley, and by the raw power of Karen Rolton as she punished anything remotely loose. Reaching the final ten overs with eight wickets in hand, Australia began to take a few risks, and lost wickets steadily. Paula Flannery was promoted from the middle order to open the innings with Rebecca Rolls, but the move backfired as Flannery proved unable to keep the score moving. With the loss of both Rolls and Emily Drumm, the Kiwis crawled to two for 43 from the first 20 overs, Flannery facing the bulk of the strike. The result was inevitable long before the final delivery.

Australia

*B.J. Clark run out (Drumm/Rolls)	..	35	(69)	†J.C. Price b Tiffen	 3	(9)
L.M. Keightley lbw b Tiffen	....	42	(95)	C.L. Fitzpatrick not out	 3	(5)
K.L. Rolton b Tiffen	....	44	(64)	B 3, L-B 6, W 12	 21	
M.A.J. Goszko b Tiffen	....	25	(35)			
M. Jones not out	....	17	(20)	(50 overs, 172 mins)	(6 wkts) 194	
L.C. Sthalekar st Rolls b Ramel	.....	4	(4)	Fall: 63 105 146 159 165 184		

J. Hayes, T.A. McGregor and E. Twining did not bat.

Bowling: Pullar 10–2–27–0; Browne 7–2–18–0; Tiffen 10–0–43–4; Mason 10–2–37–0; King 6–1–16–0; Coring 5–0–27–0; Ramel 2–0–17–1.

New Zealand

P.B. Flannery lbw b Hayes	....	36	(108)	R.J. Pullar not out	 19	(28)
†R.J. Rolls run out (Clark/Fitzpatrick)		4	(13)	F.S. King c McGregor b Hayes	 1	(10)
*E.C. Drumm lbw b McGregor	......	21	(40)	A.M. Corbin not out	 16	(32)
N. Payne c Clark b Sthalekar	....	25	(38)	B 1, l-b 2, w 2	 5	
H.M. Tiffen b Rolton	....	0	(9)			
K.A. Ramel c Fitzpatrick b Hayes	...	4	(13)	(50 overs, 160 mins)	(8 wkts) 137	
A.L. Mason run out (Clark)	....	6	(9)	Fall: 10 37 80 85 92 99 100 101		

N.J. Browne did not bat.

Bowling: Fitzpatrick 9–1–22–0; Rolton 6–0–19–1; McGregor 7–1–18–1; Hayes 10–3–17–3; Twining 8–0–29–0; Sthalekar 10–0–29–1.

Umpires: R.L. Parry and R.G. Patterson.

NEW ZEALAND v AUSTRALIA

Fourth Limited-Overs International

At Bert Sutcliffe Oval, Lincoln, March 2, 2002. New Zealand won by 22 runs. Toss: New Zealand.

New Zealand kept the series alive with a fighting 22-run victory in the first match of their home leg. With Paula Flannery involved in her fourth run-out in as many matches, the dangerous Rebecca Rolls was removed without facing a delivery, but Emily Drumm finally came into her best form. Using her trademark preference for the square boundaries, Drumm took on all the Australian bowlers and was dismissed only in the final over. She was particularly well supported by Aimee Mason, whose cameo innings was punctuated by two sixes – a rare event in women's cricket. In the final over four wickets fell in the space of five balls to stymie the chance of passing 200. Australia's reply began confidently, with Belinda Clark and Karen Rolton seemingly untroubled by the attack, but the introduction of Mason saw the tide turn. Using drift and variety, Mason deceived Rolton into presenting a return catch, and then picked up three further wickets to have Australia reeling at nine for 133. The injured Cathryn Fitzpatrick, accompanied by a runner, joined Therese McGregor at the crease and the two calmly played New Zealand out of a bonus point as they put on an unbeaten 41 in 32 minutes. New Zealand were still in the competition, but needed to pick up bonus points in both the final two matches to tie the series.

New Zealand

P. B. Flannery c Goszko b Fitzpatrick	14	(22)	
†R. J. Rolls run out (Sthalekar/Price)	0	(0)	
*E. C. Drumm run out (Clark/McGregor)	88	(121)	
N. Payne b Twining	30	(62)	
H. M. Tiffen run out (Rolton/Hayes)	10	(27)	
K. A. Ramel c Price b Sthalekar	10	(28)	
A. L. Mason b McGregor	34	(36)	
R. J. Pullar c and b McGregor	6	(3)	
A. M. Corbin not out	0	(0)	
F. S. King c Price b McGregor	0	(1)	
L-b 1, w 3	4		

N. J. Browne did not bat.

(50 overs, 167 mins)   (9 wkts) 196

Fall: 0 28 86 114 132 190 190 196 196

Bowling: Fitzpatrick 10-2-29-1; McGregor 9-1-44-3; Rolton 6-0-32-0; Hayes 10-0-32-0; Twining 5-0-23-1; Sthalekar 10-1-35-1.

Australia

L. M. Keightley c Rolls b Pullar	11	(23)	
*B. J. Clark run out (King)	43	(82)	
K. L. Rolton c and b Mason	26	(36)	
M. A. J. Goszko lbw b Tiffen	35	(61)	
M. Jones lbw b King	4	(4)	
L. C. Sthalekar c Rolls b Mason	1	(16)	
†J. C. Price c Rolls b Mason	0	(1)	
J. Hayes c Rolls b Mason	0	(6)	
T. A. McGregor not out	28	(39)	
E. Twining run out (Tiffen/Pullar)	0	(2)	
C. L. Fitzpatrick not out	17	(30)	
L-b 3, w 6	9		

(50 overs, 171 mins)   (9 wkts) 174

Fall: 21 81 95 106 117 117 119 129 133

Bowling: Pullar 10-4-14-1; Browne 2-0-16-0; Corbin 10-0-39-0; Tiffen 10-1-36-1; Mason 10-2-33-4; King 8-0-34-1.

Umpires: G. A. Baxter and B. F. Bowden.

NEW ZEALAND v AUSTRALIA

Fifth Limited-Overs International

At Bert Sutcliffe Oval, Lincoln, March 3, 2002. Australia won by 17 runs. Toss: Australia.

In the closest result to date, Australia wrapped up the series and thus gained some measure of revenge for the loss of the World Cup the previous season. Karen Rolton plundered the New Zealand attack for the first Australian half-century of the series. Belinda Clark was uncharacteristically subdued at the other end, but she proved an ideal foil for the rampant Rolton as the two added 117 runs for the second wicket. Michelle Goszko fell quickly into rhythm, and after Rolton's dismissal, she picked up the pace to push the run-rate above four runs per over. She was controversially ruled out stumped from the final ball of the innings. In the absence through injury of Cathryn Fitzpatrick, Emma Twining took the new ball, and conceded only nine runs from her first six-over spell. Rebecca Rolls played with unusual circumspection, as strategic placement of fielders denied her the boundaries she had previously scored with ease. Only Haidee Tiffen showed any inclination to attack the bowling, and while she was at the crease New Zealand had some hope of victory. In the end, however, 80 runs from the final ten overs proved beyond their reach.

Australia

*B.J. Clark c Rolls b Pullar	44 (102)	L.C. Sthalekar not out	5	(6)	
L.M. Keightley b Corbin	4 (21)	L-b 4, w 2, n-b 4	10		
K.L. Rolton run out (King)	90 (100)				
M.A.J. Goszko st Rolls b Tiffen	48 (51)	(50 overs, 168 mins)	(5 wkts) 218		
M. Jones c Flannery b Tiffen	17 (23)	Fall: 11 128 160 198 218			

†J.C. Price, J. Hayes, T.A. McGregor, E. Twining and C.I. Smith did not bat.

Bowling: Pullar 10–2–30–1; Corbin 10–1–42–1; Milliken 5–0–22–0; Tiffen 8–0–49–2; King 7–0–28–0; Mason 10–0–43–0.

New Zealand

P.B. Flannery run out (Smith/Jones)	8 (20)	R.J. Pullar b Rolton	17	(17)	
†R.J. Rolls c Goszko b Sthalekar	27 (63)	A.M. Corbin not out	8	(9)	
*E.C. Drumm c Price b Hayes	22 (39)	F.S. King not out	13	(12)	
N. Payne lbw b Hayes	2 (4)	L-b 10, b 5	15		
H.M. Tiffen b McGregor	69 (96)				
K.A. Ramel c Jones b Smith	20 (37)	(50 overs, 169 mins)	(8 wkts) 201		
A.L. Mason c Clark b Smith	0 (3)	Fall: 13 53 55 79 130 136 168 184			

L.E. Milliken did not bat.

Bowling: Twining 8–1–15–0; McGregor 10–0–48–1; Hayes 9–0–33–2; Smith 7–1–32–2; Sthalekar 6–0–28–1; Rolton 10–0–35–1.

Umpires: G.A. Baxter and D.M. Quested.

NEW ZEALAND v AUSTRALIA

Sixth Limited-Overs International

At Bert Sutcliffe Oval, Lincoln, March 6, 2002. Australia won by six wickets. Toss: New Zealand.

The final game, although technically a dead rubber, proved the best contest of the six, as both sides set new scoring records against each other, and the result hung in the balance until the final delivery. Rebecca Rolls appeared to have set her side up for victory with a stunning century in which she combined power, precision and innovation to unravel the best-laid bowling plans. With Emily Drumm she put on a record 170 for the second wicket before falling to a skied catch in the 39th over. Haidee Tiffen took up the attack, and only outstanding bowling by Cathryn Fitzpatrick and Karen Rolton kept the New Zealand total close to 250. Fitzpatrick, suffering from a strained leg muscle, bowled four overs from a short run to capture four wickets. An asking rate above five runs an over was a challenge to the Australians, who had never managed to achieve such a target against New Zealand. Lisa Sthalekar was promoted to open the batting with Belinda Clark in the absence of the out-of-form Lisa Keightley, and the pair provided a solid platform. The innings of the series, however, was played by Karen Rolton, who confirmed her status as the premier batter in women's cricket as she systematically ground the opposition bowlers down with a bewildering array of shots. Only spinners Anna Corbin and Aimee Mason were able to maintain any consistency. Melanie Jones scrambled vital runs, including a six from Rachel Pullar, and with Rolton added 146 in only 89 minutes. The final over began with six runs needed, but the pressure eased as a wayward first delivery by Tiffen allowed three leg-byes. The final shot by Rolton went straight to the keeper, but Rolls' throw missed the stumps at both ends as Rolton hobbled to safety, in pain from leg cramps and dehydration. It was a fitting end to an exciting series, which demonstrated the fighting qualities of both sides, and showcased a number of talented newcomers to international cricket.

New Zealand

P.B. Flannery run out (McGregor/Price)	5	(8)
†R.J. Rolls c Smith b McGregor	114	(120)
*E.C. Drumm run out (Smith/McGregor)	60	(111)
H.M. Tiffen b Fitzpatrick	34	(27)
N. Payne c McGregor b Fitzpatrick	16	(12)
K.A. Ramel st Price b Fitzpatrick	0	(4)
A.L. Mason run out (Goszko/Rolton)	2	(3)
R.J. Pullar run out (Clark)	2	(3)
A.M. Corbin b Fitzpatrick	4	(8)
F.S. King not out	5	(4)
L-b 5, w 5	10	
(50 overs, 176 mins) (9 wkts)	252	

L.E. Milliken did not bat.

Fall: 15 185 187 217 231 240 243 243 252

Bowling: Fitzpatrick 9–0–40–4; McGregor 10–1–42–1; Rolton 7–0–37–0; Sthalekar 7–0–40–0; Smith 5–1–28–0; Hayes 9–2–48–0; Goszko 3–1–12–0.

Australia

*B.J. Clark lbw b Pullar	52	(69)
L.C. run out (Pullar/Rolls)	33	(67)
K.L. Rolton not out	105	(102)
M.A.J. Goszko c Rolls b Mason	1	(6)
M. Jones c Milliken Tiffen	47	(56)
S.A. Cooper not out	1	(1)
L-b 7, w 6 n-b 1	14	
(50 overs, 181 mins) (4 wkts)	253	

†J.C. Price, C.L. Fitzpatrick, T.A. McGregor, J. Hayes and C.I. Smith did not bat.

Fall: 84 99 106 250

Bowling: Pullar 10–0–39–1; Corbin 10–0–36–0; Milliken 3–0–19–0; Mason 10–2–31–1; Tiffen 10–0–58–1; King 7–0–63–0.

Umpires: R.D. Anderson and G.A. Baxter.

ICC CHAMPIONS TROPHY TECHNOLOGY EXPERIMENT

The ICC decided to trial the extended use of technology in assisting umpiring decisions during the ICC Champions Trophy in Sri Lanka in September. The experimental system enables umpires to consult with the third umpire on any aspect of a decision about which they are unsure. Consultation is optional, but when it is called for, decisions are to be reached as soon as possible. The third umpire is allowed two replays of any incident before passing on information to the field umpire. Line decisions, hit wicket and boundary referrals are still decided by the television umpire, as per the present system.

The Champions Trophy was nominated for the technology trial because each Test nation was involved and all members of the ICC's elite panel of international umpires were to adjudicate. If the Champions Trophy experiment is deemed to have succeeded, the extended technology may be used in the 2003 World Cup.

PART FIVE: AUSTRALIANS OVERSEAS IN 2001-02

THE AUSTRALIANS IN SOUTH AFRICA, 2001-02

By JIM MAXWELL

At the end of the First Test, Steve Waugh said that Australia had a team of excellent cricketers. In a contest billed as the battle for the world championship of Test cricket, they had just inflicted the second-largest innings defeat in Test history. Waugh resisted the opportunity to label his team as "great", but the style and performance of the tenth official Australian touring team to South Africa was so brilliant and dazzlingly decisive that it became an increasingly tempting epithet. Their success was an amalgam of dominant batting, shrewd leadership and skilful bowling, supported by exceptional catching and fielding.

Adam Gilchrist became Australia's batting superstar, outperforming every specialist batsman with exhilarating exhibitions in all three Tests and in the limited-overs series. In five Test innings he scored 473 runs from 474 balls, including a record-breaking double-century from 212 balls in the First. He was unstoppable, scoring 138 not out from 108 balls in the Second, and was last man out for 91 in the first innings of the Third. Several of his 13 catches were spectacular, and he was the obvious choice as Player of the Series. His match-winning abilities prompted the habitually laconic Steve Waugh to observe, after the series-clinching four-wicket win in Cape Town, "I didn't see Bradman bat, but he couldn't have been better than that."

Australia's confidence and aggression overwhelmed an understrength South African team, whose captain and main strike bowler, Shaun Pollock, missed the Test series with a side-strain injury. Pollock's absence, combined with injuries to Allan Donald and Lance Klusener, weakened a squad that was trying to recover from the 3-0 drubbing in Australia. To their credit they fought back splendidly to challenge Australia at Newlands, and followed up with a meritorious victory at Kingsmead.

In the seven-match limited-overs series Australia prevailed by a convincing 5-1, with one match tied, inflicting South Africa's worst limited-overs series loss at home. The captaincy switched seamlessly from Steve Waugh to Ricky Ponting, who revelled in the opportunity. The absence of the Waugh twins, and injuries to two of Australia's most experienced players, Shane Warne and Michael Bevan, did not faze Ponting, who was shrewdly advised by Gilchrist and Darren Lehmann. South Africa were competitive, but Australia thrived on every challenge and their magnificent run-chase at Port Elizabeth sent out an unambiguous preliminary notice for the 2002-03 World Cup.

THE AUSTRALIANS IN SOUTH AFRICA, 2001-02

Standing: D.R. Martyn, S.C.G. McGill, B. Lee, R.T. Ponting, G.D. McGrath, M.L. Hayden, J.N. Gillespie, D.S. Lehmann, J.M. Buchanan (*coach*), S.R.Watson, M.E. Waugh, E.L. Alcott (*physiotherapist*). *Kneeling:* S.K.Warne, S.R. Waugh (*captain*), A.C. Gilchrist (*vice-captain*), J.L. Langer, A.J. Bichel.

The Test series followed the pattern of Australia's previous tour in 1996-97: a convincing win in the First Test, a close contest in the Second, and a consolation win for South Africa in the Third. Australia again stuck with the same 11 players in all three Tests, while South Africa chose 16 in their desperate search for a penetrative bowling combination. Andre Nel, Dewald Pretorius and David Terbrugge vainly tried to fill in for the injured Pollock, while all-rounder Andrew Hall topped the batting averages, but never looked like taking quality wickets. Paul Adams' unorthodox spin created some batting uncertainty, but he struggled to curb Gilchrist's assaults. Makhaya Ntini and Jacques Kallis were forced to carry the attack, and in these thin resources lay South Africa's major problem – of how to contain the Australian batting.

Matthew Hayden's forceful strokes alongside his aggressive accomplice Justin Langer launched the innings authoritatively. He laid the base for Australia's huge score in Johannesburg, and guided the successful run-chase in Cape Town, where he fell nine runs short of scoring centuries in five consecutive Tests. Ponting played the most responsible, mature innings of his 56-match career to carry Australia to a thrilling four-wicket win at Newlands, and his poise at No. 3 contrasted with the home side's inability to find a dominant player.

Australia's well-balanced team lacked only an all-rounder. The days of Steve Waugh chipping in with his cunning medium-pacers seem to be past, so twin brother Mark has become the occasional alternative. The maxim that five specialist bowlers are superfluous when four can do the job runs awry when partnerships prosper on slow pitches. Hence the push for the muscular all-rounder Shane Watson, who made an impression in the limited-overs matches and scored a dashing century in the Port Elizabeth tour match.

The Waughs' batting contributed usefully, but they never dominated. Steve could not find his rhythm, and Mark survived unconvincingly on the basis of his experience and elegant touch. Damien Martyn batted superbly in Johannesburg, and fielded brilliantly, turning the course of South Africa's second innings at Newlands when he ran out Neil McKenzie for 99.

The bowling of Glenn McGrath and Warne was not only sustained in its quality but remarkable in its durability. McGrath's off-stump accuracy and his ability to dismiss top-order batsmen produced 12 wickets at 18.92. Warne's probing marathon spells in the Second Test were helped by his recent diet and fitness campaign, which ensured a quicker recovery. He was transformed into the svelte all-rounder, scoring vital runs in a memorable 100th Test appearance and taking part in several lower-order partnerships. He did, however, suffer a hamstring injury at Newlands, and battled gamely through the Third Test before missing the first four limited-overs internationals.

South Africa's batting was bedevilled by inconsistency, and rarely dominated the Australian attack. Herschelle Gibbs scored their only century at Durban when the series was over, but his lapses of concentration outside the off stump were fatal against the metronomic efficiency of Australia's bowling. The Australians targeted Kallis throughout the summer, regarding his wicket as vital to triggering a domino effect on South African batting morale. Gary Kirsten, McKenzie and the new faces Ashwell Prince and Graeme Smith contributed determinedly, but the energetic batting of Jonty Rhodes was sorely missed.

Rhodes batted and fielded at his brilliant best in the subsequent limited-overs series, where he scored 338 innovative runs at 67.60. His rapid scoring in the last ten overs should have been decisive, but chasing or defending, Australia's belief in their ability to achieve victory in the limited-overs matches never wavered. The batting attack varied between the pure violence of Gilchrist's assaults, Ponting's power and the deft touches of Lehmann. Jimmy Maher grabbed his opportunity, hitting down the ground in the same confident manner of his regular partner, Hayden. Australia's out-cricket hit a peak in the opening two matches, when, defending mediocre totals, McGrath and Jason Gillespie choked the reply with outstanding opening spells. New off-spinner Nathan Hauritz impressed with his bowling control and his batting coolness in the match-levelling partnership with Maher at Potchefstroom.

Lindsay Hassett's old catchcry that "you only notice the captain when the team is losing", had a broader application for South Africa, whose leadership problems were manifold. The selection process was blurred by a quota policy, which appeared to be applied inconsistently. Diehards labelled the policy as reverse apartheid, with three, sometimes two, appearing to be the expeditious number of non-white players selected. There was no clear line of authority, and a lack of communication, which led to confusion and criticism of the management and administration. In the wake of Ali Bacher's departure to his new role as 2003 World Cup supremo, South African cricket lacked hands-on direction.

For a side that began the summer as the potential world champions, South Africa ended their campaign in a state of shock. They were overwhelmed by a confident and aggressive Australian team, who played some of the most entertaining cricket in recent memory.

AUSTRALIAN TOURING PARTY

S.R. Waugh (New South Wales) (*captain*), A.C. Gilchrist (Western Australia), A.J. Bichel (Queensland), J.N. Gillespie (South Australia), M.L. Hayden (Queensland), J.L. Langer (Western Australia), B. Lee (New South Wales), D.S. Lehmann (South Australia), S.C.G. MacGill (New South Wales), D.R. Martyn (Western Australia), G.D. McGrath (New South Wales), R.T. Ponting (Tasmania), S.K. Warne (Victoria), S.R. Watson (Tasmania) and M.E. Waugh (New South Wales).

The Australian touring party for the international limited-overs series was as follows: R.T. Ponting (Tasmania) (*captain*), A.C. Gilchrist (Western Australia), M.G. Bevan (New South Wales), A.J. Bichel (Queensland), J.N. Gillespie (South Australia), I.J. Harvey (Victoria), N.M. Hauritz (Queensland), M.L. Hayden (Queensland), B. Lee (New South Wales), D.S. Lehmann (South Australia), J.P. Maher (Queensland), D.R. Martyn (Western Australia), G.D. McGrath (New South Wales), S.K. Warne (Victoria), S.R. Watson (Tasmania).

Manager: S.R. Bernard. *Coach:* J.M. Buchanan. *Physiotherapist:* E.L. Alcott. *Fitness adviser:* J.A. Campbell. *Assistant Manager/Cricket analyst:* M.J. Walsh.

AUSTRALIAN TOUR RESULTS

Test matches – Played 3: Won 2, Lost 1.
First-class matches – Played 6: Won 3, Lost 1, Drawn 2.
Wins – South Africa (3).
Losses – South Africa.
Draws – South Africa A (2).
Limited-overs internationals – Played 7: Won 6, Lost 1, Tied 1.

TEST AVERAGES

SOUTH AFRICA – BATTING

	M	I	NO	R	HS	100	50s	Avge	Ct
A.J. Hall	2	3	1	97	70	0	1	48.50	1
H.H. Gibbs	3	6	0	287	104	1	1	47.83	2
N.D. McKenzie......	3	6	1	191	99	0	1	38.20	4
J.H. Kallis	3	6	1	184	73	0	2	36.80	4
G. Kirsten	3	6	0	192	87	0	2	32.00	2
P.R. Adams.........	2	3	1	64	35	0	0	32.00	0
G.C. Smith	2	4	0	114	68	0	1	28.50	2
A.G. Prince	3	6	0	155	49	0	0	25.83	2
M.V. Boucher.......	3	6	1	95	37	0	0	19.00	13
M. Ntini...........	3	5	0	48	14	0	0	9.60	0
D. Pretorius	1	2	1	5	5*	0	0	5.00	0
A. Nel	1	2	0	7	7	0	0	3.50	0
A.A. Donald	1	2	1	3	3*	0	0	3.00	0
N. Boje	1	2	0	5	5	0	0	2.50	0
H.H. Dippenaar......	1	2	0	3	2	0	0	1.50	0
D.J. Terbrugge	1	1	0	0	0	0	0	0.00	1

* Denotes not out.

BOWLING

	O	M	R	W	BB	5W/i	Avge
D.J. Terbrugge.........	20	3	82	4	2/21	0	20.50
P.R. Adams	63.1	1	290	10	4/102	0	29.00
J.H. Kallis	88	10	373	11	3/29	0	33.91
M. Ntini	116.5	22	459	11	4/93	0	41.73
A. Nel	30.4	6	121	2	2/121	0	60.50
A.A. Donald............	15.2	2	72	1	1/72	0	72.00
A.J. Hall.............	27.1	4	108	1	1/35	0	108.00
D. Pretorius.........	25	6	132	1	1/60	0	132.00
N. Boje	35	4	153	1	1/153	0	153.00
N.D. McKenzie	8	0	50	0	–	0	–

AUSTRALIA – BATTING

	M	I	NO	R	HS	100s	50s	Avge	Ct/St
A.C. Gilchrist	3	5	2	473	204*	2	1	157.67	13/1
R.T. Ponting	3	5	1	309	100*	1	1	77.25	4
M.L. Hayden........	3	5	0	309	122	1	2	61.80	4
M.E. Waugh	3	5	0	169	53	0	1	33.80	6
S.K. Warne	3	5	1	129	63	0	1	32.25	5
J.L. Langer	3	5	0	152	58	0	1	30.40	2
D.R. Martyn	3	5	0	146	133	1	0	29.20	3
S.R. Waugh	3	5	0	95	42	0	0	19.00	1
B. Lee	3	4	2	27	23*	0	0	13.50	1
G.D. McGrath	3	3	1	6	4*	0	0	3.00	1
J.N. Gillespie	3	3	0	4	3	0	0	1.33	1

* Denotes not out.

BOWLING

	O	M	R	W	BB	5W/i	Avge
G.D. McGrath	110.3	36	227	12	5/21	1	18.92
S.K. Warne	162	38	442	20	6/161	1	22.10
J.N. Gillespie	92	28	287	8	3/52	0	35.88
M.E. Waugh	21.5	4	78	2	2/43	0	39.00
B. Lee	95.2	10	416	10	4/82	0	41.60
S.R. Waugh	3	0	16	0	–	0	–
D.R. Martyn	4	0	15	0	–	0	–

AUSTRALIAN FIRST-CLASS TOUR AVERAGES

BATTING

	M	I	NO	R	HS	100s	50s	Avge	Ct/St
A.C. Gilchrist	5	8	3	545	204*	2	2	109.00	20/1
R.T. Ponting	5	7	1	469	120	1	2	78.17	5
D.S. Lehmann	1	1	0	60	60	1	0	60.00	0
M.L. Hayden	4	7	0	366	122	2	1	52.29	5
M.E. Waugh	5	7	0	341	110	2	1	48.71	8
J.L. Langer	5	8	0	370	161	1	1	46.25	3
S.R. Waugh	5	7	1	201	102*	0	1	33.50	2
D.R. Martyn	4	7	1	157	133	0	1	26.17	3
S.K. Warne	4	6	1	129	63	1	0	25.80	5
A.J. Bichel	1	1	0	9	9	0	0	9.00	0
B. Lee	5	7	2	33	23*	0	0	6.60	2
J.N. Gillespie	5	5	1	24	15	0	0	6.00	2
G.D. McGrath	4	3	1	6	4*	0	0	3.00	1
S.R. Watson	1	1	1	100	100*	0	1	–	0
S.C.G. MacGill	1	1	1	0	0*	0	0	–	1

Denotes not out.

BOWLING

	O	M	R	W	BB	5W/i	Avge
G.D. McGrath	125.3	45	244	17	5/17	2	14.35
S.R. Watson	22	5	60	3	2/40	0	20.00
S.K. Warne	178	40	501	22	6/161	1	22.77
A.J. Bichel	27.3	2	123	5	3/41	0	24.60
B. Lee	137.2	16	540	18	4/37	0	30.00
J.N. Gillespie	132	42	387	10	3/52	0	38.70
S.C.G. MacGill	50.3	9	208	5	4/114	0	41.60
M.E. Waugh	25.5	5	86	2	2/43	0	43.00
D.R. Martyn	8	2	22	0	–	0	–
S.R. Waugh	3	0	16	0	–	0	–

LIMITED-OVERS INTERNATIONALS

SOUTH AFRICA – BATTING

	M	I	NO	R	HS	50s	100	Avge	Ct/St	S-R
J.N. Rhodes	7	7	2	338	83	4	0	67.60	3	115.36
G.C. Smith	4	4	0	244	84	2	0	61.00	2	79.48
L. Klusener	3	3	0	162	83	2	0	54.00	0	101.25
J.H. Kallis	7	7	1	255	80*	2	0	42.50	3	80.44
N. Boje	7	6	0	183	49	0	0	30.50	3	88.41
N.D. McKenzie	5	4	0	121	67	1	0	30.25	1	74.69
H.H. Dippenaar	4	4	1	87	51	1	0	29.00	0	64.93
A.J. Hall	2	2	1	21	18*	0	0	21.00	0	91.30
H.H. Gibbs	6	6	0	104	37	0	0	17.33	2	79.39
M.V. Boucher	7	6	1	83	41*	0	0	16.60	8/2	74.11
M. Ntini	6	3	2	13	11	0	0	13.00	1	56.52
G. Kirsten	3	3	0	26	21	0	0	8.67	1	53.06
S.M. Pollock	7	6	2	34	17	0	0	8.50	4	69.39
R. Telemachus	5	3	1	4	2	0	0	2.00	0	40.00
M. Hayward	2	0	0	0	0	0	0	–	0	–
J.C. Kent	2	0	0	0	0	0	0	–	1	–

* Denotes not out.

BOWLING

	O	M	R	W	BB	5W/i	Avge
G.C. Smith	4	0	24	1	1/24	0	24.00
R. Telemachus	43	0	230	9	2/42	0	25.56
N. Boje	47.3	0	233	9	5/21	1	25.89
M. Ntini	58	5	276	9	4/33	0	30.67
S.M. Pollock	63	1	315	9	4/32	0	35.00
J.H. Kallis	61	0	345	7	2/48	0	49.29
L. Klusener	22	0	107	1	1/54	0	107.00
M. Hayward	16	0	110	1	1/58	0	110.00
A.J. Hall	7	0	41	0	–	0	–
J.C. Kent	8	0	57	0	–	0	–

AUSTRALIA – BATTING

	M	I	NO	R	HS	50s	100	Avge	Ct/St	S-R
J.P. Maher	5	4	2	160	95	1	0	80.00	5	78.05
D.S. Lehmann	5	5	1	212	910	1	1	53.00	1	91.38
R.T. Ponting	7	7	1	283	129	1	1	47.17	4	87.35
M.L. Hayden	6	6	0	255	79	2	0	42.50	4	70.83
M.G. Bevan	4	3	1	76	55	1	0	38.00	0	84.44
A.C. Gilchrist	7	7	0	258	105	1	1	36.86	13/1	89.90
D.R. Martyn	7	7	1	211	47*	0	0	35.17	1	77.01
B. Lee	4	3	1	44	28	0	0	22.00	1	107.32
A.J. Bichel	4	4	1	48	19	0	0	16.00	1	92.31
I.J. Harvey	5	4	0	43	19	0	0	10.75	2	81.13
S.R. Watson	4	4	0	37	16	0	0	9.25	2	67.27
J.N. Gillespie	6	3	1	15	11*	0	0	7.50	0	93.75
S.K. Warne	3	2	1	7	4*	0	0	7.00	1	87.50
G.D. McGrath	6	1	0	0	0	0	0	0.00	1	0.00
N.M. Hauritz	4	2	2	13	11*	0	0	–	1	61.90

* Denotes not out.

BOWLING

	O	M	R	W	BB	5W/i	Avge
B. Lee	34.1	1	199	9	4/45	0	22.11
G.D. McGrath	49.4	5	209	9	2/14	0	23.22
J.N. Gillespie	58.2	3	287	12	4/43	0	23.92
S.K. Warne.	25	0	154	5	2/44	0	30.80
D.S. Lehmann	29	0	154	4	1/22	0	38.50
I.J. Harvey	39	0	232	5	3/38	0	46.40
N.M. Hauritz	29	0	146	3	2/31	0	48.67
S.R. Watson.	27	0	154	1	1/46	0	154.00
A.J. Bichel	37	2	181	1	1/34	0	181.00
S.C.G. MacGill	29	0	0	0	–	0	–

SOUTH AFRICA A v AUSTRALIANS

At North West Cricket Stadium, Potchefstroom, February 17, 18, 19, 2002. Drawn.
Toss: Australians.

Only 36 overs were possible on the second day after a thunderstorm had washed out the first day's play at tea. In Australia's preparation for the First Test, the major batting beneficiaries were Ricky Ponting, who was at his confident best (203 minutes, 155 balls, 23 fours) and Steve Waugh, who scored his 67th first-class century (192 minutes, 145 balls, 21 fours). The home team's attack lacked penetration and patience. Their batting succumbed to Glenn McGrath's expertise with the new ball as he quickly removed Test hopefuls Graeme Smith and Jacques Rudolph, and then dismissed Daryll Cullinan, who was aiming to regain his Test place. Unheralded 24-year-old left-hander Ashwell Prince (258 minutes, 175 balls, 14 fours), who had missed most of the season with a shoulder injury, flashed and dashed through the off side, playing a defiant lone hand that earned a call-up to the Test team. In Australia's second innings, Matthew Hayden and Justin Langer gave an aggressive pointer to their likely approach in the Test series with an opening stand of 77 from 15.1 overs in only 54 minutes.

Close of play: First day, Australians (1) 3-218 (Ponting 93, S.R. Waugh 18); Second day, Australians (1) 8-351 (S.R. Waugh 91, Gillespie 4).

Australians

J.L. Langer b Hall	12	– c Prince b Henderson	45
M.L. Hayden lbw b Hall	18	– c Smith b Henderson	39
R.T. Ponting c Tsolekile b Bodi	120		
M.E. Waugh c Prince b Henderson	62		
*S.R. Waugh not out	102		
D.R. Martyn c Cullinan b Henderson	1	– (3) not out	10
+A.C. Gilchrist c Smith b Hall	16	– (5) not out	0
S.K. Warne lbw b Hall	0		
B. Lee c Smith b Hall	6	– (4) c Tsolekile b Henderson	0
J.N. Gillespie not out	5		
L-b 8, w 7, n-b 9	24	W 1	1

(98.5 overs, 399 mins)   (8 wkts dec) 366   (27 overs, 93 mins)   (3 wkts) 95
Fall: 39 52 177 271 272 319 321 332   Fall: 77 94 94

G.D. McGrath did not bat.

Bowling: *First Innings*—Nel 25–5–75–0; Langeveldt 12–4–46–0; Hall 25.7–9–97–5; Henderson 19–3–74–2; Benkenstein 4–1–15–0; Bodi 13.5–1–51–1. *Second Innings*—Nel 3–0–14–0; Henderson 13–6–41–3; Benkenstein 5–0–26–0; Bodi 6–1–14–0.

South Africa A

G.C. Smith c Ponting b McGrath	0	C.W. Henderson c Langer b McGrath	7
J.A. Rudolph b McGrath	14	C.K. Langeveldt c (sub) Lehmann	
A.G. Prince c M.E. Waugh b McGrath	92	b Gillespie	10
D.J. Cullinan c Gilchrist b McGrath	4	A. Nel not out	2
*D.M. Benkenstein c Hayden b Warne	0	B 4, n-b 6	10
A.J. Hall c M.E. Waugh b Warne	18		
G.H. Bodi c Gillespie b Lee	33	(68 overs, 291 mins)	190
†T.L. Tsolekile b Lee	0	Fall: 0 35 40 66 114 162 162 175 184 190	

Bowling: McGrath 15–9–17–5; Gillespie 17–6–44–1; Lee 15–2–55–2; Warne 16–2–59–2; M.E. Waugh 1–0–4–0; Martyn 4–2–7–0.

Umpires: I.L. Howell and R.E. Koertzen.
TV Umpire: S. Wadvalla.

SOUTH AFRICA v AUSTRALIA

First Test Match

At Wanderers Stadium, Johannesburg, February 22, 23, 24, 2002. Australia won by an innings and 360 runs. Toss: Australia. Test debut: A.G. Prince.

Australia's largest winning margin in Test cricket was South Africa's biggest defeat, eclipsing the loss by an innings and 259 runs to Lindsay Hassett's team at Port Elizabeth in 1949-50. South Africa were jolted when their captain, Shaun Pollock, withdrew with a side strain. Another blow came late on the first day when Allan Donald broke down with a hamstring injury, made a tearful exit, and subsequently announced his retirement from Test cricket. Australia's dominance was emphasised by a bravura display from Adam Gilchrist, whose thrilling exuberance yielded him the fastest Test double-century, his 212-ball extravaganza beating Ian Botham's 220-ball effort against India at The Oval in 1982.

South Africa made three changes from the side defeated at Sydney. Ashwell Prince replaced Justin Ontong, who had a hamstring injury, Andre Nel came in for the injured Pollock, and Makhaya Ntini regained a place over spinner Claude Henderson. Australia reverted to their traditional mix of pace and spin, with Jason Gillespie replacing Stuart MacGill.

In Ntini's first over Matthew Hayden's bat followed a bouncing angled delivery and edged the ball to second slip, where Jacques Kallis spilt the chance. Hayden prospered, and plundered. Justin Langer maintained a lively tempo, striking six fours as Australia raced to 46 in the 11th over. Hayden's powerful drives down the ground took him to a century from only 149 balls, while Mark Waugh forced Gary Kirsten's retirement with a pull shot that scored a cut under his right eye while fielding at short leg. Steve Waugh suffered the indignity of being spat on after making an unconvincing 32, and Damien Martyn had beer thrown on him, as both players left the field via a race that looked more appropriate for an abattoir than a distinguished sports arena. Arrests were made, security was tightened, and the race was covered. South Africa's despondency was palpable as Hayden reached his eighth Test century, collaring some undisciplined bowling with the benefit of a fast outfield. He became the fourth Australian after Bradman, Fingleton and Harvey to post four hundreds in as many Tests. His platform innings (290 minutes, 189 balls, 18 fours, two sixes) allowed Gilchrist and Damien Martyn the freedom to attack.

Gilchrist reached his fourth Test hundred just before lunch on the second day, and by tea he was 199 not out, 190 runs having come in the session. Several of his eight sixes were hit out of the ground from the hapless Nicky Boje, one of them narrowly missing a sponsor's sign that offered the prize of a gold ingot. The greatness of his innings lay in its adherence to the first principles of batsmanship, its daring resting on a firm foundation of science, not slogging. Martyn batted flawlessly and quickly after his first fifty, racing to his next from 37 balls. While Gilchrist chose his length between drives or audacious pulls, Martyn played classically through the off side, and when Ntini, having been hit for three fours in one over, went around the wicket, Martyn swayed back and flayed him past square leg for another. The partnership was pushing towards the Bradman–Fingleton sixth-wicket record of 346 when Martyn was held at third man. Steve Waugh closed the innings just after tea, when Australia had added 321 from just 55.3 overs for the day.

By stumps South Africa were in a parlous state: Gary Kirsten had left his bat dangling to his first ball from Glenn McGrath, Herschelle Gibbs misread Shane Warne's straight ball, Kallis edged droopily to slip and Neil McKenzie top-edged a hook. Prince played more bravely than regally, but his early dismissal on the third day to a sharp Hayden catch resulted in South Africa following on before lunch.

It was, as expected, a capitulation, once McGrath sorted out Kallis with his most unplayable ball of the match, after Gibbs had charged suicidally at a Warne leg-break. McGrath was on a hat-trick as he crashed through Boje and Ntini before Nel managed to survive one ball. Warne's match haul of six wickets took him past Kapil Dev as the second-highest Test wicket-taker. While statistics can obscure, those of this match were a searchlight brutally highlighting the extent of Australia's dominance: Australia lost seven wickets in scoring 652 runs in five sessions, while the home side's total occupation lasted just over three sessions and yielded just 292 runs for 20 wickets.

Man of the Match: A.C. Gilchrist.

Close of play: First day, Australia (1) 5-331 (Martyn 21, Gilchrist 25); Second day, South Africa (1) 4-111 (Prince 47, Dippenaar 2).

Australia

J.L. Langer lbw b Donald	28	S.K. Warne c McKenzie b Boje	12
M.L. Hayden c Boucher b Nel	122	B. Lee not out	4
R.T. Ponting c Boucher b Nel	39		
M.E. Waugh c Boucher b Ntini	53	B 2, l-b 14, w 4, n-b 5	25
*S.R. Waugh c Gibbs b Kallis	32		
D.R. Martyn c Kirsten b Kallis	133	(146 overs, 574 mins) (7 wkts dec)	652
†A.C. Gilchrist not out	204	Fall: 46 113 224 272 293 610 643	

J.N. Gillespie and G.D. McGrath did not bat.

Bowling: Donald 15.2–2–72–1; Ntini 33–8–124–1; Kallis 24–1–116–2; Nel 30.4–6–121–2; Boje 35–4–153–1; McKenzie 8–0–50–0.

South Africa

H.H. Gibbs lbw b Warne	34	– st Gilchrist b Warne	47
G. Kirsten c Warne b McGrath	1	– c Martyn b Gillespie	12
A.G. Prince c Hayden b Gillespie	49	– b Warne	28
J.H. Kallis c Warne b Lee	3	– c Gilchrist b McGrath	8
N.D. McKenzie c Gillespie b McGrath	16	– not out	27
H.H. Dippenaar c Gilchrist b McGrath	2	– lbw b Warne	1
*†M.V. Boucher c Gilchrist b Lee	23	– b Warne	1
N. Boje c M.E. Waugh b Gillespie	0	– c Ponting b McGrath	5
M. Ntini c S.R. Waugh b Lee	9	– b McGrath	0
A. Nel lbw b Warne	7	– c Langer b McGrath	0
A.A. Donald not out	3	– c Hayden b McGrath	0
B 4, l-b 3, n-b 5	12	W 1, n-b 3	4

(48 overs, 199 mins)	159	(38.3 overs, 152 mins) 133
Fall: 11 51 55 108 113 113 114		Fall: 20 89 98 98 107 109 122
144 155 159		122 122 133

Bowling: *First Innings*—McGrath 14–6–28–3; Gillespie 15–5–58–2; Warne 9–0–26–2; Lee 10–1–40–3. *Second Innings*—McGrath 12.3–4–21–5; Gillespie 4–1–13–1; Lee 10–2–55–0; Warne 12–3–44–4.

Umpires: S. A. Bucknor (West Indies) and R.E. Koertzen.
TV Umpire: I. L. Howell.
Referee: C. W. Smith (West Indies).

SOUTH AFRICA A v AUSTRALIANS

At St George's Park, Port Elizabeth, March 1, 2, 3, 2002. Australians won by an innings and 41 runs. Toss: Australians.

This scheduled four-day match turned into a three-day romp for the Australians. Sent in on a slow pitch, the South Africans were well placed at three for 251, with Daryll Cullinan and South African Under-19s captain Hashim Amla (208 minutes, 174 balls, 11 fours) well set after a partnership of 155. Shane Watson removed Cullinan (183 minutes, 150 balls, 11 fours), heralding a collapse as Brett Lee and Andy Bichel crashed through with the second new ball. Darren Lehmann continued the assault in another left-handed opening century partnership, while Justin Langer (352 minutes, 264 balls, 18 fours, one six), built steadily in three attractive alliances. He raised the tempo in a third-wicket partnership of 207 with Mark Waugh, whose second fifty included six fours and three sixes from only 24 balls as he raced to his 80th first-class hundred (146 minutes, 100 balls, 14 fours, three sixes). Gilchrist's cameo 56 from 60 balls inspired the hard-hitting Watson, who reached his hundred (144 minutes, 97 balls, 12 fours, three sixes) with a six over mid-wicket. The persevering Dewald Pretorius bowled impressively in an otherwise wayward attack. On Sunday an oyster-eating competition during the lunch break provided more fun for the crowd than their side's cricket. Stuart MacGill looked in need of match practice, but with Bichel and Lee again on target, he landed enough telling leg-breaks to ensure a win with 13.3 overs of the third day in hand.

Close of play: First day, South Africa A (1) 7-288 (Peterson 3, Tsolekile 0); Second day, Australians (1) 5-452 (Watson 20, Gilchrist 38).

South Africa A

G. C. Smith c Lee b Watson	28	– b MacGill	31
J. A. Rudolph c Gilchrist b MacGill	36	– c Gilchrist b Lee	11
M. Van Jaarsveld c Gilchrist b Gillespie	11	– b MacGill	29
D.J. Cullinan lbw b Watson	86	– lbw b Bichel	19
H.M. Amla b Lee	81	– b Bichel	2
J.M. Kemp b Bichel	16	– c Gilchrist b Lee	56
R.J. Peterson c Gilchrist b Lee	6	– c MacGill b Watson	9
G. H. Bodi lbw b Lee	2	– c S.R. Waugh b MacGill	45
†T.L. Tsolekile not out	0	– lbw b Bichel	6
D. Pretorius b Lee	0	– lbw b MacGill	7
C.M. Willoughby c Gilchrist b Bichel	7	– not out	0
B 1, l-b 10, w 3, n-b 14	28	B 1, l-b 1, n-b 15	17
(92.3 overs, 377 mins)	301	(60.3 overs, 261 mins)	232

Fall: 58 86 96 251 283 285 288
294 294 301

Fall: 31 70 82 96 107 127 214
219 228 232

Bowling: *First Innings*—Gillespie 15–4–33–1; Lee 14–3–37–4; Watson 16–5–40–2; Bichel 16.3–1–82–2; MacGill 28–5–94–1; M.E. Waugh 3–1–4–0. *Second Innings*—Gillespie 8–4–23–0; Lee 13–1–32–2; MacGill 22.3–4–114–4; Bichel 11–1–41–3; Watson 6–0–20–1.

Australians

J.L. Langer c Van Jaarsveld b Willoughby	. . 161	A.J. Bichel c Amla b Willoughby	 9
D.S. Lehmann lbw b Pretorius	 60	J.N. Gillespie run out (Smith/Kemp)	 15
R.T. Ponting c Kemp b Willoughby	 40	S.C.G. MacGill not out	 0
M.E. Waugh b Pretorius	 110		
*S.R. Waugh c Tsolekile b Pretorius	 4	B 4, l-b 2, w 1, n-b 12	 19
S.R. Watson not out	 100		
†A.C. Gilchrist c Van Jaarsveld b Pretorius	. 56	(116.2 overs, 491 mins)	(9 wkts dec) 574
B. Lee c Cullinan b Pretorius	 0	Fall: 103 180 387 387 391 490 490 515 563	

Bowling: Pretorius 29–1–148–5; Willoughby 29–7–101–3; Kemp 24–5–106–0; Bodi 14.2–0–85–0; Peterson 20–0–128–0.

Umpires: R.E. Koertzen and M.Z. Nanabhay.

SOUTH AFRICA v AUSTRALIA

Second Test Match

At Newlands, Cape Town, March 8, 9, 10, 11, 12, 2002. Australia won by four wickets. Toss: South Africa. Test debut: G.C. Smith, A.J. Hall, D. Pretorius.

Australia won the series just before tea on the final day when Ricky Ponting pulled a long hop from Paul Adams into the Railway Stand. His climactic blow was typical of Australia's aggressive batting throughout the match, but it followed a revival from South Africa, who were rejuvenated by some fresh talent and a more spirited approach.

The South African marketing strategists had decided that Test cricket needed the periodic accompaniment of rock music over the public address system. Apart from being almost deafening and not to everyone's taste, Queen's "We Will Rock You" disturbed Test cricket's traditional mood of serenity. Fortunately the sight of Warne leading Australia onto the field in his 100th Test drew sustained applause, and created that sense of occasion unique to major events. South Africa had made four changes to their side, introducing 21-year-old left-hander Graeme Smith, pace bowler Dewald Pretorius and all-rounder Andrew Hall, and recalling unorthodox left-arm wrist-spinner Paul Adams. Daryll Cullinan was a self-inflicted casualty. Recalled to the squad, he immediately demanded a contract from the UCB, only to withdraw when it was not offered. It was a precipitate decision that seemed to spell the end of his chequered, but sometimes brilliant, career.

Boucher's decision to bat on a pitch that was said to be slow and ideal for batting backfired when South Africa lost their first six wickets for 92. Smith and Gary Kirsten followed Herschelle Gibbs to slip catches, and Neil McKenzie was so bamboozled by Warne's leg-breaks that he left a straighter delivery that hit middle and off. In the fourth over after lunch, Glenn McGrath produced another unmissable ball to Jacques Kallis for Adam Gilchrist to take the first of four catches for the innings. Hall (187 minutes, 141 balls, 10 fours) and Adams saved the innings from total disaster in a fresh approach which added 69 runs, Adams' best Test score including a cheeky six from Warne over mid-wicket. Hall's resolute and forthright approach compensated for any shortcomings in technique and he refused to be cowed by the occasion.

By stumps Australia had scored 46 from only eight overs, with Justin Langer taking to Pretorius, whose first three overs cost 33 runs. Next morning, his attack spiralled into over-ambition, and he edged an attempted pull into his stumps. Matthew Hayden (121 minutes, 92 balls, 12 fours) top-edged a hook, but Australia eased into lunch at two for 152. In the next hour four wickets fell for only 33 runs as Ponting edged a cut, and Steve Waugh's attempt to hit the threatening Adams out of the attack ended in an embarrassing miss. Makhaya Ntini chimed in with two supporting wickets, exposing Gilchrist and the tail to the wiles of Adams. Gilchrist relished the challenge, and within an hour Australia had gained a first-innings lead and the left-hander was heading towards his sixth Test century. Warne (102 minutes, 66 balls, 10 fours, one six) drove and swung tellingly in a seventh-wicket partnership of 132, becoming the fourth player to pass 2,000 runs and 400 Test wickets behind Sir Richard Hadlee, Kapil Dev and Wasim Akram. Gilchrist rushed to his second fifty from 38 balls, scoring 62 of the 65 runs added after the fall of the seventh wicket. Adams took his 100th Test wicket, but conceded 76 runs to Gilchrist, whose blazing batting (172 minutes, 108 balls, 22 fours, two sixes) pushed Australia's lead to 143.

In their second innings South Africa at last made a substantial start as Australia relied on Warne's persevering, probing accuracy and variation to keep a measure of control. Kirsten's anchoring defiance (259 minutes, 182 balls, 11 fours) was matched by Smith (242 minutes, 147 balls, nine fours), who ignored the taunting "conversation" from the Australian fieldsmen, and watched Kallis (129 minutes, 96 balls 12 fours) play his freest innings of the series. McKenzie (307 minutes, 226 balls, 14 fours) played Warne with unceasing vigilance, sweating on the rare misdirected balls to pull or drive off the back foot. When Damien Martyn ran him out with a direct hit at the bowler's end from short cover, McKenzie became the 12th player to be run out for 99 in Tests. After this prolonged and stern resistance, South Africa then lost their last five wickets for only 42 runs. Warne celebrated his 100th Test by taking six for 161, his 21st bag of five or more wickets in an innings, and bowling 98 overs in the match.

Chasing the tenth-highest fourth-innings total in Test cricket, Australia's left-handed openers scorched past 100 inside 21 overs, maintaining their century average since The Oval in August 2001. Pretorius broke through Langer (104 minutes, 74 balls, ten fours), but not Hayden (218 minutes, 141 balls, 15 fours, one six), who was a boundary away from his ninth hundred when he chased an otherwise certain wide and edged it to Mark Boucher. Ricky Ponting kept the pursuit moving with a judicious mixture of sound defence and powerful strokes, but Adams again confounded Steve Waugh and had Martyn leg-before on the sweep. At a moment of incipient crisis, Gilchrist sustained the attack with a run-a-ball assault, and after he was dismissed for the first time in the series, a confident Warne flashed boundary hits to bring Australia within three runs of victory. Ponting (261 minutes, 160 balls, 16 fours, one six) revived memories of Ian Healy's winning six at Port Elizabeth in 1996-97 when he pounced on a ball from Adams, creating his own slice of history by raising a century and a famous win with one triumphant stroke over the square leg fence.

Man of the Match: S.K. Warne.

Close of play: First day, Australia (1) 0-46 (Langer 28, Hayden 17); Second day, South Africa (2) 0-7 (Gibbs 5, Kirsten 2); Third day, South Africa (2) 4-307 (McKenzie 28, Prince 5); Fourth day, Australia (2) 1-131 (Hayden 50, Ponting 17).

South Africa

H.H. Gibbs c M.E. Waugh b Gillespie	12	– c Ponting b Warne	39
G. Kirsten c M.E. Waugh b Lee	7	– lbw b Lee	87
G.C. Smith c Ponting b McGrath	3	– c Gilchrist b Warne	68
J.H. Kallis c Gilchrist b McGrath	23	– lbw b Warne	73
N.D. McKenzie b Warne	20	– run out (Martyn)	99
A.G. Prince c Gilchrist b McGrath	10	– c Ponting b Warne	20
*†M.V. Boucher c Gilchrist b Lee	26	– lbw b Gillespie	37
A.J. Hall c Gilchrist b Gillespie	70	– run out (Lee/Gillespie)	0
P.R. Adams c Warne b Gillespie	35	– not out	23
M. Ntini c M.E. Waugh b Warne	14	– c Langer b Warne	11
D. Pretorius not out	5	– c M.E. Waugh b Warne	0
B 4, l-b 5, n-b 5	14	B 8, l-b 3, w 2, n-b 3	16

(80 overs, 355 mins)   239   (162 overs, 683 mins)   473

Fall: 15 18 25 70 73 92 147   Fall: 84 183 254 284 350 431 433
216 229 239   440 464 473

Bowling: *First Innings*—McGrath 20–4–42–3; Gillespie 15–4–52–3; Lee 16–1–65–2; Warne 28–10–70–2; M.E. Waugh 1–0–1–0. *Second Innings*—McGrath 25–7–56–0; Gillespie 29–10–81–1; Warne 70–15–161–6; Lee 22–3–99–1; M.E. Waugh 9–3–34–0; Martyn 4–0–15–0; S.R. Waugh 3–0–16–0.

Australia

J.L. Langer b Ntini	37	– b Pretorius	58
M.L. Hayden c Hall b Kallis	63	– c Boucher b Kallis	96
R.T. Ponting c Boucher b Adams	47	– not out	100
M.E. Waugh c Gibbs b Ntini	25	– c Boucher b Ntini	16
*S.R. Waugh b Adams	0	– b Adams	14
D.R. Martyn c Boucher b Ntini	2	– lbw b Adams	0
†A.C. Gilchrist not out	138	– c McKenzie b Kallis	24
S.K. Warne c Kallis b Adams	63	– not out	15
B. Lee c Prince b Kallis	0		
J.N. Gillespie c Kallis b Adams	0		
G.D. McGrath lbw b Ntini	2		
B 2, l-b 1, w 2	5	L-b 6, n-b 5	11

(80.5 overs, 369 mins) 382   (79.1 overs, 366 mins)   (6 wkts) 334

Fall: 67 130 162 168 176 185 317 338 343 382   Fall: 102 201 251 268 268 305

Bowling: *First Innings*—Ntini 22.5–5–93–4; Pretorius 11–1–72–0; Kallis 16–2–65–2; Hall 11–1–47–0; Adams 20–1–102–4. *Second Innings*—Ntini 24–4–90–1; Pretorius 14–5–60–1; Adams 21.1–0–104–2; Hall 3–0–6–0; Kallis 17–2–68–2.

Umpires: S.A. Bucknor (West Indies) and R.E. Koertzen.
TV Umpire: D.L. Orchard.
Referee: C.W. Smith (West Indies).

SOUTH AFRICA v AUSTRALIA

Third Test Match

At Kingsmead, Durban, March 15, 16, 17, 18, 19, 2002. South Africa won by five wickets. Toss: South Africa.

South Africa regained their self-respect with a stirring and successful run-chase to achieve their highest winning fourth-innings total. Unsurprisingly, the match lacked the edge of the Newlands epic after only two rest days were allocated between the two Tests, and both sides struggled to regain their physical and mental freshness. The major casualty was Shane Warne, who showed his champion skills in South Africa's first innings, but was clearly battling fatigue and injury from there on. South Africa made only one change, replacing Dewald Pretorius with pace man David Terbrugge, the more settled composition of the side being reflected in the result.

Justin Langer began the match with a flurry of blows that dispatched a bemused Makhaya Ntini for 11 runs from his opening over before he was caught attempting an ambitious pull from the seventh ball of the innings, Terbrugge's first ball in his comeback match. Matthew Hayden seemed to lack the focus of his previous outings, and although Neil McKenzie spilt a chance in the slips at one for 47, he soon made amends with a sharp catch. Ricky Ponting (153 minutes, 100 balls, 16 fours) continued his Newlands form with some sparkling on-side boundaries, proceeding at a rate that had the punters pushing their spreads beyond 400, when Herschelle Gibbs scored a direct-hit run-out after a hazardous call from Mark Waugh ended an engaging third-wicket partnership of 108. Steve Waugh fell again to Paul Adams on an errant cut, and Mark nudged a lifting ball into the slips. Adam Gilchrist rallied the side brilliantly, dominating partnerships with Damien Martyn and Warne. He raced to his fifty in 66 balls, and, nearing his third hundred of the series with his customary audacity and flair, was the last man out (147 minutes, 107 balls, 14 fours), caught at deep mid-wicket. Australia's 315 was their lowest first-innings total in 12 Tests since England had bowled them out for 190 at Trent Bridge.

The score looked more than adequate as South Africa stumbled, then fell apart. Brett Lee began by bowling quickly and intimidatingly at Gary Kirsten, who was caught off the glove in fading light. Night watchman Adams lasted half an hour into the second day, dismissed by another athletic Hayden catch in the gully. Graeme Smith dallied outside the off stump and Gibbs (66 balls, ten fours) again lost concentration. Warne, bowling around the wicket, accepted a return catch from Jacques Kallis, then tempted catches from full tosses to Ashwell Prince and Mark Boucher. Martyn grabbed a blinding leaping left-hand catch at point to Neil McKenzie, and like the whirl at the end of a limited-overs innings, Andrew Hall and Ntini flung their bats hopefully.

Australia were batting again before tea, and Hayden's soft tap to cover in Terbrugge's first over heralded a period of batting wastefulness. Terbrugge had Langer caught behind, then gulped a Ponting top edge at long leg, ending an entertaining 32-ball cameo. Mark Waugh looked set again, but missed a straight ball from Kallis, and Martyn hooked unconvincingly to give Boucher his 200th dismissal in a record 52 Tests. Steve Waugh scrapped defiantly, but for once Gilchrist was unable to produce the necessary heroics, edging a perfectly pitched leg-cutter from Kallis. By stumps Australia had staggered to eight for 159, a lead of 307, and 17 wickets had fallen for 278 runs in the day's play. Next morning, Steve Waugh and Lee played steadily until Ntini ended the Australian resistance.

South Africa needed 334 with almost three days remaining in a match that had proceeded at high speed since Langer's manic beginning. Kirsten (187 minutes, 134 balls, 12 fours) and Gibbs (298 minutes, 197 balls, 15 fours) opened with determination and composure. Denied a rest by the side's self-destructive batting, Australia's bowlers looked flat. The break was made spectacularly when Lee gathered a Martyn return on the half-volley and shattered the bowler's stumps to run out Kirsten. Gibbs showed more restraint than usual and reached his first Test hundred against Australia. Mark Waugh's tempting off-breaks caused Graeme Smith to top-edge a pull and Gibbs to punch to Martyn at mid-wicket. Warne took his 100th wicket against South Africa, thanks to Hayden's fine running catch at wide mid-on. Had Ashwell Prince been run out in the same over backing up too far, South Africa would have been five for 232, but he survived and was there at stumps supporting Kallis. Australia's refreshed attack, armed with a new ball, could make no impression on the fourth morning, and by the time Prince edged for Mark Waugh's 173rd catch, the game was virtually over, with Kallis (159 minutes, 113 balls, 10 fours) in firm control. Later, Boucher repeated Ponting's Cape Town flourish, with a six off Mark Waugh to complete victory. South Africa's rediscovery of their competitive spirit had brought some overdue reward for their supporters.

Man of the Match: H. H. Gibbs. *Man of the Series:* A. C. Gilchrist.

Close of play: First day, South Africa (1) 1-48 (Gibbs 24, Adams 0); Second day, Australia (2) 8-159 (S. R. Waugh 34, Lee 5); Third day, South Africa (2) 4-264 (Kallis 35, Prince 8).

Australia

J.L. Langer c Kirsten b Terbrugge	11	– c Boucher b Terbrugge 18
M.L. Hayden c McKenzie b Kallis	28	– c Prince b Terbrugge 0
R.T. Ponting run out (Gibbs)	89	– c Terbrugge b Ntini 34
M.E. Waugh c Smith b Kallis	45	– b Kallis 30
*S.R. Waugh c Boucher b Adams	7	– c Kallis b Ntini 42
D.R. Martyn b Terbrugge	11	– c Boucher b Kallis 0
†A.C. Gilchrist c Smith b Adams	91	– c Boucher b Kallis 16
S.K. Warne c Boucher b Ntini	26	– c McKenzie b Adams 13
B. Lee b Ntini	0	– (10) not out 23
J.N. Gillespie c Boucher b Hall	1	– (9) c Kallis b Adams 3
G.D. McGrath not out	4	– b Ntini 0
W 2	2	B 1, l-b 3, w 1, n-b 2 7

(74.1 overs, 338 mins)	315	(49 overs, 224 mins) 186
Fall: 11 61 169 178 182 230 287		Fall: 4 19 77 90 90 114 129
289 311 315		150 186 186

Bowling: *First Innings*—Ntini 20–3–87–2; Terbrugge 16–2–61–2; Kallis 20–3–95–2; Hall 9.1–2–35–1; Adams 9–0–37–2. *Second Innings*—Ntini 17–2–65–3; Terbrugge 4–1–21–2; Hall 4–1–20–0; Adams 13–0–47–2; Kallis 11–2–29–3.

South Africa

H.H. Gibbs c Gilchrist b Gillespie	51	– c Martyn b M.E. Waugh 104
G. Kirsten c Gilchrist b Lee	21	– run out (Martyn/Lee) 64
P.R. Adams c Hayden b Lee	6	
G.C. Smith c Gilchrist b McGrath	7	– (3) c Gilchrist b M.E. Waugh 42
J.H. Kallis c and b Warne	16	– (4) not out 61
N.D. McKenzie c Martyn b Lee	25	– (5) c Hayden b Warne 4
A.G. Prince c Lee b Warne	0	– (6) c M.E. Waugh b Warne 48
*†M. V. Boucher c and b Warne	0	– (7) not out 8
A.J. Hall not out	27	
M. Ntini c McGrath b Warne	14	
D.J. Terbrugge c Gilchrist b Lee	0	
L-b 1, w 1, n-b 4	6	L-b 2, w 2, n-b 5 9

(55.2 overs, 258 mins)	167	(104.5 overs, 449 mins) (5 wkts) 340
Fall: 48 74 75 85 109 119 119 148 167 167		Fall: 142 216 218 232 331

Bowling: *First Innings*—McGrath 11–4–26–1; Lee 17.2–1–82–4; Gillespie 14–6–25–1; Warne 13–4–33–4. *Second Innings*—McGrath 28–11–54–0; Lee 20–2–75–0; Gillespie 15–2–58–0; Warne 30–6–108–2; M.E. Waugh 11.5–1–43–2.

Umpires: S. Venkataraghavan (India) and D.L. Orchard.
TV Umpire: I.L. Howell.
Referee: C.W. Smith (West Indies).

SOUTH AFRICA v AUSTRALIA

First Limited-Overs International

At Wanderers Stadium, Johannesburg, March 22, 2002. Australia won by 19 runs. Toss: Australia. International limited-overs debut: N.M. Haurtiz.

Lance Klusener's spectacular return to form enlivened a match that had looked to be over when South Africa were seven for 93. With the partisan crowd chanting his nickname, "Zulu, Zulu," he clubbed eight fours and three scudding sixes, blows reminiscent of his heroics in the 1999 World Cup semi-final. Andy Bichel, who had suffered most of the mauling, ended the onslaught when he caught him on the mid-wicket boundary. South Africa's top order had been wrecked by Jason Gillespie's three-wicket new-ball burst. Off-spinner Nathan Hauritz claimed Boeta Dippenaar in his first over, and bowled impressively as a replacement for the injured Shane Warne. Ricky Ponting's decision to bat was buoyed by Adam Gilchrist's bright opening, but on a pitch that produced variable bounce, only Darren Lehmann could match Gilchrist, and the batting lacked authority. Jonty Rhodes pulled off a stunning one-handed catch and a direct-hit run-out in a typically athletic exhibition, and Makhaya Ntini's spell underlined his sustained enthusiasm and improvement. Australia's win without the skills of their long-serving three Ws in the Waugh twins and Warne was an important first step for the new captain.

Man of the Match: J.N. Gillespie.

Australia

†A.C. Gilchrist c Boje b Ntini	37	(44)	A.J. Bichel c Telemachus b Kallis	19	(21)
M.L. Hayden c Rhodes b Kallis	27	(46)	J.N. Gillespie not out	11	(12)
*R.T. Ponting c Boje b Ntini	14	(22)			
D.R. Martyn b Telemachus	24	(56)	L-b 4, w 7, n-b 6	17	
D.S. Lehmann c Boucher b Telemachus	37	(53)			
M.G. Bevan run out (Rhodes)	18	(25)	(50 overs, 224 mins) (8 wkts)	223	
I.J. Harvey c Kallis b Ntini	19	(27)	Fall: 50 84 86 149 156 187 195 223		

N.M. Hauritz and G.D. McGrath did not bat.

Bowling: Pollock 10–0–49–0; Telemachus 7–0–45–2; Ntini 10–2–24–3; Kallis 10–0–48–2; Klusener 8–0–27–0; Boje 5–0–26–0.

South Africa

H.H. Gibbs c Hayden b Gillespie	0	(7)	N. Boje run out ((S)Lee/Bichel)	33	(48)
G. Kirsten c Gilchrist b Gillespie	2	(10)	R. Telemachus st Gilchrist b Hauritz	1	(4)
J.H. Kallis lbw b Gillespie	8	(20)	M. Ntini not out	0	(7)
H.H. Dippenaar c Gilchrist b Hauritz	51	(65)			
J.N. Rhodes c Gilchrist b Harvey	13	(21)	W 8, n-b 2	10	
†M.V. Boucher c McGrath b Harvey	3	(8)			
*S.M. Pollock c Hayden b Harvey	0	(3)	(44.4 overs, 196 mins)	204	
L. Klusener c Bichel b McGrath	83	(77)	Fall: 1 2 23 56 66 66 93 164 166 204		

Bowling: McGrath 7.4–1–26–1; Gillespie 10–0–39–3; Harvey 8–0–38–3; Bichel 9–0–70–0; Hauritz 10–0–31–2.

Umpires: I.L. Howell and B.G. Jerling.
TV Umpire: S. Wadvalla.

SOUTH AFRICA v AUSTRALIA

Second Limited-Overs International

At Centurion Park, Centurion, March 24, 2002. Australia won by 45 runs. Toss: South Africa. International limited-overs debut: S.R. Watson.

Another full house, estimated at 19,500, fell silent when Lance Klusener's innings ended. He struck four sixes, one through Glenn McGrath's hands at long-off, and two from Shane Watson full tosses that resulted in cash prizes to the skilful catchers in the crowd. His bludgeoning was more effective against pace than spin, and Darren Lehmann's tidy tempters lured a catch to deep mid-wicket. Again South Africa's top order crumbled meekly to disciplined bowling and brilliant fielding. Injuries opened opportunities for Watson, Nathan Hauritz again, and Jimmy Maher, playing his third match four years after his debut. Maher's confident, well-judged innings (180 minutes, 150 balls, 10 fours, one six) illustrated Australia's depth of talent and reminded the

South Africans of their relative shortage of the same commodity. Shaun Pollock's shrewd bowling in Australia's happy hour was matched by McGrath and Jason Gillespie in their opening spells. They forced errors with a sustained, controlled attack, taking four wickets in 12 overs. Ricky Ponting's sharp catching, and a couple of run-outs, one a direct hit to dispatch Boeta Dippenaar, completed another encouraging outing for the new captain.

Man of the Match: J.P. Maher.

Australia

†A.C. Gilchrist c Kirsten b Pollock	..	7	(11)	A.J. Bichel b Pollock 7	(7)
M.L. Hayden c Rhodes b Boje	......	38	(60)	J.N. Gillespie lbw b Pollock 4	(3)
J.P. Maher c Kallis b Telemachus	....	95	(150)	N.M. Hauritz not out 2	(4)
*R.T. Ponting c and b Boje	....	0	(1)	L-b 8, w 1, n-b 7 16	
D.R. Martyn c Boucher b Telemachus		42	(49)	—	
D.S. Lehmann not out	....	13	(18)	(50 overs, 217 mins) (8 wkts) 226	
S.R. Watson c Gibbs b Pollock	......	2	(3)	Fall: 14 99 99 192 201 206 216 220	

G.D. McGrath did not bat.

Bowling: Pollock 10–1–32–4; Ntini 9–0–43–0; Kallis 9–0–38–0; Telemachus 10–0–42–2; Klusener 4–0–26–0; Boje 8–0–37–2.

South Africa

H.H. Gibbs c Hauritz b McGrath	....	5	(14)	N. Boje c Gilchrist b Gillespie 18	(24)
G. Kirsten c Ponting b Gillespie	.....	21	(27)	M. Ntini not out 2	(6)
J.H. Kallis c Ponting b McGrath	.....	14	(17)	R. Telemachus lbw b Gillespie 2	(4)
H.H. Dippenaar run out (Ponting)	....	21	(53)		
J.N. Rhodes lbw b Gillespie	....	0	(5)	L-b 2, w 1, n-b 3 6	
†M.V. Boucher b Hauritz	....	16	(43)	—	
L. Klusener c Hayden b Lehmann	....	59	(59)	(46.2 overs, 201 mins) 181	
*S.M. Pollock run out (Ponting/Bichel)		17	(29)	Fall: 18 30 42 45 80 81 110 177 177 181	

Bowling: McGrath 7–2–14–2; Gillespie 9.2–1–43–4; Watson 6–0–21–0; Bichel 10–1–33–0; Hauritz 8–0–46–1; Lehmann 6–0–22–1.

Umpires: I.L. Howell and S. Wadvalla.
TV Umpire: K.H. Hurter.

SOUTH AFRICA v AUSTRALIA

Third Limited-Overs International

At North West Cricket Stadium, Potchefstroom, March 27, 2002. Tied. Toss: South Africa.

A dramatic tenth-wicket partnership produced the third tie in the last three years between the two leading limited-overs teams. South Africa froze in the final moments, allowing Australia to escape through the cool batting of Maher, whose six over long-on from Ntini's final delivery signalled a spirited assault which produced 36 from the last 28 balls. Needing two to win off the last ball, Hauritz drove Kallis for a single to Jonty Rhodes at deep mid-on. Pollock's reluctance to set a one-saving circle betrayed a fear that South Africa could lose. Brett Lee's express outswingers had quickly removed South Africa's opening pair before Rhodes' lively innings (95 minutes, 74 balls, six fours, one six), which included an amazing reverse sweep for six from Darren Lehmann's bowling.

Man of the Match: J.P. Maher.

South Africa

H. H. Dippenaar c Ponting b Lee	7	(14)
H. H. Gibbs c Maher b Lee	10	(15)
J. H. Kallis c Gilchrist b Gillespie	71	(101)
N. D. McKenzie c Martyn b Lehmann	37	(57)
J. N. Rhodes c Maher b Lee	83	(74)
L. Klusener c Hayden b Lee	20	(24)
†M. V. Boucher c Gilchrist b Gillespie	5	(3)

A. J. Hall not out	18	(12)
*S. M. Pollock not out	1	(1)
W 6, n-b 1	7	

(50 overs, 212 mins)   (7 wkts)   259

Fall: 11 27 105 180 222 232 256

M. Ntini and N. Boje did not bat.

Bowling: Gillespie 10–0–46–2; Lee 9–1–45–4; Watson 6–0–40–0; Bichel 10–1–44–0; Lehmann 9–0–42–1; Hauritz 6–0–42–0.

Australia

†A. C. Gilchrist c Boucher b Ntini	16	(27)
M. L. Hayden c Gibbs b Boje	79	(104)
*R. T. Ponting run out (Boje/Klusener/Boucher)	3	(11)
D. R. Martyn run out (Pollock/Boje)	35	(58)
D. S. Lehmann c Boucher b Kallis	32	(30)
J. P. Maher not out	43	(33)
S. R. Watson c Boucher b Ntini	8	(13)
A. J. Bichel b Ntini	7	(8)

B. Lee c Boucher b Ntini	8	(9)
J. N. Gillespie b Klusener	0	(1)
N. M. Hauritz not out	11	(17)
L-b 1, w 5, n-b 11	17	

(50 overs, 224 mins)(9 wkts)   259

Fall: 33 39 112 176 180 194 206 222 223

Bowling: Pollock 9–0–48–0; Ntini 10–1–33–4; Kallis 9–0–52–1; Klusener 10–0–54–1; Hall 4–0–24–0; Boje 8–0–47–1.

Umpires: K. H. Hurter and R. E. Koertzen.
TV Umpire: M. Z. Nanabhay.

SOUTH AFRICA v AUSTRALIA

Fourth Limited-Overs International

At Springbok Park, Bloemfontein, March 30, 2002. Australia won by 37 runs. Toss: Australia. International limited-overs debut: G. C. Smith.

Ricky Ponting's aggressive batting (155 minutes, 126 balls, 15 fours, one six) characterised his team's intent to establish an unbeatable position in the series. On a hot, windless day, Ponting scored his ninth limited-overs century, becoming the first Australian to achieve hundreds against every major cricket country other than Bangladesh. Darren Lehmann's clever improvisations and placements in a 91-ball partnership of 119 rushed Australia to their second-highest total against South Africa. Brett Lee drove a Jacques Kallis slower ball over long-on for six to complete a very happy hour of 88 runs from the final ten overs. After early dismissals, debutant left-hander Graeme Smith counterpunched until he was out first ball after a drinks break, edging into his stumps. Kallis and Neil McKenzie kept the required run-rate under seven an over, but Lehmann again emphasised the depth of his all-roundedness by luring Kallis into a return catch. As the rate pushed beyond eight an over, Lee hit the stumps with successive balls, and Ian Harvey took an athletic running catch to finish off the match in spectacular fashion.

Man of the Match: R. T. Ponting.

Australia

†A.C. Gilchrist b Telemachus	34	(59)		I.J. Harvey c Smith b Pollock	6	(4)
M.L. Hayden c Boucher b Telemachus	17	(30)		B. Lee not out	8	(4)
*R.T. Ponting c Pollock b Kallis	129	(126)		L-b 9, w 5, n-b 5	19	
D.R. Martyn b Boje	24	(33)				
D.S. Lehmann b Pollock	39	(37)		(50 overs, 214 mins) (6 wkts)	290	
J.P. Maher not out	14	(12)		Fall: 40 87 143 262 266 274		

J.N. Gillespie, N.M. Hauritz and G.D. McGrath did not bat.

Bowling: Pollock 10–0–59–2; Ntini 10–2–42–0; Telemachus 10–0–60–2; Kallis 10–0–67–1; Boje 7–0–36–1; Hall 3–0–17–0.

South Africa

G.C. Smith b Harvey	41	(49)		N. Boje c Gilchrist b Lee	14	(14)
G. Kirsten c Gilchrist b McGrath	3	(12)		M. Ntini b Gillespie	11	(10)
A.J. Hall c Maher b McGrath	3	(11)		R. Telemachus not out	1	(2)
J.H. Kallis c and b Lehmann	43	(51)		B 4, l-b 2, w 5, n-b 1	12	
N.D. McKenzie b Lee	67	(88)				
J.N. Rhodes c Harvey b Lee	56	(49)		(48.1 overs, 211 mins)	253	
†M.V. Boucher b Lee	0	(1)		Fall: 7 14 67 138 202 202 207		
*S.M. Pollock c Gilchrist b Gillespie	2	(3)		224 251 253		

Bowling: McGrath 8–0–20–2; Gillespie 10–1–46–2; Lee 9.1–0–63–4; Harvey 8–0–41–1; Hauritz 5–0–27–0; Lehmann 8–0–50–1.

Umpires: M.Z. Nanabhay and D.L. Orchard.
TV Umpire: B.G. Jerling.

SOUTH AFRICA v AUSTRALIA

Fifth Limited-Overs International

At Kingsmead, Durban, April 3, 2002. Day/night game. Australia won by eight wickets. Toss: Australia. International limited-overs debut: J.C. Kent.

On the best batting pitch of the series, a sell-out crowd of 21,500 watched Australia rush to a comprehensive victory in another high-scoring game with 13 balls to spare. Dropped at slip by Jacques Kallis on 11, Adam Gilchrist reached his seventh limited-overs hundred from 97 balls in 53 scoring shots. He and Matthew Hayden created a new opening partnership record for Australia against South Africa. Newcomer Jon Kent and a refreshed but inaccurate Nantie Hayward were frequently banged for fours on a fast outfield, helped by short square boundaries. Ricky Ponting and Damien Martyn finished off a superb batting exhibition. Ponting's decision to field first was based on the theory that dew would pose a problem fielding under lights. Australia kept a grip on the run-rate until Jonty Rhodes inspired a surge in the final overs. Shane Warne made his first appearance in the series, bowling economically and effectively.

Man of the Match: A.C. Gilchrist.

South Africa

G.C. Smith c Gilchrist b Warne	46	(77)		†M.V. Boucher not out	41	(42)
H.H. Gibbs c Gilchrist b Gillespie	25	(27)		*S.M. Pollock not out	6	(6)
N. Boje c and b Lee	22	(22)		B 1, l-b 4, w 7, n-b 1	13	
J.H. Kallis c Maher b McGrath	21	(41)				
J.N. Rhodes c Ponting b McGrath	76	(70)		(50 overs, 221 mins) (6 wkts)	267	
N.D. McKenzie c Gilchrist b Warne	17	(16)		Fall: 40 82 110 125 158 255		

J.C. Kent, M. Ntini and M. Hayward did not bat.

Bowling: McGrath 10–0–54–2; Gillespie 10–1–53–1; Lee 10–0–57–1; Harvey 10–0–54–0; Warne 10–0–44–2.

Australia

†A. C. Gilchrist c Kent b Ntini	105 (104)	L-b 6, w 4, n-b 6	16
M. L. Hayden b Hayward	59 (91)		—
*R. T. Ponting not out	44 (54)	(47.5 overs, 190 mins) (2 wkts)	271
D. R. Martyn not out	47 (44)	Fall: 170 180	

M. G. Bevan, J. P. Maher, I. J. Harvey, B. Lee, J. N. Gillespie, S. K. Warne and G. D. McGrath did not bat.

Bowling: Pollock 10–0–42–0; Ntini 9.5–0–51–1; Kallis 7–0–41–0; Hayward 8–0–58–1; Boje 7–0–32–0; Kent 6–0–41–0.

Umpires: B. G. Jerling and R. E. Koertzen.
TV Umpire: S. Wadvalla.

SOUTH AFRICA v AUSTRALIA

Sixth Limited-Overs International

At St George's Park, Port Elizabeth, April 6, 2002. Australia won by three wickets. Toss: South Africa.

The opening onslaught from Adam Gilchrist and Matthew Hayden spectacularly set up a remarkable victory. It was the highest winning second-innings total in 1,824 limited-overs internationals. The openers struck 81 from just 55 balls, Gilchrist racing to his fifty from only 27 deliveries. Hayden faced only 29 balls in a belligerent partnership that quietened the expectant crowd of 15,908. Thereafter the run-rate was comfortably maintained at the required six runs an over, as Ricky Ponting (151 minutes, 107 balls seven fours, two sixes) and Darren Lehmann (119 minutes, 94 balls, nine fours, one six) threaded the gaps skilfully, overwhelming some shell-shocked bowlers. South Africa had set the game alight with some dashing batting from Jacques Kallis (76 minutes, 59 balls, three fours, two sixes) and Jonty Rhodes (58 minutes, 50 balls, six fours, one six), who added 102 in the last ten overs, behind Graeme Smith (eight fours) and pinch-hitter Boje (five fours) as South Africa posted their highest limited-overs total against Australia.

Man of the Match: A. C. Gilchrist.

South Africa

G. C. Smith c Lehmann b Warne	84 (103)		
H. H. Gibbs c and b Harvey	37 (40)	L-b 5, w 2	7
N. Boje b Lehmann	47 (48)		—
J. H. Kallis not out	80 (59)	(50 overs, 196 mins) (3 wkts)	326
J. N. Rhodes not out	71 (50)	Fall: 74 157 195	

N. D. McKenzie, †M. V. Boucher, *S. M. Pollock, J. C. Kent, M. Ntini and R. Telemachus did not bat.

Bowling: McGrath 10–2–52–0; Gillespie 9–0–60–0; Harvey 9–0–64–1; Warne 7–0–58–1; Watson 9–0–47–0; Lehmann 6–0–40–1.

Australia

†A. C. Gilchrist c Ntini b Telemachus .	52	(34)	S. R. Watson run out (Boje)	11	(13)
M. L. Hayden c Pollock b Kallis	35	(29)	S. K. Warne not out	4	(1)
I. J. Harvey c Boucher b Telemachus .	4	(6)			
*R. T. Ponting c Pollock b Kallis	92	(107)	B 2, l-b 7, w 6, n-b 8	23	
D. S. Lehmann st Boucher b Smith . . .	91	(94)		—	
D. R. Martyn c Rhodes b Ntini	15	(15)	(49.1 overs, 222 mins) (7 wkts)	330	
M. G. Bevan not out	3	(4)	Fall: 81 93 104 287 312 312 326		

J. N. Gillespie and G. D. McGrath did not bat.

Bowling: Pollock 8–0–57–0; Ntini 9.1–0–83–1; Telemachus 10–0–48–2; Kallis 10–0–59–2; Boje 6–0–34–0; Kent 2–0–16–0; Smith 4–0–24–1.

Umpires: I. L. Howell and S. Wadvalla.
TV Umpire: K. H. Hurter.

SOUTH AFRICA v AUSTRALIA

Seventh Limited-Overs International

At Newlands, Cape Town, April 9, 2002. Day/night game. South Africa won on run rate. Toss: Australia.

South Africa belatedly achieved a win from a match that lacked the intensity of previous contests. There was a carefree mood that smacked of the last day at school, and Australia's run-chase faltered on some loose shots. For once, the top order failed, leaving Michael Bevan (six fours) to attempt a resuscitation with the tail. He was caught top-edging a sweep off Nicky Boje, whose five-wicket spree followed another pinch-hitting success (91 minutes, 51 balls, three fours, one six). Rain delayed the start by two hours, and Ricky Ponting's decision to field was predicated on the threat of more showers and a rain rule adjustment. The ball skidded favourably for batting, and Graeme Smith continued his excellent form, racing past fifty from 58 balls. Jonty Rhodes scampered excitedly again, striking cover-driven fours in a lively finish to the innings, capped off by Boeta Dippenaar's brace of boundaries from a weary Glenn McGrath. South Africa's win was their 14th in 16 contests at Newlands, giving their supporters some belated satisfaction. Ricky Ponting was adjudged Player of the Series. Rhodes had more impressive figures, but Ponting's captaincy in a 5-1 series triumph, together with a couple of convincing innings, clinched the award.

Man of the Match: N. Boje. *Player of the Series:* R. T. Ponting.

South Africa

G. C. Smith b Bichel	73	(78)	*S. M. Pollock c Watson b McGrath .	8	(7)
H. H. Gibbs run out (Bichel)	27	(28)	H. H. Dippenaar not out	8	(2)
N. Boje c Gilchrist b Watson	49	(51)			
J. H. Kallis c Maher b Warne	18	(28)	L-b 5, w 4	9	
J. N. Rhodes not out	39	(24)		—	
N. D. McKenzie lbw b Warne	0	(1)	(39 overs, 166 mins) (7 wkts)	249	
†M. V. Boucher c Watson b McGrath .	18	(15)	Fall: 63 134 172 180 181 225 240		

R. Telemachus and M. Hayward did not bat.

Bowling: McGrath 7–0–43–2; Lee 6–0–34–0; Bichel 8–0–34–1; Harvey 4–0–35–0; Warne 8–0–52–2; Watson 6–0–46–1.

Australia

†A. C. Gilchrist c Kallis b Pollock	7	(8)	B. Lee b Boje 28	(28)
J. P. Maher c McKenzie b Pollock	8	(10)	A. J. Bichel not out 15	(16)
S. R. Watson lbw b Pollock	16	(26)	G. D. McGrath st Boucher b Boje ... 0	(2)
M. G. Bevan c Pollock b Boje	55	(61)	B 2, l-b 7, w 4, n-b 1 14	
D. R. Martyn c Smith b Kallis	24	(19)		
*R. T. Ponting lbw b Telemachus	1	(3)	(32.3 overs, 136 mins)	185
I. J. Harvey b Boje	14	(16)	Fall: 16 16 56 95 98 125 137	
S. K. Warne b Boje	3	(7)	138 185 185	

Bowling: Pollock 6–0–28–3; Telemachus 6–0–35–1; Hayward 8–0–52–0; Kallis 6–0–40–1; Boje 6.3–0–21–5.

Umpires: K. H. Hurter and D. L. Orchard.
TV Umpire: M. Z. Nanabhay.
Series Referee: C. W. Smith (West Indies).

AUSTRALIANS IN ENGLISH CRICKET, 2001

By CATHERINE HANLEY

Professional cricket in a global context has enhanced English cricket as a major destination for Australian cricketers. They are part of a long tradition going back to the likes of Alan Marshal and Ted McDonald, but the ease of travel and the lucrativeness of contracts have increased the flow of cricketers in recent seasons, with even Test players such as Shane Warne (Hampshire) and Glenn McGrath (Worcestershire) making the trip. The importance of the experience to the players' careers and their dynamic impact on the English scene, make their performances worthy of comment.

The English season 2001 was a summer of Australian dominance, at domestic as well as international level. While the national side was beating England and Pakistan, thirteen more Australians plied their trade in county cricket, taking part in a number of different competitions. Chief among them were the first-class County Championship and the limited-overs Norwich Union League, both split into two divisions of nine teams each, with three sides to be promoted and three relegated at the end of the season. There were also three limited-overs competitions of slightly differing formats, the Cheltenham & Gloucester (C & G) Trophy, the Benson and Hedges (B & H) Cup and the Norwich Union League.

ANDY BICHEL (Worcestershire)

Many players might be overawed at the prospect of succeeding Glenn McGrath as Worcestershire's overseas player, but clearly not Andy Bichel. The Queenslander leapt heartily into the breach, and was rewarded with a triumphant season which saw him win both his county's Player of the Year awards, voted for by the club and by the supporters, as well as helping the side to promotion to the first division of the limited-overs league. He was successful in all areas of the game, taking 66 first-class and 65 limited-overs wickets – including his first hat-trick – and also enjoyed his batting, working his way up the order to as high as No. 3, scoring three Championship fifties as well as a maiden limited-overs hundred. His off-field contribution to the club was, if anything, even greater than his on-field prowess: praised by Worcestershire's coach Tom Moody for his attitude, he helped train many of the younger players at the county to ensure a firm basis for future success. It was this, as much as his runs and wickets, which persuaded the club to snap him up for another season in 2002.

	M	I	NO	R	HS	100s	50s	Avge	Ct	St	W	Avge	BB
First-class	16	24	0	627	78	0	3	26.12	5	0	66	27.33	6/44
County Championship	16	24	0	627	78	0	3	26.12	5	0	66	27.33	6/44
C & G	3	2	3	785	91	0	6	29.07	8	0	29	24.24	6/82
B & H	5	5	0	177	100	1	0	35.40	4	0	9	21.00	3/38
Norwich Union	15	12	1	148	36*	0	0	13.45	7	0	27	15.85	5/21

GREG BLEWETT (Nottinghamshire)

After his muted county season with Yorkshire in 1999, Greg Blewett had much to prove when he signed for Nottinghamshire in 2001, and he did so in style. After crashing a century on his Championship debut – only the second player to do so for the county – he obliged with four more to add to his five first-class and five limited-overs fifties. Regrettably, a combination of uninspired bowling by, and injury to, his team-mates coupled with some bad weather at the wrong times meant his sparkling form went largely unrewarded. Nottinghamshire were no more than also-rans in the second division of the Championship and had to fight for their survival in the first division of the League, needing a last-gasp win on the final day of the season, to which Blewett eased them with an unflustered contribution of 48. Despite his success, Nottinghamshire decided not to re-sign him for 2002 – not a reflection on Blewett's form, but an indication that the county preferred to bolster its thin bowling resources.

	M	I	NO	R	HS	100s	50s	Avge	Ct	St	W	Avge	BB
First-class	16	30	3	1,292	137*	5	5	47.85	24	0	6	62.33	2/20
County Championship	16	30	3	1,292	137*	5	5	47.85	24	0	6	62.33	2/20
C & G	2	2	1	28	25	0	0	28.00	1	0	0	–	–
B & H	7	7	1	264	84	0	2	44.00	3	0	4	20.75	3/41
Norwich Union	16	16	0	501	89	3	0	31.31	3	0	3	90.66	1/30

JAMIE COX (Somerset)

By his own exacting standards, Jamie Cox had a consistent rather than brilliant season with the bat. Only one century came his way, and that towards the end of the season, but he still averaged 57.45 in the first-class game and was the only Somerset player to pass 1,000 runs. His captaincy skills, however, remained undiminished, and it is hard to overestimate his contribution to the club. Despite the lack of stars in his squad he marshalled his troops astutely, guiding Somerset to runners-up in the first division of the Championship, their highest finish ever. In fact, had it not been for a slow start to the season and a somewhat aimless period in June when Cox was sidelined by a fractured thumb, the West Country side might even have gone one better. To add to this, Cox led the county to its first trophy in 18 years as they overcame the favourites Leicestershire in the final of the C & G Trophy at Lord's in September, amid scenes of great jubilation. Although 2002 is due to be his last year at Somerset, many in the county hope that he can be persuaded to stay on.

	M	I	NO	R	HS	100s	50s	Avge	Ct	St	W	Avge	BB
First-class	15	25	3	1,264	186	1	9	57.45	6	0	0	–	–
County Championship	15	25	3	1,264	186	1	9	57.45	6	0	0	–	–
C & G	4	4	1	167	63*	0	1	55.66	2	0	0	–	–
B & H	4	4	0	191	72	0	2	47.75	1	0	0	–	–
Norwich Union	12	12	1	331	76*	0	2	30.09	4	0	0	–	–

MICHAEL DI VENUTO (Derbyshire)

Derbyshire had a truly dismal season in 2001, finishing rooted to the bottom of the second division in both competitions. One of the few glimmers of sunshine amid the gloom was the form of the club's overseas player: Michael Di Venuto shouldered the often arduous burden of carrying the batting line-up with great personal success. Mid-way through the season he was promoted from his usual No. 4 to open the batting, and immediately Derbyshire started to feel the benefits: at one stage he had scored three hundreds and three fifties in seven innings trying to drag the side out of trouble. Unfortunately, nobody except his opening partner could keep up with him and the county slipped to a number of heavy defeats. Derbyshire's recent inability to hold onto its best players did not extend to Di Venuto, who was not only re-signed as overseas player for 2002 but also appointed vice-captain.

	M	I	NO	R	HS	100s	50s	Avge	Ct	St	W	Avge	BB
First-class	14	25	1	1,082	165	4	5	45.08	15	0	1	124.00	1/16
County Championship	14	25	1	1,082	165	4	5	45.08	15	0	1	124.00	1/16
C & G	1	1	1	18	18	0	0	18.00	3	0	0	–	–
B & H	5	5	0	209	108	1	0	41.80	3	0	0	–	–
Norwich Union	12	12	1	342	71	0	2	28.50	2	0	0	–	–

MURRAY GOODWIN (Sussex)

Following the exceptional performances of his predecessor at Sussex, Michael Bevan, the lower-profiled Murray Goodwin had much to prove, especially given his disappointing comeback season with Western Australia following his retirement from Test cricket. His introduction to the county game was an uninspiring soggy match where play did not get underway until the third day, but 94 runs later he had started on his path to glory. In all, seven first-class centuries and five fifties flowed from his bat, to add to another century and eight fifties in limited-overs games. Tellingly, however, the most important factor of his county season was not merely that he scored numerous elegant runs, nor that he made them at the top of the order after reluctantly agreeing to open in the absence of a specialist, but that he also seemed to coax the best performances out of his team-mates, so that their overall combined efforts saw Sussex finish the season as champion of the second division. The county was not far behind in the race for promotion in the League, either, and this is something to which Goodwin will turn his mind when he returns in 2002.

	M	I	NO	R	HS	100s	50s	Avge	Ct	St	W	Avge	BB
First-class	17	32	5	1,654	203*	7	5	61.25	8	0	0	–	–
County Championship	16	30	4	1,521	203*	6	5	58.50	8	0	0	–	–
C & G	2	2	0	105	66	0	1	52.50	0	0	0	–	–
B & H	4	4	0	222	108	1	1	55.50	1	0	0	–	–
Norwich Union	15	15	3	484	87	0	6	40.33	4	0	0	–	–

IAN HARVEY (Gloucestershire)

It was inevitable that the 2001 season would be something of an anti-climax for Ian Harvey, following the five trophies he had helped Gloucestershire win in the previous two years. There are degrees of anti-climax, though, and an appearance in the B & H Cup final at Lord's (albeit on the losing side), 70 wickets in all domestic competitions and the fastest first-class century of the season (a 61-ball dash including six sixes and 12 fours) can hardly be classed as a failure. In fact Harvey was one of the most valuable players on the circuit in terms of all-round contributions, and Gloucestershire's season looked hopeful whenever he was available. However, it floundered in his absence on international duty during the middle part of the season. This can be interpreted as a testament to his influence on the field, but that was of little consolation as the county missed out on promotion to the first division of the Championship by one place for the second season running. To compound the team's woes it was also relegated in the League, so Harvey will be playing in the second tier of both competitions in 2002 when he returns for a fourth season as Gloucestershire's overseas player.

	M	I	NO	R	HS	100s	50s	Avge	Ct	St	W	Avge	BB
First-class	10	15	2	531	130*	2	1	40.84	8	0	41	18.85	5/33
County Championship	10	15	4	531	130*	2	1	40.84	8	0	41	18.85	5/33
C & G	2	2	0	32	23	0	0	16.00	0	0	3	20.66	2/40
B & H	7	7	0	173	92	0	1	24.71	3	0	16	15.50	5/32
Norwich Union	9	9	0	226	67	0	1	25.11	1	0	10	26.10	4/42

MICHAEL HUSSEY (Northamptonshire)

Michael Hussey's first spell in county cricket is perhaps best summed up as a blaze of statistics: the highest score of the season; the highest-ever score by a Northamptonshire player; the only player to make 2,000 runs during the season, the first for the club since 1952 and the first in England since 1995; one triple hundred, two double hundreds, two further centuries – and that was just in the first-class competition. His was a lone hand, however; his team-mates were unable to keep pace with him, either in scoring or seemingly in enthusiasm, and Northamptonshire were relegated to the second division in both forms of the game. One match in particular encapsulated Hussey's herculean solo efforts throughout the season. After three winless months, he took matters into his own hands against Essex: he followed his record 329 not out in the first innings with 70 not out from 33 balls in the second, and was on the field for the duration of the match. Many of those who had asked "Mike who?" at the beginning of the season were delighted when he was not only re-engaged but also appointed captain for 2002.

	M	I	NO	R	HS	100s	50s	Avge	Ct	St	W	Avge	BB
First-class	16	30	4	2,055	329*	5	9	79.03	19	0	2	39.00	1/14
County Championship	16	30	4	2,055	329*	5	9	79.03	19	0	2	39.00	1/14
C & G	2	2	0	67	59	0	1	33.50	1	0	1	30.00	1/20
B & H	5	5	1	253	114*	1	1	63.25	3	0	1	15.00	1/15
Norwich Union	15	15	1	510	96*	0	4	36.42	4	0	0	–	–

STUART LAW (Essex)

Season 2001 marked the end of an era for Stuart Law, England's longest-serving Australian import. It was no secret that he did not see eye to eye with a number of his colleagues, and after a public outburst in which he accused his team-mates and the Essex management of stabbing him in the back, his contract was not renewed for 2002. It was a distressing end to his six-year stint at the club, which had an appalling season, finishing at the bottom of the Championship first division and two places off the foot of the League second division. It was not that Law's customary batting form deserted him, but rather that the rest of his team failed to live up to his example: at one stage in June he scored three hundreds in as many days against Lancashire, in the Championship and the League, but none of them could stave off defeat. By the time Essex played its last home game of the season it had conceded 13 first-innings deficits of more than 150, and not even Law could drag the team out of the mire. The fans of the club proved to be more loyal to Law than its employees, and he was given a standing ovation to and from the crease in his final game. He will play as Lancashire's overseas player in 2002.

	M	I	NO	R	HS	100s	50s	Avge	Ct	St	W	Avge	BB
First-class	13	23	3	1,311	153	4	8	65.55	18	0	0	–	–
County Championship	13	23	3	1,311	153	4	8	65.55	18	0	0	–	–
C & G	2	2	0	24	20	0	0	12.00	0	0	0	–	–
B & H	3	3	0	110	55	0	1	36.66	2	0	0	–	–
Norwich Union	11	10	0	300	108	1	1	30.00	5	0	0	–	–

DARREN LEHMANN (Yorkshire)

When Darren Lehmann was overlooked for the 2002 Ashes squad, many Yorkshire supporters thought Australia's loss would be their gain, and how right they were. County captain David Byas likened Lehmann's play to having Don Bradman in his side, and the South Australian steamrolled his way through virtually all opponents to guide the northern county to its first Championship for 33 years. His batting was a delight: he finished the season with the highest average of any county player, and played several innings of breathtaking proportions. Particular highlights included his 252 against Lancashire, the highest-ever score in a Roses match, and his county-record 191 from 103 balls (20 fours, 11 sixes) in a limited-overs game against Nottinghamshire, an innings which was simply awesome to behold. Yorkshire remains a parochial county, and its people have a reputation for being tough and uncompromising: unsurprising, then, that they have adopted Lehmann as one of their own. Fifteen years ago it would have been unthinkable for a foreigner to even be selected for the team, but such was Lehmann's influence during the season that he seemed the obvious choice to succeed to the vacant captaincy position for 2002.

	M	I	NO	R	HS	100s	50s	Avge	Ct	St	W	Avge	BB
First-class	13	19	2	1,416	252	5	5	83.29	6	0	12	30.66	3/13
County Championship	13	19	2	1,416	252	5	5	83.29	6	0	12	30.66	3/13
C & G	3	3	0	90	88	0	0	30.00	1	0	3	22.33	2/39
B & H	7	7	1	334	103	1	2	55.66	5	0	4	27.50	2/40
Norwich Union	15	15	1	753	191	4	2	53.78	9	0	16	21.00	3/31

MARTIN LOVE (Durham)

Consistency was the hallmark of Martin Love's first season in county cricket. The Queenslander scored just one first-class century, but was only dismissed in single figures three times: in between he amassed thirteen half-centuries to finish with an average of just over 50. Signed by Durham as a replacement for Simon Katich, who was selected in the Ashes squad, Love found his feet quickly, and, setting something of a trend, started off his season with two scores in the sixties in his opening match. His one century came in June when he showed his class to stroke his way to a second-innings 149 not out, making light of a target of 315 in 102 overs to hand the county its first win of the year. Throughout the season he also made important contributions in the limited-overs arena, ensuring Durham's promotion to the League's first division – no mean feat for a county only awarded first-class status in 1992. Although by his own high standards Love may be disappointed with his overall run tally, and by Durham's eighth place in the Championship second division, he was easily the club's highest scorer and was voted its Batsman of the Year; Durham had no hesitation in signing him up for a second season for 2002.

	M	I	NO	R	HS	100s	50s	Avge	Ct	St	W	Avge	BB
First-class	15	29	2	1,364	149*	1	13	50.51	20	0	0	–	–
County Championship	15	29	2	1,364	149*	1	13	50.51	20	0	0	–	–
C & G	3	3	0	109	51	0	1	36.33	1	0	0	–	–
B & H	4	4	0	105	59	0	1	26.25	4	0	0	–	–
Norwich Union	13	13	1	431	89	0	2	35.91	8	0	0	–	–

JIMMY MAHER (Glamorgan)

It was an up-and-down season for Jimmy Maher: Glamorgan were relegated in the Championship but promoted in the League as the second-division champions. Maher's personal fortunes also fluctuated: it took him some time to find his feet at the Welsh county, and he was in his sixth Championship match before he passed 50 for the first time. Once he got going, though, runs flowed: he scored a career-best 217 in August and also accumulated three further centuries, although none of them could help Glamorgan to a win. The other opponent he could not get the better of was the weather: approximately a quarter of all the club's Championship playing time was lost to rain, frustrating for a man coming into form, but he still managed to pass 1,000 runs for the season. Maher's personal form had more effect on his team in the limited-overs game, where Glamorgan put daylight between themselves and their nearest challengers for the second division title. He will not be around to help the county preserve its top-tier status in 2002, however, because despite his prowess and his popularity, an opening bowler was considered a more urgent need, and the county signed Mike Kasprowicz.

	M	I	NO	R	HS	100s	50s	Avge	Ct	St	W	Avge	BB
First-class	14	23	2	1,133	217	4	3	53.95	13	0	0	–	–
County Championship	14	23	2	1,133	217	4	3	53.95	13	0	0	–	–
C & G	1	1	0	30	30	0	0	30.00	1	0	0	–	–
B & H	5	5	1	182	142*	1	0	45.50	4	0	1	52.00	1/20
Norwich Union	15	15	1	453	94	0	3	32.35	7	0	0	–	–

DANIEL MARSH (Leicestershire)

To many a surprise signing, Dan Marsh was enjoying a successful spell with Leicestershire until it was cut short by injury. He fractured a cheekbone fielding at slip at the beginning of July and was unable to play for the rest of the season. By that time he had already established himself as a linchpin in the side, not only for his muscular middle-order batting – his nine first-class games yielded a century and five fifties, and he finished the season at the top of Leicestershire's averages – but also for his useful left-arm spin bowling and some breathtaking catching which turned the tide of a number of games. Subsequently overshadowed by the much-publicised exploits of his replacement,

Shahid Afridi, Marsh's contribution to his team should not be underestimated: it is worth noting than when he left, Leicestershire were unbeaten and seemingly cruising at the top of the League's first division, and that they subsequently faltered to finish second, ending the season trophyless.

	M	I	NO	R	HS	100s	50s	Avge	Ct	St	W	Avge	BB
First-class	9	16	3	600	138*	1	5	46.15	13	0	9	45.55	2/35
County Championship	9	16	3	600	138*	1	5	46.15	13	0	9	45.55	2/35
C & G	1	1	0	25	25	0	0	25.00	1	0	1	50.00	1/50
B & H	5	5	0	140	42	0	0	28.00	2	0	1	115.00	1/44
Norwich Union	5	5	2	206	97*	0	2	68.66	3	0	6	28.50	4/44

ANDREW SYMONDS (Kent)

Kent had originally signed the South African Daryll Cullinan as its overseas player for 2001, but when injury ruled him out after just three games, the county turned to his predecessor Andrew Symonds, already in England for the NatWest series and raring to go. His first-class and limited-overs contributions were more often than not in a supporting rather than a starring role, but he stood up to be counted when the pressure was on. His second-innings 125 against Leicestershire in July steered Kent towards a daunting winning target of 403, and helped guide them to third place in the Championship – something of an achievement for a team considered rank outsiders at the start of the year – and during the all-important final limited-overs game of the season he produced his best bowling figures for the county, finishing with 5/18 and a run-out to hand Kent the League trophy amid much celebration. Symonds' all-round contributions – which included holding some stunning catches, and confusing statisticians by bowling a mixture of medium-pace and off-spin – ensured that he was the county's first choice as overseas player for 2002.

	M	I	NO	R	HS	100s	50s	Avge	Ct	St	W	Avge	BB
First-class	8	12	0	563	131	2	2	46.91	13	0	10	33.30	3/28
County Championship	8	12	0	563	131	2	2	46.91	13	0	10	33.30	3/28
C & G	3	2	1	43	38*	0	0	43.00	0	0	8	7.50	5/21
B & H	0	0	0	0	0	0	0	–	0	0	0	–	–
Norwich Union	9	9	0	221	74	0	2	24.55	2	0	9	18.88	5/18

UNDER-19s WORLD CUP, 2001-02

By KEN PIESSE

Australia were undefeated on their way to their first official Under-19s World Cup title in New Zealand in February, having previously made the semi-finals in 1998 and 2000. The forthright captaincy and vibrant batting of Cameron White won generous praise, particularly from South Africa's coach and ex-international Hylton Ackerman. "He's an impressive young man, very quick thinking and has an old head on very young shoulders," he commented. The Australians had three of the four most prolific batsmen for the tournament, and White stood out with 423 runs at a strike-rate of 97.

The 16 teams contesting the Cup were divided into four groups. The standings after each side played six qualifying matches in the two Super League divisions were:

Group 1 – India, West Indies, Pakistan, Sri Lanka;

Group 2 – Australia, South Africa, New Zealand, England.

Standings for the Plate championship were:

Group 1 – Zimbabwe, Bangladesh, Kenya, Papua New Guinea;

Group 2 – Nepal, Namibia, Scotland, Canada.

The Australians declared their aggressive intention immediately by racing to six for 480 against Kenya, at Carisbrook, Dunedin. Craig Simmons thrashed 155 (115 balls, 12 fours, and 11 sixes), while Shaun Marsh was equally impressive with 125 (81 balls, 12 fours, two sixes), their third-wicket partnership of 168 coming from only 113 balls. In reply, Kenya lasted only 21 overs against the near-express pace of Aaron Bird and Robert Cassell.

Three days later, on the same ground, the Australian batting came back to earth with a thud and struggled to 200, in which George Bailey's 39 was a modest top score, against the well-directed speed of Ryan Nurse (5/28). At two for 75 in the twentieth over, the West Indies must have fancied their chances, but the varied spin attack of Xavier Doherty (3/24), Jarrod Burke (2/14 from 10 overs) and Beau Casson (3/48) worked their wiles successfully.

Against the modest Scottish attack, it was the turn of Cameron White (156 not out, 121 balls, 10 fours, four sixes) and Daniel Christian 93, 88 balls, five fours, three sixes) to make merry in a fourth-wicket partnership of 212 from 175 balls. Doherty (4/15) and Casson (3/18) flummoxed the batsmen so completely that Scotland lost its last seven wickets for 45.

Shifting to the Bert Sutcliffe Oval at Lincoln University, Christchurch, for the Super League matches, Australia's first match was against a highly fancied South African team, who put together a respectable eight for 236. But the Australian reply, led by fifties from Simmons and Bailey, was too consistent and too swift to be held in check. A comfortable victory came in the 47th over.

Australia kept their winning record intact and secured a semi-final spot when they crushed England at Hagley Oval, Christchurch. Simmons (67 from 86 balls, 10 fours) got the innings away to a good start, which was topped off by an astonishing sixth-wicket partnership between Bailey (69 not out from

74 balls, three fours, four sixes) and Adam Crosthwaite (48 not out from 26 balls, three fours, two sixes) that hammered 85 from the last six overs of the innings. At three for 112 in the 27th over, England were facing a tall order but the contrasting left-arm spin of Casson (4/33) and Burke (3/13) demolished the tail.

In the last Super League match, the Australians were initially set back on their heels by a savage opening onslaught by the New Zealand batsmen. Jesse Ryder's 70 (62 balls, six fours, three sixes) was full of authentic strokes and took the attack so belligerently to the Australians that when he was second out at 107, only 18 overs had elapsed. Doherty and Bird, in his second spell, then throttled the progress of the innings so efficiently that the innings only lasted for 46.3 overs. After the loss of two quick wickets to an attack that opened with two spinners, Marsh (70 from 97 balls, nine fours) and White (80 not out from 107 balls, eight fours) moved steadily to victory in a calm and confident third-wicket stand which yielded 139 from 184 balls.

The semi-final against the West Indians was postponed for a day after heavy rain made the Bert Sutcliffe Oval unplayable. Australia's total was founded on a thoughtful 84 (110 balls, eight fours, one six) from man of the match Simmons and an equally mature 64 (71 balls, five fours) from Marsh. The West Indians appeared well in control at two for 103 in the 22nd over but the assorted spin of Doherty, Burke and Casson overwhelmed the rest of the batting. A particularly fine 83 (123 balls, eight fours, one six) from Tonito Willett deserved much better support.

In the final against South Africa at Bert Sutcliffe Oval in Christchurch, left-hander Jarrad Burke made an undefeated century (130 balls, 11 fours) which earned him the Man of the Match award, as the Australians won comfortably by seven wickets with 29 balls remaining. Tasmanian Xavier Doherty took 2/26 from ten overs to be the equal leading wicket-taker in the tournament, with 16 (at 9.50, and conceding only 2.69 runs per over), helping to restrict the Proteas to just nine for 206. Despite a solid 51 (90 balls, six fours) from opener Greg Smith, the innings appeared to have lost its way at seven for 116 in the 34th over and it was only sensible batting from wicket-keeper Zwelibanzi Homani (52 not out from 76 balls, three fours) to raise the total to semi-respectability. Bird (4/47) made important inroads at each end of the innings. With Burke adding 74 with Simmons (34) for the first wicket and 66 with Marsh (35) for the second, the Australians were well in command from the opening overs of the run chase. The Australians played four spinners in the final: White (leg-spin), Doherty and all-rounder Burke (left-arm orthodox) and Beau Casson (left-arm wrist-spin).

All 14 members of the squad played, with White, wicket-keeper Adam Crosthwaite, Marsh and Burke the only four to play all eight matches. Crosthwaite (129), George Bailey (107) and Daniel Christian (105) all had strike-rates of over 100. Doherty, Bird and Casson each took at least 12 wickets.

The player of the championships was Zimbabwe captain and all-rounder Tatenda Taibu, who made 250 runs and took 12 wickets with his off-spin.

Australia's World Cup squad, which was chosen by Trevor Robertson (chairman), Trevor Hohns, Wayne Phillips and Brian Taber at the conclusion of the national Under-19s championships was: Cameron White (Victoria) (captain), George Bailey (Tasmania) (vice-captain), Aaron Bird (New South Wales), Jarrad Burke (New South Wales), Robert Cassell (Victoria), Beau Casson (Western Australia), Daniel Christian (New South Wales), Mark Cosgrove (South Australia), Adam Crosthwaite (Victoria), Xavier Doherty (Tasmania), Adam Fleming (New South Wales), Shaun Marsh (Western Australia), Craig Philipson (Queensland) and Craig Simmons (Western Australia).

AUSTRALIAN AVERAGES

BATTING

	M	I	NO	R	HS	100s	50s	Avge	Ct/St	S-R
D.T. Christian	4	2	1	93	93	0	1	93.00	1	105.68
G.J. Bailey	7	7	4	256	69*	0	3	85.33	3	107.11
C.L. White	8	8	2	423	156*	1	2	70.50	4	97.69
C.J. Simmons	7	7	0	399	155	1	3	57.00	2	85.62
A.J. Crosthwaite ...	8	5	3	105	48*	0	0	52.50	11/4	129.62
S.E. Marsh	8	8	0	317	125	1	1	39.62	3	82.98
J.N. Burke	8	8	1	249	100*	1	0	35.57	6	77.32
X.J. Doherty.......	7	2	1	31	23	0	0	31.00	3	52.54
M.J. Cosgrove	6	4	1	66	27	0	0	22.00	1	80.48
C.A. Philipson	3	3	0	52	32	0	0	17.33	0	57.77
B. Casson	6	3	0	34	28	0	0	11.33	2	59.64
A.L. Fleming	4	1	0	6	6	0	0	6.00	1	85.71
A.C. Bird	7	1	1	1	1*	0	0	–	1	100.00
R.J. Cassell.......	5	1	1	0	0*	0	0	–	0	0.00

* Denotes not out.

BOWLING

	O	M	R	W	BB	5W/i	Avge
X.J. Doherty............	56.2	12	152	16	4/15	0	9.50
A.C. Bird	53	6	215	15	4/47	0	14.33
B. Casson	45.2	7	181	12	4/33	0	15.08
J.N. Burke	48.2	7	142	9	3/13	0	15.77
R.J. Cassell.............	25	4	103	6	3/7	0	17.16
M.J. Cosgrove	15	1	66	2	1/7	0	33.00
D.T. Christian	17	2	91	2	1/22	0	45.50
A.L. Fleming	18	1	93	2	1/27	0	46.50
C.L. White	54	7	192	2	1/36	0	96.00

ROUND ROBIN MATCHES

AUSTRALIA v KENYA

At Carisbrook, Dunedin, January 2, 2002. Australia won by 430 runs. Toss: Kenya.

Australia

C.J. Simmons c Premji b Gore	155	(115)	†A.J. Crosthwaite not out	21	(8)
J.N. Burke c Aga b Odhiambo	45	(31)	D.T. Christian not out	0	(0)
C.A. Philipson b Aga	10	(17)	B 2, l-b 3, w 22, n-b 3	30	
S.E. Marsh c Muange b Odhiambo	125	(81)			
*C.L. White c Auma b Aga	38	(25)	(50 overs, 219 mins) (6 wkts)	480	
G.J. Bailey c Muange b Odhiambo	56	(26)	Fall: 64 100 268 371 447 462		

R.J. Cassell, A.C. Bird and X.J. Doherty did not bat.

Bowling: Luseno 9–0–62–0; Odhiambo 10–0–97–3; Bhudiya 10–0–88–0; Aga 8–0–78–2; Bhimji 9–0–95–0; Premji 1–0–18–0; Gore 2–0–37–1.

Kenya

M.N. Patel b Cassell	2	98)	A. Luseno b Doherty	18	(23)
S. Auma not out	7	(45)	J.L. Bhimji run out		
A.G. Gore b Cassell	0	(1)	(Bailey/Crosthwaite)	0	(0)
R Premji c Bailey b Cassell	3	(29)	†M.A. Ouma (absent injured)		
*R.G. Aga lbw b Bird	0	(3)	L-b 3, w 9 n-b 3	15	
T.R. Muange b Bird	0	(2)			
N. Odhiambo lbw b Bird	0	(1)	(21 overs, 88 mins)	50	
R.V. Bhudiya b Chistian	5	(17)	Fall: 4 4 9 9 18 23 50 50		

Bowling: Bird 5–1–10–3; Cassell 6–3–7–3; Christian 5–1–22–1; White 3–1–8–0; Doherty 1–1–0–1; Burke 1–1–0–0.

Umpires: G.A. Baxter and R.S. Dunne.

AUSTRALIA v WEST INDIES

At Carisbrook, Dunedin, January 23, 2002. Australia won by 42 runs. Toss: West Indies.

Australia

J.N. Burke c Holder b Nurse	12	(17)	X.J. Doherty st Matthew b Nurse	23	(49)
C.J. Simmons c Matthew b Nurse	4	(16)	A.L. Fleming c Bravo b Deonarine	6	(7)
S.E. Marsh c Bravo b Nurse	10	(11)	R.J. Cassell not out	0	(3)
G.J. Bailey c Bravo b Sammy	39	(61)			
*C.L. White run out (Holder/Matthew)	12	(17)	L-b 7, w 17, n-b 5	29	
M.J. Cosgrove c Matthew b Nurse	27	(48)			
†A.J. Crosthwaite lbw b Deonarine	10	(21)	(49.2 overs, 191 mins)	200	
B. Casson c Bravo b Deonarine	28	(51)	Fall: 20 34 44 81 94 122 139 181 193 200		

Bowling: Nurse 9.2–2–28–5; Rampaul 5–1–39–0; Sammy 10–1–36–1; Ingram 9–1–37–0; Deonarine 10–0–28–3; Holder 6–0–25–0.

West Indies

D. J. Pagon c Simmons b Doherty	 19	(31)
D. J. Bravo b Burke	 29	(50)
L. M. P. Simmons b Doherty	 1	(11)
T. A. Willett b Cosgrove	 34	(70)
*N. Deonarine c Doherty b Casson	... 8	(22)
L. T. Ingram run out (Bailey/Crosthwaite)	25	(39)
A. Holder c White b Casson	 18	(29)
D. J. G. Sammy b Burke	 0	(7)

†G. K. Matthew c Doherty b Casson	. 0	(1)
R. P. O. Nurse not out	 9	(6)
R. Rampaul c Marsh b Doherty	 1	(5)
L-b 8, w 4, n-b 2	 14	
(44.5 overs, 176 mins)	158	
Fall: 39 43 75 96 115 147 147		
147 155 158		

Bowling: Cassell 3–0–16–0; Fleming 2–0–12–0; White 10–0–29–0; Doherty 8.5–2–24–3; Burke 10–4–14–2; Casson 9–2–48–3; Cosgrove 2–0–7–1.

Umpires: G. A. Baxter and R. S. Dunne.

AUSTRALIA v SCOTLAND

At Carisbrook, Dunedin, January 25, 2002. Australia won by 229 runs. Toss: Australia.

Australia

J. N. Burke b Singh	 14	(14)
C. A. Philipson st S. Coetzer b Iqbal	.. 32	(59)
S. E. Marsh c Iqbal b Singh	 14	(24)
*C. L. White not out	156	(121)
D. T. Christian c Gray b Singh	 93	(88)
B. Casson b West	 0	(1)

M. J. Cosgrove not out	 2	(2)
B 1, l-b 3. w 11, n-b 9	 24	
(50 overs, 198 mins) (5 wkts)	335	
Fall: 21 48 107 319 331		

†A. J. Crosthwaite, A. C. Bird, X. J. Doherty and A. L. Fleming did not bat.

Bowling: Gray 9–0–60–0; Singh 10–1–63–3; West 10–0–65–1; Iqbal 10–0–48–1; McKerchar 9–0–71–0; Sheikh 2–0–24–0.

Scotland

*R. More c Crosthwaite b Bird	 0	(4)
B. T. McKerchar c White b Fleming	.. 16	(20)
M. M. Iqbal c Casson b Doherty	 23	(45)
S. Murray lbw b Bird	 5	(15)
Q. Sheikh c Crosthwaite b Doherty	... 11	(33)
K. J. Coetzer st Crosthwaite b Casson	. 24	(50)
Z. Mohammad lbw b Doherty	 0	(9)
†S. Coetzer c Fleming b Doherty	 4	(10)

H. Singh c Doherty b Casson	 2	(12)
C. M. West b Casson	 6	(5)
J. Gray not out	 1	(8)
L-b 2, w 7, n-b 5	 14	
(34.2 overs, 133 mins)	106	
Fall: 0 29 39 61 70 75 81 93 103 106		

Bowling: Bird 7–1–23–2; Fleming 8–1–34–1; Burke 5–1–10–0; Doherty 7–2–15–4; Casson 5.2–1–18–3; Christian 2–0–4–0.

Umpires: D. B. Cowie and R. S. Dunne.

SUPER LEAGUE MATCHES

AUSTRALIA v SOUTH AFRICA

At Bert Sutcliffe Oval, Lincoln, January 28, 2002. Australia won by five wickets. Toss: South Africa.

South Africa

D.J. Jacobs c and Bird	0	(3)	I. Khan c Burke b White	2	(8)
S.C. Cook run out (Crosthwaite)	48	(72)	B.L. Reddy c Bailey b Cassell	27	(18)
G.M. Smith c Crosthwaite b Cassell	1	(7)			
*H.M. Amla b Doherty	17	(33)	L-b 5, w 11, n-b 1	17	
R. De Kock b Cosgrove	37	(72)			
R.T. Bailey run out (Crosthwaite)	48	(45)	(50 overs, 188 mins) (8 wkts)	236	
R. McLaren not out	39	(42)	Fall: 2 3 49 96 130 184 192 236		

R.K. Kleinveldt and †Z. Homani did not bat.

Bowling: Bird 6–0–23–1; Cassell 5–1–24–2; Cosgrove 10–1–42–1; Doherty 10–1–38–1; White 10–3–45–1; Christian 4–0–28–0; Burke 5–0–31–0.

Australia

J.N. Burke b Smith	31	(47)	†A.J. Crosthwaite not out	7	(9)
C.J. Simmons st Homani b Khan	52	(77)			
S.E. Marsh c Cook b McLaren	22	(43)	L-b 4, w 10, n-b 2	16	
*C.L. White b Reddy	36	(42)			
G.J. Bailey not out	54	(52)	(46.4 overs, 185 mins) (5 wkts)	237	
M.J. Cosgrove b Khan	19	(12)	Fall: 57 104 125 174 214		

D.T. Christian, X.J. Doherty, A.C. Bird and R.J. Cassell did not bat.

Bowling: McLaren 9.4–1–50–1; Reddy 8–1–31–1; Kleinveldt 10–1–47–0; Smith 3–0–26–1; Khan 9–0–42–2; Bailey 7–0–37–0.

Umpires: A.L. Hill and D.M. Quested.

AUSTRALIA v ENGLAND

At Hagley Oval, Christchurch, January 30, 2002. Australia won by 116 runs. Toss: England

Australia

J.N. Burke c Bresman b Muchall	30	(64)	†A.J. Crosthwaite not out	48	(26)
C.J. Simmons st Shafayat b McMahon	67	(86)			
S.E. Marsh c Shafayat b Gilbert	22	(39)	B 1, l-b 6, w 8, n-b 5	20	
*C.L. White c Shafayat b Muchall	15	(19)			
G.J. Bailey not out	69	(55)	(50 overs, 191 mins) (5 wkts)	281	
C.A. Philipson b Gilbert	10	(14)	Fall: 98 106 133 155 189		

D.T. Christian, B. Casson, A.C. Bird and A.L. Fleming did not bat.

Bowling: Hogg 9–1–57–0; Bresnan 8–1–49–0; Gilbert 10–0–65–2; McMahon 10–0–44–1; Muchall 10–1–37–2; Patel 3–0–22–0.

England

Kadeer Ali c Crosthwaite b Christian	.	13	(15)	T.T. Bresnan c Simmons b Burke	4	(18)
N.R.D. Compton c Crosthwaite b Bird		12	(49)	C.R. Gilbert st Crosthwaite b Casson	4	(20)
*N. Peng c Marsh b Casson		57	(59)	P.J. McMahon not out	0	(3)
G.J. Murchall c Crosthwaite b Fleming		8	(26)			
S. Patel st Crosthwaite b Casson		11	(22)	L-b 4, w 9 n-b 6	19	
K.W. Hogg c Christian b Casson		1	(13)			
M.L. Pettini b Burke		6	(28)	(45.2 overs, 186 mins)	165	
†B.M. Shafayat c White b Burke		30	(25)	Fall: 28 67 83 112 115 118 144 158 165 165		

Bowling: Christian 6–1–37–1; Bird 10–2–33–1; White 7–1–18–0; Fleming 5–0–27–1; Casson 10–3–33–4; Burke 7.2–0–13–3.

Umpires: A.L. Hill and D.M. Quested.

NEW ZEALAND v AUSTRALIA

At Bert Sutcliffe Oval, Lincoln, February 1, 2002. Australia won by seven wickets. Toss: New Zealand.

New Zealand

R.J. Nicol c Bailey b White		25	(23)	P.W. Borren c Cosgrove b Doherty	10	(12)
J.D. Ryder c and b Burke		70	(62)	L.M. Burtt c White b Doherty	2	(20)
N.T. Broom lbw b Bird		20	(53)	M.D. Bates not out	1	(1)
J.W. Sheed run out (Bird)		14	(44)			
*R.L. Taylor c Crosthwaite b Bird		4	(18)	L-b 6, w 8, n-b 1	15	
B.J. Hatwell lbw b Bird		2	(7)			
†S.R. Allen run out				(46.3 overs, 184 mins)	194	
(Crosthwaite/Doherty)	..	25	(29)	Fall: 42 107 137 140 144 150 179		
I.A. Robertson c Burke b Doherty		6	(11)	187 191 194		

Bowling: Fleming 3–0–30–0; Bird 10–2–50–3; Burke 10–1–35–1; White 8–1–36–1; Casson 6–0–24–0; Doherty 9.3–1–23–3.

Australia

J.N. Burke c Sheed b Nicol		13	(12)			
C.J. Simmons run out (Bates/Allen)	..	3	(6)	L-b 1, w 8, n-b 2	11	
S.E. Marsh run out (Broom)		70	(97)			
*C.L. White not out		80	(107)	(39.3 overs, 169 mins) (3 wkts)	196	
G.J. Bailey not out		19	(17)	Fall: 5 21 160		

M.J. Cosgrove, †A.J. Crosthwaite, X.J. Doherty, B. Casson and A.C. Bird did not bat.

Bowling: Robertson 9–0–34–0; Nicol 5–0–30–1; Bates 6–0–32–0; Burtt 9.3–2–42–0; Borren 10–0–57–0.

Umpires: A.W. Cooper and E.A.R. De Silva.

SEMI-FINAL

AUSTRALIA v WEST INDIES

At Bert Sutcliffe Oval, Lincoln, February 6 (no play), 7, 2002. Australia won by 93 runs. Toss: Australia.

Australia

J.N. Burke c Willett b Nurse	4	(7)
C.J. Simmons st Simmons b Ingram	84	(110)
S.E. Marsh c Deonarine b Shillingford	19	(42)
*C.L. White c Simmons b Holder	64	(71)
G.J. Bailey st Simmons b Ingram	15	(18)
M.J. Cosgrove c Nurse b Holder	18	(20)
†A.J. Crosthwaite run out (Matthews/Ingram)	19	(17)
X.J. Doherty not out	8	(10)
B. Casson c Ingram b Nurse	6	(5)
A.C. Bird not out	1	(1)
L-b 6, w 7, n-b 1	14	
(50 overs, 214 mins) (8 wkts)	252	

R.J. Cassell did not bat.

Fall: 10 63 168 198 202 224 239 248

Bowling: Nurse 9–1–35–2; Rampaul 10–0–42–0; Shillingford 10–1–41–1; Deonarine 5–0–32–0; Matthews 4–0–32–0; Ingram 7–0–48–2; Holder 5–0–16–2.

West Indies

D.J. Pagon c Crosthwaite b Bird	12	(17)
D.J. Bravo c Burke b Cassell	4	(3)
T.A. Willett c Burke b Doherty	83	(123)
*N. Deonarine c Casson b Doherty	40	(49)
†L.M.P. Simmons run out (sub D.T. Christian)	3	(26)
L.T. Ingram run out (White/Doherty)	1	(3)
A. Holder st Crosthwaite b Casson	0	(2)
R. Matthews c Crosthwaite b Casson	0	(4)
R. Rampaul c (sub) D.T. Christian b Burke	1	(4)
R.P.O. Nurse c and b Burke	1	(9)
S. Shillingford not out	1	(2)
L-b 2, w 8, n-b 3	13	
(40 overs)	159	

Fall: 20 21 103 132 139 143 155 156 157 159

Bowling: Cassell 4–0–24–1; Bird 5–0–29–1; White 6–0–29–0; Burke 5–0–17–2; Doherty 10–2–26–2; Cosgrove 1–0–4–0; Casson 9–1–28–2.

Umpires: E.A.R. De Silva and R.S. Dunne.

FINAL

AUSTRALIA v SOUTH AFRICA

At Bert Sutcliffe Oval, Lincoln, February 9, 2002. Australia won by seven wickets. Toss: South Africa.

South Africa

G.M. Smith c Crosthwaite b Doherty	51	(90)
C. Baxter b Bird	1	(10)
S.C. Cook b Bird	5	(15)
*H.M. Amla run out (Bailey/White)	29	(34)
D.J. Jacobs c Crosthwaite b Doherty	6	(9)
R.T. Bailey run out (Doherty/Crosthwaite)	2	(7)
R. McLaren lbw b Burke	5	(21)
†Z. Homani not out	52	(76)
B.L. Reddy c Marsh b Bird	16	(23)
B.B. Kops lbw b Bird	5	(5)
I.K. Postman not out	13	(16)
B 2, l-b 7, w 6, n-b 6	21	
(50 overs, 200 mins) (9 wkts)	206	

Fall: 17 45 85 97 100 103 116 158 173

Bowling: Cassell 7–0–32–0; Bird 10–0–47–4; Doherty 10–3–26–2; White 10–1–26–2; Burke 5–0–22–1; Casson 6–0–30–0; Cosgrove 2–0–13–0.

Australia

J. N. Burke not out	100 (130)		L-b 4, w 9, n-b 1	14
C. J. Simmons b Kopps	34 (56)			
S. E. Marsh run out (Jacobs/Homani)	35 (45)		(45.1 overs, 184 mins)	(3 wkts)	209
*C. L. White b McLaren	22 (31)			
G. J. Bailey not out	4 (10)		Fall: 74 140 196	

M. J. Cosgrove, †A. J. Crosthwaite, X. J. Doherty, B. Casson, R. J. Cassell and A. C. Bird did not bat.

Bowling: Reddy 9.1–1–42–0; McLaren 10–1–35–1; Kopps 6–1–42–1; Postman 10–0–44–0; Bailey 9–0–33–0; Smith 1–0–9–0.

Umpires: E. A. R. De Silva and A. L. Hill.

PART SIX: ADMINISTRATION AND LAWS

INTERNATIONAL CRICKET COUNCIL

On June 15, 1909, representatives of cricket in England, Australia and South Africa met at Lord's and founded the Imperial Cricket Conference. Membership was confined to the governing bodies of cricket in countries within the British Commonwealth where Test cricket was played. India, New Zealand and West Indies were elected as members on May 31, 1926, Pakistan on July 28, 1952, Sri Lanka on July 21, 1981, Zimbabwe on July 8, 1992 and Bangladesh on June 26, 2000. South Africa ceased to be a member of ICC on leaving the British Commonwealth in May, 1961, but was elected as a Full Member on July 10, 1991.

On July 15, 1965, the Conference was renamed the International Cricket Conference and new rules were adopted to permit the election of countries from outside the British Commonwealth. This led to the growth of the Conference, with the admission of Associate Members, who were each entitled to one vote, while the Foundation and Full Members were each entitled to two votes, on ICC resolutions. On July 12, 13, 1989, the Conference was renamed the International Cricket Council and revised rules were adopted.

On July 7, 1993, ICC ceased to be administered by MCC and became an independent organisation with its own chief executive, the headquarters remaining at Lord's. The category of Foundation Member, with its special rights, was abolished. On October 1, 1993, Sir Clyde Walcott became the first non-British chairman of ICC.

On June 16, 1997, ICC became an incorporated body, with an executive board and a president instead of a chairman. Jagmohan Dalmiya became ICC's first president. He was succeeded at ICC's annual meeting on June 22–26, 2000 by former Australian Cricket Board chairman Malcolm Gray AM.

Officers

President: M. A. Gray. *Chief Executive:* M. Speed.
Chairman of Committees: Cricket: Sunil Gavaskar; *Development:* no appointment; *Finance and Marketing:* E. Mani; *Associate Members:* J. Rayani.

Executive Board: The six officers listed above sit on the board ex officio. They are joined by Sir John Anderson (New Zealand), P. Chingoka (Zimbabwe), S. H. Chowdhury (Bangladesh), J. Dalmiya (India), R. van Ierschot (Holland), HRH Tunku Imran (Malaysia), Lord MacLaurin (England), Tauqir Zia (Pakistan), R. Merriman (Australia), The Rev. W. Hall (West Indies), J. Ryani (Kenya), V. Malalasekera (Sri Lanka), P. Sonn (South Africa).

Constitution

President: Each Full Member has the right, by rotation, to appoint ICC's president. In 1997, India named J. Dalmiya to serve until 2000. M. A. Gray of Australia will now serve until 2003. Subsequent presidents will serve for two years.

Chief Executive: Appointed by the Council. M. Speed was appointed in June 2001.

Membership

Full Members: Australia, Bangladesh, England, India, New Zealand, Pakistan, South Africa, Sri Lanka, West Indies and Zimbabwe.

Associate Members*: Argentina (1974), Bermuda (1966), Canada (1968), Denmark (1966), East and Central Africa (1966), Fiji (1965), France (1998), Germany (1999), Gibraltar (1969), Hong Kong (1969), Ireland (1993), Israel (1974), Italy (1995), Kenya (1981), Malaysia (1967), Namibia (1992), Nepal (1996), Netherlands (1966), Papua New Guinea (1973), Scotland (1994), Singapore (1974), Tanzania (2001), Uganda (1998), United Arab Emirates (1990), USA (1965) and West Africa (1976).

Affiliate Members*: Afghanistan (2001), Austria (1992), Bahamas (1987), Bahrain (2001), Belgium (1991), Belize (1997), Bhutan (2001), Botswana (2001), Brunei (1992), Cayman Islands (1997), Cook Islands (2000), Croatia (2001), Cyprus (1999), Czech Republic (2000), Finland (2000), Greece (1995), Indonesia (2001), Japan (1989), South Korea (2001), Kuwait (1998), Lesotho (2001), Luxembourg (1998), Maldives (2001), Malta (1998), Morocco (1999), Norway (2000), Oman (2000), Philippines (2000), Portugal (1996), Qatar (1999), St Helena (2001), Samoa (2000), Spain (1992), Sweden (1997), Switzerland (1985), Thailand (1995), Tonga (2000) and Vanuatu (1995).

* Year of election shown in parentheses.

The following governing bodies for cricket shall be eligible for election.

Full Members: The governing body for cricket recognised by ICC of a country, or countries associated for cricket purposes, or a geographical area, from which representative teams are qualified to play official Test matches.

Associate Members: The governing body for cricket recognised by ICC of a country, or countries associated for cricket purposes, or a geographical area, which does not qualify as a Full Member but where cricket is firmly established and organised.

Affiliate Members: The governing body for cricket recognised by ICC of a country, or countries associated for cricket purposes, or a geographical area (which is not part of one of those already constituted as a Full or Associate Member) where ICC recognises that cricket is played in accordance with the Laws of Cricket. Affiliate Members have no right to vote or to propose or second resolutions at ICC meetings.

AUSTRALIAN CRICKET BOARD

Officers

Chairman: R. Merriman.   *Chief Executive:* J. Sutherland.

Board of Directors: R. Merriman (*chairman*), Dr A. C. Battersby, J. Clarke, W. Edwards, B. F. Freedman, R. E. Horsell, W. J Jocelyn, R. F. Merriman, D. G. Mullins, F. C. O'Connor, T. J. Robertson, A. Border, G. L. Tamblyn (*finance director*).

AUSTRALIAN CRICKETERS' ASSOCIATION

The Australian Cricketers' Association was incorporated in February 1997. It represents the collective voice of all first-class cricketers in Australia. The ACA has recently completed negotiating a Memorandum of Understanding with the Australian Cricket Board, which formalises remuneration and welfare issues between the players and their respective cricket boards within Australia. The ACA is actively involved in protecting and providing benefits to all members, particularly in the area of professional advice and secular career training.

President and Chief Executive Officer: T. B. A. May.

ADDRESSES

INTERNATIONAL CRICKET COUNCIL

M. W. Speed, The Clock Tower, Lord's Cricket Ground, London NW8 8QN (44 20 7266 1818; fax 44 20 7266 1777; website www.icc.cricket.org; e-mail icc@icc.cricket.org).

Full Members

AUSTRALIA: Australian Cricket Board, J. Sutherland, 60 Jolimont Street, Jolimont, Victoria 3002 (61 3 9653 9999; fax 61 3 9653 9900; website www.acb.com.au).

BANGLADESH: Bangladesh Cricket Board, Syed Ashraful Huq, Bangabandhu National Stadium, Dhaka 10(880 2 966 6805; fax 880 2 956 3844; e-mail bcb@bangla.net).

ENGLAND: England and Wales Cricket Board, T. M. Lamb, Lord's Ground, London NW8 8QZ (44 20 7432 1200; fax 44 20 7289 5619; website www.ecb.co.uk).

INDIA: Board of Control for Cricket in India, N. Shah, Sanmitra, Anandpura, Baroda 390 001 (91 265 431233; fax 91 265 428833).

NEW ZEALAND: New Zealand Cricket Inc., M. C. Snedden, PO Box 958, 109 Cambridge Terrace, Christchurch (64 3 366 2964; fax 64 3 365 7491; website www.nzcricket.org.nz).

PAKISTAN: Pakistan Cricket Board, Brig. Munawar Rana, Gaddafi Stadium, Ferozepur Road, Lahore 54600 (92 42 111 22 7777; fax 92 42 571 1860).

SOUTH AFRICA: United Cricket Board of South Africa, M. G. Majola, PO Box 55009, North Street, Illovo, Northlands 2116 (27 11 880 2810; fax 27 11 880 6578; website www.ucbsa.cricket.org; e-mail ucbsa@ucb.co.za).

SRI LANKA: Board of Control for Cricket in Sri Lanka, A. P. B. Tennekoon, 35 Maitland Place, Colombo 7 (94 1 691439/689551; fax 94 1 697405; e-mail: cricket@sri.lanka.net).

WEST INDIES: West Indies Cricket Board, G. Shillingford, Factory Road, PO Box 616 W, Woods Centre, St John's, Antigua (1 268 481 2450; fax 1 268 481 2498; e-mail wicb@candw.ag).

ZIMBABWE: Zimbabwe Cricket Union, M. Dudhia, PO Box 2739, Josiah Tongogara Avenue, Harare (263 4 704616; fax 263 4 729370; website www.zcu.cricket.org; e-mail zcu@mweb.co.zw).

Associate and Affiliate Members

AFGHANISTAN: Afghanistan Cricket Federation, PO Box 970, Kabul (93 23 90017; fax 92 91 287 655).

ARGENTINA: Argentine Cricket Association, D. Lord, ACA Sede Central, PTE Jose E. Uriburu 1468, Piso 3-Departamento A, Buenos Aires (54 11 4806 7306; fax 54 11 4804 5389; website cricketargentina@mail.com; e-mail cricarg@hotmail.com).

AUSTRIA: Österreichischer Cricket Verband, A. Simpson-Parker, Apollogasse 3/42, A-1070 Vienna (43 1 924 6851; website www.austria.cricket.org; e-mail austria_ cricket@yahoo.com).

BAHAMAS: Bahamas Cricket Association, S. Deveaux, Government House, PO Box N1001, Nassau (1 242 326 4720; fax 1 242 322 4659; e-mail bahamascricket@ go.com).

BAHRAIN: Bahrain Cricket Association, PO Box 2400, Manma (fax 973 234 244).

BELGIUM: Belgian Cricket Federation, M. O'Connor, Koningin Astridlaan 98, B-2800 Mechelen (32 15 331 635; fax 32 15 331 639; e-mail paul.lariviere@almo.be).

BELIZE: Belize National Cricket Association, 1128 Baracuda Street, Belize City (501 2 72201; fax 501 2 30936).

BERMUDA: Bermuda Cricket Board of Control, R. Horton, PO Box HM992, Hamilton HM DX (1 441 292 8958; fax 1 441 292 8959; e-mail bcbc@ibl.bm).

BHUTAN: Bhutan Cricket Association, PO Box 242, Thimpu (975 2322 319; fax 972 2322 753; millia@druknet.net.bt).

BOTSWANA: Botswana Cricket Association, J. Sands, Private Bag 00379, Gaborone (267 309867; fax 267 309 881; e-mail jsands@global.bw).

BRUNEI: Persatuan Keriket Negara Brunei Darussalam, S. Langton, PO Box 931, MPC-Old Airport, Berakas-BB 3577 (673 223 5834; fax 673 243 1122; e-mail mirbash@brunet.bn).

CANADA: Canadian Cricket Association, G. Edwards, 46 Port Street East, Mississauga, Ontario L5G 1C1 (1 905 278 5000; fax 1 905 278 5005; e-mail 74253.1641@compuserve.com).

CAYMAN ISLANDS: Cayman Islands Cricket Association, C. Myles, PO Box 1201 GT, George Town, Grand Cayman (1 345 244 3458; fax 1 345 949 8487; e-mail jayke@candw.ky).

COOK ISLANDS: Cook Islands Cricket Association, G. Hoskings, PO Box 139, Rarotoonga (682 29 312; fax 682 29 314).

CROATIA: Croatia Cricket Board, Kvinticka 14B, Zagreb 10 000.

CYPRUS: Cyprus Cricket Association, G. Collins, PO Box 3293, Limassol, Cyprus CY 3301 (357 662 2226; fax 357 662 2227; e-mail guttenbergs@yahoo.com).

CZECH REPUBLIC: Czech Republic Cricket Union, J. Locke, Na Berance 7/1773, 160 00 Praha 6 (420 22 432 1716; e-mail locke@cmail.cz.).

DENMARK: Dansk Cricket-Forbund, C. B. S. Hansen, Idraettens Hus, 2605 Brøndby (45 4326 2160; fax 45 4326 2163; website www.cricket.dk; e-mail dcf@cricket.dk).

EAST AND CENTRAL AFRICA: East and Central African Cricket Conference, T. B. McCarthy, PO Box 34321, Lusaka 1010, Zambia (260 1 226 228; fax 260 1 224 454; e-mail acricket@zamtel.zm).

FIJI: Fiji Cricket Association, P. I. Knight, PO Box 300, Suva (679 301 499; fax 679 301 618; e-mail fijicrick@is.com.fi).

FINLAND: Finnish Cricket Association, A. Armitage, Coats Opti Oy, Ketjutie 3, Fin-04220, Kerava (358 927 487 327; fax 358 927 487 371; e-mail andrew.armitage@coats.com).

FRANCE: Fédération Française de Baseball, Softball et Cricket, O. Dubaut, 41 rue de Fécamp, 75012 Paris (33 1 4468 8930; fax 33 1 4468 9600; e-mail edcannon@club-internet.fr).

GERMANY: Deutscher Cricket Bund, B. Fell, Luragogasse 5, D-94032 Passau (49 851 34307; fax 49 851 32815; website www.dcb-cricket.de; e-mail brimarfell@t-online.de).

GIBRALTAR: Gibraltar Cricket Association, T. J. Finlayson, 23 Merlot House, Vineyards Estate (350 79461; also fax; website www.gca.gi; e-mail thewoods@gibnet.gi).

GREECE: Hellenic Cricket Federation, C. Evangelos, Kat. Pappa 8, Corfu 49100 (30 661 47753; fax 30 661 47754; e-mail cricketadm@otenet.gr).

HONG KONG: Hong Kong Cricket Association, J. A. Cribbin, Room 1019, Sports House, 1 Stadium Path, So Kon Po, Causeway Bay (852 250 48101; fax 852 257 78486; website www.hkabc.net; e-mail hkca@hkabc.net).

INDONESIA: Indonesia Cricket Federation, Gedung BRI II, 19th Floor, Suite 1907, II Jend Sudirman No. 44-46, Jakarta (62 21 251 2660; fax 62 21 570 9455).

IRELAND: Irish Cricket Union, J. Wright, The Diamond, Malahide, Co Dublin 18 (353 1 845 0710; fax 353 1 845 5545; website www.theicu.org; e-mail typetext@eircom.net).

ISRAEL: Israel Cricket Association, S. Perlman, PO Box 65085, Tel-Aviv 61650 (972 3 642 5529; fax 972 3 641 7271; e-mail israel@cricket.org).

ITALY: Federazione Cricket Italiana, S. Gambino, Via S. Ignazio 9, 00186 Roma (39 06 689 6989; fax 39 06 687 8684; website www.crickitalia.org).

JAPAN: Japan Cricket Association, K. Matsumura, Koshi Bidg, 5F 2-11-14, Minamiaoyama Minato-ku, Tokyo 107-0062 (81 3 5772 3470; fax 81 3 5772 3471; website www.jca@cricket.ne.jp; e-mail nao720@aol.com).

KENYA: Kenya Cricket Association, H. Shah, PO Box 45870, Nairobi (254 2 766447; fax 254 2 765057; e-mail kcricket@iconnect.co.ke).

KUWAIT: Kuwait Cricket Association, Abdul Muttaleb Ahmad, PO Box 6706, Hawalli-32042 (965 572 6600; fax 965 573 4973).

LESOTHO: Lesotho Cricket Association, PO Box 964, Maseru 100, Lioli Street, Old Industrial Area, Maseru (266 313 914; fax 266 310 252; e-mail mico@ilesotho.com).

LUXEMBOURG: Federation Luxembourgeoise de Cricket, T. Dunning, 87 rue de Gasperich, L-1617 Luxembourg-Ville (352 4301 32795; fax 352 4301 35049; e-mail lcf@cricket.lu).

MALAYSIA: Malaysian Cricket Association, K. Selveratnam, 1st Floor, Wisma OCM, Jalan Hang Jebat, 50150 Kuala Lumpur (60 3 201 6761; fax 60 3 201 3878; e-mail crickmal@tm.net.my).

MALDIVES: Cricket Control Board of Maldives, Kulhivaru Ekuveni, 1st Floor, Cricket Indoor Hall, Male, Republic of Maldives (960 317 886; fax 960 310 573; e-mail ccbm@avasmail.com).

MALTA: Malta Cricket Association, M. Sacco, c/o Marsa Sports Club, Marsa HMR 15 (356 233 851; fax 356 231 809; e-mail maltacricket@yahoo.co.uk).

MOROCCO: Moroccan Cricket Association, C. Laroussi, 6 Rue Sefrou A8, Hassan-Rabat (212 7 766 453; fax 212 7 766 742; e-mail parebrabat@ megghrbenet.net.ma).

NAMIBIA: Namibia Cricket Board, L. Pieters, PO Box 457, Windhoek (264 61 263128/263129; fax 264 61 215149; e-mail rocwindk@iafrica.com.na).

NEPAL: Cricket Association of Nepal, B. R. Pandey, Heritage Plaza, 5th Floor, Kamaldi, PO Box 20291, Kathmandu (977 1 247485 ext. 252; fax 977 1 247946; e-mail bone@wlink.com.np).

NETHERLANDS: Koninklijke Nederlandse Cricket Bond, A. de la Mar, Nieuwe Kalfjeslaan 21-B, 1182 AA Amstelveen (31 20 645 1705; fax 31 20 645 1715; website www.kncb.nl; e-mail cricket@kncb.nl).

NORWAY: Norway Cricket Association, R. Gibb, Geologsvingen 11, 0380 Oslo (47 22 73 0653; also fax; e-mail bobgibb@enitel.no).

OMAN: Oman Cricket Association, A. M. Yousef, PO Box 3948, Ruwi 112, Muscat, Sultanate of Oman (968 703 142; fax 968 796 045; e-mail kanaksi@omantel.net.om).

PAPUA NEW GUINEA: Papua New Guinea Cricket Board of Control, W. Satchell, PO Box 83, Konedobu NCD, Port Moresby (675 321 1070; fax 675 321 7974; e-mail mahav@lands.gov.pg).

PHILIPPINES: Philippine Cricket Association, c/o Davies, Langdon & Search Philippines Inc., 4th Floor, 2129 Pasong Tamo, Makati City, Metro Manilla (63 2 811 2971; fax 632 811 2071; e-mail cjh@dls.com.ph).

PORTUGAL: Federação Portuguesa de Cricket, J. Simonson, PO Box 76, P-2766 Estoril Codex (351 21 444 6466; fax 351 21 924 3004; e-mail cricket@gauntlett.com).

QATAR: Qatar Cricket Association, F. H. Alfardan, PO Box 339, Dohar (974 440 8225/442 7050; fax 974 441 7468; e-mail afx@qatar.net.qa).

ST HELENA: St Helena Cricket Association, Nia Roo, New Bridge Road, Jamestown (fax 44 870 127 5517; e-mail band.niaroo@helanta.sh).

SAMOA: Samoa Cricket Association, S. Kohlhasse, Seb & Rene Sports, PO Box 9599 (685 22 790; fax 685 22 480).

SCOTLAND: Scottish Cricket Union, National Cricket Academy, MES Sports Centre, Ravelston, Edinburgh EH4 3NT (0131 313 7420; fax 0131 313 7430; website www.scu.org.uk; e-mail admin.scu@btinternet.com).

SINGAPORE: Singapore Cricket Association, A. Kalaver, 31 Stadium Crescent (South Entrance) Singapore 397639 (65 348 6566; fax 65 348 6506; e-mail cricket@singnet.co.sg).

SOUTH KOREA: Korea Cricket Association, 60-25 Hannam-Dang, Yongsam-Ku, Seoul 140 210 (82 2 3706 3001; e-mail dunnan@hlcl.com).

SPAIN: Asociacion Española de Cricket, K. Sainsbury, Casa Desiderata, VA 153, 03737 Javea, Alicante (34 96 579 4948; e-mail ksainsy@dragonet.es).

SWEDEN: Svenska Cricket Förbundet, N. Hashmi, Osbyringen 38, 163 73 Spånga, Stockholm (46 8 508 02053; fax 46 8 508 02179; e-mail naveed.hashmi@rinkeby.stockholm.se).

SWITZERLAND: Swiss Cricket Association, A. MacKay, Wingertlistrasse 22, 8405 Winterthur (41 1 839 4973/52 233 4601; fax 41 1 839 4999; e-mail alex.mackay@mackay.ch).

TANZANIA: Tanzania Cricket Association, PO Box 918, Dar es Salaam (255 22 213 0037; fax 255 22 212 3394; e-mail wizards@cats-net.com).

THAILAND: Thailand Cricket League, 12th Floor, Silom Condominium, 52/38 Soi Saladaeng 2, Silom Road, Bangkok 10500 (66 2 266 9040; fax 66 2 236 6764; e-mail ravisehgal1@hotmail.com).

TONGA: Tonga Cricket Association, 57 Hihifo Road, PO Box 297, Nuku' Alofa (676 25 888; fax 676 23 671; e-mail pmotrain@kalianet.to).

UGANDA: Uganda Cricket Association, J. Ligya, c/o National Council of Sports, Lugogo Stadium, PO Box 8346, Kampala (256 41 349550; fax 256 41 258350; e-mail ncsuga@infocom.co.ug).

UNITED ARAB EMIRATES: Emirates Cricket Board, M. Khan, Sharjah Cricket Stadium, PO Box 88, Sharjah (971 5 0646 3570; fax 971 6 533 4741; e-mail cricket@emirates.net.ae).

USA: United States of America Cricket Association, 3780 Brenner Drive, Santa Barbara, California 93105 (1 805 569 0503; fax 1 805 563 6085; e-mail president@usaca.org).

VANUATU: Vanuatu Cricket Association, M. Stafford, c/o BDO, BDO House, Lini Highway, PO Box 240, Port Vila, Vanuatu (678 22280; fax 678 22317; e-mail stafford@vanuatu.com.vu).

WEST AFRICA: West Africa Cricket Conference, Olusegun Akinlotan, Tafawa Balewa Square, Race Course, Lagos, PO Box 9309, Nigeria (234 6224 0931; fax 234 1585 0529; e-mail olusegunakinlotan@hyperia.net).

UK ADDRESSES

ENGLAND AND WALES CRICKET BOARD: T. M. Lamb, Lord's Ground, London NW8 8QZ (44 20 7432 1200; fax 44 20 7289 5619; website www.ecb.co.uk).

MARYLEBONE CRICKET CLUB: R. D. V. Knight, Lord's Ground, London NW8 8QN (44 20 7289 1611; fax 020 7289 9100. Tickets 44 20 7432 1066; fax 020 7432 1061).

AUSTRALIAN STATE CRICKET ASSOCIATION ADDRESSES

AUSTRALIAN CAPITAL TERRITORY: ACT Cricket, PO Box 3379, Manuka, Australian Capital Territory 2603 (61 2 6239 6002; fax 61 2 6295 7135).

NEW SOUTH WALES: Cricket NSW, PO Box 333, Paddington, New South Wales 2021 (61 2 9339 0999; fax 61 2 9360 6877).

QUEENSLAND: Queensland Cricket, PO Box 575, Albion, Queensland 4010 (61 7 3292 3100; fax 61 7 3262 9160).

SOUTH AUSTRALIA: South Australian Cricket Association, Adelaide Oval, North Adelaide, South Australia 5006 (61 8 8300 3800; fax 61 8 8231 4346).

TASMANIA: Tasmanian Cricket Association, PO Box 495, Rosny Park, Tasmania 7018 (61 3 6211 4000; fax 61 3 6244 3924).

VICTORIA: Victorian Cricket Association, VCA House, 86 Jolimont Street, Jolimont, Victoria 3002 (61 3 9653 1100; fax 61 3 9653 1196).

WESTERN AUSTRALIA: Western Australian Cricket Association, PO Box 6045, East Perth, Western Australia 6892 (61 8 9265 7222; fax 61 8 9221 1823).

Other Bodies

ASSOCIATION OF CRICKET UMPIRES AND SCORERS: G. J. Bullock, PO Box 399, Camberley, Surrey, GU16 5ZJ, UK (44 1276 27962).

AUSTRALIAN CRICKETERS' ASSOCIATION: Tim B. A. May, Level 46, 525 Collins Street, Melbourne, Victoria 3000 (61 3 9614 8456; fax 61 3 9620 0601).

AUSTRALIAN SCHOOLS' CRICKET COUNCIL INC: A. A. K.Gifford, 29 George Street, Avalon, New South Wales 2107 (61 2 9918 3103; fax 61 2 99187211).

BRADMAN MUSEUM: R. Mulvaney, PO Box 9994, Bowral, NSW 2576 (61 2 4862 1247; fax 61 2 4861 2536).

CRUSADERS, THE: Swan Richards, 25–31 Rokeby Street, Collingwood, Victoria, 3066 (61 3 9415 6924; fax 61 3 9417 6911)

LORD'S TAVERNERS AUSTRALIA: Keith Jones, Townhouse 1, 1-3 Wells Street, Brighton, Victoria 3186 (61 3 9593 5301)

CRICKET ASSOCIATIONS AND SOCIETIES

AUSTRALIAN CRICKET SOCIETY INC., Mr Rex Thompson (secretary), 26 Ferny Creek Avenue, Upper Ferntree Gully, Victoria 3156 (61 3 9758 4731; fax 61 3 9752 4055). There are branches of the Society in each state.

THE LAWS OF CRICKET

As updated in 2000. World copyright of MCC and reprinted by permission of MCC. Copies of the "Laws of Cricket" may be obtained from Lord's Cricket Ground or from the MCC website at www.lords.org

INDEX TO THE LAWS

THE PREAMBLE – THE SPIRIT OF CRICKET

Cricket is a game that owes much of its unique appeal to the fact that it should be played not only within its Laws but also within the Spirit of the game. Any action which is seen to abuse this spirit causes injury to the game itself. The major responsibility for ensuring the spirit of fair play rests with the captains.

1. There are two Laws which place the responsibility for the team's conduct firmly on the captain.

   Responsibility of captains

   The captains are responsible at all times for ensuring that play is conducted within the Spirit of the Game as well as within the Laws.

   Player's conduct

   In the event of a player failing to comply with instructions by an umpire, or criticising by word or action the decisions of an umpire, or showing dissent, or generally behaving in a manner which might bring the game into disrepute, the umpire concerned shall in the first place report the matter to the other umpire and to the player's captain, and instruct the latter to take action.

2. **Fair and unfair play**

   According to the Laws the umpires are the sole judges of fair and unfair play. The umpires may intervene at any time and it is the responsibility of the captain to take action where required.

3. **The umpires are authorised to intervene in cases of:**
   • time wasting
   • damaging the pitch
   • dangerous or unfair bowling
   • tampering with the ball
   • any other action that they consider to be unfair

4. **The spirit of the game involves respect for:**
   • your opponents
   • your own captain and team
   • the role of the umpires
   • the game's traditional values

5. **It is against the spirit of the game:**
   • to dispute an umpire's decision by word, action or gesture
   • to direct abusive language towards an opponent or umpire
   • to indulge in cheating or any sharp practice, for instance:
      a) to appeal knowing that the batsman is not out
      b) to advance towards an umpire in an aggressive manner when appealing
      c) to seek to distract an opponent either verbally or by harassment with persistent clapping or unnecessary noise under the guise of enthusiasm and motivation of one's side

6. **Violence**

   There is no place for any act of violence on the field of play.

7. **Players**

   Captains and umpires together set the tone for the conduct of a cricket match. Every player is expected to make an important contribution to this.

The players, umpires and scorers in a game of cricket may be of either gender and the Laws apply equally to both. The use, throughout the text, of pronouns indicating the male gender is purely for brevity. Except where specifically stated otherwise, every provision of the Laws is to be read as applying to women and girls equally as to men and boys.

LAW 1.   THE PLAYERS

1. Number of Players

A match is played between two sides, each of 11 players, one of whom shall be captain. By agreement a match may be played between sides of more or less than 11 players, but not more than 11 players may field at any time.

2. Nomination of Players

Each captain shall nominate his players in writing to one of the umpires before the toss. No player may be changed after the nomination without the consent of the opposing captain.

3. Captain

If at any time the captain is not available, a deputy shall act for him.

(a) If a captain is not available during the period in which the toss is to take place, then the deputy must be responsible for the nomination of the players, if this has not already been done, and for the toss. See 2 above and Law 12.4 (The Toss).

(b) At any time after the toss, the deputy must be one of the nominated players.

4. Responsibilities of Captains

The captains are responsible at all times for ensuring that play is conducted within the spirit and traditions of the game as well as within the Laws. See The Preamble – The Spirit of Cricket and Law 42.1 (Fair and Unfair Play – Responsibility of Captains).

LAW 2. SUBSTITUTES AND RUNNERS; BATSMAN OR FIELDER LEAVING THE FIELD; BATSMAN RETIRING; BATSMAN COMMENCING INNINGS

1. Substitutes and Runners

(a) If the umpires are satisfied that a player has been injured or become ill after the nomination of the players, they shall allow that player to have:

(i) a substitute acting instead of him in the field

(ii) a runner when batting.

Any injury or illness that occurs at any time after the nomination of the players until the conclusion of the match shall be allowable, irrespective of whether play is in progress or not.

(b) The umpires shall have discretion, for other wholly acceptable reasons, to allow a substitute for a fielder, or a runner for a batsman, at the start of the match or at any subsequent time.

(c) A player wishing to change his shirt, boots, etc. must leave the field to do so. No substitute shall be allowed for him.

2. Objection to Substitutes

The opposing captain shall have no right of objection to any player acting as substitute on the field, nor as to where the substitute shall field. However no substitute shall act as wicket-keeper. See 3 following.

3. Restrictions on the Role of Substitutes

A substitute shall not be allowed to bat or bowl nor to act as wicket-keeper or as captain on the field of play.

4. A Player for whom a Substitute has Acted

A player is allowed to bat, bowl or field even though a substitute has previously acted for him.

5. Fielder Absent or Leaving the Field

If a fielder fails to take the field with his side at the start of the match or at any later time, or leaves the field during a session of play:

(a) The umpire shall be informed of the reason for his absence.

(b) He shall not thereafter come on to the field during a session of play without the consent of the umpire. See 6 following. The umpire shall give such consent as soon as is practicable.

(c) If he is absent for 15 minutes or longer, he shall not be permitted to bowl thereafter, subject to (i), (ii) or (iii) below, until he has been on the field for at least that length of playing time for which he was absent.

  (i) Absence or penalty for time absent shall not be carried over into a new day's play.

  (ii) If, in the case of a follow-on or forfeiture, a side fields for two consecutive innings, this restriction shall, subject to (i) above, continue as necessary into the second innings but shall not otherwise be carried over into a new innings.

  (iii) The time lost for an unscheduled break in play shall be counted as time on the field for any fielder who comes onto the field at the resumption of play. See Law 15.1 (An Interval)

6. Player Returning Without Permission

If a player comes onto the field of play in contravention of 5(b) above and comes into contact with the ball while it is in play:

(i) the ball shall immediately become dead and the umpire shall award five penalty runs to the batting side. See Law 42.17 (Penalty Runs)

(ii) the umpire shall inform the other umpire, the captain of the fielding side, the batsmen and, as soon as practicable, the captain of the batting side of the reason for this action.

(iii) the umpires together shall report the occurrence as soon as possible to the Executive of the fielding side and any Governing Body responsible for the match, who shall take such action as is considered appropriate against the captain and player concerned.

7. Runner

The player acting as a runner for a batsman shall be a member of the batting side and shall, if possible, have already batted in that innings. The runner shall wear external protective equipment equivalent to that worn by the batsman for whom he runs and shall carry a bat.

8. Transgression of the Laws by a Batsman Who has a Runner

(a) A batsman's runner is subject to the Laws. He will be regarded as a batsman except where there are specific provisions for his role as a runner. See 7 above and Law 29.2 (Which is a Batsman's Ground).

(b) A batsman with a runner will suffer a penalty for any infringement of the Laws by his runner as though he himself had been responsible for the infringement. In particular he will be out if his runner is out under any of Laws 33 (Handled the Ball), 37 (Obstructing the Field) or 38 (Run Out).

(c) When a batsman with a runner is striker he remains himself subject to the Laws and will be liable to the penalties that any infringement of them demands. Additionally if he is out of his ground when the wicket is put down at the wicket-keeper's end he will be out in the circumstancs of Law 38 (Run Out) or Law 39 (Stumped) irrespective of the position of the non-striker or the runner. If he is thus dismissed, runs completed by the runner and the other batsman before the dismissal shall not be scored. However, the penalty for a No Ball or a Wide shall stand, together with any penalties to either side that may be awarded when the ball is dead. See Law 42.17 (Penalty Runs).

(d) When a batsman with a runner is not the striker:

   (i)   he remains subject to Laws 33 (Handled the Ball) and 37 (Obstructing the Field) but is otherwise out of the game.

   (ii) he shall stand where directed by the striker's end umpire so as not to interfere with play.

   (iii) he will be liable, notwithstanding (i) above, to the penalty demanded by the Laws should he commit any act of unfair play.

9. Batsman Leaving the Field or Retiring

A batsman may retire at any time during his innings. The umpires, before allowing play to proceed, shall be informed of the reason for a batsman retiring.

(a) If a batsman retires because of illness, injury or any other unavoidable cause, he is entitled to resume his innings subject to (c) below. If for any reason he does not do so, his innings is to be recorded as "Retired – not out".

(b) If a batsman retires for any reason other than as in (a) above, he may only resume his innings with the consent of the opposing captain. If for any reason he does not resume his innings it is to be recorded as "Retired – out".

(c) If after retiring a batsman resumes his innings, it shall only be at the fall of a wicket or the retirementr of another batsman.

10. Commencement of a Batsman's Innings

Except at the start of a side's innings, a batsman shall be considered to have commenced his innings when he first steps onto the field of play, provided "Time" has not been called. The innings of the opening batsmen, and that of any new batsman at the resumption of play after a call of "Time", shall commence at the call of "Play".

LAW 3.   THE UMPIRES

1. Appointment and Attendance

Before the match, two umpires shall be appointed, one for each end, to control the game as required by the Laws, with absolute impartiality. The umpires shall be present on the ground and report to the Executive of the ground at least 45 minutes before the scheduled start of each day's play.

2. Change of Umpires

An umpire shall not be changed during the match, other than in exceptional circumstances, unless he is injured or ill. If there has to be a change of umpire, the replacement shall act only as the striker's end umpire unless the captains agree that he should take full responsibility as an umpire.

3. Agreement with Captains

Before the toss the umpires shall:

> (a) ascertain the hours of play and agree with the captains:
>
>> (i)   the balls to be used during the match. See Law 5 (The Ball).
>>
>> (ii) times and durations of intervals for meals and times for drinks intervals. See Law 15 (Intervals).
>>
>> (iii) the boundary of the field of play and allowances for boundaries. See Law 19 (Boundaries).
>>
>> (iv) any special conditions of play affecting the conduct of the match.
>
> (b) inform the scorers of the agreements in (ii), (iii) and (iv) above.

4. To Inform Captains and Scorers

Before the toss the umpires shall agree between themselves and inform both captains and both scorers:

> (i) which clock or watch and back-up time piece is to be used during the match.
>
> (ii) whether or not any obstacle within the field of play is to be regarded as a boundary. See Law 19 (Boundaries).

5. The Wickets, Creases and Boundaries

Before the toss and during the match, the umpires shall satisfy themselves that:

> (i)   the wickets are properly pitched. See Law 8 (The Wickets).
>
> (ii) the creases are correctly marked. See Law 9 (The Bowling, Popping and Return Creases).
>
> (iii) the boundary of the field of play complies with the requirements of Law 19.2 (Defining the Boundary – Boundary Marking).

6. Conduct of the Game, Implements and Equipment

Before the toss and during the match, the umpires shall satisfy themselves that:

> (a) the conduct of the game is strictly in accordance with the Laws.
>
> (b) the implements of the game conform to the requirements of Laws 5 (The Ball) and 6 (The Bat), together with either Laws 8.2 (Size of Stumps) and 8.3 (The Bails) or, if appropriate, Law 8.4 (Junior Cricket).

    (c)   (i)   no player uses equipment other than that permitted. See Appendix D.

            (ii) the wicket-keeper's gloves comply with the requirements of Law 40.2 (Gloves).

7. Fair and Unfair Play

The umpires shall be the sole judges of fair and unfair play.

8. Fitness of Ground, Weather and Light

The umpires shall be the final judges of the fitness of the ground, weather and light for play. See 9 below and Law 7.2 (Fitness of the Pitch for Play).

9. Suspension of Play for Adverse Conditions of Ground, Weather of Light

    (a)   (i)   All references to ground include the pitch. See Law 7.1 (Area of Pitch).

            (ii) For the purpose of this Law and Law 15.9 (b)(ii) (Intervals for Drinks) only the batsmen at the wicket may deputise for their captain at any appropriate time.

(b) If at any time the umpires together agree that the condition of the ground, weather or light is not suitable for play, they shall inform the captains and, unless:

            (i)   in unsuitable ground or weather conditions both captains agree to continue, or to commence, or to restart play, or

            (ii) in unsuitable light the batting side wish to continue, or to commence, or to restart play, they shall suspend play, or not allow play to commence or to restart.

    (c)   (i)   After agreeing to play in unsuitable ground or weather conditions, either captain may appeal against the conditions to the umpires before the next call of Time. The umpires shall uphold the appeal only if, in their opinion, the factors taken into account when making their previous decision are the same or the conditions have further deteriorated.

            (ii) After deciding to play in unsuitable light, the captain of the batting side may appeal against the light to the umpires before the next call of Time. The umpires shall uphold the appeal only if, in their opinion, the factors taken into account when making their previous decision are the same or the condition of the light has further deteriorated.

(d) If at any time the umpires together agree that the conditions of ground, weather or light are so bad that there is obvious and foreseeable risk to the safety of any player or umpire, so that it would be unreasonable or dangerous for play to take place, then notwithstanding the provisions of (b)(i) and (b)(ii) above, they shall immediately suspend play, or not allow play to commence or to restart. The decision as to whether conditions are so bad as to warrant such action is one for the umpires alone to make. The fact that the grass and the ball are wet and slippery does not warrant the ground conditions being regarded as unreasonable or dangerous. If the umpires consider the ground is so wet or slippery as to deprive the bowler of a reasonable foothold, the fielders of the power of free movement, or the batsmen of the ability to play their strokes or to run between the wickets, then these conditions shall be regarded as so bad that it would be unreasonable for play to take place.

(e) When there is a suspension of play it is the responsibility of the umpires to monitor the conditions. They shall make inspections as often as appropriate, unaccompanied by any of the players or officials. Immediately the umpires together agree that conditions are suitable for play they shall call upon the players to resume the game.

(f) If play is in progress up to the start of an agreed interval then it will resume after the interval unless the umpires together agree that conditions are or have become unsuitable or dangerous. If they do so agree, then they shall implement the procedure in (b) or (d) above, as appropriate, whether or not there had been any decision by the captains to continue, or any appeal against the conditions by either captain, prior to the commencement of the interval.

10. Exceptional Circumstances

The umpires shall have the discretion to implement the procedures of 9 above for reasons other than ground, weather or light if they consider that exceptional circumstances warrant it.

11. Position of Umpires

The umpires shall stand where they can best see any act upon which their decision may be required.

Subject to this over-riding consideration the umpire at the bowler's end shall stand where he does not interfere with either the bowler's run up or the striker's view.

The umpire at the striker's end may elect to stand on the off side instead of the on side of the pitch, provided he informs the captain of the fielding side, the striker and the other umpire of his intention to do so.

12. Umpires Changing Ends

The umpires shall change ends after each side has had one completed innings. See Law 14.2 (Forfeiture of an Innings).

13. Consultation between Umpires

All disputes shall be determined by the umpires. The umpires shall consult with each other whenever necessary. See also Law 27.6 (Consultation by Umpires).

14. Signals

(a) The following code of signals shall be used by umpires.

(i) Signals made while the ball is in play:

Dead Ball – by crossing and re-crossing the wrists below the waist.

No-ball – by extending one arm horizontally.

Out – by raising the index finger above the head. If not out, the umpire shall call "Not out".

Wide – by extending both arms horizontally.

(ii) When the ball is dead, the signals above, with the exception of the signal for Out, shall be repeated to the scorers. The signals listed below shall be made to the scorers only when the ball is dead.

Boundary 4 – by waving an arm from side to side finishing with the arm across the chest.

Boundary 6 – by raising both arms above the head.

Bye – by raising an open hand above the head.

Commencement of Last Hour	–	by pointing to a raised wrist with the other hand.
Five Penalty Runs to be Awarded to the batting side	–	by repeated tapping of one shoulder with the opposite hand.
Five Penalty Runs to be Awarded to the fielding side	–	by placing one hand on the opposite shoulder.
Leg-bye	–	by touching a raised knee with the hand.
New Ball	–	by holding the ball above the head.
Revoke last signal	–	by touching both shoulders, each with the opposite hand.
Short Run	–	by bending one arm upwards and touching the nearer shoulder with the tips of the fingers.

(b) The umpires shall wait until each signal to the scorers has been separately acknowledged by a scorer before allowing play to proceed.

14. Correctness of Scores

Consultation between umpires and scorers on doubtful points is essential. The umpires shall satisfy themselves as to the correctness of the number of runs scored, the wickets that have fallen and, where appropriate, the number of overs bowled. They shall agree these with the scorers at least at every interval, other than a drinks interval, and at the conclusion of the match. See Laws 4.2 (Correctness of Scores), 21.8 (Correctness of Result) and 21.10 (Result not to be Changed).

LAW 4. THE SCORERS

1. Appointment of Scorers

Two scorers shall be appointed to record all runs scored, all wickets taken and, where appropriate, number of overs bowled.

2. Correctness of Scores

The scorers shall frequently check to ensure that their records agree. They shall agree with the umpires, at least at every interval, other than a drinks interval, and at the conclusion of the match, the runs scored, the wickets that have fallen and, where appropriate, the number of overs bowled. See Law 3.15 (Correctness of Scores).

3. Acknowledging Signals

The scorers shall accept all instructions and signals given to them by the umpires. They shall immediately acknowledge each separate signal.

LAW 5. THE BALL

1. Weight and Size

The ball, when new, shall weigh not less than 5½ oz/155.9g, nor more than 5¾ oz/163g; and shall measure not less than 8¹³⁄₁₆ in/22.4cm, nor more than 9 in/22.9cm in circumference.

2. Approval and Control of Balls

(a) All balls to be used in the match, having been approved by the umpires and captains, shall be in the possession of the umpires before the toss and shall remain under their control throughout the match.

(b) The umpire shall take possession of the ball in use at the fall of each wicket, at the start of any interval and at any interruption of play.

3. New Ball

Unless an agreement to the contrary has been made before the match, either captain may demand a new ball at the start of each innings.

4. New Ball in Match of More than One Days' Duration

In a match of more than one day's duration, the captain of the fielding side may demand a new ball after the prescribed number of overs has been bowled with the old one. The Governing Body for cricket in the country concerned shall decide the number of overs applicable in that country, which shall not be less than 75 overs.

The umpires shall indicate to the batsmen and the scorers whenever a new ball is taken into play.

5. Ball Lost or Becoming Unfit for Play

If, during play, the ball cannot be found or recovered or the umpires agree that it has become unfit for play through normal use, the umpires shall replace it with a ball which has had wear comparable with that which the previous ball had received before the need for its replacement. When the ball is replaced the umpires shall inform the batsmen and the fielding captain.

6. Specifications

The specifications, as described in 1 above, shall apply to men's cricket only. The following specifications will apply to

(i)   *Women's cricket*

Weight: from 4¹⁵⁄₁₆ oz/140g to 5⁵⁄₁₆ oz/151g.
Circumference: from 8¼ in/21.0cm to 8⅞ in/22.5cm.

(iii) *Junior cricket*

Weight: from 4⁵⁄₁₆ oz/133g to 5¹⁄₁₆ oz/144g.
Circumference: 8¹⁄₁₆ in/20.5cm to 8¹¹⁄₁₆ in/22.0cm.

LAW 6. THE BAT

1. Width and Length

The bat overall shall not be more than 38 in/96.5cm in length. The blade of the bat shall be made solely of wood and shall not exceed 4 ¼ in/10.8cm at the widest part.

2. Covering the Blade

The blade of the bat may be covered with material for protection, strengthening or repair. Such material shall not exceed ¹⁄₁₆ in/1.56mm in thickness, and shall not be likely to cause unacceptable damage to the ball.

2. Hand or Glove to Count as Part of Bat

In these Laws,

> (a) reference to the bat shall imply that the bat is held by the batsman.
>
> (b) contact between the ball and either
>
>> (i) the striker's bat itself, or
>>
>> (ii) the striker's hand holding the bat, or
>>
>> (iii) any part of a glove worn on the striker's hand holding the bat
>
> shall be regarded as the ball striking or touching the bat, or being struck by the bat.

LAW 7.   THE PITCH

1. Area of Pitch

The pitch is a rectangular area of the ground 22 yds/20.12m in length and 10ft/3.05m in width. It is bounded at either end by the bowling creases and on either side by imaginary lines, one each side of the imaginary line joining the centres of the two middle stumps, each parallel to it and 5ft/1.52m from it. See Laws 8.1 (Width and Pitching) and 9.2 (The Bowling Crease).

2. Fitness of the Pitch for Play

The umpires shall be the final judges of the fitness of the pitch for play. See Laws 3.8 (Fitness of Ground, Weather and Light) and 3.9 (Suspension of Play for Adverse Conditions of Ground, Weather or Light).

3. Selection and Preparation

Before the match, the Ground Authority shall be responsible for the selection and preparation of the pitch. During the match, the umpires shall control its use and maintenance.

4. Changing the Pitch

The pitch shall not be changed during the match unless the umpires decide that it is unreasonable or dangerous for play to continue on it and then only with the consent of both captains.

5. Non-turf Pitches

In the event of a non-turf pitch being used, the artificial surface shall conform to the following measurements:

> Length: a minimum of 58 ft/17.68m.
>
> Width: a minimum of 6 ft/1.83m.

See Law 10.8 (Non-turf Pitches).

LAW 8. THE WICKETS

1. Width and Pitching

Two sets of wickets shall be pitched opposite and parallel to each other at a distance of 22 yds/20.12m between the centres of the two middle stumps. Each set shall be 9 in/22.86cm wide and shall consist of three wooden stumps with two wooden bails on top.

2. Size of Stumps

The tops of the stumps shall be 28 in/71.1cm above the playing surface and shall be dome shaped except for the bail grooves. The portion of a stump above the playing surface shall be cylindrical, apart from the domed top, with circular section of diameter not less than 1⅜ in/3.49cm nor more than 1½ in/3.81cm.

3. The Bails

(a) The bails, when in position on top of the stumps,

    (i) shall not project more than ½ in/1.27cm above them.

    (ii) shall fit between the stumps without forcing them out of the vertical.

(b) Each bail shall conform to the following specifications

Overall length:	4⁵⁄₁₆ in/10.95cm
Length of barrel:	2⅛ in/5.40cm
Longer spigot:	1⅜ in/3.49cm
Shorter spigot:	1³⁄₁₆ in/2.06cm

4. Junior Cricket

In junior cricket, the same definitions of the wickets shall apply subject to the following measurements being used.

Width:	8 in/20.32cm
Pitched for Under-13:	21 yds/19.20m
Pitched for Under-11:	20 yds/18.29m
Height above playing surface:	27 in/68.58cm
Each stump	
Diameter:	not less than 1¼ in/3.18cm
	nor more than 1 ⅜ in/3.49cm
Each bail	
Overall length:	3¹³⁄₁₆ in/9.68cm
Length of barrel:	1¹³⁄₁₆ in/4.60cm
Longer spigot:	1¼ in/3.18cm
Shorter spigot:	¾ in/1.91cm

5. Dispensing with bails

The umpires may agree to dispense with the use of bails, if necessary. If they so agree then no bails shall be used at either end. The use of bails shall be resumed as soon as conditions permit.

See Law 28.4 (Dispensing with Bails).

LAW 9. THE BOWLING, POPPING AND RETURN CREASES

1. The Creases

A bowling crease, a popping crease and two return creases shall be marked in white, as set out in 2, 3 and 4 below, at each end of the pitch.

2. The Bowling Crease

The bowling crease, which is the back edge of the crease marking, shall be the line through the centres of the three stumps at that end. It shall be 8ft 8 in/2.64m in length, with the stumps in the centre.

3. The Popping Crease

The popping crease, which is the back edge of the crease marking, shall be in front of and parallel to the bowling crease and shall be 4ft/1.22m from it. The popping crease shall be marked to a minimum of 6ft/1.83m on either side of the imaginary line joining the centres of the middle stumps and shall be considered to be unlimited in length.

4. The Return Creases

The return creases, which are the inside edges of the crease markings, shall be at right angles to the popping crease at a distance of 4ft 4 in/1.32m either side of the imaginary line joining the centres of the two middle stumps. Each return crease shall be marked from the popping crease to a minimum of 8ft/2.44m behind it and shall be considered to be unlimited in length.

LAW 10. PREPARATION AND MAINTENANCE OF THE PLAYING AREA

1. Rolling

The pitch shall not be rolled during the match except as permitted in (a) and (b) below.

(a) Frequency and Duration of Rolling
During the match the pitch may be rolled at the request of the captain of the batting side, for a period of not more than seven minutes, before the start of each innings, other than the first innings of the match, and before the start of each subsequent day's play. See (d) below.

(b) Rolling After a Delayed Start
In addition to the rolling permitted above, if, after the toss and before the first innings of the match, the start is delayed, the captain of the batting side may request to have the pitch rolled for not more than seven minutes. However, if the umpires together agree that the delay has had no significant effect on the state of the pitch, they shall refuse the request for the rolling of the pitch.

(c) Choice of Rollers
If there is more than one roller available the captain of the batting side shall have the choice.

(d) Timing of Permitted Rolling
The rolling permitted (maximum seven minutes) before play begins on any day shall be started not more than 30 minutes before the time scheduled or rescheduled for play to begin. The captain of the batting side may, however, delay the start of such rolling until not less than ten minutes before the time scheduled or rescheduled for play to begin, should he so desire.

(e) Insufficient Time to Complete Rolling

If a captain declares an innings closed, or forfeits an innings, or enforces the follow-on, and the other captain is prevented thereby from exercising his option of the rolling permitted (maximum seven minutes), or if he is so prevented for any other reason, the extra time required to complete the rolling shall be taken out of the normal playing time.

2. Sweeping

(a) If rolling is to take place the pitch shall first be swept to avoid any possible damage by rolling in debris. This sweeping shall be done so that the 7 minutes allowed for rolling is not affected.

(b) The pitch shall be cleared of any debris at all intervals for meals, between innings and at the beginning of each day, not earlier than 30 minutes nor later than 10 minutes before the time scheduled or rescheduled for play to begin. See Law 15.1 (An Interval).

(c) Notwithstanding the provisions of (a) and (b) above, the umpires shall not allow sweeping to take place where they consider it may be detrimental to the surface of the pitch.

3. Mowing

(a) The Pitch

The pitch shall be mown on each day of the match on which play is expected to take place, if ground and weather conditions allow.

(b) The Outfield

In order to ensure that conditions are as similar as possible for both sides, the outfield shall be mown on each day of the match on which play is expected to take place, if ground and weather conditions allow.

If, for reasons other than ground and weather conditions, complete mowing of the outfield is not possible, the ground authority shall notify the captains and umpires of the procedure to be adopted for such mowing during the match.

(c) Responsibility for Mowing

All mowings which are carried out before the match shall be the responsibility of the ground authority.

All subsequent mowings shall be carried out under the supervision of the umpires.

(d) Timing of Mowing

(i) Mowing of the pitch on any day of the match shall be completed not later than 30 minutes before the time scheduled or rescheduled for play to begin on that day.

(ii) Mowing of the outfield on any day of the match shall be completed not later than 15 minutes before the time scheduled or rescheduled for play to begin on that day.

4. Watering

The pitch shall not be watered during the match.

5. Re-marking Creases

The creases shall be re-marked whenever either umpire considers it necessary.

6. Maintenance of Footholes

The umpires shall ensure that the holes made by the bowlers and batsmen are cleaned out and dried whenever necessary to facilitate play. In matches of more than one day's duration, the umpires shall allow, if necessary, the re-turfing of footholes made by the bowler in his delivery stride, or the use of quick-setting fillings for the same purpose.

7. Securing of Footholds and Maintenance of Pitch

During play, the umpires shall allow the players to secure their footholds by the use of sawdust provided that no damage to the pitch is caused and that Law 42 (Fair and Unfair Play) is not contravened.

8. Non-turf Pitches

Wherever appropriate, the provisions set out in 1 to 7 above shall apply.

LAW 11. COVERING THE PITCH

1. Before the Match

The use of covers before the match is the responsibility of the Ground Authority and may include full covering if required. However, the Ground Authority shall grant suitable facility to the captains to inspect the pitch before the nomination of their players and to the umpires to discharge their duties as laid down in Laws 3 (The Umpires), 7 (The Pitch), 8 (The Wickets), 9 (The Bowling, Popping and Return Creases) and 10 (Preparation and Maintenance of the Playing Area).

2. During the Match

The pitch shall not be completely covered during the match unless provided otherwise by regulations or by agreement before the toss.

3. Covering Bowlers' Run-ups

Whenever possible, the bowlers' run ups shall be covered in inclement weather, in order to keep them dry. Unless there is agreement for full covering under 2 above the covers so used shall not extend further than 5ft/1.52m in front of each popping crease.

4. Removal of Covers

(a) If after the toss the pitch is covered overnight, the covers shall be removed in the morning at the earliest possible moment on each day that play is expected to take place.

(b) If covers are used during the day as protection from inclement weather, or if inclement weather delays the removal of overnight covers, they shall be removed promptly as soon as conditions allow.

LAW 12. INNINGS

1. Number of Innings

(a) A match shall be one or two innings of each side according to agreement reached before the match.

(b) It may be agreed to limit any innings to a number of overs or by a period of time. If such an agreement is made then:

    (i) in a one-innings match it shall apply to both innings.

    (ii) in a two-innings match it shall apply to either the first innings of each side or the second innings of each side or both innings of each side.

2. Alternate Innings

In a two-innings match each side shall take their innings alternately except in the case provided for in Law 13 (The Follow-on) or Law 14.2 (Forfeiture of an Innings).

3. Completed Innings

A side's innings is to be considered as completed if:

(a) the side is all out, or

(b) at the fall of a wicket, further balls remain to be bowled, but no further batsman is available to come in, or

(c) the captain declares the innings closed, or

(d) the captain forfeits the innings, or

(e) in the case of an agreement under 1(b) above, either

    (i) the prescribed number of overs has been bowled or

    (ii) the prescribed time has expired.

4. The Toss

The captains shall toss for the choice of innings on the field of play not earlier than 30 minutes, nor later than 15 minutes, before the scheduled or any rescheduled time for the match to start. Note, however, the provisions of Law 1.3 (Captain).

5. Decision to be Notified

The captain of the side winning the toss shall notify the opposing captain of his decision to bat or to field, not later than 10 minutes before the scheduled or any rescheduled time for the match to start. Once notified the decision may not be altered.

LAW 13. THE FOLLOW-ON

1. Lead on First Innings

(a) In a two innings match of 5 days or more, the side which bats first and leads by at least 200 runs shall have the option of requiring the other side to follow their innings.

(b) The same option shall be available in two innings matches of shorter duration with the minimum required leads as follows:

      (i) 150 runs in a match of three or four days;

     (ii) 100 runs in a two-day match;

    (iii) 75 runs in a one-day match.

2. Notification

A captain shall notify the opposing captain and the umpires of his intention to take up this option. Law 10.1(e) (Insufficient Time to Complete Rolling) shall apply.

3. First Day's Play Lost

If no play takes place on the first day of a match of more than one day's duration, 1 above shall apply in accordance with the number of days remaining from the actual start of the match. The day on which play first commences shall count as a whole day for this purpose, irrespective of the time at which play starts.

    Play will have taken place as soon as, after the call of "Play", the first over has started. See Law 22.2 (Start of an Over).

LAW 14.   DECLARATION AND FORFEITURE

1. Time of Declaration

The captain of the batting side may declare an innings closed, when the ball is dead, at any time during a match.

2. Forfeiture of an Innings

A captain may forfeit either of his side's innings. A forfeited innings shall be considered as a completed innings.

3. Notification

A captain shall notify the opposing captain and the umpires of his decision to declare or to forfeit an innings. Law 10.1(e) (Insufficient Time to Complete Rolling) shall apply.

LAW 15.   INTERVALS

1. An Interval

The following shall be classed as intervals.

      (i) The period between close of play on one day and the start of the next day's play.

     (ii) Intervals between innings.

    (iii) Intervals for meals.

    (iv) Intervals for drinks.

     (v) Any other agreed interval.

All these intervals shall be considered as scheduled breaks for the purposes of Law 2.5 (Fielder Absent or Leaving the Field).

2. Agreement of Intervals

(a) Before the Toss:

    (i)   the hours of play shall be established.

    (ii) except as in (b) below, the timing and duration of intervals for meals shall be agreed.

    (iii) the timing and duration of any other interval under 1(v) above shall be agreed.

(b) In a one-day match no specific time need be agreed for the tea interval. It may be agreed instead to take this interval between the innings.

(c) Intervals for drinks may not be taken during the last hour of the match, as defined in Law 16.6 (Last hour of match – number of overs). Subject to this limitation the captains and umpires shall agree the times for such intervals, if any, before the toss and on each subsequent day not later than 10 minutes before play is scheduled to start. See also Law 3.3 (Agreement with Captains).

3. Duration of Intervals

(a) An interval for lunch or for tea shall be of the duration agreed under 2(a) above, taken from the call of "Time" before the interval until the call of "Play" on resumption after the interval.

(b) An interval between innings shall be ten minutes from the close of an innings to the call of "Play" for the start of the next innings, except as in 4, 6 and 7 below.

4. No Allowance for Interval Between Innings

In addition to the provisions of 6 and 7 below:

(a) if an innings ends when ten minutes or less remain before the time agreed for close of play on any day, there will be no further play on that day. No change will be made to the time for the start of play on the following day on account of the ten minutes between innings.

(b) if a captain declares an innings closed during an interruption in play of more than ten minutes duration, no adjustment shall be made to the time for resumption of play on account of the ten minutes between innings, which shall be considered as included in the interruption. Law 10.1(e) (Insufficient Time to Complete Rolling) shall apply.

(c) if a captain declares an innings closed during any interval other than an interval for drinks, the interval shall be of the agreed duration and shall be considered to include the ten minutes between innings. Law 10.1(e) (Insufficient Time to Complete Rolling) shall apply.

5. Changing Agreed Time for Intervals

If for adverse conditions of ground, weather or light, or for any other reason, playing time is lost, the umpires and captains together may alter the time of the lunch interval or of the tea interval. See also 6, 7 and 9(c) below.

6. Changing Agreed Time for Lunch Interval

(a) If an innings ends when ten minutes or less remain before the agreed time for lunch, the interval shall be taken immediately. It shall be of the agreed length and shall be considered to include the ten minutes between innings.

(b) If, because of adverse conditions of ground, weather or light, or in exceptional circumstances, a stoppage occurs when ten minutes or less remain before the agreed time for lunch then, notwithstanding 5 above, the interval shall be taken immediately. It shall be of the agreed length. Play shall resume at the end of this interval or as soon after as conditions permit.

(c) If the players have occasion to leave the field for any reason when more than ten minutes remain before the agreed time for lunch then, unless the umpires and captains together agree to alter it, lunch will be taken at the agreed time.

7. Changing Agreed Time for Tea Interval

(a) (i) If an innings ends when 30 minutes or less remain before the agreed time for tea, then the interval shall be taken immediately. It shall be of the agreed length and shall be considered to include the ten minutes between innings.

(ii) If, when 30 minutes remain before the agreed time for tea, an interval between innings is already in progress, play will resume at the end of the ten-minute interval.

(b) (i) If, because of adverse conditions of ground, weather or light, or in exceptional circumstances, a stoppage occurs when 30 minutes or less remain before the agreed time for tea, then unless either there is an agreement to change the time for tea, as permitted in 5 above, or the captains agree to forgo the tea interval, as permitted in 10 below, the interval shall be taken immediately. The interval shall be of the agreed length. Play shall resume at the end of this interval or as soon after as conditions permit.

(ii) If a stoppage is already in progress when 30 minutes remain before the time agreed for tea, 5 above will apply.

8. Tea Interval – Nine Wickets Down

If nine wickets are down at the end of the over in progress when the agreed time for the tea interval has been reached, then play shall continue for a period not exceeding 30 minutes, unless the players have cause to leave the field of play, or the innings is concluded earlier.

9. Intervals for Drinks

(a) If on any day the captains agree that there shall be intervals for drinks, the option to take such intervals shall be available to either side. Each interval shall be kept as short as possible and in any case shall not exceed five minutes.

(b) (i) Unless both captains agree to forgo any drinks interval, it shall be taken at the end of the over in progress when the agreed time is reached. If, however, a wicket falls within five minutes of the agreed time then drinks shall be taken immediately. No other variation in the timing of drinks intervals shall be permitted except as provided for in (c) below.

(ii) For the purpose of (i) above and Law 3.9(a)(ii) (Suspension of Play for Adverse Conditions of Ground, Weather or Light) only, the batsmen at the wicket may deputise for their captain.

(c) If an innings ends or the players have to leave the field of play for any other reason within 30 minutes of the agreed time for a drinks interval, the umpires and captains together may rearrange the timing of drinks intervals in that session.

10. Agreement to Forgo Intervals

At any time during the match, the captains may agree to forgo the tea interval or any of the drinks intervals. The umpires shall be informed of the decision.

11. Scorers to be Informed

The umpires shall ensure that the scorers are informed of all agreements about hours of play and intervals, and of any changes made thereto as permitted under this Law.

LAW 16.   START OF PLAY; CESSATION OF PLAY

1. Call of "Play"

The umpire at the bowler's end shall call "Play" at the start of the match and on the resumption of play after any interval or interruption.

2. Call of "Time"

The umpire at the bowler's end shall call "Time" on the cessation of play before any interval or interruption of play and at the conclusion of the match. See Law 27 (Appeals).

3. Removal of Bails

After the call of "Time", the bails shall be removed from both wickets.

4. Starting a New Over

Another over shall always be started at any time during the match, unless an interval is to be taken in the circumstances set out in 5 below, if the umpire, after walking at his normal pace, has arrived at his position behind the stumps at the bowler's end before the time agreed for the next interval, or for the close of play, has been reached.

5. Completion of an Over

Other than at the end of the match:

(a) if the agreed time for an interval is reached during an over, the over shall be completed before the interval is taken except as provided for in (b) below.

(b) when less than two minutes remain before the time agreed for the next interval, the interval will be taken immediately if either

(i)   a batsman is out or retires, or

(ii) the players have occasion to leave the field

whether this occurs during an over or at the end of an over. Except at the end of an innings, if an over is thus interrupted it shall be completed on resumption of play.

6. Last Hour of Match – Number of Overs

When one hour of playing time of the match remains, according to the agreed hours of play, the over in progress shall be completed. The next over shall be the first of a minimum of 20 overs which must be bowled, provided that a result is not reached earlier and provided that there is no interval or interruption in play. The umpire at the bowler's end shall indicate the commencement of this 20 overs to the players and the scorers. The period of play thereafter shall be referred to as the last hour, whatever its actual duration.

7. Last Hour of Match – Interruptions of Play

If there is an interruption in play during the last hour of the match, the minimum number of overs to be bowled shall be reduced from 20 as follows.

(a) The time lost for an interruption is counted from the call of "Time" until the time for resumption of play as decided by the umpires.

(b) One over shall be deducted for every complete three minutes of time lost.

(c) In the case of more than one such interruption, the minutes lost shall not be aggregated; the calculation shall be made for each interruption separately.

(d) If, when one hour of playing time remains, an interruption is already in progress:

    (i) only the time lost after this moment shall be counted in the calculation.

    (ii) the over in progress at the start of the interruption shall be completed on resumption of play and shall not count as one of the minimum number of overs to be bowled.

(e) If, after the start of the last hour, an interruption occurs during an over, the over shall be completed on resumption of play. The two part-overs shall between them count as one over of the minimum number to be bowled.

8. Last Hour of Match – Intervals Between Innings

If an innings ends so that a new innings is to be started during the last hour of the match, the interval starts with the end of the innings and is to end ten minutes later.

(a) If this interval is already in progress at the start of the last hour, then to determine the number of overs to be bowled in the new innings, calculations are to be made as set out in 7 above.

(b) If the innings ends after the last hour has started, two calculations are to be made, as set out in (c) and (d) below. The greater of the numbers yielded by these two calculations is to be the minimum number of overs to be bowled in the new innings.

(c) Calculation based on overs remaining:

    (i) At the conclusion of the innings, the number of overs that remain to be bowled, of the minimum in the last hour, to be noted.

    (ii) If this is not a whole number it is to be rounded up to the next whole number.

    (iii) Three overs to be deducted from the result for the interval.

(d) Calculation based on time remaining:

    (i) At the conclusion of the innings, the time remaining until the agreed time for close of play to be noted.

    (ii) Ten minutes to be deducted from this time, for the interval, to determine the playing time remaining.

(iii) A calculation to be made of one over for every complete three minutes of the playing time remaining, plus one more over for any further part of three minutes remaining.

9. Conclusion of a Match

The match is concluded:

(a) as soon as a result, as defined in sections 1, 2, 3 or 4 of Law 21 (The Result), is reached.

(b) as soon as both

(i) the minimum number of overs for the last hour are completed, and

(ii) the agreed time for close of play is reached unless a result has been reached earlier.

(c) if, without the match being concluded either as in (a) or in (b) above, the players leave the field, either for adverse conditions of ground, weather or light, or in exceptional circumstances, and no further play is possible thereafter.

10. Completion of Last Over of Match

The over in progress at the close of play on the final day shall be completed unless either

(i) a result has been reached, or

(ii) the players have occasion to leave the field. In this case there shall be no resumption of play, except in the circumstances of Law 21.9 (Mistakes in Scoring), and the match shall be at an end.

11. Bowler Unable to Complete an Over During Last Hour of Match

If, for any reason, a bowler is unable to complete an over during the last hour, Law 22.8 (Bowler Incapacitated or Suspended During an Over) shall apply.

LAW 17. PRACTICE ON THE FIELD

1. Practice on the Field

(a) There shall be no bowling or batting practice on the pitch, or on the area parallel and immediately adjacent to the pitch, at any time on any day of the match.

(b) There shall be no bowling or batting practice on any other part of the square on any day of the match, except before the start of play or after the close of play on that day. Practice before the start of play:

(i) must not continue later than 30 minutes before the scheduled time or any rescheduled time for play to start on that day.

(ii) shall not be allowed if the umpires consider that, in the prevailing conditions of ground and weather, it will be detrimental to the surface of the square.

(c) There shall be no practice on the field of play between the call of "Play" and the call of "Time", if the umpire considers that it could result in a waste of time. See Law 42.9 (Time-Wasting by the Fielding Side).

(d) If a player contravenes (a) or (b) above he shall not be allowed to bowl until at least five complete overs have been bowled by his side after the contravention. If an over is in progress at the contravention he shall not be allowed to complete that over nor shall the remaining part-over count towards the five overs above.

2. Trial Run-Up

No bowler shall have a trial run-up between the call of "Play" and the call of "Time" unless the umpire is satisfied that it will not cause any waste of time.

LAW 18.   SCORING RUNS

1. A Run

The score shall be reckoned by runs. A run is scored:

(a) so often as the batsmen, at any time while the ball is in play, have crossed and made good their ground from end to end.

(b) when a boundary is scored. See Law 19 (Boundaries).

(c) when penalty runs are awarded. See 6 below.

(d) when "Lost ball" is called. See Law 20 (Lost Ball).

2. Runs Disallowed

Notwithstanding 1 above, or any other provisions elsewhere in the Laws, the scoring of runs or awarding of penalties will be subject to any disallowance of runs provided for within the Laws that may be applicable.

3. Short Runs

(a) A run is short if a batsman fails to make good his ground on turning for a further run.

(b) Although a short run shortens the succeeding one, the latter if completed shall not be regarded as short. A striker taking stance in front of his popping crease may run from that point also without penalty.

4. Unintentional Short Runs

Except in the circumstances of 5 below:

(a) if either batsman runs a short run, unless a boundary is scored the umpire concerned shall call and signal "Short run" as soon as the ball becomes dead and that run shall not be scored.

(b) if, after either or both batsmen run short, a boundary is scored, the umpire concerned shall disregard the short running and shall not call or signal "Short run".

(c) if both batsmen run short in one and the same run, this shall be regarded as only one short run.

(d) if more than one run is short then, subject to (b) and (c) above, all runs so called shall not be scored.

If there has been more than one short run the umpire shall inform the scorers as to the number of runs scored.

5. Deliberate Short Runs

(a) Notwithstanding 4 above, if either umpire considers that either or both batsmen deliberately run short at his end, the following procedure shall be adopted:

   (i) The umpire concerned shall, when the ball is dead, warn the batsman or batsmen that the practice is unfair, indicate that this is a first and final warning and inform the other umpire of what has occurred.

   (ii) The batsmen shall return to their original ends.

   (iii) Whether a batsman is dismissed or not, the umpire at the bowler's end shall disallow all runs to the batting side from that delivery other than the penalty for a No ball or Wide, or penalties under Laws 42.5 (Deliberate Distraction or Obstruction of Batsman) and 42.13 (Fielders Damaging the Pitch), if applicable.

   (iv) The umpire at the bowler's end shall inform the scorers as to the number of runs scored.

(b) If there is any further instance of deliberate short running by either of the same batsmen in that innings, when the ball is dead the umpire concerned shall inform the other umpire of what has occurred and the procedure set out in (a)(ii) and (iii) above shall be repeated. Additionally, the umpire at the bowler's end shall:

   (i) award five penalty runs to the fielding side. See Law 42.17 (Penalty Runs).

   (ii) inform the scorers as to the number of runs scored.

   (iii) inform the batsmen, the captain of the fielding side and, as soon as practicable, the captain of the batting side of the reason for this action.

   (iv) report the occurrence, with the other umpire, to the Executive of the batting side and any governing body responsible for the match, who shall take such action as is considered appropriate against the captain and player or players concerned.

6. Runs Scored for Penalties

Runs shall be scored for penalties under 5 above and Laws 2.6 (Player Returning Without Permission), 24 (No-ball), 25 (Wide Ball), 41.2 (Fielding the Ball), 41.3 (Protective Helmets Belonging to the Fielding Side) and 42 (Fair and Unfair Play).

7. Runs Scored for Boundaries

Runs shall be scored for boundary allowances under Law 19 (Boundaries).

8. Runs Scored for Lost Ball

Runs shall be scored when "Lost ball" is called under Law 20 (Lost Ball).

9. Batsman Dismissed

When either batsman is dismissed:

(a) any penalties to either side that may be applicable shall stand but no other runs shall be scored, except as stated in 10 below. Note, however, Law 42.17(b) (Penalty Runs).

(b) 12(a) below will apply if the method of dismissal is Caught, Handled the Ball or Obstructing the Field. 12(a) will also apply if a batsman is Run Out, except in the circumstances of Law 2.8 (Transgression of the Laws by a Batsman Who Has a Runner) where 12(b) below will apply.

(c) the not out batsman shall return to his original end except as stated in (b) above.

10. Runs Scored When a Batsman is Dismissed

In addition to any penalties to either side that may be applicable, if a batsman is

(a) dismissed Handled the Ball, the batting side shall score the runs completed before the offence.

(b) dismissed Obstructing the Field, the batting side shall score the runs completed before the offence.

If, however, the obstruction prevents a catch from being made, no runs other than penalties shall be scored.

(c) dismissed Run Out, the batting side shall score the runs completed before the dismissal.

If, however, a striker with a runner is himself dismissed Run Out, no runs other than penalties shall be scored. See Law 2.8 (Transgression of the Laws by a Batsman Who Has a Runner).

11. Runs Scored When a Ball Becomes Dead

(a) When the ball becomes dead on the fall of a wicket, runs shall be scored as laid down in 9 and 10 above.

(b) When the ball becomes dead for any reason other than the fall of a wicket, or is called dead by an umpire, unless there is specific provision otherwise in the Laws, the batting side shall be credited with:

  (i) all runs completed by the batsmen before the incident or call, and

  (ii) the run in progress if the batsmen have crossed at the instant of the incident or call. Note specifically, however, the provisions of Laws 34.4(c) (Runs Permitted From Ball Lawfully Struck More Than Once) and 42.5(b)(iii) (Deliberate Distraction or Obstruction of Batsman), and

  (iii) any penalties that are applicable.

12. Batsman Returning to Wicket he has Left

(a) If, while the ball is in play, the batsmen have crossed in running, neither shall return to the wicket he has left, except as in (b) below.

(b) The batsmen shall return to the wickets they originally left in the cases of, and only in the cases of:

  (i) a boundary.

  (ii) disallowance of runs for any reason.

  (iii) the dismissal of a batsman, except as in 9(b) above.

LAW 19. BOUNDARIES

1. The Boundary of the Field of Play

(a) Before the toss, the umpires shall agree the boundary of the field of play with both captains. The boundary shall if possible be marked along its whole length.

(b) The boundary shall be agreed so that no part of any sight-screen is within the field of play.

(c) An obstacle or person within the field of play shall not be regarded as a boundary unless so decided by the umpires before the toss. See Law 3.4(ii) (To Inform Captains and Scorers).

2. Defining the Boundary – Boundary Marking

(a) Wherever practicable the boundary shall be marked by means of a white line or a rope laid along the ground.

(b) If the boundary is marked by a white line:

    (i) the inside edge of the line shall be the boundary edge.

    (ii) a flag, post or board used merely to highlight the position of a line marked on the ground must be placed outside the boundary edge and is not itself to be regarded as defining or marking the boundary. Note, however, the provisions of (c) below.

(c) If a solid object is used to mark the boundary, it must have an edge or a line to constitute the boundary edge.

    (i) For a rope, which includes any similar object of curved cross section lying on the ground, the boundary edge will be the line formed by the innermost points of the rope along its length.

    (ii) For a fence, which includes any similar object in contact with the ground, but with a flat surface projecting above the ground, the boundary edge will be the base line of the fence.

(d) If the boundary edge is not defined as in (b) or (c) above, the umpires and captains must agree, before the toss, what line will be the boundary edge. Where there is no physical marker for a section of boundary, the boundary edge shall be the imaginary straight line joining the two nearest marked points of the boundary edge.

(e) If a solid object used to mark the boundary is disturbed for any reason during play, then if possible it shall be restored to its original position as soon as the ball is dead. If this is not possible, then:

    (i) if some part of the fence or other marker has come within the field of play, that portion is to be removed from the field of play as soon as the ball is dead.

    (ii) the line where the base of the fence or marker originally stood shall define the boundary edge.

3. Scoring a Boundary

(a) A boundary shall be scored and signalled by the umpire at the bowler's end whenever, while the ball is in play, in his opinion:

    (i) the ball touches the boundary, or is grounded beyond the boundary.

(ii) a fielder, with some part of his person in contact with the ball, touches the boundary or has some part of his person grounded beyond the boundary.

(b) The phrases "touches the boundary" and "touching the boundary" shall mean contact with either

(i) the boundary edge as defined in 2 above, or

(ii) any person or obstacle within the field of play which has been designated a boundary by the umpires before the toss.

(c) The phrase "grounded beyond the boundary" shall mean contact with either

(i) any part of a line or a solid object marking the boundary, except its boundary edge, or

(ii) the ground outside the boundary edge, or

(iii) any object in contact with the ground outside the boundary edge.

4. Runs Allowed for Boundaries

(a) Before the toss, the umpires shall agree with both captains the runs to be allowed for boundaries. In deciding the allowances, the umpires and captains shall be guided by the prevailing custom of the ground.

(b) Unless agreed differently under (a) above, the allowances for boundaries shall be six runs if the ball having been struck by the bat pitches beyond the boundary, but otherwise four runs. These allowances shall still apply even though the ball has previously touched a fielder. See also (c) below.

(c) The ball shall be regarded as pitching beyond the boundary and six runs shall be scored if a fielder:

(i) has any part of his person touching the boundary or grounded beyond the boundary when he catches the ball.

(ii) catches the ball and subsequently touches the boundary or grounds some part of his person beyond the boundary while carrying the ball but before completing the catch. See Law 32 (Caught).

5. Runs Scored

When a boundary is scored:

(a) the penalty for a No Ball or a Wide, if applicable, shall stand together with any penalties under any of Laws 2.6 (Player Returning Without Permission), 18.5(b) (Deliberate Short Runs) or 42 (Fair and Unfair Play) that apply before the boundary is scored.

(b) the batting side, except in the circumstances of 6 below, shall additionally be awarded whichever is the greater of:

(i) the allowance for the boundary.

(ii) the runs completed by the batsmen, together with the run in progress if they have crossed at the instant the boundary is scored. When these runs exceed the boundary allowance, they shall replace the boundary for the purposes of Law 18.12 (Batsman Returning to Wicket He Has Left).

6. Overthrow or Wilful Act of Fielder

If the boundary results either from an overthrow or from the wilful act of a fielder the runs scored shall be:

(i) the penalty for a No-ball or a Wide, if applicable, and penalties under any of Laws 2.6 (Player Returning Without Permission), 18.5(b) (Deliberate Short Runs) or 42 (Fair and Unfair Play) that are applicable before the boundary is scored, and

(ii) the allowance for the boundary, and

(iii) the runs completed by the batsmen, together with the run in progress if they have crossed at the instant of the throw or act.

Law 18.12(a) (Batsman Returning to Wicket He Has Left) shall apply as from the instant of the throw or act.

LAW 20.   LOST BALL

1. Fielder to Call "Lost Ball"

If a ball in play cannot be found or recovered, any fielder may call "Lost Ball". The ball shall then become dead. See Law 23.1 (Ball is Dead). Law 18.12(a) (Batsman Returning to Wicket He Has Left) shall apply as from the instant of the call.

2. Ball to be Replaced

The umpires shall replace the ball with one which has had wear comparable with that which the previous ball had received before it was lost or became irrecoverable. See Law 5.5 (Ball Lost or Becoming Unfit for Play).

3. Runs Scored

(a) The penalty for a no-ball or a wide, if applicable, shall stand, together with any penalties under any of Laws 2.6 (Player Returning Without Permission), 18.5(b) (Deliberate Short Runs) or 42 (Fair and Unfair Play) that are applicable before the call of "Lost ball".

(b) The batting side shall additionally be awarded, either

(i) the runs completed by the batsmen, together with the run in progress if they have crossed at the instant of the call, or

(ii) six runs,

whichever is the greater.

4. How Scored

If there is a one-run penalty for a no-ball or for a wide, it shall be scored as a no-ball extra or as a wide as appropriate. See Laws 24.13 (Runs Resulting from a No-ball – How Scored) and 25.6 (Runs Resulting from a Wide – How Scored). If any other penalties have been awarded to either side, they shall be scored as penalty extras. See Law 42.17 (Penalty Runs).

Runs to the batting side in 3(b) above shall be credited to the striker if the ball has been struck by the bat, but otherwise to the total of byes, leg byes, no-balls or wides as the case may be.

LAW 21.   THE RESULT

1. A Win – Two-Innings Match

The side which has scored a total of runs in excess of that scored in the two completed innings of the opposing side shall win the match. Note also 6 below. A forfeited innings is to count as a completed innings. See Law 14 (Declaration and Forfeiture).

2. A Win – One-Innings Match

The side which has scored in its one innings a total of runs in excess of that scored by the opposing side in its one completed innings shall win the match. Note also 6 below.

3. Umpires Awarding a Match

(a) A match shall be lost by a side which either

    (i) concedes defeat, or

    (ii) in the opinion of the umpires refuses to play and the umpires shall award the match to the other side.

(b) If an umpire considers that an action by any player or players might constitute a refusal by either side to play then the umpires together shall ascertain the cause of the action. If they then decide together that this action does constitute a refusal to play by one side, they shall so inform the captain of that side. If the captain persists in the action the umpires shall award the match in accordance with (a)(ii) above.

(c) If action as in (b) above takes place after play has started and does not constitute a refusal to play

    (i) playing time lost shall be counted from the start of the action until play recommences, subject to Law 15.5 (Changing Agreed Times for Intervals).

    (ii) the time for close of play on that day shall be extended by this length of time, subject to Law 3.9 (Suspension of Play for Adverse Conditions of Ground, Weather or Light).

    (iii) if applicable, no overs shall be deducted during the last hour of the match solely on account of this time.

4. A Tie

The result of a match shall be a tie when the scores are equal at the conclusion of play, but only if the side batting last has completed its innings.

5. A Draw

A match which is concluded, as defined in Law 16.9 (Conclusion of a Match), without being determined in any of the ways stated in 1, 2, 3 or 4 above, shall count as a draw.

6. Winning Hit or Extras

(a) As soon as a result is reached, as defined in 1, 2, 3 or 4 above, the match is at an end. Nothing that happens thereafter shall be regarded as part of it. Note also 9 below.

(b) The side batting last will have scored enough runs to win only if its total of runs is sufficient without including any runs completed before the dismissal of the striker by the completion of a catch or by the obstruction of a catch.

(c) If a boundary is scored before the batsmen have completed sufficient runs to win the match, then the whole of the boundary allowance shall be credited to the side's total and, in the case of a hit by the bat, to the striker's score.

7. Statement of a Result

If the side batting last wins the match, the result shall be stated as a win by the number of wickets still then to fall. If the other side wins the match, the result shall be stated as a win by runs. If the match is decided by one side conceding defeat or refusing to play, the result shall be stated as "Match conceded" or "Match awarded" as the case may be.

8. Correctness of a Result

Any decision as to the correctness of the scores shall be the responsibility of the umpires. See Law 3.15 (Correctness of Scores).

9. Mistakes in Scoring

If, after the umpires and players have left the field in the belief that the match has been concluded, the umpires discover that a mistake in scoring has occurred which affects the result, then, subject to 10 below, they shall adopt the following procedure.

(a) If, when the players leave the field, the side batting last has not completed its innings, and either

    (i) the number of overs to be bowled in the last hour has not been completed, or

    (ii) the agreed finishing time has not been reached,

then unless one side concedes defeat the umpires shall order play to resume.

If conditions permit, play will then continue until the prescribed number of overs has been completed and the time remaining has elapsed, unless a result is reached earlier. The number of overs and/or the time remaining shall be taken as they were when the players left the field; no account shall be taken of the time between that moment and the resumption of play.

(b) If, when the players leave the field, the overs have been completed and time has been reached, or if the side batting last has completed its innings, the umpires shall immediately inform both captains of the necessary corrections to the scores and to the result.

10. Result Not to Be Changed

Once the umpires have agreed with the scorers the correctness of the scores at the conclusion of the match – see Laws 3.15 (Correctness of Scores) and 4.2 (Correctness of Scores) – the result cannot thereafter be changed.

LAW 22. THE OVER

1. Number of Balls

The ball shall be bowled from each wicket alternately in overs of six balls.

2. Start of an Over

An over has started when the bowler starts his run-up or, if he has no-run up, his delivery action for the first delivery of that over.

3. Call of "Over"

When six balls have been bowled other than those which are not to count in the over and as the ball becomes dead – see Law 23 (Dead Ball) – the umpire shall call "Over" before leaving the wicket.

4. Balls Not to Count in the Over

(a) A ball shall not count as one of the six balls of the over unless it is delivered, even though a batsman may be dismissed or some other incident occurs before the ball is delivered.

(b) A ball which is delivered by the bowler shall not count as one of the six balls of the over:

(i) if it is called dead, or is to be considered dead, before the striker has had an opportunity to play it. See Law 23 (Dead Ball).

(ii) if it is a no-ball. See Law 24 (No-Ball).

(iii) if it is a wide. See Law 25 (Wide Ball).

(iv) if it is called dead in the circumstances of either of Laws 23.3 (vi) (Umpire Calling and Signalling "Dead ball") or 42.4 (Deliberate Attempt to Distract Striker).

5. Umpire Miscounting

If an umpire miscounts the number of balls, the over as counted by the umpire shall stand.

6. Bowler Changing Ends

A bowler shall be allowed to change ends as often as desired, provided only that he does not bowl two overs, or parts thereof, consecutively in the same innings.

7. Finishing an Over

(a) Other than at the end of an innings, a bowler shall finish an over in progress unless he is incapacitated, or he is suspended under any of Laws 17.1 (Practice on the Field), 42.7 (Dangerous and Unfair Bowling – Action By the Umpire), 42.9 (Time-Wasting by the Fielding Side), or 42.12 (Bowler Running on the Protected Area After Delivering the Ball).

(b) If for any reason, other than the end of an innings, an over is left uncompleted at the start of an interval or interruption of play, it shall be completed on resumption of play.

8. Bowler Incapacitated or Suspended During an Over

If for any reason a bowler is incapacitated while running up to bowl the first ball of an over, or is incapacitated or suspended during an over, the umpire shall call and signal "Dead ball". Another bowler shall complete the over from the same end, provided that he does not bowl two overs, or parts thereof, consecutively in one innings.

LAW 23. DEAD BALL

1. Ball is Dead

(a) The ball becomes dead when:

(i) it is finally settled in the hands of the wicket-keeper or the bowler.

(ii) a boundary is scored. See Law 19.3 (Scoring a Boundary).

(iii) a batsman is dismissed.

(iv) whether played or not it becomes trapped between the bat and person of a batsman or between items of his clothing or equipment.

(v) whether played or not it lodges in the clothing or equipment of a batsman or the clothing of an umpire.

(vi) it lodges in a protective helmet worn by a member of the fielding side.

(vii) there is a contravention of either of Laws 41.2 (Fielding the Ball) or 41.3 (Protective Helmets Belonging to the Fielding Side).

(viii) there is an award of penalty runs under Law 2.6 (Player Returning Without Permission).

(ix) "Lost ball" is called. See Law 20 (Lost Ball).

(x) the umpire calls "Over" or "Time".

(b) The ball shall be considered to be dead when it is clear to the umpire at the bowler's end that the fielding side and both batsmen at the wicket have ceased to regard it as in play.

2. Ball Finally Settled

Whether the ball is finally settled or not is a matter for the umpire alone to decide.

3. Umpire Calling and Signalling "Dead Ball"

(a) When the ball has become dead under 1 above, the bowler's end umpire may call "Dead ball", if it is necessary to inform the players.

(b) Either umpire shall call and signal "Dead ball" when:

(i) he intervenes in a case of unfair play.

(ii) a serious injury to a player or umpire occurs.

(iii) he leaves his normal position for consultation.

(iv) one or both bails fall from the striker's wicket before he has the opportunity of playing the ball.

(v) he is satisfied that for an adequate reason the striker is not ready for the delivery of the ball and, if the ball is delivered, makes no attempt to play it.

(vi) the striker is distracted by any noise or movement or in any other way while he is preparing to receive or receiving a delivery. This shall apply whether the source of the distraction is within the game or outside it. Note, however, the provisions of Law 42.4 (Deliberate Attempt to Distract the Striker). The ball shall not count as one of the over.

(vii) the bowler drops the ball accidentally before delivery.

(viii) the ball does not leave the bowler's hand for any reason other than an attempt to run out the non-striker before entering his delivery stride. See Law 42.15 (Bowler Attempting to Run out Non-striker Before Delivery).

(ix) he is required to do so under any of the Laws.

4. Ball Ceases to Be Dead

The ball ceases to be dead – that is, it comes into play – when the bowler starts his run up or, if he has no run up, his bowling action.

5. Action on Call of "Dead Ball"

(a) A ball is not to count as one of the over if it becomes dead or is to be considered dead before the striker has had an opportunity to play it.

(b) If the ball becomes dead or is to be considered dead after the striker has had an opportunity to play the ball, except in the circumstances of 3(vi) above and Law 42.4 (Deliberate Attempt to Distract Striker), no additional delivery shall be allowed unless "No-ball" or "Wide" has been called.

LAW 24. NO-BALL

1. Mode of Delivery

(a) The umpire shall ascertain whether the bowler intends to bowl right-handed or left-handed, and whether over or round the wicket, and shall so inform the striker. It is unfair if the bowler fails to notify the umpire of a change in his mode of delivery. In this case the umpire shall call and signal "No-ball".

(b) Underarm bowling shall not be permitted except by special agreement before the match.

2. Fair Delivery – The Arm

For a delivery to be fair in respect of the arm the ball must not be thrown. See 3 below.

Although it is the primary responsibility of the striker's end umpire to ensure the fairness of a delivery in this respect, there is nothing in this Law to debar the bowler's end umpire from calling and signalling "No-ball" if he considers that the ball has been thrown.

(a) If, in the opinion of either umpire, the ball has been thrown, he shall

(i) call and signal "No-ball".

(ii) caution the bowler, when the ball is dead. This caution shall apply throughout the innings.

(iii) inform the other umpire, the batsmen at the wicket, the captain of the fielding side and, as soon as practicable, the captain of the batting side of what has occurred.

(b) If either umpire considers that after such caution a further delivery by the same bowler in that innings is thrown, the umpire concerned shall repeat the procedure set out in (a) above, indicating to the bowler that this is a final warning. This warning shall also apply throughout the innings.

(c) If either umpire considers that a further delivery by the same bowler in that innings is thrown:

(i) the umpire concerned shall call and signal "No-ball". When the ball is dead he shall inform the other umpire, the batsmen at the wicket and, assoon as practicable, the captain of the batting side of what has occurred.

(ii) the umpire at the bowler's end shall direct the captain of the fielding side to take the bowler off forthwith. The over shall be completed by another bowler, who shall neither have bowled the previous over nor be allowed to bowl the next over. The bowler thus taken off shall not bowl again in that innings.

(iii) the umpires together shall report the occurrence as soon as possible to the Executive of the fielding side and any governing body responsible for the match, who shall take such action as is considered appropriate against the captain and bowler concerned.

3. Definition of Fair Delivery – The Arm

A ball is fairly delivered in respect of the arm if, once the bowler's arm has reached the level of the shoulder in the delivery swing, the elbow joint is not straightened partially or completely from that point until the ball has left the hand. This definition shall not debar a bowler from flexing or rotating the wrist in the delivery swing.

4. Bowler Throwing Towards Striker's End Before Delivery

If the bowler throws the ball towards the striker's end before entering his delivery stride, either umpire shall call and signal "No-ball". See Law 42.16 (Batsmen Stealing a Run). However, the procedure stated in 2 above of caution, informing, final warning, action against the bowler and reporting shall not apply.

5. Fair Delivery – The Feet

For a delivery to be fair in respect of the feet, in the delivery stride:

(i) the bowler's back foot must land within and not touching the return crease.

(ii) the bowler's front foot must land with some part of the foot, whether grounded or raised, behind the popping crease.

If the umpire at the bowler's end is not satisfied that both these conditions have been met, he shall call and signal "No-ball".

6. Ball Bouncing More Than Twice or Rolling Along the Ground

The umpire at the bowler's end shall call and signal "No-ball" if a ball which he considers to have been delivered, without having previously touched the bat or person of the striker, either

(i) bounces more than twice, or

(ii) rolls along the ground

before it reaches the popping crease.

7. Ball Coming to Rest in Front of Striker's Wicket

If a ball delivered by the bowler comes to rest in front of the line of the striker's wicket, without having touched the bat or person of the striker, the umpire shall call and signal "No-ball" and immediately call and signal "Dead ball".

8. Call of "No-Ball" for Infringement of Other Laws

In addition to the instances above, an umpire shall call and signal "No-ball" as required by the following Laws.

>   Law 40.3 – Position of wicket-keeper,
>   Law 41.5 – Limitation of on-side fielders,
>   Law 41.6 – Fielders not to encroach on the pitch,
>   Law 42.6 – Dangerous and unfair bowling,
>   Law 42.7 – Dangerous and unfair bowling – action by the umpire,
>   Law 42.8 – Deliberate bowling of high full pitched balls.

9. Revoking a Call of "No-Ball"

An umpire shall revoke the call of "No-ball" if the ball does not leave the bowler's hand for any reason.

10. No-Ball to Over-ride Wide

A call of "No-ball" shall over-ride the call of "Wide ball" at any time. See Law 25.1 (Judging a Wide) and 25.3 (Call and Signal of "Wide Ball").

11. Ball Not Dead

The ball does not become dead on the call of "No-ball".

12. Penalty for a No-Ball

A penalty of one run shall be awarded instantly on the call of "No-ball". Unless the call is revoked, this penalty shall stand even if a batsman is dismissed. It shall be in addition to any other runs scored, any boundary allowance and any other penalties awarded.

13. Runs Resulting from a No Ball – How Scored

The one run penalty for a no-ball shall be scored as a no-ball extra. If other penalty runs have been awarded to either side, these shall be scored as in Law 42.17 (Penalty Runs). Any runs completed by the batsmen or a boundary allowance shall be credited to the striker if the ball has been struck by the bat; otherwise they also shall be scored as no-ball extras. Apart from any award of a five-run penalty, all runs resulting from a no-ball, whether as no-ball extras or credited to the striker, shall be debited against the bowler.

14. No-Ball Not to Count

A no-ball shall not count as one of the over. See Law 22.4 (Balls Not to Count in the Over).

15. Out from a No-Ball

When "No-ball" has been called, neither batsman shall be out under any of the Laws except 33 (Handled the Ball), 34 (Hit the Ball Twice), 37 (Obstructing the Field) or 38 (Run Out).

LAW 25. WIDE BALL

1. Judging a Wide

(a) If the bowler bowls a ball, not being a no-ball, the umpire shall adjudge it a wide if according to the definition in (b) below, in his opinion, the ball passes wide of the striker where he is standing and would also have passed wide of him standing in a normal guard position.

(b) The ball will be considered as passing wide of the striker unless it is sufficiently within his reach for him to be able to hit it with his bat by means of a normal cricket stroke.

2. Delivery Not a Wide

The umpire shall not adjudge a delivery as being a wide

(a) if the striker, by moving, either

(i) causes the ball to pass wide of him, as defined in 1(b) above, or

(ii) brings the ball sufficiently within his reach to be able to hit it with his bat by means of a normal cricket stroke.

(b) if the ball touches the striker's bat or person.

3. Call and Signal of "Wide Ball"

(a) If the umpire adjudges a delivery to be a wide he shall call and signal "Wide ball" as soon as the ball passes the striker's wicket. It shall, however, be considered to have been a wide from the instant of delivery, even though it cannot be called wide until it passes the striker's wicket.

(b) The umpire shall revoke the call of "Wide ball" if there is then any contact between the ball and the striker's bat or person.

(c) The umpire shall revoke the call of "Wide ball" if a delivery is called a "No-ball". See Law 24.10 (No-Ball to Over-ride Wide).

4. Ball Not Dead

The ball does not become dead on the call of "Wide ball".

5. Penalty For a Wide

A penalty of one run shall be awarded instantly on the call of "Wide ball". Unless the call is revoked (see 3 above), this penalty shall stand even if a batsman is dismissed, and shall be in addition to any other runs scored, any boundary allowance and any other penalties awarded.

6. Runs Resulting From a Wide – How Scored

All runs completed by the batsmen or a boundary allowance, together with the penalty for the wide, shall be scored as wide balls. Apart from any award of a five-run penalty, all runs resulting from a wide ball shall be debited against the bowler.

7. Wide Not to Count

A wide shall not count as one of the over. See Law 22.4 (Balls Not to Count in the Over).

8. Out From a Wide

When "Wide ball" has been called, neither batsman shall be out under any of the Laws except 33 (Handled the Ball), 35 (Hit Wicket), 37 (Obstructing the Field), 38 (Run Out) or 39 (Stumped).

LAW 26. BYE AND LEG-BYE

1. Byes

If the ball, not being a no-ball or a wide, passes the striker without touching his bat or person, any runs completed by the batsmen or a boundary allowance shall be credited as byes to the batting side.

2. Leg-Byes

(a) If the ball, not having previously touched the striker's bat, strikes his person and the umpire is satisfied that the striker has either

    (i)   attempted to play the ball with his bat, or

    (ii) tried to avoid being hit by the ball,

then any runs completed by the batsmen or a boundary allowance shall be credited to the batting side as leg-byes, unless "No-ball" has been called.

(b) If "No-ball" has been called, the runs in (a) above, together with the penalty for the no-ball, shall be scored as no-ball extras.

3. Leg-Byes Not to Be Awarded

If in the circumstances of 2(a) above, the umpire considers that neither of the conditions (i) and (ii) has been met, then leg-byes will not be awarded. The batting side shall not be credited with any runs from that delivery apart from the one-run penalty for a no-ball if applicable. Moreover, no other penalties shall be awarded to the batting side when the ball is dead. See Law 42.17 (Penalty Runs).

The following procedure shall be adopted.

(a) If no run is attempted but the ball reaches the boundary, the umpire shall call and signal "Dead ball", and disallow the boundary.

(b) If runs are attempted and if:

    (i)   neither batsman is dismissed and the ball does not become dead for any other reason, the umpire shall call and signal "Dead ball" as soon as one run is completed or the ball reaches the boundary. The batsmen shall return to their original ends. The run or boundary shall be disallowed.

    (ii) before one run is completed or the ball reaches the boundary, a batsman is dismissed, or the ball becomes dead for any other reason, all the provisions of the Laws will apply, except that no runs and no penalties shall be credited to the batting side, other than the penalty for a no-ball if applicable.

LAW 27. APPEALS

1. Umpire Not to Give Batsman Out Without an Appeal

Neither umpire shall give a batsman out, even though he may be out under the Laws, unless appealed to by the fielding side. This shall not debar a batsman who is out under any of the Laws from leaving his wicket without an appeal having been made. Note, however, the provisions of 7 below.

2. Batsman Dismissed

A batsman is dismissed if either

> (a) he is given out by an umpire, on appeal, or

> (b) he is out under any of the Laws and leaves his wicket as in 1 above.

3. Timing of Appeals

For an appeal to be valid it must be made before the bowler begins his run-up or, if he has no run-up, his bowling action to deliver the next ball, and before "Time" has been called.

The call of "Over" does not invalidate an appeal made prior to the start of the following over provided "Time" has not been called. See Laws 16.2 (Call of Time) and 22.2 (Start of an Over).

4. Appeal of "How's That?"

An appeal "How's That?" covers all ways of being out.

5. Answering Appeals

The umpire at the bowler's end shall answer all appeals except those arising out of any of Laws 35 (Hit Wicket), 39 (Stumped) or 38 (Run Out) when this occurs at the striker's wicket. A decision "Not out" by one umpire shall not prevent the other umpire from giving a decision, provided that each is considering only matters within his jurisdiction.

When a batsman has been given not out, either umpire may, within his jurisdiction, answer a further appeal provided that it is made in accordance with 3 above.

6. Consultation By Umpires

Each umpire shall answer appeals on matters within his own jurisdiction. If an umpire is doubtful about any point that the other umpire may have been in a better position to see, he shall consult the latter on this point of fact and shall then give his decision. If, after consultation, there is still doubt remaining the decision shall be "Not out".

7. Batsman Leaving his Wicket Under a Misapprehension

An umpire shall intervene if satisfied that a batsman, not having been given out, has left his wicket under a misapprehension that he is out. The umpire intervening shall call and signal "Dead ball" to prevent any further action by the fielding side and shall recall the batsman.

8. Withdrawal of an Appeal

The captain of the fielding side may withdraw an appeal only with the consent of the umpire within whose jurisdiction the appeal falls and before the outgoing batsman has left the field of play. If such consent is given the umpire concerned shall, if applicable, revoke his decision and recall the batsman.

9. Umpire's Decision

An umpire may alter his decision provided that such alteration is made promptly. This apart, an umpire's decision, once made, is final.

LAW 28.   THE WICKET IS DOWN

1. Wicket Put Down

(a) The wicket is put down if a bail is completely removed from the top of the stumps, or a stump is struck out of the ground by:

  (i)   the ball.

  (ii) the striker's bat, whether he is holding it or has let go of it.

  (iii) the striker's person or by any part of his clothing or equipment becoming detached from his person.

  (iii) a fielder, with his hand or arm, providing that the ball is held in the hand or hands so used, or in the hand of the arm so used.

The wicket is also put down if a fielder pulls a stump out of the ground in the same manner.

(b) The disturbance of a bail, whether temporary or not, shall not constitute its complete removal from the top of the stumps, but if a bail in falling lodges between two of the stumps this shall be regarded as complete removal.

2. One Bail Off

If one bail is off, it shall be sufficient for the purpose of putting the wicket down to remove the remaining bail, or to strike or pull any of the three stumps out of the ground, in any of the ways stated in 1 above.

3. Remaking the Wicket

If the wicket is broken or put down while the ball is in play, the umpire shall not remake the wicket until the ball is dead. See Law 23 (Dead Ball). Any fielder, however, may

  (i) replace a bail or bails on top of the stumps.

  (ii) put back one or more stumps into the ground where the wicket originally stood.

4. Dispensing with Bails

If the umpires have agreed to dispense with bails, in accordance with Law 8.5 (Dispensing with Bails), the decision as to whether the wicket has been put down is one for the umpire concerned to decide.

(a) After a decision to play without bails, the wicket has been put down if the umpire concerned is satisfied that the wicket has been struck by the ball, by the striker's bat, person, or items of his clothing or equipment separated from his person as described in 1(a)(ii) or 1(a)(iii) above, or by a fielder with the hand holding the ball or with the arm of the hand holding the ball.

(b) If the wicket has already been broken or put down, (a) above shall apply to any stump or stumps still in the ground. Any fielder may replace a stump or stumps, in accordance with 3 above, in order to have an opportunity of putting the wicket down.

LAW 29.   BATSMAN OUT OF HIS GROUND

1. When Out of His Ground

A batsman shall be considered to be out of his ground unless his bat or some part of his person is grounded behind the popping crease at that end.

2. Which is a Batsman's Ground?

(a) If only one batsman is within a ground:

    (i) it is his ground.

    (ii) it remains his ground even if he is later joined there by the other batsman.

(b) If both batsmen are in the same ground and one of them subsequently leaves it, (a)(i) above applies.

(c) If there is no batsman in either ground, then each ground belongs to whichever of the batsmen is nearer to it, or, if the batsmen are level, to whichever was nearer to it immediately prior to their drawing level.

(d) If a ground belongs to one batsman, then, unless there is a striker with a runner, the other ground belongs to the other batsman irrespective of his position.

(e) When a batsman with a runner is striker, his ground is always that at the wicket-keeper's end. However, (a), (b), (c) and (d) above will still apply, but only to the runner and the non-striker, so that that ground will also belong to either the non-striker or the runner, as the case may be.

3. Position of Non-Striker

The batsman at the bowler's end should be positioned on the opposite side of the wicket to that from which the ball is being delivered, unless a request to do otherwise is granted by the umpire.

LAW 30.　BOWLED

1. Out Bowled

(a) The striker is out *Bowled* if his wicket is put down by a ball delivered by the bowler, not being a no-ball, even if it first touches his bat or person.

(b) Notwithstanding (a) above he shall not be out Bowled if before striking the wicket the ball has been in contact with any other player or with an umpire. He will, however, be subject to Laws 33 (Handled the Ball), 37 (Obstructing the Field), 38 (Run Out) and 39 (Stumped).

2. Bowled to Take Precedence

The striker is out Bowled if his wicket is put down as in 1 above, even though a decision against him for any other method of dismissal would be justified.

LAW 31.　TIMED OUT

1. Out Timed Out

(a) Unless "Time" has been called, the incoming batsman must be in position to take guard or for his partner to be ready to receive the next ball within three minutes of the fall of the previous wicket. If this requirement is not met, the incoming batsman will be out, *Timed Out*.

(b) In the event of protracted delay in which no batsman comes to the wicket, the umpires shall adopt the procedure of Law 21.3 (Umpires awarding a match). For the purposes of that Law the start of the action shall be taken as the expiry of the three minutes referred to above.

2. Bowler Does Not Get Credit

The bowler does not get credit for the wicket.

LAW 32. CAUGHT

1. Out Caught

The striker is out *Caught* if a ball delivered by the bowler, not being a no-ball, touches his bat without having previously been in contact with any member of the fielding side and is subsequently held by a fielder as a fair catch before it touches the ground.

2. Caught to Take Precedence

If the criteria of 1 above are met and the striker is not out Bowled, then he is out Caught, even though a decision against either batsman for another method of dismissal would be justified. Runs completed by the batsmen before the completion of the catch will not be scored. Note also Laws 21.6 (Winning Hit or Extras) and 42.17(b) (Penalty Runs).

3. A Fair Catch

A catch shall be considered to have been fairly made if:

(a) throughout the act of making the catch:

    (i) any fielder in contact with the ball is within the field of play. See 4 below.

    (ii) the ball is at no time in contact with any object grounded beyond the boundary.

The act of making the catch shall start from the time when a fielder first handles the ball and shall end when a fielder obtains complete control over the ball and over his own movements.

(b) the ball is hugged to the body of the catcher or accidentally lodges in his clothing or, in the case of the wicket-keeper, in his pads. However, it is not a fair catch if the ball lodges in a protective helmet worn by a fielder. See Law 23 (Dead Ball).

(c) The ball does not touch the ground, even though the hand holding it does so in effecting the catch.

(d) a fielder catches the ball after it has been lawfully struck more than once by the striker, but only if the ball has not touched the ground since first being struck.

(e) a fielder catches the ball after it has touched an umpire, another fielder or the other batsman. However, it is not a fair catch if the ball has touched a protective helmet worn by a fielder, although the ball remains in play.

(f) a fielder catches the ball in the air after it has crossed the boundary provided that:

    (i) he has no part of his person touching, or grounded beyond, the boundary at any time when he is in contact with the ball.

    (ii) the ball has not been grounded beyond the boundary. See Law 19.3 (Scoring a Boundary).

(g) the ball is caught off an obstruction within the boundary, provided it has not previously been decided to regard the obstruction as a boundary.

4. Fielder Within the Field of Play

(a) A fielder is not within the field of play if he touches the boundary or has any part of his person grounded beyond the boundary. See Law 19.3 (Scoring a Boundary).

(b) six runs shall be scored if a fielder:

    (i) has any part of his person touching, or grounded beyond, the boundary when he catches the ball.

    (ii) catches the ball and subsequently touches the boundary or grounds some part of his person over the boundary while carrying the ball but before completing the catch.

See Laws 19.3 (Scoring a Boundary) and 19.4 (Runs Allowed for Boundaries).

5. No Runs to Be Scored

If the striker is dismissed Caught, runs from that delivery completed by the batsmen before the completion of the catch shall not be scored, but any penalties awarded to either side when the ball is dead, if applicable, will stand. Law 18.12(a) (Batsman Returning to Wicket He Has Left) shall apply from the instant of the catch.

LAW 33.   HANDLED THE BALL

1. Out Handled the Ball

Either batsman is out *Handled the Ball* if he wilfully touches the ball while in play with a hand or hands not holding the bat unless he does so with the consent of the opposing side.

2. Not Out Handled the Ball

Notwithstanding 1 above, a batsman will not be out under this Law if:

(i) he handles the ball in order to avoid injury.

(ii) he uses his hand or hands to return the ball to any member of the fielding side without the consent of that side. Note, however, the provisions of Law 37.4 (Returning the Ball To a Member of the Fielding Side).

3. Runs Scored

If either batsman is dismissed under this Law, any runs completed before the offence, together with any penalty extras and the penalty for a no-ball or wide, if applicable, shall be scored. See Laws 18.10 (Runs Scored When a Batsman is Dismissed) and 42.17 (Penalty runs).

4. Bowler Does Not Get Credit

The bowler does not get credit for the wicket.

LAW 34.   HIT THE BALL TWICE

1. Out Hit the Ball Twice

(a) The striker is out *Hit The Ball Twice* if, while the ball is in play, it strikes any part of his person or is struck by his bat and, before the ball has been touched by a fielder, he wilfully strikes it again with his bat or person, other than a hand not holding the bat, except for the sole purpose of guarding his wicket. See 3 below and Laws 33 (Handled the Ball) and 37 (Obstructing the Field).

(b) For the purpose of this Law, "struck" or "strike" shall include contact with the person of the striker.

2. Not Out Hit the Ball Twice

Notwithstanding 1(a) above, the striker will not be out under this Law if:

(i) he makes a second or subsequent stroke in order to return the ball to any member of the fielding side. Note, however, the provisions of Law 37.4 (Returning the Ball to a Member of the Fielding Side).

(ii) he wilfully strikes the ball after it has touched a fielder. Note, however, the provisions of Law 37.1 (Out Obstructing the Field).

3. Ball Lawfully Struck More Than Once

Solely in order to guard his wicket and before the ball has been touched by a fielder, the striker may lawfully strike the ball more than once with his bat or with any part of his person other than a hand not holding the bat.

Notwithstanding this provision, the striker may not prevent the ball from being caught by making more than one stroke in defence of his wicket. See Law 37.3 (Obstructing a Ball from Being Caught).

4. Runs Permitted from Ball Lawfully Struck More Than Once

When the ball is lawfully struck more than once, as permitted in 3 above, only the first strike is to be considered in determining whether runs are to be allowed and how they are to be scored.

(a) If on the first strike the umpire is satisfied that either

(i) the ball first struck the bat, or

(ii) the striker attempted to play the ball with his bat, or

(iii) the striker tried to avoid being hit by the ball

then any penalties to the batting side that are applicable shall be allowed.

(b) If the conditions in (a) above are met then, if they result from overthrows, and only if they result from overthrows, runs completed by the batsmen or a boundary will be allowed in addition to any penalties that are applicable. They shall be credited to the striker if the first strike was with the bat. If the first strike was on the person of the striker they shall be scored as leg-byes or no-ball extras, as appropriate. See Law 26.2 (Leg-Byes).

(c) If the conditions of (a) above are met and there is no overthrow until after the batsmen have started to run, but before one run is completed:

(i) only subsequent completed runs or a boundary shall be allowed. The first run shall count as a completed run for this purpose only if the batsmen have not crossed at the instant of the throw.

(ii) if in these circumstances the ball goes to the boundary from the throw then, notwithstanding the provisions of Law 19.6 (Overthrow or Wilful Act of Fielder), only the boundary allowance shall be scored.

(iii) if the ball goes to the boundary as the result of a further overthrow, then runs completed by the batsmen after the first throw and before this final throw shall be added to the boundary allowance. The run in progress at the first throw will count only if they have not crossed at that moment; the run in progress at the final throw shall count only if they have crossed at that moment. Law 18.12 (Batsman Returning to Wicket He Has Left) shall apply as from the moment of the final throw.

(d) If, in the opinion of the umpire, none of the conditions in (a) above have been met then, whether there is an overthrow or not, the batting side shall not be credited with any runs from that delivery apart from the penalty for a no-ball if applicable. Moreover, no other penalties shall be awarded to the batting side when the ball is dead. See Law 42.17 (Penalty Runs).

5. Ball Lawfully Struck More Than Once – Action By The Umpire

If no runs are to be allowed, either in the circumstances of 4(d) above, or because there has been no overthrow and:

(a) if no run is attempted but the ball reaches the boundary, the umpire shall call and signal "Dead ball" and disallow the boundary.

(b) if the batsmen run and:

(i) neither batsman is dismissed and the ball does not become dead for any other reason, the umpire shall call and signal Dead Ball as soon as one run is completed or the ball reaches the boundary. The batsmen shall return to their original ends. The run or boundary shall be disallowed.

(ii) a batsman is dismissed, or if for any other reason the ball becomes dead before one run is completed or the ball reaches the boundary, all the provisions of the Laws will apply except that the award of penalties to the batting side shall be as laid down in 4(a) or 4(d) above as appropriate.

6. Bowler Does Not Get Credit

The bowler does not get credit for the wicket.

LAW 35.   HIT WICKET

1. Out Hit Wicket

The striker is out *Hit Wicket* if, while the ball is in play, his wicket is put down either by the striker's bat or person as described in Law 28.1(a)(ii) and (iii) (Wicket Put Down either:

(i) in the course of any action taken by him in preparing to receive or in receiving a delivery, or

(ii) in setting off for his first run immediately after playing, or playing at, the ball, or

(iii) if he makes no attempt to play the ball, in setting off for his first run, providing that in the opinion of the umpire this is immediately after he has had the opportunity of playing the ball, or

(iv) in lawfully making a second or further stroke for the purpose of guarding his wicket within the provisions of Law 34.3 (Ball Lawfully Struck More Than Once).

2. Not Out Hit Wicket

Notwithstanding 1 above, the batsman is not out under this Law should his wicket be put down in any of the ways referred to in 1 above if:

(a) it occurs after he has completed any action in receiving the delivery, other than as in 1(ii), (iii) or (iv) above.

(b) it occurs when he is in the act of running, other than in setting off immediately for his first run.

(c) it occurs when he is trying to avoid being run out or stumped.

(d) it occurs while he is trying to avoid a throw-in at any time.

(e) the bowler after starting his run-up, or his bowling action if he has no run-up, does not deliver the ball. In this case either umpire shall immediately call and signal "Dead ball". See Law 23.3 (Umpire calling and signalling "Dead ball").

(f) the delivery is a no-ball.

LAW 36. LEG BEFORE WICKET

1. Out LBW

The striker is out *LBW* in the circumstances set out below.

(a) The bowler delivers a ball, not being a no-ball and

(b) the ball, if it is not intercepted full pitch, pitches in line between wicket and wicket or on the off side of the striker's wicket, and

(c) the ball not having previously touched his bat, the striker intercepts the ball, either full-pitch or after pitching, with any part of his person, and

(d) the point of impact, even if above the level of the bails, either

　　(i) between wicket and wicket, or

　　(ii) is either between wicket and wicket or outside the line of the off stump, if the striker has made no genuine attempt to play the ball with his bat, and

(e) but for the interception, the ball would have hit the wicket.

2. Interception of the Ball

(a) In assessing points (c), (d) and (e) in 1 above, only the first interception is to be considered.

(b) In assessing point (e) in 1 above, it is to be assumed that the path of the ball before interception would have continued after interception, irrespective of whether the ball might have pitched subsequently or not.

3. Off Side of Wicket

The off side of the striker's wicket shall be determined by the striker's stance at the moment the ball comes into play for that delivery.

LAW 37.   OBSTRUCTING THE FIELD

1. Out Obstructing the Field

Either batsman is out *Obstructing the Field* if he wilfully obstructs or distracts the opposing side by word or action. It shall be regarded as obstruction if either batsman wilfully, and without the consent of the fielding side, strikes the ball with his bat or person, other than a hand not holding the bat, after the ball has touched a fielder. See 4 below.

2. Accidental Obstruction

It is for either umpire to decide whether any obstruction or distraction is wilful or not. He shall consult the other umpire if he has any doubt.

3. Obstructing a Ball from Being Caught

The striker is out should wilful obstruction or distraction by either batsman prevent a catch being made.

This shall apply even though the striker causes the obstruction in lawfully guarding his wicket under the provisions of Law 34.3 (Ball lawfully struck more than once).

4. Returning the Ball to a Member of the Fielding Side

Either batsman is out under this Law if, without the consent of the fielding side and while the ball is in play, he uses his bat or person to return the ball to any member of that side.

5. Runs Scored

If a batsman is dismissed under this Law, runs completed by the batsmen before the offence shall be scored, together with the penalty for a no-ball or a wide, if applicable. Other penalties that may be awarded to either side when the ball is dead shall also stand. See Law 42.17(b) (Penalty Runs).

If, however, the obstruction prevents a catch from being made, runs completed by the batsmen before the offence shall not be scored, but other penalties that may be awarded to either side when the ball is dead shall stand. See Law 42.17(b) (Penalty Runs).

6. Bowler Does Not Get Credit

The bowler does not get credit for the wicket.

LAW 38.   RUN OUT

1. Out Run Out

(a) Either batsman is out *Run Out*, except as in 2 below, if at any time while the ball is in play

(i) he is out of his ground and

(ii) his wicket is fairly put down by the opposing side.

(b) (a) above shall apply even though "No-ball" has been called and whether or not a run is being attempted, except in the circumstances of Law 39.3(b) (Not Out Stumped).

2. Batsman Not Run Out

Notwithstanding 1 above, a batsman is not out Run out if:

(a) he has been within his ground and has subsequently left it to avoid injury, when the wicket is put down.

(b) the ball has not subsequently been touched again by a fielder, after the bowler has entered his delivery stride, before the wicket is put down.

(c) the ball, having been played by the striker, or having come off his person, directly strikes a helmet worn by a fielder and without further contact with him or any other fielder rebounds directly on to the wicket. However, the ball remains in play and either batsman may be Run out in the circumstances of 1 above if a wicket is subsequently put down.

(d) he is out Stumped. See Law 39.1(b) (Out Stumped).

(e) he is out of his ground, not attempting a run and his wicket is fairly put down by the wicket-keeper without the intervention of another member of the fielding side, if "No-ball" has been called. See Law 39.3(b) (Not Out Stumped).

3. Which Batsman is Out

The batsman out in the circumstances of 1 above is the one whose ground is at the end where the wicket is put down. See Laws 2.8 (Transgression of the Laws by a Batsman Who Has a Runner) and 29.2 (Which is a Batsman's Ground).

4. Runs Scored

If a batsman is dismissed Run Out, the batting side shall score the runs completed before the dismissal, together with the penalty for a no-ball or a wide, if applicable. Other penalties to either side that may be awarded when the ball is dead shall also stand. See Law 42.17 (Penalty Runs).

If, however, a striker with a runner is himself dismissed Run Out, runs completed by the runner and the other batsman before the dismissal shall not be scored. The penalty for a no-ball or a wide and any other penalties to either side that may be awarded when the ball is dead shall stand. See Laws 2.8 (Transgression of the Laws by a Batsman Who Has a Runner) and 42.17(b) (Penalty Runs).

5. Bowler Does Not Get Credit

The bowler does not get credit for the wicket.

LAW 39. STUMPED

1. Out Stumped

(a) The striker is out *Stumped* if

    (i) he is out of his ground, and

    (ii) he is receiving a ball which is not a no-ball, and

    (iii) he is not attempting a run, and

    (iv) his wicket is put down by the wicket-keeper without the intervention of another member of the fielding side. Note Law 40.3 (Position of Wicket-Keeper).

(b) The striker is out Stumped if all the conditions of (a) above are satisfied, even though a decision of Run Out would be justified.

2. Ball Rebounding from Wicket-Keeper's Person

(a) If the wicket is put down by the ball, it shall be regarded as having been put down by the wicket-keeper if the ball

    (i) rebounds on to the stumps from any part of his person or equipment, other than a protective helmet, or

    (ii) has been kicked or thrown on to the stumps by the wicket-keeper.

(b) If the ball touches a helmet worn by the wicket-keeper, the ball is still in play but the striker shall not be out Stumped. He will, however, be liable to be Run Out in these circumstances if there is subsequent contact between the ball and any member of the fielding side. Note, however, 3 below.

3. Not Out Stumped

(a) If the striker is not out Stumped, he is liable to be out Run Out if the conditions of Law 38 (Run Out) apply, except as set out in (b) below.

(b) The striker shall not be out Run Out if he is out of his ground, not attempting a run, and his wicket is fairly put down by the wicket-keeper without the intervention of another member of the fielding side, if "No-ball" has been called.

LAW 40.   THE WICKET-KEEPER

1. Protective Equipment

The wicket-keeper is the only member of the fielding side permitted to wear gloves and external leg guards. If he does so, these are to be regarded as part of his person for the purposes of Law 41.2 (Fielding the Ball). If by his actions and positioning it is apparent to the umpires that he will not be able to discharge his duties as a wicket-keeper, he shall forfeit this right and also the right to be recognised as a wicket-keeper for the purposes of Laws 32.3 (A Fair Catch), 39 (Stumped), 41.1 (Protective Equipment), 41.5 (Limitation of On Side Fielders) and 41.6 (Fielders Not to Encroach on the Pitch).

2. Gloves

If the wicket-keeper wears gloves as permitted under 1 above, they shall have no webbing between fingers except that a single piece of flat non-stretch material may be inserted between index finger and thumb solely as a means of support. This insert shall not form a pouch when the hand is extended.

3. Position of Wicket-Keeper

The wicket-keeper shall remain wholly behind the wicket at the striker's end from the moment the ball comes into play until

    (a) a ball delivered by the bowler either

        (i) touches the bat or person of the striker, or

        (ii) passes the wicket at the striker's end

or

(b) the striker attempts a run.

In the event of the wicket-keeper contravening this Law, the umpire at the striker's end shall call and signal "No-ball" as soon as possible after the delivery of the ball.

4. Movement By the Wicket-keeper

It is unfair if a wicket-keeper standing back makes a significant movement towards the wicket after the ball comes into play and before it reaches the striker. In the event of such unfair movement by the wicket-keeper, either umpire shall call and signal "Dead ball". It will not be considered a significant movement if the wicket-keeper moves a few paces forward for a slower delivery.

5. Restriction on Actions of Wicket-Keeper

If the wicket-keeper interferes with the striker's right to play the ball and to guard his wicket, the striker shall not be out, except under Laws 33 (Handled the Ball), 34 (Hit the Ball Twice), 37 (Obstructing the Field) or 38 (Run Out).

6. Interference with Wicket-Keeper by Striker

If, in playing at the ball or in the legitimate defence of his wicket, the striker interferes with the wicket-keeper, he shall not be out, except as provided for in Law 37.3 (Obstructing a Ball from Being Caught)

LAW 41. THE FIELDER

1. Protective Equipment

No member of the fielding side other than the wicket-keeper shall be permitted to wear gloves or external leg guards. In addition, protection for the hand or fingers may be worn only with the consent of the umpires.

2. Fielding the Ball

A fielder may field the ball with any part of his person but if, while the ball is in play he wilfully fields it otherwise:

(a) the ball shall become dead and 5 penalty runs shall be awarded to the batting side. See Law 42.17 (Penalty Runs).

(b) the umpire shall inform the other umpire, the captain of the fielding side, the batsmen and, as soon as practicable, the captain of the batting side of what has occurred.

(c) the umpires together shall report the occurrence as soon as possible to the Executive of the fielding side and any governing body responsible for the match who shall take such action as is considered appropriate against the captain and player concerned.

3. Protective Helmets Belonging to the Fielding Side

Protective helmets, when not in use by fielders, shall only be placed, if above the surface, on the ground behind the wicket-keeper and in line with both sets of stumps. If a helmet belonging to the fielding side is on the ground within the field of play, and the ball while in play strikes it, the ball shall become dead. Five penalty runs shall then be awarded to the batting side. See Laws 18.11 (Runs Scored When Ball Becomes Dead) and 42.17 (Penalty Runs).

4. Penalty Runs Not Being Awarded

Notwithstanding 2 and 3 above, if from the delivery by the bowler the ball first struck the person of the striker and if, in the opinion of the umpire, the striker neither

    (i) attempted to play the ball with his bat, nor

    (ii) tried to avoid being hit by the ball,

then no award of five penalty runs shall be made and no other runs or penalties shall be credited to the batting side except the penalty for a "No-ball" if applicable. See Law 26.3 (Leg-Byes Not to Be Awarded).

5. Limitation of On-Side Fielders

At the instant of the bowler's delivery there shall not be more than two fielders, other than the wicket-keeper, behind the popping crease on the on side. A fielder will be considered to be behind the popping crease unless the whole of his person, whether grounded or in the air, is in front of this line. In the event of infringement of this Law by the fielding side, the umpire at the striker's end shall call and signal "No-ball".

6. Fielders Not to Encroach on the Pitch

While the ball is in play and until the ball has made contact with the bat or person of the striker, or has passed the striker's bat, no fielder, other than the bowler, may have any part of his person grounded on or extended over the pitch. In the event of infringement of this Law by any fielder other than the wicket-keeper, the umpire at the bowler's end shall call and signal "No-ball" as soon as possible after the delivery of the ball. Note, however, Law 40.3 (Position of Wicket-Keeper).

7. Movement by Fielders

Any significant movement by any fielder after the ball comes into play and before the ball reaches the striker is unfair. In the event of such unfair movement, either umpire shall call and signal "Dead ball". Note also the provisions of Law 42.4 (Deliberate Attempt to Distract Striker).

8. Definition of Significant Movement

    (a) For close fielders anything other than minor adjustments to stance or position in relation to the striker is significant.

    (b) In the outfield, fielders are permitted to move in towards the striker or striker's wicket, provided that 5 above is not contravened. Anything other than slight movement off line or away from the striker is to be considered significant.

    (c) For restrictions on movement by the wicket-keeper see Law 40.4 (Movement By Wicket-Keeper).

LAW 42.   FAIR AND UNFAIR PLAY

1. Fair and Unfair Play – Responsibility of Captains

The responsibility lies with the captains for ensuring that play is conducted within the spirit and traditions of the game, as described in The Preamble – The Spirit of Cricket, as well as within the Laws.

2. Fair and Unfair Play – Responsibility of Umpires

The umpires shall be the sole judges of fair and unfair play. If either umpire considers an action, not covered by the Laws, to be unfair, he shall intervene without appeal and, if the ball is in play, shall call and signal "Dead-ball" and implement the procedure as set out in 18 below. Otherwise the umpires shall not interfere with the progress of play, except as required to do so by the Laws.

3. The Match Ball – Changing Its Condition

(a) Any fielder may:

  (i) polish the ball provided that no artificial substance is used and that such polishing wastes no time.

  (ii) remove mud from the ball under the supervision of the umpire.

  (iii) dry a wet ball on a towel.

(b) It is unfair for anyone to rub the ball on the ground for any reason, interfere with any of the seams or the surface of the ball, use any implement, or take any other action whatsoever which is likely to alter the condition of the ball, except as permitted in (a) above.

(c) The umpires shall make frequent and irregular inspections of the ball.

(d) In the event of any fielder changing the condition of the ball unfairly, as set out in (b) above, the umpires after consultation shall:

  (i) change the ball forthwith. It shall be for the umpires to decide on the replacement ball, which shall, in their opinion, have had wear comparable with that which the previous ball had received immediately prior to the contravention.

  (ii) inform the batsmen that the ball has been changed.

  (iii) award five penalty runs to the batting side. See 17 below.

  (iv) inform the captain of the fielding side that the reason for the action was the unfair interference with the ball.

  (v) inform the captain of the batting side as soon as practicable of what has occurred.

  (vi) report the occurrence as soon as possible to the executive of the fielding side and any governing body responsible for the match, who shall take such action as is considered appropriate against the captain and team concerned.

(e) If there is any further instance of unfairly changing the condition of the ball in that innings, the umpires after consultation shall:

  (i) repeat the procedure in (d)(i), (ii) and (iii) above.

  (ii) inform the captain of the fielding side of the reason for the action taken and direct him to take off forthwith the bowler who delivered the immediately preceding ball. The bowler thus taken off shall not be allowed to bowl again in that innings.

  (iii) inform the captain of the batting side as soon as practicable of what has occurred.

  (iv) report the occurrence as soon as possible to the executive of the fielding side and any governing body responsible for the match, who shall take such action as is considered appropriate against the captain and team concerned.

4. Deliberate Attempt to Distract Striker

It is unfair for any member of the fielding side deliberately to attempt to distract the striker while he is preparing to receive or receiving a delivery.

(a) If either umpire considers that any action by a member of the fielding side is such an attempt, at the first instance he shall:

    (i) immediately call and signal "Dead ball".

    (ii) warn the captain of the fielding side that the action is unfair and indicate that this is a first and final warning.

    (iii) inform the other umpire and the batsmen of what has occurred. Neither batsman shall be dismissed from that delivery and the ball shall not count as one of the over.

(b) If there is any further such deliberate attempt in that innings, by any member of the fielding side, the procedures, other than warning, as set out in (a) above shall apply. Additionally, the umpire at the bowler's end shall:

    (i) award five penalty runs to the batting side. See 17 below.

    (ii) inform the captain of the fielding side of the reason for this action and, as soon as practicable, inform the captain of the batting side.

    (iii) report the occurrence, together with the other umpire, as soon as possible to the executive of the fielding side and any governing body responsible for the match, who shall take such action as is considered appropriate against the captain and player or players concerned.

5. Deliberate Distraction or Obstruction of Batsman

In addition to 4 above, it is unfair for any member of the fielding side, by word or action, wilfully to attempt to distract or to obstruct either batsman after the striker has received the ball.

(a) It is for either one of the umpires to decide whether any distraction or obstruction is wilful or not.

(b) If either umpire considers that a member of the fielding side has wilfully caused or attempted to cause such a distraction or obstruction he shall

    (i) immediately call and signal "Dead ball".

    (ii) inform the captain of the fielding side and the other umpire of the reason for the call.

Additionally,

    (iii) neither batsman shall be dismissed from that delivery.

    (iv) Five penalty runs shall be awarded to the batting side. See 17 below. In this instance, the run in progress shall be scored, whether or not the batsmen had crossed at the instant of the call. See Law 18.11 (Runs Scored When Ball Becomes Dead).

    (v) the umpire at the bowler's end shall inform the captain of the fielding side of the reason for this action and, as soon as practicable, inform the captain of the batting side.

(vi) the umpires shall report the occurrence as soon as possible to the executive of the fielding side and any governing body responsible for the match, who shall take such action as is considered appropriate against the captain and player or players concerned.

6. Dangerous and Unfair Bowling

(a) Bowling of Fast Short-Pitched Balls

(i) The bowling of fast short-pitched balls is dangerous and unfair if the umpire at the bowler's end considers that by their repetition and taking into account their length, height and direction they are likely to inflict physical injury on the striker, irrespective of the protective equipment he may be wearing. The relative skill of the striker shall be taken into consideration.

(ii) Any delivery which, after pitching, passes or would have passed over head height of the striker standing upright at the crease, although not threatening physical injury, is unfair and shall be considered as part of the repetition sequence in (i) above. The umpire shall call and signal "No-ball" for each such delivery.

(b) Bowling of High Full-Pitched Balls

(i) Any delivery, other than a slow paced one, which passes or would have passed on the full above waist height of the striker standing upright at the crease is to be deemed dangerous and unfair, whether or not it is likely to inflict physical injury on the striker.

(ii) A slow delivery which passes or would have passed on the full above shoulder height of the striker standing upright at the crease is to be deemed dangerous and unfair, whether or not it is likely to inflict physical injury on the striker.

7. Dangerous and Unfair Bowling – Action by the Umpire

(a) In the event of dangerous and/or unfair bowling, as defined in 6 above, by any bowler, except as in 8 below, at the first instance the umpire at the bowler's end shall call and signal "No-ball" and, when the ball is dead, caution the bowler, inform the other umpire, the captain of the fielding side and the batsmen of what has occurred. This caution shall continue to apply throughout the innings.

(b) If there is a second instance of such dangerous and/or unfair bowling by the same bowler in that innings, the umpire at the bowler's end shall repeat the above procedure and indicate to the bowler that this is a final warning. Both the above caution and final warning shall continue to apply even though the bowler may later change ends.

(c) Should there be a further instance by the same bowler in that innings, the umpire shall:

(i) call and signal "No-ball".

(ii) direct the captain, when the ball is dead, to take the bowler off forthwith. The over shall be completed by another bowler, who shall neither have bowled the previous over nor be allowed to bowl the next over. The bowler thus taken off shall not be allowed to bowl again in that innings.

(iii) report the occurrence to the other umpire, the batsmen and, as soon as practicable, the captain of the batting side.

(iv) report the occurrence, with the other umpire, as soon as possible to the Executive of the fielding side and to any governing body responsible for the match, who shall take such action as is considered appropriate against the captain and bowler concerned.

8. Deliberate Bowling of High Full-Pitched Balls

If the umpire considers that a high full pitch which is deemed to be dangerous and unfair, as defined in 6(b) above, was deliberately bowled, then the caution and warning prescribed in 7 above shall be dispensed with. The umpire shall:

(a) call and signal "No-ball".

(b) direct the captain, when the ball is dead, to take the bowler off forthwith.

(c) implement the remainder of the procedure as laid down in 7(c) above.

9. Time-Wasting by the Fielding Side

It is unfair for any member of the fielding side to waste time.

(a) If the captain of the fielding side wastes time, or allows any member of his side to waste time, or if the progress of an over is unnecessarily slow, at the first instance the umpire shall call and signal "Dead ball" if necessary and

(i) warn the captain, and indicate that this is a first and final warning.

(ii) inform the other umpire and the batsmen of what has occurred.

(b) If there is any further waste of time in that innings, by any member of the fielding side, the umpire shall either

(i) if the waste of time is not during the course of an over, award five penalty runs to the batting side. See 17 below, or

(ii) if the waste of time is during the course of an over, when the ball is dead, direct the captain to take the bowler off forthwith. If applicable, the over shall be completed by another bowler, who shall neither have bowled the previous over nor be allowed to bowl the next over. The bowler thus taken off shall not be allowed to bowl again in that innings.

(iii) inform the other umpire, the batsmen and, as soon as practicable, the captain of the batting side of what has occurred.

(iv) report the occurrence, with the other umpire, as soon as possible to the executive of the fielding side and to any governing body responsible for the match, who shall take such action as is considered appropriate against the captain and team concerned.

10. Batsman Wasting Time

It is unfair for a batsman to waste time. In normal circumstances the striker should always be ready to take strike when the bowler is ready to start his run-up.

(a) Should either batsman waste time by failing to meet this requirement, or in any other way, the following procedure shall be adopted. At the first instance, either before the bowler starts his run-up or when the ball is dead, as appropriate, the umpire shall:

(i) warn the batsman and indicate that this is a first and final warning. This warning shall continue to apply throughout the innings. The umpire shall so inform each incoming batsman.

(ii) inform the other umpire, the other batsman and the captain of the fielding side of what has occurred.

(iii) inform the captain of the batting side as soon as practicable.

(b) if there is any further time wasting by any batsman in that innings, the umpire shall, at the appropriate time while the ball is dead:

(i) award five penalty runs to the fielding side. See 17 below.

(ii) inform the other umpire, the other batsman, the captain of the fielding side and, as soon as practicable, the captain of the batting side of what has occurred.

(iii) report the occurrence, with the other umpire, as soon as possible to the executive of the batting side and to any governing body responsible for the match, who shall take such action as is considered appropriate against the captain and player or players and, if appropriate, the team concerned.

11. Damaging the Pitch – Area to be Protected

(a) It is incumbent on all players to avoid unnecessary damage to the pitch. It is unfair for any player to cause deliberate damage to the pitch.

(b) An area of the pitch, to be referred to as "the protected area", is defined as that area contained within a rectangle bounded at each end by imaginary lines parallel to the popping creases and 5ft/1.52m in front of each and on the sides by imaginary lines, one each side of the imaginary line joining the centres of the two middle stumps, each parallel to it and 1ft/30.48cm from it.

12. Bowler Running on the Protected Area After Delivering the Ball

(a) If the bowler, after delivering the ball, runs on the protected area as defined in 11(b) above, the umpire shall at the first instance, and when the ball is dead:

(i) caution the bowler. This caution shall continue to apply throughout the innings.

(ii) inform the other umpire, the captain of the fielding side and the batsmen of what has occurred.

(b) If, in that innings, the same bowler runs on the protected area again after delivering the ball, the umpire shall repeat the above procedure, indicating that this is a final warning.

(c) If, in that innings, the same bowler runs on the protected area a third time after delivering the ball, when the ball is dead the umpire shall:

(i) direct the captain of the fielding side to take the bowler off forthwith. If applicable, the over shall be completed by another bowler, who shall neither have bowled the previous over nor be allowed to bowl the next over. The bowler thus taken off shall not be allowed to bowl again in that innings.

(ii) inform the other umpire, the batsmen and, as soon as practicable, the captain of the batting side of what has occurred.

(iii) report the occurrence, with the other umpire, as soon as possible to the executive of the fielding side and to any governing body responsible for the match, who shall take such action as is considered appropriate against the captain and bowler concerned.

13. Fielder Damaging the Pitch

(a) If any fielder causes avoidable damage to the pitch, other than as in 12(a) above, at the first instance the umpire shall, when the ball is dead:

(i) caution the captain of the fielding side, indicating that this is a first and final warning. This caution shall continue to apply throughout the innings.

(ii) inform the other umpire and the batsmen.

(b) If there is any further avoidable damage to the pitch by any fielder in that innings, the umpire shall, when the ball is dead:

(i) award five penalty runs to the batting side. See 17 below.

(ii) inform the other umpire, the batsmen, the captain of the fielding side and, as soon as practicable, the captain of the batting side of what has occurred.

(iii) report the occurrence, with the other umpire, as soon as possible to the executive of the fielding side and any governing body responsible for the match, who shall take such action as is considered appropriate against the captain and player or players concerned.

14. Batsman Damaging the Pitch

(a) If either batsman causes avoidable damage to the pitch, at the first instance the umpire shall, when the ball is dead:

(i) caution the batsman. This caution shall continue to apply throughout the innings. The umpire shall so inform each incoming batsman.

(ii) inform the other umpire, the other batsman, the captain of the fielding side and, as soon as practicable, the captain of the batting side.

(b) If there is a second instance of avoidable damage to the pitch by any batsman in that innings:

(i) the umpire shall repeat the above procedure, indicating that this is a final warning.

(ii) additionally he shall disallow all runs to the batting side from that delivery other than the penalty for a no-ball or a wide, if applicable. The batsmen shall return to their original ends.

(c) If there is any further avoidable damage to the pitch by any batsman in that innings, the umpire shall, when the ball is dead:

(i) disallow all runs to the batting side from that delivery other than the penalty for a no-ball or a wide, if applicable.

(ii) additionally award five penalty runs to the fielding side. See 17 below.

(iii) inform the other umpire, the other batsman, the captain of the fielding side and, as soon as practicable, the captain of the batting side of what has occurred.

(iv) report the occurrence, with the other umpire, as soon as possible to the executive of the batting side and any governing body responsible for the match, who shall take such action as is considered appropriate against the captain and player or players concerned.

15. Bowler Attempting to Run Out Non-striker Before Delivery

The bowler is permitted, before entering his delivery stride, to attempt to run out the non-striker. The ball shall not count in the over. The umpire shall call and signal "Dead ball" as soon as possible if the bowler fails in the attempt to run out the non-striker.

16. Batsmen Stealing a Run

It is unfair for the batsmen to attempt to steal a run during the bowler's run up. Unless the bowler attempts to run out either batsman – see 15 above and Law 24.4 (Bowler Throwing Towards Striker's End Before Delivery) – the umpire shall:

(i) call and signal "Dead ball" as soon as the batsmen cross in any such attempt.

(ii) return the batsmen to their original ends.

(iii) award five penalty runs to the fielding side. See 17 below.

(iv) inform the other umpire, the batsmen, the captain of the fielding side and, as soon as practicable, the captain of the batting side of the reason for the action taken.

(v) report the occurrence, with the other umpire, as soon as possible to the executive of the batting side and any governing body responsible for the match, who shall take such action as is considered appropriate against the captain and player or players concerned.

17. Penalty Runs

(a) When penalty runs are awarded to either side, when the ball is dead the umpire shall signal the penalty runs to the scorers as laid down in Law 3.14 (Signals).

(b) Notwithstanding any provisions elsewhere in the Laws, penalty runs shall not be awarded once the match is concluded as defined in Law 16.9 (Conclusion of a Match).

(c) When five penalty runs are awarded to the batting side, under either Law 2.6 (Player Returning Without Permission) or Law 41 (The Fielder) or under 3, 4, 5, 9 or 13 above, then:

(i) they shall be scored as penalty extras and shall be in addition to any other penalties.

(ii) they shall not be regarded as runs scored from either the immediately preceding delivery or the following delivery, and shall be in addition to any runs from those deliveries.

(iii) the batsmen shall not change ends solely by reason of the five-run penalty.

(d) When five penalty runs are awarded to the fielding side, under Law 18.5(b) (Deliberate Short Runs), or under 10, 14 or 16 above, they shall be added as penalty extras to that side's total of runs in its most recently completed innings. If the fielding side has not completed an innings, the five penalty extras shall be added to its next innings.

18. Players' Conduct

If there is any breach of the Spirit of the Game by a player failing to comply with the instructions of an umpire, or criticising his decisions by word or action, or showing dissent, or generally behaving in a manner which might bring the game into disrepute, the umpire concerned shall immediately report the matter to the other umpire.

The umpires together shall:

(i) inform the player's captain of the occurrence, instructing the latter to take action.

(ii) warn him of the gravity of the offence, and tell him that it will be reported to higher authority.

(iii) report the occurrence as soon as possible to the executive of the player's team and any governing body responsible for the match, who shall take such action as is considered appropriate against the captain and player or players, and, if appropriate, the team concerned.

REGULATIONS OF THE INTERNATIONAL CRICKET COUNCIL

Extracts

1. Standard Playing Conditions

In 2001, the ICC Cricket Committee amended its standard playing conditions for all Tests and one-day internationals to include the new Laws of Cricket. The following playing conditions were to apply for three years from September 1, 2001:

Duration of Test Matches

Test matches shall be of five days' scheduled duration and of two innings per side. The two participating countries may:

(a) Provide for a rest day during the match, and/or a reserve day after the scheduled days of play.

(b) Play on any scheduled rest day, conditions and circumstances permitting, should a full day's play be lost on any day prior to the rest day.

(c) Play on any scheduled reserve day, conditions and circumstances permitting, should a full day's play be lost on any day. Play shall not take place on more than five days.

(d) Make up time lost in excess of five minutes in each day's play due to circumstances outside the game, other than acts of God.

Hours of Play, Intervals and Minimum Overs in the Day

1. Start and cessation times shall be determined by the home board, subject to there being six hours scheduled for play per day (Pakistan a minimum of five and a half hours).

(a) Play shall continue on each day until the completion of a minimum number of overs or until the scheduled or rescheduled cessation time, whichever is the later. The minimum number of overs to be completed, unless an innings ends or an interruption occurs, shall be:

    (i) on days other than the last day - a minimum of 90 overs (or a minimum of 15 overs per hour).

    (ii) on the last day - a minimum of 75 overs (or 15 overs per hour) for playing time other than the last hour when a minimum of 15 overs shall be bowled. All calculations with regard to suspensions of play or the start of a new innings shall be based on one over for each full four minutes. (Fractions are to be ignored in all calculations except where there is a change of innings in a day's play, when the over in progress at the conclusion shall be rounded up.) If, however, at any time after 30 minutes of the last hour have elapsed both captains (the batsmen at the wicket may act for their captain) accept that there is no prospect of a result to the match, they may agree to cease play at that time.

    (iii) Subject to weather and light, except in the last hour of the match, in the event of play being suspended for any reason other than normal intervals, the playing time on that day shall be extended by the amount of time lost up to a maximum of one hour. The minimum number of overs to be bowled shall be in accordance with the provisions of this clause (i.e. a minimum of 15 overs per hour) and the cessation time shall be rescheduled accordingly.

(iv) If any time is lost and cannot be made up under (a)(iii), additional time of up to a maximum of one hour per day shall be added to the scheduled playing hours for the next day, and subsequent day(s) as required. Where appropriate, the first 30 minutes (or less) of this additional time shall be added before the scheduled start of the first session and the remainder to the last session. Where it is not possible to add this time before the scheduled start, the timing of the lunch and tea intervals will be adjusted to provide a scheduled two-and-a-half-hour session and not affect the start time. On any day's play, except the last day, when the scheduled hours have been completed but the required number of overs have not been bowled, and weather or bad light causes play to be abandoned, the remaining overs shall be made up on the next or subsequent days. On any one day, a maximum of 15 additional overs shall be permitted. When additional time is added to subsequent day(s), no scheduled day's play shall exceed seven hours. The length of each session is subject to Law 15. Timings can be altered at any time on any day if time is lost, not necessarily on that day. The captains, umpires and referee can agree different timings under those circumstances before play starts on any day.

(b) When an innings ends, a minimum number of overs shall be bowled from the start of the new innings. The number of overs to be bowled shall be calculated at the rate of one over for each full four minutes to enable a minimum of 90 overs to be bowled in a day. The last hour of the match shall be excluded from this calculation (see (a) (ii)).

Where a change of innings occurs during a day's play, in the event of the team bowling second being unable to complete its overs by the scheduled cessation time, play shall continue until the required number of overs have been completed.

2. The umpires may decide to play 30 minutes (a minimum eight overs) extra time at the end of any day (other than the last day) if requested by either captain if, in the umpires' opinion, it would bring about a definite result on that day. If the umpires do not believe a result can be achieved, no extra time shall be allowed. If it is decided to play such extra time, the whole period shall be played out even though the possibility of finishing the match may have disappeared before the full period has expired. Only the actual amount of playing time up to the maximum 30 minutes' extra time by which play is extended on any day shall be deducted from the total number of hours of play remaining and the match shall end earlier on the final day by that amount of time.

Use of Lights

If, in the opinion of the umpires, natural light is deteriorating to an unfit level, they shall authorise the ground authorities to use the available artificial lighting so that the match can continue in acceptable conditions. The lights are only to be used to enable a full day's play to be completed as provided for in Clause 1 above. In the event of power failure or lights malfunction, the existing provisions of Clause 1 shall apply.

Dangerous and Unfair Bowling: The Bowling of Fast, Short-Pitched Balls: Law 42.6

1.   (a) A bowler shall be limited to two fast, short-pitched deliveries per over.

(b) A fast, short-pitched ball is defined as a ball which passes or would have passed above the shoulder height of the batsman standing upright at the crease, but not clearly above the batsman's head so that it is so high it prevents him from being able to hit it with his bat by means of a normal cricket stroke.

(c) The umpire at the bowler's end shall advise the bowler and the batsman on strike when each fast short-pitched ball has been bowled.

(d) For the purpose of this regulation, a ball that passes clearly above head height, other than a fast, short-pitched ball, that prevents the batsman from being able to hit it with his bat by means of a normal cricket stroke shall be a no-ball.

(e) Any fast, short-pitched delivery called no-ball under this condition shall count as one of the allowable short-pitched deliveries in that over.

2. In the event of a bowler bowling more than two fast, short-pitched deliveries in an over, the umpire at the bowler's end shall call and signal "no-ball" on each occasion. The umpire shall call and signal "no-ball" and then tap the head with the other hand.

If a bowler delivers a third fast, short-pitched ball in one over, the umpire must call no-ball and then invoke the procedures of caution, final warning, action against the bowler and reporting as set out in Law 42.7. The umpires will report the matter to the ICC referee who shall take such action as is considered appropriate against the captain and bowler concerned. The above Regulation is not a substitute for Law 42.6 (as amended below), which umpires are able to apply at any time:

The bowling of fast, short-pitched balls is unfair if the umpire at the bowler's end considers that, by their repetition and taking into account their length, height and direction, they are likely to inflict physical injury on the striker, irrespective of the protective clothing and equipment he may be wearing. The relative skill of the striker shall also be taken into consideration.

The umpire at the bowler's end shall adopt the procedures of caution, final warning, action against the bowler and reporting as set out in Law 42.7. The ICC referee shall take any further action considered appropriate against the captain and bowler concerned.

New Ball: Law 5.4

The captain of the fielding side shall have the choice of taking a new ball any time after 80 overs have been bowled with the previous ball. The umpires shall indicate to the batsmen and the scorers whenever a new ball is taken into play.

Ball Lost or Becoming Unfit for Play: Law 5.5

The following shall apply in addition to Law 5.5:

However, if the ball needs to be replaced after 110 overs for any of the reasons above, it shall be replaced by a new ball. If the ball is to be replaced, the umpires shall inform the batsmen.

Judging a Wide: Law 25.1

Law 25.1 will apply, but in addition:

For bowlers attempting to utilise the rough outside a batsman's leg stump, not necessarily as a negative tactic, the strict limited-overs wide interpretation shall be applied. For bowlers whom umpires consider to be bowling down the leg side as a negative tactic, the strict limited-overs wide interpretation shall be applied.

Practice on the Field: Law 17

In addition to Law 17.1:

> The use of the square for practice on any day of any match will be restricted to any netted practice area on the square set aside for that purpose.

Fieldsman Leaving the Field: Law 2.5

If a fielder fails to take the field with his side at the start of the match or at any later time, or leaves the field during a session of play, the umpire shall be informed of the reason for his absence, and he shall not thereafter come on to the field during a session without the consent of the umpire. The umpire shall give such consent as soon as practicable. If the player is absent from the field longer than eight minutes, he shall not be permitted to bowl in that innings after his return until he has been on the field for at least that length of playing time for which he was absent. In the event of a follow-on, this restriction will, if necessary, continue into the second innings. Nor shall he be permitted to bat unless or until, in the aggregate, he has returned to the field and/or his side's innings has been in progress for at least that length of playing time for which he has been absent or, if earlier, when his side has lost five wickets. The restrictions shall not apply if he has suffered an external blow (as opposed to an internal injury such as a pulled muscle) while participating earlier in the match and consequently been forced to leave the field, nor if he has been absent for exceptional and acceptable reasons (other than injury or illness).

ICC CODE OF CONDUCT

1. The captains are responsible at all times for ensuring that play is conducted within the spirit of the game as well as within the Laws.

2. Players and/or team officials shall at no time engage in conduct unbecoming to their status which could bring them or the game of cricket into disrepute.

3. Players and/or team officials must at all times accept the umpire's decision and not show dissent at the umpire's decision.

4. Players and/or team officials shall not verbally abuse, assault, intimidate or attempt to assault or intimidate any umpire, spectator, referee, player or team official. Nor shall any player or team official engage in any conduct towards or speak to any other player, umpire, spectator, referee or team official in a manner which offends, insults, humiliates, intimidates, disparages or vilifies the other person on the basis of that other person's race, religion, colour, descent or national or ethnic origin.

5. Players and/or team officials shall not use crude or abusive language nor make offensive gestures.

6. Players and/or team officials shall not disclose or comment publicly upon any alleged or actual breach of this Code, whether by themselves or any other person to whom the Code applies, or upon any hearing, report or decision arising from such an alleged or proven breach.

7. Players and/or team officials shall not at any time breach any ICC regulation which may be in force from time to time.

8. Players and/or team officials shall not make any public pronouncement or media comment which is detrimental either to the game of cricket in general; or to a particular tour whether or not they are personally involved with the tour; or to relations between the home boards of competing teams.

9. Players and/or team officials shall be required to report to the captain and/or team manager any approach made to them by a bookmaker or any other corrupt approach or knowledge of such approach made to any other player or team official.

10. Players and/or team officials shall not bet on matches nor otherwise engage in conduct of the nature described in Appendix A of the ICC Code of Conduct Commission Terms of Reference and in the paragraphs below. For conduct in breach of this rule, the penalties to be considered are set out below, for individuals who have:

    i. Bet on any match or series of matches, or on any connected event, in which such player, umpire, referee, team official or administrator took part or in which the Member country or any such individual was represented (penalty (a));

    ii. Induced or encouraged any other person to bet on any match or series of matches or on any connected event or to offer the facility for such bets to be placed (penalty (b));

    iii. Gambled or entered into any other form of financial speculation on any match or on any connected event (penalty (a));

    iv. Induced or encouraged any other person to gamble or enter into any other form of financial speculation on any match or any connected event (penalty (b));

    v. Was a party to contriving or attempting to contrive the result of any match or the occurrence of any connected event (penalty (c));

    vi. Failed to perform on his merits in any match owing to an arrangement relating to betting on the outcome of any match or on the occurrence of any connected event (penalty (c));

    vii. Induced or encouraged any other player not to perform on his merits in any match owing to any such arrangement (penalty (c));

    viii. Received from another person any money, benefit or other reward (whether financial or otherwise) for the provision of any information concerning the weather, the teams, the state of the ground, the status of, or the outcome of, any match or the occurrence of any connected event unless such information has been provided to a newspaper or other form of media in accordance with an obligation entered into in the normal course and disclosed in advance to the cricket authority of the relevant Member country (penalty (b));

    ix. Received any money, benefit or other reward (whether financial or otherwise) which could bring him or the game of cricket into disrepute (penalty (d));

    x. Provided any money, benefit or other reward (whether financial or otherwise) which could bring the game of cricket into disrepute (penalty (d));

    xi. Received any approaches from another person to engage in conduct such as that described above, and has failed to disclose the same to the chief executive officer of the home board of his member country or to the ICC chief executive (penalty (e)); or

    xii. Is aware that any other player or individual has engaged in conduct, or received approaches, such as described above, and has failed to disclose the same to the chief executive officer of the home board of his member country or to the ICC chief executive (penalty (e));

    xiii. Has received or is aware that any other person has received threats of any nature which might induce him to engage in conduct, or acquiesce in any proposal made by an approach, such as described above, and has failed to disclose the same to the chief executive officer of the home board of his member country or to the ICC chief executive (penalty (e));

xiv. Has engaged in any conduct which, in the opinion of the Executive Board, relates directly or indirectly to any of the above paragraphs (i to xiii) and is prejudicial to the interests of the game of cricket (penalty (e)).

Penalties:

(a) Ban for a minimum of two years and a maximum of five years. In addition, a fine may be imposed, the amount to be assessed in the circumstances.

(b) Ban for a minimum of two years and a maximum of five years if a bet was placed directly or indirectly for the benefit of the individual; otherwise, a ban for a minimum of 12 months. In addition, a fine may be imposed, the amount to be assessed in the circumstances.

(c) Ban for life (a minimum of 20 years).

(d) Ban for a minimum of two years and a maximum of life. In addition, a fine may be imposed, the amount to be assessed in the circumstances.

(e) Ban for a minimum of one year and a maximum of five years. In addition, a fine may be imposed, the amount to be assessed in the circumstances.

Note: The terms of Appendix A are almost identical to paragraphs (i) to (xiv) above, except that they are stated to apply to any player, umpire, referee, team official or administrator connected with any Test, one-day international or representative match after July 1, 1993.

11. Players and/or team officials shall not use or in any way be concerned in the use or distribution of illegal drugs.

AUSTRALIAN CRICKET BOARD
PLAYING CONDITIONS, 2001-02

Note: This section is an abridged version of the full Playing Conditions Booklet of the Australian Cricket Board. Some parts have been omitted.

TEST MATCH
PLAYING CONDITIONS 2001-02

Except as modified for one-day internationals and in the section on other tour matches, these playing conditions shall apply to all tour matches.

1. Laws of Cricket

Except as varied hereunder the Laws of Cricket (2000 Code) shall apply.

2. Duration of Matches

Test matches shall be of five days' scheduled duration, and of two innings per side. The two participating countries may:

(a) Provide for a rest day during the match, and/or a reserve day after the scheduled days of play.

(b) Play on any scheduled rest day, conditions and circumstances permitting, should a full day's play be lost on any day prior to the rest day.

(c) Play on any scheduled reserve day, conditions and circumstances permitting, should a full day's play be lost on any day. Play shall not take place on more than five days.

(d) Make up time lost in excess of five minutes in each day's play due to circumstances outside the game other than acts of God.

Other tour matches shall be as scheduled as in the tour program authorised by the Australian Cricket Board.

3. Hours of Play, Intervals and Minimum Overs in the Day

3.1 Start and Cessation Times

3.1.1 Test Series
New South Wales, South Australia, Tasmania and Victoria

Session 1	11.00 a.m. – 1.00 p.m.
Lunch	1.00 p.m. – 1.40 p.m.
Session 2	1.40 p.m. – 3.40 p.m.
Tea	3.40 p.m. – 4.00 p.m.
Session 3	4.00 p.m. – 6.00 p.m.

Queensland

Session 1	10.00 a.m. – 12.00 p.m.
Lunch	12.00 p.m. – 12.40 p.m.
Session 2	12.40 p.m. – 2.40 p.m.
Tea	2.40 p.m. – 3.00 p.m.
Session 3	3.00 p.m. – 5.00 p.m.

Western Australia

Session 1	10.30 a.m. – 12.30 p.m.
Lunch	12.30 p.m. – 1.10 p.m.
Session 2	1.10 p.m. – 3.10 p.m.
Tea	3.10 p.m. – 3.30 p.m.
Session 3	3.30 p.m. – 5.30 p.m.

3.1.2 Minimum Overs in the Day in Test Matches

(a) Play shall continue on each day until the completion of a minimum number of overs or until the scheduled or re-scheduled cessation time, whichever is the later. The minimum number of overs to be completed, unless an innings ends or an interruption occurs, shall be:

(i) On days other than the last day – a minimum of 90 overs (or a minimum of 15 overs per hour).

(ii) On the last day – a minimum of 75 overs (or a minimum of 15 overs per hour) for playing time other than the last hour when Clause (e) below shall apply.

(iii) **Additional Hour:** Subject to weather and light, except in the last hour of the match, in the event of play being suspended for any reason other than normal intervals, the playing time on that day shall be extended by the amount of time lost up to a maximum of one hour. In these circumstances, the minimum number of overs to be bowled shall be in accordance with the provisions of this clause, i.e. a minimum of 15 overs per hour and the cessation time shall be re-scheduled accordingly.

(iv) If play has been suspended for 30 minutes or more prior to the commencement of the scheduled tea interval, the tea interval shall be delayed for half an hour.

(v) If any time is lost and cannot be made up under (iii) above, additional time of up to a maximum of one hour per day shall be added to the scheduled playing hours for the next day, and subsequent day(s) as required (to make up as much lost time as possible). Where appropriate the first 30 minutes (or less) of this additional time shall be added prior to the scheduled start of the first session, and the remainder shall be added to the last session.

In circumstances where it is not possible to add this additional time prior to the scheduled start of the first session, the timing of the lunch and tea intervals will be adjusted to provide a scheduled 2-hour session and not affect the start time.

On any day's play, except the last day, when the scheduled hours of play have been completed, but the required number of overs have not been bowled and weather or bad light causes play for that day to be abandoned, the remaining overs on that day shall be made up on the next or subsequent days (refer (v) above for timings). On any one day, a maximum of 15 additional overs shall be permitted.

When additional time is added to subsequent day(s), no scheduled day's play shall exceed seven hours. The length of each session of play under this experimental condition is subject to the provisions of Law 15.

Under Law 15.5 timings can be altered at any time on any day if playing time is lost, not necessarily on that day. The captains, umpires and the referee can agree different timings under those circumstances before play starts on any day.

(b) When an innings ends a minimum number of overs shall be bowled from the start of the new innings. The number of overs to be bowled shall be calculated at the rate of one over for each full four minutes to enable a minimum of 90 overs to be bowled in a day. The last hour of the match shall be excluded from this calculation when Clause (e) shall apply.

Where a change of innings occurs during a day's play, in the event of the team bowling second being unable to complete its overs by the scheduled cessation time, play shall continue until the required number of overs have been completed.

Where there is a change of innings during a day's play (except at lunch or tea), two overs will be deducted from the minimum number of overs to be bowled.

(c) Except in the last hour of the match, for which Clause (e) makes provision, if play is suspended due to adverse weather or light for more than one hour in aggregate on any day, the minimum number of overs shall be reduced by one over for each full four minutes of the aggregate playing time lost.

(d) On the last day, if any of the minimum of 75 overs, or as recalculated, have not been bowled when one hour of scheduled playing time remains, the last hour of the match for the purposes of Clause (e) shall be the hour immediately following the completion of those overs.

(e) Law 16.6, 16.7 and 16.8 will apply except that a minimum of 15 overs shall be bowled in the last hour and all calculations with regard to suspensions of play or the start of a new innings shall be based on one over for each full four minutes (refer (i) below). If, however, at any time after 30 minutes of the last hour have elapsed both captains (the batsmen at the wicket may act for their captain) accept that there is no prospect of a result to the match, they may agree to cease play at that time.

(f) Notwithstanding any other provision, there shall be no further play on any day, other than the last day, if a wicket falls or a batsman retires or if the players have occasion to leave the field during the last minimum over within two minutes of the scheduled or re-scheduled cessation time or thereafter.

(g) An over completed on resumption of a new day's play shall be disregarded in calculating minimum overs for that day.

(h) Except on the final day, if in the event of ground, weather or light conditions causing a suspension of play and/or if the players are already off the field at the re-scheduled cessation time or any time thereafter, stumps shall be drawn.

(i) Fractions are to be ignored in all calculations regarding the number of overs, except where there is a change of innings in a day's play, when the over in progress at the conclusion shall be rounded up.

(j) The scoreboard shall show:
– the total number of overs bowled with the ball currently in use; and
– the minimum number of overs remaining to be bowled in a day.

(k)   Penalties shall apply for slow over-rates (refer ICC Code of Conduct).

3.2   Extra Time

The umpires may decide to play 30 minutes (a minimum of eight overs) extra time at the end of any day (other than the last day) if requested by either captain if, in the umpires' opinion, it would bring about a definite result on that day (this is in addition to the maximum one hour's extra time provided for in 3.1.1 (a) (iii) above). If the umpires do not believe a result can be achieved no extra time shall be allowed.

If it is decided to play such extra time on one or more of these days, the whole period shall be played out even though the possibility of finishing the match may have disappeared before the full period has expired.

Only the actual amount of playing time up to the maximum 30 minutes extra time by which play is extended on any day shall be deducted from the total number of hours of play remaining, and the match shall end earlier on the final day by the amount of time by which play was previously extended under this clause.

3.3   Use of Lights

If in the opinion of the umpires, natural light is deteriorating to an unfit level, they shall authorise the ground authorities to use the available artificial lighting so that the match can continue in acceptable conditions.

The lights are only to be used to enable a full day's play to be completed as provided in Clause 3 – Hours of Play, Intervals and Minimum Overs in the Day.

In the event of power failure or lights malfunction, the existing provisions of Clause 3 "Hours of Play, Intervals and Minimum Overs in the Day" shall apply.

3.4   Luncheon Interval

Law 15.6 shall be replaced by the following: Of 40 minutes duration from or at the conclusion of the over in progress at the agreed time for the luncheon interval. Where an innings concludes, or there is a break in play, within 10 minutes of the scheduled or re-scheduled interval, the interval will commence at that time and be limited to 40 minutes.

3.5   Tea Interval

Tea shall be of 20 minutes duration from or at the conclusion of the over in progress at the agreed time for the tea interval subject to the provisions of Law 15.

Law 15.8 shall be replaced by the following:

If at the scheduled time for the tea interval, the ninth wicket of the innings in progress is already down, or it falls at, or after that time, or falls when less than two minutes remain before that time, play will continue for a period of 30 minutes unless the players have cause to leave the field of play, or the innings is concluded earlier.

3.6   Intervals for Drinks

The provisions of Law 15.9 shall be strictly observed except that under conditions of extreme heat the umpires may permit extra intervals for drinks.

An individual player may be given a drink either on the boundary edge or at the fall of a wicket, on the field, provided that no playing time is wasted. No other drinks shall be taken onto the field without the permission of the umpires. Any player taking drinks onto the field shall be dressed in proper cricket attire.

3.7   Time Keeping

Add the following paragraph to Law 3.4: The host country may provide for the ringing of a bell and shall inform the visiting country at the start of the tour. The bell will be rung 5 minutes before the termination of an interval, when the umpires shall go to the wickets.

3.8   Other Matches: Wherever possible, the above conditions should apply to all matches. However, the Home Board with the agreement of the visiting Country's Board, may provide for local variations for matches other than Test and One Day International matches. In the case of one-day matches, starting and finishing times (and interval times) may be altered on any scheduled playing day with the prior approval of the State authority, the ACB and the touring team Manager.

State players shall be bound by the terms of the ACB Code of Behaviour.

Touring players shall be bound by Law 42.18 and/or the terms of the ICC Code of Conduct for Players and Team Officials.

The local State Association shall appoint a representative to meet with the umpires and captains prior to the commencement of the match to secure uniform interpretation of these playing conditions and to adjudicate, if necessary, should there be any dispute.

4.   Law 1.3 Captain

The following shall apply in addition to Law 1.3 (a):

The deputy must be one of the nominated players.

5.   Appointment of Umpires

The following shall apply in place of Laws 3.1 and 3.2:

For as long as ICC maintains an international panel of umpires, the following rules for the selection and appointment of Test match umpires shall be followed as far as it is practicable to do so:

(a)   ICC will establish each year a panel of up to 20 umpires nominated by the Test countries and will appoint one umpire from that panel to stand in each Test match.

(b)   The home board shall appoint a committee for the purpose of nominating the other umpire to officiate in each Test match in its country.

(c)   Test match umpires will be nominated by this committee from those umpires officiating in first-class matches during the current season.

(d)   As long as possible before each Test match, ICC will advise the home board of the name of its appointee and the home board will advise the manager of the touring team of both umpires' names.

(e)   The home board shall also appoint a third umpire who shall act as the emergency umpire and officiate in regard to TV replays. Such appointment must be made from the panel of umpires used by the home board for international matches.

(f)   Neither team will have a right of objection to an umpire's appointment.

(g)   The sole authority for handling media enquiries shall be the ACB Media Manager or a nominee appointed by the board.

6.   Substitutes

6.1   Law 2.5 Fielder Absent or Leaving the Field

Law 2.5 shall apply as modified:

If a fielder fails to take the field with his side at the start of the match or at any later time, or leaves the field during a session of play, the umpire shall be informed of the reason for his absence, and he shall not thereafter come onto the field during a session of play without the consent of the umpire. (See Law 2.6 as modified.) The umpire shall give such consent as soon as practicable. If the player is absent from the field for longer than eight minutes:

(i)   the player shall not be permitted to bowl in that innings after his return until he has been on the field for at least that length of playing time for which he was absent. In the event of a follow-on, this restriction will, if necessary, continue into the second innings.

(ii) the player shall not be permitted to bat unless or until, in the aggregate, he has returned to the field and/or his side's innings has been in progress for at least that length of playing time for which he has been absent or, if earlier, when his side has lost five wickets.

The restriction in (i) and (ii) above shall not apply if the player has suffered an external blow (as opposed to an internal injury such as a pulled muscle) whilst participating earlier in the match and consequently been forced to leave the field. Nor shall it apply if the player has been absent for very exceptional and wholly acceptable reasons (other than injury or illness).

In the event of a fieldsman already being off the field at the commencement of an interruption in play through ground, weather or light conditions, he shall be allowed to count any such stoppage time as playing time, provided that he personally informs the umpires when he is fit enough to take the field had play been in progress.

6.2   Law 2.6 – Player Returning without Permission

Law 2.6 shall apply except that: The reference to 'Governing Body' shall be replaced by 'ICC Match Referee' in 2.6 (iii).

7.   Law 3.8 and Law 3.9 – Fitness of Ground, Weather and Light

Add the following to Law 3.8:

If conditions during a rain stoppage improve and the rain is reduced to drizzle, the umpires must consider if they would have suspended play in the first place under similar conditions. If both on-field umpires agree that current drizzle would not have caused a stoppage, then play shall resume immediately. In these circumstances the provisions of Laws 3.9 (b)(i) and 3.9 (c)(i) shall not apply.

The umpires shall disregard any shadow on the pitch from the stadium or from any permanent object on the ground.

If a shadow from the fielder falls across the strikers half the pitch, the fielder must remain stationary from the time the bowler commences his run up until the striker has received the ball. In the event of a fielder moving before the striker receives the ball, the umpire shall call and signal 'dead ball' if he considers the striker has been disadvantaged by the action

8.   The Ball

8.1   Law 5 – The Ball

The following shall apply in place of Law 5.2:

The home board shall provide cricket balls of an approved standard for Test cricket and spare used balls for changing during a match which shall also be of the same brand. Wherever possible the home board will make available more than one make of approved ball and the captains may agree as to the make to be used. In the event of disagreement between the captains, the home board shall decide by the toss of a coin. The fielding captain or his nominee may select the ball with which he wishes to bowl from the supply provided by the home board. The fourth umpire (or third umpire when no fourth umpire is appointed) shall take a box containing at least six new balls to the dressing room and supervise the selection of the ball.

The umpires shall retain possession of the match ball(s) throughout the duration of the match when play is not actually taking place. During play umpires shall periodically and irregularly inspect the condition of the ball and shall retain possession of it at the fall of a wicket, a drinks interval, at the end of each over, or any other disruption in play.

Note: The Kookaburra "Turf" brand ball has been approved by the Australian Cricket Board.

8.2 Law 5.4 – New Ball in Match of More than One Day's Duration

The following shall apply in place of Law 5.4:

The captain of the fielding side shall have the choice of taking a new ball any time after 80 overs have been bowled with the previous ball. The umpires shall indicate to the batsman and the scorers whenever a new ball is taken into play.

8.3 Law 5.5 – Ball Lost or Becoming Unfit for Play

The following shall apply in addition to Law 5.5:

However, if the ball needs to be replaced after 110 overs for any of the reasons above, it shall be replaced by a new ball. If the ball is to be replaced, the umpire shall inform the batsmen.

8.4 Law 5.6 – Specifications

Law 5.6 shall not apply.

9. Law 6 – The Bat

Add the following sentence to Law 6.1:

The blade of the bat shall have a conventional "flat" face.

10. Law 7 – The Pitch

10.1 Law 7 – The Pitch

In addition to the Law 7.3, the following will apply:

Captains, umpires, the referee and groundsmen should co-operate to ensure that, prior to the start of any day's play, no-one bounces a ball on the pitch or strikes it with a bat to assess its condition or for any other reason, or causes damage to the pitch in any other way.

Prior to the start of play on any day, only the captain and team coach may walk on the pitch to assess its condition. Spiked footwear is not permitted.

Prior to the commencement of a day's play, one TV commentator and camera crew of the official licensed TV broadcaster(s) (but not news crew) may be permitted to inspect the pitch and surrounds subject to the following:

- a ball must not be bounced on the pitch

- a key or knife may only be inserted in the pitch in the area between the popping and bowling creases

In the event of any dispute, the referee in consultation with the home board will rule and his ruling will be final.

10.2 Law 7.4 Changing the Pitch

The following shall apply in place of Law 7.4:

1   In the event of a pitch being considered too dangerous for play to continue in the estimation of the match umpires, they shall stop play and immediately advise the match referee.

2   The match umpires and referee shall consult with both captains.

3   If the captains agree, play shall resume.

4   If the decision is not to resume play, the match umpires shall consider one of the following options:

   •   whether the existing pitch can be repaired. Repair work will only be considered if there has been malicious damage to a non-crucial part of the pitch;

   •   whether the alternative pitch can be used (but see above);

   •   whether the match has to be abandoned.

5   When such a decision is made, the ground authority shall make a public announcement as soon as possible following that decision.

6   In the event of a decision being taken in favour of 4(a) or 4(b) above, the supervision of the remedial or new preparatory work shall be the responsibility of the match umpires and the representative of the ground authority.

7   The re-scheduled starting time and the re-scheduled cessation time, together with any make-up procedures in either the existing or experimental regulations, shall be the responsibility of the match umpires.

8   In the event that the existing pitch can be made playable after suitable remedial work (4(a) above) the match shall continue from the point stopped.

9   If a new pitch is prepared (4(b) above), the match shall be re-started from the first ball (but see above).

10   If the decision is to abandon the match (4 (c) above), the relevant officials from the boards involved shall agree on whether the match can be replayed within the existing tour schedule.

10.3 Law 7.5 – Non-turf Pitches

Law 7.5 shall not apply.

11. Law 8 – The Wickets

The following shall apply in addition to Law 8.2:

For televised matches the home board may provide a slightly larger cylindrical stump to accommodate the stump camera. When the larger stump is used, all three stumps must be exactly the same size.

12. Law 9.3 – The Popping Crease

Law 9.3 shall apply, except that the reference to "a minimum of 6 ft" shall be replaced by "a minimum of 15 yards".

13. Law 10 – Preparation and Maintenance of Playing Area

13.6 Maintenance of Foot Holes – Law 10.6 will apply but add:

The umpires shall see that wherever possible and whenever it is considered necessary, action is taken during all intervals in play to do whatever is practicable to improve the bowlers' foot holes. As soon as possible after the conclusion of each day's play, bowlers' foot holes will be repaired.

Note: Watering the Outfield

In order that the condition of the outfield can be maintained throughout the duration of a match, oval managers/curators must first be granted approval by both captains to water the outfield after any day's play.

Such approval shall not be unreasonably withheld.

14. Law 11 – Covering the Pitch – Before and During a Match

In place of Law 11.2, 11.3 and 11.4, the following shall apply:

In all matches, the pitch shall be entirely protected against rain up to the commencement of play and for the duration of the period of the match. It shall be wholly covered at the termination of each day's play or providing the weather is fine, within a period of two hours thereafter.

The covers shall be removed no earlier than 5.00 a.m. and no later than 7.00 a.m. on each morning of the match (including the rest day) provided it is not raining at the time, but they will be replaced if rain falls prior to the commencement of play.

Note: The covers must totally protect the pitch and also the pitch surroundings, a minimum five metres either side of the pitch and any worn or soft areas in the outfield, as well as the bowlers' run-ups to a distance of at least 10 metres.

Attention is drawn to Clause 7.

15. Drying of Pitch and Ground

(a) Prior to tossing for choice of innings the artificial drying of the pitch and outfield shall be at the discretion of the groundsman. Thereafter and throughout the match the drying of the outfield may be undertaken at any time by the groundsman, but the drying of the affected area of the pitch shall be carried out only on the instructions and under the supervision of the umpires. The umpires shall be empowered to have the pitch dried without reference to the captains at any time they are of the opinion that it is unfit for play.

(b) The umpires may instruct the groundsman to use any available equipment, including any roller for the purpose of drying the pitch and making it fit for play.

Note: An absorbent roller may be used to remove water from the covers including the cover on the match pitch.

16. Law 12 – Innings

Law 12.1 (a) shall apply as modified:

(a) A match shall be two innings per side subject to the provisions of Law 13.1.

Law 12.1 (b) and 12.3 (e) shall not apply.

17. Law 13 – The Follow-On

Add the following to Law 13.1:

If the provision of Clause 3.1 (a) (v) is applied the additional time is regarded as part of that day's play for the purpose of Law 13.3, i.e. it is the number of days remaining and not the total number of hours available.

18. Law 17 – Practice on the Field

Add the following to Law 17.1:

The use of the square for practice on any day of any match will be restricted to any netted practice area on the square set aside for that purpose.

19. Law 18 – Scoring Runs

Law 18.5 shall apply, except that the reference to 'Governing Body' shall be replaced by 'ICC Match Referee' in 18.5(b)(iv).

20. Law 19 – Boundaries

Add the following to Law 19.1:

All boundaries must be designated by a rope of similar object of a minimum standard as authorised by the ICC from time to time. Where appropriate the rope should be a required minimum distance (3 yards minimum) inside the perimeter fencing or advertising signs. For grounds with a large playing area, the maximum length of boundary should be used before applying the minimum three yards between the boundary and the fence.

The playing area shall be a minimum of 140 yards from boundary to boundary square of the pitch. The pitch shall be a minimum 60 yards from one boundary square of the pitch. When this minimum distance is used, the pitch has to be a minimum 80 yards from the opposite square boundary. The straight boundary at both ends of the pitch shall be a minimum of 60 yards. Distances shall be measured from the centre of the pitch to be used.

Any ground on which a Test or One Day International has been played prior to 1st July 1995 which does not conform with these minimum dimensions shall be exempt from this playing condition. Any new ground must conform to these minimum dimensions.

If an unauthorised person enters the playing arena and handles the ball, the umpire at the bowler's end shall be the sole judge of whether the boundary allowance should be scored or the ball be treated as still in play or called dead ball if a batsman is liable to be out as a result of the unauthorised person handling the ball. See Law 19.1 (c).

Sight screens shall be provided at both ends of all grounds. Advertising shall be permitted on the sight screen behind the striker, providing it is removed for the subsequent over from that end.

21. Law 21 – The Result

Law 21 shall apply with the following:

Any query on the result of the match as defined in Law 21.1, 21.3, 21.4, 21.5, 21.8 and 21.10 shall be resolved as soon as possible and a final decision made by the umpires at close of play.

22. Law 22 – The Over

Law 22.5 shall apply with the following:

Whenever possible the third umpire or TV umpire shall liaise with the scorers and if possible inform the on-field umpires if the over has been miscounted.

23. Law 24 – No Ball

Law 24.1 (b) shall be replaced by the following:

The bowler may not deliver the ball underarm. If a bowler bowls a ball underarm the umpire shall call and signal dead ball, and the ball is to be re-bowled overarm.

24. Law 24.2 – Fair Delivery – The Arm

Law 24.2 shall apply, except that the reference to "Governing Body" shall be replaced by "ICC Match Referee":

25. Law 25.1 – Judging a Wide

Law 25.1 will apply, but in addition:

For bowlers attempting to utilise the rough outside a batsman's leg stump, not necessarily as a negative tactic the Strict Limited Over Wide Interpretation shall be applied.

    For bowlers whom umpires consider to be bowling down the leg side as a negative tactic, the Strict Limited Over Wide interpretation shall be applied.

26. Law 32 – Caught

Add the following to Law 32.1:

The striker is out under this Law if the ball is deflected from his bat onto the helmet he is wearing and a fair catch is taken. Runs may be scored off deflections from the batsman's or fielder's helmet.

27. Helmets

The following will apply to the batsman:

A batsman may call for a helmet to be brought out to him at any time. He must then wear or carry it personally all the time while play is in progress, or can have it taken off the field at the fall of a wicket, or at the end of an over, or at any drinks interval.

    In all cases, no actions involving helmets are to waste playing time. Umpires are not to hold helmets.

28. Law 41 – The Fielder

Law 41 shall apply with the following:

The exchanging of protective equipment between members of the fielding side on the field shall be permitted provided that the umpires do not consider that it constitutes a waste of playing time. A batsman may only change other items of protective equipment (e.g. batting gloves, etc.) provided that there is no waste of playing time.

29. Law 41.2 – Fielding The Ball

Law 41.2 shall apply, except that the reference to 'Governing Body' shall be replaced by 'ICC Referee' in 41.2 (c).

30. Law 42.3 – The Match Ball – Changing its Condition

Law 42.3 shall apply, and penalty runs shall be awarded, as defined in this Law.

    In addition, the umpires shall report the incident to the referee under the

Code of Conduct. Law 42.3 shall apply as modified:

(1) That the reference to 'Governing Body' shall be replaced by 'ICC match referee' in 42.3 (d) (vi).

(2) Delete Law 42.3 (e) (ii) and replace with the following:

(3) Inform the captain of the fielding side of the reason for the action taken.

And in addition to Law 42.3:

In the event that a ball has been interfered with and requires replacement the batsman at the wicket shall choose the replacement ball from a selection of six other balls of various degrees of usage (including a new ball) and of the same brand as the ball in use prior to the contravention.

31. Law 42.4 – Deliberate Attempt to Distract Striker

Law 42.4 shall apply, and penalty runs shall be awarded, as defined in this Law.

In addition, the umpires shall report the incident to the referee under the Code of Conduct. Law 42.4 shall apply as modified:

(1) that the reference to 'Governing Body' shall be replaced by 'ICC match referee' in 42.4 (b) (iii).

32. Law 42.5 – Deliberate Distraction or Obstruction of Batsman

Law 42.5 shall apply, and penalty runs shall be awarded, as defined in this Law. In addition, the umpire shall report the incident to the referee under the Code of Conduct.

Law 42.5 shall apply as modified:

(1) that the reference to 'Governing Body' shall be replaced by 'ICC Match Referee' in 42.5 (b) (vi).

33. Law 42.6 – Dangerous and Unfair Bowling – The Bowling of Fast Short-Pitched Balls

Law 42.6 (a) (ii) shall be replaced by the following:

1. Law 42.6 (a) shall be replaced by the following:

   (a) A bowler shall be limited to two fast short-pitched deliveries per over.

   (b) A fast short-pitched ball is defined as a ball which passes or would have passed above the shoulder height of the Batsman standing upright at the crease, but not clearly above the batsman's head so that it is so high it prevents him from being able to hit it with his bat by means of a normal cricket stroke.

   (c) The umpire at the bowlers end shall advise the bowler and the batsman on strike when each fast short pitched delivery has been bowled.

   (d) In addition, for the purpose of this regulation, a ball that passes clearly above head height of the batsman, other than a fast short-pitched ball as defined in (b) above, that prevents him from being able to hit it with his bat by means of a normal cricket stroke shall be a No ball.

2. (a) In the event of a bowler bowling more than two fast short-pitched deliveries in an over as defined in (b) above, the umpire at the bowlers end shall call and signal no ball on each occasion. A differential signal shall be used to signify a fast short pitched delivery. The umpire shall call and signal No ball and then tap the head with the other hand.

(b) If a bowler delivers a third fast short pitched ball in an over, the umpire, after the call of No ball and when the ball is dead, shall caution the bowler, inform the other umpire, the captain of the fielding side and the batsmen at the wicket of what has occurred. This caution shall apply throughout the innings.

(c) If there is a second instance of the bowler being no balled in the innings for bowling more than two fast short pitched deliveries in an over, the umpire shall advise the bowler that this is his final warning for the innings.

(d) Should there be any further instance by the same bowler in that innings, the umpire shall call and signal No ball and when the ball is dead direct the captain to take the bowler off forthwith. If necessary, the over shall be completed by another bowler, who shall neither have bowled the previous over nor be allowed to bowl the next over.

(e) The bowler thus taken off shall not be allowed to bowl again in that innings.

(f) The umpire will report the occurrence to the other umpire, the batsmen at the wicket and as soon as possible to the captain of the batting side.

(g) The umpires will then report the matter to the ICC Match Referee who shall take such action as is considered appropriate against the captain and the bowler concerned. (Refer also to Law 42.1 Fair and Unfair Play - Responsibility of the Captains.)

The above is not a substitute for ICC Playing Condition 34 below which umpires are able to apply at any time.

34. Dangerous and Unfair Bowling

Regardless of any action taken by the umpire as a result of a breach of clauses 33, 35 or 36 the following shall apply at any time during the match.

The bowling of fast short-pitched balls is unfair if the umpire at the bowler's end considers that by their repetition and taking into account their length, height and direction, they are likely to inflict physical injury on the striker, irrespective of the protective clothing and equipment he may be wearing. The relative skill of the striker shall also be taken into consideration.

In the event of such unfair bowling, the umpire at the bowler's end shall adopt the following procedure:

(a) In the first instance the umpire shall call and signal "no ball", caution the bowler and inform the other umpire, the captain of the fielding side and the batsmen of what has occurred.

(b) If this caution is ineffective, he shall repeat the above procedure and indicate to the bowler that this is a final warning.

(c) Both the above caution and final warning shall continue to apply even though the bowler may later change ends.

(d) Should the above warnings prove ineffective the umpire at the bowler's end shall:

    (i) At the first repetition call and signal "no ball" and when the ball is dead direct the captain to take the bowler off forthwith and to complete the over with another bowler, provided that the bowler does not bowl two overs or part thereof consecutively. See Law 22.8 (Bowler Incapacitated or Suspended during an Over).

    (ii) Not allow the bowler, thus taken off, to bowl again in the same innings.

(iii) Report the occurrence to the captain of the batting side as soon as the players leave the field for an interval.

(iv) Report the occurrence to the Executive of the fielding side and to the ICC match referee responsible for the match who shall take any further action which is considered to be appropriate against the Captain and the Bowler concerned. (Refer also to Law 42.1 Fair and Unfair Play - Responsibility of the Captains.)

35. Law 42.6 (b) – The Bowling of Fast, High, Full-Pitched Balls

Law 42.6 (b) shall apply as modified:

(a) Any delivery, other than a slow paced one, which passes or would have passed on the full above waist height of the striker standing upright at the crease is deemed dangerous and unfair, whether or not is it likely to inflict physical injury on the striker.

(b) A slow delivery which passes or would have passed on the full above shoulder height of the striker standing upright at the crease, is to be deemed dangerous and unfair, whether or not it is likely to inflict physical injury on the striker.

(c) In the event of a bowler bowling a high full pitched ball as defined in (a) and (b) above (i.e. a beamer), the umpire at the bowler's end shall adopt the following procedure:

(d) In the first instance the umpire shall call and signal No ball and when the ball is dead, caution the Bowler and issue a first and final warning. The umpire shall inform the other umpire, captain of the fielding side and the Batsman of what has occurred.

(e) At the first repetition call and signal no ball and when the ball is dead direct the captain of the fielding side to take the Bowler off forthwith and to complete the over with another Bowler, provided that the Bowler does not bowl two overs or part thereof consecutively.

(f) Not allow the Bowler, thus taken off, to bowl again in the same innings.

(g) At the first opportunity report the occurrence, with the other umpire, to the captain of the batting side and the ICC match referee responsible for the match who shall take any further action which is considered to be appropriate against the Captain and the Bowler concerned. (Refer also to Law 42.1 Fair and Unfair Play - Responsibility of the Captains.)

36. Law 42.8 – Deliberate Bowling of High Full-Pitched Balls

Law 42.8 shall apply as modified:

If the umpire considers that a high full pitch, which is deemed dangerous and unfair as defined in clause 35, was deliberately bowled, then the caution and warning process shall be dispensed with. The umpire at the bowlers end shall:

(a) Call and signal no ball

(b) When the ball is dead, direct the captain to take the bowler off forthwith

(c) Not allow the bowler to bowl again in that innings

(d) Complete the over with another Bowler, provided that the Bowler does not bowl two overs or part thereof consecutively.

(e) At the first opportunity report the occurrence, with the other umpire, to the captain of the batting side and the ICC match referee responsible for the match who shall take any further action which is considered to be appropriate against the Captain and the Bowler concerned. (Refer also to Law 42.1 Fair and Unfair Play – Responsibility of the Captains.)

37. Action by Umpires

Law 42.7 shall be replaced by the following:

The Bowling of Fast Short Pitched Deliveries, Dangerous and Unfair Bowling, The Bowling of High Full Pitched Balls and Deliberate Bowling of High Full Pitched Balls.

Please note that should the umpires initiate the caution and warning procedures set out in Clauses 33, 34, 35 and 36, such cautions and warnings are to be cumulative.

Should a bowler be cautioned under clause 33 (More than 2 deliveries above shoulder height in an over) and then infringe under clause 34 (Dangerous and Unfair Bowling) or clause 35 (High Full Pitched Balls) he will not be started again on a first caution – it will be his final warning.

38. Law 42.9 – Time-Wasting by the Fielding Side

Law 42.9 shall apply, and penalty runs shall be awarded, as defined in this Law. In addition, the umpires may report the incident to the referee under the Code of Conduct. Law 42.9 shall apply as modified:

(a) If there is any further waste of time in that innings, by any member of the fielding side the umpire shall:

(1) Delete Law 42.9 (b) (ii)

(2) Call and signal Dead Ball

(3) That reference to 'Governing Body' shall be replaced by 'ICC Match Referee in 42.9 (b) (iv)

39. Law 42.10 – Batsman Wasting Time

Law 42.10 shall apply, and penalty runs shall be awarded, as defined in this Law. In addition, the umpires may report the incident to the referee under the Code of Conduct.

The provisions of Law 42.10 (b) shall apply, except as modified:

(a) If there is any further time wasting by any batsman in that innings, the umpire shall, at the appropriate time while the ball is dead:

(1) Call and signal dead ball

(2) That the reference to 'Governing Body' shall be replaced by 'ICC Match Referee' in 42.10 (b) (iii).

40. Law 42.12 – Bowler Running on the Protected Area after Delivering the Ball

Law 42.12 shall apply, except that the reference to "Governing body" shall be replaced by "ICC match referee".

41. Law 42.13 – Fielder Damaging the Pitch

Law 42.13 shall apply, except that the reference to 'Governing Body' shall be replaced by 'ICC match referee' in 42.13 (b) (iii).

42. Law 42.14 – Batsman Damaging the Pitch

Law 42.14 shall apply, except that the reference to 'Governing Body' shall be replaced by 'ICC match referee' in 42.14 (c) (vi).

43. Law 42.16 – Batsmen Stealing a Run

Law 42.16 shall apply, except that the reference to 'Governing Body' shall be replaced by 'ICC match referee' in 42.16 (v).

44. Law 42.18 – Players' Conduct

Law 42.18 shall apply, except that the reference to "Governing body" shall be replaced by "ICC match referee" in 42.18 (iii).

45. "Hitting Up"

Teams are required to observe Ground Authority regulations and to exercise the utmost care and caution when engaging in practice and pre-match warm-up and "hitting-up" activities so as to avoid the risk of injury to members of the public, damage to the centre wicket region and to perimeter fencing.

VB SERIES
PLAYING CONDITIONS, 2001-02

Test Match Playing Conditions and the Laws of Cricket (2000 Code) shall apply, except as varied below.

1. Duration of Matches

One-day international matches shall be of one day's scheduled duration. The participating countries in a series may provide for a reserve day on which an incomplete match may be replayed (but not continued from the scheduled day). The matches will consist of one innings per side and each innings will be limited to 50 six-ball overs. A minimum of 25 overs per team shall constitute a match.

2. Hours of Play, Intervals and Minimum Overs in the Day

There will be two sessions of three and a half hours each, separated by a 45-minute break.

2.2 Interval Between Innings

The innings of the team batting second shall not commence before the scheduled time for commencement of the second session unless the team batting first has completed its innings at least 30 minutes prior to the scheduled interval, in which case a ten-minute break will occur and the team batting second will commence its innings and the interval will occur as scheduled.

Where play is delayed or interrupted the umpires will reduce the length of the interval as follows:

Time Lost	Interval
Up to 60 minutes	30 minutes
Between 60 and 120 minutes	20 minutes
More than 120 minutes	10 minutes

Note: Refer also to the provisions of Clause 4.2

2.3   Intervals for Drinks: Two drinks breaks per session shall be permitted, each one hour ten minutes apart. The provisions of Law 15.9 shall be strictly observed except that under conditions of extreme heat the umpires may permit extra intervals for drinks.

An individual player may be given a drink either on the boundary edge or at the fall of a wicket, on the field, provided that no playing time is wasted. No other drinks shall be taken onto the field without the permission of the umpires. Any player taking drinks onto the field shall be dressed in proper cricket attire.

2.4   Extra Time: Provision has been made for up to 15 minutes of extra official playing time in day matches and up to 45 minutes in day/night matches – refer 4.2.1 (a) and 4.2.3.

3.   Appointment of Umpires

(a)   The home board shall appoint both on-field umpires from those umpires officiating in first-class matches during their current season.

(b)   The home board shall also appoint a third umpire who shall act as the emergency umpire and officiate in regard to TV replays. Such appointment must be made from the panel of umpires used by the home board for international matches.

4.   Length of Innings

4.1   Uninterrupted Matches

(a)   Each team shall bat for 50 overs unless all out earlier. A team shall not be permitted to declare its innings closed.

(b)   If the team fielding first fails to bowl the required number of overs by the scheduled time for cessation of the first session, play shall continue until the required number of overs has been bowled.

Unless otherwise determined by the referee, the innings of the team batting second shall be limited to the same number of overs bowled by it at the scheduled time for cessation of the first session. The over in progress at the scheduled cessation time shall count as a completed over. The interval shall not be extended and the second session shall commence at the scheduled time.

The referee may increase the number of overs to be bowled by the team bowling second if, after consultation with the umpires, he is of the opinion that events beyond the control of the bowling team prevented that team from bowling the required number of overs by the scheduled time for the cessation of the innings of the team batting first.

(c)   If the team batting first is all out and the last wicket falls at or after the scheduled time for the interval, the innings of the team batting second shall be limited to the same number of overs bowled to the team batting first at the scheduled time for the interval (the over in which the last wicket falls to count as a complete over).

(d) If the team batting first is dismissed in less than 50 overs, the team batting second shall be entitled to bat for 50 overs except as provided in (c) above.

(e) If the team fielding second fails to bowl 50 overs or the number of overs as provided in 4.1 (b), (c) or (d) by the scheduled cessation time, the hours of play shall be extended until the required number of overs has been bowled or a result achieved.

(f) Penalties shall apply for slow over-rates (refer ICC Code of Conduct for Players and Team Officials).

4.2 Delayed or Interrupted Matches

4.2.1 General

(a) The object shall always be to re-arrange the number of overs so that both teams have the opportunity of batting for the same number of overs. A team shall not be permitted to declare its innings closed.

A minimum 25 overs have to be bowled to the side batting second to constitute a match, subject to the provisions of Clause 4.1 (b).

The calculation of the number of overs to be bowled shall be based on an average rate of 14.28 overs per hour in the total time available for play. If a reduction of the number of overs is required, any recalculation must not cause the match to be rescheduled to finish earlier than the original cessation time. This time may be extended to allow for one extra over for both teams to be added if required.

(b) If the team fielding second fails to bowl the required number of overs by the scheduled cessation time, the hours of play shall be extended until the overs have been bowled or a result achieved.

(c) The team batting second shall not bat for a greater number of overs than the first team unless the latter has been all out in less than the agreed number of overs.

(d) Fractions are to be ignored in all calculations regarding the number of overs.

4.2.2 Delay or Interruption to the Innings of the Team Batting First

(a) If the number of overs of the team batting first is reduced, a fixed time will be specified for the completion of the first session, as calculated by applying the provisions of Clauses 2.2 and 4.2.1 (a).

(b) If the team fielding first fails to bowl the required number of overs by the scheduled time for cessation of the first session, play shall continue until the required number of overs has been bowled, and 4.1 (b) shall apply.

(c) If the team batting first is all out and the last wicket falls at or after the scheduled time for the interval, 4.1 (c) shall apply.

4.2.3 Delay or Interruption to the Innings of the Team Batting Second

If there is a suspension in play during the second innings, the overs shall be reduced at a rate of 14.28 overs per hour for time lost, except that, when the innings of the team batting first has been completed prior to the scheduled or rescheduled time for the interval between innings, the reduction of overs will not commence until an amount of time equivalent to that by which the second innings started early has elapsed.

The hours of play shall be extended by the amount of time lost up to a maximum of 15 minutes in day matches and up to 45 minutes in day/night matches. Calculations because of any time lost thereafter shall be as per 4.2.1 (a).

5.   Restrictions on the Placement of Fieldsmen

5.1   Two semi-circles shall be drawn on the field of play. The semi-circles have as their centre the middle stump at either end of the pitch. The radius of each of the semi-circles is 30 yards (27.5m). The ends of each semi-circle are joined to the other by a straight line drawn on the field on the same side of the pitch.

The field restriction area should be marked by continuous painted white lines or "dots" at five-yard (4.5 m) intervals, each "dot" to be covered by a white plastic or rubber (but not metal) disc measuring seven inches (18 cm) in diameter.

5.2   At the instant of delivery, there may not be more than five fieldsmen on the leg side.

5.3   For the first 15 overs only two fieldsmen are permitted to be outside the field restriction marking at the instant of delivery.

5.4   For the remaining overs only five fieldsmen are permitted to be outside the field restriction marking at the instant of delivery.

5.5   Two inner circles shall be drawn on the field of the play. The circles have as their centres the centre point of the popping crease at either end of the pitch. The radius of each of the circles is 15 yards (13.72 m). The field restriction area should be marked by "dots". The segment for the circles reserved for the slip positions shall not be demarcated.

In the first 15 overs there must be a minimum of two stationary fieldsmen within the 15-yard field restriction of the striker at the instant of delivery. When a fast bowler is bowling the two stationary fieldsmen may be permitted to stand deeper than 15 yards (in the undemarcated area) provided only that they are standing in slip, leg slip and gully positions.

5.6   In circumstances where the number of overs for the team batting first is reduced, the number of overs in regard to the restrictions in 5.3 and 5.5 above shall be reduced proportionally in a ratio of 15:50 (30%) in accordance with the table below. Fractions are to be ignored in all calculations regarding the number of overs.

Total overs in innings	No. of overs for which fielding restrictions in 5.3 and 5.5 above will apply
25-26	7
27-29	8
30-33	9
34-36	10
37-39	11
40-43	12
44-46	13
47-49	14
50	15

5.7   Where the number of overs for the team batting second is reduced (including under the provisions of Clause 4.1 (b) and/or 4.1 (c) above), the restrictions in 5.3 and 5.5 above will apply for the same proportion of the second innings as applied in the first innings (fractions to be ignored).

5.8   In the event of an infringement of any of the above fielding restrictions, the square leg umpire shall call and signal "no ball".

6.   Number of Overs per Bowler

No bowler shall bowl more than ten overs in an innings.

In a delayed or interrupted match where the overs are reduced for both teams or for the team bowling second, no bowler may bowl more than one-fifth of the total overs allowed. This restriction shall not apply to the team fielding second where the provisions of Clause 4.1(b) have been applied.

Where the total overs is not divisible by five, one additional over shall be allowed to the maximum number per bowler necessary to make up the balance.

In the event of a bowler breaking down and being unable to complete an over, the remaining balls will be bowled by another bowler. Such part of an over will count as a full over only in so far as each bowler's limit is concerned.

The scoreboard shall show the total number of overs bowled and the number of overs bowled by each bowler.

7.   No-Ball

A bowler shall be allowed to bowl one short pitched delivery per over (not being a wide or a no-ball).

A fast short pitched delivery is defined as a ball that passes or would have passed above the shoulder height of the striker standing upright at the crease, but not clearly above the batsman's head. (refer Test Match clause 33).

In the event of the bowler bowling more that one fast short pitched delivery in an over, the umpire shall call and signal "No-ball". The penalty shall be one run for the no ball, plus any runs scored from the delivery.

The above regulation is not a substitute for Law 42.6 which umpires may apply at any time.

Note - the provisions of one allowable fast short pitched delivery per over shall be superseded by the provisions of Clause 8 – Wide Bowling.

8.   Wide Bowling – Judging a Wide

Umpires are instructed to apply a very strict and consistent interpretation in regard to this Law in order to prevent negative bowling wide of the wicket.

Any offside or legside delivery which in the opinion of the umpire does not give the batsman a reasonable opportunity to score shall be called a wide. As a guide, on the leg side a ball landing clearly outside the leg stump going further away shall be called a wide.

A penalty of one run for a wide shall be scored. This penalty shall stand in addition to any other runs which are scored or awarded. All runs which are run or result from a wide ball which is not a no ball shall be scored as wide balls.

9.   The Ball

The home board shall provide cricket balls of an approved standard for one-day international cricket and spare used balls for changing during a match which shall also be of the same brand.

The fielding captain or his nominee may select the ball with which he wishes to bowl from the supply provided by the home board. The fourth umpire (or third umpire when no fourth umpire is appointed) shall take a new box containing at least six new balls to the dressing room and supervise the selection of the ball.

The umpires shall retain possession of the match ball(s) throughout the duration of the match when play is not actually taking place. During play umpires shall periodically and irregularly inspect the condition of the ball and shall retain possession of it at the fall of a wicket, a drinks interval, at the end of each over, or any other disruption in play.

Where day/night matches are scheduled, white balls will be used in all matches (including day matches) in a series. Each fielding team shall have one new ball for its innings.

In the event of a ball being lost during play or, in the opinion of the umpires, being unfit for play through normal use, the umpires shall allow it to be replaced by one that in their opinion has had a similar amount of wear.

In the event of a ball becoming wet and soggy as a result of play continuing in inclement weather or it being affected by dew, or a white ball becoming significantly discoloured and in the opinion of the umpires being unfit for play, the ball may be replaced by a ball that has had a similar amount of wear, even though it has not gone out of shape.

If the ball is to be replaced, the umpire shall inform the batsmen. Either bowler or batsman may raise the matter with the umpires and the umpires' decision as to a replacement or otherwise will be final.

Kookaburra "Turf" (white) brand balls as approved by the Australian Cricket Board will be used in all matches.

10. The Result

10.1 A result can be achieved only if both teams have had the opportunity of batting for at least 25 overs, subject to the provisions of Clause 4.1(b) and 4.2.2 (b), unless one team has been all out in less than 25 overs or unless the team batting second scores enough runs to win in less than 25 overs.

All matches in which both teams have not had an opportunity of batting for a minimum of 25 overs shall be declared "no result".

10.2 Tie

In matches in which both teams have had the opportunity of batting for the agreed number of overs, subject to the provision of Clauses 4.1 (b) and 4.2.2 (b), the team scoring the higher number of runs shall be the winner. If the scores are equal, the result shall be a tie and no account shall be taken of the number of wickets which have fallen.

10.3 Delayed or Interrupted Matches – Calculation of the Target Score

If, due to suspension of play after the start of the match, the number of overs in the innings of either team has to be revised to a lesser number than originally allotted (minimum 25 overs unless the provisions of 4.1 (b) or 4.2.2 (b) apply), then a revised target score (to win) should be set for the number of overs which the team batting second will have the opportunity of facing. This revised target is to be calculated using the current Duckworth/Lewis method. The target set will always be a whole number and one run less will constitute a tie.

11. Points

11.1 Preliminary Matches

In a competition with three or four Full Members and with a final match or series, the home board may institute a points system as follows:

Win	4
Tie or No Result	2
Loss	0
Bonus Point	1

In the event of the teams finishing on equal points, the right to play in the final match (or series) will be determined as follows:

- the team with the most number of wins
- the team with the most number of wins over the other team(s).
- the team with the highest number of bonus points
- the team with the highest net run rate.

In a match declared as no result, run rate is not applicable

11.2 Net Run-Rate

A team's net run-rate is calculated by deducting from the average runs per over scored by that team throughout the competition, the average runs per over scored against that team throughout the competition.

In the event of a team being all out in less than its full quota of overs, the calculation of its net run-rate shall be based on the full quota of overs to which it would have been entitled and not on the number of overs in which the team was dismissed.

Only those matches where results are achieved will count for the purpose of net run rate calculations. Where a match is abandoned, but a result is achieved under Duckworth/Lewis, for net run rate purposes Team 1 will be accredited with Team 2's Par Score on abandonment off the same number of overs faced by Team 2. Where a match is concluded but with Duckworth/Lewis having been applied at an earlier point in the match, Team 1 will be accredited with 1 run less than the final Target Score for Team 2 off the total number of overs allocated to Team 2 to reach the target.

11.3 Bonus Points

The team that achieves a run rate of 1.25 times that of the opposition shall be awarded one bonus point. A team's run rate will be calculated by reference to the runs scored in an innings divided by the number of overs faced. Refer Appendix 3.

11.4 Final Match or Series

If no result is achieved in a final on the scheduled day of play, the match shall be replayed on the scheduled reserve day. If no result is achieved in the replay on the reserve day, the match shall be declared drawn.

In the event of a drawn final, the prize money will be shared equally between the two competing teams.

In a best of three-final series, a third match will always be played where neither team has a clear two-match advantage after the scheduled completion of the second match.

For the determination of the final series no reference will be made to preliminary match results, wins or run-rates.

In the event of a tied final series, the prize money will be shared equally between the two competing teams.

Note: In a best of three final series, a third match will always be played where neither team has a clear two match advantage after the scheduled competition of the second match. For the determination of the final series no reference will be made to preliminary match results, wins or run rates. In the event of a tied final series, the prizemoney will be shared equally between the two competing teams.

12. Day/Night Matches

(a) Pads and players' and umpires' clothing shall be coloured.

(b) Sightscreens shall be black.

(c) If during a day/night or a day match played with black sightscreens and white balls, in the opinion of the umpires, natural light is deteriorating to an unfit level, they may authorise the ground authority to use the available artificial lighting so that the match can continue in acceptable conditions.

PURA CUP COMPETITION
PLAYING CONDITIONS, 2001-02

1. Laws of Cricket

Except as varied hereunder the Laws of Cricket (2000 Code) shall apply.

2. Duration of Matches

Matches shall be four days scheduled duration.

3. Start and Cessation Times

3.1 The following playing times shall apply to therse specific matches

20-24 MARCH 2002 PURA CUP FINAL

As daylight saving time is still in operation, if the Final is played in Queensland, play will commence at 10.00am; in New South Wales, Victoria, Tasmania or South Australia at 11.00am; in Western Australia at 10.30am.

3.2 Daylight Saving Time

Daylight saving will commence in Tasmania on 7 October 2001 and in New South Wales, Victoria and South Australia on 28 October 2001. Daylight saving will conclude on 31 March 2002.

3.3 Hours of Play

Any State wishing to change the hours of play must first obtain approval from the ACB.

4. Minimum Overs in the Day

(a) Play shall continue on each day until the completion of a minimum number of overs or until the scheduled or re-scheduled cessation time, whichever is the later.

The minimum number of overs to be completed, unless an innings ends or an interruption occurs, shall be:

  (i) on days other than the last day - a minimum of 96 overs (or a minimum of 16 overs per hour).

  (ii) on the last day - a minimum of 80 overs (or a minimum of 16 overs per hour) for playing time other than the last hour of the match when Clause (e) below shall apply.

  (iii) Additional Hour: Subject to weather and light, except in the last hour of the match, in the event of play being suspended for any reason other than normal intervals, the playing time on that day shall be extended by the amount of time lost up to a maximum of one hour. In these circumstances, the minimum number of overs to be bowled shall be in accordance with the provisions of this clause i.e. a minimum of 16 overs per hour and the cessation time shall be rescheduled accordingly.

  (iv) If play has been suspended for 30 minutes or more prior to the commencement of the scheduled or rescheduled tea interval, the tea interval shall be delayed for half an hour.

  (v) If any time is lost and cannot be made up under (iii) above, additional time of up to a maximum of one hour per day shall be added to the scheduled playing hours for the next day, and subsequent day(s) as required (to make up as much lost time as possible). Where appropriate the first 30 minutes (or less) of this additional time shall be added prior to the scheduled start of the first session, and the remainder shall be added to the last session.

In circumstances where it is not possible to add this additional time prior to the scheduled start of the first session, the timing of the lunch and tea intervals will be adjusted to provide a scheduled 2 1/2 hour session and not affect the start time.

On any day's play, except the last day, when the scheduled hours of play have been completed, but the required number of overs have not been bowled and weather or bad light causes play for that day to be abandoned, the remaining overs on that day shall be made up on the next or subsequent days (refer (v) above for timings). On any one day, a maximum of 16 additional overs shall be permitted.

When additional time is added to subsequent day(s), no scheduled days play shall exceed 7 hours. The length of each session of play is subject to the provisions of Law 15.

Under Law 15.5 timings can be altered at any time on any day if playing time is lost, not necessarily on that day. The captains, umpires and the local State Association can agree different timings under those circumstances before play starts on any day.

(b) When an innings ends a minimum number of overs shall be bowled from the start of the new innings. The number of overs to be bowled shall be calculated at the rate of one over for each full 3.75 to enable a minimum of 96 overs to be bowled in a day. The last hour of the match shall be excluded from this calculation when Clause (e) shall apply.

Where a change of innings occurs during a day's play, in the event of the team bowling second being unable to complete its overs by the scheduled cessation time, play shall continue until the required number of overs have been completed.

Where there is a change of innings during a day's play (except at lunch or tea or when play is suspended due to unfit ground, weather or light conditions or for exceptional circumstances), 2 overs will be deducted from the minimum number of overs to be bowled.

(c) Except in the last hour of the match, for which Clause (e) makes provision, if play is suspended due to adverse weather or light for more than one hour in aggregate on any day, the minimum number of overs shall be reduced by one over for each full 3.75 minutes of the aggregate playing time lost.

(d) On the last day, if any of the minimum of 80 overs, or as recalculated, have not been bowled when one hour of scheduled playing time remains, the last hour of the match for the purposes of Clause (e) shall be the hour immediately following the completion of those overs.

(e) Laws 16.6, 16.7 and 16.8 will apply except that a minimum of 16 overs shall be bowled in the last hour and all calculations with regard to suspensions of play or the start of a new innings shall be based on one over for each full 3.75 minutes (refer (i) below). If, however, at any time after 30 minutes of the last hour have elapsed both Captains (the batsmen at the wicket may act for their Captain) accept that there is no prospect of a result to the match, they may agree to cease play at that time.

(f) Notwithstanding any other provision, there shall be no further play on any day, other than the last day, if a wicket falls or a batsman retires or if the players have occasion to leave the field during the last minimum over within 2 minutes of the scheduled or re-scheduled cessation time or thereafter.

(g) An over completed on resumption of a new day's play shall be disregarded in calculating minimum overs for that day.

(h) Except on the final day, if in the event of ground, weather or light conditions causing a suspension of play and/or if the players are already off the field at the re-scheduled cessation time or any time thereafter, stumps shall be drawn.

(i) Fractions are to be ignored in all calculations re the number of overs except where there is a change of innings in a day's play, when the over in progress at the conclusion shall be rounded up.

(j) The scoreboard shall show:

– the total number of overs bowled with the ball currently in use: and

– the minimum number of overs remaining to be bowled in a day;

– the number of overs above or below the target overs for the innings.

(k) Penalties shall apply for not achieving over rates.

Subject to the provisions of Clause 4 (Minimum Overs in the Day), over rates shall be assessed on 16 overs per hour, ie a minimum of 96 overs in a six hour day, subject to the following deductions:

2 minutes	for every wicket taken
4 minutes	for one drinks break taken in any session
actual time	where treatment by authorised medical personnel is required on the ground and/or for a player leaving the field due to serious injury.

Overs will be calculated at the end of the match. For each over short of the target number, 0.1 shall be deducted from the team's match points.

For the purpose of calculation of penalties.

(a) the scheduled last hour of the match, as defined in clause 4 (e) shall be excluded.

(b) a maximum allowance of 20 overs in any hour shall apply

In the event of a match finishing within 3 scheduled playing days, penalties for not achieving the required over rates shall not apply, regardless of the hours played on those days.

A Commissioner appointed by the ACB will hear and determine all appeals against penalties imposed.

For the purpose of determining whether the fielding side has fallen short of the target number of overs, umpires may take into account any factor they consider relevant, including whether inclement weather has adversely affected the ability of the fielding side to comply with the required over rate.

Appeals shall be lodged within 14 days of the completion of the match.

The onus shall be on the appellant to prove that the umpires have erred in their assessment of time allowances. Video evidence where available may be produced by the appellant in support of the appeal.

Umpires will be required to record all delays and stoppages on the appropriate form.

30. The Result

Match Points

(i)	For an outright win after leading on the first innings	6 Points
(ii)	For an outright win after a tie in the first innings	6 Points
(iii)	For an outright win after being behind on the first innings	6 Points
(iv)	For a tie where both teams have completed two innings (irrespective of the first innings result)	3 Points
(v)	For a first innings lead (to be retained even if beaten outright)	2 Points
(vi)	For an outright loss after leading on the first innings	2 Points
(vii)	For a tie on the first innings (and no outright result)	1 Point each
(viii)	For an outright loss after a tie in the first innings	1 Point
(ix)	For a loss on the first innings	Nil
(x)	For an outright loss after being behind on the first innings	Nil
(xi)	Abandoned or drawn matches with no first innings result	Nil
(xii)	Abandoned match due to negligence (see Clause 19)	

Law 21 shall apply with the following:

Any query on the result of the match as defined in Law 21.1, 21.3, 21.4, 21.5, 21.8, and 21.10 shall be resolved as soon as possible and a final decision made by the umpires at the close of play.

Qualifying For The Final

The two teams which have highest aggregate of points at the end of a season shall play off in a final for the Pura Cup for that season (refer clause 58).

In the event of an equality of points the higher number of outright wins will determine the positions on the Pura Cup table.

Should there be equality in both points and wins, the positions shall be determine by average calculated thus:

(i) divide the total number of runs scored by a State by the total number of wickets lost by it.

(ii) divide the total number of runs scored against a State by the total number of wickets taken by it.

(iii) divide the former (i) by the latter (ii)

(iv) The team having the higher percentage shall be considered to have the better performance.

For the purpose of the calculations and for individual averages a team declaring its innings closed shall be deemed to have lost only the number of wickets which have actually fallen.

For the purpose of the calculations the provisions of Clause 30 shall apply.

Note: It is possible for a team to record a negative points tally on the Pura Cup table as a result of penalties incurred under the provision of Clause 4.

55. Interpretation of Playing Conditions

55.1 Uniform Interpretation

The local state association shall be responsible to ensure uniform interpretation of these playing conditions and to adjudicate, if necessary, should there be any dispute.

55.2 Contrived Result

1. The ACB shall have the power to investigate a game or the actions of the captains of the teams or any player involved in a match, if it suspects reasonably that the competing states with or without the assistance of any other person or club have colluded to contrive the result of a match. If the ACB decides to carry out an investigation, it will conduct such inquiries as it sees fit and invite submissions about the match or the conduct of either captain or any player, and will give the opportunity to be heard to interested parties, including representatives of both teams involved.

2. If the ACB finds that the teams, officials, captains or players have colluded unfairly to contrive the outcome of a match, to the detriment of any other team in the competition, the ACB may in its absolute discretion do one or more of the following:

    (a) fine a team, captain or player;

    (b) suspend a captain from playing in any match or matches;

    (c) disallow any points earned by a team in respect of the match;

    (d) amend any points earned by a team in the match; or

    (e) take such other action as is deemed appropriate by the ACB.

    For the purpose of this playing condition, "colluded unfairly to contrive the outcome of a match" means an agreement designed to contrive the outcome of a match in favour of a particular team or to achieve a result which is unfair to any of the other teams in the same competition. The operation of this playing condition is not intended to prevent competing captains from making aggressive declarations with a view to giving either side the chance of achieving an outright win.

58. Pura Cup Final

Except as varied hereunder ordinary Pura Cup playing conditions shall apply.

58.1 Duration of Match

(a) The Pura Cup Final shall be of five days scheduled duration.

(b) If immediately prior to the commencement of the scheduled last hour of the match a cumulative total of at least six hours scheduled play has been lost on account of weather, light, pitch or ground, then one extra day shall be added.

(c) If the match has not commenced by 2.40 pm on the fourth day then the match shall revert to a first innings match played under ordinary conditions (i.e. total playing time remaining is 15 hours or less including the extra day as in (b) above).

58.2 Over Rates

As per Test Match Playing Conditions Clause 3. That is, the initial minimum of overs shall be 90 calculated at one over for each complete four minutes.

58.3 Penalties for not Achieving Over Rates

Overs will be calculated at the end of the match. For each over short of the target number 5%, of each players match fee in the fielding side (excluding twelfth man) is to be deducted for the first five overs and 10% per over thereafter.

58.4 Venue

The State whose team finishes on top of the points table at the conclusion of the preliminary matches shall have the choice of venue, provided that this venue is acceptable to the Australian Cricket Board. Should the State waive this right, the choice shall be offered to the State whose team finishes second. Otherwise the decision shall be made by the Board.

58.5 Umpires

The Umpires for the Final shall be appointed by the Board and must be members of the National Umpires Panel.

58.6 Referee

ACB will appoint a Referee for the Final

58.7 Result

The team finishing second must defeat the team finishing first outright to win the Pura Cup; except where 58.1(c) above applies, whereby the match shall revert to a first innings result.

Note: If the Final is drawn or tied, the team finishing at the top of the points table prior to the Final shall be declared the winner of the Pura Cup.

ING CUP
PLAYING CONDITIONS, 2001-02

Pura Cup Playing Conditions and the Laws of Cricket (2000 Code) shall apply except as varied below.

1. Duration of Matches and Composition of Team

1.1 Mercantile Mutual Cup matches shall be of one day's scheduled duration. The matches will consist of one innings per side and each innings will be limited to 50 six-ball overs. A minimum of 15 overs per team shall constitute a match (finals a minimum of 25 overs per team).

1.2 A team shall consist of twelve players.

Eleven fieldsmen only shall be on the field of play at any one time.

One player in each side shall not be permitted to bat.

Interchange of fieldsmen without restriction is permitted, provided no playing time is wasted.

1.3. Replacement player

- Should any player during a match be required by ACB for playing duties elsewhere, that requirement shall take precedence.

- The player's Association will then be able to select a like player as the replacement for the remainder of the match concerned.

- The player's Association will submit nominations for the replacement player to the opposing team Captain for approval which must not be unreasonably withheld.

- If after a replacement player has been chosen the replaced player's services are no longer required by ACB, the player may resume his place in the Team only if his replacement has not either batted or bowled in his absence. Otherwise the player may take no further part in the match and the replacement player must continue in his stead.

2. Hours of Play and Intervals

2.1.1 Final

Time and venue to be determined by ACB.

2.1.2 Venues

If it is necessary for ACB to transfer a match, the hours of play applying to the new venue shall be determined by ACB.

There will be two sessions of 3½ hours each.

2.2 Interval between Innings

The innings of the team batting second shall not commence before the scheduled time for commencement of the second session unless the team batting first has completed its innings at least 30 minutes prior to the scheduled interval, in which case a ten-minute break will occur and the team batting second will commence its innings and the interval will occur as scheduled.

Where play is delayed or interrupted the umpires will reduce the length of the interval as follows:

Time Lost	Interval
Up to 60 minutes	30 minutes
Between 60 and 120 minutes	20 minutes
More than 120 minutes	10 minutes

Note: Refer also to the provisions of Clause 4.2.

2.3 Intervals for Drinks

Two drinks breaks per session shall be permitted, each one hour ten minutes apart. The provisions of Law 15.9 shall be strictly observed except that under conditions of extreme heat the umpires may permit extra intervals for drinks.

An individual player may be given a drink either on the boundary edge or at the fall of a wicket, on the field, provided that no playing time is wasted. No other drinks shall be taken onto the field without the permission of the umpires. Any player taking drinks onto the field shall be dressed in proper cricket attire.

2.4 Extra Time

Provision has been made for up to 15 minutes of extra official playing time and up to 45 minutes in day/night matches – refer 4.2.1 (a) and 4.2.3.

11. Points

11.1 Preliminary Matches

Win   4

Tie or No Result   2

Loss   0

11.2 Bonus Points

The team that achieves a run-rate of 1.25 times that of the opposition shall be awarded one bonus point.

A team's run-rate will be calculated by reference to the runs scored in an innings divided by the number of overs faced.

Where matches are shortened and targets revised using the Duckworth/Lewis system, bonus run-rates and defensive targets are derived as a function of the revised target score and maximum overs.

In the event of the teams finishing on equal points, the right to play in the final match will be determined as follows:

- The team with the most number of wins
- The team with the most number of wins over the other team(s)
- The team with the highest number of bonus points
- The team with the highest net run-rate

In a match declared no result, run-rate is not applicable.

11.3 Net Run-Rate

A team's net run-rate is calculated by deducting from the average runs per over scored by that team throughout the competition, the average runs per over scored against that team throughout the competition.

In the event of a team being all out in less than its full quota of overs, the calculation of its net run-rate shall be based on the full quota of overs to which it would have been entitled and not on the number of overs in which the team was dismissed.

Only those matches where results are achieved will count for the purpose of net run rate calculations. Where a match is abandoned, but a result is achieved under Duckworth/Lewis, for net run rate purposes Team 1 will be accredited with Team 2's Par Score on abandonment off the same number of overs faced by Team 2. Where a match is concluded but with Duckworth/Lewis having been applied at an earlier point in the match, Team 1 will be accredited with 1 run less than the final Target Score for Team 2 off the total number of overs allocated to Team 2 to reach the target.

12. Penalty for not Bowling Required Overs

If the team fielding second fails to bowl the required number of overs by the scheduled time for cessation of the second session, play shall continue until the required number of overs has been bowled or a result achieved.

Unless determined otherwise the referee, after consultation with the match umpires and the scorers, shall award a penalty of six runs per over to the batting side for each over short of the required number at the scheduled, or re-scheduled, cessation time.

12.1 If the team fielding second fails to bowl the required number of overs by the scheduled time for cessation of the session, play shall continue until the required number of overs has been bowled or a result achieved.

Unless determined otherwise by the Referee, after consultation with the match umpires and the scorers, a penalty of six (6) runs per over shall be awarded to the batting side for each over short of the required number at the scheduled, or rescheduled, cessation time.

The over in progress at the cessation time shall count as a complete over.

18. Final

18.1 Venue

The Final shall be played at a venue to be determined by ACB.

18.2 Tie

If there is a tie in the Final, the teams competing in the Final shall be declared joint winners.

18.3 No Result

If no result is achieved in the Final on the scheduled day of play, the match shall be replayed on the reserve date as scheduled.

In the event of a no result in the Final (including the reserve day), the team finishing on top of the points table at the end of the preliminary matches shall be declared the winner.

18.4 Reserve Date

Monday February 25, 2002.

AUSTRALIAN CRICKET BOARD CODE OF BEHAVIOUR

PREAMBLE

Cricket is a game that owes much of its unique appeal to the fact that it is to be played not only within its Laws, but also within the spirit of the game. Any action seen as abusing this spirit causes injury to the game itself.

Embracing the spirit of the game means playing fairly and exhibiting respect for opponents, fellow team members, the umpires and the game's traditional values such as graciousness in defeat and humility in victory.

Cricket has a distinct place in Australian society and history. As an element in Australia's national identity, cricket plays a significant role. This status brings with it particular responsibilities for players and officials to conform to high standards of fair play and personal behaviour on and off the field.

This Code of Behaviour is intended to protect and enshrine such important qualities and standards so that all may continue to enjoy the game of cricket now and in the future.

SECTION 1: RULES FOR BEHAVIOUR

Laws of Cricket and spirit of the game

1.   Players must obey the **Laws of Cricket** and play within the spirit of the game.

2.   The captain and team coach must use their best efforts to ensure that their team complies with Rule 1 of this Section.

Unbecoming behaviour

3.   Players and officials must not at any time engage in behaviour unbecoming to a representative player or official that could bring the game of cricket into disrepute or be harmful to the interests of cricket.

Assaults

4.   Players and officials must not assault or attempt to assault:

    a)   another player or official, or

    b)   a spectator or other person attending a match to which this Code applies.

Intimidation of umpires and dissent

5.   Players and team officials must not intimidate an umpire and must accept the umpire's decision. Players and team officials must not show dissent from the umpire's decision.

Crude or abusive behaviour and racial or religious vilification

6.   (a)   Players and officials must not use crude or abusive language or make crude or abusive gestures.

    (b)   Players and officials must obey the ACB's Racial and Religious Vilification Code as amended from time to time.

Anti-doping policy

7.   Players and officials must obey the Anti-Doping Policy as amended from time to time.

Betting, match-fixing and corruption

8.   Players or officials must not, directly or indirectly, engage in the following conduct:

    (a)   bet, gamble or enter into any other form of financial speculation on any cricket match or on any event connected with any cricket match;

    (b)   induce or encourage any other person to bet, gamble or enter into any other form of financial speculation on any cricket match or on any event connected with any cricket match or to offer the facility for such bets to be placed;

    (c)   be a party to contriving or attempting to contrive the result of any cricket match or the occurrence of any event connected with any cricket match in exchange for any benefit or reward (other than a benefit or reward received from his home board);

    (d)   fail to perform on his merits in any cricket match for any reason whatsoever (including, in particular, owing to an arrangement relating to betting on the outcome of any cricket match or on the occurrence of any event connected with any cricket match) other than for legitimate tactical reasons in relation to that cricket match;

(e) induce or encourage any player not to perform on his merits in any cricket match for any reason whatsoever (including, in particular, owing to an arrangement relating to betting on the outcome of any cricket match or on the occurrence of any event connected with any cricket match) other than for legitimate tactical reasons in relation to that cricket match;

(f) for benefit or reward (whether for himself or any other person), provide any information concerning the weather, the state of the ground, a team or its members (including, without limitation, the team's actual or likely composition, the form of individual players or tactics), the status or possible outcome of any cricket match or the possible occurrence of any event connected with any cricket match other than in connection with bona fide media interviews and commitments;

(g) engage in any other form of corrupt conduct in relation to any cricket match or event connected with any cricket match;

(h) fail to promptly disclose to the Chief Executive Officer of the ACB that he has received an approach from another person to engage in conduct such as that described in paragraphs (a) to (g) above (such disclosure to be in writing and include full particulars of any such approach);

(i) fail to promptly disclose to the Chief Executive Officer of the ACB that he knows or reasonably suspects that any current or former player or official or any other person has engaged in conduct, or been approached to engage in conduct, such as that described in paragraphs (a) to (g) above (such disclosure to be in writing and include full particulars of any such knowledge or suspicion);

(j) fail to promptly disclose to the Chief Executive Officer of the ACB that he has received, or is aware or reasonably suspects that another player or official or any other person has received, actual or implied threats of any nature in relation to past or proposed conduct such as that described in paragraphs (a) to (g) above (such disclosure to be in writing and include full particulars of any such knowledge or suspicion); or

(k) engage in conduct that relates directly or indirectly to any of the conduct described in paragraphs (a) to (j) above and is prejudicial to the interests of the game of cricket.

Clothing, footwear and equipment

9. While playing Matches, training, attending official functions or acting in an official or representative capacity for cricket, players and officials must wear and use only that clothing, footwear and equipment approved by or on behalf of the ACB. The wearing or display of a commercial motif or logo (whether on clothing, equipment or directly on part of the body) not expressly permitted under the Playing Conditions or otherwise approved in writing by or on behalf of the ACB is not permitted.

Detrimental public comment

10. Players and officials must not make any public or media comment which is detrimental to the interests of the game or to a tour or series of matches in which they are or are likely to be involved. Without limitation, players and officials will breach this Rule 10 if, by making such comment in the circumstances, they:

   (a) denigrate a country in which they are or are likely to be touring or officiating;

   (b) denigrate the home country of a touring team against which they are or are likely to be playing or in respect of which they are or are likely to be officiating;

   (c) make detrimental comment upon the prospects of selection in any team of any player or upon the selection of any team when made; or

   (d) make detrimental comment upon the prospects of appointment of any team official or to the appointment of that person to another official capacity or upon the appointment when made.

Comment on disciplinary proceedings

1. Players and officials must not make any public disclosure of or any public or media comment upon:

   (a) any report made to the Commission alleging a breach of this Code or of any appeal from a decision of the Commission;

   (b) he proceedings of any hearing of a report or appeal before the Commission; or

   (c) the decision of the Commission in relation to a report or appeal.

SECTION 2: THE CODE OF BEHAVIOUR COMMISSION

Establishment

1. A Code of Behaviour Commission is established.

Powers

2. The Commission is empowered to:

   (a) hear and decide reports and appeals brought under this Code and penalise any breaches;

   (b) hear and decide complaints referred to it under the Racial and Religious Vilification Code and penalise any breaches; and

   (c) deal with any other matter referred to it by the ACB.

SECTION 4: HEARINGS

Procedure

1. The Commission will hold a hearing into each report made to it. Where appropriate, the Commission may hear more than one report simultaneously where those reports are in respect of the same or related behaviour.

2. The hearing of a report in relation to on-field behaviour (other than a report made by the Chief Executive Officer of the ACB pursuant to Rule 2 of

Section 3) will be held promptly after the person against whom the report is made has been informed of the making of the report and its details. In the normal course of events and subject to the availability of a Commissioner, such reports will be heard on the day of the making of the report and no later than the commencement of the next match in which the player or official is scheduled to participate. The Commission may grant an adjournment of the hearing where the player or official demonstrates that an adjournment is essential in order to be given a fair opportunity to prepare a defence. The hearing of a report by the Chief Executive Officer of the ACB pursuant to Rule 2 of Section 3 will be held as soon as practicable after the report has been lodged, having regard always to the requirements to accord procedural fairness to the player or official concerned.

SECTION 5: PENALTIES

1. Subject to Rule 5 of this Section, in the event the Commission decides that any person has breached this Code of Behaviour, it will apply one or more of the following penalties:

    (a) Ban the person from representing Australia in international competition or in any other cricket activity;

    (b) Ban the person from (in the case of a player) being selected in a team or (in the case of an official) being involved in any team or match;

    (c) Ban the person from holding (or continuing to hold) any position within the ACB or a State or Territory Cricket Association (including as an employee or officer);

    (d) Fine the person;

    (e) Direct that the person make reparation for damage caused by that person to any property;

    (f) Require the person to undergo counselling for a specified time;

    (g) Require the person to perform voluntary service to cricket or the community;

    (h) Reprimand the person.

2. Subject to Rule 3 and Rule 5 of this Section, when imposing any penalty upon a person who has breached the Code, the Commission may take into account any circumstance it considers relevant, including the following:

    (a) the seriousness of the breach;

    (b) the harm caused by the breach to the interests of cricket;

    (c) the person's seniority and standing in the game;

    (d) remorse shown by the person and the prospect of further breaches;

    (e) the prior record of the person in abiding by this Code, the ICC Code of Conduct and any similar code of behaviour; and

    (f) the impact of the penalty on the person, including the person's capacity to pay a fine as evidenced by the proportion of the person's annual income from the ACB or a state or territory cricket association that the proposed fine represents.

AUSTRALIAN CRICKET BOARD
RACIAL AND RELIGIOUS VILIFICATION CODE

1. Purpose of Code

The purpose of this Code is to:

1. Recognise the commitment of the Australian Cricket Board to the elimination of racial and religious vilification of players.

2. Establish a framework for handling complaints made by players who believe they have been subjected to racial or religious vilification by another player.

2. Conduct Covered by the Code

A player who is participating in a match under the jurisdiction or auspices of the ACB will not engage in any conduct, act towards or speak to any other player in a manner which offends, insults, humiliates, intimidates, threatens, disparages or vilifies the other player on the basis of that player's race, religion, colour, descent or national or ethnic origin.

THE ACB'S POSITION ON DOPING

2.1 The ACB condemns the use of performance-enhancing drugs and doping practices in sport. The use of performance-enhancing drugs and doping practices is contrary to the ethics of sport and potentially harmful to the health of athletes.

The only legitimate use of drugs in sport is under the supervision of a physician for a clinically justified purpose.

2.2 The ACB aims to prevent the use of performance-enhancing drugs and doping practices in cricket by:

(a) imposing effective sanctions on persons who commit doping offences;

(b) educating and informing persons about drugs in sport; and

(c) supporting the drug-testing programs and education initiatives of the Australian Sports Drug Agency and other drug-testing authorities.

PART SEVEN: MISCELLANEOUS

CHRONICLE OF 2001-02

By Shane Erickson

AUGUST

7 Adam Gilchrist is named as Australia's stand-in captain for the Fourth Test of the Ashes series, replacing the injured Steve Waugh. Ricky Ponting is named as his deputy. **10** Sussex police are called to a burglary at the pavilion of the Hove County Cricket Ground after £1,200 worth of equipment is stolen from the Australian team's dressing room. Adam Gilchrist and Ricky Ponting score centuries as Australia beat Sussex in their final county tour match. **11** Queensland fast bowler Ashley Noffke returns home from the Ashes tour after injuring his right ankle against Sussex. **14** South African fast bowler Allan Donald announces he has come out of Test retirement in a bid to play Australia later in the year. Simon Katich is picked for his Test debut, replacing the injured Steve Waugh for the Fourth Test. **16** Ricky Ponting scores a long overdue century in the rain-affected opening day of the Fourth Test. **18** Glenn McGrath becomes the third Australian player to take 350 Test wickets after capturing 7/76 in the Fourth Test. **20** Following the refusal of the MCC to hand over the original Ashes urn to the Australians, Steve Waugh wants to create Australia's own Ashes trophy by burning the bails after the final Test at The Oval. Mark Butcher scores an unbeaten 173 to lead England to a surprise six-wicket win over Australia in the Fourth Test. **21** Christchurch, New Zealand is announced as the venue of the Under-19s World Cup beginning in January 2002. **22** Michael Slater breaks ranks and reveals to a Sydney radio station that he has been dropped for the final Test, to be replaced by Justin Langer. **23** Steve Waugh makes an astonishing recovery to be fit for the final Test at The Oval. Justin Langer impresses with 102 in his first Test of the tour. **24** Steve Waugh scores a gutsy unbeaten 157 in Australia's first innings total of four for 641 declared. **25** Geoff Marsh is appointed the new Zimbabwean coach, taking over from Carl Rackemann. Shane Warne becomes the sixth bowler in Test history to take 400 wickets. **27** An anonymous group of businessmen who bought five letters written by Sir Donald Bradman to former Australian captain Greg Chappell donate them to the Bradman Foundation. Australia claim a 4-1 series win after defeating England by an innings and 25 runs to confirm their lead at the head of the ICC Test Championship table. Man of the Series Glenn McGrath picks up five second-innings wickets to top the bowling for the series with 32. **28** Steve Waugh reclaims the No.1 spot in the PricewaterhouseCoopers cricket ratings for Test batsmen, while Glenn McGrath receives the highest rating of any bowler for nearly 20 years. **31** New ICC conditions specify the mandatory use of lights, where available, for all Test matches, a no-ball penalty for short-pitched deliveries not allowing a batsman to make contact with a normal cricket stroke in Test matches, the provision to bowl one bouncer per over in limited-overs internationals, and a new bonus points system for limited-overs tournaments.

SEPTEMBER

6 Shane Warne predicts Michael Slater will return to Test cricket "stronger and better" following his axing during the Ashes series. **11** Zimbabwean Andy Flower becomes the first wicket-keeper to occupy the No. 1 position in the PricewaterhouseCoopers ratings for batsmen. Steve Waugh is now second. **16** The ICC Anti-Corruption Unit led by Lord Condon visits South Africa for a series of meetings linked to security planning and the prevention of corruption during the 2003 World Cup. **17** New Zealand asks Australia to expand the itinerary of its November and December tour to compensate for the cancellation of a tour of Pakistan amid security concerns. **18** Former ACB Director and Test cricketer Barry Shepherd dies, aged 64. **19** South Africa's 1-0 series win over Zimbabwe moves their average to just 0.12 behind Australia. **21** Bob Merriman is named Chairman of the ACB at the annual general meeting in Melbourne after long-serving Dennis Rogers does not seek re-election. **30** Steve Waugh begins a course of blood-thinning tablets after problems with the leg injury suffered on the Ashes tour. It is rumoured he is suffering from deep vein thrombosis.

OCTOBER

1 Victorian coach John Scholes resigns just six days before the first match of the season. **2** A Melbourne court hears that West Indian fast bowler Marlon Black lost his place in international cricket as well as an income of $100,000 following an attack on him earlier in the year outside Colonial Stadium. **3** Steve Waugh confirms he is suffering from deep vein thrombosis but expects to be fit for the First Test against New Zealand in five weeks. The long flight back from the Ashes tour apparently contributed to the formation of a blood clot in his injured calf muscle. **5** Former Australian Test batsman, ICC match referee and 1965 Wisden Cricketer of the Year, Peter Burge, dies, aged 69. **6** Injured New Zealand trio Chris Cairns, Dion Nash and Daniel Vettori return from lengthy lay-offs to be named in the squad to tour Australia. **7** The ING Cup begins with New South Wales crushing Victoria by 123 runs at the Memorial Oval, Bankstown. **10** Victoria appoint Michael O'Sullivan as coach for season 2001-02. **16** New Zealand captain Stephen Fleming helps dig his side out of trouble with an unbeaten 133 on the first day of their opening tour match against the Queensland Academy of Sport. **17** The ICC welcomes the judgement by Justice Frank Kirk-Cohen that upholds the life ban imposed on Hansie Cronje from playing and coaching at first-class and international level. **19** A hat-trick to Victorian Ian Harvey cannot prevent South Australia from taking first-innings points in their Pura Cup clash at the Adelaide Oval. **21** New Zealand spinner Daniel Vettori is stretchered from Manuka Oval with a badly sprained ankle following a fall in the three-day match against the ACT President's XI. **23** Daniel Vettori is forced home just two weeks before the First Test. **26** Jason Gillespie records career-best figures of 8/50 for South Australia against New South Wales at the Sydney Cricket Ground. **31** Andy Bichel is included in the 12-man squad for the First Test against New Zealand.

NOVEMBER

2 New Zealand's Nathan Astle records a first-class highest score of 223 against Queensland at the Brisbane Cricket Ground. **3** Steve Waugh notches up 84 on his return to cricket for Sydney club Bankstown. **5** The ICC introduces tough new security measures to combat corruption, including TV cameras covering entrances and exits to players' dressing rooms. **7** Daniel Vettori makes a stunning return from injury and is picked to play in the First Test. **8** The ACB announces that Australian Test shirts will now include the players' initials and cap number on the front. Justin Langer and Matthew Hayden get Australia off to a dream start with an opening partnership of 224 in the First Test. **10** The United Arab Emirates upset an Australian team of ex-international players in their Hong Kong Cricket Sixes game. **11** New Zealand captain Stephen Fleming records his fourth duck from his last six Test innings in Australia as Jason Gillespie rips open the Kiwi top order. **12** The First Test ends in a thrilling draw after four days of rain-affected play. **14** Steve Waugh announces, along with a bat sponsorship worth $750,000 over three years, his intention of continuing into his 40th year to complete "unfinished business" by winning a Test series in India. **20** Australian coach John Buchanan agrees to a new two-year contract taking him through to spring 2003. **21** Steve Waugh comes out in support of match referee Mike Denness's decision to fine and place a suspended Test ban on Indian star Sachin Tendulkar for misconduct in the Test series in South Africa. **22** Australia get off to a strong start in the Second Test in Hobart, scoring six for 411 on the opening day. Pakistani speedster Shoaib Akhtar is picked for his Sydney grade debut for Mosman Cricket Club. **23** Veteran fast bowlers Allan Donald and Steve Elworthy are selected in the South African squad to tour Australia but there is no room for Daryll Cullinan. **26** The Second Test ends in a draw after rain permits only 86 minutes of play on the final day. **30** On the first day of the third and deciding Test, New Zealand lose five for 75 in the last hour to finish at seven for 293 at stumps.

DECEMBER

2 Tasmania score their highest-ever score against Victoria (nine for 527 declared) on the third day of the Pura Cup game in Hobart. **4** A seesawing final day of the Third Test between Australia and New Zealand sees Australia hold on for a draw at seven for 381 chasing 440 for victory. Australian bowler Brett Lee is fined 75 per cent of his match fee after breaching the ICC's Code of Conduct during the Test. **5** Australian captain Steve Waugh suggests Australia will have to raise their game or risk losing the upcoming series against South Africa as the visitors open their tour of Australia with a victory against an ACB Chairman's XI by 48 runs in a 50-over match in Perth. **9** Australia opt for two spinners in the squad for the First Test against South Africa, choosing Stuart MacGill to partner Shane Warne. **10** South African Jacques Kallis continues his great form in preparation for the Test series with a century on the final day of the drawn tour match against Western Australia. **14** South African Claude Henderson takes three important wickets on the opening day of the First Test in Adelaide. New South Wales win the national Under-19s championship for 2001-02 after triumphing in a thrilling final against Queensland by 22 runs in Newcastle. **15** South Australian skipper Darren Lehmann becomes the greatest run-scorer in Australian domestic first-class cricket, surpassing his former skipper Jamie Siddons's record of 10,643 runs. **16** South African cricket and government officials deny a claim by Australian journalists that Makhaya Ntini was selected to play for South Africa because selectors were obliged to pick two non-white players for the Adelaide Test. **18** Shane Warne and Glenn McGrath bowl South Africa out for 128 and secure victory in the opening Test in Adelaide. Queensland head into the Christmas break on top of both the Pura and ING Cup points tables. **20** Stuart MacGill produces figures of 5/125 including 3/0 from seven deliveries for New South Wales against South Africa. **23** Pressure mounts on South African all-rounder Lance Klusener after scoring a pair against New South Wales. **24** Australian fast bowler Jason Gillespie is forced out of the Second Test against South Africa with a shoulder injury. Uncapped Western Australian fast bowler Brad Williams replaces him in the squad. **26** Day one of the Boxing Day Test is reduced to just 40 overs due to rain. **29** Australia win the Second Test by nine wickets with a day to spare and clinch the three-match series to retain world champion status. Steve Waugh is fined half of his match payment after showing dissent following a run-out decision by umpire Darrell Hair. **31** Lance Klusener is dropped for the Third Test and returns home. His replacement is left-arm spinner Nicky Boje.

JANUARY

2 Australia score five for 308 on the opening day of the Sydney Test, however the real story surrounds the selection of Justin Ontong for the South Africans. United Cricket Board president Percy Sonn vetoes the selection of Jacques Rudolph in line with a UCB principle that there should be opportunities "for people of colour who have been previously disadvantaged". **3** South Africa is forced to follow on some 400 runs behind on the second day of the Third Test. **5** Australia seal a 3-0 series whitewash after defeating South Africa by ten wickets on the fourth day at the SCG. **6** A hat-trick to New South Wales bowler Nathan Bracken is not enough to save New South Wales from losing their ING Cup match against Victoria at the MCG. **11** New Zealand win the opening match of the VB Series by 23 runs in Melbourne despite defending a target of just 199. **12** Glenn McGrath is suspended for one match after being found guilty of dissent during Australia's clash with New Zealand, while Brad Williams is ruled out for a month with a fractured right thumb. **13** Australia crash to no wins from two starts after losing to South Africa by four wickets at the MCG. **14** Western Australian keeper Ryan Campbell is called in to the Australian squad to replace Adam Gilchrist after he returns home for personal reasons. **17** Australia's hopes of reaching the VB Series finals receive another blow after losing to New Zealand by 23 runs at the SCG. **19** New Zealand notch up a four-wicket victory over South Africa at the Gabba thanks mainly to a century from Chris Cairns. **20** Australia break their VB Series duck with a hard-fought 27-run victory over South Africa at the Gabba. **22** Australia continue their form reversal with a resounding victory over South Africa at the SCG to move into second place on the table. **23** Victorian and Australian fast bowler Paul Reiffel retires from first-class cricket after 14 years at the top level including 35 Tests and 92 limited-overs internationals. **27** South Africa are back in contention for the VB Series after a 93-run victory over New Zealand at the Adelaide Oval. **29** New Zealand captain Stephen Fleming is charged with dissent during Australia's amazing two-wicket win over the Kiwis with just three balls to spare at the MCG.

FEBRUARY

1 South Africa are the first team to advance to the finals of the VB Series with a crushing 67-run victory over New Zealand in Perth. **2** Australia miss out on the VB Series finals despite a 33-run victory over South Africa. The Australians needed a bonus point to advance. **4** The ACB takes no action against captain Steve Waugh after a hostile ending to his WACA post-match media conference in which he swore under his breath and muttered that some journalists were "on thin ice". **6** South Africa win the opening final of the VB Series, thrashing New Zealand by eight wickets at the MCG. **7** Australia advance to the finals of the Under-19s World Cup in New Zealand after defeating West Indies in the semi-final. **8** South Africa take out the VB Series after defeating New Zealand by six wickets in the final at the SCG. **9** Australia win the Under-19s World Cup with a seven-wicket victory over South Africa. Australian Jarrad Burke scores an unbeaten 100. **11** Matthew Hayden tops off a sensational 12 months by being named the 2002 Allan Border Medallist. **12** India's Sachin Tendulkar replaces Australia's Michael Bevan as No.1 in the world limited-overs international batting rankings while Australian Glenn McGrath maintains his position as the best bowler. **13** Steve Waugh is axed as Australia's limited-overs captain for the series in South Africa starting in March. Waugh says he sees his sacking as "a setback and a challenge". **14** Western Australian Michael Hussey collects $200,000 after connecting with a sponsor's sign in a day-night game against New South Wales at the WACA. **16** Tasmanian Ricky Ponting is named captain of the Australian limited-overs team for the tour of South Africa and Zimbabwe with Adam Gilchrist his deputy. **17** Queensland earn the right to host the ING Cup final against New South Wales with victory over South Australia. **18** The ACB confirms that the Victoria Police are investigating allegations of blackmail. **19** The ACB reveals blackmail allegations centre around accusations that Shane Warne inappropriately kissed a girl on Queensland's Gold Coast. Warne denies the accusations. **20** Australia beat New Zealand by 53 runs in the opening match of the women's cricket series in Adelaide. **21** New South Wales batsman Graeme Rummans withdraws from the ING Cup final after testing positive to the banned masking agent probenecid. **22** Matthew Hayden's century leads the Australians to a dominant position on the first day of the First Test against South Africa, while Allan Donald injures a hamstring. Darren Lehmann is named limited-overs player of the series for the second year running. **23** Adam Gilchrist scores an unbeaten 204 from just 212 balls – the fastest Test double-century – in Australia's first innings of seven for 652 declared. **24** South Africa crash to the second-biggest defeat of all time, losing the First Test by an innings and 360 runs inside three days. New South Wales win back-to-back limited-overs cups, defeating Queensland by 19 runs. **25** Allan Donald announces his retirement from Test cricket after being plagued by injury over the past two years. **28** Victorian Brad Hodge reaches 5,000 domestic first-class runs with his century against Western Australia at the MCG.

MARCH

1 The ACB Anti-Doping Committee fines New South Wales batsman Graeme Rummans $2,000 and suspends him from all forms of cricket for one month after he tested positive for a banned substance. **3** Western Australia record the greatest comeback in domestic first-class cricket history, beating Victoria by 37 runs after following on 275 runs behind. **4** Mark Waugh loses his spot in the limited-overs side for the series in South Africa and Zimbabwe. **5** After being selected for the Second Test, Daryll Cullinan is dropped after he demands an "A Category" contract until 2003. **8** Brett Lee bowls the fastest delivery ever recorded by speed gun, clocking 157.4 km/h on the first day of the Second Test in Cape Town. **10** Adam Gilchrist pushes his Test average beyond 60, scoring 138 not out from 108 balls. **11** Michael Slater is recalled to the New South Wales side and made captain for its closing game of the Pura Cup season. **12** Australia clinch the Test series against South Africa and retain the Test Championship title with a four-wicket victory. Shane Warne is named Man of the Match in his 100th Test. New Zealand's Nathan Astle breaks the record Adam Gilchrist set in February, scoring a Test double-century off only 153 balls against England in Christchurch. **16** Defending champions Queensland will host Tasmania in the Pura Cup final after both sides secure outright wins in their final matches. **18** South Africa avoid a whitewash against Australia, securing a five-wicket win in the final Test. Sri Lanka is confirmed as the venue of the ICC Champions Trophy in September. **20** Brad Hodge and Jimmy Maher are named joint winners of the 2001-02 Pura Cup Player of the Series, sharing the $8,000 award. **21** Shane Warne is ruled out of the first two limited-overs internationals against South Africa with a hamstring strain. **22** Australia win the opening limited-overs international against South Africa by 19 runs at the Wanderers. Queensland reach four for 253 at stumps on the opening day of the Pura Cup final in Brisbane. **24** Australia defeat South Africa by 45 runs at Centurion Park, Jimmy Maher top scoring with 95. **26** Queensland clinch their third successive first-class title and their fifth in eight years, thrashing Tasmania by 235 runs in the Pura Cup final. Andrew Symonds is named man of the match with six wickets and scores of 91 and 32. **27** Australia's last-wicket pair of Jimmy Maher and Nathan Hauritz score 17 from the last two overs to snatch a tie in the third international against South Africa in Potchefstroom. Australia withdraws from the tour of Zimbabwe, citing safety and security concerns. **30** Australia wins the fourth international in Bloemfontein to take an unbeatable 3-0 lead in the seven-match series. Ricky Ponting scores 129 for the tourists.

APRIL

1 Queensland's most successful leader, Stuart Law, stands down as captain following their Pura Cup championship win, citing family reasons for his decision. **3** The ACB announces that Melbourne and Brisbane will host the Super Challenge II series between Australia and Pakistan in June 2002. Australia take an unassailable 4-0 lead against South Africa with an eight-wicket victory at Kingsmead, thanks mainly to Adam Gilchrist, who scored 105 from 104 balls. **5** Adam Gilchrist, Jason Gillespie and Damien Martyn win selection among the five Cricketers of the Year in the 2002 edition of Wisden Cricketers' Almanack. **6** Australia record the highest-ever winning score by a team batting second in limited-overs internationals to beat South Africa by three wickets. **10** South Africa end their losing streak with a 65-run victory over Australia in the rain-affected final international at Cape Town. The Australians win the series 5-1. **13** Prize money of \$US5 million is announced for the 2002-03 World Cup tournament. The winners will pocket \$US2 million. **18** Sri Lankan off-spinner Muttiah Muralitharan is to be flown to Melbourne for examination by specialists to ascertain whether his shoulder requires surgery after injuring it while fielding in the Sharjah Cup final. Pakistan won the final by 217 runs. **21** Andy Bichel takes 9/93 in an innings for Worcestershire against Gloucestershire. **29** Cairns and Darwin are announced as Australia's newest Test cricket venues, with the ACB set to schedule winter Test matches for both cities as early as 2003. **30** Former Australian vice-captain David Hookes is named as Victoria's new coach on a two-year contract. He replaces Michael O'Sullivan after a troubled season for Victorian cricket. Shane Warne reaches an out-of-court settlement with the Melbourne *Herald-Sun* over a false match-fixing allegation.

MAY

1 An unprecedented seven revisions are made to the annual list of ACB contract holders. Michael Slater, Damien Fleming and Colin Miller are among six former international players out of favour. **6** Adam Gilchrist becomes the first regular No. 7 batsman to top the PricewaterhouseCoopers Test batting rankings after his superb form against South Africa took his average to 60. **8** New Zealand's tour of Pakistan is prematurely ended after a bomb kills 14 people outside the team's hotel in Karachi. None of the tour party was injured. The blast prompts the ACB to consider cancelling their tour of the country in September. **14** Shane Warne says he won't go to Pakistan if Australia's cricket tour goes ahead. "If it was tomorrow and we were going, I wouldn't be going, no way", he said. Australia's cricketers are named the best team in world sport at the Laureus World Sports Awards in Monte Carlo. **18** New South Wales land a major recruiting coup, announcing Simon Katich will be leaving his native Western Australia to join them next season. **21** The careers of Damien Fleming and Colin Miller seem finished after being overlooked by Victoria for contracts. **24** Steve Waugh is discharged from a Sydney hospital after undergoing minor surgery on his left ankle. **27** Adam Gilchrist tarnishes his image after being charged by the ACB with making statements detrimental to the sport. The charges follow a Melbourne AFL club luncheon where Gilchrist questions the legality of Sri Lankan spinner Muttiah Muralitharan's bowling action. **30** Adam Gilchrist receives a formal reprimand for his comments regarding Muttiah Muralitharan's bowling action. **31** Axed Victorian pace man Damien Fleming signs a two-year deal with South Australia.

JUNE

1 Former South African captain Hansie Cronje dies when his plane crashes in the Outeniqua Mountains on its approach to George in South Africa's Southern Cape.

3 Glenn McGrath returns to the top of PricewaterhouseCooper's list of the world's best bowlers by just one point over Muttiah Muralitharan. Adam Gilchrist is still rated the best batsman. **6** The Victorian government pledges $77 million and the MCC $13 million towards the MCG redevelopment, which will increase the ground's capacity to 100,000. **12** Australia win the opening game of the Super Challenge II series by seven wickets under the roof of Melbourne's Colonial Stadium. The battle of the two fastest bowlers in the world never eventuates, with both Brett Lee and Shoaib Akhtar left out of their teams. **13** ICC Elite Panel umpire Steve Bucknor breaks the world record for umpiring appearances as he officiates in his 67th Test, between England and Sri Lanka at Old Trafford. **15** Brett Lee and Shoaib Akhtar are included for the second game of the Super Challenge II series in Melbourne. Pakistan win the hard-fought match by two wickets. **19** A superb bowling performance by Shoaib Akhtar (5/25) helps Pakistan to a series-winning victory by 91 runs over Australia at the Gabba. **20** A mini-World Cup for women is to be played in New Zealand in 2003 with Australia, India and England joining the hosts for a 14-game series starting in January. **24** Australian limited-overs captain Ricky Ponting enters hospital in Melbourne to undergo surgery to repair stress fractures in his left foot. **27** The Pakistan and Australian cricket boards are forced to explore different options after Pakistan refuses to reschedule the October Test series between the countries. **28** Adam Gilchrist and Matthew Hayden join four other players as the nominees for the Federation of International Cricketers Association's Cricketer of the Year award to be announced in July.

JULY

1 Pakistan announces that a three-nation series involving New Zealand and Australia in August and a Test series with Australia in October will now be played outside the country. This follows fears for player safety. **2** Australia re-schedules its tour of Zimbabwe originally planned for April 2002 to mid-2004 because of civil unrest. Colin Miller announces his retirement after 17 years of first-class cricket. **9** Australia and New Zealand agree in principle to play Pakistan in a triangular one-day series to be staged in Kenya in August. **10** Former Australian fast bowler Paul Reiffel announces he will join the umpiring ranks next season, beginning initially in first-grade district matches. **11** Adam Gilchrist is recognised by his international peers as the Cricketer of the Year, receiving the award from the Federation of International Cricketers Association at a ceremony in London. **18** Australia confirm their availability for the August triangular one-day series moved from Pakistan to Kenya, but New Zealand pull out due to a busy international schedule. **19** Queensland off-spinner Nathan Hauritz is the only addition to the 13 players who took part in the June Super Challenge II series for the approaching limited-overs series against Pakistan in Kenya and the ICC Champions Trophy in Sri Lanka during September. **22** The Pakistan Cricket Board confirms that Kenya will replace New Zealand in the triangular series to be played in Nairobi.

OBITUARIES

By WARWICK FRANKS

ANTONIO (later HOWARD), PEGGY, died on January 11, 2002 at the North Park Hospital in the suburb of Bundoora in Melbourne, the city where she had been born on June 2, 1917. Regarded by many as one of the best spin bowlers in the history of Australian women's cricket, she was known as "the girl Grimmett", which underlined the regard in which her skills were held. The daughter of a Chilean-born dock-worker who died when she was just over a year old, she joined the Collingwood women's club and progressed so rapidly that she played for Victoria at the age of 15. She also played for a team from Nelson Raymond's Shoe Factory, where she worked as a box maker and whose owners were enthusiastic supporters of women's cricket in Melbourne. Her slight build and short stature (153 cm) were no impediment to her development, as she learned quickly and practised assiduously under the tutelage of club cricketer Eddie Conlon. She rapidly developed into an attacking yet controlled slow bowler who mixed her leg-spin with off-breaks, supplemented by a top-spinner and an occasional wrong'un. Match figures of 10/48 in the state match against the English tourists ensured that in December 1934 Antonio appeared in the inaugural women's Test at Brisbane, and at the age of 17 she took the first wicket to be captured by an Australian when she dismissed Betty Snowball. In the Third Test of that series, at Melbourne, she was both persistent and dangerous in returning figures of 6/49.

The financial support of James McLeod, a senior executive in the shipping firm of McIlwraith McEachern, enabled her to make the 1937 tour of England. There she was even more successful, exploiting the fallibility of the English women against the flighted ball turning from the leg, securing 19 wickets at 11.15 in the three-Test series. In the First Test at Northampton her 6/51 and 3/40 were vital contributions to Australia's first Test victory, while in the next Test at Blackpool she took 3/34 and 5/31. Her batting developed during the tour to the extent that she made 103 not out against Kent and her highest Test score of 37 in the second innings at The Oval, where she joined Hazel Pritchard (66) in an important third-wicket partnership which helped to put the match beyond England's reach. Believing that the game was being turned into a relentless grind, she retired at the beginning of the next season. She married Eddie Howard in 1943, their family ultimately consisting of four children, 11 grandchildren and four great-grandchildren. Her skill and delight in the game, coupled with an unassuming personal charm, have ensured her a permanent place as a key figure in the history of Australian women's cricket.

	M	I	NO	R	HS	100s	50s	Avge	Ct	St	W	Avge	BB
Tests	6	12	1	128	37	0	0	11.64	0	0	31	13.90	6/49

BALL, THOMAS EDWARD, died on January 13, 2002 at Cairns. Born on the tableland at Atherton on December 3, 1921, Tom Ball gained favourable attention for his performance against a team of New South Wales and Queensland first-class players brought to Cairns by Bill Ives in 1940, when he took 2/47 and 2/41. Lean and lithe, he held the seam upright, cutting rather than swinging the ball, and generating genuine speed from an approach of only 12 paces. These qualities were much in evidence in two Country visits to Brisbane in 1945 and 1946 where gave a number of prominent Brisbane batsmen an uncomfortable time. He was selected for Queensland Country's match against the MCC tourists at Gympie in December 1946 and took 5/69, including the wickets of Denis Compton and Joe Hardstaff as he and Len Johnson restricted the tourists to a modest 282. The Queensland selectors saw him as the answer to their prayers for a strike bowler and he responded with five wickets in the last two Sheffield Shield games of the season. In the opening game of the first match of the 1947-48 season, against New South Wales at the Gabba, Ball's 3/57 in the first innings included the scalps of Arthur Morris and Keith Miller. He missed the southern tour of that season following an accidental fall by his pregnant wife, and subsequently paid the price for his inability to move to Brisbane because of his secure employment in Cairns as an engine driver with the Queensland Railways. In this context, his story is yet another example of the way in which the tyranny of distance has worked against many country cricketers of real quality. Ball had started his Cairns cricket with Rovers and continued to be a dominating force with both the Marist Cricket Club and CYMS until his retirement in the mid-1960s. A gifted natural and all-round athlete, he captained Cairns at hockey and soccer and ran the 100 yards in ten seconds at a number of athletics meetings. In all of his sports he had a reputation as a companionable competitor who had high standards of personal sporting integrity.

	M	I	NO	R	HS	100s	50s	Avge	Ct	St	W	Avge	BB
First-class	3	4	1	11	9	0	0	3.67	1	0	8	27.63	3/57
Dom. first-class	3	4	1	11	9	0	0	3.67	1	0	8	27.63	3/57

BESSEN, MERVYN OSACAR, died on 13 July, 2002, at Mandurah, south of Perth. Born at Tambellup, in the Great Southern district of Western Australia on 29 August, 1913, Merv Bessen was educated at Albany High School before working the family farming property between Tambellup and Kojonup. He was a well-built (180 cm and 73kg) left-hand batsman whose footwork was an outstanding feature of his free-stroking approach. A prolific scorer in country cricket, he was prominent in a number of Country Week carnivals in Perth, showing his ability to make runs at the next level of competition. In February, 1934, for example, he made 108 against Geraldton No. 2 for Dumbleyung, while, three years later, he was in a rich vein of form, scoring 101 not out against Waddington and 113 not out against the Lake Grace side. A week earlier, he had made two fifties and a century in the Great Southern carnival. Bessen scored another century in the 1940 carnival, against Narrogin. His brother, Frank (1911-2000) was also made his presence felt with the bat in these carnivals with a number of big innings. Bessen's only game for the Western Australia was against the Australian team on its way to England for the 1938 tour, making him one of those rare examples in Australian first-class cricket of a player being chosen for his state without having appeared in the metropolitan competition of that state. In its first innings, his side were in real trouble at six for 76 but Bessen made a sensible and composed 39, joining with Tony Zimbulis (33) in a partnership of 66 which redressed the balance a little before number 10 batsman Gordon Eyres lashed 41 in 17 minutes, including 24 from one Frank Ward over.

He was also a gifted country Australian Rules football player with Tambellup, but did make city appearances in this sport, playing 29 games at half-forward for Subiaco in the Western Australian Football League between 1937 and 1949. Later in life, he became a noted lawn bowler, being singles champion of both the Tambellup and Floreat Park clubs. During World War Two he served in the 24th Signals Brigade of the Ninth Division in North Africa, the Middle East and New Guinea.

	M	I	NO	R	HS	100s	50s	Avge	Ct	St	W	Avge	BB
First-class	1	2	0	40	39	0	0	20.00	0	0	0	–	–

BREMNER, COLIN DAVID, died on June 13, 2002 at Canberra. Born in the Melbourne suburb of Hawthorn on January 29, 1920, and educated at Scotch College, Bremner played for three seasons and 38 matches with the Colts side in the Melbourne District competition as a wicket-keeper, where he made an immediate impact as a safe and stylish performer behind the stumps. From 1940-41 to 1947-48 he played a further 18 games with Hawthorn–East Melbourne but found a regular first-grade spot difficult to hold because of the presence of the Victorian and Australian keeper Ben Barnett. His 56 first-grade games underlined his lack of pretension as a batsman as they brought him only 155 runs at 5.34. His skill with the gloves, however, was shown in his 52 catches and 65 stumpings; in 1940-41, for example, he took only two catches but effected 18 stumpings, making a substantial contribution to leg-spinner Colin Duncan's 52 wickets for the season. During the war he trained as a flying officer with the Royal Australian Air Force before being posted to England in 1943 where he undertook operations over Germany and occupied Europe. Bremner played for the RAAF team and acted as understudy to Stan Sismey in the Services side in England in 1945, as well as playing several matches in India and Australia. He kept wickets for the Dominions against England at Lord's in late August 1945, stumping Wally Hammond in each innings. Bremner had worked as an accountant with T&G Assurance from 1937 to 1941 and rejoined the company after the war. In 1951 he resigned to rejoin the RAAF, and in October 1952 he received the Queen's Commendation for Valuable Service in the Air. Subsequently, he participated in the British atomic tests in Australia before achieving the rank of wing commander with RAAF Staff Intelligence during the 1960s, ultimately retiring with the rank of group captain.

	M	I	NO	R	HS	100s	50s	Avge	Ct	St	W	Avge	BB
First-class	7	9	6	8	4*	0	0	2.66	4	6	0	–	–

BURGE, PETER JOHN PARNELL, died on October 5, 2001 at Main Beach, Southport, on Queensland's Gold Coast. Born in the inner Brisbane suburb of Kangaroo Point on May 17, 1932, Burge made a towering contribution to Queensland cricket, both on and off the field. Moreover, in the first half of the 1960s he was an integral part of the Australian batting line-up, his 160 at Leeds in 1964 being of such a memorable quality that *Wisden* compared it to Stan McCabe's 232 at Nottingham in 1938. He had blossomed early, scoring his first century for Buranda State School at the age of nine, then spending three years in the first eleven at the Church of England Grammar School, during which time he scored a century against Victoria in the 1945-46 interstate schoolboys' carnival in Sydney. In 1949-50 he began a lifetime's association with Eastern Suburbs, playing for them for 20 years, as well as acting as treasurer from 1950 to 1956 and again from 1962 to 1974, service which he was recognised by the award of life membership in 1967. The club's ground at Bottomley Park was named in his honour, as was the ground at Wellington Point when the club merged with Redlands. He had a ready mentor in his father, Jack (1903–57) who had played with the club and gone on to be a leading Queensland cricket administrator.

Selected for Queensland's last match of the 1952-53 season, Burge showed a mature temperament when he came in with his side at five for 76, chasing South Australia's 355, and proceeded to make a dogged 54 in 145 minutes, adding 116 for the sixth wicket with Jim Bratchford (143). In the second innings he made a more uninhibited 46. When the powerful New South Wales side visited Brisbane for the opening match of the next Sheffield Shield season, he showed his mettle with a powerful 103 against an attack led by Ray Lindwall, Keith Miller and Richie Benaud. At this time he was a useful wicket-keeper, a fact which he underlined with two smart stumpings off the leg-spinner Brian Flynn while he was deputising for the injured Don Tallon. So handsomely did he make his mark in state cricket that he was selected for the final Test of the 1954-55 Ashes series and for the succeeding tour of the West Indies, a side managed by his father. This period in his career was also marked by an anomalous pattern of consistent and convincing scoring for Queensland contrasted with inconsistent performances at Test level, and he was unable to cement a place in the Australian side, even though the selectors were reluctant to turn their backs on him permanently. He began the 1956 tour of England with successive innings of 99, 131 and 61 but was dropped after three unproductive Tests in a sodden and spin-tormented summer, although he played three times against India on the way home. Tours to South Africa in 1957-58 and to Pakistan and India in 1959-60, interspersed with a home series against England, produced only sporadic Test appearances, so that when the West Indians arrived in 1960-61, it seemed that Burge's Test career may have been on permanent hold. Thirteen Tests spread over five years had produced only 442 runs at an unprepossessing average of 26.00 and only three fifties in 19 innings.

When Neil Harvey was forced to miss the Fourth Test because of a pulled leg muscle, weight of runs forced the selectors to turn once more to Burge. He had recently batted for three minutes over seven hours in making 240 against South Australia at Adelaide, joining with Ken Mackay (156) in adding a then record for Queensland of 295 for the third wicket. Against Western Australia in Perth he made 103 and 55 in a low-scoring match on a difficult pitch. The final two Tests saw a transformed Burge at this level; he made 215 runs in four innings and the power of his frame (183 cm and 85 kg) was reflected in batting of a commanding maturity. Gone were the inconsistency and tentativeness and in their place was a player who could destroy an attack

with the ferocious power of his driving. Perhaps most symptomatic of his arrival as a Test batsman was his use of the sweep against the spinners; previously it had been a weakness but now it was an instrument of domination. In England in 1961 he played two crucial Test innings. At Lord's, Australia crumbled to four for 19 chasing 69 for victory as the malign influence of the infamous ridge in the pitch made itself manifest. Burge's response was to revive the innings with a series of fearless and booming drives in scoring 37 not out to secure victory for Australia. In the final Test at The Oval he made a commanding 181 in 350 minutes, sweeping the off-spinner David Allen to distraction in the process.

At the domestic level, he continued to be prolific. In 1962-63, against South Australia at Brisbane, Burge (163) and Tom Veivers (137) added a record 295 for the fourth wicket. He began the 1963-64 season at the Gabba with Queensland's highest individual innings of 283 (447 minutes, 414 balls, one six, 42 fours) which he made out of 468 runs scored while he was at the wicket against a New South Wales attack containing six Test bowlers. As Burge was wont to emphasise, Bob Simpson replied with 359 and Queensland's total of 613 was overhauled by 48, but he followed this innings with an even more spectacular 205 not out (285 minutes, 271 balls, 31 fours) in the next match, against Western Australia again at the Gabba, dominating an unfinished fourth-wicket partnership of 256 with Graham Bizzell (81). A senior member of the 1964 team to England, he played one of the indelible innings of Test cricket at Leeds, where Australia had crumbled to seven for 178 and were still a distant 90 runs from overhauling the England first innings. He then received staunch support from Neil Hawke and Wally Grout who each contributed 37 to successive partnerships of 105 and 89 as Burge dismantled the attack with an exhibition of controlled batting power which produced 160 in 315 minutes with 22 fours. It also contributed to his being named by Wisden as one of its Five Cricketers of the Year in the 1965 edition.

Appointed Queensland captain in 1964-65, he was unable tour the West Indies in 1965 and, just before the last Ashes Test of 1965-66, he announced that he was unavailable for the next season's tour of South Africa. Consequently, he finished his Test career as 12th man in that Test. Burge retired from first-class cricket after the southern tour in 1967-68 but was persuaded to play a final home match against Western Australia. His farewell hand was a defiant and commanding 100, made while 52 were being snicked and scraped at the other end. He finished with 7,627 runs for Queensland at 56.08, placing him fifth in the aggregates for the state. He was also one of the few

Australians to have been given out "handled the ball" when, against New South Wales at Sydney in 1958-59, he instinctively threw up a hand and caught the ball after it had hit his pad and ballooned into the air.

There followed three decades of energetic involvement in cricket administration beginning with a decade as a Queensland selector from 1968-69, while in 1990 he became a vice-president of the Queensland Cricket Association and from 1994 was on the board of Queensland Cricket, contributions recognised with the award of life membership in 1989. In 1991-92 he was one of the early appointees to the ICC Referees Panel, where he quickly established a reputation as a candid and respected official in the 25 Tests and 63 limited-overs internationals over which he presided. In July 1994 at Lord's, Burge did not hesitate to reprimand the England captain, Mike Atherton, over the so-called "dirt in the pocket" incident. His stature as a cricketer and the force of his personality are reflected in the life memberships bestowed on him by the MCC, Queensland Cricket, the Brisbane Cricket Ground Trust and the Queensland Cricketers' Club. In 2000, he was one of the first and most obvious selections in Queensland's Team of the Century.

An accountant by profession, he was provided with secure employment by the cricket-loving Harry Bolton, of J.L. Rawlings Bolton & Co., now Bentleys Queensland. A devotee of harness racing, he expressed his interest in the sport by an extensive succession of administrative posts from 1969 until his death, including holding office with Brisbane's Albion Park Harness Club, the Queensland Harness Racing Board, the TAB of Queensland, the Australian Harness Racing Council and the Interdominion Harness Racing Council. In 1997 he was made a Member of the Order of Australia (AM) for his services to cricket and harness racing. Bob Merriman, chairman of the Australian Cricket Board, aptly referred to him as "one of the game's finest servants", yet both on and off the ground he was also one of its undoubted masters.

	M	I	NO	R	HS	100s	50s	Avge	Ct	St	W	Avge	BB
First-class	233	354	16	14,640	283	38	66	47.53	166	4	1	120.00	1/0
Tests	42	68	8	2,290	181	4	0	38.16	23	0	0	–	–
Dom. first-class	83	138	12	7,084	283	22	31	56.22	70	3	0	–	–

BURTON, JACK RICHARD, died on October 30, 2001 at the northern Adelaide suburb of Elizabeth Vale. Born at Cleve, on the Eyre Peninsula, on November 3, 1923, Burton gave four years of service in the Australian army during World War Two. A prominent local cricketer, he took two wickets for Combined Country against the South Australian Cricket Association after the 1947-48 Country Carnival. The following winter Norwood Football Club drew him to the city with an offer designed to exploit his reputation as a gifted country footballer. Although he went no further with his football, East Torrens snapped him up as a cricketer, relishing the prospects that his large frame (six feet five inches – 195 cm) offered as a bowler of lively pace who could make the ball lift unpleasantly. Burton, however, made an immediate mark as a batsman as he clubbed 61 in 28 minutes against West Torrens, including 28 from successive Bruce Dooland overs. In 1950-51 he shifted to Prospect where, in 1951-52, his form (42 wickets for the season at 16.45) was good enough for him to be taken on the eastern states tour two weeks after he was married. He only appeared against New South Wales, where his single expensive wicket was that of century-maker Jim de Courcy. He retired during the 1953-54 season because of work commitments at John Martin's department stores, having scored 639 runs at 11.83 and taken 150 wickets at 21.10 in first-grade cricket.

	M	I	NO	R	HS	100s	50s	Avge	Ct	St	W	Avge	BB
First-class	1	2	0	8	8	0	0	4.00	0	0	1	118.00	1/118
Dom. first-class	1	2	0	8	8	0	0	4.00	0	0	1	118.00	1/118

BUTTSWORTH, WALLACE FRANCIS, died on May 22, 2002 at Milton, on the south coast of New South Wales. Born on January 21, 1917 at North Perth, Wally Buttsworth had a short cricket career before moving to Melbourne to embark on a career in Australian

Rules football with Essendon, where his skill was such that shortly after his death he was named in the club's team of the century. He played cricket with North Perth from the 1934-35 season, his solid frame (185cm and 91 kg) allowing him to become a punishing player in front of the wicket and returning him 682 runs at 32.73 from 25 matches for the club. He was taken on the 1937-38 tour to the eastern states where he was 12th man in the first game against Victoria. Against New South Wales, in the three-day match which has been mysteriously denied first-class status, he batted at No. 7, driving his way to 41 in a sixth-wicket partnership of 70 with Frank Alexander. In the second match against Victoria, he top-scored with a careful 35 (112 minutes, two fours) in his side's total of 137, following this up with 25 in a third-wicket partnership of 59 with Jack Shea in the second innings. Soon after, he moved to take up a football contract with Essendon, who had been impressed by his work with West Perth, but that club would not release him from his contract, forcing him to wait until the 1939 season to make his debut with the Dons. Between then and 1948, he played 188 games at centre half-back and appeared in the premiership sides of 1942 and 1946, as well as three losing grand final teams (1941, 1943 and 1947), plus the drawn game of 1948. Buttsworth won his club's Best and Fairest Award in both 1945 and 1947, while in the latter year *Sporting Life* named him in its all-Australian football team. Having played and coached in the Riverina district of New South Wales, he returned to serve on the Essendon committee from 1961 to 1970, by which time he had taken up lawn bowls so skilfully that he was to play for Victoria. His cricket in Melbourne was subsumed by his footballing activities, his appearances being restricted to a work team in a local competition. Initially, he had worked as a fireman in Melbourne, before owning a taxi truck in later years. His father, Frederick Richard (1880-1974) played seven games of cricket for Western Australia between 1920-21 and 1925-26 before umpiring 17 first-class matches in Perth between 1928-29 and 1938-39, while a younger brother, Frederick James (1927-), represented Western Australia eight times between 1947-48 and 1949-50.

	M	I	NO	R	HS	100s	50s	Avge	Ct	St	W	Avge	BB
First-class	2	4	0	62	35	0	0	15.50	1	0	0	–	–

CHARLES, PETER RICHARD, died on April 20, 2002 at the suburb of Wooloowin in Brisbane, the city where he had been born at Herston on July 26, 1955. A left-arm pace bowler, he played with Northern Suburbs while training as a teacher, before his transfer to the central Queensland coal-mining town of Blackwater. While teaching there, he travelled each weekend to Rockhampton to play cricket, his speed and fire earning him selection in the Queensland Country team which met the West Indians at Toowoomba in December 1979. On a dicey pitch, the Country team managed only 96, a total slightly augmented by the dozen runs that Charles heaved from No. 11. With the ball, he caused a sensation by dismissing Gordon Greenidge and Viv Richards before a run had been scored and his later removal of Larry Gomes meant that the West Indians, at four for 35, were teetering at the edge of an improbable defeat. Collis King restored a sense of perspective but Charles finished with a return of 3/43 in the visitors' ultimate seven for 124. Later in the 1980s he joined the coaching staff of Queensland Cricket, becoming its first Development Officer, while in 1991 he took up the first such appointment in North Queensland when he moved to Townsville. Three years later he returned to Brisbane as Development Manager for Queensland before returning to teaching at Nudgee College.

COATS, JAMES, died at a nursing home in the south-eastern Brisbane suburb of Wynnum West on June 8, 2002. Born at the inner southern suburb of Annerley on February 26, 1914, he was a member of the Queensland State Primary Schoolboys team which travelled to Sydney to play their New South Wales counterparts in February 1928. He was later educated at Brisbane Grammar School, following which he made an immediate impression with the Northern Suburbs club when he scored 432 runs at 30.85 in 1933-34, his first full season in first-grade cricket. Next season, he acted as 12th man in the Colts' match against New South Wales but the selectors waited until 1937-38 to call him into the state side for the southern tour. In his first appearance, against Victoria, he top-scored in the second innings with 46, combining with Col Loxton in a second-wicket partnership of 72 in 67 minutes. In the other two matches, he gave glimpses of what might be, but failed to make substantial scores. Acting as 12th man in the last match of the season, against Victoria at the Gabba, was his last state appearance, despite a long and prolific club career. A ruggedly effective batsman with the ability to drive powerfully, Coats played with Northern Suburbs until 1953-54, scoring 6,285 runs at 29.64 and taking 79 wickets at 18.41, 26 of them in the one season, 1944-45, when he also put together 630 runs. At the end of that season, he played for The Rest in a two-day game against Queensland in which he made 111 and joined with former New South Wales player Jack Fitzpatrick in a fourth-wicket partnership of 220. In 1939-40 he had raced to a spectacular 217 against Western Suburbs, an innings which remained a club record until Robbie Kerr made 218 not out in 1985-86. He subsequently captained Norths from 1946-47, leading from the front with 614 runs at 47.23 in 1947-48 and 518 runs at 43.16 the next season. His service to the club was recognised by the award of life membership in 1952. From 1954-55 he played two seasons as captain and coach of the Colts' side in the Brisbane competition, a club with whom he had spent a season in 1936-37. During World War Two, Coats joined the Australian Army and was drafted to supply where he reached the rank of warrant officer. Having studied accountancy, he spent over two decades with the Australian Guarantee Corporation Ltd from the early 1930s before operating a milk delivery run for some years from 1955.

	M	I	NO	R	HS	100s	50s	Avge	Ct	St	W	Avge	BB
First-class	3	6	0	127	46	0	0	21.17	0	0	0	–	–
Dom. first-class	3	6	0	127	46	0	0	21.17	0	0	0	–	–

COTTON, EDWARD KENNETH, died on March 26, 2002, at the southern Sydney suburb of Kogarah. Despite a brief career with his state, Ted Cotton's long service as a grade player and coach made him an outstanding example of the kind of cricketer who takes delight and satisfaction from contributing far more to the game than he ever takes from it. Eloquent testimony to his standing and qualities came from his close friend and grade rival Brian Booth, who nominated Cotton as one of his first selections in any team of players he would most like to play with or against. Born on August 8, 1927 at the inner suburb of Paddington, he was educated at Sydney's St Mary's Cathedral School and made his initial appearance in first grade for the Paddington club in 1947-48. He bowled at a lively fast-medium pace and had the ability to swing and cut the ball sufficiently to be a penetrative member of the attack. A genuine all-rounder, he was a methodical and organised batsman who eschewed the flamboyant approach in favour of sound defence and judicious shot selection. In November 1951 he was selected for New South Wales Colts in the Sydney Gregory Cup match against Queensland at Sydney, in which he contributed 50 to a fifth-wicket partnership of 114 with Noel Hughes (69). In 1952-53 he appeared twice for the state while its Test players were on duty against the South Africans. 1953-54 was a bountiful grade season for Cotton, as he scored 778 runs and took 43 wickets, performances which led to his selection in a full-strength state side for the last two Sheffield Shield matches of the season. In the first of these he made an unbeaten 49 as his side beat Western Australia by six wickets. He was retained in the side for the opening match against Queensland at Brisbane in 1954-55 where he shared the new ball with Keith Miller. Coming in with his side at seven for 329, chasing the home side's 405, Cotton batted grittily for 152 minutes in making 41 and helping Jim Burke (137) to add 118. The long innings, however, exacerbated a finger injury that he had sustained in a match played at Gunnedah on the way north and he was unable to resume batting on the fourth morning. One further match, against Victoria at Melbourne, in which his 35 was the highest score in his team's first innings, completed his first-class career, although he continued to be selected in the state squad until the 1958-59 season.

Cotton was an integral member of the Paddington side until it was amalgamated with Glebe after the 1964-65 season. He then moved to the south of Sydney to become a foundation member of the new Sutherland side, for whom his experience and tactical acumen were invaluable. His captaincy was an important factor in the club's reaching the first-grade final in 1966-67, its second season in the competition. He finished his career with five seasons of ripe achievement with both bat and ball, signing off with 466 runs at 38.83 and 31 wickets at 17.97 in 1969-70 and skilfully leading an inexperienced side to victory in the Rothmans limited-overs knockout competition. In the last match of the previous season he had taken 9/24 against Gordon. In his 23 seasons in first grade he scored 7,559 runs at 28.10 and took 587 wickets at 18.12. Cotton then gave dedicated service as a thoughtful and respected coach, beginning immediately with his club's A.W. Green Shield side in 1970-71. In 1983-84 he was appointed coach of the New South Wales Under-19s side, his charges including Mark Taylor, Mark and Steve Waugh, and Gavin Robertson. His tenure continued until 1991-92, during which time Adam Gilchrist, Michael Slater and Shane Lee also received the benefit of his guidance. Cotton returned to Sutherland in the capacity of assistant coach for five seasons from 1995-96, during which period various of the club's sides won six premierships. Having been made a life member during his time with Paddington, he was awarded the same honour by Sutherland in June 2000, a fitting tribute to over 30 years of service to the club. His wife, Shirley, represented Australia at the 1956 Olympic Games in the discus, while his daughter, Lisa, was named Tasmania's Women's Hockey Coach of the Year in 1995 and 1996. Having worked in his father's newsagency from the time he left school until 1956, he then joined Williamson Croft Pty Ltd, which was later absorbed by Dulux Australia Ltd, and spent 33 years as one of their industrial representatives.

	M	I	NO	R	HS	100s	50s	Avge	Ct	St	W	Avge	BB
First-class	6	9	2	191	49*	0	0	27.28	3	0	2	87.50	1/26
Dom. first-class	6	9	2	191	49*	0	0	27.28	3	0	2	87.50	1/26

ELLIS, DONALD GEORGE, died on September 4, 2001 at Launceston, the city where he had been born on October 5, 1917. Educated at Charles Street School, "Sconny" Ellis was a slightly-built left-arm medium-pacer whose subtle variations of pace and movement reaped him a harvest of wickets in Launceston cricket. After an initial season with the Launceston club, he played with South, North and West Launceston, captaining West when he was only 21. He returned to the Launceston club in 1942-43, immediately underlining his value with innings figures of 10/19, including a hat-trick, and helping the club win three premierships in the next six seasons. His best season was 1945-46 when he took 78 wickets at 8.16, including six returns of five wickets or more in an innings. It was during this season that the Tasmanian selectors gave their sole recognition of his talents when he was selected to play against the Australian Services team in Hobart. After going wicketless in the visitors' first innings, he took 3/56, including Cec Pepper, in the second. Batting at No. 11, he joined Arthur Lovett and the pair held firm for the last few minutes of the match to extract a draw for their side. Ellis retired after the 1948-49 season, having taken 256 wickets at 14.39 for Launceston, including five wickets in an innings 15 times. He subsequently became a skilled trout fisherman and a proficient rifle shot. A clerk and computer operator with the Tasfibre Corporation, he was held in high esteem by Terry Cowley, one of Tasmania's best post-war bowlers, who regarded Ellis as a versatile and skilful bowler.

	M	I	NO	R	HS	100s	50s	Avge	Ct	St	W	Avge	BB
First-class	1	2	1	9	6*	0	0	9.00	0	0	3	50.33	3/56

GARDNER, CHARLES ALLAN, died on December 9, 2001 in Melbourne, having just passed his 93rd birthday. Born in the bayside suburb of Brighton East on October 28, 1908, Gardner and his twin brother Norman were educated at East Bentleigh State School. Despite his small frame (165 cm and 65 kg) he became a blacksmith and subsequently turned out for Melbourne Cricket Club where he gained a reputation as an uncertain starter who was an attractive strokemaker with a penchant for the cut shot, both square and late. A sparkling and undefeated 142 in only 150 minutes against University in January 1934 earned him a place in the state team a month later for two matches against the touring Western Australians. In the first of these, batting at No. 4, Gardner made a fluent 78 in 123 minutes, partnering the flamboyant Arthur Allsopp (146) in a partnership of 187 before retiring hurt with a badly-strained back muscle. A fortnight later, he made only 13 and 12, although in the first innings he again joined Allsopp in a second-wicket partnership of 53. In a first-grade career with Melbourne CC which stretched from 1932-33 to 1943-44, his 96 matches produced 1,811 runs at 23.21. Subsequently, he was a successful coach in suburban cricket, particularly with the Bentleigh team, and had a half-length turf pitch and practice nets set up in his back yard so he could supervise his players on the spot. By this time, he was reading gas meters, later being promoted to inspector in his section.

	M	I	NO	R	HS	100s	50s	Avge	Ct	St	W	Avge	BB
First-class	2	3	1	108	78	0	1	54.00	0	0	0	–	–

HARBURG, CLIVE HENRY, died on July 21, 2002 at the Brisbane suburb of Birkdale, eight days after his 90th birthday. Born on July 13, 1912 in the western Queensland town of Roma, Harburg's voice has become immortal because of his description of the closing minutes of the Tied Test between Australia and West Indies at the Gabba on December 14, 1960. Another famous commentator, Alan McGilvray, had been given permission to catch an early plane back to Sydney because, with Australia at six for 92 shortly before tea and still needing another 141, it appeared that either the visitors would wrap up proceedings smartly or the match would fade away to a draw. His departure left Harburg and Michael Charlton to share the ball-by-ball commentary interspersed with expert observations from Johnny Moyes. Thus it was Harburg who described the closing stages of the magnificent seventh-wicket partnership of 134 between Alan Davidson and Richie Benaud, which ended in the penultimate over of the day, following which three wickets, including two run-outs, and six runs were scored in the seven balls bowled by Wesley Hall before Joe Solomon threw the wicket down from side-on for the second time to finish the Test in a tie. In all of this pandemonium, it was the calm, measured and mellifluous tones of Harburg which created a vivid and accessible set of word pictures for the countless thousands of Australians listening around the country. Subsequently, a story circulated that the commentary team was so befuddled by the tension of the finish that Harburg broadcast the wrong result and was ordered to re-tape it for posterity by the formidable General Manager of the Australian Broadcasting Commission, Charles Moses, who was anxious to preserve the national broadcaster's reputation for infallibility. Harburg firmly and convincingly denied the veracity of the tale, insisting that it was utterly apocryphal.

Educated at Brisbane Grammar School, he began his broadcasting career at Longreach shortly before World War Two, during which he saw service with the RAAF as a radar operator in the south-west Pacific. He joined the ABC in 1945 as a general announcer based in Brisbane and became the founding editor of the organisation's Queensland sporting service in 1947. His was the voice of cricket from the Gabba, both at Sheffield Shield and Test level, for over two decades. In addition, he called both codes of rugby and a number of Davis Cup challenge rounds from Brisbane's Milton courts, as well as being part of the ABC's broadcasting team for the 1956 Olympic Games in Melbourne. He was also part of a national commentary team for a number of the royal tours in the 1950s and 1960s. Harburg resigned in 1969 and then spent a decade as a member of the War Pensions Entitlement Tribunal. He explained his approach to sports commentary by insisting that he took it as a privilege to be invited into the listener's home, a privilege that required him to be informative, courteous and, above all, a reliable and discreet source of authoritative information.

HARTEN, JAMES THOMAS, died on September 11, 2001 at the Brisbane suburb of Everton Hills. Jim Harten was born in the inner suburb of Windsor on November 11, 1924, and educated at St James' College, Fortitude Valley. He joined Valley Cricket Club in 1939-40, becoming the epitome of the dedicated and skilled grade cricketer. Between 1941-42 and 1967-68, he made a club record 234 first-grade appearances, which produced 7,452 runs at 27.20, the highest aggregate for the club until Brett Henschell overhauled it in 2000-01. In addition, he took 112 wickets at 18.25 and held 108 catches, besides serving three spells as captain between 1949-50 and 1962-63. His service to the club was recognised by the bestowing of life membership on him in 1957-58 and his acting as patron from 1976 to 1997. Harten was a solid, well-organised batsman who was particularly strong off the front foot, and sold his wicket dearly. He was treated churlishly by the state selectors, who made him 12th man for two matches at the end of the 1948-49 season and then once more at the beginning of the next season. He finally made his debut against South Australia at home in January 1950 when, batting at No. 6, he was tragically run out, having put on 59 with Bill Brown, who went on to make 190 in his last Sheffield Shield match. After one further game he was declared surplus to requirements, but his riposte was to continue scoring plentiful and determined runs in grade cricket. Having been a storeman with the Queensland Railways from 1939 to 1954, Harten subsequently became secretary of the Railways Institute until his retirement in 1988.

	M	I	NO	R	HS	100s	50s	Avge	Ct	St	W	Avge	BB
First-class	2	3	0	30	160	0	0	10.00	3	0	0	–	–
Dom. first-class	2	3	0	30	160	0	0	10.00	3	0	0	–	–

HOLLIOAKE, BENJAMIN CAINE, died in a car accident at South Perth on March 23, 2002. Born in Melbourne on November 11, 1977, Ben Hollioake was raised in England until his mid-teenage years and educated at Millfield School in Somerset. His family then returned to Australia where he completed his schooling at Perth's Wesley College. Having first appeared for Surrey at the end of 1996, next season he seized the imagination of the England selectors as an all-rounder who could bat with dash and who could swing the ball each way at a lively pace. Thus, after a handful of first-class games, he appeared at Lord's in 1997 in a limited-overs international against Australia. Batting at No. 3, his 63 from 45 balls sent Glenn McGrath and Shane Warne packing and paved the way for an England victory. Later that summer he was selected for the Trent Bridge Test at the age of 19 years 269 days, the youngest England debutant since Brian Close in 1949. Adam, his older brother by six years, also played his first Test in this match. Ben's potential was further recognised by being named Young Cricketer of the Year for 1997 by the Cricket Writers' Club. By this time he had played rugby union for Somerset and represented the West of England at hockey. Ben fell victim to the England selection policy of choosing many but recalling few and only played one further Test, against Sri Lanka at The Oval in 1998. His own form was too spasmodic to force any change of mind, and it seemed as though he had been consigned to the role of intermittent appearances in England's limited-overs side. Nevertheless, he had been included in the squad which toured Zimbabwe, India and New Zealand as part of the side's preparations for the 2003 World Cup, although a knee injury prevented him from playing in the series of matches in New Zealand. He had maintained his links with Perth cricket, turning out for the Melville, North Perth and South Perth clubs.

	M	I	NO	R	HS	100s	50s	Avge	Ct	St	W	Avge	BB
First-class	75	114	6	2,794	163	3	14	25.87	68	0	126	33.45	5/51
Tests	2	4	0	44	28	0	0	11.00	2	0	4	49.75	2/105

KING, DARRYL JAMES, died on March 3, 2002 at his home at Buderim, on Queensland's Sunshine Coast. Born on June 6, 1942 at East Brisbane, the tall (183 cm) King was educated at St Laurence's Christian Brothers' College in South Brisbane where he made an eye-catching century at the age of eight. Having spent four years in his school's first eleven, he joined the Eastern Suburbs club in 1959-60, where his free-flowing strokeplay earned him selection in the state Colts' side for the 1960-61 Sydney Gregory Cup match in Sydney. His 72 was the highest score in a consistent Queensland batting performance and, over the next two seasons, he was successively vice-captain and captain of the side. Having made a single unsuccessful appearance in the state side in 1962-63, consistent grade performances allowed him to regain his place for the last two matches of the 1965-66 Sheffield Shield season. In the latter of these, against South Australia at Brisbane, King played two contrastingly successful hands. In the first innings, he cracked 56 in only 77 minutes, joining Keith Ziebell (53) in a swift fifth-wicket partnership of 101. Queensland faced a deficit of 119 and King's second innings 65 not out in 199 minutes helped the home side set the visitors an ultimately unattainable target. Next season, he made a composed 66 (206 minutes, six fours) at home against New South Wales, adding 112 for the second wicket with Sam Trimble (92) but he was unable to convert several subsequent promising starts into substantial scores and was dropped after the southern tour. He continued with Easts until 1968-69, retiring with nearly 2,743 runs at 25.64 to his credit. A talented all-round sportsman, King played first-grade rugby union, squash, tennis and baseball in the Brisbane area. Having trained and practised as a solicitor, since the mid-1970s he had been manager and then director of a property management and consulting company on the Sunshine Coast.

	M	I	NO	R	HS	100s	50s	Avge	Ct	St	W	Avge	BB
First-class	8	14	2	310	66	0	3	25.83	3	0	0	–	–
Dom. first-class	8	14	2	310	66	0	3	25.83	3	0	0	–	–

LANGSFORD, TRICIA, died on March 16, 2002 at the northern Sydney suburb of Wahroonga. Born on October 9, 1971 in Sydney, she was educated at Ravenswood School for Girls at Gordon, where she was a member of the tennis team in each of her six years at the school. Trish played club cricket with Kuring-gai where her all-round ability saw her named as Player of the Year in both 1990-91 and 1992-93. An obvious selection for her state in the 1991-92 national championships, she topped both the bowling aggregates and averages with 17 wickets at 9.88 and made valuable runs in the middle order. Her lively medium-pace deliveries were enhanced by her ability to swing the ball appreciably, while her batting revealed her as an elegant strokemaker of flair and judgment. As a result, the *ABC Australian Cricket Almanac* named her as one of its four women players of the year. Next season, she top-scored with 59 and took 2/26 in an unavailing effort to stop the South Australians achieving a second successive national title. In 1993-94 she captained the Australian Under-23s side against their New Zealand counterparts in three limited-overs matches and an unofficial Test for the Dive–Lamason Youth Challenge Cup. The Test was ruined by rain, but the Australians won all the one-dayers, two of them at a canter, Langsford's captaincy harnessing the talents of such future stars as Karen Rolton, Olivia Magno, Jo Garey and Julia Price. In addition to her cricket, she played first-grade hockey and tennis in Sydney.

A graduate in Human Movement, Langsford became a development officer with the New South Wales Women's Cricket Association but in 1994 she was diagnosed as suffering from a rare and virulent form of multiple sclerosis. Naturally, she was unable to take her place as captain of the national Under-23s side on its tour of India at the end of that year. The rapid progress of the disease soon meant that she required permanent specialist care. In 1999 her family and friends established what is now known as the Trish Multiple Sclerosis Research Foundation which has the aim of promoting research aimed at the cure and prevention of the disease. The tragedy of her early death was leavened slightly by the universal admiration which her warmth and courage inspired in others.

McFARLINE, PETER MUIR, died on April 7, 2002 in Melbourne. Born at Sale, in Victoria's Gippsland, on March 27, 1945, he cut his journalistic teeth at the Courier-Mail in Brisbane. It was in Melbourne, however, particularly in the columns of the Age, that he established his reputation as a journalist whose first passion was cricket, but whose knowledge and enthusiasm took him into many other sports, and even to a stint during the 1980s in Washington for the Herald and Weekly Times. A skilful investigative journalist, McFarline combined impeccable sources with the ability to break big stories. Perhaps the biggest was the schism of World Series Cricket in 1977, whose machinations he charted in tandem with Alan Shiell of Adelaide. His work on the episode produced two substantial books on the episode: *A Game Divided* (1977) and *A Testing Time* (1979) in which his detestation of the World Series phenomenon continued to be cogently expressed. While at the height of his powers he was diagnosed with syringomyelia, a degenerative condition which slowly robbed him of the ability to move independently. McFarline spent the last seven years of his life in hospital, years made marginally bearable by the unceasing devotion of his wife, Dell, and his own grinding, unflinching stoicism and courage in refusing to allow illness to deny him the ability to observe and analyse the cricket world. Against the odds, he collaborated with the colossus of Australian football, Ron Barassi, to produce Barassi: *The Life behind the Legend* (1995). In 1998, the Melbourne Press Club bestowed on him one of its Quills awards, for lifetime achievement, while in the Queen's Birthday Honours list for 2002, he was awarded a Medal in the Division of the Order of Australia (OAM) for services to journalism, particularly sports journalism. Because of McFarline's illness and death, the award was made effective from May 10, 2000.

McMAHON, JOHN WILLIAM JOSEPH, died on May 8, 2001 in North London. Born at Balaklava in South Australia's mid-north on December 28, 1917, Jack McMahon was an orthodox slow left-armer who would occasionally produce an outrageously-turning ball out of the back of his hand. Having played with the Adelaide CC from 1938-39 to 1941-42, taking 58 wickets at 26.00, he then turned out in one game for Port Adelaide in 1943-44. He stayed on in England after World War Two, and played 84 matches for Surrey between 1947 and 1953, his most productive season being 1948 when he took 91 wickets at 28.07, including 8/46 against Northamptonshire at The Oval. Thereafter, he found it more difficult to hold a regular place in the side because of the prolific presence of Tony Lock, and moved to Somerset, for whom he made 115 appearances between 1954 and 1957. Despite the workload caused by his county's chronically fragile batting, he became a respected member of the county scene, equalling his best innings figures, against Kent at Yeovil in 1955, and taking 103 wickets at 25.57 in 1956. Throughout his career, he remained a consistently modest batsman, very much in the mould of Horace Hazell, whose spinning tradition he continued in the county. He was sacked by Somerset in 1957, despite having taken 86 wickets at 23.10 before the axe fell. It is not clear whether his thirst or his forthrightness gave more offence to the county committee. Despite an outcry from loyal team-mates and outraged supporters, the committee remained obdurate, and McMahon returned to clerical work in London, where, in later years, he penned occasional contributions to *Wisden Cricket Monthly*.

	M	I	NO	R	HS	100s	50s	Avge	Ct	St	W	Avge	BB
First-class	201	285	125	989	24	0	0	6.18	109	0	590	27.60	8/46

MARSHALL, GEOFFREY THOMAS, died on January 2, 2001, at his home in the southern Brisbane suburb of Mount Gravatt. Born on October 3, 1928 at Degilbo, near Bundaberg, Geoff Marshall turned to umpiring in 1951-52 after a severe back injury ended his career as a promising young country cricketer. So rapidly did his skill and judgment make an impression that in January 1955, at the age of 26, he was appointed to the first of six first-class matches in which he officiated at the Gabba. Four of these matches involved visiting South Australian Sheffield Shield teams. After the 1958-59 season, continued back problems forced him to retire from umpiring. After teacher training at Kelvin Grove Teachers' College, Marshall pursued a career in the Queensland primary schools, serving from 1956 to 1982 as principal of Saville Road State School in Brisbane, before spending six years in regional educational administration.

POLLARD, JACK ERNEST, died at the Royal North Shore Hospital in the Sydney suburb of St Leonards on May 25, 2002. For over 40 years, the prolific and wide-ranging Pollard had devoted himself to chronicling Australian sports and pastimes; his energy and success were such that for many years he was one of the few full-time authors of sports books in this country. Although cricket and rugby union were his favourite subjects, he turned his attention to rugby league, Australian Rules, tennis, golf, lawn bowls, fishing, shooting, horse racing, surfing and skin diving. In the 1970s and 1980s, he used his wide-ranging knowledge to publish books on such diverse areas as crafts, pottery, birds, whale watching and the keeping of pets. Born in the south-western Sydney suburb of Campsie on July 31, 1926, his Depression childhood was not easy, particularly after his father left the family when Pollard was seven. He became a copy boy on the Sydney *Daily Telegraph* before joining the army just before the end of World War Two. Following two years in Japan as an army journalist, where he became sports editor of the armed services newspaper, in 1946 he travelled to England where, from 1947 to 1956, he worked for Australian Associated Press, covering sport and foreign affairs. The sporting highlights of his work there were his coverage of the 1948 Australian cricket tour of England and the Helsinki Olympic Games in 1952. He returned to Australia to cover the 1956 Melbourne Olympics for the Packer group, but resigned as a full-time journalist in 1959 in order to devote himself to writing, editing and publishing sports books.

Pollard's journalistic background helped him to develop an accessible and readable style which was combined with an instinct for the tastes of the sports market. In addition, he built a substantial research collection of printed material and photographs which allowed him to write with insight and authority. Amongst his cricket books, he edited one of the most successful of Australian cricket anthologies, *Six and Out* (1964), and wrote the encyclopaedic *Australian Cricket: The Game and the Players* (1982) for which he became only the second Australian cricket writer, after Ray Robinson, to be awarded the English Cricket Society's Jubilee Award. This book proved to be a training run for his four-volume *Complete History of Australian Cricket* (1995). In turn, he showed his willingness to encourage other cricket writers by donating the Jack Pollard Trophy for the annual winner of the literary award of the Australian Cricket Society. His services to sports writing were recognised in 1992 when he was awarded the Medal of the Order of Australia. He would have appreciated the symmetry of both his first and last books having had the tennis player Lew Hoad as their subjects, together with the wry significance that his last book was his 87th.

PUCKETT, CHARLES WILLIAM, who died on January 21, 2002 at the southern Adelaide suburb of Morphett Vale, made his first Sheffield Shield appearance at the age of 36. He was a key factor in Western Australia winning the trophy at their first attempt and wore with distinction the sobriquet "The Iron Man" which aptly caught his indestructible value to his state. His family emigrated to Adelaide 12 months after his birth on February 21, 1911 at Beddington Corner, near Mitcham in Surrey, where his father was a glove maker who had also been a groundsman at The Oval. Educated at Burnside High School, Puckett made his initial sporting mark as a gifted catcher in baseball, representing South Australia from 1931 to 1935 and winning the initial Capps Medal in 1936 for the best and fairest Adelaide baseballer. In 1937 he moved to Melbourne where he represented both Essendon and Victoria and won the Lansdown Medal, before accepting a job offer from C.P. Smith, managing director of the *West Australian*, who was keen to secure his catching skills for the Western Australian team. Smith's discernment was rewarded by Puckett representing his new state from 1938 to 1954, captaining the side in his final season, and being chosen in the Australian team in 1948 and 1952. In 1939, he also completed a hat-trick of state best and fairest baseball awards by winning the Smith prize in Western Australia. His older brother, Tom, was a South Australian baseballer, besides being a selector and umpire at state level, while a younger brother, Jim, represented both South Australia and Western Australia as a pitcher.

Until his move to Perth, cricket had been an undemanding summer diversion for Puckett, but in 1939-40 he joined the West Perth club and performed with such effect that he topped the Perth pennant bowling aggregates with 82 wickets and was selected against South Australia towards the end of the season. By the time he retired at the end of the 1954-55 season, he had taken 668 wickets (the eighth-highest return in Perth pennant cricket) at 11.56 and had headed the bowling aggregates or averages nine times. After serving in the Australian army as a physical training and unarmed combat instructor during World War Two, Puckett took 5/126 from 37 overs against Wally Hammond's 1946-47 MCC team. This lion-hearted performance brought him selection for an Australian XI at Melbourne, by which time acute judges of the game such as R. S.

Whitington and Tom Goodman were endorsing the class of his bowling. Soon after, he felt compelled to return to Adelaide to see his ailing parents, but men of influence in Western Australian cricket, such as WACA secretary-treasurer Harry Guy, were convinced that Puckett was integral to their team's performance in its first Sheffield Shield season and successfully secured his return to Perth by organising a job for him in the sports department of the Harris Scarff Sandover store, from whence he would be released for cricket as required.

Puckett was a multi-skilled cricketer long before that ugly term came into vogue. Bowling at a disconcertingly peppery fast-medium pace, his stock ball in a well-furnished store was a controlled outswinger. He gained even greater variety after his new state captain, Keith Carmody, encouraged him to widen his repertoire by cutting his pace to bowl slow-medium off-cutters and even off-spinners, depending on the state of the pitch. His value was further enhanced by the stamina which enabled him to bowl for long periods without ever becoming dully mechanical, stamina which may have been produced by his reputed habit of engaging in four-hour bowling spells at practice. In the match against Queensland at Brisbane, which Western Australia had to win outright in order to win the 1947-48 Sheffield Shield, Puckett bowled unchanged for 23 overs to take 6/48, finishing with a winning burst of 5/9 from his final six overs, thus making good his promise to his captain, "I'll bowl till my arm drops off." That performance gave him 24 wickets at 24.79 from four matches, figures which he eclipsed in 1949-50 when he claimed 32 wickets at 18.85.

As a batsman, he liked to draw on his baseball skills and hit the ball hard, high and often and against Victoria at Melbourne in 1951-52 he came in at seven for 96 and lathered 75 out of 115 in 99 minutes. In addition, he was a versatile fieldsman equally at home behind or in front of the wicket, possessing safe hands and a strong, accurate arm. He once asserted that he "liked a run in the country to keep fit", as if 20 or 30 overs of bowling had not already honed his physical fitness.

The enormity of his contribution to the embryonic Western Australian Shield side can be gauged from the fact that in his career of 22 matches, he bowled more than a third of his team's overs and took almost a third of its wickets, with the remaining load and spoils being divided among 23 other bowlers. Given the presence in the Australian team of his time of bowlers such as Ray Lindwall, Keith Miller, Bill Johnston and Ern Toshack, and the then eastern states habit of viewing Western Australian cricketers as not being worth a second glance, Puckett's only national recognition came with selection for the 1949-50 tour of New Zealand by Bill Brown's "second" side. It was there that he turned in the performance which gave him most satisfaction: 5/24 from 24 overs at Dunedin, against an Otago side which included Bert Sutcliffe, an achievement which is a reminder of what a formidable proposition he would have been in English conditions. Puckett remained consistently effective, retiring at the end of the 1952-53 season at the age of 42. Only a few months earlier, he had welcomed Jack Cheetham's South Africans by taking 5/119 from 37.2 marathon overs, thus continuing his tradition of success against touring teams. In 1960, he returned to Adelaide, secure in the knowledge that he had helped to foster Western Australia in a crucial period of its cricket history and imbued with a bowling ethic that is simple and unanswerable. In responding to the question as to which batsman worried him most, he replied: "None of them. I always believed that if I worked hard enough I could get them out." His services were recognised when he became the first Western Australian player to be granted a testimonial match, against Richmond Cricket Club in 1954.

His son, Maxwell Charles Puckett (1935–1991) played one match for South Australia in 1964-65 as a right-arm medium-fast bowler. In addition, he played baseball as a pitcher for Western Australia from 1955 to 1957 and South Australia from 1961 to 1965, and was selected in the Australian teams of 1956, 1957, 1961, 1964 and 1966, besides being a member of the Olympic team at Melbourne in 1956.

	M	I	NO	R	HS	100s	50s	Avge	Ct	St	W	Avge	BB
First-class	37	57	13	643	75	0	1	14.61	24	0	158	25.58	6/35
Dom. first-class	22	39	9	481	75	0	1	16.03	13	0	113	24.96	6/35

SHEPHERD, BARRY KEITH, died on September 17, 2001 at Fremantle. Barry Shepherd's pugnacity as a batsman was complemented by his perspicacity as a captain. When he first played for Western Australia, the euphoria of winning the Sheffield Shield at the first attempt was but a distant glow; in its place was the sense of being consigned to the backwater of limited participation in the competition, exacerbated by meagre and fitful doses of success. When he retired, he had by both practice and precept instilled a new sense of purpose and professionalism which saw the westerners on the cusp of becoming a dominating force in Australian cricket. In contrast, the Australian selectors of the time were unable or unwilling to recognise his manifold talents, and his nine Test calls were a wanton denial of an outstanding talent. Fortunately, in later years his coaching and administrative talents were given freely and tapped copiously at both the state and national levels.

Born at Donnybrook in the south-west of Western Australia on April 23, 1937, Shepherd was an outstanding schoolboy sportsman at Perth's Scotch College. His skills at hockey saw him quickly selected for the state, and his prowess at Australian Rules football provoked interest from at least one Melbourne club. Success in school cricket and with the South Perth club led to his selection for the state at the age of 18, and he became the first Western Australian-born player to make a century on debut in a Sheffield Shield match. His 103 not out (273 minutes, five fours) in the second innings against Queensland at Perth in 1955-56 had begun with his side at six for 87 in its second innings and staring down the barrel of overwhelming defeat against an attack led by Ray Lindwall and Ron Archer. There followed, however, a determined seventh-wicket partnership of 156 between Shepherd and Keith Carmody (78) which made the game secure. Over the next three seasons he established himself as a substantial presence on the Sheffield Shield scene, revealing a capacity for punishing strokes which grew out of a sound technique and a firm defence. Unfortunately, in successive seasons from 1959-60, Shepherd slipped into a trough of low scores which cost him a place in the side to Pakistan and India and in the 1961 Ashes tour.

In 1961-62 he was made captain of the Western Australian side, the additional responsibility appearing to be a tonic, as he was immediately back to making runs plentiful in quantity and rich in quality, his 212 not out against Queensland at Perth even eclipsing the panache of his partner Rohan Kanhai. As captain, he set about instilling new expectations of professionalism and commitment, hammering home the belief that this was how the traditional Sheffield Shield powers could be challenged and beaten. His approach involved the honing of Western Australia's abundant supply of speed and swing, preaching the virtues of tougher and more purposeful batting, and promoting skilful and sure fielding as an attacking weapon. Shepherd himself embodied this approach; his powerful frame with its daunting forearms and shoulders announced that his batting was built on power and resistance rather than subtlety and ease. He had the ability to impose himself on any attack and his trademark strokes were powerful drives and hammer blow shots square of and behind the wicket.

In the 1962-63 season, with its Ashes visit from Ted Dexter's team, Shepherd found the richest vein of form of his career as he passed 1,000 runs for the season. He played contrasting innings for an Australian XI against the tourists at Melbourne, batting solidly for over five hours in making 114 and then finishing the match with a rollicking undefeated 91 in 137 minutes. A week later, on the same ground against Victoria, he made an even more spectacular 219 in 231 minutes from only 198 balls, his destruction of the attack being so complete that he registered hundreds in both the second and third sessions of the opening day. This sheer weight of achievement propelled him into the Test team, but the pattern of the season suggested that his hold on a Test spot would be tenuous. After spending the first two Tests carrying the drinks, he replaced Peter Burge for the Third Test at Sydney, and immediately played an innings of marked maturity. Batting at No. 6, he had to deal with Fred Titmus at his most subtle and demanding, but made his unconquered 71 in 204 minutes out of 132 scored while he was at the wicket. His solidity kept a teetering innings together and earned Australia a valuable lead of 40 on the first innings. This performance did not spare him from being dropped after the next Test, to be replaced, ironically, by Burge.

Next season included a tour by South Africa and Shepherd seemed to be at the apogee of his achievement. He greeted the tourists with a neat 100 not out for Western Australia, had another spell as 12th man in the First Test, but then held his Test spot for the rest of the series. In the Second Test at Melbourne his 96 ensured that the 219 opening stand by Bill Lawry and Ian Redpath was not squandered, while in the Fourth Test at Adelaide he produced a fine double of 70 and 78 in a losing cause. Yet despite 1,087 runs for the season, he was not selected for the 1964 tour of England, the selectors' deliberate disregard of the scope of his achievement being difficult to fathom. Shepherd did make the 1964-65 tour to the West Indies but his first-class career closed at the age of 28 when, after the 1965-66 season, he was transferred to New South Wales as the state manager of Rothman's, a company for whom he eventually became chief executive. Significantly, it was in this season that he led his side to second place on the Sheffield Shield table, his 35 Shield games as captain preparing the way for Western Australia to claim the trophy in 1967-68 and then to repeat that success at regular intervals.

Shepherd's influence continued to be exercised in a positive and forthright manner through his long commitment to and involvement in the administration of the game. In 1979, he joined the Western Australian Cricket Association's Executive Committee, serving until 2000 when he retired as one of the association's vice-presidents. His contribution to the state's cricket was recognised by the award of life membership of the WACA in 1985. During this period Shepherd was a moving force in the establishment of the annual international match at Lilac Hill and was active in seeing off moves to deprive Perth of its Test status. From 1988 he spent 12 years as a director at the Australian Cricket Board, serving on the board's Executive, Umpires Appointments and Interstate Cricket Committees. A lifetime of service to cricket was recognised in 1999 when he was awarded the Medal in the Division of the Order of Australia (OAM). In his latter years he struggled with severe diabetes which was exacerbated by the affliction of an eating disorder. His condition necessitated the amputation of one leg in 2000 and the other leg six weeks before his death. Shepherd was, in many ways, a mirror image of Peter Burge, whose obituary also appears in these columns. As batsmen, they exuded the ability to tame all kinds of bowlers; indeed, they probably spent the first half of the 1960s competing for the same batting spot in the Australian team. Their solid and imposing physique bespoke a natural authority, yet their competitive drive was kept in perspective by innately companionable natures. After their playing careers finished, they made a substantial contribution to the game through their extensive involvement in its administration. To lose two players of such stature in such a short time is a sad but timely reminder of the richness of Australia's cricket heritage.

	M	I	NO	R	HS	100s	50s	Avge	Ct	St	W	Avge	BB
First-class	110	186	20	6,834	219	15	36	41.16	72	0	4	85.75	1/1
Tests	9	14	2	502	96	0	5	41.83	2	0	0	–	–
Dom. first-class	75	127	13	4,934	219	11	26	43.28	51	0	3	96.67	1/1

TOVEY, EDWARD RICHARD, died at the Sydney suburb of St Leonards on May 31, 2002. Born at King's Cross on Christmas Day 1930, Dick Tovey was educated at Newington College, which he represented at cricket, rugby union and athletics. In his final year at school he was chosen to keep wickets for the GPS First XI before joining the Paddington club, where his consistent form behind the stumps gained him selection for the state Colts' side against Queensland Colts in successive seasons from 1953-54. In the first of these matches, he gave an entertaining display of his batting talents as he made a second innings 69, dominating a fifth-wicket partnership of 99 in only 56 minutes with Bill Watson. In 1956 the firm of James North, for whom he worked as a sales representative, transferred him to Brisbane, where he found a place with the South Brisbane club. He played for Queensland against his old state in the opening Sheffield Shield match of the 1957-58 but was dropped after an uncharacteristically poor match with the gloves. In 1959 he was again transferred, this time to Auckland, where he played with the Papatoetoe club and represented Auckland over three seasons in the Plunket Shield, his presence being an important factor in his side's victory in the 1963-64 season. Apart from his 21 dismissals (20 caught and one stumped) in the five competition matches, he contributed valuable runs, most particularly a second innings 69 against Northern Districts at Auckland which enabled Auckland to win by eight runs despite being dismissed for 69 in their first innings. Tall for a keeper (180 cm), Tovey was both elegant and safe behind the stumps, a sure sense of anticipation removing the need for him to dive and sprawl. Moreover, he was a late example of the keeper who was both able and willing to stand up to the quicker bowlers, a practice which cramped and harried the opposing batsmen. After returning to Sydney, he rose to be general manager of his firm, retiring in 1978 and spending two decades offering his sales expertise and experience as a consultant.

	M	I	NO	R	HS	100s	50s	Avge	Ct	St	W	Avge	BB
First-class	13	21	4	238	62	0	1	14.00	35	7	0	–	–
Dom. first-class	1	2	0	18	18	0	0	9.00	0	1	0	–	–

TURNER, HERBERT WILFRED, died on February 24, 2002, in the Victorian city of Bendigo. Born at nearby Woodvale on July 6, 1921, Herb Turner found his skills as a boilermaker required in Melbourne during World War Two. With his cricketing and football ability he quickly made his mark with the Carlton club, making his initial first-grade cricket appearance in 1942-43 and being an integral member of the 1945-46 and

1947-48 premiership sides. His nickname "Stumpy" drew attention to his nuggety frame (170 cm and 73 kg); possessing powerful forearms, he refused to be staked to the crease and used his left-handed batting to take the attack to the bowlers. The Victorian selectors took some interest in him in the 1948-49 season, but only to the extent that he became an expert drinks carrier, acting as 12th man in four matches during the season. In January that season, Turner made a forthright 97 in 111 minutes in the Second XI match against New South Wales, an innings which set up a substantial victory for his side. A month later, he made his first-class debut against Western Australia at Melbourne, hitting 96 in 160 minutes in an innings flecked with powerful driving and savage pulling. Batting at No. 6, he was last out, having dominated proceedings to the extent that his runs came out of 165 made while he was at the wicket. The next season was punctuated with another three matches as 12th man but, restored to the side for the last two matches, he made 50 on a difficult Sydney pitch against New South Wales and a scintillating 78 against Queensland at the Gabba. After starting 1950-51 carrying the drinks for the eighth time he made a number of promising starts during the rest of the season, reaching 20 in six of his nine innings, but went no further than 45 not out against Queensland at Melbourne. Turner continued with Carlton until 1955-56, finishing with 4,947 runs at 32.33 from 161 matches, and was awarded life membership for his services to the club, before returning to Bendigo where he was an active coach with Eaglehawk and Calgully clubs over the next decade. He was also an important member of the Carlton football side, playing as a wingman in the 1945 premiership team and appearing as a rover and in the forward pocket in the 1947 team which again claimed the flag. In 84 games for Carlton between 1944 and 1949, Turner kicked 102 goals, and in 1950 he turned out for Hawthorn in another ten matches.

	M	I	NO	R	HS	100s	50s	Avge	Ct	St	W	Avge	BB
First-class	12	20	1	632	96	0	3	33.26	3	0	1	16.00	1/16
Dom. first-class	11	18	1	559	96	0	3	32.88	3	0	0	–	–

WEIR, HAROLD STANLEY, died on June 11, 2002 at the age of 98, in a nursing home at Maryborough, Queensland, having worn with dignity and distinction his status as Queensland's longest-lived cricketer. Born on April 23, 1904 at nearby Croydon Junction (later renamed Baddow), Stan Weir was educated at the Central Boys' State School in Maryborough, subsequently joining the Tinana club for whom he played all his local cricket. A prolific left-handed all-rounder at this level, he was an attractive batsman who bowled at a sprightly medium pace. Early in the 1929-30 season, he took part in the Country trial matches in Brisbane, following which he was selected as a member of the first state Colts' side to visit Sydney. He batted attractively, scoring 36 at No. 3 in each innings, adding 61 for the second wicket with Roy Levy (91) on his first visit to the crease, but bowled 14 wicketless overs. A month later, against Harold Gilligan's MCC side, he was a late replacement in a Queensland side hit by the unavailability of Otto Nothling, the captain, and the withdrawal of six other selected players. Although the home side beat the injury-riddled visitors by five wickets, Weir batted only in the first innings, scoring three at No. 6, and not being called on for a single over by Leo O'Connor, the Queensland skipper, despite his use of six other bowlers. In 1930-31, he scored 55 for North against South in a Country trial match; thereafter he continued to be an integral part of the Maryborough representative side and his own club. He joined the Woocoo Shire Council immediately on leaving school and spent all his working life there, ultimately retiring as shire clerk. In his retirement, he was a familiar figure as he kept himself fit with long walks around his home city; moreover, his accurate memory and agile mind were important resources in recording the history of Maryborough and its cricket.

	M	I	NO	R	HS	100s	50s	Avge	Ct	St	W	Avge	BB
First-class	1	1	0	3	3	0	0	3.00	0	0	0	–	–

CRICKET BOOKS, 2001-02

By JAMIE GRANT

When 21-year-old Robert Rose began the 1973-74 Sheffield Shield season for Victoria with an innings of 118 not out and 88, many knowledgeable cricket watchers identified him as a future Test player. The season before, he had made 48 against Dennis Lillee's bowling on the MCG, batting in such a manner as to suggest that he might provide a solution to Australia's then persistent lack of suitable opening batsmen. Rose was not out on 23 in Victoria's last Shield match of the season, a victory over New South Wales on January 22, 1974. Less than a month later he was driving his Volkswagen at night on a notoriously hazardous stretch of road near the country town of Bacchus Marsh, on his way home from a day at the Ballarat races, when the car left the road and rolled over several times. Though "there wasn't a mark on his body", Rose suffered severe spinal damage in the accident, and was left a quadriplegic. After a quarter-century of ever-increasing distress, both physical and psychological, which he bore with courage, he died as a result of side-effects of his condition in 1999. *Rose Boys* (Allen & Unwin, \$29.95), by Robert Rose's younger brother Peter, is an account of that cruelly abbreviated life, and of the effect the tragedy had on all of the Rose family. It does not purport to be a cricket book, and indeed the story it tells, and the impressive manner of its telling, mean that the book has a wider appeal than the specialised confines of the cricket community, but for cricketers it will have a particular significance.

Though Bob Rose, Robert's father, was one of the greatest of all Australian Rules footballers, and Robert, too, played football for Collingwood and Footscray, cricket was always as important a sport as the winter game for the Rose family (in the 1970s, this reviewer encountered uncles and cousins of Robert Rose on the field at various levels of junior and District cricket in Melbourne). Even before his accident, it was apparent that Robert's talent, for all his versatility, was weighted towards cricket. Afterwards, cricket-watching and the company of cricketers came to be among his foremost consolations.

Thus there is a great deal about the game of cricket in Peter Rose's book, from descriptions of childhood backyard contests to well-informed eye-witness accounts of innings in first-class matches. Though by his own admission no sportsman himself – he is, perhaps improbably for one of his family, a highly-regarded poet, editor and intellectual – Peter Rose is able to take the reader behind the scenes for the various levels of cricket his brother was involved in, and by doing so he provides many useful insights into the thoughts and actions of top-class sportsmen. The consequences of the accident make Robert Rose's life a condensed version of the empty, frustrating fate which awaits many such sportsmen when their playing careers come to an end; the loss of both physical activity and the adulation which accompanies it throws many of these players back onto their own inner resources, which, as David Frith has shown in his explorations of cricket's suicides, can often prove lacking. In Rose's case, that lack was overcome only after many difficulties, which are detailed by Peter Rose with a clear-eyed candour which make this book one of the most powerful memoirs readers in any genre could hope to encounter, and which entitles it to be considered the most notable cricket book of the past 12 months even though it is not intended to be a cricket book.

Gideon Haigh's *The Big Ship* (Text Publishing, \$60), on the other hand, purports to be a cricket book when in fact it is something more. Haigh is one of Australia's finest social historians, who simply happens to use cricket as a window into the whole of Australian society in the period which coincided, in this case, with the life of one of Australia's foremost captains, Warwick Armstrong. As the dates concerned are between 1879 and 1947, it should not be surprising that Haigh has been unable to speak – as he did in his previous biography-cum-social-history, *Mystery Spinner* – with witnesses who had seen Armstrong in action. Instead, he supplies abundant quotations from the newspaper reports of the time, and these are often as much to be relished for their style as for their informative content.

When Armstrong began his career in international cricket, the administration of the sport was entirely in the hands of private promoters, and Haigh is as usual particularly absorbed by the financial ramifications of the haphazardly arranged early tours (in which "amateur" players like W. G. Grace were paid more than the "professionals") and of the controversial foundations of the Australian Cricket Board and more formal competitive structures throughout the country. Before Federation, of course, it might not have been feasible to establish such a board; its setting-up created a situation which was the reverse of the player rebellion against the board in 1977, as the new board constituted in effect a rebellion of administrators against the player-organised international tours which had gone before. Armstrong, like many of the leading players of the time, preferred the earlier arrangements on the grounds that they could be more financially profitable, and he was one of the signatories to a letter sent to the board which led to a fist-fight in the boardroom.

The lead-up to that colourful climax is meticulously documented by Haigh, though some readers might be content with less detail than he supplies; similarly, when Haigh describes the tremendous weight which led to Armstrong being given the nickname which is this book's title, he also details the chemical processes which could make a man grow fat ("alcohol is a great builder of bulk. One gram of ethanol produces seven calories of energy – fat produces nine, sugar and protein merely four"), and the health risks associated with obesity ("coronary heart disease, high blood pressure, diabetes and osteoarthritis") when most cricket lovers would feel that being told how much he weighed (140 kilograms, or 22 stone) would suffice. Still, Haigh's thoroughness is far preferable to its opposite – found in some of the other titles to be reviewed in these pages – and if some of the facts he has set down may seem superfluous, many more are of great interest, so that *The Big Ship* is a worthy addition to Haigh's already formidable body of published work.

A book with the title *At the Heart of English Cricket* (Fairfield Books, $50) would seem an unlikely prospect for inclusion on a list of the year's Australian cricket books. Yet Stephen Chalke's quasi-biography of Geoffrey Howard manages to do so because a great part of it concerns one of the more dramatic Ashes Test series to be contested in Australia. Howard, who was then the Secretary of Lancashire County Cricket Club, was the manager of the English (or MCC) touring party of 1954-55. The book begins not with its subject's early life, as would a conventional biography, but at Woolloongabba in November 1954, with the words, "What was Len Hutton thinking?"

The idea of an interview with the then 92-year-old Howard must have promised, at best, a magazine profile when Chalke first undertook it; what he discovered, instead, while looking in a back room for photographs, was a box full of the "letters he had written home every day from his three tours". The freshness of these letters and their closeness to the action and the inner-most thoughts of some of the central figures in the 1954-55 Test series make this a uniquely absorbing book. The structure Chalke has devised – alternating chapters which are devoted to a detailed, and vivid, account of each of the Tests with flashbacks to Howard's early life and developing career, first as a cricketer and then as an administrator – is calculated to sustain tension in both strands of the narrative.

Chalke writes elegantly in the connecting passages he is called on to supply, but the strength in this exceptional book lies in the personality of Howard himself, which emerges through the letters, extensively quoted from, and through the comments he made in his interviews with Chalke; he strikes one as a man of rare qualities, efficient and imaginative as a manager, intelligent and yet modest about his achievements. To

Australian readers familiar with other accounts of the 1954-55 series, the most surprising feature of this book may be the portrait of Len Hutton which emerges through Howard's reminiscences. Hutton has been portrayed traditionally as a ruthless, calculating leader, as willing as Douglas Jardine had been to exploit the limits of cricket's laws, but to Howard he was a lonely, unhappy figure, anxious about the prospect of defeat, and so depressed on the eve of the Third Test (which England were to win in sensational circumstances) that he refused to get out of his hotel bed. "I can see Len now," Howard recalls. "He was sitting up in his bed with a woollen vest on, staring at the wall."

Another English writer who might seem an improbable inclusion in the company of Australia's cricket writers is Simon Hughes, the former Middlesex and Durham pace bowler. In *Yakking Around the World* (Simon & Schuster, $24.95), though, he writes about his times as a visiting player in Perth, Sydney and Auckland, and in the process offers some insight into the structure and standards of grade and first-class cricket in Australia and New Zealand. He is more perceptive about Perth than about Sydney, it must be added, and the degree to which his amusing, well-written book can be an example of cricket writing rather than something else is debatable. Much of it comprises a fairly superficial travelogue, enlivened by a blow-by-blow (literally) account of the author's love life, so that the work it most nearly resembles is the *Memoirs of Casanova*. Similar boasting is often heard in changing rooms all over the world, but some readers might take the view that the activities he describes are just not cricket.

Another book with a somewhat tenuous claim to being Australian – despite its title and subject-matter – is *Men of Waugh*, by Norman Geras (self-published, $27.50). Geras is a Zimbabwe-born academic at an English university who became a passionate supporter of the Australian cricket team as a young boy, when his homeland was not among the Test-playing nations. In 2001, as he had done in 1997, Geras attended each day of the season's Ashes Tests, recorded his impressions, and published them as a book – all at his own expense. It would of course have been most improbable for a commercial publisher to have supported his project, as he is neither a former Test cricketer nor a high-profile sporting journalist. His enterprising spirit, refusing to be deterred by commercial convention, is to be admired, but unfortunately his prose style is so flat and his observations are so banal that his book might as well have been written by a former Test cricketer.

The death of Don Bradman last year predictably provoked an outpouring of exploitation, disguised as mourning, of Australia's most successful cricketer. In *Bradman's Best* (Random House, $29.95), Roland Perry, Bradman's "biographer", has produced a shoddily written, mistake-ridden collection of a dozen profiles of past players who constituted, according to Perry, Bradman's idea of the best cricket team of all time. The claim is less than plausible. To start with, Bradman himself is included in the side, when modesty should have forbidden it, and then the first 11 names are a bizarrely unbalanced selection, with only four specialist batsmen, a wicket-keeper not especially noted for his batting at No. 6, and, if one counts the all-rounder at No. 5, Garfield Sobers, as three bowlers in one, a total of eight bowlers. Yet the great West Indian teams of the 1980s needed only four bowlers to dismiss all opposition, and likewise Bradman's own Invincibles habitually used only four, with some help from the all-rounders. A team that needs eight bowlers is one that has been kept in the field for too long to have any chance of winning. Bradman, unfortunately, is not here to account for the choices Perry has attributed to him.

On the scale of Bradman exploitation, Alan Eason is at the opposite end to Perry: his fascination with what he calls "Bradmania" is motivated only by personal satisfaction – "I wrote this tome for myself" he announces in the Introduction – and not by commercial greed. A percentage of the proceeds from *The A-Z of Bradman* (published by the author, 105 Ninth Avenue, Austral NSW 2171, $40) are to be donated to charity. Eason is an accountant and a professional crossword compiler, and this unusual combination of occupations is reflected in the format and the content of his "tome", with its numerical and cross-referencing obsessions. Only "a brave soul", he says of his own book, would attempt "to read it from cover to cover"; it aims instead at "the quintessential dipper".

Another book which should appeal to the "dipper" is Kersi Meher-Homji's *Dramatic Debuts and Swan Songs* (ABC Books, \$27.95). "Dramatic" is a word which embraces many possibilities, so that Meher-Homji must necessarily be selective; among the dramas he chooses to describe, unsurprisingly are Bradman's Swan Song duck (somewhat of a mixed metaphor), the century debuts of Australian players such as Doug Walters and Greg Chappell, and of subcontinental batsmen such as Javed Miandad and Mohammad Azharuddin, and the 16-wicket debuts of Bob Massie and Narendra Hirwani. A more unpredictable inclusion is the Swan Song of Denise Annetts, who scored 148 not out in her last innings for the Australian women's Test team, only to be omitted from the side – so she maintained – on the grounds that she was not a lesbian. Fortunately, such stringent selection criteria do not apply to the men's team. A list of batsmen who made centuries in their first or last Tests, and of bowlers who took either seven wickets in an innings or ten wickets in a match, is appended; if anything about these lists is revealing, it might be the high proportion of "dramatic debutants" who were scarcely heard of again after their initial success.

The "dipping" reader will also be attracted to Jim Maxwell's *Stumps* (Hardie Grant, \$29.95). Best known as the voice of cricket on ABC radio (in that role, in the opinion of this listener, he has surpassed his celebrated mentor, Alan McGilvray, having added a dimension of humour which was seldom heard from the founder of radio cricket commentary), he is also the editor of the *ABC Cricket Book*, which is, despite its title, a magazine; though written by only one person, *Stumps* could be taken for a magazine, too. Its layout, with abundant illustrations, "boxes" and "breakouts", might prove distracting for readers who want to follow Maxwell's thoughts on Australia's recent Test series against West Indies, India and England, or who hope for a conventional memoir of Maxwell's early days and career in public broadcasting. While both of these topics are covered in this book, the format makes it easier for the reader to dip in and out of them rather than going from cover to cover. A magazine-like sub-heading on the front cover promises that Maxwell will deal with "Sledging, Slogging, Scandal, Success – The Way I See It"; it has to be said that there are no startling insights into any of these matters on the pages inside: everything is as condensed as an on-air radio comment, whereas at least for this reviewer it would have been of great interest to see Maxwell expound at length on those ideas he is only able to touch upon briefly before the bowler comes in to deliver another ball.

Could anyone alive read Charles Davis's *Test Cricket in Australia 1877–2002* (published by the Author, \$99) from cover to cover? It seems unlikely; and yet this is a magnificent production, and a supreme instance of historical research and the statistician's craft. It consists simply of scores and averages for every Test series played in Australia, with a minimal text introducing each series. "The traditional published style of scorecards", Davis asserts, is "outdated". Thus he has devised "a layout for a Test scoresheet with the aim of presenting as much information as practicable on an A4 page with as much clarity as possible". Unfortunately, for this format to become universal all cricket books in the future will have to be printed on A4-sized pages, which would be cumbersome and expensive. His new format is indeed fascinating and packed with information, though many cricket lovers may find it confusing and weighted with too much detail (do we really need to know, for example, that in the drawn Fifth Test in 1954-55 W. J. Watson took 20 balls to make a score of 3?). However, subsequent editions of this work will need closer attention to proof-reading, in both the introductory text and the Player Register at the back of the book, where a listing of "bowler type" appears to put Brett Lee in the same category as Colin Miller, and describes Adam Gilchrist as a medium-pacer.

Sam Anderson, it seems, was a wicket-keeper who could bowl. On the North Coast of New South Wales he was a legendary figure in the years between the two World Wars; in *Dusky Legend* (Northern Rivers Press, $18) Maurice Ryan tells the story of a famous Aboriginal cricketer who was not allowed, because of his race, to prove his ability at the highest levels of the game. Anderson was the grandfather of the well-known Aboriginal writer Ruby Langford, who supplies a foreword to this somewhat sketchy biography – it is sketchy because little verifiable material exists about its subject. Scorecards have survived for three representative matches Anderson played in for the Richmond–Tweed region against the New South Wales state team; in each of the first two matches (in 1922 and 1924) Anderson took four wickets, while in the third (in 1928), as wicket-keeper, he caught Don Bradman before the future Test player had scored. Maurice Ryan wrote to Bradman in the hope of obtaining more information about this match, only to receive the reply "the truth is I can't remember a single incident about the match in question".

Currency Lads (The Cricket Publishing Company, $48), by Max Bonnell, is a multiple biography of four pioneering figures from the early history of Test cricket. In 1884, T. W. Garrett, R. C. Allen, S. P. Jones and R. J. Pope were the first four batsmen in the order for Sydney University's team; Garrett and Jones were then current Australian Test players, while Allen and Pope were each to play a single Test in the next few years. All four had much in common at the time, having come from comfortable middle-class families and attended private schools before enrolling at the university. The lives of Garrett, Allen and Pope were to remain entwined for the rest of their long lives (Garrett was the youngest of the four when he died at the age of 85, a life-span nine years briefer than Allen's), but Sammy Jones, about whom Bonnell writes with a certain

TEST CRICKET
IN AUSTRALIA
1877-2002

By Charles Davis

The ultimate record of
Australian Test matches.

Match descriptions with
detailed scorecards,
including batting times, 4s,
6s, for over 95% of all
individual innings.

544pp, Hardcover, $99.
Contact Charles Davis 03 9459 6834.
PO Box 39, Rosanna 3084.
Email: sportstats@iprimus.com.au
For more info check the website:
www.sportstats.com.au
Also avail. Roger Page Cricket Books

"An extremely valuable historical document, and a fine read." (Allan Miller)

relish, moved to New Zealand at the end of his playing days, becoming cricket coach at Auckland Grammar, a position he retained for 35 years even though it was somewhat beneath his abilities. Jones was the unfortunate young batsman, in his first Test, who was run out by W. G. Grace when he left his crease to "pat down a defect in the pitch"; later, he was omitted from Australian teams for reasons, Bonnell deduces, which had less to do with cricket than with his off-field behaviour. Only Garrett, of the four, had an extended Test career, and his achievements were solid rather than spectacular. Allen was an uncle of the English Test captain G. O. B. Allen. Pope became a leading eye surgeon, and was a man of many parts, playing rugby, tennis and golf at high levels, speaking three languages, and being an accomplished musician and a noted art collector. In recounting the lives of these four cricketers, Bonnell, like Gideon Haigh, brings all of their world to life, providing as many insights into the Australian society of the late nineteenth century as into the foundations of Australian cricket.

CRICKET AND THE MEDIA, 2000-01

By ALEX BUZO

DOORKNOBS AND DROPPINGS

"Cricket, cricket, cricket! Dead, dead, dead!" said the clue-giver at the trivia contest in March 2001, and the answer was Don Bradman. A year later if the answer was "The Waughs", the clue would have been "Cricket, cricket, cricket! Dropped, dropped, dropped!" It was not enough to die; you had to be dropped to make page one.

The big story was the omission of Mark and Steve Waugh from the Australian limited-overs side and it highlighted the role of the real superstars of the year: the selectors. Having sacked the coach from the panel and abolished the convention of the three-man players' committee on tour, the selectors went on tour themselves, where they also doubled as commentators. At more than one point in South Africa, the commentary box was staffed entirely by selectors – Allan Border, Trevor Hohns, Omar Henry, Mike Procter.

Henry and Procter had to contend with their own problems, including the perception that race had superseded merit in the South African team, but luckily for all concerned, Makhaya Ntini and Roger Telemachus soon proved they were not "quota quicks" and got among the wickets. "Prockie" then made an extraordinary outburst, saying that South Africa had improved enormously under Mark Boucher as captain. Was he talking as commentator or was this something left over from the selection table? At the end of the series it was announced that Procter would become a match referee and he was replaced as a selector by fellow commentator Pat Symcox.

Why did they sack Steve Waugh, Border was asked on *Inside Cricket*. "Make-up of the team and forward planning," he replied, adding, "When I put the phone down I felt physically ill." There was some evidence here for the view that the 2002-03 World Cup campaign had already begun.

With Border and Hohns behind the microphone, at least the criticism of the media was halted – indeed, the only way to stop the abuse seemed to be to put the selectors on television and keep them there. After a press conference back in Australia, Steve Waugh had called his interrogators "a bunch of dickheads", while a bloodied Michael Slater hurled his helmet down in front of the working press after being hit by a bouncer. "I hope you're satisfied, you pricks!" yelled Slats.

It was cosier on *Inside Cricket*, where David Hookes thanked ACB head James Sutherland for his help and support throughout the season. While there should not necessarily be an adversarial atmosphere in relations between the Board and the media, it did emphasise how different things are in the world of cricket coverage. Those who believe that independent analysis is the most satisfactory outcome for both player and fan were certainly sent packing in 2001-02. It was only in the print media that traditional journalistic values – such as avoiding any appearance of conflict of interest or confusion of roles – were given a whirl, and there is no evidence the fans were more appreciative.

In the print media as well, the "Waugh droppings" were the main story. As with the Chappells, one brother is a talented stylist, while the other is a mentally strong hatchet-man but, as Galileo proved, when you drop balls of unequal weight from a tower, they still hit the ground at the same time. A new literary form, the mezzanine obituary, made its appearance, pioneered by Trevor Marshallsea in the Fairfax press: "When Waugh [Mark] trudged off Kingsmead after making 30 on Saturday afternoon, it was almost certainly the final act …"

Peter Roebuck of *The Age* was in no doubt that the Waughs had gone for good ("Australia has chosen its team for the next World Cup"), while Phil Wilkins in the

Sydney Morning Herald (home of the headline "The Baggy Green St Valentine's Day Massacre") wrote this of Steve Waugh on February 14: "The old wolf stalked into Melbourne's Crown Casino at the head of the Australian team on Monday night, grim and unsmiling, padding along the VIP red carpet as if it were a minefield." Roebuck then came back for a second spell with "His body has thickened and his footwork slowed" and concluded with an oxymoronic flourish: "Eternity is approaching its end."

Mike Coward in the *Australian* was less sentimental: "For much too long, the selectors were so seduced by [Mark] Waugh's beauty as a batsman, they effectively allowed him to do as he liked." As for the "old wolf", Steve looked far from unsmiling as he accepted the Laureus award for the world's best sporting team at a more congenial casino – Monte Carlo – and appeared to be smirking at a press conference afterwards. It was a grim smirk, not in the least bit smarmy, but a smirk nonetheless. Only romanticists and tragics believe the Australian cricket captain is more powerful than a locomotive and more important than the Prime Minister, but by the end of the season the job seemed to have lost authority in almost everyone's eyes. There were some victories, however, and the Laureus was one.

Earlier in the season, it had been a friskier Steve Waugh who had treated the idea of anti-corruption cameras in the dressing room with satire: "There might be a few practice cricket balls going around the dressing room and they might hit one of those cameras." He even raised the prospect of a final "passage to India" in 2004 when he would be 39. "It will end in tears," predicted Chip le Grand in the *Australian*. By the end of the South African tour it was a sadly incredulous skipper who responded to the "dropping story" at Sydney airport on March 22: "I find this pretty amazing. We've just won a series 5-1 but nobody's asked me about that. I think the priorities are wrong somewhere. Australian cricket is going really well."

The first person to raise the prospect of sacking the Waughs had been David Hookes, and this provoked Peter Frilingos on Foxtel's *The Back Page*. "You've killed Lassie twice," he exclaimed, to which Hookes replied, "Bambi." He went on to point out that no one on "700 grand a year" was going to retire and that sackings would dominate cricket news for some time to come. The days when "Wallaby" Bob Cowper left the game prematurely to pursue a business career (successfully, as it turned out; he finished up in Monte Carlo permanently) are over. Cricket is a business career.

The other player dropped, Andrew Symonds, told *The Age* the whole atmosphere was bad for team morale, as everyone now feared the axe. This inspired a wonderful piece in the *Sydney Morning Herald* by Gavin Robertson, with the classic aphorism, "As a general rule, politics within great teams is minimal, politics in mediocre teams is rife." First there was Raymond Robertson-Glasgow and now we have Gavin Robertson-Tolstoy. The general rule was certainly borne out in Ian Botham's new memoirs, where he claimed to have earned the gratitude of his team-mates by obeying vice-captain Willis's orders to run out skipper Boycott.

For the new boy, finger-spinner Nathan Hauritz, there was a welcome of sorts. Not since Gordon Bray's "He's in for a try! He's doing a PhD on the reproductive cycle of the ewe!" has there been such a rampant CV as this one by Peter Roebuck: "As befits a young man delivered by Carl Rackemann's mother, Hauritz is a proper cricketer and varies his pace craftily as he plies a trade frowned upon down under, making it respectable."

I wonder what old offies Greg Matthews and Tom Veivers think of that – not to mention the current Gavin Robertson, the late Ian Johnson and the long-fingered Hugh Trumble. Old new boy Darren "Boof" Lehmann was piped aboard by Mike Haysman on Foxtel ("I played with him back when the Dead Sea was just sick") and Roebuck, who described Boof and Warney as "Warriors who trot around cheerfully though without undue alacrity". Ian Harvey was probably not thrilled when South African commentators claimed, "Australia are searching for a genuine all-rounder; your bits-and-pieces man gets exposed at this level" and disparaged his running between wickets ("He turns like the Queen Mary"). Only Michael Bevan was universally praised when he returned to the one-day team after a "rotation" spell. The *Daily Telegraph* promptly hailed him as "The Pyjama Picasso" and satisfied the quality buffs by not spelling it "Pycasso".

Under this ill-fated rotation process, Australia lost its first three limited-overs games in the VB Series competition, and that started the "droppings" controversy, which culminated in Ricky Ponting's ascension to the captaincy. "When did you first sense leadership potential in Punter?" Hookes asked Border on Inside Cricket. "From the word go," was AB's unhesitating answer.

This Fox Sports program also covered the Pura Cup in some detail, including a hilarious interview with Stuart Law, who captained the Queenslanders to victory in the final and took a glorious running catch. "Lucky I wasn't drug-tested," said Law. Another Pura star, Simon Katich, noted the changing face of the speed-friendly WACA: "It doesn't harden up on day two or day three any more. It's more of a pudding, like a normal pitch." Katich then announced he would be a visitor when next he braved the WACA; he was moving to New South Wales and the Spin City that is the SCG.

The next rung down, grade cricket, is not covered in much detail by the mainstream media – except for the semi-final between North Sydney and UTS–Balmain, which finished up in court after "horizontal rain" appeared to have fallen on Drummoyne Oval when Norths arrived after a dry week to begin their innings. It was reminiscent of the "block of ice on a good length" scandal in the 1969 Melbourne district semi-final between Carlton and University, in which the Carlton bowlers, Barry Knight and Barney Jones (father of Dean) cleaned up – although neither was accused outright of leaving the ice on the pitch the night before University began their innings, and indeed were praised by some pundits for their immaculate length.

"The Sydney Cricket Association final begins today with more pre-publicity than the competition has had since a boy named Bradman batted for St George," wrote Andrew Stevenson in the *Sydney Morning Herald*. In this case, the winner was not cricket, it was Fairfield–Liverpool, and very easily, too; as David Sygall explained in the *Sun-Herald*, "The North Sydney players looked tired after spending hours in the field yesterday, having earned the right to contest the final less than 24 hours before it started." The match was played at neutral Bankstown Oval – where the semi-final had been completed – but as a contest, the final got out at Redfern.

After Sydney's Black December, Grey January and dry autumn (except for that freakish night in Drummoyne), the action made a welcome shift to South Africa, and a bigger shift in media terms, to pay television from free-to-air, or "Freda Ware", as they say on talkback radio. Channel Nine's coverage of the domestic season had been pretty much the same as it had been for the last 25 years, although there was much speculation about whether the modern McGilvray, Richie Benaud, the undisputed voice of summer, was going to retire at the age of 71.

Whoever replaces him will have lingering memories to dispell. Mike Haysman left Australia in 1985, but his commentary in South Africa was still full of Benaudian cadences – "It's been a commanding performance, this … I can promise you …" The 12th Man canvassed possible replacements for Benaud – including the hyper-barbaric Darrell Eastlake – in a very funny double CD, but in the end the Willow King signed on for another season. Some scribes speculated that Simon O'Donnell and Ian Healy were going to succeed to the throne in 2003-04 but now that Mark Taylor has thrown away his chewing gum and learned to make himself understood, there was quiet money going his way.

Always verbally inventive, Taylor claimed that "Claude Henderson has disrailed the Australian innings" and finally explained just what the under-thatched New Zealander Chris Harris bowls while he appears to look at the square-leg umpire. Were they fast spinners or slow seamers? "I call them doorknobs," said Tayls, "because he looks as if he's turning a doorknob when he bowls them." It may have been an unenlightening explanation, but it was certainly the most imaginative piece of commentary of the season.

The much younger (by 14 years) brother of "Rich", John Benaud stepped down from the New South Wales selection process and nominated Steve Waugh as selector material, so there could be redemption (and media commitments) ahead for these brothers who were born only four minutes apart. John Benaud had been an Australian selector and wrote a classic, definitive book on the subject called *Matters of Choice* (1997), so it was quite a "wrap".

Another job that became vacant was coach of Victoria, but not for long. As soon as the season ended, it was announced that David Hookes was the new appointment. "The only job in sport you haven't got is mine," exclaimed *Back Page* chairman Mike Gibson, while Peter Fitzsimons asked if the Croweaters felt they had been betrayed. "I couldn't give a stuff what people in Adelaide think," was Hookesy's brisk reply. "What happens if there's a big story," pressed Fitzsimons; "Say, the sacking of Shane Warne – will you break it first on your radio program?" Hookes glared at the big fella. "There's already been a big story – the dropping of Damien Fleming – and I didn't break it," said the former South Australian.

At season's end the now-traditional charges of sledging were levelled at Australia, this time by South African debutant Graeme Smith, who was involved in several on-field disputes. As Gordon Bray said elsewhere, "Temperatures are fraying out there." Even the crowd got involved in sledging, with one placard making the extravagant claim, "Ntini's weenie is bigger than Bichel's pickle." At least it made a change from "Your missus is a dud root" or the answer to "Why are you so fat?" (Every time I have sex with your wife she gives me a biscuit).

The end of summer did not mean the end of cricket, however, and the ACB programmed three limited-overs internationals against Pakistan for Melbourne Docklands Stadium and the Gabba in June – right in the middle of the World Cup soccer, or football ("food bowl") as SBS prefers to call it. It would take a special kind of embittered fantasist to believe that *The Age* got its name by taking the last three letters from "disparage", but ... the cap does fit sometimes. The Super Challenge was given a bucketing ("this winter frolic ... a Truman Show") and cold water was poured on the Clash of the Speedsters: "Akhtar is almost always broken down and Lee is almost always out of form," wrote Greg Baum. In the event, Akhtar swung the decider with 5/25 at the Gabba, and his apparent coat of arms – spreadeagled stumps on a green background with a bowed Anzac exiting right – continued to be seen.

The first match at Colonial Stadium attracted under 12,000, which led Baum to conclude that "discerning Melbourne is not so easily sold". Ex-Melburnian Keith Miller once said of his home town, "If you put on two girls playing hopscotch you'd get a crowd of 20,000." The International Challenge at Colonial did not disprove this theory outright, but its abrupt appearance reminded us that cricket is a serial, not a series. The only continuity was provided by new skipper Ponting, who displayed his mastery of press conferences by describing the 2-1 defeat as "a good wake-up call".

We know now that cricket is a summer game, but where do flies and match referees go in winter? Morocco appears to be the answer. Mike Procter was sent there and reported the stadium at Tangier was fit for Test match play. Like Webster's Dictionary, cricket appears to be Morocco-bound, where it is to be hoped that the locals give a stuff. Presumably, discerning Tangier cannot be easily sold, but a fair dinkum contest in warm weather may just tip the scales, win over those curmudgeons at *The Age* and attract big parties of tourists from Melbourne. From there, who knows what will be the limit.

AUSTRALIAN CRICKET MEMORABILIA, 2001-02

By STEPHEN W. GIBBS

The commercial cricket auction forum in Sydney has changed recently, with the merging of Lawson's Auctioneers with Menzies International to form Lawsons–Menzies, and Wemyss, which began in Australia in 1996, being taken over by Cromwell's of the UK. The effect of these changes is fewer auctions in Sydney featuring cricket memorabilia and the items being offered generally having a higher value. Christie's Australia and Charles Leski, both based in Melbourne, continued to conduct their regular (and in Leski's case, frequent) auctions, with choice pieces often on offer.

The salesroom value of the "baggy green" Australian cricket cap has encouraged more of these iconic bits of apparel into the market place. Caps owned by Ted a'Beckett sold for $8,500 (1928-29 series) and $5,250 (1931-32 series). The Test cap worn by Gary Cosier fetched $4,000 while Jack Fingleton's 1938 cap reached $5,500. Lindsay Hassett's cap fetched an astounding $22,000 and two caps of Greg Chappell were sold for $16,000 each.

The sale of Greg Chappell's material at Christie's in July 2001 and subsequently at Leski's in October 2001 seemed like a clear-out of his entire garage, with golfing trophies and mugs included in the offerings. Buyer interest in his collection was mixed except for his "baggy greens"; an archive of his personal cricket and business papers selling for $20,000; and two irate letters from Sir Donald Bradman to Chappell dated 1977 and 1978 which sold for $16,000. These letters were subject to critical comment and threatened legal action from the Bradman Museum in Bowral. They were subsequently passed on by the buyers to the Museum out of respect to Bradman.

Significant items from such recent Test cricketers as Craig McDermott (his first Test blazer going for $1,500), Gary Cosier, Geoff Marsh and more material from Alan Connolly were offered with varying degrees of interest and sales results. Material from deceased cricketers was of more interest, with Jack Ryder and Ted a'Beckett prominent. A small archive of items from pre-World War II Test cricketer Ross Gregory attracted interest, his wartime diary featuring in the offering which sold for $4,200 to a collector in England.

Charles Leski in Melbourne continues to conduct his regular auctions of cricket material with something for everybody. Twelve of 14 of the 1897 Cameo Famous Cricketers badges set realised $2,000 and a full set of 1901 Cameo English Cricketers badges brought $1,300. A proof strip of twelve matchbox labels from the 1950 Duncan's Yacht Safety Matches showing the 1950 Australian Test squad including Hassett, Lindwall and Harvey sold for $140.

Autograph material featured strongly in sales. A signed letter from Charles Bannerman dated 1921 went for $1,650; one from William Murdoch dated 1882 sold for $1,750; a 1922 signed letter from Monty Noble realised $575, as did a handwritten and signed 1927 telegram from Archie Jackson; lastly, a Hugh Trumble letter of 1924 sold for $440. The perennially popular 1948 team was again represented with an autograph album of 59 signatures including all 17 of that tour going for $1,050, contrasting with the $2,250 gained by an official 1948 teamsheet with 16 signatures (lacking Lindwall) plus the usual Barnes handstamp. A version of the latter with all 17 signatures gained $3,500, proving that completeness and presentation are everything to a collector.

Bradman memorabilia continues to be released largely through the auspices of the Bradman Museum in Bowral. The Museum now has tight control over the use and commercial association of the Bradman name thanks to the Australian government which, in October 2000, included the Bradman name in the Corporations Law Register, thus controlling its use. Examples of Bradmania were limited editions of mugs, famous photographs and an attractive Wedgwood porcelain sculpture of him raising his bat and doffing his cap (an issue of 2,000, 27 cm high at $995). The pose is similar to the stance of the new bronze figure of Bradman in the garden area of the Museum in Bowral.

Bradman items from the auction houses included an unworn pair of cricket trousers branded "The Don Bradman Autograph Model" size six and a half, which sold for $650. The latest book on Bradman by new cricket author Alan Eason took an interesting A–Z style and to further expand the universe of Bradman-related items a limited issue of a Bradman rose was released during 2002 to follow a variety of pansy, "The Lady Jessie Bradman", released in 2001.

Some rarely seen printed items were offered during the year. Leski's sold a copy of *The Australian Cricketers' Guide for 1870-71* edited by T. W. Wills (Padwick number 3361) for $6,250 and great excitement was shown in a copy for season 1874-75 which was described in the catalogue as "possibly unique". It sold for $17,000! In March 2002, *The Australian Cricketer's Guide for 1856-57* edited by H. Biers and W. Fairfax (Padwick 3360), the catalogue stating that only three copies were known to be in private hands worldwide, sold for an impressive $13,000, but the Sands & Kenny (Victorian) *Cricketer's Guide for 1859-60* edited by J. B. Thompson (Padwick 3377) was passed in at $6,000.

Signed bats were also offered. A bat from the 1930 Jack Ryder testimonial match with 24 signatures went below estimate at $3,750 and a bat from the 1932-33 match in Perth between the MCC team and a Combined Eleven realised $4,000, again below estimate. A Gunn & Moore bat with 235 signatures including the 1921 Australian and England teams, the 1948 Australians, the 1960-61 West Indians and a total of 18 Australian Test captains realised $12,000. In contrast, a bat featuring 28 players from the 1989 Ashes series sold for $800.

The collecting market in Australia is very strong, with domestic retirement funds becoming available for ageing cricket collectors to use. The weak Australian dollar also attracts interest from overseas, particularly the UK, where buyers' pounds seem to stretch a long way. The 2001 Ashes series generated extra bidding interest, which is again expected with the Ashes series of 2002-03, and with rising prices, cricket memorabilia is currently a better investment than shares.

Prices stated are exclusive of buyer's premium and GST.

FIXTURES, 2003-03

Note: At time of publication all fixtures were correct.
Timetables are subject to change without notice.

ENGLAND AND SRI LANKA TO AUSTRALIA
2002-03 INTERNATIONAL SEASON

2002
October
Tue 22	Chairman's XI v England	Lilac Hill
Thu 24 – Fri 25	Western Australia v England	Perth
Mon 28 – Wed 30	Western Australia v England	Perth

November
Sat 2 – Mon 4	Queensland v England	Brisbane
Fri 15 – Sun 17	Australia A v England	Hobart

December
Fri 8	New South Wales v England	Sydney
Sun 8	Australia A v England	Sydney
Tue 10	Prime Minister's XI v England	Canberra
Fri 13	Australia v England (day/night)	Sydney
Sun 15	Australia v England (day/night)	Melbourne
Tue 17	Sri Lanka v England (day/night)	Brisbane
Fri 20	Sri Lanka v England (day/night)	Perth

2003
January
Wed 8	Bradman XI v England	Bowral
Sat 11	Australia v England	Hobart
Sun 12	Australian Country XI v England	Bundaberg
Mon 13	Sri Lanka (day/night) v England	Sydney
Fri 17	Sri Lanka (day/night) v England	Adelaide
Sun 19	Australia (day/night) v England	Adelaide

Test Series

2002
November
Thu 7 – Mon 11   First Test – Australia v England   Brisbane
Thu 21 – Mon 25   Second Test – Australia v England   Adelaide
Fri 29 – Dec. Tue 3 Third Test – Australia v England   Perth

December
Dec 26 – Dec 30   Fourth Test – Australia v England   Melbourne

2003
January
Thu 2 – Mon 6   Fifth Test – Australia v England   Sydney

VB Series

2002
December
Fri 13   Australia v England (day/night)   Sydney
Sun 15   Australia v England (day/night)
Melbourne
Tue 17   England v Sri Lanka (day/night)   Brisbane
Fri 20   England v Sri Lanka (day/night)   Perth
Sun 22   Australia v Sri Lanka (day/night)   Perth
2003
January
Thu 9   Australia v Sri Lanka (day/night)   Sydney
Sat 11   Australia v England   Hobart
Mon 13   England v Sri Lanka (day/night)   Sydney
Wed 15   Australia v Sri Lanka (day/night)   Brisbane
Fri 17   England v Sri Lanka (day/night)   Adelaide
Sun 19   Australia v Sri Lanka (day/night)   Adelaide
Tue 21   Australia v Sri Lanka (day/night)   Melbourne
Thu 23   First Final (day/night)   Sydney
Sat 25   Second Final (day/night)   Melbourne
Mon 27   Third Final (if required) (day/night)   Adelaide

2002-03 PURA CUP

2002
October

Tue 15 – Fri 18	South Australia v Victoria	Melbourne
Wed 16 – Sat 19	Queensland v New South Wales	Brisbane
Fri 25 – Sun 28	South Australia v New South Wales	Adelaide
Wed 30 – Nov. 2	Victoria v Tasmania	Melbourne

November

Thu 7 – Sun 10	Victoria v Queensland	Melbourne
Fri 8 – Mon 11	New South Wales v Tasmania	Sydney
Fri 8 – Mon 11	Western Australia v South Australia	Perth
Fri 15 – Mon 18	Queensland v Tasmania	Brisbane
Fri 15 – Mon 18	New South Wales v South Australia	Sydney
Fri 15 – Mon 18	Western Australia v Victoria	Perth
Fri 22 – Mon 25	Victoria v South Australia	Melbourne
Fri 22 – Mon 25	Tasmania v New South Wales	Hobart
Sun 24 – Wed 27	Queensland v Western Australia	Brisbane

December

Sun 8 – Wed 11	Western Australia v Tasmania	Perth
Thu 19 – Sun 22	New South Wales v Victoria	Sydney
Thu 19 – Sun 22	Tasmania v Queensland	Hobart
Thu 19 – Sun 22	South Australia v Western Australia	Adelaide

2003
January

Fri 3 – Mon 6	Western Australia v Queensland	Perth
Wed 15 – Sat 18	Tasmania v Victoria	Hobart
Sun 19 – Wed 22	Queensland v South Australia	Brisbane
Thu 23 – Sun 26	New South Wales v Western Australia	Newcastle

February

Tue 4 – Fri 7	South Australia v Queensland	Adelaide
Wed 5 – Sat 8	Victoria v New South Wales	Melbourne
Wed 5 – Sat 8	Tasmania v Western Australia	Hobart
Thu 27 – March 2	Queensland v Victoria	Brisbane
Thu 27 – March 2	Tasmania v South Australia	Hobart
Thu 27 – March 2	Western Australia v New South Wales	Perth

March

Thu 6 – Sun 9	New South Wales v Queensland	Sydney
Thu 6 – Sun 9	Victoria v Western Australia	Melbourne
Thu 6 – Sun 9	South Australia v Tasmania	Adelaide
Fri 14 – Wed 19	Final	T.B.A

2002-03 ING CUP

2002
October

Sun 13	New South Wales Blues v Queensland Bulls	North Sydney
Sat 18	Southern Redbacks v Victorian Bushrangers	Adelaide
Sun 19	Queensland Bulls v New South Wales Blues	Brisbane
Sun 27	Queensland Bulls v Tasmanian Tigers	Brisbane

November

Sat 2	Southern Redbacks v New South Wales Blues	Adelaide
Sun 3	Victorian Bushrangers v Tasmanian Tigers	Melbourne
Wed 6	Western Warriors v Southern Redbacks (day/night)	Perth
Fri 29	Queensland Bulls v Western Warriors (day/night)	Brisbane
Fri 29	Southern Redbacks v Tasmanian Tigers (day/night)	Adelaide

December

Sun 1	New South Wales Blues v Victorian Bushrangers	Sydney
Fri 6	Victorian Bushrangers v Southern Redbacks (day/night)	Melbourne
Fri 6	Western Warriors v Tasmanian Tigers (day/night)	Perth

2003
January

Jan 1	Tasmanian Tigers v New South Wales Blues	Hobart
Jan 1	Western Warriors v Queensland Bulls (day/night)	Perth
Sun 5	Tasmanian Tigers v Southern Redbacks	Hobart
Fri 10	Victorian Bushrangers v Western Warriors (day/night)	Melbourne
Fri 17	Queensland Bulls v Southern Redbacks (day/night)	Brisbane
Sun 19	New South Wales Blues v Western Warriors	Coffs Harbour
Sun 19	Tasmanian Tigers v Victorian Bushrangers	Hobart
Sun 26	Victorian Bushrangers v Queensland Bulls	Melbourne
Fri 31	Queensland Bulls v Victorian Bushrangers (day/night)	Brisbane

February
Sat 1	Southern Redbacks v Western Warriors	Adelaide
Sun 2	New South Wales Blues v Tasmanian Tigers	Drummoyne
Sat 8	Southern Redbacks v Queensland Bulls	Adelaide
Sun 9	Victorian Bushrangers v New South Wales Blues	Melbourne
Sun 9	Tasmanian Tigers v Western Warriors	Hobart
Wed 12	Western Warriors v New South Wales Blues (day/night)	Perth
Fri 14	Western Warriors v Victorian Bushrangers (day/night)	Perth
Sat 15	Tasmanian Tigers v Queensland Bulls	Hobart
Sun 16	New South Wales Blues v Southern Redbacks	Sydney
Sun 23	Final	T.B.A.

WOMEN'S CRICKET AUSTRALIA
2002-02 PROGRAMME

National Matches

2002
November
Sat 16 – Sun 17	South Australia v New South Wales	Adelaide Oval No. 2
Sat 23 – Sun 24	Queensland v South Australia	Albion
Sat 23 – Sun 24	Western Australia v Victoria	Perth

December
Sat 7 – Sun 8	New South Wales v Victoria	Bankstown/ Mosman
Sat 7 – Sun 8	South Australia v Western Australia	Adelaide
Mon 9 – Fri 13	Second XI Championships	Melbourne
Sat 14 – Sun 15	Western Australia v Queensland	Perth
Mon 16 – Fri 20	Under 15 Championships	Sydney
Sat 28 – Sun 29	Queensland v New South Wales	Albion
Sat 28 – Sun 29	Victoria v South Australia	Richmond

2003
January
Fri 3 – Fri 10	Under-19s Championships	Canberra
Sat 11 – Sun 12	New South Wales v Western Australia	Bowral
Sat 11 – Sun 12	Victoria v Queensland	Regional Victoria
Tue 14	Youth Limited-Overs International	Bowral
Wed 15	Youth Limited-Overs International	Bowral
Sat 18 – Mon 20	Final	T.B.A.

February

Wed 12	Australia Youth v England	Brisbane
Thu 13	Australia Youth v England	Brisbane
Sat 15 – Tue 18	First Test – Australia v England	Brisbane or Albion
Sat 22 – Tue 25	Second Test – Australia v England	Sydney or
		Regional Qld
Sun 23 – Fri 28	Under-17's Championships	Adelaide

2003 CRICKET WORLD CUP

PRELIMINARY ROUND

Pool A: Australia, Pakistan, India, England, Zimbabwe, Netherlands, Namibia.

2003
February

Mon 10	Zimbabwe v Namibia	Harare
Tue 11	Australia v Pakistan	Johannesburg
Wed 12	India v Netherlands	Paarl
Thu 13	Zimbabwe v England	Harare
Sat 15	Australia v India	Centurion
Sun 16	England v Netherlands	East London
Sun 16	Pakistan v Namibia	Kimberley
Wed 19	England v Namibia	Port Elizabeth
Wed 19	Zimbabwe v India	Harare
Thu 20	Australia v Netherlands	Potchefstroom
Sat 22	England v Pakistan	Cape Town
Sun 23	India v Namibia	Pietermaritzburg
Mon 24	Zimbabwe v Australia	Bulawayo
Tue 25	Pakistan v Netherlands	Paarl
Wed 26	England v India	Durban
Thu 27	Australia v Namibia	Potchefstroom
Fri 28	Zimbabwe v Netherlands	Bulawayo

March

Sat 1	Pakistan v India	Centurion
Sun 2	Australia v England	Port Elizabeth
Mon 3	Namibia v Netherlands	Bloemfontein
Tue 4	Zimbabwe v Pakistan	Bulawayo

Pool B: South Africa, Sri Lanka, West Indies, New Zealand, Bangladesh, Kenya, Canada.

February

Sun 9	South Africa v West Indies	Cape Town
Mon 10	Sri Lanka v New Zealand	Bloemfontein
Tue 11	Bangladesh v Canada	Durban
Wed 12	South Africa v Kenya	Potchefstroom
Thu 13	West Indies v New Zealand	Port Elizabeth
Fri 14	Sri Lanka v Bangladesh	Pietermaritzburg
Sat 15	Kenya v Canada	Cape Town
Sun 16	South Africa v New Zealand	Johannesburg
Tue 18	West Indies v Bangladesh	Benoni
Wed 19	Sri Lanka v Canada	Paarl
Fri 21	New Zealand v Kenya	Nairobi
Sat 22	South Africa v Bangladesh	Bloemfontein
Sun 23	West Indies v Canada	Centurion
Mon 24	Sri Lanka v Kenya	Nairobi
Wed 26	New Zealand v Bangladesh	Kimberley
Thu 27	South Africa v Canada	East London
Fri 28	Sri Lanka v West Indies	Cape Town

March

Sat 1	Kenya v Bangladesh	Johannesburg
Mon 3	New Zealand v Canada	Benoni
Mon 3	South Africa v Sri Lanka	Durban
Tues 4	West Indies v Kenya	Kimberley

SUPER SIX ROUND

March

Fri 7	A1 v B1 (1st Pool A v 1st Pool B)	Centurion
Fri 7	A2 v B2	Cape Town
Sat 8	A3 v B3	Bloemfontein
Mon 10	A2 v B1	Johannesburg
Tue 11	A1 v B3	Port Elizabeth
Wed 12	A3 v B2	Bloemfontein
Fri 14	A2 v B3	Centurion
Sat 15	A3 v B1	East London
Sat 15	A1 v B2	Durban

SEMI-FINALS

March

| Tue 18 | 1st Super Six v 4th Super Six | Port Elizabeth |
| Thu 20 | 2nd Super Six v 3rd Super Six | Durban |

FINAL

March

| Sun 23 | | Johannesburg |